Western Civilization

BEYOND BOUNDARIES

Western Civilization

BEYOND BOUNDARIES

Sixth Edition

Thomas F. X. Noble
University of Notre Dame

Barry Strauss
Cornell University

Duane J. Osheim
University of Virginia

Kristen B. Neuschel
Duke University

Elinor A. Accampo
University of Southern California

David D. Roberts
University of Georgia

William B. Cohen
Late of Indiana University

WADSWORTH
CENGAGE Learning

Australia • Brazil • Japan • Korea • Mexico • Singapore • Spain • United Kingdom • United States

WADSWORTH
CENGAGE Learning™

Western Civilization: Beyond Boundaries,
Sixth Edition
Thomas F. X. Noble, Barry Strauss, Duane J. Osheim, Kristen B. Neuschel, Elinor A. Accampo, David D. Roberts, William B. Cohen

Senior Publisher: Suzanne Jeans

Senior Sponsoring Editor: Nancy Blaine

Associate Editor: Adrienne Zicht

Editorial Assistant: Emma Goehring

Senior Media Editor: Lisa Ciccolo

Executive Marketing Manager:
Diane Wenckebach

Marketing Coordinator: Lorreen Pelletier

Marketing Communications Manager:
Christine Dobberpuhl

Senior Content Project Manager: Jane Lee

Senior Art Director: Cate Rickard Barr

Senior Print Buyer: Judy Inouye

Senior Rights Acquisition Account Manager:
Mollika Basu

Production Service: Elm Street Publishing
Services

Text Designer: Henry Rachlin

Senior Photo Editor: Jennifer Meyer Dare

Cover Designer: Harold Burch

Cover Image: *The Blessings of Good
Government* (detail). Mural, early
14th century by Ambrogio Lorenzetti.
Erich Lessing/Art Resource, NY

Text Credits: Page 751: Excerpts from *A Room
of One's Own* by Virginia Woolf, copyright
1929 by Harcourt, Inc. and renewed 1957 by
Leonard Woolf, reprinted by permission of
the publisher.

Compositor: Integra Software Services Pvt. Ltd.

For product information and technology assistance, contact us at
Cengage Learning, Customer & Sales Support, 1-800-354-9706

For permission to use material from this text or product,
submit all requests online at **www.cengage.com/permissions**.
Further permissions questions can be e-mailed to
permissionrequest@cengage.com.

Library of Congress Control Number: 2009934607

ISBN-13: 978-1-424-06782-4
ISBN-10: 1-424-06782-0

Wadsworth
20 Channel Center Street
Boston, MA 02210
USA

Cengage Learning is a leading provider of customized learning solutions with
office locations around the globe, including Singapore, the United Kingdom,
Australia, Mexico, Brazil, and Japan. Locate your local office at
international.cengage.com/region.

Cengage Learning products are represented in Canada by Nelson Education, Ltd.

For your course and learning solutions, visit **www.cengage.com.**

Purchase any of our products at your local college store or at our preferred
online store **www.ichapters.com.**

Printed in the United States of America
1 2 3 4 5 6 7 13 12 11 10 09

BRIEF CONTENTS

CONTENTS

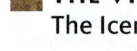

30 A Continuing Experiment: The West and the World Since 1989 851

MAPS

DOCUMENTS

THE VISUAL RECORD

PREFACE

An old adage says that each generation must write history for itself. If the adage is true, then it would also be true that each generation must teach and learn history for itself. The history, of course, does not change, although new discoveries come to light all the time. What does change is us, each succeeding generation of us. What causes us to change, and thus to experience and understand history in ever new ways, are the great developments of our own times. Think of the world-changing events of the last century: two world wars, the Great Depression, the cold war, nuclear weapons, the civil rights movement, the women's movement, the explosion in scientific knowledge, and the media revolutions involving radio and television, the computer, and the Internet. The pace of change has accelerated in our time, but the process of change always affects people's view of their world.

As we launch the sixth edition of this book we are once again acutely aware of the need to address big questions in ways that make sense to teachers and students right now, in the world we live in today. As these words are being written, the news is full of reports from Afghanistan, Iraq, Iran, Darfur, Somalia, and North Korea. The world's economy is in a perilous state. The United States has elected an African American as its president. In such circumstances we might well ask, What is the West; what is Western? Some believe that we are engaged in a "Clash of Civilizations." Is one of these Western Civilization? If so, who or what is its adversary? The West is sometimes understood geographically and sometimes culturally. For most people, the West means western Europe. And yet western Europe itself is the heir of the peoples and cultures of antiquity, including the Sumerians, Egyptians, Persians, Greeks, Romans, Jews, Christians, and Muslims. In fact, Europe is the heir of even earlier civilizations in Asia and Africa. As a cultural phenomenon, "Western" implies many things: freedom and free, participatory political institutions; economic initiative and opportunity; monotheistic religious faiths (Judaism, Christianity, and Islam); rationalism and ordered thought in the social, political, and philosophical realms; an aesthetic sensibility that aspires to a universal sense of beauty. But the West has felt free to evoke tradition as its guiding light and also to innovate brilliantly, to accommodate slavery and freedom simultaneously, and to esteem original thought and persecute people who deviate from the norm. "Western" indeed has meant many things in various places at different times. This book constantly and explicitly attempts to situate its readers in place, time, and tradition.

Another big question is this: What exactly is civilization? No definition can win universal acceptance, but certain elements of a definition are widely accepted. Civilization is the largest unit within which any person might feel comfortable. It is an organizing principle that implies common institutions, economic systems, social structures, and values that extend over both space and time. Cities are crucial; with cities emerge complex social organizations that involve at least a minimal division of labor. Some people work in the fields, some in the home. Soldiers defend the city, and artisans provide its daily goods. Governing institutions have a wide measure of acceptance and have the ability to enforce their will. Civilizations also develop religious ideas and authorities; literatures and laws that may be oral or written; monumental architecture, especially fortifications, palaces, and temples; and arts such as music, painting, and sculpture. Every civilization enfolds many cultures, a term that may be applied to the full range of expressions of a people in a given place and time. So, for example, the cultures of Egypt, Greece, and Rome were distinctive but all fit under the broad umbrella of Western Civilization.

Western Civilization has had an influence on almost every person alive today. The West deserves to be studied because its tale is compelling, but it demands to be studied because its story has been so central to the development of the world in which we live. Many of the world's dominant institutions are Western in their origin and in their contemporary manifestations—most notably parliamentary democracy. Commercial capitalism, a Western construct, is the world's dominant form of economic organization. The Internet, fast food, and hip-hop music are all western in origin but world-wide in reach today.

Until a generation or so ago, Western Civilization was a staple of college and university curricula and was generally studied in isolation. Although it was, and is, important for us to know who we are, it is also important for us to see that we have changed in dramatic ways and that we can no longer understand ourselves in isolation from the world around us. Accordingly, this book repeatedly sets the experience of the West into its global context. This is not a World History book. But it is a book that sees Western Civilization as one significant segment of the world's history.

BASIC APPROACH

Nearly two decades ago the six original authors of *Western Civilization: Beyond Boundaries* set out to create a textbook for a course that would, as a total effort, inform students about essential developments within a tradition that has powerfully, though not always positively, affected everyone in the contemporary world. Although each of us found something to admire in all of the existing textbooks, none of us was fully happy with any of them. We were disappointed with books that claimed "balance" but actually stressed a single kind of history. We regretted that so many texts were uneven in their command of recent scholarship. Although we were convinced of both the inherent interest of Western Civilization and the importance of teaching the subject, we were disconcerted by the celebratory tone of some books, which portrayed the West as resting on its laurels instead of creatively facing its future.

We decided to produce a book that is balanced and coherent; that addresses the full range of subjects that a Western Civilization book needs to address; that provides the student reader with interesting, timely material; that is up-to-date in terms of scholarship and approach; and that is handsome to look at—in short, a book that helps the instructor to teach and the student to learn. We have kept our common vision fresh through frequent meetings, correspondence, critical mutual readings, and expert editorial guidance. The misfortune of the untimely death of one member of our team has brought us the fortune of a new colleague who has inspired and challenged the rest of us in new ways. Because each of us has focused on his or her own area of specialization, we believe that we have attained a rare blend of competence, confidence, and enthusiasm. Moreover, in moving from plans for a first edition to the preparation of a sixth, we have been able to profit from the experience of using the book, the advice and criticism of dozens of colleagues, and the reactions of thousands of students.

Western Civilization is a story. Therefore, we aimed at a strong chronological narrative line. Our experience as teachers tells us that students appreciate this clear but gentle orientation. Our experience tells us, too, that an approach that is broadly chronological will leave instructors plenty of room to adapt our narrative to their preferred organization, or to supplement our narrative with one of their own.

Although we maintain the familiar, large-scale divisions of a Western Civilization book, we also present some innovative adjustments in arrangement. For instance, we incorporate a single chapter on Late Antiquity, the tumultuous and fascinating period from about A.D 300 to 600 that witnessed the transformation of the Roman Empire into three successors: Byzantine, Islamic, and European. One chapter studies those three successors, thereby permitting careful comparisons. But we also assign chapters to some of the greatest issues in Western Civilization, such as the Renaissance, the age of European exploration and conquest, the Scientific Revolution, and the industrial transformation. Our twentieth-century chapters reflect an understanding of the last century formed in its closing years rather than in its middle decades. What is new in our organization represents adjustments grounded in the best scholarship, and what is old represents time-tested approaches.

In fashioning our picture of the West, we took two unusual steps. First, our West is itself bigger than the one found in most textbooks. We treat the Celtic world, Scandinavia, and the Slavic world as integral parts of the story. We look often at the lands that border the West—Anatolia/Turkey, western Asia, North Africa, the Eurasian steppes—in order to show the to-and-fro of peoples, ideas, technologies, and products. Second, we continually situate the West in its global context. Just as we recognize that the West has influenced the rest of the world, we also carefully acknowledge how the rest of the world has influenced the West. We begin this story of mutual interaction with the Greeks and Romans, carry it through the European Middle Ages, focus on it in the age of European exploration and conquest, and analyze it closely in the modern world of industry, diplomacy, empire, immigration, and questions of citizenship and identity.

Another approach that runs like a ribbon throughout this textbook involves balance and integration. Teachers and students, just like the authors of this book, have their particular interests and emphases. In the large and diverse American academy, that is as it should be. But a textbook, if it is to be helpful and useful, should incorporate as many interests and emphases as possible. For a long time, some said, Western Civilization books devoted excessive coverage to high politics—"the public deeds of great men," as an ancient Greek writer defined the historian's subject. Others felt that high culture—all the Aristotles and Mozarts—was included to the exclusion of supposedly lesser figures and ordinary men and women. In the 1970s, books began to emphasize social history. Some applauded this new emphasis even as they debated fiercely over what to include under this heading.

In this book, we attempt to capture the Western tradition in its full contours, to hear the voices of all those who have made durable contributions. But because we cannot say everything about everybody at every moment, we have had to make choices about how and where to array key topics within our narrative. Above all, we have tried to be integrative. For example, when we talk about government and politics, we present the institutional structures through which power was exercised, the people who possessed power as well as the people who did not, the ideological foundations for the use of power, and the material conditions that fostered or hindered the real or the would-be powerful. In other words, instead of treating old-fashioned "high politics" in abstract and descriptive ways, we take an approach that is organic and analytical: How did things work? Our approach to the history of women is another example. A glance at this book's table of contents and then at its index is revealing. The former reveals very few sections devoted explicitly and exclusively to women. The latter shows that women appear constantly in every section of this book. Is there a contradiction here? Not at all. Women and men have not been historical actors in isolation from one another. Yet gender, which is relational, reciprocal, and mutual, is an important variable that has shaped individual and collective experience. Hence we seek to explain why certain political, economic, or social circumstances had differing impacts on men and women, and how such conditions led them to make different choices.

Similarly, when we talk of great ideas, we describe the antecedent ideas from which seemingly new ones were built up, and we ask about the consequences of those ideas. We explore the social positions of the authors of those ideas to see if this helps us explain the ideas themselves or gauge their influence. We try to understand how ideas in one field of human endeavor prove to be influential in other fields. For instance, gender is viewed as connected to and part of the larger fabric of ideas including power, culture, and piety.

We invite the reader to look at our narrative as if it were a mosaic. Taken as a whole, our narrative contains a coherent picture. Viewed more closely, it is made up of countless tiny bits that may have their individual interest but do not even hint at the larger picture of which they are parts. Finally, just as the viewer of a mosaic may find his or her eye drawn especially to one area, feature, color, or style, so too the reader of this book will find some parts more engaging or compelling than others. But it is only because there is, in this book as in a mosaic, a complete picture that the individual sections make sense, command our attention, excite our interest.

One word sums up our approach in this book: "balance." We tell a good story, but we pause often to reflect on that story, to analyze it. We devote substantial coverage to the typical areas of Greece, Rome, Italy, France, Great Britain, and so forth, but we say more about western Europe's frontiers than any other book. We do not try to disguise our Western Civilization book as a World History book, but we take great pains to locate the West within its global context. And we always assume that context means mutuality and reciprocity. We have high politics and big ideas alongside household management and popular culture. We think that part of the fascination of the past lies in its capacity to suggest understandings of the present and possibilities for the future.

Our subtitle, "Beyond Boundaries," is intended to suggest growth, challenge, and opportunity. The West began in Mesopotamia but soon spread to all of western Asia. Gradually the Greeks entered the scene and disseminated their ideas throughout the Mediterranean world. The Romans, always heirs of the Greeks, carried ideas and institutions from Britain to Mesopotamia. As the Roman order collapsed, Rome's imprint was left on a small segment of Europe lying west of the Rhine and south of the Danube. Europeans then crashed through those boundaries to create a culture that extended from Iceland to the Russian steppes. At the dawn of the modern age Europe entered into a complex set of commercial, colonial, military, and political relations with the rest of the globe. Our contemporary world sees Western influences everywhere. No western "boundary" has ever been more than temporary, provisional.

DISTINCTIVE FEATURES

To make this book as accessible as possible to students, we have constantly been aware of its place in a program of teaching and learning. In the preceding paragraphs something has been said about this book's distinctive substantive features and how, we believe, they will contribute to the attainment of a deeper understanding of Western Civilization, as well as of its importance and place in the wider history of the earth's peoples. Teaching and learning also involve pedagogical techniques and innovations. We have attended conscientiously to pedagogical issues from the start, and we have made some significant changes in this edition.

Our chapters have always begun with a vignette that is directly tied to an accompanying picture. These vignettes alert the reader to one or more of the key aspects of the chapter. Thus the readers have encountered a thematic introduction that evokes interest while pointing clearly and in some detail to what follows.

To make our chapter introductions more effective, which means to give students greater confidence as they proceed through the book, we have taken numerous steps. First, as in past editions, we reviewed and revised our opening vignettes to connect text and picture more closely and to use both to invite the reader into the chapter.

Second, the first page of each chapter contains a succinct Outline that immediately and dramatically tells the reader what he or she is going to encounter in the following pages. Third, the chapter introductions conclude with a list of Focus Questions that both echo the introduction and set the reader off on the right path into the following pages. Fourth, as the student begins to read the chapter proper, a Chronology serves as yet another orientation to the material contained in the chapter. Subject-specific chronologies still appear in various parts of the book, but we felt readers would benefit from a chronological guide at the beginning of each chapter.

In this edition, we have repeated each Focus Question at the head of the section to which it pertains. At the end of each major section, we provide a succinct Section Summary. Each chapter concludes with a Chapter Summary that reiterates the Focus Questions and then briefly answers them once again.

As a complement to text coverage, a ready reference, and a potential study guide, all of the Key Terms have been gathered into a Glossary included in the website that accompanies the book. For this edition, we have also placed definitions on the pages where the Key Terms first appear.

In addition to this fundamental attention to chapter themes and contents, we have sought to improve the book's teachability by adding a pronunciation guide. Whenever we use an unfamiliar name or term, we show the reader how to pronounce it. Instead of using the intricate rules of phonetics, we provide commonsense guides to pronunciation in parentheses directly following the word.

This edition is a bit shorter than its predecessors. Relevance, "teachability," and "learnability" were our guides in streamlining our coverage at many points. Virtually every chapter experienced some slimming in the interest of keeping major points and themes front and center.

Having always been conscious of this book's physical appearance, we have this time adopted a dynamic, single-column design to enhance the reader's experience of the book. Attractively laid-out pages, a handsome full-color design, engaging maps, and beautifully reproduced pictures enhance the book's appearance. In keeping with our desire to integrate the components of the book into a coherent whole, we carefully anchor the maps and pictures into the volume. Our maps, always chosen and conceptualized by the authors, have for the sixth edition been completely redesigned to make them fresher, more attractive, and more informative. Map captions have been carefully written, and revised, to make them effective elements of the book's teaching program. The same is true of the pictures: the authors selected them, worked with the book's designers to place them advantageously (and not just decoratively), and wrote all the captions. For this edition, we paid particular attention to reviewing all the captions and to revising many of them. All of the maps are cross-referenced in the text, some of them several times, and the text often refers directly to the pictures.

From the start, every chapter in this book has had boxed documents, one of which treated a "global" theme, as well as a two-page feature entitled "Weighing the Evidence." For this edition, we thought hard about our features and decided to take some decisive steps to make them work better for teachers and students. First, we reduced the number of features to three per chapter. Second, we introduced a uniform structure and format. One feature, entitled "The Global Record," presents a significant document that sets some aspect of Western Civilization within the global perspective. These documents are substantial, are carefully introduced, and conclude with study questions. Another feature is called "The Written Record." This feature contains a significant document relevant to the text materials then under discussion with a careful introduction and study questions. The third feature is called "The Visual Record." This feature represents a reconceptualization of our former "Weighing the Evidence" feature. Most of those features did focus on visual evidence, but now the Visual Record features all do so. As with the Global Record and Written Record features, the Visual Records have helpful questions. Whereas the Weighing the Evidence features always concluded our chapters, now the Visual Records are placed into the chapters at the most appropriate position. For the fifth edition, we cast a careful eye over all the Visual Record features and prepared eight new ones, and for the sixth edition, we have prepared two new ones. Finally, we took two last steps. We deleted the "Looking Ahead" sections because reviewers suggested that this "telegraphing" of what was to come might confuse the student reader as to what he or she has just read. And we moved the "Suggested Readings" to the book's website.

ORGANIZATION AND CONTENT CHANGES

Throughout the book, the authors have made changes to improve the narrative and to incorporate new ways of talking about particular topics. Chapter 1 has been trimmed by cutting the short section "The First Cities" and by eliminating the larger section "Widening Horizons: The Levant and Anatolia, 2500–1150 B.C." The original subsection "War Abroad, Reform at Home, 1786–1075 B.C." has been divided into two separate sections and the material on the Amarna Archives and the Hittites has been moved to the new "War Abroad" section.

Chapter 2 gained a new main section, "Traders Invent the Alphabet: Canaanites and Phoenicians, ca. 1400–450 B.C.," with new subsections on "The Canaanite City-States, ca. 1400–1200 B.C." and "The Phoenicians, ca. 1050–450 B.C." Material on the Phoenicians, formerly found under "Assyrians and Babylonians," has been moved to the new section. These revisions create sharper focus and clearer organization. A new Visual Record feature, "The Siege of Lachish," has been introduced. The entire main section on "Early Greece" has been moved to Chapter 3, once again in the interest of sharpening the focus.

In Chapter 5, two subsections, "The Roman Household" and "Patrons and Clients," have been combined and shortened into one new section entitled "Families and Patronage." The sections on Roman expansion, both in Italy and in the wider Mediterranean, have been recast as follows: The former section on "The Latin League and Beyond" has been replaced by a section entitled "Keeping the Peace," which has been moved to the section "Republican Expansion: The Conquest of Italy, ca. 509–265 B.C." The sections on "Rome Versus Carthage: The Punic Wars, 264–146 B.C." and "Victories in the Hellenistic East, ca. 200–133 B.C." have been combined into one new section, "Punic Wars and the Conquest of the Greek East." The sections on "The Gracchi" and on "Marius and Sulla" have been recast as "Reformers and Revolutionaries." Chapter 6 has a new Written Record feature on "Boudicca's Revolt."

Chapter 8 has been substantially revised. The long and largely introductory section "Catholic Kingdoms in the West" has been deleted. Its material, much abbreviated, has been recast as the opening subsection, "Medieval Europe takes Shape," under the main section "The Rise of the Carolingian Empire." This main section includes revised and trimmed subsections entitled "The Carolingian Dynasty," "Carolingian Government," "The Carolingian Renaissance," and "The Fragmentation of Charlemagne's Empire." The former subsections "Social Patterns" and "The Experiences of Women" have been combined into a new section, "Social Patterns."

In Chapter 12, the section "Renaissance Court and Society" has been revised as "Politics and Renaissance Culture." In Chapter 14, the map "Reform in Germany, 1517–1555" has been replaced by a new map, "The Global Empire of Charles V." Chapter 15 has been significantly reorganized. The material in the subhead "The Failure of the Invincible Armada" has been moved into the section on "The Formation of the United Provinces." Material from the former subhead "Henry IV and the Fragile Peace" has been moved into the section "Decades of Civil War." The main heading "Religious and Political Conflict in Central and Eastern Europe" has been recast as "The Holy Roman Empire and the Thirty Years' War." The subheads in this main section have been revised, shortened, and renamed. The social and cultural sections of this chapter have been revised and reorganized. One old map 15.4 ("Two Empires in Eastern Europe, ca. 1600") has been deleted. In Chapter 16, material on "The Dutch War" has been moved into the section on "The Burdens of War and the Limits of Power." The section on "Competition Around the Baltic" has been tightened.

Chapter 17 has a new subsection, "Women Scientists and Institutional Constraints," and the former section on "Pierre Bayle" has been revised as "Skepticism and the Spread of Scientific Rationality" to signal the central issues more clearly. Similarly, in Chapter 18, the old section "Adam Smith and David Hume" has been recast as "Economic Thought and the Scottish Enlightenment." Some subsections within the former section on "Monarchy and Constitutional

Government" have been eliminated and the whole section reorganized under "Monarch and Parliament in Great Britain." The subheads in the rest of this chapter have been revised, and two main headings "The Widening World of Commerce" and "Economic Expansion and Social Change" have been eliminated with some of their material reorganized and placed in other sections and other material retained under the new main heading "The Widening World of Trade and Production." Finally, this chapter acquires the new main heading "The Widening World of Warfare" that pulls together military history issues. In Chapter 19, several minor subheads have been shortened and combined into other sections, but a new subhead on "Revolution in the Atlantic World" has been added to the section "The Legacy of Revolution for France and the World" and an old section, "The View from Britain," has been deleted. In general, the revisions in Chapters 15 to 19 aim to gather like with like, to streamline the narrative, and to make topics more explicit.

Two important sections in Chapter 20 have been renamed: "Advances in the Cotton Industry" to "Mass Production" and "Iron, Steam, and Factories" to "New Energy Sources and Their Impacts." Several small, fifth-edition subheads have been incorporated into the larger section on "The Spread of Industry to the Continent." The former subhead "The Working Classes and Their Lot" has been renamed "Social Class and Family Structure," which also gained some material from the deleted section "Industrialization and the Family." This chapter acquired a new Visual Record feature, "St. Giles," while material from the former Visual Record "Collective Action" has been creatively reintegrated into the chapter.

Chapters 21 and 22, which deal with the tangled political history of the nineteenth century, received significant attention in this edition. The first major heading in Chapter 21, "The Congress of Vienna," has been reorganized under a heading entitled "Restoration and Reaction." This move permits new subheads, "The Congress of Vienna," "Restored Monarchs in Western Europe," "Eastern Europe," and "Spain and Its Colonies," to carry the political story effectively down to 1830. Then, the former main heading "Restoration, Reform, and Reaction" has been recast as "The Quest for Reform." In other words, the chapter now establishes Europe's restored regimes and then looks inside them to understand their internal political dynamics. Accordingly, the old heading "Western Europe: From Reaction to Liberalism, 1815–1830" has been deleted because its essential material has already been presented. The chapter does receive a new heading entitled "The Revolution of 1830 and the July Monarchy in France," but a number of smaller subheads have been eliminated and their material redistributed. In Chapter 22, the former main heads "Italian Unification, 1859–1870" and "German Unification, 1850–1871" have been combined into one major section, "Forging New States," that itself contains subsections on the main stages in Italian and German unification subordinated to central themes. The main heading on "The Emergence of New Political Forms in the United States and Canada, 1840–1880" has been eliminated, along with its maps. As in earlier chapters, the aim has been to streamline and focus the narratives in these two as well.

In Chapter 23, some headings received new titles, for instance "The Declining Aristocracy" became "The Adapting Aristocracy," while "The Workers' Lot" shifted to "Improving Conditions Among the Workers and the Poor." The former main heading "Social and Political Initiatives" has been deleted with its most important material, particularly "Educational and Cultural Opportunities," redistributed elsewhere. Old Map 23.1, "European Rails, 1850–1880," has been cut.

Chapter 24 has a new title: "Imperialism and Escalating Tensions, 1880–1914." Its first main heading, "The New Imperialism and the Spread of Europe's Population," has been changed to "The New Imperialism and the Spread of Europe's Influence." This change permitted deletion of the subsection on "Overseas Migration and the Spread of European Values." A new subhead on "Unanticipated Consequences: Rebellion and Colonial War" has been added. Former Map 24.3, "European Migrations," has been replaced by a new map on the Ottoman Empire. In Chapter 25, two maps (25.1 and 25.2) have been combined into one new map called "The War in Europe, 1914–1918," and a new map has been added, "The European Peace Settlement and the Peace in the Middle East." In Chapter 26, one main head, "Weimar Germany and the Trials of New Democracies," has been renamed "The Trials of the New Democracies." In Chapter 28, the main heading "The Victory of Nazi Germany, 1939–1941" received a new title, "German Military Successes, 1939–1941." In Chapter 29, the subhead "The Energy Crisis and the Changing Economic Framework" has been moved under the main heading "Prosperity and Democracy in Western Europe." The subhead "New Nations in Asia" has been deleted with its most important information transferred to "The Varieties of Decolonization."

Our attempt to bring the story up to date means that Chapter 30, as always, received considerable attention. This begins with a new opening photo and vignette on the financial crisis, the meeting of the G-20 in London in April 2009. Several subheads received new titles, for example "Origins of the Union" became "Renewing the Union," "War Crimes Tribunals" became "War Crimes Trials," "Unemployment and Economic Challenges in Western Europe" became "Responding to New Economic Challenges," and "Immigration, Assimilation, and the New Right" became "Immigration, Assimilation, and Citizenship." The subhead "The Post-Communist Experiment" has been expanded with new material on Vladimir Putin and the confrontation between Russia and Georgia. One subhead, "Consensus in the Established Democracies" was deleted. The last section, "The West in the Global Age," has been rewritten, especially the subsection "Questioning the Meaning of the West."

ANCILLARIES

Instructor Resources

PowerLecture CD-ROM with ExamView® and JoinIn® This dual platform, all-in-one multimedia resource includes the Instructor's Resource Manual; Test Bank, revised to reflect the new material in the text by Dolores Grapsas of New River Community College (includes key term identification, multiple-choice, short answer, essay, and map questions); Microsoft® PowerPoint® slides of both lecture outlines and images and maps from the text that can be used as offered, or customized by importing personal lecture slides or other material; and *JoinIn®* PowerPoint® slides with clicker content. Also included is ExamView, an easy-to-use assessment and tutorial system that allows instructors to create, deliver, and customize tests in minutes. Instructors can build tests with as many as 250 questions using up to 12 question types, and using ExamView's complete word-processing capabilities, they can enter an unlimited number of new questions or edit existing ones.

HistoryFinder This searchable online database allows instructors to quickly and easily download thousands of assets, including art, photographs, maps, primary sources, and audio/video clips. Each asset downloads directly into a Microsoft® PowerPoint® slide, allowing instructors to easily create exciting PowerPoint presentations for their classrooms.

Instructor's Resource Manual Prepared by Janusz Duzinkiewicz of Purdue University North Central, the Instructor's Resource Manual has been revised to reflect the new material in the text. This manual has many features, including instructional objectives, chapter outlines and summaries, lecture suggestions, suggested debate and research topics, cooperative learning activities, and suggested readings and resources. The Instructor's Resource Manual is available on the instructor's companion site.

WebTutor™ on Blackboard® With WebTutor's text-specific, pre-formatted content and total flexibility, instructors can easily create and manage their own custom course website. WebTutor's course management tool gives instructors the ability to provide virtual office hours, post syllabi, set up threaded discussions, track student progress with the quizzing material, and much more. For students, WebTutor offers real-time access to a full array of study tools, including animations and videos that bring the book's topics to life, plus chapter outlines, summaries, learning objectives, glossary flashcards (with audio), practice quizzes, and weblinks.

WebTutor™ on WebCT® With WebTutor's text-specific, pre-formatted content and total flexibility, instructors can easily create and manage their own custom course website. WebTutor's course management tool gives instructors the ability to provide virtual office hours, post syllabi, set up threaded discussions, track student progress with the quizzing material, and much more. For students, WebTutor offers real-time access to a full array of study tools, including animations and videos that bring the book's topics to life, plus chapter outlines, summaries, learning objectives, glossary flashcards (with audio), practice quizzes, and weblinks.

Student Resources

Book Companion Site A website for students that features a wide assortment of resources, which have been revised to reflect the new material in the text, to help students master the subject matter. The website, prepared by David Paradis of the University of Colorado, Boulder, includes a glossary, flashcards, crossword puzzles, tutorial quizzes, essay questions, weblinks, and suggested readings.

CL eBook This interactive multimedia eBook links out to rich media assets such as video and MP3 chapter summaries. Through this eBook, students can also access self-test quizzes, chapter outlines, focus questions, chronology and matching exercises, essay and critical thinking questions (for which the answers can be emailed to their instructors), primary source documents with critical thinking questions, and interactive (zoomable) maps. The CL eBook is available on ichapters.

Wadsworth Western Civilization Resource Center Wadsworth's Western Civilization Resource Center gives your students access to a "virtual reader" with hundreds of primary sources including speeches, letters, legal documents and transcripts, poems, maps, simulations, timelines, and additional images that bring history to life, along with interactive assignable exercises. A map feature including Google Earth™ coordinates and exercises will aid in student comprehension of geography and use of maps. Students can compare the traditional textbook map with an aerial view of the location today. It's an ideal resource for study, review, and research. In addition to this map feature, the resource center also provides blank maps for student review and testing.

Rand McNally Historical Atlas of Western Civilization, 2e This valuable resource features over 45 maps, including maps that highlight classical Greece and Rome; maps document European civilization during the Renaissance; follow events in Germany, Russia, and Italy as they lead up to World Wars I and II; show the dissolution of Communism in 1989; document language and religion in the western world; and maps that describe the unification and industrialization of Europe.

Document Exercise Workbook Prepared by Donna Van Raaphorst, Cuyahoga Community College. A collection of exercises based around primary sources. This workbook is available in two volumes.

Music of Western Civilization Available free to adopters, and for a small fee to students, this CD contains many of the musical selections highlighted in the text and provides a broad sampling of the important musical pieces of Western civilization.

Exploring the European Past A collection of documents and readings that give students first-hand insight into the period. Each module also includes rich visual sources that help put the documents into context, helping the students to understand the work of the historian.

Writing for College History, 1e Prepared by Robert M. Frakes, Clarion University. This brief handbook for survey courses in American history, Western Civilization/European history, and world civilization guides students through the various types of writing assignments they encounter in a history class. Providing examples of student writing and candid assessments of student work, this text focuses on the rules and conventions of writing for the college history course.

The History Handbook, 1e Prepared by Carol Berkin of Baruch College, City University of New York and Betty Anderson of Boston University. This book teaches students both basic and history-specific study skills such as how to read primary sources, research historical topics, and correctly cite sources. Substantially less expensive than comparable skill-building texts, *The History Handbook* also offers tips for Internet research and evaluating online sources.

Doing History: Research and Writing in the Digital Age, 1e Prepared by Michael J. Galgano, J. Chris Arndt, and Raymond M. Hyser of James Madison University. Whether you're starting down the path as a history major, or simply looking for a straightforward and systematic guide to writing a successful paper, you'll find this text to be an indispensible handbook to historical research. This text's "soup to nuts" approach to researching and writing about history addresses every step of the process, from locating your sources and gathering information, to writing clearly and making proper use of various citation styles to avoid plagiarism. You'll also learn how to make the most of every tool available to you—especially the technology that helps you conduct the process efficiently and effectively.

The Modern Researcher, 6e Prepared by Jacques Barzun and Henry F. Graff of Columbia University. This classic introduction to the techniques of research and the art of expression is used widely in history courses, but is also appropriate for writing and research methods courses in other departments. Barzun and Graff thoroughly cover every aspect of research, from the selection of a topic through the gathering, analysis, writing, revision, and publication of findings presenting the process not as a set of rules but through actual cases that put the subtleties of research in a useful context. Part One covers the principles and methods of research; Part Two covers writing, speaking, and getting one's work published.

Reader Program Cengage Learning publishes a number of readers, some containing exclusively primary sources, others a combination of primary and secondary sources, and some designed to guide students through the process of historical inquiry. Visit Cengage.com/history for a complete list of readers.

Custom Options Nobody knows your students like you, so why not give them a text that is tailor-fit to their needs? Cengage Learning offers custom solutions for your course—whether it's making a small modification to *Western Civilization: Beyond Boundaries* to match your syllabus or combining multiple sources to create something truly unique. You can pick and choose chapters, include your own material, and add additional map exercises along with the *Rand McNally Atlas* to create a text that fits the way you teach. Ensure that your students get the most out of their textbook dollar by giving them exactly what they need. Contact your Cengage Learning representative to explore custom solutions for your course.

ACKNOWLEDGMENTS

The authors have benefited throughout the process of revision from the acute and helpful criticisms of numerous colleagues. We thank in particular: **Stephen Andrews,** Central New Mexico Community College; **Sascha Auerbach,** Virginia Commonwealth University; **Jonathan Bone,** William Paterson University; **Kathleen Carter,** High Point University; **Edmund Clingan,** Queensborough Community College/CUNY; Gary Cox, Gordon College; **Padhraig Higgins,** Mercer County Community College; **John Kemp,** Meadows Community College; **Michael Khodarkovsky,** Loyola University; **William Paquette,** Tidewater Community College; **David Paradis,** University of Colorado, Boulder; **Sandra Pryor,** Old Dominion University; **Ty Reese,** University of North Dakota; **Michael Saler,** University of California, Davis; **Janette VanBorsch,** Midlands Technical College; and **Matthew Zembo,** Hudson Valley Community College.

Each of us has benefited from the close readings and careful criticisms of our coauthors, although we all assume responsibility for our own chapters. Barry Strauss has written Chapters 1–6; Thomas Noble, 7–10; Duane Osheim, 11–14; Kristen Neuschel, 15–19; and David Roberts, 25–30. Originally written by William Cohen, Chapters 20–24 have been substantially revised and updated by Elinor Accampo.

Many colleagues, friends, and family members have helped us develop this work as well. Thomas Noble continues to be grateful for Linda Noble's patience and good humor. Noble's coauthors and many colleagues have over the years been sources of inspiration and information. He also thanks several dozen teaching assistants and more than 4,000 students who have helped him to think through the Western Civilization experience.

Barry Strauss is grateful to colleagues at Cornell and at other universities who offered advice and encouragement and responded to scholarly questions. He would also like to thank the people at Cornell who provided technical assistance and support. Most important have been the support and forbearance of his family. His daughter, Sylvie; his son, Michael; and, above all, his wife, Marcia, have truly been sources of inspiration.

Duane Osheim thanks family and friends who continue to support and comment on the text. He would especially like to thank colleagues at the University of Virginia who have engaged him in a long and fruitful discussion of Western Civilization and its relationship to other cultures. They make clear the mutual interdependence of the cultures of the wider world. He particularly wishes to thank H. C. Erik Midelfort, Arthur Field, Brian Owensby, Joseph C. Miller, Chris Carlsmith, Beth Plummer, and David D'Andrea for information and clarification on a host of topics.

Kristen Neuschel thanks her colleagues at Duke University for sharing their expertise. She is especially grateful to Sy Mauskopf, Bill Reddy, John Richards, Tom Robisheaux, Alex Roland, Barry Gaspar, and Peter Wood. She also thanks her husband and fellow historian, Alan Williams, for his wisdom about Western Civilization and his support throughout the project, and her children, Jesse and Rachel, for their patience and interest over many years.

Elinor Accampo is deeply indebted to the late Bill Cohen whose chapters in the first four editions offered a model of expertise and prose, and she continues to carry on what he originated with pride and respect. She owes special thanks to Kristen Neuschel and Rachel Fuchs for friendship and advice, to her daughter, Erin Hern, for her expert input as a consumer of college textbooks, and, as always, to her husband Robert Hern for his encouragement and enduring support.

David Roberts wishes to thank Sheila Barnett, Vici Payne, and Brenda Luke for their able assistance and Walter Adamson, Timothy Cleaveland, Karl Friday, Michael Kwass, John Morrow, Miranda Pollard, Judith Rohrer, John Short, William Stuek, and Kirk Willis for sharing their expertise in response to questions. He also thanks Beth Roberts for her constant support and interest and her exceedingly critical eye.

The first plans for this book were laid in 1988, and over the course of twenty-one years there has been remarkable stability in the core group of people responsible for its development. The author team lost a member, Bill Cohen, but Elinor Accampo stepped into Bill's place with such skill and grace that it seemed as though she had been with us from the start. Our original sponsoring editor, Jean Woy, moved up the corporate ladder but never missed an author meeting with us. Through five editions we had the pleasure of working with production editor Christina Horn and photo researcher Carole Frohlich. For this edition Jane Lee and Catherine Schnurr filled those roles, and we are grateful for their efforts. Our sponsoring editor for more than a decade, Nancy Blaine, has been a tower of strength. She believes in us, as we believe in her. We have been fortunate in our editors, Elizabeth Welch, Jennifer Sutherland, Julie Swasey, and Adrienne Zicht. All these kind and skillful people have elicited from us authors a level of achievement that fills us at once with pride and humility.

Thomas F. X. Noble

ABOUT THE AUTHORS

Thomas F. X. Noble   After receiving his Ph.D. from Michigan State University, Thomas Noble taught at Albion College, Michigan State University, Texas Tech University, and the University of Virginia. In 1999 he received the University of Virginia's highest award for teaching excellence and in 2008 Notre Dame's Edmund P. Joyce, C.S.C., Award for Excellence in Undergraduate Teaching. In 2001 he became Robert M. Conway Director of the Medieval Institute at the University of Notre Dame and in 2008 chairperson of Notre Dame's history department. He is the author of *The Republic of St. Peter: The Birth of the Papal State, 680–825; Religion, Culture and Society in the Early Middle Ages; Soldiers of Christ: Saints and Saints' Lives from Late Antiquity and the Early Middle Ages; From Roman Provinces to Medieval Kingdoms; Images, Iconoclasm, and the Carolingians;* and *Charlemagne and Louis the Pious: Five Lives.* He was a member of the Institute for Advanced Study in 1994 and the Netherlands Institute for Advanced Study in 1999–2000. He has been awarded fellowships by the National Endowment for the Humanities (twice) and the American Philosophical Society. He was elected a Fellow of the Medieval Academy of America in 2004.

Barry Strauss   Professor of history and Classics at Cornell University, Barry Strauss holds a Ph.D. from Yale. He has been awarded fellowships by the National Endowment for the Humanities, the American School of Classical Studies at Athens, The MacDowell Colony for the Arts, the Korea Foundation, and the Killam Foundation of Canada. He is the recipient of the Clark Award for excellence in teaching from Cornell. He is Chair of Cornell's Department of History, Director of Cornell's Program on Freedom and Free Societies, and Past Director of Cornell's Peace Studies Program. His many publications include *Athens After the Peloponnesian War: Class, Faction, and Policy, 403–386 B.C.; Fathers and Sons in Athens: Ideology and Society in the Era of the Peloponnesian War; The Anatomy of Error: Ancient Military Disasters and Their Lessons for Modern Strategists* (with Josiah Ober); *Hegemonic Rivalry from Thucydides to the Nuclear Age* (co-edited with R. New Lebow); *War and Democracy: A Comparative Study of the Korean War and the Peloponnesian War* (co-edited with David R. McCann); *Rowing Against the Current: On Learning to Scull at Forty; The Battle of Salamis, the Naval Encounter That Saved Greece – and Western Civilization; The Trojan War: A New History;* and *The Spartacus War.* His books have been translated into six languages. His book *The Battle of Salamis* was named one of the best books of 2004 by the Washington Post.

Duane J. Osheim   A Fellow of the American Academy in Rome with a Ph.D. in History from the University of California at Davis, Duane Osheim is professor of history at the University of Virginia. He has held American Council of Learned Societies, American Philosophical Society, National Endowment for the Humanities and Fulbright Fellowships. He is author and editor of *A Tuscan Monastery and Its Social World; An Italian Lordship: The Bishopric of Lucca in the Late Middle Ages; Beyond Florence: The Contours of Medieval and Early Modern Italy;* and *Chronicling History: Chroniclers and Historians in Medieval and Renaissance Italy.*

Kristen B. Neuschel   After receiving her Ph.D. from Brown University, Kristen Neuschel taught at Denison University and Duke University, where she is currently associate professor of history and Director of the Thompson Writing Program. She is a specialist in early modern French history and is the author of *Word of Honor: Interpreting Noble Culture in Sixteenth-Century France* and articles on French social history and European women's history. She has received grants from the Josiah Charles Trent Memorial Foundation, the National Endowment for the Humanities, and the American Council of Learned Societies. She has also received the Alumni Distinguished Undergraduate Teaching Award, which is awarded annually on the basis of student nominations for excellence in teaching at Duke.

Elinor A. Accampo   Professor of history and gender studies at the University of Southern California, Elinor Accampo completed her Ph.D. at the University of California, Berkeley. Prior to her career at USC, she taught at Colorado College and Denison University. She specializes in modern France and is the author of *Blessed Motherhood; Bitter Fruit: Nelly Roussel and the Politics of Female Pain in Third Republic France;* and *Industrialization, Family, and Class Relations: Saint Chamond, 1815–1914.* She has also published *Gender and the Politics of Social Reform in France* (co-edited with Rachel Fuchs and Mary Lynn Stewart) and articles and book chapters on the history of reproductive rights and birth control movements. She has received fellowships and travel grants from the German Marshall Fund, the Haynes Foundation, the American Council of Learned Societies, and the National Endowment for the Humanities, as well as an award for Innovative Undergraduate Teaching at USC.

David D. Roberts After receiving his Ph.D. in modern European history at the University of California, Berkeley, David Roberts taught at the Universities of Virginia and Rochester before becoming professor of history at the University of Georgia in 1988. At Rochester he chaired the Humanities Department of the Eastman School of Music, and he chaired the History Department at Georgia from 1993 to 1998. A recipient of Woodrow Wilson and Rockefeller Foundation fellowships, he is the author of *The Syndicalist Tradition and Italian Fascism; Benedetto Croce and the Uses of Historicism; Nothing but History: Reconstruction and Extremity After Metaphysics; The Totalitarian Experiment in Twentieth-Century Europe: Rethinking the Poverty of Great Politics;* and *Historicism and Fascism in Modern* Italy, as well as two books in Italian and numerous articles and reviews. He is currently Albert Berry Saye Professor of History *Emeritus* at the University of Georgia.

Western Civilization

BEYOND BOUNDARIES

CHAPTER OUTLINE

Origins, to ca. 3000 B.C.

Mesopotamia, to ca. 1600 B.C.

Egypt, to ca. 1100 B.C.

Male and Female Statuettes

Early Dynastic Period, Mesopotamia. (Iraq Museum, Baghdad/Scala/Art Resource, NY)

The Ancestors of the West

T heir huge staring eyes peer out across the centuries. He has long hair, a flowing beard, and a pleated skirt. She has short black hair and wears a simple dress and cloak that go down to her ankles. The man is taller and broader and grabs our attention with his big hair and his hands clasped in prayer. The woman seems modest and may originally have had a child beside her. They represent one of history's oldest couples, dating back to about 2500 B.C.

The powerful gaze of their inlaid alabaster eyes is a way of looking toward heaven. In fact, the couple may have represented gods. Certainly, they did not lack for company, to judge from the dozen other figurines and busts found with them, most of them smaller than the couple and are probably priests and worshipers. One is inscribed with a name, no doubt of an important person. They all come from a temple in the ancient Mesopotamian city of Eshnunna (modern Tell Asmar in Iraq), where they had been placed as an offering to the gods. The statuettes show us that early civilization was religious, artistic, literate, structured by rank and status, and fascinated by the relationship between men and women.

The world of 2500 B.C. had already seen the most momentous inventions in human history. They began approximately 100,000 years ago, when the first modern humans evolved from humanlike ancestors. Human beings wrestled with an often-hostile environment, engaging in a continuing series of experiments, until beginning about 10,000 B.C., they learned how to plant crops and tame animals. The shift from a food-collecting to a food-producing economy dramatically increased the amount of human life that the earth could support. Then between 3500 and 3000 B.C., in parts of what is today the Middle East, human society reached a new stage. These complex societies were marked by inequality and governed by states whose administrators used the first written records. In short, these societies had achieved civilization.

What we call Western civilization, however, was still more than two thousand years away. As a term, *Western civilization* is imprecise, inviting disagreement about its definition and about the lands, peoples, and cultures that it embraces at any given time. In the strictest sense, Western civilization means the "West," and that, in turn, has traditionally meant the lands and peoples of western Europe.

Initially, however, the West embraced the Greek and Roman peoples, plus the foundational monotheistic religions of Judaism and Christianity. These first Westerners, in turn, borrowed many ideas and institutions from the earlier civilizations of western Asia and Egypt. (These civilizations are sometimes referred to as the ancient Near East.) Indeed, civilization began in those lands and came only relatively late to Europe.

Western Asia and Egypt contributed greatly to the cultures of Greece and Rome and to the religious visions of the Jews and Christians. Yet, those earlier civilizations are

FOCUS QUESTIONS

- How did the earliest human beings adapt to their environments and create the first civilizations?

- What were the Mesopotamians' major contributions to government, religion, and art and culture?

- How did the king's power affect various aspects of Egyptian society?

This icon will direct you to additional materials on the website: www .cengage.com/history/ noble/westciv6e

e See our interactive eBook for map and primary source activities.

3

sufficiently different from the West and its society, politics, and religion that they are better considered as ancestors or forerunners of the West rather than as its founders. (For a longer discussion of the definition of Western civilization, see the Preface.)

So, after briefly surveying the origins of the human species, the historian of the West must begin with the emergence of civilizations, after 3500 B.C., in two great river valleys: the valley of the Tigris (TY-gris) and Euphrates (yoo-FRAY-tees) in Mesopotamia (today, Iraq and Syria), and the valley of the Nile in Egypt. Impressive in their own right, Mesopotamia and Egypt influenced a wide range of other early civilizations in western Asia and northern Africa, including the Hittites and the Canaanite city-states.

ORIGINS, TO CA. 3000 B.C.

How did the earliest human beings adapt to their environments and create the first civilizations?

The earth is old; modern human beings are young; and civilization is a recent innovation. Scientists have made great strides in explaining human origins, but great disagreement still reigns. We can be more certain about the series of processes, beginning around 10,000 B.C., that led to the emergence of civilization by 3500 to 3000 B.C. The period studied in this chapter includes both prehistory—the term often used for time before the invention of writing—and recorded history. Writing appeared last among the complex of characteristics that marks the emergence of civilization.

Over a period of several thousand years, humans abandoned a mobile existence for a sedentary one. They learned to domesticate animals and to cultivate plants. They shifted from a food-collecting economy to a predominantly food-producing economy. They developed the first towns, from which, over several millennia, the first urban societies slowly evolved. The result— the first civilizations, found in western Asia and Egypt—laid the groundwork on which later would be built the founding civilizations of the West: the Greeks, Romans, and Hebrews.

The First Human Beings

Anatomically modern human beings, *Homo sapiens sapiens*—genus *Homo*, species *sapiens*, subspecies *sapiens*—first appeared about 100,000 years ago, but the human family is much older. Also known as **hominids**, the human family includes many ancient and extinct species.

Africa is the cradle of humanity. The first hominids appeared in Africa's tropics and subtropics over 4 million years ago. By 2.5 million years ago, they had evolved into creatures who invented the first technology, simple stone tools. Prehistory is traditionally referred to as the Stone Age because stone was the primary medium from which hominids made tools. The hominids were migratory: not less than 1.6 million years ago and perhaps much earlier, they appeared in East Asia and the eastern edge of Europe. The next important stage in human evolution is *Homo erectus* ("upright person"), a hominid with a large brain who used more complex stone tools and may have acquired language. The appearance of *Homo erectus* is usually dated to 1.8 million years ago, but a recent discovery in China may date *Homo erectus* as early as 2.25 million years ago.

About 800,000 years ago, another species of early humans lived in Europe. They are sometimes known as *Homo heidelbergensis* ("Heidelberg person") from the discovery spot of a jaw bone near Heidelberg, Germany. Beginning about 400,000 years ago, Europe was home to the ancestors of the best-known archaic people, the Neandertals. Neandertals lived in Europe and western Asia until about 30,000 years ago. They had strong and stocky physiques, perhaps an adaptation to the rugged climate of the Ice Age, the period of fluctuating cycles of warm and cold, beginning about 730,000 years ago and ending only about 10,000 years ago, an era when glaciers ebbed and flowed. Yet, the Neandertals were no brutes, as they are usually imagined to be. They were, for example, among the first people to bury their dead, often with grave offerings—for example, flint, animal bones, or flowers—which suggest they were sensitive enough to mourn their losses. Recent research shows that Neandertals were both clever enough to use tools to attack one another and caring enough to nurse their wounded back to health.

hominids The primate family *Hominidae*, which includes humans. The modern human being, *Homo sapiens sapiens*, is the only species of this family still in existence.

Neandertals, however, were not modern humans. The most recent research suggests that all anatomically modern humans are descended from a single African ancestor. About 89,000 years ago, the *Homo sapiens sapiens*, from whom we are all descended, was born in Africa. About 70,000 years ago, descendants of that person left Africa for the other continents.

Modern humans entered Europe about 35,000 years ago. Within 5,000 years, Neandertals had disappeared—whether through war, disease, or an inability to compete with modern humans, we do not know. The first modern humans tended to be taller and less muscular than Neandertals. They also used their hands more precisely and walked more efficiently, and they lived longer. The modern human skull, with its high forehead and tucked-in face, is distinctive, but differences between the modern and archaic human brain are a matter of scholarly debate. What no one debates, however, is that, with the disappearance of Neandertals, modern humans put into effect a revolution in culture.

The Revolution in Human Culture, ca. 70,000–10,000 B.C.

Before the emergence of modern humans, people had relatively little ability to change the natural environment. Modern humans changed that. They exploited natural resources, largely by means of technology and organization. Thus, they began the process of human manipulation of the environment that—sometimes brilliantly, sometimes disastrously—has remained a leading theme of the human experience ever since. The key to this change was a dramatic increase in the amount and complexity of information being communicated— what might be called the first information revolution. The twin symbols of the revolution are cave paintings and notations made on bone, signs that humans were thinking about their environment and their experiences.

CHRONOLOGY

ca. 4.4 million years ago	Earliest hominids
800,000 years ago	First humans in Europe
ca. 100,000 years ago	*Homo sapiens sapiens*
40,000–10,000 B.C.	Upper Paleolithic era
10,000–2500 B.C.	Neolithic era
3500–3000 B.C.	First civilizations
3500–3100 B.C.	First writing in Mesopotamia
3300–3200 B.C.	First writing in Egypt
ca. 3200 B.C.	Unification of Nile Valley
2800–2350 B.C.	Early Dynastic Period
2695–2160 B.C.	Egyptian Old Kingdom
2500–2350 B.C.	Cuneiform texts from Ebla
2025–1786 B.C.	Egyptian Middle Kingdom
1650–1180 B.C.	Hittite Old, Middle, and New Kingdoms
1550–1075 B.C.	Egyptian New Kingdom
1450–1300 B.C.	First international system
1250–1150 B.C.	Sea Peoples invade

(All dates in this chapter are approximate.)

Chauvet Cave Art This black-painted panel shows horses, rhinoceroses, and wild oxen. The purpose of cave paintings is unknown, but perhaps they served as illustrations of myths or as attempts to control the environment through magic. (Courtesy, Jean Clottes/ Ministère de la Culture)

It was long thought that these dramatic changes began in Europe about 40,000 B.C.* Recently, however, they have been traced to southern Africa, probably more than 70,000 years ago. The discovery there of carefully worked bone tools and stone spearheads pinpoints the dawn of modern human technology. Still, it is not in Africa, but elsewhere, that we can best trace the early evolution of the modern human mind. Europe from about 40,000 to about 10,000 B.C. provides reliable evidence of the life and the culture of early human hunter-gatherer societies, which survived by a food-collecting economy of hunting, fishing, and gathering fruits and nuts. This period is sometimes called the Upper Paleolithic (Greek for "Old Stone") era. Then, around 10,000 B.C., a second revolution began in western Asia: the invention of a food-producing economy through the domestication of animals and the cultivation of crops. The period from about 10,000 to 3000 B.C. is sometimes called the Neolithic (Greek for "New Stone") era.

Archaeology tells us something about early people's way of life. So do analogies from contemporary anthropology, for even today, a few people still live in hunter-gatherer societies in isolated corners of the globe. An educated guess is that early humans lived in small groups, of maybe twenty-five to fifty persons, related by kinship or marriage. Early **hunter-gatherers** moved from place to place, following the seasonal migration of game, but by the eve of the invention of agriculture, some hunter-gatherers had settled down in villages. Modern cases suggest that work was usually, but not always, divided by sex. Usually, women gathered plants and cared for children and elders, while men went hunting. In some modern cases, however, women hunt as well or better than men, and that might have been the case in Paleolithic times too.

It was probably common for men and women to pair off, have children, and establish a family, much as marriage is a near-universal practice among humans today. Compared with other animals, humans produce extremely dependent infants requiring years of attention. To ensure the survival of the young to adulthood, men as well as women may have needed to play a role in child rearing.

Early people found shelter by building huts or, frequently, by living in caves or rock shelters—hence, our notion of the "caveman." Caves offered shelter, could be heated, and made a naturally good vantage point for observing prey and hostile humans. In the Upper Paleolithic era, about 30,000 years ago, caves were the site of the earliest representational art. The most spectacular Upper Paleolithic paintings discovered so far have been found in caves in southern France (for example, at Lascaux [lass-CO] and at Chauvet [show-VAY] Cave) and in Spain (at Altamira). European cave paintings of animals, such as the bison, horse, reindeer, and woolly mammoth (a huge, extinct member of the elephant family with hairy skin and long, upward-curving tusks), attest to early human artistic skill.

Other early art includes engravings on stone of animals, birds, and stylized human females, as well as female figurines carved from ivory or bone. Usually represented with exaggerated breasts or buttocks, the carvings are called Venus figurines, after Venus, the Roman goddess of love. They may represent an attempt to control fertility through magic.

Upper Paleolithic craftsmanship is as impressive as the art. The early human tool kit included the first utensils in such easily worked materials as antler and ivory. Stone tools became longer and more varied. The first stone and bone spear points, the first bows and arrows, and the first bone needles and awls (probably for sewing animal skins) all appeared.

Hunting was a communal enterprise. Related families probably joined together in clans, which in turn may have formed tribes. Many scholars think of these groups as patriarchal (literally, "ruled by the father"), that is, with the family governed by the father, and the tribe by a male headman or chief. Yet, some later myths (for example, among the ancient Greeks) envision women as the rulers of prehistoric society. Today, some historians see the possibility of matriarchy (literally, "rule by the mother") in the Venus figurines but that is not firm evidence of matriarchy. If chiefs were generally male, as in later periods, some tribes may have had no chief at all, following the decision of the community rather than an individual leader.

hunter-gatherers　Food-collecting society in which people live by hunting, fishing, and gathering fruits and nuts, with no crops or livestock being raised for food.

---

* We follow the traditional practice in the West of expressing historical dates in relation to the birth of Jesus Christ (actually, to a now discredited calculation of his birth date, because in fact Jesus was not born in A.D. 1; see page 159). Dates before his birth are labeled B.C. (which stands for "before Christ"), and dates after his birth are labeled A.D. (*anno Domini*, Latin for "in the year of the Lord"). A widely used alternative refers to these dates as B.C.E. ("before the common era") and C.E. ("of the common era").

The Coming of Agriculture, ca. 10,000–5000 B.C.

The human invention of agriculture was dramatic, meriting the name **Neolithic Revolution** that scholars sometimes give it. Yet if dramatic, the invention spread slowly and unevenly. In most areas, hunting and fishing continued to be a major source of food, even though agriculture fed more people. Agriculture was first invented sometime after 10,000 B.C. in western Asia, then discovered again independently in other parts of the world. By 5000 B.C., information about the new practices had spread so widely that farming could be found in many places around the world.

The story begins about 13,000 B.C., when humans began to specialize in the wild plants they collected and the animals they hunted. They had good reason to do so because hunter-gatherer society had become increasingly complex, and in some places, permanent settlements had appeared. There were now probably more mouths to feed, requiring more food. The next step is not surprising: learning how to domesticate plants and animals.

The first animals to be domesticated were probably dogs because they were useful in hunting. Then came sheep, goats, and cattle. Wheat and barley were the first plants that humans learned to grow, followed by legumes (beans). With males occupied in hunting, it may well have been females who first unraveled the secrets of agriculture.

Domestication began in a crescent-shaped zone of land of dependable annual rainfall. The region stretches west to east from what is today southern Jordan to southern Iran: scholars call it the Fertile Crescent (see **MAP 1.1**). With domestication came small agricultural settlements, which were increasingly common after 7000 B.C. Thus was born the farming village, probably the place that most people have called home since the spread of agriculture around the world.

Neolithic Revolution
Human discovery and spread of agriculture, between about 10,000 and 5000 B.C. People first domesticated dogs and other animals and then learned how to cultivate crops.

🌐 MAP 1.1—Western Asia

The Neolithic Revolution began after 10,000 B.C. in the Fertile Crescent, an arc-shaped region of dependable annual rainfall. In this area between the Tigris and Euphrates Rivers known as Mesopotamia, the world's first urban civilization took root about 3500 to 3000 B.C.

Scholars once thought of Neolithic villages as simple places devoted to subsistence agriculture, with no craft specialization, and as egalitarian societies lacking social hierarchies. In recent years, new evidence and a rethinking of older information have altered this picture considerably. A Neolithic village site in eastern Anatolia (modern Turkey), for example, provides evidence of metalworking (of copper) and specialization of labor (in beadmaking) from approximately 7000 to 6000 B.C. The site also contains the world's earliest known example of cloth, probably linen, woven around 7000 B.C. Artwork shows men wearing loincloths and headdresses, women wearing pants and halter tops, and both sexes wearing jewelry.

The Neolithic town of Çatal Hüyük (CHAH-tal Her-yerk) in south-central Anatolia (see **Map 1.1**) had six thousand people in 6000 B.C., making it by far the largest settlement in its time. It was probably a trading center and perhaps a religious shrine. Carbonization from fire has preserved many objects showing Çatal Hüyük's sophistication, including woven fabrics, obsidian (a sharp volcanic glass used in tools), mirrors, wooden vessels, and makeup applicators.

Agriculture made human populations richer and more numerous, but it also bred disease and probably increased the scale of war. More men than ever before were available to fight because agriculture proved to be so efficient a source of food that it freed people for specialized labor—including war.

Evidence of war comes from Jericho (JEH-rih-co). Located in Palestine near the Dead Sea (see **Map 1.1**), Jericho may be the oldest continuously settled community on earth. Around 7000 B.C., Jericho was a town surrounded by massive walls 10 feet thick and 13 or more feet high, about 765 yards long, and probably enclosing an area of about 10 acres. The most prominent feature of the walls was a great tower 33 feet in diameter and 28 feet high with an interior stairway. Inside the walls lived a densely packed population of about two thousand people.

This is not to say that war in Neolithic times was sophisticated. Indeed, it was probably more a matter of group skirmishes and sporadic raids than of systematic warfare. Spanish rock art shows a confrontation between two groups of archers, one following what seems to be a leader. The scene may be a ritual rather than a violent conflict, but we have evidence, too, of actual bloodshed. The earliest known evidence of what may have been organized warfare comes from a cemetery in Sudan dating from 12,000 to 4500 B.C. Of fifty-nine human skeletons there, nearly half died violently, including women and children.

Neolithic and Copper Age Europe, 7000–2500 B.C.

Europe was one day to become the center of Western civilization, but the region lagged behind its neighbors at first. Innovations from the east reached Europe after 7000 B.C. and slowly transformed it. At the same time, Europeans developed their own unique culture.

Europe The westernmost peninsula of Eurasia, Europe is one of the world's seven continents. Civilization came late to Europe, although the continent was destined to become the center of the West.

Today, "Europe" has a political meaning, referring to specific countries or to the European Union, but its most basic meaning is geographical. The term **Europe** refers to a vast peninsula of the Eurasian continent with several distinct regions. Southern Europe is made up of a rugged and hilly Mediterranean coastal strip, linked to northern Africa and western Asia by the sea and by similarities in climate and landscape. High mountains are found in the Alps of south-central Europe, from which chains of lower mountains radiate toward the southwest and southeast. Northern Europe, by contrast, consists in large part of a forested plain, indented here and there by great rivers. In the southeast, the plain, or steppe, becomes open and mostly treeless. The eastern boundaries of Europe are, in the north, the Ural Mountains and, in the south, the Caucasus Mountains. Georgia, Armenia, and Azerbaijan are all considered parts of Europe.

Before 7000 B.C., Europeans lived a traditional hunter-gatherer existence. Then came farming, which was introduced in southeastern Europe around 7000 B.C. by migrants from western Asia. Agriculture expanded across Europe between about 6000 and 4500 B.C., but not until 2500 B.C. did the majority of Europeans adopt a food-producing way of life. Yet, Europe was hardly static in the meantime. The era of European prehistory from 4500 to 2500 B.C. is known as the Late Neolithic Age, or the Copper Age, because copper came into use on the Continent during this time, as did gold.

Between about 3500 and 2500 B.C., Copper Age Europe grew in sophistication. The urbanization of Mesopotamia (in modern-day Iraq; see **Map 1.1**) had an impact on southeastern Europe, which supplied raw materials for western Asia. Greece underwent the greatest transformation, to the extent that it developed its own urban civilization by about 2000 B.C. (see Chapter 2). The recent discovery of a Copper Age corpse, preserved in the ice of the Italian Alps, opens a window into northern Italian society of about 3200 B.C. (See the feature, "The Visual Record: The Iceman and His World.")

On Europe's northern and western edges, people began to set up megaliths—stone tombs and monuments—often of huge blocks. Such monuments may illustrate an awareness of time created by the spread of agriculture, with its seasonal rhythms. In Britain, megalithic architecture reached its peak with Stonehenge, built in stages from about 2800 to 1500 B.C. This famous monument consists of a circle of stones oriented precisely on the rising sun of midsummer—a sign both of early Europeans' interest in the calendar and of their skill in technology.

The Emergence of Civilization, 3500–3000 B.C.

Civilization comes from the Latin word *civitas*, meaning "commonwealth" or "city." Yet, it is not the city but the state that marks the first civilizations, which began in Mesopotamia and Egypt between 3500 and 3000 B.C. Cities played a major role in Mesopotamia but were less important in Egypt. Civilization allowed human beings to think big. A large and specialized labor force, organized by a strong government, made it possible to expand control over nature, improve technology, and trade and compete over ever widening areas. An elite class emerged that was able to pursue ever more ambitious projects in art and thought and to invent systems of writing. In short, the advent of civilization in the fourth millennium B.C. marked a major turning point. Thereafter, the human horizon expanded forever.

Civilization arose in Iraq, in the valley between the Tigris and Euphrates Rivers (see **Map 1.1**), a region that the Greeks named Mesopotamia (literally, "between the rivers"). At around the same time or shortly afterward, civilization also began in the valley of the Nile River in Egypt. Both Mesopotamia and Egypt are home to valleys containing alluvial land—that is, a relatively flat area where fertile soil is deposited by a river. Although these civilizations each developed largely independently, some borrowing between the two took place.

The first states emerged through a process of action and reaction. In order to feed rulers, priests, and warriors, farmers worked harder, used better techniques, and increased the amount of land under cultivation. Meanwhile, both the number and variety of settlements increased.

Along with states, came writing, which developed between about 3500 and 3100 B.C. in Egypt and Mesopotamia. The growth of writing from simple recordkeeping can be traced step by step. Before writing, Mesopotamian people used tiny clay or stone tokens to represent objects being counted or traded. By 3500 B.C., with 250 different types of tokens in use, the system had grown unwieldy enough for people to start using signs to indicate tokens. It was a short step to dropping

THE DEVELOPMENT OF WRITING

The Maltese Female
The "Sleeping Lady," a terra-cotta statuette of the late fourth millennium B.C. from Malta, shows a reclining woman, perhaps a goddess or priestess. Her double-egg–shaped buttocks are thought to symbolize fertility or regeneration. (Erich Lessing/Art Resource, NY)

The Iceman and His World

On September 19, 1991, a German couple went hiking in the Italian Alps. At 10,530 feet above sea level, in a mountain pass, they thought they had left civilization and its problems behind until they stumbled on an unexpected sight: the body of a dead man lying in the melting ice. Nor was that their only surprise. At first they thought the corpse was the victim of a recent accident. When the authorities arrived, however, the body was discovered to be very old. A helicopter was ordered, and the body was brought to a research institute in Innsbruck, Austria. When the investigators were through, it was clear that the hikers had chanced upon one of the most remarkable archaeological discoveries of the century.*

He was 5,300 years old. The Iceman—as the corpse has become known—is a natural mummy, preserved under the snow: the oldest known remains of human flesh. If that weren't striking enough, consider the clothes and extensive gear that survived with him—they are a window into the European world of about 3200 B.C. The most difficult and most fascinating question is this: Who was the Iceman?

His body offers an introduction. The Iceman stood 5 feet 2 inches tall. He was in his mid-40s and probably had a beard. Genetic testing shows that he was a European, a close relative of modern northern and alpine Europeans. His sinewy frame points to a life of hard work, and scientific tests indicate other difficulties. His growth was arrested by periods of illness, grave hunger, or metal poisoning. His teeth are badly worn, the result perhaps of chewing dried meat or, alternatively, of working leather. He may have undergone a kind of acupuncture; at any rate, he is tattooed, which in some cultures is a medical treatment rather than a form of decoration. He has several broken ribs, which indicates either damage under the ice, mishandling when the body was discovered, or an ancient accident or fight.

The Iceman died violently. The story began in a valley south of the mountains one spring day—pollen analysis specifies the season. There the Iceman ate goat meat and vegetables. Then he decided to climb into the mountains, perhaps to escape after a fight. At least several days before he died, the Iceman received a severe cut on his right hand from a rough blade, which should indicate trouble.

In the mountains the Iceman enjoyed his very last meal, consisting of red deer and some cereals. Soon afterwards he encountered someone who shot him in the shoulder with an arrow. The arrow struck a major artery, which caused the Iceman to bleed to death within minutes. Who killed the Iceman and why? We don't know. Some evidence suggests that as many as four people attacked him but not all scholars agree about that.

Whoever killed the Iceman pulled out the shaft and left the arrowhead in his victim. Nor did the killer take any of the

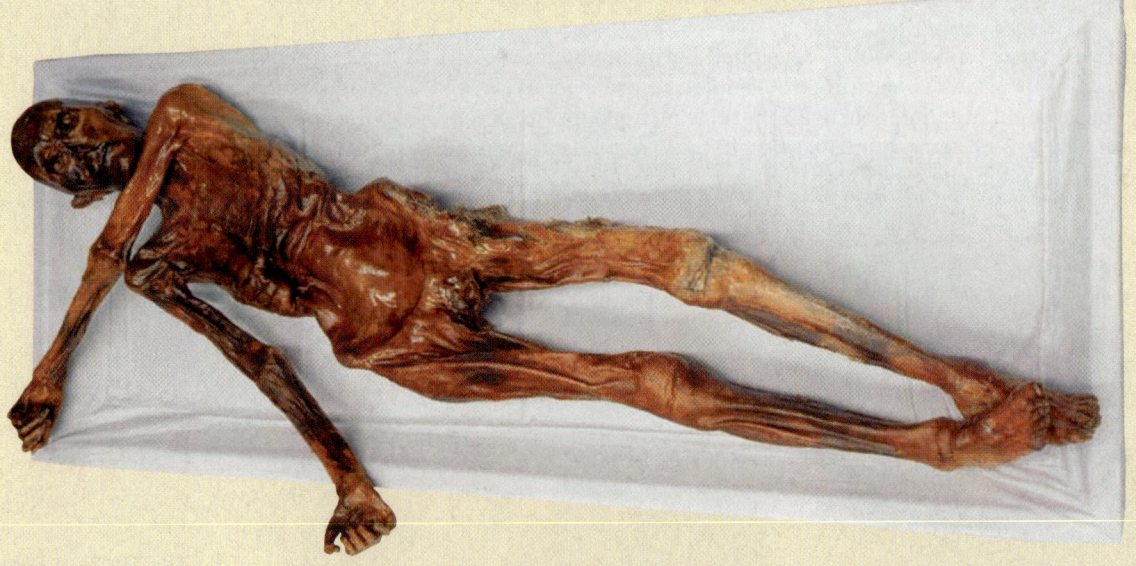

Mummy of Iceman (Copyright Photo Archives, South Tyrol Museum of Archaeology)

cuneiform First writing system in Mesopotamia, consisting of wedge-shaped impressions in soft clay. Named from the Latin word for "wedge-shaped," it was developed about 3500–3100 B.C.

the tokens and placing the signs on a clay tablet by making indentations in the clay with a reed stylus: writing. New words were soon added through pictographs (pictures that stand for particular objects). The pictographs evolved into ideograms—that is, abstract symbols that are no longer recognizable as specific objects and thus can be used to denote ideas as well as things.

In the centuries following its introduction, Mesopotamian writing became standardized. Scholars call the signs **cuneiform**, from the Latin for "wedge-shaped," a good description of what early writing looks like (see **FIGURE 1.1**). In its first centuries, cuneiform was used almost

Iceman's valuable gear, which may suggest that he didn't want to be caught with any of the dead man's property. Today that gear provides tantalizing clues to the Iceman's social status. Look at the artist's drawing. A woven grass or reed cape lies over the Iceman's deerskin coat, which in turn covers a leather loincloth and garter, held in place by a leather belt. A bearskin hat, skin leggings, and calfskin shoes, stuffed with grass for insulation, complete his wardrobe. The Iceman and his contemporaries knew how to dress for the cold weather of the mountains.

The Iceman carries a rich tool kit. Notice his copper ax and 6-foot-long bow, made of yew, the best wood then available for making bows. A quiver (arrow case), two birch-bark containers, a waist pouch, and a frame—probably part of a backpack—hang from his body. Among his items of equipment are flint tools (including a dagger, a retouching tool, and a scraper); a piece of net; two birch-fungus-like "polypores" threaded on a leather thong, probably used as a natural antibiotic; and fourteen arrows, all, oddly, broken. In short, it appears that the Iceman was equipped with a state-of-the-art mountain survival kit of his day. It is not clear why he carried broken arrows, but he would not have had time to change his gear before he fled.

Scholars differ about the Iceman's occupation. Educated guesses range from to a herdsman to a hunter to a trader to a warrior to an outlaw to a shaman (a priest who uses magic). The Iceman's complex weapons and well-made clothing point to a sophisticated culture. The copper ax is the key to that culture and its relationship with the wider world. Similar axes have been found in northern Italian tombs in Remedello, about 240 miles south of the Alps. Before the discovery of the Iceman, archaeologists believed that Italians learned the metalwork technology needed for such an ax from Anatolia, where similar pieces of metalwork are dated to approximately 2700 to 2400 B.C. Hence, the Remedello culture was usually also dated to that period. The discovery of the Iceman means that Remedello must be backdated by about five hundred years. It is clear, then, that by about 3200 B.C., northern Italians not only borrowed from the more advanced eastern Mediterranean areas but also created their own original technology and culture. Thus, a small object (a copper ax), placed within a larger body of evidence (Italian and Anatolian met-

Artist's Rendition of the Iceman   (© Michael Rothman)

alwork), permits broad generalization about the interaction and independence of ancient cultures.

QUESTIONS

1. What do the Iceman's clothing, tools, and weapons tell us about his society?

2. How do modern, scientific tests add to our knowledge of the Iceman?

3. How does the discovery of the Iceman change our understanding of the relationship between Europe and Anatolia about five thousand years ago?

4. How skilled at technology was Copper Age Europe?

5. What role did violence play in prehistoric human relations?

---

* For an introduction to the Iceman, see Brenda Fowler, *Iceman: Uncovering the Life and Times of a Prehistoric Man Found in an Alpine Glacier* (Chicago: University of Chicago Press, 2001); Stephen S. Hall, "Last Hours of the Iceman," *National Geographic* (July 2007), http://ngm.nationalgeographic.com/2007/07/iceman/hall-text/1; James H. Dickson, Klaus Oeggl, and Linda L. Handley, "The Iceman Reconsidered," *Scientific American* (May 2003); and <http://www.mummytombs.com/mummylocator/featured/otzi.htm>.

---

entirely for economic records or commercial transactions. Then it was used to record offerings to the gods. By 2350 B.C., cuneiform had evolved into a mixed system of about six hundred signs, most of them phonetic (syllabic), with relatively few ideograms.

Egyptian writing developed independently, beginning around 3300 to 3200 B.C.: It was not derived from or related to cuneiform. Whether writing began in Egypt or Mesopotamia, therefore, is an open question. What is clear, however, is that writing was invented to meet economic rather than creative needs. In Egypt, the earliest writing includes records of the delivery of linen

papyrus   Paperlike writing material used by the ancient Egyptians, Greeks, and Romans. Made primarily in Egypt from the papyrus plant, it was durable, flexible, and easy to write on.

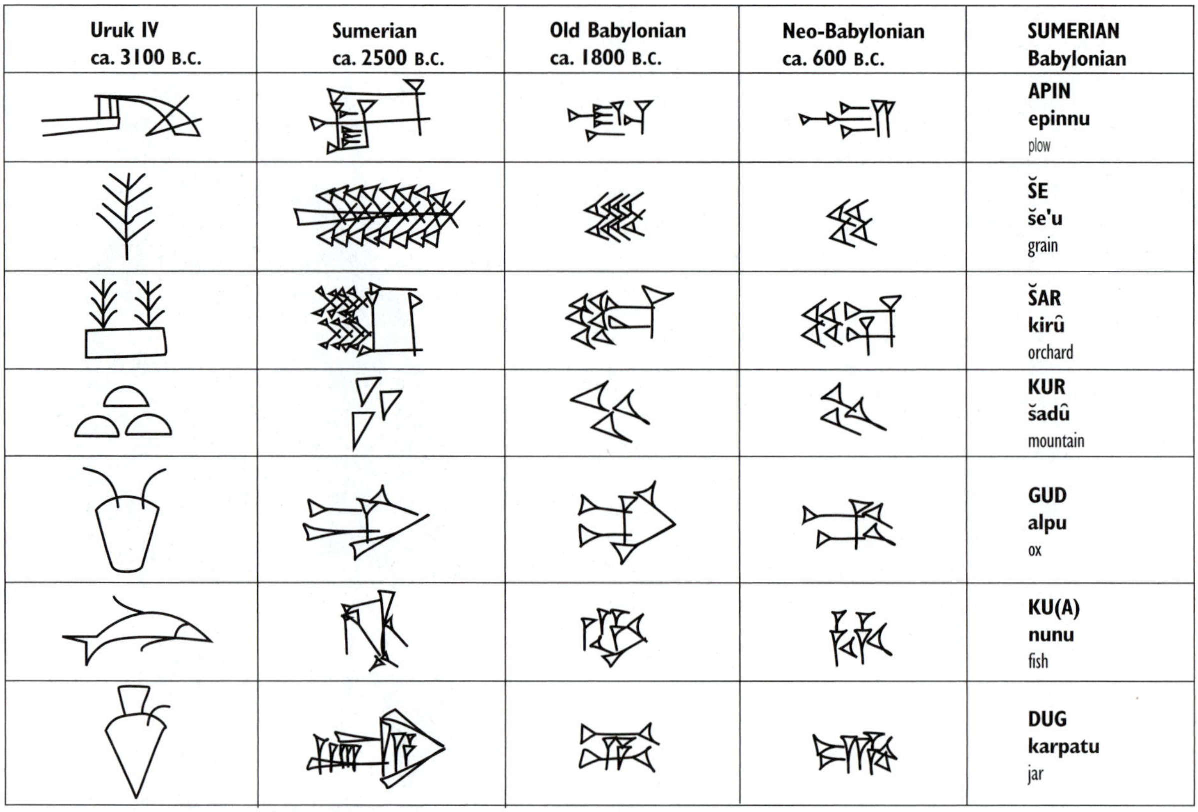

Uruk IV ca. 3100 B.C.	Sumerian ca. 2500 B.C.	Old Babylonian ca. 1800 B.C.	Neo-Babylonian ca. 600 B.C.	SUMERIAN Babylonian
				APIN **epinnu** plow
				ŠE **še'u** grain
				ŠAR **kirû** orchard
				KUR **šadû** mountain
				GUD **alpu** ox
				KU(A) **nunu** fish
				DUG **karpatu** jar

■ **FIGURE 1.1—Early Mesopotamian Writing**

The pictographs of early writing evolved into a system of phonetic syllables and abstract symbols. Simplified and standardized, this writing was *cuneiform*, or "wedge-shaped." Over time, it was adapted from Sumerian to Babylonian and other languages throughout western Asia.

(From *Babylon*, by Joan Oates. Published by Thames and Hudson Ltd., 1978. Reprinted by permission of the publisher.)

and oil as taxes to King Scorpion I (ca. 3250 B.C.). The writing consists of early *hieroglyphs* (literally, "sacred carvings"), a system of pictures and abstract signs that represent sounds or ideas, later to become more formal and standardized.

Either Egyptian or a Mesopotamian language called Sumerian was the first written language. They are the earliest known of the many thousands of human languages that have existed in history. Most belong to large groupings of related languages called language families. Egyptian, for instance, is part of the Afro-Asiatic family of languages. Sumerian, in contrast, stands on its own; it cannot be reliably classified into any language family.

Incising cuneiform on clay was much clumsier than writing with pen and ink on **papyrus**, as became possible in Egypt. The papyrus plant grew in the Nile marshes and it was the source of the ancient world's favorite writing material. (Our word *paper* comes from "papyrus," although modern paper comes from a different source, trees.) Nonetheless, cuneiform was flexible enough to be used for poetry as well as for bookkeeping. Moreover, cuneiform became the standard script in western Asia for several thousand years. Clumsy it may have been, but cuneiform was writing, and writing is both a catalyst for change and the historian's best friend. Mesopotamia after 3000 B.C. was dynamic, sophisticated, and, best of all, intelligible to us.

SECTION SUMMARY

- Anatomically modern human beings are called *Homo sapiens sapiens* and first appeared about 100,000 years ago.

- Humans lived by hunting animals and gathering nuts and berries until agriculture was invented shortly after 10,000 B.C. in western Asia.

- Early Europeans were skilled metalworkers and architects, but they lagged behind the more advanced regions, Egypt and Mesopotamia.

- The first civilizations in Mesopotamia and Egypt emerged between 3500 and 3000 B.C. and probably contained the first cities.

- Civilization meant bigger and more complex societies, with specialized labor forces, strong governments, and well-structured armies.

- Along with cities came writing, which developed independently in Egypt and Mesopotamia between about 3500 and about 3100 B.C.

MESOPOTAMIA, TO CA. 1600 B.C.

What were the Mesopotamians' major contributions to government, religion, and art and culture?

After 3000 B.C., the people of Mesopotamia flourished. They experimented in government, in cooperation and conflict among different ethnic groups, in law, and in the working out of class and gender relations. Keenly aware of human limitations and vanity, they sought divine justice, as their literary and religious texts show. Their engineering skill, mathematics, and astronomy set ancient science on an upward path. In later centuries, Western civilization would build on these foundations, and then take off in new directions.

The fertile Tigris-Euphrates plain had to be tamed by would-be farmers. Most of the soil was either so dry or so marshy that agriculture required considerable irrigation and drainage—that is, the use of channels, dikes, or dams to control floodwaters and improve the fertility of the land. Making matters worse, Mesopotamia was also given to extreme heat and scorching winds. Some scholars argue that the very hostility of Mesopotamia's environment generated the cooperation and control that civilization requires.

Archaeologists sometimes refer to the third and second millennia in the eastern Mediterranean and western Asia as the Bronze Age. In this period, people mastered the technology of making bronze, an alloy of copper and tin, and bronze frequently replaced stone as a primary material for everyday use.

The City-States of Sumer

Though their culture is long dead, the Sumerians live on. Whenever someone today counts the minutes, debates politics, or quotes the law, the Sumerians live, for these are all legacies of that ingenious society.

The dominant inhabitants of Mesopotamian civilization in its first flowering are named **Sumerians**. Present in southern Mesopotamia by 3200 B.C., and probably earlier, the Sumerians entered their great age in the third millennium B.C., when their **city-states** enjoyed a proud independence (see **MAP 1.1**).

The formative era of Mesopotamian civilization is known as the Uruk Period (ca. 3800–3200 B.C.), after one of its major archaeological sites. During the Uruk Period, the Sumerians invented the wheel and the plow, planted the first orchards—of dates, figs, or olives—and developed the first sophisticated metal-casting processes. They built some of the first cities, for example, Uruk. They expanded the size of territories and populations, the scale of war, the complexity of society, and the power of government. Finally, as if to cap a period of remarkable change, at the end of the Uruk Period, the Sumerians invented cuneiform writing.

By the period that scholars have named the Early Dynastic Period (2800–2350 B.C.), named for the first royal dynasties (ruling families), large Mesopotamian cities had grown to the point where they might cover 1,000 acres surrounded by more than five miles of walls, within which lived about fifty thousand people. Such cities were part of a network of thirty such city-states. It was a web of culture, commerce, and competition, sometimes leading to war. The system was bigger, more complex, and more technologically advanced than any predecessor. Hence, the city-states of Mesopotamia may be called the first civilization.

It was a land of cooperation and conflict. The Sumerian cities had much in common: language, literature, arts and sciences, and religion. Yet, the cities often quarreled, often over farmland boundaries or water rights. Each city had its own urbanized area and surrounding agricultural land irrigated by canals. Cities traded with one another and with the outside world. The primary political units of southern Mesopotamia for most of the third millennium B.C., Sumerian city-states were an incubator of civilization.

A history of Sumerian government begins in the Early Dynastic Period, because good evidence for earlier times is lacking. Historians once labeled these cities as temple-states, governed by priests, but there is no proof of that. Certainly, the first Sumerian temples were wealthy and powerful. Each city had at least one temple, the house of its patron god and the common symbol of the community.

By the Early Dynastic Period, around 2800 B.C., political power in a Sumerian city rested largely with its Council of Elders, whose members were probably wealthy landowners. Some

Sumerians Dominant inhabitants of Mesopotamia in the third millennium B.C. They established the world's first civilization, thirty flourishing city-states with a common culture, commerce, and tendency to make war on one another.

city-states State consisting of an independent city and the surrounding territory under its control. Early examples were the Sumerian city-states in the third millennium B.C.

scholars argue that the council shared power with a popular assembly, creating, in effect, a bicameral legislature and perhaps even a primitive democracy. But this is just a theory.

Ordinary people enjoyed only limited freedom. Even if they owned their own land, farmers often had to provide forced labor for the state as a kind of taxation—maintaining the vast Mesopotamian irrigation system, for example. There was also apparently a large group of semi-free people who owned no land of their own but worked others' land. Finally, there were slaves—that is, people who could be bought and sold. Slaves were not numerous because there was no policing system to catch runaways. Slaves were usually foreign prisoners of war, but some were local people who had been sold into slavery to pay off a debt; often poor parents sold their own children (especially daughters).

By about 2700 B.C., political power shifted. War between cities became chronic and many felt the times demanded a strong hand. The new ruler was not a Council of Elders but rather a "big man" (*lugal*) or, less often, a "governor" (*ensi*)—that is, a king or, occasionally, a queen. Kings and queens sponsored irrigation works, raised fortification walls, restored temples, and built palaces, but the monarch was first and foremost a warrior.

One of the earliest Sumerian kings, dating from ca. 2700–2600 B.C., was Gilgamesh (GIL-ga-mesh) of Uruk, a hero of epic poetry whom many scholars consider a genuine historical personage. In the cities of Ur and Lagash, the king's wife was often a power in her own right. Kish was ruled by Ku-baba (r. ca. 2450 B.C.), history's first recorded reigning queen.

Though warriors, Sumerian monarchs also recognized a responsibility for promoting justice. History's earliest known reformer of law and society was Uru-inim-gina, king of Lagash around 2400 B.C. Surviving documents describe Lagash as a city in which wealthy landowners interfered with the temples and oppressed the poor, and in which royal administrators mistreated ordinary people. Uru-inim-gina attempted to manage the bureaucracy, protect the property of humble people, and guard the temples. He also put into effect the first known wage and price controls. Uru-inim-gina's proclaimed intention was to promote impartial justice, a goal that he expressed in the formula "[the king] will protect the mother that is in distress, the mighty man shall not oppress the naked and the widow." No doubt he also wanted to weaken independent sources of power threatening royal authority. As it turned out, Lagash was conquered only a few years after Uru-inim-gina's reign. His reforms nonetheless survived as the precedent for a long Mesopotamian tradition of royal lawgiving.

Conquest and Assimilation, ca. 2350–1900 B.C.

The poor and hardy peoples of the desert and the mountains coveted Mesopotamia's wealth. They attacked: some from without, by raising armies and assaulting cities, while others immigrated and climbed to power from within the Sumerian city-states. The attackers were sufficiently impressed by Sumerian culture to adopt a great many Sumerian customs and ideas. The most successful attacker was Sargon (r. 2371–2316 B.C.), who rose from nowhere to a high position under the king of the city of Kish before founding his own capital city, Agade (ah-GAH-day). Notice that Sargon was a native speaker not of Sumerian but of Akkadian.

The Akkadians were originally a seminomadic people who lived as shepherds on the edge of the desert. They had begun settling in the northern cities of southern Mesopotamia by the end of the Uruk Period, in a part of southern Mesopotamia known as Akkad. Their language, Akkadian, belongs to the Semitic group of languages, a subfamily of the Afro-Asiatic language family. Semitic languages include Arabic and Hebrew.

As commander of one of history's first professional armies, Sargon conquered all of Mesopotamia, and his power extended westward along the Euphrates and eastward into Iran. Rather than rule conquered peoples directly, the Akkadians generally were satisfied with loose control, as long as they could monopolize trade. They adopted Sumerian religion and wrote Akkadian in cuneiform.

Akkadian Bronze This stern-faced, life-size cast-bronze head, with its stylized ringleted beard and carefully arranged hair, shows Mesopotamian craftsmanship at its finest. Thought by some to be Sargon (r. 2371–2316 B.C.) or Naramsin (r. ca. 2250–2220 B.C.), it was deliberately mutilated in ancient times. (Scalar/Art Resource, NY)

Sargon's son inherited his throne. His dynasty boasted that it reigned over "the peoples of all lands" or "the four quarters of the earth." Sargon proved to be one of western Asia's most influential figures because his ideal of universal rule would continue to inspire future conquerors.

Assimilation was another lasting Akkadian legacy. Although Sargon made Akkadian the language of administration, he made many concessions to Sumerian practices. For instance, his daughter Enkheduanna (en-khe-du-AN-na), whom he appointed high priestess at Ur and Uruk, wrote poetry in Sumerian, is still quoted often in later Sumerian texts. The first known woman poet, Enkheduanna celebrated the union of Sumerians and Akkadians.

As a political reality, Akkadian rule proved short-lived, but assimilation survived as a cultural ideal. Around 2200 B.C., the Akkadian kingdom broke up into a series of smaller successor states. Then, after a century of rule by invaders from the east, the Sumerians returned to power under the Third Dynasty of Ur (2112–2004 B.C.). Far from stripping away Akkadian influence, the new Sumerian rulers spoke of themselves as "kings of Sumer and Akkad." The title would have a long and potent history: For the next fifteen hundred years, many of the great kings of western Asia would use it, in recognition of a common Mesopotamian society.

After renewed turmoil in Mesopotamia around 2000 B.C., a new kingdom emerged in the south under the rule of the Amorites around 1900 B.C. The Amorites were Semitic speakers and shared Mesopotamian culture and traditions. Babylon, northwest of Ur in the central part of Mesopotamia, became the Amorite capital. From Babylon, Amorite kings issued cuneiform decrees that, although written in a Semitic language, drew heavily on Sumerian material.

Hammurabi's Code

The most famous Amorite king, Hammurabi (r. 1792–1750 B.C.) ruled in Babylon about six hundred years after Sargon. Much of his forty-two-year reign was devoted to creating a Mesopotamian empire. He was a careful administrator who ushered in an era of prosperity and cultural flowering. He is most famous for the text known as **Hammurabi's Code**. Although the work was less a "code" than a collection listing various crimes and their punishments—a kind of treatise on justice glorifying Hammurabi's qualities as a judge—we shall use the familiar name. Hammurabi's Code became both a legal and a literary classic, much copied in later times.

Hammurabi's Code offers a portrait of Mesopotamian society. The document contains nearly three hundred rulings in cases ranging from family to commercial law, from wage rates to murder. The administration of justice in Mesopotamia was entirely practical: We find no notion of abstract absolutes or universal principles, not even a word for "law."

Though occasionally less harsh than earlier law codes, which date as far back as around 2100 B.C., Hammurabi's Code was by no means lenient. Whereas earlier codes were satisfied with payment in silver as recompense for crime, Hammurabi's Code was the first to stipulate such ruthless penalties as mutilation, drowning, and impaling. It also introduced the law of retaliation for wounds: "If a man has destroyed the eye of a member of the aristocracy: they shall destroy his eye. If he has broken his limb: they shall break the (same) limb." Moreover, children could be punished for the crimes of their parents.

The code was inscribed in forty-nine vertical columns on a stone stele about 7½ feet high and displayed in a prominent public place. Thus, Hammurabi's Code symbolized the notion that the law belonged to everyone. Although ordinary people could not read, it was possible for them to find a patron who could. Yet, the societies of western Asia and Egypt were anything but egalitarian, and Hammurabi's society was no exception. Punishments were class-based: Crimes against a free person, for example, received harsher treatment than crimes against a slave or a semi-free person. Debt seems to have been a serious and widespread problem, frequently leading to debt slavery. While women could own and inherit property and testify in court, the code tended to enshrine the power of the male head of the family.

Hammurabi's Code An influential collection of various crimes and punishments, this work was named for the famous Amorite king Hammurabi (r. 1792–1750 B.C.).

Divine Masters

The Sumerians were polytheists—that is, they had many gods—and their gods (like the later gods of Greece) were anthropomorphic, or human in form. Indeed, Sumerian gods were thought to be much like humans, by turns wise and foolish, except that they were immortal and superpowerful. Many Sumerian gods represented the forces of nature: An, the sky-god; Enki, the earth-god and freshwater-god; Enlil, the air-god; Nanna, the moon-god; and Utu (Semitic, Shamash), the sun-god. Other Sumerian gods embodied human passions or notions about the afterlife: Inanna (Semitic, Ishtar), goddess of love and war; and Ereshkigal, goddess of the underworld.

The Sumerians sometimes envisioned their gods holding an assembly, much like a boisterous Sumerian assembly. The Sumerians and Akkadians considered Enlil, city-god of Nippur, to be the chief god. The Babylonians replaced him with Marduk, city-god of Babylon.

Every Mesopotamian city had its main temple complex, the most striking feature of which was a *ziggurat*, or stepped tower. Constructed originally as simple raised terraces, ziggurats eventually became seven-stage structures. Unlike the pyramids of Egypt, ziggurats were not tombs but "stairways" connecting humans and the gods.

The keynote of Mesopotamian religion was pessimism. It is not surprising that the Mesopotamians, living in a difficult natural environment, regarded the gods with fear and awe. Although the gods communicated with humans, their language was mysterious. To understand the divine will, the Mesopotamians engaged in various kinds of divination: They interpreted dreams, examined the entrails of slaughtered animals, and studied the stars (which stimulated great advances in astronomy, as we will see).

Most people expected nothing glorious in the afterlife, merely a shadowy existence. It was thought that with a person's last breath, his or her spirit embarked on a long journey to the Netherworld, a place under the earth. More than one Mesopotamian text describes the Netherworld as the "Land-of-no-return" and "the house wherein the dwellers are bereft of light, / Where dust is their fare and clay their food, / Where they see no light, residing in darkness."[1] The dead resided there permanently, though in some texts their spirits return to earth, often with hostile intent toward the living.

Archaeological evidence indicates a possible shift in such attitudes toward death, at least on the part of the Mesopotamian upper classes, by the late third millennium B.C. The kings and nobles of the Third Dynasty of Ur were buried with rich grave goods and with their servants, who were apparently the victims of human sacrifice following the master's death. Perhaps the rulers now expected to have the opportunity to use their wealth again in a comfortable immortality, possibly influenced by Egyptian ideas (see pages 19–21).

Arts and Sciences

The people of Mesopotamia were deeply inquisitive. They focused on the beginning and the end of things. "How did the world come into being?" and "What happens to us when we die?" are perhaps the two basic questions of their literature. Consider, for example, the Babylonian creation epic, known from its first line as *Enuma Elish* ("When on high"). An epic poem is the story of heroic deeds, in this case, the deeds of the gods of order, who triumphed over the forces of chaos. Another important Babylonian literary form, known as wisdom literature, responded to life's ups and downs with teachings that are sometimes simple, sometimes sophisticated. It proved eventually to influence the wisdom literature of the Hebrew Bible.

Epic of Gilgamesh The best-known example of Mesopotamian literature, the *Epic of Gilgamesh* is one of the earliest known poems and, in its original form, may date back to the Sumerians ca. 2500 B.C.

The best-known example of Mesopotamian literature is the ***Epic of Gilgamesh***. Frequently translated and adapted by various western Asian peoples, *Gilgamesh* might originally have been a Sumerian work dating to about 2500 B.C. Gilgamesh, king of Uruk, was probably a real historical person, but the poem concerns his fictionalized personal life. The main themes are friendship, loss, and the inevitability of death. As king, Gilgamesh is a tyrant; Enkidu arrives and puts him in his place, and then the two become close friends and comrades in arms. Enkidu's untimely death makes Gilgamesh aware of his own mortality. Distraught by his friend's passing, Gilgamesh goes on a vain quest for immortality. The *Epic of Gilgamesh* contains stories that presage the later biblical Eden and Flood narratives; there is little doubt but that those narratives found their way from Mesopotamia to the Hebrew Bible. (See the feature, "The Written Record: Heroism and Death in Mesopotamia.")

Cuneiform spread beyond Mesopotamia to Anatolia and the Levant (le-VANT)—the geographic region consisting today of such countries as Syria, Lebanon, Israel, Palestine, and Jordan. One cultural advance took place at Ebla (EH-bla) (modern Tell Mardikh), in northern Syria, where the world's earliest known dictionaries were written down between 2500 and 2300 B.C. A prosperous city, Ebla was known for commerce and artisanry as well as scholarship.

The Mesopotamians, meanwhile, made advances in mathematics, astronomy, medicine, and engineering. The Sumerians had two systems of numbers: a decimal system (powers of ten) for administration and business and a sexagesimal system (powers of sixty) for weights and mathematical or astronomical calculations. Like the Babylonians, we still divide hours by

Heroism and Death in Mesopotamia

The Epic of Gilgamesh sheds light on notions of gender and power in Mesopotamia. Men such as King Gilgamesh and his friend Enkidu have heroic adventures and risk death. Women lead quieter lives but are wiser and more realistic, as the following excerpts show. Here Gilgamesh, who wanders in his grief over the death of Enkidu, comes to the cottage of the tavernkeeper Siduri.

Who are you? You are no one that I know. / I am Gilgamesh, who killed Humbaba / And the bull of heaven with my friend.

If you are Gilgamesh and did those things, why / Are you so emaciated and your face half-crazed?

I have grieved! Is it so impossible / To believe? He pleaded. / My friend who went through everything with me / Is dead!

No one grieves that much, she said. / Your friend is gone. Forget him. / No one remembers him. He is dead Enkidu. Enkidu. Gilgamesh called out:

Help me. They do not know you as I know you?

Then she took pity on him / And let him enter and lie down and rest. / She gave him her bed to fall into and sleep / And rubbed his back and neck and legs and arms / When he was coming out of sleep, still muttering / About the one "who went with me through everything." / Like those old people who forget their listeners / Have not lived through their past with them, / Mentioning names that no one knows. / Enkidu, whom I loved so much, / Who went through everything with me / He died—like any ordinary man. / I have cried both day and night. / I did not want to put him in a grave. / He will rise, I know, one day. / But then I saw that he

was dead. / His face collapsed within / After several days, / Like cobwebs I have touched / With my finger.

She wiped his face with a moist cloth / Saying: Yes yes yes yes, / As she made him cooler / Trying to help him forget / By the steady softness of her flesh. / She moved her lips across his chest / And caressed the length of his tired body / And lay over him at night until he slept.

You will never find an end to grief by going on, / She said to the one half sleeping at her side, / Leaning forward to wipe the perspiration from his face. / His eyes were open though his whole self felt asleep / Far off alone in some deep forest / Planted in his flesh / Through which he felt his way in pain / Without the help / Of friends. / She spoke as to a child who could not understand / All the futility that lay ahead / Yet who she knew would go on to repeat / Repeat repeat the things men had to learn. The gods gave death to man and kept life for / Themselves. That is the only way it is. / Cherish your rests; the children you might have; / You are a thing that carries so much tiredness.

QUESTIONS

1. What differences between men and women appear in this excerpt?
2. Why is it so hard for Gilgamesh to accept Enkidu's death?
3. Is Siduri's view of the gods pessimistic or realistic?

sixty today. Furthermore, our modern system of numerical place-value notation—for example, the difference between 42 and 24—is derived, through Hindu-Arabic intermediaries, from the Babylonian system. The Babylonians were adept at arithmetic and could solve problems for which we would use algebra. A millennium before the Greek mathematician Pythagoras (who claimed to have studied the Mesopotamian tradition) proved the validity of the theorem that bears his name, they were familiar with the proposition that in a right triangle the square of the longest side is equal to the sum of the squares of the other two sides. In the first millennium B.C., the Babylonians developed a sophisticated mathematical astronomy (see page 34). As early as the seventeenth century B.C., they made systematic, if not always accurate, recordings of the movements of the planet Venus.

In medical matters, they demonstrated considerable critical ability. Physicians made advances in the use of plant products for medicines and in very rudimentary surgery. The Babylonians had a simple pregnancy test of moderate accuracy, for example, and their surgeons were experienced at setting broken bones. When they became ill, however, most people in Mesopotamia set more store by magic and incantations than by surgery or herbal medicine.

SECTION SUMMARY

- Approximately thirty city-states of southern Mesopotamia spoke Sumerian and flourished in the third millennium B.C.
- Sargon, an Akkadian, conquered the Sumerian cities of Mesopotamia and united them in one kingdom.
- Hammurabi's Code (1792–1750 B.C.), one of the earliest collections of laws, reveals the inequality and harshness of Mesopotamian society.
- Mesopotamians were religious, believed in many gods, and expected only a grim and shadowy Netherworld after death.
- Mesopotamia's rich culture excelled in mathematics, astronomy, and epic poetry.

EGYPT, TO CA. 1100 B.C.

How did the king's power affect various aspects of Egyptian society?

From Babylon to the valley of the Nile River was about 750 miles by way of the caravan routes through Syria southward—close enough to exchange goods and customs but far enough for a distinct Egyptian civilization to emerge. As in Sumer, civilization in Egypt arose in a river valley, but Egypt was much earlier than Mesopotamia in becoming a unified kingdom under one ruler. Moreover, ancient Egypt survived as a united and independent kingdom for over two thousand years (to be sure, with some periods of civil war and foreign rule). Egypt made great strides in a variety of areas of human achievement, from the arts to warfare. Western civilization borrowed much from Egypt, especially in technology and religion.

Ancient Egypt is a product of the unique characteristics of the Nile River (see **MAP 1.2**). Yet, most of Egypt is desert. Today, only about 5 percent is habitable by humans, including a few oases, the Nile Delta, and the Nile Valley itself, which extends about 760 miles from Cairo to Egypt's modern southern border: Upper Egypt, a long and narrow valley never more than about 14 miles wide. North of Cairo, in "Lower Egypt," the Nile branches out into the wide, low-lying delta before flowing into the Mediterranean Sea.

Divine Kingship

The fertility of the Nile River gave ancient Egypt a prosperous economy and optimistic culture. The river's annual floods, which took place during late summer and autumn, were generally mild and predictable. With less human effort than was required in Mesopotamia, the floodwaters could be used to irrigate most of the farmland in the Nile Valley. As a result, Egyptian agriculture was one of the wealthiest in the ancient world.

No wonder many Egyptians considered change as undesirable. Even death appeared to be a minor event compared with the eternal regularity of the Nile, which may help explain the prominence in Egyptian religion of belief in the afterlife. In addition, the static outlook helped promote the idea of an absolute, all-powerful, and all-providing king—namely, **pharaoh**.

Agriculture and settled village life emerged in Egypt around 5000 B.C. By 4000 B.C., villages had grown into towns, each controlling a strip of territory. By about 3100 B.C., Egyptian communities up and down the Nile Valley had cleared marshes and expanded the amount of land under cultivation, which in turn could support a larger population. The Nile Valley became one unified kingdom of Egypt, with a capital city perhaps at Memphis.

The new kingdom had monumental architecture, writing, and a king. For several centuries, Egyptians consolidated their institutions. Although few specifics are known about this Archaic Period (3200–2695 B.C.), it clearly laid the groundwork for the next era. Around 2700 B.C., a remarkable, distinctive, and relatively well-documented period of creativity began.

The history of third- and second-millennium B.C. Egypt is usually divided into three distinct eras of great prosperity:

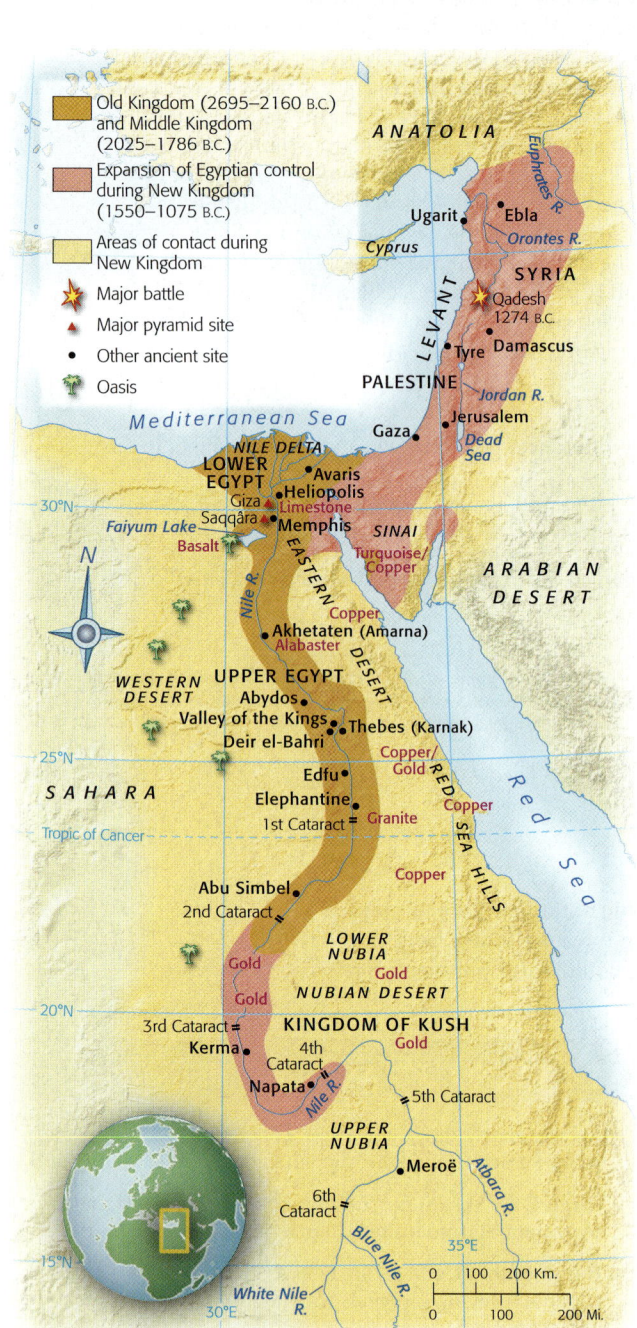

🌐 **MAP 1.2—Ancient Egypt and the Levant**
The unique geography of the Nile Valley and its fertile soil left a stamp on ancient Egypt. Egypt enjoyed trade and cultural contact—and sometimes went to war—with nearby lands such as Nubia and the Levant.

the Old Kingdom (2695–2160 B.C.), the Middle Kingdom (2025–1786 B.C.), and the New Kingdom (1550–1075 B.C.). Each kingdom is subdivided into dynasties, that is, ruling families. Between the kingdoms, central authority broke down in the Intermediate Periods. Broadly speaking, the Old Kingdom was an era of spectacular creativity and originality, symbolized by the building of the Great Pyramids; the Middle Kingdom, an era of introspection and literary production; and the New Kingdom, an era in which Egypt's traditional isolation gave way to international diplomacy and expansion.

Egypt's was the first government in recorded history to govern a large territory. Indeed, a chart of Egypt's power structure would look like a pyramid, with a broad base of laborers and artisans supporting a small commanding elite. The holder of the highest point of power was considered so important that, for centuries, Egyptians referred to the office rather than to the person, calling it "the Great House"—in Egyptian, *per-aa*, or "pharaoh," as the ruler himself (or occasionally herself) was eventually called.

Egyptian kingship was sacred monarchy. In Mesopotamia, the king generally claimed to have been appointed by the gods. In Egypt, pharaoh was deemed to *be* a god. The most dramatic symbol of the king's divinity was a building—or, rather, a series of buildings—the pyramids. The ancients built thirty-five major and many smaller pyramids, of which the best known are the Great Pyramids of Giza—three gigantic, perfectly symmetrical limestone tombs. Now, nearly five thousand years later, the pyramid of King Khufu (r. 2589–2566 B.C., better known by his Greek name, Cheops) is still the largest all-stone building in human history. Near the Great Pyramids stands the Great Sphinx, a human headed lion carved out of a rock outcropping, perhaps representing Khufu's son, King Khafre (r. 2558–2532 B.C.; Greek name, Chephren), for whom the second pyramid at Giza was built.

pharaoh Ancient Egyptians' title for their king, an absolute, all-powerful, and all-providing ruler.

Great Pyramids of Giza　Royal funerary monuments of three Egyptian kings of the twenty-sixth century B.C., the pyramids symbolize the power and ambition of the Old Kingdom. The pyramid of King Khufu (or Cheops, rearmost in the photo) is still the largest all-stone building in human history.　(Hisham Ibrahim/Photodisc/Getty Images)

The pyramids were not just monuments to an ego, but also temples where the king would continue to be worshiped and served in the afterlife. The structures served a political purpose as well. When the Great Pyramids were constructed, the kingdom of Egypt was still young and fragile. By building a pyramid, the king made a statement of his power—an eloquent, simple, and irrefutable statement. The sheer size of the Great Pyramids demonstrated the king's ability to organize a vast labor force. Indeed, the encampment of workers at Giza may have been the largest gathering of human beings to that date.

In theory, the king owned all the land, but in practice, Egypt's economy was a mixture of private enterprise and centralized control. The king delegated authority to a large group of officials, including governors, mayors, military commanders, judges, treasurers, engineers, agricultural overseers, scribes, and others. The highest official was the vizier, a sort of prime minister who had more day-to-day power than pharaoh himself.

The essence of good government was what the Egyptians called *ma'at*, whose basic meaning is "order"—in government, society, or the universe; *ma'at* can also mean "truth" or "justice." Egypt had a well-functioning system of judges who heard lawsuits, and it probably also had a detailed law code, although few written laws survive.

Life and Afterlife

Egyptian life was full of religious practices, from daily rituals and seasonal festivals to ethical teachings and magic. Egyptian religion tended toward *syncretism*—that is, the blending of mutually opposed beliefs, principles, or practices. For example, Egyptian mythology taught variously that the sky was a cow, was held up by a god or by a post, or was a goddess stretched over the earth. No one was troubled by such inconsistencies, as a modern worshiper might be, because Egyptians believed that a fundamental unity underlay the varieties of nature.

Egypt's religion had many greater and lesser deities, including human, animal, and composite gods. Various animals, from cats and dogs to crocodiles and serpents, were thought to represent the divine. Important deities included Thoth, the moon-god and god of wisdom; Nut, goddess of the sky; Ptah, a creator-god; Osiris, who invented agriculture and became lord of the dead; Horus, son of Osiris, a sky-god imagined as a giant falcon; and Isis, wife of Osiris and mother of Horus, a mother-goddess. Temples were numerous and lavish.

Egyptian religion focused on the afterlife. Unlike the Mesopotamians, the Egyptians believed that death could be a pleasant continuation of life on earth. Hence, they actively sought immortality. The wealthy built tombs that were decorated with paintings and inscriptions and stocked with cherished possessions for use after death. The most cherished possession of all was

Egyptian Book of the Dead   This scene from a lavishly illustrated papyrus shows a dead person's appearance before a divine court of judgment. His heart is being weighed in the balance to determine his fate in the afterlife.   (Courtesy of the Trustees of the British Museum)

the body, and the Egyptians provided for its preservation through their mastery of the science of embalming—thus, the Egyptian mummies.

Reserved for the king and his officials in the Old Kingdom, the afterlife became, as it were, democratized by the Middle Kingdom. By the Middle Kingdom, even ordinary Egyptians believed they could enjoy immortality after death, as gods, as long as they could purchase for their graves funerary texts containing the relevant prayers. The texts emphasize ritual—incantations, magic spells, prayers—as the key to eternal life. Yet, from time to time, we find other texts, especially from the Middle Kingdom, that say that ritual is not enough; ethical behavior also is required. New Kingdom texts describe the details of a dead person's appearance before a divine court for judgment. The sinless are admitted into eternal life in the kingdom of the blessed. The guilty, their heavy hearts devoured by a beast, suffer a second, final death.

Egyptian women did not enjoy equal status with men, but they had more freedom than women in other ancient societies, particularly in legal matters. As in Mesopotamia, so in Egypt, a woman could buy or sell, bequeath or inherit, sue or testify in court, but a married Egyptian woman, unlike her eastern sisters, could do so without a male guardian's approval. A married woman in Egypt remained legally independent. She could own property without her husband's involvement. But how often did women exercise such privileges? Egyptian women worked in agriculture and trade, in the textile and perfume industries, in dining halls, and in entertainment, but they were rarely managers. Women also served as priestesses of various kinds. Yet, in Egypt, as elsewhere, women were expected to make the home the focus of their activities.

War Abroad, 1786–ca. 1150 B.C.

The humane attitudes of the Middle Kingdom were swept away after about 1700 B.C., when Semitic-speaking immigrants from Canaan*—the Hyksos (HICK-sos)—conquered much of Egypt. In many ways gentle conquerors, the Hyksos worshiped Egyptian gods, built and restored Egyptian temples, and intermarried with natives. As foreigners, however, the Hyksos were unpopular. Eventually, a war launched from Upper Egypt, which had retained a loose independence, drove the Hyksos out.

The first restored Egyptian ruler of the New Kingdom was Ahmose I (r. 1550–1525 B.C.). His Egypt proved to be a new Egypt indeed. The Hyksos had brought advanced military technology to Egypt, including the horse-drawn war chariot, new kinds of daggers and swords, and the composite bow. Made of laminated materials, including wood, leather, and horn, the composite bow could hit a target at 600 yards.

Warlike, expansionist, and marked by a daring attempt at religious reform, the New Kingdom's Eighteenth Dynasty (1540–1293 B.C.) has long held a special fascination for historians. One of the dynasty's memorable names is that of Queen Hatshepsut (HAT-shep-soot). Widow of Thutmose II (r. 1491–1479 B.C.), Hatshepsut first served as regent for her young stepson and then assumed the kingship herself (r. 1479–1457 B.C.). Other Egyptian queens had exercised royal power before, but Hatshepsut was the first to call herself king. Although Hatshepsut dispatched Egyptian armies to fight, her reign is best known for peaceful activities: at home, public works and temple rebuilding; abroad, a commercial expedition over the Red Sea to the "Land of Punt" (perhaps modern Somalia, in eastern Africa).

After her death, Hatshepsut was succeeded by her stepson, Thutmose III (r. 1479–1425 B.C.). Late in his reign, he tried to erase his stepmother's memory by having Hatshepsut's statues destroyed and her name expunged from records—an attempt, perhaps, to cut off a claim to the throne by her supporters. A warrior pharaoh, Thutmose III, led his dynasty's armed expansion in western Asia and northern Africa. Thutmose won his greatest victory during his first campaign, at the Battle of Megiddo in Canaan in 1457 B.C. (see **Map 1.2**), where Egypt's triumph prevented the kingdom of Mitanni from expanding southward. Egypt now ruled an empire with territory in Nubia and Canaan.

The years from about 1450 to about 1300 B.C. marked a period of peace among the great powers from Egypt to Anatolia and Mesopotamia—what historians call the first international system.

---

* Canaan is an ancient name for the lands currently called Israel, Palestine, and coastal Syria and Lebanon.

The arts of peace are illustrated in surviving treaties and letters between monarchs, many of which come from Amarna.

The Amarna Archives (mid-fourteenth century B.C.), written in Akkadian cuneiform, illustrate formal communication among states. Rulers of great powers addressed each other as "brother," while Canaanite princes called pharaoh "my lord and my Sun-god" and assured him that they were "thy servant and the dirt on which thou dost tread." The texts reveal a system of gift exchange and commerce, politeness and formality, alliance and dynastic marriage, subjects and governors, rebels and garrisons. Because of a rough equality of power, no king was likely to defeat the others, so the parties avoided all-out war. They preferred instead to compete by jockeying for allies among the small Canaanite border states.

Sometimes, the competition turned into war. By the late fourteenth century B.C., Egypt had a new rival abroad, the **Hittites**, who had built a great empire in Anatolia. The Hittites were masters of the horse and rank among the leading charioteers of what was the golden age of chariot battle. They made full use of Anatolia's mineral wealth and made a limited number of iron weapons as well as the more usual bronze.

The Hittite state was vibrant if often divided. Hittite kings were powerful, but they had to deal with a strong nobility. Hittite queens and queen mothers often had considerable power. Puduhepa (pu-du-HE-pa), wife of King Hattusilis (hat-tu-SIL-is) III (r. 1278–1250 B.C.), played a memorable role in state affairs. Some of her prayers were written down and survive to this day.

Hittite is the oldest recorded Indo-European language, the language group to which English belongs. Thousands of Hittite texts have survived. They paint a picture of a sophisticated society with rich traditions in law, scholarship, poetry, and religion. One thing that stands out in their texts is the Hittites' vivid sense of history.

During the Hittite New Kingdom (ca. 1380–1180 B.C.), the Hittites' power extended into Syria and northern Mesopotamia (see **MAP 1.3**), which became the arena of conflict with

Hittites Builders of a great empire in Anatolia in the Late Bronze Age, the Hittites fought Egypt to a standstill and made history's first peace treaty between equals. Hittite is the oldest recorded Indo-European language, the language group to which English belongs.

🌐 **MAP 1.3—The International System, ca. 1500–1250 B.C.**

This era of competing kingdoms and city-states witnessed considerable war, especially between Egypt and the Hittites for control of the Canaanite states. Yet it was also a period of international trade, diplomacy, and, from 1450 to 1300 B.C., peace.

Peace and Brotherhood

After the stalemate at Qadesh (1274 B.C.) the kings of Egypt and the Hittites (referred to below as Hatti) agreed to make peace permanently. The result was a landmark of history, the first peace treaty between equals. A copy of this treaty is displayed in the United Nations building in New York City.

Preamble

P1 (A obv. 1–3) [The treaty which] Ramses, [Beloved] of Amon, Great King, King [of Egypt, Hero, concluded] on [a tablet of silver] with Hattusili, [Great King], King of Hatti, his brother, in order to establish [great] peace and great [brotherhood] between them forever. . . .

Purpose of Treaty; Previous Relations

P3 (A obv. 7–13) I have now established good brotherhood and good peace between us forever, in order likewise to establish good peace and good brotherhood in [the relations] of Egypt with Hatti forever. As far as the relations of the Great King, King of Egypt, [and] the Great King, King of Hatti, are concerned, from the beginning of time and forever [by means of a treaty] the god has not allowed the making of war between them. . . .

Future Relations

P4 (A obv. 13–18) And Ramses, Beloved of Amon, Great King, King [of Egypt], has indeed created <it> (the relationship) [on] this [day] by means of a treaty upon a tablet of silver, with [Hattusili], Great King, King of Hatti, his brother, in order to establish good peace and good brotherhood [between them] forever. He is [my] brother, and I am his brother. <He is at peace with me>, and I am at peace with him [forever. And] we will create our brotherhood and our [peace], and they will be better than the former brotherhood and peace of [Egypt with] Hatti. P5 (A obv. 19–21) Ramses, Great King, King of Egypt, is in good peace and good brotherhood with [Hattusili], Great King of Hatti. The sons of Ramses, Beloved of Amon, <Great King>, King of Egypt, will be at peace and [brothers with] the sons of Hattusili, Great King, King of Hatti, forever.

And they will remain as in our relationship of brotherhood [and of] peace, so that Egypt will be at peace with Hatti and they will be brothers like us forever.

Non-aggression

P6 (A obv. 22–27) And Ramses, Beloved of Amon, Great King, King of Egypt, for all time shall not open hostilities against Hatti in order to take anything from it. And Hattusili, Great King, King of Hatti, for all time shall not open hostilities against Egypt in order to take [anything] from it. The eternal regulation which the Sun-god and the Storm-god made for Egypt with Hatti is intended <to provide> peace and brotherhood and to prohibit hostilities between them. . . .

Defensive Alliance

P7 (A obv. 27–30) And if someone else, an enemy, comes against Hatti, and Hattusili, [Great King, King of Hatti], sends to me: "Come to me to my aid against him," then [Ramses, Beloved] of Amon, Great King, King of Egypt, must send his infantry and his chariotry and they will defeat [his enemy and] take revenge for Hatti.

P8 (A obv. 31–33) And if Hattusili, Great King, King of Hatti, [becomes angry] with his own [subjects], after they have offended against him, and he sends to Ramses, Great King, King of Egypt, on account of this, then Ramses, Beloved of Amon, must send his infantry and his chariotry, [and] they will destroy all with whom he is angry. . . .

[The next two paragraphs repeat these obligations but with the roles of the two kings reversed.]

Fugitives

. . . P18 (A obv. 60–64) [And if] a single man flees from [Hatti, or] two men, [or three men, and they come to] Ramses, Beloved [of Amon, Great King, King] of Egypt, his brother, [then Ramses], Beloved of Amon, Great King, [King of Egypt, must seize them and send them] to Hattusili, his brother [. . .]—for they are brothers. But [they shall not punish them for] their offenses. They shall [not] tear out [their tongues or their eyes]. And [they shall not mutilate(?) their ears or [their] feet. [And they shall not destroy(?) their households, together with their wives] and their sons.

QUESTIONS

1. What does the treaty mean by "good brotherhood and good peace"?
2. In what ways does the treaty display more concern for kings than for their subjects?
3. What punishments were usually given to fugitives from justice?

Source: "Peace and Brotherhood" from Gary Beckman, *Hittite Diplomatic Texts*, 2/e, pp. 96–99. Copyright © 1999. Reprinted by permission of Society of Biblical Literature.

Egypt. The most dramatic episode was the Battle of Qadesh in northern Syria in 1274 B.C., where twenty thousand Egyptian troops faced seventeen thousand Hittites. Qadesh is the first well-documented battle in history. Since neither of the two evenly matched powers managed to conquer the other, they made peace. The treaty between them still survives, and it is the oldest surviving peace treaty between equals. (See the feature, "The Global Record: Peace and Brotherhood.")

Egyptian Queen This elegant, red granite statue of the pharaoh Hatshepsut (r. 1479–1457 B.C.) is one of the few to depict her as a woman. She is usually shown as a man, complete with beard, to symbolize her royal power. Centuries later the proportions and carving techniques of Egyptian stone sculpture would influence the Greeks, although Greek artists chose less to copy the Egyptians than to try to outdo them (see the photo on page 64).
(Brian Brake/Photo Researchers, Inc.)

Amarna reform Term for the ancient Egyptian king Amenhotep IV's seizure of power from temple priests by replacing the god Amun-Re with Aten and renaming himself Akhenaten.

However, peace was temporary. Between about 1200 and 1150 B.C., the international system came to a crashing end. From Mesopotamia to Greece, from Anatolia to Egypt, one state after another collapsed. Surviving evidence is fragmentary, but it suggests that both foreign and domestic problems were devastating. Raiders and invaders beset the eastern Mediterranean in this period. Called "Sea Peoples" by the Egyptians, they attacked both on land and at sea. We do not know precisely who they were. In addition, some evidence of regional famine and climatic change indicates that natural causes may have led to disruption and rebellion.

Whatever the cause, what followed would prove to be a different world. Yet the end of the international system did not result in the disappearance of ancient cultures. Although new peoples appeared and old peoples changed, both continued to borrow from the cultures that had flowered before 1200 B.C.

Reform at Home and Its Aftermath, 1352–1075 B.C.

Empire brings power, and power often causes conflict. In imperial Egypt during the fourteenth century B.C., kings and priests struggled over authority. Consider the Amarna (a-MAR-na) reform, named for a major archaeological site at the modern town of Tell el-Amarna.

The **Amarna reform** was carried out by Thutmose III's great-great-grandson, King Amenhotep IV (r. 1352–1336 B.C.). Earlier, the god Amun-Re had become the chief deity of the New Kingdom. As supporters of imperialism, his temple priests had been rewarded with enough land and wealth that their power now rivaled pharaoh's own. Amenhotep IV responded by forbidding the worship of Amun-Re and replacing him with the god Aten, the solar disk. The king changed his own name to Akhenaten ("pleasing to Aten"). He also created a new capital city: Akhetaten (modern Amarna). Akhenaten's wife, Nefertiti, figures prominently in Amarna art, and she too may have played an important role in the reform.

The reformers gained power, but we need not doubt their sincerity. Contemporary literature suggests intense religious conviction in Aten as a benevolent god and one who nurtured not only Egypt but all countries. Although the Aten cult focuses on one god, only Akhenaten and his family were permitted to worship Aten directly; the rest of the Egyptian population was expected to worship the god through pharaoh.

Bold as the reform was, it was too radical to last. After Akhenaten's death, his son-in-law and successor, Tutankhaten (r. 1336–1327 B.C.) restored good relations with the priests of Amun-Re, which he signaled by changing his name to Tutankhamun. The Amun-Re cult was revived, the Aten cult was abolished, and the city of Akhetaten was abandoned.

Arts and Sciences in the New Kingdom

The Egyptians were superb builders, architects, and engineers. In addition to pyramids and irrigation works, they constructed monumental royal tombs, palaces, forts, and temples, and they erected looming obelisks. At their best, Egyptian architects designed buildings in harmony with the unique landscape—one of the reasons for the structures' lasting appeal. Their most original and enduring work was done in stone. Stone temples, for example, culminated in the imposing pillared structures of the New Kingdom. That period also saw the construction of rock-cut temples, the most famous of which is Ramesses II's (r. 1279–1213 B.C.) project at Abu

Hittite God   This figurine in gold, standing only 1.5 inches high, represents Hittite art of the Old Kingdom (ca. 1650–1450 B.C.). The clothes, shoes, and conical hat are typical of Hittite depictions of gods.   (Louvre, Paris, France/Réunion des Musées Nationaux/Art Resource/NY)

Simbel (see **MAP 1.2**). In front of the temples sit four colossal statues of Ramesses, also carved out of rock. Obelisks were slender, tapering pillars carved of a single piece of stone. Inscribed with figures and hieroglyphs, and usually erected in pairs in front of a temple, obelisks were meant to glorify the sun-god.

Throughout history, royal courts have excelled as patrons of the arts; the Egyptian court was one of the first and greatest. Egyptian craftsmen were master goldsmiths, glassmakers, and woodworkers. The major arts are well represented in tombs, which were decorated with rich, multicolored wall paintings, the first narrative depictions.

Sculpture was another art form in which Egyptians excelled. Carved in stone, wood, or metal, Egyptian sculpture is a study in contrasts. The body posture is usually rigid and stiff, the musculature only sketchy; the face, in contrast, is often individualistic, the expression full of character and drawn from life. Statues represent kings and queens, gods and goddesses, husbands and wives, adults and children, officials, priests, scribes, and animals.

Ancient Egyptian literature is notable for its variety. Religious subjects, historical and commemorative records, technical treatises in mathematics and medicine, and secular stories survive alongside business contracts and royal proclamations. Egyptian writing is best known for hieroglyphs. Elaborate and formal, hieroglyphs were generally used after the Archaic Period only for monuments and ornamentation. Two simplified scripts served for everyday use.

The people who built the pyramids had to be skilled at arithmetic and geometry. Egyptians were able to approximate pi (the ratio of the circumference of a circle to its diameter) and to solve equations containing one or two unknowns. The Egyptian calendar was also a remarkable achievement. Based on observation of the star Sirius, the Egyptian calendar, with its 365-day year, approximates the solar calendar. Corrected to 365 1/4 days, it survives to this day as the calendar of Europe, the Americas, and much of the rest of the world.

Egyptian medical doctors were admired in antiquity and in demand abroad. They knew how to set a dislocated shoulder and used a full battery of splints, sutures, adhesive plasters, elementary disinfectants (from tree leaves), and burn treatments (fatty substances). One Egyptian treatise offers something like modern triage, dividing diseases into three categories: treatable, possibly treatable, and untreatable. Egyptian doctors may have done postmortem dissection in order to understand the human body better.

SECTION SUMMARY

- The Nile River, with its dependable annual flooding, gave ancient Egypt fertile soil, economic prosperity, and an optimistic worldview.

- Egypt invented the idea of worshiping the king as a god; eventually, the king became known as pharaoh.

- Egyptians believed in a happy afterlife after death, as long as the gods judged that the dead person had led a life without sin.

- Egypt's New Kingdom was a great military power that expanded into southwest Asia.

- The earliest known Indo-European civilization is that of the Hittites, who established a great kingdom in today's Turkey and left thousands of documents.

- The conflicts between Hittites and Egyptians led to history's first great system of diplomacy, its first well-documented battle (Qadesh), and its first peace treaty between equals.

- The Amarna reform of the 1300s was history's first great struggle between church and state.

- The Egyptians excelled at architecture, such as the pyramids, as well as at sculpture and medicine, and they invented the solar calendar that we still use (in revised form) today.

- We are not sure why, but the great civilizations of the ancient Near East all either declined, split apart, or collapsed not long after 1200 B.C.

CHAPTER SUMMARY

The earliest human beings, probably beginning before 70,000 B.C., invented human culture—that is, they developed communications well enough that people could cooperate and exploit their natural environment by means of technology. Next came the move from a food-collecting to a food-producing economy. After beginning in the Fertile Crescent region of western Asia shortly after 10,000 B.C., food production spread to Europe beginning around 7000 B.C. Over the thousands of years following the invention of agriculture, human society became more complex and won increasing control of the natural environment. The result was the emergence of civilization in Egypt and Mesopotamia after 3500 B.C. The first cities appeared in Mesopotamia about 3500 B.C. and maybe even earlier. Writing was invented independently in Mesopotamia and Egypt between 3500 and 3000 B.C. In Mesopotamia, the Sumerians and Akkadians flourished in city-states, which were eventually conquered and united into a kingdom. The Mesopotamians wrote the first law codes, including the famous Hammurabi's Code (1792–1750 B.C.). Mesopotamians were religious, believed in many gods, and expected only a grim and shadowy Netherworld after death. Mesopotamia's rich culture excelled in mathematics, astronomy, and epic poetry.

Egyptian society and culture was focused on the king. Egypt invented the idea of worshipping the king as a god; eventually, the king became known as pharaoh. Early Egypt was relatively peaceful and inward-looking, but after a period of foreign rule, the newly liberated Egypt of the New Kingdom was a great military power that expanded into southwest Asia. The Egyptians excelled at architecture, such as the pyramids, as well as at sculpture and medicine, and they invented the solar calendar that we still use (in revised form) today.

Our language, English, belongs to the Indo-European language group; the first known Indo-European civilization is that of the Hittites, the dominant power in Anatolia from 1650 to 1180 B.C. The conflicts between Hittites and Egyptians led to history's first great system of diplomacy, its first well-documented battle (Qadesh), and its first peace treaty between equals. The great civilizations of the ancient Near East all either declined, split apart, or collapsed not long after 1200 B.C. Although this destruction is often attributed to the Sea Peoples, the cause is still uncertain.

FOCUS QUESTIONS

- How did the earliest human beings adapt to their environments and create the first civilizations?

- What were the Mesopotamians' major contributions to government, religion, and art and culture?

- How did the king's power affect various aspects of Egyptian society?

 This icon will direct you to additional materials on the website: www .cengage.com/history/ noble/westciv6e

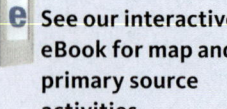 **See our interactive eBook for map and primary source activities.**

KEY TERMS

hominids (p. 4)
hunter-gatherers (p. 6)
Neolithic Revolution (p. 7)
Europe (p. 8)
cuneiform (p. 10)

papyrus (p. 11)
Sumerians (p. 13)
city-states (p. 13)
Hammurabi's Code (p. 15)

Epic of Gilgamesh (p. 16)
pharaoh (p. 19)
Hittites (p. 22)
Amarna reform (p. 24)

NOTES

1. James B. Pritchard, ed., *Ancient Near Eastern Texts Relating to the Old Testament*, 3d ed., with Supplement (Princeton, N.J.: Princeton University Press, 1969), p. 107.

CHAPTER OUTLINE

Bull from Ishtar Gate, Babylon
(Bildarchiv Preussischer Kulturbesitz/Art Resource, NY)

The Ship, the Sword, and the Book: Western Asia ca. 1500–400 B.C.

The bull in brick relief shown on the left symbolizes power even today, twenty-six hundred years after it was molded and glazed. About 4 feet high, this bull was one of several dozen figures of bulls and dragons that decorated the massive Ishtar Gate, which led through the inner town wall of Babylon (BAB-eh-lon) into the palace. The gate represents only a small part of a magnificent reconstruction of the city by the Neo-Babylonian kings who ruled western Asia around 600 to 539 B.C.

Imagine the king's surprise had he known that under his nose an obscure prophet—we know him only as "Second Isaiah" (eye-ZAY-ah)—was preaching a bold message to his compatriots, a conquered people living in exile in Babylon. Isaiah reminded them that Yahweh (YAH-way), their god, was a god of justice and mercy—the one and only true god of the entire world—and that Yahweh had chosen the king of mountainous, backward Persia to conquer western Asia and redeem Yahweh's people. The Neo-Babylonian king might have laughed at the idea. Yet the Persians, under Cyrus the Great, conquered Babylon in 539 B.C. and proclaimed the freedom of Yahweh's people—the Jews—to return to Palestine and re-establish the Temple to their god in the city of Jerusalem (juh-ROO-suh-lem). They did so, and around this time, they wrote down their religious and historical traditions in large sections of what would become the Hebrew Bible, or Old Testament.

It was a momentous development, because the Hebrew Bible founded the West's religious tradition. Along with Greece and Rome, ancient Israel may be considered one of the three founders of the West. Greece began the western tradition of philosophy and politics; Rome began Western law and administration. Israel gave the West ethical monotheism, the idea that God is one and that everything he does is good.

In contrast to ancient Israel, the other peoples studied in this chapter are all ancestors of the West: the Phoenicians and other Canaanites, the Neo-Babylonians and the other great empires of the era, the Assyrians and Persians. Traders or conquerors, they came to power through merchant ships or by the sword, but once in power they spread civilization, serving as conduits through which the achievements of earlier civilizations were transmitted. They spread trading networks that brought the alphabet to the Greeks, which would prove essential to preserving the brilliant culture that later developed in Greece. They built great empires whose institutions were eventually transformed into notions of mass citizenship under law and justice in a universal empire by the third founder of the West, Rome.

The first half of the first millennium B.C., therefore, left a divergent legacy to the West. On the one hand, new empires arose that were more systematically organized, farther-flung, and more diverse ethnically than those created before. On the other hand, prophets and poets looked in new and deeper ways into the human soul.

FOCUS QUESTIONS

- Who were the Phoenicians and what did they contribute to Western civilization?

- What made the first-millennium B.C empires of the Assyrians, Neo-Babylonians, and Persians so much more effective than earlier empires?

- What was the religious experience of ancient Israel, and what is its legacy today?

This icon will direct you to additional materials on the website: www.cengage.com/history/noble/westciv6e

See our interactive eBook for map and primary source activities.

In this chapter we look at the deeply influential developments in empire, religion, and thought forged in the first half of the first millennium B.C. At the same time, we consider the peaceful expansion in this era, through trade and colonization, particularly under the Phoenicians. Finally, we examine the material innovation that has earned the period the title "Iron Age."

TRADERS INVENT THE ALPHABET: CANAANITES AND PHOENICIANS, CA. 1400–450 B.C.

Who were the Phoenicians and what did they contribute to Western Civilization?

Canaan (CAY-nan) is an ancient name for the lands currently called Israel, Palestine, Lebanon, and Syria. Often eclipsed by Egypt, Mesopotamia, and the Anatolian kingdoms, the Canaanite (CAY-nan-ites) city-states made important contributions to the West. Not only did they take part in the first international system of states, the era documented by the Amarna Archives ca. 1450–1300 B.C., but they also served as the cradle of Western writing systems. After surviving the invasions of the Sea Peoples, the Canaanite city-states on the coast prospered in the first millennium B.C. Now known as Phoenicians, they were great sailors who planted colonies throughout the Mediterranean and spread the alphabet.

The Canaanite City-States, ca. 1400–1200 B.C.

Canaanite centers thrived both inland and on the Mediterranean coast. The first flowering of Canaanite civilization came in the third millennium B.C. at such sites as Ebla, but Ebla's greatest days were behind it after being conquered around 2000 B.C. To find a much more vibrant city in Syria after 2000 B.C., we need only look at the coast and the city of **Ugarit** (see **MAP 1.3**). Ugarit (OO-ga-rit) was a thriving Mediterranean port, especially around 1400 to 1180 B.C. It was located in what is today Syria, at the modern Ra's Shamrah, near today's port of Latakia. Further south, in what is today Lebanon, other Canaanite cities also existed in the second century B.C., such as Tyre, Sidon, Byblos, and Beirut.

A multiethnic city, Ugarit's cosmopolitanism made it distinctive among western Asian city-states. As a trading center, it linked ships coming from the eastern Mediterranean island of Cyprus or the Anatolian ports with land caravans heading to Babylonia. The native inhabitants of Ugarit spoke a Semitic language. The merchants of Ugarit, however, were often foreigners, and the bazaars echoed with a multitude of languages. In its heyday, Ugarit housed documents written in at least four different languages.

Ugarit played an important role in the spread of one of history's most important writing systems: the **alphabet**. Unlike the pictographic or syllabic systems of Mesopotamia, Egypt, and China, in an alphabet each letter—that is, written symbol—stands for one sound in a spoken language or for several closely related sounds such as the "s" in "say" and the "s" in "was." In the 1300s B.C., scribes in Ugarit developed an alphabet. It was not the first alphabet, however. In Egypt, in the desert west of the Nile, limestone inscriptions have recently been found in a Semitic script with Egyptian influences. Dated to about 1900 to 1800 B.C., during the Middle Kingdom, the writing is now recognized as the earliest known example of an alphabet.

We do not know whether that alphabet was invented by Egyptians or by speakers of a Semitic language that were visiting Egypt, nor do we know if that alphabet influenced Ugarit. What is clear is that Ugaritic scribes invented thirty cuneiform signs as an alphabet to write their Semitic language. Later adapted by the Phoenicians and, through them, the Greeks, the Ugaritic alphabet is the source of the Roman alphabet, used today by English and many other languages around the world.

The Phoenicians, ca. 1050–450 B.C.

Ugarit was destroyed by the Sea Peoples ca. 1180 B.C. Most Canaanite cities survived, however. After the invasions of the Sea Peoples and others, the Canaanites' once-large territory was reduced to a narrow strip along the Mediterranean in the area of modern Lebanon and northern Israel (see **MAP 2.2** on page 41). Between 1050 and 750 B.C., the inhabitants of the area flourished;

Ugarit A thriving, cosmopolitan Mediterranean port in what is today Syria, whose scribes developed an alphabet in the 1300s B.C.

alphabet A set of letters (written symbols) each of which represents roughly one sound in a spoken language.

historians call them, as did the ancient Greeks, "Phoenicians." Their purple-dyed textiles gave the Greeks their word for the color purple: *Phoenician*. Besides textiles, the Phoenicians exported the famous cedars of Lebanon for shipbuilding.

In the Hebrew Bible, the **Phoenicians** (fuh-NEESH-anz) loom large as merchants and seamen, as "traders the world honored" (Isaiah 23:8). Phoenicians were Canaanites, speakers of a Semitic language and heirs to the civilization that had prospered in Ugarit around 1400 B.C. (see page 30).

The Phoenicians were master shipbuilders and sailors. Around 600 B.C., their ships accomplished the first known circumnavigation of Africa. Around 450 B.C., they made the first known commercial sailing trip to the British Isles. Some scholars think they even reached Brazil. The most lasting Phoenician achievement at sea, however, was the planting of colonies in the Mediterranean, probably beginning in the ninth century B.C. Apparently, the colonies left a deep imprint. A recent genetic study shows that as many as 1 in 17 men living today on the coasts of North Africa and southern Europe may be directly descended from the Phoenicians.

Phoenician colonies were located in Cyprus, North Africa, Sicily, Malta, Sardinia, Italy, southern France, and Spain and Portugal. Many of their colonies eventually became independent states. The greatest Phoenician colony was Carthage (CAR-thidge), founded by the city of Tyre around 750 B.C. It was the major port city of the western Mediterranean for much of the next thousand years. There was also a Phoenician colony at the western gateway to the Mediterranean, at Gibraltar.

Phoenician culture was open to outside influences. Phoenician religious art is full of Egyptian sphinxes, coffins that look like mummy cases, and women wearing wigs in the style of Egypt's New Kingdom. But Phoenician art also contains Near Eastern seals and figures out of Greek myths.

Phoenician traders introduced advanced material goods, slaves, and possibly law codes to the Greeks. It was probably from the Phoenicians, whose alphabet derived from Ugarit, that the Greeks adapted their alphabet, probably shortly after 800 B.C.

One aspect of Phoenician culture is less attractive: child sacrifice. The Hebrew Bible, as well as Greek and Roman writers, state that Phoenician and other Canaanite parents sacrificed a child, especially their first-born child, to a god in return for divine favor. Many Phoenician archaeological sites contain an area with large numbers of infant burials. While skeptics consider that evidence only of infant mortality, most scholars hold it as confirmation of the literary record.

Around 750 B.C., the Phoenician city-states lost their independence to the Assyrians, and in later years Neo-Babylonians, Persians, and other foreign conquerors followed. But Phoenician culture survived—at home, in the colonies, and among the many Mediterranean peoples influenced by it. The result, though unintended, was that Phoenician colonists exported the civilization of western Asia to the western Mediterranean.

CHRONOLOGY

ca. 1900–1800 B.C.	Earliest known alphabet
ca. 1400–1180 B.C.	Height of Ugarit
1250–1150 B.C.	Sea Peoples invade the eastern Mediterranean
1180 B.C.	Ugarit destroyed
1075–656 B.C.	Third Intermediate Period in Egypt
ca. 1050–750 B.C.	Height of Phoenician city-states
1004–928 B.C.	Reigns of David and Solomon
722 B.C.	Assyrians conquer kingdom of Israel
612 B.C.	Conquest of Nineveh ends Assyrian power
598 B.C.	Neo-Babylonians conquer kingdom of Judah
559–530 B.C.	Reign of Cyrus the Great
550–330 B.C.	Achaemenid Persian Empire
539 B.C.	Cyrus conquers Babylon; permits Jews to return to Palestine
ca. 425 B.C.	Judean assembly accepts the Torah
701 B.C.	Siege and destruction of Lachish

Phoenicians Canaanites whose civilization flourished about 1050–750 B.C. in present-day coastal Syria, where they established major trading ports. Master sailors, they planted colonies around the Mediterranean, many of which, including Carthage, became independent states.

ASSYRIANS, NEO-BABYLONIANS, AND PERSIANS, CA. 1200–330 B.C.

What made the first-millennium B.C empires of the Assyrians, Neo-Babylonians, and Persians so much more effective than earlier empires?

A ncestors of the West, three great multiethnic empires emerged between the 800s and 500s B.C. Ruthless soldiers, brutal conquerors, and innovative administrators, the Assyrians established an empire in western Asia and Egypt during the ninth through seventh centuries B.C. They were followed in turn by a Neo-Babylonian empire in the late seventh and sixth centuries.

🌐 **MAP 2.1—The Assyrian and Persian Empires**

In the 660s B.C., the Assyrians ruled the largest empire the ancient world had seen, extending from the Tigris to the Nile. The Persian Empire was even greater. Around 500 B.C., it reached from its heartland in southwestern Iran westward to Macedonia and eastward to India.

However, neither of these was as successful or as durable as the empire of the Persians (ca. 550–330 B.C.). At its height, the Persian Empire stretched from central Asia and northwest India in the east to Macedonia and Libya in the west (see **MAP 2.1**). Persia's vast empire was loosely governed by a Persian ruling elite and its native helpers. Unlike the ironfisted Assyrians, the Persians were relatively tolerant and respectful of their subjects' customs. Many of Persia's kings were followers of Zoroastrianism, an ethical and forceful religion. A period of relative peace in most of Persia's domains from the 530s to the 330s B.C. fostered widespread economic prosperity.

The Persians borrowed the administrative methods of the Assyrians and Medes (meedz) and the long-established officialdom of Babylon and built a new and durable imperial government. Their official art stressed the unity of the peoples of the empire under Persian leadership. Persian rule represented the greatest success yet in implementing the notions of universal kingship that dated back to Sargon of Agade (r. 2371–2316 B.C.) (see page 14). In turn, Persia transmitted the idea of absolute kingship to later ambitious rulers, from Alexander the Great to the caesars of Rome and from the Byzantine emperors to the Muslim caliphs.

Assyrians and Neo-Babylonians

Assyrians Warlike people who ruled the ancient Near East during the first millennium B.C. Their innovations included using cavalry as their main striking force and having weapons and armor made of iron.

The **Assyrians** already had a long history as a military and commercial power in the Bronze Age. They lived in what is today northern Iraq and spoke a Semitic language. Around 1200 B.C., their state collapsed during that era of international crisis (see page 24), but they held on to a small homeland of about 5,000 square miles, roughly the size of Connecticut. The toughened survivors emerged with an aggressive, expansionist ideology.

Assyria's greatest successes came in the eighth and seventh centuries. One by one, states large and small fell—Babylonia, Syria, the kingdom of Israel, Cilicia in southern Anatolia, even Egypt (though Assyrian rule there lasted only a generation). Assyria became the first state to rule the two great river valleys of the ancient Near East, the Nile and the Tigris-Euphrates (see **MAP 2.1**).

The Assyrians were warriors. Ashur, their main deity, was a war-god. Theirs was an ideology of power, conquest, and control. The key to Assyria's success was its army—100,000 to 200,000 men strong—which made an unforgettable impression on observers and foes. The Israelite prophet Isaiah of Jerusalem ("First Isaiah") said of Assyrian soldiers: "[Their] arrows are sharpened, and all their bows bent, their horses' hoofs are like flint, their chariot wheels like the whirlwind. Their growling is like that of a lion" (Isaiah 5:28–29). He might have added that Assyrian spearmen, archers, and cavalrymen were equipped with weapons and armor of iron.

Thanks to new heating and cooling techniques, metal smiths in the ancient world produced an alloy of carbon and iron that was harder and more durable than bronze. It was also easier to obtain since iron ore is widespread—unlike tin, an essential element of bronze. Iron tools and weapons were often stronger and cheaper than their bronze predecessors, which opened up new technical and military possibilities.

Adding to its might, Assyria was the first major state to employ regular cavalry units (rather than charioteers) as the main strike force. The Assyrians were also excellent engineers, adept at taking walled cities by siege.

In addition, the Assyrians displayed superb organizational skills. The central standing army was supplemented with draftees conscripted from around the empire. Provinces were kept small to prevent the emergence of separate power bases, and independent-minded nobles were regularly checked by the kings.

To control the restive subjects of their far-flung empire, the Assyrians met rebellion with ferocious reprisals. Disloyal cities were attacked and, if need be, destroyed. Sculptured reliefs and inscriptions were set up to show, often in gruesome detail, the fate awaiting Assyria's enemies. We see or read of cities burned to the ground; of men flayed alive, even though they had surrendered, and walls covered with their skin; and of piles of human skulls. (See the feature, "The Visual Record: The Siege of Lachish" on pages 44–45.)

The Assyrians also engaged in mass deportations. They uprooted the people of a conquered country, resettled them far away—often in Assyria itself—and colonized their land with Assyrian loyalists. The so-called Ten Lost Tribes of Israel—the people of the northern Israelite kingdom (see page 41)—were conquered by Assyria in 722 B.C., and many of them were transported to Mesopotamia, where they disappeared from history. (Those who remained in Israel mixed with colonists, and the new group became known, and scorned, as Samaritans.)

Assyrian policy was the result of careful calculation. The political goal was to punish rebellion; the economic goal was to create a varied labor force. For example, although it is estimated that the Assyrians deported several million people, they deported not whole populations but a carefully chosen cross section of professions. They also deported entire families together, to weaken deportees' emotional ties to their former homes.

Assyria's success also was due in part to the relative weakness of other powers. After a period of great warrior-pharaohs and builder-pharaohs during the Nineteenth Dynasty (ca. 1291–1185 B.C.), Egypt suffered a series of weak kings who lost power to the priests of Amun during the Twentieth Dynasty (ca. 1185–1075 B.C.). When the Twentieth Dynasty ended in 1075 B.C., the New Kingdom ended with it, and regional conflict between the Nile Delta and Upper Egypt broke out.

Egypt was at the mercy of factions and invaders for much of the Third Intermediate Period (1075–656 B.C.). Around 950, for example, the kingship came into the hands of Libyan mercenaries. From the eighth century on, their rule was challenged, in turn, by invaders from the south, rulers of a new Nubian kingdom called Kush (see **MAP 1.2** on page 18). Kushite pharaohs governed Egypt

Assyrian Winged Genie This alabaster relief comes from a temple of the Assyrian king Ashurnasirpal II (r. 883–859 B.C) at his capital of Calah (Nimrud). The figure holds an incense pouch in one hand and a pine cone in the other, perhaps symbols of the tree of life. (The Metropolitan Museum of Art, Gift of John D. Rockefeller, Jr., 1931 [31.72.1])

Phoenician Ivory   This delicately carved plaque of a cow and calf, just 3 inches high, illustrates the wealth of artistic talent at the disposal of the Phoenicians, whose civilization reached its peak between 1050 and 750 B.C.   (Iraq Antiquities Department)

from around 719 until 656, when they withdrew back south. It was they who faced the Assyrian attacks in 671 and 667.

The conquest of Egypt marked imperial Assyria's greatest extent—and its overextension (see **Map 2.1**). A coalition army consisting of soldiers from a new Babylonian kingdom and from the Medes (who had formed a powerful state in Iran) conquered Nineveh (NIN-eh-veh), the Assyrian capital, in 612 B.C. and defeated the remnants of the Assyrian army in battles in 609 and 605. Few of its subjects mourned the empire's passing.

The destruction of Assyria led to revival for Babylon, whose rulers attempted to recapture the glories of Hammurabi's day (see page 15). For a short period, until the Persian conquest in 539 B.C., the **Neo-Babylonian** dynasty (founded in 626 B.C.), as it is known today, and the Medes of Iran were the dominant military forces in western Asia. The Neo-Babylonian king Nebuchadrezzar II (neh-boo-khad-REZ-zar) conquered the kingdom of Judah (in southern Palestine) in 598 and destroyed Jerusalem, its capital, in 586. He deported many thousands of Judeans to Babylon, an event remembered by Christians and Jews as the Babylonian Captivity. Most of the rest of western Asia also fell to Nebuchadrezzar's troops. His most enduring achievement was rebuilding Babylon on a grand scale. In addition to the city's numerous temples, shrines, and altars, he created the so-called Hanging Gardens celebrated by later Greek writers. They describe the structure as a large terraced complex that Nebuchadrezzar built for his queen, although it may have been a plant-covered ziggurat.

The Neo-Babylonians and Assyrians both made great strides in astronomy. Their primary motive was not scientific but religious—that is, a belief in astrology (the study of the movements of heavenly bodies in the belief that they influence human affairs). Astrology led to advances in the scientific observation of the heavens. Assyrian priests had produced relatively accurate circular diagrams (astrolabes) that showed the positions of the major constellations, stars, and planets over the course of the year. By 600 B.C., Assyrian and Neo-Babylonian astronomers could predict solstices, equinoxes, and lunar eclipses.

Neo-Babylonians   Rulers of western Asia between 612 and 539 B.C., who elaborately rebuilt Babylon, creating the famous Hanging Gardens. They destroyed Jerusalem, deporting many Judeans in what is known as the Babylonian Captivity.

Astronomy in Mesopotamia reached its heights in the centuries after 500 B.C. The zodiac, a diagram showing the movement of the sun and planets relative to the constellations, was invented in Persian-ruled Babylon in the fourth century B.C. In the third and second centuries B.C., when Babylonia was under Hellenistic Greek rule, native scientists made impressive advances in mathematical astronomy, composing tables that could be used to calculate movements of the moon and planets. More sophisticated mathematical astronomy would not be produced in the West until the Scientific Revolution of the sixteenth century A.D.

Building the Persian Empire

A thousand miles east of Phoenicia, a great empire took root. Indo-European–speaking peoples, the Medes and Persians arrived in what is now western Iran, probably around 1500 B.C., but perhaps not until 900 B.C. The two peoples were closely related in language and customs. The Medes lived in the central Zagros Mountains. The Persians made their homeland farther south in Anshan (modern Fars). At first, the Medes ruled the Persians, but in 550 B.C., the tables were turned when the Medes were suddenly conquered by the young Persian king Cyrus the Great (r. 559–530 B.C.).

Persian Empire   Vast, prosperous, and law-abiding West Asian empire, from about 550 to 330 B.C., it represented the greatest success yet of a universal kingship. The Persians also built the first great navy.

It took Cyrus only twenty years to conquer most of western Asia and much of central Asia. Within five years of his death in 530 B.C., his son and successor, Cambyses (kam-BYE-seez) (r. 530–525 B.C.), added Egypt and Libya. Cambyses' successor, Darius (dah-RYE-us) (r. 521–486 B.C.), corralled northwestern India and Thrace. The frontier regions, especially Egypt, were often in revolt, and the attempt of Darius and his successor, Xerxes (ZURK-seez) (r. 486–465 B.C.), to extend Persian rule to Greece ended in failure (see pages 69–70). But the Achaemenid **Persian Empire** (named after a legendary founder, Achaemenes) survived for two hundred years, until a Greco-Macedonian army under Alexander the Great, king of Macedon (r. 336–323 B.C.), destroyed it.

Let us consider several reasons for the success of Achaemenid (ah-KEE-men-id) Persia. The first was military prowess. Persia was ruled by a warrior-aristocracy whose traditional values, according to the Greek historian Herodotus, were "riding, hunting, and telling the truth." The state was able to field a huge army of about 300,000 men, conscripted from the various subject peoples. Although the resultant hodgepodge of soldiers from across the empire did not always fight as a unit, a crack infantry group, called the 10,000 Immortals, provided a solid core. The Persians excelled as bowmen and cavalrymen. Following the Assyrians, they made cavalry into the decisive strike force of the battlefield, assigning a more minor role to chariotry. Persia was even more innovative at sea, where it had its subjects build the first great navy. Although Persians served as marines and sometimes as commanders, the rowers and seamen were usually Phoenicians or Greeks.

The second reason for Persia's success was political. Unlike the Assyrians, the Persians considered generosity and tolerance to be more effective than terrorism and brutality. As Cyrus prepared to attack Babylon, he portrayed himself as the champion of the traditional Babylonian religion, and Babylon surrendered to him without a fight. Cyrus also emphasized his continuity with earlier Mesopotamian history by adopting the traditional title of "King of Sumer and Akkad." He did not hesitate to break with Assyrian and Neo-Babylonian population transfers, as witnessed in his edict permitting the Jewish exiles in Babylon to return to Judea.

The third reason for Persia's success was its skill at administration and organization. Darius played a crucial role in reorganizing the imperial administration and finances. Like the Assyrian Empire, the Persian domain was divided into provinces, called *satrapies* (SAY-truh-peez). Each of the twenty satrapies was a unit of administration and tax collection. For the first time, taxes could be paid with a stable, official coinage: the gold daric (named after Darius) and the silver shekel. Coins had been invented in the kingdom of Lydia in western Asia Minor in the seventh century B.C. Croesus (CREE-sus) (r. 560–547 B.C.), Lydia's king, was known for his wealth—hence, the expression "rich as Croesus"—before Cyrus conquered him in 547 B.C.

The provincial governors, or *satraps*, were powerful, often quasi-independent figures, but the king tried to keep a firm hand on them. Each province had a royal secretary and was visited regularly by traveling inspectors called "the king's eyes." A network of good roads radiated from the capital cities of Susa and Persepolis. The most famous road, the so-called Royal Road, stretched 1,600 miles from western Iran to western Anatolia (see **Map 2.1**). Covering the whole distance took most travelers three months, but the king's relay messenger corps could make the trip in a week, thanks to a series of staging posts furnished with fresh horses.

Another unifying element was a society that was law-abiding and prosperous. Darius proclaimed in an inscription that he had fostered the rule of law: "These countries [of the empire] showed respect toward my law; as was said to them by me, thus it was done." Darius and other Persian kings helped create the conditions for compliance and security by taking an interest in the economy. For example, they opened to commercial traffic Persian roads and a canal connecting the Red Sea and the Nile.

Language, too, built unity. Not Persian, which relatively few people spoke, but Aramaic, the most widespread language of western Asia, became the empire's basic language of commerce and administration. A Semitic language related to Hebrew, Aramaic was first used by the Aramaeans (air-uh-MAY-unz), a nomadic people who settled in northern Syria about 1100 B.C. and ruled an area extending into Mesopotamia before succumbing to Assyrian conquest about 725 B.C. The Aramaeans dominated the overland trade routes, which, combined with the simple and easily learned Aramaic alphabet, contributed to the spread of their language. Aramaic facilitated the development of literacy and recordkeeping. Aramaic would become the common language of western Asia for over a thousand years, until Arabic replaced it; Jesus of Nazareth was to be its most famous native speaker.

The King of Kings

Persia's empire had several weaknesses. First, Cyrus had bequeathed a legacy as a charismatic war leader. Feeling the need to live up to his example, his successors sometimes undertook ambitious and expensive expeditions that failed, such as wars with the

Achaemenid Persian Silver   This silver rhyton (drinking vessel) is in the shape of a griffin, a mythological animal that is part lion and part eagle. Persian rulers commanded the talents of western Asia's best artists and craftsmen, silversmiths among them.   (Courtesy of the Trustees of the British Museum)

Scythians (a tough nomadic people in Ukraine) and the Greeks. Second, however mild Persian rule, however peaceful and prosperous, it was still ruled by foreigners and it still involved taxation. Persian officials, military garrisons, and colonists were found—and were resented—in every corner of the empire. Native resentment, particularly in Egypt, and the independence of certain satraps led to intermittent provincial revolts.

The exaltation of the Persian king served as a counterweight to rebellious tendencies. From Darius on, the Persian monarch tried to overawe his officials with his majesty and might. The "King of Kings," as the monarch called himself, sat on a high, gold and blue throne, dressed in purple, decked out in gold jewelry, wearing fragrant oils and cosmetics, and attended by corps of slaves and eunuchs (castrated men employed in high positions). Although he was not considered a god, he had to be treated with reverence. Persians spoke of the king's *khvarna*, his "kingly glory," a mysterious aura of power. Anyone who came into the royal presence had to approach him with a bow to the ground, face-down.

Impressive as the court ceremonial was, Persian kings were not all-powerful. They were bound by the rule of law and by the considerable power of Persia's proud nobility, on whom they relied to fill the top administrative positions. Competing factions of ministers, wives, concubines, eunuchs, and sons often brought intrigue and discord to court, especially in the fourth century B.C., a time of frequent rebellion.

Royal authority was symbolized in the decoration of the great palaces at Susa and Persepolis, a project begun by Darius I and completed by his son and successor, Xerxes. The Susa palace, the larger of the two, reflected the universality of the empire in the variety of hands that built it. Craftsmen from east and west took part in the construction. (See the feature, "The Global Record: The Subject Peoples of a Multicultural Empire.") The Persepolis palace, too, displayed the heterogeneity of the empire in its architecture. The palace was placed on a terrace, as in

Frieze at Persepolis This sculptured relief lines the stairway to the audience hall of King Darius (r. 521–486 B.C.). It depicts Persian nobles, well groomed and formally dressed, carrying flowers for the New Year's feast. (Ronny Jaques/Photo Researchers)

The Subject Peoples of a Multicultural Empire

The Persian Empire ruled more people than ever before, and the kings were proud of that. This inscription from the capital city of Susa, dated probably about 520 B.C., emphasizes the participation of a variety of peoples, from India to Egypt and the Aegean Sea, in the construction of King Darius's palace.

§2. I am Darius, the Great King, the king of kings, king of the lands, king of this earth, son of Hystaspes, an Achaemenid. And Darius the king says: "Ahura Mazda, who is the greatest of the gods, has created me, has made me king, has given me this kingdom, which is great, and which has good horses and good men. By the favor of Ahura Mazda, my father Hystaspes and Arsames, my grandfather, were both alive when Ahura Mazda made me king on this earth. Thus it was the desire of Ahura Mazda to choose me as his man on this entire earth, he made me king on this earth. I worshipped Ahura Mazda. Ahura Mazda brought me aid. What I ordered (to be done), this he accomplished for me. I achieved all of what I did by the grace of Ahura Mazda.

§3. "This palace which I built at Susa: its materials were brought from afar. The earth was dug down deep, until the rock was reached in the earth. When the excavation had been made, then rubble was packed down, some 40 cubits (ca. 65 feet) deep, another (part) 20 cubits deep. On that rubble the palace was constructed. And that earth, which was dug deep, and that rubble, which was packed down, and the sun dried bricks, which were molded, the Babylonian people—they performed (these tasks).

§4. "The cedar timber was brought from a mountain called Lebanon. The Assyrian people brought it to Babylon. From Babylon the Carians and Ionians brought it to Susa. The sissoo-timber was brought from Gandara and from Carmania. The gold which was worked here was brought from Sardis and from Bactria. The precious stone lapis lazuli and carnelian which was worked here was brought from Sogdiana. The precious stone turquoise, which was worked here, this was brought from Chorasmia. The silver and the ebony were brought from Egypt. The ornamentation with which the wall was adorned was brought from Ionia. The ivory which was worked here was brought from Ethiopia, and from India and from Arachosia. The stone columns which were worked here were brought from a village called Abiradu, in Elam. The stonecutters who worked the stone were Ionians and Sardians. The goldsmiths who worked the gold were Medes and Egyptians. The men who worked the wood were Sardians and Egyptians. The men who worked the baked brick were Babylonians. The men who adorned the wall were Medes and Egyptians."

§5. Darius the king says: "At Susa a very excellent work was ordered, a very excellent work was brought to completion. May Ahura Mazda protect me, and Hystaspes my father and my country."

QUESTIONS

1. What does Darius consider to be special signs that heaven favored him? Why does he choose these signs?

2. List all the different materials in the palace and all the different ethnic groups that brought them to Susa. What do you think was the most valuable material? Least valuable?

3. How does the variety of peoples and materials demonstrate Darius's power?

Source: From *The Persian Empire from Cyrus II to Artaxerxes I* (*LACTOR* 16), translated and edited by Maria Brosius, Copyright 2000 London Association of Classical Teachers. Reprinted by permission of L.A.C.T.

Mesopotamia, but contained columned halls as in Egypt, with Assyrian-style column capitals or tops. In Persepolis, a frieze of sculpted relief panels lining a monumental stairway leading to the palace emphasized the king's vast power. The panels depict an endless procession of the peoples of the world paying homage to the King of Kings: from the nobility to the Immortals, to Median and Persian soldiers, to tribute-bearing subjects from the ends of the earth. The overall feeling of the scene is static, as if the Persian Empire would last forever.

Zoroastrianism

Like ancient Israel, Persia developed a highly ethical religion in the first millennium B.C. From obscure beginnings, **Zoroastrianism** (zoh-roh-AS-tree-un-izm) became the religion of Persia that persisted until the Muslim conquest in the seventh century A.D. Although largely extinct in today's Iran, an Islamic country, Zoroastrianism still survives in small communities elsewhere, primarily in India. Some scholars argue that Zoroastrian beliefs eventually influenced Judaism and Christianity, as well as Roman paganism and Indian Buddhism.

It is easier to describe ancient Zoroastrianism in broad strokes than in detail, partly because the religion changed radically over the course of its ancient history, and partly because relatively little information survives before A.D. 300. This much is clear: The religion was founded by a great reformer and prophet named Zarathustra (*Zoroaster* in Greek). Zarathustra (zah-ruh-THOOS-truh) lived in

Zoroastrianism Religion founded about 1000–550 B.C. by the Persian prophet Zarathustra (*Zoroaster* in Greek). Zoroastrians believe in a supreme deity and a cosmic contest between good and evil within each individual.

SECTION SUMMARY

- Iron arms and armor, engineering skill, organizing ability, and brutality all helped build Assyria's empire, at its height in the 660s B.C.

- The Neo-Babylonian kingdom (626–539 B.C.) was famous for its Hanging Gardens and astronomers.

- Phoenicia's outstanding sailors spread the alphabet and established the great city of Carthage.

- From their homeland in Iran, the Persians built the ancient world's largest empire yet, the Achaemenid Empire (ca. 550–330 B.C.).

- Rather than try to "Persianize" the empire, the Persian kings emphasized the variety of peoples under their rule.

- Zoroastrianism, an ethical religion emphasizing the struggle between good and evil, flourished in Achaemenid Persia.

eastern Iran. His teachings survive in the *Gathas* ("Songs"), a portion of the Zoroastrian holy book called the *Avesta*. Some scholars date Zarathustra as late as 550 B.C.; others prefer an earlier date, 750 or even 1000 B.C.

Zarathustra's society was dominated by warriors whose religion consisted of blood cults, violent gods, animal sacrifice, and ecstatic rituals in which hallucinogens were eaten. Zarathustra rejected such violent practices in favor of an inward-looking, intellectual, and ethical religion. He favored ceremonies involving fire, considered a symbol of purity. Zarathustra was not a strict monotheist like the Jews, but he did emphasize the power of one god over all people, the supremely good and wise creator of the universe, whom he called Ahura Mazda ("Wise Lord"). Unlike the Jews, Zarathustra considered the problem of evil to be the central question of religion. If god was one, good, and omnipotent, how could evil exist?

Zarathustra's answer might be called *ethical dualism* (dualism is the notion of a grand conflict between good and evil). Ahura Mazda had twin children: the Beneficent Spirit and the Hostile Spirit. Each spirit had made a free choice: one for the "truth" and the other for the "lie"—that is, one for good and the other for evil. Every human being faces a similar choice between good and evil. "Reflect with a clear mind—man by man for himself—upon the two choices of decision, being aware to declare yourselves to Him before the great retribution," says Zarathustra.[1] Indeed, humanity is caught in a great cosmic struggle in which individuals are free to make a momentous choice. Zarathustra distinguished between two states of being: the spiritual and the material. The more a person pursued spiritual purity, the greater was the person's ability to choose good rather than evil.

Zarathustra held a linear conception of history, similar to that in the Hebrew Bible. His religion is marked by a strong *eschatology* (interest in the end of the world) as well as *soteriology* (belief in a savior). He believed that one day, through an ordeal by fire, Ahura Mazda would judge all the people who had ever lived. Those who had chosen good would be rewarded, and those who had chosen evil would be punished. Then would follow a Last Judgment in which the dead would be transfigured and restored to a glorious bodily existence. There would be, Zarathustra promised, "long destruction for the deceitful but salvation for the truthful." The notion of a savior who would initiate the Last Judgment is an early Zoroastrian belief, if perhaps not a doctrine of Zarathustra himself.

In later centuries, Zarathustra's followers eased his uncompromising rejection of Iranian paganism. Under the leadership of priests, known as *magi* (MAY-jye) in western Iran, the religion changed considerably. Lesser deities beneath Ahura Mazda were added to the Zoroastrian pantheon, in part, to suit the religion to the needs of the huge, multicultural Persian Empire.

It is tempting to attribute Cyrus's policy of toleration to the ethical teachings of Zarathustra, but it is uncertain whether Cyrus was Zoroastrian. We are on firmer ground with later Persian kings, particularly Darius I, who had an image of himself alongside Ahura Mazda carved on the face of an Iranian cliff. In an accompanying inscription Darius announces: "For this reason Ahura Mazda bore aid, and the other gods who . . . [exist], because I was not hostile, I was not a Lie-follower, I was not a doer of wrong—neither I nor my family. According to righteousness I conducted myself."[2]

ISRAEL, CA. 1500–400 B.C.

What was the religious experience of ancient Israel, and what is its legacy today?

In the first millennium B.C., a small, often-conquered people turned imperialism on its head. Human achievement is meaningless, they argued; only the power of divinity matters. There is only one god, they said; all other gods are false. The one true god had revealed himself not to the awesome, imperialistic Assyrians, but to the less powerful Hebrews—ancient Jews. They founded the Western tradition of religion. The God of ancient Israel eventually gave rise

to the God of Christianity and of Islam, as well as of modern Judaism.

The Hebrews, also known as Israelites, had existed as a people since about 1200 B.C. and perhaps for centuries earlier. They spoke a Semitic language.

The Hebrew Bible as a Historical Record

As literature and as religious teaching, the Bible is the most influential single text in the history of Western civilization. As a source of history, however, it presents difficulties. Many Jews and Christians today believe that God gave the Hebrew Bible (called the Old Testament by Christians) in its entirety to the Jewish people at Mt. Sinai. In addition, Jews believe that unwritten laws were handed down at Sinai as well, and that these laws were preserved via oral tradition across the generations. Scholars argue differently. They believe that the Hebrew Bible is man-made and that it is based on written sources that probably date back at least as far as the early Israelite monarchy of about 1000 B.C. Other parts of the Hebrew Bible are probably the product of an oral tradition, and the nature, antiquity, and reliability of that tradition are the subject of much scholarly debate.

Israelite Seal This seal stone, which shows a roaring lion, was used by a man named Shema, an official of King Jeroboam of Israel. The stone was used to make an impression in hot wax, creating a seal on a document. (Reuben and Edith Hecht Collection, University of Haifa, Israel/Erich Lessing/Art Resource, NY)

Archaeological evidence from the area of ancient Israel; a small number of inscriptions, that is, writings on stone or other durable material (almost all after 800 B.C.); and some information in Greek and Roman literary sources provide an alternative source of information. Yet, little of that alternative evidence sheds light on the period before about 1200 B.C., and it offers only partial insight into the later period. The historian needs both to pay attention to the Bible and to consider its nature.

The Hebrew Bible reached something close to its current form a century or two before the birth of Christ. It consists of three main sections: (1) the **Torah** (TOE-rah), also known as the Pentateuch, or five books of Moses (that is, the first five books of the Bible); (2) the Prophets, that is, the "historical" books of the early prophets (Joshua, Judges, Kings, and Chronicles) and the books of the later prophets (Isaiah, Jeremiah, Ezekiel, and the twelve "minor prophets"); and (3) the Writings, various books of poetry, proverbs, and wisdom literature.

Torah First five books of the Bible. Accepted as sacred by the Hebrews around 425 B.C., it relates the working out of God's pact, or covenant, with the Hebrews, his chosen people.

The books of the Hebrew (and Christian) Bible are canonical: one by one, each was accepted by established authority as sacred. Two key dates stand out in the canonization of the Hebrew Bible: 622 B.C. and about 425 B.C. On the first date, Josiah, king of Judah (see page 41), assembled "the entire population, high and low" to swear to obey "the scroll of the covenant which had been discovered in the house of the Lord" (the scroll probably was Deuteronomy, now the fifth book of the Torah). On the second date, a similar assembly of the people, called by the religious leader Ezra, swore to accept the five books of the Torah that had by then been assembled. The introduction of the Torah (literally, "teaching") made its worshipers into what they have been ever since: "a people of the Book," as the Muslims would put it centuries later. The written tradition and literacy became central to the Hebrews.

The Hebrews are the first people we know of to have a single national history book. That book was written not as secular history, but as sacred history. It is the story of the working out of God's pact, or **covenant**, with the Hebrews, his chosen people. All ancient peoples told stories of their semidivine foundation. Only the Hebrews imagined the nation created by an actual treaty between the people and their God.

covenant As told in the Hebrew Bible, the pact God made with Abraham, the first patriarch of Israel. In return for the land of Canaan and the promise of becoming a great nation, the Israelites agreed to worship no other gods.

The central fact of human existence in the Hebrew Bible is God's covenant with the Hebrews. Because of the covenant, history has meaning. History is the story of the success or failure of the Hebrew people in carrying out God's commandments. The focus is on the individual: on individual people taking actions that have not just moral, but military and political consequences that unfold over time.

Many of the themes, narrative details, and styles of writing in the Hebrew Bible derive from earlier cultures. The biblical Flood story, for example, seems to have been modeled on a similar flood in the *Epic of Gilgamesh* (see page 17). Biblical poems in praise of God are often similar to Egyptian poems in praise of pagan gods, and biblical wisdom literature (that is, works containing proverbs and rules of conduct) often recalls Egyptian or Babylonian parallels. In spite of such borrowings, the Hebrew Bible is dramatically different from its predecessors because it subordinates everything to one central theme: God's plan for humanity and, in particular, for his chosen people—the Hebrews.

The Emergence of Hebrew Monotheism, ca. 1500–600 B.C.

We first hear of the Hebrews, outside of the Bible, in an inscribed monument of the New Kingdom Egyptian pharaoh Merneptah (r. 1224–1214 B.C.). After a military expedition into Canaan (CAY-nan), pharaoh declared triumphantly that "Israel is laid waste." Most scholars accept this as evidence of an Israelite presence in Canaan, but the question is how did they get there? The Bible says that the **Israelites** settled Palestine by conquering its earlier inhabitants. Most scholars now reject that account. Archaeological evidence suggests, rather, a more complex process. The Israelites, it seems, were a combination of three groups: armed conquerors, shepherds who gradually entered the country and later settled down to farming, and dispossessed and oppressed Canaanites who rebelled against their masters.

From such sources, the Israelites may have emerged. The Bible, however, tells a different story of Israelite origins. Although much of it is credible, none of it is confirmed by nonbiblical sources. Still, the biblical story of Israelite origins has been so influential in later Western culture that we must examine it. If one follows the Bible, Hebrew history began sometime during the period 2000 to 1500 B.C., with the patriarchs, or founding fathers. Abraham, the first patriarch, migrated to Canaan from the city of Haran in northern Mesopotamia. A seminomadic chieftain, Abraham settled on territory north and west of the Dead Sea, where he grazed his herds. Seminomadic clans in the region frequently made long migrations in antiquity, so the biblical account of Abraham and his descendants, Isaac and Jacob, is plausible.

The Bible, however, emphasizes the implausible: Abraham's extraordinary decision to give up Mesopotamian polytheism for belief in one god. This god commanded Abraham to leave Haran; indeed, he made a treaty, or covenant, with Abraham. In return for Abraham's faith, said the god, "As a possession for all time I shall give you and your descendants after you the land in which you are now aliens, the whole of Canaan, and I shall be their God" (Genesis 17:8). Abraham was not a strict monotheist: Although he worshiped only one god, he did not deny the existence of other gods. (See, for a comparison, the discussion of Akhenaten on page 24.) Nevertheless, he took a giant step on the road to pure **monotheism** by coming to believe that only one god rules *all* peoples.

According to the Bible, the next important step took place several hundred years later. In a time of famine in Canaan, many of Abraham's descendants left for prosperous Egypt. At first, they thrived there, but in time, they were enslaved and forced to build cities in the Nile Delta. Eventually, Moses, a divinely appointed leader, released the Hebrews from bondage in Egypt and led them back toward Canaan and freedom.

The Exodus ("journey out," in Greek), as this movement has been called, is a rare example of a successful national liberation movement in antiquity. Among those who accept its historicity, a date in the thirteenth century B.C. is frequently assigned to the Exodus. According to the Bible, the Exodus marked the key moment of another covenant, this time between the god of Abraham and the entire Israelite people. At Mount Sinai (SYE-nye), traditionally located on the rugged Sinai Peninsula between Egypt and Palestine, the Israelites are said to have first accepted as their one god a deity whose name is represented in Hebrew by the letters corresponding to YHWH. YHWH is traditionally rendered in English as "Jehovah," but "Yahweh" is more likely to be accurate. The Israelites accepted Yahweh's laws, summarized by the Ten Commandments. In return for obedience to Yahweh's commandments, they would be God's chosen people, his "special possession; . . . a kingdom of priests, . . . [his] holy nation."

The **Ten Commandments** are both more general and more personal than the laws of Hammurabi's Code. They are addressed to the individual, whom they commit to a universal standard. They emphasize prohibitions, saying more about what one should *not* do than about what one should do. The first three commandments establish Yahweh as the sole god of Israel, prohibit any sculpture or image of God, and forbid misuse of the divine name. The next two commandments are injunctions to observe the seventh day of the week (the Sabbath) as a day free of work and to honor one's parents. The sixth and seventh prohibit destructive or violent acts

Israelites People who settled on the eastern shore of the Mediterranean around 1200 B.C., or perhaps earlier. Their belief in one God directly influenced the faith of Christians, Muslims, and modern Jews.

monotheism Belief that there is only one God. The Hebrew Bible places this belief as originating about 2000–1500 B.C., when God commanded Abraham to give up Mesopotamian polytheism for belief in one God.

Ten Commandments According to the Hebrew Bible, these ten basic ethical and religious rules were given by God to Moses and the Israelites at Mt. Sinai. They have played an immensely influential role in Judaism and Christianity.

against neighbors, in particular adultery and killing. The final three commandments regulate community life by prohibiting stealing, testifying falsely, and coveting another man's wife or goods. In contrast to the starkness of the Ten Commandments, an enormous amount of detailed legal material is also found in the Hebrew Bible.

Many scholars doubt whether Hebrew monotheism emerged as early as the thirteenth century. In any case, the Bible makes clear that many ordinary Hebrews remained unconvinced. For centuries afterward, many Israelite worshipers deemed Yahweh their greatest god but not their only god. Unready for the radical innovation that monotheism represented, they carried out the rituals of various Canaanite deities, whom they worshiped on hilltop altars. Forging a national consensus for monotheism took centuries.

From the thirteenth to the late eleventh century B.C., the Hebrews were governed by a series of tribal leaders, referred to as "judges" in the Bible, but eventually the military threat posed by the Philistines (FILL-uh-steenz) persuaded the tribes to accept a centralized monarchy. The Philistines were one of the Sea Peoples, those raiders and invaders who beset the eastern Mediterranean in the Late Bronze Age. The Philistines had settled on the Palestinian coast where they prospered and eventually, seriously endangered Israel. The first Israelite king, Saul (r. ca. 1020–1004 B.C.), had some success against them but eventually fell in battle along with his son, Jonathan. The next king, David (r. 1004–965 B.C.), a former mercenary captain for the Philistines, defeated them decisively.

A recent discovery may provide archaeological evidence of the early Israelite monarchy. A fortress near Jerusalem provides the earliest example of Hebrew script yet discovered, dating from about 1050–970 B.C. The text contains the words "judge," "slave," and "king." It was written in ink on a piece of pottery. The work of a trained scribe, it might be a legal text, although further study is needed to be sure.

David was Israel's greatest king. He extended the kingdom into parts of modern Jordan, Lebanon, and Syria and conquered the Canaanite city of Jerusalem, which he made Israel's capital. David's son and successor, Solomon (r. 965–928 B.C.), was also a great king, a centralizer who moved from a loose kingship toward a tightly organized monarchy. His most famous accomplishment was the construction of the magnificent Temple in Jerusalem. The Temple priesthood and sacrifices became the focus of the national cult of Yahweh. Previously, that focus had been a humble, movable wooden chest known as the Ark of the Covenant.

Solomon's reign represented the high-water mark of the power of the Israelite monarchy. Under his successors, the monarchy was split into a large northern kingdom of Israel with a capital at Samaria and a smaller southern kingdom of Judah (JOO-duh) centered on Jerusalem (see **MAP 2.2**). In 722 B.C., the Assyrians conquered the kingdom of Israel and deported its inhabitants. Judah survived, first as a state controlled by Assyria, and then as an independent power.

The religious history of the period of the two kingdoms (928–722 B.C.) and the Judean survivor-state (722–587 B.C.) is marked by an intense drive toward monotheism. The kings of Judah in the seventh century B.C., especially Hezekiah (r. 715–686 B.C.) and Josiah (r. 640–609 B.C.), aggressively attacked the worship of all gods other than Yahweh and all centers of Yahweh worship other than the Temple in Jerusalem. The kings also began the process of canonizing the Hebrew Bible. Ambitious and independent, Hezekiah

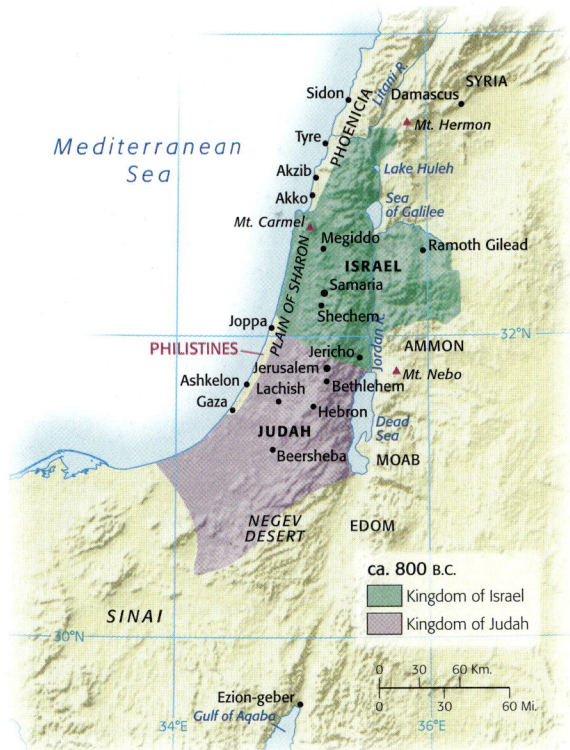

🌐 **MAP 2.2—Ancient Israel**

The Israelites settled in the Canaanite hill country west of the Jordan River and the Dead Sea after 1200 B.C. (*top map*). Control of Israelite territory after 928 B.C. was shared between two monarchies (*bottom map*): the kingdoms of Israel (conquered by the Assyrians in 722 B.C.) and Judah (conquered by the Babylonians in 598 B.C.).

joined in a revolt against Assyria that was brutally suppressed in 701 B.C. and almost cost him his kingdom.

The Judean kings could not have succeeded without the help of the prophets, who were prominent from approximately 900 to 500 B.C. Seers, uttering divinely inspired predictions, were universal figures in ancient religion. No other culture of antiquity, however, has anything like the Hebrew prophets: charismatic, uncompromising, terrible figures who announced God's anger and ultimate forgiveness. The prophets remind us of the most radical spiritual teachings of Israel: absolute monotheism, an insistence on righteousness, contempt for materialism and worldly power, love of the powerless. They often supported the kings but did not shrink from confronting authority and insisting on uncompromising justice. Among them were Amos, a humble shepherd who preached the superiority of righteousness to ritual; Jeremiah, who prophesied the destruction of Jerusalem as punishment for the people's idolatry; and Isaiah, who predicted the coming of a savior who would inaugurate a new day of universal peace and justice.

A characteristic story of the prophets is the confrontation between Elijah, perhaps the most famous prophet, and Ahab, king of Israel (r. 871–852 B.C.). Ahab coveted the vineyard of one Naboth, but Naboth refused Ahab's offer to buy it. Spurred on by his wife, Jezebel, Ahab trumped up charges against Naboth, who was unjustly stoned to death. Ahab then confiscated the vineyard. God sent Elijah to declare to Ahab that, as punishment for committing murder, "dogs will lick [Ahab's] blood" and that of his family (1 Kings 21:19). In a remarkable scene, we witness not only Elijah's courage in confronting the king, but also the king's surrender and repentance before Elijah's spiritual authority. Ahab (though not Jezebel) humbles himself and is spared, but his son and successor, King Ahaziah, who is equally wicked, is punished with a fatal injury. The Western tradition of civil disobedience owes much to the courage of the Hebrew prophets.

Exile and Return, 598–ca. 400 B.C.

The prophets taught the people of Judah how to survive. They correctly predicted ruin and exile and the promise that divine providence would guarantee return. The Judeans clung to this message with remarkable tenacity. Indeed, they had to, for between 598 and 586 B.C., the Neo-Babylonians conquered Judah, destroying Jerusalem and the Temple. The cultural, political, and economic elite was deported eastward to Babylon. Those who could do so fled for safety in the opposite direction, westward to Egypt. The dispirited remnant in Palestine shared their land with colonists from neighboring regions, with whom they intermarried and among whom their religion all but disappeared.

And that, given the usual fate of exiled and uprooted peoples in antiquity, should have been that. Yet, not only did the Judeans in the Babylonian Captivity persevere in their religious loyalty; they actually returned to Palestine in large numbers.

The Neo-Babylonian rulers allowed Judean deportees to continue to practice their religion. Judaeans in Babylon were not slaves; rather they rented land on royal estates, and some became prosperous. Although some Babylonian Judeans assimilated to local ways, many continued a Judean religious life. Communal worship was observed in open places, perhaps with associated buildings. Some scholars argue that synagogues ("gatherings" in Greek), modest centers of prayer and study that have been the focus of Jewish worship ever since, first emerged in Babylon. It is also possible that the exiles put together the Torah in something like its current form. Elders led the community, while prophets continued to speak out: Two examples are Ezekiel, who preached the restoration of the Temple, and the man known to us only as "Second Isaiah" (Isaiah 40–66). Second Isaiah emphasized the universal aspect of the god of Israel, who made empires rise and fall and would bring the exiles home from far-off Babylon.

The Temple in Jerusalem was rebuilt around 515 B.C., only seventy years after its destruction. This remarkable turn of events was possible partly because of the Persians, who conquered Babylon in 539 B.C. and proclaimed the freedom of the Judeans to rebuild their Temple in Jerusalem. Still, Persian benevolence would not have been enough if the Judean elite had not kept the faith burning among the exiles.

Second Isaiah's message points to a second important development among the exiles of Judah. As striking as the return to Palestine was the survival of large numbers of Judeans as an unassimilated people outside of Judah—in other words, as Jews. The terms *Jew* and *Jewish* began to be used in the fifth century B.C. For the first time, membership in a community of worship was divorced from residence. Jewish communities flourished in Babylon, Persia, and Egypt, but the members often chose not to become Babylonians, Persians, or Egyptians. From the sixth century

B.C. on, a majority of Jews were living outside Palestine, and the Jewish Exile, or Diaspora ("dispersion"), became a permanent fact of history.

The People of the Covenant

Equality, limited government, and the rule of law under God were basic Israelite political principles. Eventually, they would become fundamental political ideals for many in the West, and they would be applied not only to Israelites, but to all people.

According to Israelite belief, God made humans in his own image. Thus, all individuals were equal in a fundamental sense; all were bound by God's law. A king who disobeyed this law was illegitimate. Indeed, Israel was ambivalent at best about the institution of kingship, which was tolerated as an evil made necessary only by the country's many armed enemies. God's covenant with the Hebrews was a religious contract with political consequences, rendering God the only true king of Israel. Far from being gods themselves, or even God's representatives, Israel's kings were merely God's humble servants.

Israelite egalitarianism was restricted to men. Israelite women usually could not own or inherit property, as women could in Hammurabi's Babylon; or sue in court, as women could in pharaonic Egypt; or initiate a divorce, as women could in Classical Athens (see page 69). The powerful goddesses of other ancient cultures were absent in Israel. Women participated in the rituals of early Israelite religion and the original Temple (ca. 940–586 B.C.) but were segregated in a separate women's courtyard in the rebuilt Temple (ca. 515 B.C.–A.D. 79) and kept out of Temple ritual. Indeed, the perspective of the Hebrew Bible is predominantly male. Consider just two examples. First, of the 1,426 names in the Hebrew Bible, 1,315 are male; only 111 women's names appear, about 9 percent of the total.[3] Second, only men and boys can bear the sign of the Lord's covenant with Israel—that is, circumcision.

Nevertheless, Israelite women claimed honor as mothers and partners in running the household. The Hebrew Bible states that woman (as exemplified by Eve, the first woman) was created as "a suitable partner" for man (Genesis 2:18, 20). Reproduction and hence motherhood assume great importance in the Hebrew Bible; the Lord enjoins humans to "be fruitful and multiply" (Genesis 1:28). The Bible also commands that children honor both their father and their mother: The two parents are equal in parental authority (Exodus 20:12).

The Hebrew Bible sometimes displays sympathy for and insights into the strategies that women used to counter the abuses of male power. Rebecca, for instance, thwarts her husband Isaac's plan to give his blessing to their son Esau. As the eldest, Esau was entitled to this honor, but Rebecca preferred her younger son Jacob, and she saw to it that he and not Esau obtained her husband's blessing.

Only about a half dozen women in the Hebrew Bible served as leaders of Israel, but that is more than in the literature of most other ancient cultures. Deborah (ca. 1125 B.C.), for example, a charismatic Israelite prophet, organizes an army that destroys the forces of a Canaanite commander. In a later book, Esther, a Hebrew woman, becomes the wife of a Persian king whom the Bible calls Ahasuerus (probably Xerxes, r. 485–465 B.C.). Esther works ferociously at the Persian court to defeat a conspiracy to wipe out her people, and she saves them. The Book of Ruth (date uncertain) tells the story of a selfless and loyal woman, Ruth, who rescues her mother-in-law, Naomi, from ruin and poverty. The Bible celebrates Ruth as Naomi's "devoted daughter-in-law, who has proved better to you [Naomi] than seven sons." (See the feature, "The Written Record: Ruth.")

Israelite culture prized women for their cunning, courage, and perseverance—qualities that allowed the people to survive. Military prowess was highly valued in men, but their inner qualities were appreciated as well. Schooled in defeat and exile, many Israelites came to the conclusion that "wisdom is better than weapons of war" (Ecclesiastes 9:18). Thus, the Hebrew Bible stresses God's primary interest in goodness of soul: "The Lord does not see as man sees; men judge by appearances, but the Lord judges by the heart" (1 Samuel 16:7). The God of Israel prized righteousness above wealth, might, sacrifice, or ritual.

One might say that Israelite law reflected a similar tension between power and righteousness. On the one hand, just as the God of Israel was omnipotent and jealous, so the law of Israel was meant to be comprehensive and forceful. Capital punishment existed for murder, rape, incorrigible rebelliousness of a son against his parents, adultery by a married woman (both she and her lover were to be executed), a woman's loss of her virginity before marriage, and other offenses. Harsh punishment was mandated for Canaanite towns taken by siege: The entire population was to be killed so as not to corrupt Israel with their religious practices.

The Siege of Lachish

From the distance, it looks like one of the foothills that surround it. Up close, though, it can be clearly seen for what it is: Tel Lachish, the mound of the biblical city of Lachish. It is a link in the chain of evidence that tells one of the most remarkable stories in biblical history.*

Lachish was a great city, a royal fortress, and second only to Jerusalem in its importance to the kingdom of Judah (928–587 B.C.). In 701 B.C., the Assyrians under King Sennacherib (r. 704–681 B.C.) besieged Lachish and took it by force. The siege of Lachish is unique in early biblical history for the wealth of independent corroborating sources. In addition to reports in the Hebrew Bible are many Assyrian written documents. Furthermore, Sennacherib commemorated his victory by depicting the siege and recording the spoils in carved reliefs that he erected in his royal palace at Nineveh. Finally, the mound itself has been excavated, allowing a striking comparison of the archaeological and pictorial evidence of a siege in the biblical period.

Originally a Canaanite town, Lachish was fortified by the Israelite kings because of its strategic location. It sits southwest of Jerusalem in the Judean foothills, dominating the road between the Judean hills to the east and the Philistine coast to the west (see **MAP 2.2**). By the reign of King Hezekiah of Judah (r. 715–686 B.C.), one of the most prominent kings of the House of David, Lachish was a large garrison city constructed on a monumental scale. It included inner and outer rings of thick walls, a massive gate complex, many houses and shops, and, in the center, a palace-fort surrounded by earthen ramps.

Having seen Assyria turn the kingdom of Israel into an occupied province, Hezekiah knew that he was facing the greatest power of the region. Nevertheless, he joined Egypt and the Philistine cities in a revolt soon after Sennacherib came to the throne in 704 B.C. Sennacherib responded by attacking the rebels in 701. The Hebrew Bible states: "In the fourteenth year of the reign of Hezekiah, Sennacherib king of Assyria attacked and took all the fortified cities of Judah" (2 Kings 18:13). We can read the results of the campaign in one of Sennacherib's inscriptions:

"As to Hezekiah, the Jew, he did not submit to my yoke. I laid siege to 46 of his strong cities, walled forts and to the countless small villages in their vicinity, and conquered (them) by means of well-stamped (earth-) ramps, and battering-rams brought (thus) near (to the walls) (combined with) the attack by foot-soldiers, (using) mines, breeches as well as sapper work [that is, digging away foundations]." Hezekiah bowed to Assyrian power. He gave up territory (though not Jerusalem) and agreed to an increase in tribute, which now amounted to "30 talents of gold, 800 talents of silver, precious stones, antimony, large cuts of red stone, couches inlaid with ivory, elephant-hides, ebonywood, boxwood and all kinds of valuable treasures, his own

daughters, concubines, male and female musicians." So the Assyrian inscription records.

The Lachish reliefs (in Sennacherib's palace) offer a vivid picture of the attack on the city. Lachish was well fortified and well defended, but the Assyrians were experts in taking cities by storm. The reliefs show the camp of the attackers, Assyrian archers and slingers advancing on the city, battering rams and siege engines in action against the walls, flaming chariots thrown down by the defenders, and, after the city was taken, captives impaled on sharp stakes.

Look at the artist's reconstruction of an Assyrian assault on the city, based on the archaeological evidence. The soldiers are climbing a massive siege ramp that the Assyrians built against a "vulnerable" point in the city walls. The excavators of Lachish found the ramp, consisting of a level of stones cemented together over a core of boulders. It is the oldest siege ramp so far discovered in the ancient world. In and around the city the excavators found other evidence of the battle: hundreds of arrowheads, many sling stones, a number of pieces of bronze sheet mail used in armor, and what may be the crest of a helmet worn by one of the Assyrian spearmen shown attacking the city walls in the Lachish reliefs. Most dramatic, the excavators discovered about seven hundred skeletons, evidently civilians killed during the Assyrian attack and then buried in mass graves outside the city. Three of the individuals were trepanned—that is, they were operated on before death by removing a portion of their skulls. Perhaps this represents a last attempt, evidently futile, to save the lives of the wounded.

The Lachish reliefs also depict rows of captives and deportees marching toward Sennacherib on his throne. Look at this detail of the relief, showing a large Judean family leaving Lachish for exile. They are allowed to bring cattle with them, and a woman and child are permitted to ride on a wagon. The Assyrians claimed to have deported 200,150 people from Judah, of whom many men ended up as slave laborers working on Sennacherib's palace.

As for Lachish, it was burned to the ground, as the excavations confirm. Sometime in the seventh century the city was restored and refortified. Lachish was destroyed again, however, in 598 B.C., during the first of two military campaigns in Judah by Nebuchadrezzar, the Neo-Babylonian king. The excavators found a group of pottery sherds with ink inscriptions (called *ostraca*) in old Hebrew script, dating to just before that destruction. This unique set of documents in classical Hebrew writing consists of letters to a man named Yaush, the military governor of Lachish. They testify, among other things, to the worship of Yahweh, to the signal system linking the fortresses of Judah, and to the practices of the scribal profession. Once again, the city's misfortune has proved illuminating to students of the past.

Artist's Reconstruction of an Assyrian Assault on Lachish (Drawing by Gert le Grange, from David Ussishkin, *The Conquest of Lachish by Sennacherib* [Tel Aviv: Tel Aviv University, Institute of Archaeology, 1982], p. 123. Reproduced by permission.)

Detail of the Assyrian Conquest of Lachish, a Relief from the Palace of Sennacherib (British Museum/Erich Lessing/Art Resource, NY)

QUESTIONS

1. What makes the evidence for the siege of Lachish unique in biblical history?

2. What are the various sources of evidence for the siege of Lachish?

3. Why was the city of Lachish so important to the kingdom of Judah?

4. What do we learn about the siege of Lachish from the Assyrian Lachish Reliefs?

5. What information about the siege of Lachish does archaeology at Tel Lachish reveal?

*In much of what follows about Lachish (LAH-kish), I rely on the discussion in David Ussishkin, *The Conquest of Lachish by Sennacherib* (Tel-Aviv: Tel-Aviv University, Institute of Archaeology, 1982).

Ruth

*Some parts of the Hebrew Bible prohibit intermarriage. The Book of Ruth, however, praises marriage between Judean men and women from neighboring Moab (modern Jordan; see **Map 2.2**). This excerpt illustrates such unions, as it does the problem of food shortages, which were a special burden for widows.*

Once, in the time of the Judges when there was a famine in the land, a man [Elimelech] from Bethlehem in Judah went with his wife [Naomi] to live in Moabite territory. . . .

Elimelech died, and Naomi was left a widow with her two sons. The sons married Moabite women, one of whom was called Orpah and the other Ruth. [After ten years the sons died.] . . . Then Naomi, bereaved of her two sons as well as of her husband, got ready to return to her own country with her daughters-in-law, because she had heard in Moab that the Lord had shown his care for his people by giving them food. Accompanied by her two daughters-in-law she left the place where she had been living and they took the road leading back to Judah.

Naomi said to her daughters-in-law, "Go back, both of you, home to your own mothers. May the Lord keep faith with you, as you have kept faith with the dead and with me; and may he grant each of you the security of a home with a new husband." And she kissed them goodbye. They wept aloud and said, "No, we shall return with you to your people." But Naomi insisted, "Go back, my daughters, go; for I am too old to marry again. But if I could say that I had hope of a child, even if I were to be married tonight and were to bear sons, would you, then, wait until they grew up? Would you on their account remain unmarried? No, my daughters! For your sakes I feel bitter that the Lord has inflicted such misfortune on me." At this they wept still more. Then Orpah kissed her mother-in-law and took her leave, but Ruth clung to her.

"Look," said Naomi, "your sister-in-law has gone back to her people and her God. Go, follow her." Ruth answered, "Do not urge me to go back and desert you. Where you go, I shall go, and where you stay, I shall stay. Your people will be my people, and your God my God. Where you die, I shall die, and there be buried. I solemnly declare before the Lord that nothing but death will part me from you." When Naomi saw that Ruth was determined to go with her, she said no more. [They returned to Naomi's hometown, Bethlehem, in Judah.]

Naomi had a relative on her husband's side, a prominent and well-to-do . . . [man named] Boaz. One day Ruth the Moabite asked Naomi, "May I go to the harvest fields and glean [collect excess grain] behind anyone who will allow me?" "Yes, go my daughter," she replied. So Ruth went gleaning in the fields behind the reapers. [She met Boaz in his fields.] . . .

Boaz said to Ruth, "Listen, my daughter: do not go to glean in any other field. Do not look any farther, but stay close to my servant-girls. Watch where the men reap, and follow the gleaners; I have told the men not to molest you. Any time you are thirsty, go and drink from the jars they have filled." She bowed to the ground and said, "Why are you so kind as to take notice of me, when I am just a foreigner?" Boaz answered, "I have been told the whole story of what you have done for your mother-in-law since the death of your husband, how you left father and mother and homeland and came among a people you didn't know before. The Lord reward you for what you have done. . . ."

[Eventually, Boaz marries Ruth; their great grandson would be Israel's greatest king, David.]

QUESTIONS

1. In this excerpt, what are the various ways in which people cope with hunger and famine?

2. Why does Ruth, a foreign widow, stay with her mother-in-law and go to Judah?

3. Why does Boaz admire and eventually marry Ruth?

Source: *Revised English Bible* © Oxford University Press and Cambridge University Press, 1989. Reprinted by permission of Cambridge University Press.

SECTION SUMMARY

- The Bible, including the Hebrew Bible (called Old Testament by Christians) and the Christian New Testament, is the single most influential text in Western civilization.
- The central theme of the Hebrew Bible is God's covenant with his chosen people—the Hebrews.
- Hebrew monotheism evolved between the 1200s and 600 B.C. with tribal leaders, kings, and prophets each playing a major role.
- Jews, deported to Babylon after 598 B.C., maintained their religion and some returned home after the Persians conquered Babylon in 539 B.C.
- Equality, limited government, and the rule of law under God were Israelite political notions that have greatly influenced the later West.

On the other hand, by taking intention into account, Israelite law echoed a note already present in Mesopotamia. The so-called Law of the Goring Ox, for instance, allowed a person to go unpunished for owning an ox that gores a person to death, unless the owner knew beforehand that the animal was dangerous. If the owner did know, however, the owner had to be put to death. Israelite law, moreover, demonstrated a belief in the sanctity of human life by prohibiting human sacrifice. An Israelite had to be ready in his or her heart (but *only* in his or her heart) to sacrifice his or her child to Yahweh, as Abraham was willing to sacrifice Isaac when Yahweh so commanded. After ascertaining Abraham's willingness to obey, even to the point of sacrificing his son, Yahweh freed Isaac from the altar and supplied a ram as a substitute offering. Israelite monotheism thus broke with its Canaanite neighbors and rejected human sacrifice, as did the religions later derived from it.

CHAPTER SUMMARY

T he first half of the first millennium B.C. witnessed dramatic developments among both the ancestors of the West and its founders. Canaanite city-states, known as the Phoenicians, created trading networks and spread colonies across the entire length of the Mediterranean Sea. The ships of these great sailors circled Africa and reached faraway Britain. Closer to home, they influenced the culture of Greece, to whom they imparted the alphabet. The Greek alphabet, derived from the Phoenician alphabet, in turn, led to the Roman alphabet, the basis of the English alphabet today.

A new form of empire appeared. New military technology, the frank adoption of brutal and inhumane methods, and improvements in administration led to the creation of the Assyrian Empire, stretching from western Iran to Palestine and briefly even to Egypt. After short-lived hegemonies by Neo-Babylonians and Medes, the Persians established an empire that was larger, better organized, and more tolerant than the empire of the Assyrians. Multi-ethnic, far-flung, and claiming to be universal, such an empire would one day be brought into the Western tradition of Rome.

The most important developments of the era, however, were not in commerce, weaponry, or imperialism, but in new conceptions of the nature and meaning of human life. The Israelites conquered Palestine and, even after losing it, held on to their identity by means of a tenacious belief in one god. They broke with tradition by insisting that their god was merciful and just. Omnipotent, God gave history meaning and direction. The purpose of life, in the Israelite view, was to serve God by acting righteously. The new religion laid the foundation for Judaism as well as Christianity and Islam. The Jews wrote down their religious and historical traditions in a book that, along with the Christian New Testament, proved to be the most influential single text in the history of the West: the Hebrew Bible.

FOCUS QUESTIONS

- Who were the Phoenicians and what did they contribute to Western civilization?

- What made the first-millennium B.C. empires of the Assyrians, Neo-Babylonians, and Persians so much more effective than earlier empires?

- What was the religious experience of ancient Israel, and what is its legacy today?

KEY TERMS

Ugarit (p. 30)

alphabet (p. 30)

Phoenicians (p. 31)

Assyrians (p. 32)

Neo-Babylonians (p. 34)

Persian Empire (p. 34)

Zoroastrianism (p. 37)

Torah (p. 39)

covenant (p. 39)

Israelites (p. 40)

monotheism (p. 40)

Ten Commandments (p. 40)

 This icon will direct you to additional materials on the website: www .cengage.com/history/ noble/westciv6e

e See our interactive eBook for map and primary source activities.

NOTES

1. S. Insler, *The Gāthās of Zarathustra: Acta Iranica*, 8 (Leiden: E. J. Brill, 1975), p. 33.

2. Roland G. Kent, *Old Persian: Grammar, Texts, Lexicon* (New Haven, Conn.: American Oriental Society, 1950), p. 132.

3. Carol L. Meyers, "Everyday Life: Women in the Period of the Hebrew Bible," in *The Women's Bible Commentary*, ed. Carol A. Newsom and Sharon H. Ringe (Louisville, Ky.: Westminster/ John Knox Press, 1992), p. 245.

CHAPTER OUTLINE

Athenian Acropolis, with Pnyx Hill in Foreground
(Julia M. Fair)

The Greeks in the Polis to ca. 350 B.C.

It is dawn. The light reveals a hillside in the city of Athens, a natural auditorium. Its rocky slopes, visible in the photograph opposite, would have been covered, beginning about 500 B.C., with wooden benches facing a platform cut into the rock. The six thousand men gathered there constitute a diverse group, ranging from farmers to philosophers, from dockyard workers to aristocrats. As they take their seats, these, the citizens of Athens, watch priests conducting prayers and offering a sacrifice. Then all eyes turn to the individual who mounts the platform—a herald. His booming voice asks the question that marks the start of business: "Who wishes to speak?" Someone rises to address the assembly. It is the first democracy in history—and the central laboratory in this great experiment in participation.

The assembly meeting recalls the defining features of what was, in its era, the characteristic political institution in much of Greece: the *polis* (plural, *poleis*). The polis dominated Greek life between ca. 750 and ca. 350 B.C., an era that is sometimes called the Hellenic Period. By the time the polis emerged, Greece was old. Two great civilizations had already risen and fell in Greek lands, the Minoans and Mycenaeans. Now, several centuries after their fall, the polis appeared, and its dawn was marked by a great cultural achievement. Around 725 B.C., Homer composed his two great epic poems, the *Iliad* and the *Odyssey*. These poems preserved many of the religious and historical traditions of Greece's earlier period. Yet, in their focus on the individual, they also heralded a new era, one that would differ greatly from the palace economies and warrior kingdoms of Bronze Age Greece.

Usually translated as "city-state," the polis is better understood as "citizen-state." The polis was the product of communal activities—whether in the assembly, the military, or the theater—undertaken by its members: its citizens. Not every polis was a democracy, but every polis emphasized cooperative activities whose participants enjoyed at least a measure of equality. Every polis also sought a balance between the group and the individual, be that person the speaker, a military hero, or a freethinker.

Balance is a difficult state to achieve, however, and the equilibrium of the polis was frequently disturbed by tension and exclusion. Greek democracy failed to grant equal rights to women or immigrants, and it depended on slave labor. Relations among poleis were less often a matter of cooperation than of war. Although the Greeks created magnificent religious architecture, a portion of their intellectual elite came to the conclusion that the gods were of little importance in explaining the universe. Whereas one leading polis, Sparta, was a paragon of militarism, obedience, and austerity, scorning the life of the mind, another, Athens, prided itself on freedom and cultural attainments. Yet, the Greeks made the most even of such tensions, exploring them in literary genres—tragedy, comedy, history, and

FOCUS QUESTIONS

- How did early Greece develop before the polis and what light do the Homeric poems shed on its history?
- What was the Greek polis, and how did it develop in Sparta, Athens, and Corinth in Archaic Greece?
- How did Western individualism and rationalism take root in Archaic Greece?
- What was Athenian democracy and how did it clash with Sparta in the Peloponnesian War?
- How did tragedy, comedy, philosophy, and history all begin and develop in the culture of Classical Greece?

This icon will direct you to additional materials on the website: www.cengage.com/history/noble/westciv6e

See our interactive eBook for map and primary source activities.

philosophy—that focused on the polis as a central theme. Creative tensions also marked Greek achievements in sculpture, painting, and architecture.

The era of the polis proved to be a defining moment in Western history. Although the Greeks of this era borrowed much from neighboring cultures, they were remarkably original. In the mid-first millennium B.C., the monotheistic religious heritage of the West first emerged among the Jews. During that same era, the Greeks founded the Western tradition in a broad range of culture, including politics; philosophy; literary genres, such as comedy, tragedy, and history; and the visual and plastic arts of painting, sculpture, and architecture. The Jews and the Greeks represent two poles of Western culture: the sacred and the worldly, revelation and reason.

BEFORE THE POLIS: EARLY GREECE, TO CA. 725 B.C.

How did early Greece develop before the polis and what light do the Homeric poems shed on its history?

"La Parisienne" This masterpiece of Minoan art shows a priestess in a long robe, with her hair tied in a special knot. A fresco from Knossos, it was dubbed "the Parisian lady" because of its elegance. (Erich Lessing/Art Resource, NY)

The ancient Greek genius reached its height in the Classical period (480–323 B.C.), but it is already visible in the *Iliad* (IL-ee-ud) and the *Odyssey* (ODD-uh-see), the epic poems of Homer. Homer's poems shaped Greece's national identity and provided the basis of Greek education. Homer probably lived around 725 B.C., but his works have roots in the civilization that had flourished in Greece a thousand years earlier. Along with the discoveries of archaeologists, Homer's poems provide evidence for the rise and fall of two great civilizations: the Minoans on the island of Crete and the Mycenaeans on the Greek mainland (see **MAP 3.1**).

Minoans and Mycenaeans, 3000–1180 B.C.

Europe's first civilization appeared in what is today Greece, on the Aegean island of Crete (KREET) around 2000 B.C., and soon spread to the Greek mainland. Civilization came relatively late to Greece, but in comparison with Egypt or western Asia, Greece is not a hospitable land. It is mountainous, dry, and contains little cultivable farmland. Yet, it was destined for greatness.

Cretan civilization would influence early Greece considerably, but in 2000 B.C., Crete was not yet a Greek-speaking island. The Cretans of that era were literate and used a syllabary, or a writing system of syllables that form words, known as "Linear A." Although we know its language is not Greek, we do not know what it is. Most of the evidence of Cretan civilization comes from the excavations of the island's palaces—monumental structures that first appeared at various locations on Crete around 2000 B.C. and reached their height between 1800 and 1490 B.C. Scholars call the palace builders and their civilization "**Minoan** (mih-NO-un)," after King Minos of later Greek myth. He was supposed to have ruled a great sea empire from his palace at Knossos (see **MAP 3.1**).

The Minoan palaces were not merely royal residences but centers of administration, religion, and economics. The largest palace, Knossos sprawled across 3 acres. It was built around a large central court, probably used for public ceremonies and surrounded by a mazelike structure of staterooms, residence quarters, storage rooms, workshops, and bathrooms, interconnected by corridors, ramps, and stairways. The Minoans exploited Crete's natural wealth in agriculture and timber and set up a trading network from the Levant to Sicily. A Minoan settlement flourished on the Aegean island of Thera, 70 miles north of Crete (see **MAP 3.1**). This settlement was destroyed sometime in the late 1600s B.C. by one of the most violent volcanic eruptions ever. It might have given rise to the legend of Atlantis, the city that sank beneath the sea.

Peace and prosperity are themes of Minoan culture, yet Minoan civilization came to a violent and relatively sudden end. All of the palaces except Knossos were destroyed around 1490 B.C.; Knossos fell around 1375 B.C. The archaeological evidence strongly supports the notion of an invasion, but by whom? To find the answer, let us look to the Greek mainland.

Around 1700 B.C., the sleepy Greek mainland suddenly appears to have burst into power and prosperity. So, we can conclude from a series of burial sites, especially those found at Mycenae (see **MAP 3.1**), where the tombs of kings and queens contain a treasure house of objects in gold and other precious metals. The inhabitants of Mycenae (my-SEE-ne) were Greek-speakers. They and the wider civilization they represent are called Mycenaean (My-suh-NEE-un). The **Mycenaeans** had arrived in Greece sometime between 2300 and 1700 B.C., either through migration or invasion.

Warriors at heart, the Myceneans went on raids, around the Aegean, aimed at acquiring loot and prestige. Around 1490 B.C., they achieved their greatest feat: the conquest of Crete. The Mycenaeans adopted the Minoans' palace economy and wide trading network.

Mycenaean civilization was at its height between about 1400 and 1180 B.C. A Mycenaean royal household was organized to produce textiles, arms, and armor, with raw materials provided by the common people. Our knowledge of the palace economy comes primarily from thousands of clay tablets inscribed by palace scribes around 1200 B.C. They are written in a script scholars call "Linear B," an early form of Greek consisting of a combination of syllabary and ideograms (a system of symbols that stand for words or ideas).

It appears likely that Mycenaean Greece suffered from a combination of internal weakness and foreign invasion similar to that experienced by most of the eastern Mediterranean around 1250 to 1150 B.C., the era of the Sea Peoples (see page 24). By 1180 B.C., most of the fortified sites had been destroyed. Afterward, only a few people continued to live in the old towns.

Homer and History

The era from the fall of Mycenae to the rise of the Greek city-states is often referred to as the Greek Dark Ages. New archaeological evidence renders the period less dark but no less gloomy: The evidence shows depopulation, poverty, and invasion. Northern Greeks, probably Dorians, came south, driving out or dominating the Mycenaean Greeks. Many Mycenaean refugees migrated eastward around 1000 B.C. to the Aegean coast of Anatolia, which was destined to become an important center of Greek culture.

In spite of its material poverty, Dark Age Greece produced notable painted pottery and preserved an oral tradition of poetry handed down from the Mycenaean era. After 800 B.C., more settled and more prosperous times led to dramatic changes in politics, warfare, and culture. Around 725 B.C., Greece reached a milestone in literary artistry that heralded a new age: the epic poetry of Homer.

Had ancient Greece produced a Bible, the *Iliad* and the *Odyssey* of **Homer** would have been its two Testaments. Only Hesiod (HEE-see-ud), a poet who lived around 700 B.C., had as much influence on later generations, but his poems (*Theogony* and *Works and Days*), though composed in the epic tradition, were shorter than Homer's and less dramatic. Homer's and Hesiod's poems inspired and educated the Greeks—a large part of a Greek boy's education consisted of learning to recite Homer from memory. Homer's poems shaped Greece's national identity by praising its heroes and by looking back toward the glory days of the Mycenaeans.

CHRONOLOGY	
ca. 750 B.C.	Greek colonization of Magna Graecia begins
ca. 725 B.C.	Sparta conquers Messenia
ca. 675 B.C.	Pheidon becomes tyrant of Argos
ca. 625 B.C.	Sappho active as poet
594 B.C.	Solon is archon in Athens
ca. 560 B.C.	Pisistratus becomes tyrant of Athens
508 B.C.	Cleisthenes begins reforms in Athens
499 B.C.	Ionians revolt against Persia
490 B.C.	Battle of Marathon
480–479 B.C.	Persia invades Greece
477 B.C.	Delian League founded
460–429 B.C.	Pericles at peak of power
458 B.C.	Aeschylus's *Oresteia* first performed in Athens
431–404 B.C.	Peloponnesian War
399 B.C.	Trial of Socrates
395–386 B.C.	Corinthian War
371 B.C.	Battle of Leuctra

Minoan Society that flourished between 2000 and 1490 B.C. on the Aegean island of Crete, where Greece's first civilization appeared. Their sophisticated culture and economy were administered from their magnificent palaces.

Mycenaeans Militaristic people from the Greek mainland who conquered the Minoans around 1490–1375 B.C. Mycenaean civilization was a center of Bronze Age culture until its destruction around 1100 B.C.

Homer Greatest ancient Greek poet, credited as the author of the epics the *Iliad* and the *Odyssey*, both written during the eighth century B.C. His dramatic stories inspired, moved, and educated the Greeks.

🌐 Map 3.1—Aegean Greece

The Minoan civilization (height: ca. 1800–1490 B.C.) and Mycenaean civilization (height: ca. 1400–1180 B.C.) flourished in turn in the Aegean region during the second millennium B.C. The center of Minoan civilization was the island of Crete. A mainland people, the Mycenaeans conquered Minoan Crete around 1490 B.C.

The *Iliad* and the *Odyssey* focus on the Trojan War and its aftermath. The *Iliad* is set in the tenth year of the conflict. The long war leads to a quarrel between Greek chieftains: Agamemnon, king of Mycenae and the leader of the expedition, and Achilles (uh-KILeez), the greatest Greek warrior. The most prominent Trojans, King Priam and his eldest son, Hector, are less petty but suffer the greater ruin. The *Odyssey* is the story of the Greek hero Odysseus (oh-DIS-ee-us) and his struggle to return home to his kingdom after a twenty-year absence, ten years at Troy and ten years wandering homeward. It also focuses on the loyalty and ingenuity of Odysseus's wife, Penelope, who saves the household in his absence, and the maturation of their son, Telemachus (te-LEH-muh-kus), who helps his father regain his kingdom.

Homer's poems look back, but did the Trojan War really happen? That is a controversial subject, but both archaeology and the evidence of inscriptions suggest that the answer is probably yes. Troy really existed: It was a big, wealthy city, strategically located near the entrance to the Hellespont (or Dardanelles), the straits that lead toward the Black Sea. The king of Troy was attached politically to the Hittite empire, and his city had strong trading relations with the Mycenaean Greeks. But Mycenaeans turned quickly from trade to war. Troy was destroyed violently in the period 1210–1180 B.C., possibly by Mycenaean warriors.

Homer lived in a Greek city in Ionia (eye-OH-nee-uh), a region of the western coast of Anatolia (see **Map 3.2**). Although Homer lived centuries after the end of Troy, he resided in an area whose culture had been affected by Troy and its neighbors. Homer could have drawn some of his material from native populations and traditions. Besides, Homer worked in a continuous,

Lion Gate at Mycenae
Carved about 1250 B.C. above the main gate of the citadel's massive walls, the lions—flanking a column, their front paws resting on altars—probably represent royal authority. Inside the walls is Grave Circle B, a royal burial site. (Dmitrios Harissiadis. From the Photographic Archives of the Benaki Museum)

Greek, poetic tradition going back to the Mycenaean Age, that gave him knowledge of a society that was long gone by his day. His poems are a combination of accurate details of Mycenaean palace life, historical fiction, and details of his own, much later society.

Homer focuses on the elite. Homeric men and women hold aristocratic values and tend to look down on ordinary people. But society in Homer's day was more level and egalitarian. Except for a small number of traders and craft specialists who lived in towns, most Greeks lived in villages and hamlets. Most farmed or herded pigs, goats, or sheep, and most were free. The people of each community were called the *demos* (DEE-mus); the leading men, *basileis* (bah-see-LAYS). *Basileis* means "kings," but it is more accurate to understand them as chiefs.

The main activity of Homer's basileis is warfare. The *Iliad* consists largely of a series of battlefield contests. Since women did not take part in battle, they are not presented as men's equals, but Homer's women are neither timid nor helpless. Penelope, for example, personifies female resourcefulness: By refusing to marry until she has finished weaving a shroud for Odysseus's elderly father, and then by unraveling every night what she has woven during the day, she puts the noble suitors off for years. She is as concerned with honor as any Homeric man. By refusing to accept an offer of marriage while Odysseus might still be alive, Penelope does honor to her own good name and to her husband's.

SECTION SUMMARY

- The Minoans built Greece's first civilization, centered on the island of Crete around 2000–1375 B.C.

- Greek-speakers arrived in Greece about 2300–1700 B.C. and established the wealthy and warlike Mycenaean civilization on the mainland, at its height about 1400–1180 B.C.

- From 1100 to 800 B.C., between the fall of Mycenaean civilization and the rise of the city-states, Greece was largely poor and illiterate.

- Homer did not live until 725 B.C. or later, but an oral tradition of poetry, going back to Mycenaean times, means that the *Iliad* and *Odyssey* are based on a kernel of historical truth.

- Homer expresses the heroic and aristocratic values of elite men and women that would influence Greek antiquity for centuries.

Both in Mycenaean times and in Homer's day, the Greeks were polytheists. The gods figure prominently in early Greek poetry, but they are less powerful than the Hebrew God, less immediate, and less interested in the inner life of men and women. Already emerging at the beginning of the Greek cultural tradition was the belief that became the hallmark of ancient Greece: that "man is the measure of all things," as the thinker Protagoras would declare in the fifth century B.C.

The gods embody the values of a warrior society that put a premium on *arête* (ah-reh-TAY), meaning warrior prowess or excellence. Because they were thought to live on Mount Olympus, a 9,500-foot-high peak in northern Greece (see **MAP 3.1**), the Greek gods were called the Olympians. The "household" of the Olympians—modeled on a noble's household—included Zeus (ZOOS), a sky god and the "father of gods and men," and his consort, Hera; Zeus's brother, Poseidon, god of the sea, earthquakes, and horses; Ares, god of war; and Aphrodite, goddess of love. Also in the "household" were Zeus's children: Athena, goddess of wisdom and cunning; Hephaestus, god of craftsmen; Hermes, god of travelers and thieves; Apollo, god of disease and healing; and Artemis, goddess of the hunt, of maidens, and of childbirth.

arête Originally meaning "warrior prowess" or "excellence," *arête* was a key term of ancient Greek culture. It evolved over the centuries to apply to politics and philosophy and to women as well as men.

Loyalty to the family played an important role in social relations. A person's obligations to kin included the duty to avenge crime or murder. Friendship, cemented by an exchange of gifts, was another important social institution. Even humble peasants prided themselves on hospitality.

Such values served Homeric society well. Although they would survive in later centuries, they would be challenged after 700 B.C. by the increasing emphasis on public life as the Greek city-state evolved.

SOCIETY AND POLITICS IN ARCHAIC GREECE, CA. 750–500 B.C.

What was the Greek polis, and how did it develop in Sparta, Athens, and Corinth in Archaic Greece?

Archaic Greece Period of ancient Greek history from around 700 to 500 B.C.

Historians usually call the era in Greek history from roughly 750 to 500 B.C. the "Archaic period." **Archaic Greece** was a patchwork of hundreds of separate city-states, tribal leagues, and monarchies (see **MAP 3.2**). Nevertheless, it displayed a distinctive style and outlook, not only in art, but also in politics, military arrangements, technology, economics, literature, and religion.

The Archaic era laid the groundwork for much of lasting importance in Western civilization. Archaic Greece witnessed the simultaneous growth of individualism and a tight community spirit, the emergence of social cohesion despite a continual state of war, and the coexistence of deep religious piety and the West's first nontheistic philosophy. The Archaic period also saw the origin of characteristic Western types of governmental regimes—tyranny, oligarchy, and the first steps toward democracy—and of fundamental Western notions of citizenship and the rule of law.

Agriculture, Trade, Colonization, and Warfare

An observer of ninth century B.C. Greece would hardly have predicted greatness of that poor, illiterate society of small settlements and low-level trade. Yet, everything began to change in Greece in the eighth century B.C. It was out of these changes that a new communal institution emerged: the **polis** (PO-liss).

polis Term for an ancient Greek city-state, a system that reached its height around 700–300 B.C.

Change was a product of peace, which stimulated a sharp population rise. In response, the economy shifted from herding to farming, a more efficient source of food. Seeking new agricultural land in the rocky Greek peninsula, farmers terraced hillsides and drained marshes. The typical agricultural unit was the family farm. Most farms were small and roughly equal in size, and so served to stimulate social and political equality.

🌐 **MAP 3.2—Archaic and Classical Greece**

The region of the Aegean Sea was the heartland of Greek civilization around 750 to 350 B.C. The mountainous terrain, rugged coastline, and numerous islands encouraged political fragmentation.

Greek commerce, too, was expanding. Shortly before 800 B.C., Greeks from the island of Euboea, perhaps following the example of Phoenician merchants and seafarers who had been casual traders in Greece for a century (see pages 30–31), established a trading post in Syria at Al-Mina, at the end of the chief caravan route from Mesopotamia (see **MAP 3.3**). Shortly afterward, Euboeans established another trading post in the west, on an island in the Bay of Naples in Italy. In both east and west, Greek merchants sought iron and luxury goods. What they offered in return was probably silver, of which ancient Greece had rich deposits, and slaves.

From commerce, it was but a short step to colonization in order to siphon off the extra mouths created by population growth. In colonization as in trade, the Greeks may have followed the Phoenicians, who had begun establishing colonies probably in the ninth century B.C. Between about 750 and 500 B.C., the Greeks founded colonies throughout the Mediterranean and the Black Sea, planting nearly as many cities as already existed in Greece (see **MAP 3.3**). Colonization in Italy and Sicily began in earnest around 750 B.C.; in the northeast Aegean perhaps a generation later; in the Sea of Marmara (in modern Turkey) about 680 B.C.; in North Africa around 630 B.C.; and in the Black Sea about 610 B.C. In the far west, Massalia (modern Marseilles, France) was established about 600 B.C. Southern Italy and Sicily, whose climate and landscape recalled the Aegean, were especially intense areas of Greek settlement, so much so that the Romans later

🌐 MAP 3.3—Phoenician and Greek Colonization

Both the Phoenicians (beginning perhaps after 900 B.C.) and the Greeks (beginning around 750 B.C.) established numerous colonies on the coasts of the Mediterranean and Black Seas.

called the region *Magna Graecia* ("Great Greece"). Greek colonization spread urban civilization westward, especially into Italy.

One important consequence of foreign contact was the introduction to Greece of the alphabet, borrowed from the Phoenicians shortly after 800 B.C. The Greeks made one significant addition to the Phoenician alphabet by adding vowels. Vowels are not essential to reading a Semitic language, but an Indo-European language like Greek would be almost indecipherable without them. The alphabet spread rapidly and widely after 750 B.C. Literacy underlay the achievements in poetry, philosophy, and the law that Archaic Greece has left behind. However, so few people could read and write well that ancient Greece remained primarily an oral culture.

Another consequence of foreign contact was the introduction of new military technology, which the increase in wealth allowed the Greeks to adopt. Social changes, furthermore, fostered new tactics on the battlefield. The result was the **hoplite phalanx** (HOP-lite FAY-lanks), a tightly ordered unit of heavily armed, pike-bearing infantrymen. The phalanx not only became the dominant military force in Archaic Greece, but, with relatively few changes in equipment and tactics, it remained supreme on land in Greece, western Asia, and other Mediterranean regions for centuries, until its defeat by a Roman army in 197 B.C.

hoplite phalanx
Battlefield tactic of Archaic Greece that relied on a tightly ordered unit of heavily armed, pike-bearing infantrymen.

The phalanx emerged through a process of evolution rather than in a revolutionary leap. Before 800 B.C., single combat among the basileis appears to have decided battles. Around 800 to 750 B.C., armies began to include more men, fighting in close formation. Around 700 B.C., came new armaments. The result was the phalanx. The heavily armed infantryman (hoplite) of the fighting unit (phalanx) wore bronze armor on his shins and chest and a bronze helmet with a narrow opening for eyes and mouth. He carried a heavy wooden shield in his left hand. His weapons were a pike—a heavy, wooden, iron-tipped thrusting spear at least 9 feet long—and a short, iron stabbing sword.

The men of the phalanx were arranged in close ranks, normally four to eight deep. Soldiers stood together in line, each man's shield overlapping his neighbor's. Hoplite combat involved set battles—head-to-head, army-against-army, all-or-nothing affairs—rather than individual skirmishes or guerrilla raids. Battle usually consisted of a charge followed by a grueling contest. The men in the front line pounded the enemy with their pikes, while the men in the rear pushed forward. Finally, one side would give way and run. The victors stayed and erected a trophy.

Greek hoplite warfare rested on deep societal roots. Only independent men of means could afford hoplite armor. Thanks to the spread of the family farm, such men were common in Greece by around 700 B.C. Hoplites were amateur soldiers. Most were full-time farmers outside the fighting season, which lasted only for the summer months. The notion of the farmer-soldier, independent and free, would have a lasting impact on Western political thought. So would the warrior values of what became a way of life in Greece.

Unlike in Homer, whose warriors sought aretê mainly for personal and familial honor, hoplites fought for the community. According to the poet Tyrtaeus (ca. 650 B.C.), a good soldier's death brought glory, not only to his father, but also to his city and his countrymen. Although the battlefield remained the favored arena for displays of aretê, the assembly or the council house became increasingly acceptable as an alternative.

Characteristics of the Polis

The polis was both a product of the changes of the eighth century B.C. and a stimulus for change. As an urban settlement, the polis existed as early as the ninth or even the tenth century B.C., but its intense communal spirit did not emerge until around 750–700 B.C.

Polis came to denote not just a city, but the community as a whole, corresponding roughly to a country or nation. One crude gauge of the centrality of the polis is the number, not to mention the significance, of words the Greeks derived from it: among them, *polites* (citizen), *politeia* (constitution), *politeô* (to govern), *ta politika* (politics), and *politikos* (politician).

Most poleis (PO-lays) were small, many less than 100 square miles in size. Athens was one of the largest. Its territory, known as Attica (see **MAP 3.4**), covered 1,000 square miles (approximately the size of Rhode Island). At its height (ca. 430 B.C.), the population of Athens was about 400,000, but a typical polis contained only between 5,000 and 10,000 people. The philosopher Aristotle (AR-is-tot-il) (384–322 B.C.) wrote that an ideal polis should be small enough that the citizens know one another personally.

The polis consisted of two parts: the urban area, which usually was tiny, and the surrounding countryside, where most people lived. From the earliest times, the urban public space included both a defensible hill (preferably with a water supply), called a "high city" (*acropolis* [uh-CROP-uh-liss]), and a "gathering place" (*agora* [AH-go-rah]), used as a marketplace and meeting area.

Hoplites   A detail from a Corinthian vase of 625 to 600 B.C. shows pike-wielding hoplites closed in battle over a fallen comrade. In this image as elsewhere, Greek artists rendered warriors seminude and fighting in small groups, but in reality hoplites went into battle wearing heavy armor and fought in large units.   (Louvre/Réunion des Musées Nationaux/Art Resource, NY)

There was at least one temple. After 500 B.C., stone buildings, including council houses, theaters, covered porticoes, gymnasia, and baths, became increasingly common.

What distinguished the early polis, however, was not its buildings but its spirit. As the poet Alcaeus (b. ca. 630 B.C.) puts it, "Not houses finely roofed or the stones of walls well-built, nay nor canals and dockyards, make the polis, but men able to use their opportunity."

The Greeks came to call the polis a "common thing" (*koinon*). It belonged to its people, not to a few nobles or to a king or a god. As early as about 700 B.C., important public documents were inscribed in stone. Acts of state were attributed not to a personified polis but to the community—for example, not to Thera but to "the Thereans," not to Sybaris but to "the Sybarites." The emphasis is on the plurality.

The emphasis was on equality as well. The polis developed an ethos of moderation. The ideal citizen was thought to be neither rich nor poor but of moderate means. Women were not considered citizens and were excluded from taking part in politics. Yet, women's behavior was considered important to the polis. For example, some poleis passed laws against extravagant jewelry or unrestrained mourning (mourning the dead was considered women's work).

In theory, all citizens were supposed to be roughly similar, but this was not always true in practice, as the politics of the early polis makes clear.

Corinth and Tyranny

Trade and colonization inspired change at home, for one thing, making increasing numbers of Greeks into seafarers and so generating wealth. Centrally located Corinth became a great seaport and the wealthiest city in mainland Greece. And Corinth was in the forefront of political change.

Political change followed economic trends. Although some Greeks shot to the top of the economic ladder, many of these newly rich lacked the status of the elite basileis. In order to claim a share, the newly rich seem to have made common cause with the independent farmers who staffed the hoplite phalanx. The result was tyranny.

Tyrant originally referred not to an arbitrary and oppressive ruler but rather to a champion of the people. Having overthrown a narrow and entrenched aristocracy, tyrants were popular at first. *Tyrant* did not become a negative word before roughly 550 B.C., when the people soured on the second and third generation of tyrants.

Greek tyranny began in Argos, a polis in the northeastern Peloponnesus (pel-uh-puh-NEE-suss), around 675 B.C. (see **Map 3.2**). The first tyrant was an Argive named Pheidon. By 660 B.C., tyranny had spread to nearby Corinth. During the seventh and sixth centuries B.C., all the major Greek poleis except Sparta became tyrannies.

Much of what the tyrants did, especially in the first generation, was popular and progressive. It appears that they had the support of the prosperous farmers who fought in the phalanx. Tyrants stimulated the economy by founding colonies on trade routes, standardizing weights and measures, and encouraging the immigration of skilled craftsmen from other poleis. They built temples and instituted festivals, providing both jobs and leisure-time activities.

When tyrants passed power on to their sons, however, the second generation tended to rule oppressively. Buoyed by the discontent of the demos, the basileis regrouped and tried to take back power. One second-generation tyrant advised accordingly: To maintain power, a tyrant should "lop off the tallest ears of grain"—that is, execute or exile aristocrats in order to deny leaders to the opposition. However, the tide of discontent was not to be stopped. Few tyrannies lasted beyond the third generation, when they were overthrown and replaced by oligarchy (literally, "rule by the few") or, less often, by democracy (literally, "power of the people"). By 500 B.C., tyranny had disappeared from most of Greece.

Sparta

Sparta was located in Laconia, a fertile valley in the south-central Peloponnesus, in the southern part of mainland Greece, and seemed destined by geography for prosperity but not for glory (see **Map 3.2**). Yet Sparta proved to be a powerful model of citizenship and constitutionalism, virtue and community, austerity and militarism.

Sparta was closed and secretive, which makes its history difficult to write. Scholarship has lifted the veil a little, however. For example, Spartans believed that their unique way of life was created all at once by the legendary lawgiver Lycurgus in the 700s B.C. Archaeological evidence, however, suggests gradual innovations in Sparta rather than revolutionary change, beginning around 650 B.C., and it is by no means clear that there ever was a Lycurgus.

The foundations of the Spartan regime were laid around 650 B.C., when a three-part class system emerged. Helots (HEL-uts), unfree laborers who worked the land, were at the lowest level. In the middle ranks were *perioikoi* (roughly, "neighbors"), who were free but under the thumb of the highest class. At the top stood Similars, who were the only full citizens. We do not know the number of helots, but we do know that they vastly outnumbered the other two classes.

GOVERNMENT

Compared with individuals of the other classes, a Similar had a good life. If male and over age 30, he had the right to attend the assembly and to hold public office. Each male Similar, moreover, was given a basic allotment of land worked by helots, which freed him to fight. As the name implies, Similars were alike but not equal. Wealthy Similars owned more land than the basic allotment.

Although Sparta is remembered as a conservative society, the idea of a large group of men sharing power was radical in its day. When the system began around 650 B.C., Similars numbered about nine thousand. What gave them their clout and prestige? The Similars were probably hoplites, the backbone of Sparta's army.

In the mid-seventh century B.C., Sparta depended on its army to keep the helots down. Most helots were Messenians, whose land had been conquered by Sparta in about 725 B.C. Although fellow Greeks, Messenians were forced to work for the conquerors. Sparta profited, but it now faced a security problem. The restive helots had to be policed, and a revolt sometime between 675 and 650 B.C. almost succeeded. To keep Messenia, Sparta needed a crack army; to get that, Sparta made all its hoplites into Similars.

Sparta was no democracy, however. The ancients classified the Spartan government as "mixed" because it combined monarchy, oligarchy (that is, rule by an elite few), and popular government. The assembly of Similars was the popular element, but its powers were limited. Real power was shared among those Similars who were kings, elders, and *ephors* (overseers), men generally belonging to a few wealthy families.

The elite did not lead lives of luxury, however, at least not after around 550 B.C., when austerity became the order of the day. Society was reordered to promote military discipline. For example, the Spartans' diet was famous for its simplicity. The preferred food was a black broth of pork cooked in its own blood and spiced with salt and vinegar. To discourage consumption, Sparta issued no coins; the official "currency" consisted of heavy and clumsy iron skewers. Since the outside world was considered corrupt, Sparta engaged in little trade and admitted few foreigners to its territory—and those who were admitted were subject to periodic expulsion.

SOCIETY

Whereas other poleis offered little or no formal public education, Sparta schooled its sons from childhood to be soldiers—a system known as the *agoge* (ahgo-GAY) ("upbringing"). Limited to male Similars, the agoge created a life cycle unique in Greece. At birth, babies were examined by public inspectors. Those who were considered deformed or unfit were "exposed"—that is, they were abandoned without food or shelter. The victims might die, but they might also be sold into slavery or even secretly adopted. (Other Greeks also practiced exposure of infants, but the choice was a family matter, not public policy.) Surviving children were raised at home up to the age of 7, at which point, boys left the family to be boarded with a "herd" of their age-mates. For the eleven years from age 7 to age 18, a boy went through rigorous training. On the theory that good soldiers should be strong and silent, boys learned only enough reading and writing for practical ends—for example, to transmit messages to and from military headquarters.

Many boys between the ages of 18 and 20 served in the *krypteia* (secret service), living secretly in the hills of Messenia, where they survived by hunting, foraging, and stealing. They spied on the ever rebellious Messenian helots, whom they could kill freely because every year Sparta declared war on helots. By age 20, all Similars had become hoplites, and they continued to serve in the army until age 60. Supported by helot labor, they devoted all their time to fighting and training the next generation.

Sparta offered more opportunities to elite women than did other Greek states. For example, unlike most Greek girls, Spartan girls received a public education—limited, however, to physical training, which was thought to strengthen females for

Spartan Woman This bronze statuette (4¾ inches tall) from Laconia (ca. 530 B.C.) shows a woman running. Unlike other Greek women, elite Spartan women underwent physical education. Although their personal freedom was limited, women in Sparta suffered fewer restrictions than their counterparts in democratic Athens. (C.M. Dixon/Ancient Art & Architecture Collection Ltd)

Spartan Women

Spartan women were famous in antiquity for their freedom, but male observers differed as to whether the results were good or bad. In the following excerpts, Aristotle (384–322 B.C.) criticizes Spartan women, whereas Plutarch (ca. A.D. 50–120), a Greek scholar living in the Roman Empire, praises them.

Aristotle Complains

. . . The legislator [Lycurgus] wished the city as a whole to be hardy, and this is manifest in terms of the men; but he thoroughly neglected it in the case of the women, who live licentiously in every respect and in luxury. Wealth will necessarily be honored in a regime of this sort, particularly if they are dominated by women, as is the case of most stocks that are fond of soldiering and war. . . . This was the case with the Spartans, and many matters were administered by the women during the period of their [imperial] rule [405–371 B.C.]. And yet what difference is there between women ruling and rulers who are ruled by women? For the result is the same . . .

Now this laxness concerning women appears to have arisen among the Spartans in a way that is quite reasonable. They spent much time away from their own land when they were at war. . . . As for the women, they say Lycurgus attempted to lead them toward the laws, but they were resistant, and he gave it up. . . . That what is connected with the women is not finely handled would seem not only to create an inappropriateness in the regime in its own terms, as was said earlier, but to contribute to their greed. For next to what has just been said, one must censure what pertains to the disparity in possessions. For it has happened that some of them possess too much property, and others very little; hence the territory has come into the hands of a few. . . . Indeed, nearly two fifths of the entire territory belongs to women, both because many have become heiresses and because large dowries are given.

Plutarch Counters

Aristotle claims wrongly that he [Lycurgus] tried to discipline the women but gave up when he could not control the considerable degree of license and power attained by women because of their husbands' frequent campaigning. . . . Lycurgus rather showed all possible concern for . . . [women] too. First he toughened the girls physically by making them run and wrestle and throw the discus and javelin. Thereby their children in embryo would make a strong start in strong bodies and would develop better, while the women themselves would also bear their pregnancies with vigour and would meet the challenge of childbirth in a successful, relaxed way. He did away with prudery, sheltered upbringing and effeminacy of any kind. He made young girls no less than young men grow used to walking nude in processions, as well as to dancing and singing at certain festivals with the young men present and looking on . . .

There was nothing disreputable about the girls' nudity. It was altogether modest, and there was no hint of immorality. Instead it encouraged simple habits and an enthusiasm for physical fitness, as well as giving the female sex a taste of masculine gallantry, since it too was granted equal participation in both excellence and ambition.

QUESTIONS

1. According to Aristotle, how and why do Spartan women misbehave?
2. How does Plutarch defend Spartan women?
3. Which author offers more evidence for his case?

Sources: From Aristotle, *The Politics*, trans. Carnes Lord, 1984, pp. 74–75. Reprinted by permission of the publisher, the University of Chicago Press; From *Plutarch on Sparta*, translated with an introduction and notes by Richard J. A. Talbert (Penguin Classics, 1988). Translation, Introduction and Notes copyright © Richard J. A. Talbert 1988. Reproduced by permission of Penguin Books Ltd.

childbearing. The sight of girls running, wrestling, and throwing the discus and javelin, which was common in Sparta, was unthinkable elsewhere in Greece. So was Sparta's unique recognition of the risks of maternity. Like Spartan men who died in battle, Spartan women who died in childbirth were allowed to have their names inscribed on their tombstones. All other Spartan burials were anonymous.

Spartan women were relatively more independent than women elsewhere in Greece. With the men consumed by military training or warfare, women ran the day-to-day operations of life, controlling the helot farmworkers and servants, and raising the girls and the very small boys. Spartan women also had the advantage of being able to inherit property, unlike Athenian women. (See the feature, "The Written Record: Spartan Women.")

Beginning around 550 B.C., Sparta used its military might to build up a network of alliances (dubbed the "Peloponnesian League" by scholars) in the Peloponnesus and central Greece. It may seem paradoxical that a society that feared foreigners, as Sparta did, became the *hegemon* (HEJ-uh-mahn) (literally, "leader") of an extensive alliance system, but Sparta's fear made its leadership slow and careful. Sparta intervened in the wider world only to prevent threats from arising on the horizon, and usually only after a great deal of debate and with the utmost caution.

By around 500 B.C., every Peloponnesian polis except Argos was an ally of Sparta, and in central Greece, Thebes came aboard shortly thereafter. Until its breakup after the Peloponnesian War (431–404 B.C.; see pages 70–72), the Peloponnesian League was the dominant land power in Greece and, after the defeat of Persia in 480 B.C., in the entire eastern Mediterranean.

Sparta exemplified community spirit and respect for law. The people of Sparta, as the historian **Herodotus** (he-ROD-uh-tus) (ca. 485–425 B.C.) quotes a Spartan king, "are free . . . , but not entirely free; for they have a master, and that master is Law, which they fear." Sparta was also an exemplar of equality—limited equality, to be sure, but equality extended to a wider group than ever before in Greece. The notion of the Similars, moreover, contains the germ of the idea of the citizen: a free member of the political community who, unlike a subject, has rights as well as duties. Few other poleis could match the stability and sense of civic duty fostered by Sparta. In the realms of equality and citizenship, however, Sparta was eventually outstripped by Athens. In the realm of liberty, Athens wrote a new chapter in Western history.

Early Athens

Around 650 B.C., the basileis of the Pedion, or Attic, Plain, who proudly called themselves the Eupatrids ("well-fathered men"), ruled Athens (see **MAP 3.4**). They served in one-year magistracies and afterward became life members of the Areopagus (ar-ee-OP-uh-gus), a council of elders named for its meeting place on the "hill of Ares." This aristocratic council dominated both politics and justice, for it also served as a court. The demos (DEE-mus) (the people) met in an

🌐 **MAP 3.4—Attica**
Mountains and plains alternate in the 1,000-square-mile area of ancient Attica. The Long Walls connecting Athens with the port city of Piraeus were built around 450 B.C.

assembly. Probably from early times on, the assembly had, in theory, supreme lawmaking power as well as authority over war and peace, but voting was by shouting, and few people challenged Eupatrid wishes.

By 632 B.C., the aristocrats faced trouble in Athens as elsewhere because of corruption, economic change, and assertive hoplites. A failed attempt that year to establish a tyranny left the forces for change eager. In 621 B.C., a loose coalition opposed to Eupatrid rule forced a codification of the laws, which were then issued in writing. This Code of Draco (DRAY-co), named for its main drafter, was infamous for its harsh provisions (hence, our adjective *draconian*); it was written, a later commentator suggested, "not in ink but blood." Yet, Draco's Code seems only to have whetted an appetite for change. A wealthy non-Eupatrid elite of hoplites was emerging, grown rich exporting olive oil. Some were merchants; most were prosperous farmers. They now wanted political power. As for ordinary Athenians, they typically worked small family farms. Over the years, bad harvests and soil exhaustion had sent many into debt. Those who had pledged their land as collateral became known as *hektemoroi* ("sixth-parters"), probably because they owed one-sixth of their crops to their creditors. Other farmers sank even further into debt and had only themselves or their children as collateral. Some ended up as slaves, sometimes sold abroad. Because both rich and poor Athenians had grievances against the Eupatrids, revolution was in the air.

Solon Statesman of early Athens, he transformed Greek society through mediation, moderation, respect for law, and measures that liberated the poor and downtrodden.

Enter **Solon** (ca. 630–560 B.C.), who was appointed to the emergency position of sole *archon* (chief officer) for one year, probably 594 B.C. A Eupatrid who had become a merchant, Solon (SO-lun) understood both the old and the new elite, and he was sympathetic to ordinary Athenians as well. As his surviving writings show, Solon was a moderate. He could have become tyrant, but he preferred to be a mediator.

Solon reformed both economics and politics. Many of his measures were aimed at encouraging Athenian trade, and they led to a commercial boom. More important, Solon helped ordinary people by the "shaking off of burdens," measures that abolished the institution of *hektemorage* and probably canceled some debts. He also abolished the practice of making loans on personal surety and set up a fund to redeem Athenians who had been sold into slavery abroad. By freeing the hektemoroi, Solon ensured Athens a large class of independent small farmers.

Solon made fundamental changes in Athenian government, too. He changed qualifications for office from birth to wealth, a boon to the non-Eupatrid elite. He established four census classes based on agricultural production. Most offices were reserved for men of property, but the poorest class, known as *thetes*, could participate in the assembly and courts. Solon probably established the Council of 400, which prepared the assembly's agenda. He is probably also responsible for setting a regular schedule of council and assembly meetings and for replacing the assembly's voice votes with the counting of hands.

Solon's moderation, respect for law, and liberation of the poor and downtrodden are milestones in Greek history. Without his reforms, it is doubtful that democracy could have later taken root in Athens. Yet Solon's work also had an unexpected byproduct: the growth of slavery in Athens. Though booming, the Athenian economy lost its cheap labor when Solon freed debt slaves and hektemoroi. The solution was to buy slaves abroad and import them to Athens. The island city-state of Chios led the way; it was the first Greek polis to organize a slave trade and always had a large slave population (see **MAP 3.2**). After Solon, Athens joined Chios as a society that depended on slave labor. Unlike helots, slaves could be bought and sold and were often uprooted, and the system was better policed than in earlier societies.

In the centuries after Solon, slavery became widespread in Athens. Some slaves served in agriculture, some labored under miserable conditions in Athenian silver mines, and some were engaged in commerce or the military (where some rowers were slaves). Most, however, worked as domestics or in small workshops as, for example, metalworkers or furniture makers. The vast majority of slaves were non-Greek. Most were prisoners of war; some were victims of pirates or debtors from states where, unlike Athens, citizens might end up in debt slavery. Thrace (roughly, modern Bulgaria) and Anatolia were the main sources of slaves, but some slaves came from North Africa and other Mediterranean regions.

Living conditions for slaves were usually poor and those in the silver mines were abysmal. Emancipation, however, was more common in Athens than in the American South before 1865. A few ex-slaves even rose to positions of wealth and power in Athens. A striking and unusual case is that of Pasion (d. 370 B.C.). Originally a slave employee of a banking firm, he bought his freedom and became the wealthiest Athenian banker of his day, as well as an Athenian citizen.

If free Athenians had any moral doubts about slavery, they went unrecorded. Yet, there was much dissatisfaction with Solon's reforms, since his middle way satisfied neither Eupatrids nor champions of the free poor. After years of conflict, around 560 B.C., advocates of radical reform established a tyranny under Pisistratus (pie-SIS-trah-tus) (ca. 600–528 B.C.). He and his sons held power for forty of the next fifty years.

Supported by the common people, the Pisistratids exiled many Eupatrids and confiscated and redistributed their land. Pisistratus kept the façade of Solon's reforms while ensuring that loyal supporters held all key offices.

The tyranny was a stable regime that witnessed prosperity at home and the expansion of Athenian influence abroad. Yet, Pisistratus's dynasty lasted only two generations and was deposed in 510 B.C. Athens's elites by birth and wealth were ready to establish an oligarchy, but the way was open for an unexpected development: the emergence of popular government.

SECTION SUMMARY

- Trade, colonization, and the invention of the Greek alphabet and of the hoplite phalanx all contributed to the emergence of the polis around 750–700 B.C.
- The polis was a community of citizens that emphasized participation and equality.
- Corinth is the best example of a polis where new wealth led to the emergence of the first tyrants—originally, popular champions.
- Sparta's austere and militaristic society turned boys into soldiers and trained girls to be tough and assertive wives and mothers.
- Solon's reforms freed the poor, but unintentionally laid the foundations for the growth of slavery.

THE CULTURE OF ARCHAIC GREECE

How did Western individualism and rationalism take root in Archaic Greece?

While one trend in Archaic culture was communal solidarity, as reflected in the hoplite phalanx, another was the opposite: a growing elevation of individualism. Increased prosperity and mobility (social, geographic, and political) during the Archaic period encouraged the breakdown of old ties and left some people with a sense of their uniqueness. Archaic poetry and sculpture both demonstrate this new consciousness of the self.

Meanwhile, although most Archaic Greeks celebrated religion, a small group of thinkers expressed religious doubts. While monumental stone temples and international centers for divination were being erected to honor the pantheon of gods, Greek thinkers began to move away from divine and toward abstract and mechanistic explanations of the universe. Their defection marked the start of the Western philosophical tradition.

Revealing the Self: Lyric Poetry and Sculpture

Between approximately 675 and 500 B.C., the dominant Greek literary form was lyric poetry. This genre consisted of short poems written in a variety of styles but sharing a willingness to experiment, sometimes by revealing private feelings, sometimes by commenting on politics. Epic poetry, by contrast, was longer, grander in theme and tone, and less personal.

Homer never speaks directly about himself, and Hesiod reveals only a few personal details. In contrast, Archilochus (ar-KIL-uh-kus) of Paros (ca. 700–650 B.C.), the earliest known of the lyric poets, flaunts the self. Born on the Cycladic island of Paros, Archilochus was the son, perhaps the illegitimate son, of a noble. He was a mercenary soldier (that is, he fought for pay for a foreign city) and a colonist before returning home and dying in a hoplite battle against a neighboring island. The varied subjects of Archilochus's poetry include love, travel, and war. Much of his poetry is satire, sometimes mocking and ironic, sometimes vicious and abusive. Archilochus takes a cynical and detached view of hoplite ideals, freely admitting that he once tossed away his shield to escape the battlefield: "And that shield, to hell with it! Tomorrow I'll get me another one no worse."[1]

Sappho of Lesbos (ca. 625 B.C.) is also famous as a private poet, one who composed unmatched descriptions of intimate feelings, among them love for other women. Sappho (SAF-foh) is one of the few women poets of antiquity whose work has survived—very little, unfortunately, but enough to show that she was educated, worldly, and versed in politics. Like a modern experimental poet, she uses language self-consciously. Sappho's sensuality comes through in a description of her feelings at seeing a woman whose company she desires talking with a man: her heart shakes, her tongue is stuck, her eyes cannot see, her skin is on fire. "I am greener than grass," Sappho writes. "I feel nearly as if I could die."[2]

Sappho Ancient Greek poet from the island of Lesbos, she wrote odes, wedding songs, and hymns expressing intimate feelings, including love for other women.

Sappho discusses female sexuality, a subject that Greek elite culture, dominated by males, tended to ignore. We know little about the sexuality of Greek women or of non-elite males. Among the male elite, romantic love in Archaic and **Classical Greece** was homosexual love or, to be precise, *pederasty* ("boy love"). The ideal relationship was supposed to involve a man in his twenties and a boy in his teens. The male elite was, strictly speaking, bisexual. By age 30, a man was expected to marry and raise a family. Perhaps bisexuality prevailed among elite females as well; Sappho, for example, eventually married and had a child.

Another sign of the interest in the personal in Archaic Greece is the growing attention paid to the depiction of the human body, both in painting (most of the surviving examples are painted pottery) and in sculpture. Archaic artists displayed increasing skill and sensitivity in depicting the human form. The rich marble deposits in Greek soil gave sculptors promising material; baked clay (terra cotta) and bronze were other common sculptural media.

Early Archaic marble sculpture (seventh century B.C.) was strongly influenced by the way Egyptian sculpture represented the human body. Like Egyptian statuary, early Greek sculpture tended to be formal and frontal. Over the course of the seventh and sixth centuries B.C., Greek sculptors experimented with a greater variety of poses and with increasing realism in showing musculature and motion. This realism, however, was expressed within limits, for the favorite subject of Archaic sculptors was not ordinary people but idealized, beautiful youth. The goal was to show people not as they were but as they might be.

Athenian Kore This statue of a young woman (*kore*) exemplifies Archaic Greek sculpture's interest in the idealized human form. Note the slight smile, the carefully coifed hair, and the elaborate clothes. Influenced by contemporary Egyptian statues, Greek sculptors nonetheless created a new and original style.
(Nimatallah/Art Resource, NY)

Classical Greece Period of ancient Greek history from about 480 to 323 B.C.

Religious Faith and Practice

The Olympian gods who had been worshiped in the Mycenaean era survived in later ages, adapted to fit new political and social conditions. In the Archaic period, accordingly, the Olympian gods became gods of the polis.

Although the Olympians were revered throughout Greece, each polis had its patron deity, as well as its favorite heroes or demigods. Devotees considered it important to build a "house"—that is, a temple—for the local patron god or at least for his or her statue. The first temples were built of wood; the earliest stone temple, a temple of Apollo at Corinth, was built around 550 B.C.

Temples were rectangular structures with long sides on the north and south, short sides on the east and west, a colonnade around all four sides, and a pitched roof. The columns were based loosely on those of Egyptian architecture. Greek temples faced east so sunlight would illuminate the interior, which consisted of two rooms: a small treasury, open to the west, and a larger main chamber, in which a statue of the deity stood. The interior decoration of the temple was simple. Outside, however, brownish red roof tiles, painted sculpture above the colonnade and in the pediments (the area between the gables and the front and rear doorways), and terra-cotta roof ornaments created a festive and lively effect. The bare white ruins seen today are misleading.

The emphasis on exterior decoration reflects the way a Greek temple was used. The main ceremony took place outside. A long altar stood in front of the temple where on feast days temple priests would sacrifice animals (pigs, goats, lambs, and, less often, bulls) on the altar. Only the thighs would be burned for the gods. The rest of the meat would be boiled and distributed to worshipers. Under the tyrants, the number of such days was increased greatly, as a concession to the common people.

As in other ancient cultures, so in Greece, divination was an important element of religion. Divination was institutionalized in *oracles*, places where a god or hero might be consulted for advice. The most famous Greek oracle was that of Apollo at Delphi (DEL-fye) in central Greece. At Delphi, Apollo spoke through the Pythia, a priestess who went into a trance. The utterances of Apollo at Delphi were known for being ambiguous. Because different people might interpret them in different ways, Apollo could not be blamed after the fact if things did not turn out as the listener expected. Politicians and poleis regularly consulted Delphi about public policy.

Archaic thinkers pondered the theme of divine justice. In Archaic literature, we see less of the petty squabbling among the gods than in Homer and more of Zeus's majesty and justice. Although the wicked might seem to prosper, Zeus eventually punishes them or their descendants.

Archaic writers delighted in portraying human emotions, but they had no confidence about the human ability to master emotions. In Archaic literature, people are weak and insignificant; their fortune is uncertain and mutable. Further, the gods are jealous of human success. People who aim too high are guilty of *hubris*—arrogance with overtones of violence and transgression. Hubris inevitably brings *nemesis*, "punishment" or "allotment." The safest course is for a person to be pious and humble.

So, Archaic religion taught a humbling, even pessimistic, lesson. Yet, its teachings were not always heeded. The pages of Archaic history are full of people who aimed high and sought success with seemingly little worry or dire consequences. In Ionia (see **MAP 3.2**), one group of Greek thinkers made a radical break with Archaic religion and invented speculative philosophy.

The Origins of Western Philosophy

Abstract, rationalistic, speculative thinking emerged in Greece during the sixth century B.C. The first developments took place in Miletus (my-LEE-tus), an Ionian city. It is often said that the thinkers of Miletus (the Milesians) and their followers in other parts of Ionia invented philosophy. So they did, but we must be precise about what this means.

The Ionians were not the first to ask questions or tell stories about the nature and origins of the universe; virtually every ancient people did so, nor did the Ionians invent science. They conducted no experiments. By 600 B.C., moreover, mathematics, astronomy, medicine, and engineering had been thriving for over two thousand years in Egypt and Mesopotamia, a heritage with which the Ionians were familiar and from which they borrowed.

The real importance of the Ionians is as pioneers of rationalism. They began the movement away from anthropomorphic or divine explanations and toward an abstract and mechanistic explanation of the universe. Later Greek philosophers were rarely (if ever) atheists, but they took for granted what the Ionians labored to establish: the primacy of human reason.

The Ionians saw themselves as students of nature—*physis* (from which the word *physics* is derived). Although they also commented on morality and politics, their interest in natural phenomena is what makes the Ionians significant. In their own day, the Ionians were called "wise men" (*sophoi*); to a later generation, they were "lovers of wisdom," *philosophoi* (from which *philosopher* comes).

Thales (THAY-leez), the first Milesian thinker, made a name for himself by successfully predicting a solar eclipse in 585 B.C. He is credited with founding Greek geometry and astronomy. Little survives of his writings or those of the other Milesians, but it is clear that he created the first general and systematic theory about the nature of the universe. According to Thales, the primary substance, the element from which all of nature was created, was water. He emphasized the mobility of water and its ability to nourish life.

A reply followed soon. Around 550 B.C., Anaximander of Miletus wrote the first known book of prose in Greek, expounding his own philosophy of nature. He attacked Thales for oversimplifying the dynamism of nature. Anaximander accepted Thales' monist assumption—that all matter originated from one primary substance—but he called the substance "the unlimited" or "the undefined" rather than water. A third Milesian, Anaximenes, replied that the primary substance might be unlimited but it was not undefined. It was air, whose properties of condensation and rarefaction symbolized the dynamic and changing nature of things.

Humble as these theories might seem today, they represent a dramatic development: an open and critical debate among thinkers, each of whom was proposing an abstract and rational model of the universe. Many scholars have speculated about the origins of this development. Why Miletus? Why the sixth century B.C.? There are no sure answers, although certain influences have been suggested. Among them are Miletus's contacts on the trade routes with sophisticated Babylon, the proximity of Ionia to non-Greek peoples and the resulting Milesian appreciation of variety and complexity, and the search for law and order in contemporary Greek political life and its extension to the philosophical plane.

In its second generation, early Greek philosophy moved to other Ionian cities and then migrated westward across the Mediterranean. Heracleitus (her-uh-CLY-tus) of Ephesus (ca. 500 B.C.) proposed fire as the primary substance. Although fire was ever changing, it had an underlying coherence. According to Heracleitus, this paradox nicely symbolized the nature of the universe. He summed up the importance of change by the aphorisms "All things flow" and "You cannot step into the same river twice." The universe witnessed a constant struggle of opposites, yet an essential unity and order prevailed. To describe this order, Heracleitus used the term *logos* (LOH-gos). This key concept of Greek philosophy is difficult to translate; among other definitions, *logos* can mean "word," "thought," "reason," "story," or "calculation." The term *logos* embodies the importance of reason in ancient Greek civilization.

Heracleitus's contemporary, Pythagoras (py-THAGuh-russ) of Samos, was both a rationalist and a religious thinker. On the one hand, Pythagoras was a mathematician who discovered the numerical ratios determining the major intervals of the musical scale—that is, the range of sound between high and low. It is less certain if, as tradition has it, he discovered the so-called Pythagorean theorem—that in a right triangle the hypotenuse squared is equal to the sum of the squares of the other two sides.

On the other hand, Pythagoras believed that the purity of mathematics would improve the human soul. Just as he had imposed numerical order on the musical scale, so could philosophers understand the entire universe through number and proportion. The resulting knowledge was no mere academic exercise, but a way of life. Pythagoras devoted himself to "observation" or "contemplation"—to *theoria* (from which *theory* comes).

In Magna Graecia (southern Italy), Pythagoras founded a religious community. Its members observed strict secrecy, but it appears that they abstained from meat because they believed in the kinship of all living things. They also believed in the reincarnation of the human soul, though not necessarily into a human body.

The early Greek philosopher whose work is most fully preserved is Parmenides (par-MEN-uh-deez) of Elea in Magna Graecia. Parmenides (b. ca. 515 B.C.) completely distrusted the senses. He believed that reality was a world of pure being: eternal, unchanging, and indivisible, comparable to a sphere. To Parmenides, change was a mere illusion. Parmenides, therefore, is the first Western philosopher to propose a radical difference between the world of the senses and reality. This fundamental strain of Western thought would be taken up by Plato and his followers and then passed to Christianity.

To sum up, in philosophy, as in so many other endeavors, the Archaic Greeks were great borrowers and even greater innovators who left a profound mark on later ages. By the late sixth century B.C., Archaic Greece was poised on the brink of a revolution that would give birth to the Classical period of Greek civilization.

SECTION SUMMARY

- Lyric poetry and Archaic sculpture display a groundbreaking interest in individual feelings and the human body.

- Archaic Greek religion was pessimistic. It feared human arrogance (*hubris*) and divine punishment (*nemesis*).

- Western philosophy began in Ionia in the 500s B.C.

- The first philosophers were rationalists who offered abstract and mechanistic explanations of nature.

CLASSICAL GREECE

What was Athenian democracy and how did it clash with Sparta in the Peloponnesian War?

demokratia Term coined in Athens in the fifth century B.C. to describe the city's system of direct government.

The word **democracy** comes from the Greek **demokratia** (deh-mo-kra-TEE-uh), coined in Athens early in the fifth century B.C. *Demokratia* literally means "the power (*kratos*) of the people (*demos*)." Modern democracy is characterized by mass citizenship, elections, and representative government. Athenian *demokratia*, in contrast, was a direct democracy in which elections mattered less than direct participation, citizenship was restricted, women were excluded from politics, immigrants could rarely become citizens, and citizens owned slaves and ruled an empire. Modern democracies are big, but Athens encompassed only 1,000 square miles. Modern democracies emphasize individual rights, but Athens placed the community first. Yet Athenian *demokratia* established principles enshrined in democracy today: freedom, equality, citizenship without property qualifications, the right of most citizens to hold office, and the rule of law.

The young democracy's greatest achievement was to spearhead Greece's victory over the Persian invaders in 480 B.C. After that victory, Athens became Greece's leading sea power. Yet Sparta remained the superior land power, and the two poleis were soon locked in a cycle of competition and war. The result nearly destroyed Athenian democracy. Even more serious, it undermined Greece's very independence.

The Development of Demokratia, 508–322 B.C.

In Athens after Pisistratid rule, conditions were ripe for revolution. Solon had left a society of independent small farmers, while the Pisistratids had strengthened the ranks of immigrants and weakened the Eupatrids. Elite leaders nonetheless tried to establish an Athenian oligarchy. We may imagine strong popular opposition.

Ironically, a Eupatrid, Cleisthenes (KLICE-the-neez) (d. ca. 500 B.C.), led the revolution. Originally, Cleisthenes aimed to head the oligarchy, but his rivals shut him out of power. He turned then to the demos, whose leader he became. The watchwords of the day were *equality* and *mixing* (that is, mixing people from different regions of Attica in order to break down local, aristocratic power bases).

Frightened by the assertive populace, the oligarchs called for Spartan military assistance, but to no avail: Cleisthenes rallied the people to victory. The Athenian triumph proved, in Herodotus's opinion, "that equality is an excellent thing, not in one way only but in many. For while they were under a tyranny, [Athenians] were no better at fighting than any of their neighbors, but once they were rid of tyrants they became by far the best."[3]

Cleisthenes extinguished Eupatrid power once and for all by attacking its local bases of support. For example, he abolished the four traditional tribes and apportioned the people among ten new tribes. The tribes formed the basis of a new Council of 500 to replace Solon's Council of 400. The council was divided into ten tribal units, each serving as a kind of executive committee for one of the ten months of the civic year.

The centerpiece of the government was the assembly, some of whose members, emboldened by the new spirit of equality, now spoke up for the first time. The new Council of 500, like its predecessor, prepared the assembly's agenda, but assemblymen felt free to amend it. Only the Areopagus council remained a privileged preserve.

The last and most unusual part of the Cleisthenic system was ostracism, a sort of annual *un*popularity contest that received its name from the pieces of broken pottery (*ostraka*) on which the names of victims were chiseled. The "winner" was forced into ten years of exile, although his property would not be confiscated. Ostracism was meant to protect the regime by defusing factionalism and discouraging tyrants. Judging by Athens's political stability, it worked.

In 508 B.C., the poorest Athenians had relatively little power in Cleisthenic government, but changes by the 450s made Athens even more democratic. During that period, the oldest principle

Greek Trireme *Olympias* is a hypothetical reconstruction of an Athenian war galley of about 400 B.C. Rowed by 170 oarsmen arranged on three decks, the trireme fought by ramming an enemy ship with the bronze ram attached to its bow. (John Coates/Trireme Trust Foundation)

of Greek politics came to the fore: Whoever fights for the state governs it. To counter the Persian threat against Greece in the 480s (see page 70), Athens built a great navy. The standard ship was a trireme (TRY-reem), an oared warship rowed by 170 men on three decks. The core of the rowers consisted of thetes, the poorest free men in Athens. Just as hoplites supported new regimes in Greece after 700 B.C., so rowers supported new regimes in Greece after 500 B.C.

A second revolution occurred around 461 B.C., when Ephialtes (d. ca. 460 B.C.) and his young associate **Pericles** (ca. 495–429 B.C.) targeted the last bulwark of privilege, the Areopagus. They stripped away the council's long-standing supervisory powers over the regime and redistributed those powers to the Council of 500 and the people's court. The decade of the 450s B.C. saw another innovation: payment for public service, specifically for jurors, who received a half-drachma (perhaps half a day's wages) for a day of jury duty. Eventually, other public servants also received pay. Conservatives complained bitterly because they perceived, rightly, that state pay made political activity by poor people possible. State pay was, an Athenian said, "the glue of demokratia."

Demokratia became closely connected with Pericles (PAIR-ih-kleez), who inherited the constituency of Ephialtes after his assassination around 460 B.C. For much of the next thirty years, Pericles dominated Athenian politics. An aristocrat who respected the common people, an excellent orator who benefited from an education in philosophy, an honest and tireless worker, and a general who led in peace as well as war, Pericles was a political giant. Under his leadership, demokratia became firmly entrenched as the government and way of life in Athens.

Pericles was much influenced by a woman, Aspasia (uh-SPAY-see-uh). She belonged to the small group of noncitizen women called *hetairai*, or courtesans (that is, prostitutes patronized by men of wealth and status). An educated woman from Miletus, Aspasia was Pericles' mistress and bore him a son. Aspasia and Pericles gathered around them a glittering circle of thinkers and artists. Some say that Aspasia even influenced Pericles' political decisions.

Athenian democracy survived, with occasional oligarchic intrusions, for 150 years after Pericles' death. During those years, it became more institutionalized and cautious, but it also became more thoroughly egalitarian.

How Demokratia Worked

Unlike most modern democracies, Athenian demokratia was direct and participatory. Pericles once claimed that in Athens, "people pay attention both to their own household and to politics. Even those occupied with other activities are no less knowledgeable about politics."[4] This is part boast, but only part. Large numbers of ordinary citizens attended the assembly from time to time and held public office or served on the Council of 500 for a year or two.

GOVERNMENT The central institution was the assembly. Open to all male citizens over age 20, assembly meetings were held in the open air, on a hillside seating several thousand on benches (see the photograph on page 48). In the fourth century B.C., the assembly gathered a minimum of forty times per year, about once every ten days.

The assembly heard the debates of the day. It made decisions about war and peace, alliance and friendship; it conferred honors and issued condemnations; it passed decrees relating to current issues and set up commissions to revise fundamental laws. In the assembly, top orators addressed the people, but everyone, however humble, was theoretically entitled to speak.

The judicial branch consisted of courts, which, with a few exceptions, were open to all citizens, no matter how poor. Aristotle or a member of his school comments that "when the people have the right to vote in the courts, they control the constitution." Juries were large, commonly consisting of several hundred men chosen by lottery; small juries, it was felt, were easily bribed. After a preliminary hearing, cases were decided in a single day.

The executive consisted of the Council of 500 and some seven hundred public officials (also, under Athens's empire in the fifth century B.C., several hundred others living abroad). All male citizens over age 30 were eligible to serve. Most public officials were chosen by lottery, which put rich and poor, talented and untalented, on an equal footing. To guard against installing incompetents or criminals, all officials had to undergo a scrutiny by the council before taking office and an audit after the term. Most magistracies, moreover, were boards, usually of ten men, so even if a bad man managed to pass this scrutiny, he would be counterbalanced by his colleagues. Only generals and treasurers were chosen by election.

Pericles Leader of fifth century B.C. Athens, he established Athens as a great center of art and literature as well as a great empire.

Athens had a weak executive and no president or prime minister. Generals and orators led debates and sometimes exercised great influence, but ordinary people set the agenda and made the decisions by taking votes at each assembly meeting. On the local level, every deme (county) had an annually chosen executive and a deme assembly of all citizens.

So novel and populist a system of government has not been without critics, either in antiquity or today. Some have charged that the Athenian people were uneducated, emotional, and easily swayed by oratorical tricks. Others say that demokratia degenerated into mob rule after the death of Pericles. Still others complain about the lack of a system of formal public education, which denied many citizens equality of opportunity.

Another serious charge against Athenian demokratia is that it was democracy for an elite only. Adult male citizens never amounted to more than one-tenth of the population, approximately 40,000 out of a total population—men, women and children, resident aliens, and slaves—of about 400,000. To become a citizen, a boy at age 18 had to prove that he was the legitimate son of a citizen father and a citizen maternal grandfather. Girls were never officially registered as citizens. Although the term *citizeness* existed, Athenian citizen women were usually referred to as "city women." Resident aliens rarely attained citizenship.

WOMEN AND RESIDENT ALIENS

In the fifth and fourth centuries B.C., Athens had a large population of foreigners. Some were transient. Others were officially registered resident aliens, or *metics* (MEH-tiks). Metics came by the thousands from all over the Greek world and beyond. Some, like Aristotle (a native of a Greek colony in Macedonia [mah-suh-DOE-nee-uh]), were attracted by the city's schools of philosophy, but most came because of its unparalleled economic opportunities. Metics could not own land in Athens, and they had to pay extra taxes and serve in the Athenian military. Nevertheless, they prospered in Athenian commerce and crafts.

Athenian women were excluded from politics and played only a modest role in commerce as small retailers. In legal matters, women were almost always required to be represented by a male guardian. Demokratia also promoted an ideal of the male as master of his household. Women were expected to be obedient and remain indoors.

Practice, however, was another matter. As Aristotle asks rhetorically, "How is it possible to prevent the wives of the poor from going out?" *Poor* is a synonym for *ordinary* in ancient Greek. Ordinary women could not stay at home because they had work to do in the city or fields. Ordinary houses, moreover, were small and cramped, and in the Mediterranean heat, women could not stay inside all the time.

We occasionally get glimpses, sometimes more, of Athenian women resisting or working behind the scenes to correct male mistakes. An inheritance case reveals a woman go-between interceding among her quarreling male relations. Greek comedy shows women mocking male pretensions and establishing sisterly friendships. A woman who brought a large dowry into a marriage could use it and the threat of divorce to influence her husband (the dowry had to be returned to the woman's father or guardian if there was a divorce). In short, Athenian women had some access to the world outside the household and some influence within the household. There existed, nonetheless, a real disparity in power between men and women.

Athenian demokratia lacked many features of modern democracy, including a notion of human rights, the mass naturalization of immigrants, gender equality, the abolition of slavery, and public education. To its small citizen body, however, Athenian demokratia offered freedom, equality, and responsibility, as well as a degree of participation in public life seldom equaled. Demokratia was a model of what democracy could be, but not of who could take part.

The Persian Wars, 499–479 B.C.

In 500 B.C., Sparta, hegemon of the Peloponnesian League, was the most prominent power of the Greek mainland. Across the Aegean Sea in Anatolia, the Greek city-states had been under Persian rule for two generations, since Cyrus the Great's conquest in the 540s B.C. In 499 B.C., however, events began to unfold that not only would revolutionize that balance of power, but also would throw the entire eastern Mediterranean into two hundred years of turmoil.

Led by Miletus, the Ionian Greek city-states rose in revolt against Persia in 499 B.C. Athens sent troops to help, but despite initial successes, Athens reconsidered the alliance and withdrew its forces. The Ionian coalition broke down thereafter and was crushed by Persia. Miletus was besieged and destroyed, but otherwise, Persia was relatively lenient in Ionia.

Amazon Queen This red-figure Athenian cup (ca. 440 B.C.) shows the Greek warrior Achilles about to slay the Amazon queen Penthesilea during the Trojan War, in which she fought on Troy's side. She was a symbol of feminine courage and beauty. (Staatliche Antikensammlungen und Glyptothek, Munich)

Upstart Athens, however, could not go unpunished. In 490 B.C., Darius I sent a large naval expedition against Athens. About 25,000 infantrymen and 1,200 cavalrymen (with horses) landed at Marathon, some 24 miles from the city of Athens (see **Map 3.4**). Athens sent 10,000 men (including 1,000 allies) to defend Marathon, and a great battle ensued.

Persian overconfidence and the superiority of the Greek phalanx over Persia's loosely organized infantrymen won Athens a smashing victory. Persia suffered 6,400 casualties, Athens only 192. (The story, unconfirmed, that a messenger ran from the battlefield to the city of Athens with the news, "Rejoice, we conquer!" is the inspiration for the modern marathon race, a slightly longer distance of about 26 miles.) After the battle, Athens experienced a burst of confidence that propelled it to power and glory.

Meanwhile, Persia sought a rematch. After Darius's death in 486, his son and successor, Xerxes, amassed a huge force of about a thousand ships and several hundred thousand soldiers and rowers. Athens, under the leadership of Themistocles (ca. 525–460 B.C.), prepared by building a fleet of two hundred ships. Athens joined Sparta and twenty-nine other poleis in the Hellenic League of defense, with Sparta in overall command. Most poleis either stayed neutral or, like Thebes and Argos, collaborated with Persia. The Greeks had only three-hundred-plus ships and about fifty thousand infantrymen.

Persia invaded Greece in 480 B.C. and won the opening moves. At the narrow pass of Thermopylae in central Greece (see **Map 3.2**), the Persians outflanked and crushed a small Spartan army, who died fighting to the last man, including their king, Leonidas. This sacrifice added to the Spartan reputation for courage but left the road south open. Abandoned by its defenders, Athens was sacked.

The tide then turned. The Greeks lured the Persian fleet into the narrow straits between Athens and Salamis. The Persians could not use their numerical superiority in this confined space, and the Greeks had the home advantage. The result was a crushing Persian defeat under the eyes of Xerxes himself, who watched the battle from a throne on a hillside near the shore.

Because their sea links to the Levant had been cut, Xerxes and the remainder of the Persian fleet left for home. Soon afterward, the united Greek army, under Spartan leadership, defeated Persian forces on land at Plataea (just north of Attica; see **Map 3.2**) in 479 B.C. At about the same time, the Greek fleet defeated a reorganized Persian fleet off the Anatolian coast. The victorious Greeks sailed the coast and liberated the Ionians. Not only did Persia fail to conquer the Greek mainland, but it also lost its eastern Aegean empire.

Greeks did not remember the invader fondly. After 480, they thought of Persians not merely as enemies but as barbarians—that is, cultural inferiors. (See the feature, "The Global Record: The Enemy as Barbarian.") At the same time, Greeks became more conscious of their own common culture.

Struggles to Dominate Greece, 478–362 B.C.

The Greek unity forged by the struggle against Persia was fragile and short-lived. What followed was a constant struggle in diplomacy and war among city-states, usually arranged in leagues under hegemons.

Following the Greek victory over Persia, Athens expanded its power as hegemon of a new security organization. Founded on the island of Delos in the Aegean Sea, the so-called Delian League aimed both at protecting Greek lands and at plundering Persian territory. The number of allies grew from about 150 in 477 B.C. to about 250 in 431 B.C., at the height of the league.

Because they feared entanglement outside the Peloponnesus, most Spartans preferred to leave the Aegean to Athens. Some Spartans, nonetheless, watched with unease and jealousy as Athenian power boomed.

The Enemy as Barbarian

Classical Greeks no longer regarded the enemy as honored rivals, as Homer's heroes had regarded Trojans. Rather, they looked down on the enemy as a barbarian. Greece's archenemies, the Persians, were portrayed as indulgent, effeminate, emotional, slavish, cruel, and dangerous. Consider the contrasting portraits of Persians and Greeks in these excerpts from the historian Herodotus's account of Persia's invasion of Greece in 480 B.C.

The Persians

He [King Xerxes of Persia] then prepared to move forward to Abydos, where a bridge had already been constructed across the Hellespont from Europe to Asia. . . . It was here not long afterwards that the Greeks under Xanthippus the son of Ariphron took Artayctes the Persian governor of Sestos, and nailed him alive to a plank—he was the man who collected women in the temple of Protesilaus at Elaeus and committed various acts of sacrilege. This headland was the point to which Xerxes' engineers carried their two bridges from Abydos—a distance of seven furlongs. . . . The work was successfully completed, but a subsequent storm of great violence smashed it up and carried everything away. Xerxes was very angry when he learned of the disaster, and gave orders that the Hellespont should receive three hundred lashes and have a pair of fetters thrown into it. And I have heard before now that he also sent people to brand it with hot irons. He certainly instructed the men with the whips to utter, as they wielded them, the following words: "You salt and bitter stream, your master lays this punishment upon you for injuring him, who never injured you. But Xerxes the King will cross you, with or without your permission. No man sacrifices to you, and you deserve the neglect by your acrid and muddy waters"—a highly presumptuous way of addressing the Hellespont, and typical of a barbarous nation. In addition to punishing the Hellespont Xerxes gave orders that the men responsible for building the bridge should have their heads cut off. This unseemly order was duly carried out . . .

The Greeks

To the Spartan envoys . . . [the Athenians] said: "No doubt it was natural that the Lacedaemonians [Spartans] should dread the possibility of our making terms with Persia; nonetheless it shows a poor estimate of the spirit of Athens. Were we offered all the gold in the world, and the fairest and richest country the earth contains, we should never consent to join the common enemy and bring Greece into submission. There are many compelling reasons to prevent our taking such a course, even if we wish to do so: the first and greatest is the burning of the temples and images of our gods—now mere heaps of rubble. It is our bounden duty to avenge this desecration with all the power we possess—not to clasp in friendship the hand that wrought it. Again, there is the Greek nation—the common blood, the common language; the temples and religious ritual; the whole way of life we understand and share together—indeed, if Athens were to betray all this it would not be well done. We would have you know, therefore, if you did not already know it, that we will never make peace with Xerxes so long as a single Athenian remains alive."

Quote.

QUESTIONS

1. Find at least three examples in these passages of Persian barbarism.

2. By deciding to make war instead of negotiating peace, are the Athenians barbarians or civilized people?

3. Does Herodotus offer convincing proof that the Persians are more barbarous than the Greeks? Is he fair?

Source: From *The Histories* by Herodotus, translated by Aubrey de Sélincourt, revised with introductory matter and notes by John Marincola (Penguin Classics 1954, Second revised edition 1996). Translation copyright 1954 by Aubrey de Sélincourt. This revised edition copyright ©John Marincola 1996. Reproduced by permission of Penguin Books Ltd.

Afraid of the new titan, the major allied states rebelled, beginning with Thasos in 465 B.C., but Athens crushed each rebellion. Sometimes after surrender, rebels were executed and their wives and children sold into slavery. Allied complaints began to stir Sparta. A conflict loomed between Greece's greatest land power, Sparta, and Greece's greatest sea power, Athens.

The Peloponnesian War, as this conflict is known today, came in 431 B.C. and lasted intermittently until 404 B.C. The war proved bloody and bitter. Battles between huge fleets, economic warfare, protracted sieges, epidemic disease, and ideological struggle produced a devastating war. It was clear that the Greeks could not maintain their unity against Persia; indeed, they appeared to be destroying themselves.

In this era, both democratic Athens and oligarchic Sparta sought to promote their respective ideologies. Some unfortunate states became ideological battlegrounds, often at great cost of life. In Corcyra (modern Corfu; see **Map 3.5**), for example, bloody civil war marked a series of coups and countercoups in the 420s B.C.

Given Spartan supremacy on land and Athenian mastery of the sea, it is not surprising that the Peloponnesian War remained undecided for a decade and a half. The balance of power shifted only after an Athenian blunder, an expedition to conquer Sicily (415–413 B.C.) that became a quagmire and then a disaster, leading to total defeat and thousands of Athenian casualties. In

MAP 3.5—Greece in the Peloponnesian War

During the long and bloody Peloponnesian War (431–404 B.C.), much of the Greek world was divided into two camps: one led by Sparta, the other by Athens.

the aftermath, most of the Athenian empire rose in revolt. Persia re-emerged and intervened on Sparta's side—in return for Sparta's restoration of Ionia to Persia, an ironic counterpoint to Sparta's role in driving Persia from Greece in 479. Athens, nevertheless, was sufficiently wealthy and plucky to hold out until 404 B.C.

Sparta won the Peloponnesian War, but establishing a new Greek order proved beyond its grasp. Spartans were soldiers, not diplomats; infantrymen, not sailors; and commanders, not public speakers. They made poor leaders. Sparta took over Athens's former empire and quickly had a falling-out with its allies: Persia, Corinth, and Thebes.

In addition, Sparta suffered a vast decline in the number of citizens. The original nine thousand Similars of the seventh century B.C. had dropped to only about fifteen hundred in 371 B.C. The main problem seems to have been greed. Rich Spartans preferred to get richer by concentrating wealth in fewer hands, rather than open the elite to new blood. Thousands of men could no longer afford to live as elite soldiers.

The result was military disaster. In 371 B.C., the Boeotian army crushed the Spartans at the Battle of Leuctra, killing a thousand men (including four hundred Similars) and a Spartan king. In the next few years, Boeotia invaded the Peloponnesus, freed the Messenian helots, and restored Messenia to independence, after some 350 years of bondage. It was a fatal blow to Spartan power, but Boeotia, too, was exhausted and its main leaders were dead. None of the Greek city-states had been able to maintain hegemony.

SECTION SUMMARY

- Democracy or "people power" (*demokratia*) began in ancient Greece, and Athens was the most influential Greek democracy.

- Athenian democracy was direct and participatory for adult male citizens, but women, resident aliens, and slaves were all denied citizen rights.

- Persia's massive invasion of mainland Greece in 480–479 B.C. was defeated by a coalition led by Sparta and Athens.

- The Greek *poleis* then turned on each other in a series of wars that lasted about a century.

- Sparta defeated Athens in the most intense phase of these conflicts, known today as the Peloponnesian War (431–404 B.C.).

THE PUBLIC CULTURE OF CLASSICAL GREECE

How did tragedy, comedy, philosophy, and history all begin and develop in the culture of Classical Greece?

The word *classical* means "to set a standard." The culture of Greece between 480 and 322 B.C. proved so influential in the later West that it may justly be called classical. Classical Greek culture was public culture. Poets were not inward-looking or alienated figures. Rather, to quote the Athenian playwright Aristophanes (air-ih-STOF-uh-neez) (ca. 455–385 B.C.), they were "the teachers of men," who commented on contemporary public debate. (As the quotation might also suggest, men, especially citizens, dominated public life.) Dramas were performed in a state theater at state religious festivals. The philosopher Socrates (sock-ruh-TEEZ) (469–399 B.C.) discussed philosophy in marketplaces and gymnasia. It was not private individuals, but the public, that was the major patron of sculpture and architecture.

Public life, accordingly, is the central theme of Classical Greek art and literature. In tragedy, for example, regardless of the particular hero or plot, the same character always looms in the background: the polis. The Classical historians Herodotus, Xenophon, and especially Thucydides focus on public affairs rather than private life. Classical philosophy ranged from biology to metaphysics, but it never forgot politics.

Religion and Art

A hallmark of Classical culture is the tension between the religious heritage of the Archaic period and the worldly spirit of the Classical age. The Classical period was a time of prosperity, political debate, and military conflict. "Wonders are many on earth, and none more wondrous than man,"

The Parthenon   The temple of Athena Parthenos ("the Maiden") on the Athenian Acropolis, the Parthenon was dedicated in 438 B.C. One of the largest and most complex Greek temples, it was built of fine marble. The partially restored ruins symbolize the wealth, power, and greatness of Classical Greece.   (William Katz/Photo Researchers)

The Parthenon

The Parthenon, completed in 432 B.C., dominates both the skyline of Athens and the historical imagination of the West. The building's fine marble and Classical proportions symbolize the free, confident, and united society that one might expect of Periclean Athens, the world's first democracy (see the photograph on page 73). A close look, however, suggests a more complex story. The Parthenon's sculpture offers glimpses of the tensions behind the Classical façade.

The temple of Athena Parthenos ("the Maiden"), as the Parthenon is formally known, was a public project of Greece's wealthiest city-state, leading naval power, and premier

Centaur Struggling with Lapith, Parthenon Metope, South Side
(Courtesy of the Trustees of the British Museum)

democracy. Athenians spared no expense on its construction. Sculpture included a gold and ivory statue of the goddess Athena inside the temple and, on the outside, statuary in each pediment (the triangular space under the eaves) and sculptured reliefs running around the building above the exterior and interior colonnades.

So lavish a program of art demonstrated Athenian wealth, but also served an educational purpose: to illustrate basic Athenian values. Because every Athenian male was expected to fight for the city when called on, militant competition is a central theme. Above the exterior colonnade, for example, ninety-two separate panels of relief sculpture depict gods and heroes fighting foes, such as giants and centaurs.

See the detail from the south wall. It shows a fight between a human male and a centaur, a mythological creature who was half-man, half-beast. Both the man and the centaur are powerful, but the centaur is old and ugly, while the man is young and handsome. The man fights fairly, while the centaur makes a savage attack with arm and forelegs. The man belongs to a Greek people known as the Lapiths. According to myth, the centaurs attacked the Lapiths during a wedding celebration, but they were driven off by the Lapith men, led by the bridegroom and his Athenian friend, the hero Theseus.

To a real-life Athenian observer, the triumph of the Lapiths might have symbolized Athens's victory over the Persians. It was easy to make the connection because the Parthenon was in effect a war memorial as well as a temple. When the Persians invaded Athens in 480 B.C., they destroyed the temples on the Acropolis. For forty years after Greece's victory, Athens left the Acropolis empty as a reminder of Persian barbarism. Then Pericles sponsored a building program of new temples, of which the Parthenon was the grandest.

Delian League funds were diverted to pay for the new buildings, which raised controversy. Ironically, democratic Athens used allied money,

said the Athenian tragedian Sophocles (sof-uh-KLEEZ) (ca. 495–406 B.C.). Yet Sophocles was a deeply religious man who also believed that people were doomed to disaster unless they obeyed the laws of the gods.

Classical religion was less sure of itself than its Archaic predecessor. A few people even questioned the very existence of the gods, although most Greeks wanted religion to be adapted to the new age, not discarded altogether. Thus, Athenian religion was tailored to the needs of a democratic and imperial city. In the 440s B.C., under Pericles' leadership, Athens embarked on a vast, ambitious, and expensive temple-building project, using Delian League funds and serving as a large public employment program. Temples were built in and around the city, most notably on the Athenian Acropolis. (See the feature, "The Visual Record: The Parthenon.")

To adapt religion to a new age, new cults also were introduced. The most popular was the worship of Asclipius, god of healing. Traditionally a minor figure, Asclipius became enormously popular beginning in the late fifth century B.C., perhaps in response to the high mortality of the Peloponnesian War. Outside Athens, large shrines to Asclipius became pilgrimage centers in the fourth century B.C. for ailing people in search of a cure.

Four Women in Procession, Parthenon Frieze, East Wall (Louvre/Réunion
des Musées Nationaux/Art Resource, NY)

From both of these pieces, we may detect Athenian commonplaces about gender. Young women were expected to be maidenly, reserved, and modest. Their bodies were to be kept private. Young men were expected to be outgoing and assertive. Although men wore clothes in public, they exercised naked in gymnasia, wrestling grounds, and stadiums, competing in a healthy activity considered to be effective preparation for war.

The historian finds subtler messages in the two scenes. For example, however constrained the role of women, their very presence in the frieze is significant. Women were not permitted to attend the Athenian assembly, but they participated in the rituals and festivals that played so large a role in Athenian public life. Notice, for instance, the two girls shown in the back who are carrying ritual vessels.

Scholars disagree about the subject of the procession in the frieze. Most scholars argue that the subject is the Pan-Athenaic procession, held once every four years to honor Athena. The people depicted are said to be the people of Athens—a daring novelty, considering that all previous Greek temple sculpture was restricted to gods, heroes, and mythological figures. Some scholars view the scene as an illustration of a legend from the early history of Athens. In either case, one thing is clear: The Parthenon sculptures depict the Athenians the way they wanted to see themselves—as courageous, pious, and public-spirited.

earmarked for defense, to glorify itself. Some people considered that oppressive.

The sculpture above the interior colonnade is a continuous band, or frieze, around the four sides of the building, and it illustrates a procession. Warriors aplenty, primarily cavalrymen but also hoplites and charioteers, compose the lineup. Like the Lapith, the cavalrymen are depicted without clothes, and so they embody the ideal of strong bodies in the service of the polis.

Not all of the men in the interior frieze are warriors, though. Women, too, are depicted. See the detail from the east wall. Look at the four women shown here. The women are on foot, clothed and in solemn procession. The heavy folds of their robes, the hands held at their sides, and the expression on the one visible face all suggest calm and decorum.

QUESTIONS

1. In what sense is the Parthenon an example of public education in democratic Athens?

2. What does the Parthenon have to say about gender in Athens?

3. What does the Parthenon have to say about Greek-Persian relations?

Women played a major role in Classical Athenian religion. They were priestesses in more than forty major cults. They participated each year in many festivals, including several reserved only for women. One such festival, the Thesmophoria, a celebration of fertility held each autumn, featured a three-day encampment of women on a hillside in the city, right beside the Athenian assembly amphitheater. Women also attended public funeral orations in honor of soldiers who had died in battle. They probably attended plays as well.

In art, Classical sculptors completed the process begun by their Archaic forebears of mastering the accurate representation of the human body. In anatomical precision, Classical Greek sculpture was the most technically proficient sculpture the world had seen. Like Archaic sculpture, it was not, however, an attempt to portray humans "warts and all" but rather an idealization of the human form.

The Sophists and Socrates

Success in democratic politics required knowledge of oratory. This demand was met in the late fifth century B.C. by the arrival in Athens of professional teachers of *rhetoric*, the art of speaking. They

Sophists Professional teachers of rhetoric and other subjects in the mid-fifth century B.C., whose training of ambitious young Athenians challenged the stability of standard values and established institutions. Today, "sophist" has come to mean "twister of words."

were known as **Sophists** (SOF-ists) (from a word meaning "instruct" or "make wise"). Sicilian Greeks invented rhetoric around 465 B.C. by drawing up the rules of argument. For a fee—rarely small and sometimes astronomical—Sophists taught young Athenians the art of speaking. Their curriculum consisted not only of rhetoric, but also of the rudiments of linguistics, ethics, psychology, history, and anthropology—in other words, any aspect of "human nature" that might help an aspiring politician. Within a few years, most ambitious young Athenians of prosperous families were studying with Sophists.

At their best, Sophists sharpened young minds. Athenian tragedians, historians, and philosophers all benefited from sophistic teaching. Protagoras (b. ca. 485 B.C.), perhaps the best-known Sophist, summed up the spirit of the age in his famous dictum, "Man is the measure of all things"—an appropriate credo for the interest in all things human that is apparent in Classical literature and art. There is, however, a more troubling side to the Sophists. As teachers of rhetoric, they taught respect for success, not for truth. Thus, they acquired a reputation as word-twisters who taught men how to make "the weaker argument defeat the stronger."

Much to the distress of conservatives, Sophists drew a distinction between *nomos*, a word that means "law" or "convention," and *physis*, which means "nature." The distinction had revolutionary potential. In general, Sophists had little respect for the established order, or nomos. They considered it mere convention. A great man trained by a Sophist might rise above convention to realize the limitless potential of his nature, or physis. If he used his skill to overturn democracy and establish a tyranny, so much the worse for democracy. Indeed, the Sophists trained both unscrupulous democratic politicians and many of the oligarchs who launched coups d'état against Athenian democracy at the end of the fifth century B.C. As a result, *sophist* became a term of abuse in Athens and remains so to this day.

Classical Greek advances in rhetoric, therefore, were as problematic as they were brilliant. The Sophists influenced many different branches of thought. Consider, for example, the work of the philosopher Democritus (dee-MOCK-ruh-tus) (b. ca. 460 B.C.). Democritus was not a Sophist, but he shared the common Sophistic notion that the reality of nature was far more radical than conventionally thought. He concluded that all things consisted of tiny, indivisible particles, which could be arranged and rearranged in an infinite variety of configurations. He called these particles *atoma*, "uncuttable" (from which the word *atom* is derived).

The physicians of the Aegean island of Cos are known as Hippocratics, from Hippocrates (hih-POKruh-teez) (b. ca. 460 B.C.), the first great thinker of their school. If they were not directly influenced by the Sophists, they shared similar habits of thought. Like the Sophists, the Hippocratics were religious skeptics. They considered disease to be strictly a natural phenomenon in which the gods played no part. Hippocratic medicine was noteworthy for its methodology, which emphasized observation and prognosis (the reasoned prediction of future developments). The Hippocratics were the most rigorously naturalistic physicians to date, although no more successful in healing illness than earlier practitioners.

In the fifth century B.C., not all thinkers welcomed the Sophists. Their most notable critic, and the greatest of all fifth century B.C. philosophers, was **Socrates** (469–399 B.C.). Unlike the Sophists, he charged no fees, had no formal students, and did not claim to teach any positive body of knowledge. His main virtue, he believed, was his awareness of his ignorance. Unlike the Sophists, most of whom were metics, Socrates was an Athenian citizen.

Socrates Ancient Greek philosopher, he was a founder of the Western philosophical tradition and is credited with the "Socratic method" of learning.

Socrates, however, resembled the Sophists in his attention to political theory. Like any good Athenian citizen, Socrates served in the military—as a hoplite during the Peloponnesian War. He had his doubts about democracy, which he considered inefficient and uneducated. He preferred rule by a wise elite. Nonetheless, Socrates was too loyal an Athenian to advocate revolution.

Yet Socrates made many enemies because of his role as a self-styled "gadfly." He stung the pride of Athens's leaders by demonstrating their ignorance. Mistakenly considered a Sophist by the public because of his unconventional opinions, Socrates was tried, convicted, and executed in 399 B.C. by an Athenian court for alleged atheism and "corrupting the young." The Athenian public soon had second thoughts, and the trial of Socrates is usually considered one of history's great miscarriages of justice, as well as one of Athenian democracy's greatest blunders.

Socrates was trained in the Ionian natural philosophy tradition. He went beyond it, as the Roman thinker Cicero later said, by bringing philosophy "down from the heavens into the streets"; he changed the emphasis from the natural world to human ethics. Like most Greeks, Socrates believed that the purpose of life was the pursuit of aretê. Unlike his contemporaries, however, he did not consider aretê to be primarily excellence in battle or in public life, but rather excellence in philosophy. One became good by studying the truth, which is part of what Socrates meant by his saying "Virtue (aretê) is knowledge." He also meant that no one who truly understood goodness would ever choose to do evil.

Teach people well, Socrates says, and they will behave morally. Socrates has gone down in history as an inspiring teacher, despite his protestations of not teaching anything. His emphasis was not on research or writing, and in fact, he refused to write anything down. He believed that truth can be found only in persons, not through books—that philosophy requires a thoughtful verbal exchange. His favorite technique was to ask people difficult questions. Teaching that relies on inquiry is still called the "Socratic method."

Plato and Aristotle

Because Socrates never wrote anything down, we are dependent on others for our knowledge of him. Fortunately for us, he inspired students who committed his words and ideas to paper. Socrates' most distinguished student, and our most important source for his thought, was Plato (427–348 B.C.), who in turn was the teacher of Aristotle (384–322 B.C.). Together, these three men laid the foundations of the Western philosophical tradition. They were thinkers for the ages, but each was also a man of his times.

Socrates grew up in confident Periclean days. **Plato** (PLAY-toe) came of age during the Peloponnesian War, a period culminating in the execution of Socrates. Shocked and disillusioned, Plato turned his back on public life, although he was an Athenian citizen. Instead of discussing philosophy in public, Plato founded a private school in an Athenian suburb, the Academy. Plato held a low opinion of democracy, and when he did intervene in politics, it was not in Athens but in far-off Syracuse (in Sicily). Syracuse was governed by a tyranny, and Plato hoped to educate the tyrant's heir in philosophy—a vain hope, as it turned out.

In an attempt to recapture the stimulating give-and-take of a conversation with Socrates, Plato did not write straightforward philosophical treatises, but instead dialogues or speeches. All of Plato's dialogues have more than one speaker, and in most, the main speaker is named "Socrates." Sometimes this figure is the historical Socrates, sometimes merely a mouthpiece for ideas Plato wished to explore.

Socrates This figure emphasizes the colorful character of one of ancient Greece's greatest philosophers. Note his advanced age, unrefined face, and simple clothing. (Erich Lessing/Art Resource, NY)

A voluminous writer, Plato is not easily summarized. The word that best characterizes his legacy, though, is *idealism*, of which Plato is one of Western philosophy's greatest exponents. Like Parmenides, Plato distrusted the senses. Truth exists, but comes only by training the mind to overcome commonsense evidence. The model for Plato's philosophical method is geometry. Just as geometry deals not with this or that triangle or rectangle but with ideal forms—with a pure triangle, a pure rectangle—so the philosopher could learn to recognize purity. A philosopher would not, say, compare aretê in Athens, Sparta, and Persia; a philosopher would understand the meaning of pure, ideal aretê. No relativist, Plato believed in absolute good and evil.

Philosophy is not for everyone, according to Plato. Only a few people have the necessary intelligence and discipline. In the *Republic*, perhaps his best-known work, Plato displays his idealism and its political consequences. He envisioned a society whose elite would study philosophy and attain enlightenment. They would understand the vanity of political ambition but would accept the responsibility of governing the masses. Plato never makes clear precisely why they should assume this burden. Perhaps he was enough of a traditionalist, in spite of himself, to consider a citizen's responsibility to the polis to be obvious. In any case, Plato's ideal state was one in which philosophers would rule as kings, benevolently and unselfishly.

The ideal state would be like a small polis: self-sufficient and closed to outside corruption like Sparta, but committed to the pursuit of things intellectual like Athens. Society would be divided into three classes—philosophers, soldiers, and farmers—with admission to each class based on merit rather than heredity. Poetry and drama would be censored. Plato advocated public education and toyed with more radical notions: not only gender equality, but also the abolition of the family and private property, which he felt led to disunity and dissension.

Plato's ideas have always been controversial, but rarely ignored. The writings of his great student Aristotle better suited contemporary tastes. Originally from Macedonia, **Aristotle** spent

Plato Ancient Greek philosopher and student of Socrates, he is best known for his work, the *Republic*.

Aristotle Ancient Greek philosopher, student of Plato and tutor of Alexander the Great. His scientific writings were the most influential philosophical classics of Greek and Roman civilization and remained so during the Middle Ages.

most of his life in Athens, first as a student at the Academy, then as founder of his own school, the Lyceum (lie-SEE-um). Like Plato, Aristotle wrote dialogues, but none survive. His main surviving works are treatises, largely compilations by students of his lecture notes. One of the most wide-ranging intellectuals, Aristotle thirsted for knowledge. His writings embrace politics, ethics, poetry, botany, physics, metaphysics, astronomy, rhetoric, zoology, logic, and psychology.

Though influenced by Plato's idealism, Aristotle was a far more practical, down-to-earth thinker. His father had been a doctor, which may account for Aristotle's interest in applied science and in biology and the biological method. Unlike Plato, Aristotle placed great emphasis on observation and fieldwork and on classification and systemization.

Aristotle agreed with Plato about the existence of absolute standards of good and evil, but he emphasized the relevance of such standards to everyday life. Unlike Plato, Aristotle considered the senses important guides. Change, he believed, was not an illusion, but rather an important phenomenon. Aristotle's view of change was teleological—that is, he emphasized the goal (*telos* in Greek) of change. According to Aristotle, every organism changes and grows toward a particular end and is an integral and harmonious part of a larger whole. The entire cosmos is teleological, and each and every one of its parts has a purpose. Behind the cosmos was a principle that Aristotle called "the unmoved mover," the supreme cause of existence.

Aristotle defined an object's aretê as the fulfillment of its inherent function in the cosmos. The aretê of a horse, for example, was to be strong, fast, and obedient; the aretê of a rose was to look beautiful and smell sweet. As for the aretê of a human being, Aristotle agreed with Plato: Only the philosopher achieved true aretê. As a pragmatist, however, Aristotle did not imagine philosophers becoming kings. Even so, he did not advocate democracy, which he considered mob rule. Instead, he advocated a government of wealthy gentlemen who had been trained by philosophers—not the best regime imaginable but, in Aristotle's opinion, the best one possible.

Aristotle believed that men had stronger capacities to make judgments than women and so should rule over them. He condemned states like Sparta that accorded power to women. (See the feature, "The Written Record: Spartan Women," on page 60.) Hence, Aristotle would be cited in later centuries to justify male dominance. Ironically, however, Aristotle was more enlightened on gender issues than most of his contemporaries. For example, he believed that since women played a crucial role in the family, they should receive education in morality.

Aristotle may be the single most influential thinker in Western history. His scientific writings not only were the most influential philosophical classics of Greece, and of Rome as well, but they remained so during the Middle Ages in the Arabic and Latin worlds. It took nearly two thousand years for serious rivals to challenge Aristotle's supremacy.

Athenian Drama

Perhaps the greatest art form that emerged in the polis was drama. Modern comedy and tragedy find distant ancestors in Athens's theater of Dionysus, named for the god of unrestraint, liberation, and wine. Comedy and tragedy began in religious festivals honoring Dionysus (also known as Bacchus) but quickly became an independent forum for comment on public life. Ancient drama was poetry, not prose. Because it highlighted the relation of the individual to the community, drama proved to be the most suitable poetic medium for the ideology of the polis.

tragedy Serious play with an unhappy ending. Greek tragedy emerged and reached its height in the fifth century B.C. in the works of Aeschylus, Sophocles, and Euripides.

According to ancient tradition, **tragedy** was first presented at the Dionysian festival in Athens by Thespis in the 530s B.C. (hence, the word *thespian* for "actor"). The first surviving tragedy dates from the 470s B.C., the first surviving comedy from the 420s B.C. A play in the fifth century B.C. consisted of a chorus (a group of performers working in unison) and three individual actors, who played all the various individual speaking parts. Plays were performed in an open-air theater on the south hillside of the Acropolis. Enormously popular, drama spread all over Greece, and eventually, most poleis had a theater.

Classical Athenian tragedy was performed at the annual Dionysia in March. Each playwright would submit a trilogy of plays on a central theme, plus a raucous farce to break the tension afterward. Comedies, which were independent plays rather than trilogies, were performed both at the Dionysia and at a separate festival held in winter. Wealthy producers competed to outfit the most lavish and impressive productions. Judges would award prizes for the best plays—a typical reflection of Greek competitiveness.

Tragedy is not easy to define, except generally: a serious play with an unhappy ending. Perhaps a short tag from the playwright Aeschylus (ESS-kih-luhs) can be said to sum up tragedy: *pathos mathei*, "suffering teaches." The essence of tragedy is what has been called the tragic sense of life: the nobility in the spectacle of a great man or woman failing but learning from failure. In *Oedipus the Tyrant* (ca. 428 B.C.) by Sophocles, for example, the hero unknowingly kills his father and

Theater at Delphi　Open to the air, an ancient Greek theater contained tiers of stone benches above a circular area where the action took place, behind which backdrops could be erected. The audience often had a view of stirring scenery that, at Delphi, included the temple of Apollo and the valley below.　(Vanni/Art Resource, NY)

unknowingly marries his mother. Oedipus cannot escape the consequences of his deeds, but he can react to his fate with dignity and heroism; he can try to understand it. Oedipus loses his power as tyrant and goes into exile, but he retains a degree of honor. He carries out his own punishment by blinding himself. As Aristotle observed, tragedy derives its emotional power from the fear and pity that it evokes and from the purification of the senses (*katharsis*) that it leaves in its aftermath.

The great period of Attic tragedy began and ended in the fifth century B.C. Aeschylus (525–456 B.C.), Sophocles (ca. 495–406 B.C.), and Euripides (ca. 485–406 B.C.) were and are considered the three giant playwrights. Although other tragedians wrote plays, only the works of these three men have survived. Aeschylus was perhaps the most pious of the three. His plays—notably the trilogy of the *Oresteia* (the *Agamemnon*, the *Libation Bearers*, and the *Eumenides*), the only surviving tragic trilogy, dating from 458 B.C.—take as their central question the justice of Zeus. The subject is the myth of the House of Atreus—in particular, the murder of King Agamemnon by his much-wronged wife, Clytemnestra, and her murder in turn by their son, Orestes, avenging his father. Aeschylus casts this primitive saga into an epic of the discovery of justice. In fulfillment of the will of Zeus, Athena puts an end to vengeance killings and institutes the supposed first court of law: the court of the Areopagus in Athens.

Sophocles, too, was interested in divine justice. His tragedies focus on the relationship between the individual and the community. Heroic individuals have a spark of the divine in them, but their towering virtues are threats to ordinary people. In *Antigone* (ca. 442 B.C.), for example, the heroine refuses to compromise with injustice. Her late brother had committed treason, for which his corpse is denied burial—the standard Greek punishment. Antigone, however, insists on following a higher law, Zeus's law, which demands that all bodies be buried. Turmoil, disorder, and death ensue, but Antigone stays true to principle.

Of the three tragedians, Euripides (yoo-RIP-uhdeez) is the least traditional and the most influenced by the Sophists. His plays reflect the disillusionment of the Peloponnesian War era. Euripides was more impressed by divine power than by divine justice. The central gods of Aeschylean drama are Zeus the father and Apollo the lawgiver, while Sophocles focuses on semidivine heroes, but Euripides' major deities are Dionysus and Aphrodite, goddess of erotic passion. In the *Bacchae*

(406 B.C.), for example, an arrogant young king named Pentheus is punished for refusing to recognize the power of Dionysus (Bacchus). When he goes to the hills to spy on drunken women, called "Bacchae," who are worshiping the god, he ends up as their prisoner. Driven to frenzy by Dionysus, the women do not recognize the king. Indeed, Pentheus's own mother, one of the Bacchae, mistakes him for an animal and kills him.

The changes in tragedy from Aeschylus to Euripides reflect the changes in Athens as first imperial arrogance and then the Peloponnesian War took their moral toll. Aeschylus's trust in the community's goodness gives way, first to a focus on the individual struggling to be good, and then to a fundamental doubt about the possibility of goodness. The civic order, celebrated so confidently at the end of the *Oresteia* (458 B.C.), looks less certain in Sophocles' *Oedipus* (ca. 428 B.C.), and by the time of Euripides' *Bacchae* (406 B.C.), seems feeble.

Comedy Play with a happy ending. Greek comedy emerged and reached its first height in the fifth century B.C. in the works of Aristophanes.

Comedy, too, was invented in Athens in the Classical period. Like tragedy, comedy offers a moral commentary on contemporary Athenian life. Unlike tragedy, which is usually set in the past and takes its characters from mythology, Athenian comedy (the so-called Old Comedy) is set in the present and pokes fun at politicians and public figures.

The greatest writer of comedy in the fifth century B.C. was Aristophanes (ca. 455–385 B.C.). His extant plays are lively, ribald, even scatological, and full of allusions to contemporary politics. Aristophanes loved to show the "little guy" getting the better of the powerful and women deflating the pretensions of men. In *Lysistrata* (411 B.C.), his best-known play, he imagines the women of Greece stopping the Peloponnesian War by going on a sex strike, which forces the men to make peace.

Historical Thought and Writing

Herodotus Credited, along with Thucydides, of founding history-writing in the West. The word *history* comes from the word *historiai* used by Herodotus.

Thucydides Ancient Greek historian; with Herodotus, a founder of history-writing in the West.

Like drama, history flourished in the exciting intellectual atmosphere of classical Athens. Indeed, its two greatest historians, **Herodotus** (ca. 485–425 B.C.) and **Thucydides** (ca. 455–397 B.C.), are among the founders of history-writing in the West. This judgment is not meant to discount the contributions of, for example, the Hittites or Hebrews, or the chronicles, inventories, and genealogies of early Greece. Herodotus and Thucydides, however, are more rationalistic than their predecessors, and their subject matter is war, politics, peoples, and customs—what we think of as the stuff of history-writing today. Indeed, the word *history* comes from a word used by Herodotus, *historiai*, meaning "inquiries" or "research."

The works of Herodotus (*The Histories*) and Thucydides (*The Peloponnesian War*) have unifying themes. The thread through *The Histories* is the cyclical rise and fall of empires. Herodotus sees the Persian Wars as merely one episode in a vast historical drama. Again and again, hardy, disciplined peoples conquered their neighbors, grew wealthy, were corrupted by a life of luxury, and were eventually conquered in turn. Success made people arrogant, driving them to commit injustices, which were eventually punished by Zeus. The breadth of Herodotus's vision is noteworthy. A native of Halicarnassus (a polis on the southwestern coast of Anatolia; see **MAP 3.5**), Herodotus traveled widely, eventually settling in Athens. He wrote not only about Greeks, but also about Persians, Egyptians, and a host of other peoples in Europe, Asia, and Africa. (See the feature, "The Global Record: The Enemy as Barbarian," on page 71.)

Only a child at the time of the Persian Wars, Herodotus gathered information by interviewing older people in various countries, as well as by checking what limited written public records existed. Herodotus also wrote about previous centuries and places he had not visited, but with uneven accuracy. He could rarely resist a good story, and alongside solid research are tall tales, unconfirmed accounts, and myths.

Thucydides, by contrast, prided himself on accuracy. He confined himself mainly to writing about an event that he had lived through and participated in: the Peloponnesian War. A failed Athenian general, Thucydides spent most of the Peloponnesian War in exile, carefully observing, taking notes, and writing.

Like Herodotus, Thucydides was influenced by the grandeur of Classical tragedy. He also shows the signs of the Sophist movement, especially in the finely crafted speeches he includes in his writing. Thucydides' great theme is the disastrous effect of war on the human soul. In Thucydides' opinion, Periclean Athens was a high point in the history of civilization. The strain of prolonged war, however, destroyed Athens's moral fiber as well as its empire.

SECTION SUMMARY

- The culture of Greece during 480–322 B.C. is called classical because it has proved influential throughout the history of the West.

- Classical Greek sculpture was the most technically proficient sculpture seen yet, and it set a standard for all future work.

- The Athenian Socrates changed the emphasis of Greek philosophy from nature to human ethics.

- The idealist philosopher Plato and his more practical student, Aristotle, are the most influential philosophers of the West.

- Comedy and tragedy were invented in Athens, flourished in public festivals, and offered a moral commentary on contemporary life.

- Herodotus and Thucydides are among the founders of history-writing in the West.

CHAPTER SUMMARY

Western philosophy, science, politics, sculpture, painting, and literary genres, such as comedy, tragedy, and history, all emerged in Archaic and Classical Greece.

The focus of ancient Greek life between ca. 750 and ca. 350 B.C. was the polis. Trade, colonization, and the invention of the Greek alphabet and of the hoplite phalanx all contributed to the emergence of the polis around 750–700 B.C. Earlier, in the Bronze Age, Minoan and Mycenaean kingdoms had ruled Greek lands. Homer evoked their memory brilliantly in the *Iliad* and *Odyssey* around 725 B.C. but, by then, the spirit of Greek civilization had changed radically. The Bronze Age kingdoms were palace economies, dominated by a noble elite. The polis was a city-state that emphasized participation and equality and invented the idea of the citizen.

Archaic Sparta developed Greece's best citizen-army whose job was to prevent helot uprisings or attacks from abroad. Sparta's stable government and austere culture fostered the idea that public duty is more important than private advantage. Archaic Corinth is the prime example of tyranny, a widespread form of government in Greece in which new wealth led to the emergence of popular champions. Archaic Athens developed, thanks to Solon's reforms, a large class of independent small farmers. They later turned out to be the backbone of democracy. Solon unintentionally created conditions for the growth of slavery.

The culture of Archaic Greece was the seedbed of Western individualism and rationalism. Lyric poetry emphasized individual emotion, and Archaic sculpture focused on the human body. Although Archaic Greece was a religious society, it also gave rise to the first philosophers. They lived in Ionia in the 500s B.C. and offered a nontheological explanation of nature.

Democracy or "people power" (*demokratia*) began in ancient Greece, and the Athenian version is best known. Athenian democracy was direct and participatory but limited to adult males. Classical Greece was a period of intense war. Athens and Sparta united to lead a Greek coalition that defeated Persia's invasion in 480–479 B.C. Afterward, the two poleis turned on each other, most violently in the Peloponnesian War (431–404 B.C.). With its democracy, freedom, and high culture, Athens stands for one aspect of the achievement of the polis; with its hierarchy, militarism, and citizen virtue, Sparta stands for another.

Classical Greek culture has proved influential again and again in the history of the West. Athens became Greece's cultural center. Here, comedy and tragedy were invented, history-writing was founded, sculpture reached a peak of proficiency in showing the human body, and philosophy changed its emphasis from nature to human ethics. The philosophers Socrates, Plato, and Aristotle are among the West's greatest thinkers.

FOCUS QUESTIONS

- How did early Greece develop before the polis and what light do the Homeric poems shed on its history?

- What was the Greek polis, and how did it develop in Sparta, Athens, and Corinth in Archaic Greece?

- How did Western individualism and rationalism take root in Archaic Greece?

- What was Athenian democracy and how did it clash with Sparta in the Peloponnesian War?

- How did tragedy, comedy, philosophy, and history all begin and develop in the culture of Classical Greece?

KEY TERMS

Minoan (p. 51)

Mycenaeans (p. 51)

Homer (p. 51)

arête (p. 54)

Archaic Greece (p. 54)

polis (p. 54)

hoplite phalanx (p. 56)

Solon (p. 62)

Sappho (p. 63)

Classical Greece (p. 64)

demokratia (p. 66)

Pericles (p. 68)

Sophists (p. 76)

Socrates (p. 76)

Plato (p. 77)

Aristotle (p. 77)

tragedy (p. 78)

comedy (p. 80)

Herodotus (p. 80)

Thucydides (p. 80)

 This icon will direct you to additional materials on the website: www.cengage.com/history/noble/westciv6e

e See our interactive eBook for map and primary source activities.

NOTES

1. Charles Rowan Beye, *Ancient Greek Literature and Society*, 2d ed. (Ithaca, N.Y.: Cornell University Press, 1987), p. 78.

2. Ibid., p. 79.

3. Herodotus, *The Histories*, trans. Barry S. Strauss.

4. Thucydides, *The Peloponnesian War*, trans. Barry S. Strauss.

CHAPTER OUTLINE

Philip and Alexander

The Hellenistic Kingdoms, 323–30 B.C.

Hellenistic Culture

The Turn Inward: New Philosophies, New Faiths

Stag Hunt Pebble mosaic from Pella
(HIP/Art Resource, NY)

Alexander the Great and the Spread of Greek Civilization, ca. 350–30 B.C.

The young men in the pebble mosaic shown opposite wield ax and sword against the stag whom they are hunting. The artist, named Gnosis, was a master at rendering perspective and drama. Clearly, no expense was spared on the work, dated around 325 B.C. Both the vigor of the scene and the quality of the craftsmanship symbolize the spirit of a young man who was born in Pella, the Macedonian (mah-seh-DOE-nee-un) capital where the mosaic was displayed: That man was Alexander the Great. Alexander was a fearless warrior and one of the most brilliant generals in the history of the world. In just twelve years, he conquered all the territory between Greece and India, as well as Egypt.

Alexander created new realities of power as king of Macedon (r. 336–323 B.C.). A northeastern Greek kingdom that had previously been only a fringe power, Macedon rose meteorically under Alexander's father, Philip II (r. 359–336 B.C.), to become the leading military power in Greece. Philip was a brilliant and ambitious general, but Alexander outstripped him.

Alexander laid the foundations of a new Greek world: the world of the Hellenistic (hel-len-IS-tik) period (323–30 B.C.), in which Hellenic, or Greek, language and civilization spread and were transformed. This era was distinct in many ways from the preceding Hellenic period (ca. 750–323 B.C.). In Hellenistic times, Macedonians and Greeks replaced Persians as the ruling people of Egypt and western Asia. Large numbers of Greek-speaking colonists moved south and east. Governed by Macedonian dynasties, Egypt and the Levant became integral parts of the Greek world and remained so until the Arab conquest in the seventh century A.D. Greek-speaking kingdoms thrived briefly as far east as modern Afghanistan and Pakistan.

Conquest put huge amounts of wealth into Greek hands. Alexander and his successors built great new cities: Antioch (AN-tee-ock) in Syria, Pergamum in Anatolia, Seleucia (seh-LOO-she-uh) in Mesopotamia, and, greatest of all, Alexandria in Egypt. Trade increased and expanded southward and eastward. In political life, individual cities continued to be important, but federal leagues (that is, unions of city-states) and monarchies ruled most of the Greek-speaking world.

Material and political expansion led to unanticipated cultural changes, which may be summarized as a turn inward. Frequently finding themselves among strange peoples, the Greeks sought comfort in new philosophies, religions, and modes of literary and artistic

FOCUS QUESTIONS

- How did Macedon under Philip and Alexander conquer both the Greek city-states and the Persian Empire?

- What new states emerged as a result of Alexander's conquests and how did they integrate Greek settlers with native peoples?

- How did Greek civilization spread during the Hellenistic era, and what were the main trends in literature, science, and art?

- What new philosophies and religions emerged in the Hellenistic period?

This icon will direct you to additional materials on the website: www.cengage.com/history/noble/westciv6e

See our interactive eBook for map and primary source activities.

expression. Many of these new cultural forms emphasized people's emotions and intentions, not simply their actions. Science, meanwhile, flourished under royal patronage, as did the emerging discipline of literary criticism. The prestige of royal women tended to promote improvements in the overall status of Greek women.

Hellenistic Greeks boasted of having created one world—a common, or ecumenical (from the Greek *oikoumene* [oy-koo-men-AY], "inhabited"), region. In truth, that world was complex. Native cultures flourished, while Greeks adapted and Hellenized a number of Egyptian and Asian deities.

Hellenistic Greek contact with one native culture in particular—Judaism—proved to have a lasting impact on the West. Under the impact of the Greeks, Judaism became more self-conscious and placed a greater emphasis on salvation, martyrdom, and individual study and prayer. Some Jews resisted Greek culture, others adopted it, and still others resolved to convert Greeks to Judaism. Reshaped by its contacts with the Greeks, Hellenistic Judaism was poised to transform Western religion.

PHILIP AND ALEXANDER

How did Macedon under Philip and Alexander conquer both the Greek city-states and the Persian Empire?

The Hellenistic world was founded by two conquerors: Philip II of Macedon (382–336 B.C.) and his son, Alexander III, known as Alexander the Great (356–323 B.C.). After a century of indecisive warfare among the Greek city-states, Philip swept south and conquered them in twenty years. In even less time, Alexander conquered Egypt and all of western Asia as far east as modern India. The legacy of these impressive conquests was to spread Greek civilization and to change it, both of which consequences were revolutionary developments.

The Rise of Macedon

Macedon Weaker, less culturally advanced state on Greece's northern border that was unified and led to power by Philip II and Alexander the Great.

Philip II King of Macedon and father of Alexander the Great, he was a brilliant soldier and statesman who conquered the Greek world.

Macedon was a border state, long weaker than its more advanced neighbors but capable of learning from them and ultimately of conquering them. Though rich in resources and manpower, Macedon lacked the relatively efficient organization of the polis. Several dialects of Greek were spoken, some unintelligible to southern Greeks, who considered Macedonians "barbarians" (from the Greek *barbaros*, meaning "a person who does not speak Greek"). Ordinary Macedonians lived hardy lives, while the king and the royal court inhabited a sophisticated capital city, Pella, where they sponsored visits by leading Greek artists and writers. **Philip II** confounded Greek stereotypes of Macedonian barbarism by turning out to be a brilliant soldier and statesman—a man of vast ambition, appetite, and energy. Although vain, lustful, and a hard drinker, he was also an excellent orator and general. Philip's goals were to make himself dominant in Macedon and then, after neutralizing opposition in Greece, to conquer the Persian Empire, or at least its holdings in Anatolia. He accomplished all but the last.

Philip owed success to his army, a well-trained, professional, year-round force. Macedon, with its plains and horses, was cavalry country, and Philip raised cavalry to a new level of importance. In battle, the Macedonian phalanx would first hold the enemy phalanx until the cavalry could find a weak spot and break the enemy line. Then, the phalanx would attack and finish the job. Macedonian hoplites carried extra-long pikes to keep the enemy at a distance. Philip also mastered the technology of siegecraft, raising it to a level unseen since Assyrian days (see pages 31–32).

Philip used his army effectively. After capturing a gold mine in Thrace (modern Bulgaria), he turned to the Greek city-states nearby. Olynthus, the most important, fell in 348 B.C. Led by the Athenian Demosthenes (de-MOSS-thuh-neez) (ca. 385–322 B.C.), the central and southern Greek city-states prepared to make a stand, but it was too late. By 338 B.C., when an Atheno-Theban army met the Macedonians, Philip had already won over much of the Greek world through diplomacy, bribes, and threats. His complete military victory at Chaeronea, in central Greece, was followed up with a lenient settlement in which all the Greeks except Sparta acknowledged Philip's hegemony (see **Map 4.1**). The polis would no longer decide the fate of the eastern Mediterranean.

In 336 B.C., Philip was murdered by a disgruntled courier, and the invasion of the Persion Empire fell to his 20-year-old son, Alexander, the new king.

Alexander the Conqueror

Alexander III of Macedon (r. 336–323 B.C.), better known as **Alexander the Great**, is as famous in art as in literature, in romance as in history, in Iran and India as in Europe and America. Yet, the evidence for the historical Alexander is poor. After his untimely death at age 32, contemporaries wrote histories and memoirs, but none has survived. Several good historical accounts, based on earlier texts, are extant, but none was written less than three hundred years after Alexander's day. (See the feature, "The Written Record: Virtues and Vices of Alexander the Great.") Alexander, moreover, was not only a legend in his own time, but also a master propagandist. Many of the incidents of his life took place in remote regions or among a few individuals, and they tended to grow with the telling.

Still, Alexander's virtues are clear. He was charismatic, handsome, intelligent, and well educated; as a teenager he had Aristotle himself as a private tutor. Alexander was ruthless as well as cultured. He brought a team of Greek scientists along with him on his expedition through the Persian Empire. He founded twenty cities. One of those cities was born in 331 B.C., at the site of a fishing village in the northwestern part of Egypt's delta. Alexander and his advisers planned a great trading center and the new city, called Alexandria, later grew into the largest city in the Mediterranean.

Alexander certainly had vices as well. He began his reign with a massacre of his male relatives. He destroyed the great cities of Thebes and Tyre and had their inhabitants killed or sold into slavery. He burned Persepolis, Persia's capital, to the ground. He massacred large numbers of civilians during his campaigns in central Asia.

For all his varied interests, Alexander was first and foremost a warrior. Battlefield commander of the Macedonian cavalry at age 18, he devoted most of the rest of his life to warfare. As a leader of men, Alexander was popular and inspiring, and he shared risks with his troops. Knowing the value of propaganda, he told the Greeks that he was fighting a war of revenge for Persia's invasion of Greece in 480 B.C.

On the eve of invasion, Persia vastly outnumbered Macedon on both land and sea. Darius III of Persia was rich; Alexander's treasury was virtually empty. The Macedonian expeditionary force was short on supplies. The peoples in Persia's multiethnic empire were restive, but so too were Alexander's Greek allies, the mainstay of his fleet. One of Darius's advisers proposed a naval campaign to raise a revolt in Greece and force the Macedonians home. How, then, did Alexander propose to conquer Persia?

The answer was the Macedonian army. Although Alexander invaded Anatolia with only about thirty-five thousand men, they were the fastest-marching, most experienced, and most skilled army in the eastern Mediterranean. If Persia would fight the Macedonians in a set battle, Alexander might be confident of victory—and proud Persia insisted on fighting. As expected, Macedon won the war in three great battles (see **Map 4.1**): at the Granicus River in

CHRONOLOGY

359–336 B.C.	Reign of Philip II of Macedon
ca. 342–292 B.C.	Life of playwright Menander
338 B.C.	Greece falls to Philip at Battle of Chaeronea
336–323 B.C.	Reign of Alexander the Great
331 B.C.	Battle of Gaugamela completes Persian defeat
323–275 B.C.	Wars of the Successors
313 B.C.	Zeno founds Stoic philosophy in Athens
312 B.C.	Seleucus I conquers Babylon
304 B.C.	Ptolemy I king of Egypt
294 B.C.	Museum founded in Alexandria
276 B.C.	Antigonus Gonatas king of Macedon
263 B.C.	Kingdom of Pergamum founded
ca. 246 B.C.	Parthia revolts from Seleucids
ca. 245 B.C.	Bactria gains independence
244–222 B.C.	Reforms of Agis and Cleomenes in Sparta
ca. 225 B.C.	Eratosthenes of Cyrene calculates earth's circumference
217 B.C.	Battle of Raphia brings Palestine under Ptolemies
167–142 B.C.	Maccabean revolt in Judea
146 B.C.	Antigonid Macedonia becomes a Roman province
64 B.C.	Seleucid Syria becomes a Roman province
30 B.C.	Ptolemaic Egypt becomes a Roman province

Alexander the Great King of Macedon and conqueror of the Persian Empire, he spread Greek civilization to western Asia, Egypt, and India.

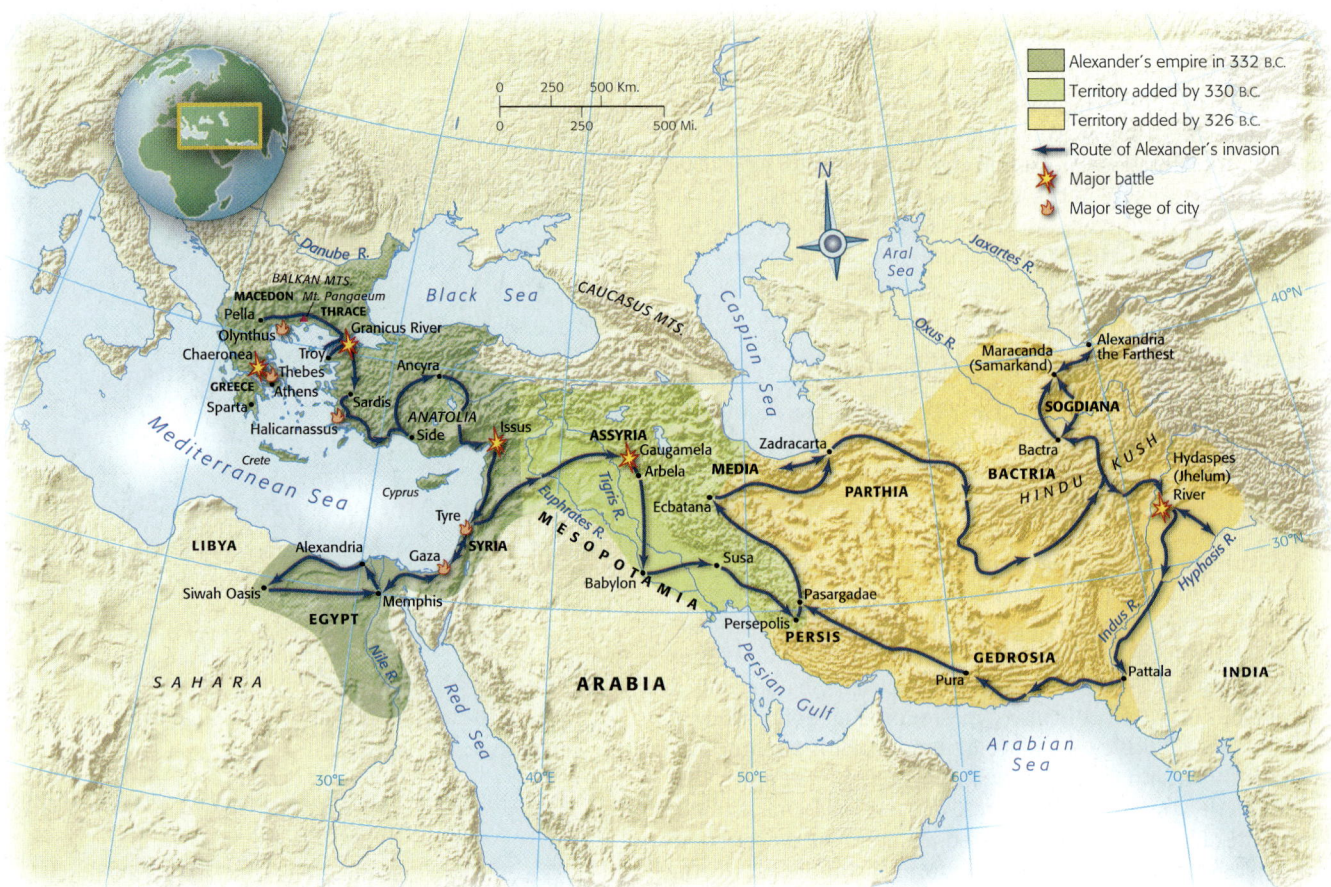

🌐 **MAP 4.1—Conquests of Philip and Alexander**

Between 359 and 323 B.C., the armies of Macedon conquered first the Greek city-states and then the Persian Empire. Macedonian power extended from Greece and Egypt eastward to modern India.

Anatolia (334 B.C.), at Issus in Syria (333 B.C.), and at Gaugamela in Mesopotamia (331 B.C.). By 328 B.C., Alexander's claim to be king of Persia was sealed with blood and iron.

Having conquered the Persian heartland, Alexander turned eastward and fought for seven more years. Alexander pushed his army not only into the eastern parts of the Persian Empire but beyond, into India, which had not been controlled by Persia since the early fifth century B.C. The Macedonians won a big victory there in 326 B.C., near the Hydaspes River (modern Jhelum River), over the army of King Porus, which had as many as two hundred elephants (see **MAP 4.1**). Alexander's infantry suffered heavy casualties before inflicting enough wounds on the elephants to make them uncontrollable. Alexander wanted to continue eastward, perhaps as far as the Bay of Bengal, but his exhausted and homesick men mutinied and forced Alexander to turn back.

Meanwhile, Alexander tightened the screws of power. He turned on the proud and independent Macedonian nobility via a series of conspiracy trials, purges, and assassinations. Alexander offended Macedonians by demanding that they bow down to him, Persian style. He offended Greek city-states by insisting that they deify him. "If Alexander wishes to be a god, let him be" was the concise reply of the Spartans, but Alexander had set a precedent for both Hellenistic monarchs and Roman emperors.

Another theme of Alexander's later career is his policy of fusion. In 325 B.C., Alexander began training an army of thirty thousand Persians and dismissed a large number of Macedonian troops. He forced his commanders to marry Persian women, just as he himself did. He publicly prayed for "concord and a partnership in rule between Greeks and Persians." Many Macedonians

🌐 **MAP 4.2—Hellenistic Kingdoms, Leagues, and City-States, ca. 240 B.C.**
After Alexander's death, his empire lost its political unity. Great new cities and kingdoms arose in the lands he had conquered.

would have preferred to keep their former enemy at arm's length, but Alexander sought a new power base independent of the Macedonian nobility.

Alexander died in Babylon in June 323 B.C., a month before he turned 33, probably of malarial fever, although some contemporaries suspected poison and some historians have suggested drunkenness. Alexander did not name a successor. The Macedonian generals fought a long and bloody round of wars over the spoils of empire. Not until some fifty years later, in 275 B.C., was it clear that three large kingdoms—Macedon (under the Antigonid dynasty), Ptolemaic (tol-eh-MAY-ik) Egypt, and the Seleucid (seh-LOO-sid) realm—would inherit most of Alexander's empire. The rest was divided among small kingdoms, federal leagues, and independent city-states (see **MAP 4.2**).

In the long run, Alexander's life was far more influential than his death. His conquests did nothing less than lay the foundations of the Hellenistic world. Whether it was exalting a savior or debunking a hero, much of Hellenistic culture centered on the myth of heroism that Alexander had engendered. Historians who insist that the individual is insignificant will rarely have a more challenging refutation than Alexander.

SECTION SUMMARY

- Macedon rose to power under King Philip and conquered the Greek city-states.

- Alexander was a brilliant soldier and leader of the most skilled army in the eastern Mediterranean, created by his father Philip.

- Alexander and the Macedonians won, thanks to Persia's proud but foolish decision to fight the enemy in pitched battles.

- A march into India, increasing despotism, and a policy of fusion of Greeks and Macedonians all marked Alexander's last years.

- By conquering the Persian Empire, Alexander ushered in a new age in Greek history: the Hellenistic era.

Virtues and Vices of Alexander the Great

Writing in the second century A.D., four centuries after Alexander's death, the historian Arrian composed from earlier accounts what is now the best surviving history of Alexander. A military man himself, Arrian appreciated Alexander's skills but was not blind to his flaws.

Alexander died in the 114th Olympiad, in the archon ship of Hegesias at Athens [June 323 B.C.]. He lived, as Aristobulus tells us, thirty-two years and eight months, and reigned twelve years and eight months. He had great personal beauty, invincible power of endurance, and a keen intellect; he was brave and adventurous, strict in the observance of his religious duties, and hungry for fame. Most temperate in the pleasures of the body, his passion was for glory only, and in that he was insatiable. He had an uncanny instinct for the right course in a difficult and complex situation, and was most happy in his deductions from observed facts. In arming and equipping troops and in his military dispositions he was always masterly. Noble indeed was his power of inspiring his men, of filling them with confidence, and, in the moment of danger, of sweeping away their fear by the spectacle of his own fearlessness. When risks had to be taken, he took them with the utmost boldness, and his ability to seize the moment for a swift blow, before the enemy had any suspicion of what was coming, was beyond praise. No cheat or liar ever caught him off guard, and both his word and his bond were inviolable. Spending but little on his own pleasures, he poured out his money without stint for the benefit of his friends.

Doubtless, in the passion of the moment Alexander sometimes erred; it is true he took some steps towards the pomp and arrogance of the Asiatic kings: but I, at least, cannot feel that such errors were very heinous, if the circumstances are taken fairly into consideration. For, after all, he was young; the chain of his successes was unbroken, and, like all kings, past, present, and to come, he was surrounded by courtiers who spoke to please, regardless of what evil their word might do. On the other hand, I do indeed know that Alexander, of all the monarchs of old, was the only one who had the nobility of heart to be sorry for his mistakes.... In the course of this book I have, admittedly, found fault with some of the things which Alexander did, but of the man himself I am not ashamed to express ungrudging admiration.

QUESTIONS

1. What are Alexander's main virtues, according to Arrian?
2. In what way does Arrian find fault with Alexander?
3. For Arrian, what is the "bottom line" about Alexander?

Source: From *The Campaigns of Alexander* by Arrian, translated Aubrey de Sélincourt, revised with an introduction and notes by J. R. Hamilton (Penguin Classics, 1958, revised edition 1971). Copyright © the Estate of Aubrey de Sélincourt, 1958. Introduction and Notes copyright © J. R. Hamilton, 1971. Reproduced by permission of Penguin Books Ltd.

Alexander Mosaic   This detail of a Roman-era mosaic from Pompeii shows Alexander the Great in battle, probably at Issus. Shining in his battle armor, Alexander is bareheaded, with a wide-eyed, intense gaze betokening his power. The larger scene includes the Persian king Darius, fleeing in his chariot.   (Scala/Art Resource, NY)

THE HELLENISTIC KINGDOMS, 323–30 B.C.

What new states emerged as a result of Alexander's conquests and how did they integrate Greek settlers with native peoples?

Variety, flexibility, and the creation of a new elite to transmit Greek culture compose the Hellenistic political legacy. Hellenistic political units ranged from multiethnic kingdoms to small, ethnically homogeneous city-states (see **Map 4.2**). The Greek peninsula saw both a monarchy, with republican leanings, as well as experiments in federalism and social revolution. In Asia and Egypt, a new ruling elite emerged, consisting both of Greeks and Macedonians and of natives. Although the first group tended to dominate high office, natives were by no means excluded. The immigrants wanted land, wealth, or adventure. Their paths were smoothed by a new ideology that identified being Greek less with loyalty to an individual city than with participation in a common Greek civilization.

Although the Hellenistic world became relatively peaceful after 275 B.C., conflict among the kingdoms continued. Generally waged at a low level of intensity, with bribes and diplomacy as weapons, the conflict nonetheless sometimes broke out into major battles. A number of small states emerged in Anatolia, notably Pergamum, whose wealthy rulers were patrons of literature and art, and Galatia (guh-LAY-shuh), carved out by Celtic invaders from Europe.

Colonialism, Greek Style

Many Greeks and Macedonians emigrated during the fourth and third centuries B.C., but we do not know how many. The few available statistics indicate a significant migration but not a mass exodus. By the second century B.C., the colonizing impulse had diminished in Greece and Macedon, but a large number of Jews left war-torn Judea, particularly for Egypt. Ptolemaic Egypt and the Seleucid realm were also the most common destinations for Greek and Macedonian migrants.

Greek migrants could take advantage of a new definition of being Greek that had begun to emerge even before Alexander's conquests. Isocrates (eye-SOCK-rah-teez) (428–338 B.C.), an Athenian thinker, redefined Greek identity by promoting the idea that Greece was not a collection of city-states but a civilization. "The people we call Hellenes"—that is, Greeks—he wrote, "are those who have the same culture as us, not the same blood."[1]

The ideal of Greek culture made it easier for the migrants to maintain a Greek identity. For that matter, it was now possible for foreigners to become Greek by learning the Greek language and literature. The number of Hellenized foreigners was relatively small, yet their very existence marked a break from the Classical polis, where even a resident genius, such as Aristotle, could not obtain Athenian citizenship because he was not of Athenian descent.

The Greek language also served as a common denominator, along with Aramaic, both of which became the languages of trade in the eastern Mediterranean. To get a sense of the importance of Isocrates' redefinition of **Hellenism**, consider that one of the most famous Greek-speakers of all antiquity was Paul, the Christian apostle who was born a Jew in Tarsus, a city in southern Anatolia.

Hellenism Term used to designate ancient Greece's language, culture, and civilization.

Immigrants sought to realize dreams of prosperity or adventure. Although agriculture was the main economic pursuit, trade, industry, finance, administration, and military service also offered opportunities.

In the Ptolemaic and Seleucid realms, administration was a joint effort of both immigrants and natives. The upper ranks of government were dominated by Greeks and Macedonians, while native elites usually held low- or mid-level government positions. Especially after about 200 B.C., some natives even reached high office. Others worked in the traditional native administrative structures that survived largely intact in the new kingdoms—for example, as judges or village headmen or priests.

To create a hereditary military group in the countryside, Ptolemy (TOL-eh-mee) I settled his soldiers on land grants there. Native Egyptians were excluded from the army at first, although they served as policemen, but by the second century B.C., the dynasty needed native

Egyptians too as soldiers. In return, natives now received land, tax breaks, and the right to call themselves Hellenes. Their Hellenism sometimes just scratched the surface, but other times it went deeper.

An Egyptian named Plenis, a villager in Middle Egypt in the late second century B.C., is a good example. Plenis was a tenant farmer on a royal estate and a priest in a local Egyptian cult. Like his father before him, Plenis served as a soldier in the Ptolemaic army. Plenis could write Greek as well as Egyptian, and he even used a Greek name: Dionysius, son of Kephalas.

Temples, which often administered large estates, represented important sources of local power. Because priests shaped local opinion, they demanded royal patronage. Both **Ptolemies** and **Seleucids** complied: from Babylon to Edfu, money poured into temple-building and renovation.

The Seleucids addressed the security needs of their far-flung realms by establishing over seventy colonies extending to central Asia. Some colonies were civilian, but most were military, composed of retired or reserve soldiers, mostly Greeks or Macedonians, but also Jews and other non-Greek peoples. Colonists received land allotments. Greek-style public buildings were erected, and some cities were laid out according to a rectilinear grid reminiscent of the Classical polis. The gymnasium attained a great practical and symbolic importance as both the center of Greek culture and the preparatory school for entry into the elite. The Hellenistic gymnasium offered education in literature, philosophy, and oratory as well as athletics.

Some Seleucid colonies developed into flourishing Greek cities, particularly in Anatolia and on the coast of Syria. Greek urbanization should not create the false impression, however, that the Seleucids were motivated by some civilizing mission. They were not. They established colonies to increase their power.

Economic Expansion

Immigration and colonization were not the only sources of new economic opportunities. At the beginning of the Hellenistic era, Alexander turned the huge gold and silver reserves of Persia into coinage and released it onto the market virtually all at once. The result was about seventy-five years of inflation, but also a commercial boom. In particular, money largely replaced barter in Egypt, which increased production and trade, helping to render Egypt an economic powerhouse. Another stimulus to trade was the creation of thriving new Hellenistic cities, especially Alexandria with its great harbors, canals, marketplaces, and infrastructure of banks, inns, courts, and shipbuilding facilities.

During Hellenistic times, commerce tended to shift from Greece proper to Anatolia and Egypt (see **MAP 4.3**). The island of Rhodes, located off the southwest tip of Anatolia, grew into a major trading center, especially for grain. The Rhodian aristocracy grew rich off taxes and duties, wisely reinvesting a portion of the profits in naval infrastructure (such as arsenals and dockyards) and in campaigns against pirates. Egypt, too, had many products to trade. Grain was the most important, but textiles, glass, papyrus, and luxury goods were also significant. A network of canals connecting Alexandria to the Nile and the Red Sea beyond made trading possible with Sudan, Arabia, and India.

The Seleucid kingdoms controlled trade routes to the east. Commerce benefited from good roads, safe sea travel between the Persian Gulf and India, and a unified royal coinage. The Seleucids traded agricultural goods and manufactured products for spices from India and Arabia. In the first century B.C., they even imported silk from China. The kingdom of Pergamum, which stretched inland from Anatolia's northwest coast, exported its rich agricultural products, as well as the local gray-blue building stone and, as an alternative to Egyptian papyrus, parchment.

Slavery was an important part of the Hellenistic social and economic scene. Although war and piracy were the main sources of enslavement, some people were born into slavery. In Sicily and southern Italy, slaves worked huge plantations, but eastern Mediterranean slaves were commonly found in the household or in administration, and in cities rather than in the countryside. Many unfree laborers worked on farms in Egypt and western Asia. Following the pre-Greek traditions of those regions, they were generally tenant farmers tied to kings or potentates rather than outright slaves.

Ptolemies Dynasty founded by Ptolemy I and ruled by Egyptian kings; it was the wealthiest, most sophisticated, and longest lasting of the Hellenistic kingdoms.

Seleucids Dynasty founded by Seleucus and governed by rulers of Anatolia from 312 to 64 B.C., it established seventy colonies throughout the Near East.

🌐 **MAP 4.3—The Eastern Mediterranean, ca. 200 B.C.**

The great Hellenistic powers contended for control of this vibrant, turbulent, and prosperous region. Conflict centered on Palestine and the Aegean islands, the rulership of which frequently changed hands.

Map legend:
- Seleucid Monarchy
- Ptolemaic Monarchy
- Antigonid Monarchy
- Pergamene Monarchy
- Other Greek states and Hellenized kingdoms
- Roman allies and dependents

On some plantations, conditions for slaves were harsh enough to lead to mass uprisings. It was not unusual, however, for domestic or administrative slaves to buy their freedom, sometimes using savings they were allowed to keep, sometimes borrowing money from the master or from friends. Greeks enslaved fellow Greeks, but often, it seems, with guilty consciences; they frequently made special efforts to help Greek slaves win their freedom. Even in bondage, therefore, Greeks had special privileges.

Macedon and Greece

Macedon was the last of the three great Hellenistic kingdoms to emerge from civil war after Alexander's death. Not until 276 B.C. was Antigonus Gonatas, grandson of Alexander's general Antigonus the One-Eyed, established firmly on the throne. His Antigonid (an-TIG-on-id) dynasty lasted about a century, when the Romans conquered Macedon.

True to the traditions of Macedon, the **Antigonids** projected an image of simplicity and toughness. As a young man, Antigonus had studied the new school of Stoic philosophy in Athens (see pages 103–104). As king, he devoted himself to the Stoic dictates of duty, describing his office as "noble servitude" and his diadem as a mere "rag." Antigonus shared the traditional Macedonian ambition to dominate the Greek city-states, but he faced rival powers. Besides Ptolemaic Egypt, there was the kingdom of Epirus in northwestern Greece and two new federal leagues in the south, the Aetolians (ay-TOL-ee-unz) (north of the Corinthian Gulf) and the Achaeans (uh-KEE-unz) (in the Peloponnesus; see **MAP 4.3**).

The new leagues were dominated by the wealthy; they were not democracies. Yet, the leagues interest us as models of federalism that would one day influence the founders of the

Antigonids Dynasty founded by Antigonus Gonatas in 276 B.C. and governed by Macedonian rulers for about 140 years, until the Roman conquest.

Tanagra Figurine   A terra-cotta (baked clay) statuette of around 320 B.C. shows a modestly dressed woman wearing a hat and carrying a fan. Named for its place of manufacture in Greece, this popular style of figure demonstrates the Hellenistic taste for ordinary, household themes.   (Bildarchiv Preussischer Kulturbesitz/Art Resource, NY)

United States. The Achaeans, for example, successfully balanced local and federal authorities. Affiliated cities kept their own constitutions while recognizing federal jurisdiction. The federal government consisted of a governing general (both president and commander-in-chief) and ten subordinate magistrates, an executive council, and a general assembly.

Extremes of wealth and poverty, problems of debt, and class conflict challenged Hellenistic Greece. Athens remained a vibrant democracy until the late third century B.C., when the oligarchic upper classes finally won the upper hand for good. The wealthy now contributed less to the public good in taxes and amassed private fortunes instead. Still, they usually made just enough concessions to avoid full-scale revolution.

Sparta was an exception. In the late third century B.C., a social revolution was launched from above by Agis and Cleomenes, two Spartan kings working together. After defeat in the fourth century B.C., Sparta had become impoverished (see page 72). The reformers now offered debt relief, redistribution of land, and restoration of Classical Spartan austerity and equality. Popular in Sparta, the revolution threatened to spread elsewhere. Peloponnesian oligarchs called in Macedonian forces, which crushed Sparta in 222 B.C. and ended the revolution.

Ptolemaic Egypt

The wealthiest, most sophisticated, and longest-lasting Hellenistic kingdom was Ptolemaic Egypt. One of Alexander's great generals, Ptolemy (d. 283 B.C.), founded a dynasty that lasted until Rome annexed Egypt in 30 B.C., after the suicide of the last ruler of the line, Queen Cleopatra (see pages 133–134). By then, Rome had already conquered or annexed all the other Hellenistic kingdoms.

Unlike the Antigonids, the Ptolemies gloried in wealth and grandeur. Ptolemy I showed the way to his successors when he had Alexander's funeral procession hijacked on its way to Macedonia and established a tomb and then a cult in the capital city, **Alexandria**—a Greek hero-shrine in the land of the pyramids. Ptolemy I made arrangements to have himself proclaimed "savior god" after his death; his successors, less reticent, took divine honors while still alive.

Like the pharaohs, the Ptolemies intervened in the Egyptian economy on a massive scale. Putting to use the science of the Museum, the great institute in Alexandria (see pages 96–97), the Ptolemies sponsored irrigation and land reclamation projects, the introduction of new crops (for example, new varieties of wheat), and the greatly expanded cultivation of old ones (such as grapes for wine).

Most of the people of Egypt made their living in agriculture, either as independent small farmers or as tenants on large estates. Government enriched itself through taxes, rents, demands for compulsory labor, state monopolies (on such diverse items as oils, textiles, and beer), and various internal tolls and customs duties. The result was boom times under strong kings and queens in the third century B.C. Egypt became the most prosperous part of the Hellenistic world, and Alexandria became the wealthiest, most populous city in the Mediterranean, as well as its literary capital (see **MAP 4.3**). In the second century B.C., however, continued economic prosperity was derailed by decline, which created conditions for revolt.

To defeat the Seleucids at the Battle of Raphia in Gaza in 217 B.C., the Ptolemies had to enroll thousands of Egyptians in the Macedonian phalanx, because of a shortage of Greek mercenaries. Emboldened by their new military power, people in Upper Egypt soon broke into armed revolt against the government in far-off Alexandria. Rival kings appeared in the south, and unrest continued for about a century.

To advance their cause, the rebels inflamed anti-Greek sentiment. High taxes and regional rivalries, however, probably carried

Egyptians Versus Greeks in a Temple

This second-century B.C. papyrus, a petition to the authorities from a Greek worshiper of Serapis, provides insight into relations between Greeks and Egyptians in Hellenistic Egypt. It shows how Greeks lived in the temple at Memphis in order to worship Serapis, a Hellenized Egyptian god (see page 105). It also depicts violence and hostility across ethnic lines.

To Dionysius, general and one of the "friends" [of the king], from Ptolemy son of Glaucias, a Macedonian, one of those "held in detention" [that is, on a voluntary, religious retreat] for twelve years in the great Temple of Serapis in Memphis. As I have suffered grave injustice and my life has been frequently endangered by the temple cleaners whose names are listed below, I am taking refuge with you in the belief that in this way I would best secure justice. For on . . . [November 9, 161 B.C.] they came to the temple of Astarte, which is in the sanctuary, and in which I have been living "in detention" for the number of years mentioned above; some of them had stones in their hand and others sticks, and they tried to force their way in, in order to seize the opportunity to plunder the temple and to put me to death because I am a Greek, like men laying a plot against my life. But when I anticipated them and shut the door of the temple, and shouted to them to withdraw in peace, they did not go away even so. When Diphilus, one of the worshipers held "in detention" by Serapis besides me, expressed indignation at their conduct in such a temple, they pushed him back, handled him very roughly and beat him up, so that their lawless brutality was clear for all to see. When these same men treated me in the same way in . . . .[November 163 B.C.], I immediately addressed a petition to you, but as I had no one to look after the matter further, they were let off scot-free and became even more arrogant. I therefore ask you, if you please, to order them to be brought before you, so that they may receive the punishment they deserve for all these misdeeds. Farewell.

QUESTIONS

1. What is the complaint of Ptolemy, son of Glaucias, about? Is this the first time he has made such a complaint?

2. Why was Ptolemy unable to get justice before? What does this tell us about the way petitions were handled by the government?

3. Why were Ptolemy and Diphilus attacked? What does the attack indicate about Greek-Egyptian relations in second century B.C. Egypt?

Source: Adapted from M. M. Austin, *The Hellenistic World from Alexander, to the Roman Conquest: A Selection of Ancient Sources in Translation*, 2/e, 2006, p.536. Reprinted with the permission of Cambridge University Press.

---

more weight than nationalism in the minds of most people. Although friction between immigrants and natives sparked from time to time, most Egyptians accepted the Ptolemies as pharaohs as long as they brought peace and prosperity. (See the feature, "The Global Record: Egyptians Versus Greeks in a Temple.")

And the Ptolemies reasserted their power. In 196 B.C., for example, Ptolemy V Epiphanes celebrated his coronation in full pharaonic ceremonial in Memphis. Egyptian priests commemorated the occasion in a decree written in Egypt's traditional language of kingship in a trilingual inscription (Greek, hieroglyphic, and demotic—ordinary—Egyptian). This inscription, discovered by French soldiers in 1799 and dubbed the Rosetta stone (named for the place where it was found), led to the modern European deciphering of hieroglyphics.

Despite the frictions, evidence points to native settler cooperation, especially in the countryside, where intermarriage and bilingualism became common. Many an ordinary Greek became fully assimilated to Egyptian ways, and even wealthy, sophisticated, urban Greeks adopted a smattering of Egyptian customs. By 98 B.C., assimilation was evident in the cultural hybrid of a group of 18- and 19-year-old male youths who received traditional Greek military and literary training but prayed to Egypt's crocodile-god.

Alexandria Thriving Hellenistic city in northern Egypt founded by Alexander the Great in 332 B.C.

Western Asia

The kingdom founded by Alexander's general Seleucus (suh-LOO-kus) (ca. 358–281 B.C.) experienced shifting borders and inhabitants. The Seleucid kingdom began when Seleucus took Babylon in 312 B.C. and ended in 64 B.C. when Syria became a Roman province. Many territorial changes occurred in between. The first three kings ruled a domain stretching from the Aegean to Bactria (BACK-tree-uh) (modern Afghanistan), but by the early second century B.C., most of the Iranian Plateau and lands eastward had been lost. At its height, in the third century B.C., the Seleucid kingdom had three nerve centers: Ionia (in western Anatolia), with a capital at Sardis; Syria, with a capital at Antioch; and Babylonia, whose capital was Seleucia-on-the-Tigris (near modern Baghdad; see **MAP 4.2**).

The far-flung and multiethnic Seleucid lands presented an enormous administrative challenge. The kings took over the Persian system of satraps (provincial governors), taxes, and royal roads and post (see page 35), to which they added a Macedonian-style army, a common coinage, and a Hellenistic ruler cult. The chief Seleucid innovation was the establishment of colonies. Greek and Macedonian soldiers and administrators dominated, but natives also filled bureaucratic slots.

Antioch Located near the present-day Turkish-Syrian border, it was the greatest of the cities founded by Seleucus, a general of Alexander the Great.

The greatest Seleucid city was **Antioch**, which became one of the wealthiest and most luxurious of all eastern Mediterranean cities; only Ptolemaic Alexandria outstripped it. The intellectual and artistic capital of Greek Asia in Hellenistic times, however, was not Antioch but Pergamum, in northwestern Anatolia (see **MAP 4.3**).

The rulers of Pergamum, the Attalid dynasty of kings, carved out a small kingdom that became independent of the Seleucids in 263 B.C. and fell into Roman hands in 133 B.C. The Attalids made Pergamum into a showplace of Greek civilization, a would-be second Athens. As in Athens, public building was focused on a steep acropolis. The upper city of Pergamum

Laocoön This famous statue group of the second or first century B.C. shows the Trojan priest Laocoön and his sons being strangled by snakes sent by the gods. The scene's emphasis on extreme emotion is typical of Hellenistic art. (Scala/Art Resource, NY)

was laid out on hillside terraces, rising to a palace and fortified citadel. One of the terraces housed the famous Pergamum Altar, a huge monument to an Attalid victory over the Celts, who first invaded Anatolia in 278 B.C. and whose advance the Attalids checked. They could not, however, stop the Celts from settling in central Anatolia, where they created their kingdom of Galatia.

Pergamum was famous for its sculptors and for a library second only to Alexandria's. Pergamene writers focused on scholarship, to the exclusion of poetry, perhaps as a result of the influence of Stoic philosophers, who disapproved of poetry's emotionalism.

The Greco-Indian Interaction

The Seleucids' hold on Alexander's vast eastern domains turned out to be temporary. A new Persian dynasty, the Parthians (PAR-thee-unz), achieved independence in the mid-third century B.C. and over the next century, extended westward into Mesopotamia. But to the east, Bactria remained Greek, if not Seleucid. From the mid-third century B.C., an independent Greek **Bactria** prospered (see **Map 4.2**).

Vivid evidence of Greek colonization in Bactria comes from the site of Aï Khanum (its ancient name is unknown) in northern Afghanistan. This prosperous and populous city contained many reminders of Greece, among them a gymnasium, theater, and library. A pillar in the gymnasium was inscribed in the mid-third century B.C., with 140 moral maxims from Delphi in Greece, over 3,000 miles away.

In the second century B.C., Bactrian kings extended their rule into the Indus River valley and the Punjab, a region with a modest Greek presence since the fifth century B.C., when the Persians settled Greek mercenaries there. Virtually no literary evidence survives, but monuments and, particularly, coins demonstrate Greco-Indian cultural interaction. For example, some coins from the second century B.C. show bilingual inscriptions in Greek and Indian languages. Their designs include a variety of Indian religious motifs, such as the lotus plant, symbol of Lakshmi, goddess of wealth and good fortune. Indians admired Hellenistic astronomy; one text goes so far as to say that Greek scientists should be "reverenced like gods."

The Hellenistic world seems to have intrigued King Asoka (uh-SO-kuh) (r. ca. 270–230 B.C.), who ruled almost the entire Indian subcontinent. Asoka is best remembered as a religious reformer. A convert to Buddhism, he played a major role in its spread, which proceeded under the slogan of *dhamma*— that is, "morality" or "righteousness." One of his inscriptions apparently records embassies, aimed at spreading Buddhism, to the Hellenistic kingdoms.[2]

The envoys apparently found few converts, for it is difficult to find any trace of Buddhism in Hellenistic Greek culture, at least outside the Greco-Indian kingdoms. There, one of the most powerful Greek rulers, Menander Soter Dikaios (r. ca. 155–130 B.C.), may have converted to Buddhism in the mid-second century B.C. But certain aspects of Indian religion—especially India's powerful currents of asceticism, mysticism, and monasticism—interested Greek intellectuals around the Mediterranean in Hellenistic and Roman times. Observers on Alexander's expedition, Hellenistic envoys, merchants, and philosophers in search of Eastern wisdom all served as conduits between East and West. One of the most influential was Megasthenes, a Seleucid ambassador to the court of Asoka's grandfather, who published his *Indika*, a description of India, around 300 B.C.

Bactria Bactria flourished as an independent Greek-ruled state in what is today Afghanistan, beginning in the mid-third century B.C., and expanded into what is today India and Pakistan.

A Greek-Influenced Indian Statue This figure of a *bodhisattva* ("enlightened one") belongs to the Gandharan school, which was heavily influenced by Hellenistic sculpture. The statue's proportions, facial features, and draped clothing particularly recall Hellenistic motifs, suggesting that it may be the work of a Greek sculptor. (Photograph courtesy of the Royal Ontario Museum, © ROM)

SECTION SUMMARY

- Greek and Macedonian colonists and their descendants dominated the army and administration in the Ptolemaic and Seleucid kingdoms, but natives played a role as well.

- Greek culture made only a small impact in the multiethnic kingdoms of the Ptolemies and Seleucids; native cultures flourished.

- The Antigonid dynasty of Macedon and federal leagues joined city-states as prominent features of Hellenistic Greek political life.

- Ptolemaic Egypt, with its capital of Alexandria, was the wealthiest, most sophisticated, and longest lasting Hellenistic kingdom.

- Seleucid Antioch and Attalid Pergamum were new and thriving cities of Hellenistic southwest Asia.

- Hellenistic Greek kingdoms prospered for centuries in parts of Afghanistan, India, and Pakistan.

Yet, the degree to which this interest influenced Greek and Roman culture is debatable. Although ancient writers mention Greek or Roman philosophers who were attracted by Indian culture, modern scholars tend to be cautious. The ancients had a weakness for tall tales and exotic stories. For example, the great Neo-Platonic philosopher Plotinus (A.D. 235–270) is reported to have traveled with the Roman emperor Gordian's army eastward, hoping in vain to reach India. Some scholars see Indian influence in Plotinus's mysticism and pantheism, but others dismiss the idea.

Central Asian nomads overran Bactria in the late second century B.C. The Hellenistic kingdoms of India and Pakistan, however, survived until about the time of Christ, and some Greek communities lasted until the fifth century A.D. The Gandharan sculptors who flourished in a formerly Greek-ruled region in about A.D. 200 used Greek artistic techniques to depict Buddhist subjects, which might suggest the impact of Indian culture on the remaining Greek population.

HELLENISTIC CULTURE

How did Greek civilization spread during the Hellenistic era, and what were the main trends in literature, science, and art?

The capital of Egypt, Alexandria, was also the main laboratory for transforming Hellenistic Greek culture and so facilitating its spread. By the first century B.C., Alexandria was a city of half a million or more inhabitants. It was one of the largest and wealthiest cities in the world. The bulk of the people were Egyptian, but Greeks and Jews made up large minorities, and no one would have been surprised, in this cosmopolitan center, to see an Indian or a Celt, an Italian or a Persian.

Archaeologists today, looking for submerged parts of the city in Alexandria harbor, have found Egyptian sphinxes and obelisks, as well as Greek statues. Written sources portray a picture of social change in the elite, an increase in leisure time, a growth in educational opportunities for both sexes, royal patronage of culture, and the value of even a limited knowledge of Greek literature as the ticket to advancement.

Athens and Alexandria

In 294 B.C., King Ptolemy I invited the deposed tyrant of Athens, Demetrius of Phalerum, to found an institution of culture in Alexandria. Demetrius had studied with Aristotle's successor at the Lyceum, Theophrastus (the-uh-FRAS-tus) (ca. 370–288 B.C.), a practical man interested in compiling and cataloging knowledge.

Museum Literally "House of the Muses," the Museum was Alexandria's most important scholarly and scientific center. It included the Library, which housed the world's largest collection of Greek writing.

The new institution was called the **Museum** (literally, "House of the Muses," or the home of the female deities who inspired creativity). The Museum was a residence, study, and lecture hall for scholars, scientists, and poets. It was also a research center to keep the king's engineers up to date on new technology for warfare and agriculture. One of the Museum's key components was the Library, in its day, the largest collection of Greek writing in the world. In the third century B.C.—at the height of the Ptolemaic kingdom—the Library contained 700,000 papyrus rolls, the equivalent of roughly 50,000 modern books. Its nearest competitor, at Pergamum, contained less than a third as many rolls. The Library reflects the growth of the Hellenistic reading and writing public. The names of over a thousand writers of the Hellenistic era survive, and after 300 B.C., anthologies, abridgments, and school texts multiplied.

Though modeled on Athens's Lyceum, the Museum represented a break from the public culture of the Classical period. The residents of the Museum were an elite, dependent on royal patronage and self-consciously Greek and not Egyptian. One wit dismissed them as pedants and "fatted fowls that quarrel without end in the hen coop of the Muses."

The background to Alexandrian literature is Hellenistic Athenian literature, which diverged sharply from its Classical roots. The greatest Hellenistic Athenian writer, a man famous throughout the ancient world, was Menander (ca. 342–292 B.C.). He was the master of a style of comedy called "New Comedy," as distinguished from the "Old Comedy" of Aristophanes, which had flourished a century earlier (see page 80). Where Old Comedy was raucous and ribald, New Comedy was restrained; where Old Comedy focused on public matters such as war and politics, New Comedy was domestic and private. New Comedy was typical of the turn away from public life in Hellenistic times.

Menander wrote over seventy plays, but only one complete work has survived, *Dyskolos* (*The Grouch*). There are also large excerpts from several other comedies, as well as Roman imitations. Menander favored stock plots and stock characters: the boastful soldier, the clever slave, the dashing but inept young man, the sweet maiden, and the old miser. Within those limitations, Menander created realistic and idiosyncratic characters. As a Hellenistic critic asked rhetorically: "O Menander and Life, which of you imitated the other?"

Like Menander, Alexandrian writers spurned public themes, but in Alexandria, the characteristic literary figure was not the playwright but the critic: a professional man of letters. Adopted by the Romans, Alexandrian critical standards have influenced the West to this day.

Of the three greatest Alexandrian writers, two—Callimachus (305–240 B.C.) and Apollonius of Rhodes (b. ca. 295 B.C.)—worked at the Library; the third, Theocritus (ca. 300–260 B.C.), probably lived on a stipend from the Ptolemies. Popular for centuries, Callimachus was probably the most influential, the complete Hellenistic poet. A native of Cyrene (see **MAP 4.2**) who came to Alexandria as a schoolteacher, Callimachus worked in the Library to compose a virtually universal history of all recorded Greek (and much non-Greek) knowledge.

Callimachus was a prolific writer, but he aimed at brevity: "Big book, big evil" was his maxim. While earlier Greek poets were usually austere and public-minded, Callimachus preferred the private, the light, and the exotic. "Don't expect from me a big-sounding poem," he writes. "Zeus thunders, not I."[3] Callimachus was an expert at the pithy statement in verse—the epigram.

Another major Alexandrian writer was Callimachus's student Apollonius of Rhodes. His major work was the epic poem *Argonautica* (ar-go-NAW-tih-kuh) (*Voyage of the Argo*). The subject is the legend of Jason and the heroes who travel on the ship *Argo* to the Black Sea, in pursuit of the Golden Fleece (the skin of a winged ram). With the help of the princess Medea, who falls in love with Jason, the heroes succeed and return home safely after numerous adventures.

The most striking thing about Apollonius is his doubt about the very possibility of heroism. Apollonius's Jason is no hero of old. Whereas Homer describes Odysseus as "never at a loss," Apollonius describes Jason as "helpless." Men move the action in the *Iliad* and the *Odyssey*; Jason depends on a woman, Medea, for his success. Indeed, much of the *Argonautica* focuses on Medea and her love for Jason. All in all, the *Argonautica* is less a traditional epic than a romance.

Theocritus, a native of Syracuse, composed thirty-one subtle and refined poems, conventionally known as idylls. The best known poems focus on country life. They are the first known pastoral poems; indeed, Theocritus probably invented the genre. Through his Roman admirers, Theocritus's love of nature has exerted a powerful hold on the Western literary imagination.

Outside the Museum, Alexandria had a lively popular culture, much of it Egyptian or influenced by Egyptian models. A glimpse of this culture is offered in the seven surviving mimes, or farces, of an obscure writer named Herondas or Herodas. Though written in literary Greek, they discuss commonplace subjects—shopping for shoes, tourism, lawsuits, and beatings at school—and titillating themes, such as adultery and prostitution.

Advances in Science and Medicine

The Ptolemies not only reaped practical benefits in military and agricultural technology from their Museum, but also became the patrons of a flourishing period in the history of pure scientific inquiry. They unwittingly promoted a split between philosophy and science that has

Street Musicians The lively scene of a mixed group of young and old, male and female, recalls the jaunty mimes popular with the Hellenistic public. A mosaic from about 100 B.C., the artwork comes from a private villa in the Greco-Italian city of Pompeii. (Museo Archeologico Nazionale, Naples, Italy/Erich Lessing/Art Resource, NY)

characterized much of Western culture since. Antigonid patronage of ethical and political philosophy helped keep Athens preeminent in those fields. In contrast, the study of science tended to shift to Alexandria and to Pergamum in Anatolia and, far to the west, Syracuse, a flourishing Hellenistic city in Sicily. Hellenistic science benefited from several factors, including the era's wealth, improved communications and literacy, continued warfare, and cross-fertilization between Greek and non-Greek traditions.

MATHEMATICS Some of the best-known figures of Hellenistic science were mathematicians. In his *Elements*, the Alexandrian Euclid (active ca. 300 B.C.) produced a systematic study of geometry that was hugely influential in both Western and Islamic civilizations.

Archimedes The greatest ancient Greek mathematician, Archimedes of Syracuse (287–212 B.C.) calculated the approximate value of pi (the ratio of a circle's circumference to its diameter) and invented the water snail (also known as Archimedes' screw).

But the greatest mathematician of Greek antiquity was a Sicilian Greek, **Archimedes** (ar-kuh-MEE-deez) of Syracuse (287–212 B.C.). Among other things, Archimedes calculated the approximate value of pi (the ratio of a circle's circumference to its diameter) and made important discoveries in astronomy, engineering, optics, and other fields. Although Archimedes looked down on practical things as "ignoble and vulgar," he was a notable inventor. His most important invention was the water snail, also known as Archimedes' screw—a device to raise water for irrigation. Created by Archimedes during a stay in Egypt, the screw made it possible to irrigate previously barren land, as did the ox-driven water wheel, another innovation of this period.

Advances in mathematics promoted advances in astronomy. Aristarchus of Samos (active ca. 275 B.C.) is known for his heliocentric hypothesis, which confounded tradition by having the earth revolve around the sun, instead of the sun around the earth. He was right, but Hellenistic astronomy lacked the data to prove his theory, so its rejection was not unreasonable at the time. Eratosthenes (er-uh-TOSS-the-neez) of Cyrene (active ca. 225 B.C.) was saddled with the frustrating nickname of "Beta" (the second letter of the Greek alphabet) because he was considered second best in every branch of study. This "second best" nonetheless calculated through simple geometry an extraordinarily accurate measurement of the earth's circumference.

MEDICINE

Hellenistic medicine thrived in Alexandria. Both Greece and Egypt had long-established medical traditions, but the key to medical advance was the dissection of human cadavers in Alexandria, a first in the history of science. In Greece, as in many ancient societies, religious tradition demanded that dead bodies not be mutilated. But in the frontier atmosphere of early Alexandria, this traditional taboo lost much of its force. Although Egyptians did not practice dissection, they did practice embalming, which may have helped Alexandrian Greeks overcome the prohibition against cutting open the human body.

The leading scientific beneficiary was Herophilus (her-AH-fih-lus) of Chalcedon (ca. 320–250 B.C.), a practicing physician in Alexandria. Among his achievements was the recognition (against Aristotle) that the brain is the center of the nervous system, a careful dissection of the eye, the discovery of the ovaries, and the description of the duodenum, which he named (*duodenum* is a Latin translation of a Greek word meaning "twelve fingers," describing the organ's length). In addition, Herophilus developed a detailed theory of the diagnostic value of measuring pulse rates.

ENGINEERING

Hellenistic technology has long fascinated and frustrated scholars. The great engineers invented both numerous engines of war and various "wonderworks" to amuse the royal court. Among the latter were mechanical puppets and steam-run toys. Given these advances, why did the Greeks achieve neither a scientific revolution, along the lines of the one begun in the early modern era by thinkers such as Copernicus and Galileo, nor an industrial transformation, such as was ushered in by the steam engine around A.D. 1800? Historians are not entirely sure but can venture a guess. Greek machine-making technology was not as sophisticated as that of eighteenth-century Europe. The prevalence of slavery in antiquity discouraged laborsaving machines; steam was used only for playthings and gadgets.

Perhaps the most important point is the Greek attitude toward nature. Whereas Jews and Christians learned from the Bible that human beings have dominion over nature, thereby making possible the conclusion that it is appropriate to conquer nature, the Greeks thought in more restricted terms. They believed that nature set limits, that a virtuous person tried to follow nature, not subdue it. Thus, Greek engineers were not inclined to make the revolutionary changes that their modern counterparts have promoted.

Men and Women in Art and Society

Like Hellenistic literature, Hellenistic art attests to changing male attitudes toward women and toward gender issues. The portrait of Jason and Medea in Apollonius's *Argonautica* makes fun of masculine pretensions and celebrates the triumph of female intelligence. It also presents a sympathetic portrait of a woman's romantic desire for a man, as does Theocritus's work. In the Classical period, depictions of romantic love were generally restricted to relationships between males. Accordingly, statues of naked males were common, but women were almost always depicted clothed. Hellenistic sculpture, by contrast, affords many erotic examples of the female nude.

There are indications that the Hellenistic Greek male of the elite was much more willing than his Classical predecessor to see lovemaking as a matter of mutuality and respect. Classical vase-painting often depicts heterosexual lovemaking with a lusty and explicit mood. In contrast, in Hellenistic vase-painting, the emphasis is more often on tenderness and domesticity. Hellenistic men wrote with sensitivity about satisfying a woman's needs and desires. The vogue for representations of Hermaphrodite (her-MAF-ro-dyte), the mythical creature who was half-female and half-male, may suggest a belief that the feminine was as important a part of human nature as the masculine.

Many a Hellenistic artist or writer seems to be as interested in emotion as in action and to focus on the inner as much as on the outer life. Hellenistic art often depicts women, children, and

Images of Cleopatra

"*Cleopatra's nose: if it had been shorter, the whole face of the earth would have changed*," wrote the French Blaise Pascal (1623–1662). He does Cleopatra an injustice. It was not a pretty face and classical features that enabled her to win the throne of Egypt (r. 51–30 B.C.), to obtain first Julius Caesar and then Mark Antony as ally and lover, and finally to come close to gaining control of the Roman Empire. Intelligence, daring, charm, and extraordinary diplomatic skill account for Cleopatra's success.

Let us consider the queen's manipulation of her public image—no mean task, given the fragility of Ptolemaic power in the first century B.C. Within Egypt, the monarch had to satisfy several different ethnic groups. Most important were the Greeks and Macedonians—who dominated government, the military, and the economy—and the native Egyptian majority. Daughter of Ptolemy XII (r. 80–51 B.C.), Cleopatra was supposed to rule jointly with her brother, but they had a falling-out. She grabbed the throne from him and then from another brother and thus had to assert her legitimacy. Also, Ptolemaic Egypt had to project an image of unity to the Romans, who were threatening to annex it as they had the other Hellenistic monarchies.

Bronze Coin of Cleopatra   (Courtesy of the Trustees of the British Museum)

Cleopatra, like earlier Ptolemaic monarchs, met these challenges by presenting two faces to the world. To the Greeks and Romans, she was a Hellenistic monarch; to the Egyptians, she was an ancient pharaonic queen. Look first at the bronze coin of Cleopatra issued at Alexandria probably in the 30s B.C. The queen is shown as a young woman. Her hair, tied in a bun at the nape of her neck, is in the so-called melon style often seen in Hellenistic female portraits. She wears a diadem (royal headband), its ends hanging behind her neck. More commonly worn by Hellenistic kings than by queens, the diadem signifies Cleopatra's claim to authority.

So does the queen's profile. She is portrayed with a prominent chin, a large mouth, and a rugged nose. These features may not be the standard attributes of beauty, but they are precisely the features that mark coin portraits of Cleopatra's father. By emphasizing Cleopatra's physical similarity to her father, the portrait artist perhaps subtly suggests her right to sit on his throne.

The side of the coin not shown here is far from subtle: Its legend states clearly in Greek, "Queen Cleopatra." The illustration is of an eagle and thunderbolt and a double cornucopia (horn of plenty) entwined with a diadem. The eagle and thunderbolt recall the Greek god Zeus, and the two cornucopias suggest fertility and prosperity. All are recurrent symbols of Ptolemaic royalty. The coin thus portrays Cleopatra as a Greek monarch, the worthy heir of her father. It would have been an effective image in Alexandria, a city dominated by Greeks and visited by Romans, but not in the countryside, especially south of the Nile Delta, in Upper Egypt, an area that was primarily Egyptian. Following dynastic custom, Cleopatra changed her image there.

In Upper Egypt, earlier Ptolemies frequently had been represented in stone in traditional pharaonic style, and they were great restorers of ancient Egyptian temples and builders of new ones. Look at the sculptural relief from the temple of the Egyptian cow-goddess Hathor at Dendera in Upper Egypt. The temple was a monumental structure initiated and underwritten by Ptolemy XII. Cleopatra, his daughter, added an enormous relief on the outside of the rear wall. Carved into the stone are two persons carrying offerings for Egyptian deities. The persons are Cleopatra (*left*) and her son Ptolemy XV Caesar, who ruled with his mother from 44 to 30 B.C. Alleged to be the illegitimate son of Julius Caesar, Ptolemy XV was commonly known as

domestic scenes. Representations of warriors are as likely to focus on their unrestrained emotions as on their soldierly self-control.

Hellenistic women enjoyed small improvements in political and legal status and bigger improvements in economic and ideological status. Greek women, particularly in the elite, benefited from the spread of monarchy. Queens and princesses had more power than female commoners in city-states. Also, in the new cities, as in many a frontier society, women were permitted to inherit and use property more often than in old Greece.

horn of Amon. Caesarion is shown as a pharaoh, wearing the double crown of Upper and Lower Egypt. Mother and son offer incense to the local deities. The small figure between Caesarion and Cleopatra is his *ka*, or soul.

Cleopatra's face is in profile, but otherwise has very little in common with her portrait on the Alexandrian coin. Although the features are stylized pharaonic commonplaces, the shape of her head perhaps echoes the elegant and graceful relief portraits of Hatshepsut (r. 1479–1457 B.C.), the most famous female pharaoh before Cleopatra. Cleopatra commissioned other artworks and monuments in the native style in the Nile Valley. This was the custom of her dynasty, and Cleopatra had absorbed its traditions, but she stands second to none of the Ptolemies in shrewdness and subtlety. She was the only Ptolemaic monarch to learn to speak Egyptian, and she was the only one to come even close to gaining the upper hand over Rome. As the artifacts shown here indicate, she was able to put on an Egyptian face as easily as a Greek one, but she never lost sight of her true interests.

Relief of Cleopatra and Caesarion (Erich Lessing/Art Resource, NY)

Caesarion, or "little Caesar." At Dendera, however, he and his mother are shown neither as Romans nor as Greeks but as Egyptians.

Look closely at Cleopatra. She wears a long body-hugging robe. On her head is a royal headdress with symbols of the Egyptian gods: the lyre-shaped cow horns and sun-disk of Hathor, the tall plumes of Isis, and the ram's

QUESTIONS

1. Why did Cleopatra need to show two faces to the world?
2. Does Cleopatra's coin emphasize her good looks? Why or why not?
3. What image of herself does Cleopatra present at the Temple of Hathor at Dendera? Why?

It was an era of powerful queens: Olympias, Alexander the Great's mother, played kingmaker after her son's death. Arsinoe II Philadelphus was coruler of Egypt with her husband (who was also her brother) for five years at the height of Ptolemaic prosperity around 275 B.C. The most famous Hellenistic woman, Cleopatra VII, was queen of Egypt from 51 to 30 B.C. Although she was the lover of two of the most powerful men in the world, the Romans Julius Caesar and Mark Antony, Cleopatra was no exotic plaything. Rather, she was a brilliant and ambitious strategist who nearly succeeded in winning a world empire for her family. (See the feature, "The Visual Record: Images of Cleopatra.")

Writers in the new Hellenistic cities often described freedom of movement for women. Theocritus and Herondas, for example, show women visiting a temple or a show. In Hellenistic Athens, aristocratic fathers put up inscriptions in honor of their daughters who had participated in the cult of Athena. Although women generally continued to need a male guardian to represent them in public, in some situations, at least in Egypt (where the evidence is most plentiful), a woman could represent herself. A woman could petition the government on her own behalf. Widows and mothers of illegitimate children could give their daughters in marriage or apprentice their sons. A few cities granted women citizenship and even permitted them to hold public office.

Some Hellenistic cities admitted women to the gymnasium, previously a male preserve. Heretofore, only Sparta had promoted physical education for women, but by the first century A.D., women were even competing in the great Pan-Hellenic games. Gymnasia were also centers of education in music and reading. One consequence of growing literacy was the re-emergence of women poets and the first appearance of women philosophers in the West. Before dying at age 19, Erinna, who lived on the Aegean island of Telos during the late fourth century B.C., wrote the *Distaff*, a poem in memory of her childhood friend Baucis. This three-hundred line poem, famous in antiquity, describes the shared experiences of girlhood. Hipparchia (hih-PAR-kee-uh) of Maroneia (b. ca. 350 B.C.), like her husband, Crates of Thebes, studied Cynic philosophy. The Cynics, like another philosophical school, the Epicureans, supported a measure of equality between women and men. Hipparchia and Crates led an itinerant life as popular teachers and the Hellenistic equivalent of counselors or psychologists.

Much of the explanation for the relative freedom of elite women lies in the new economic power of this group. The new cities generally imposed fewer restrictions on women's economic roles than had Classical poleis such as Athens. In many cities, women could sell land, borrow money, and decide whether their husbands could make loans or contracts on the strength of their dowries. Free women could manumit slaves as well.

Hellenistic women never attained the equality that sometimes exists between men and women today, but they did enjoy genuine improvements in status. Men and women played new roles in a changed, complex world. The new Hellenistic philosophies and religions attempted to address that complexity.

Aphrodite of Cnidos This 7½-foot-tall marble statue is a Roman copy of an original by Praxiteles (ca. 350–330 B.C.). Perhaps the most famous of Hellenistic female nudes, the statue was housed in a special shrine where it could be viewed in the round to accommodate all the interest it generated. (Nimatallah/Art Resource, NY)

SECTION SUMMARY

- Alexandria's Museum (a research institute) and Library were the focal point of much of Hellenistic literature and science.

- The playwright Menander and the poets Callimachus, Apollonius of Rhodes, and Theocritus represent the Hellenistic era's turn away from civic and heroic themes.

- Mathematics, astronomy, and medicine are all fields in which notable advances were made in the Hellenistic era, thanks in part to royal patronage.

- Philosophy and science first became separate disciplines, as they are today.

- Hellenistic women experienced real, though limited, improvements in status and power.

THE TURN INWARD: NEW PHILOSOPHIES, NEW FAITHS

What new philosophies and religions emerged in the Hellenistic period?

The events of the Hellenistic era—emigration, a trend from independent city-states to monarchies and federal leagues, new extremes of wealth and poverty, and contact with foreign peoples and customs—all generated uncertainty. In response, Greek culture was spread and transformed. As literacy expanded, more Greeks than ever before could participate in cultural debate. New philosophies and religions arose to meet new spiritual concerns, generating ideas that would be influential for centuries.

The meeting of Jews and Greeks proved to be just as significant. Challenged by Greek conquest, Greek colonization, and their own migration to Greek lands, Jews alternately embraced Hellenism and engaged in resistance, both cultural and armed. In the process, first Judaism and then Hellenism were changed forever.

Hellenistic Philosophy

Although the polis lost its military and political preeminence in the fourth century B.C., philosophy continued to thrive. It was, however, much changed. With the city-state losing significance as a focus of loyalty, and with the Greek-reading public growing in size and geographic extent, Hellenistic philosophy paid less and less attention to politics. Since Hellenistic science tended to become a separate discipline from philosophy, philosophers focused on ethics, the discovery of the best way to live. The essence of the good life, most philosophers agreed, was peace of mind, or freedom from troubles. Hellenistic philosophy won a wide following; indeed, for many people, primarily in the elite, philosophy became a way of life, even a religion.

CYNICISM

Several competing philosophical schools emerged, beginning with Cynicism (SIN-uh-sizm). Never a widespread philosophy, Cynicism is nonetheless important as a precursor of the two most popular doctrines, Stoicism and Epicureanism. Skepticism rejected the main philosophies and proposed instead a commonsense attitude toward ethics.

The first Cynic was Diogenes (dye-AH-juh-neez) of Sinope (ca. 400–325 B.C.). An exile in Athens, Diogenes developed a philosophy that rejected all conventions. People find happiness, he decided, by satisfying their natural needs with simplicity. Accordingly, Diogenes chose a life of poverty. A beggar in rags, he delighted in shocking conventional morality. Famous for wit and shamelessness, he was nicknamed "Dog" (*kuon*) because the Greeks considered dogs to be shameless animals; his followers were called "Doglike" (*kunikoi*, whence the name *Cynic*).

STOICISM

Although he founded no school, Diogenes cast a wide shadow. Among those whom he indirectly influenced was Zeno (ZEE-no) (335–263 B.C.), who began one of the most important philosophical systems of antiquity: Stoicism (STO-ih-sizm). Zeno came to Athens in 313 B.C. from Citium in Cyprus, a multiethnic city; he was possibly of Phoenician origin. Influenced by both Cynicism and Socratic philosophy, Zeno developed his own doctrines, which he taught in the *Stoa Poikile* ("Painted Porch," hence the name *Stoic*), a public building.

Like Plato and Aristotle, Zeno sought an absolute standard of good on which to base philosophical decisions. He found it in the divine reason (*logos*), which he considered the principle of the universe and the guide to human behavior. The best life was spent in pursuit of wisdom—that is, a life of philosophy. Only that rare and forbidding figure, the Sage, could truly attain wisdom; ordinary people could merely progress toward it through study and the attempt to be free from all passion.

Stoicism may seem harsh. It is not surprising that *stoical* has come to describe austere indifference to pain. In some ways, however, Stoicism was comforting. The **Stoics** were empiricists—that is, they trusted the evidence of the senses, an attitude that they thought would inspire confidence and security. They believed in human brotherhood—led, to be sure, by a Greek-speaking elite. Since brothers have a duty to one another, the Stoics argued that a good person should play an active role in public life.

Stoics Believers in a philosophical system begun in Athens by Zeno, which emphasized the pursuit of wisdom, the reliability of sensory experience, and freedom from all passion.

The Stoics emphasized the inner life. They believed that intentions matter. This was an important departure from Greek tradition, which tended to emphasize the outcome of an action, not its motivation. Stoicism also departed from traditional Greek localism, embracing a more cosmopolitan outlook. "This world is a great city, [and] has one constitution and one law," wrote Philo of Alexandria (30 B.C.–A.D. 45), a Stoic and a Jew. Many Stoics believed in a natural law or law of nations—that is, that overarching and common principles governed international relations.

With its emphasis on duty and order, Stoicism became popular with Greek ruling elites, and eventually with the Romans, who used its concept of a universal state to justify their empire. Many Stoic principles were later embraced by early Christian writers.

EPICUREANISM

Epicurus (341–270 B.C.), an Athenian citizen, founded his philosophical school at around the same time as Zeno founded Stoicism. There were other similarities: Both schools were empiricist and materialist (that is, they tended to trust the evidence of the senses), both sought peace of mind, and both inspired widespread followings. Epicurus, however, taught not in a public place but in a private garden. Whereas the Stoics encouraged political participation, the **Epicureans** counseled withdrawal from the rough-and-tumble of public life. "Calm" and "Live in hiding" are famous Epicurean (eh-pi-kyuh-REE-un) maxims.

Epicureans Adherents of the Athenian philosopher Epicurus, they emphasized the avoidance of pain and the pursuit of intellectual pleasure.

Epicurus's materialism is based on the atomic theory of Democritus (see page 76). It envisions a thoroughly mechanistic universe in which the gods exist but play no active role in events. Individuals need fear neither fickle deities nor an unhappy afterlife because the soul is merely a combination of atoms that ceases to exist after death. The purpose of life was the avoidance of pain and the pursuit of pleasure. The latter was called hedonism (from *hedone*, Greek for "pleasure"), but not, as the word has come to mean today, indulgence in food, drink, or sex. Instead, Epicureans meant intellectual pleasure. Friendship and fraternity were Epicurean ideals—the private analogs, as it were, of Stoic brotherhood.

The Epicureans raised eyebrows and sometimes ire, occasionally suffering persecution by the state. They were accused of atheism and sensuality. Classical Greek philosophy defined virtue as the highest good. The Epicurean emphasis on pleasure, even spiritual pleasure, seemed perverse to some. Yet, Epicureanism was simple, sure of itself, and practical, and it offered both friendship and a sense of community. It became a popular philosophy, especially among the wealthy.

SKEPTICISM

Skepticism (SKEP-tih-sizm) was founded by Pyrrho of Elis (ca. 360–270 B.C.), a Greek who traveled with Alexander to India. Like Stoics and Epicureans, Skeptics sought peace of mind. They rejected those thinkers' conclusions, however, on the grounds that they were dogmatic—that is, based not on positive proof but merely on opinion (*doxa*). Considering the senses unreliable, Skeptics rejected the commonsense approach of Stoics and Epicureans. They preferred to suspend judgment on the great philosophical questions (hence, our term *skepticism* for a doubting state of mind). Whoever was able to do so could accept the customs of the community, avoid politics, and thereby obtain peace of mind.

The Mystery Religions

The name "mystery religion" comes from the Greek word for "secret." A mystery religion initiated worshipers into secret teachings. Long a feature of Greek religion, the **mystery religions**—there were several different ones—grew very popular in Hellenistic times. They offered relief similar to that of the philosophical schools: ethical guidance, comfort, release from worries, reassurance about death, and a sense of unity. The rise of the mystery religions went along with the decline of the traditional Greek religion of the Olympian gods.

mystery religions Popular Hellenistic cults, featuring the initiation of worshipers into secret doctrines, they replaced the traditional Greek religion of the Olympian gods.

The old Greek gods came under attack on every front in the Hellenistic era. The newly divinized kings stole their spotlight, while philosophers criticized the Olympians as primitive and immoral. Scholarship got into the act as well. Around 300 B.C., Euhemerus of Messene wrote that Zeus and others were not gods, but merely great kings of the past who were rewarded with deification, much as a Hellenistic monarch might be.

The Olympians retained their temples, but the rituals seemed hollow and antiquarian. What was to replace them? Of the several new religious movements that marked the age, three stand out: the divinization of kings, the cult of Tyche (Fortune), and the mystery religions.

Under the Ptolemies and Seleucids, ruler-worship became standard procedure. Some no doubt considered it just a patriotic formality, while others prayed to the god-king or god-queen to intercede for them in heaven. Meanwhile, the old Greek city-states, especially democracies, bristled. "To transfer to men the honor due to the gods," said one Athenian playwright, "is to dissolve the democracy."

He might have said as much about the Hellenistic cult of Tyche (TOO-kay) (Fortune or Luck), often worshiped as a goddess, sometimes as the protector of a particular city. The most famous example was the Tyche of Antioch, personified as a statue of a woman wearing the battlements of the city on her head as a kind of crown—a very popular statue, to judge by the many copies found around the Hellenistic world.

Various mystery religions flourished. In Athens, the cult of Demeter, goddess of fertility, had long been celebrated in the suburb of Eleusis, and it grew in popularity. Those who took part in the ceremonies received promises of life after death.

New mystery religions from outside Greece grew even more popular, particularly the Hellenized Egyptian cults of Serapis and of Isis. Created under Ptolemy I, Serapis (SEH-ruh-pis) was meant to combine Osiris, the Egyptian god of the afterlife, with Apis, the god of the Nile flood. Serapis also suggested Pluto, the Greek god of the underworld. Hence, it is an early example of the common Hellenistic practice of religious syncretism, or fusion. Despite its roots, Serapis-worship had little appeal to native Egyptians, but the god became popular in the Greek world as the patron of healing and sailing.

Another traditional Egyptian deity, Osiris's wife, Isis (EYE-sis), also became a popular Greek and, later, Roman goddess. Called the Goddess of Ten Thousand Names, Isis was said to symbolize all the female deities of antiquity. Hers was a cult of the afterlife and of the suffering but tender and loving mother; she was particularly popular among women. Thus, under Ptolemaic sponsorship, ancient Egyptian cults were reworked and spread throughout the Greek-speaking world, circulating such notions as the suffering mother, the Last Judgment, and blessed eternal life after death. Early Christianity was much influenced by such Greco-Egyptian religious notions, but it was more directly the product of debate and ferment within Hellenistic Judaism.

A Cretan Dream Interpreter in Egypt A painted stele (ca. 200 B.C.) advertises the services of a Greek in Memphis near the Temple of Serapis, a Greco-Egyptian god. The inscription and pediment are Greek, while the pilasters, women, and sacred bull (facing an altar) are Egyptian. (Egyptian Museum, Cairo)

Hellenistic Judaism

Few consequences of Alexander's conquests had so lasting an impact as the mixing of Greeks and Jews. When Alexander conquered it in 332 B.C., Judea had been a Persian province for 200 years. Now, the fates of Greeks and Jews grew intertwined.

Jewish responses to Greek culture varied. At one extreme stood the Hellenizers, who admired Greek culture and wanted to assimilate to it. At the other extreme were traditionalists, who defended Jewish law as interpreted by scholars and rabbis. Their disagreement led to war, which broke out as follows.

After Alexander's death, Hellenistic Judea was governed first by the Ptolemies until 200 B.C., then by the Seleucids, until the establishment of an independent Jewish state in 142 B.C., which came in turn under Roman control in 63 B.C. The Greeks were not absentee rulers. Rather, they established a large number of Greek colonies in and around Judea, especially under the Seleucids. Many Jews, especially wealthy ones, adopted some degree of Greek culture. Some Hellenizers gave up Jewish customs altogether for the Greek gymnasium, theater, and political institutions. With the help of the Seleucid king Antiochus IV Epiphanes (r. 175–163 B.C.), Jewish Hellenizers in 175 B.C. had Jerusalem proclaimed a Greek polis; they built a gymnasium at the foot of the Temple Mount. They looted the Temple's treasury. In 167 B.C., they attacked the essence of Judaism by outlawing

Bronze Coin with Menorah   This issue of Mattathias Antigone (r. 40–37 b.c.), the last Hasmonean king, is an early example of the use of the seven-branched candelabrum as the symbol of the Jewish people. A similar candelabrum was used in the Temple of Jerusalem.   (Erich Lessing/Art Resource, NY)

Maccabees   Traditionalist Jews led by the Hasmonean family, who, in 167 b.c., revolted against Hellenizing laws and influences.

Sabbath observance, prohibiting circumcision, and rededicating the Temple to Olympian Zeus, to whom they sacrificed pigs.

The traditionalists, however, rallied the Jewish masses into opposition. Soon a guerrilla revolt began in the countryside, led by the Hasmonean family, also known as the **Maccabees**, whose successes are celebrated today by Jews during the holiday of Hanukkah. The guerrilla movement developed into a disciplined armed uprising, which restored all Jewish religious practices and rededicated the Temple. The revolt also forced the Seleucids to tolerate an independent state under the Hasmonean dynasty. Jewish independence lasted from 142 b.c., until the Roman conquest in 63 b.c.

During the struggle over Hellenism, new elements of lasting significance became part of Judaism. First, the Jews developed a literature of spiritual resistance to the foreigner. This literature was apocalyptic—that is, it claimed to reveal dramatic, heretofore secret truths. Drawing on both biblical and Mesopotamian traditions, Jewish apocalyptic writing predicted a future cataclysm, when a royal redeemer would evict the foreigner and establish a new kingdom of Israel. The redeemer was often identified with another notion that first became popular in this era: the Messiah (literally, "anointed one"), someone anointed with oil signifying his election as king, a descendant of King David, who would save Israel. Another new aspect of Hellenistic Judaism was martyrdom, the notion of the holy sacrifice of one's life for a religious cause. There was also a growing belief in a final Judgment Day and resurrection, when God would raise the meritorious dead to live again on earth in their own bodies.

Hellenistic Judaism was diverse. Various sects each proposed its own version of Judaism. Among these sects were the Sadducees (SAJ-oo-seez) (the disciples of one Tzadok), a wealthy establishment group for whom the rituals of the Temple in Jerusalem were the heart of Judaism. Their opponents were the Pharisees (FAIR-ih-seez) (from the Hebrew *perushim*, "those who separate themselves," that is, in order to observe the laws of ritual purity). The Pharisees believed that the written law of the Hebrew Bible needed to be supplemented by an oral tradition that they traced back to Moses and Mt. Sinai. They saw themselves as the only true interpreters of that tradition. They proposed a kind of guided democratization of Judaism, emphasizing study and prayer in small groups under their leadership. Eventually, after several centuries, the Pharisees prevailed: they are the ancestors of modern Judaism. A third group was the Essenes (EH-seenz), generally identified with the Qumran (koom-RAHN) community in the Judean desert (see page 160).

Most Jews of the Hellenistic era lived outside Judea. Some had left voluntarily in search of wealth or adventure, while others had been taken captive in various wars. The Diaspora had spread into (among other places) Syria, Anatolia, the Greek mainland, Babylon, and Egypt, where a strong Jewish presence during the Persian period grew even stronger, particularly in Alexandria. Jews served the Ptolemies as soldiers, generals, bureaucrats, and tax collectors. They also prospered in private enterprise. Hostility to Jews by some Greeks and Egyptians spawned the first anti-Semitic literature. Sporadic violence at times broke into riots and persecution. Yet, there was also considerable admiration among Greek intellectuals for what they saw as Jewish virtue and antiquity.

Greek was the common tongue of Diaspora Jews. Between around 300 and 100 b.c. in Alexandria, the Hebrew Bible was translated into Greek. Known as the Septuagint, or Seventy, from the number of translators who, legend has it, labored on the project, this text made the Bible accessible to a Jewish community increasingly unable to understand Hebrew or Aramaic. In later centuries, the Septuagint became the Old Testament of Greek-speaking Christians.

Foreign conversions and immigration into the Diaspora began to change the meaning of the word *Jew*. The word came to mean less "inhabitant of Judea" than "practitioner of Judaism."

SECTION SUMMARY

- Philosophy changed its emphasis from politics to ethics and won a wide following in the Greek-speaking elite.

- Stoicism, austere and public-spirited, and Epicureanism, which called for withdrawal into private life, were the most popular Hellenistic philosophies.

- The traditional Olympian religion of Greece declined, while so-called mystery religions, which offered secret teachings, grew popular.

- While some Jews adopted the Greek customs of their Seleucid rulers, traditionalists revolted and reestablished an independent Jewish state in Palestine.

- Most Jews in the Hellenistic era lived outside Palestine, in the Diaspora, where they had frequent contacts with other peoples.

CHAPTER SUMMARY

As king, Philip built a state and an army that allowed Macedon to conquer the Greek city-states and prepared to invade the Persian Empire. Upon Philip's assassination, his son Alexander replaced him and led an army of invasion. Although outnumbered and out-spent by Persia, the Macedonians won because of their army. As Alexander's empire stretched into India, he became despotic and he planned a fusion of Greeks and Persians. His conquests laid the foundation of the Hellenistic age.

After fifty years of war following Alexander's death, several new states emerged: The most important were Macedonia under the Antigonid dynasty, Egypt under the Ptolemies, and western Asia under the Seleucids. Hellenistic Greek kingdoms were founded in lands as far away as Afghanistan, Pakistan, and India, and they lasted for centuries. Greek and Macedonian colonists to the Ptolemaic and Seleucid kingdoms dominated the army and administration, but there was some room for natives. But few natives adopted Greek ways, and native culture thrived in these multiethnic empires. New cities, such as Alexandria, Antioch, and Pergamum, were flourishing centers of commerce and culture.

Under royal patronage, the Museum (a research institute) and Library were founded in Alexandria and became a focus of Hellenistic literature and science. Hellenistic writers turned away from civic life and heroic themes toward private life and ordinary events. Hellenistic science flourished and there were great achievements in mathematics, astronomy, and medicine. Hellenistic women made small gains in status and power, compared to earlier Greek women.

New beliefs emerged as faith in the Olympian gods declined. Ethics replaced politics as the focus of philosophy. The two most popular new philosophical schools were Stoicism and Epicureanism, the first austere and public-spirited, the second emphasizing withdrawal into private life. So-called mystery religions, which offered secret teachings, drew a wide public. Greeks and Jews came into increasing contact, both in the Diaspora and in Palestine, where Ptolemaic and Seleucid kings ruled in turn. Jews were divided into various schools of thought, with Hellenizers and traditionalists representing the two poles of opinion.

FOCUS QUESTIONS

- How did Macedon under Philip and Alexander conquer both the Greek city-states and the Persian Empire?

- What new states emerged as a result of Alexander's conquests and how did they integrate Greek settlers with native peoples?

- How did Greek civilization spread during the Hellenistic era, and what were the main trends in literature, science, and art?

- What new philosophies and religions emerged in the Hellenistic period?

KEY TERMS

Macedon (p. 84)
Philip II (p. 84)
Alexander the Great (p. 85)
Hellenism (p. 89)
Ptolemies (p. 90)

Seleucids (p. 90)
Antigonids (p. 91)
Alexandria (p. 93)
Antioch (p. 94)
Bactria (p. 95)
Museum (p. 96)

Archimedes (p. 98)
Stoics (p. 103)
Epicureans (p. 104)
mystery religions (p. 104)
Maccabees (p. 106)

 This icon will direct you to additional materials on the website: www .cengage.com/history/ noble/westciv6e

NOTES

1. Isocrates, "Panegyricus," trans. H. I. Marrou, in *A History of Education in Antiquity*, trans. George Lamb (New York: Mentor Books/New American Library, 1956), p. 130.

2. Romila Thapar, *As'oka and the Decline of the Mauryas* (Oxford: Oxford University Press, 1961), p. 256.

3. Quoted in Charles Rowan Beye, *Ancient Greek Literature and Society*, 2d ed. (Ithaca, N.Y.: Cornell University Press, 1987), p. 265.

See our interactive eBook for map and primary source activities.

5

CHAPTER OUTLINE

Before the Republic, 753–509 B.C.

The Early and Middle Republic at Home, ca. 509–133 B.C.

The Early and Middle Republic Abroad, ca. 509–133 B.C.

The Late Republic and Its Collapse, 133–31 B.C.

The Forum, Rome
(Alinari/Art Resource, NY)

Rome, From Republic to Empire

ere is the Roman Forum. We are standing in the heart of the ancient city, near the arch of the emperor Septimius Severus, looking south toward two columns that once held statues of great citizens. Beyond them are the Sacred Way, Rome's oldest street, and the three elegant columns of the Temple of Castor and Pollux. In the background, beyond a market and vaulted warehouse, is the Palatine Hill. The photograph takes us from an arch celebrating military triumph to ruins evoking citizenship and piety, to a reminder of the everyday needs of the masses of Rome, and finally, to a historic hill. On this hill, shepherds founded the city of Rome, and on this hill, centuries later, emperors lived. We see, in short, the civic center of the city destined to give the Western world many of its fundamental ideas about government and empire. It may well be the single most important public space in the history of the world.

The ancient Romans were a practical people. Virgil (70–19 B.C.), for example, the greatest Roman poet (see page 143), celebrates not his countrymen's artistry or cultivation, but rather their pragmatic accomplishments:

> For other peoples will, I do not doubt,
> still cast their bronze to breathe with softer features,
> or draw out of the marble living lines,
> plead causes better, trace the ways of heaven
> with wands and tell the rising constellations;
> but yours will be the rulership of nations,
> remember, Romans, these will be your arts:
> to teach the ways of peace to those you conquer,
> to spare defeated peoples, tame the proud.[1]

The Romans turned an Italian city-state into one of the largest empires in history, including all the countries of the Mediterranean, as well as large parts of western Asia and of northern and central Europe. By holding this empire for centuries and by promoting prosperity in every corner, Rome planted in what would become Britain, France, Germany, and Spain (among other places) the seeds of the advanced civilizations of the Mediterranean.

Rome is no less important for its influence on the Western civic tradition. Much of the modern vocabulary of politics, from *president* to *inauguration* to *forum*, can be traced back to Rome. After an early period of monarchy, Rome was for centuries a republic (Latin, *res publica*, literally "public thing"), before becoming essentially a monarchy again under the Caesars. The Roman Republic mixed popular power with government controlled by wealthy landowners. The government was divided into three branches, which created a system of

FOCUS QUESTIONS

- What was early Rome like and how was it shaped by relations with its neighbors?

- How was the Roman Republic governed, and how did that government shape the Western political tradition?

- How did Rome conquer an empire?

- How did the unintended consequences of conquest on Rome lead to a revolution that destroyed the Republic?

This icon will direct you to additional materials on the website: www .cengage.com/history/ noble/westciv6e

See our interactive eBook for map and primary source activities.

checks and balances that tended toward consensus. The result was efficiency and, for centuries, stability.

Roman politicians sought to control ordinary citizens, but in some ways were more flexible than Greek democrats. Unlike Greece, Rome extended its citizenship to a large population, first throughout Italy and then across its entire empire. The modern nation-state with its mass citizenship owes much to Rome. Indeed, although Rome was not democratic, modern democracy—that is, popular government with a large population, whose officials are elected by the people—has roots in the Roman Republic as well as in the Greek city-state.

Fueled by fear, ambition, and greed, Roman expansion generated its own momentum. Rome's arrogance matched its success: In consolidating power over huge territories, the Romans committed atrocities, enslaved whole peoples, and destroyed cities with little provocation. Ironically, military success slowly undermined both Rome's political stability at home and the socioeconomic basis of its army. Meanwhile, the Romans showed great open-mindedness in borrowing from other societies, in particular, from the Greeks, to whom the Republic owed great cultural debts. Also fascinating is the shrewdness and generosity with which the Romans shared their citizenship with the elites whom they had conquered, thereby winning their loyalty and strengthening Rome's grip on their territories.

Historians conventionally divide the Republic into three periods: Early (509–287 B.C.), Middle (287–133 B.C.), and Late (133–31 B.C.). This chapter begins with the origins of the city of Rome in the early first millennium B.C. and then traces the Republic from its foundation to its imperial conquests to its collapse under their weight. Success spoiled Rome. The unintended consequences of conquest on Rome's society, politics, and culture led to a revolution that, in the century beginning in 133 B.C., saw the Republic's downfall.

BEFORE THE REPUBLIC, 753–509 B.C.

What was early Rome like and how was it shaped by relations with its neighbors?

Romulus Legendary founder of Rome in 753 B.C., whose name supplies a convenient etymology for the city, he may have really existed, as archaeology suggests.

The ancient Romans believed that their city was founded on April 21, 753 B.C., by **Romulus**, a descendant of refugees from the Trojan War. Although the name "Romulus" supplies a convenient origin for "Rome," we cannot take the story at face value. Nevertheless, archaeology shows that by the eighth century B.C. Rome was already on its way to being a city and it had a king. Archaeologists have recently discovered a palace in the Forum from this era. They have also found traces of sanctuaries and a defensive wall. Nearby stands the Palatine Hill, one of the seven hills on which Rome would cluster and the place where tradition puts the settlement of 753 (see inset, **MAP 5.2**, on page 122). Archaeologists have recently found fortification walls on the Palatine from ca. 750 B.C., which lends support to tradition. They have also found an underground chamber there that some would identify with the cave where, according to legend, Romulus was nursed by a she-wolf. In any case, the first settlers on the hills of Rome came even earlier, around 1000 B.C., as pottery and graves show.

Archaeological evidence raises some basic questions: What were Rome's origins, and how did it grow? Are seeds of Roman greatness visible in its early history? By examining the data of archaeology and of those elements in ancient historiography that seem to be based on accurate tradition, we can answer these questions, at least in outline.

The First Romans and Their Neighbors

Italy is a long peninsula, shaped roughly like a boot, extending about 750 miles from the Alps into the Mediterranean (see **MAP 5.1**). In the far north, the high Alps provide a barrier to the rest of

Europe. To the east, the Adriatic Sea separates Italy from modern Slovenia and Croatia; to the west, the Tyrrhenian Sea faces the large islands of Sardinia and Corsica (and the smaller but iron-rich island of Elba) and, beyond, the coasts of France and Spain. Off the "toe" of the Italian boot, and separated from the mainland by a narrow, 3-mile strait of water, is the large island of Sicily, rich farm country in ancient times. Sicily is only 90 miles from North Africa. In short, Italy is centrally located in the Mediterranean. It was both a target for conquerors and a springboard for conquest.

Italy contained some of the ancient Mediterranean's most fertile and metal-rich land. From the watershed of the Po and Adige Rivers in the north, the agriculturally rich plains of Etruria (modern Tuscany), Latium (the region of Rome), and Campania (the region of Naples) unfold southward down Italy's west coast. Although the Apennine (AP-puh-nine) mountains run north-south along most of the Italian peninsula, they are low compared with the Alps and contain many passes, permitting the movement of armies.

A sensational recent archaeological discovery opens a window into second millennium B.C. Italy. Poggiomarino is a prehistoric village consisting of houses that were built on oak pilings and separated by canals. The village, located on a river near Naples, was inhabited from around the 1500s B.C. to around 700 B.C. A masterpiece of prehistoric engineering, the village covered at least 7 acres and was a center of bronze production.

In the first millennium B.C., Italy was a hodgepodge of peoples and languages. They included the Etruscans in the north, Greek colonists in southern Italy and in Sicily, and such mountain peoples as the Sabines and the Samnites. The Samnites spoke Oscan, an Indo-European language, as did the Campanians, who lived around Naples, and the Lucanians, who lived in south-central Italy. Both the Samnites and the Lucanians were warlike peoples who conquered their neighbors before finally being conquered by Rome. (See the feature, "The Visual Record: From Poseidonia to Paestum.")

Latium (LAY-shum) was home to a number of small Latin-speaking towns, one of them Rome. In the fifth century B.C., another important people arrived on the Italian scene: Celts (called Gauls by the Romans), large numbers of whom crossed the Alps and settled in northern Italy after roughly 500 B.C. Most of these various peoples spoke Indo-European languages, of which **Latin**, the language of the Romans (as well as other peoples of Latium), was one.

Rome's location in Italy was central and protected. Located 15 miles inland on the Tiber (TY-ber), the largest river on Italy's west coast, Rome had access to the sea. A midstream island makes Rome the first crossing place upstream from the Tiber's mouth, which offered the Romans freedom of movement north and south. Yet strategically, Rome was protected. It was far enough from the sea to be safe from raiders and pirates. And its seven hills offered a natural defense—from nature as well as humans, because the Tiber often flooded its banks.

In the eighth century B.C., Archaic Rome (as the pre-Republican period is called) began to change from a large village into a city. By the sixth century B.C., Rome had streets, walls, drains, temples, and a racetrack. What caused the transformation? Perhaps the key factor was contact with Magna Graecia (MAG-nuh GREE-shuh), the Greek colonies to the south (see **MAP 5.1**). Established in the eighth and seventh centuries B.C., the colonies transported westward the sophisticated urban civilization of the eastern Mediterranean (see pages 55–56).

CHRONOLOGY

753–509 B.C.	Monarchy (traditional dates)
509–287 B.C.	Early Republic
449 B.C.	Law of the Twelve Tables
338 B.C.	Latin League dissolved; Roman citizenship extended
289 B.C.	First Roman coinage (traditional date)
287–133 B.C.	Middle Republic
264–146 B.C.	Punic Wars
240 B.C.	First play produced at Rome
197 B.C.	Rome defeats Macedonian phalanx
146 B.C.	Rome destroys Carthage and Corinth
133–31 B.C.	Late Republic
133–121 B.C.	The Gracchi
107–78 B.C.	Marius and Sulla
73–71 B.C.	Spartacus's revolt
66–62 B.C.	Pompey's eastern campaigns
63 B.C.	Consulship of Cicero
58–51 B.C.	Caesar conquers Gaul
44 B.C.	Caesar assassinated
31 B.C.	Antony defeated at Actium; Octavian in power

Latin Indo-European language of ancient Rome and its empire, from which today's Romance languages developed.

🌐 **MAP 5.1—Early Italy and Region of City of Rome**
Early Italy comprised a variety of terrain and peoples. Rome is located in the central Italian region of Latium. The Alps separate Italy from northern Europe. The Apennine mountain range runs almost the entire length of the Italian peninsula. Much of the rest of Italy is fertile plain.

Etruscans Inhabitants of twelve loosely confederated city-states north of Rome; they were conquered by the Romans by the early third century B.C.

Less well understood is the impact on early Rome of its neighbors to the north, the **Etruscans** (ee-TRUS-kunz). The twelve Etruscan city-states were organized in a loose confederation centered in Etruria (ee-TROO-ree-uh). They grew rich from the mining of iron, copper, and silver, from piracy, from trade, and from a network of influential Etruscan emigrants throughout central Italy, probably including Rome's last three kings (traditionally dated 616–509 B.C.).

The Etruscans were brilliant, wealthy, and warlike. We know less about them than we would like, from their language, which is only partly understood, to their origins, which probably lay in Italy but possibly in Anatolia. Etruscan power extended to many places in central, northern, and even southern Italy. Many scholars argue that the Etruscans conquered pre-Republican Rome, but the evidence does not support that theory. Rather, an Etruscan nobleman, Lucius

Etruscan Tomb Painting This wall painting from Tarquinia shows a married aristocratic couple at a banquet. The style of the figures is derived from Greek art, but the depiction of husband and wife dining on the same couch is characteristically Etruscan. (National Museum, Tarquinia/Scala/Art Resource, NY)

Tarquinius Priscus, migrated to Rome and was eventually elected king. Under him and his son (or perhaps grandson), Lucius Tarquinius Superbus, who was Rome's last king, Etruscan culture left an impact on Rome. For example, the Tarquins sponsored several building projects in Rome, including the great Temple of Jupiter on the Capitoline Hill in the center of Rome. But scholars disagree as to whether the Etruscan impact on Roman culture was superficial or deep.

At least we can be sure that the Etruscans were great artists and architects and very religious. They believed that it was possible to learn the will of the gods by interpreting the sight and sound of lightning and thunder and by carefully examining the internal organs, especially the liver, of sacrificial animals. Etruscan elite women had high status compared with their Greek or Roman counterparts. Etruscan women kept their own names, and Etruscan children bore the names of both parents. In addition, Etruscan elite women were permitted to attend athletic contests in spite of the presence of naked male athletes.

The Roman Monarchy

Tradition says that Rome was ruled by seven kings before the foundation of the Republic. Although the number of kings may be a later invention, their existence is undoubted. In addition to traces of the monarchy in Republican institutions, there is archaeological proof: A form of the Latin word *rex* ("king"), for example, has been found inscribed on a Roman monument from the early sixth century B.C. The king's power, called *imperium* (from *imperare*, "to command"), was very great, embracing religious, military, and judicial affairs.

The king was advised by a council of elders, called the "fathers" (*patres* in Latin) or the "senate" (*senatus*, from *senex*, "old man"). In theory, the senate was primarily an advisory body, but in practice, it was very powerful. Senators were the heads of the most important families in Rome, so the king rejected their advice at his peril. Romans spoke of the senate's *auctoritas* (from which our word "authority" comes), a quasi-religious prestige.

From Poseidonia to Paestum

Between them, the elegant Greek painting and the rough Roman bronze statue shown here sum up the history of the ancient city of Paestum. Paestum is located in southern Italy, about 200 miles south of Rome. It was a port and commercial center in a rich farming region on the Gulf of Salerno. Founded as the Greek colony of Poseidonia around 600 B.C., Paestum ended up as a thriving Roman city after being conquered by the Romans in 273 B.C. In between (410–273 B.C.), Paestum was overrun and ruled by the Oscan-speaking Lucanian warriors of southern Italy. Somehow, no matter who ruled it or what it was called, Paestum managed to flourish. Its remains present a picture of the wealth, high civilization, and ethnic diversity of first millennium B.C. Italy.

Look first at the painting from Greek-era Poseidonia of the man reclining on a couch. He wears a wreath and is holding a lyre in his right hand. He is one of ten men, in a series of paintings, shown participating in a *sumposion*, or "wine party," a typical gathering of aristocratic Greek culture. (Ironically, we get our word *symposium*, or "academic meeting," from this ancient, alcoholic merrymaking.) His manicured beard and trim physique identify him as a member of the leisure class.

A superb example of ancient painting, it was discovered on the outskirts of Paestum in 1968 and dates to 480/470 B.C. It is part of one of five tomb paintings from the Tomb of the Diver, named after the painting, on the lid of the tomb, of a young man in the act of diving, perhaps a symbol of the journey into the underworld.

The artistic style, the clothing, and the sumposion are all Greek. Yet the practice of painting a tomb and the use of diving as a symbol of death are Etruscan in origin. Thus, the paintings demonstrate the cultural mix of Greek Italy.

This sums up the experience of Poseidonia well, because the city grew rich as a commercial center between the Etruscans and the Greeks farther south. Poseidonia's Greekness is underlined by its excellent Doric temples; the ruins of these are among the best such ruins in the world today. Also of note is the Greek-style rectangular

A Guest Holding a Lyre (painting from Tomb of the Diver, Paestum) (Scala/Art Resource, NY)

Most senators were patricians (puh-TRIH-shunz), as early Rome's hereditary aristocracy was known. The rest of the people, the bulk of Roman society, were called plebeians (pleh-BEE-unz). Plebeians were free; most were ordinary people, though some were wealthy. Patricians monopolized the senate and priesthoods, and they did not intermarry with plebeians. The Romans called these two social classes **orders**. Both in the monarchy and, later, in the Republic, most wealthy Romans were landowners.

orders An order is a social class whose members share a common rank.

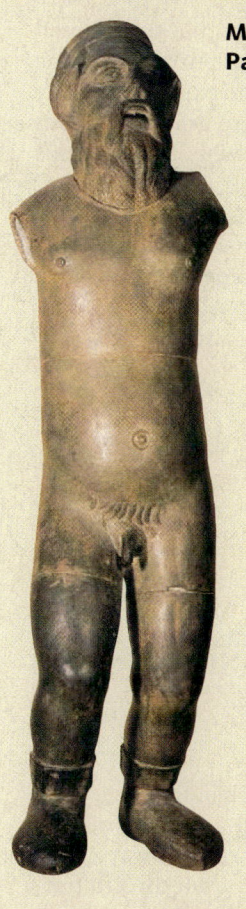

Marsyas (bronze statue, Paestum) (Scala/Art Resource, NY)

the local elite. Many non-elite inhabitants of Paestum no doubt lost land to the settlers.

Meanwhile, both the landscape and the politics of the city were transformed. The agora of Poseidonia became the forum of Paestum, on whose sides were built Roman-style buildings, including a council hall and a temple of Jupiter (like the temple on Rome's Capitoline Hill). Eventually, Paestum would acquire an amphitheater and Roman baths.

Paestum also acquired a copy of a famous Roman work of art, the bronze statue of Marsyas, which is reproduced here. This statue dates to the mid-third century B.C. It was cast in imitation of a well-known statue of Marsyas in Rome and erected at the center of Paestum on the west side of the forum.

For the Romans, Marsyas symbolized liberty. He was a character from Greek mythology and had been adopted by the prominent plebeian family of Marcius Rutilus to symbolize the victory of the plebeians in their struggle with the patricians.

The statue's right hand would have been raised in a gesture of authority. His calves are ringed by metal bands, like the legs of a slave, except that the chains of slavery have been broken off. For the citizens of Paestum, the statue celebrated their identification with Rome, their liberation from Lucanian rule, their privileged status as Latin colonists, and perhaps their freedom from economic need as landholders in a fertile territory.

The statue of Marsyas is considered today to be one of the most important works of the new culture of an Italy dominated by Rome. But it is many other things as well: It symbolizes the combined plebeian-patrician elite of Rome and its success in extending Roman power throughout the peninsula. It demonstrates the continued importance of Greek culture, since Marsyas was a Greek character, but it also shows the flexibility with which the Roman elite adapted Greek symbols for its own purposes. And it reminds us of the willingness of the Romans to trample on local customs and impose Roman culture throughout Italy.

QUESTIONS

1. How does the history of Paestum illustrate the ethnic diversity of first millennium B.C. Italy?

2. What light on the life of a Greek colony is shed by the Tomb of the Diver?

3. What does the statue of Marsyas symbolize about Roman rule in Italy?

public space, with its central agora, three broad avenues, and thirty-two cross streets, as well as the strong walls.

Under the Lucanian conquerors, Poseidonia continued the traditions of tomb painting and cultural interchange. Many Lucanian tomb paintings from the town survive, and they illustrate a lively mix of Greek and Italic styles.

After Poseidonia was conquered by Rome in 273 B.C., it became known as Paestum and acquired the status of a Latin colony. As soldiers and sailors, the citizens of Paestum defended Roman interests in southern Italy. In return, and because they were Latin colonists, they enjoyed the privileges of free trade with Rome and intermarriage with Romans, as well as the more theoretical possibility of becoming Roman citizens by moving to Rome (but only after leaving a son in the colony). The citizens consisted of around five thousand Roman and Latin settlers, as well as

The whole people, probably both patricians and plebeians, met in an assembly organized in thirty local units, or *curiae*, hence, the name *curiate assembly*. Although the assembly's numbers were large, its powers were limited. Before becoming law, resolutions of the assembly required approval by the senate.

Early Rome was a class-based society, but it was open to foreigners. Among others, Etruscans, Sabines, and Latins—as the inhabitants of other Latin-speaking towns are called—came to settle in Rome. Foreigners, at first, had low status, but they gained equality around 550 B.C., for pragmatic purposes. Rome needed soldiers to fight its wars; in order to expand the body of loyal infantrymen, the immigrants were granted citizenship—a reform traditionally associated with King Servius Tullius (578–535 B.C.).

Servius probably introduced to Rome the hoplite phalanx (see page 56), with immigrants included in its ranks. The changes in the army contributed to the process that, within several generations of Servius's reform, took Rome from monarchy to republic.

THE EARLY AND MIDDLE REPUBLIC AT HOME, CA. 509–133 B.C.

How was the Roman Republic governed, and how did that government shape the Western political tradition?

Tradition says that the Roman Republic was established in 509 B.C., when the kings were overthrown. Nowadays, scholars envision a long process rather than a single, dramatic upheaval. In either case, the Republic differed from the monarchy in two basic ways. First, the Republic stood for liberty, which for the Romans meant both freedom from the arbitrary power of a king and freedom to participate in public affairs. Second, the Republic was a commonwealth, in Latin, *res publica* (rays POO-blee-kuh), literally "public thing," as opposed to *res privata*, "private thing," as the Romans characterized monarchy. As a kingdom, Rome belonged to the royal family, but as a republic, it belonged to the Roman people. In theory, the Roman people were sovereign—that is, the people ruled the state.

res publica Latin for "public thing," it was the Romans' concept of their republic, which uniquely influenced Western political institutions.

But which people? This is a key question because the Romans did *not* embrace another principle that might seem to follow from liberty: equality. Rather, they believed in order, balance, and competition, all of which are central themes of Roman Republican history. Roman society and culture, moreover, were conservative. Once the young Republic had its new values in place, it tried to maintain those values over the centuries, with little change.

We know relatively little about the Early Republic (509–287 B.C.) but enough to know that it witnessed centuries of social and political conflict. The Middle Republic (287–133 B.C.) was a shorter and better documented period of relative consensus at home and massive expansion abroad. Social and political conflict broke out again with a vengeance in the Late Republic (133–31 B.C.), ultimately rendering the Republic a deathblow.

Political Institutions

The best and most even-handed ancient analyst of Roman politics is the historian Polybius (po-LIH-bee-us) (ca. 200–118 B.C.). A Greek and former hostage who lived in Rome, Polybius observed his adopted city with an outsider's careful eye. Polybius argued that in the Middle Republic of his day, Rome was a "mixed constitution," balancing the power of the masses with the authority of the elite. The result was a strong and stable state.

senate In the ancient Roman Republic and Empire, the influential and powerful council of elders.

Polybius divides Roman political institutions into three branches: executive, deliberative, and legislative. The American founders adopted a similar division, but they combined the legislative and deliberative functions and added a judicial branch. In Rome the executive branch also administered justice. Rome's executive branch was made up of magistrates—that is, public officials; the deliberative branch consisted of the Roman senate; and the legislative branch was composed of four different assemblies of the people.

Executive power lay in the hands of Rome's powerful magistrates. They were elected and not chosen by lottery, as in Greek democracy. Election required campaigning, which in turn took money and connections. Magistracies were time-consuming jobs but offered no salary, unlike in Greek democracy. Thus, only a wealthy few could afford to hold public office in Rome.

Eager for strong magistrates, but afraid that power corrupts, Romans imposed the principles of *collegiality* and *annuality* on their officials. Every magistrate had one or more colleagues and held office for only one year. The chief magistrates were eventually called consuls, of which there were two. Each consul had the power to veto the other's actions. Like the former king, each consul had *imperium*, the power to issue commands and order punishments, including execution.

From about 500 B.C. to about 300 B.C., other public offices were created to help the consuls as administration grew more complex. In addition, the Romans elected two censors, older men chosen once every few years for eighteen month terms. At first, their job was to supervise the census, the military register of citizens that recorded each man's property class. Later, the censors became, as it were, supervisors of public morals, since they could punish "bad" citizens.

The Republic's government adapted flexibly to trying circumstances. In times of emergency, for example, the Republic turned power over to a single magistrate. The dictator, as he was called, made binding decisions, but he held office for only six months.

The Roman **senate** guided and advised the magistrates. During most of the Republic, the senate consisted of three hundred men, all former magistrates and each of whom served for life. Senators possessed great authority. They supervised public expenditures and were, for all practical purposes, in charge of foreign policy.

Only the assemblies of the people could make laws. There were four assemblies: the curiate assembly, the centuriate assembly, the council of the plebs, and the tribal assembly. Roman assemblies combined democratic and nondemocratic features. On the one hand, all decisions were made by majority vote, and only after speeches or campaigning. Assembly meetings were often preceded by public meetings, typically in the Forum, which featured lively debate. Women, free noncitizens, and even slaves could attend. On the other hand, voting took place by groups, and those groups were unrepresentative. Furthermore, in contrast to Greece, assembly participants stood rather than sat down and received no salary for attendance.

Although the curiate assembly of the monarchy survived, in the Republic, it had a largely ceremonial role. The centuriate assembly held real power: It elected magistrates, voted on laws and treaties, accepted declarations of war and peace, and acted as a court in cases of treason, homicide, and appeals of the magistrates' decisions. But this assembly was dominated by wealthy men, especially the equestrians, or cavalrymen. The poorest men, known as *proletarii* ("breeders"), often did not have even the chance to vote.

The two other assemblies were the council of the plebs and the tribal assembly. The tribal assembly eventually replaced the plebs and, in fact, became Rome's main legislative body in the third century B.C., outstripping the centuriate assembly in making laws. To understand the evolution and workings of the tribal assembly, we turn now to the class conflicts in Rome during the fifth through third centuries B.C.

A Clear Sign of Power   The lictor, or official, depicted in this bronze statuette (ca. first century A.D.) accompanied Roman magistrates, who had *imperium*, the power to issue punishments resulting in execution. That power is visible in the fasces—an ax in a bundle of wooden rods bound with straps—that he holds.   (Courtesy of the Trustees of the British Museum)

Conflict of the Orders, 494–287 B.C.

Social and political conflict between the patricians and plebeians severely tested the Roman state in the fifth century. There were only 136 patrician families in 509 B.C., but they dominated the Early Republic. The plebs, in contrast, comprised masses of peasants and a tiny number of men who, though prosperous, were not patricians. Plebeian artisans, traders, and shopkeepers made up only a small part of the population. The various plebeian groups each wanted to break patrician power. Wealthy plebeians wanted access to high office, from which they had been largely excluded. Ordinary plebeians demanded relief from debt, redistribution of land, and codification and publication of the law. For a century and a half, the two groups of plebeians worked together, writing an important chapter in the history of political resistance.

Debt and hunger loomed large as concerns of ordinary plebeians. If a free man could not repay a loan, he had to work off what he owed, often for the rest of his life. Plebeians wanted this harsh system abolished. The average farm was too small to feed a family, so most peasants depended on public land for farming and grazing. Time and again throughout Republican history, however, public land was taken by the wealthy, who denied access to the poor. The only plebeian hope was to change the system.

The plebeians organized themselves as a kind of state within the state, complete with their own assembly (the council of the plebs) and officials (the tribunes of the plebs). The decisions of the council of the plebs, called *plebiscita* (from which *plebiscite* comes), were binding only on the plebs; they did not receive the full force of law for over two hundred years. Yet, the plebs did not retreat. On several occasions during the Early Republic, they resorted to secession: The plebs, as a whole, left the city, often for the Aventine Hill, where they stayed until their grievances were addressed (see inset, **MAP 5.2**).

The ten tribunes (TRIB-yoonz), elected annually by the plebs, were the people's champions. A tribune's house stood open to any plebeian who needed him, and he could not leave the city limits. Inside the city of Rome, a tribune also had the right to veto any act of the magistrates, assembly, or senate that harmed plebeians. In return, the plebs swore to treat the tribunes as sacrosanct and to lynch anyone who harmed them.

But the patricians struck back. They controlled important priesthoods and had many supporters in the military. Furthermore, the new tribal assembly, created around the same time as the council of the plebs, used a system of representation that heavily favored landowners, such as patricians. The tribal assembly elected lower magistrates and, like the centuriate assembly, voted on laws and acted as a court of appeals.

Still, the plebeians pressed onward and forced concessions from the patricians, until finally the patricians retreated. They decided to neutralize the poor by meeting the main demands of the plebeian elite. The outcome was a new nobility that combined patricians and well-to-do plebeians. The patricians had decided to compromise to keep most of their privileges. The personnel changed, but the elite maintained power in Rome.

A key moment came in 449 B.C., with publication of the law code known as the "Twelve Tables," eventually, if not at first, on twelve bronze tablets in the Forum. By modern standards, the code was tough and primitive, but its very existence was a plebeian victory because published law was accessible and dependable. Unfortunately, the complex legal procedure remained a secret of the priests for another 150 years, which meant that no poor man could go to court without the help of a rich patron.

Continued plebeian pressure slowly yielded other gains through the fourth century B.C. Around 445 B.C., the patricians accepted patrician-plebeian intermarriage, but it took nearly another eighty years, until 367 B.C., until they agreed to plebeian consuls. That same year saw a debt-relief law, and further debt relief came in 326 B.C.

Finally, in 287 B.C., the patrician and plebeian **orders** were formally merged, and a law called the "lex Hortensia" made decisions of the council of the plebs and the tribal assembly binding on the whole community, including patricians. Rome's new, combined patrician-plebeian elite was based on wealth, not heredity. Most Romans were non-elite, but at least they had won something: debt relief, access to the published laws, increased power for their assembly, and, most important, protection from arbitrary power.

Families and Patronage

The family was the basic unit of Roman society and a model of political authority, both foreign and domestic. Elite Roman families stuck together and wielded great power.

The Latin word *familia* is broader in meaning than the English word *family*. Better translated as "household," it connotes slaves, animals, and property, as well as the members of a nuclear family and their ancestors or descendants. In theory, though not always in practice, the Roman household was an authoritarian institution governed by a male; thus, the familia is an example of patriarchy.

The legal head of the familia was the ***paterfamilias*** (pah-ter-fah-MIL-ee-us)—the oldest living male, usually the father. Roman respect for the paterfamilias stemmed from Roman esteem for ancestors, who were more important than in Greek culture. All patricians and some plebeians belonged to a *gens* (plural, *gentes*), a kinship group that traced its ancestry back to a purported common ancestor. All Roman males had a personal and a family name, and patricians and elite plebeians also had a third (middle) name, indicating their gens—for example, Gaius Julius Caesar, whose personal name "Gaius" was followed by the gens name "Julius" and the familia name "Caesar."

According to Roman law, the paterfamilias had supreme power within the household. He had the right to sell family members into slavery. A son, no matter how old, was always legally subject to the authority of a living paterfamilias. However, practice was more complex than theory. Roman fathers rarely used their power to kill an errant wife or child. The sources are full of fathers who showed affection, love, and even indulgence toward their children. Moreover, Roman women usually married in their late teens and men in their late twenties. Given the low life expectancies, it was common for a man of 25 to have already buried his father. Many, perhaps even most, adult males were independent of a paterfamilias.

Unlike men, Roman women never became legally independent, even on the death of a paterfamilias. Instead of receiving a personal name, a daughter was called by the name of her father's gens. For example, Gaius Julius Caesar's daughter was called Julia; if Caesar had had a second daughter, she would have been Julia Secunda ("Julia the Second"). Although fathers were expected to support all male children, they had to support only the first of their daughters. In other words, they were free to "expose" additional daughters—that is, leave them in the open to die or, as was perhaps more likely, to be adopted or raised as a slave. A father also arranged a daughter's marriage and provided her with a dowry. In theory, again, the customs suggest a most severe relationship, but the evidence shows considerable father-daughter affection, including married daughters who sought advice or aid from their fathers.

Most women in early Rome married *cum manu* (kum MAN-oo) (literally, "with hand"); that is, they were "handed over" to their husbands, who became their new paterfamilias. Even so, Roman wives and mothers had more prestige and freedom than their counterparts in Classical Greece. Legends of early Rome mention some elite women of influence who were peacemakers, negotiators, or catalysts of quarrels among men. Roman women regularly shared meals and social activities with their parents and were expected to take an interest in their husbands' political lives.

Roman society was modeled on the hierarchy of the Roman family. At the center of things stood patrons and clients. *Patron* (derived from *pater*, "father") means "defender" or "protector." *Client* means "dependent." Roman society consisted of pyramidal and hereditary patron-client networks. Most patrons were in turn clients of someone more powerful; only a few men stood at the top of the pyramid. Various paths led to the status of client. A peasant in need of help on his farm might ask a wealthy neighbor to become his patron. A freed slave became the client of his former owner. A conquered foe became the client of the victorious general.

Patron and client helped each other in various ways. A patron might provide a client with food, with property for a dowry, or with legal assistance.

paterfamilias Oldest living male in an ancient Roman family, who had supreme legal power within the household.

Shrine of a Wealthy Household This painting from Pompeii shows the spirit of the paterfamilias in a toga, which is wrapped around his head in keeping with the Roman procedures of sacrifice. He is flanked by the spirits of departed ancestors. A snake symbolizes fertility. (Alinari/Art Resource, NY)

In return, a client owed his patron his vote and his presence in public on important occasions—possession of a large clientele signified prestige and power.

Cloaked in an elaborate language of goodwill, the patron-client relationship was considered a matter of *fides* (FEE-days) ("good faith" or "trustworthiness"). Romans spoke not of a client submitting to a patron's power, but rather of a client "commending himself" to the patron's fides. A patron spoke not of his clients, but of his "friends," especially if they were men of standing or substance.

Patronage played an important role in domestic politics and in foreign affairs. Experience as patrons schooled Roman leaders in treating the peoples they conquered as clients, often as personal clients. Moreover, the Roman state sometimes took foreign countries into its collective "fides"—much as a patron did a client—thus, allowing Rome to extend its influence without the constraints of a formal alliance.

Religion and Worldview

If we knew nothing about early Roman religion, we could deduce much about it from the familia and patronage. We could expect to find an emphasis on powerful fathers and binding agreements, and both are indeed present. The task of a Roman priest, whether an official of the state or an individual paterfamilias, was to establish what the Romans called the "peace of the gods." Roman cults aimed at obtaining the gods' agreement to human requests, at "binding" the gods—the Latin term for which is *religio.*

The earliest Roman religion was animistic—that is, it centered on the spirits that, the Romans believed, haunted the household and the fields and forests and determined the weather. The spirit of the hearth was Vesta; of the door, Janus; of the rain and sun, Jupiter (later identified with the Greek sky-god and the father-god Zeus), and of the crops and vegetation Mars (later identified with the Greek war-god Ares). The Romans believed that these spirits needed to be appeased—hence, the contractual nature of their prayers and offerings. Over the years, as a result of Greek influence, anthropomorphism (that is, the worship of humanlike gods and goddesses) replaced Roman animism.

Roman state religion grew out of house religion. Vesta, the hearth-goddess, became goddess of the civic hearth; Janus, the door-god, became god of the city's gates; Jupiter became the general overseer of the gods; and Mars became the god of war. When trade and conquest brought the Romans into contact with foreign religions, the Romans tended to absorb them. The senate screened and sometimes rejected new gods, but by and large, Roman religion was tolerant and inclusive.

The Republic sponsored numerous priestly committees, or colleges, to secure the peace of the gods. Originally restricted to patricians, most of the highest priesthoods were opened to plebeians by law in 300 B.C. Although some priesthoods were full-time jobs, most left the officeholder free to pursue a parallel career as a magistrate or a senator. The two most important priestly colleges were the augurs (AW-gers), who were in charge of foretelling the future from omens and other signs, and the pontiffs, who exercised a general supervision of Roman religion. The chief pontiff, the *pontifex maximus* (PON-tih-fex MAX-ih-mus), was the head of the state clergy. He was chosen by election. The pontiffs alone controlled the interpretation of the law until the fourth century B.C. The Romans allowed priests to interpret the law on the theory that an offense against humans was also an offense against the gods.

There were also two colleges of priestesses: those of Ceres, goddess of fertility and death, and those of the Vestal Virgins. The six Vestals tended the civic hearth and made sure that its fire never went out. They served, as it were, as wives of the whole community, as guardians of the civil household. The Vestals were the only Roman women not under the authority of a paterfamilias. Chosen between the ages of 6 and 10 by the pontifex maximus, they had to remain virgins while they served or face death, but enjoyed honorable retirement after thirty years.

Roman ideology promoted simple and austere farmers' virtues—discipline, hard work, frugality, temperance, and the avoidance of public displays of affection, even between spouses. Such virtues underlined the difference between the Republic and the kings, with their luxury and sophistication. At the same time, these virtues papered over class distinctions between rich and poor and so promoted stability.

Other Roman ideals included the supreme virtue of the household, *pietas*—devotion and loyalty to the familia, the gods, and the state. Household duties and gender obligations were defined clearly. Women were to be modest, upright, and practical. Men were to project *gravitas* ("weight" or "seriousness"), never lightness or levity. A serious man would display self-control and constancy, the ability to persevere against difficult odds. The masculine ideal was *virtus* (literally, "manliness"), which indicated excellence in war and government.

Roman men who attained virtus considered themselves entitled to the reward of *dignitas*, meaning not only public esteem, but the tangible possession of a dignified position and official rank—in short, public office. The ultimate test of virtus, however, was in battle. Rome's wars supplied ample occasion to display it.

SECTION SUMMARY

- Republican government consisted of three branches: executive, deliberative, and legislative.

- The magistrates, the senate, and the assemblies were Rome's three main political institutions.

- The Conflict of the Orders led to debt relief for the poor and a combined patrician-plebeian nobility for the rich.

- The Roman household, headed by the *paterfamilias*, was a model of political authority.

- Roman society was made up of networks of patrons and clients.

- Romans idealized *pietas*, that is, loyalty to household, the gods, and the Republic.

THE EARLY AND MIDDLE REPUBLIC ABROAD, CA. 509–133 B.C.

How did Rome conquer an empire?

At the beginning of the Republic (ca. 509 B.C.), Roman territory comprised about 500 square miles. By 338 B.C., Rome controlled the 2,000 square miles of Latium and was moving north into Etruria and south into Samnite country. Three-quarters of a century later, in 265 B.C., Rome controlled all of the Italian peninsula south of an imaginary line from Pisae (modern Pisa) to Ariminum (modern Rimini), an area of about 50,000 square miles (see **MAP 5.2**). By 146 B.C., Roman provinces included Sicily, Cisalpine Gaul (northernmost Italy), Sardinia, Corsica, and Spain (divided into two provinces). Once great Carthage was the Roman province of Africa (roughly, modern Tunisia), and once-mighty Macedon was the province of Macedonia, whose governor was also effectively in charge of Greece. The Seleucid kingdom was free but fatally weakened. Rome was the supreme power between Gibraltar and the Levant. It was the greatest empire of the ancient West. How and why had Rome, from its humble beginnings as a local power, reached this breathtaking height?

Republican Expansion: The Conquest of Italy, ca. 509–265 B.C.

Romans maintain that they conquered an empire without ever committing an act of aggression. When war was declared, a special college of priests informed the gods that Rome was merely retaliating for foreign injury. True, the Romans were frequently attacked by others, but often only after provocative behavior by Rome had left its rivals little choice.

Rome's early conquests reveal many of its lasting motives for expansion. No doubt, lust for conquest played a part, as did fear and hatred of outsiders, but self-control and shrewdness were stronger Roman characteristics. Greed, particularly land-hunger, was a perennial theme. Sometimes a domestic political motive was at work, for foreign adventure was a convenient way of deflecting plebeian energies. Perhaps the most significant factors, however, were the personal ambitions of a warrior elite and the presence of conflict in early Italy.

Victory in battle promised both prestige and booty and the political success that might follow. Military achievement brought unique acclaim. For example, certain victorious generals were allowed to celebrate a **triumph**; no such ceremony rewarded the feats of peacemakers or distinguished judges or other public benefactors. The triumphant general rode a chariot through the city to the Temple of Jupiter on the Capitoline Hill. He was accompanied by his troops, by the spoils of victory, including famous captives, and by the magistrates and senators.

WHY ROME FOUGHT

triumph Elaborate procession through the streets of ancient Rome to salute a general's victory over a foreign army.

🌐 Map 5.2—Roman Italy, ca. 265 B.C.
Rome controlled a patchwork of conquered territory, colonies, and allied states in Italy, held together by a network of treaties and of roads. The city of Rome (*inset*) was built on seven hills beside the Tiber River.

In the harsh environment of Italian states, Rome could not have survived without the willingness to fight. Yet, what began as a pragmatic response to present dangers, hardened into a habit of meeting even remote threats with force. In the fourth century B.C., having gained control of Latium, Rome considered the Samnites of central and southern Italy to be a potential threat. In the third century B.C., once Rome controlled Italy, it felt threatened by Carthage. After Carthage, the threat of Macedon was squelched, and after Macedon, Seleucid Syria, and so on.

Though flexible and far-reaching, Roman diplomacy sometimes ended up in war. Rome made formal alliances with some states, granting protection in return for obedience and troops or ships when needed by Rome. Short of a formal commitment, however, Rome might accept a state "into its fides"—that is, treat the state as a client. The result was only a moral, and not a legal, commitment, which sometimes sufficed to frighten any would-be aggressor from harassing Rome's new friend. If not, Rome had to go into battle to prove its trustworthiness as a patron.

Rome organized its military resources well. The Roman military camp was a more regular and systematic place than anything seen since Assyrian days. Beginning in the fourth century B.C., Rome began to give its soldiers regular pay; this and the distribution of conquered land improved morale. Even more significant for Rome's military success was the willingness to utilize foreign military technology.

Borrowed from the Greeks in the sixth century B.C., the hoplite phalanx suited Rome on the relatively level ground of Latium but fared poorly in the rugged Apennines against the Samnites. Following a major defeat in 321 B.C., the Romans adopted with great success the Samnites' equipment and tactics.

Unlike the phalanx, which overpowered the enemy by fighting as one thickly massed unit, a Roman **legion** was flexible and adaptable. Legions were divided into units of thirty maniples ("handfuls"), which were subdivided into sixty centuries (literally "hundreds," although the number of men per century varied); each century was commanded by a centurion. The semi-independence of the maniples, each with its own commander and banner, created a more maneuverable army than that of the phalanx and one better suited for mountain fighting. When it went into battle, it drew up into three lines. If one line failed, there were two more lines to turn to. Unlike hoplites, who engaged the enemy at short range, legionnaires first threw their

HOW ROME FOUGHT

legion Ancient Roman battle formation in which many semi-independent groups broke their enemies' order with javelins at long range, then charged with sword and shield.

The Appian Way Named for the censor Appius Claudius Caecus, who proposed its construction, Rome's first great road was built in 312 B.C. during the Samnite Wars. It originally ran 132 miles from Rome to Capua and was extended an additional 234 miles, probably by 244 B.C., to Brundisium, on Italy's southern Adriatic coast. (F. H. C. Birch/Sonia Halliday Photographs)

javelins at long range. Then, having broken the enemy's order, they charged and fought with sword and shield.

Rome used victory wisely. It treated its allies with a combination of generosity and firmness, beginning with its fellow Latin states. Rome was the leading power in Latium, where it led in an alliance known as the Latin League. Under Roman leadership, the Latin League successfully defended Latium's borders against a series of enemies during the fourth and fifth centuries B.C. But eventually, Rome had to confront a bitter two-year-long Latin revolt (340–338 B.C.).

The year 338 B.C. marked a turning point. Defeated peoples in the ancient world were often executed or enslaved, but not now. The Latin League was dissolved. Some of its member states were annexed, but their inhabitants became Roman citizens, not slaves; others retained independence and alliance with Rome though no longer with one another. The non-Latin allies of the former rebels were also annexed, but they received the unique halfway status of "citizenship without suffrage." They had all the rights of Roman citizenship except the vote; they also maintained local self-government. The settlement of 338 B.C. broke new ground by making it possible for Rome and its former enemies to live together on the basis of relative equality.

The settlement also set a precedent. As Rome conquered Italy, some privileged cities (called *municipia*) received the status of citizenship without suffrage. Others remained independent but were tied to Rome by alliance. Romans often annexed a portion of the land of these states.

If municipia were the carrots of Roman imperialism, the stick was a network of military roads and colonies in Italy, which kept Rome's eye on potential rebels. Roman roads allowed the swift movement of troops and linked a network of colonies in strategic areas. The inhabitants, Roman and Latin, owed military service to Rome.

In later years, Italians would complain about treatment by Rome, but compared with Roman provinces outside Italy, they had a privileged status. Romans too would complain about allied demands for equality, but Rome received, from its allies, a huge pool of military manpower. They staffed the armies that conquered the Samnites, Etruscans, and Gauls, all of whom came into Rome's orbit by the early third century B.C. Manpower abundance won Rome's war (280–276 B.C.) against the Greek general Pyrrhus (PIR-us) of Epirus (319–272 B.C.), who invaded southern Italy. Although Pyrrhus won battle after battle, he was unable to match Roman willingness to sustain casualties. Pyrrhus's seeming victories, therefore, turned out to be defeats, which sent him home to Greece disappointed and left us with the expression "Pyrrhic victory."

As for Rome, by 265 B.C., it emerged as the ruler of all of Italy south of the Pisae-Ariminum line (see **MAP 5.2**). One might say that Rome unified Italy, although Italy was less a unity than a patchwork of Roman territory and colonies and of diverse cities, states, and peoples each allied to Rome by separate treaties.

Punic Wars and Conquest of the Greek East

The conquest of Italy made Rome one of two great powers in the central Mediterranean. The other was Carthage (CAR-thidge). Founded around 750 B.C. by Phoenicians from Tyre, Carthage controlled an empire in North Africa, Sicily, Corsica, Sardinia, Malta, the Balearic Islands, and southern Spain. (The adjective *Phoenician* is *Punicus* in Latin, hence, the term *Punic* [PYOO-nik] for *Carthaginian*.) Like Rome, Carthage was guided by a wealthy elite, but it was mercantile in character rather than agrarian. Rome was a land power, Carthage a sea power. Rome had virtually no navy. Carthage commanded a great war fleet, and its merchant ships dominated the western Mediterranean and played a major role in the east.

Carthage had many strengths. It was an economic powerhouse. The Carthaginians exploited the mineral-rich mines of Spain. They were the first Mediterranean people to organize large-scale plantations of slaves for the production of single crops. Carthage also boasted brilliant generals, especially in the Barca family, whose most famous member was Hannibal (HAN-uh-bull) (247–183 B.C.). Carthage might have seemed the favorite at the outbreak of its long wars with Rome in 264 B.C., yet Carthage was weaker and Rome was stronger than it seemed.

Unlike Rome, Carthage did not have a citizen army. The commanders were Carthaginian, but most of the soldiers were mercenaries and of questionable loyalty. Unlike Rome, which treated its Italian allies well, Carthage showed contempt for its troops, who repaid the favor by revolting often. Carthage fielded large armies, but not as large as Rome's.

At the start of the **Punic Wars**, Rome had no navy or commanders to match the Barca family, but it proved adaptable, tenacious, and ruthless. To win the First Punic War (264–241 B.C.), for

Punic Wars Three wars during which the Roman Empire eventually destroyed Carthage.

Carthaginian Craftsmanship These pendants of male heads are made of colored glass and come from Carthage. The Phoenicians and their colonists excelled in glasswork as a medium for the production of luxury goods. (Erich Lessing/Art Resource, NY)

example, Rome not only built a navy, but outlasted the enemy in a long and bloody conflict. After initially granting a mild peace treaty, Rome took advantage of later Carthaginian weakness to seize Sardinia and Corsica and to demand an additional indemnity.

Forced to give in to Rome's demands, Carthage decided to build a new and bigger empire in Spain, beginning in 237 B.C., under Barca family leadership. With Spain's rich silver and copper mines in its hands, Carthage once again posed a threat so, in the mid-220s B.C., Rome challenged Carthaginian power in Spain. The new Carthaginian commander, 27-year-old Hannibal Barca, was not to be cowed, however, and the Second Punic War broke out (218–201 B.C.).

Carthage was willing to fight because Hannibal promised a quick and decisive victory. Because Carthage no longer had a fleet, the Romans felt secure in Italy; Hannibal surprised them by marching overland to Italy, making a dangerous passage across the Alps. He even took war elephants with him, although most of them died along the way. A tactical genius, Hannibal reckoned that with his superior generalship, he could defeat the Romans in battle and cause them enormous casualties, and he was right. Hannibal's forces dominated the battlefield. Among his victories was the Battle of Cannae in Apulia (southeastern Italy), where, in 216 B.C., Carthage gave Rome the bloodiest defeat in its history, killing perhaps fifty thousand Romans.

But huge casualties alone could not bring Rome to its knees. Nor did many of Rome's allies revolt, as Hannibal had hoped. Most stood by Rome, which had treated them relatively well in the past. After Cannae, Rome's leadership followed a cautious strategy of harassment, delay, refusal to fight, and attrition. Hannibal was stymied by an enemy who lost battles but refused to surrender. In addition, Hannibal did not have the power to take the city of Rome.

A new Roman military star now emerged: Publius Cornelius Scipio (SIP-ee-o) (236–183 B.C.), a Roman who finally understood Hannibal's tactics and matched them. First, Scipio conquered Carthage's Spanish dominions, and then, he forced Hannibal back to North Africa for a final battle in 202 B.C. near Zama (in modern Tunisia). Scipio won the battle and gained the surname Africanus ("the African"). Hannibal ended his days in exile from Carthage, fighting for the Seleucids in their unsuccessful war against Rome.

The peace settlement of 201 B.C. stripped Carthage of its empire. Yet, soon its economy rebounded, reviving old Roman fears of Carthage's political ambitions. In the Third Punic War (149–146 B.C.), Rome mounted a three-year siege under the leadership of Scipio Aemilianus (185–129 B.C.), and destroyed the city of Carthage in 146 B.C. Approximately a century later, Carthage was resurrected as a Roman colony and became one of the empire's greatest cities. In the meantime, it was left desolate, its people killed or enslaved.

Rome emerged from the Punic Wars as the greatest power in the Mediterranean. It had acquired new provinces in Sicily, Sardinia, Corsica, Spain, and North Africa (where Carthage's

🌐 **MAP 5.3—Roman Expansion, 264–44 B.C.**
Wars against Carthage, the major Greco-Macedonian powers, Gauls, Germans, North Africans, and other peoples brought Rome an empire on three continents.

former territory was annexed as the province of Africa). Exhausted as it was, Rome immediately leaped into a long conflict in Greece and Anatolia. The king of Macedon, Philip V (r. 221–179 B.C.), had made an alliance with Hannibal after Cannae, which left Rome with a score to settle. Rome won a relatively quick and easy victory when, in 197 B.C., the legions crushed the Macedonian phalanx at Cynoscephalae in central Greece (see **MAP 5.3**). The age of the phalanx was over; the legion had defeated it decisively.

Rome had hoped to impose a patron-client relationship on Greece and Macedon, thereby avoiding having to sustain a permanent military presence, but the independent-minded Greeks refused to submit to Roman domination. Several years of tension followed, only to lead to renewed wars. First the Seleucids, under the ambitious king Antiochus III (r. 223–187 B.C.), moved into the Greek peninsula and challenged Rome for hegemony. It was in this war that Hannibal took a small, doomed part. Roman forces made short work of the enemy. Driven out not only from Greece, but from Anatolia as well, the Seleucids in effect recognized Roman supremacy in the Mediterranean (188 B.C.).

Then came another two rounds of war that pitted Rome against a resurgent Macedon and various Greek states (171–167 and 150–146 B.C.). Victorious in both wars, Rome deprived the Greeks and Macedonians of their independence. Wherever democracy had survived in Greece, it was replaced with oligarchy. In 146 B.C., Rome destroyed Corinth, one of Greece's wealthiest cities, as a warning against further rebellion. For the next two centuries, Rome would pay little attention to its Greek province except to tax it.

By annexing Carthage, Macedon, and Greece in the mid-second century B.C., Rome created a dynamic for expansion around the entire Mediterranean. Before the century was over, southern Gaul was annexed, and Rome had gained a foothold in Asia. The kingdom of Pergamum (northwestern Anatolia) had supported Rome throughout Rome's wars in the east. When Attalus III of Pergamum died without an heir in 133 B.C., he surrendered his kingdom to the Roman people, who made it into a province of Asia.

Two great Hellenistic states remained independent: the Seleucid kingdom, that is, Syria, and Ptolemaic Egypt. Rome frequently interfered in their affairs, however, and no one was surprised when, in the first century B.C., they too were annexed.

The Socioeconomic Consequences of Expansion

Expansion led to big and unintended changes in Rome's society, economy, and culture. Already wealthy, the Roman elite now came into fabulous riches. Huge profits awaited the generals, patrons, diplomats, magistrates, tax collectors, and businessmen who followed Rome's armies. In Italy, most profits were in the form of land; the provinces offered not only land, but also in slaves, booty, and graft. One of the worst grafters, Gaius Verres, governor of Sicily from 73 to 71 B.C., was prosecuted by Cicero (see page 135) for allegedly extorting tens of thousands of pounds of silver from his province. However, even Cicero skimmed off several thousand pounds of silver as governor of the province of Cilicia (southern Anatolia) from 51 to 50 B.C.

The first Roman coinage, traditionally dated to 289 B.C., facilitated commercial transactions. Previously, the Romans had made do with barter, uncoined bronze, and cast bronze bars, but now they imitated the workmanship and style of Greek coins. Equally prominent in the homes of wealthy Romans were Greek metalwork, jewelry, art objects, and other luxury goods. Conservatives bemoaned the decline of Roman austerity, but they fought a rear-guard action.

Ordinary Romans needed no reminder of the virtues of austerity, for they did not share in the elite's profit from Roman expansion. Indeed, a century of warfare—from the outbreak of the Punic Wars in 264 B.C. to the destruction of Carthage and Corinth in 146 B.C.—pushed the Roman people to the breaking point. Hannibal's invasion ruined much of the farmland of southern Italy and reduced Italian manpower considerably. Yet, most people would have soon rebounded from these problems if they had not faced other serious troubles.

Conscription had become the norm. The average term of military service, between ages 17 and 46, was six years; the maximum term was twenty years. Because experienced legionnaires were at a premium, commanders did not want to release them from service. But the longer a man served, the harder it was for his wife and children to keep the family farm running. A patron might have helped, but most patrons, in fact, added to the problem through the introduction to Italy of large-scale agricultural entrepreneurship.

A revolution in the Italian countryside brought ruin on the free peasantry of Italy. Wealthy Romans wanted to invest in large landed estates, or *latifundia* (lat-uh-FUN-dee-uh), worked by slaves. These estates were either mixed farms (most often devoted to cultivating vines, olives, and grain) or ranches (establishments where animals were raised for meat, milk, and wool). One devotee of the latter was the prominent conservative Marcus Porcius Cato (KAY-toe) (234–149 B.C.), known as **Cato the Censor**. Cato argued that there were only three ways to get rich: "pasturage, pasturage, and pasturage." All a would-be entrepreneur needed was land, which Rome had conquered a huge amount of in Italy. Called public land, Rome's new territory belonged to the Roman people, but an individual was legally entitled to claim about 320 acres as his own. Many entrepreneurs flouted the law, however, and grabbed much more than their fair share of public land. In addition, they often forced families of absent soldiers off private land, either by debt foreclosure or by outright violence. Sometimes, families would leave the land for the city, but usually they stayed as tenants.

Cato the Censor Name given to Marcus Porcius Cato, a Roman general and statesman. He was the first Roman historian to write in Latin.

The last two centuries B.C. witnessed the transformation of Roman rural society from one of independent farmers to one in which slave labor played a major role. By the end of the first century B.C., Italy's slave population was estimated at two million, about a third of the peninsula's total. Prisoners of war and conquered civilians provided a ready supply of slaves. Most worked in agriculture or mining, and their treatment was often abominable; the fewer house slaves were usually better off.

There were few escape routes from poverty. Before about 170 B.C., poor Romans were sometimes able to find land in colonies, but by 170 B.C., Rome had established all the colonies in Italy that its security demanded. A displaced farmer who wanted to compete in the labor market would have found it difficult to underbid cheap slave labor. In any case, Roman ideology frowned on wage labor by citizens. Nor was it practical for a poor farmer to sue a wealthy patron who seized his land, because a plaintiff himself had to bring the accused into court.

The situation of the Italian peasantry was becoming increasingly miserable by the mid-second century B.C. As one modern scholar has put it, "In conquering what they were pleased to call the world, the Romans ruined a great part of the Italian people."[2]

The Impact of Greece on Rome and Its Empire

Rome learned much from its new encounters with foreign peoples—and from none more than the Greeks. Wealthy Romans cultivated interests in Greek art, literature, rhetoric, and speculative thought; poor and rich alike enjoyed Greek drama. Before the mid-third century B.C., Roman literature was virtually nonexistent. An oral tradition of songs, ballads, and funeral oratory kept alive the deeds of the famous, for writing was generally restricted to commercial and government records and inscriptions. In short, the Romans conquered Italy without writing about it.

Contact with the Greek cities brought changes. Large numbers of Roman soldiers in Magna Graecia (southern Italy and Sicily) were introduced to comedy, tragedy, mimes, and sophisticated song lyrics, and many developed a permanent taste for them. It is no accident that the first production of a drama at Rome took place in 240 B.C., the year after the end of the First Punic War. Afterward, the annual production of such dramas became standard procedure.

No one could accuse the Romans of rushing headlong into a new age, however. The authorities continued to look down on theater as emotional and corrupt. They did not allow the building of a permanent theater in Rome until 55 B.C., nor did the Roman elite readily become playwrights or poets. The first gentleman poet in Rome, Lucilius (180–102 B.C.), did not arrive until the second century B.C., and he was a Latin, not a Roman. His predecessors, the founders of Latin literature, were all of low social status; little of their work survives.

The two great early Latin playwrights are Titus Maccius Plautus (ca. 254–184 B.C.) and Publius Terentius Afer, today known as Terence (ca. 195–159 B.C.). Both of them wrote comedies on the model of the great Greek playwright Menander (see page 97). Plautus was a poor man from northern Italy who learned his Latin in Rome; Terence was a North African slave, educated and freed in Rome. Twenty-one plays by Plautus and six by Terence survive. Plautus's plays are generally slapstick farces. They are set in Greece, not Rome, in part, out of escapism (many were written during the Second Punic War), in part, out of the censorial demands of the Roman authorities. They nonetheless reveal much about Roman society. Terence's plays are more subtle than Plautus's, indicating the growing sophistication of Roman theatergoers.

Latin prose developed more slowly than did poetry and drama. The first histories by Romans, composed after the Second Punic War, were written in Greek, for Latin lacked the vocabulary or the audience for history. Cato the Censor was the first historian of Rome to write in Latin. His *Origines*, of which we have only remnants, recounted Roman history from the origin of the city to about 150 B.C. The earliest surviving Latin prose work is Cato's *On Agriculture*.

In the traditional education of a Roman aristocrat, parents and close family friends played the primary role. Although this practice continued, wealthy Romans in the second century B.C. began acquiring Greek slaves to educate their sons in the Greek language and Greek literature. Soon Greek freedmen began setting up schools offering the same subjects. Before long, similar Latin grammar schools also opened.

One of the forms of Greek literature that appealed most to the practical-minded Romans was rhetoric. Roman orators studied Greek models, and many would say that they eventually outdid the Greeks. Cato was the first Roman to publish his speeches, and he also wrote a book on rhetoric. Both gave impetus to the spread of sophisticated rhetoric in Rome.

Scipio Aemilianus, conqueror of Carthage in 146 B.C., not only had a distinguished political and military career; he also served as patron of a group of prominent statesmen and soldiers who shared his love of Hellenism. Among the writers whom they supported were the playwright Terence, the poet Lucilius, the historian Polybius, and the Stoic philosopher Panaetius (ca. 185–109 B.C.). The Stoic emphases on duty, wisdom, and world brotherhood appealed both to Rome's traditional ideology and to its more recent acquisition of empire. Yet, not all Romans shared Scipio's admiration of Greek culture; Cato, for example, was famously ambivalent.

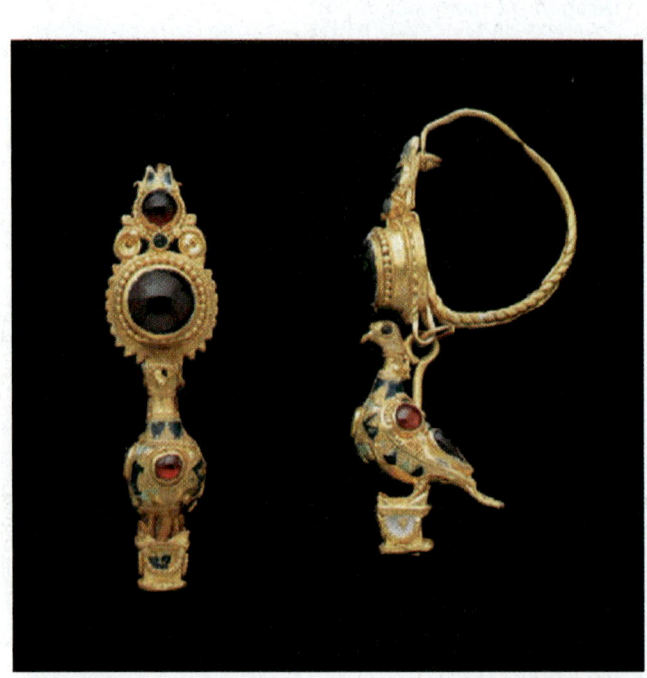

Luxurious Earrings   A wealthy Roman woman might have been proud to wear these refined and expensive gold earrings, produced in a Greek city of southern Italy in the second century B.C. Only 2 inches long, each earring shows a dove standing on a small, garland-trimmed base.   (Pair of earrings with pendant doves, Greek, Hellenistic period, 150–100 B.C.; gold, garnet, and glass paste; L. 5.2 cm. Courtesy of the Museum of Fine Arts, Boston, Harriet Otis Cruft Fund, 68.5a.b)

Cornelia, Scipio Aemilianus's mother-in-law, is an example of the political importance of elite women. She was an educated lover of Hellenism who wrote letters that existed several hundred years later as examples of elegant Latin prose. Her villa in the resort of Misenum on the Bay of Naples was well known for the distinguished guests whom she received there. When her husband, an outstanding statesman and general, died, Cornelia chose to remain a widow. One of the men who tried to change her mind was no less a figure than the king of Egypt. The widow spent her time managing her own estate and supervising the education of her two sons, the future tribunes Tiberius and Gaius Gracchus.

Although Cornelia's privileges were extraordinary, she is nonetheless a reminder of the opportunities that imperial expansion offered to wealthy Roman women. Marriage practices are one example of change. Few women were married *cum manu* anymore—that is, handed over by their fathers to their husbands. A woman's father or nearest male relative, not her husband, was most likely to be her paterfamilias, which meant that a husband's control over his wife's dowry was limited. The result was more freedom, at least for wealthy women.

SECTION SUMMARY

- The flexible infantry formation, known as the legion, was the key to Roman success in battle.

- Rome consolidated its control of Italy by wisely treating its allies with a mixture of firmness and generosity, including the extension of Roman citizenship.

- The strength of Rome's alliance led to success in the Punic Wars with Carthage and then drew Rome into conquering all the Hellenistic Greek states.

- Military expansion brought fabulous riches to the Roman elite, brought misery to the peasants of Italy, and established a slave system of two million people.

- Conquest of and contact with Greek civilization led to the rise of Latin literature.

Cornelia   Mother of the Gracchi, Cornelia was an influential elite woman whose letters served as models of Latin prose style.

THE LATE REPUBLIC AND ITS COLLAPSE, 133–31 B.C.

How did the unintended consequences of conquest on Rome lead to a revolution that destroyed the Republic?

A citizen of the Roman Republic in the mid-second century B.C. might have looked forward to a long and happy future for his country, unaware that the Republic—after 350 years of expansion—was about to begin a century of domestic and foreign unrest that would bring down the whole system. Why and how did the Republic collapse? More than a century of warfare weighed heavily on the ordinary people of Italy—the Romans and allied peasants whose farms were ruined while they were off fighting. The Roman elite was bitterly divided over what to do about the problems of the peasants. One group wanted to redistribute land on behalf of the poor; another group had no sympathy for them.

By the Late Republic, the city of Rome was crowded: Scholars estimate the number of inhabitants to have reached one million by the end of the first century B.C. The government had to take charge of the grain supply. But elite politicians exploited the issue for partisan purposes. Once before, during the struggle between the patrician and plebeian orders in the Early Republic, the elite had been similarly divided and had resolved its differences through compromise (see page 118). In the Late Republic, however, ambitious nobles were no longer willing to subordinate themselves to the community. It was not long before competing armies of land-hungry peasants, thwarted from above, were marching across Italy.

Reformers and Revolutionaries

Many Romans fretted over the military dimension of the agrarian crisis. In modern societies, draftees are often the poorest people. In Rome, military service was a prestigious activity, so a property qualification was imposed and the poor were not drafted. As fewer and fewer potential soldiers could afford to own property, however, during the second century, it became necessary to reduce the property qualification several times. If the free peasantry continued its decline, Rome would either have to drop the property qualification for the military altogether or stop fielding armies. Clearly, something had to be done.

Gracchi Led by Tiberius Sempronius Gracchus and later his brother Gaius, this ancient Roman faction challenged the conservative senate on behalf of the poor.

Into the breach stepped Tiberius Sempronius Gracchus (GRAK-us) (d. 133 B.C.), one of the ten tribunes for the year 133 B.C. The son of Cornelia, and a distinguished general and ambassador (also named Tiberius), Tiberius belonged to the eminent **Gracchi** (GRAK-eye) family. He seemed an excellent spokesperson for a group of prominent senators who backed land reform to restore Rome's peasant soldiers.

Tiberius's proposed law restored the roughly 320-acre limit to the amount of public land a person could own (plus an exception for a man with two sons, who was allowed to hold about 667 acres). A commission was to be set up to redistribute land to the poor, in small lots that were to be inalienable—that is, the wealthy could not buy them back. The former landowners would be reimbursed for improvements they had made, such as buildings or plantings.

The proposal was moderate, but wealthy landowners repudiated it outright. Many senators suspected that Tiberius wanted to set himself up as a kind of superpatron, buoyed by peasant supporters. Senators also disliked his pushy and heavy-handed legislative tactics. Finally, Tiberius broke with custom by running for a second consecutive term as tribune. While the tribal assembly prepared to vote on the new tribunes, some senators led a mob to the Forum and had Tiberius and three hundred of his followers clubbed to death.

This shocking event marked the first time in the Republic that a political debate was settled by bloodshed in Rome itself. Tiberius's killers had not merely committed murder, but had attacked the traditional inviolability of the tribunes. The ancient sources agree that it was the beginning of a century of revolution. Over the next hundred years, violence grew as a weapon of politics in the Republic.

The land commission went ahead with its work, even without Tiberius. His younger brother, Gaius (GUY-us) (d. 121 B.C.) became tribune himself in 123 B.C. Gaius expanded Tiberius's coalition, adding to it supporters from the equestrian order and the urban populace, mainly composed of slaves and freedmen. He gave the plebs cheap grain at subsidized prices. The equestrians were wealthy landowners, similar to senators in most respects except for their failure to have reached the senate; they yearned for political power. A small but important group of equestrians was engaged in commerce and tax collection in the provinces. The senate regulated their activities through the so-called extortion courts, which tried corruption cases. Gaius staffed those courts with equestrians. Alluding to the new equestrian power, Gaius remarked, "I have left a sword in the ribs of the senate."

Gaius sponsored an extension of his brother's agrarian law, new colonies, public works, and relief for poor soldiers. Eventually, he ran aground on a plan to include the Italian allies as beneficiaries of reform—a farsighted notion, but one unpopular with the Roman people, who were jealous of their privileges. A riot by his supporters led the senate to pass a declaration of public emergency, empowering officials to use any means necessary to protect the state.

One of the consuls had Gaius and 250 of his followers killed. Another 3,000 Gracchans were executed soon thereafter. The Gracchan land commission gave land to approximately 75,000 citizens. The law, however, was amended to permit the resale of redistributed land, and the commission itself was abolished. With the wealthy poised to buy land back, the settlers' future was uncertain. The senatorial oligarchy was back in control.

Or so it seemed. In fact, Roman politics had become an unstable brew. In time, it became clear that the Gracchi had divided the political community into two loose groupings. On one side were the *optimates* (op-tee-MAH-tayz) ("the best people"; singular, *optimas*), conservatives who asserted the rule of the senate against popular tribunes and the maintenance of the estates of the wealthy in spite of the agrarian crisis. On the other side were the *populares* (pah-poo-LAH-rayz) ("men of the people"; singular, *popularis*), who challenged the rule of the senate in the name of relief of the poor. The populares were not democrats. Like the optimates, they were Roman nobles who believed in hierarchy, but, like the Gracchi, they advocated the redistribution of wealth and power as a way of restoring stability and strengthening the military.

By 100 B.C., Rome's agrarian crisis had become a full-scale military crisis, too. Roman armies under senatorial commanders fared poorly, both in Numidia (modern North Africa) and in southern Gaul against Germanic invaders (see **MAP 5.3**). The situation was saved by an outsider to established privilege, an equestrian named Gaius Marius (157–86 B.C.), the first member of his family to be elected consul, for 107 B.C. This "new man" proved to be a military reformer and a populeris. Marius made several moves to streamline and strengthen the Roman army: Camp followers were reduced in number, and individual soldiers were made to carry their own equipment. To meet the Germans, who attacked in overwhelming waves, maniples—the tactical subunits of a legion—were reorganized and combined into larger units called cohorts, rendering the army firmer and more cohesive. Most important, Marius abandoned altogether the property qualification for the military. As a result, Roman soldiers were no longer peasants doing part-time military service, but rather landless men making a profession of the military.

Politically, they became a force to be reckoned with. As an indispensable general, Marius demanded and won six elections to the consulship, unconstitutional though that was. Furthermore, after gaining victories in North Africa and Gaul, Marius championed his soldiers. In 100 B.C., he asked that land be distributed to them. The senate refused, but its triumph was temporary. The poor recognized that only military leaders, such as Marius, would give them land. As a result, ordinary Romans, who were all now eligible for the army, transferred their loyalty from the senate to their commanders.

Two new wars weakened the Republic further. First, its Italian allies rose against Rome in a bloody and bitter struggle from 91 to 89 B.C., known as the "Social War," that is, war with the *socii* ("allies"). The allies fought hard, and Rome, in order to prevail, had to concede to them what they had demanded at the outset: full Roman citizenship. The other conflict of this period pitted Rome against Mithridates (120–63 B.C.), a rebellious king in northern Anatolia with great ambitions. Mithridates conquered Roman territory in western Anatolia and slaughtered the numerous Italian businessmen and tax collectors there. He invaded Thrace and Greece, where he found great support. Once again a military man rose to save the day for Rome: Marius's former lieutenant, Lucius Cornelius Sulla Felix (ca. 138–78 B.C.), consul for the year 88 B.C.

Sulla was as ambitious as Marius, but he came from the opposite political camp: He was a patrician and an optimas. The two became deadly rivals. The two men's troops fought over the issue of the command against Mithridates. Sulla's forces won the first round by marching on Rome, but after they left for the east, Marius's men retook the city and settled scores. Victorious over Mithridates, Sulla returned to Italy in 83 B.C. and engaged in all-out civil war. Sulla defeated Marius's men in battle (minus Marius himself, who had died in 86), then sealed his victory by executing his political opponents, as many as two thousand men. Their land was confiscated and sold to Sulla's friends. Sulla also confiscated the land of any Italian community that had opposed him and gave it to his veterans, about eighty thousand men.

Having assumed the long-dormant office of dictator—but without a time limit on his tenure—Sulla attempted to restore the senatorial rule of pre-Gracchan days. To do this, he greatly weakened the tribunate and strengthened the senate, whose size he doubled, from about three hundred to about six hundred members.

Sulla retired in 79 B.C. and died a year later. His hope of restoring law and order under the senate died with him. The populares soon regained enough strength to restore the old powers of the tribunes. Discontent smoldered among the men whose land Sulla had confiscated. Equally serious, many senators, aspiring to what Sulla had done and not to what he had said, pursued personal power, not the collective interests of the senate.

Caesar

At first, the dominant leader after Sulla was the optimas Pompey the Great (106–48 B.C.), a brilliant general and a supporter of Sulla. Young Pompey (POM-pee) went from command to command: He put down an agrarian rebellion in Italy and a rebellion in Spain, cleared the Mediterranean of pirates, defeated Mithridates again after that able king started another war, and added rich conquests to the empire in Anatolia, Syria, Phoenicia, and Palestine. In the fifties B.C., however, the tide began turning in favor of Gaius Julius **Caesar** (100–44 B.C.), an even more gifted general and politician—indeed, perhaps one of history's greatest. A populfrom the issue, Caesar (SEE-zer) had family connections to Marius. Caesar's career depended on his oratory, his boldness, and his sheer talent at war and politics. Caesar conquered Gaul, gained a foothold in Britain, and laid the foundations of Roman rule in Egypt (see **MAP 5.3**).

While the elite of the Late Republic struggled to maintain order and secure power, ordinary people struggled for survival. Violence had become a way of life in rural Italy. Many once-prosperous farmers, dispossessed peasants, and runaway slaves ended up as robbers or bandits. It was also an era of slave revolts, the most serious of which lasted from 73 to 71 B.C., under the leadership of Spartacus, a Thracian gladiator who had once served as a Roman allied soldier. An able commander, Spartacus beat nine separate Roman armies in two years before finally

Caesar   Roman general gifted at war and politics, he was named dictator in 49 B.C. and was later assassinated by the members of the senate in 44 B.C.

Bust of Julius Caesar This marble sculpture accurately conveys the conqueror's firmness of expression and perhaps his intelligence—but not his looks, since Caesar was bald. (Vatican Museums/Scala/Art Resource, NY)

suffering defeat. (See the feature, "The Written Record: Spartacus's Slave Revolt.") At the same time, Rome also faced major wars in its provinces.

Pompey and Caesar sought alliances with other families by marrying influential women or by becoming their lovers. In 80 B.C., for example, Pompey divorced his first wife to advance his career by marrying Aemilia, Sulla's stepdaughter. Aemilia was not only married at the time, but pregnant by her first husband. Soon after her divorce and remarriage, she died in childbirth. Caesar had many lovers, among whom, there was the queen of Egypt, Cleopatra (see pages 100–101). Caesar had a penchant for certain Egyptian institutions, such as the Egyptian calendar, and he toyed with becoming a monarch himself, an inclination that Cleopatra perhaps encouraged.

Another of Caesar's lovers was Servilia, stepsister of Marcus Porcius Cato (Cato the Younger, 95–46 B.C.), great-grandson of the famous censor (see page 127). She was also the mother of Brutus, the man who would eventually help murder Caesar.

Pompey was an optimas, Caesar a popularis, but the two of them agreed that they, not the senate or the assemblies, should dominate Rome. Each man's ambition was more important to him than any political principles. In 60 B.C., they entered into a pact with a third ambitious noble, Marcus Licinius Crassus (d. 53 B.C.). Known today as the "First Triumvirate," this coalition amounted to a conspiracy to run the state. Their individual ambitions rebuffed by the senate, each man had an agenda that could be achieved by pooling resources in the triumvirate: for Pompey, ratification of his acts in the east and land for his veterans; for Caesar, who became consul for 59 B.C., a long period of command in Gaul and a free hand in his behavior there; for Crassus, a rebate for the tax collectors of Roman Asia, whom he championed, and eventually, a command in Syria to make war on Parthia (the new Persian Empire).

Having achieved its goal, the triumvirate did not long survive, but its very existence shows how little the Republic now meant. Crassus died in an inglorious defeat against the Parthians at Carrhae in Syria in 53 B.C. (see **MAP 5.3**). Frightened by Caesar's stunning victories in Gaul, Pompey returned to the senatorial fold, now led by Cato the Younger. Cato and his supporters stood for the traditional rule of the senatorial oligarchy. In 49 B.C., they ordered Caesar to give up his command in Gaul, but instead, Caesar marched on Italy with his army. Italy's northern boundary was marked by a tiny stream called the Rubicon; when Caesar defiantly crossed it, he declared, "The die is cast." Indeed it was, for civil war. Caesar swept to victory against the senate's army, led by Pompey, at Pharsalus in Greece in 48 B.C. Pompey fled but was assassinated. The complete destruction of the senate's forces took until 45 B.C.

The years of civil war took Caesar from Spain to Anatolia. During the fighting, he showed the qualities that made him great: He was fast, tough, smart, adaptable, and a risk-taker. He was a diplomat, too, offering mercy to any of his enemies who joined him. A talented writer, Caesar published two books about his military campaigns—*On the Gallic War* and *On the Civil War*—the latter appearing after his death. These works glorified Caesar's conquests and defended his decision to wage civil war. (See the feature, "The Global Record: Caesar on the Gauls.")

Back in Rome, Caesar sponsored a huge number of reforms. His political goal was to elevate Italians and others at the expense of old Roman families. To achieve this, Caesar conferred Roman citizenship liberally, on all of Cisalpine Gaul (northernmost Italy), as well as on certain provincial towns. He enlarged the senate from six hundred to nine hundred, adding his supporters, including some Gauls, to the membership. Caesar sponsored social and economic reforms, too, including reducing debt and founding the first colonies outside Italy, where veterans and poor citizens were settled. He undertook a grand public building program in the city of Rome. Caesar's most long-lasting act was to introduce the calendar of 365¼ days, on January 1, 45 B.C. Derived from the calendar of Egypt, it is known as the Julian calendar.

Caesar did not hide his contempt for Republican constitutional formalities. By accepting a dictatorship for life, he offended conservatives; by flirting with the title of king, he infuriated them. His career ended abruptly on March 15, 44 B.C. (the Ides of March by the Roman calendar), when sixty senators stabbed him to death. The assassination took place in the portico attached to the Theater of Pompey, in front of a statue of Pompey himself, where the senate was meeting that day. It had been eighty-nine years since the murder of Tiberius Gracchus.

Spartacus's Slave Revolt

Spartacus's revolt was the third and most famous of three great slave rebellions that rocked Italy and Sicily between 135 and 71 B.C. The revolt itself was not a success; all of the slaves were either imprisoned or killed. But Spartacus terrified the Roman elite and became a powerful symbol of the struggle for freedom to all who were oppressed. This account, by the ancient writer Appian, illustrates his fight.

At about this same time, at the city of Capua in Italy, gladiators were being trained to fight in spectacles. Spartacus, a Thracian whom the Romans had imprisoned and then sold to be trained as a gladiator, had once fought as a soldier for the Roman army. He persuaded about seventy of the enslaved men to risk a break for freedom rather than to allow themselves to be put on display for the entertainment of others. Using force to overcome their guards, the men made their escape. The fugitives armed themselves with wooden clubs and daggers that they seized from travelers on the roads nearby, and then rushed to take refuge on Mount Vesuvius. Many fugitive slaves and even some free men from the surrounding countryside came to this place to join Spartacus. They began to stage bandit raids on nearby settlements. Spartacus had his fellow gladiators Oenomaus and Crixus as his two subordinate commanders. Since Spartacus divided the profits of his raiding into equal shares, he soon attracted a very large number of followers . . .

[Spartacus wins victories in southern and northern Italy.] With the 120,000 men under his command, he began a march on Rome. So that traveling would be as light as possible, he torched all unnecessary supplies, killed all prisoners of war, and slaughtered all pack animals. Many deserters from the Roman army came to him, but he accepted none of them. The consuls made a stand against him in a place in the land of Picenum. Another great armed struggle took place here and the Romans were defeated again. Spartacus changed his mind about an attack on Rome. He decided that he was not ready for an all-out battle and that his whole army was not yet properly armed for regular warfare. Moreover, so far no city had come over to his side, but only slaves, deserters, and the flotsam and jetsam of humanity . . .

[After many successes and some defeats, Spartacus is forced into a final battle with a Roman army led by Crassus.] Since so many tens of thousands of desperate men were involved, the result was a protracted battle of epic proportions. Spartacus took a spear wound in his thigh. Collapsing on one knee, he held his shield up in front of him and fought off those who were attacking him, until he and the large number of men around him were finally surrounded and cut down. The rest of his army was thrown into disarray and confusion and was slaughtered in large numbers. The killing was on such a scale that it was not possible to count the dead. The Romans lost about a thousand men. The body of Spartacus was never found. When the survivors among Spartacus's men, who were still a large number, fled from the battle, they went up into the mountains, where they were pursued by Crassus's forces. Splitting themselves into four groups, they continued to fight until all of them had perished—all, that is, except six thousand of them, who were taken prisoner and crucified along the whole length of the highway that ran from Capua to Rome.

QUESTIONS

1. Why do you think Spartacus attracted so many followers?

2. Why do you think Spartacus was able to defeat the Romans time and again? Why do you think he finally failed?

3. What evidence does the passage offer to show that Spartacus and his men were brave and determined?

Source: *Spartacus' Slave Revolt from Spartacus and the Slave Wars: A Brief History with Documents.* Translated, edited and with an Introduction by Brent D. Shaw. Copyright © 2001 by Bedford/St. Martin's. Used with permission of Bedford/St. Martin's.

The assassins called themselves Liberators, believing that they were freeing themselves from tyranny just as the founders of the Republic had done centuries before. Indeed, one of the chief conspirators, Marcus Junius Brutus (ca. 85–42 B.C.), claimed descent from Lucius Junius Brutus, traditional leader of the revolt against the Tarquins that was thought to have established the Republic. Like his co-conspirator, Gaius Longinus Cassius (d. 42 B.C.), Brutus had been a magistrate, military officer, and provincial administrator.

The assassination of Caesar threw Rome back into turmoil. Civil war followed for the next thirteen years. The Liberators and Caesar's partisans fought to settle whether the Senate or a dictator would rule Rome. Then, after they defeated the Senate, the two leading Caesarians struggled over power. The final conflict pitted Mark Antony (Marcus Antonius, ca. 83–30 B.C.), Caesar's chief lieutenant and the man who inherited his love affair with Cleopatra, against Octavian (Gaius Julius Caesar Octavianus, 63 B.C.–A.D. 14), Caesar's grandnephew and adopted son and heir to Caesar's name and his huge fortune. At first, it looked as if Antony had the upper hand

Caesar on the Gauls

Julius Caesar (ca. 100–44 B.C.) advertised his achievements in conquering Gaul (58–51 B.C.) in his Commentaries on the Gallic War. The book focuses on battles and negotiations, but here Caesar discusses the society of the Gauls (also known as Celts). He depicts the inhabitants as superstitious and warlike.

In the whole of Gaul two types of men are counted as being of worth and distinction. The ordinary people are considered almost as slaves: they dare do nothing on their own account and are not called to counsels. When the majority are oppressed by debt or heavy tribute, or harmed by powerful men, they swear themselves away into slavery to the aristocracy, who then have the same rights over them as masters do over their slaves. Of the two types of men of distinction, however, the first is made up of the druids (priests), and the other of the knights.

The druids are involved in matters of religion. They manage public and private sacrifices and interpret religious customs and ceremonies. Young men flock to them in large numbers to gain instruction, and they hold the druids in great esteem. For they decide almost all disputes, both public and private: if some crime has been committed, if there has been murder done, if there is a dispute over an inheritance or over territory, they decide the issue and settle the rewards and penalties. If any individual or group of people does not abide by their decision, the druids ban them from sacrifices. This is their most severe punishment. Those who are banned in this way are counted among the wicked and criminal: everyone shuns them and avoids approaching or talking to them, so as not to suffer any harm from contact with them. . . .

Druids are not accustomed to take part in war, nor do they pay taxes like the rest of the people. . . . The principal doctrine they attempt to impart is that souls do not die but after death cross from one person to another. Because the fear of death is thereby set aside, they consider this a strong inducement to physical courage. Besides this, they debate many subjects and teach them to their young men—for example, the stars and their movements, the size of the universe and the earth, the nature of things, and the strength and power of the immortal gods.

The second class is that composed of the knights. When necessity arises and some war flares up—which before Caesar's arrival used to happen almost every year, so that they were either on the offensive themselves or fending off attacks—they are all involved in the campaign. Each man has as many retainers and dependents about him as is appropriate to his status in terms of his birth and resources. This is the sole form of power and influence they know.

The whole of the Gallic nation is much given to religious practices. For this reason those who are afflicted with serious illnesses and those who are involved in battles and danger either offer human sacrifice or vow that they will do so, and employ the druids to manage these sacrifices. For they believe that unless one human life is offered for another, the power and presence of the immortal gods cannot be propitiated.

QUESTIONS

1. According to Caesar, who were the druids, and what did they do? How did they help the Gauls succeed as warriors? How did the druids differ from the knights?

2. What was the status of ordinary people in Gaul?

3. What do you think Caesar and his readers thought of the Gauls' practice of human sacrifice?

Source: Caesar on the Gauls from *Julius Ceasar, Seven Commentaries on the Gallic War with an Eighth Commentary by Aulus Hirtius,* translated by Carolyn Hammong. Copyright © 1996 Oxford University Press. By permission of Oxford University Press.

because Octavian was young and inexperienced, was not a general, and was cursed with poor health. Octavian was, however, a man of unusual cunning and prudence. His forces defeated Antony and Cleopatra at the naval battle of Actium (off northwestern Greece) in 31 B.C.; their suicides followed shortly. The Roman world held its breath to see how Octavian would govern it.

The World of Cicero

Cicero Philosopher, writer, and statesman who was Rome's greatest orator.

Marcus Tullius **Cicero** (106–43 B.C.) is one of the best known figures of all antiquity. His enormous body of writings provides a vivid, detailed, and sometimes damning picture of Roman life at the end of the Republic. They demonstrate both Rome's genius for flexibility and its limits.

Like Marius, Cicero (SIS-er-o) was a wealthy equestrian from the central Italian town of Arpinum who, as consul (in 63 B.C.), became a "new man." Unlike Marius, Cicero was an optimas and defender of the senate. He was, however, ready for compromise with the equestrians, from whose ranks he himself had arisen. He made his name by successfully leading the opposition to Lucius Sergius Catilina, a down-and-out patrician who organized a debtors' revolt in Etruria; the army smashed the rebellion.

Young Cicero studied philosophy and oratory in Greece. As an adult, he produced writings that made the Latin language a vessel for the heritage of Greek thought, even if he never equaled the originality of Plato or Aristotle. Cicero produced over a hundred speeches, of which about sixty survive; several works on speech-writing; philosophical works; poetry, of which little survives; and numerous letters. After his death in 43 B.C., his immense correspondence was published, with little censored.

Politics in the Late Republic was loud and boisterous. The elite prided itself on free speech and open debate. In senate deliberations, court cases, and public meetings in the Forum that preceded assembly votes, oratory—sometimes great oratory—was common.

POLITICS, SOCIETY, AND LAW

Elite women benefited from increased freedom and greater educational opportunities in the Late Republic, which made it possible for women, as well as men, to study oratory. Private tutors were common among the aristocracy, and girls often received lessons alongside their brothers. Girls sometimes also profited from a father's expertise. A particularly dramatic case is that of Hortensia, daughter of Quintus Hortensius Hortalus (114–50 B.C.), a famous orator and rival of Cicero. An excellent speaker herself, Hortensia defied tradition by arguing successfully in the Roman Forum, in 42 B.C., against a proposed war tax on wealthy women.

Ordinary people lacked the education and freedom to express themselves in the manner of a woman like Hortensia, but a less civilized means of expression was open to them: the political gang. Brawls and violence between the rival groups of Clodius, a supporter of Caesar, and Milo, a supporter of the senate, became increasingly common in the fifties B.C. As dictator, Caesar abolished the gangs.

Cicero's works provide evidence of a key development in the practice of Roman law. Often unheralded, what Cicero's contemporaries did was invent the notion of the legal expert, a person devoted to explaining and interpreting the law. Roman law needed interpretation because it was complex and intricate. Much of it was the work not of legislators, but of magistrates, who issued annual statements setting forth how their courts would work. The unsystematic and sometimes contradictory result cried out for someone to make sense of it. Enter the jurisconsults, legal interpreters who emerged in the third and second centuries B.C. At first, they had no special standing, but in the first century B.C., they became true jurists; their interpretations began to be considered authoritative. No earlier Mediterranean society had a professional class of legal experts, but no earlier society had faced issues as complicated and turbulent, or had grown to three million citizens, as the Roman Republic did in the mid-first century B.C. The Western tradition of legal science has its roots in Rome.

Rome's political system, unlike its legal system, did not adapt flexibly to changing circumstances. The disenfranchised of the Late Republic had reasonable goals: land for those who had fought for their country and admission to the senate of a wider group. Yet the old elite resisted both. Cicero's solution was to build on Sulla's reforms by uniting the senatorial and equestrian orders and by widening the Roman ruling class to include the elite of all Italy. The expanded ruling class could close ranks and establish *otium cum dignitate*, "peace with respect for rank." Cicero's proposed new order was distinctly hierarchical.

A NEW ELITE?

In the turbulent times of the Late Republic, the Roman elite often turned to the Hellenistic philosophers. The poet Lucretius (loo-CREE-shus) (ca. 94–55 B.C.) describes the Epicurean ideal of withdrawal into the contemplative life in a long didactic epic called *On the Nature of Things*. Most elite Romans, however, including Cicero, preferred the activist philosophy of Stoicism (see pages 103–104). Cicero put forth a generous view of human brotherhood. He argued that all people share a spark of divinity and are protected by natural law. Consequently, all persons have value and importance and should treat others generously. Such ideas would be influential in the new Roman Empire when, under the leadership of Augustus, fair treatment of provincials was a major theme. For Cicero, however, these ideas existed more as theory than as practice.

Cicero did not hide his lack of sympathy for his fellow citizens who were poor. In one speech, he castigated "artisans and shopkeepers and all that kind of scum"; in a letter, he complained about "the wretched half-starved populace, which attends mass meetings and sucks the blood of the treasury." Cicero also made his disdain for democracy clear: "The greatest number," he said, "should not have the greatest power."

Elitist as Cicero's views were, they were by no means extremist. Cassius, Brutus, and the other Liberators had little interest in even Cicero's limited compromises. Their stubbornness proved

SECTION SUMMARY

- After the Gracchi brothers' failed attempts at reform, the Roman poor threw their support to new patrons, military leaders who raised private armies to win land for their followers and glory for themselves.

- The general Marius turned Rome's citizen soldiers into professionals, and then fought a civil war against another general, Sulla.

- The next generation of Roman politics was divided into factions led by Pompey and Caesar, leading to another civil war.

- Caesar reformed Rome as dictator for life before being assassinated.

- The great orator Cicero symbolizes the rough-and-tumble of civilian politics in the Late Republic.

to be their downfall, for dispossessed peasants and ambitious equestrians transferred their loyalties to Julius Caesar and, later, to Augustus. One of Caesar's supporters, Sallust (86–ca. 34 B.C.), wrote biting and bitter works of history that indicted the greed and corruption of the optimates, whom he blamed for the decline of the Republic. In any case, peace was not restored, for the generation of Liberators was wiped out in renewed civil war, and a new generation emerged, weary for peace.

CHAPTER SUMMARY

Rome was destined to provide Western civilization with many basic notions about government and empire, but Rome sprang from humble origins. A central Italian village at first, Rome was urbanized after contact with more sophisticated neighbors, especially Greeks and Etruscans. Rome became a monarchy and then a republic.

In the Early and Middle Republic, Rome was a mixed constitution. It combined popular power with control by an oligarchy. Government was shared by the magistrates, the senate, and the assemblies. The so-called Conflict of the Orders brought debt relief for the poor and a combined patrician-plebeian nobility for the rich. Roman society was composed of a network of households tied in patron-client relationships. The ingrained hierarchy of the Roman social and cultural system helped keep politics stable.

FOCUS QUESTIONS

- What was early Rome like and how was it shaped by relations with its neighbors?

- How was the Roman Republic governed, and how did that government shape the Western political tradition?

- How did Rome conquer an empire?

- How did the unintended consequences of conquest on Rome lead to a revolution that destroyed the Republic?

The elite channeled popular energies into protecting the young Republic from its numerous rivals in central Italy. Greed and ambition, as well as fear, were powerful motives of Rome's military expansion. Rome conquered most of Italy by 265 B.C., then fought the bloody Punic Wars against Carthage (264–201, 148–146 B.C.) and conquered all the Hellenistic Greek states (201–30 B.C.).

Rome consolidated its control of Italy by wisely treating its allies with a mixture of firmness and generosity. By extending Roman citizenship, Rome gave them a stake in continued Roman hegemony. Having defeated all opponents near and far, Rome seemed to have won absolute security by the mid-second century B.C. Yet, its strength was deceptive. Contact with Greek culture liberated the Romans from ruder, peasant ways, but also loosened previous restraints. A huge influx of slaves made acquisition of large estates profitable, at the expense of Italy's peasant farmers. The result was a growing and dangerous social instability with military and political ramifications. After the Gracchis' failed reform attempts, the poor threw their support to new patrons, military leaders who raised private armies to win land for their followers and glory for themselves. First Marius and Sulla, then Caesar and Pompey, led Roman armies against each other in civil war.

KEY TERMS

Romulus (p. 110)

Latin (p. 111)

Etruscans (p. 112)

orders (p. 114)

res publica (p. 116)

senate (p. 116)

paterfamilias (p. 119)

triumph (p. 121)

legion (p. 123)

Punic Wars (p. 124)

Cato the Censor (p. 127)

Cornelia (p. 129)

Gracchi (p. 130)

Caesar (p. 131)

Cicero (p. 134)

 This icon will direct you to additional materials on the website: www .cengage.com/history/ noble/westciv6e

NOTES

1. From *The Aeneid of Virgil*, trans. Allen Mandelbaum. Copyright © 1971 by Allen Mandelbaum. Reprinted by permission of Bantam Books, a division of Bantam Doubleday, Dell Publishing Group, Inc.

2. P. A. Brunt, *Social Conflicts in the Roman Republic* (New York: Norton, 1971), p. 17.

See our interactive eBook for map and primary source activities.

6

CHAPTER OUTLINE

Augustus and the Principate, 31 B.C.–A.D. 68

The Roman Peace and Its Collapse, A.D. 69–284

Early Christianity

Ara Pacis (detail), Rome
(Scala/Art Resource, NY)

Imperial Rome, 31 B.C.–A.D. 284

The imperial family of Rome walks in stately procession to a sacrifice: Livia, wife of Augustus, first of the emperors; his daughter, Julia; Julia's husband, Agrippa; and various cousins and in-laws and their children. They are formally dressed in togas and gowns, heads wreathed. The men and women gaze seriously; the boys and girls have impish looks, betraying thoughts of mischief as they hold their parents' hands. They are all carved in stone, one of several sculptured reliefs decorating the walls of a public monument in Rome. Dedicated on Livia's birthday in 9 B.C., the monument shown here illustrates the propaganda themes of the new regime, among them, the happy family as a symbol of peace after generations of civil war. The senate, which had commissioned the monument, called it the *Ara Pacis Augustae*, or "Altar of Augustan Peace."

Having made peace was no idle boast on Augustus's part. Not only did he end the Roman revolution, but he began a period of two hundred years of prosperity and stability in the Roman Empire. Augustus took advantage of Rome's war-weariness to create a new government out of the ruins of the Republic. Like the Early Republic's leaders, Augustus displayed a genius for compromise. Although he retained the final say, he shared a degree of power with the senate. He made financial sacrifices to feed the urban poor and distribute farms to landless peasants. He ended Rome's seemingly limitless expansion and stabilized the borders of the empire. He began to raise the provinces to a status of equality with Italy.

The *pax Romana* (PAHKS ro-MAHN-uh) ("Roman peace"), at its height between A.D. 96 and 180, was an era of enlightened emperors, thriving cities, intellectual vitality, and artistic and architectural achievement in an empire of 50 million to 100 million people. Yet, it was also an era of slavery. More positively, the Roman peace was a period of heightened spirituality. In the peaceful and diverse empire, ideas traveled from people to people, and the religious beliefs of an obscure sect from western Asia began to spread around the Mediterranean and into northern Europe. The new religion was Christianity.

After 180, Rome slowly passed into a period marked in turn by bad emperors, civil war, inflation, plague, invasion, and defeat. After reaching a low point around 235 to 253, Rome's fortunes began to improve under reformers who would forge a stronger and different empire.

FOCUS QUESTIONS

- How did Augustus establish a new imperial government to replace the Roman Republic? Why was he so successful?

- What was life like in the era of the Roman peace? Why did peace end during the third century A.D.?

- What were the origins of Christianity, and how did it fare among the other religions of the Roman world?

This icon will direct you to additional materials on the website: www.cengage.com/history/noble/westciv6e

See our interactive eBook for map and primary source activities.

AUGUSTUS AND THE PRINCIPATE, 31 B.C.–A.D. 68

How did Augustus establish a new imperial government to replace the Roman Republic? Why was he so successful?

Augustus Honorific title of Gaius Julius Caesar Octavianus, whose forty-five-year rule laid the foundations of two hundred years of prosperous Roman peace.

In 31 B.C., Gaius Julius Caesar Octavianus (63 B.C.–A.D. 14), or Octavian, as **Augustus** was then known, stood at the top of the Roman world. His forces had defeated those of Mark Antony and Cleopatra at the Battle of Actium in northwestern Greece, whereupon, his two chief enemies committed suicide. Few could have predicted the vision and statesmanship that Octavian now displayed. He spent the next forty-five years healing the wounds of a century of revolution. He did nothing less than lay the foundations of the prosperous two centuries enjoyed by the empire under the Roman peace (see **MAP 6.1**).

The Political Settlement

Octavian was both astute and lucky. He was lucky in the length and violence of the civil wars. After Actium, most of his enemies were dead, so establishing the one-man rule that he claimed was necessary to restore stability was relatively easy. He was also lucky to live to be nearly 80—he had plenty of time to consolidate his rule. He was a cagey man and a sharp judge of others. Octavian learned the lesson of Caesar's greatest mistake. He understood that the Roman elite, however weakened, was still strong enough to oppose a ruler who flaunted monarchical power. To avoid a second Ides of March, therefore, Octavian was infinitely diplomatic.

🌐 **MAP 6.1—The Roman World in the Early Empire**

Many modern cities are built on the sites of Roman foundations, evidence of the immense extent of the Roman Empire at its height.

Historians accurately call Octavian Rome's first emperor, but he avoided terms like emperor or dictator. Instead, Octavian took the title of *princeps* (PRIN-keps) ("first citizen"), an old title of respect in the senate. From *princeps* comes **Principate** (PRIN-sih-pate), a term often used to describe the constitutional monarchy of the "Early Empire," the name that historians have given to the period from 31 B.C. to A.D. 192. Four years after Actium, in 27 B.C., the senate granted Octavian the honorific title *augustus*, symbolizing the augmentation, or increase, of his authority. He was also known as *Caesar* and *divi filius* ("son of a god"), which tied him to Julius Caesar. Another name, *imperator* ("commander" and, later, "emperor"), recalled the military might that Augustus (as we shall henceforth call him) could call on, if needed.

In 27 B.C., Augustus proclaimed "the transfer of the state to the free disposal of the senate and the people"—that is, the restoration of the Republic. Remembering similar claims by Sulla and Julius Caesar, few Romans were likely to believe this, and few would have wanted the Republic restored in any case. They, no doubt, appreciated their ruler's tact, however.

Two strokes of genius marked the new regime. First, Augustus held power without monopolizing public office. He held the civil authority of the tribunate without being a tribune and the military authority of provincial generals without holding a specific command. Generalships remained open to ambitious men as long as they accepted Augustus's power. Second, the new government divided the provinces between Augustus and the senate. To check any new would-be Caesar, Augustus kept for himself the frontier provinces, with the main concentration of armies, as well as grain-rich Egypt (which Rome had annexed after Actium). The local commanders were loyal equestrians who owed their success to Augustus. Most of the other provinces continued to be ruled as before, by senators serving as governors.

Augustus wanted advice without dissent. He used the senate, or rather a committee of senators and magistrates, as a sounding board; the group evolved into a permanent advisory body. Ordinary senate meetings, however, lost their old freedom of speech because of informers and the emperor's secret agents. The popular assemblies fared even worse, as their powers were limited and eventually transferred to the senate. Nor would unruly crowds be tolerated. Augustus established the city of Rome's first police force and also stationed there his own personal guard. Called the praetorians (pre-TOR-ee-unz), or Praetorian Guard, the name used for a Roman general's bodyguard, the guard would play a crucial role in future imperial politics.

More important for the public good, Augustus established the first civil service, consisting of a series of prefectures—or departments—supervising, for example, the city watch, the grain supply, the water supply, the building of roads and bridges, tax collection, and the provisioning of the armies. Equestrians and freedmen were prominent in these prefectures and in provincial government, so they enthusiastically supported the Principate.

Although one may speak loosely of "imperial bureaucracy," neither Augustus nor his successors ever established a tight administrative grip on their far-flung empire. As in all ancient empires, Roman government tended to be decentralized and limited. In an age in which few public officials received a salary, bribes were winked at.

The Economic and Social Settlement

The old Roman ruling class made its peace with Augustus, but some never forgave him for ending their ancient privileges. The conservative historian Tacitus (TASS-ih-tus) (ca. A.D. 55–117) looked back wistfully to the Late Republic as a golden era of freedom, eloquence, and "the old sound morality." Even Tacitus, however, was forced to admit that most people in the Roman world welcomed and admired the Principate. The reason is simple: Augustus and his

CHRONOLOGY	
31 B.C.	Octavian defeats Antony and Cleopatra at Actium
27 B.C.	Augustus establishes Principate
14 B.C.–A.D. 68	Julio-Claudian dynasty
19 B.C.	Death of Virgil
ca. A.D. 27–30	Ministry of Jesus
ca. 67	Death of Paul of Tarsus
69–96	Flavian dynasty
70	Temple in Jerusalem destroyed
79	Eruption of Vesuvius
96–180	The "Five Good Emperors"
ca. 117	Death of Tacitus
193–235	Severan dynasty
ca. 200	Mishnah and New Testament each completed
212	Almost all free inhabitants of empire awarded Roman citizenship
235–284	Period of military anarchy

Principate The constitutional monarchy of the Early Roman Empire, from 31 B.C. to A.D. 192.

successors brought peace and prosperity after a century of disasters under the Late Republic. The Augustan period enjoyed affluence, especially in Italy; the other provinces caught up with Italy by the second century A.D. Agriculture flourished with the end of civil war. Italian industries became leaders in exports. Italian glass bowls and windowpanes, iron arms and tools, fancy silver eating utensils and candlesticks, and bronze statues and pots circulated from Britain to central Asia.

The city of Rome's urban poor, many of them freedmen, enjoyed a more efficient system of free grain distribution under Augustus and a large increase in games and public entertainment—the imperial policy of "bread and circuses" designed to content the masses. Augustus also set up a major public works program, which provided jobs for the poor. He prided himself on having found Rome "a city of brick" and having left it "a city of marble."

The perennial problem of the Late Republic had been land-hunger, which drove peasants into the arms of ambitious generals. Augustus kept his troops happy by compensating 300,000 veterans with land, money, or both, often in new overseas colonies. At first, he paid from his own private sources; after A.D. 6, he made the rich pay via new taxes. The result kept the peace, but many nonsoldiers in Italy remained poor, as of course, did the huge number of slaves.

As for the renegade commanders who had bedeviled the Late Republic, Augustus cut their potential power base by reducing the size of the army, gradually cutting the number of legions from over sixty to twenty-eight. The total size of the army, including light infantry and cavalry, was about 300,000. This reduction lightened Rome's tax burden but left Augustus with little room to expand the empire. In A.D. 9, Rome lost three legions to a native revolt against Rome's plan to extend its rule in Germany as far east as the Elbe River. Short of manpower, Augustus had to accept the Rhine River as Rome's new German frontier (see **MAP 6.1**).

Imperial defense remained a major issue. Strong Roman armies were a necessity along the hostile European frontier. On the friendlier border in western Asia and northern Africa, Augustus and his immediate successors set up client kingdoms, such as Judea and Armenia, to protect Roman territory.

To promote his ideology of renewal, Augustus sponsored social legislation embodying the old Republican virtues. He passed a series of laws encouraging marriage and childbearing and discouraging promiscuity and adultery. Such legislation was so flagrantly disobeyed that in 2 B.C., Augustus made an example of his own daughter, Julia (39 B.C.–A.D. 14), his only child, whose adulteries were the talk of Rome. As punishment, she was banished to a barren islet.

Augustus's era marks the beginning of the classical period of Roman jurisprudence, during which the professionalism that had begun to mark Roman law in the Late Republic became a permanent fact. It was probably Augustus who established the practice, followed by later emperors, of granting a few distinguished jurists the exclusive right to issue legal opinions "on behalf of the princeps." He ensured, therefore, that experts guided the administration of justice. The first law school was opened in Rome under Augustus. Roman jurists adapted Roman law to the practices of the provinces. Although various local legal systems remained in use, the international system of Roman law was also used widely in the provinces.

In religion, too, Augustus was a legislator and reformer. He restored once-neglected cults and temples in order to appear as Rome's savior. He would probably have approved when, after his death, he was deified, just as Julius Caesar had been. Even while he was still alive, Augustus was worshiped in the provinces as a god—in both the East, where the cult of Roma and Augustus grew in popularity, and the West, where centers of emperor-worship were established at the sites of Lyon and Cologne (see **MAP 6.1**). The imperial cult, an important part of state propaganda until the empire became Christian in the fourth century A.D., was well underway.

Deification, whether formal or informal, was a heady brew, but Augustus deserved it more than most. He not only ended the Late Republican era of civil wars, but established the Roman Empire on a completely new footing. Republican freedom was gone, but the emperor and bureaucrats brought stability. The peace of the Augustan Principate would last, with few interruptions, for two hundred years. Few people in history have created order so successfully.

The Culture of The Augustan Age

Like *Periclean*, the adjective *Augustan* (aw-GUS-tin) has come to signify an era of literary and artistic flowering. In both periods, strong elements of classicism shaped the arts—that is, an attempt to project heroic and idealized values, the values that the rulers of each epoch wished to promote. Both prose and poetry flourished under Augustus. The emperor and his close adviser Maecenas (d. 8 B.C.) were patrons of a number of important poets, chief among them Virgil (70–19 B.C.) and Horace (65–8 B.C.). The historian Livy (59 B.C.–A.D. 17), who wrote his history of Rome from the founding of the city to 9 B.C. under Augustus, also elicited the princeps's interest. All three writers contributed to the Augustan renewal and rededication of Rome.

In many ways, **Virgil** (VER-jill) speaks for his contemporaries. In the *Eclogues*—poems that, following an Alexandrian model (see page 97), have rustic settings—Virgil describes the miseries of the civil wars and the blessings of peace under Augustus. "A god created this peace for us; for he will always be a god to me," one character says. In the Fourth Eclogue, Virgil speaks of the birth of a child to usher in a restored Golden Age. At the Council of Nicaea in A.D. 325 (see page 175) and later, this poem was given a Christian interpretation. In the *Georgics*, Virgil describes the glories of Italian agriculture, which, thanks to Augustus, could be practiced peacefully again.

Virgil's masterpiece is an epic poem, the *Aeneid* (ee-NEE-id), "the story of Aeneas," the legendary Trojan founder of Rome, or at least of the Latin town from which Rome's founders eventually came. Legend also makes Aeneas the ancestor of Augustus. Thus, the *Aeneid* indirectly celebrates Augustus, often considered Rome's second founder. The poem explores the pain and burden, as well as the glory, of empire.

If Virgil's work has the grandeur of marble, Horace's poems—*Odes, Epodes, Satires, Epistles*, and *Ars Poetica* (*Art of Poetry*)—are more like finely cut gems. They tend to be polished, complex, and detached. Like Virgil, Horace explores the themes of war and peace and praises Augustus. "With Caesar [Augustus] holding the lands, I shall fear neither turmoil nor violent death," declares one of the *Odes*. Both Horace and Virgil successfully adapted Greek models and, in the process, created something new. Few writers have had a greater influence on the later Western literary tradition.

Only 35 of the original 142 books of Livy's ambitious history have survived. Livy (LIV-ee) is both a master storyteller and a superb ironist. His anecdotes of Roman history are vivid and told in a grand rhetorical style. Livy is our major source for the Roman monarchy and Early Republic,

Virgil Roman poet whose works, including the *Aeneid*, contributed to the Augustan renewal.

Mosaic of the Doves
This exquisite mosaic shows a number of doves drinking from or positioned around a gilded bronze basin on a marble pedestal. Derived from a Hellenistic work from Pergamum, this mosaic comes from a wealthy house in Pompeii. (Scala/Art Resource, NY)

although his account of early Rome is long on myth and short on fact. Nevertheless, Livy is not merely an entertaining stylist; he engages in frank, subjective judgments intended to inspire both patriotism and reflection on the ironies of history.

Another patron of writers in Augustus's circle was Messalla, himself an orator as well as a statesman. Love poetry was his special interest. Among the poets Messalla supported were Ovid, best known for works on love and mythology; Tibullus, an elegist; and his ward, Sulpicia. Although little survives of Sulpicia's work, more of her work exists than of any other Roman woman. She describes her passion for one Cerinthus: "a worthy man ... at last a love ... of such a kind that my shame, Gossip, would be greater if I kept it covered than if I laid it bare."[1]

Augustus and his entourage were also great patrons of the arts and of architecture, which they considered propaganda tools. They sponsored many major building projects throughout the empire, especially in Rome, which gained temples, a new Forum of Augustus, the Theater of Marcellus, the Baths of Agrippa, the Pantheon, and the Mausoleum of Augustus.

The Julio-Claudians

Under Augustus and his successors, most Romans enjoyed the benefits of stable, effective, and peaceful government. The emperors presented their household to the world as the ideal family, the very model of social order. Behind the walls of the palace, however, dwelt a troubled reality.

Augustus had only one child, Julia, from his first marriage, which ended in divorce. In 38 B.C., Augustus took as his second wife **Livia** (58 B.C.–A.D. 29), who divorced her husband to marry Augustus, even though she was pregnant with their second son. Livia (LI-Vee-uh) did not bear Augustus children. Seeking a male successor, Augustus used Julia as a pawn in a game of dynastic marriage, divorce, and remarriage, but to no avail. Julia's first two husbands both predeceased her, as did two sons, each of whom Augustus had adopted. (In Rome, it was common for a man without a birth son to adopt a son.) In the end, Augustus was forced to choose as successor, and adopt, a man he disliked, Tiberius (ty-BEER-ee-us) (42 B.C.–A.D. 37), Livia's elder son.

Livia was among the most powerful women in Roman history. One of Augustus's main advisers, she pursued her own agenda brutally but deftly in order to secure the succession for Tiberius. Livia's enemies accused her of poisoning many people, including Julia's husbands and sons; her own grandson, Germanicus (a brilliant general whose popularity threatened Tiberius's); and even Augustus himself, who died in bed after a short illness in A.D. 14.

From A.D. 14 to 68, Rome was ruled by other emperors from Augustus's family. The dynasty, known as the **Julio-Claudians**, consisted of Augustus's stepson Tiberius, great-grandson Caligula, grandnephew Claudius, and great-great-grandson Nero. For many elite Romans, this era was one of decadence, scandal, and oppression of the old nobility, but ordinary people continued to enjoy good government.

The reign of Tiberius (r. 14–37) was later remembered by the elite for its treason trials and murders. The senate complained as it steadily lost power to the princeps. The Roman masses grumbled because Tiberius cut back on games and building projects. But despite his shortcomings, Tiberius was a skilled and prudent administrator. He wisely drew back from war on the borders, reduced taxes and spending, and promoted honesty among provincial governors.

His successor, his nephew Gaius (r. 37–41), nicknamed Caligula (ca-LIG-yoo-luh) ("Baby Boots," after the boots he had worn as a little boy in his father's army camp), humiliated the senate. It was bad enough that he tried to have himself declared a living god. On top of that, he appointed his favorite horse not only high priest of a new cult in his honor, but also a member of the senate. Caligula raised taxes and accused people of treason in order to confiscate property. He wanted to have his statue erected in the Temple at Jerusalem, and he would have done so, but he was assassinated first, the victim of a high-level conspiracy. After his death, the senate debated restoring the Republic, but it was not to be.

Caligula's uncle, Claudius, was named emperor by the Praetorian Guard, which forced the senate to support him. Physically handicapped, Claudius (r. 41–54) was often the butt of jokes, but he was a man of substance: a historian, politician, and priest and someone fully versed in the cunning ways of his family. An activist emperor, he expanded the imperial offices with their powerful freedmen; oversaw the construction of an artificial harbor at Rome's silt-clogged port of Ostia; and conquered Britain, where Roman arms had not

Livia Wife of Augustus, she was suspected of poisoning several family members, including Augustus himself.

Julio-Claudians Dynasty of Roman emperors founded by Augustus and ruling from A.D. 14 to 68.

Boudicca's Revolt

What made the British revolt against Rome of A.D. 60–61 famous was its leader—a woman. She was Boudicca, queen of the Iceni people. In the following accounts, two Roman writers, Cassius Dio (ca. A.D. 164–after 229) and Tacitus (ca. A.D. 56–after 117), play up the queen's transgression of gender norms.

Cassius Dio

… a terrible disaster occurred in Britain. Two cities were sacked, eighty thousand of the Romans and of their allies perished, and the island was lost to Rome. Moreover, all this ruin was brought upon the Romans by a woman, a fact which in itself caused them the greatest shame. An excuse for the war was found in the confiscation of the sums of money that Claudius had given to the foremost Britons; for these sums, as Decianus Catus, the procurator of the island, maintained, were to be paid back. This was one reason for the uprising; another was found in the fact that Seneca, in the hope of receiving a good rate of interest, had lent to the islanders 40,000,000 sesterces that they did not want, and had afterwards called in this loan all at once and had resorted to severe measures in exacting it.

… But the person who was chiefly instrumental in rousing the natives and persuading them to fight the Romans, the person who was thought worthy to be their leader and who directed the conduct of the entire war, was Boudicca, a Briton woman of the royal family and possessed of greater intelligence than often belongs to women. … In stature she was very tall, in appearance most terrifying, in the glance of her eye most fierce, and her voice was harsh; a great mass of the tawniest hair fell to her hips; around her neck was a large golden necklace; and she wore a tunic of diverse colors over which a thick mantle was fastened with a brooch. This was her invariable attire.

Tacitus

Prasutagus, king of the Iceni, famed for his long prosperity, had made the emperor his heir along with his two daughters, under the impression that this token of submission would put his kingdom and his house out of the reach of wrong. But the reverse was the result. … First, his wife Boudicca was scourged, and his daughters outraged. … Roused by these insults and the dread of worse, reduced as they now were into the condition of a province, they flew to arms and stirred to revolt the Trinobantes and others who, not yet cowed by slavery, had agreed in secret conspiracy to reclaim their freedom.

…

[After months of revolt, a great battle looms.] Boudicca, with her daughters before her in a chariot, went up to tribe after tribe, protesting that it was indeed usual for Britons to fight under the leadership of women. "But now," she said, "it is not as a woman descended from noble ancestry, but as one of the people that I am avenging lost freedom, my scourged body, the outraged chastity of my daughters. Roman lust has gone so far that not our very persons, nor even age or virginity, are left unpolluted. But heaven is on the side of a righteous vengeance. … They will not sustain even the din and the shout of so many thousands, much less our charge and our blows. If you weigh well the strength of the armies, and the causes of the war, you will see that in this battle you must conquer or die. This is a woman's resolve; as for men, they may live and be slaves."

Nor was Suetonius [the Roman commander] silent at such a crisis. Though he confided in the valour of his men, he yet mingled encouragements and entreaties to disdain the clamours and empty threats of the barbarians. "There," he said, "you see more women than warriors. Unwarlike, unarmed, they will give way the moment they have recognized that sword and that courage of their conquerors, which have so often routed them. … "

[When the battle began, the Romans routed the enemy. Boudicca died shortly thereafter, either because of illness (Cassius Dio) or because she poisoned herself (Tacitus).]

QUESTIONS

1. What impression of Boudicca does each historian offer?
2. How do the two historians differ about the causes of the revolt?
3. What does each account reveal about Roman categories of gender?

Sources: Cassius Dio, *Roman History*, 62.1–2, Loeb Classical Library translation, vol. ix 1925, public domain, http://penelope.uchicago.edu/Thayer/E/Roman/Texts/Cassius_Dio/62*.html; Tacitus, *The Annals*, Translated by Alfred John Church and William Jackson Brodribb, *The Internet Classics Archive*, http://classics.mit.edu/Tacitus/annals.10.xiv.html.

intervened since Julius Caesar's forays in 55 to 54 B.C. (See the feature, "The Written Record: Boudicca's Revolt.")

Claudius's death may have been the result of poisoning by his wife, who was also his niece, Agrippina (a-grip-PIE-nuh) the Younger (15–59); in any case, her son by a previous marriage, Nero, became emperor (r. 54–68). Nero's scandalous behavior rivaled Caligula's, and his treason trials outdid Tiberius's. After a great fire destroyed half of Rome in 64, Nero mounted a big

Agrippina the Younger This statue shows the mother of the emperor Nero praying. It is carved in basanite, a stone whose use is typical of the imperial Roman taste for art objects in exotic materials. (Courtesy, Mondadori Electa S.P.A.)

rebuilding program, including a 300-room villa for himself, and was accused of having started the fire. He found a scapegoat for the fire in the members of a small religious sect, the Christians, whom he persecuted. Ordinary Romans supported Nero because he gave them good government. He was unpopular with the senators and, more serious, with the army, because he failed to pay all his troops promptly. Confronted with a major revolt in 68, Nero committed suicide.

The next year, 69, witnessed Rome's first civil war in about a century. Three men claimed the imperial purple after Nero. A fourth, Vespasian (ves-PAY-zhun) (Titus Flavius Vespasianus, r. 69–79), commander of the army quelling a revolt in the province of Judea, was able to make his claim stick. Peace was restored, but not the rule of Augustus's family. Vespasian founded a new dynasty, the Flavians (r. 69–96), which was followed in turn by the Nervo-Trajanic (r. 96–138) and Antonine (r. 138–192) dynasties. The ultimate tribute to Augustus may be that his regime was stable enough to survive the extinction of his family.

SECTION SUMMARY

- Augustus, Rome's first emperor, shared a degree of power with the senate, while keeping the armies firmly under his control.

- Augustus gave Rome its first civil service and first police force; he gave Italy prosperity; he began to raise the status of the provinces.

- Augustus reduced military spending and compromised with Rome's enemies in order to stabilize the frontiers.

- The poets Virgil and Horace and the historian Livy are among the great writers of the flourishing culture of Augustan Rome.

- Although they included such scandalous figures as Nero, the Julio-Claudian emperors (A.D. 14–68) delivered peaceful and effective government.

THE ROMAN PEACE AND ITS COLLAPSE, A.D. 69–284

What was life like in the era of the Roman peace? Why did peace end during the third century A.D.?

Much about Rome in the second century A.D. appears attractive today. Within the multiethnic empire, opportunities for inhabitants to become part of the elite were increasing. The central government was on its way to granting Roman citizenship to nearly every free person in the empire, a process completed in the year 212. The emperors emphasized sharing prosperity and spreading it through the provinces. Italy was no longer the tyrant of the Mediterranean, but merely first among equals. To be sure, rebellions were crushed, but few people rebelled. This period, known as the **pax Romana**, or "Roman peace," seems particularly golden in contrast with what followed: the disastrous and disordered third century A.D., in which the empire came close to collapse, but survived because of a radical and rigid transformation.

pax Romana   Latin for "Roman peace," the term refers to the period of peace and prosperity in the Roman Empire from A.D. 69 to 180.

The Flavians and the "Good Emperors"

The **Flavian** dynasty of Vespasian (r. 69–79) and his sons Titus (r. 79–81) and Domitian (r. 81–96) provided good government, and their successors built on their achievements. Unlike the Julio-Claudians, Vespasian hailed not from the old Roman nobility, but from an equestrian family from an Italian town. A man of rough-and-ready character, Vespasian is supposed to have replied when Titus complained that a new latrine tax was beneath the dignity of the Roman government, "Son, money has no smell." Unlike his father and brother, Domitian reverted to frequent treason trials and persecution of the aristocracy, which earned him assassination in 96, although the empire as a whole enjoyed peace and sound administration under his reign.

Flavian   Dynasty of the Roman emperors Vespasian, Titus, and Domitian, whose rule was a time of relative peace and good government.

The so-called Five Good Emperors are Nerva (r. 96–98), Trajan (r. 98–117), Hadrian (r. 117–138), and the first two Antonines, Antoninus Pius (r. 138–161) and Marcus Aurelius (r. 161–180). They exemplify the principle of merit. Trajan, a Roman citizen born in Spain, was Rome's first emperor from outside Italy. Hadrian and Marcus Aurelius also came from Spain, and Antoninus Pius from Gaul. Each of the Five Good Emperors, except Marcus Aurelius, adopted the most competent person, rather than the closest relative, as his son and successor, thus elevating duty over sentiment. Marcus Aurelius, a deeply committed Stoic, gave full vent to his sense of duty in his *Meditations*, which he wrote in Greek while living in a tent on the Danube frontier, where he fought long and hard against German raids. Antoninus was surnamed "Pius" (Dutiful) because he was devoted to his country, the gods, and his adoptive father, Hadrian.

The Five Good Emperors made humaneness and generosity the themes of their reigns. Trajan, for example, founded a program of financial aid for the poor children of Italy. They also went to great lengths to care for the provinces. These emperors not only commonly received petitions from cities, associations, and individuals in far-off provinces, but answered them. Yet, humaneness does not mean softness. Hadrian, for instance, ordered a revolt in Judea (132–135) to be suppressed with great brutality.

Like the Julio-Claudians, the Five Good Emperors advertised their wives to the world as exemplars of traditional modesty, self-effacement, and domesticity. In fact, they were often worldly, educated, and influential. Trajan's wife, Plotina, for example (d. 121 or 123), acted as patron of the Epicurean school at Athens, whose philosophy she claimed to follow. She advised her husband on provincial administration as well as dynastic matchmaking. Hadrian's wife, Sabina, traveled in her husband's entourage to Egypt (130), where her aristocratic Greek friend, Julia Balbilla, commemorated the trip by writing Greek poetry, which she had inscribed alongside other tourists' writings on the leg of one of two statues of Amenhotep III at Thebes.

A darker side of the second century empire was the problem of border defense. Augustus and the Julio-Claudians had established client kingdoms where possible, to avoid the expense and political dangers of raising armies. The emperors of the day tended to be more aggressive on the borders than their predecessors. They moved from client kingdoms to a new border policy of stationary frontier defense. Expensive fortification systems of walls, watchtowers, and trenches were built along the perimeter of the empire's border and manned with guards. A prominent example is Hadrian's Wall, which separated Roman Britain from the enemy tribes to the north. Stretching 80 miles, the wall required fifteen thousand defense troops.

The most ambitious frontier policy was that of Trajan, who crossed the Danube to carve out the new province of Dacia (modern Romania) and who used an excuse to invade Parthian Mesopotamia. He won battles as far away as the Persian Gulf, but he lost the war. As soon as his army left, Mesopotamia rose in revolt, followed by Germany. Trajan's reign marked the empire's greatest geographic extent, but Trajan had overextended Rome's resources. When he died, his successor, Hadrian, had to abandon Trajan's province of Mesopotamia (see **Map 6.1**).

Prosperity and Romanization in the Provinces

Compared with a modern economy, the Roman economy was underdeveloped. Most people worked in agriculture, employed primitive technology, and lived at a subsistence level. Even so, the Roman Empire experienced modest economic growth during the first two centuries A.D. The chief beneficiaries were the wealthy few, but ordinary people shared in the economic expansion. In addition to stability and peace, several other factors encouraged economic development. The western provinces witnessed the opening of new lands to agriculture, where improved techniques were applied, thereby meeting increased agricultural demand from the growing cities of the region. Changes in Roman law aided commerce by making it easier to employ middlemen in business transactions. Travel and communications were relatively easy and inexpensive.

PROSPERITY Trade boomed, as an archaeological discovery in the Italian city of Pisa (PEE-zuh) recalls. Nineteen Hellenistic and Roman ships were found at the site of the ancient harbor, beginning in 1999. Several are merchant ships, both coastal freighters and small harbor craft. One of the ships was filled with amphoras (storage jars), still stacked in neat rows and filled with wine and sand. Both of those goods came from the region of the Bay of Naples, whose sand was used for concrete that could set underwater. The finds, which seem to date from the mid-second century A.D., offer a vivid picture of trade along the coast of Italy. When the cargo was unloaded at Pisa, the ships probably picked up the local grain and marble, which was shipped in turn to Rome.

Rome was an economic magnet, but so, to a lesser extent, were all cities, and the second century A.D. was a great age of city life. New cities were founded far from the Mediterranean. They began as veterans' colonies, market towns, and even army camps, and some grew into cities of permanent importance in European history: Cologne (Colonia Claudia Agrippinensis), Paris (Lutetia Parisiorum), Lyon (Lugdunum), London (Londinium), Mérida (Emerita Augusta), Vienna (Vindobona), and Budapest (Aquincum).

Whether old or new, cities attracted large elite populations. In the Principate, ambitious people wanted to live in great cities, in emulation of the greatest city of the empire, Rome, which was by Augustus's day a city of perhaps a million people. In cities, men competed for positions as magistrates, in imitation of the two consuls, or for seats on the local town council, often called a *curia* (KYOO-ree-uh), like the senate in Rome. Town councilors were called *decurions* (day-KYOO-ree-uns) and known collectively as the *curial order.* Decurions played one-upmanship in sponsoring public buildings in the Roman style—one man endowing a new forum, another a triumphal arch, a third a library, a fourth an amphitheater, and so on. From Ephesus in Anatolia to Colchester in Britain, from Mainz in Germany to Leptis Magna in Libya, a Roman could find familiar government institutions, architecture, and street plans.

Unlike men, women did not usually hold magistracies, but wealthy women of the empire could and did lavish money on public projects. Women endowed temples and synagogues, amphitheaters and monumental gateways, games and ceremonies. They were rewarded with wreaths, front-row seats, statues, priesthoods, and inscriptions honoring them as "most distinguished lady," "patron," and even "father of the city."

Double Portrait, Pompeii   This wall painting from a house joined to a bakery depicts a married couple, possibly the wealthy baker P. Paquius Proculus and his wife. The portraiture is realistic. The couple carries symbols of education: She holds wax tablets and a stylus (pen), while he grasps a sealed scroll.   (Scala/Art Resource, NY)

The buildings were visible examples of Romanization, although the Romans did not use the term. If they had, it would have had a limited meaning because the emperors neither would nor could impose a cultural uniformity on their subjects. The empire was too big and ancient technology too primitive for that. The total population of the empire consisted of between 50 million and 100 million people, most of whom lived in the countryside. The small and largely urbanized Roman administration had little direct contact with most people. So, for example, only a minority of the inhabitants of the empire spoke Latin; in the East, Greek was the more common language of administration. Millions of people spoke neither Greek nor Latin. Celtic, Germanic, Punic, Tamazight (Berber), Coptic, Aramaic, and Syriac were other common languages in Roman domains. In short, the empire lacked the unity of a modern nation-state.

What, then, besides buildings and language might "Romanization" entail? One index has already been suggested: the participation of provincials in the central government, even as emperor. By around A.D. 200, for example, about 15 percent of the known Roman equestrians and senators came from North Africa. By this time, the senate was no longer dominated by Italians, but was representative of the empire as a whole.

Participation in government implies another index of Romanization—the extension of Roman citizenship outside Italy to magistrates, decurions, or even whole cities. Citizens took Roman names reflecting the emperor or Roman official who had enfranchised them. Thus, the provinces were full of Julii, Claudii, and Flavii, among others.

The spread of Roman customs is another measure of Romanization. For example, the gladiatorial shows that Romans loved became popular from Antioch to England. Combats between gladiators advertised both Roman culture and Roman brutality. (See the feature, "The Visual Record: Gladiators.")

By the same token, native customs might be adopted by Romans. Consider the case of Egypt, where, in the late 1990s, archaeologists discovered a vast Roman-era cemetery about 230 miles southwest of Cairo, in the Bahriya Oasis. The population was Romanized here. Yet, the cemetery, with its dozens of gilded mummies from the first and second centuries A.D., shows the persistence of the mummification processes of the pharaohs.

Another ambiguous symbol of Romanization is found in A.D. 212. In a law known as the *Constitutio Antoniana*, the emperor Caracalla (r. 211–217) rendered nearly all of the free inhabitants of the empire Roman citizens. On the one hand, the law is a historical landmark. Near-universal Roman citizenship was a kind of halfway point between ancient empire and modern mass democracy. On the other hand, the *Constitutio Antoniana* was something of a gimmick. It was probably less an instrument of unification than of taxation, for citizens had a heavier tax burden than noncitizens.

The Roman army, by contrast, did promote Romanization. In antiquity, as today, military service offered education and social mobility. Only citizens could join the legions; non-Romans served as auxiliaries. They received Roman citizenship after completing their regular term of service, twenty-five years. Non-Italians had, and took, the opportunity to rise high in the army or government. This was all to Rome's credit. Yet, as Italians became a minority in the Roman army, and as ever larger numbers of frontier peoples were recruited, it became conceivable that someday the army might abandon its loyalty to Rome.

Roman Law on Class and Marriage

Roman law is one of the ancient world's most influential and enduring legacies. Logical, practical, orderly, and—within the limits of a society of patriarchal fathers and of slaves and masters—relatively fair, Roman law has influenced the legal systems of most Western countries and many non-Western countries. The law governing Roman citizens was called *ius civile*, or "civil law." Originally, this term covered a very broad range of legal matters, but in the empire, its meaning was narrowed to private matters. Criminal law became a separate category.

The law helped Rome administer its empire. Roman law was not universal, and noncitizens continued to use their own laws for local matters, but the governors used Roman law to run their provinces, so local elites became familiar with it. Like so many Roman customs, the law was both hierarchical and flexible. Let us consider two areas in which the law affected daily life: class and marriage.

The law reflected Roman society's ingrained social inequality. Traditional classes, such as senators and equestrians, survived to be joined by the new distinction between citizens and noncitizens. Even when all free people became Roman citizens, another important division maintained

Gladiators

Historians and novelists write about them, filmmakers portray them, revolutionaries salute them, and a few years ago, television athletes claimed to be American updates of them. They are gladiators, literally men who carried a gladius, or sword. They fought to the death as entertainment, and they enraptured the Roman Empire.

Gladiators took part in so-called games or combat before large crowds. Armed with various specialized weapons, they fought each other and sometimes wild animals. Some unfortunates were thrust into fights with no weapons at all. The audience, seated in rank order, ranged from slaves to senators to the emperor himself. There was nothing tame about what they had come to see. Consider the word *arena*, referring to the site of the games. It literally means "sand," which is what covered the floor—and soaked up the blood.

Our fascination with the gladiator is nothing compared to the Romans'. Everybody in Rome talked about gladiators. At **Pompeii**, graffiti celebrated a star of the arena whom "all the girls sigh for." Jokes poked fun at gladiators, philosophers pondered their meaning, and literature is full of references to them.

Gladiatorial images decorated art around the empire, from mosaics to household lamps. Look at this mosaic from a Roman villa in Germany, one of several mosaic panels on the floor of the building's entrance hall, depicting scenes from the arena. The illustration shows a *retiarius*, or net-and-trident bearer, fighting a better-armed *secutor*, literally "pursuer," under the watchful eyes of a *lanista*, or trainer. As was typical, the retiarius wears no armor except for a shoulder piece protecting his left side. To defend himself against the dagger wielded by the secutor (in the mosaic, hidden behind the shield), the retiarius had to be fit enough to be able to keep moving. The difference between various types of gladiators would have been as obvious to a Roman as the difference between a catcher and a pitcher is to a baseball fan today.

As for the amphitheaters where gladiatorial combats took place, they were as common in Italy and the Roman Empire as skyscrapers are in a modern city. Look, for example, at this photograph of the amphitheater in the city of El Djem in modern Tunisia (the Roman province of Africa). Built of high-quality local stone in the third century A.D., the structure was meant to have sixty-four arches, but it was never

Roman Amphitheater, El Djem, Tunisia   (Adina Tovy/Robert Harding World Imagery)

completed. The openings in the floor permitted animals to be released into the arena. A large amphitheater like this one held at least thirty thousand spectators, and the largest amphitheater of all, the Flavian Amphitheater—or Colosseum—at Rome, seated around fifty thousand. Amphitheaters were less common in the east, but the fans there also were loyal, so the games went on—in theaters.

Most gladiators were condemned criminals, prisoners of war, or slaves bought for the purpose. The most famous slave gladiator was Spartacus, a Thracian. Along with seventy-seven other gladiators in the Italian city of Capua, Spartacus instigated a slave rebellion that attracted thousands and shook Italy for two years (73–71 B.C.).

Yet, some gladiators were free men who volunteered for a limited term of service. Once even the emperor Commodus (r. 180–192) served, to the disgust of other Roman nobles, who found the arena fascinating but low-class. The gladiator was part warrior, part athlete, part showman, and part butcher. Yet, there was something of the pagan priest in the gladiator, too, for his was a solemn profession. Every gladiator took an oath to endure being burned, bound, beaten, and killed by the sword. They began each combat by greeting the official in charge (in Rome, the emperor) in this way: "We who are about to die salute you."

Students of the Romans find it hard to believe that they adored such a murderous sport, in which dozens and occasionally hundreds of men might die in a single day, to the roar of the crowds. Yet, perhaps the arena makes us uncomfortable not so much because it is foreign, but because it is familiar. Although we no longer flock to games in which men kill each other, we do go in droves to blood sports such as boxing, and we pack hockey rinks to watch men regularly give each other concussions. Modern people no longer kill animals in the arena for sport, but we hunt, fish, go on big-game safaris, watch cockfights, and, in Spain, kill bulls and occasionally get killed by them.

Besides, perhaps our discomfort reflects our instinctive understanding of the symbolism of the arena. The games were brutal, but so was the empire. Rome had brought peace to three continents, but it had done so by brandishing a sword, and it kept the peace by its readiness to fight. The arena kept Romans tough and warlike, or so an intellectual could argue, as does Pliny the Younger, who describes gladiatorial games:

[The games] inspired a glory in wounds and a contempt of death, since the love of praise and desire for victory could be seen, even in the bodies of slaves and criminals. (*Panegyric* 33)

Arguably, the arena also contributed to public order. This was no small achievement, since the imperial army could not police a population of 50 million to 100 million, and few places had even the elementary police force that the city of Rome did. The violence that bloodied the amphitheater stepped into the breach by reminding criminals—or those defined as criminals—what punishment awaited

Gladiator Mosaic, Nennig, Germany (Bildarchive Preussischer Kulturbesitz/Art Resource, NY)

them. Rob or kill, and you might end up in the arena. Refuse to worship the emperor, and you might be fed to the lions, as Christians were from time to time. Rebel against Rome, and you might find yourself on a chain gang building a new amphitheater, as tradition says thirty thousand prisoners of the First Jewish Revolt (A.D. 66–70) did. The result was the Colosseum.*

Occasionally pagan, as well as Christian, writers condemned gladiatorial games. Seneca the Younger (ca. 4 B.C.–A.D. 65), for example, criticized them for inciting greed, aggression, and cruelty. Yet, so popular was Rome's theater of power that gladiators and their games were not abolished until around A.D. 400.

QUESTIONS

1. What does the scene on the mosaic show, and what does it indicate about the Roman public's interest in gladiators?

2. What were the main features of the amphitheater at El Djem?

3. How might gladiatorial games have contributed to public order in the Roman Empire?

---

* The preceding two paragraphs lean heavily on the fine discussion in Colin Wells, *The Roman Empire*, 2d ed. (Cambridge, Mass.: Harvard University Press, 1995), pp. 248–255.

class distinctions: the division between *honestiores* (in general, the curial order) and *humiliores* (everyone else). Previously, Roman citizens enjoyed certain privileges, such as exemption from flogging by officials, but now citizens who were *humiliores* tended to lose those privileges.

The most basic legal distinction was that between free and slave—and the empire contained millions of slaves. A third category, ex-slaves or freedmen, also became increasingly important. Freedmen owed service to their former masters, who became their patrons. A few freedmen grew rich in commerce or wielded enough power in imperial administration to lord it over even Roman aristocrats. The result was strong elite hostility toward freedmen, which is often reflected in Roman literature. Witness the stereotype of the vulgar freedman, embodied in Trimalchio in the *Satyricon* (suh-TEER-uh-con), a novel by Petronius (first century A.D.). Trimalchio had more estates than he could remember and so much money that his wife counted it by the bushel-load.

As regards marriage, Roman family law was strict and severe in principle. In practice, however, it often proved pragmatic and even humane, as demonstrated by three cases: elite marriages, slave marriages, and soldiers' marriages.

As in the Late Republic, so in the Early Empire, most Roman women married without legally becoming members of their husbands' families—or their children's. This gave women a degree of freedom from their husbands, but it left elite women, who owned property, with a problem: Technically that property was controlled by their fathers or brothers. Yet, society recognized a woman's wish to leave her property to her children, and imperial law increasingly made it possible for her to do so—although the conservative Romans waited until the sixth century A.D. before abolishing completely the rights of greedy uncles. Another case is a mother's right to have a say in her children's choice of marriage partner. This maternal prerogative became accepted social practice, even though Roman law gave women no such right.

Roman slaves married and had children, but they had to do so in the face of both legal and practical obstacles. Roman law gave slaves no right to marry, and it made slave children the property of the owner of the slave mother. Owners could and did break up slave families by sale. Even if a slave was freed, the law expressed far more concern with the continuing obligations

Roman Slaves   This first-century A.D. wall-painting from Herculaneum, Italy shows Roman ladies with their slave hairdressers. Note the elaborate hairstyle of the seated woman.   (Erich Lessing/Art Resource, NY)

of freedmen to their former masters than with the rights of slave families. Yet, during the Early Empire, cracks appeared in the wall of law that allowed slave families to slip through.

For example, although the law insisted that a slave be age 30 before being freed, it made an exception for an owner who wished to free a female slave younger than 30 in order to marry her. To take another example, the law conceded that slave children owed devotion and loyalty (*pietas*) to their slave parents.

Career soldiers, from at least the time of Augustus on, could not marry, probably on the grounds of military discipline. Yet, many soldiers cohabited anyhow, often with noncitizen women in the areas where they served, and frequently, children were the result. Not until the reign of Septimius Severus (SEH-ver-us) (r. 193–211) were soldiers permitted to marry formally, and then, only after twenty-five years of service. Yet, commanders had permitted cohabitation for two centuries, and the law too made concessions now and then. For example, the Flavians gave soldiers a degree of freedom to make wills, which could allow them to leave property to illegitimate children. Various emperors gave soldiers the privilege, on discharge, to legalize a marriage with a noncitizen, which ordinary Romans were not permitted to do.[2]

The Culture of the Roman Peace

In Latin poetry, the century or so after the death of Augustus (roughly A.D. 18–133) is often referred to as the "Silver Age," a term sometimes applied to prose as well. The implication is that this period, though productive, fell short of the golden Augustan era. It might be fairer to say that the self-confidence of the Augustan writers did not last. As the permanence of monarchy became clear, many in the elite looked back to the Republic with nostalgia and bitterness. Silver Age writing often takes refuge in satire or rhetorical flourish.

The Silver Age was an era of interest in antiquities and in compiling handbooks and encyclopedias; it was also an era of self-consciousness and literary criticism. In the first two centuries A.D., Roman writers came from an ever greater diversity of backgrounds and wrote for an ever wider audience, as prosperity and educational opportunities increased.

Many writers of the era pursued public careers, which offered access to patronage. The historian **Tacitus**, for instance, became governor of the province of Asia. Prominent literary families emerged, such as that of Pliny (PLIH-nee) the Elder (A.D. 23–79), an encyclopedic author on natural science, geography, history, and art; and his nephew, Pliny the Younger (ca. A.D. 62–ca. 113), an orator and letter writer. The most notable literary family is that of Seneca the Elder (ca. 55 B.C.–A.D. 40), a historian and scholar of rhetoric; his son, Seneca the Younger (ca. 4 B.C.–A.D. 65); and Seneca the Younger's nephew, the epic poet Lucan (A.D. 39–65).

Tacitus Roman historian of the "Silver Age," his greatest works were *The Histories* and *The Annals*.

Born in Cordoba, Spain, the younger Seneca moved at an early age to Rome, where he became a successful lawyer and investor. He was banished in A.D. 41 for alleged adultery with a sister of Caligula. Recalled in 49, he was tutor to the young Nero. When Nero became emperor in 54, Seneca became one of his chief advisers and helped bring good government to the empire. Seneca eventually fell out of favor, however, and was forced first into retirement and then, in A.D. 65, into suicide. He had been the major literary figure of his age, a jack-of-all-trades: playwright, essayist, pamphleteer, student of science, and noted Stoic philosopher.

A literary career was safer under the Five Good Emperors. Consider Tacitus and his contemporary, the poet Juvenal (JOO-veh-nal) (ca. A.D. 55–130). Juvenal's *Satires* are bitter and brilliant poems offering social commentary. He laments the past, when poverty and war had supposedly kept Romans chaste and virtuous. Amid "the woes of long peace," he says, luxury and foreign ways had corrupted Rome. Like many a critic who blames society's troubles on marginal groups, Juvenal launches harsh attacks on women and foreigners. Tacitus, too, is sometimes scornful of women.

Yet, if he is biased on matters of gender, Tacitus is far from ethnocentric. Few historians have expressed graver doubts about the value of their country's alleged success. For example, Tacitus highlighted the simple virtues of the Germanic tribes, so different from the sophisticated decadence of contemporary Rome. Nostalgia for the Republic pervades his two greatest works, *The Histories*, which covers the civil wars of A.D. 69, and *The Annals* (only parts of which survive), chronicling the emperors from Tiberius through Nero. A masterpiece of irony and pithiness, Tacitus's style makes an unforgettable impression on the reader.

Plutarch (PLOO-tark) (ca. A.D. 50–120), whose *Parallel Lives of Noble Greeks and Romans* later captured the imagination of Shakespeare, is probably the best-known pagan writer of the first two centuries A.D. Plutarch was a Roman citizen from Greece who wrote in Greek. Like Livy, Plutarch emphasizes the moral and political lessons of history. A careful scholar, Plutarch found his true calling in rhetorical craftsmanship—polished speeches and carefully chosen anecdotes. As in Rome, rhetoric was the basis of much of Greek literary culture in this period.

Another star of Greek culture at this time was the physician Galen of Pergamum (A.D. 129–?199). In his many writings, Galen (GAY-len) was to medicine what Aristotle had been to philosophy: a brilliant systematizer and an original thinker. He excelled in anatomy and physiology and proved that the arteries, as well as the veins, carry blood. He was destined to have a dominant influence on European medicine in the Middle Ages.

The Crisis of the Third Century, A.D. 235–284

Leaving the relative calm of the second century A.D. behind, the third century Roman Empire descended into crisis. Barbarian invasions, domestic economic woes, plague, assassinations, brigandage, urban decline—the list of Rome's problems is dramatic. The empire went "from a kingdom of gold to one of iron and rust," as one writer put it, summing up Roman history after the death of Marcus Aurelius in 180, when the seeds of the **third-century crisis** were sown.

third-century crisis Period from A.D. 235 to 284, when the Roman Empire suffered barbarian invasions, domestic economic problems, plague, assassinations, and urban decline.

Stability first began to slip away during the reign of the last of the Antonines, Marcus Aurelius's birth son, Commodus (KOM-uh-dus) (r. 180–192), a man with Nero's taste for decadence and penchant for terrorizing the senatorial elite. His predictable assassination led to civil war, after which Septimius Severus, commander of the Danube armies, emerged as the unchallenged emperor (r. 193–211). He founded the Severan dynasty, which survived until 235.

Severan reformers attempted to reestablish the empire on a firmer footing, but they only brought the day of crisis nearer. The main theme of Septimius's reign was the transfer of power—from the senate to the army and from Italy to the provinces. To extend the Roman frontier in North Africa and western Asia, Septimius expanded the army and improved the pay and conditions of service. These measures might have been necessary, but Septimius went too far by indulging in war with Parthia (197–199)—unnecessary war, because the crumbling Parthian

Hadrian's Wall   Built in A.D. 122–126, this extensive structure protected Roman England from raids by the tribes of Scotland. It represents the strategy of stationary frontier defense.   (Roy Rainford/Robert Harding World Imagery)

Syria Between Rome and Persia

Rome and Persia fought three great battles in western Asia in A.D. 244, 252, and 260, all resounding victories for Persia under King Shapur I (r. ca. 241–272). In the first selection Shapur celebrates his success in an inscription carved in rock near Persepolis. The second selection provides a Greek view of what Syria's inhabitants endured when Shapur "burned, ruined and pillaged" in A.D. 252. It comes from the Thirteenth Sibylline Oracle, a verse commentary on contemporary events, purporting to be ancient prophecy.

The Persian Inscription

I, the Mazda worshipping lord Shapur, king of kings of Iran and non-Iran, whose lineage is from the Gods. . . .

When at first we had become established in the empire, Gordian Caesar raised in all of the Roman Empire a force from the Goth and German realms and marched on Babylonia against the Empire of Iran and against us. On the border of Babylonia at Misikhe, a great "frontal" battle occurred. Gordian Caesar was killed and the Roman force was destroyed. And the Romans made Philip Caesar. Then Philip Caesar came to us for terms, and to ransom their lives, gave us 500,000 denars, and became tributary to us. . . .

And Caesar lied again and did wrong to Armenia. Then we attacked the Roman Empire and annihilated at Barbalissos a Roman force of 60,000 and Syria and the environs of Syria we burned, ruined and pillaged all. In this one campaign we conquered of the Roman Empire fortresses and towns . . . a total of 37 towns with surroundings.

In the third campaign when we attacked Carrhae and Urhai [Edessa] and were besieging Carrhae and Edessa Valerian Caesar marched against us. He had with him a force of 70,000. . . .

And beyond Carrhae and Edessa we had a great battle with Valerian Caesar. We made prisoner ourselves with our own hands Valerian Caesar and the others, chiefs of that army, the praetorian prefect, senators; we made all prisoners and deported them to Persis.

And Syria, Cilicia and Cappadocia we burned, ruined and pillaged. . . .

And men of the Roman Empire, of non-Iranians, we deported. We settled them in the Empire of Iran. . . .

We searched out for conquest many other lands, and we acquired fame for heroism, which we have not engraved here, except for the preceding. We ordered it written so that whoever comes after us may know this fame, heroism, and power of us.

The Sibylline Oracle

. . . the evil Persians. . . .

. . . the Persians, arrogant men. . . .

. . . the arrow-shooting Persians . . . Now for you, wretched Syria, I have lately been piteously lamenting; a blow will befall you from the arrow-shooting men, terrible, which you never thought would come to you. The fugitive of Rome will come, waving a great spear; crossing the Euphrates with many myriads, he will burn you, he will dispose all things evilly. Alas, Antioch, they will never call you a city when you have fallen under the spear in your folly; he will leave you entirely ruined and naked, houseless, uninhabited; anyone seeing you will suddenly break out weeping. . . .

Alas . . . they will leave ruin as far as the borders of Asia, stripping the cities, taking the statues of all and razing the temples down to the all-nourishing earth.

QUESTIONS

1. According to Shapur's inscription, what were Rome's misdeeds toward Persia? According to the *Sibylline Oracle*, what were Persia's misdeeds toward Rome?

2. How did Persia retaliate, according to Shapur's inscription and according to the *Sibylline Oracle*? How and why do the two accounts differ?

3. Which account do you find more convincing? Why?

Source: Inscription: Richard N. Frye, trans., *History of Ancient Iran* (Munich: C. H. Beck's che Verlagsbuchhandlung, 1984), pp. 371–372. Reprinted by permission of Richard N. Frye. Oracle: D. S. Potter, trans., *Prophecy and History in the Crisis of the Roman Empire* (Oxford: Clarendon Press, 1990), p. 175.

---

kingdom was too weak to threaten Rome. What the war did accomplish, however, was to inspire the enemy's rejuvenation under a new Eastern dynasty, the **Sassanids** (SASS-uh-nids).

The Sassanid Persians spearheaded increased pressure on Rome's frontiers. The Sassanids overran Rome's eastern provinces and captured the emperor Valerian himself in 260. (See the feature, "The Global Record: Syria Between Rome and Persia.") The caravan city of Palmyra (in Syria) took advantage of Rome's weakness to establish independence; its most famous leader was the queen Zenobia. Meanwhile, three Germanic tribes, the Alamanni, the Franks, and the Goths, hammered the empire from the north.

Fending off invasions at opposite fronts stretched Rome to the breaking point. To pay for defense, the emperors devalued the currency, but the result was massive inflation. As if this were not bad enough, a plague broke out in Egypt at midcentury and raged through the empire for fifteen years, compounding Rome's military manpower problems.

Sassanids A Persian dynasty (A.D. 224–651) that greatly strengthened Persian power and threatened Roman rule in western Asia.

Assassinations and civil wars shook the stability of the government. Between 235—when the last Severan emperor, Severus Alexander, was murdered—and 284, twenty men were emperor, however briefly in some cases. Civilians suffered in the resulting disorder.

SECTION SUMMARY

- The Flavian dynasty (A.D. 69-96) and the so-called Five Good Emperors (96-180) brought Rome a long era of stability and good government.

- A modest prosperity, an upturn in trade, and a flourishing city life all characterized the Roman Empire of the first two centuries A.D.

- Most of the empire's 50-100 million inhabitants lived in the countryside and had little contact with Rome, but the urban elite often adopted Roman ways.

- Pragmatic, orderly, and relatively fair, Roman law is one of antiquity's great legacies.

- The historian Tacitus, the poet Juvenal, the essayist and scholar Plutarch, and the man of letters and philosophy Seneca the Younger are among the great writers of Rome's so-called Silver Age.

- Invasions, plague, inflation, crime, and political assassination were among the many woes that made the third century A.D. a period of crisis for the Roman Empire.

Yet, the empire rebounded, which is a tribute to Roman resilience as well as a sign of the disunity and lack of staying power among the empire's enemies. Recovery began during the reign of Gallienus (r. 253-268), who instituted a series of reforms. Gallienus excluded senators from high military commands and replaced them with professionals. Moreover, he began a new, more modest policy of border defense. The Romans now conceded much of the frontier to the enemy and shifted to a defensive mode: Fortified cities near the frontier served as bases from which to prevent deeper enemy penetration into Roman territory. They also concentrated mobile armies at strategic points in the rear, moving them where needed. Thanks to his new policies, Gallienus inflicted defeats on the Alamanni and the Goths. By 275, Aurelian (r. 270-275) had checked the Goths decisively and reconquered the eastern provinces, including Palmyra.

Gallienus's new military and border policies pointed the way to imperial reorganization, but they remained to be completed by the two great reforming emperors at the end of the third century and the beginning of the fourth: Diocletian (r. 284-305) and Constantine (r. 306-337), subjects of the next chapter. When their work was done, the new Roman Empire of Late Antiquity might have been barely recognizable to a citizen of the Principate.

EARLY CHRISTIANITY

What were the origins of Christianity, and how did it fare among the other religions of the Roman world?

Increasing contact between Rome and its western provinces served to plant Roman cities, Roman law, and the Latin language (or its derivatives) in western Europe. As Rome, in turn, owed much to other Mediterranean peoples, so the Roman Empire transported ancient Mediterranean civilization to northern and western Europe. No feature of that civilization was to have a greater historical impact than the religion born in Tiberius's reign: Christianity.

Christianity began in the provincial backwater of Palestine among the Jews, whose language, Aramaic, was understood by few in Rome. It immediately spread to speakers of the two main languages of the empire, Greek and Latin, and the new movement addressed the common spiritual needs of the Roman world. By the reign of Diocletian, Christians had grown from Jesus's twelve original followers to perhaps millions, despite government persecution (see **MAP 6.2** on page 159). In the fourth century A.D., Christianity unexpectedly became the official religion of the entire Roman Empire, replacing polytheism—one of the most momentous changes in Mediterranean history. We turn to that change in the next chapter; here we consider the career of Jesus and the early spread of the Christian Gospel (literally, "Good Tidings"). But first, to set the stage, we look at other religions of the Roman Empire.

Mystery Religions

The Romans were polytheists. They did not try to impose one religion on the empire. Instead, Romans were usually willing to accept new gods, as long as their worshipers took part in the patriotic emperor cult. New religions spread widely during the first three centuries A.D. Besides Christianity and Judaism, the most important religions were Greek mystery cults, the cults of Isis and Mithras, and Manichaeism. These religions displayed a tendency toward syncretism, often borrowing rites, doctrines, and symbols from one another.

Greek mystery cults included the cults of Dionysus, the god of wine, and of Demeter, the goddess of grain, who was worshiped at annual ceremonies at Eleusis, a town outside Athens. The "mystery" consisted of secret rites revealed only to initiates. In the case of Demeter, the rites apparently had something to do with the promise of eternal life.

The cult of Isis derived from the ancient Egyptians' worship of Isis (see page 105), her brother and husband, Osiris, and their son, Horus. Like the cult of Demeter, its central theme was eternal life, through resurrection achieved by moral behavior in this life. Isis, the "Goddess of Ten Thousand Names," was portrayed as a loving mother, and elements of Isis were later syncretized in the cult of the Virgin Mary. Isis's followers marched in colorful, and at times terrifying, parades through Roman streets, flagellating themselves as a sign of penitence.

Although men joined in the worship of Isis, the cult appealed particularly to women. The goddess's popularity crossed class lines; devotees ranged from slaves to one Julia Felix, whose estate at Pompeii included a garden shrine to Isis and Egyptian statuettes. By contrast, the worship of Mithras (MYTH-rus) was dominated by men, and especially by soldiers. Mithras, a heroic Persian god of light and truth, also promised eternal life. His worshipers believed that Mithras had captured and killed a sacred bull, whose blood and body were the source of life. Accordingly, Mithraism focused on bull sacrifice carried out in a vaulted, cavelike temple called a *Mithraeum*. Initiates were baptized with bull blood and participated in various other rituals, among them a sacramental meal. Their moral code advised imitating the life of their hero.

Manichaeism (MAN-ih-kee-izm) also originated in Persia, but later, in the third century A.D. Its founder, the Persian priest Mani, was martyred by conservative religious authorities. Manichaeism attempted to be the true synthesis of the religious beliefs of the period, recognizing not only Jesus, but also Zoroaster and Buddha, as prophets. The main tenet of Manichaeism was philosophical dualism, which emphasized the universal struggle between good (Light) and evil (Darkness). According to believers, the world had been corrupted by Darkness, but eventually the Light would return. In the meantime, good Manichaeans were to attempt to lead pure lives. Manichaeism was a powerful religious force for two centuries, and its believers were spread as far as India. The great theologian Augustine even flirted with it before becoming a Christian.

A new philosophy that developed in the same intellectual world as these Roman religions was Neo-Platonism (nee-oh-PLAY-ton-ism), which was founded by Plotinus (ploh-TIE-nus) (A.D. 209–270). Using the works of Plato as a starting point, Plotinus developed a philosophy in which the individual could first seek inner unity and then achieve oneness with the supreme unity of what Plotinus called the One or the Good. By this, he meant an intangible and impersonal force that is the source of all values. Like the mystery cults, Plotinus's philosophy promised a kind of salvation. Neo-Platonism was destined to have a great influence on Western thought.

Jesus of Nazareth

Christianity begins with **Jesus of Nazareth**. For all its historical importance, Jesus' life is poorly documented. The main source of information about it is the New Testament books of Matthew, Mark, Luke, and John. Jesus left no writings of his own. Early Christians, however, wrote a great deal. Between the second and fourth centuries A.D., Christians settled on a holy book consisting of both the Hebrew Bible, called the "Old Testament" by Christians, and a collection of writings about Jesus and his followers, called the "New Testament." The four **Gospels** provide commanding accounts, but they do not agree on all details. The Gospel according to Mark, probably the earliest Gospel, was most likely written about forty years after Jesus' crucifixion; several of the letters written by Paul of Tarsus (see pages 161–162) date from the 40s A.D.; and the earliest non-Christian sources are later in date and are scanty.

No personality has generated as much discussion among Western scholars as has Jesus. Many would distinguish the Jesus of theology, the object of faith, from the Jesus of history, the man who really lived in first century Palestine. Recent work argues that the historical Jesus must be understood within the Judaism of his day—or rather the Judaisms, because it was an era of debate and disagreement about how to be a Jew. Within two centuries, the lines hardened. By A.D. 200, two new religions had emerged: Orthodox Christianity and **rabbinic Judaism**. The

Jesus of Nazareth
Founder of Christianity. To his followers, he was Christ, "the anointed one," foretold in the Hebrew Bible as the redeemer of Israel who would initiate the kingdom of heaven.

Gospels One of the four canonical, that is, authoritative books of the New Testament that describes the birth, life, ministry, crucifixion, and resurrection of Jesus.

rabbinic Judaism
Main form of Judaism, which emerged during the first century A.D. under the leadership of the rabbis. It clarified Jewish practice, elevated the oral law to equal authority with the written Torah, and enabled Judaism to evolve flexibly.

Mithras Sacrificing the Bull, copy of a Roman original (stone). This sculpted relief comes from an underground sanctuary along the Rhine frontier (in modern Germany). It shows the hero-god Mithras sacrificing a bull, the central symbol of Mithraism. Actual bull sacrifices were carried out in a temple known as a Mithraeum. (Saalburgmuseum, Romerkastell-Saalburg, Hessen, Germany/ Bildarchiv Steffens/The Bridgeman Art Library)

proponents of both religions claimed to be the rightful heirs of the biblical covenant. However, in Jesus' day, that outcome could hardly have been foreseen.

THE JEWISH BACKGROUND

Jesus was born a Jew. A speaker of Aramaic, he may also have known at least some Greek, widely spoken by both Jews and non-Jews in the several Hellenized cities of Palestine. To his followers, Jesus was Christ—"the anointed one" (from the Greek *Christos*), the man anointed with oil and thus marked as the king of Israel. They considered him the Messiah (from the Hebrew for "anointed one"), foretold in the Hebrew Bible, who would redeem the children of Israel and initiate the kingdom of heaven. The popularity of his teachings led to a clash with Jewish and Roman authorities in Jerusalem, the capital city of Judea, and to his execution. His mission began, however, in a corner

PALESTINE IN THE
TIME OF CHRIST,
CA. A.D. 30

- Roman Empire, ca. A.D. 200
- • Selected center of early Christianity
- • Other city
- → St. Paul's journey to Italy, A.D. 59–62

🌐 **MAP 6.2—The Expansion of Christianity to A.D. 200**

After its origin in Palestine, early Christianity found its main centers in the Greek-speaking cities of the Roman East. Missionaries such as Paul also brought the new faith to the Latin-speaking West, as well as to Ethiopia and Mesopotamia.

of the Jewish world, in the northern region of Galilee (GAL-uh-lee), where he lived in the town of Nazareth (NAZ-uh-reth) (see inset, **MAP 6.2**). Jesus was probably born not long before the death in 4 B.C. of Herod, the Roman-installed client-king of Judea. (The date of A.D. 1 for Jesus's birth, a mistaken calculation of Late Antiquity, does not accord with the data in the New Testament.) At around age 30, Jesus was baptized by the mysterious preacher John the Baptist. Soon afterward, Herod Antipas, the Romans' client-king of Galilee, ordered the execution of John. John had preached that God's kingdom was about to arrive—a time of universal perfection and an end of misery. In preparation, sinful humankind needed to repent. Just how much influence John had on Jesus is a matter of debate.

The most popular group among Palestinian Jews, the Pharisees, focused on the spiritual needs of ordinary folk (see page 106). The Pharisees believed that the written law of the Hebrew Bible was supplemented by oral tradition, as interpreted by generations of Jewish sages and scholars. They saw themselves as the guardians of that tradition. The Pharisees emphasized charity toward the poor and spoke in parables—vivid allegories that made their teaching accessible.

Another movement within Judaism at the time was Essenes, who lived apart from society in pursuit of a new covenant with God. The community at Qumran in the Judean desert, whose history is documented in the Dead Sea Scrolls, ancient texts discovered in 1947, was probably Essene. The tenets of Qumran included frugality, sharing, participating in a sacred communal meal, and avoiding oath-taking. Adherents anticipated the coming of the Messiah and an end of days in which God would punish the wicked.

JESUS' TEACHING   There are both similarities and differences between Jesus' teaching and contemporary doctrines of Palestinian Judaism. Like the Essenes, he spoke of the Messiah, but he did not withdraw from the world as the Essenes did; instead, Jesus immersed himself in it. Like the Pharisees, Jesus strongly criticized the pillar of the Jewish establishment, the Sadducees, the priests and wealthy men who saw the Temple at Jerusalem and its rites as the heart of Judaism. Also like the Pharisees, Jesus rejected the growing movement of the Zealots (ZELL-ots), advocates of revolt against Roman rule, although there were Zealots among his followers. Unlike the Pharisees, however, Jesus believed that he could interpret the Hebrew Bible on his own authority, without the consent of the sages and scholars of Jewish tradition. Jesus rejected the need to follow the letter of Jewish law. Inward purity became the key principle, as reflected in Jesus' statement to his disciples (that is, his close followers): "Whoever does not accept the kingdom of God like a child will never enter it" (Mark 10:15). Only an adult could become expert in Jewish law, but it is probably easier for a child than for an adult to attain spiritual innocence.

Jesus argued that the kingdom of God, which John the Baptist had said was coming soon, was actually already beginning to arrive. Moreover, Jesus said that he himself, acting through the direct order of God, could forgive sins. He said, "the Son of Man has authority on earth to forgive sins" (Mark 2:10). He emphasized the notion of God as a loving and forgiving father. He often spoke in parables and announced himself through miracles, particularly faith healing. He welcomed marginalized groups, including prostitutes and lepers.

The Good Shepherd   This ceiling painting comes from a Christian catacomb in Rome dating before A.D. 284. The pastoral image, common in the early church, recalls Christ's ministry. It symbolizes both his beneficence and his sacrifice, as well as his closeness to ordinary people.   (Scala/Art Resource, NY)

Jesus' teaching is typified in the Sermon on the Mount, addressed to his many followers in Galilee. He praised the poor and the humble and scorned the pursuit of wealth instead of righteousness. "Blessed are the poor in spirit;/the kingdom of Heaven is theirs" (Matthew 5:3). He called for generosity and forgiveness, recalling the traditional Jewish golden rule—to treat others as one would like to be treated. He said that prayer, fasting, and acts of charity should be conducted in private, not in public, in order to emphasize purity of motive. He called on his followers to endure persecution in order to spread his teachings: "You are light for all the world," he told them (Matthew 5:14).

Jesus spoke with conviction and persuasiveness—with "authority," as his followers said. He traveled from place to place; in Galilee, they greeted him as king. For some, this was a purely spiritual designation; others planned an overthrow of Roman rule, although Jesus rejected that course of action. In any case, his teachings won him hostility from some Pharisees, who considered his claim of authority to be heretical and his claim to be able to forgive sins blasphemous, and from Sadducees stung by his criticisms. Neither group accepted Jesus as the Messiah. It should be emphasized, nevertheless, that most of Jesus' followers were Jewish.

Jesus challenged central authority by going to Jerusalem and teaching and healing in the Temple under the eyes of the men whom he criticized. Nor did he confine his opposition to words: He drove merchants and money changers away from the Temple precincts by overturning their tables and perhaps even threatening them with a whip. Jesus attracted large crowds of followers, at least some of whom were armed. Jewish authorities feared trouble, and so did the overlords of Judea, the Romans. The governor, Pilate (Pontius Pilatus), had already endured vehement Jewish objections to the display in Jerusalem of an imperial medallion and of an inscription that seems to have asserted Augustus's divinity. Pilate had no need of further uproar. Temple police and Roman soldiers were called on to arrest Jesus quietly.

JESUS IN JERUSALEM

Jesus' subsequent trial and execution have always been controversial. The New Testament emphasizes the role of the Jewish leadership and the Jerusalem mob in Jesus' death. Written after the First Jewish Revolt (A.D. 66–70), however, the Gospels may reflect anti-Jewish sentiment in the empire. Crucifixion, the method used to execute Jesus, was a Roman penalty (the traditional Jewish method was stoning), and Jesus was executed by Romans, not Jews. Jesus probably appeared in informal and hurried proceedings before both the Jewish Council and Pilate. He suffered slow death by crucifixion on Golgotha (Calvary) Hill, just outside the city. It was a spring Friday, on the eve of the Passover festival, around A.D. 30.

Paul of Tarsus

According to the Gospel writers, Jesus died on a Friday and rose from the dead on Sunday, an event commemorated by Christians at Easter. He is said to have then spent forty days on earth, cheering and commissioning his disciples in Galilee and working miracles, before finally ascending to heaven. Heartened, the disciples returned to Jerusalem and spread Jesus' teachings.

Jesus' followers preached in synagogues, private households, and even the Temple, and to speakers of Greek as well as of Aramaic. Their movement spread, in the 30s and 40s A.D., throughout Palestine and into Syria. In Jerusalem, Christians were known as Nazarenes—that is, followers of Jesus of Nazareth; it was at Antioch in Syria that they were first called "men of Christ" (*christianoi*).

THE APOSTLES

The leaders of the movement were known as apostles, from the Greek *apostolos*, "one who is sent" and who enjoys the authority of the sender. The apostles believed that Jesus had sent them and given them authority. The apostles included Jesus' original followers, or disciples. The most prominent disciple was Peter, a Galilean fisherman whom Jesus endowed with particular authority. According to a reliable tradition, Peter eventually went to Rome, whose church he headed and where he died as a martyr in A.D. 64.

It was not clear at first that Christians would form a new religion separate from Judaism. Although the Sadducees and Jewish civil officials were hostile, Christians found much support among the Pharisees. Some Christians, however, contemplated a radical break; among

PAUL'S FAITH

Paul of Tarsus Christian apostle and saint, under whom Christianity began its complete separation from Judaism.

them no one was more important than **Paul of Tarsus** (d. A.D. 67?). Only Jesus himself played a greater role than Paul in the foundation of Christianity. A remarkable figure, Paul embodied three different and interlocking worlds. Born with the name of Saul, he was a Jew of the Diaspora from the southern Anatolian city of Tarsus. Paul was a native speaker of Aramaic and knew Hebrew and Greek. His father was one of the few Jews to attain Roman citizenship, a privilege that Paul inherited. Paul's heritage speaks volumes about the multiethnic and multicultural nature of the Roman peace, and his religious odyssey speaks volumes more (see **MAP 6.2**).

At first, Paul joined in the persecution of the Christians, whom he considered blasphemous. Around A.D. 36, however, he claimed to see a blinding light on the road to Damascus, a vision of Jesus that convinced him to change from persecutor to believer. It was a complete turnaround, a *conversio* ("conversion"), to use the Latin word that would grow so important in years to come. Saul changed his name to Paul and became a Christian.

He also changed what being a Christian meant. The key to Paul's faith was not so much Jesus' life, although that was a model for Christian ethics, as it was Jesus' death and resurrection. Jesus' fate, Paul wrote, offered all humanity the hope of resurrection, redemption, and salvation. Paul retained his belief in Jewish morality and ethics but not in the rules of Jewish law. Following the law, no matter how carefully, would not lead to salvation; only faith in Jesus as Messiah would.

Such doctrines bespoke a break with Judaism, as did Paul's attitudes toward converts. Hellenistic Judaism had long reached out to Gentiles. Some became Jews. Others remained Gentiles: Scattered throughout the cities of the Roman Empire, they were known as "God-fearers"—that is, they accepted the moral teachings of Judaism but refrained from following strict dietary laws, circumcision, and other Jewish rituals. Seneca the Younger, writing in the 60s, complains about the spread of Judaism: "The customs of this accursed race have gained such influence that they are now received throughout the world."[3]

The Jerusalem church baptized converts and considered them Jews, but Paul considered them not Jews but, rather, converts in Christ. For Pauline Christians, circumcision, dietary laws, and strict observance of the Sabbath were irrelevant. From the late forties to the early sixties A.D., Paul tirelessly undertook missionary journeys through the cities of the Roman East and to Rome itself. He aimed to convert Gentiles, and so he did, but many of his followers were Hellenized Jews and "God-fearers."

JUDAISM

Paul started Christianity on the road to complete separation from Judaism. Events over the next century widened the division. First, while Pauline churches prospered, departing ever more from Jewish customs, the Jerusalem church was decimated. Jewish authorities persecuted its leaders, and after Rome's suppression of the First Jewish Revolt and destruction of the Jerusalem Temple in A.D. 70, the rank and file of Palestinian Jews rallied to the Pharisees. Second, Jews and Christians, competing for converts, emphasized their respective differences. Third, although many Jews made their peace with Rome in A.D. 70, enough Jewish-Roman hostility remained to lead to uprisings in the Diaspora in 115 and to the Second Jewish Revolt in 132 to 135. Both were suppressed mercilessly by Rome, and Judaism became ever more stigmatized among Gentiles.

Bereft of the Temple at Jerusalem, Judaism nonetheless thrived as a religion. The rabbis, the religious leaders of the Pharisees, kept Judaism alive. After both A.D. 70 and 135, the Romans made the rabbis responsible for Jewish self-government in Palestine but Roman persecutions continued. The rabbis left their mark on history, however, not in administration, but in an intellectual movement. Continuing in the tradition of the Pharisees, the rabbis emphasized the notion of the "dual Torah," elevating the oral law to equal authority with the written law of the Hebrew Bible.

Because of the fragility of the Jewish community under the Romans, the rabbis decided to write the oral law down for the first time. The basic text of rabbinic Judaism is the Mishnah (MISH-nuh) (ca. A.D. 200), a collection of the oral law. During the next three centuries, rabbis would compile commentaries and analysis of the Mishnah in a collection known as the Gemara. Together, the Mishnah and the Gemara comprise the Talmud, which, for rabbinic Judaism, is the essence of the oral law. In rabbinic Judaism lies the basis of the medieval and modern forms of the Jewish religion.[4]

Expansion, Divergence, and Persecution

Although Jesus' mission was mainly in the countryside, early Christianity quickly became primarily an urban movement. Through missionary activity and word of mouth, the religion slowly spread. It was concentrated in the Greek-speaking East, but by the second century A.D., Christian communities dotted North Africa and Gaul and, beyond Roman boundaries, appeared in Parthian Iraq and in Ethiopia (see **Map 6.2**).

By around A.D. 200, an orthodox (Greek for "right thinking") **Christianity** had emerged. Rooted in Judaism, it was nonetheless a distinct and separate religion that found most of its supporters among Gentiles. A simple "rule of faith," emphasizing the belief in one God and the mission of his son, Jesus, as savior, united Christians from one end of the empire to the other. Christianity attracted both rich and poor, male and female; its primary appeal was to ordinary, moderately prosperous city folk. Believers could take comfort from the prospect of salvation in the next world and in a caring community in the here and now. Christians emphasized charity and help for the needy, even for strangers; Greco-Roman society rarely helped those outside of the family. A Christian writer justly described a pagan's amazed comment on Christian behavior: "Look how they love each other." Most early Christians expected Christ's return—and the inauguration of the heavenly kingdom—to be about to happen.

Early churches were simple and relatively informal congregations that gathered for regular meetings. The liturgy, or service, consisted of readings from the Scriptures (the Old and New Testaments), teaching, praying, and singing hymns. Baptism was used to initiate converts. The Lord's Supper, a communal meal in memory of Jesus, was a major ritual. The most important parts of the meal were the breaking and distribution of bread at the beginning and the passing of a cup of wine at the end; these recalled the body and blood of Christ. As organizational structures emerged (see pages 173–175), churches in different cities were in frequent contact with one another, discussing common concerns and coordinating doctrine and practice.

Just as Jewish women were not rabbis, so early Christian women did not hold the priesthood. Jewish women, however, did hold office in the synagogue, and Christian women likewise served as deaconesses. Both endowed buildings and institutions. For example, consider the Italian Jewish woman Caelia Paterna, an officeholder honored by her congregation as "mother of the synagogue of the people of Brescia." Or the two Christian deaconesses, both slaves, whom Pliny the Younger tortured during his governorship of the Anatolian province of Bithynia (buh-THIN-ee-uh) in about A.D. 110 in an attempt to extract information about the worrisome new cult. Deaconesses played an active part in church charities and counseling and could also preach sermons.

As Christianity spread, its troubles with the authorities deepened. For one thing, Christians met in small groups, a kind of assembly that conservative Romans had long suspected as a potential source of sedition. More troubling, however, was Christians' refusal to make sacrifices to the emperor. The Romans expected all subjects to make such sacrifices as a sign of patriotism. The only exception was the Jews, who were permitted to forgo the imperial cult because their ancestral religion prohibited them from worshiping idols. The Christians, however, were a new group, and the Romans distrusted novelty.

As a result, the emperors considered Christianity at best a nuisance and at worst a threat. Christians were tested from time to time by being asked to sacrifice to the emperor; those who failed to do so might be executed, sometimes in the arena. More often, however, the Romans tacitly tolerated Christians as long as they kept their religion private. Christians could not proselytize in public places, put up inscriptions or monuments, or build churches. Christianity thus spread under severe restrictions, but spread it did, particularly in the cities of the East. The willingness of martyrs to die for the faith made a strong impression on potential converts. Although the number of Christians in the empire is not known, it is clear that by the late third century, they were a significant and growing minority.

Christianity Sect originally rooted in Judaism that emerged as a fully separate religion by around A.D. 200. It emphasized belief in one God and the mission of his son, Jesus of Nazareth, as savior.

SECTION SUMMARY

- The cult of Demeter, the cult of Isis, Mithraism, and Manichaeism are among the mystery religions that spread in the Roman Empire during the first three centuries A.D.

- Jesus was born a Jew and was hailed by his followers as the Messiah or redeemer foretold in the Hebrew Bible.

- Jesus' teachings emphasized purity of soul, humility, charity, and the endurance of persecution to spread the word.

- Paul of Tarsus played an enormous role in spreading faith in Jesus outside the Jewish world, but Christianity took a long time to separate from its Jewish roots.

- By around A.D. 200, Orthodox Christianity had emerged as a systematic set of beliefs and a fully distinct religion from Judaism.

- The Roman peace provided the conditions for the spread of Christianity.

CHAPTER SUMMARY

The Roman Republic collapsed under the weight of political maneuvering, judicial murders, gang skirmishes, and civil war. A shrewd and sickly outsider, Octavian, confounded expectations by creating a new empire that would enjoy two centuries of stability; as Augustus, he served as its first emperor. Augustus reconciled the senatorial class by sharing a degree of power, but he guaranteed peace by keeping most of the armies in his own hands. He wisely reduced military spending and compromised with Rome's enemies to stabilize the frontiers. He solved the problem of rebellious soldiers by raising taxes to provide farms for veterans. Perhaps most important, he began a new policy toward the provinces, which were slowly raised to equality with Italy. In short, Augustus initiated the prosperous Roman peace. Under imperial patronage, culture flourished in the Augustan Age, including such writers as Virgil, Horace, and Livy. Augustus's successors, the Julio-Claudian emperors, included scandalous figures like Nero, but nevertheless, they delivered peaceful and effective government.

The Flavian dynasty (A.D. 69–96) and the so-called Five Good Emperors (96–180) brought Rome a long era of stability and good government. In the provinces, the Roman peace made possible an era of architectural and literary flowering. It was a prosperous era, but not for everyone, as slavery remained widespread. Rome was a multiethnic empire whose inhabitants increasingly mixed with one another and exchanged ideas. Latin literature flourished in its so-called Silver Age, and so did the practical and relatively fair-minded system that was Roman law, one of antiquity's greatest legacies. The Roman peace did not last forever: invasions, plague, inflation, crime, and political assassination were among the many woes that made the third century A.D. a period of crisis for the Roman Empire.

The cult of Demeter, the cult of Isis, Mithraism, and Manichaeism are among the mystery religions that spread in the Roman Empire during the first three centuries A.D. But the most important religion of the empire turned out to be Christianity, which began with Jesus of Nazareth. Born a Jew and hailed by his followers as the Messiah, Jesus taught humility, charity, and endurance of persecution to spread the word. The most important early Christian was Paul of Tarsus, who spread faith of Jesus outside the Jewish world. By around A.D. 200, Christianity had emerged as a systematic and fully distinct religion from Judaism.

FOCUS QUESTIONS

- How did Augustus establish a new imperial government to replace the Roman Republic? Why was he so successful?

- What was life like in the era of the Roman peace? Why did peace end during the third century A.D.?

- What were the origins of Christianity, and how did it fare among the other religions of the Roman world?

 This icon will direct you to additional materials on the website: www .cengage.com/history/ noble/westciv6e

KEY TERMS

Augustus (p. 140)

Principate (p. 141)

Virgil (p. 143)

Livia (p. 144)

Julio-Claudians (p. 144)

pax Romana (p. 147)

Flavian (p. 147)

Pompeii (p. 152)

Tacitus (p. 153)

third-century crisis (p. 154)

Sassanids (p. 155)

Jesus of Nazareth (p. 157)

Gospels (p. 157)

rabbinic Judaism (p. 157)

Paul of Tarsus (p. 162)

Christianity (p. 163)

NOTES

1. Mary R. Lefkowitz and Maureen B. Fant, trans., *Women's Life in Greece & Rome: A Source Book in Translation*, 2d ed. (Baltimore: Johns Hopkins University Press, 1992), p. 9.

2. Based on Susanne Dixon, *The Roman Family* (Baltimore: Johns Hopkins University Press, 1992), pp. 36–60.

3. Seneca, *De Superstitione*, trans. Menachem Stern, in *Greek and Latin Authors on Jews and Judaism*, vol. 1 (Jerusalem: Israel Academy of Sciences and Humanities, 1976), p. 431.

4. See Lawrence H. Schiffman, *From Text to Tradition: A History of Second Temple and Rabbinic Judaism* (Hoboken, N.J.: Ktav Publishing House, 1991), pp. 1–16.

e See our interactive eBook for map and primary source activities.

7

Santa Maria Maggiore
Santa Maria Maggiore (or Saint Mary Major) looks today much as it did when it was built. It was Rome's first church dedicated to Mary, the mother of Jesus. (Erich Lessing/Art Resource, NY)

The World of Late Antiquity, 284–ca. 600

The reigns of Diocletian (284–305) and Constantine (306–337) inaugurated a period that scholars now label "Late Antiquity." For many years, educated people, often taking their lead from the elegant and influential *Decline and Fall of the Roman Empire* by the British historian Edward Gibbon (1737–1794), believed that, beset by insurmountable problems, the Roman Empire "fell" in the fifth century. With that fall, such a view insisted, the glories of classical civilization gave way to the gloom of the "Dark Ages." Today, on the contrary, specialists in the period from roughly 300 to 600 see vigor and achievement. They emphasize continuity and coherence over calamity and collapse. No one denies that the Roman world of 600 was different from the Roman world of 300. But recent scholarship stresses how the Romans themselves created a stable framework for change. No catastrophic time, place, or event marked the "fall of Rome."

The magnificent church of Santa Maria Maggiore in Rome was dedicated by Pope Sixtus III in 432. This building encapsulates many of the themes we shall encounter in this chapter. How is it that a pope, a Christian bishop, had the power and resources to construct such a building in the empire's capital? For centuries, only emperors had built on such a scale. In architectural form, the building is a basilica, the traditional name for the rectangular halls that served the Romans well for public business. Now, the Christian church was adapting an old Roman form to its own purposes. Moreover, the beautiful mosaics and frescoes reveal ways in which the church was adapting Roman crafts and artistic motifs to its needs. In 410, Rome was sacked by barbarians and yet, within twenty years, the city's resources had rebounded sufficiently to make a building like this possible. In other words, this building itself testifies to the profound processes of continuity and change that are the hallmarks of Late Antiquity.

FOCUS QUESTIONS

- What were the most important reforms of Diocletian, Constantine, and their successors, and what roles did those reforms play in saving and transforming the empire?

- How and why did a Roman and Catholic Church emerge in Late Antiquity?

- Who were the "barbarians," and what kinds of relations did Romans and barbarians have in Late Antiquity?

- What challenges did the eastern empire face and what were some of its major contributions?

- How did women and men, elites and ordinary people, urban dwellers and farmers experience continuity and change in Late Antiquity?

 This icon will direct you to additional materials on the website: www.cengage.com/history/noble/westciv6e.

 See our interactive eBook for map and primary source activities.

REBUILDING THE ROMAN EMPIRE, 284–395

What were the most important reforms of Diocletian, Constantine, and their successors, and what roles did those reforms play in saving and transforming the empire?

The third-century Roman Empire had lurched from crisis to crisis. Decisive action was needed if Rome was to survive. The chronic civil wars had to be brought to an end. The army needed to be reformed and expanded to meet new threats on the frontiers. And the economy had to be stabilized to bring in the revenue the government needed for administrative and military reforms.

Rome was fortunate in raising up two rulers, Diocletian (dy-oh-KLEE-shun) and Constantine, with more than fifty years of rule between them, who understood the empire's problems and legislated energetically to address them. Although these rulers thought of themselves as traditional Romans, they actually initiated a far-reaching transformation of the Roman Empire.

The Reforms of Diocletian (r. 284–305)

The son of a poor Dalmatian farmer, Diocletian rose through the ranks of the army until he attained a key position in the emperor's elite guards. When the emperor was murdered, the soldiers elevated Diocletian to the imperial office.

tetrarchy Government ruled by four leaders. It was established about 293 by Emperor Diocletian to address the Roman Empire's political instability, huge size, and complexity.

In about 293, Diocletian devised a regime that historians call the **tetrarchy** (see **MAP 7.1**). Diocletian intended the tetrarchy (teh-TRAR-kee), "government by four," to address the empire's political instability and huge size, as well as to promote experienced men and provide an orderly succession to the imperial office. First, Diocletian decided to divide the empire into eastern and western halves, and he appointed an imperial colleague for the West. Ruling from Nicomedia and retaining the position of senior emperor, he took charge of the wealthy and militarily threatened eastern half of the empire. Diocletian and his colleague each selected a subordinate official who would eventually succeed to the imperial office. The advantage of the tetrarchy was that it yielded

🌐 **MAP 7.1—Diocletian's Division of the Roman Empire, 286**

Diocletian divided the empire into eastern and western halves; each half was divided into two prefectures. Thus, four regions, rulers, and bureaucratic administrations replaced the ineffective rule of one man.

four men of imperial rank who could lead armies and make decisions in political and administrative matters.

Historians call the regime instituted by Augustus in 31 B.C. the "Principate" (see page 141) because the emperor pretended to be the "first citizen" and heir of the Republican magistrates, even though his real power depended on control of the army. By contrast, Diocletian abandoned all pretense of being a magistrate. Scholars call his regime the "Dominate," from the Latin *Dominus*, "lord and master." Diocletian adopted Eastern, especially Persian, habits, such as wearing a gilded cloak and a jeweled diadem, sprinkling gold dust in his hair, sitting on an elevated throne, rarely appearing in public, and requiring those who approached to prostrate themselves before him. Diocletian succeeded in enhancing the prestige of the imperial office but did so at the price of making the emperor more remote from his subjects.

The empire had some fifty provinces, which varied greatly in size, population, wealth, strategic importance, and degree of Romanization, but the imperial administration was made up largely of aristocratic amateurs and numbered only a few hundred men when Diocletian ascended the throne. Rome had traditionally asked for relatively little from its empire—primarily taxes, military recruits, and loyalty. Local authorities generally did the tax collecting and military recruiting, with little interference from imperial agents.

Diocletian increased the number of officials and doubled the number of provinces by dividing old, large provinces into smaller ones. He then organized groups of provinces into thirteen dioceses and joined the dioceses into four prefectures. Diocletian subordinated each prefecture to a tetrarch and equipped each prefecture with a force of military, legal, financial, and secretarial officials headed by a praetorian prefect. By 350, the number of officers from the provincial to the prefectorial level had risen from a few hundred to thirty-five or forty thousand. Diocletian wished to fill the bureaucracy with trained administrators instead of with wealthy senators and equestrians, who viewed government service as a means of enriching themselves and advancing the interests of their families.

Diocletian also attended to Rome's military problems. His major initiative was to build his army to 450,000 men. Diocletian also built new forts along the frontiers and improved the roads that supplied frontier defenders. He systematically incorporated barbarians into the army, a step that led to a blurring of the distinction between Romans and barbarians. Military service had long been attractive to people in the empire because it provided Roman citizenship as well as a secure income. After 212, almost every free man in the empire enjoyed automatic citizenship. As a result, noncitizen barbarians living along the frontiers found the army attractive. As the proportion of barbarian soldiers and officers in the army grew, its culture and ethos began to change.

Diocletian's reforms required more income from taxes. Thus, Diocletian attempted to regularize the tax system in the empire. The government conducted a census to identify all taxpayers and assessed the productive value of land. To address the mounting inflation of the third century, Diocletian issued, in 302, the Edict of Maximum Prices, which froze the costs of goods. Virtually the whole cost of the Roman system continued to fall on agriculture, in particular on small farmers. Diocletian's reform of the tax structure brought in more revenue, but it also caused hardships. A rising tax burden threatened those who were most vulnerable. And with more officials handling vastly greater sums of money, corruption ran rampant. Most people never saw the emperor, but they saw too much of his tax-gouging local minions.

The rationale behind Diocletian's reforms is easy to understand; their results were less easy to anticipate. The actions were costly in three unintended respects: moral, social, and economic. The emperors had always been military dictators, but Diocletian removed all pretenses that they

CHRONOLOGY

284–337	Reforms of Diocletian and Constantine
300–400	Origins and spread of Christian monasticism
324–360	Foundation and development of Constantinople
325–553	First five ecumenical councils of the Christian church
350s–ca. 600	Age of the Church Fathers
370s–530s	Beginnings of the Germanic kingdoms inside the Roman Empire
379–395	Reign of Theodosius I, last emperor of a united empire
408–450	Reign of Theodosius II; consolidation of eastern Roman Empire
410	Visigoths sack Rome
412–418	Visigoths settle in Gaul
429	Vandals begin conquest of North Africa
440–604	Development of the Roman papacy
450–600	Anglo-Saxons settle in Britain
476	Last Roman emperor in the West deposed
481–511	Clovis founds Frankish kingdom
493	Beginning of Ostrogothic kingdom in Italy
527–565	Reign of Justinian I

Tetrarchy　Ideal and reality are both evident in this sculpture of the tetrarchy. The rulers, depicted equal in size, embrace one another but also bare their weapons—to one another and to the world.　(Scala/Art Resource, NY)

served at the behest of the Roman people. His frankness may have enhanced the aura of the imperial office, but it also loosened the ties between the ruler and his subjects. By reducing the official duties of the senatorial order, Diocletian alienated an influential group of about two thousand leading citizens. The enlarged imperial administration necessarily impinged on the autonomy of cities and their local leaders, for three centuries the key components of the imperial system. Finally, the expanded administration and army cost dearly in real cash. That cash had to be extracted from an empire that was in serious economic distress.

The Reforms of Constantius I (r. 306–337)

Diocletian's careful plans for the imperial succession collapsed almost immediately after his voluntary retirement in 305. When Diocletian's Western colleague (Constantius I) died in 306, his troops reverted to the hereditary principle and declared his son, Constantine, emperor. Until 324, Constantine's power was shared or contested, and from 324 to 337, he ruled alone over a reunited empire, although he made his sons subordinates in various parts of the empire. This compromise between the hereditary and tetrarchal systems persisted for the next two centuries.

Constantine knew the system well and maintained the administrative structure that Diocletian had introduced. Constantine continued the eastward shift of power by creating a second imperial capital in the East. In 324, he selected an old Greek city, Byzantium (bizz-AN-tee-um), and renamed it after himself, "Constantine's polis" or Constantinople (modern Istanbul). Byzantium's location, more than its size, wealth, or fame, recommended it. The city straddled military roads between the eastern and western halves of the empire, overlooked crucial trade lanes to and from the Black Sea region, and was well sited to respond to threats along both the Balkan and the eastern frontiers (see **MAP 7.1**).

In financial affairs, too, Constantine's work echoed his predecessor's. He issued a new gold *solidus*, the principal currency in the Roman Empire. This coin promoted monetary stability in the Mediterranean world for nearly a thousand years. Unfortunately, both a stable currency and Diocletian's price controls braked, but could not stop, the headlong rush of inflation.

In military affairs, Constantine believed that Rome's frontiers stretched too far to be held securely by garrisons, so he expanded the use of mobile field armies. These armies, recruited largely (as under Diocletian) from barbarians living along or beyond the frontiers, were stationed well inside the borderlands so that they could be mobilized and moved quickly to any threatened point. They were given their own command structures, under officers called "Masters of the Soldiers." The praetorian prefects were deprived of their military responsibilities and became exclusively civilian officials. The separation of civilian and military command made sense administratively and politically because it meant that no individual could combine the command of an army with the authority of a government post.

Whereas Diocletian will always be remembered for launching the last persecution of Christianity (303–305), Constantine legalized the new faith. Each man's motivation has evoked scholarly controversy. Diocletian was a Roman of conventional piety, who seems to have been convinced that the presence of Christian soldiers in his army offended the ancestral gods and denied victory to the Roman troops. Constantine's mother, Helena, was a devout Christian, and there were Christians in his father's court circle. In 312, while marching toward Rome to fight one of his rivals, Constantine believed that he saw in the sky a cross accompanied by the words "In this sign you shall

Chi-Rho

conquer." Persuaded, Constantine put a chi-rho (from the first two letters of *Chrestos*, "Christ" in Greek) monogram on his soldiers' uniforms. He defeated his foe at the Milvian Bridge near Rome, and, certain that Christ had assured his victory, he and his Eastern colleague issued the **Edict of Milan** in 313, granting Christianity full legal status in the empire.

Diocletian's persecution had been harsh and systematic. He ordered churches to be closed and the Scriptures seized, arrested members of the clergy, and required all citizens to make a public act of sacrifice in a temple. Constantine did far more than merely stop the persecution or legalize Christianity. He granted the church tax immunities, exempted the clergy from military and civic obligations, and provided money to replace books and buildings that had been destroyed in the persecution. He and his mother sponsored the construction of impressive churches, such as Saint Peter's in Rome and the Church of the Holy Sepulcher over the traditional site of Christ's tomb in Jerusalem.

Edict of Milan   Issued jointly by Constantine and his colleague Licinius, it granted freedom of worship to all and restored properties seized from the Christian church during Diocletian's persecution.

Old Saint Peter's   Constantine I erected this huge five-aisled basilica over the presumed place of burial of the apostle Peter. This was the first Christian basilica erected over a saint's place of burial. The prominence of Peter, Rome, and the popes caused the church to be widely emulated.   (Scala/Art Resource, NY)

Scholars have long debated the strategic and political wisdom of Constantine's arrangements. Moving experienced troops away from the frontiers may have invited, rather than deterred, attacks. Recruiting barbarians into the field armies and leaving frontier defenses to barbarian auxiliaries may have created divided loyalties and conflicts of interest. One certain result of the reforms of Diocletian and Constantine was the militarization of Roman society—the transformation of the Roman Empire into a vast armed camp. The financial resources of that empire were now largely devoted to maintaining an expensive military establishment that was socially diverse and potentially politically volatile. Christians were still a minority of the population in Constantine's lifetime, so his legalization and patronage of the new faith may have been visionary but offended the elites of his day.

Diocletian and Constantine responded with imagination to the third-century crisis. They created a new kind of rulership and a new type of imperial regime. Constantine erected a statue of himself in Rome that was more than 30 feet high; its head alone was about 8 feet tall. This statue is an indicator of the late antique imperial ideology. Constantine's size in stone serves to emphasize a distance that the viewer cannot articulate but cannot help feeling. The huge statue does not so much depict Constantine, as proclaim emperorship. The majesty of Constantine and his long, productive reign, in conjunction with Diocletian's success and longevity, stands in stark contrast to the troubles of the third century. But we may ask, as contemporaries did, whether order was purchased at too high a price in terms of personal freedom.

The Fourth-Century Empire: A Fragile Stability

Diocletian and Constantine considered themselves to be Roman traditionalists, but their wide-ranging reforms had actually introduced deep changes in the Roman system. When Constantine died in 337, the Roman Empire was more peaceful and stable than it had been throughout the crisis-ridden third century. But Rome's rulers were now more despotic; Rome's government was bigger, more intrusive, and more expensive; and Rome's military was larger and increasingly barbarian in composition. The open question in 337 was whether Rome would revert to the chaos of the third century or continue along the path marked out by the reforms of Diocletian and Constantine.

Succession to the imperial office remained a troubling issue, despite the introduction of the tetrarchy. Constantine had employed a combination of the tetrarchal and dynastic systems. He had three subordinates, all of them his sons. Constantine's sons had no heirs of their own, and when the last of them died in 361, the army turned to Julian (331–363), Constantine's nephew. Julian was a great leader and a man who looked out for his troops. Julian ruled for only two years before he was killed fighting in Mesopotamia. Because Julian had no heirs, the army controlled the succession. The choice fell on Valentinian (r. 364–375) and his brother, Valens (r. 364–378). Valentinian ruled in the west, his brother in the east. Valentinian established a dynasty that ruled the Roman world for ninety-one years (364–455). In 378, when Valens was killed in battle, Valentinian's sons sent their brother-in-law, Theodosius (thee-oh-DOE-zhus) I (r. 379–395), who had risen through the military ranks in Spain, to the east to restore order.

Until his own death in 395, Theodosius was the most powerful man in the Roman world and, after 392, sole ruler. He enjoyed the confidence of the people and the army—the former because he was exceptionally competent and honest and the latter because he was an old military man and a superb general. He divided the empire between his two sons without dynastic or military challenge. His branch of the family lived on until the deaths of Theodosius II in the East in 450 and Valentinian III in the West in 455.

Following the reforms of Diocletian and Constantine, the army was supposed to protect the empire, not play a role in Roman politics. Events proved otherwise. In the 340s, the Romans faced a renewed threat in the east from Persia, where an ambitious king sought to revive the glories of his ancestors. The Romans did not take this Persian threat lightly, for they knew that in the Persians, they faced an old and formidable foe. In the west, Rome faced one serious challenge from the Visigoths (discussed later in this chapter). These military provocations inevitably enhanced the role of the army in public life and elevated military concerns over civilian ones.

The fourth century did not witness the kinds of intensive reforms that characterized the reigns of Diocletian and Constantine, but emperors did introduce many modest measures, some of which had outcomes very different from those intended by their implementers. One example may stand for many.

Valentinian I wanted to make military careers more attractive and soldiers' lives more comfortable. To achieve these ends, he proposed providing soldiers with plots of land and seed grain. He aimed to supplement soldiers' pay, to tie them more securely to a particular region, and to make them more loyal to him. This creative idea complemented earlier military reforms.

Nonetheless, Valentinian's program angered the senators, who were still rich and influential. They agitated against the reform because, they said, the emperor was spending too much time worrying about the army, and he was depriving them of lands they desired. The senators also complained that the new program was expensive. They were right. To pay for land and seed, Valentinian had to raise taxes.

Higher taxes were especially unpopular in the cities, where the burden of collecting them fell on the *decurions*, the main local officials who composed the town councils. From the time of Valentinian in the late fourth century, evidence points to a steady decline in loyalty to Rome among these provincial urban elites. One great success under the Principate involved the regime's ability to win over local elites all over the empire. Now, a military reform whose rationale was clear and defensible actually provoked suspicion and disloyalty among senators and decurions.

In the late fourth century, the empire may have numbered 50 million to 60 million inhabitants. Of these, not more than 5 million to 10 million lived in towns. Because Roman government was based on towns, the actual capacity of the Roman administration to keep track of, tax, coerce, and Romanize the population as a whole was limited. Nevertheless, as the Roman Empire became an increasingly militarized state, its towns were being dominated by central authorities as never before, and its rural population was being pressed hard by tax policies necessitated by larger civil and military structures. The reforms of Diocletian and Constantine continued to provide the framework within which these changes took place.

When Theodosius died in 395, the Roman world seemed reasonably secure. The families of Constantine and Valentinian had produced effective rulers. Frontiers faced ominous threats, but for the moment, conditions appeared stable. Programs of institutional and economic reform continued, generally along the lines marked out by Diocletian and Constantine.

SECTION SUMMARY

- Diocletian and Constantine enhanced the prestige of the imperial office but made it more remote and despotic.
- Diocletian and Constantine expanded and redeployed the army but turned the empire into an armed camp.
- Diocletian and Constantine increased taxes and stabilized the currency.
- Diocletian and Constantine expanded the government and made it more effective, yet also more intrusive.
- Diocletian persecuted, but Constantine legalized Christianity.

THE CATHOLIC CHURCH AND THE ROMAN EMPIRE, 313–604

How and why did a Roman and Catholic Church emerge in Late Antiquity?

While Rome's rulers were trying to stabilize the state during the fourth century, the empire was experiencing a dynamic process of religious change. The formerly small and persecuted communities of Christians were achieving majority status in the Roman world. The Christianization of the empire's population (see **MAP 7.2**), first in towns, and then in the countryside, and the emergence of the Catholic Church as an institutional structure were two of the greatest transformations of the ancient world. Many Christians, now able to practice their faith publicly, discovered that they had sharp disagreements with one another on points of doctrine. Attempts to resolve those controversies entangled the church with the Roman authorities and strengthened the bishops of Rome. Moreover, numerous Christians—monks and nuns—sought a life of perfection away from the bustle of the world.

Emperors, Bishops, and Heretics

heresy An opinion that goes against religious or political doctrine and beliefs.

Arianism A term for the teaching of Arius and the beliefs of his followers, who believed that Jesus Christ, as "the first born of all creation," was generated by the Father, not coeternal with him. Their teachings challenged the doctrine of the Trinity.

Constantine discovered that his support of the church drew him into heated disputes over doctrine and **heresy**. *Heresy* comes from a Greek word meaning "to choose." Heretics are persons who choose teachings or practices that religious or state authorities deem wrong. The two greatest and most difficult heresies of Late Antiquity involved the central doctrines of Christianity: the deity of Jesus Christ himself and the relationship between his divine and human natures.

Christian belief holds that there is one God, who exists as three distinct but equal persons: Father, Son, and Holy Spirit. But around 320, a priest of Alexandria, Arius (AIR-ee-us) (ca. 250–336), began teaching that Jesus was the "first born of all creation." Christians had long been stung by the charge that their monotheism was a sham, that they really worshiped three gods. **Arianism**, as the faith of Arius and his followers is called, preserved monotheism by making Jesus slightly subordinate to the Father. Arianism won many adherents.

Constantine was scandalized by disagreements over Christian teachings and distressed by riotous quarrels among competing Christian factions. He dealt with religious controversies by summoning individual theologians to guide him and by assembling church councils to debate controversies and reach solutions. In 325, at Nicaea (Ny-SEE-uh), near Constantinople (see **MAP 7.2**),

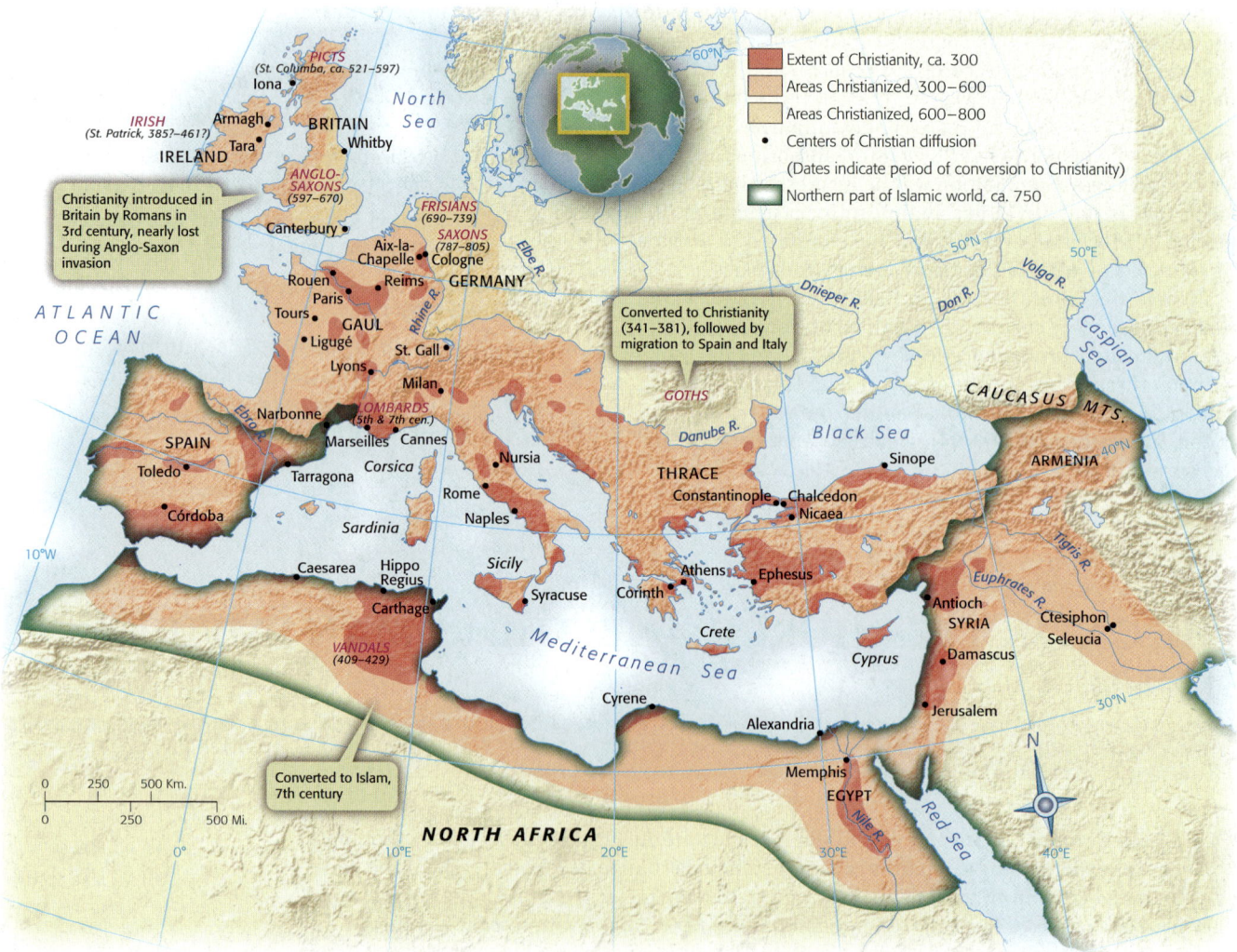

🌐 **MAP 7.2—The Spread of Christianity to A.D. 600**
From its beginnings in Palestine (see **MAP 6.2** on page 159), Christianity, while still illegal, spread mainly in heavily urbanized regions. After Constantine legalized Christianity, the faith spread into every corner of the Roman world.

the emperor convened a council of more than two hundred bishops, the largest council that had met up to that date. The **Council of Nicaea** condemned Arius and his teachings. The bishops issued a creed, or statement of beliefs, which maintained that Christ was "one in being with the Father," coequal and coeternal.

Religious unity remained elusive, however. The Council of Nicaea's attempt to eliminate Arianism was unsuccessful in the short term. Constantius II (r. 337–361), Constantine's son and successor in the eastern half of the empire, was an avowed Arian, as were some later emperors. For more than forty years, Rome's rulers occasionally embraced a faith that had been declared heretical. It was during this time that the Visigothic priest Ulfilas entered the empire, was converted to Arian Christianity, and returned to spread this faith among his people. Arian Christianity spread widely among the barbarian peoples living along the empire's frontiers. By the time those people began to enter the empire in significant numbers (see pages 179–180), catholic Christianity, universal (for that is what *catholicos* means) Christianity proclaimed by councils and emperors, had triumphed over Arianism, leaving the barbarians as heretics.

One emperor—Constantine's nephew Julian—made a last-ditch attempt to restore paganism during his short reign. He did not resort to persecution but forbade Christians to hold most government or military positions or to teach in any school. Although Christianity had been legalized only in 313, by the 360s, it was too well entrenched to be barred from the public sphere, and Julian's pagan revival died with him.

In the fifth century, Monophysitism (literally one-nature-ism) emerged as a result of bitter quarrels between Christian thinkers in Alexandria and Antioch. Theologians were struggling to find a way to talk about the divine and human natures in Christ. Some emphasized one nature, some the other. In 451, an emperor called a new council at Chalcedon (KAL-see-dun) to deal with the issue of Monophysitism. At Chalcedon, the theologians condemned the Monophysites, who emphasized Christ's divine nature, and pronounced that Jesus Christ was true God and true man—that he had two authentic natures. By 451, the Roman world had a large Catholic majority that derived its teachings from Nicaea and Chalcedon and heretical minorities who believed themselves to be the true Catholics.

The Institutional Development of the Catholic Church, ca. 300–600

The earliest Christian communities were urban and had three kinds of officials, whose customary titles in English are *bishop, priest,* and *deacon*. Deacons were responsible for charitable works and for arranging meetings. Bishops and priests presided at celebrations—most prominently the Eucharist (or Holy Communion, as it came to be called)—preached, and taught. Distinctions between bishops and priests developed over time. Towns often had many independent Christian groups, each headed by a priest. By about 200, as a sign of unity and authority, the eldest priest came to be called "overseer," the literal meaning of *bishop*. As more people converted, as the church acquired property, and as doctrinal quarrels began to cause divisions among the faithful, bishops began to be influential local officials. By the late fourth century, the bishops in the major cities of the empire were called *metropolitan bishops*, or sometimes *archbishops*, and they had responsibility for territories often called *dioceses*. The church was adapting to its own purposes the administrative geography of the Roman Empire—another sign of change and continuity in Late Antiquity. (See the feature, "The Global Record: Christianity Arrives in Nubia.")

From its earliest days, the Christian community had espoused the doctrine of *apostolic succession*. In other words, just as Jesus had charged his apostles with continuing his earthly ministry, that ministry was passed on to succeeding generations of Christian bishops and priests through the ceremony of ordination. When one or more bishops laid their hands on the head of a new priest or bishop, they were continuing an unbroken line of clerics that reached back through the apostles to Jesus himself. The bishops of Rome coupled this general notion of apostolic succession with a particular emphasis on the original primacy of Peter, in tradition, the leader of the apostles and the first bishop of Rome. The theory of "Petrine Primacy" was based on Matthew's Gospel (16:16–18), where Jesus founded his church on Peter, "the Rock," and conferred upon him the keys to the kingdom of heaven. The theory held that just as Peter had been the leader of the apostles, so the successors to Peter, the bishops of Rome, continued to be the leaders of the

Council of Nicaea The first "ecumenical" or "all-the-world council." Several more ecumenical councils would meet in Late Antiquity to deal with major heresies.

THE EMERGENCE OF THE ROMAN PAPACY

Christianity Arrives in Nubia

In the early fifth century, a Constantinopolitan lawyer, Socrates Scholasticus (389–450), wrote an Ecclesiastical History, drawing upon many earlier sources. In the following passage, he recounts the introduction of Christianity into "India," by which he means Nubia, or what is basically today Ethiopia. This document presents the first evidence for Christianity in Africa.

A certain philosopher, Meropius, was determined to acquaint himself with the country of the Indians. Having taken with him therefore two youths to whom he was related…Meropius reached the country by ship;…he touched at a certain place which had a safe harbor, for the purpose of procuring some necessaries. It so happened that a little before that time the treaty between the Romans and Indians had been violated. The Indians, therefore, having seized the philosopher and those who sailed with him, killed them all except his two youthful kinsmen; but sparing them from compassion for their tender age, they sent them as a gift to the king of the Indians. He, pleased with the personal appearance of the youths, made one of them, whose name was Edesius, cup-bearer at his table; the other, named Frumentius, he entrusted with the care of the royal records. The king dying soon after, left them free, the government devolving on his wife and infant son. Now the queen seeing her son thus left in his minority, begged the young men to undertake the charge of him, until he should become of adult age. The youths accepted the task, and entered on the administration of the kingdom. Frumentius controlled all things and made it a task to enquire whether among the Roman merchants trafficking with that country, there were any Christians to be found: and having discovered some, he informed them who he was, and exhorted them to select and occupy some appropriate places for the celebration of Christian worship. In the course of a little while he built a house of prayer; and having instructed some of the Indians in the principles of Christianity, they fitted them for participation in the worship. On the young king's reaching maturity, Frumentius and his associates resigned to him the administration of public affairs … and sought permission to return to their own country. Both the king and his mother entreated them to remain; but being desirous of revisiting their native place, they could not be prevailed on, and consequently departed. Edesius for his part hastened to Tyre to see his parents and kindred; but Frumentius arriving at Alexandria, reported the affair to Athanasius, who had recently been made bishop, and acquainted him with his wanderings and the hopes Indians had of receiving Christianity. He also begged him to send a bishop and clergy there, and by no means to neglect those who might thus be brought to salvation. Athanasius … requested Frumentius himself to accept the bishopric, declaring that he could appoint no one more suitable than he was. Accordingly this was done; Frumentius invested with episcopal authority, returned to India and became there a preacher of the Gospel, built several churches, and aided by divine grace, he performed various miracles, healing with the souls also the bodily diseases of many.

QUESTIONS

1. By what routes would a person be likely to sail to Nubia, and how would Frumentius have traveled from Nubia to Alexandria?

2. What impressions does this text give you of the knowledge possessed by Romans of the peoples outside the empire?

3. Do Frumentius and Edesius remind you of Moses?

4. What techniques did Frumentius use to institute Christianity in Nubia?

Source: Socrates Scholasticus, *The Ecclesiastical History*, Book 1, chapter 19, in Philip Schaff and Henry Wace, eds., *A Select Library of Nicene and Post-Nicene Fathers of the Christian Church*, Second Series, Volume 2, 1978. By kind permission of Continuum International Publishing Group.

church as a whole. By the late fourth century, the bishop of Rome was usually addressed as *papa*, or "pope" in English. The growing authority of the bishop of Rome within the church is the most striking organizational process of the fourth and fifth centuries.

Growing numbers of Christians, the increasing prominence of the clergy, and doctrinal quarrels drew emperors more deeply into the public life of the church. Between 378 and 381, Theodosius virtually outlawed the pagan cults, thereby making Christianity and Judaism the only legal religions, and required all Christians to believe as the bishop of Rome did, in the hope of imposing religious unity. Unity under Roman leadership was essential, Theodosius said, because Peter had transmitted the unblemished faith directly to Rome, and Peter's successors had preserved it there. The bishops of Rome took an ambivalent view of Theodosius's laws. They were glad to have the emperor's support but they did not wish for their authority or teaching to rest on imperial decrees. Theodosius's actions reflect the growing power of the bishop of Rome and demonstrate the degree to which the state and the church were becoming intertwined. The decrees themselves failed to achieve the unity Theodosius desired.

Ever since Nicaea, councils, with active participation by the emperors, had settled major disagreements in the church. Pope Leo I (r. 440–461) began to assert papal prerogatives. He had sent representatives to the Council of Chalcedon bearing his doctrinal formulation. Leo insisted that, as the bishop of Rome, he had full authority to make decisions in doctrinal controversies. The emperor skillfully steered Leo's "Tome" to acceptance by the council, but to appease many Eastern bishops, who felt that too much authority was being claimed by the pope, the emperor also encouraged the council to assert that the bishop of Constantinople (or patriarch, as he was often called) was second in eminence and power to the bishop of Rome. Leo, the greatest exponent of "Petrine Primacy" though not its originator, objected strenuously to the Council of Chalcedon's procedures. He disliked the prominent role of the emperor, complained that Eastern bishops had no right to challenge his doctrinal authority, and particularly opposed the elevation of Constantinople's status.

A generation later, Pope Gelasius I (r. 492–496) sent a sharply worded letter to the emperor Anastasius (r. 491–518), who had intervened in a quarrel between the Catholics and the still-numerous Monophysites. Gelasius protested the emperor's intervention. He told the emperor that the world was governed by the "power" of kings and by the "authority" of priests. Ordinarily, the pope said, the jurisdictions of kings and priests are distinct. In a controversy between them, however, priestly authority must have precedence, because priests are concerned with the salvation of immortal souls, whereas kings rule only mortal bodies. Gelasius was telling the emperor to stay out of theology, but he was implying much more. His opposition of the words *power*—meaning mere police power, the application of brute force—and *authority*—legitimacy, superior right—was of great importance. Gelasius elevated the church, with the pope at its head, above the whole secular regime, with the emperor at its head. But Gelasius had no means of coercing emperors. Moreover, many clergy in the eastern Mediterranean refused to accept the idea that the pope had supreme authority in either doctrine or church government.

Pope Gregory I "the Great" (r. 590–604) exemplifies the position of the papacy as Late Antiquity drew to a close. Gregory was the scion of an old senatorial family. He had risen through several important positions in the Roman administration, but then decided to abandon public life, sell off his family's property, and pursue a life of spiritual retreat. Soon, however, the Roman people elected him pope. His reputation for holiness was important to his election, but so too were his impeccable social credentials and wide political connections. Rome was threatened by the Lombards (a barbarian group that had entered Italy in the 560s), the local economy was in a shambles, and relations with the imperial government had been strained. Gregory did not wish to be elected pope, but given his conventional Roman sense of duty and obligation, he had little choice but to accept the office. Immediately, he undertook dangerous diplomatic measures to ward off the Lombard threat, sought improved relations with the emperor, and put the local economy on surer footing. He reorganized the vast estates of the church to place their products and revenues at the disposal of the Romans. In the absence of effective imperial administration in and around Rome, Gregory also began to attend to urban services and amenities, such as streets, aqueducts, and baths.

The rise of the pope in the church as a whole was paralleled by the rise of bishops throughout the empire. By the year 400, members of the social elite were everywhere entering the clergy and rising to its highest offices. This capture of the elite was the final, decisive factor in the triumph of Christianity.

THE ROLE OF THE ELITE

The clergy was an outlet for the talents and ambitions of the elite. For some time, senators had been excluded from military offices and reduced in civilian influence, and decurions were growing dissatisfied with public service. The *episcopal* office (that is, the office of bishop) was desirable to prominent men for many reasons. It was prestigious. Bishops wore distinctive clothing when officiating and were addressed by special titles—traditional Roman marks of respect. They had opportunities to control patronage in the way that prominent Romans always had done. They could intervene on behalf of individuals at the imperial court. They controlled vast wealth, as the generosity of pious Christians put more resources at their disposal. By the middle of the fifth century, the dominant person in most towns was the bishop, not a civilian official. The bishops, however, were the same persons, from the same families, who had once dominated local society through civic service. The overall effect of these social changes was dramatic in the long run, but it happened very gradually.

The change from a secular to an ecclesiastical elite in Roman cities even led to alterations of the topography of the cities themselves. The elite usually financed local building projects, such as temples, basilicas, forums, and amphitheaters. Such benefactions declined sharply during the tumultuous third century. The fourth century at first saw little building on private initiative, but then came the construction of Christian cathedrals (a bishop's church, from *cathedra*, the chair or seat of the bishop's authority), episcopal residences, and other churches. Such buildings, as a rule, were not placed in the old city centers, which had associations with the pagan past. Instead, they were placed on the edges of populated districts. In the future, these Christian centers served as poles around which ancient towns were reconfigured. The Roman elites built to show pride in their cities and to promote themselves. This did not change in Late Antiquity, but this time, the elites were bishops or rich Christians, and the buildings were religious—look again at Santa Maria Maggiore on page 170.

The Rise of Christian Monasticism

monasticism A way of life involving the renunciation of worldly pleasures and the embrace of a life of prayer and solitude. Monasticism arose in fourth-century Egypt and spread all over the Roman world.

For some men and women, the call of the Gospel was radical. They yearned to escape the world and everything that might come between them and God. To do so, many of them embraced a new way of life—**monasticism**. Christian monks and nuns developed a theology and an institution that were among the most creative and long-lived achievements of Late Antiquity.

The practice of rigorous self-denial (*askesis*) was common to several religious and philosophical sects in antiquity—for example, the Pythagoreans and the Stoics—and was well known among the Jews in the time of Christ, as the Essenes show (see page 160). Ascetics believed that if they could conquer the desires of the body, they could commune with the supernatural beings who were greater and purer than humans, encumbered by lust for food, drink, knowledge, sex, and adventure. Sometimes ascetic practices were adopted by tightly knit groups, sometimes by heroic solitaries.

The founder of Christian monasticism was a young Egyptian layman, named Anthony (d. 356). At age 19, Anthony gave away all his possessions and took up, in the Egyptian desert, a life of prayer and renunciation. His spiritual quest became famous, and many disciples flocked to him. Finally, he decided to organize these seekers into a very loose community. His followers remained in solitude except for worship and meals. Anthony's form of monasticism is called *eremitic*, from the Greek *heremos*, or "desert," hence, the word *hermit*.

eremitic monasticism
An especially austere, solitary form of asceticism.

Pachomius (pack-OH-mee-us) (290–346) created a more communal form of monastic life. A former Roman soldier, he was baptized a Christian in 313 and retired to the Egyptian desert, where he studied with a hermit. Eventually Pachomius founded a community, which before long had grown to thousands of members. Perhaps because of his military background, or because his religious instincts favored order and unity, Pachomius wrote the first Rule, or code for daily living, for a monastic community. He organized most aspects of his community by designing a common life based on routines of private prayer, group worship, and work. By the time of his death, Pachomius led nine male and two female communities. Pachomius's pattern of monasticism is called *cenobitic* (sen-oh-BIT-ik), from the Greek for "common life." People living this common life were called *monks*, and the place where they lived was called a *monastery*. The head of the community was designated the *abbot*, a word meaning "father." In later times, the term *abbess*, meaning "mother," was coined for the woman who led a female community.

cenobitic monasticism
From the Greek *koinos bios*, common life, this form of monasticism was communal.

Monasticism spread from Egypt by means of texts, such as the *Life of Anthony* (a late antique "best seller"), collections of the wise sayings of famous desert abbots, and books written by persons who went to Egypt seeking a more perfect life—among whom were several prominent women. One attraction of monasticism among the devout was that it seemed to be a purer form of Christian life, uncorrupted by the wealth, power, and controversy of the hierarchical church. Many pious women embraced monasticism at least partly because they could not be ordained priests. Positions in monasteries, including that of abbess, provided responsible roles for talented women. Monasticism gave women a chance to choose a kind of family life different from the one available in households dominated by fathers and husbands.

Eremitic monasticism was prominent in Palestine and Syria and eventually throughout the Greek-speaking world. Eastern monasticism produced a great legislator in Basil (330–379), whose Rule was the most influential in the Orthodox Church (see page 193). Generally, these monks assembled only for weekly worship and otherwise ate, prayed, and worked alone.

Eremitic monasticism arrived in the West in the person of Martin of Tours (336–397). Like Pachomius, Martin was a Roman soldier who, after his military service, embraced both

Christianity and asceticism. Even though he was elected bishop of Tours, Martin kept to his rigid ascetic life. Martin's form of monasticism influenced many in the western regions of the Roman world, but set especially deep roots in Ireland. There, the whole organization of the church was based on monasteries. At Kildare, the abbess Brigid (d. 523) had more authority than the local bishop.

In the West, cenobitic monasticism became the dominant pattern. Benedict of Nursia (480–545) abandoned his secular career to pursue a life of solitary prayer in a mountain cave. Benedict's piety attracted a crowd of followers, and in about 520, he established a monastery at Monte Cassino, 80 miles south of Rome. The Rule he drafted for his new community is marked by shrewd insights into the human personality. It emphasizes the bond of mutual love among the monks and obedience to the abbot. The Rule assigns the abbot wide powers but exhorts him to exercise them gently. The Rule allows monks a reasonable diet and decent, though modest, clothing. Although providing for discipline and punishment, the Rule prefers loving correction. In later centuries, Benedict's Rule dominated monastic life.

Monasticism was a conscious alternative and an explicit challenge to the civic world of classical antiquity. Monks and nuns did not seek to give their lives meaning by serving the state or urban communities. They went into remote places to serve God and one another. They sought not to acquire, but to abandon. Spiritual wisdom was more important to them than secular learning, and they yearned for acknowledgment of their holiness, not recognition of their social status. Still, monasticism was sometimes controversial. Whereas many people admired and emulated these holy men and women, others disputed their claims to elite spiritual status.

At the dawn of Late Antiquity, the church was persecuted and struggling. By the end of the period, the church was rich and powerful, its leaders were prominent and prestigious, and in the monasteries, at least, its spiritual fervor was deep. This change was gradual but fundamental.

SECTION SUMMARY

- Imperial legislation and church councils imposed a universal, a catholic, form of Christianity.

- The church developed a hierarchy of officers over which the bishops of Rome gradually achieved preeminence.

- Christians disagreed strongly on basic teachings, such as the Trinity (God is Father, Son, and Holy Spirit) and the divine and human natures of Jesus Christ.

- Some men and women rejected the values of the late antique world and embraced the monastic life of prayer and renunciation, achieving in the process a new kind of status: holiness.

THE RISE OF GERMANIC KINGDOMS IN THE WEST, CA. 370–530

Who were the "barbarians," and what kinds of relations did Romans and barbarians have in Late Antiquity?

The years from the 370s to the 530s were decisive in the history of the Roman Empire in the West. This period saw the transformation of Rome's western provinces into several Germanic kingdoms, most of which maintained some formal relationship with the eastern Roman Empire. Roman encounters with the barbarians took many different forms, ranging from violent conflict to peaceful accommodation. The key point to understand is that although the barbarians supplanted Roman rule in the West, they did so slowly and often with Roman permission and assistance.

Invasions and Migrations

Individual groups of barbarians did invade the empire in various places at different times, but there was never a single, coordinated barbarian invasion of the Roman world that had well-formulated objectives. The Romans and barbarians did not face one another as declared enemies. Indeed, peaceful encounters outnumbered violent confrontations in the history of Romano-barbarian relations. The Romans had long traded with the barbarian peoples, carried out complicated diplomacy with them, and recruited them into their armies. Barbarian veterans were settled in most provinces of the empire.

If we cannot label one grand movement as "the barbarian invasions," we must also avoid the idea that the barbarians were naturally nomadic and migratory. Holding this view would tempt us to see the entry of the barbarians into the empire as one stage in a long process of human movement. Archaeological evidence collected to date makes it clear that the barbarians were settled agriculturists. They lived in villages, farmed the surrounding country, and raised livestock. If barbarians moved from one place to another, their movement must be explained with reference to specific developments and cannot be attributed to migratory habits.

Few images of the ancient world are more fixed in the popular imagination than the overrunning of the Roman Empire by hordes of barbarians who ushered in a dark age. The Romans inherited the word *barbarian* from the Greeks, who had divided the world between those who spoke Greek and those who did not. Barbarians were literally babblers, foreigners who spoke an unknown language.

Who were the barbarians? Linguists classify them as speakers of Germanic languages. The Germanic peoples can be differentiated from the Celts and Slavs with whom they shared much of central and eastern Europe, but apart from some minor linguistic variations, it is difficult to distinguish one Germanic group from another.

What are we to make of the profusion of names offered to us by our sources: Franks, Saxons, Vandals, Visigoths, Ostrogoths, Lombards, Burgundians? The Romans referred to the Germanic peoples as tribes, but that does not mean that they were actually groups of related people. Every Germanic "tribe" was a confederation, and these confederations formed, dissolved, and reformed many times. The confederations were formed either by powerful leaders who coerced less powerful people to join them or by groups of villages that banded together to protect themselves from aggressive neighbors. As a tribe was forming, its constituent peoples would intermarry and adopt the language, law, and lifestyle of the dominant group.

Incorporating the Barbarians

The transformation of the western Roman Empire began as a result of an unexpected set of events involving the Huns, nomadic warriors from the central Asian steppes. (See the feature, "The Written Record: Two Views of the Huns.") After plundering the frontiers of Persia and China for centuries, they turned west in search of booty and tribute. In 374 or 375, they fell on the Ostrogoths, who lived near the Black Sea, and frightened the **Visigoths**, who requested permission to cross the Danube and enter the empire.

Visigoths A "West" Germanic people who coalesced along the Danube frontier in the fourth century, allied with the Romans, eventually entered the empire, sacked Rome in 410, and finally established a kingdom in Gaul.

Because of dynastic quarrels and military challenges, the Romans delayed responding to the Visigoth request. Fearful of the Huns, the Visigoths crossed the Danube on their own and then asked if they might settle in the Balkans. Reluctantly, Valens (VAY-lenz) (r. 364–378) agreed but postponed permanent arrangements. While the government considered how to deal with the Visigoths, local authorities sold them food at exorbitant prices and even traded dog meat for Gothic children, who were then enslaved. When the Visigoths revolted, Valens foolishly marched north to meet them with a small force. The Visigoths defeated his army and killed him at Adrianople in 378.

The history of the Visigoths presents an instructive example of Romano-Germanic relations. They had served as auxiliary troops entrusted with defending a stretch of the Danube frontier for a long time when they requested permission to enter the empire in 376. They did not cross the border as part of a massive invasion but because they were sorely threatened. In 382, Theodosius marched east to pacify the situation. He agreed to grant the Visigoths what they had been demanding: land to settle on and a Roman military title—that is, official status—for their king. A spokesman for Theodosius explained the emperor's motives: "Which is better: To fill Thrace with corpses or with farmers? To fill it with graves or with people? To travel through wilderness or cultivated land? To count those who have perished or those who are ploughing?"

For about thirty years, the Visigoths struggled to improve the terms of their settlements in the Balkans. Alaric (AL-uh-rik), the Visigothic king after 395, grew tired of unfulfilled promises and forced matters by attacking Italy. In 410, the Visigoths sacked Rome. The taking of the city for the first time in eight hundred years shocked the entire Roman world and has loomed large for centuries in people's ideas about the "fall" of the Roman Empire. Actually, it was a ploy by Alaric to improve the terms of his already official status. Alaric died in 410, and his brother led

Two Views of the Huns

The dread and disgust inspired by the Huns is well captured in the first passage, from the Roman historian Ammianus Marcellinus. The second passage, from a surviving fragment of the history of Priscus, shows the Huns in quite a different light. Only rarely can we contrast two different views, and these documents permit us to do so.

(a)

From the moment of their birth they make deep gashes in their children's cheeks, so that when in due course hair appears its growth is checked by the wrinkled scars; as they grow older this gives them the unlovely appearance of beardless eunuchs. They have squat bodies, strong limbs, and thick necks, and are so prodigiously ugly and bent that they might be two-legged animals. Their shape, however disagreeable, is human. They have no use for seasoned food, but live on the roots of wild plants and the half-raw flesh of any animal, which they warm a little by placing it between their thighs and the backs of their horses. They have no buildings to shelter them. They wear garments of linen or of the skins of field-mice stitched together. Once they have put their necks into some dingy shirt they never take it off or change it until it rots and falls to pieces. They have round caps of fur on their heads, and protect their hairy legs with goatskins. They are ill-fitted to fight on foot, and remain glued to their horses, hardy but ugly beasts, on which they sometimes sit like women to perform their everyday business and they even bow forward over their beasts' narrow necks to enjoy a deep and dreamy sleep.

(b)

[The Roman ambassadors] came upon a very large village in which the dwelling of Attila was said to be more notable than those elsewhere. It had been fitted together with highly polished timbers and encircled with a wooden palisade, conceived not for safety but for beauty. Next to the king's dwelling that of Onegisus [chief minister to Attila] was outstanding, and it also had a circuit of timbers but was not embellished with towers in the same way as Attila's. Not far from the enclosure was a large bath. . . . Maidens came to meet Attila as he entered this village, advancing before him in rows under fine white linen cloths stretched out to such a length that under each cloth, which was held up by the hands of the women along either side, seven or even more girls walked. There were many such formations of women under the linen cloths, and they sang Scythian songs. When he [Attila] came near the house of Onegisus, the wife of Onegisus came out with a host of servants, some bearing dainties and others wine, greeted him and asked him to partake of the food which she had brought for him with friendly hospitality. To gratify the wife of his intimate friend, he ate sitting on his horse, the barbarians accompanying him having raised the silver platter up to him. Having also tasted the wine, he went on to the palace, which was higher than the other houses and situated on a high place.

QUESTIONS

1. How do these two accounts differ in tone, emphasis, and details?

2. Leaving aside the question of whether these accounts are true, what impressions do you think they would have made on the Romans? What impressions were they intended to make?

3. How do the public rituals of the Huns compare with those of the Romans?

Sources: Excerpt (a): Ammianus Marcellinus, *The Later Roman Empire* (A.D. *354–378*), 31.2, ed. and trans. Walter Hamilton (Harmondsworth, U.K.: Penguin, 1986), pp. 411–412. Excerpt (b): Priscus, Fragment 8, in C. D. Gordon, *The Age of Attila: Fifth-Century Byzantium and the Barbarians* (Ann Arbor: University of Michigan Press, 1961), pp. 84–85.

the Visigoths north into southern Gaul. For good measure, the new Visigothic king captured the Western emperor's sister, Galla Placidia, and forced her to marry him. However objectionable this act must seem, the Visigoths viewed it as a further demonstration of their loyalty to Rome and their determination to effect a satisfactory new treaty.

In 418, the Roman government gave in. A treaty permitted the Visigoths to settle in southern Gaul, with Toulouse as their base of operations. They were assigned the task of protecting the area from marauding bands of brigands. In return for their service, the Visigoths were given land allotments and a portion of Roman tax receipts as pay.

The Visigoths' treaty with Rome made theirs the first Germanic kingdom on Roman soil. From 418 to 451, the Visigoths served Rome loyally and earned the respect of the Gallo-Roman aristocrats among whom they ruled. Between 466 and 484, the Visigothic kingdom in Gaul reached its high point and continued to receive official recognition from Roman rulers. Southern

Gaul, one of Rome's oldest provinces, gradually passed from the hands of the Roman bureaucracy and the local nobility into the control of the Visigoths.

While they were dealing with the Visigoths, the Roman authorities realized that the Huns, who had settled in the Danube basin after driving the Visigoths into the empire, were a serious menace. They raided the Balkans, preyed on trade routes that crossed the region, and demanded tribute from the Eastern emperor. In 434, the fearsome warrior Attila murdered his brother and became sole ruler of the Huns. In return for a huge imperial subsidy, he agreed to cease raiding the Balkans. At the same time, a Roman general in Gaul concluded an alliance with the Huns in an attempt to use them to check the expansion of the Burgundians, an allied people who lived in the central Rhineland.

Together, Attila and the Romans routed the Burgundians, but Attila realized the weakness of the Roman position in the West. He attacked Gaul in 451 and was stopped only by a combined effort of Romans, Visigoths, Burgundians, and Franks. The soldiers who defeated the Huns were all called "Romans."

More Kingdoms: The End of Direct Roman Rule in the West

To meet threats in Gaul and elsewhere, the Romans had begun pulling troops out of Britain in the fourth century and abandoned the island to its own defense in 410. Thereafter, raiding parties from Scotland and Ireland, as well as seaborne attackers—called "Saxons" by contemporaries because some of them came from Saxony in northern Germany—ravaged Britain. The British continually appealed to the military authorities in Gaul for aid, but to no avail. Between 450 and 600, much of southern and eastern Britain was taken over by diverse peoples whom we call the "Anglo-Saxons." The newcomers jostled for position with the Celtic Britons, who were increasingly confined to the north and west of the island. Amid these struggles was born the legend of King Arthur, a Briton who defended his people and led them to victory. Gradually, several small kingdoms emerged. Although Britain retained contacts with Gaul, the island had virtually no Roman political or institutional inheritance.

Valentinian III (r. 425–455) was born in 419 and became emperor of the West as a 6-year-old. Even when he came of age, his court was weakened by factional strife, and his regime was dominated by military men. After Valentinian, the western empire saw a succession of nonentities, the last of whom was deposed by a Germanic general in 476. Ruling in Italy, he simply sent the imperial regalia to Constantinople and declared that the West no longer needed an emperor. This is all that happened in 476, the traditional date for the "fall" of the Roman Empire.

After the vast coalition defeated the Huns in Gaul in 451, the remaining Roman authorities in the Paris region discovered that the Visigoths were expanding north of the Loire River into central Gaul. To check this advance, the Roman commander in Paris forged an alliance with the Franks. The Franks, long Roman allies, had been expanding their settlements from the mouth of the Rhine southward across modern Holland and Belgium since the third century.

The fortunes of the Frankish kingdom, indeed of all of Gaul, rested with Clovis. He became king of one group of Franks in 481 and spent the years until his death in 511 subjecting all the other bands of Franks to his rule. He gained the allegiance of the Frankish people by leading them to constant military victories that brought territorial gains, plunder, and tribute. The greatest of Clovis's successes came in 507, when he defeated the Visigoths and drove them over the Pyrenees into Spain.

Clovis was popular, not only with the Franks, but also with the Gallo-Roman population, for three reasons. First, Clovis and the Romans had common enemies: Germanic peoples still living beyond the Rhine and pirates who raided the coast of Gaul. Second, whereas most of the Germanic peoples were Arian Christians, the majority of the Franks passed directly from paganism to Catholicism. Thus, Clovis and the Gallo-Romans had a shared faith that permitted Clovis to portray his war against the Visigoths as a kind of crusade against heresy. Third, Clovis eagerly sought from Constantinople formal recognition and titles, appeared publicly in the dress of a Roman official, and practiced such imperial rituals as distributing gold coins while riding through crowds. The Frankish kingdom under Clovis's family—called "Merovingian," from the name of one of his semilegendary ancestors—became the most successful of all the Germanic realms.

Several early Germanic kingdoms were short-lived. The Burgundian kingdom, which had once prompted the Romans to ally with the Huns, was swallowed up by the Franks in the 530s. The Vandals, who crossed the Rhine in 406 and headed for Spain, crossed to North Africa in 429 (see **Map 7.3**). They were ardent Arians, who persecuted the Catholic population. They refused imperial offers of a treaty on terms similar to those accepted by other Germanic peoples, and they constantly plundered the islands of the western Mediterranean and the Italian coast, even sacking Rome in 455. Roman forces from Constantinople eliminated the Vandals in 534.

The Ostrogoths, who had been living in Pannonia since the 370s as subjects of the Huns, began to pose a threat to the eastern empire after Attila's death. In 493, the emperor decided to send them to Italy to recover that area for the imperial government. The government at Constantinople was familiar with the Ostrogoths' king, Theodoric, because he had been a hostage there for several years

Theodoric conquered Italy quickly and set up his capital in Ravenna, the swamp-surrounded and virtually impregnable city that had sheltered the imperial administration for much of the fifth century. Through the force of his personality, and by a series of marriage alliances, Theodoric became the dominant ruler in western Europe. In Italy, he promoted peace, stability, and good

🌐 **Map 7.3—The Germanic Kingdoms, ca. 530**

By 530, the western provinces of the Roman Empire (compare **Map 6.1** on page 140) had evolved into Germanic kingdoms. Just as Roman provincial boundaries had changed numerous times, the existence and extent of Germanic kingdoms were also impermanent.

Amalasuntha, Daughter of Theodoric   This ivory plaque (ca. 530) depicts Amalasuntha in the way that Roman consuls and emperors had long been depicted on their assumption of office. Since the late fifth century, empresses had been depicted this way, too. Amalasuntha projects an image of legitimacy.   (Kunsthistorisches Museum, Vienna)

government. Still, Theodoric had two strikes against him. First, he and his people were Arians. Second, although the population of Italy was accustomed to having an imperial court dominated by barbarians and to having Germanic military men as the real powers in the state, they had never been directly ruled by a barbarian, and some of them could not accept Theodoric. By the 520s, Theodoric grew increasingly suspicious and dictatorial.

When Theodoric died, his daughter Amalasuntha (498–535) served as regent for her son Athalaric from 526 to 534 and then briefly served as queen. A contemporary said that she was beautiful and well educated. She favored the Romans in Italy and promoted cultural fusion. For this, she angered the Goths, who deposed and then murdered her. Her death was Justinian's pretext to launch the Gothic Wars (535–554), which put an end to the Ostrogothic kingdom.

By the 530s, the western Roman Empire had vanished, the conclusion of a process initiated by the entry of the Visigoths into the Balkans in 376. Of all the peoples who had contested for a share of Rome's legacy, only the Franks in Gaul, the Visigoths in Spain, and the Anglo-Saxons in Britain had created durable political entities.

Why did the Roman government perish in the West? Beginning with Diocletian, Rome's best rulers were resident in and concerned mainly about the East. The Visigoths and other peoples were settled in their own kingdoms on Roman soil instead of being enrolled in and dispersed among Roman army units. Also during Diocletian's rule, the army was increasingly Germanized, and Germanic military men gained high offices in the state. Those leaders often dominated imperial courts and negotiated the series of treaties that submitted former provinces to barbarian peoples. Provincial elites had long been accustomed to having prominent Germans in their midst. The new situation was not unusual to them. Churchmen readily embraced the Catholic Franks and tolerated Arians, such as the Visigoths, when they promoted peace and good government without abusing the Catholic population.

Old and New in the West

Each realm was led by a king who usually appeared in two distinct guises. To his people, the king was the military leader. The essential bond of unity among each Germanic people was loyalty to the leader, who repaid his followers in booty, tribute, land, legal protection, and military security. To the Romans, the king appeared as an ally and magistrate. Almost all Germanic kings bore Roman titles, such as *consul* or *patrician*, and in these officially conferred titles resided the authority necessary to govern Roman populations. The kings also succeeded to a long line of Germanic Masters of the Soldiers, the title of the highest military officers in a prefecture. Each monarchy was led by a dynasty—for example, the Merovingians among the Franks—that was preeminent in wealth and possessed a sacral aura not unlike that of the Roman emperors.

The most common local officials were counts, a combined civilian-military position that made its first appearance in the fifth century. Initially a direct representative of the emperor, a count had financial, judicial, and military responsibilities. Local notables, usually great landowners, initially resented counts but gradually aspired to the office. Kings were careful to promote important locals, both Romans and their own people, to the office of count.

Local administration remained based in cities and towns. Taxes continued to be paid to royal governments throughout the sixth century. Provincial populations did not find this policy odd or unjust. Their taxes had always gone primarily to pay for the Roman military establishment, and the monarchies were the heirs of that establishment. Latin persisted as the language of administration. Until the end of Late Antiquity, notaries continued to draw up wills, records of land transactions, and legal documents of all kinds. Law codes issued by the Germanic kingdoms were largely adaptations of Roman provincial law. The legal conditions under which most people lived stayed pretty much the same. In sum, people's daily lives changed surprisingly little as a result of the replacement of Roman provinces by Germanic kingdoms.

SECTION SUMMARY

- The Romans had long-standing relations with the Germanic barbarians living beyond their frontiers.

- The barbarian "tribes" were actually loose confederations of peoples, which achieved coherence only in kingdoms inside the empire.

- The Visigoths' change from allies, to enemies, and back to allies of the Romans is an instructive example of Romano-barbarian relations.

- The barbarian kingdoms retained many public and private aspects of Roman life.

THE ROMAN EMPIRE IN THE EAST, 395–565

What challenges did the eastern empire face and what were some of its major contributions?

The creation of the tetrarchy at the end of the third century separated the eastern and western halves of the Roman Empire administratively. In theory, there was only one empire, ruled by one senior emperor, but in practice, the Eastern and Western courts followed different policies in many areas, notably in their relations with the barbarians. Fundamental cultural differences also distinguished East from West. The East was more populous, more heavily urbanized, and more prosperous. The eastern Mediterranean was Greek in culture and livelier intellectually than the West. The eastern empire survived, as the western empire was being parceled out into kingdoms.

Constantinople and Its Rulers

Constantius II (r. 337–361), Constantine's son and successor in the East, began making Constantinople a truly imperial city. He gave "New Rome" its own senate and urban magistrates, placing the city on an equal constitutional footing with Rome. Constantinople did not have an ancient aristocracy, so Constantius had to create a senatorial order. This he did by recruiting some Romans and promoting prominent and cultivated persons from cities in the eastern half of the empire, thereby forging bonds between the capital and its hinterland. Constantius and his successors also built palaces, public buildings, and churches to give the city a truly imperial character (see **Map 7.4**).

The greatest ruler was Theodosius II (r. 408–450), who enjoyed the longest imperial reign in Roman history. Through skillful diplomacy and the occasional application of force, he managed to keep the eastern empire free of serious Germanic incursions and the Persians at bay in Mesopotamia. To protect his capital on the landward side, he built massive walls, whose ruins are impressive even today. He promoted learning in the city and both added and beautified important buildings. Theodosius and his family made the new capital a real intellectual center.

Born in 401, Theodosius ascended the throne as a child. Throughout his life, the two greatest influences on him were his sister, Pulcheria (399–453), and his wife, Athenais-Eudoxia (ca. 400–460). Theodosius's moderate religious policy owed much to his wife, while his deep personal piety seems attributable to his sister. Pulcheria achieved the appointment and dismissal of imperial officers, guided foreign policy, and patronized scholars and churchmen. Only rarely do surviving sources permit us to observe the activities of imperial women. The cases of Pulcheria and Eudoxia hint at how much we do not know.

Theodosius's greatest achievement was his law code of 438. The most comprehensive collection of Roman law yet produced, this code brought together all Roman laws issued since Constantine and arranged them in systematic fashion. The principal Germanic kingdoms were

🌐 MAP 7.4—Constantinople in Late Antiquity

Protected by the sea, the Golden Horn, and its massive landward walls, Constantine's new city was an impregnable fortress for a thousand years. Note how the city was equipped with palaces, forums, wide thoroughfares, and other urban amenities.

(*Source:* The Cambridge Illustrated History of THE MIDDLE AGES, *edited by Robert Fossier, translated by Janet Sondheimer. Copyright* © 1989. Used by permission of Cambridge University Press.)

established just after the Theodosian code was issued. From this text, and from the Roman institutional structures that employed it, the barbarians were taught the rule of law and regulations for the conduct of daily affairs.

The Emperor Justinian (r. 527–565)

After Theodosius II died in 450, the eastern empire endured seventy-seven years of rule by military men who lacked the culture, vision, or administrative capacity of their predecessors. But they preserved the empire and kept its government functioning. It was from these rough soldiers that **Justinian** emerged to become the greatest ruler of Late Antiquity. (See the feature, "The Visual Record: The Ravenna Mosaics.")

Justinian was born in an Illyrian village (Croatia, today), entered the army, and secured high office under his illiterate uncle Justin, who had likewise risen from the peasantry to the imperial office (r. 518–527). Justinian surrounded himself with remarkable people and gave them considerable latitude. In 525, he flouted convention by marrying the actress Theodora (ca. 497–548). A woman of intelligence, imagination, and great courage, Theodora was one of Justinian's key

Justinian Emperor of the eastern empire, he is best known for his law code and for overseeing the construction of the Church of Hagia Sophia.

Theodosian Walls By 413, Theodosius II had erected a massive set of walls, extending more than four miles, to protect Constantinople on the landward side. The wall system consisted of a double set of walls with brick facings and rubble-filled interiors. The main walls (shown here) were about 35 feet high with towers about every 240 feet. (Sonia Halliday Photographs)

advisers. Contemporaries believed that she guided the emperor's religious policy. She certainly spent lavishly on charitable activities, not least, on homes for former prostitutes. Justinian also identified and promoted such previously obscure figures as the gifted general Belisarius (bel-uh-SAR-ee-us), the administrative genius John the Cappadocian, and the greatest legal mind of the age, Tribonian (tree-BONE-ee-un).

Almost immediately on assuming the throne, Justinian put John the Cappadocian to work reforming an administration that had been little altered in two centuries, despite vast changes in the scope of the empire. John worked particularly to secure tighter control of provincial administrators, to ensure a steady flow of tax revenue, and to eliminate official corruption. Tribonian and a commission were assigned the task of producing the first comprehensive collection of Roman law since that of Theodosius II in 438. Between 529 and 533, Justinian issued his code, the *Corpus Iuris Civilis* in several parts. Justinian's code, based on the idea that law should "give everyone his due," is the most influential legal collection in human history. It summarizes a thousand years of legal work, remained valid in the eastern empire until 1453, and has subsequently influenced almost every legal system in the modern world.

Not long after undertaking his legal and administrative reforms, Justinian launched an ambitious attempt to reunite the empire by reconquering its lost western provinces. Belisarius retook Africa from the Vandals and Italy from the Ostrogoths. Justinian also landed an army in Spain in an unsuccessful attempt to wrest Iberia from the Visigoths.

Justinian's ability to sustain major campaigns in the West was limited by the need to ward off constant threats in the East. The empire faced new enemies—Bulgars and Slavs—in the Balkans

donations to the church and populace. Still, by both personal conviction and a sense of official duty, Justinian desired religious unity. Justinian was mildly Monophysite, and his wife was enthusiastically so. Justinian tried again and again to find a compromise that would bring all parties together. His church council of 553 assembled amid high hopes, but his proposed doctrinal compromises alienated the clergy in Syria, Egypt, and Rome.

To create a monument equal to his lofty vision of the empire, Justinian sought out two great mathematicians, Anthemius of Tralles and Isidore of Miletus. He charged them to design a church that would represent the place where heaven and earth touched. Regular meetings in this place of the emperor, the patriarch, and the people gave repeated symbolic confirmation of the proper ordering of the state. There is no evidence that Justinian dictated the form of his church—the Church of Hagia Sophia (AYE-yuh so-FEE-yuh)—but the fact that he did not turn to any of the city's regular builders suggests that he was not looking for a conventional basilica. Tradition says that when Justinian first saw his new church he said "Solomon, I have outdone thee."

Hagia Sophia Interior view of Hagia Sophia, the church of "Holy Wisdom," built by Justinian between 527 and 532. The church combines traditional Roman features and stunning new elements. When Constantinople fell to the Turks in 1453, this church became a mosque, an Islamic house of worship. In the early twentieth century, it became a museum. (Werner Forman/Art Resource, NY)

Hagia Sophia was the largest Christian church until the construction of new Saint Peter's in Rome (1503–1614). The building begins with a square just over 100 feet on a side, 70 feet above which are four great arches. Two of the arches are solid and form the nave walls of the church; the other two give way to semicircular continuations of the nave. Above the main square is a dome that seems to float on the blaze of light that pours through its windows. The inside is a riot of color, achieved by marble fittings in almost every imaginable hue and by the mysterious play of light and shadow. The effect of the whole is disorienting. The space in most basilicas is ordered, controlled, and elegant. The space in Hagia Sophia is horizontal and vertical, straight and curved, square and round. The inside is by turns dark and light, purple and green, red and blue. It is indeed as if one has entered a realm that is anchored to this world but gives access to another.

It is appropriate that in assessing his church, Justinian should have looked backward to Solomon, the Hebrew king who built Jerusalem's Temple. Justinian was a traditional, backward-looking ruler. His concern for the administrative minutiae of his empire would have made perfect sense to Diocletian. His combination of military and diplomatic initiatives would have been appreciated by Theodosius I, whose namesake, Theodosius II, would have admired Justinian's legal code. In his religious policies, especially his quest for unity, Justinian drew from a deep well of imperial precedent. Even in his attempt to restore direct rule in Rome's former western provinces, Justinian showed himself a traditionalist.

Hagia Sophia　Constructed during the reign of the emperor Justinian, this church in Constantinople was the largest Christian church until the construction of Saint Peter's in the sixteenth century.

SECTION SUMMARY

- As the western empire was disappearing, the eastern empire experienced two centuries of capable, enlightened leadership.
- Constantinople was developed into a magnificent capital city.
- East Roman rulers continued to reform the administration and tax system.
- Both Theodosius II and Justinian made important contributions to the development of Roman law.

SOCIETY AND CULTURE IN LATE ANTIQUITY

How did women and men, elites and ordinary people, urban dwellers and farmers experience continuity and change in Late Antiquity?

During these centuries of the ascendancy of the eastern Roman Empire, and the splintering of the western, the daily lives of men and women of every social class changed relatively little in terms of power relationships and economic opportunities. Nevertheless, provincial elites, members of the clergy, and barbarians gained unprecedented influence. Ordinary farmers, the overwhelming majority of the population, experienced changes in their legal status but not in their material well-being. Secular intellectual life lost most of its vitality, but a vibrant Christian culture flourished in the writings of the Church Fathers. Christianity added yet another element to the diversity that always characterized the Roman world.

Social Hierarchies and Realities

Roman society had long been hierarchical, and from Republican times, Rome had been governed by a hereditary class. Although the members of this class affected a style of life that set them apart, they were never a closed caste. First, they did not reproduce themselves very effectively. About two-thirds of the Roman aristocracy was replaced every century—a typical pattern in premodern societies. This turnover created significant opportunities for social mobility. Second, just as the empire had been born in a social transformation that brought the Italian aristocracy into the Roman governing class, so Late Antiquity was characterized by a transformation that brought provincial elites and barbarians into the framework of power. Paradoxically, social change was always masked as social continuity, because when new men reached the top, they tried to embrace the culture and values of those whom they had replaced.

Three ideals guided the lives of elite men: *otium, amicitia*, and *officium*. *Otium*, "leisure," meant that the only life worth living was one of withdrawal in which the finer things in life—literature especially—could be cultivated. *Amicitia*, "friendship," implied several things. It could mean the kinds of literary contacts that the thousands of surviving letters from Late Antiquity reveal. Friendship also could mean patronage. The doorstep of every noble household was crowded every morning with hangers-on who awaited their patron's small offerings and any commands as to how they might do his will. *Officium*, "duty," was the sense of civic obligation that Roman rulers communicated to the provincial upper classes.

Aristocrats governed in both public and private ways. Though gradually excluded from key military and administrative posts, nobles did not lose their influence. They used their wealth to win or reward followers, bribe officials, and buy verdicts. In towns, decurions controlled local market privileges, building trades, police forces, fire brigades, and charitable associations. Their public and private means of persuasion and intimidation were immense. In the West, in the growing absence of an imperial administration, Roman public power did not so much "decline and fall" as find itself privatized and localized. Patronage and clientage in Roman society had a benevolent dimension, but they also revealed the raw realities of power.

In Roman society, power was everything, and those who lacked power were considered "poor," regardless of their financial status. On this reckoning, much of the urban population was poor because they lacked access to the official means of coercion and security that the notables enjoyed. Merchants, artisans, teachers, and others were always vulnerable because their social, political, or economic positions could change at a moment's notice. They lacked the influence to protect themselves.

Most citizens of the late antique world can be classed as farmers, but this categorization is misleading because it lumps together the greatest landowners and the poorest peasants. Late Antiquity saw a trend in the countryside that continued into the Middle Ages: Freedom and slavery declined simultaneously. In uncertain times, many small farmers handed over their possessions to local notables and received them back in return for rents in money or in kind. They became *coloni*, "tenants." Their patrons promised to protect them from lawsuits and from severe economic hardship. More and more, these coloni were bound to their places of residence and forced to perform services or pay fees that marked their status as less than fully free. At the same time, many landlords who could no longer afford to house, feed, and equip slaves gave them their freedom and elevated them to the status of coloni. Probably, the day-to-day lives of the great mass of the rural population and their position at the bottom of the social hierarchy changed very little.

Women's lives are not as well known to us as men's. "Nature produced women for this very purpose," says a Roman legal text, "that they might bear children and this is their greatest desire." Ancient philosophy held that women were intellectually inferior to men, science said they were physically weaker, and law maintained that they were naturally dependent. In the Roman world, women could not enter professions, and they had limited rights in legal matters. Christianity offered women opposing models. There was Eve, the eternal temptress through whom sin had fallen on humanity, and then there was Mary, the virginal mother of God. The Bible also presented readers with powerful, active women, such as Deborah and Ruth, and loyal, steadfast ones, such as Jesus' female disciples.

Girls usually did not choose their marriage partners. Betrothals could take place as early as age 7 and lawful marriages at 12. Most marriages took place when the girl was around 16; husbands were several years older. A daughter could reject her father's choice only if the intended man was unworthy in status and behavior. Women could inherit property from their fathers and retained some control over their marital dowries. Divorce was possible but only in restricted cases. A divorced woman who had lost the financial security provided by her husband and father was at a distinct disadvantage legally and economically unless she had great wealth.

Christianity brought some interesting changes in marriage practices. Since the new faith prized virginity and celibacy, women now had the option of declining marriage. The church at Antioch supported three thousand virgins and widows. Christian writers tried to attract women to the celibate life by emphasizing that housework was drudgery. Christianity required both men and women to be faithful in marriage, whereas Roman custom had permitted men, but not women, to have lovers, prostitutes, and concubines. Christianity increased the number of days when men and women had to abstain from sex. Ancient cultures often prohibited sexual intercourse during menstruation and pregnancy, but Christianity added Sundays and many feast days as forbidden times. Further, Christianity disapproved of divorce, which may have accorded women greater financial and social security, although, at the cost of staying with abusive or unloved husbands.

Traditionally women were not permitted to teach in the ancient world, although we do hear of women teachers, such as Hypatia of Alexandria (355–415), renowned for her knowledge of philosophy and mathematics. Until at least the sixth century, the Christian church had deaconesses who had important responsibilities in the instruction of women and girls. Medical knowledge was often the preserve of women, particularly in areas such as childbirth, sexual problems, and "female complaints."

Christianity also affected daily life. Churchmen were concerned that women not be seen as sex objects. They told women to clothe their flesh, veil their hair, and use jewelry and cosmetics in moderation. Pious women no longer used public baths and latrines. Male or female, Christians thought and lived in distinctive new ways. All Christians were sinners, and so all were equal in God's eyes and equally in need of God's grace. Neither birth, wealth, nor status was supposed to matter in this democracy of sin. Theological equality did not, however, translate into social equality.

The church also introduced some new status distinctions. Holiness became a badge of honor, and holy men and women became Late Antiquity's greatest celebrities. After their death, they were venerated as saints. Sanctuaries were dedicated to them, and people made pilgrimages to their tombs to pray and seek healing from physical and spiritual ailments. Thus, in some ways, Christianity produced a society the likes of which the ancient world had never known, a society in which the living and the dead jockeyed for a place in a hierarchy that was at once earthly and celestial. But in other ways, Christianity reoriented traditional Roman patron-client relations so that client sinners in this world were linked to sanctified patrons in heaven.

The Quest for a Catholic Tradition

By the middle of the fifth century, the Nicene Creed, first spelled out in 325, had taken definitive shape; it is still recited regularly in many Christian churches. With the Council of Nicaea, we see the first clear evidence that people were striving for a *catholic*, a universal, form of Christianity. Strictly speaking, catholic Christianity would be the one form professed by all believers. It is no accident that the Catholic Church grew up in a Roman world steeped in ideas of universality. The most deeply held tenet of Roman ideology was that Rome's mission was to civilize the world and bend it to Roman ways. As we have seen, however, it proved impossible to attain or impose a single set of beliefs.

One intriguing development in Late Antiquity is the emergence of several Christian communities claiming fidelity to a universal, or catholic, tradition. The Latin Christian church in the West clung tightly to the doctrinal formulations of Nicaea and Chalcedon and took its bearings from Latin church writers. In the eastern Mediterranean, writers tended to use the word *Orthodox*, which means "right believing" but also carries clear implications of catholicism, or "universality." The Orthodox Church centered primarily on the emperors and patriarchs, used Greek, and followed Greek Christian writers. The Coptic Church in Egypt was Monophysite, followed the teachings of the patriarchs of Alexandria, and used the Coptic language. The Jacobite Church, mildly Monophysite, was originally strong in Syria, from which it spread to Mesopotamia and beyond. Each of these churches produced a literature, art, and way of life that marked its members as a distinct community. These traditions did not reflect the emergence of something new in Late Antiquity so much as a Christian reinterpretation of very old cultures and ideals. Each of these traditions exists today.

Christianity drew much from the pagan and Jewish environments within which it grew, but its fundamental inspiration was the collection of writings called in modern times the Bible. It was understood to be a collection of sacred writings, and the individual items in that collection had different meanings. From the second century, Christian writers began trying to define a canon, a definitive list of genuine Old and New Testament scriptures. It was widely recognized that without an official, standardized set of Christian writings, there could be no uniformity of Christian belief. This process of determining authentic Scripture was not completed until the middle of the fifth century.

While the search was underway for an authoritative list of books, it was also necessary to try to get uniform versions of the books that were being pronounced canonical. The Greek East used the Greek version of the Old Testament and the Greek New Testament. But that version was unsuitable in the West, where Latin was the principal tongue. Late in the fourth century, Pope Damasus (DAM-uh-sus) commissioned Jerome (331–420), a man who had renounced his wealth for a life of monasticism and scholarship, to prepare a Latin version based on a new translation of the Hebrew Scriptures and Greek New Testament. Jerome's version was called the **Vulgate Bible** because it was the Bible for the "people" (*vulgus*), who knew Latin.

Vulgate Bible   Prepared by Jerome in the late fourth century, it was a Latin translation of the Hebrew Scriptures (Old Testament) and the Greek New Testament.

Sarcophagus of Junius Bassus Junius Bassus, prefect of Rome, died in 359 and was laid to rest in this splendid sarcophagus (from the Greek "body eater"). Three points are important: First, as members of the Roman elite became Christian, they could afford to employ the finest craftsmen. Second, as Christianity became legal, it could search for artistic expression. Third, these Old and New Testament scenes proclaim Christ's divinity but, in an age of intense theological quarrels, glide over his humanity. Compare Santa Maria Maggiore on page 170. (Scala/Art Resource, NY)

The development of a scriptural canon paralleled the elaboration of a creedal statement that would set down precisely what Christians believed. As we have seen, the Councils of Nicaea and Constantinople defined the nature of the Trinity, and Chalcedon formulated the relationship between the human and divine natures of Christ. There were also debates about the nature of the priesthood, the structure and authority of the church, and the problem of human free will. Practical questions came up, too. How could Christians fulfill the moral demands of their faith while living in a world whose values were often at odds with church teachings?

Answers to these kinds of questions were provided by a group of Greek and Latin writers who are called the "Church Fathers" and whose era is called "patristic" (from *patres*, the Latin word for "fathers"). In versatility and sheer output, they have few rivals at any time. Their intellectual breadth was matched by their elegant style and trenchant reasoning.

Many Christian writers addressed the problems of moral living in the world. In his treatise, *On Duties*, Ambrose of Milan (339–397) attempted to Christianize the public ethos that Cicero had spelled out many years before in his book of the same name. Cicero talked of citizens' obligations to one another and to the law and the need for those in power to be above reproach in the conduct of their personal lives. Ambrose reinterpreted these obligations as duties that Christians owed to one another because of their common worship of God.

Pope Gregory I wrote *The Pastoral Rule* to reformulate Cicero's and Ambrose's ideas in ways that made them relevant to society's Christian leaders, the clergy. John Chrysostom (KRIH-sus-tum) (347–407), a patriarch of Constantinople and one of the most popular and gifted preachers of Late Antiquity (his name means "golden tongued"), bitterly castigated the immorality of the imperial court and aristocracy: By setting a bad example, they endangered the souls of their subjects.

Boethius (bow-EE-thee-us) (480–524) illustrates contemporary themes well. Descended from one of Rome's oldest families, he held high offices but eventually earned the enmity of Theodoric the Ostrogoth, who imprisoned and executed him. He was a prolific writer, whose Latin translations of Greek philosophical texts bequeathed those writings to the Middle Ages. In his most famous book, *The Consolation of Philosophy*, written while he was in prison, Boethius describes how the soul could rise through philosophy to a knowledge of God. Once again, we see the classical and the Christian blended in a new synthesis.

Saint Augustine and the Christian Tradition

The most influential Christian thinker after Saint Paul was **Augustine of Hippo** (354–430). Augustine was born in North Africa to a pagan father and a Christian mother. His family was of modest means, but at great sacrifice, they arranged for him to receive the best education available. He embarked on a career as a professor of rhetoric. Augustine fell under the spell of Ambrose and embraced the Christianity that his mother, Monica, had been urging on him throughout his life. Later, Augustine chronicled his quest for truth and spiritual fulfillment in his *Confessions*, a classic of Western literature. In 395, Augustine became a bishop and, until his death, served the wider Christian world, with a torrent of writings.

Not a systematic thinker, Augustine never set out to provide a comprehensive exposition of the whole of Christian doctrine. Instead, he responded to problems as they arose. Crucial among these were the relationship between God and humans, the nature of the church, and the overall plan of God's creation.

In the early fifth century, some people believed that they could achieve salvation by the unaided operation of their own will. Augustine responded that although God did indeed endow humankind with free will, Adam and Eve had abused their will to rebel against God. Ever since that first act of rebellion, a taint, called by theologians "original sin," predisposed all humans to continual rebellion, or sin, against God. Only divine grace can overcome sin, and only by calling on God can people receive grace. Here was a decisive break with the classical idea of humanity as good in itself and capable of self-improvement, perhaps even perfection, in this world.

Some North African heretics taught that sacraments celebrated by unworthy priests are invalid. Augustine believed that the validity of the church's sacraments—those ritual celebrations that are considered to be channels for the communication of grace, of God's special aid and comfort to the faithful—does not depend on the personal merit of the minister. They depended on the grace of God. To Augustine, God alone is perfect. Clergy, rulers, and churches are all human institutions, all more or less good in particular circumstances.

To many adherents of the traditional Roman religion, the sack of Rome by the Visigoths in 410 was repayment for Rome's abandonment of its traditional gods. To refute them, Augustine wrote the most brilliant and difficult of all his works, *The City of God*. This book is a theology of history. Augustine sees time not as cyclical—the traditional classical view—but as linear. Since the creation of the world, a plan has been in operation—God's plan—and that plan will govern all human activity until the end of time. History is the struggle between those who call on divine grace, who are redeemed, who are citizens of the City of God, and those who keep to the ways of the world, who persist in sin, who live in the earthly city. One may observe the unfolding of the divine plan by seeing how much of the earthly city has been redeemed at any given time.

Even though the Roman Empire was officially Christian, Augustine refused to identify his City of God with it. Nor would he say that the church and the City of God were identical. What he did say was that the sack of Rome was a great irrelevance because many kingdoms and empires had come and gone and would continue to do so, but only the kingdom of God was eternal and, in the long run, important. To a Roman people whose most cherished belief held that the world would last exactly as long as Rome's dominion, Augustine's dismissal of Rome's destiny sounded the death knell of the classical worldview.

Augustine also addressed the problem of education. He regarded salvation as the goal of life but realized that people have to carry on with their ordinary occupations. He also knew that almost the entire educational establishment was pagan in design and content. Education was confined mainly to the elite, who sought schooling partly to orient themselves within their cultural tradition and partly to gain employment, often in the imperial or urban service. This education had three mainstays. Latin or Greek grammar—rarely both—was the first. Augustine, for instance, knew little Greek, and by the sixth century, few people in the East knew Latin. The second mainstay of education was rhetoric, once the art of public speaking but now, increasingly, literary criticism. The third was dialectic, or the art of right reasoning. In Late Antiquity, public schools were fast disappearing as the need for them slipped away. But the church still needed educated persons, so it provided schools in cathedrals and monasteries.

In a treatise entitled *On Christian Doctrine*, Augustine expressed some ideas about education that proved influential for a millennium. He argued that everything a person needs to know to achieve salvation is contained in the Bible. But the Bible, written in learned language, is full of difficult images and allusions. How is an ordinary person to learn what he or she needs to know

Augustine of Hippo
North African bishop and influential Christian thinker, he authored the *Confessions* and *The City of God*.

SECTION SUMMARY

- Despite dramatic political changes, Late Antiquity witnessed relatively little social or economic change.

- Christianity did, however, introduce many changes in morals and values.

- Late Antiquity presents us with the paradox of multiple "Catholic" traditions, that is, different Christian groups who believed that their tradition was universal.

- In the Latin and Greek churches, a catholic tradition was built upon a canon of sacred writings, a creed, and the writings of the Church Fathers.

- The greatest intellectual of Late Antiquity was Saint Augustine, who wrote on theology, history, and education.

in order to master this great book of life? Only by getting some schooling, and that education would inevitably be in the classical languages and literatures. Augustine's attitude toward classical learning was that it was useful only to the extent that it equipped individuals to read the Bible, to understand it, and to seek salvation. Classical culture had no intrinsic merit. It might give pleasure, but it was equally likely to be a distraction or a temptation to immorality.

The Italian writer Cassiodorus (ca. 485–580) gave this Augustinian interpretation of the classical heritage its definitive statement in his treatise, *On Divine and Human Readings*. His treatise served as a kind of annotated bibliography and curriculum of the major writings on school subjects, such as grammar, rhetoric, and dialectic, and on biblical commentary. For centuries, schools organized on Augustine's and Cassiodorus's model did an estimable job of preparing the clergy to carry out their functions.

CHAPTER SUMMARY

When the late antique period opened, Rome's vast and diverse empire was beset with innumerable political, military, and economic problems. The classical culture that had evolved over centuries in the Mediterranean world seemed to have lost much of its vigor and appeal. But energetic rulers, such as Diocletian and Constantine, undertook half a century of intense military, economic, and administrative reform. On religious issues, the rulers differed—Diocletian persecuted Christians while Constantine legalized the new faith. Their reforms put the empire on firm footing while simultaneously changing forever the basic nature of the Roman state.

The fourth century was a period of religious change for the empire. Church officials attempted to resolve disagreements over Christian teachings with ecumenical councils, but religious unity was never fully achieved. Further attempts to resolve controversies strengthened the power of the bishops and created the new role of the papacy. As the power of the pope increased, so too did the role of the elite. However, some men and women yearned to escape the trappings of the world and turned toward a new way of life—monasticism.

In 300, barbarians were a worrisome threat along the northern frontiers of the empire. By 600, barbarians had created, from Britain to Spain, a succession of kingdoms, the most successful of which owed great debts to Rome. The barbarians did not appear suddenly in Late Antiquity. Rome knew these people and had traded, fought, and allied with them for centuries. The barbarians did not come to destroy Rome but to join it, to benefit from it, to learn its ways. The creation of the barbarian kingdoms was, in many ways, one of Rome's most creative political acts.

In the eastern empire, Constantinople rose to become a truly imperial city under the emperors Theodosius and Justinian. Justinian's code, which collected and organized Roman law, is the most influential legal collection in history. Equally impressive was the construction of a new Christian church, the Hagia Sophia. Yet despite these achievements, Justinian had to deal with new enemies, expensive military campaigns, and a devastating plague.

FOCUS QUESTIONS

- What were the most important reforms of Diocletian, Constantine, and their successors, and what roles did those reforms play in saving and transforming the empire?

- How and why did a Roman and Catholic Church emerge in Late Antiquity?

- Who were the "barbarians," and what kinds of relations did Romans and barbarians have in Late Antiquity?

- What challenges did the eastern empire face and what were some of its major contributions?

- How did women and men, elites and ordinary people, urban dwellers and farmers experience continuity and change in Late Antiquity?

While these centuries were a period of great political and religious change, the daily lives of men and women stayed remarkably unchanged. Society was hierarchical and most of the population was categorized as poor. Christianity brought some changes to social practices, such as marriage and relationships between men and women. Believers strived for a universal, or catholic, form of Christianity and this led to the development of a scriptural canon. New writings on Christianity, from Saint Augustine and others, also helped to shape beliefs.

KEY TERMS

tetrarchy   (p. 168)

Edict of Milan   (p. 171)

heresy   (p. 174)

Arianism   (p. 174)

Council of Nicaea   (p. 175)

monasticism   (p. 178)

eremitic monasticism
   (p. 178)

cenobitic monasticism
   (p. 178)

Visigoths   (p. 180)

Justinian   (p. 186)

Hagia Sophia   (p. 191)

Vulgate Bible   (p. 193)

Augustine of Hippo   (p. 195)

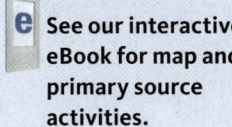 This icon will direct you to additional materials on the website: www .cengage.com/history/ noble/westciv6e.

See our interactive eBook for map and primary source activities.

8

CHAPTER OUTLINE

The Islamic East

The Byzantine Empire

The Rise of the Carolingian Empire

Early Medieval Economies and Societies

The Great Mosque of Cordoba
(Christopher Rennie/Robert Harding World Imagery)

Early Medieval Civilizations, 600–900

This chapter treats three areas and histories: the Islamic East, the Byzantine Empire, and the Latin West. For each, the seventh century was an era of dramatic change, the eighth century a period of reform and consolidation, and the ninth century a time of upheaval. A new imperial tradition developed in all three areas. Muslims, Orthodox Christians, and Catholics all believed themselves to be chosen by God, and their rulers defined themselves as God's earthly agents. In all three realms, the interaction of local traditions and the Roman past produced new forms of central government that would prove influential for centuries. Commercial ties began to transform the Mediterranean world into a community of peoples who needed to balance mutual interests with bitter rivalries.

The Great Mosque of Cordoba, erected by Abd ar-Rahman in 786–787, at first glance, appears much like a late antique building: elegant columns, arches arranged in arcades, rectangular space. But this is a *mosque*, an Islamic house of worship, and it was built in Spain, one of Rome's oldest provinces. We saw in Chapter 7 that Spain had fallen to the Visigoths in the sixth century and that Justinian had been unable to reconquer the region. Between 711 and 716, an army of Arabs and North African tribesmen overwhelmed Spain and inaugurated seven centuries of Islamic rule on the Iberian Peninsula. A time traveler transported to the Mediterranean world of 600 would almost certainly have predicted only two heirs to Rome: the eastern empire and the kingdoms of the barbarian West. It is extremely unlikely that our intrepid wanderer would have foreseen one of the most dramatic developments in the history of Western civilization: the rise of the Arabs and their Islamic faith.

The Great Mosque serves as a remarkable reminder of how much changed—and how much remained the same—in the early Middle Ages. Arches and arcades graced classical architecture for more than a millennium. But Cordoba's arches are horseshoe shaped, a minor innovation. The arches incorporate alternating bands of red and cream-colored stone. These shapes and colors may be local traditions, an imitation of the Roman aqueduct at Mérida, Byzantine imports, or Syrian characteristics. The building is basilican in shape. In a basilica, the space is oriented to the area where officials presided—to an altar when the basilica is a church. In a mosque, the space is oriented to the *qibla* wall—the wall facing Mecca, the birthplace of Muhammad and Islam. The elements of the Great Mosque were old, but the overall effect was new.

The period from 600 to 900 is commonly called the "early Middle Ages." What does this term mean? In the seventeenth century, a Dutch scholar wrote of the *Medii Aevi*, the "Middle Times" that lay between antiquity and the dawning modern world. The name stuck.

FOCUS QUESTIONS

- What were the most important factors in the rise of the Arab peoples and the Islamic faith?

- Why did a distinctive civilization that can be called "Byzantine" emerge?

- What were the greatest achievements of the Carolingians and why were they so successful compared to the other states that survived Rome's collapse in the West?

- What were the chief similarities and differences among the early medieval civilizations?

This icon will direct you to additional materials on the website: www .cengage.com/history/ noble/westciv6e.

See our interactive eBook for map and primary source activities.

As a label for the post-Roman world, "Middle Ages" (whose adjectival form is "medieval") has become traditional. The fact that we no longer talk of an abrupt and catastrophic "fall" of the Roman Empire means that we no longer use the word *medieval* in negative ways.

THE ISLAMIC EAST

What were the most important factors in the rise of the Arab peoples and the Islamic faith?

Muhammad Prophet and founder of Islam. He began receiving revelations to preach about Allah in around 610. Before his death, he had converted most of Arabia.

Ancient writers took little notice of the Arabs, who inhabited the Arabian peninsula and lands to the north. Around 600, the prophet **Muhammad** (570–632) appeared among them preaching a faith old in its basic elements but new in its formulation. With unprecedented spiritual and military fervor, converts to that new faith conquered territories from Spain to the frontiers of China. Slowly, they built an imperial system with a coherent government and ideology. At the same time, cultural elites began forging a new civilization out of the ethnic, religious, and historical diversity of that vast realm.

Arabia Before Muhammad

The Arab world in 600 was large and turbulent. Long dominated by the Roman and Persian Empires, the region had no large-scale political entities. People belonged to close-knit clans, or extended families, that formed tribes. In theory, tribes were groups of people tracing descent from a known ancestor; in reality—and in this, Arab and Germanic peoples were alike—tribes were complex groups of relatives, allies, and political or economic clients.

The Arab East was also economically intricate and fragile. Bedouins (Arabs who were nomadic pastoralists) provided for their own needs from their herds of sheep and goats, from small-scale trading in towns, and from regular raids on one another and on caravans. Some farmers worked the land, but in many areas, soils were too poor and rain was too infrequent to support agriculture. Cities supported traders who carried luxury goods, such as spices, incense, and perfumes, from the Indian Ocean region and southern Arabia along caravan routes to the cities of the eastern Mediterranean. These traders formed the economic and political elite of Arabia, and they led the tribes. Mecca, dominated by the powerful Quraysh (KOOR-aysh) tribe, was the foremost city of Arabia.

A solution to the competition among tribes and towns for control of trade routes was the institution of *harams* (HAR-ahms), or sanctuaries—places where contending parties could settle disputes peacefully. Mecca was one of the chief harams in Arabia, and its founding was attributed to the Israelite patriarch Abraham and one of his sons, Ishmael. The focus of the sanctuary was the black stone shrine known as the Kaaba (KAH-bah), founded by Abraham, according to Arab tradition. For centuries, people from all over Arabia had made pilgrimages to Mecca, to the Kaaba, supposedly following Abraham's example.

The region's ethnic and religious composition was complicated, too. The Roman world was overwhelmingly Christian, although there were many kinds of Christians. The Persian realm was officially Zoroastrian, but it had Jewish, Christian, Manichaean, and Buddhist minorities. The Arabs themselves were generally pagans, but Arabia had Jewish and Christian minorities.

The Prophet and His Faith

Muhammad was born in 570 to a respectable, though not wealthy or powerful, clan of the Quraysh tribe. His father died before he was born, his mother shortly afterward, leaving Muhammad under the care of his grandparents and an uncle. Like many young Meccans, he entered the caravan trade. By the time he was 20, Muhammad had such a reputation for competence and moral uprightness that he became financial adviser to a wealthy Quraysh widow, Khadija (KAH-dee-ah) (555–619). Though older than Muhammad, she became his wife in 595, and they had a loving marriage until her death.

In 610, Muhammad received the first of many revelations that commanded him to teach all people a new faith that called for an unquestioned belief in one god, Allah, and a deep commitment to social justice for believers. Muhammad began teaching in Mecca, but he converted few people outside his own circle; his wife was his first convert. Some Meccans were envious of Muhammad. Others feared that his new faith and new god might call into question the legitimacy of the shrines in Mecca and jeopardize the traditional pilgrimages to the Kaaba and the trade that accompanied them. By 619, Muhammad's well-connected wife and uncle were dead, and his position was precarious.

At this juncture, citizens from Medina, a smaller trading community wracked by dissension among pagan Arabs, Jews, and followers of Muhammad, asked Muhammad to establish a haram there. In the summer of 622, small groups of Muhammad's disciples made their way to Medina, and, in September, Muhammad joined them. His journey from Mecca to Medina, the *hijra* (HEEZH-rah), marks the beginning of a new era, symbolized to this day in the Arab world by a calendar that dates "In the year of the Hijra."

Although Muhammad was fully in control in Medina, Mecca retained his attention. In addition to his sentimental attachment to Mecca, its political and economic importance was critical to his emerging desire to convert all of Arabia. His followers began attacking Meccan caravans and battled with the Meccans several times in the 620s. In 630, Muhammad and many of his followers returned to Mecca in triumph. Muhammad left the Quraysh in control, and he retained the Kaaba as a focus of piety. After making local arrangements, he returned to Medina and set about winning over the bedouins of the Arabian desert. By the time Muhammad died in 632, he had converted most of Arabia (see **Map 8.1**).

To what exactly had Muhammad and his followers converted? At the most basic level, people were asked to surrender completely to Allah, the one true God—that is, they were asked to make *al-Islam*, "the surrender." Those who surrendered became *Muslims* and joined the *umma muslima* (OO-mah MOOSE-lee-mah), a completely new kind of community in which membership depended only on belief in Allah and acceptance of Muhammad as Allah's prophet. No longer were one's bonds confined to a particular clan, tribe, or town. All members of the umma were understood to have personal and communal responsibility for all other members. Because of the experience of the hijra, Islam was a religion of exile, of separation from the ordinary world, and of reliance on God.

The basic teachings of Islam are traditionally described as **Five Pillars**: (1) the profession of faith, "There is no God but Allah and Muhammad is His Prophet"; (2) individual prayer five times daily, plus group prayer at noon on Friday in a *mosque*, a Muslim house of prayer; (3) the sunup-to-sundown fast for one month per year; (4) the donation of generous alms to the poor; and (5) a pilgrimage to Mecca at least once in a person's lifetime. These pillars are still the central requirements of Islam.

In the early decades the pillars sustained a faith that stressed strict monotheism and practices that affirmed Islam and built up a sense of community. At certain times of the day, all Muslims everywhere bowed in prayer, with their heads facing toward Mecca. Everyone paid alms, creating thereby a feeling of solidarity among all members of the umma. Mecca itself and the experience of pilgrimage were central to all Muslims.

Originally, there was no elaborate theology, intricate doctrinal mysteries, creed, or clergy. Men called *imams* led the Friday prayers in the mosque and usually offered sermons that applied Muslim teaching to the issues of the day, but Islam involved no ordained priesthood, as in Judaism or Christianity, and no hierarchy, as in the Christian churches.

Muhammad always insisted that he transmitted a direct, verbal revelation, not his own interpretations. That revelation came in the form of "recitations" that make up the **Quran** (koo-RAHN), the Scriptures of Islam. Not long after Muhammad's death, his closest followers arranged

CHRONOLOGY

570–632	Life of Muhammad
597	Pope Gregory I sends missionaries to England
610–641	Reign of Heraclius in Byzantium
622	Hijra
632–733	Muslim conquests
661–750	Umayyad caliphate
664	Council of Whitby
711–716	Muslim conquest of Spain
726–787, 815–842	Byzantine iconoclasm
750	Founding of Abbasid caliphate
751	Lombard conquest of Ravenna
755–756	Foundation of Papal States
755–774	Frankish conquest of Lombards
757–796	Reign of Offa of Mercia
768–814	Reign of Charlemagne
780s–860s	Carolingian Renaissance
786–809	Reign of Harun al-Rashid
800	Imperial coronation of Charlemagne
843	Treaty of Verdun creates three Frankish kingdoms
867–886	Reign of Basil I

Five Pillars The basic beliefs and practices of Islam.

Quran Containing Allah's revelations to Muhammad, it constitutes the scriptures of Islam.

🌐 **MAP 8.1—Arab Conquests to 733**

This map vividly illustrates the spectacular gains by the Arabs in the time of Muhammad, under the first caliphs, and under the Umayyads. Later slow, steady gains in Africa, central Asia, and India expanded the empire even farther. Muslim conquest did not at first mean widespread conversion to Islam; Egypt, for example, was not majority Muslim before the tenth century.

the recitations into 114 *Suras*, or chapters. The Quran contains legal and wisdom literature, like the Hebrew Scriptures, and moral teaching, like the Christian New Testament. It also prescribes regulations for diet and for personal conduct.

For example, the Quran forbids alcohol and gambling, censures luxury and ostentation, and imposes strict sexual restraints on both men and women. (See the feature, "The Written Record: The Message of the Quran.") The Quran permitted a man to have up to four wives if he could care for them and would treat them equitably. A Muslim woman, however, was given her dowry outright, and multiple marriages may have meant that relatively more Muslim women could gain a measure of security.

Initially, the Quran was interpreted rather freely within the umma, doubtless because there was no clergy to impose a uniform interpretation. After the Prophet's death, some people felt the need for an authoritative teaching—as early Christians had felt the need for a canon of Christian scripture and teaching—and their efforts resulted in the collections called the *sunna*, which means roughly "good practice"—that is, the words and customs of Muhammad himself. Crucial in the development of the sunna were the *hadith*, the "sayings" of the Prophet, the comments he sometimes made about how God's revelation was to be understood and applied. Extant compilations of the sunna date from the ninth century, and scholars are not sure what portion of them derives authentically from the age of the Prophet.

The Arab Conquests

Muhammad's death brought a crisis. Who or what was to succeed him? In 632, the Meccan elite chose Abu Bakr as *caliph* (KAY-lif), or "successor to the Prophet." Abu Bakr was elderly, an early convert to Islam, and a former secretary to Muhammad. He and his three successors down to 661 (Umar, Uthman, and Ali) were all Meccans, relatives of the Prophet by marriage, and early converts. Islamic tradition calls them the "Rightly Guided Caliphs."

The Message of the Quran

The Quran consists of 114 Suras, literally the "steps" (we might say chapters) by which one rises to knowledge of Allah. The earliest versions of the Quran were equipped with a running commentary. The first four extracts here illustrate the simplicity and elegance of Muslim prayer and the absolute transcendence of Allah. The last two extracts demonstrate the profound sense of religious continuity that marked Muhammad's teaching.

Sura 1

In the name of Allah, Most Gracious, Most Merciful. / Praise be to Allah, the Cherisher and Sustainer of worlds; / Most Gracious, Most Merciful. / Master of the Day of Judgment. / Thee do we worship and Thine aid we seek. Show us the straight way, the way of those on whom Thou hast bestowed Thy grace, Thou whose portion is not wrath, and who do not go astray.

Sura 4.171

O People of the Book! Commit no excesses in your religion, nor say of Allah anything but truth. Christ Jesus the son of Mary was a messenger of Allah … so believe in Allah and in His messengers. Say not "Trinity" … for Allah is One God. Glory be to Him for He is exalted above having a son. To Him belong all things in the heavens and on earth.

Sura 3.84

Say ye: We believe in Allah, and the revelation given to us, and to Abraham, Ismail, Isaac, Jacob and the descendants (children of Jacob), and that given to Moses and to Jesus and that given to all prophets from their Lord, but we make no difference between one and another of them, and we bow to Allah.

Sura 2.87

We gave Moses the book and followed him up with a succession of messengers; We gave Jesus the son of Mary clear signs and strengthened him with the Holy Spirit.

Sura 48

If the People of the Book rely upon Abraham, let them study his history. His posterity included both Israel and Ismail. Abraham was a righteous man of Allah, a Muslim, and so were his children. Abraham and Ismail built the Kaaba as the house of Allah and purified it, to be a centre of worship for all the world: For Allah is the God of all peoples.

Sura 56

God's truth is continuous, and His prophets from Adam, through Noah and Abraham, down to the last of the prophets, Muhammad, form one brotherhood. Of Imran father of Moses and Aaron sprang a woman, who devoted her unborn offspring to Allah. That child was Mary the mother of Jesus. Her cousin was the wife of the priest Zakariya, who took charge of Mary. To Zakariya, in his old age, was born a son Yahya, amid prodigies: Yahya was the herald of Jesus the son of Mary and was known as John the Baptist.

QUESTIONS

1. What can you discern from these suras about the similarities and differences among Islam, Christianity, and Judaism?

2. Who are the "people of the book"? Why do you think they matter?

3. How is Allah portrayed in these suras?

Source: *The Meaning of the Holy Qur'an*, new edition with revised translation, commentary, and newly compiled comprehensive index by Abdullah Yusuf Ali. Amana Publications, 1988.

Abu Bakr left his successor, Umar, a united Arabia (see **MAP 8.1**), no small feat in that fractious world. Umar began the lightning conquests by the Arabs of much of the Roman and Persian Empires. He initiated the policy of granting choice positions in the expanding **caliphate**, the Arab empire, to old converts and of ranking them according to precedence in conversion. As the old elite divided up the new provinces of the caliphate, some of them became *emirs* (governors), and others became lower administrators. Arab administrators then collected from all conquered people personal taxes and land taxes. Converts to Islam paid only land taxes. Arab settlers paid no taxes and received salaries from the taxes paid by others.

Umar was murdered by a slave in 644, leaving his successor, Uthman, a huge empire to administer. A great centralizer, Uthman chose emirs, regulated the finances of the provinces, and authorized the preparation of the definitive text of the Quran. In attempting to preserve the advantages of the old Meccan elite, Uthman alienated many people, particularly in Egypt, Syria, and Iraq, who had benefited from conquest and who guarded jealously their newfound local wealth and power. Uthman was murdered in 656 and replaced by Ali, Muhammad's son-in-law, whose goal was to create a truly Islamic government by emphasizing the religious side of

caliphate The name for the territory conquered by Muhammad's successors and for the governmental regime they established.

Coin of Empress Irene This gold *nomisma* of the empress Irene was struck between 797 and 802. The text reads "Irene, Empress." Note the craftsmanship of the Byzantine moneyers. (Courtesy of the Trustees of the British Museum)

in Italy, except for the areas around Naples and Sicily. In 827, Muslims seized Sicily, and in the ensuing decades, they subjected southern Italy to continuous raids and occasional conquests.

After Constantine V's death, unsettled conditions prevailed until Irene (ca. 752–803) succeeded in 780, first as regent for her son and then as empress—the only woman to rule Byzantium in her own right. Irene was a skilled politician, but under her, the army grew restive because she preferred to make treaties, sometimes on unfavorable terms, than to send troops into the field. She did not trust the military's loyalty. Moreover, Irene had to contend with a foolish son who spent his time trysting with ladies of the court rather than attending to his official duties. In 797, Irene had him blinded, ironically in the very palace chamber where she had given birth to him. This was not a barbaric act in the Byzantine way of thinking. By mutilating Constantine VI, she merely rendered him unfit to rule: Roman ideology held that only a physically perfect person could reign; the alternative would have been to murder him. In any case, Irene's credibility sank to nothing, and in 802, she was deposed by a wily old soldier, Nicephorus (nye-SEFF-for-us) (r. 802–811).

For two generations, Byzantium suffered through short reigns, usurpations, political unrest, and military reverses. In 867, a rough soldier, Basil I (r. 867–886), seized the throne and, like Heraclius and Leo III before him, reversed the fortunes of the state. He established a new dynasty, the "Macedonian," and for the first time in years won important military victories. This dynasty ruled effectively until the eleventh century.

New Forms of Government

Even as its territory was shrinking, Byzantium undertook military and administrative reforms, revised its laws, and refocused its culture, particularly its religious practices. In the early Middle Ages, a distinctive "Byzantium" emerged in place of Rome.

Leo III and Constantine V are reminiscent of Diocletian and Constantine, or of Justinian. They energetically brought to completion military reforms that had been pursued intermittently since the late sixth century. These reforms amounted to a major administrative change. For centuries, Rome had recruited, trained, and paid professional troops out of tax revenues; they even used tax revenues to settle barbarian soldiers in their midst. Leo and Constantine put the finishing touches on a new "theme" system.

Men from frontier regions were now recruited and settled on farms in military districts called *themes*. All themes, whether land-based army ones or sea-based naval ones, were under the command of a leader who was simultaneously the civil and military chief of his theme. The farmer-soldiers did not pay taxes on their farms but discharged their obligation to the state by personal service. Henceforth, the thematic armies (see **MAP 8.2**) formed the backbone of the Roman system. The new system demanded less tax revenue and fewer bureaucrats. The empire was smaller than in the past and needed a different kind of army: Smaller squadrons concentrated near the threatened frontier regions in Anatolia and the Balkans rather than large armies that were expensive to maintain and cumbersome to transport over long distances.

There were other reforms, too. Leo issued the *Ecloga* (ECK-low-guh), the first major revision and updating of Roman law since Justinian's. Leo and Constantine also instituted far-reaching reforms in imperial administration, which had changed little in centuries. Roman bureaucracy had consisted of a few large departments headed by officials with immense responsibilities and power. The revised Byzantine system was characterized by a profusion of departments under officers who had little real power. The emperor neutralized the bureaucrats by drawing them from all social classes, paying them well, and giving them pompous titles and lots of public recognition, all the while dividing their responsibilities, curbing their influence, and making them dependent on himself.

The Birth of Byzantine Culture

Byzantine culture came to be increasingly defined by the church. The massive Arab conquests that stripped Byzantium of so much territory also removed the ancient patriarchates of

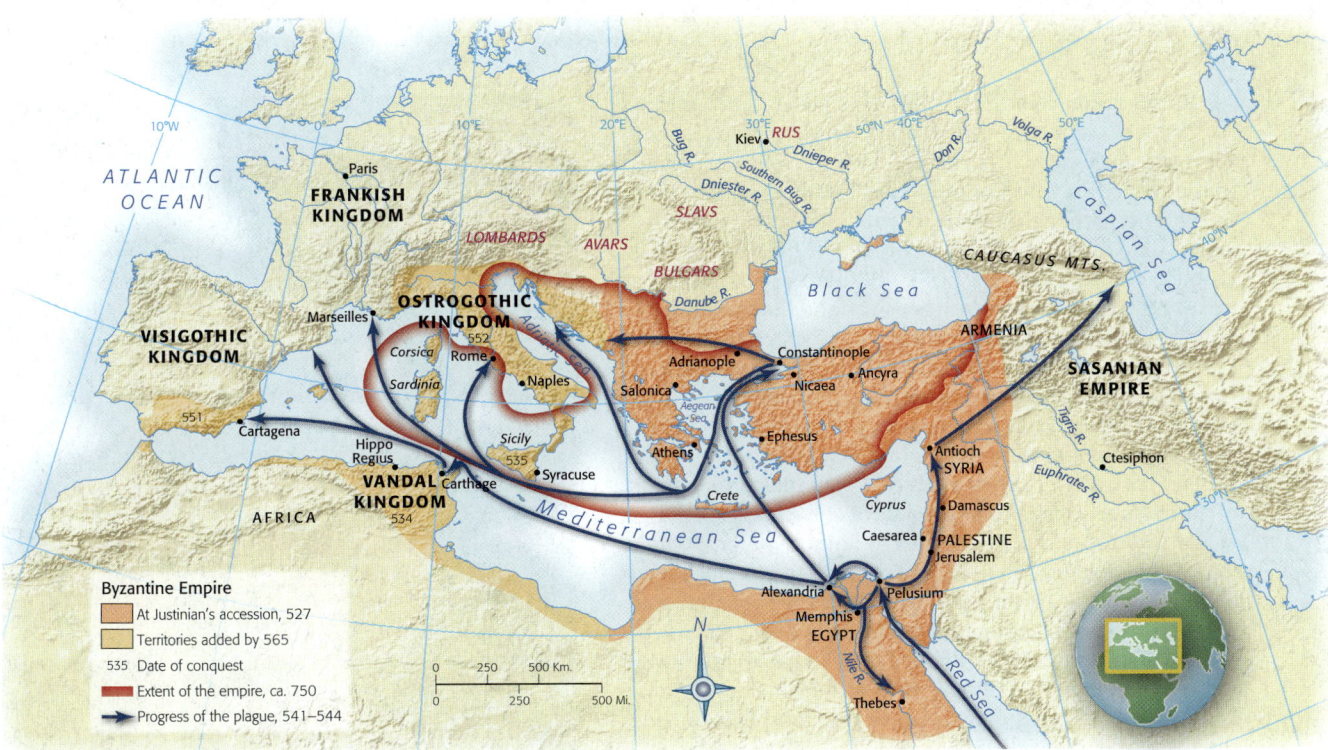

🌐 MAP 8.2—The Byzantine Empire in the Eighth and Ninth Centuries

After suffering tremendous territorial losses to the barbarians and Arabs, the Byzantine Empire transformed its military, institutional, and cultural structures to create a regime that lasted until it was conquered by Crusaders in 1204. This map shows the Byzantium's major institutional innovation.

Alexandria, Jerusalem, and Antioch from effective contact with Constantinople. Often, in the past, the empire had been disturbed by severe theological quarrels generated by the differing views held in the several patriarchates. These disputes had been disruptive, but they had also prompted a great deal of learned religious writing. Now, deprived of this stimulus, Byzantium turned inward.

Monasticism gradually assumed a more prominent place in religious life. So many members of elite families sought to become monks that some emperors actually tried to limit entry into the religious life. Byzantine monks tended to be deeply learned, intensely critical of the patriarchs of Constantinople—whom they regarded as worldly and political—and opposed to imperial interference in the church.

In 726, Emperor Leo III embarked on a bold new religious policy: **iconoclasm**. For centuries, a beautiful and inspiring religious art had been emerging that troubled the emperor. Leo, a man of simple but fervent piety, believed that the presence of religious images, called "icons," in churches and public places was offensive to God. Moreover, Leo was convinced that the military disasters suffered by the empire in recent years were attributable to divine displeasure at the violation of Moses' prohibition of "graven images." Accordingly, he and his son banned religious images. They and some of their more enthusiastic followers even destroyed a few of them. Hence, they were called "iconoclasts," which means "image breakers." Iconoclasm was officially proclaimed by a church council in 754, repudiated by another council in 787, proclaimed again in 815, and then definitively rejected in 843.

Iconoclasm had several important consequences in its own time and reveals important aspects of emerging Byzantium to the modern observer. Iconoclasm was categorically rejected as heretical by the popes. This difference drove a sharp wedge between Eastern and Western Catholics. The debates over iconoclasm finally sharpened Byzantine thinking on the role and function of art in religious life. To this day, the icon plays a more prominent role in religious devotion in the East than in the West. (See the feature, "The Visual Record: Icons.") Moreover, the battle over iconoclasm evoked some of the most sophisticated Greek religious writing since Late Antiquity. Writers produced learned treatises in defense of religious art that drew on Greek

iconoclasm Literally means "image breaking"; it describes the rejection or destruction of religious pictures called "icons."

Icons

The word icon comes from the Greek eikōn, which means "image." Scholarly conventions, however, tend to use the term to signify a particular kind of religious image that emerged in Late Antiquity and became prominent in Byzantium. Although large frescoes or mosaics can be called icons, the word is typically restricted to panel paintings painted with encaustic (en-COST-ik). This is a technique that involves mixing pigment with beeswax and then heating the painted surface to fuse the painting to the surface.

Icons portrayed saints, the Virgin Mary, and sometimes Jesus Christ. They were believed to be genuinely holy, to capture, in some mysterious way, the holiness of the person whom they represented. Icons may have arisen from funeral portraits, or they may have been miniature versions of much larger images on the walls of churches. One of the earlier examples of icons relates to Saint Symeon Stylites (STILL-ee-tays) (ca. 390–459). Symeon was a recluse who lived for many years on top of a pillar in the Syrian desert. After his death, his reputation for holiness drew many people to worship at his tomb. Soon, people began to take away pictures of Symeon. We hear that in far-off Rome, shopkeepers affixed icons of Symeon to the doorposts outside their shops to ward off evil.

Eventually, Byzantine armies carried icons into battle and hung them over the walls of Constantinople to repel enemy attacks. Some churches became famous for their icons. Individuals possessed icons, too, and carried them around in sacks or installed them in their houses. People touched, kissed, or caressed icons to invoke the power of the person who was at once portrayed and spiritually present in the icon. Icons were believed to ward off demons, to heal illnesses, to overcome complications in pregnancy, and to secure victory in lawsuits—among many other uses to which they were put.

Pictured here is an icon of Saint Peter from the monastery of Saint Catherine in Sinai. It is one of the oldest surviving icons, believed to date back to the sixth century. Let us note some of its formal characteristics. Peter is depicted frontally and the background is indistinct, as if Peter is removed from earthly time and space. Peter is represented holding keys, which symbolize the keys to the kingdom of heaven mentioned by Christ. Notice that Peter's eyes look out hauntingly, taking in everything, yet are not focused on anything in particular. This feature, too, gives the icon a sense of timelessness, and of holiness. The style of this

Icon of Saint Peter from Saint Catherine's, Mount Sinai (Alexandria-Michigan-Princeton Archaeological Expedition to Mount Sinai/Roger Wood/Corbis)

icon is very similar to that of a consular diptych. When the emperor named two men consuls each year, they often had

patristic writing (see pages 203–204) and on ancient Greek philosophy in ways that sharply differentiated Byzantine and Western religious thought.

As the Byzantines turned more and more deeply into their own traditions, they exposed other differences between themselves and the West. Some of these were important, such as the dispute over the so-called *filioque.* In the East, people believed that the Holy Spirit proceeded "from the Father." In the West, people said that the Holy Spirit proceeded "from the Father *and from the Son*" (*filioque* in Latin). Greek monks shaved the front of their heads, whereas Western monks shaved a circlet on the top. The Greek church used leavened (with yeast) bread

Khludov Psalter (Courtesy, State Historical Museum, Moscow [Khludov] Psalter, cod.Gr. 129 d)

portraits done. In such a portrait, one consul was front and center, while medallions above or beside him depicted the other consul, the emperor, and the empress. In this icon, Peter is likewise shown with three medallions: Christ in the center, Mary on the viewer's right, and Saint John the Evangelist on the viewer's left. One can see right away how ancient artistic motifs were being adapted to new purposes in Christian art.

In the eighth century, Byzantium's emperors initiated a policy of iconoclasm; literally, "icon-breaking." Many icons were destroyed, some were simply removed from view, while still others were whitewashed. The emperors believed that icons violated the biblical prohibition of "graven images" (Exodus 20:4). They felt that God had forsaken the empire because of idolatry and that only by removing the offending pictures could divine favor be won again. The monastery of Saint Catherine, where the icon of Saint Peter was, and still is, was so remote that iconoclasm did not touch it (see **Map 2.2**, top, on page 41). Eventually, iconoclasm came to an end and icons were restored to their honored position in Byzantium, and later in all the lands religiously influenced by the Byzantines. For an example of a Russian Orthodox icon, see the Virgin of Vladimir in Chapter 9 (page 251).

Iconoclasm was a particularly bitter episode in Byzantine history. There were polemical writings on all sides. Byzantine artists also commented on the controversy. In this image from the early-ninth-century Khludov Psalter—a psalter is a book containing the psalms—you can see two pictures. One is of a crucifixion. It is placed opposite verse 22 in Psalms 68 (modern 69): "They gave me also gall for my food and vinegar for my thirst." Note the soldier on Jesus' left (the viewer's right) who is holding up a sponge soaked in vinegar. But note too the soldier on Jesus' right (the viewer's left). This is the figure, later named Longinus, who pierced Jesus' side with a spear. Now look at the lower image. Depicted here is a man whitewashing an icon of Christ. The message is clear and powerful. Just as Longinus had tortured Jesus, so too do the iconoclasts.

We learned in Chapter 7 (see "The Visual Record: The Ravenna Mosaics" on pages 188–189) that art could serve propaganda purposes. The Ravenna mosaics were large and public. Some icons were also large and public, but many more were small and private. And the picture from the Khludov Psalter is tiny and very private, very intimate. But it conveys well the depth of anger provoked by iconoclasm, by an attack on Byzantium's revered icons.

QUESTIONS

1. What kinds of ideas enter your mind when you hear words like icon, or iconic?

2. How does the icon of Saint Peter compare with the diptych-like representation of Amalasuntha on page 184?

3. How well do the images from the Khludov Psalter convey their message?

in worship, whereas the Western church used unleavened bread. Taken together, these differences amounted to a sharpening of the divide between Christian groups whom we may now label "**Orthodox**" and "Roman Catholic." Neither group wished to see a division in the Christian world, but physical separation and independent cultural evolution were producing two different traditions.

With its new geographic shape, institutional structure, and its Orthodox faith, Byzantium was at once something old and something new. In official Byzantine ideology, the Roman Empire had always been one and inseparable. With its indebtedness to classical and Christian traditions,

Orthodox The Christian faith of Byzantium. It is known for its use of Greek, inclusion of icons in worship, and adherence to the Greek Church Fathers.

SECTION SUMMARY

- The Byzantine Empire faced hard challenges from Persians and then Muslims in the east; from Slavs, Avars, and Bulgars in the Balkans; and from Lombards in Italy.

- The "theme" system was a comprehensive and effective revision of the empire's traditional governmental structure.

- Byzantine culture was based on the Greek language, the Greek Church Fathers, Orthodox religious traditions, and distinctive local practices.

there can be no question that Byzantium was a part of the West. But in its reduced size, constantly threatened frontiers, and Orthodox traditions, Byzantium was going to have a somewhat different future than the portions of the West situated inside Rome's former western provinces. As was the case in the Muslim world, the seventh and ninth centuries were acutely tumultuous in Byzantium, whereas the eighth was marked by consolidation and achievement.

THE RISE OF THE CAROLINGIAN EMPIRE

What were the greatest achievements of the Carolingians and why were they so successful compared to the other states that survived Rome's collapse in the West?

In the West, the seventh century also was marked by challenges, the eighth century by innovation and accomplishment, and the ninth century by new threats and, in some areas, near collapse. The social and political heritages of both the Germanic and the Roman past interacted with Christianity and the church to produce the third early medieval civilization: Western Europe. Crucial to these developments were the evangelization of the countryside, the growth of an ecclesiastical hierarchy, the shift of papal interests away from the Mediterranean world toward Western Europe, and the evolving relationship between royal governments and the Catholic Church. The decisive political development in Western Europe was the rise, among the Franks, of the Carolingian family whose most famous member was Charlemagne. Yet, as the seventh century dawned, the Franks had several potential rivals. One by one, those rivals encountered insurmountable challenges.

Medieval Europe Takes Shape

In Spain, the Visigothic monarchy never recovered from its devastating defeat by Clovis at Vouillé in 507 (see Chapter 7). The kings managed to create a capital at Toldeo, to issue sophisticated law codes that owed much to Roman law, and to adopt symbolic trappings of rulership, such as thrones and crowns. In 589, the Visigoths formally converted from Arianism to Catholicism, a step that helped social and cultural cooperation. In a churchman, such as Isidore of Seville (560–636), Visigothic Spain produced a scholarly polymath whose works were influential for centuries. Nevertheless, intense rivalries within the Visigothic aristocracy and between the aristocrats and the kings engendered constant struggles that left Spain vulnerable to an attack by Arab-led Berbers (North African tribesmen and recent converts to Islam). Between 711 and 716, Spain was almost completely overrun and conquered.

In Italy, the Lombards, who had entered the peninsula after the conclusion of the Gothic Wars, were never able to build a cohesive kingdom. No dynasty could establish itself permanently, and the kings, ruling from Pavia in the north, could not control the large, powerful duchies of Benevento and Spoleto in the center and south. Lombard, Italy, produced memorable writers, impressive law codes, and influential art and architecture. But the Lombards could not contend with their foes. The Lombards confronted a Byzantine presence in parts of Italy and, as the Byzantine grip loosened, the popes began to rally the Italians and also turned to the Franks for help. Pippin III, Charlemagne's father, campaigned in Italy in 755 and 756 and forced the Lombards to hand over to the papacy the territories that they had conquered at Byzantium's expense. These campaigns fatally weakened the Lombards, and Charlemagne finally conquered their kingdom and took its crown for himself in 774. The lands, which the Franks guaranteed to the popes, formed the basis for the Papal States, a political entity in central Italy that endured many changes over time and survives today as Vatican City. The papal claim to territorial rule was based at least in part on the *Donation of Constantine*, a document probably written in the

760s, but claiming to represent a donation to the papacy by Constantine of rule in the West after he departed for Constantinople.

The period between 600 and 900 saw only the faint beginnings of political consolidation in the British Isles. In Ireland, Wales, and Scotland, there were numerous tiny kingdoms that constantly struggled with each other. In England, the Anglo-Saxons were slowly settling into seven kingdoms (see **MAP 8.3**). Leadership within England shifted from one of these kingdoms to another. In the late eighth century, one king, Offa of Mercia (r. 757–796) was called "king of all the English." England may have been heading toward some form of political consolidation when, in 793, the Vikings began what would be more than a century of devastating raids and conquests. Continued political unification in England was delayed until Alfred the Great (r. 871–899) ascended the throne of Wessex. He rallied the English and began the long, slow political recovery that bore fruit in the tenth century.

In the areas of religion and culture, however, the British Isles were distinctive and influential. Isolated groups of Christians survived in Ireland from Roman times, but tradition says that St. Patrick (360?–431?) effectively Christianized the island and initiated its ecclesiastical organization. Political rivalries among Irish clans led one prominent exile, St. Columba, to flee Ireland, settle on the Isle of Iona off the coast of Scotland, and begin the conversion of the local Picts (as the inhabitants of Scotland were called). Working from this northern base, Irish missionaries began spreading Christianity southwards in England. Meanwhile, in 597, Pope Gregory I sent Augustine and a group of monks to Kent, in southeastern England, where they established a base at Canterbury. From that base, Augustine's successors began spreading Christianity northwards. In 664, a council was held at the monastery of Whitby, then under the powerful abbess Hilda (614–680). The council decided that Roman, and not Irish, customs would be accepted by the English church. A few years later, the pope sent Theodore (r. 668–690), as Archbishop of Canterbury, and he organized the English church along traditional Roman lines. All the while, nobles had been founding monasteries and from these centers the real work of converting the English countryside was underway. The conversion of England to Christianity was fostered by women. Most convents had aristocratic abbesses who presided over complex enterprises and often schools. The Vikings were eventually disruptive to the English church too.

Nevertheless, at several centers, and notably at the monasteries of Wearmouth and Jarrow, an impressive Christian culture emerged. Schools were established and libraries were built up. The greatest product of those schools was Bede (673–735). A profoundly learned man and prolific author, Bede wrote commentaries on the Bible, and popularized the use of A.D. dating. He is best known for his *Ecclesiastical History of the English Church and People*, a comprehensive history of the emergence of both England's kingdoms and church. Bede commanded a superb Latin style.

The Carolingian Dynasty

Clovis and the Franks created the most effective of the early Germanic kingdoms. During the seventh century, that kingdom, too, experienced difficulties but did not disappear. Just as Roman aristocrats had borne the ancient heritage into the Middle Ages, so now a Frankish family, called "Carolingian" from the name of its greatest member, Charlemagne, assembled the talent and resources of the Frankish realm in a new way. Charlemagne reformed his government and church, patronized learning, and resurrected the western empire. Early medieval civilization reached its culmination in the work of Charlemagne and his dynasty.

When Clovis died in 511, he divided his realm among his sons, and thereafter, several kingdoms coexisted. The Merovingian royal families feuded constantly, sought to expand at

Lindisfarne Gospels: Opening Page of the Gospel According to Matthew　In the last years of the seventh century in the north of England, scribes and painters produced this exquisite book, which combines the artistic styles of the Mediterranean and Celtic worlds. (British Library)

MAP 8.3—The Carolingian World

The territory over which Charlemagne exerted direct or indirect control was vast. The areas beyond the Rhine and Danube, never part of the Roman Empire, became under the Carolingians a permanent part of Western civilization. The Treaty of Verdun (see inset), signed by Charlemagne's grandsons in 843, was the first and most important of many divisions of the Carolingian Empire that eventually led to the emergence of France and Germany.

one another's expense, and drew local aristocracies into their battles. Nevertheless, the *idea* of a single kingdom of the Franks persisted. Kings and aristocrats in the small kingdoms competed for leadership of the realm as a whole. The flourishing culture of late antique Gaul was largely gone, but a creative Christian monastic culture was growing up in all parts of the Frankish kingdom. The seventh century, in other words, was a time when the late antique regime was slowly changing into the medieval regime.

The Carolingian family appeared in history just after 600 and thereafter monopolized the office of mayor of the palace (sort of a prime minister) to the king in Austrasia (the easternmost kingdom; see **MAP 8.3**). The Carolingians were the boldest and wealthiest family in Austrasia (aw-STRAY-zhuh), perhaps in the Frankish world. Within two generations, they unified the Frankish realm and increased their own power.

The Carolingians formed alliances with powerful noble families in many regions. They waged war against the enemies of the Franks to restore the territorial integrity of the kingdom. Charles Martel (d. 741), Charlemagne's grandfather, led the Frankish forces that put an end to Arab raiding in Gaul, defeating a large force near Poitiers in 733. With booty from their wars, tribute from conquered peoples, spoils taken from recalcitrant opponents, and even lands seized from the church, the Carolingians attracted and rewarded more and more followers until no one was a match for them. The Carolingians also allied themselves very early with leading churchmen, both episcopal and monastic. They aided missionaries in the work of converting central Germany, thereby expanding Frankish influence in that area.

For years, the Carolingians were content with the office of mayor of the palace. Then in 749, Pippin III (son of Charles Martel) decided to send envoys to the pope to ask whether it was right that the person who had all the power in the land of the Franks was not the king. The pope responded that this situation ran counter to the divine plan. Accordingly, in 751, the last Merovingian king was deposed, and Pippin was elected in his place (r. 751–768). Pippin had prepared his usurpation very carefully with his Frankish supporters, but he appealed to the pope to make it appear that he had become king with divine approval and not by crude seizure. Three years later, the pope visited the Frankish kingdom, where he crowned and anointed Pippin and his sons, including Charlemagne. (The practice of anointing the head of a ruler with holy oil, which renders the recipient sacred, dates back to the kings of Israel. The head and hands of Catholic bishops also were anointed. The anointing of rulers and churchmen persisted throughout the Middle Ages and into the modern world.) The pope also forbade the Franks ever to choose a king from a family other than the Carolingians and received from their new favorites a promise of aid in Italy.

Charlemagne (Carolus Magnus, "Charles the Great" in Latin) was a huge man, and his stature has grown in European history and legend. Like all great leaders, Charlemagne (r. 768–814) was complex. He spoke and read Frankish, Latin, and some Greek but never learned to write. He promoted Christian morality but perpetrated unspeakable brutalities on his enemies and enjoyed several concubines. Many battles were fought in his name, but he rarely accompanied his armies and fought no campaigns that are remembered for strategic brilliance. Determination and organization were the hallmarks of his forty-six-year reign.

Charlemagne's first major achievement was the articulation of a new ruling ideology in the Latin West. In capitularies (kuh-PITCH-u-lar-eez)—royal executive orders—of 789, Charlemagne required all males to swear an oath of allegiance to him, and he compared himself to a biblical king in his responsibility to admonish, to teach, and to set an example for his people. He referred to the people of his realm as a "New Israel," a new chosen people. Interestingly, this chosen people was not exclusively Frankish. No distinctions were to be made among Franks or Bavarians or Saxons. Everyone was to be equal in allegiance to the king and in membership in a sort of Augustinian City of God.

Einhard (ca. 770–840), Charlemagne's friend and biographer, reports that Augustine's *City of God* (see page 195) was the king's favorite book. The king understood it to mean that two opposing domains contended for power on earth: a City of God consisting of all right-thinking Christians—the "New Israel"—and a City of Man consisting of pagans, heretics, and infidels. This idea is similar to the Islamic umma (see page 201). To Charlemagne and his advisers, it was obvious that as God was the sole legitimate ruler in heaven, Charlemagne was the sole legitimate and divinely appointed ruler on earth.

Modern readers may think that Charlemagne had crossed a boundary between church and state. It is crucial to understand that to Charlemagne, as to his Muslim and Byzantine contemporaries, no such boundary existed. Church (or religion) and state were complementary attributes of a polity whose end was eternal salvation, not military security or personal fulfillment. Charlemagne's ideological legacy was twofold: It created possibilities for bitter struggles later in the Middle Ages between secular rulers and ecclesiastical powers about the leadership of Christian society and it made it hard to define the state and its essential purposes in other than religious terms.

The most disputed event in the reign of Charlemagne was his imperial coronation in Rome on Christmas Day in 800. It is important to separate how this event happened from what it meant to the participants. In April 799, some disgruntled papal bureaucrats and their supporters attacked Pope Leo III (r. 795–816) in an attempt to depose him. Leo escaped and then traveled all the way to Saxony, where the king was camped with his army. Charlemagne agreed to restore the pope to Rome and, as his ally and protector, to investigate those who had attacked him. No real offenses could be proved against the pope, who appeared publicly in Rome to swear that he had done nothing wrong. Everything was handled to avoid any hint that the pope had been put on trial. When Charlemagne went to Saint Peter's Basilica on Christmas, he prayed before the main altar. As he rose from prayer, Pope Leo placed a crown on his head, and the assembled Romans acclaimed him as emperor.

Debate over this coronation arises from a remark of Einhard, who said that if Charlemagne had known what was going to happen, he would not have gone to church that day, even though it was Christmas. Einhard's point was not that Charlemagne did not wish to be emperor. For at least fifteen years, prominent people at the Carolingian court had been addressing Charlemagne in imperial terms in letters, treatises, and poems. Moreover, some were saying that because of

Charlemagne The greatest ruler of the early Middle Ages and a major figure in European lore and legend.

Irene's usurpation (see page 208), the imperial throne was vacant—implying that a woman could not truly rule. What Einhard did mean was that Charlemagne saw himself as a Frankish and Christian emperor, not as a *Roman* emperor. The imperial office dignified his position as leader of the Frankish "Israel." Charlemagne did not wish to be beholden to the pope or to the Romans.

Charlemagne continued his program of legal and ecclesiastical reform and put the finishing touches on some military and diplomatic campaigns. In 806, he divided his empire among his three legitimate sons. Two of them died, so in 813, he made Louis his sole heir and successor. Charlemagne outlived most of the friends and companions of his youth and middle age. He outlived four wives and many of his children. Old and alone, ill and lame, he died in early 814.

Charlemagne's legacy was great. He brought together the lands that would become France, Germany, the Low Countries, and northern Italy and endowed them with a common ideology, government, and culture. He provided a model that Europeans would look back to for centuries as a kind of golden age. His vast supraregional and supra-ethnic entity, gradually called "Christendom," drew deeply on the universalizing ideals of its Roman, Christian, and Jewish antecedents but was, nevertheless, original. With its Roman, Germanic, and Christian foundations, the Carolingian Empire represented the final stage in the evolution of the Roman Empire in the West. (See the feature, "The Global Record: 'Persian' Visitors to the Court of Charlemagne.")

Carolingian Government

Charlemagne accomplished much through the sheer force of his personality and his boundless energy. But he also reformed and created institutional structures. These helped him to carry out his tasks, guaranteed a measure of permanence to his reforms, and created government patterns that lasted in many parts of Europe until the twelfth century.

The king (or emperor—the offices differed little in practical importance) was the heart of the system. In theory, the king ruled by God's grace and did not have to answer for his conduct to any person. In reality, the king necessarily sought consensus through a variety of means. The king controlled vast lands, which gave him great wealth of his own and also the means to reward loyal followers. By controlling appointments to key positions, the king required men to come to him for power, wealth, and prestige.

The Eastern contemporaries of the Carolingians relied on large numbers of carefully trained, paid civil servants. In contrast, the Carolingians employed a limited number of men who were tied to them by bonds of familial and personal allegiance. The Carolingian court included several ceremonial officers and a domestic staff, all desirable positions. For example, the constable, an officer in charge of transporting the royal entourage, was usually a great aristocrat; the real work of the office was carried out by underlings. The treasurer was the keeper of the king's bedchamber, where the royal treasure chest was kept. Several chaplains, whose primary duty was to see to the spiritual needs of the court, kept official records. The queen controlled the domestic staff and the stewards who managed the royal estates.

Local government was mainly entrusted to counts. About six hundred counts, and several times that number of minor officials, managed the empire. As in Merovingian times, the counts were administrative, judicial, and military officials. Most came from prominent families, and the office increased the wealth and importance of its holders. Counts had to promulgate and enforce royal orders and preside in regular sessions of local courts. They got one-third of the fines, so the zealous pursuit of justice was in their interest.

The royal court and the localities were linked in several ways. Under Charlemagne and his successors, it became usual for all major officers, whether secular (counts and their subordinates) or ecclesiastical (bishops and abbots), to be **vassals** of the king. Vassals solemnly pledged loyalty and service to the king. Vassalage drew on both Roman and Germanic customs. Patron-client ties had always been socially and politically important among the Romans, and the allegiance of warriors to a chief was a key Germanic bond. But by connecting personal loyalty with public office, Charlemagne created something essentially new. Only a few thousand men, a tiny fraction of the total population, were vassals at any time. They constituted the political and social elite.

Another connection between the king and his local agents was the assembly that met in various places once or twice a year. In theory, all free men could attend these gatherings, which sometimes had separate secular and ecclesiastical sessions, to advise the king on matters of great importance, such as war and peace or legal reforms. In practice, only the vassals had the means or the interest to ensure their presence. Most of the great Carolingian reforms were formulated in these assemblies by cooperation between the king and his most important subjects.

vassals Generally high-status men who pledged personal loyalty to a lord in return for public offices and material benefits.

"Persian" Visitors to the Court of Charlemagne

In the 880s a monk named Notker wrote the Deeds of Charles the Great. The work is not a continuous historical narrative but instead a lengthy series of anecdotes, including this one about some "Persian" (probably, in fact, Arab) envoys to Charlemagne. The story is fanciful but revealing of attitudes prevalent in the West. In reading, one has to work through the flattery and exaggeration.

Envoys of the Persians were sent to him. They arrived in the last week of Lent. They were announced to the emperor but he put off seeing them until the eve of Easter. On the special feast that incomparable man was decked out incomparably and he ordered the people from the race that had once seemed terrible to all the world to be introduced. To them the most excellent Charles seemed amazing before all others, as if they had never seen a king or an emperor. He received them kindly and bestowed on them this gift: As if they were one of his children they had permission to go wherever they wished, look over anything whatsoever, and ask about or investigate anything. They jumped excitedly at the chance to be near him, to look upon him, to admire him; they valued this more than the riches of the East. They climbed up to the balcony that ran around the basilica and looked down on the clergy and soldiers but coming back again and again to the emperor they were unable to keep from laughing on account of their immense joy and they clapped their hands, saying "Before we have only seen men of clay but now we have seen men of gold."

At dawn Charles, unable to tolerate idleness or leisure, prepared to go hunting in the forest for bison or wild oxen, and to take along the Persian envoys. When they saw those huge animals they were struck with terror and turned in flight. But the hero Charles was unperturbed and sat on his bold horse as he approached one of them, drew his sword, and tried to cut right through its neck. But his blow was in vain. The monstrous beast tore through the boot and leg-wrap of the king and grazed his leg with the tip of his horn, rendering him a little slower than he was before. Angered by this slight wound, the beast fled safe and sound into a valley made tough by trees and rocks. Just about everyone in the service of the lord wanted to take off their leggings but he stopped them.

The Persians also brought the emperor an elephant, monkeys, balsam, nard, and various ointments, spices, perfumes, and different medicines to such an extent that the East seemed emptied and the West, filled. When they had begun to become extremely familiar with the emperor, one day they were a little sillier than usual, heated up with strong white-beer, and they spoke these words in jest to Charles, who was always armed with seriousness and sobriety: "Your power, O Emperor, is very great but much less than the report of your power that is spread in the eastern kingdoms." On hearing this, Charles concealed his great indignation and asked them with a smile "Why do you speak so, my sons? Or why do things seem so to you?" So they went back to the beginning and told him everything that had happened to them in these lands across the sea saying "We Persians, or Medes, and Armenians, Indians, Parthians, Elamites, and all the peoples of the East, fear you much more than our own ruler Harun. What should we say about the Macedonians or Achaeans? Nowadays they fear the pressure of your greatness more than they do the waves of the Ionian Sea. The peoples of all the islands through which we passed on our journey were as ready and determined in your service as if they had been raised in your palace and honored with huge favors."

QUESTIONS

1. How likely do you think it is that "Persian" visitors would have been so dazzled by Charlemagne?

2. Reading between the lines, so to speak, what does this document tell you about Frankish attitudes toward Arabs?

3. What aspects of this story seem most credible to you?

Source: Notker Balbulus, *Gesta Karoli*, 2.8, ed. Reinhold Rau (Darmstadt: Wissenschaftliche Buchgesellschaft, 1975), pp. 386–390. Translated by Thomas F. X. Noble.

The assemblies served to defuse dissension, but the king also brought his power to bear locally by traveling widely. The monarchy possessed estates all over the heartlands of the kingdom, and the royal entourage often moved from one place to another. Monasteries and cathedrals provided hospitality to the king. As the royal party traveled about the realm, they were able to check on local conditions and to compel local officials to comply with royal wishes.

In 788, Charlemagne began to build a palace at Aachen (AH-ken), and in the last twenty years of his life, he usually resided there (see **Map 8.3**). The later Carolingian rulers all tended to have fixed residences, as did the Byzantines and the Abbasids. In adopting fixed residences and elaborate court rituals, the Carolingians may have been returning to Roman precedents or copying their contemporaries to appear as sophisticated as they. Elegant courts and intricate rituals project an aura of grandeur that enhances people's respect for their rulers. It is no accident that a key innovation of Charlemagne's reign coincided with his permanent residence in Aachen. In the late 780s, he began to send out pairs of roving inspectors, or *missi dominici* (MISS-ee doe-MEE-nee-kee), envoys of the lord king. Their function was to see that royal orders were being observed, that counts were dispensing justice honestly, and that persons of power were not oppressing the powerless.

The Carolingian Renaissance

Charlemagne's reforms culminated in a revival of learning that scholars have named the **Carolingian Renaissance** (*renaissance* is French for "rebirth"). Charlemagne's fundamental ideas are revealed by the constant use in contemporary sources of words, such as *rebirth, renewal, reform*, and *restoration*. Charlemagne, his advisers, and his successors looked back for inspiration to Christian and papal Rome, to Saint Peter and Constantine, and to the Church Fathers. To them, the rebirth of Western society as a "New Israel" was equivalent to the theological rebirth of an individual in baptism. The Carolingians were the driving force behind intellectual growth in their era.

To accomplish his objectives, Charlemagne required every cathedral and monastery to establish a school. To set up and run those schools, he summoned to his court many of the most able and influential intellectual figures of the day, among them Franks, such as his biographer Einhard, grammar teachers from Italy, and Visigothic theologians from the Spanish border. His most famous recruit was the Anglo-Saxon Alcuin (AL-kwin) (735–804), the most learned man of his day and the heir of Bede and of the brilliant culture of Northumbria.

Much of the work of Alcuin and his associates was devoted to producing textbooks and to teaching elementary knowledge. Charlemagne was convinced that people needed to be taught the basic truths of Christianity if he were to accomplish his task of leading them to salvation. A massive effort was thus undertaken to copy manuscripts of the Bible and the writings of the Latin Church Fathers. These books, the essential resources for the whole program, needed to be disseminated as widely as possible. The process of copying was facilitated by a new script, Caroline minuscule. The Frankish convent at Chelles was a renowned center for the copying of manuscripts.

Alcuin recognized that Charlemagne could place more resources at his disposal than anyone else and had the will to do so. Alcuin also saw the long-term benefits that would come from his work. Alcuin's pupils spread out in the next generation to create a network of schools that went right on multiplying across the ninth century. That is a powerful legacy. And Alcuin did more than just teach. He wrote learned works and poetry and was for twenty years Charlemagne's most trusted adviser.

With his plan, personnel, and schools in place, Charlemagne took many concrete steps. He secured from Rome a copy of the authoritative canon law of the church. Charlemagne also got from the pope a *sacramentary*, a service book for worship in cathedral churches. Charlemagne sought an authoritative copy of the *Rule of St. Benedict*, and after study and commentary, this Rule was imposed on all monasteries in the kingdom.

Secular reforms mirrored religious ones. Orders regularized the management of all royal estates. Charlemagne attempted to update local law codes and to make them as uniform as possible. Not since Rome had governments possessed either the interest in or the means to promote such centralization. It is striking that in the eighth century, the caliphate, the Byzantine Empire, and the Carolingian Empire were engaged in similar centralizing activities.

Versatility was a hallmark of Carolingian learning. In the Frankish world, aristocratic women secured some learning, and one, Dhuoda, wrote in 841 a manual of advice for her son that conveys biblical and patristic teachings as well as practical wisdom. Various scholars excelled at poetry, history, and biography. Biblical studies and theology attracted a lot of attention. One figure who personifies the Carolingian Renaissance is the

Ivory Cover of the Lorsch Gospels In 810, the monks at Lorsch produced a Gospel book and probably its covers, too. This cover (front or back? scholars are not sure) is now in London. It depicts an enthroned Mary with Jesus on her lap, flanked by Zacharias and his son, John the Baptist. The ivory carving is of such exquisite quality that scholars long refused to believe that this was not a late antique work. (Victoria & Albert Museum, London/Art Resource, NY)

Visigoth Theodulf (ca. 760–821). He came to court in about 790 and served thereafter as a missus, royal adviser, abbot of several monasteries, and bishop of Orléans. He issued important legislation for his diocese. He was the foremost Old Testament expert of his day and the only one who knew Hebrew. He wrote the official Frankish response to Byzantine iconoclasm. He also composed theological treatises, many letters, and dozens of poems. At Germigny (JHER-mee-nee), he designed a church that is a masterpiece of early Carolingian architecture.

Carolingian art is a crowning glory of the age. Several distinct currents inspired and informed Carolingian art. Most prominent were the animal and geometric decorative motifs of Irish and Anglo-Saxon art; the elegance, formality, and sense of composition of classical art; basic elements of style from Byzantine painting; actual scenes from papal Rome; and the mysteries of Christian theology. Every element was borrowed, but the finished product was new.

Architecture shows the same trends. Charlemagne's palace complex at Aachen has parallels in imperial Constantinople, papal Rome, and Ostrogothic Ravenna. Workers and building materials were fetched from all over the empire. From 768 to 855, 27 cathedrals were built, along with 417 monasteries and 100 royal residences. For basic buildings, the Carolingians adapted the basilica. The classical basilica was a horizontal building, but the Carolingians, by altering the western end and façade (the "westworks"), added the dimension of verticality. In Romanesque and Gothic architecture this innovation would have a long career (see pages 281–286).

The Fragmentation of Charlemagne's Empire, 814–887

The Carolingian Empire did not outlive the ninth century. By the end of the ninth century, small political entities had replaced the unified Carolingian Empire. Size and ethnic complexity contributed to the dissolution of the empire, as did dynastic squabbling and new waves of attacks.

The empire included many small regions—Saxony, Bavaria, Brittany, and Lombardy, for example—that had their own resident elites, linguistic traditions, and distinctive cultures, which had existed before the Carolingians came on the scene and persist to this day. The Merovingian and Carolingian periods were basically a unifying intrusion into a history characterized by regional diversity. The Carolingians made heroic efforts to build a common culture and to forge bonds of unity, but the obstacles were insuperable.

Another key issue in the breakup of the Carolingian Empire was political and dynastic. The Carolingians regularly tried to create subkingdoms for all their legitimate sons while preserving the imperial title for one of them. Unfortunately, younger sons rarely yielded to their older brothers, and the bonds of loyalty among cousins, nephews, and grandchildren grew weak. Frequent divisions of the empire, or of segments of it, placed local nobilities in the difficult position of changing their allegiance frequently and of jeopardizing their offices and landholdings.

In the Treaty of Verdun in 843 (see inset, **MAP 8.3**), the three grandsons of Charlemagne—Charles the Bald, Louis the German, and Lothair—divided the empire into three realms: the West Frankish, the East Frankish, and the Middle Kingdoms. After fierce battles among the brothers, each appointed forty members to a study commission that traversed the empire to identify royal properties, fortifications, monasteries, and cathedrals so that an equitable division of these valuable resources could be made. Each brother needed adequate resources to solidify his rule and to attract or hold followers. The lines drawn on the map at Verdun did not last even for a generation. Nevertheless, large West Frankish and East Frankish Kingdoms emerged, swallowed the Middle Kingdom, and created a framework for the future France and Germany.

On the frontiers of the Carolingian Empire, new political entities began to appear. Before the ninth century, Scandinavia had known only small-scale political units under local chieftains and their trusted followers. Economic and political pressure from the Carolingians gradually began to push both Denmark and Norway in the direction of greater political consolidation. A single Danish monarchy has a continuous history from the late ninth century, and Norway's monarchy dates from the early tenth.

To the east of the Carolingian Empire lay a vast swath of Slavic lands. The Carolingians fought, allied, and traded with these peoples for decades. Charlemagne destroyed the Avar khanate in the Danube basin in campaigns between 788 and 804. By the middle of the ninth century, the princes of Great Moravia dominated the region and played a complicated diplomatic game between the East Frankish rulers and the Byzantine emperors. To the east of the Moravians, the Bulgarians profited from the Avar, and then the Carolingian, collapse to expand their kingdom. For two centuries, the Bulgarians dominated the northern Balkans and threatened Byzantium.

The most durable consequence of this political restructuring along the eastern frontier of the Frankish world was religious. In 863, on an invitation from Moravia and in hopes of countering the Franks, the Byzantine emperor sent the missionaries Cyril (826–869) and Methodius (805–884) into eastern Europe. The emperor hoped to erect an Orthodox union of his own realm, the southern Slavs, and the newly converted Bulgarians. Likewise, he was seeking a diplomatic bulwark between the Bulgarians in the East and the Franks in the West. Unfortunately for Byzantium, Cyril and Methodius agreed with the pope to introduce Roman Catholic Christianity in return for the pope's permission to use the Slavonic language in worship. Cyril and Methodius were formidable linguists who created a religious literature in "Church Slavonic" that went far toward creating a new cultural realm in central Europe.

Finally, a new wave of attacks and invasions contributed decisively to the fragmentation of the Carolingian Empire. In the middle decades of the ninth century, Muslims, Vikings, and Magyars wreaked havoc on the Franks.

Based in North Africa and the islands of the western Mediterranean, Muslims attacked Italy and southern France. The Byzantines lost Sicily to raiders from North Africa in 827 and found themselves seriously challenged in southern Italy. In the 840s, Muslims raided the city of Rome. These same brigands preyed on trade in the western Mediterranean and even set up camps in the Alps to rob traders passing back and forth over the mountains.

"From the fury of the Northmen, O Lord, deliver us," was a plaintive cry heard often in ninth-century Europe. Those Northmen were Vikings, mainly Danes and Norwegians, seeking booty, glory, and political opportunity. Most Viking bands were formed by leaders who had lost out in the dawning institutional consolidation of the northern world. Some were opportunists who sought to profit from the weakness of Carolingian, Anglo-Saxon, and Irish rule. Vikings even began settling and initiated their own state-building activities in Ireland, England, northwestern France ("Normandy"—the region of the Northmen), and Rus (early "Russia").

Magyars, relatives of the Huns and Avars who had preceded them into eastern Europe, were accomplished horsemen whose lightning raids, beginning in 889, hit Italy, Germany, and even France. East Frankish Carolingians tried to use the Magyars as mercenaries against the troublesome Moravians. In the end, the Magyars destroyed the incipient Moravian state and raided with impunity.

All of these attacks were unpredictable and caused local regions to fall back on their own resources rather than look to the central government. Commerce was disrupted everywhere. Schools, based in ecclesiastical institutions, suffered severe decline. The raids represented a thousand pinpricks, not a single deadly sword stroke.

Even though the Carolingian Empire itself disintegrated, the idea of Europe as "Christendom," as a single political-cultural entity, persisted. The Latin Christian culture, promoted by Carolingian schools and rulers, set the tone for intellectual life until the twelfth century. Likewise, Carolingian governing structures were inherited and adapted by all of the successor states that emerged in the ninth and tenth centuries. In these respects, the Carolingian experience paralleled the Roman, and the Islamic and Byzantine, too. A potent, centralizing regime disappeared but left a profound imprint on its heirs. For hundreds of years, Western civilization would be played out inside the lands that had been Charlemagne's empire and between those lands and their Byzantine and Muslim neighbors.

SECTION SUMMARY

- The Carolingian family rose steadily to power, first as mayors of the palace, then as kings, and finally, as emperors.

- Charlemagne instituted far-reaching governmental innovations and reforms intended to make his power effective and to unify the lands under his rule.

- Carolingian rulers launched a cultural revival, called the Carolingian Renaissance, which aimed to master and then communicate basic Christian teachings.

- The Carolingian Empire broke down because of geographic diversity, political disunity, and new waves of invasion.

EARLY MEDIEVAL ECONOMIES AND SOCIETIES

What were the chief similarities and differences among the early medieval civilizations?

The economic and social history of the early Middle Ages provides additional evidence of the similarities among the three early medieval civilizations, while also revealing differences. Overall, the world remained rural, society was hierarchical, and women were excluded from public power. Although broad political frameworks changed, the lives of most people changed rather little.

Trade and Commerce

In the simplest terms, trade is a mechanism for exchanging goods from one person or group to another. There are many such exchange mechanisms. The Roman government, for example, moved large amounts of goods from the center of the empire to the frontiers to supply its armies. Roman, Byzantine, and Islamic governments raised taxes in one place, bought goods in another, and then consumed their purchases someplace else. Tribute and plunder were also effective exchange mechanisms, as were diplomatic gifts: A caliph, for example, sent Charlemagne an elephant.

The most common exchanges were intensely local, but several major trading networks operated during the early Middle Ages. In the East, Mesopotamia was linked by rivers to the Persian Gulf, East Africa, and southern Asia; by land and sea to Byzantium; and by land and rivers to the Black Sea region, Slavic Europe, and the Baltic. Byzantines traded mainly by sea. The whole Mediterranean was open to them, and from the Black Sea, they received the products of the Danube basin. The Muslim world was fundamentally a land empire that had relatively poor roads and primitive wheeled vehicles, so transport considerations were crucial: A caravan of some five hundred camels could move only one-fourth to one-half the cargo of a normal Byzantine ship.

The West had many trade routes. The Rhône-Saône river system carried goods, as did the land routes through the Alpine passes. The North and Baltic Seas were the hubs of a network that linked the British Isles, the whole of the Frankish north (by means of its rivers), the Rhineland, Slavic Europe, Byzantium, and the Muslim world. The Danube was also a major highway. The major trade networks intersected at many points. Despite religious and ideological differences, Rome's three heirs regularly traded with one another. Recent research has documented hundreds of east-west and north-south contacts across the early medieval period.

Food and other bulk goods never traveled very far because the cost was prohibitive. Most towns were supplied with foodstuffs by their immediate hinterlands, so the goods that traveled long distances were portable and valuable. Cotton and raw silk were transported to the

Oseberg Ship   Discovered in 1880, the Oseberg ship was buried in Norway in (probably) the tenth century. The ship may have belonged to a king and contained the remains of Queen Asa. It is 70 feet long and 16 feet wide. Its crew would have been thirty to forty men.   (Christophe Boisvieux/Terrra/Corbis)

Mediterranean, where they were made into cloth in, respectively, Egypt and Byzantium. Paper and pottery were transported around the caliphate. Asian spices and perfumes were avidly sought everywhere. The Byzantines traded in silk cloth, fine ivories, delicate products of the gold- and silversmiths' art, slaves, and naval stores. Byzantium, with its large fleet, usually controlled the Black and Mediterranean Seas. Reduced in prosperity, the empire could no longer dictate trade terms to subject peoples and competed badly with the Muslims. Trade in the West was partly in high-value luxury goods, but mainly in ordinary items, such as plain pottery, raw wool, wool cloth, millstones, weapons, and slaves. Some Anglo-Saxon nuns owned ships and invested in commercial activities to support their convents. Almost all aspects of the cloth industry were in women's hands.

Town and Countryside

To think of the ancient world is to think of cities, but to think of the medieval world is to envision forests and fields. Actually, 80 to 90 percent of people in antiquity lived in rural settings, and in the early Middle Ages, the percentage was not much higher. What changed was the place occupied by towns in the totality of human life. Fewer government functions were based in towns, cultural life was less bound to the urban environment, and trade in luxuries, which depended on towns, declined.

Towns in the West often survived as focal points of royal or, more often, ecclesiastical administration. A cathedral church required a large corps of administrators. Western towns were everywhere attracting *burgs*, new settlements of merchants, just outside their centers. Few Western towns were impressive in size or population. Rome may have numbered a million people in the time of Augustus, but only about thirty thousand lived there in 800. Paris had perhaps twenty thousand inhabitants at that time. These were the largest cities by far in Catholic Europe.

In the Byzantine East, apart from Constantinople, the empire had a more rural aspect after the Muslims took control of the heavily urbanized regions of Syria, Egypt, and parts of Anatolia in the seventh century. The weakening of the caliphate in the second half of the ninth century was a spur to renewed urban growth in the Byzantine Empire. In provincial cities, population growth and urban reconstruction depended heavily on military conditions: Cities threatened by Arabs or Bulgarians declined.

The Arabs were great city-builders. Baghdad—four times larger in area than Constantinople, with a million residents to the latter's 400,000—was created from scratch. The most magnificent city in the West was Cordoba, the capital of Muslim Spain. Its population may have reached 400,000, and its Great Mosque, begun in 786, held 5,500 worshipers, more than any Latin church except Saint Peter's. The city had 900 baths, 1,600 mosques (Rome had about 200 churches), 60,000 mansions, and perhaps 100,000 shops. Its libraries held thousands of books, while the largest Carolingian book collections numbered a few hundred.

Agriculture nevertheless remained the most important element in the economy and in the daily lives of most people in all three realms. Farming meant primarily the production of cereal grains, which provided diet staples such as bread, porridge, and beer. Regions tended to specialize in the crops that grew most abundantly in local circumstances. For example, olives and grapes were common in the Mediterranean area, whereas cereals predominated around the Black Sea and in central Gaul. Animal husbandry was always a major part of the rural regime. English sheep provided wool and meat. In Frankish and Byzantine regions, pigs, which were cheap to raise, supplied meat, but for religious reasons, pork was almost absent in the Muslim East—Islam adopted the Jewish prohibition against it.

A key development in the Frankish West was the appearance of a bipartite estate, sometimes called a **manor**. On a bipartite estate, one part of the land was set aside as *demesne* [duh-MEEN]), and the rest was divided into tenancies. The demesne, consuming from one-quarter to one-half of the total territory of the estate, was exploited directly for the benefit of the landlord. The tenancies were generally worked by the peasants for their own support. The bipartite estate provided the aristocrats with a livelihood, while freeing them for military and government service.

Estates were run in different ways. A landlord might hire laborers to farm his reserve, paying them with money exacted as fees from his tenants. Or he might require the tenants to work a certain number of days per week or weeks per year in his fields. The produce of the estate might be gathered into barns and consumed locally or hauled to local markets. The reserve might be a separate part of the estate, a proportion of common fields, or a percentage of the harvest. The tenants might have individual farms or work in common fields. Although the manor is one of the

manor A common term for an agricultural estate that typically had its lands divided between the manor's lord and dependent peasants.

most familiar aspects of European life throughout the Middle Ages, large estates with dependent tenants also were evolving in the Byzantine and Islamic worlds.

Social Patterns

Most of the surviving medieval records were written by elite members of society and reveal little about the middle and lower orders of society. Nevertheless, certain similarities are evident in the social structures of all levels in all three societies. The elites tended to be large landholders, to control dependent populations, and to have access to government offices. There were regional differences, too. Scholars ranked higher in Byzantium and the caliphate than in the West; churchmen, especially bishops, were powerful in Christian societies but had no counterparts in Muslim ones. Literature, surely reflecting social realities, portrays the cultivated Muslim gentleman in the Abbasid period. This social type, marked by learning, good manners, and a taste for finery, does not appear in Byzantium or in the West until the twelfth century.

Women were bound to the same social hierarchies as men. Predictably enough, women had few formal, public roles to play. Their influence, however great, tended to function in the private sphere, rarely revealed to us by sources that stem from the public realm of powerful men. Aristocratic women had opportunities and power that were denied ordinary women. Irene ruled at Byzantium as empress. Frankish and Anglo-Saxon queens were formidable figures in their realms. Carolingian queens managed the landed patrimony of the dynasty—dozens of huge estates with tens of thousands of dependents. The combination of a lack of evidence and the rigorous exclusion of women from public life in the Islamic world means that virtually no Muslim women emerge as distinct personalities in the early Middle Ages.

One example of the problems in the evidence concerning women relates to church roles. Women could not hold priestly office, and although deaconesses served at Hagia Sophia in the sixth century, they disappeared soon after and had long before vanished in the West. Religious power could come from personal sanctity as well as holding office. One study of some 2,200 saints from the early Middle Ages finds only about 300 females. It was hard for women to gain recognition as saints. And if a woman became a saint, her holiness was inevitably described either as "manly"—an extreme ascetic was praised for having the strength and courage of a man—or as beautiful, virginal, and domestic—in other words, with female stereotypes.

The middling classes show some disparities among the regions. Merchants, for example, often rose through the social ranks to become great aristocrats in Muslim society. Islamic society often evinced great mobility because of its restless, expanding nature and because Islamic ideology rejected distinctions in the umma. In Byzantium, traditional Roman prejudices against merchants and moneymaking activities persisted. Thus, rich merchants whose wealth gave them private influence frequently lacked public power and recognition. In the West, merchants were neither numerous nor powerful in the Carolingian period. In some towns, moreover, commerce was in the hands of Jews, always outsiders in a militantly Christian society.

Merchants were not the only people occupying the middle rungs of the social ladder. All three societies, in fact, possessed both central elites and provincial elites. Service at the Carolingian, Byzantine, or Abbasid court counted for more than service in a provincial outpost. It was one thing to be abbot of a great monastery and quite a different thing to preside over a poor, tiny house. The thematic generals in Byzantium were lofty personages; their subordinates held inferior positions. The vassals of a Carolingian king formed a real aristocracy, but vassals were of decidedly lower rank.

Degrees of freedom and local economic and political conditions shaped the lives of peasants. In all three societies, some farmers were personally free and owed no cash or labor services to anyone but the central government. In areas such as Abbasid Iraq, ordinary free farmers led a comfortable life. In the Frankish world, most peasants existed outside the dawning manorial system. They were free, and if they lived in areas of good land and political security, such as the Paris basin, their lives most likely were congenial. Byzantine peasants, though free, often lived in areas of military danger, and in some parts of the Balkans, they eked out a living from poor soils. Highly taxed and perpetually endangered, they may have viewed their freedom as small compensation for their economic and personal insecurity. All peasants were alike in their subjection to political forces over which they had no control.

At the bottom of the social scale everywhere were slaves. Christianity did not object to slavery in general but forbade the enslavement of Christians. Islam likewise prohibited Muslims from enslaving other Muslims. Slaves, therefore, tended to be most common in pagan societies—Scandinavia, for example—or in frontier regions where neighboring pagans could be captured and sold. There were more slaves in the Muslim world than in Byzantium, which had, in turn, more than the West.

SECTION SUMMARY

- The early Middle Ages witnessed the elaboration of several major trading networks that made ordinary and luxury goods available over long distances.

- Cities continued to play important roles in the life of the Islamic and Byzantine worlds but played comparatively little role in western Europe.

- Arab, Byzantine, and European societies were elitist and hierarchical. Merchants were less important in Europe than elsewhere. Agriculture was dominant everywhere.

- Women played important political, social, and economic roles in all societies, but women's lives were hedged with restrictions.

The domestic sphere is a difficult realm to enter. In Byzantium and the West, families rarely arranged marriages for more than one or two daughters. Others remained single or entered convents. Women at all social levels tended to pass from the tutelage of their fathers to that of their husbands. In antiquity, a suitor usually paid a fee, or "bride price," to his prospective wife's father and then endowed his wife with a "morning gift," money or possessions of her own. Gradually, this practice changed to a system whereby a bride's father paid a dowry to her future husband. Thus, a wife who was cast aside could be left impoverished, for in most places, the law did not permit her to inherit land if she had brothers. Females were such valuable property in the marriage market that rape was an offense not against a girl but against her father. A man could divorce, even kill, his wife for adultery, witchcraft, or grave robbing and then marry again. A woman could usually gain a divorce only for adultery, and she could not remarry. For the vast majority of women, daily life was hedged about with legal limitations and personal indignities.

CHAPTER SUMMARY

We have traced three parallel histories in the development of early medieval civilizations: that of the Arabs and Islam; that of the Byzantines; and that of Western Europe and the Carolingians. Muhammad was a great teacher who emphasized *al-Islam*, surrender to Allah. He taught a faith that may be summarized in the "Five Pillars" of Islam. Both internal and external factors contributed to the lightning conquests of Islam in the century after Muhammad's death, spreading Islam and Arab rule from Spain to the frontiers of China. Islamic culture was rooted in the religious teachings of the *ulama* and in the scholarship of those who tackled Greek and Persian learning.

The Byzantine Empire faced hard challenges from Persians and then Muslims in the east, from Slavs, Avars, and Bulgars in the Balkans, and from Lombards in Italy. The Byzantine Empire in the early Middle Ages was much smaller than the Roman Empire that preceded it. The "theme" system was a comprehensive and effective revision of the empire's traditional governmental structure. A distinctive Byzantine culture was based on the Greek language, the Greek Church Fathers, Orthodox religious traditions, and distinctive local practices.

FOCUS QUESTIONS

- What were the most important factors in the rise of the Arab peoples and the Islamic faith?

- Why did a distinctive civilization that can be called "Byzantine" emerge?

- What were the greatest achievements of the Carolingians and why were they so successful?

- What were the chief similarities and differences among the early medieval civilizations?

Visigothic Spain suffered from religious, political, and military disunity, while Italy developed three stable regions: a Lombard and then Frankish north; a papal center; and a Byzantine and then Muslim south. In the British Isles, the conversion to Catholic Christianity and the development of ecclesiastical organization were forces for unity and cultural achievement. In the British Isles, political development in the Celtic regions was slow, but England began emerging as a coherent political entity under ambitious and effective kings.

The Carolingian family rose steadily to power, first as mayors of the palace, then as kings, and finally as emperors. The greatest Carolingian, Charlemagne, instituted far-reaching governmental innovations and reforms intended to make his power effective and to unify the lands under his rule. Carolingian rulers launched a cultural revival, called the Carolingian Renaissance, which aimed to master and then communicate basic Christian teachings. The Carolingian Empire broke down because of geographic diversity, political disunity, and new waves of invasion.

The early Middle Ages witnessed the elaboration of several major trading networks that made ordinary and luxury goods available over long distances. Cities continued to play important roles in the life of the Islamic and Byzantine worlds but played comparatively little role in western Europe except as ecclesiastical centers. Arab, Byzantine, and European societies were elitist and hierarchical. Merchants were less important in Europe than elsewhere. Agriculture was dominant everywhere. Women played important political, social, and economic roles in all societies, but women's lives were hedged by legal limitations, social conventions, and religious restrictions.

KEY TERMS

Muhammad (p. 200)

Five Pillars (p. 201)

Quran (p. 201)

caliphate (p. 203)

Papal States (p. 207)

iconoclasm (p. 209)

Orthodox (p. 211)

Charlemagne (p. 215)

vassals (p. 216)

Carolingian Renaissance (p. 218)

manor (p. 222)

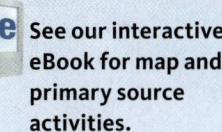 This icon will direct you to additional materials on the website: www.cengage.com/history/noble/westciv6e.

See our interactive eBook for map and primary source activities.

9

Bayeux Tapestry
The tapestry (ca. 1077) depicts the fleet of William the Conqueror of Normandy sailing to England in 1066.   (Erich Lessing/Art Resource, NY)

The Expansion of Europe in the High Middle Ages, 900–1300

The picture to the left represents one small section of the Bayeux Tapestry, a narrative account—in words and illustrations—of the conquest of England in 1066 by Duke William of Normandy. This scene is an apt introduction to the central theme of this chapter: expansion.

This section of the 230-foot-long tapestry depicts William setting sail for England. Already successful in Normandy, William was about to claim the throne of England. He gathered soldiers from all over western France and boldly crossed the English Channel. Leaving nothing to chance, he transported horses, too, as you can see in the picture.

One group of Normans conquered England, while another seized control of southern Italy. Still other Normans played a decisive role in the period's most prominent manifestation of expansion: the Crusades. Meanwhile, certain Scandinavians settled Iceland and Greenland to the west, while others founded the first state on Russian soil. Spanish Christians pushed back the Muslims in Iberia. From the Baltic to the Balkans, Slavic rulers founded new states and pressed hard against their neighbors. German rulers crossed the Alps into Italy, French kings reached the Pyrenees, and English monarchs pushed into Wales, Scotland, and Ireland. Seldom has Europe's political geography expanded so dramatically as during the High Middle Ages.

Between 900 and 1300, Europe's population began one of its longest periods of sustained growth. People brought more land under cultivation, introduced new crops, and made agriculture more efficient. Villages, towns, and cities grew in number and size. Trade expanded in every material and in every direction.

Europe witnessed the reemergence of centralizing monarchies in France, England, and Spain. Some new realms, such as Denmark and Hungary, built strong central governments. And an explosion of new states occurred along the frontiers of the old Carolingian Empire.

The "West" began taking on a more *western European* character. The Crusades complicated relations between Christian Europeans and Muslims, and both the Crusades and increasing religious differences alienated western Europe from Byzantium, and Roman Catholics from Orthodox believers. The center of Western civilization became more and more anchored to northwestern Europe. And that same western Europe was expanding to influence lands in Scandinavia and the Slavic world that had played no role at all in the West's classical, Mediterranean phase. The High Middle Ages repeatedly posed the question: Where is the West?

FOCUS QUESTIONS

- In how many different realms of life do you see signs of growth and innovation, of expansion?

- What did Germany, Italy, and France owe to the Carolingian past? How alike and different were these areas by 1300?

- What were the chief dynamics in the development of medieval Britain?

- How did new states emerge in Spain, Scandinavia, and the Slavic world, and how do those states compare with their western neighbors?

- What basic factors contributed to the rise, persistence, and eventual decline of the crusading movement?

 This icon will direct you to additional materials on the website: www .cengage.com/history/ noble/westciv6e.

See our interactive eBook for map and primary source activities.

ECONOMIC EXPANSION

In how many different realms of life do you see signs of growth and innovation, of expansion?

The economic expansion of Europe is manifest in many kinds of evidence that are more often qualitative than quantitative. Medieval people did not keep the kinds of records of births, deaths, population, or business activity that modern states routinely accumulate. After about 1000, every available indicator points to a growing population and an expanding scale and sophistication of economic activity.

The Growing Population

The population of Europe began rising slowly in the Carolingian period and may have doubled between 1000 and 1200 to 60 million. In regions where family size can be estimated, fertile marriages were producing on the average 3.5 children in the tenth century and from 6 to 7 in the twelfth. People were also living longer than their forebears. Studies of aristocrats, high clergy, and soldiers show that a surprising 40 percent of them were over 40 years old. Male life expectancy was surely longer than female because of the dangers of childbirth, always the great killer of women in the premodern world. The general trend is clear: more babies being born, more infants living into adulthood, more adults living longer.

Everywhere in Europe new land was brought into cultivation. More than half of the French documents relating to land in the twelfth century show new land being brought under the plow. Thousands of acres of forest were cut down. Marshes were reclaimed from the sea. Some 380,000 acres were drained along the western coast of France and probably twice that amount in both Flanders and England. This activity is inexplicable without assuming a growing number of mouths to feed.

Agriculture benefited from a warmer and drier climate through this whole period. Not a single vegetable blight was recorded. Food was more abundant and more nutritious. Animals were increasingly reared for their meat, and higher meat consumption meant more protein in the diet. Beans and other legumes, also rich in protein, were more widely cultivated. People of every class and region were almost certainly eating better and living longer and healthier lives.

Technological Gains

The eleventh century was a decisive period in the spread of new technologies in Europe. Innovations occurred in agriculture, transportation, mining, and manufacturing. Agricultural changes came first as a rising population created an increased demand for food that could be met only by new practices. By the late twelfth century, an acre of farmland in a fertile region was probably yielding a crop three to four times larger than in the Carolingian era. Given the combination of more land under cultivation and more yield per acre, the overall gains in the food supply were enormous.

The increases can be accounted for in several ways. Horses were more frequently used as draft animals. They did, in a day, a third or half again as much work, hauling loads farther and faster than oxen. Thus, fewer people could, with horses, cultivate more land than their predecessors managed with oxen. In addition, they could cultivate the land more frequently and increase yields because more seed would fall on more finely plowed soil. The dissemination of the horse collar made possible the expanded use of horses—older forms of harnesses suitable for the low-slung, broad-shouldered ox would have choked a horse.

Plows, too, were improved. The light wooden scratch plow used by the Romans was satisfactory for the thin soils of the Mediterranean region but barely disturbed the heavy soils of northern Europe. The invention of a heavy wheeled plow with an iron plowshare and a moldboard was a real breakthrough. The iron plowshare cut deep furrows, and then the moldboard turned and aerated the soil. This heavy plow allowed farmers to exploit good soils more fully without exhausting the ground too rapidly. Perhaps introduced into Carolingian Europe from the Slavic world, this plow was widely adopted from the eleventh century.

Wider adoption of nitrogen-fixing crops, such as peas and some kinds of beans, retarded soil exhaustion and also put more protein in the diet. Leaving land fallow also avoided soil exhaustion. In the early Middle Ages, this meant setting aside about half of the arable land every year (the two-field system) or working the land intensively for a few years and then moving on. By the twelfth century, three-field schemes of crop rotation were common. Under the three-field system, two-thirds of the arable land saw nearly constant use. The amount of an estate under cultivation rose from 50 to 67 percent.

Surplus produce was intended mainly for the growing towns. To supply that market, improvements in transportation were necessary. Kings often passed laws to secure the safety of highways, and popes three times (in 1097, 1132, and 1179) threatened highwaymen—robbers who preyed on travelers—with excommunication. Landlords required their dependents to maintain roads and bridges. Many stone bridges were constructed in France between 1130 and 1170 because wooden bridges were so vulnerable to fire. Indeed, fire destroyed the bridge at Angers (in western France) five times between 1032 and 1167.

Transport improved not only because of safer roads, but also thanks to better vehicles. The old two-wheeled cart, drawn by oxen, began giving way to the sturdy four-wheeled, horse-drawn wagon. Because greater quantities of foodstuffs could be moved farther and faster, urban communities could be supplied from larger areas. This was a crucial factor in enabling cities to grow and in providing urban residents with a predictable and diverse range of foods.

Seaborne trade expanded, too. The stern rudder, better sails, the compass (in use by 1180), and better navigational charts facilitated sea travel, as did the growing use of larger ships. An Italian fleet sailed to Flanders in 1277, and within a few years the old overland trade routes began a decline that was not reversed until the invention of the railroad in the nineteenth century.

At any time of year, travel was difficult and costly. Few dared to venture across the Alps in the winter, and the northern seas, especially the passage around Denmark, were treacherous in cold weather. Even in the relatively calm Mediterranean, the Venetians refused to send out their trading fleet between November and March. Overland trade was impeded by snow, rain, mud, and highwaymen, who would rob travelers on the road. Governments tried to restrain robbers, but no one could change the weather.

There were notable improvements in both the quarrying of stone and the mining of metals. Mines were not deep because people lacked the means to keep the shafts and galleries free of water. Still, the exploitation of surface veins of ore—principally iron, but also tin and silver—intensified, to supply the increased demand for plowshares, tools, weapons, construction fittings, and coins. Stone quarrying, the most common form of mining in the Middle Ages, benefited directly from more efficient stone saws and indirectly from improvements in transport. Better techniques in stonecutting, construction, and conveyance help to explain, for example, the increase in the number of England's stone religious buildings from sixty to nearly five hundred in the century after 1050.

Forms of Enterprise

Agricultural specialization became common. People began to cultivate intensively those crops that were best suited to local conditions. The area around Toulouse, for example, concentrated on herbs from which blue and yellow dyes were made. The central regions of France focused on cereal grains, while the Bordeaux and Burgundy regions emphasized the grapes that produced wine. Northern Germany specialized in cattle raising; northern England favored sheep.

Agricultural specialization helps to explain the growth in trade everywhere (see **Map 9.1**). For certain commodities, local trade continued to flourish. Italian wines and olive oil, for example, only moved from countryside to town within a region. The same was true of French or English grains. However, French wines were much prized throughout Europe, especially in England, and certain

CHRONOLOGY	
862	Founding of Kiev
870–930	Settlement of Iceland
962	Imperial coronation of Otto I
987	Accession of Hugh Capet in France
988	Kievan Rus accept Orthodox Christianity
1016	Conquest of England by Cnut
1066	Norman Conquest of England
1073–1085	Pontificate of Gregory VII
1078	Decree against lay investiture
1085	Spanish reconquest of Toledo
1086	*Domesday Book*
1096–1099	First Crusade
1122	Concordat of Worms
1171	Henry II of England invades Ireland
1176	Battle of Legnano
1198–1216	Pontificate of Innocent III
1202–1204	French drive English out of Normandy
1203	Fourth Crusade
1212, 1214	Battles of Las Navas de Tolosa and Bouvines
1215	Magna Carta
1265	First Parliament in England
1294–1303	Quarrel between Boniface VIII and Philip IV
1295	Model Parliament

Heavy Wheeled Plow   The improved plow, the horse collar, and the cooperative labors of many peasants in preparing the fields led to an agricultural boom in the European countryside. (Bibliothèque nationale de France)

products, such as English wool and Flemish cloth, were carried far and wide. Salt fish from the Baltic found its way all over the continent. Lumber traveled across the Mediterranean to the wood-poor Muslim world. Spain produced warhorses. Southern Europe supplied the northern demand for spices, oranges, raisins, figs, almonds, and other exotic foodstuffs. Caen, in Normandy, sent shiploads of its beautifully colored and textured stone to England for the construction of churches and monasteries. Rising population, higher productivity, and greater prosperity added up to a larger volume of goods moving farther and more frequently.

Whether for fuel, or for ships and buildings, the demand for wood grew steadily. Wood exemplifies the expansion and interconnectedness of the medieval economy and society. Forests were essential to daily life, providing the wood for houses, fences, and fuel in villages and towns. Animals, especially pigs, were grazed at the edges of the forest to permit as much land as possible to be dedicated to food crops. Wild animals were hunted in the forest. For aristocrats, hunting was as much for sport as for food. For poorer rural people, however, wild game made up a significant part of the regular diet. The forest was also a plentiful source of fruits, nuts, and honey. Thus, the decision to cut down a stand of trees was a serious one.

MAP 9.1—European Resources and Trade Routes, ca. 1100

In an age of expansion, some products were consumed locally, but many others were transported over longer and longer distances. Commercial connections expanded, too, creating several interlocking networks.

Major route of trade and commerce
Grain-growing region
Wine-producing region
Coal Primary product

ATLANTIC OCEAN

North Sea

Baltic Sea

Caspian Sea

Black Sea

Mediterranean Sea

Adriatic Sea

CAUCASUS MTS.
CARPATHIAN MTS.
ALPS
PYRENEES

Volga R.
Don R.
Dnieper R.
Vistula R.
Danube R.
Rhine R.
Rhône R.
Ebro R.
Tigris R.
Euphrates R.

Baghdad
Damascus
Beirut
Jerusalem
Acre
Famagusta
Cyprus
Candia
Crete
Rhodes
Ephesus
Phocea
Trebizond
Constantinople
Varna
Kaffa
Tana
Sarkel
Itil
Bulgar
Derbent
Novgorod
Pskov
Reval
Riga
Smolensk
Kiev
Lvov
Cracow
Visby
Stockholm
Bergen
Danzig
Lübeck
Magdeburg
Frankfurt an der Oder
Prague
Nuremberg
Vienna
Augsburg
Frankfurt am Main
Utrecht
Bruges
Lille
Ypres
London
Hull
Chester
Ipswich
Boston
Bristol
Southampton
Dublin
Paris
Dijon
Besançon
Lyons
Arles
Marseilles
Tours
Bordeaux
Albi
Toulouse
Bayonne
Barcelona
Valencia
Murcia
Almeria
Málaga
Cadiz
Honein
Bougie
Bône
Tunis
Lisbon
Palma
Balearic Is.
Sardinia
Cagliari
Corsica
Sicily
Syracuse
Malta
Naples
Rome
Orvieto
Siena
Florence
Bologna
Ancona
Barletta
Ragusa (Dubrovnik)
Venice
Padua
Ferrara
Milan
Pavia
Parma
Genoa
Lucca

Furs
Wax
Copper
Iron
Silver
Tin
Salt
Wool
Coal
Wood
Alum

TABLE 9.1

Population Increases In Italian Cities, 1200–1300

City	1200	1300	Percentage Increase
Florence	15,000	96,000	+640%
Siena	19,000	52,000	+274%
Pisa	20,000	38,000	+190%

Source: Adapted from Malcolm Barber, *The Two Cities: Medieval Europe, 1050–1320*, p. 270. Copyright © 1992. Reprinted by permission of the publisher, Routledge, an imprint of the Taylor & Francis Group.

The Roles of Cities and Towns

All over Europe, towns grew impressively in size and importance. **TABLE 9.1** shows the growth of three Italian cities. Such growth also occurred in cities in Flanders, such as Bruges and Ghent, and in Paris, London, and other cities that were becoming national capitals. Ghent expanded its city walls five times between 1160 and 1300, a sure sign of growth even in the absence of population figures. Similar forces were operating in the countryside. In 1100, about 11 fortified villages surrounded Florence, but by 1200, the city was ringed by 205 such villages.

For the first time since Late Antiquity, cities were becoming centers for many activities. Governments, which required larger staffs of trained personnel, settled in towns. Schools and eventually universities (see pages 280–282) were urban institutions. Mercantile, industrial, ecclesiastical, and legal organizations were located in towns. Towns began to compete with royal and aristocratic courts as literary centers, and cathedrals, the great buildings of the age, were exclusively urban.

A novelty of the twelfth century was the emergence of the Champagne fairs as a meeting point for the commerce of north and south. Since the early Middle Ages, a few locations hosted permanent fairs, and many places sponsored occasional fairs. By the middle of the twelfth century, however, the spices, silks, and dyes of the Mediterranean, the wool of England, the furs and linens of Germany, and the leather products of Spain began to be sold in a series of six fairs held in the Champagne region of France from spring to autumn.

guilds Voluntary associations of people who shared common crafts or trades.

One distinctive urban phenomenon was the rise of **guilds**. The guilds had many functions. Their main purpose was economic: to regulate standards of production, to fix prices, and to control membership in their respective trades. But as towns grew larger and more impersonal, these associations of people engaged in similar occupations fostered a sense of belonging, a feeling of community. Members tended to live in the same areas and to worship together in a parish church. Growing wealth in general, coupled with fierce local pride, produced building competitions whose results are still visible in the huge neighborhood churches that survive in most European towns. The guilds indulged in elaborate festivals and celebrations, which sometimes turned into drunken debauches despite being held to honor saints. The guilds also assisted members who fell on hard times, saw to their funeral expenses, and provided for widows and orphans.

The guilds had a damaging impact on women. As more economic activity came under the umbrella of the guild structures, women were more systematically excluded from guild membership. Usually, women could become guild members only as wives or widows. They could not open economic enterprises of their own, although they were workers in many trades. Despite a growing, diversifying economy, women were increasingly denied opportunities, although later centuries would find women establishing their own guilds.

Changing Economic Attitudes

As medieval society generated more wealth and populations concentrated in cities, people who were relatively well-off became more conscious of those who were less fortunate. Moralists began to argue that the poor were a special gift of God to the rich, who could redeem their own souls by generous charitable benefactions. Most towns established schemes of poor relief. But the numbers of poor people grew so rapidly, particularly in large towns, that helping seemed hopeless, and some gave up trying. Hospitals, for example, began to refuse abandoned babies for fear that they would be deluged with them.

Efforts to alleviate the condition of the poor constituted one ethical concern of medieval thinkers, but two issues attracted even more attention. First, theologians and lawyers alike discussed the "just price," the price at which goods should be bought and sold. Christian teaching had long held that it was immoral to hoard food during a famine or knowingly to sell a damaged item. But what was the correct price in ordinary circumstances? A theological view, often dismissed as unrealistic, held that items could be sold for only the cost of the materials in them and the labor absolutely necessary to produce them. A commercial view, often dismissed as immoral, insisted that a fair price was whatever the market would bear, regardless of costs or consequences. A working consensus held that a just price was one arrived at by bargaining between free and knowledgeable parties.

The other ethical issue concerned usury, the lending of money at interest. Christian writers were always hostile to commercial enterprise, and they had plenty of biblical warrant for their view. Psalm 15 warned that no one can be blameless "who lends his money at usury." Luke's Gospel admonished Christians to "give without expecting to be repaid in full." Luke actually forbade the profit that makes most commercial enterprises possible. In the twelfth century, churchmen began to be much more assiduous in their condemnations of usury, a practice that had been winked at for centuries. Gradually, thinkers began to defend usury on the grounds that a person who lent money incurred a risk and deserved to be compensated for that risk.

Investment demands credit, and credit requires some payback for the lender. Even in the face of deep hostility, credit mechanisms spread in thirteenth-century Europe. They were held up to minute scrutiny by theologians and popular preachers and were found to be evidence of man's sinfulness, acquisitiveness, and greed. But all these practices persisted, fueled by the expansion of the European economy, and began putting individual profit alongside community interest at the heart of social and economic thought.

SECTION SUMMARY

- Europe's population grew dramatically until the late 1200s, owing to better diets and more plentiful foods.
- Technological gains came with wider use of horses, improved plows, and more productive farming techniques.
- Many regions began to specialize in growing or manufacturing products, and this local specialization prompted larger-scale trade.
- Economic growth widened the gap between rich and poor and induced theologians to write about the just price and usury.

THE HEIRS OF THE CAROLINGIAN EMPIRE: GERMANY, ITALY, AND FRANCE

What did Germany, Italy, and France owe to the Carolingian past? How alike and different were these areas by 1300?

The scope of political and institutional life expanded everywhere between 900 and 1300. In 900, the Carolingian Empire was collapsing. By 1300, France had emerged as a large, stable kingdom, and Italy had turned into several reasonably coherent regional entities. The most surprising political development within the old Carolingian lands, indeed within Europe as a whole, was Germany's rise to a premier position in the tenth century and then its long, slow decline. The states that evolved out of the Carolingian Empire faced common challenges: the achievement of territorial integrity; the growing responsibility of the central government; complicated political relations among kings, aristocrats, and churchmen; and the elaboration of new ideas about the state and its responsibilities.

Germany and the Empire, 911–1272

From the ninth century to the present, no state in Europe has been less stable territorially and politically than Germany and the German Empire. Two issues are paramount: the role of dynastic and territorial instability in German history and German rulers' complex, contentious relations with the leaders of the church.

The Treaty of Verdun (see page 219) created something essentially new in 843: an East Frankish kingdom. Frankish rulers had long claimed authority over some of the lands that eventually became Germany, but before 843, no unified kingdom had ever existed in the territories east of the Rhine River (see **Map 9.2**). The lands had no tradition of common or unified rule and there was no single "German" people. Roman culture had barely penetrated into German lands, and Christian culture was recent. "Germany" had—has—no natural frontiers.

GERMANY'S LAND AND RULERS

After the last East Frankish Carolingian died in 911, the dukes, or leaders, of Germany's major regions chose one of their number as king. Under varying circumstances, the dukes chose kings from different families several times: Saxons (or Ottonians) in 919; Salians in 1024; and Staufer in 1138. This record of frequent dynastic change might be contrasted with the situation in France (see pages 244–245), where one family reigned from 987 to 1328.

At the beginning of Saxon rule, Germany comprised five duchies: Saxony, Franconia, Lorraine, Swabia, and Bavaria. German romantic tradition regarded the dukes as the heroic leaders of distinct

🌐 **MAP 9.2—Germany and Its Duchies, ca. 1000–1200**

The chief political dynamic in Germany was a contest for power between the kings and the dukes. The duchies emerged in the ninth and tenth centuries and outlived one dynasty of kings after another.

ethnic communities, the so-called Tribal Duchies. The dukes were actually the descendants of local rulers introduced by the Carolingians. They were wealthy and powerful; they contested with kings for control of the bishops and abbots in their duchies; and sometimes they managed to make vassals out of the lower ranks of the aristocracy in their territories, effectively denying kings connections with these people. In sum, the dukes were extremely jealous of their independence.

When the Saxons came to power, they attempted to control one or more of these duchies. Hoping to win new territories and distract troublesome aristocrats, the Saxons began Germany's centuries-long drive to the east, into Slavic Europe. In 955, Otto I gained power and prestige when he led a combined German force to victory against the Magyars at Lechfeld.

The Saxons also tried to control the church, especially bishops and abbots, to gain the allegiance of powerful and articulate allies. In 962, Otto I, who had begun expanding into Italy in 952, was crowned emperor in Rome by the pope. The imperial title conferred two benefits on the German kings: It gave them immense prestige and power that owed nothing to the dukes, and it raised the possibility of securing huge material resources in Italy, where, as emperors, they did not have to share power the way they did in Germany. The marriage of Otto II to a Byzantine princess was a sign of Germany's growing stature. Their son, Otto III, sponsored a brilliant court, patronizing writers and painters. When he died in 1002, Germany was the preeminent land in Europe.

After 1002, dynastic instability plagued Germany. For example, when Henry III, died in 1056, he left behind a 6-year-old heir and a decade of civil war. Military expansion virtually ceased, and powerful aristocrats struggled with one another and with their kings. Chief among these aristocrats were the dukes, who had chafed under Saxon and Salian efforts to control them. When Henry IV came of age in 1066, he faced opposition on all sides, controlled no duchies, was not yet emperor, and had lost much of his father's control of the church. When he tried to make church appointments in the traditional way, he encountered the fierce opposition of the newly reformed papacy in the person of Pope Gregory VII (r. 1073–1085). Their battles inaugurated the so-called investiture controversy, which lingered on until 1122, when both of the original foes were long dead.

In the twelfth century, the Salian dynasty died out. With the accession of Frederick Barbarossa ("Red Beard") in 1152, a new family, the Staufer, consolidated its hold on the German throne. Frederick, based in Swabia, patiently worked to get other dukes to recognize his overlordship, even though he was powerless to demand payments or services from them. His plan was slowly to build up the idea that the king was the highest lord in the land (a plan that his French and English contemporaries used effectively). In 1158, Frederick summoned representatives of the major Italian cities to demand full recognition of his regalian, or ruler's, rights. These included military service; control of roads, ports, and waterways; administration of tolls, mints, fines, vacant fiefs, and confiscated properties; appointment of magistrates; construction of palaces; and control of mines, fisheries, and saltworks. Frederick's attempts to control northern Italy resulted in the creation of the Lombard League, a union of Italian cities that inflicted a humiliating defeat on German forces at Legnano (len-YAN-oh) in 1176.

Frederick also struggled for more than twenty years to get the popes to recognize his claim to the imperial office, which he viewed as a source of prestige and as a legitimation of his right to rule Italy. When he spoke of his "Holy Roman Empire," he meant that his power came from God himself and from the Romans via Charlemagne. The handsome, energetic, and athletic Frederick accomplished much, and he might have done more had he not drowned in Anatolia in 1190, while on his way to the Third Crusade.

In 1197, Germany's heir was an infant, Frederick II (r. 1212–1250), who had been born in Sicily. His mother, Constance, had no standing in Germany and little influence in Italy. Accordingly, she placed her son under the tutelage of Pope Innocent III (r. 1198–1216). By the time Frederick came of age, he so despaired of governing Germany that he conceded the "Statute in Favor of the Princes," which lodged royal power in ducal hands in return for a vague acknowledgment of his overlordship. Frederick concentrated his own efforts in Italy. Although he made good progress, he faced constant opposition from the popes, who were unwilling to trade a German ruler with interests in Italy for an essentially Italian ruler with interests in Germany. When Frederick II died in 1250, effective central authority in both Germany and Italy collapsed.

A long-lived dynasty might have made a difference. Germany did have great rulers: Otto I, Otto III, Frederick Barbarossa, and even Frederick II were the equals of any contemporary ruler. But repeated changes of ruling family in the context of a fragile political regime provided repeated opportunities for fragmentation. The German monarchy had a very limited territorial base and unimpressive government institutions. The Saxons were based in the north, the Salians in the center, and the Staufer in the south. Thus, continuity of rule was constantly threatened by huge dynastic, institutional, and geographical challenges. Germany's involvement with Italy and quest for the imperial title have occasioned no end of controversy. To some, royal involvement in Italy signals a failure to deal imaginatively with Germany itself. To others, the quest for prestige, power, and money in Italy was actually a creative solution to the monarchy's relative impotence in Germany.

The key issue in the relations between Germany's rulers and the church is the investiture controversy. In the middle of the eleventh century, a group of ardent church reformers, who were committed to improving the moral and intellectual caliber of the clergy all over Europe, targeted the chief

Rulers of Medieval Germany

Saxons

Henry I (919–936)

Otto I (936–973)

Otto II (973–983)

Otto III (983–1002)

Henry II (1002–1024)

Salians

Conrad II (1024–1039)

Henry III (1039–1056)

Henry IV (1056–1106)

Henry V (1106–1125)

Staufer

Conrad III (1138–1152)

Frederick Barbarossa (1152–1190)

Henry VI (1190–1197)

Frederick II (1212–1250)

THE INVESTITURE CONTROVERSY

Henry IV, Duchess Matilda of Tuscany, and Abbot Hugh of Cluny The embattled Henry IV here implores Matilda, a tremendously wealthy landowner and ally of Pope Gregory VII, to intercede with the pope. The powerful abbot of Cluny looks over the scene protectively. Written documents do not portray women's power as vividly as this image does. (Biblioteca Apostolica Vaticana)

RexrogatAbbatem:MathildimSupplicatAtq;

lay investiture A term for the appointment ("investiture") of members of the clergy by laymen.

impediment to reform: the control of church appointments by laymen—or **lay investiture**, as they called it. Gregory VII prohibited lay investiture. This brought the reformers into direct conflict with the Salians, who, like their predecessors back to Charlemagne, believed that they reigned supreme in the "City of God." These German rulers stood, in their own view, nearest to God in a great hierarchy; the clergy occupied the rungs beneath them in human society. Thus, the king was God's specially chosen agent on earth, and the higher clergy were the king's natural helpers in governing the realm. To the reformers, the proper organization of society was just the opposite: The clergy, with the pope at its head, stood nearest to God, with secular monarchs subordinate to the church.

Alongside ideological struggles, the particular quarrel over the appointment of churchmen mushroomed into a general struggle for leadership in Christian society. In Germany, the struggle between Henry IV and Gregory VII became a pretext for ducal and aristocratic opposition to the king. Henry expended time and resources in Italy trying in vain to control Rome and the pope. (See the feature, "The Written Record: The Issues in the Investiture Controversy.")

The Concordat of Worms (VORM), concluded in 1122 between Henry V (r. 1106–1125) and Pope Calixtus II (r. 1119–1124), brought the investiture controversy to an end. The decree stipulated that the election of bishops should be free and conducted according to church law. Only after a man had been duly elected bishop could a king, or emperor, invest him with the symbols and offices of secular authority. The Concordat was a blow to the German political system as it had existed for centuries. When Otto III died in 1002, Germany was powerful and confident. When Henry V died in 1125,

The Issues in the Investiture Controversy

These two documents illustrate the range of issues involved in the conflict between the emperor Henry IV and Pope Gregory VII. The first excerpt is from a long letter written by Henry in 1076. The second is a decree issued by Gregory in 1078.

Henry Denounces the Pope

Henry, king not by usurpation but by the holy ordination of God, to Hildebrand, not now pope but false monk:

Such greeting as this you have merited through your disturbances, for there is no rank in the church on which you have brought, not honor but disgrace, not blessing but curse. To mention only a few notable cases, you have dared to assail the holy rulers of the church, archbishops, bishops, and priests, and you have trodden them underfoot like slaves ignorant of what their master is doing;…you have regarded them as knowing nothing, yourself as knowing all things.…

We have endured all this in our anxiety to save the honor of the apostolic see, but you have mistaken our humility for fear and have ventured to attack the royal power conferred on us by God, and threatened to divest us of it. As if we had received our kingdom from you! As if the kingdom and empire were in your hands, not God's! For our Lord Jesus Christ did call us to the kingdom.…You have assailed me who, though unworthy of anointing, have nevertheless been anointed to the kingdom and who, according to the traditions of the holy fathers, are subject to the judgment of God alone.…The true pope Peter exclaims "Fear God, honor the king." But you, who do not fear God, dishonor me, His appointed one…

Gregory Strikes Back

You, therefore, damned by this curse and by the judgment of all our bishops and ourselves, come down and relinquish the apostolic chair which you have usurped. I, Henry, king by the grace of God, together with all our bishops, say to you: "Come down, come down, to be damned throughout all eternity."

Inasmuch as we have learned that, contrary to the ordinances of the holy fathers, the investiture of churches is, in many places, performed by lay persons, and that from this cause many disturbances arise in the church by which the Christian religion is degraded, we decree that no one of the clergy shall receive the investiture of a bishopric, abbey, or church from the hand of an emperor, or king, or of any lay person, male or female. If anyone shall presume to do so, let him know that such investiture is void by apostolic authority, and that he himself shall lie under excommunication until fitting satisfaction shall have been made.

QUESTIONS

1. On what foundations does Henry IV challenge Gregory VII?

2. How does Gregory see the issues?

3. What aspects of medieval thought and politics made this quarrel possible?

Source: Slightly adapted from James Harvey Robinson, *Readings in European History*, vol. 1 (Boston: Ginn, 1904), pp. 279–281, 275.

Germany was weak, disunited, and searching for new bases of authority. With its promise, undoubted achievements, and yet ultimate failure, Germany is the political mystery of medieval Europe.

The Varying Fortunes of Italy

The history of Italy has always been played out in three regions: north, central, and south. The Carolingians and the Germans after them laid a heavy hand on northern Italy. In the center of the peninsula, the Papal States was the key player. Outsiders always dominated the south, but their identities changed often.

The rise of **communes** (see **Map 9.3**) owed much to the period's economic expansion. Merchants and artisans were gaining in wealth and anxious to have some say in the government of their cities. At the same time, bishops and counts contested each other for power and began to grant fiefs to vassals in the town's surrounding countryside. Landed and commercial wealth produced a volatile mix.

Communes began as sworn associations of the local nobility—landed lords—and their vassals. Commune members swore to uphold one another's rights and called themselves the *popolo*, or "people," although the people as a whole had nothing to do with the early communes. A commune accorded a high degree of participation to its members in choosing leaders and in assembling to vote on matters of common concern. The leaders of the early communes were usually

THE COMMUNAL MOVEMENT

communes Self-governing Italian towns.

🌐 MAP 9.3—The Communal Movement in Italy

Beginning in the late eleventh century, many towns in northern Italy, some in the central regions, and a very few in the south erected communal forms of government. This distribution reflects the relative wealth of north and south and the power of the popes in the center. North of the Alps, only Flanders and northern France experienced comparable communal movements.

called *consuls*—a deliberate attempt to evoke the Roman past. Usually elected for a single year, the consuls varied in number from four to twenty in different cities. The consuls proposed matters to an assembly for ratification. By the 1140s, every significant city in northern and central Italy had a commune. One by one, cities either refused to recognize papal or imperial overlordship or else renegotiated the terms under which they would acknowledge the rule of their historic masters. The working out of this ongoing relationship was a major development in the history of the Italian cities in the twelfth century.

By the late twelfth century, the consular communes were still governed by oligarchies of men whose wealth and power came from land, trade, and industry. Guild interests, however, gained in prominence at the expense of the landed groups among whom the communal movement had arisen, and ordinary workers began to clamor for participation. The communes were becoming increasingly volatile and violent.

One solution to this potential crisis was the introduction of the *podestà* (poe-des-TAH), a sort of city manager chosen by the local oligarchy. The podestà often came from the outside, served for a set period (usually six months or a year), and underwent a careful scrutiny at the conclusion of his term. He was expected to police the city as well as defend it. Normally, he could not be a property owner in the town, marry into local society, or dine privately with any citizen. By the middle of the thirteenth century, some podestàs were becoming virtual professional administrators. One man, for example, was elected sixteen times in nine cities over a period of thirty-four years, four times in Bologna alone.

The Italian commune was a radical political experiment. Everywhere else in medieval Europe, power was thought to radiate downward—from God, the clergy, the emperor, the king. In a commune, power radiated upward from the popolo to its leaders. For several centuries, the Italian city was arguably the most creative institution in the Western world.

The key power in central Italy was the papacy, and the main political entity was the Papal States. In the political turmoil of the tenth and eleventh centuries, the papacy lost a great deal of territory. Throughout the twelfth and thirteenth centuries, therefore, a basic objective of papal policy was to recover lost lands and rights. This quest to restore the territorial basis for papal power and income helps explain why the popes so resolutely opposed German imperial influence in Italy.

The most striking development pertaining to the papacy is the expansion of its institutions. The **Papal Monarchy** is meant to characterize a church whose power was increasingly centralized in the hands of the popes. In Rome, the pope presided over the *curia*, the papal court. The College of Cardinals, potentially fifty-three in number, formed a kind of senate for the church. They elected the popes (by majority after 1059 and by a two-thirds majority after 1179), served as key advisers, headed the growing financial and judicial branches of the papal government, and often served as legates, papal envoys. Lateran Councils met often and gathered the clergy from all over Europe to legislate for the church as a whole. The hierarchical structure of the church became more visible as ecclesiastical business tended to accumulate in Rome.

High medieval popes also reserved to themselves certain jurisdictional and coercive prerogatives. Popes could excommunicate persons—that is, exclude them from the sacraments of the church and the community of Christians. This was a form of social death in that excommunicated persons could not eat, converse, or socialize with others. Popes could lay a territory under interdict. This decree forbade all religious services except baptisms and burials and was designed to bring maximum pressure to bear on a particular individual. Finally, popes could invoke the inquisition. Despite horror stories about the inquisition, this was a judicial mechanism fully rooted in Roman law and widely used in the medieval West. Basically, an inquisition involved churchmen taking sworn testimony in an attempt to discover heresy.

THE FATE OF SOUTHERN ITALY

From the ninth century on, the region south of Rome was contested among Byzantines, North African Muslims, and local potentates. In 1026, Norman pilgrims, bound for the Holy Land, landed in southern Italy, where local people enlisted them in the fight against the Muslims. Initially opposed to the Normans, the papacy later allied with their leader as a counterweight against the Germans.

From his capital at Palermo, Roger II "the Great" (r. 1130–1154), ruled a complex state that blended Byzantine, Lombard, and Norman structures. Perched advantageously at the juncture

Coronation of Roger II in Sicily, 1130 Roger's coronation by Jesus Christ makes a powerful ideological statement: He owes his office to no earthly power. The cultural crosscurrents of Sicily are visible: Roger is depicted more like a Byzantine emperor than a Western king. The inscriptions above his head ("Rogerios Rex") and next to Christ's are in Greek, not Latin. Beside Christ's head are the customary Greek abbreviations **IC** (the first and last letters of **I**esu**S**) and **XP**, for **ChR**istos. (The original surely contains the full XP symbol.) (Scala/Art Resource, NY)

THE PAPAL MONARCHY

Papal Monarchy
A term meant to signify the enlarged and centralized papal government beginning in the twelfth century.

Important Popes During the High Middle Ages
Gregory VII (1073–1085)
Urban II (1088–1099)
Innocent III (1198–1216)
Boniface VIII (1294–1303)

of the Latin, Greek, and Arab worlds, the Norman court was more advanced in finance and bureaucratic administration than any of its European contemporaries. No one forgot for a moment, however, that the Normans were primarily great warriors. A chronicler said of the Normans, "They delight in arms and horses."

Once the popes had defeated Frederick II, they decided to look for more pliant allies in the south. They invited a succession of French and Spanish princes to assume the Crown, thus touching off long-standing rivalries in the area. A profusion of outsiders always dominated southern Italy.

Capetian France, 987–1314

When the Treaty of Verdun created the West Frankish Kingdom in 843, no one knew what the future of France might be. Referring to France's tremendous diversity, the twentieth-century French leader Charles de Gaulle once quipped, "It is impossible to govern a country with 325 kinds of cheese." During the late ninth century and much of the tenth, the area suffered cruelly from constant waves of Viking attacks and from repeated failures of the Carolingian family to produce adult heirs to the throne. At the end of the tenth century, however, the Carolingians were replaced by the Capetians (kuh-PEE-shunz), the family of Hugh Capet (r. 987–996). The Capetians ruled France for more than three hundred years—an impressive achievement in light of the repeated failure of German dynasties.

CAPETIAN PRESTIGE

From the very beginning, the Capetian kings of France sought to preserve the royal office, increase its prestige, and consolidate its political base. Hugh Capet inaugurated the tradition of crowning his son as his successor during his own lifetime. This meant that when the old king died, a new king was already in place and the nobility could not easily meddle in the succession. Robert II (r. 996–1031) displayed the "royal touch," a ceremony in which the king was believed to be able to cure people of scrofula (a common respiratory ailment) by touching them. No French nobleman ever laid claim to such miraculous powers. Capetian kings capitalized on their control of the old, rich, prestigious, and centrally located city of Paris. The kings promoted the shrine of Saint Denis, the legendary first bishop of Paris, as a kind of "national" shrine for France. Louis VII (r. 1137–1180) began to make elegant tours of the country to put himself, his office, and his sparkling entourage on display. In Louis IX (r. 1226–1270), the Capetian family actually produced a saint of the Catholic Church—Saint Louis.

BUILDING THE CAPETIAN KINGDOM

The Capetians initially controlled no more than Paris and its immediate region. They contested for control of this region with a number of ambitious and aggressive families, finally ground them down, and made the Île-de-France one of the best-governed regions in all of France. The kings also controlled about two dozen bishoprics and some fifty monasteries in northern France. This power base gave the kings unrivaled opportunities to extend their influence and, in turn, to build up a cadre of loyal and articulate supporters. Although French kings provoked a few battles with the papacy, France experienced no investiture controversy.

France's territorial expansion was tightly connected to military success. The background to French military success is complicated. The counts of Anjou (see **MAP 9.4**), through war and marriage, secured control of almost two-thirds of France. Decisive was the marriage of Henry of Anjou to Eleanor of Aquitaine. To make things even more complicated, in 1154, Henry became king of England through his mother, a granddaughter of William the Conqueror (see below). For two generations, the king of France hammered away at this "Angevin Empire." In 1204, Philip II of France (r. 1180–1223) defeated King John of England (r. 1199–1216) and laid claim to the French holdings of the Angevins—but not to England.

Southeastern France was gained by wars of a different kind. In the last decades of the twelfth century, much of the south became a hotbed of the Albigensian (al-buh-JEN-see-un) heresy—an important religious movement (see page 267). Some Catholic locals and many churchmen urged the kings to undertake military action against the heretics. The French kings bided their time until they had the resources to deal with this turbulent region. Under Louis VIII (r. 1223–1226) and Louis IX, the French monarchy finally extended its authority to France's Mediterranean coast.

The Capetian Kings of France	
Hugh Capet (987–996)	Philip II (1180–1223)
Robert II (996–1031)	Louis VIII (1223–1226)
Henry I (1031–1060)	Louis IX (1226–1270)
Philip I (1060–1108)	Philip III (1270–1285)
Louis VI (1108–1137)	Philip IV (1285–1314)
Louis VII (1137–1180)	

🌐 **MAP 9.4—French Territorial Principalities, ca. 1200**

As the Carolingian West Frankish Kingdom (see **MAP 8.3** on page 214) broke down and feudal bonds proliferated, many territories arose under counts and dukes. Their struggles to impose control locally and to fight off royal supervision animated French history.

The chief political dynamic in France was the contest for power between the kings and the territorial princes (see **MAP 9.4**). At stake was the monarchy's ability to introduce effective rule into the lands won in all those battles. The territorial princes were locally powerful magnates, rather like the German dukes. But whereas Germany comprised five major duchies, France had a dozen or more territorial principalities.

The territorial princes also faced localized rivalries for power and influence. Countless individuals built castles (see the feature, "The Visual Record: The Medieval Castle"), brutally subjected local peasants, and became lords. Sometimes these individuals were the vassals of the territorial princes—say, the dukes of Normandy or the counts of Anjou—and sometimes they had vassals of their own. In the Carolingian world, the number of vassals was small, their fidelity reasonably solid, and their services reliable. By 1100, the number of vassals was immense, their fidelity was constantly shifting, and they tended to provide only local military service. Scholars call this shift from effective Carolingian government to myriad local lordships a **feudal revolution**. For the kings of France to re-create central government, they had to overcome the disruptive tendencies of this revolution and then consolidate institutions.

In the twelfth and thirteenth centuries, the Capetians followed a few basic policies to increase their ability to govern. They circumvented the local lords as much as possible. When they won military victories, the kings did not dole out the seized lands to lords as new fiefs but instead kept them in their own hands, or in the hands of family members. The kings introduced into these lands new officials, called bailiffs or provosts, who were of modest social background, had no personal ties to their assigned regions, often had some schooling in law, and were intensely loyal to the kings. By the time of Louis IX, officials called *enqueteurs* (on-KEH-tur) were sent around the country to

STRATEGIES OF CAPETIAN GOVERNMENT

feudal revolution   A term that refers to the proliferation of lord-vassal bonds as key elements of governmental and social control.

The Medieval Castle

Storybook castles, in the manner of Disneyland, figure prominently in almost everyone's idea of the Middle Ages. The reality was different. Medieval castles were generally small, stark, and uncomfortable, not beautiful and romantic.

Castles represent a stage in the history of both dwellings and fortifications. Initially, castles were private, residential, and military. A consideration of these three elements will place the castle in historical context and illustrate what historians learn from the impressive ruins that dot the landscape of Europe and the crusader states.

The first medieval castles were constructed in the tenth century. The French word *château* (from the Latin *castellum*) means "great house," signifying the castle's residential purpose. Powerful aristocrats erected castles not just as their principal dwellings, but also as a base for securing and extending their social and political influence. From his castle, a lord could dominate the surrounding region. The castle also sheltered the lord's immediate dependents temporarily in the event of an attack and his military retainers more or less permanently.

A few castles were built exclusively for military purposes. In 1110, Crusaders captured a strategic plateau rising 2,000 feet above the main road from inner Syria to the Mediterranean. Between 1142 and 1205, Crusaders continually expanded the fortifications of the castle pictured here, the "Krak des Chevaliers" (from Syriac *karka*, meaning "fortress," and the Old French word for "horsemen"). This castle fell to Muslim attackers in 1271. The techniques of fortification developed in the crusader East influenced castle building in Europe.

The medieval city of Murviedro, Spain, takes its name from the Latin *mures veteres* (old walls). In 1871, the city was given back its ancient name, Sagunt. The hilltop above ancient Saguntum (attacked by Hannibal, thus affronting the Romans and providing a pretext for the Second Punic War between Rome and Carthage; see page 124–125) reveals fortifications from the prehistoric, Carthaginian, Roman, Visigothic, and Muslim periods. The most spectacular visible remains date from the Muslim period, between 900 and 1098, when El Cid captured the site.

Krak des Chevaliers, Syria, ca. 1200 (Robert Harding World Images)

Muslim Fortress of Murviedro, Valencia, Spain, Eleventh Century
(Institut Amatller d'Art Hispanic)

Castles took many forms. From 900 to 1200, the "motte and bailey" castle was the most common. A lord commanded his dependents to dig a circular ditch and heap the dirt into a mound (the motte). The ditch, together with a wooden palisade—a fencelike wall—was the bailey. A wooden tower was often built atop the mound. Some castles included an elaborate series of mounds, ditches, and wooden walls, but usually these structures were quite simple.

As siege techniques improved (catapults could hurl projectiles weighing 600 pounds), the wooden building of the bailey began to be replaced by stone. By 1150 or 1200, stone towers (*donjons*, from the Latin *dominium* for "lordship") were only the inner portion—the "keep"—of a more complicated structure of walls, towers, and gates. It was not unusual for walls to be 75 or 100 feet high. Because of the growing power of bombarding engines, castle walls often had to be made thicker. Towers built at 40- or 50-foot intervals projected beyond the walls so that defenders armed with bows and arrows could fire at attackers along the length of a castle wall. Look at the spacing of the towers in the castles pictured here. At Krak des Chevaliers, we see one of the earliest examples of a double ring of walls. Two walls made it more difficult for attackers to take the keep and permitted defenders to battle invaders from inside both the inner and the outer walls.

To allow people to enter and leave, castles had gate towers, usually with two gates, one on the outside and one on the inside. Intricate systems of winches, cranks, and counterweights regulated the raising and lowering of the gates. Speedy operation was essential. Some castles had small "sally ports" from which soldiers could make a rapid dash to attack a besieging enemy.

When possible, lords sited their castles on the edges of cliffs, because fewer sides were open to assault and a garrison of modest size could defend the remaining walls. Krak sits on an impressive natural site. The fortress of Murviedro, perched on a hilltop, commands the surrounding territory. Rulers and conquerors from Roman to modern times have exploited this dominating site. To walls and natural defenses were sometimes added ditches.

Much can be learned from the number of castles in a particular area. The presence of numerous small castles across the countryside suggests an extreme decentralization of power in that place and time. Remains of several hundred castles have been found in France alone; and England, in 1100, boasted a castle every 10 miles. Conversely, areas with only a few large, strategically sited castles were likely subject to greater central control. Careful mapping of the known locations of castles can tell historians a great deal about the structure of social and political relationships.

Castles both contributed and responded to developments in military technology, such as more powerful catapults. Stone castles proliferated as Europe grew wealthier and as quarrying technology improved. Castles grew larger as monarchies, rather than private individuals, built them. Like cathedrals, massive state-funded castles tended to be built by professionals rather than by local laborers.

Both fortifications and magnificent dwellings have existed in Western civilization for millennia. From about 900 to 1200, the castle met the needs of a politically dominant warrior-aristocracy for a private residence with military significance. In later centuries, the castle, as a château, retained its private and residential nature but lost much of its military character to garrisoned fortresses in the service of kings and princes.

QUESTIONS

1. Who built castles and why did they build them?

2. What were the essential characteristics of a castle?

3. How does a castle differ from a residence?

inspect the work of bailiffs and provosts. Such roles had been unheard of since the Carolingian *missi dominici* (see page 217–218). Louis also began to issue *ordonnances*, what might be called executive orders, which were binding on all the land under the king's control. These precepts are reminiscent of Carolingian capitularies (see page 215).

If in 1000 France was a land of innumerable tiny lordships, then by 1300, it was the best-governed kingdom in Europe. Indicative of France's position is the outcome of two battles between King Philip IV (r. 1285–1314) and Pope Boniface VIII (r. 1294–1303). First, Philip attempted to tax the French clergy, and then, he sought to bring a bishop before his court. Boniface angrily objected to Philip's intervention in ecclesiastical affairs. But things had changed drastically since the fateful confrontation between Henry IV and Gregory VII. Boniface had to back down. In 1300, France was the largest, richest, and best-governed kingdom in Europe. French culture and language were increasingly dominant. Considering France's situation in 900, and compared with Germany's in 1300, these were impressive achievements.

THE BRITISH ISLES

What were the chief dynamics in the development of medieval Britain?

In the British Isles, expansion had three dimensions: the tremendous growth of the English government, England's relentless push into the Celtic world, and the emergence of states in the Celtic world. England is smaller than France or Germany and more homogeneous in population, culture, and language than either of them, or than Italy. Nevertheless, England faced some acute dynastic, military, and political challenges. Moreover, England shared an island with two Celtic neighbors, Wales and Scotland, whose inhabitants were close kin to the people of England's neighboring island, Ireland (see **MAP 9.5**).

Viking and Norman Invasions in England

Alfred's (see page 213) descendants ruled England for more than a century. They gradually rolled back the frontier of the "Danelaw," the areas of eastern and northern England controlled by Viking settlers (mainly Danes, hence the name). Alfred and his successors built strong central institutions. All free men in the realm owed allegiance to the king and could, in principle, be called to the militia, or *fyrd* (FEERD). The great men of the realm attended meetings of the royal council, or *witan* (WHIT-un), which was partly a court of law and partly a deliberative body. The king could issue writs—executive orders rather like Carolingian capitularies. The Danegeld— literally "money for the Danes"—was originally collected solely in times of danger and then slowly transformed into a regular tax. All of England was divided into shires, and each shire had a royally appointed officer, the *shire-reeve* (or sheriff).

Late in the tenth century, English leadership failed in the face of a severe threat from a new generation of Vikings. The powerful king of Denmark, Swein Forkbeard, conquered England in 1014, but survived his conquest by only two years. His son Cnut then ruled from 1016 to 1035, at which point power passed to Cnut's sons. Cnut was simultaneously king of Denmark and England, and for a time of Norway, too. He wed his daughter to Emperor Henry III and himself to Emma, the widow of the last English king. He was cultured, Christian, and an acquaintance of the pope.

When Cnut's sons died in 1042, without heirs, the English nobles called over from Normandy Edward, called "the Confessor," the son of the last English king. Edward, who was unusually pious, had taken a vow of chastity. Because he was not going to have an heir, claimants to the English throne began jockeying for position. Edward seems to have promised his throne to William, the duke of Normandy. Most of the English nobles preferred Harold of Wessex, one of their number. In Norway, Harald (who became known as Hardrada, or "Hard-Ruler") prepared to make a claim as Cnut's rightful heir. Harold of Wessex defeated Hardrada, only to be defeated in turn at Hastings by William.

🌐 **Map 9.5—Northern and Eastern Europe, ca. 1200**
Apart from Germany, the core states of Europe emerged inside the former Roman frontiers or right alongside them. After 900, an arc of new states emerged, from the Celtic realms and Iceland in the west, to Scandinavia in the north, to the western, southern, and eastern Slavs in eastern Europe.

Neither Cnut nor William, known as "the Conqueror" (r. 1066–1089), desired to dismantle or replace the old English institutions. But William had won England by conquest, and he did introduce some changes. He turned most of the estates in England into fiefs and distributed them among some 180 of his most loyal followers. Each of these vassals held his fief in return for a fixed quota of soldiers for the royal army. To raise the approximately five thousand soldiers required by William, each of his vassals had to create vassals of his own. The technical name for this process of vassals creating vassals is *subinfeudation*. In 1087, William exacted the Salisbury Oath, which established the principle of liege homage (LEEGE AHM-idge), according to which the king was the final lord of all vassals. To avoid creating territorial principalities on the French model, William scattered his vassals' holdings around the kingdom. Finally, to learn as much as he could about his new kingdom, and about the fiefs he had assigned to his followers, William conducted a massive survey of England that resulted in 1086 in the *Domesday Book*, named for the Day of Judgment, against which there was no appeal. No comparable survey of any state was accomplished until the American census of 1790.

The Development of English Law and Government

William was succeeded by two of his sons in turn, William II (r. 1089–1100) and Henry I (r. 1100–1135). Henry's only son drowned in a shipwreck, and the English nobles would accept neither his daughter Matilda as their queen nor her husband, Geoffrey of Anjou, as their king. Most of the English elite were Normans, and the Normans and Angevins were old foes. Consequently, the English turned in 1135 to a French prince, Stephen of Blois, who was a grandson of William the Conqueror through a daughter. Stephen I died childless in 1154 and bequeathed his kingdom to Henry of Anjou, the son of Geoffrey and Matilda, who ruled as Henry II (r. 1154–1189).

Henry was as much a French prince as an English king. From his father, mother, and wife (Eleanor of Aquitaine; see page 240), he had inherited a large part of France and was much preoccupied with his continental realm. He constantly battled his four sons for control of these vast French holdings. Two of these sons eventually became king. Richard I, also known as "Richard the Lionhearted" (r. 1189–1199), was a dashing prince who spent only ten months in England, preferring to pass his time on crusade or campaigning in France. John (r. 1199–1216) was defeated by France's Philip II, inducing contemporaries to mock him as "John Lackland" and "John Softsword."

Just as Viking and Norman rulers built on the solid foundations of the Anglo-Saxon state, so the Anglo-Normans and Angevins retained and expanded those very foundations. They refined the financial machinery of the English government, the Exchequer, named for the checkerboard table on which the accounts were reckoned. They vastly improved the judicial institutions. Henry I began to send itinerant justices around the realm. He brought the royal court, with its swift, fair, and competent justice, within the reach of most people, and he made royal justice more attractive than the justice available in local lords' courts. This expansion of the work of the royal courts led to the emergence of a common law in England—a law common to all people, courts, and cases.

England's relations with the church fell somewhere between Germany's and France's in both intensity and outcome. Anglo-Saxon kings generally enjoyed cordial relations with the church on a traditional Carolingian model. William the Conqueror controlled the church with an iron hand but introduced reforms and reformers who were acceptable to Rome. Archbishop Anselm of Canterbury and Henry I had a quarrel that lasted several years, but they finally mended their differences in a settlement that anticipated the terms of the Concordat of Worms. Henry II was always anxious to extend the influence of his courts. In 1164, he decided that "criminous clerks," or members of the clergy who had committed a crime, should be judged in royal courts. The archbishop of Canterbury, Thomas Becket (ca. 1118–1170), protested that clerics could be tried only in church courts. Although the two sides came to a reconciliation, a band of overly zealous knights murdered Becket, believing that they were doing the king's bidding. In fact, the crime so outraged the church and the public that Henry had to back down on criminous clerks and give up some authority to Rome. Despite these religious quarrels, however, England experienced no investiture controversy.

John's conflict with the church resulted in far more dramatic changes for England. The loss of Normandy had been costly in terms of prestige and resources. In difficult circumstances, John got into a row with Pope Innocent III because he refused to admit to England the pope's candidate for archbishop of Canterbury. Eventually, he submitted because Innocent had laid England under interdict and John needed the pope's support for his planned war of revenge against Philip II of France. True to his nickname, "Softsword," John lost and thus ended his quarrel with Rome.

With John's defeat and capitulation, the barons of England had had enough. These barons (a general name for the upper ranks of English society) were increasingly upset that an expanding royal government limited their influence. In 1215, a large group of disgruntled barons forced King John to sign the

Important Kings of England	
Alfred (871–899)	William II (1089–1100)
Ethelred II (978–1016)	Henry I (1100–1135)
Cnut (1016–1035)	Stephen I (1135–1154)
Edward the Confessor (1042–1066)	Henry II (1154–1189)
Harold of Wessex (1066)	John (1199–1216)
William I (the Conqueror) (1066–1089)	Edward I (1272–1307)

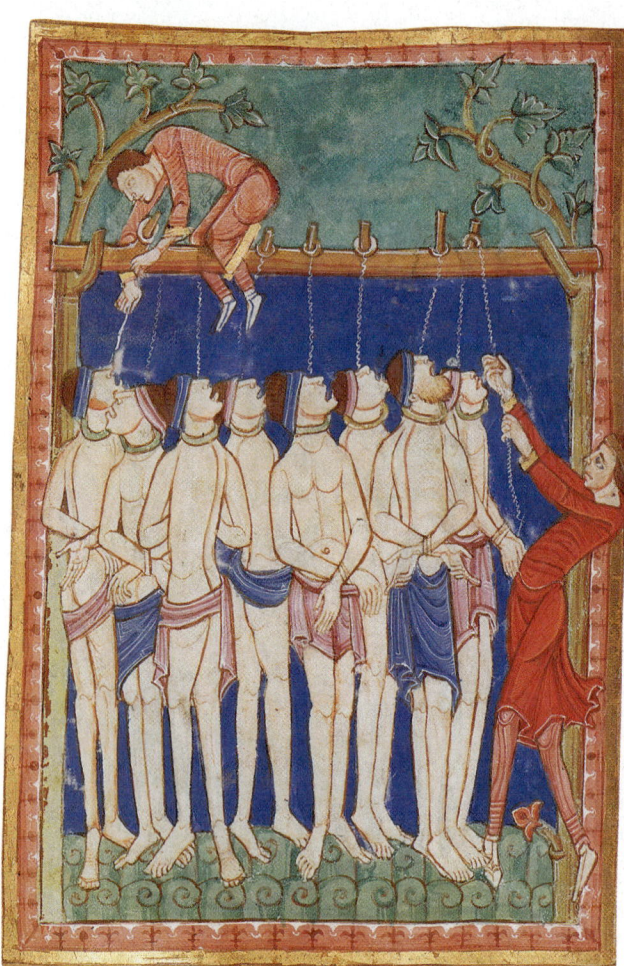

Swift and Certain Justice This picture from about 1130 depicts some of the forty-four thieves hung by Sheriff Ralph Basset in 1124. As a common law spread throughout England, criminals were more likely to be caught and punished. (The Pierpont Morgan Library, New York/Art Resource, NY)

Magna Carta, or "Great Charter" (so called because it was written on an unusually large sheet of parchment). This document required the king to respect the rights of feudal lords, not abuse his judicial powers, and consult his "natural" advisers—that is, the barons.

John tried to wiggle out of the Magna Carta, but he died in 1216, leaving only a minor heir, and the barons exacted many concessions from the regency government. When Henry III came of age in 1234, he struggled to win a limited application of the Magna Carta. The barons, on the contrary, wanted a voice in devising royal policy, especially military policy, in light of recent defeats. They also wished to have some say in naming the king's closest advisers and in controlling the work of the king's agents, especially judges. This tension between king and barons led to several meetings of the royal court, often called *parliaments*, a French word meaning, roughly, "talking together." Initially, these meetings had no fixed rights or procedures, no set group of attendees, and no defined role. The kings viewed them as clever political devices to win support for royal policies. The barons viewed them as opportunities to play a real role in a government that had been marginalizing them. The English were groping to find a way to build consultation into their system.

The reign of Edward I (1272–1307) sums up the achievements of England's rulers in the High Middle Ages. He issued numerous statutes, laws that bear comparison with Louis IX's *ordonnances* (see page 241)—which earned him the nickname "the English Justinian." He worked skillfully with the newly emerging Parliament. And like other English rulers before him, Edward balanced political and military accomplishments, bravely fighting for years on the Welsh and Scottish frontiers.

Magna Carta 1215 English document that sets limits on the power of the king.

parliaments Initially expanded meetings of the royal court intended to secure consensus for royal policies.

The Celtic Realms

When the Romans appeared on the scene, Celtic peoples could be found in virtually every region from Ireland to Anatolia. Most Celts were absorbed by more numerous and powerful Germanic and Slavic peoples. It was in the British Isles that the most durable and distinctive Celtic regions evolved into Ireland, Wales, and Scotland. Two essential dynamics characterized each of these regions: Tiny political entities gradually turned into larger kingdoms; and, relations between England and the Celtic realms were everywhere contentious (see **Map 9.5**).

In each of the Celtic realms, the movement toward greater unity was opened by the efforts of powerful, ambitious leaders to subjugate numerous well-entrenched local potentates, many of whom had expanded their power during the period of Viking invasions. In Ireland, Brian Boru (r. 976–1014) became the first ruler to exercise real authority over most of the island. In Wales, Rhodri the Great (d. 898) and Howell the Good (d. 950) were the first rulers to gain at least nominal authority over the whole of the land. Although disunity is a continuous theme of Scottish history, the centuries after the reign of Kenneth MacAlpin (843–858) reveal the slow creation of a national tradition.

The course of development in the Celtic lands was disrupted by the English in the eleventh and especially the twelfth centuries. The Norman Conquest of England brought adventurers to the frontiers of Wales and Scotland. Sometimes these continental knights advanced with the support of William the Conqueror and his sons, but more often, they looked to wild frontier regions for opportunities to escape tight control. In Wales, some Normans allied with various local princes who resented the growing power of the Welsh kings. Henceforth, the actual power of Welsh rulers varied greatly, and English kings usually claimed some authority over the region. Scottish kings managed to enlist a good many Norman knights into their service, but this recruitment effort angered the English kings and spurred them to greater intervention. Civil disturbances in Ireland induced King Rory O'Connor (r. 1156–1186) to turn to King Henry II of England for mercenaries to help him establish his power. But by 1171, Henry had invaded Ireland himself and inaugurated the complicated English involvement that persists to this day.

Edward I of England intervened repeatedly in the Celtic world. In 1277, he invaded Wales with the intention of totally subduing the Welsh. He built immense castles, whose ruins are still impressive today. Edward also made his son the Prince of Wales—still the title of the heir to the British throne. Between 1100 and 1260, England and Scotland went to war four times, and Edward resolved to put an end to this struggle by annexing Scotland. The Scots, however, rallied to the standard of Robert Bruce (r. 1306–1329), a dashing knight who managed to free Scotland for centuries.

SECTION SUMMARY

- England's kings survived several changes of dynasty (compare Germany) without making fundamental changes in English society or government.

- English kings built on Anglo-Saxon precedents to secure revenues, extend the work of the royal courts, and limit the power of the barons.

- English kings brought constant pressure to bear on the Celtic realms that surrounded England, in the process retarding political development in these regions.

Howell the Good This picture of Howell, from a manuscript of his laws, depicts him wearing a crown, holding a scepter, and sitting on a tufted throne that looks like a palace. These are key symbols of rule. (The National Library of Wales)

THE GROWTH OF NEW STATES

How did new states emerge in Spain, Scandinavia, and the Slavic world, and how do those states compare with their western neighbors?

The proliferation of new states constitutes one of the most remarkable examples of expansion in high medieval Europe. In Spain, Christian rulers waged a steady war of reconquest against the Islamic caliphate of Cordoba that led to the emergence of the kingdoms of Portugal, Castile, and Aragon. In Scandinavia, mighty leaders built durable kingdoms in Denmark, Norway, and Sweden. Local rulers created a band of new Slavic states running from the Baltic to the Balkans. To the east of those Slavic realms, around the city of Kiev, the Scandinavian Rus founded the first state on Russian soil. Between 900 and 1300, the geographic range of Europe's political entities more than doubled.

Reconquista and Kingdom Building in Spain

Historians perceive two driving forces in the rich and colorful history of medieval Spain. One is the bloody experience of several centuries of war along an expanding frontier. The other is the constant interplay within the Iberian Peninsula of three vibrant cultures: Christian, Jewish, and Muslim. We describe the first of these forces in this chapter and the second in the next.

After 1002, unified Muslim rule in Spain began breaking down, affording an unprecedented opportunity to the Christians living in the north of the peninsula. King Sancho I (r. 1000–1035) of Navarre launched an offensive against the Muslims. This war, carried on intermittently until the fifteenth century, is called the **Reconquista** (ray-con-KEE-stuh), the "Reconquest."

Before Sancho died, he divided his realm among his sons; thus, the kingdoms of Aragon and Castile arose alongside Navarre. Castile advanced the Reconquista. In 1085, its forces captured the Muslim stronghold and old Visigothic capital of Toledo, an important moral and strategic victory. Now, the Reconquista began moving on three fronts (see **MAP 9.6**). In the east, the emerging kingdom of Aragon-Catalonia advanced along the Mediterranean coast. In the center, León-Castile pressed hard against al-Andalus. In the west, the nascent kingdom of Portugal became a factor in Iberian politics. Christian successes, and the reconquest of Toledo, led the retreating Muslims to summon aid in the 1150s from militant North African Muslims. The Christian advance temporarily stopped.

Reconquista The name for the centuries-long battle of Christians against Muslims in Spain.

MAP 9.6—The Christian Reconquista of Muslim Spain
From slow beginnings in the ninth century to the epochal Battle of Las Navas de Tolosa (1212), the Christians in Spain pushed back the Muslim frontier and built durable states behind it.

Alfonso the Wise   The Spanish king Alfonso X, depicted here in a thirteenth-century manuscript from Spain, is judging his Muslim and Christian subjects. Alfonso's reputation for impartiality was important in his culturally diverse realm.   (Biblioteca de El Escorial/Laurie Platt Winfrey)

In the early thirteenth century, Pope Innocent III stirred up crusading zeal and lent encouragement to clerics and nobles in Spain who wished to reopen hostilities against the Muslims. In 1212, a combined Castilian-Aragonese army won a decisive victory at Las Navas de Tolosa, south of Toledo. The victory of Las Navas de Tolosa was a great turning point in Spanish history. The outcome of the Reconquista, which did not conclude until the fifteenth century, was never again in doubt.

Twelfth-century Spanish kings, especially in Castile, imposed hereditary rule and exacted oaths of allegiance from their free subjects. The kings tried to force powerful nobles to become their vassals. In the thirteenth century, Spain produced kings of genius, especially Alfonso X (r. 1252–1284) of Castile. These rulers were pious men, genuinely inspired by the ideal of the Crusades (discussed later in this chapter) and zealous in the promotion of the church. They also were hardheaded rulers. Aragon-Catalonia became the greatest naval power of the western Mediterranean and a formidable economic power. Military victories brought as well a flow of booty and a supply of lands to reward the nobles who spent their energy on the frontier rather than on attacking the king. These kings built strong central governments. Increasingly, they used professional officers in key government posts and dispatched roving officials from the court to check on local rulers. Alfonso issued a major law book for the whole of Castile. The Cortes, a representative assembly made up primarily of urban notables, began forging an alliance between the king and the towns. Iberia was not united in the thirteenth century, but it had evolved into four coherent blocks: a small and impotent Muslim region in Valencia and Granada, and three vibrant kingdoms centered on Portugal, Castile, and Aragon.

Scandinavia

Europe's expanding map saw new states in Scandinavia, the Roman name for the lands that became Denmark, Norway, and Sweden. Although the faint beginnings of political consolidation in Denmark can be traced to the Carolingian period, actual development of the states of Scandinavia dates from the tenth and eleventh centuries. Overseas expansion played one key role in northern political development. Another was the slow achievement of political unity by kings who had to overcome powerful local interests (see **Map 9.5**).

The sea, not the land, is the great fact of Scandinavian history. Norway has more than 1,000 miles of coastline, and no point in Denmark is more than 35 miles from the sea. Scandinavia did not offer opportunities for large, land-based kingdoms or empires, but the sea provided Scandinavians with a wide scope for activities.

Because the sea made exit from Scandinavia so easy, and because the whole region had absolutely no tradition of unified government, kings had a hard time establishing their power. Essentially, kings were war leaders with loyal bands of followers. Territorial states were thus built up as powerful leaders persuaded or forced more and more men to join them. Denmark's was the first of the northern monarchies to emerge in the early tenth century. Norway's monarchy arose a little later in the tenth century, but for much of the eleventh century, Norway was under Danish control. As the Danes fell more and more under German influence in the eleventh century, Norway managed to break free. Sweden's monarchy was the last to emerge in the northern world; it was not fully stable until the twelfth century, but by 1300, it had become the most powerful.

Christianity came rather late to Scandinavia, with the first missionaries entering the region in the ninth century and widespread conversion ensuing in the eleventh. Norway's King Olaf (r. 1016–1028), affectionately remembered as Saint Olaf, was the first northern king who actively promoted Christianization. Scandinavian kings viewed the church as a useful adjunct to their power. They cooperated in creating bishoprics on the assumption that members of the high clergy would be educated, talented allies in the process of building central governments. Ironically, the church was a stabilizing force in Scandinavia during the very years when the investiture controversy wreaked havoc in Germany.

The Slavic World

In eastern Europe, between the Elbe and Dnieper (NEE-per) Rivers, lived numerous peoples customarily called Slavs. Partly because of language differences and partly because of the areas in which these people settled, scholars divide them into western, southern, and eastern Slavs. These peoples were never conquered by the Romans, assimilated few influences from the classical world, and received Christianity later than western Europe. Still, as states began emerging in eastern Europe, they exhibited many of the same problems that older and more westerly states had encountered: shifting frontiers, clashes between ambitious rulers and powerful nobles, and outside military and cultural influences (see **Map 9.5**).

The first western Slavic state was Great Moravia, created in the 830s by capable dukes, while the Carolingian Empire was experiencing civil wars. Moravia's early promise was cut short in 906 by the Magyars. Also in the late ninth century, the Přemysl (PURR-em-ih-sill) dynasty forged a kingdom in Bohemia that lasted through the Middle Ages, although for long periods, it was under German domination.

The greatest of the western Slavic states was Poland. In the 960s and 970s, Duke Mieszko (mee-ESH-koe) (d. 992) unified a substantial territory and received Christianity from Rome. The first action created the Polish state, and the second anchored Poland firmly within the orbit of the Latin West. Mieszko's descendants, the Piast dynasty of kings, ruled until the kingdom was divided in 1138. For more than two centuries, Polish development was retarded as weak rulers contested for power with local magnates, who themselves were successfully subordinating both peasants and men of middling status.

The creation of a Hungarian state played a decisive role in dividing the western and southern Slavs. The Magyars were disruptive raiders from the 880s until their defeat by Otto I in 955. After that disaster, the Magyars concentrated on building a state within the Danube basin, the home base from which they had launched their raids. The Magyars blended with the local Slavs. King (later Saint) Stephen (r. 997–1038), who received Christianity from Rome, was the real founder of Hungary. Like Poland, Hungary was attached to the Latin West. Stephen's family, the Arpads, ruled in Hungary for centuries. They built ruling centers at Buda and Esztergom, created an impressive territorial organization, and promoted the growth of the church.

The southern Slavs built a band of states that extended across the Balkans. The first, reaching back to the seventh century, was Bulgaria. The Bulgars were a Turkic people who first led and then merged into the local Slavic population. The first Bulgarian state lasted until the early eleventh century, when the Byzantines, who had suffered many defeats at Bulgarian hands, destroyed it. By the late twelfth century, when Byzantium itself had weakened, a new Bulgarian state emerged, but its rulers never had the firm control that their predecessors had wielded. Under Khan Boris (r. 852–879), Bulgaria made the momentous decision to accept Orthodox Christianity from Constantinople instead of Roman Catholicism, despite the pope's best efforts. To the west of Bulgaria lay Serbia, a region dominated until the fourteenth century by Bulgaria and Byzantium. The region accepted Orthodox Christianity. To the west of Serbia lay Croatia. Croatia managed to preserve itself and evade the clutches of Hungary, Byzantium, and Venice. By 1107, however, Croatia was incorporated by Hungary. Owing to Italian and Hungarian influences, Croatia became Roman Catholic.

Virgin of Vladimir   The holiest icon of Russia, once the miraculous protector of the city of Vladimir and later of Moscow, this image was painted in Constantinople in 1131. Rus, and later Russian, icons tended to follow Byzantine traditions very closely.   (Scala/Art Resource, NY)

The Mongol Khan Writes to the Pope

Alarmed, like many of his contemporaries, by the Mongol onslaught, Pope Innocent IV (r. 1243–1254) sent missionaries to try to convert the Mongol khan Guyuk to Christianity. Large groups of Mongols had only recently converted to Christianity. Innocent not only did not get the answer he was hoping for, but he must have been shocked by Guyuk's haughty reply in 1246.

We, by the power of the eternal heaven, Khan of the great Ulus [compare the Islamic umma; see page 201], Our Command: This is a version sent to the great pope that he may know and understand in the Muslim [actually, Persian] tongue, what has been written. If he reaches you with his own report, You, who are the great pope, together with all the princes, come in person to serve us. You have also said that supplication and prayer have been offered by you, that I might find a good entry into baptism. This prayer of yours I have not understood. Other words which you have sent me: "I am surprised that you have seized all the lands of the Magyar [i.e., Hungarians] and the Christians. Tell us what their fault is." These words of yours I have also not understood. The eternal God has slain and annihilated these lands and peoples, because they have neither adhered to Chingis [Jenghiz] Khan, nor to the Khagan, both of whom have been sent to make known God's command, nor to the command of God. Like your words, they also were impudent, they were proud and they slew our messengers. How could anybody seize or kill by his own power contrary to the command of God?

Though you likewise say that I should become a trembling Nestorian [probably the only form of Christianity well known to the Mongols] Christian, worship God, and be an ascetic, how do you know whom God absolves, in truth to whom He shows mercy? How do you know that such words as you speak are with God's sanction? From the rising of the sun to its setting, all the lands have been made subject to me. Who could do this contrary to the command of God?

Now you should say with a sincere heart: "I will submit and serve you." You yourself, at the head of all the princes, come at once to serve and wait upon us! At that time I shall recognize your submission.

If you do not observe God's command, and if you ignore my command, I shall know you as my enemy. Likewise, I shall understand you. If you do otherwise, God knows what I know.

QUESTIONS

1. How does Guyuk try to convince Innocent that he and he alone has God's favor?

2. Do you think that Guyuk was, literally or figuratively, diplomatic?

3. Suppose that we had Innocent's response to Guyuk (we do not). What might he have said in reply?

Source: Christopher Dawson, *Mission to Asia*, pp. 85–86, copyright © 1980, published by Sheed & Ward.

The creation of the major eastern Slavic state is shrouded in mystery and legend. It seems that in 862, a Swedish Viking named Rurik and his followers, called Varangians, established or seized a trading camp at Novgorod. A few years later, Oleg (r. 879–912) took over Kiev and made it his base of operations. Thus was founded Kievan Rus, a state that, like Hungary and Bulgaria, began with an outside, elite leadership over a local Slavic majority.

Kiev was ruled by grand dukes who pursued four basic policies. They created a vast trading network that linked Germany, Scandinavia, Byzantium, and the caliphate. They shared power with regional nobles who built up several important towns of their own. They received Orthodox Christianity from Constantinople in 988. And, finally, they struggled to defend Kiev, indeed Rus territory as a whole, from wave after wave of invaders from the eastern steppes.

Kievan Rus was destroyed by the Mongols. These were a loose coalition of pastoral nomads from Mongolia (lands lying east of the Caspian Sea and north of China) and Turkic soldiers. The charismatic leader Jenghiz Khan (1154–1227) turned the Mongols into an invincible fighting force. He and his successors built an empire stretching from China to eastern Europe. In 1221, the Mongols began their attacks on Rus, and in 1240, Kiev fell. Jenghiz Khan's empire was divided into several khanates on his death, with Rus dominated by the Golden Horde, so called because of the splendid golden tent from which they ruled. Throughout the West, people were alarmed by the Mongol onslaught. (See the feature, "The Global Record: The Mongol Khan Writes to the Pope.")

SECTION SUMMARY

- The Reconquista motivated Spanish kings to military victories and political consolidation.

- Although Scandinavian Vikings were influential and disruptive, large-scale states began to emerge in Denmark, Norway, and Sweden.

- Slavic states emerged from resolute local action (Poland, Bohemia) or from a fusion of elite outsider and dependent local populations (Hungary, Bulgaria, Rus).

- Christianity expanded everywhere, sometimes Roman Catholic (Spain, Scandinavia, Poland, Hungary) and sometimes Orthodox (Bulgaria, Rus).

THE CRUSADES

What basic factors contributed to the rise, persistence, and eventual decline of the crusading movement?

In 1096, an army of Christian knights who called themselves pilgrims left Europe to liberate the Holy Land from the Muslim "infidel." This was the first of many **Crusades**, so called because the warriors were *crucesignati*, "signed by the cross." By the late eleventh century, Europe was a fortress that had marshaled its resources for an attack on the world around it. Europe's expanding population, economic dynamism, political consolidation, and buoyant optimism made possible not only the First Crusade, but also many more over two centuries.

Crusades Armed pilgrimages intended to recover the Holy Land from the "infidel."

The Background: East and West

With the accession in 867 of the Macedonian dynasty in the person of Basil I, the Byzantine Empire experienced a period of vigorous, successful rule that lasted until 1025. Although the Macedonians fostered striking cultural achievements, carried out significant administrative reforms, and established the kind of tight control of the church that had been so elusive in the iconoclastic era (see page 209), they were primarily great soldiers. Along the Balkan frontier, the Macedonian rulers kept both the Bulgarians and Kievan Rus at bay while also neutralizing many smaller Slavic principalities. In the West, the Macedonians maintained an effective diplomacy with Venice that permitted lucrative commercial opportunities in the Adriatic. In the East, the Macedonian rulers profited from the gradual dissolution of the Abbasid caliphate by expanding their frontier in Anatolia.

By contrast, throughout the ninth and tenth centuries, the ability of the caliphs in Baghdad to control their vast empire declined precipitously. Egypt and North Africa escaped Baghdad's control almost completely, and religious strife between Sunni and Shi'ite Muslims further destabilized the Islamic state.

After Basil II's death in 1025, Byzantium suffered a long period of short reigns and abrupt changes in policy. In the capital, factional squabbling swirled around the imperial court, and in the person of Patriarch Michael Cerularius (r. 1043–1058), the church sought to break out from two centuries of domination. When, in 1054, Cerularius and Pope Leo IX (r. 1049–1054) quarreled so bitterly over ecclesiastical customs that they excommunicated each other, a deep schism opened between the Catholic and Orthodox Churches that still exists.

It was in these divisive circumstances that the Seljuk Turks appeared on the eastern frontier of Anatolia. Bands of Turks, peoples from central Asia, had been serving the caliphs as mercenaries since the ninth century. With new leaders at their head, and with both the caliphate and the empire distracted, the Turks broke into Anatolia with a vengeance. In 1071 at Manzikert, a skirmish between Byzantine and Turkish soldiers turned into a rout in which Byzantium lost an army, an emperor, and the Macedonian reputation for military prowess.

Ever since the emergence of the Turkish threat in the early eleventh century, the Byzantines had been seeking mercenary help. The imperial defeat at Manzikert made their search more urgent and led to appeals to the West. In 1095, Emperor Alexius Comnenus (r. 1081–1118) pleaded with Pope Urban II (r. 1088–1099) for mercenary help against the Turks.

To most people in western Europe, the Turkish threat to Byzantium mattered little. What *did* alarm Westerners was Turkish attacks on pilgrims to Jerusalem. The popes saw in the plight of the Byzantines and of Western pilgrims some opportunities to manifest their leadership of the church. The papacy also wanted very much to heal the Roman-Orthodox rift. The popes, therefore, placed a high value on aiding the Byzantines.

A crusade was perfectly consonant with the ethos of the knights of western Europe, born and trained to fight. The age's literature glorified war and warriors. But churchmen had for some years been advancing an ideal of Christian knighthood that stressed fighting God's enemies. In the late tenth century, first in France and then in many other places, movements arose called the "Peace of God" or the "Truce of God." These movements sought to prevent war in certain seasons, such as around Christmas and Easter, and on Sundays. Peace movements also attempted to outlaw fighting near churches, protect noncombatants, and soften the treatment of enemies and captives. Together, the movements induced knights to fight non-Christians outside Europe.

Along with religious zeal, a quest for fame and fortune motivated many young men whose political prospects at home were limited.

The "Pilgrimage" to Jerusalem

Pope Urban II received Alexius's envoys in 1095 and then left Italy for France. He was actually a fugitive because Henry IV controlled Rome. In November at Clermont, Urban delivered a rousing speech to a vast Christian assembly. He ignored the Eastern emperor's appeal for aid and instead promised salvation to soldiers who would enlist in a great struggle to free the Holy Land. The crowd acclaimed his words with a shout of "God wills it!"

By 1096, four large armies, which eventually swelled to perhaps a hundred thousand men—mostly French knights, with a smattering of troops from other parts of Europe—assembled under the leadership of the pope's legate. The forces were to rendezvous at Constantinople, where they seem to have expected a cordial imperial welcome and all necessary assistance. Alexius, however, took a rather different view. A ragtag band of ordinary people preceding the Crusaders had torn through the Balkans like a plague of locusts. The crusading armies themselves sorely taxed the imperial authorities, who spent a lot of time and money arranging their passage from the frontier of Hungary to the gates of Constantinople. Finally, Alexius wanted mercenaries to fend off Turks in Anatolia, not armed pilgrims intent on liberating Palestine (see **Map 9.7**).

After receiving nominal promises of loyalty and the return or donation of any lands captured, Alexius moved the Crusaders into Anatolia. Almost immediately, the Latin army defeated a Turkish force, thus earning a valuable, though short-lived, reputation for invincibility. The troops then entered Syria and laid siege to Antioch, which did not fall until 1098. At this point, rivalries among the Crusaders came into the open. One force went to the frontier of Armenia and carved out a principality.

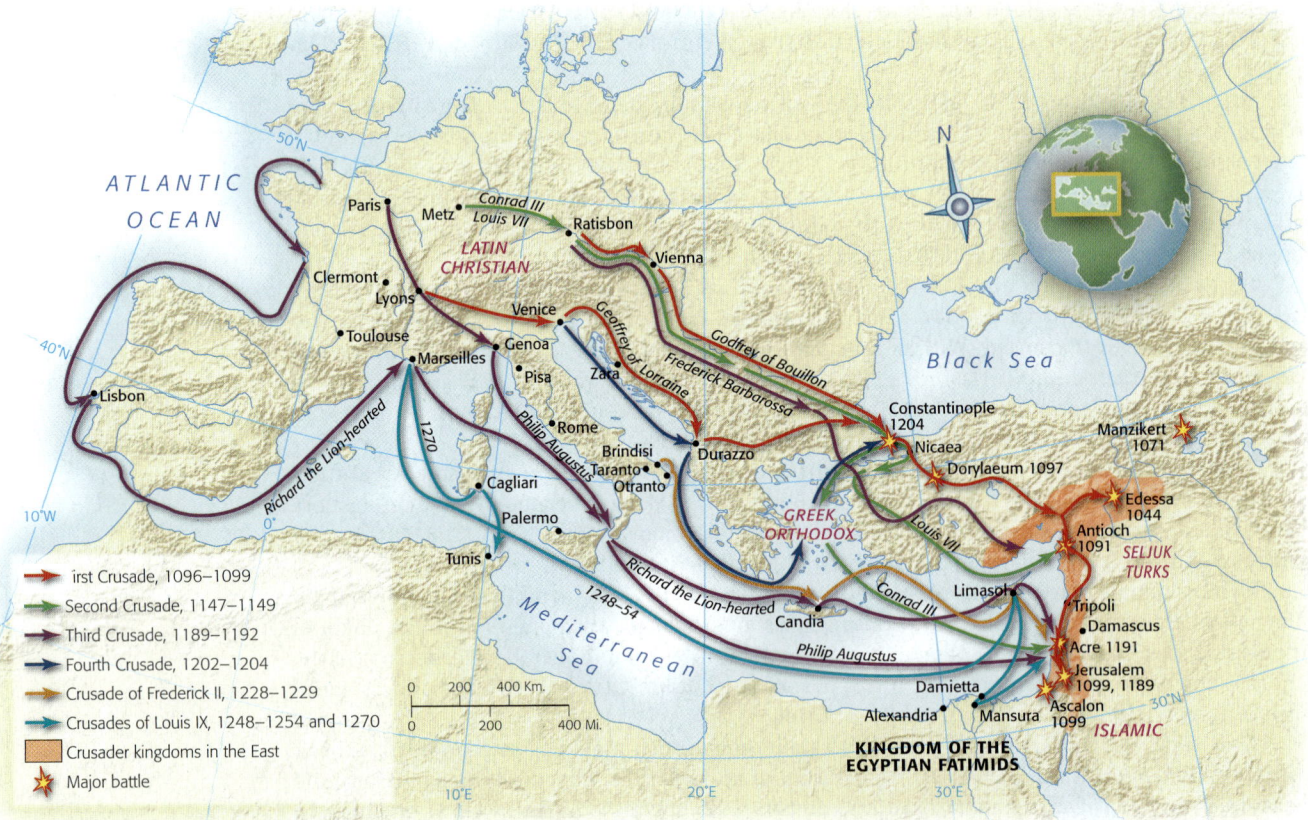

🌐 Map 9.7—The Crusades

The long-standing Western interest in the Holy Land is vividly illustrated by the Crusades. Note the numerous routes taken, lands traversed, destinations attained, and points of cultural encounter.

One of the Normans leaders kept Antioch for himself. The main army pressed on to Jerusalem and, after a short but fierce siege, conquered it in July 1099. A Muslim historian describes the scene:

> In the Masjid [Mosque] al-Aqsa the Franks slaughtered more than 70,000 people, among them a large number of Imams and Muslim scholars, devout and ascetic men who had left their homelands to live lives of pious seclusion in the Holy Place. The Franks stripped the Dome of the Rock [the Mosque of Umar, near the al-Aqsa mosque, pictured on page 205] of more than forty silver candelabra, each of them weighing 3,600 drams [almost 40 pounds], and a great silver lamp weighing forty-four Syrian pounds, as well as a hundred and fifty smaller candelabra and more than twenty gold ones, and a great deal more booty.[1]

Godfrey of Bouillon, leader of the troops that had "liberated" Jerusalem, was named "Advocate of the Holy Sepulcher" and became ruler of the Christians in the East. He lived only a short time, however, and was replaced by his brother, Baldwin, as king of Jerusalem in 1100.

Judged on its own terms, the First Crusade was a success. The Holy Land was retaken from the infidel, and the pilgrim routes were passable once more. Entirely uncertain, however, were the prospects of the crusader states, the future course of Western relations with Byzantium, and the reaction of the Islamic world once it recovered from its initial shock.

The Later Crusades

Crusading was intended to protect the Holy Land and keep open the pilgrim routes to Jerusalem. The creation of the small crusader states in the hostile environment of Syria and Palestine made continued crusading almost inevitable. In 1144, the tiny crusader state at Edessa on the Armenian frontier fell to a Muslim army. Although the news saddened Europeans, it took immense efforts by the papacy and other religious leaders to launch another crusade. Finally, Conrad III of Germany and Louis VII of France agreed to lead it, but the Second Crusade accomplished little. Its one achievement was an accident. In 1147, an army of English, French, and Flemish soldiers who were proceeding to the Holy Land by sea put in on the Iberian coast and captured Lisbon. This opened a new front in the Reconquista and laid the foundations for the later kingdom of Portugal (see **MAP 9.7**).

The papacy called for the Third Crusade when Saladin (sah-lah-DEEN) (1138–1193), a powerful local leader typical of the disintegrating Abbasid caliphate, recaptured Jerusalem in 1187. It is a measure of the force of the crusading ideal that the greatest crowned heads of the day—Frederick Barbarossa, Philip II, and Richard the Lionhearted—answered the call. Only Frederick did so enthusiastically, but he died en route in 1190, while Philip returned home in 1191, and Richard in 1192. Because neither Richard nor Philip would stay in Palestine to fight Saladin, this crusade merely won access to Jerusalem for pilgrims.

Disappointed with the results of the Third Crusade, Innocent III began calling for another crusade immediately on his election in 1198. Popular preachers summoned an army, once again largely French, and the pope and the Fourth Crusade's military leaders engaged the Venetians to construct a fleet of war and transport ships. In less than eighteen months, they produced 50 galleys and 450 transports, a tribute to the awesome capabilities of the Venetian shipyards.

Ships, however, were expensive, and the Venetians drove hard bargains. When too few Crusaders and too little money appeared, the Venetians suggested that the Crusaders could discharge some of their debt by recapturing from the Hungarians the formerly Venetian port of Zara on the Dalmatian coast. This idea outraged the pope, but he could do little about it. Then into the camp of the Crusaders came a pretender to the Byzantine throne, who promised that if the Crusaders would help him to claim his patrimony, he would contribute to the cost of the Crusade. The Venetians urged the indebted Crusaders to accept this offer, and, to the horror of Innocent III, the Fourth Crusade turned to Constantinople.

Once in Constantinople, the Crusaders learned that their new ally had few friends in the Byzantine capital, but the venture hardly collapsed. The Venetians saw an opportunity to expand business opportunities in the East, and the soldiers welcomed a chance to plunder the Mediterranean's greatest city and to avenge what they regarded as a century of Byzantine perfidy. Thus, the Fourth Crusade captured not Jerusalem but Constantinople. Until 1261, the Eastern and Western churches were reunited under papal leadership, and substantial tracts of the Balkans fell to Western knights under a "Latin emperor" of Constantinople.

In later decades, popes began to take a more active role in planning crusades. No pope wanted to lose control of a crusade as Innocent had done, and all popes saw that the liberation of Jerusalem required a solid base of operations in the eastern Mediterranean. Egypt was the objective of the

Fifth (1218–1221) and Sixth (1248–1250) Crusades. Despite a few victories, the Crusaders could not win a secure base. No further crusades to the East were organized in the thirteenth century. In 1291, Acre, the last Crusader stronghold, fell, and the original crusading era ended.

The Aftermath of the Crusades

Why did the Crusades end? There are several reasons. By the late thirteenth century, more violence was being directed inward against heretics and political foes of the papacy than outward against the alleged enemies of Christendom itself. As rulers became more sophisticated and controlled more territory, they had less interest in the intangible benefits of crusading, such as prestige. Whereas the cities of Italy once needed to open up Mediterranean ports, now they wished to secure comparative advantage over one another. The Christian ideals of poverty, charity, and service were incompatible with warfare. Literary images provide another insight into the decline of the Crusades. After 1300, we are less likely to read about a Christian knight fighting honorably for God and king than about a gentleman of manners seeking the favor of a fair lady.

Crusading was brutal. Soldiers and their clerical companions spent years away from their homes and families, endured scorching Mediterranean heat, and suffered shortages of food and basic supplies. The vulnerable crusader states never received enough settlers to be viable communities, and consequently, intermarriage with locals was common and gradually produced a hybrid culture that was neither European nor Middle Eastern. Warfare was constant on all sides. When Crusaders conquered a town, they executed many locals. When Muslims recaptured a town, they did the same.

An examination of the crusading movement as a whole reveals more losses than gains. The Crusades exported many violent men from Europe, but it is not clear that Europe became a less violent place. As might be expected, the Crusades devastated relations between Christian Europe and the Muslim world. The Fourth Crusade mortally wounded Byzantium and worsened the already tense standoff between the Catholic and Orthodox Churches. Crusading zeal was directed deliberately against heretics and coincidentally against Jews. The Jewish populations of several towns were massacred on the eve of the First and Second Crusades. The Crusades did not create anti-Semitism, but they aggravated it. Some women, particularly in France, from which the majority of all Crusaders came, may have enjoyed momentary benefits in terms of control of land, wealth, and people while their husbands were away. But the long-term trend in feudal society was disadvantageous to women, and the Crusades did not change that. Finally, the Crusades may have done as much to disrupt Mediterranean trade as to promote it. Italian urban rivalries took the place of Latin-Muslim-Byzantine ones. That a single new product, the apricot, entered Europe in the crusading era seems small reward for such a huge effort.

SECTION SUMMARY

- Weakness and disunity in the Byzantine Empire and the caliphate were important background factors in the Crusades.

- Heightened religious zeal in western Europe along with growing papal leadership were also significant background factors.

- Mixed motives stood behind the initial Crusades: The Byzantines wanted mercenaries to fight in Anatolia, the popes wanted to extend their authority and free the Holy Land, urban Italians sought commercial opportunities, and western knights sought both worldly glory and eternal reward.

- The momentum of the early crusading movement could not be sustained over a long time, and the Holy Land was not definitively liberated

CHAPTER SUMMARY

Between 900 and 1300, Western civilization expanded as never before in human, material, geographical, and political terms. Europe's population grew dramatically until the late 1200s, owing to better diets and more plentiful foods. Technological gains came with wider use of horses, improved plows, and more productive farming techniques. Many regions began to specialize in the products that they grew or made, and this local specialization prompted larger-scale trade. Towns came to play a larger role in almost all aspects of economic and social life. Economic growth widened the gap between rich and poor and induced theologians to write about the just price and usury.

German political development was impeded by short-lived dynasties, territorial complexity, and battles with the papacy. From being Europe's greatest state in the tenth century, Germany declined into weakness in the thirteenth. Italy experienced the communal movement in the north, the consolidation of the Papal States and Papal Monarchy in the center, and the continued fragmentation of the south, where foreigners ruled. Differences among these three zones are characteristic of Italian history. France had a prestigious and long-lived royal dynasty, patient territorial expansion, and a slowly, steadily centralizing government. By 1300, France was the most powerful state in Europe.

England's kings survived several changes of dynasty (compare Germany) without having to make fundamental changes in English society or government. English kings built on Anglo-Saxon precedents to secure revenues, extend the work of the royal courts, and limit the power of the barons.

English kings brought constant pressure to bear on the Celtic realms that surrounded England, in the process, retarding political development in these regions and involving themselves in dangerous and costly ventures. By 1300, England was a unified and well-governed kingdom.

The growth of new states is an impressive achievement of the High Middle Ages. The Reconquista motivated Spanish kings to military victories and political consolidation. Although Scandinavian Vikings were influential and disruptive, large-scale states began to emerge in Denmark, Norway, and Sweden. Slavic states emerged from resolute local action (Poland, Bohemia) or from a fusion of elite outsider and dependent local populations (Hungary, Bulgaria, Rus). Christianity expanded everywhere, sometimes Roman Catholic (Spain, Scandinavia, Poland, Hungary) and sometimes Orthodox (Bulgaria, Rus). The "West" was a lot bigger in 1300 than it had been in 900.

The Crusades represent a key sign of western Europe's expansion. Weakness and disunity in the Byzantine Empire and the caliphate were important background factors in the Crusades. Heightened religious zeal in western Europe along with growing papal leadership were also significant background factors. Mixed motives stood behind the initial Crusades: The Byzantines wanted mercenaries to fight in Anatolia, the popes wanted to extend their authority and free the Holy Land, urban Italians sought commercial opportunities, and western knights sought both worldly glory and eternal reward. The momentum of the early crusading movement could not be sustained over a long time, and the Holy Land was not definitively liberated.

FOCUS QUESTIONS

- In how many different realms of life do you see signs of growth and innovation, of expansion?

- What did Germany, Italy, and France owe to the Carolingian past? How alike and different were these areas by 1300?

- What were the chief dynamics in the development of medieval Britain?

- How did new states emerge in Spain, Scandinavia, and the Slavic world, and how do those states compare with their western neighbors?

- What basic factors contributed to the rise, persistence, and eventual decline of the crusading movement?

KEY TERMS

guilds (p. 232)

lay investiture (p. 236)

communes (p. 237)

Papal Monarchy (p. 239)

feudal revolution (p. 241)

Magna Carta (p. 247)

parliaments (p. 247)

Reconquista (p. 249)

Crusades (p. 253)

 This icon will direct you to additional materials on the website: www.cengage.com/history/noble/westciv6e.

NOTES

1. Slightly adapted from the *Gesta Francorum*, trans. August C. Krey, in *The First Crusade* (Princeton, N.J.: Princeton University Press, 1921), p. 257.

See our interactive eBook for map and primary source activities.

CHAPTER OUTLINE

The Confirmation of the Rule of Saint Francis, 1223
Pope Honorius III confirms the revised version of Francis's Rule. (Scala/Art Resource, NY)

Medieval Civilization at Its Height, 900–1300

This painting by Giotto di Bondone depicts Pope Honorius III confirming the Rule of Saint Francis in 1223. Saint Francis kneels humbly before the pope, along with several of his Franciscan followers. Note the simplicity of their dress, especially as compared with the regal clothing worn by the pope and his bishops. The plain brown robes are recognized as the traditional clothing of Franciscans, who lived according to the scriptural ideals of poverty, preaching, and service. Unlike monastic orders who withdrew from the world, the Franciscans pledged themselves to working among Europe's outcasts—the poor, the sick, and the old.

The Franciscans, and similar orders, such as the Dominicans, led one of the most powerful religious movements of the Middle Ages. Yet, they were just one part of the religious climate of the period. Several social and religious movements, including heretical movements and religious communities of women, also emerged during the twelfth and thirteen centuries.

We know about Saint Francis and others from many Latin documents and from Italian ones. The culture of the High Middle Ages saw Latin cede some space to the *vernacular* languages. Religious themes were still foremost in writings of all kinds, but adventures, romances, and other works dedicated to secular themes were gaining in prominence. Intellectual life was broadened by encounters with long-lost Greek texts and with the writings of Jewish and Muslim scholars. Universities owed much to earlier cathedral and monastic schools but were new institutions—one of medieval Europe's greatest, and most durable, inventions.

The previous chapter concentrated on the economic foundations of society and on the ways in which people organized themselves politically. This chapter begins by introducing the increasingly complex social structures within which people lived and then turns to a study of what those people thought, said, and built.

FOCUS QUESTIONS

- Into what principal social groups were the people of high medieval Europe organized?
- Why did some spiritual movements result in heresy, while others ended in new religious orders?
- What signs do you find of an expanding intellectual climate in high medieval Europe?
- What were the hallmarks of vernacular culture?

This icon will direct you to additional materials on the website: www .cengage.com/history/ noble/westciv6e.

See our interactive eBook for map and primary source activities.

THE TRADITIONAL ORDERS OF SOCIETY

Into what principal social groups were the people of high medieval Europe organized?

Alfred the Great (r. 871–899) of England and two French bishops said that a kingdom needed "men of prayer, men of war, and men of work." This threefold division reveals the way the elite looked at the world. It provided neat places for the clergy, warrior-aristocrats, and peasants. The clergy and the nobility agreed that they were superior to the "workers," but fierce controversies raged over whether ultimate leadership in society belonged to the "prayers" or the "fighters."

By the time this three-part view of society was fully established in the West, it had begun to fit social realities less well. It excluded townspeople, who were becoming ever more important. Town residents worked for a living, of course, but only farmers were considered "workers." Alfred and the bishops did not speak about women, and they consciously excluded minorities, chiefly Jews.

Those Who Pray: The Clergy

As the church promoted its own vision of the three-part ordering of society, it assigned primacy to the prayers—its own leaders. Within the clergy, however, sharp disagreements arose over whether the leading prayers were the monks in the monasteries or the bishops in their cathedrals. Whereas in the Carolingian world the clergy served occasionally as an avenue of upward social mobility for talented outsiders, in the High Middle Ages, church offices were usually reserved for the younger sons of the nobility.

Cluny A monastery in France that became a model for religious reform.

In the aftermath of the Carolingian collapse, a great spiritual reform swept Europe. It began in 910 when Duke William of Aquitaine founded the monastery of **Cluny** (CLUE-nee) in Burgundy on land that he donated (see **Map 9.4** on page 290). At a time when powerful local families dominated almost all monasteries, Cluny was a rarity because it was free of all lay and episcopal control and because it was under the direct authority of the pope. Cluny's abbots were among the greatest European statesmen of their day and became influential advisers to popes, French kings, German emperors, and aristocratic families.

Cluny placed great emphasis on liturgical prayer. The monks spent long hours in solemn devotions and did little manual work. Because Cluniac prayer was thought to be especially effective, nobles all over Europe donated land to Cluny and placed local monasteries under Cluniac control. Many independent monasteries also appealed to Cluny for spiritual reform. By the twelfth century hundreds of monasteries had joined in a Cluniac order. Individual houses were under the authority of the abbot of Cluny, and their priors had to attend an annual assembly. Although the majority of houses reformed by Cluny were male, many convents of nuns also adopted Cluniac practices.

Cluny promoted two powerful ideas. One was that the role of the church was to pray for the world, not to be implicated deeply in it. The other was that freedom from lay control was essential if churches were to concentrate on their spiritual tasks.

The same spiritual forces that motivated the Cluniacs inspired Bishop Adalbero of Metz in 933 to promote the restoration of Benedictine practices in the dilapidated Lorraine monastery of Gorze (GORTZ-eh). Customs at Gorze resembled those at Cluny, and they spread widely in Lorraine, Germany, and England. The Gorze reform was well received by kings and nobles; its aim was not so much to withdraw from the world as to improve it. Monks from the Gorze and Cluniac traditions bitterly condemned clerical immorality and inappropriate lay interference in the church. They preached against clerical marriage and simony, the buying and selling of church offices.

Reformers in the more ascetic eremitic tradition (see pages 178–179) desired more profound changes. They criticized the monastery at Cluny, saying that it had become too opulent and successful, and the monastery at Gorze because it seemed too immersed in worldly affairs. A desire to build new communities according to their vision of the apostolic church, featuring a life of poverty, self-denial, and seclusion, captivated the ascetics. Thus, the eleventh and early twelfth centuries saw a proliferation of both male and female experiments in eremitic monasticism. Other Europeans believed that the apostolic calling demanded not only an austere regimen of personal renunciation, but also an active life of Christian ministry. Cathedral clergy, called canons, adapted the Rule of Saint Augustine so that they could live a communal life and also carry out priestly duties.

The greatest critics of the Cluniac tradition, and the real monastic elite of the early twelfth century, were the Cistercians. In 1098, Abbot Robert left his Burgundian monastery of Molesme (MOE-lem) because he believed it had abandoned the strict teachings of Saint Benedict. He founded a new monastery at Cîteaux (SEE-toe) in Burgundy. This house was to follow the Benedictine Rule literally and to refuse all secular entanglements: lands, rents, and servile dependents. So rigorous and poor was the community that it struggled until a charismatic young Burgundian nobleman named Bernard (1090–1153) joined in 1112. Through his writing, preaching, and personal example, Bernard dominated the religious life of Europe in his lifetime. By the end of the twelfth century, there were about five hundred Cistercian (from the Latin for *Cîteaux*) monasteries in Europe. Initially, the Cistercians wished to be an order of adult men. They successfully avoided admitting young boys, but by 1200, they had authorized about one hundred convents of Cistercian nuns.

And it was not just the Cistercians and the traditional Benedictines who attracted women. The twelfth century saw many new communities of women from England to eastern Europe. The age's growing prosperity and population contributed both potential nuns and healthy endowments, but the key factor was that women were responding to the spiritual forces of the age in the same way men were.

With the monastic clergy gaining so much in prestige and visibility, the episcopal clergy countered with its own view of society. Surely, the bishops agreed, spiritual, moral, and intellectual improvement were desirable. Likewise, it was time to end the grossest examples of lay interference in the church. But precisely because so many bishops came from great families and were so well connected, they were less inclined to be rigid about the line of demarcation between lay and clerical responsibilities. In Germany, for example, the king's chapel recruited young noblemen to train them as clerics and to inculcate in them the policies and ethos of the court. Many of these chaplains were appointed to bishoprics and then advanced the king's interests in their new ecclesiastical areas of authority. They were often men of spiritual depth and resented what they regarded as monastic carping about their worldliness.

It was the special responsibility of the clergy to look after the moral order of society. In the turbulent world of gentlemen warriors, the church had its own ideas about what a perfect "fighter" should do. The English bishop and scholar John of Salisbury (d. 1180), reflecting on knighthood in the twelfth century, concluded that it existed "to protect the church, to attack infidelity, to reverence the priesthood, to protect the poor, to keep the peace, to shed one's blood and, if necessary, to lay down one's life for one's brethren."

Turning large numbers of violent young men into servants of the church was a tall order for the clergy, and they had only limited success. One strategy that worked was the creation of military orders. The Palestine-based Knights of St. John, or Hospitallers, and Knights of the Temple, or Templars, are the major examples. The Hospitallers started near Jerusalem as a foundation under Benedictine auspices dedicated to charitable works and care of the sick. They evolved into a monastic order using a version of the Rule of Saint Benedict and devoted themselves to the defense of pilgrims to the Holy Land. The Templars were men living under religious rule and sworn to protect the small states created by the Crusaders (see pages 255–256). These military orders measured up very well to the clergy's idea of what a perfect knight should be.

The clergy could also regulate disputes in society. For example, when a community was divided by a difficult conflict that demanded resolution, it might turn to the *ordeal*—a judicial procedure that sought divine judgment by subjecting the accused to a physically painful or dangerous test. An accused person might walk a certain distance carrying hot iron or plunge a hand into a boiling cauldron to pluck out a pebble. The resulting wounds would be bandaged for a set time and then examined. If they were healing, the person was considered innocent; if they were festering, the person was considered guilty. The clergy officiated at ordeals until the papacy forbade their participation in 1215.

CHRONOLOGY

ca. 900	*Beowulf*
910	Foundation of Cluny
940–1003	Gerbert of Aurillac
960–1028	Fulbert of Chartres
d. 970	Roswitha of Gandersheim
1000–1088	Berengar of Tours
ca. 1033–1109	Anselm of Canterbury
ca. 1050–1150	Maturation of the Romanesque
1079–1142	Peter Abelard
1090–1153	Bernard of Clairvaux
1098	Foundation of Cîteaux
1098–1179	Hildegard of Bingen
ca. 1100	*Song of Roland*
1135–1183	Chrétien de Troyes
1170–1221	Dominic de Guzman
ca. 1177–1213	Mary of Oignies
1181–1226	Francis of Assisi
1184	Waldensians declared heretics
1194–1253	Clare of Assisi
1208	Albigensian Crusade launched
1210–1280	Mechtild of Magdeburg
1225–1274	Thomas Aquinas
1265–1321	Dante Alighieri

Those Who Fight: The Nobility

In recent years, scholars have spilled a sea of ink trying to define the medieval nobility. The matter is important because even though the nobility constituted only a small minority of the total population, nobles were the ruling class. To appreciate their crucial role, we need to consider the nobles' lifestyle and ethos.

Reconstruction of Cluny A view of the monastic complex at Cluny in the early twelfth century. Note the basilica (the largest church in Europe until the sixteenth century), the cloister (to the left, actually south, of the basilica, with its dormitory in the foreground and refectory opposite the basilica), and the workshops. (Based on a drawing from *Cluny des Églises et la Maison du Chef d'Ordre*, by R. J. Conant. Courtesy, Medieval Academy of America)

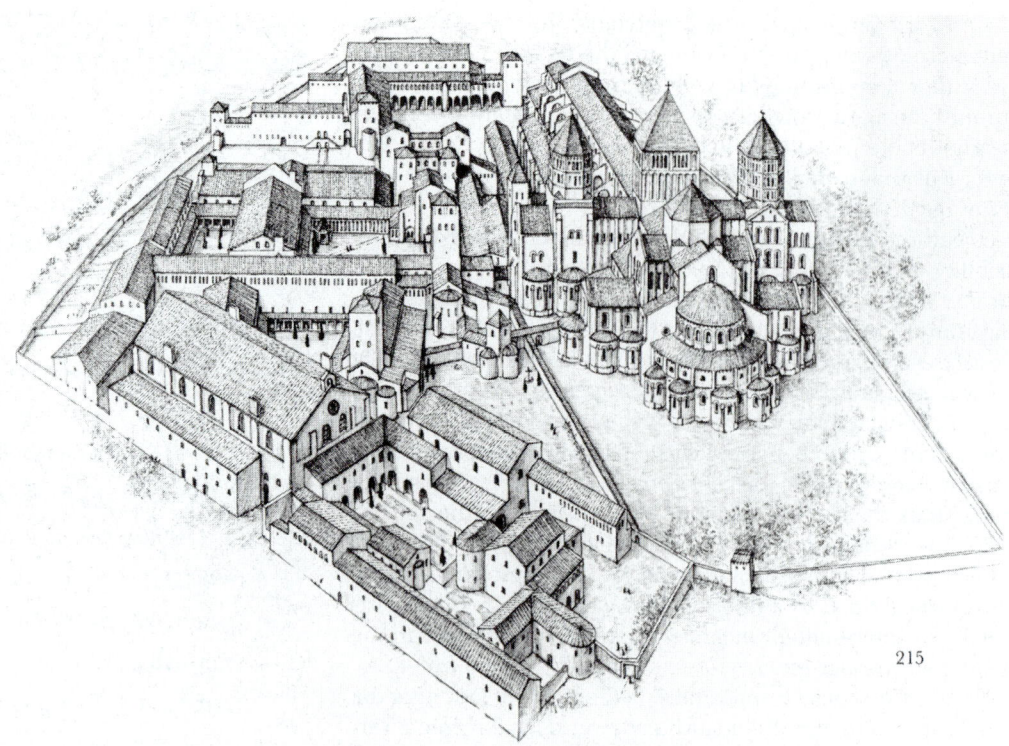

215

In English, the word *noble* can be either an adjective or a noun. More commonly, it is an adjective, as in a "noble sentiment" or a "noble deed." Before the twelfth century, the Latin *nobilis* was almost exclusively an adjective. The word pertained to certain desirable personal qualities. Then, gradually, the word became a noun and pertained to a certain kind of person.

In the ideal case, a noble was a well-born, cultivated, office-holding soldier. In the earlier Middle Ages, many men held offices without necessarily being considered noble. Virtually all free men were expected to be soldiers, but few of them ranked as nobles. It was in the century or so following the feudal revolution (see page 240–241) that these distinct elements were fused into a single social order.

In a world in which lords were everywhere extending their power, military prowess became more valuable. At the same time, the need for horses and for more expensive arms and armor made it almost impossible for ordinary freemen to be soldiers. Likewise, ambitious lords who wished to expand their influence were looking for ways to use their resources to gain followers. These trends came together as lords granted to their followers either military gear or lands, which would generate the income necessary to obtain arms and horses. We call those followers "vassals" and the lands they obtained "fiefs." Vassalage became a widespread institution all over Europe, and fief-holding became a normal accompaniment to vassalage.

Vassals and fiefs bring to mind the concept of *feudalism* or the term *feudal system*. As we saw in Chapter 9, England, France, and, to a lesser degree, Germany and Italy were in some respects feudal realms. That is, lords, right up to the king, secured some personal and political services from vassals in return for material rewards, often landed estates called fiefs. Today, historians are reluctant to use the term *feudal system* because across Europe, and through many centuries, there was nothing systematic about how services were obtained or discharged.

Contemporary sources often call vassals "knights." Knights rarely boasted high birth or venerable ancestry, nor were they initially officeholders appointed by kings or emperors. Moreover, they were not wealthy and did not enjoy the lavish lifestyle that one might expect from nobles. Across the eleventh and twelfth centuries, knights saw their status change, in part because they mimicked the behavior of the nobles, who themselves accepted the necessity of military ability.

All over Europe, especially where royal power was ineffective, both knights and nobles secured tighter control of peasant labor. This process provided knights and nobles with the money to build castles and to acquire fine possessions. As governments expanded their competence, these nobles and knights often held high offices, or if they did not, they pressured kings to concede such offices to them. Lords also tended to gather their lands into coherent blocks and to name themselves after the castles they built on their lands. Families also began to produce genealogies tracing their ancestry to relatives in the distant past and to kings if at all possible. At the same time, families began to practice primogeniture—that is, reserving their lands, castles, and titles to the *primus genitus*, or "firstborn" son.

This allotment of the choicest inheritances to a shrinking group turned loose a large number of younger sons. Many of them entered the clergy, a tendency that helps to explain the rising aristocratic character of the church. This was not a punishment. Sons were not "dumped" on the church. Clerical careers were prestigious and relatively comfortable. But more numerous than clerics were the young men who were without an estate and who lacked the means to secure a bride and to form a family of their own. These men traipsed about Europe looking for fame and fortune, or failing that, a lord to serve. Many of these "young" men were 30 or 40 years old. They were called young because they had not yet established themselves.

By 1200, the nobility was a group identified by the profession of arms, the holding of office, a consciousness of family traditions, and an elevated lifestyle. A specific ethos—chivalry—belonged to the nobility. Today, chivalry is often thought of as either an elaborate code of conduct regulating relations between the sexes or the value system behind the literary image of dashing knights in shining armor saving damsels in distress from fire-breathing dragons. Actually, its very name derives from *cheval*, French for "horse," the classic conveyance of a knight. Chivalry began as the code of conduct for mounted warriors.

Chivalry highly esteemed certain masculine, militant qualities. Military prowess was the greatest of chivalric virtues. A knight who was not a great warrior was useless. Literature of the time exalts the knight who slays fearsome beasts or the hero who single-handedly overwhelms impossible numbers of the enemy. Openhanded generosity was another key virtue. The truly noble person engaged in sumptuous display to manifest his power, to show concern for his dependents, and to enlarge his entourage. Medieval literature is full of rich banquets and stunning presents. Knights were obsessed with their honor, their reputations. They sought glory, the better to win a lord or a bride or, if a lord already, to attract followers. Chivalry also emphasized loyalty, the glue that held feudal society together.

What role was left to noblewomen in a world of chivalry and lordship? By the late eleventh century, three developments adversely affected the position of aristocratic women. First, the elaboration of the chivalric ethos defined most key social and political roles as military and "manly" and thereby excluded women. By the middle of the twelfth century, it was rare for a woman to hold a castle and unheard of for one to ride to arms. Second, the consolidation of lineages by aristocratic families accompanied a moral campaign by the church to promote monogamous, unbreakable marriages. This situation subordinated women's freedom in the marriage market to the dynastic and patrimonial demands of great families. Third, the spread of lordship, with its intricate network of personal and proprietary relationships based on military service, tended to deprive women of independent rights over land.

But every rule has its exceptions. As noble families married off fewer of their daughters to noblemen, "extra" daughters accounted in part for the dramatic increase in the number and size of convents. Convents of aristocratic nuns were places where women could be highly educated and almost entirely in control of their own affairs. Matilda, daughter of the German empress Adelaide, was abbess of Quedlinburg, mistress of vast estates in northern Germany, and a dominant figure in German politics. But knights looking for brides would often marry the younger daughters of noblemen, because if they could establish a household, any children born of that marriage could lay claim to the noble lineage of their maternal grandfathers.

Less predictably, Gaita, wife of a Norman prince in Italy, fought in helmet and armor alongside her husband, as did Duchess Agnes of Burgundy. And let us reflect on the career of Adela of Blois (ca. 1067–1137). She was the daughter of William the Conqueror, the wife of a powerful French count, and the mother of King Stephen I of England. In addition to regularly accompanying her husband as he administered his county, Adela founded monasteries, promoted religious reform, hosted Pope Paschal II, helped to reconcile her brother Henry I with the archbishop of Canterbury (thus averting an English investiture controversy), issued formal legal judgments, held fairs, and skillfully negotiated the aristocratic politics of western France after her husband's death. Adela is unusual because we know so much about her. In other words, noblewomen in high medieval society may often have led interesting, active lives, but there are few surviving records to document this.

Those Who Work: The Peasants

The peasants were the "workers" in the three-part model. An extremely diverse segment of society, "peasants" ranged from slaves to free persons of some means. Except in frontier zones, where victims were available and religious scruples diminished, slaves declined dramatically in numbers during the tenth and eleventh centuries (as illustrated by the shift in meaning of the classical Latin *servus* from "slave" to "serf"). Serfs, persons bound to the soil, constituted the majority of the peasants, although their legal and social statuses differed considerably from place to place. In the twelfth century, serfdom was disappearing in France, even as its terms were hardening in central and eastern Europe. Serfdom was a mixture of economic, legal, and personal statuses. The serf could be flogged in public, could be set upon by dogs, was excluded from many judicial proceedings, required approval to contract a marriage, and was denied the right to bear arms.

The tenth and eleventh centuries were decisive in the reshaping of rural society. As lordships of all kinds and sizes formed in the countryside, they drew communities of people. Castles were critical. Powerful men generally sited their castles in close proximity to wood, water, and iron. (See the feature, "The Visual Record: The Medieval Castle" on pages 242–243 in Chapter 9.) People from a fairly wide area settled in the vicinity of the castle. Many, originally free, commended themselves to the local lord by handing over their properties and receiving them back in return for rents or personal services. Other people fell into dependent status through military or economic misfortune. What eventually emerged was the manor, an institution best described as a powerful lord controlling the lives of an often large number of dependents. He required payments and services from them and regulated their ordinary disputes. His control was simultaneously public and private.

A minor castellan, or lord of a castle, might control only a small manor and would probably be the vassal of a great lord. A powerful landed lord, on the other hand, would generally control many manors and would often give some of them to retainers as fiefs. In other words, the reorganization of the countryside affected the nobility and the peasantry and created parallel sets of vertical bonds of association: feudal lords and vassals entered into political bonds; lords and peasants entered into economic bonds.

The structure of individual manors, and the dues owed by peasants, varied tremendously across Europe. Certain trends were fairly consistent, however. As the economy expanded, as trade brought more and different products into Europe, and as a more consciously aristocratic lifestyle spread, the nobility began to want disposable cash. Thus, in many places corvées (KOR-vay) (labor services) were commuted into cash payments. Peasants were required to pay rent from their own holdings instead of working on the lord's lands. But lords still needed provisions, so they sometimes split peasant payments into cash and kind. The lord could also extract money from his peasants by requiring them to use his mill and oven and then charging them gristing and baking fees.

The trend everywhere, however, was for labor services to diminish. In one region in northern France, twelfth-century peasants owed only three corvées of two days each per year for harvesting and haymaking. Elsewhere, peasants might still be required to haul crops to market or to keep roads, bridges, and buildings in repair. On many estates where the menfolk had been largely freed from corvées, the women might still have to work in the lord's house washing laundry, sewing, plucking fowl, cooking, minding dogs, and tending to other household chores.

In the expanding economy of the eleventh and twelfth centuries, the peasants grew more prosperous, and their lords constantly sought new ways to extract the fruits of that prosperity. Peasants thus began to band together to demand that "customs" be observed. These customs were more or less formal agreements spelling out the terms under which work and fees would be arranged. In general, life improved for the peasants in terms of both legal status and living conditions.

The European village was a key product of the tenth and eleventh centuries. People who originally gathered together around a castle for security and livelihood began to form a durable human community. Their church and graveyard helped to reinforce the community by tying together the living and the dead and by giving the village a sense of memory and continuity. Peasants generally worked only 250 to 270 days per year, so they had a good deal of time for festivals and celebrations. Births, baptisms, betrothals, and deaths provided opportunities for the community to come together and affirm its mutual ties. Market days and sessions of the lord's court also assembled the village. Villagers needed to cooperate in many of the operations of daily life. They shared tools, plow teams, and wagons. They performed their corvées together. The peasants experienced much less social differentiation than the nobility, and so, less tension.

The status of women in peasant society tended to be, in legal theory and in daily reality, the same as that of men at a time when the status of aristocratic women was fragile. Marriage contracts from northern Italy show that brides often entered marriages with a complement of valuable tools. This suggests that peasant women retained some control over their own personal property and also reminds us that the huge gains in rural productivity were almost certainly attributable in part to the work and ingenuity of women.

Those Left Out: Townspeople and Jews

The three-part model excluded two important groups of people. The first neglected group consisted of the increasingly numerous citizens of Europe's growing towns. Obviously, people in towns worked, but the prejudices of the aristocracy were rural, so the only "workers" deemed necessary to the smooth functioning of the social order were farmers. In the second group were Europe's principal religious minority, the Jews. Jews could be found almost everywhere, although they constituted only about 1 percent of the population as a whole and, outside of Rome and parts of Spain, formed no single community numbering more than 1,500 to 2,000.

The central factor in the growth of towns was the rise in the productivity and profitability of medieval agriculture. For the first time in history, a regular and substantial farm surplus could support an urban population that did not produce its own food. Increased local exchange, coupled with the relentless growth of a money economy, meant there were fortunes to be made and cash to be spent. Some of that cash was spent on luxury and exotic products that increasingly became the objects of far-flung commercial networks. A good part of the cash was spent by rural nobles, who earned it from rents, booty, and the profits of the private exercise of public power. When those nobles moved into towns, they created opportunities for merchants, craftsmen, day laborers, domestic servants, and professional people, such as notaries and lawyers. This was particularly true in Europe's most heavily urbanized regions: Flanders, southern France, and northern Italy. The key point is that the growth of the medieval city and of its human community began in the medieval countryside.

Town society was hierarchical, but its structures were new, ill-defined, and flexible. Rich men built up bands of followers who supported them in urban politics, protected their neighborhoods, and occasionally raided the houses of their enemies in the next neighborhood. Relatives, friends, neighbors, people from a common rural district, or those engaged in similar trades tended to worship together in particular churches, observe certain festivals, and look after one another's families.

San Gimignano The towers of this Tuscan city reveal the concentrated and competitive nature of power in the Italian communes. Most of these towers date from around 1300. (Scala/Art Resource, NY)

In the rapidly changing world of the tenth and eleventh centuries, towns provided numerous opportunities for women. In urban industries, such as clothmaking, tanning, laundering, and brewing, women sometimes managed and even owned enterprises. Apart, perhaps, from finance and the law, distinctions between male and female roles were not as sharp in towns as in rural areas.

If urban men and all women stood in an ambiguous relationship to the ideals of the male, rural, aristocratic elite, we can hardly imagine what it must have been like for Jews. Jewish communities had existed in most European towns since antiquity. Then, because the Byzantine and Islamic worlds vacillated between persecution and toleration, many Jews migrated to western Europe, with the largest numbers settling in northern France and the German Rhineland. Paris had northern Europe's largest Jewish community, perhaps two thousand people in the twelfth century. Many cities had Jewish populations numbering two hundred to three hundred, but groups of forty to fifty were common. Although some Jews in Italy, Spain, and Germany owned farms and vineyards, most Jews settled in cities, where they could live and worship in community with other Jews. Urban clusters also provided strength in numbers for people who could at any moment fall victim to persecution and whose power was not based on landholding.

Three of the most important developments in high medieval Europe were disastrous for Jews. First, the growth of the European economy, with its attendant urban and commercial expansion, brought countless Christians into the practice of trade, an occupation dominated by Jews since Late Antiquity. As Jews were excluded from commercial opportunities, they were more and more confined to moneylending. Jews had been moneylenders before the economic surge of the High Middle Ages, but the expanding economy made financial operations more widespread than ever before. Given that, as we saw in Chapter 9, Christian moralists considered handling money to be the Devil's work, the visibility of Jews as moneylenders brought them much criticism, although they were never alone in this practice.

The second phenomenon that adversely affected Jews was the reform of the church. With so much attention being paid to the proper Christian life and the correct organization of the church, it was inevitable that more attention would be directed to the one prominent group in Western society that was not Christian.

Third, the Crusades unleashed vicious attacks on Jews. As crusading armies headed east in 1096, they visited unspeakable massacres on the Jewish communities of several German towns. This awful process was repeated on the eve of the Second Crusade in 1146–1147 and again just before the third in 1189. Popular frenzy identified the Jews as Christ-killers and equated them with Muslims as the enemies of Christianity. In fact, and despite grotesque and groundless stories about Jews kidnapping and ritually killing Christian children, Jews everywhere wished to live in peace with their Christian neighbors and to be left alone to observe their distinctive religious, dietary, and social customs.

The Jews were not without sympathetic champions, however. From the time of Gregory I (r. 590–604), the papacy urged peaceful coexistence and prayers for Jewish conversion. In the twelfth and thirteenth centuries, popes forcefully reminded Christians that while converting Jews was highly desirable, Jews were to be tolerated and left in peace. The Carolingians protected the Jews, and some kings in succeeding centuries repeated or even expanded upon Carolingian legislation.

Jews were vulnerable to attack at almost any time from people who simply disliked them or who owed them money. In 1181, Philip II of France, always on the lookout for income, had his henchmen arrest Jews and confiscate their possessions. In 1182, he expelled them from royal lands. Across the thirteenth century, French kings accorded the Jews less and less protection and often abused them financially. In 1306, Philip IV expelled the Jews from France after confiscating their goods. In England, the story is much the same. The ever-needy Henry II laid crushing taxes on the Jews in 1171. In 1189 in London and in 1190 in York, massive riots stirred by false rumors raged against the Jewish populations. In 1290, Edward I seized Jewish possessions and expelled Jews from the country. Royal protection of German Jews was reasonably effective until the death of Frederick II in 1250, after which time local princes often repudiated debts to Jewish lenders and appropriated Jewish property.

SECTION SUMMARY

- Among the elite, society was divided into "those who pray," "those who fight," and "those who work."

- Constant waves of monastic reform modeled good spiritual behavior.

- Warrior-nobles were the governing class, marked by chivalry, their distinctive ethos.

- Peasants did much of the "work" in medieval society and generally found their lives improving.

- Townspeople enjoyed expanding opportunities but always suffered under the prejudices of landholding elites.

- In religious life, urban occupations, and rural pursuits, women experienced some improvements in their conditions of life.

- The condition of Europe's Jews grew progressively dangerous.

SOCIAL AND RELIGIOUS MOVEMENTS, CA. 1100–1300

Why did some spiritual movements result in heresy, while others ended in new religious orders?

Twelfth- and thirteenth-century Europe witnessed several social movements unlike any that had occurred before. Spurred by increasingly intrusive governments, economic dislocation, and spiritual turmoil, they involved large numbers of people; cut across lines of gender, wealth, status, and occupation; and appeared in many places. Most of these movements had cohesive beliefs, even ideologies, and well-determined goals. They are the first large-scale social movements in European history.

Heretics and Dissidents

The canon lawyer Gratian (see page 267) defined *heresy* as a situation in which "each man chooses for himself the teaching he believes to be the better one"—that is, he ignores official doctrines. For Gratian and his like-minded contemporaries, faith was not an individual matter. Unity of belief was crucial in a catholic ("universal") Christian Europe. In the twelfth century, the church reacted ever more strictly to challenges to its teachings or to its exclusive right to teach. The effort by the church to define its law, theology, and bureaucratic procedures with greater precision drew lines more sharply than ever before between what was and was not acceptable.

Heretics did not see themselves as secessionists from the true church. They saw themselves as its only representatives. Church teachings always encountered a degree of popular skepticism. Not everyone believed, for example, that Jesus was born of a virgin or that he was true God and true man. But such doubts had not previously led to mass defections. Before the middle of the twelfth century, challenges to the church came from men—as far as we can tell, the ringleaders were all men—who saw themselves as inspired reformers.

Tanchelm (TANK-elm) of Antwerp preached between 1100 and 1115 in the Netherlands. He scandalized the mainstream by calling churches brothels and clerics whores. He rejected the sacraments and the payment of tithes. Although Tanchelm was radical and pugnacious, his ideas constituted a fairly coherent program of criticism. Like many others, he was concerned about the immorality and wealth of the church. But Tanchelm and his followers went even further. The heretic distributed his nail and hair clippings as relics of a sort, and in a bizarre public ceremony he "married" a statue of the Virgin Mary.

Coherent movements of much larger proportions emerged later in the century. In 1173, Waldo, a rich merchant of Lyon, decided to sell all his property, give the proceeds to the poor, and embrace a life of poverty and preaching. Waldo was motivated by the same quest for the apostolic life that had animated the eremitic movement of the eleventh century. But there was a difference: He was a layman. Waldo attracted many followers (known as Waldensians), and in 1179, Pope Alexander III (r. 1159–1181) scrutinized him closely, found his beliefs to be essentially correct, and approved his vow of poverty. But the pope commanded Waldo to preach only when invited to do so by bishops. The bishops, jealous about their own power, extended no such invitations.

Waldo and his "Poor Men of Lyon" went right on preaching and in 1184 were formally declared heretics. Until this point it was not their ideas so much as their appropriation of a clerical duty, preaching, that had set the church against them. From this time on, however, the Waldensians became more radical in their attacks. Waldensian communities exist to this day.

The most serious of the popular heretical movements was Catharism (from the Greek *katharos*, meaning "pure"). Because there were numerous Cathars near the southern French town of Albi, the whole movement is sometimes called "Albigensian." In fact, Cathars could be found all over Europe, although they did cluster in northern Italy and southern France. Cathars were the religious descendants of Mani (see page 157), a third-century Persian who taught an extreme dualism that featured polarities in almost all things: good-evil, love-hate, flesh-spirit. Extreme Cathars abstained from flesh in all ways: They were vegetarians and renounced sexual intercourse so as not to produce offspring—that is, more flesh. Cathar ideas had spread widely in the West by the 1140s. Catharism attracted many converts when Nicetas, the Cathar bishop of Constantinople, visited northern Italy and southern France between 1166 and 1176. People of every station joined the new church, which, in its own view, was the only true church.

The Catholic Church sent isolated preachers against the Cathars, but with little success. In 1198 and 1203, Pope Innocent III organized systematic preaching tours in southern France, but these, too, lacked solid results, and in 1208, the pope's legate was murdered by a man who was sympathetic to the Cathars. The killing led to the launching of the Albigensian Crusade, a loosely structured military action that lasted into the 1260s. Although the crusade itself was largely over by the 1220s, violence against Albigensians sputtered for decades: a massacre in 1244 and inquisitorial campaigns in 1246 and again in 1256 to 1257. Isolated resisters struggled on into the fourteenth century.

Albigensians denounced the clergy of their day as rich and corrupt. These teachings attracted urban dwellers who resented the wealth and pretensions of the clergy—the same people who followed Waldo. Nobles may have been drawn to the movement because it gave them opportunities to take possession of extensive tracts of church lands, something the investiture controversy had denied them. In addition, embracing Catharism may have been a way for nobles to resist the increasing encroachment of the government of far-off Paris. The Albigensians also attracted many women. Unlike the Catholic Church, which denied clerical, preaching, and teaching offices to women, the heretical sects tended to permit women to hold leading roles.

The Albigensians, like the Waldensians, were driven by the same spiritual zeal and desire for ecclesiastical reform that moved many of their contemporaries. They differed from other would-be reformers in that they did not seek to reform the Catholic Church from within but departed from it or insisted that they alone represented it. Thus, these heretical movements marked the first serious challenge to the ideology of a uniformly "catholic" Christendom since Late Antiquity.

Reform From Within: The Mendicant Orders

Traditional monastic orders continued to win adherents, but their interpretation of the apostolic life meant ascetic withdrawal from the world, not pastoral work and preaching. Laymen who wished both to embrace poverty and to preach fell under the suspicion of the ecclesiastical authorities. Early in the thirteenth century, a new movement arose, the mendicants (literally, beggars). Mendicants were men who aimed to preach, to be poor, and to create formal but noncloistered religious orders. Though similar to the heretics in many ways, they submitted willingly to ecclesiastical authority.

Francis of Assisi   An Italian layman who renounced his wealth and founded a religious order dedicated to charitable works.

The mendicant phenomenon began when **Francis of Assisi** (1181–1226), the son of a rich Italian merchant, decided to renounce the wealth and status that were his birthright. He carried out his renunciation in a most public display before the bishop of Assisi (uh-SEE-zee) in 1206. Francis had gradually grown tired of a life of ease and luxury, but he also experienced a blinding moment of spiritual insight when, by chance, his eyes fell on the passage in the Scriptures in which Christ commanded the rich young ruler, "Go, sell all you have, and follow me." Francis stripped himself naked so that "naked he might follow the naked Christ."

For a few years, Francis wandered about Italy begging for his meager sustenance, repairing churches, caring for the sick, and preaching repentance to all who would listen. By 1210, he had attracted many followers, and together, they set out to see Innocent III to win approval. After considering the matter for a while, Innocent decided to approve the new order of friars (that is, "brothers," from the Latin *fratres*) as long as they would accept monastic tonsure—a ritual haircut signifying submission—profess obedience to the pope, and swear obedience to Francis. The pope was genuinely won over by Francis himself, but he also sensed that by permitting the formation of the Franciscan order, he could create a legitimate and controllable repository for the explosive spiritual forces of the age.

Francis prepared a simple Rule based on his understanding of the scriptural ideals of poverty, preaching, and service. Alarmed by the vagueness of the first Rule and by the extraordinary influx of new members, the papal curia in 1223 prevailed on Francis to submit a revision that stressed order, a hierarchy of officials, and a novitiate—a regularized period of training for new members. Somewhat disappointed by this regulated formality, Francis withdrew more and more from the world and lived reclusively in the hills near Assisi.

After Francis died, the issues of property, power, education, and ordination provoked deep controversies within his order. Usually called "Franciscan," Francis's order is technically the "Friars Minor." The movement had begun among laymen, but over time, more Franciscan brothers became ordained priests. Franciscans established schools in most great cities, and by the middle of the thirteenth century, some of Europe's greatest intellects were Franciscans.

In the 1230s, papal legislation had alleviated strict poverty by permitting the order to acquire property to support its work. Nevertheless, the issue of property continued to spark controversy among the Franciscans.

The other major mendicant order was the Dominican, a product of very different experiences than the Franciscan. Its founder, **Dominic de Guzman** (1170–1221), was the son of a Spanish nobleman. He became a priest and later a cathedral canon. While traveling, he saw firsthand the Albigensian heresy in southern France, and in 1206, he went to Rome to seek permission to preach against the heretics. The Albigensian Crusade began in 1208, but Dominic's methods were those of persuasion, not coercion.

Albigensian criticisms of the ignorance, indifference, and personal failings of the clergy could never be applied to Dominic and his fellow preachers. Dominic and his followers were supported enthusiastically by the bishop of Toulouse, who saw how useful these zealous preachers of unblemished lives could be. In 1215, Dominic, with his bishop's assistance, attempted to form a new order, but by that time, Rome had forbidden the creation of new orders for fear of heresy or uncontrollable diversity. Thus, Dominic's "Order of Preachers" (the proper name for the "Dominicans") adopted the Rule of Saint Augustine, which many communities of cathedral canons had been using since the eleventh century.

In 1217, Dominic presided at the first general meeting of the order. The Dominicans decided to disperse, some going to Paris, some (including Dominic) to Rome, and some to other cities in Europe. Henceforth, the order saw its mission as serving the whole church. Dominican schools were set up all over Europe, and the order acquired a reputation for learning and scholarship. The Dominicans were voluntarily poor, but the order was never rent by a controversy over property as the Franciscans were.

Both the Franciscan and Dominican orders reflected a widespread desire to emulate the apostolic life of the early church by poverty and preaching. Both submitted to legitimate authority. Francis's religious vision of charity and service was the product of a heartfelt need for repentance and renewal. This concern for the soul often caused Franciscans to serve as missionaries. Dominic set out to save the church from its enemies. He desired preachers who were sufficiently learned that they could combat the errors of heretics. Both men saw the need for exemplary lives. Francis was a more charismatic figure than Dominic, and his apostolate to the urban poor was more compelling. By 1300, Franciscan houses outnumbered Dominican by 3 to 1. The mendicants were the greatest spiritual force in high medieval Europe.

Dominic de Guzman
A Spanish nobleman who preached against Albigensian heretics and founded a religious order dedicated to preaching.

Communities of Women

The religious forces that attracted men drew women as well. Traditional orders, however, tended to be hostile toward women. Cluniacs and Cistercians struggled to keep women out of their ranks. The wandering preachers of the twelfth century, without exception, acquired women as followers, but the usual results were either segregation of the women in cloisters or condemnation of the whole movement.

In 1212, Francis attracted the aristocrat Clare of Assisi (1194–1253), who was fleeing from an arranged marriage. She wanted to live the friars' life of poverty and preaching, and Francis wanted to assist her. Aware that the sight of women begging or preaching would be shocking, in 1215, he gave Clare and his other female followers their own rule. Clare became abbess of the first community of the "Poor Clares." Though cloistered and forbidden to preach, the Clares lived lives of exemplary austerity and attracted many adherents.

Beguines (BAY-geenz) were communities of women who lived together, devoted themselves to charitable works, but did not take vows as nuns. The Beguine movement grew from the work in Nivelles, near Liège (lee-EZHE), of Mary of Oignies (ca. 1177–1213). She was drawn to the ideals of voluntary poverty and service to others. So strong was the pull that she renounced her marriage, gave away all her goods, worked for a while in a leper colony, and thought of preaching against the Cathars. Instead, she formed a community.

Groups of Beguines appeared all over the Low Countries, western Germany, and northern France. This was the first exclusively women's movement in the history of Christianity. Beguines sometimes vowed poverty and sometimes did not. They sometimes cloistered themselves into communities and sometimes taught and served the poor and outcast. They neither challenged the officials and teachings of the church nor demanded a right to preach. As laywomen, they did not give rise to scandal as noncloistered nuns would have. They were content to have power over their own lives and communities but not seek a voice in the wider world around them.

The Parting of Mary from the Apostles Duccio di Buoninsegna lived from the middle of the thirteenth century to 1318 or 1319. He did his finest work in Siena, including a huge altarpiece, one of whose panels depicts the touching scene of Mary taking leave of the apostles just before her death. Note the clever way Duccio has arranged the figures and how he balances Saint Paul, standing in the doorway, with Mary, reclining on the bed. (Scala/Art Resource, NY)

Thirteenth-century Europe knew more female than male mystics, and female mysticism tended to focus on Jesus, especially on His presence in the Eucharist. This is the first religious devotion that can be shown to have been more common to women than to men. Most of the mystics were either nuns or Beguines. As the clergy was defining its own prerogatives more tightly, and excluding women more absolutely from the exercise of formal public power, female communities provided a different locus for women's activity.

Women who spent their lives in community with other women reveal, in their writings, none of the sense of moral and intellectual inferiority that was routinely attributed to women by men and often by women themselves. Women who were in direct spiritual communion with God acquired, as teachers, mediators, and counselors in their communities, power that they simply could not have had outside those settings.

SECTION SUMMARY

- Some men and women who opposed the wealth and immorality of some clerics, and who wished to preach and teach, veered off into heresy.

- The Mendicants—Franciscans and Dominicans, chiefly—led holy lives, worked among the poor or preached against heretics, and always had the approval of the papacy.

- Several religious movements were especially popular among women and constituted the first women's movements in the history of Christianity.

LATIN CULTURE: FROM SCHOOLS TO UNIVERSITIES

What signs do you find of an expanding intellectual climate in high medieval Europe?

As in the late antique and Carolingian periods, courts and churches were the greatest patrons of artists and authors. But in this age of expansion, the number and geographic spread of such patrons increased dramatically. By 1150, the church comprised 50 percent more bishoprics and about three times as many monasteries as it had in 900. In 1300, monarchies reigned in many places—Scandinavia and the Slavic world, for example—where none had existed in 900 (see **MAP 10.1**). In addition to an increase in the sheer amount of cultural activity,

🌐 **MAP 10.1—Europe, ca. 1230**

By the early thirteenth century, the European states that would exist into modern times were clearly visible, although each would continue to undergo changes. To gain a sense of the evolution of Europe, compare this map with **MAPS 6.1, 7.3,** and **8.3.**

the years between 900 and 1300 also witnessed innovations. Logic replaced grammar at the heart of the school curriculum. Latin letters remained ascendant, but literature in many vernacular (native) languages began to appear in quantity and quality. Romanesque art and architecture were fresh and original interpretations of their Carolingian ancestors. Europe's incipient urbanization produced the first stirrings of a distinctively urban culture. In one of those cities, Paris, a new kind of academic institution emerged—the university—which was arguably the period's greatest legacy to the modern world.

The Carolingian Legacy

Political dislocation and constant attacks in the ninth and tenth centuries initially deprived schools and masters of the Carolingian patronage that they had enjoyed for a century or more. The Carolingians left firm enough foundations in a few centers for intellectual life to continue, but the scale of activity between 900 and 1050 was smaller than before. Three examples serve to capture the spirit of the age that set the stage for the High Middle Ages.

Gerbert of Aurillac (DJAIR-bear of OR-ee-ak) (940–1003) was the most distinguished intellect of his age. He left his home in Aquitaine to study in Spain and Italy before settling in Reims, in northern France, where he was a teacher and then briefly a bishop. He attracted the attention of the emperor Otto III and spent some time at the German court, earning appointments as abbot of Bobbio, bishop of Ravenna, and, finally, pope. Gerbert followed Carolingian tradition in being a collector of manuscripts and critic of texts, but he departed from older traditions in his interest in mathematics and in his study of logic—the formal rules of reasoning that, in the Western tradition, trace back over many thinkers to Aristotle (see page 77–78).

Fulbert of Chartres (FULL-bear of SHART), Gerbert's finest pupil, elevated the cathedral school of Chartres to the paramount place in academic Europe. Fulbert (960–1028) wrote letters in elegant Latin and composed fine poems. He carried on his master's literary interests more than his scientific ones, and well into the twelfth century, Chartres remained a major center of literary studies.

Another figure of interest is the aristocratic German nun Roswitha of Gandersheim (d. 970). She wrote poems on saints and martyrs, as well as a story about a priest who sold his soul to the Devil. In her mature years, Roswitha wrote Latin plays in rhymed verse based on the Roman writer Terence. In these plays, she refashioned tales from Roman and biblical history to convey moral truths.

The Study of Law

Law was a field of major innovation. The increasing sophistication of urban life demanded a better understanding of law. The growing responsibilities of the church called for orderly rules, and the church's frequent quarrels with secular rulers demanded careful delineations of rights and responsibilities. Governments issued more laws and regulations than at any time since antiquity.

In Bologna, Irnerius (d. ca. 1130), a transplanted German and protégé of Emperor Henry V, began teaching Roman law from the Code of Justinian (see pages 186–187). This legal work culminated in the publication in 1140 of the *Decretum* of the Bolognese monk Gratian (GRAY-shun). The most comprehensive and systematic book of **canon law** yet written, Gratian's work remained authoritative for centuries.

canon law The law of the church (as distinguished from civil law). It is based on papal decrees and the rulings of church councils.

Throughout the twelfth century, canon lawyers studied and wrote commentaries on Gratian's *Decretum*. These legists are called "decretists." Gratian had systematically collected earlier papal *decretals* (official pronouncements), but popes continued to issue them. Several collections of these new decretals were prepared in the thirteenth century, and the scholars who studied these later decrees are called "decretalists." The church thus produced a vast corpus of law and legal commentary.

England was precocious in creating a common law, a single law applied uniformly in its courts. But English law was based on the careful accumulation of legal decisions—or precedents—and not on the routine application of the provisions of a law code. There were many law codes elsewhere. Alfonso X of Castile issued the *Siete Partidas*, a comprehensive law code largely reliant on Roman law. Prince Iaroslav (d. 1054) is reputed to have issued the first version of the laws of Kievan Rus. Byzantine law was revised under the Macedonian dynasty.

Greek, Arab, and Jewish Contributions

Norman and German settlement in southern Italy and Sicily, the Reconquista in Spain, the Crusades, and the creation of Italian communities in many Mediterranean cities brought European thinkers face-to-face with the intellectual traditions of Classical Greece, Islam, and medieval Judaism. Between 1100 and 1270, almost the whole corpus of Aristotle's writings, virtually unknown in the West for a millennium, became available. Arab commentaries on Aristotle, as well as Jewish philosophical and theological works, began to circulate. The presence of all these texts and currents of thought was decisive in expanding the range and raising the level of Western thought.

Prior to about 1100, only a few of Aristotle's writings, primarily some of his early writings on logic, had been available in the West. Gradually, scholars recovered Aristotle's full treatment of logic, then his scientific writings, and finally his studies of ethics and politics. Aristotle's books posed a number of problems for Christian scholars. What relationship exists between the Christian faith and reason? Aristotle taught that the universe is eternal and mechanistic. His thought left no room for creation or for the continuing role of a Creator. For Christian thinkers, Aristotle asked questions that demanded answers: Were the Scriptures true? Did God create the world as Genesis said? Did God continue to intervene in this world?

Two major Arab thinkers were particularly influenced by the vast Aristotelian corpus. Ibn-Sina (980–1037), called Avicenna (ah-vih-SENN-uh) in the West, was drawn to the fundamental problem of how to understand the relationship between objects that exist in the world and the knowledge of those objects that is formed and held in the human mind. (See the feature, "The Global Record: The Making of an Arab Scholar.") Ibn Rushd (1126–1198), called Averroes (uh-VERR-oheese), wrote no fewer than thirty-eight commentaries on the works of Aristotle, and at least fifteen of these were translated into Latin in the thirteenth century. Among many contributions, Averroes particularly tried to clarify the relationship between truths acquired through the exercise of reason and truths that depend on divine revelation. His contemporaries and many later scholars understood him to teach the "double truth": Truths about the natural world are more or less accessible to everyone depending on a person's intellectual ability. Revealed truths, however, are available only to the most enlightened.

Spain and northern France were both important centers of Jewish thought. In Spain, some Jewish thinkers also grappled with Aristotle. Solomon ibn Gebirol (1021–1070), called Avicebron, wrote *The Fountain of Life*, a treatise that attempted to reconcile Aristotle with the Jewish faith by finding a role for God in communicating knowledge to every human mind. The greatest of all medieval Jewish thinkers, Moses ben Maimon (1135–1204), called Maimonides (my-MON-uh-deez), wrote *A Guide for the Perplexed*. The perplexed he had in mind were those who had trouble reconciling the seemingly opposed claims of reason and faith. Maimonides taught a doctrine very close to Averroes's double truth.

Solomon ben Isaac (1040–1105), called Rashi, was educated in Jewish schools in the Rhineland and then set up his own school in Troyes (TWAH). He became the most learned biblical and Talmudic scholar of his time, indeed one of the wisest ever. The Talmud was a detailed and erudite commentary on the scriptural studies of the ancient rabbis. Christian scholars who wished to know the exact meaning of passages in the Bible sometimes consulted Rashi and his successors.

From Persia to Spain to France, then, countless thinkers were engaged in serious reflection on the mechanics of knowing, the nature of reality, the relationship between reason and faith, and the meaning and significance of revelation. In the years just around 1100, Latin Christian scholars began to encounter this torrent of thought and writing.

Muslim Scholars in a Garden   From a thirteenth-century Iraqi manuscript, this picture shows literary men in a pleasure garden. Beasts are driving a water wheel to refresh them, and a lute player accompanies their poetry with music.   (Bibliothèque nationale de France)

The Development of Western Theology

Carolingian schools had focused on grammar—that is, on the basic foundations of language. Gradually, logic supplanted grammar at the center of both intellectual interests and school curricula. Eventually, the wider application of logic produced a new intellectual style and also evoked bitter criticisms.

Berengar (ca. 1000–1088), master of the school of Tours, wrote a treatise that denied Christ's presence in the Eucharist—the Communion bread and wine received by Catholics and Orthodox Christians in the celebration of the mass. This position was heretical. Ordinarily, churchmen would have refuted Berengar simply by quoting various passages from the Scriptures or from the writings of the Church Fathers, along with conciliar pronouncements about the consecrated elements. Berengar's claim was finally proved false, at least to the satisfaction of his opponents, by Archbishop Lanfranc of Canterbury (1010–1089) who used Aristotelian logical argumentation to dispose of Berengar's heretical arguments.

Anselm (ca. 1033–1109), Lanfranc's successor as archbishop of Canterbury, developed an ingenious logical proof for the existence of God. The French theologian and philosopher Peter

The Making of an Arab Scholar

These excerpts from the engaging life of Avicenna (980–1037) reveal not only his remarkable intellectual attainments but also his ongoing encounter with Greek thought. Avicenna was deeply influenced by Aristotle, and, in turn, his writings influenced Jewish and Christian writers who were also coming to grips with the greatest of Greek philosophers. His writings on medicine were authoritative until the seventeenth century.

My father was from Balkh and moved from there to Bukhārā [now Turkmenistan]…where I was given teachers of the Quran and polite letters [literature, especially poetry]. By the time I was ten years old I had mastered the Quran and so much of polite letters as to provoke wonderment. My father decided to send me to a certain grocer who knew Indian arithmetic so that I could learn it from him. Then Abu Abdallah al-Natili, who claimed to be a philosopher, came to Bukhara. My father lodged him in our house in the hope that I would learn something from him. Before he came I was studying jurisprudence…and I was one of the best pupils. Then, under the guidance of al-Natili, I began to study the *Isagoge* [a commentary on some of Aristotle's works]. Thus I learned from him the broad principles of logic, but he knew nothing of the subtleties. Then I began to read books and study commentaries on my own until I mastered logic. I also read the geometry of Euclid. Then I passed on to the *Almagest* [Ptolemy's second-century astronomical treatise]. Eventually I busied myself with the study of the [treatises] and other commentaries on physics and metaphysics [subjects treated at great length by Aristotle and by Avicenna's Arab predecessors, especially al-Farabi], and the doors of knowledge opened before me. Then I took up medicine and began to read books written on this subject. Medicine is not one of the difficult sciences, and in a very short time I undoubtedly excelled in it, so that physicians of merit studied under me. At the same time I carried on debates and controversies in jurisprudence. At this point I was sixteen years old.

I resumed the study of logic and all parts of philosophy. During this time I never slept a whole night through and I did nothing but study all day long. Whenever I was puzzled by a problem…I would go to the mosque, pray, and ask the Creator of All to reveal to me that which was hidden from me and to make easy for me that which was difficult. Then at night I would return home, put a lamp in front of me, and set to work reading and writing.

I returned to the study of divine science. I read the book called *Metaphysics* [by Aristotle], but could not understand it, the aim of its author remaining obscure for me. I read the book forty times, until I knew it by heart, but I still could not understand its meaning or its purpose. Then one afternoon I happened to be in the market of the booksellers, and a crier was holding a volume in his hand and shouting the price. I bought it and found that it was Abu'l Nasr al-Farabi's book explaining the meaning of the *Metaphysics*. I returned to my house and made haste to read it. Immediately the purposes of this book became clear to me because I already knew it by heart. I was very happy at this, and the next day I gave much alms to the poor in thanksgiving to Almighty God.

In my neighborhood there lived a man who asked me to write him an encyclopedic work on all the sciences. I compiled the *Majmu* for him and named it after him. In it I dealt with all sciences other than mathematics. I was then twenty-one years old.

QUESTIONS

1. In what academic subjects was Avicenna particularly interested?
2. In what ways was Avicenna's education like and unlike that received by students in Europe?
3. How did faith and reason play complementary roles in Avicenna's education?

Source: Bernard Lewis, ed., *Islam: From the Prophet Muhammad to the Capture of Constantinople*, vol. 2, 1974, pp. 177–181. Reprinted by permission of Oxford University Press.

Abelard (1079–1142) used logic to reconcile apparent contradictions in the Scriptures and in the writings of the Church Fathers. Anselm and Abelard were not skeptics. Anselm's motto was "Faith seeking understanding."

Bernard of Clairvaux
A church reformer, adviser to rulers, and conservative intellectual who opposed the wide application of logic.

Hildegard of Bingen
A German Benedictine abbess and prolific author.

For conservatives, such as **Bernard of Clairvaux** (see page 260) and **Hildegard of Bingen** (1098–1179), however, faith and immediate divine inspiration were primary. To them, logical approaches to divine truth were the height of arrogance. Hildegard—well educated, musically gifted, and knowledgeable in medical matters—was perhaps the most profound psychological thinker of her age. More than anyone before her, Hildegard opened up for discussion the feminine aspects of divinity. She, like Bernard, believed that God was to be found deep within the human spirit, not in books full of academic wrangling.

The future lay with Anselm and Abelard, however. Anselm was the most gifted Christian thinker since Augustine. He wrote distinguished works on logic, and his theological treatise, *Why God Became Man* (ca. 1100), served for three hundred years as the definitive philosophical and theological explanation of the incarnation of Christ, the central mystery of the Christian faith.

Peter Abelard was a more colorful figure. He argued rudely and violently with all his teachers, though in the end, he was probably more intelligent than any of them. He rose to a keener understanding of Aristotle than anyone in centuries, and he developed a sharper sense of both the power and the limitations of language than anyone since the Greeks. He concerned himself with ethics, too, and was one of the first writers to see intention as more important than simple action.

Abelard seduced and then secretly married Heloise, one of his pupils and the daughter of an influential Paris churchman. Heloise's relatives castrated Abelard for his refusal to live openly with his wife. Abelard then arranged for Heloise to enter a convent, and he joined a monastic community, where he continued writing and teaching. The two carried on a voluminous correspondence that reveals Heloise as a first-rate philosophical thinker and one of her age's most knowledgeable connoisseurs of Classical literature. Some of Abelard's more imaginative ideas earned him formal ecclesiastical condemnations in 1121 and 1140. He popularized the schools of Paris, however, and attracted to them promising scholars from all over Europe.

Abelard and several of his contemporaries engaged in one of the first widespread intellectual debates in Western history, the quarrel over "universals." *Universal* is the philosophical name for a concept that applies to more than one seemingly related object. To illustrate: May we agree that you are reading a book right now? May we further agree that the book you are reading is not identical to any other book on your bookshelf? And may we go one step further and agree that no book on your bookshelf is exactly like any other book on that shelf? So, why do we call all of these objects books? "Book" is here the universal that we are trying to understand.

A medieval "realist," whose thought may be traced back to Plato, would say that there is a concept, let us call it "bookness," that exists in our minds before we ever encounter any particular object that we label a book. Just as no book is ever identical to any other, so too, no specific book is a perfect representation of that concept "bookness." The concept is fully real, and all representations of it in the world are mere hints, suggestions of a more perfect reality.

A medieval "nominalist," on the contrary, would say that "book" is merely a name (*nomen* in Latin, whence nominalism) that we apply to objects that we deem to bear sufficient similarity to one another that they can be adequately captured by one name. But only each particular book is fully real.

With the emergence of the problem of universals, we enter fully into a new intellectual approach that has long been called "Scholasticism." This word has come to have many different meanings, but at the most basic level, it describes a movement that attempted to show that Christian theology is inherently rational, that faith and reason need not be contradictory or antithetical. Scholasticism also implies a certain systematization of thought. Gratian's attempt to organize all of canon law rationally and systematically was a Scholastic exercise. Twelfth-century biblical scholars tried to produce a single, systematic commentary on the Bible. In 1160, Peter Lombard produced the *Four Books of Sentences*, a comprehensive treatment of all of Christian theology.

Thomas Aquinas (1225–1274) was the greatest of the Scholastics, the most sensitive to Greek and Arab thought, and the most prolific medieval philosopher. A Dominican friar, Thomas was educated at Naples, Cologne, and Paris. Apart from brief service at the papal court, he spent the years after 1252 teaching and writing in Paris. His two most famous works are the *Summa Contra Gentiles* and the *Summa Theologiae*. A *summa* is an encyclopedic compendium of carefully arrayed knowledge on a particular subject. One might think of Gratian's and Peter Lombard's works as precursors to the great summas of the thirteenth century. Thomas's first summa addresses natural truth—that is, the kinds of things that any person can know through the operation of reason. His second summa is a summation of the revealed truths of the Christian faith.

Thomas's works are distinctive for two reasons. First, no one before him had so rigorously followed the dialectical method of reasoning through a whole field of knowledge, not just a particular problem. For thousands of pages, Thomas poses a question, suggests answers, confronts the answers with objections, refutes the objections, and then draws a conclusion. Then, he repeats the process. Second, Thomas carefully distinguishes between two kinds of truths. On the one hand are *natural truths*, truths (even theological ones) that anyone can know (or so Thomas thought)—for example, that God exists. On the other hand are *revealed truths*, truths that can be known (if not understood) only through faith in God's revelation—for example, the Trinity or the incarnation of Christ. Thomas maintains that natural and revealed truths simply cannot contradict one another because God is ultimately the source of both. If a natural truth—for example,

Thomas Aquinas
A Dominican theologian and the greatest of the Scholastics.

summa A compendium of knowledge within a particular field.

The Triumph of St. Thomas This painting by Benozzo Gozzoli (1349) for the church of Santa Caterina in Pisa, Italy, is idealized but still reveals much that is true. Above Thomas are four evangelists and two church fathers; to Thomas's right and left stand Plato and Aristotle; at Thomas's feet Averroes crouches, vanquished. Thomas was seen as the great synthesizer of philosophical and theological knowledge. (Scala/Art Resource, NY)

Aristotle's contention that the world is eternal—appears to contradict a revealed truth, the natural truth is wrong. Thomas was accused by some contemporaries of applying reason too widely, and after his death some of his ideas were condemned by the church. But he actually steered a middle path between intellectual extremes. In this respect, Thomas was like Maimonides and Averroes.

The University

In the early decades of the twelfth century, students gathered wherever famous teachers might be found. Such teachers—figures like Peter Abelard—clustered in a few centers, and the students congregated there as well. The last decades of the twelfth century saw a swarm of masters and students in Paris. Like members of secular guilds (see page 232), the masters organized. The University of Paris was the result of their efforts. By 1300, universities had formed elsewhere in France, as well as in Italy, England, and western Germany.

Several forces drove masters to organize. They wanted to negotiate with the bishop's chancellor, the traditional head of all schools in an episcopal city. They wanted to regulate the curriculum that students followed and to prescribe the requirements for entry into their own ranks. They also desired to set the fees to be charged for instruction. By 1209, the bishop of Paris, the pope, and the king of France had granted formal recognition to the university.

In Bologna, the university developed a little differently. Here the students came primarily to study law, after already acquiring a basic education. These law students were usually older and more affluent than students elsewhere, and foreign to Bologna. Consequently, in Bologna, the university arose from a guild of students who united to set standards in fees and studies and to protect themselves against unscrupulous masters.

Women and Medicine in Twelfth-Century Salerno

Late in the twelfth century, an anonymous author compiled three lengthy medical texts into one that came to be called the "Trotula." The second of these treatises, "On the Cures of Women," was almost certainly written by a woman named Trota. For centuries, scholars argued that a woman could not have written the widely disseminated Trotula because women could neither study nor teach in the Salerno schools. Absolutely nothing is known about Trota herself, but her text presents an intriguing question: How was she able to acquire vast learning in the Greek, Arab, and Persian medical traditions? Perhaps Trota "practiced" medicine. Whatever the case, most of her text involves either physical appearance or problems connected with menstruation and childbirth. Trota's treatise put her ahead of her time, but just maybe there were other women like her, concealed by ignorance and prejudice.

There are some women who, when they come to their time of menstruation, have either no or very few menses. For these, we proceed thus. Take root of the red willow with which large wine jars are tied and clean them well of the exterior bark, and, having pulverized them, mix them with wine or water and cook them, and in the morning give them in a potion when it has become lukewarm.

To those giving birth with difficulty we give aid in this manner. We should prepare a bath and we put the woman in it, and after she leaves let there be a fumigation of spikenard and similar aromatic substances. For strengthening and for opening the birth canal, let there be sternutatives [substances that induce sneezing] of white hellebore well ground into a powder. For just as Copho [a twelfth-century Salerno medical teacher] says, the organs are shaken and the uterus ruptures and thus the fetus is brought out and comes out.

For making the face red, take root of red and white bryony and clean it and chop it finely and dry it. Afterward, powder it and mix it with rose water, and with cotton or a very fine cloth we anoint the face and it induces redness.

For the woman having a naturally white complexion, we make a red color if she lacks redness, so that with a kind of fake or cloaked whiteness a red color will appear as if it were natural.

For freckles of the face which appear by accident, take root of bistort and reduce it to powder, and cuttlefish bones and frankincense, and from all these things make a powder. And mix with a little water and smear it, rubbing, on the (face) in the morning…until you have removed the freckles.

An ointment for whitening the face. Take two ounces of the very best white lead, let them be ground; afterward let them be sifted through a cloth, and that which remains in the cloth, let it be thrown out. Let it be mixed in with rainwater and let it cook until the consumption of the water, which can be recognized when we see it almost completely dried out. Then let it be cooled. And when it is dried out and cooled, let rose water be added, and again boil it until it becomes hard and thick, so that from it very small pills can be formed. And when you wish to be anointed, take one pill and liquefy it in the hand with water and then rub it well on the face, so that the face will be dried. Then let it be washed with pure water, and this will last for eight days.

QUESTIONS

1. Does it make sense that a medical treatise by a woman would emphasize issues of particular concern to women?

2. Why do you suppose that scholars long refused to believe that a woman could have written this book?

3. Do you detect in Trota's writing evidence of experimental, empirical science?

Source: Monica H. Green, ed. and trans., *The Trotula: A Medieval Compendium of Women's Medicine* (Philadelphia: University of Pennsylvania Press, 2001), pp. 117–119, 139, 141, 163. Reprinted by permission of the University of Pennsylvania Press.

Universities were known for certain specializations: Paris for arts and theology, Bologna for law, Salerno in Italy and Montpellier in France for medicine, Oxford for mathematical and scientific subjects. Still, the basic course of study was similar. At Paris, a young scholar came to the city, found lodgings where he could, and attempted to find a master who would guide him through the arts curriculum. These boys might be in their early teens or several years older, depending on their earlier education and financial resources. The arts course, which was the prerequisite to all higher faculties, usually lasted from four to six years. The bachelor's degree was a license to teach, but a bachelor who wished to teach in a university needed to go on for a master's degree. The master's degree required at least eight years of study (including the baccalaureate years), which culminated in a public oral examination. Some masters went on to become doctors in theology, law, or medicine. A doctorate required ten to fifteen years of study.

Student life was difficult. In many ways, students were always foreigners. Although their presence in a town enhanced its prestige, townspeople exploited them by charging exorbitant prices for food and rent. Students' own behavior was not always above reproach. There was surely some truth in the frequently lodged charge that students were noisy, quarrelsome, given to drinking, and excessively fond of prostitutes. England's Oxford and Cambridge were unique in always providing residential colleges for students; Paris got one later, and the mendicants often established houses of study. Typically, though, students were on their own.

Students had to work very hard. The arts curriculum demanded a thorough acquaintance with all the famous texts of grammar, logic, and rhetoric. Higher studies added more Aristotle, particularly his philosophical writings. In theology, the students had to master the Scriptures, the principal biblical commentaries from patristic times to the present, and the *Four Books of Sentences*. In medicine, the ancient writings of Galen and Hippocrates were supplemented by Arab texts as well as by observation and experimentation.

The basic method of teaching provides yet another definition of Scholasticism—that is, the method of studying in the schools. The teacher started by reciting a short piece of a set text, carried on with the presentation and discussion of many authoritative commentaries on that text, and concluded with his own explanations. The teacher then presented another passage of the set text and repeated the whole process. This education focused on standard books and accepted opinions and required students to remember large amounts of material.

In principle, universities were open to free men, but in practice, they were restricted to those who had the means to attend them. Women were not accepted at universities, either as students or as teachers. It was generally thought, by men, that learning made women insubordinate. Lacking the required education, women were denied entry into the learned professions of theology, law, and medicine, despite the fact that many rural and some urban medical practitioners were women. Nevertheless, women commonly possessed and transmitted knowledge of both folk remedies and scientific medicine. Trota of Salerno, who probably lived in the twelfth century, wrote a knowledgeable treatise, *On the Care of Women*. (See the feature, "The Written Record: Women and Medicine in Twelfth-Century Salerno.") Documents from medieval Naples record the names of twenty-four women surgeons between 1273 and 1410. How these women were educated is utterly unknown.

SECTION SUMMARY

- Latin studies in literature, law, theology, and philosophy remained important.

- Europe's expansion brought scholars into increasing contact with ancient Greek, Jewish, and Arab thought.

- The increasing prominence of logic drove theology and philosophy to the center of the curriculum and led to the production of majestic summas.

- Formed as guilds of either masters or students, universities were among the most original and durable medieval achievements.

THE VERNACULAR ACHIEVEMENT

What were the hallmarks of vernacular culture?

A major achievement of high medieval civilization, from Iceland to Kievan Rus, was the appearance of rich literatures in native tongues. Vernacular, from the Latin *vernaculus*, meaning "home-born" or "domestic," is the name for the languages other than Latin—say, English or French. Although Latin remained the language of the clerical elite, writers of vernacular prose and poetry produced some of the greatest works in Western literature.

Literatures and Languages

The number of people who commanded Latin was always a minority in western Europe, just as native Greek-speakers were a minority in Byzantium. As Latin, beginning in Late Antiquity, slowly evolved into the Romance (from Roman) languages, people who used what eventually became French, Italian, and Spanish had some advantages over the people in Celtic, Germanic, or Slavic lands, where the languages bore no obvious relationship to Latin. Persons who spoke Old French in their towns and villages would have had an easier time learning Latin than people who spoke Irish or Polish. Nevertheless, vernacular literatures began to appear at roughly the same time all over Europe, between about 800 and 1000.

Many writers continued to use Latin for several centuries. University scholars continued to compose their learned treatises in the ancient tongue, but now often in a style that was less ornate than before. Most law books and public documents were still in Latin, but in a "vulgar" Latin that was reasonably close to the vernacular in areas where Romance languages were spoken. Technical manuals—on farming and animal husbandry, on warfare and armaments, or on law and government—were prepared in Latin, too, but again in a style that was far more accessible than that of their ancient models. Popular literature—poetry, history and biography, and romance and adventure—was still often written in Latin. Some of this material was serious, but some breathed a light and carefree spirit. The anonymous German known as the Archpoet (d. 1165) wrote poems about drinking and womanizing. These lines are typical of his work:

> In the public house to die
> Is my resolution;
> Let wine to my lips be nigh
> At life's dissolution:
> That will make the angels cry,
> With glad elocution
> "Grant this drunkard, God on high,
> Grace and Absolution!"[1]

No less insouciant were the authors of biting satires, such as the anonymous *The Gospel According to the Silver Marks*, which parodies the wealth and greed of the papal curia.

The literary masterpieces of the High Middle Ages are almost entirely written in vernacular languages. The epic poem *Beowulf* is the first classic of English literature. We do not know who wrote it or when it was written. Scholars now usually place it in the ninth or possibly the tenth century. The story focuses on three great battles fought by the hero, Beowulf. The first two are against the monster Grendel and Grendel's mother, who have been harrying the kingdom of an old ally of Beowulf's family; the third is against a dragon. *Beowulf* is a poem of adventure and heroism, of loyalty and treachery. It treats lordship, friendship, and kinship. Themes of good and evil resound throughout. The poem is barely Christian, but nevertheless, deeply moral. It speaks, in a mature, vigorous, and moving language, to and for the heart of a warrior society.

Beowulf is the best-known Anglo-Saxon work but by no means the only one. Several volumes of elegiac and lyric poetry, mostly on religious themes, also survive. And Anglo-Saxon writers produced chronicles, legal materials and charters, and at least one large collection of homilies.

Some fragments of poetry in Old French survive from the ninth century, but the great *chansons de geste* ("songs of deeds," or celebrations of the great) appeared in the eleventh century. Undoubtedly, they were transmitted orally for a long time before they were written down. The best is the *Song of Roland*, written around 1100. In 778, as Charlemagne's army was returning from Spain, Basques raided the baggage train and killed Count Roland. By 1100, this obscure event, long kept alive in oral traditions, had been transformed into a heroic struggle between Charlemagne and his retinue and an army of countless thousands of "paynim," who are crude caricatures of Muslims.

Like *Beowulf*, the *Song of Roland* is a story about loyalty and treachery, bravery in the face of insuperable odds, and the kindness and generosity of leaders. Both take us into a man's chivalric world, where females are all but absent. The two works do not show us personal hopes, fears, or motivations. What pours forth is the communal ethos and the dominant values of the elite, male social group. Although *Beowulf* is lightly clothed in Christianity, the *Song of Roland* is thickly vested in the faith.

Southern France, in the middle and late twelfth century, added something new to Western literature: the love lyrics of the troubadours. This poetry, composed by both men and women, profoundly influenced an age and created the literary movement that has long been called "courtly love." **Chivalry** was initially a code for men interacting with other men. In the world of courtly love, chivalry became an elaborate set of rules governing relations between men and women.

Courtly love had several sources. The classical poet Ovid (43 B.C.–A.D. 17?), who wrote *The Art of Love*, a manual of seduction, was one. Another was the lyrical poetry of Muslim Spain. Ironically, feudal values such as loyalty and service played a critical role as men became, in effect, love vassals. Platonic ideas made some contribution, too, particularly the notion that

chivalry   Beginning as the dominant ethos of the warrior-nobility, it changed into rules governing relations between men and women.

any love in this world could be only a pale imitation of real love. The courtly poets sang of *fin' amours*, a pure love in contrast to the mere lust of the masses. A lover cherished an unattainable lady. He would do anything for the merest display of pleasure or gratitude on her part, as we see in these lines from Bernart de Ventadorn, court poet of the counts of Toulouse in the late twelfth century:

> *Down there, around Ventadorn, all my friends*
> *have lost me, because my lady does not love me;*
> *and so, it is right that I never go back there again,*
> *because always she is wild and morose with me.*
> *Now here is why the face she shows me is gloomy and full of anger:*
> *because my pleasure is in loving her and I have settled down to it.*
> *She is resentful and complains for no other reason.*[2]

Male troubadours placed women on pedestals and, in ballads, worshiped them from afar. Women troubadours took a different line. Women's poems were more realistic, human, and emotionally satisfying. Castellozza (KAHS-teh-lohtz-eh) (b. ca. 1200), the southern French wife of a Crusader, idealized not at all when she wrote these lines:

> *Friend, if you had shown consideration,*
> *meekness, candor and humanity,*
> *I'd have loved you without hesitation,*
> *but you were mean and sly and villainous.*

And she did not assign the active role exclusively to the man:

> *Handsome friend, as a lover true*
> *I loved you, for you pleased me*
> *But now I see I was a fool*
> *for I've barely seen you since.*[3]

Count William IX of Poitou (1071–1127) was among the first of the troubadours, and his daughter, Eleanor of Aquitaine, brought the conventions of this poetry and point of view to the French and Angevin courts. She and her daughters were the greatest literary patrons of the late twelfth century. The wives of kings and nobles, who were frequently away from home, maintained stunning courts and cultivated vernacular literature.

The courtly literature of northern France broke new ground in both forms and content. The romance and the lay were the chief new forms. Both drew on Classical literature, the heroic Germanic past, and the Arthurian legends of the Celtic world to create stories of love and adventure. The romance usually develops a complex narrative involving several major characters over a long time. The lay is brief and focuses on a single incident. The most famous twelfth-century writer of romance was Chrétien de Troyes (1135–1183), the court writer of Marie of Champagne, the daughter of Eleanor of Aquitaine. The greatest writer of lays was Marie de France, who wrote at the Angevin court in the 1170s.

The romances and lays explore the contradictions and tensions in a variety of human relationships. Loyalty and honor make frequent appearances. Lancelot, a paragon of knightly virtue, desperately loves his lord Arthur's wife, Guinevere. What is he to do? How can he be loyal to his lord, to his love, and to himself? What will he do when a single course of action brings both honor and dishonor? In the epics, speeches are made to swords, to horses, or sometimes to no one in particular; the points being made are universalized. In the romances, credible human beings struggle to resolve powerful and conflicting emotional and moral dilemmas.

France led the way in the production of vernacular literature, but French models did not inspire slavish imitation. This is seen most clearly in the work of the master of all vernacular writers, Dante Alighieri (DAHN-tay ah-lih-GYAIR-ee). Dante (1265–1321) began as a poet in *la dolce stil nuova*, "the sweet new style," which came from France and captivated Italians. But he moved beyond it in many ways. Dante was a man of extraordinarily wide learning and reading. He is best known for one of the masterpieces of world literature, *The Divine Comedy*.

The secret of the *Comedy*'s success is not easy to grasp. It is a long and difficult poem, but it is also humorous, instructive, and moving. In an exquisitely beautiful Italian, Dante took the most advanced theology and philosophy of his time, the richest poetic traditions, a huge hoard of stories, many contemporary events, and a lot of common sense and wove them into an allegorical presentation of the journey of the whole human race and of the individual lives of all people.

Accompanied by the Roman poet Virgil (see page 143), Dante travels through Hell and Purgatory, commenting along the way on the condition of the people he meets. Then, because Virgil is a pagan and only Dante's true love can accompany Dante into Paradise, Beatrice, the love of Dante's youth, joins him for a visit to Heaven. The poet's central metaphor is love; the love he feels for Beatrice symbolizes the love God feels for the world. Dante canvasses humanity from the pits of Hell, which he reserved for traitors, to the summit of Paradise, where a man inspired by pure love might, despite his sinfulness, dare to look into the face of God.

Although the romances and lays were by no means the exclusive preserve of the elite, very little is known about popular literature. Two exceptions are the mystery play and women's devotional writing. Mystery plays made their first appearance in the eleventh century. The liturgy of the church, which formally reenacted the life of Christ, was confined to the clergy. But this limitation did not prevent troupes of actors from staging, on church porches or village greens, scenes from the life of Christ in simple, direct language. Such plays served as both a form of popular entertainment and a device for teaching elementary Christian ideas. The female religious movements of the age gave rise to works in the vernacular. Mechtild of Magdeburg (1210–1280), a German Beguine, wrote *The Flowering Light of Divinity*, a mystical, allegorical account of the marriage between God and a spiritual woman. The vernaculars opened avenues of expression to women, who were normally denied Latin learning.

Innovations in Architecture

Romanesque, "in the Roman style," is a term that was coined in the nineteenth century to characterize the architecture and, to a lesser extent, the painting of the period between the waning of Carolingian art and the full emergence of **Gothic** art in the late twelfth century. Today, scholars view the Romanesque style as a transition between Carolingian and Gothic.

At several places in Ottonian Germany, a return of political stability led to the construction of churches. Ducal dynasties and women of the imperial family were among the most generous patrons. The Germans developed a distinctive architectural style marked by very thick walls, alternating piers and columns in the nave, and galleries. As this architectural style spread all over Europe in the eleventh century, it produced true Romanesque, a style that differed from Roman and Carolingian styles, mainly in the greater internal height and space made possible by vaulting (see **FIGURE 10.1**). To the rectangular elegance of the classical basilica and the height of the Carolingian westworks (see page 219), Romanesque builders added a refined verticality. Among the distinctive features of Romanesque churches were their wall paintings and frescoes, sculpture, reliquaries, pulpits, and baptisteries—in short, their exuberant decoration and ornament.

It is surely no coincidence that Gothic art and architecture emerged just as the West was absorbing the rediscovery of Euclid's mathematical writings and applying the intensely ordered logic of Aristotle to everything from legal problems to theological mysteries. One of the most familiar images of the Middle Ages is the inspiringly beautiful Gothic cathedral. It is thus ironic that the word *Gothic* first appeared in the sixteenth century as a term of derision for what was then regarded as an outmoded style so ugly that only the horrible conquerors of Rome, the Goths, could have been responsible for it. The name stuck, but today, it simply identifies a period in European architecture, sculpture, and painting that began in the middle of the twelfth century and that in some places lasted until the early sixteenth century.

Gothic is a French invention. It was Abbot Suger (SOO-jhay) (1085–1151) of Saint-Denis, a monastery outside Paris, who, in rebuilding his basilica beginning in 1135, consciously sought a new style. He desired to achieve effects of lightness, almost weightlessness, in the stonework of his church and to admit large amounts of light to create a dazzling and mysterious aura on the inside. The

Romanesque The name assigned to architecture "in the Roman style" that dominated the period from about 900 to 1150.

Gothic The name assigned to the architecture that emerged in twelfth-century France, spread all over Europe, and dominated construction until the fifteenth century.

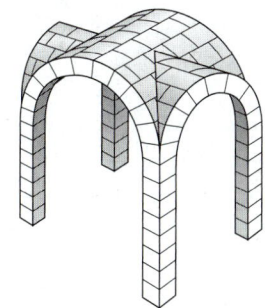

Barrel vault   Groin vault

■ **FIGURE 10.1—The Structure of Romanesque Architecture**

The basic structural element of Romanesque architecture was the barrel vault, which, when two were joined at right angles, formed a groin vault. These vaults produced great height and strength but gave buildings a massive, fortresslike appearance.

(Source: Anne Shaver-Crandell, *The Middle Ages*. Copyright © 1982 Cambridge University Press. Reprinted with permission of Cambridge University Press.)

Romanesque Interior, Saint Sernin, Toulouse The interior space of Saint Sernin is elegant, high, and well-ordered. But its typical Romanesque effect—from "barrel" vaulting—is that of a tunnel. Massive piers support the gallery and roofing above. (Éditions Gaud)

Bible often uses images of light to refer to God, and Suger wished to give expression to those images in the house of God for which he was responsible.

Suger produced something startlingly original by combining a number of elements that had long been in use—three in particular: A *pointed arch* is more elegant than a round one; it also permits the joining of two arches of identical height but different widths, which, in turn, permits complex shapes and sizes (see **FIGURE 10.2**). The *ribbed vault* is lighter and more graceful than the barrel and groin vaults characteristic of Romanesque architecture; it also exerts less stress and facilitates experimentation with shapes. Finally, *point support*—basically, the support of structural elements at only certain points—permits the replacement of heavy, stress-bearing walls with curtains of stained glass. (See the feature, "The Visual Record: Stained Glass.")

The points of support might be massive internal piers or intricate skeletal frameworks, called *buttresses*, on the outside of the church. These three elements—pointed arch, ribbed vault, and point support—produce a building that is characterized by verticality and translucency. The desired effect is one of harmony, order, and mathematical precision.

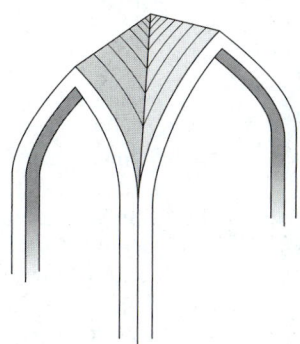

■ **FIGURE 10.2—The Structure of Gothic Architecture**

The adoption of pointed arches, an import from the Islamic world, let Gothic builders join structures of identical height but different widths (something that barrel and groin vaulting could not do; see Figure 10.1 on page 281). The resulting structures were high, light, airy, and visually interesting.

(Source: Anne Shaver-Crandell, *The Middle Ages*. Copyright © 1982 Cambridge University Press. Reprinted with permission of Cambridge University Press.)

Gothic Interior, Chartres Cathedral   Looking down the early-thirteenth-century nave of Chartres Cathedral provides an opportunity to visualize each of the major building components of Gothic architecture: pointed arch, ribbed vault, point support. The desired verticality is evident.   (Éditions Gaud)

Stained Glass

To walk into one of Europe's great churches is to enter a realm of mystery and beauty produced by the play of light—the brilliant light of the morning sun, the softer glow of the evening sun, the muted tones of a cloudy day—on thousands of square feet of colored glass. This mystery and beauty were created intentionally in Europe in the High Middle Ages. But the magnificent surviving medieval windows are not important solely for their beauty. Their images provide unique and crucial insights into religious and secular life.

Pictured here are two thirteenth-century cathedral windows. The one from Canterbury depicts that city's great bishop and martyr, Thomas Becket. A large window at Chartres depicts Saint Lubin, a sixth-century bishop of the city who was the patron saint of the town's inn and tavern keepers, and Noah, according to the Bible the first planter of grapevines. Here, in a window donated by the vintners guild, we see barrels of wine being hauled to market.

Many of Canterbury's windows represent aspects of the life of the murdered archbishop. The one pictured here shows Thomas as a bishop, not as a martyr. He is wearing a miter, the traditional headgear of a bishop. He also wears a *pallium*, a white wool band sent to a new archbishop by the pope. Becket's vestments are green, the most common liturgical color of the religious year (others were white, purple, and red). This window, then, would have served to remind people of their beloved bishop as he was in life, not martyrdom.

In Chartres, wine was important to the church because of its use in mass, and it was also a staple of the local economy. Accordingly, the vintners are portrayed in twenty-three of this window's forty-one panels. By comparison, most guilds are depicted only once in the windows they donated. These windows remind us, as they reminded contemporaries, of how these magnificent buildings fitted into the daily life of their communities. Religious devotions and secular preoccupations blended in one spot.

Glass is made by heating silica, found naturally in sand, flint, and quartz, to a very high temperature and then fusing the molten silicate with a borate or phosphate, often obtained from ashes produced by burning natural substances. Colored glass was made by adding metal oxides to the molten mixture. Iron oxide produced red, copper oxide produced green, and cobalt produced blue. Such glass, called "pot glass," tended to be opaque, obviously unsuitable for windows. To achieve greater translucency, glassmakers made "flashed glass" by fusing at low temperatures a layer of colored liquid to the

Canterbury, Thirteenth-Century Window: Thomas Becket (Sonia Halliday Photographs)

surface of a panel of clear glass. Although fine glass vessels were made in a number of places, notably in Venice and the Rhineland, the large sheets of colored glass used for church windows were commonly manufactured in Lorraine and Normandy.

To make a stained glass window, a master glazier first drew a cartoon—a sort of rough draft—on a flat board, or perhaps on a piece of parchment. He then cut pieces of

Chartres, Thirteenth-Century Window: Story of Saint Lubin (© Clive Hicks)

colored glass into various irregular shapes according to his design. To produce facial features, folds in garments, or other details, the glazier painted the inner sides of the colored glass pieces with dark-colored paints and then fired them at low temperatures to produce an enamel-like effect. You can see this patina on Thomas's face. Once the glazier had all his pieces cut and placed, he joined them together by means of lead strips that were H shaped. If you look closely, you can see the pieces of glass, lead stripping, and painted details in the images on these pages. The whole picture was then fitted into a metal frame and mounted in a window opening.

Documents first mention the use of glass in church windows in the sixth century. The oldest surviving fragments of stained glass date from the ninth century, and the oldest complete windows from around 1100. With large Romanesque churches, and even more with the huge Gothic churches, came opportunities to use more and more glass. First, the greater height of Romanesque buildings meant that tall windows could be placed high up in the nave walls. Then, the structural innovations of Gothic architecture that removed stress, and hence stone, from the walls permitted them to become vast expanses of glass. Chartres Cathedral has 176 windows. Many high medieval churches had windows more than 50 feet high.

So far, we have looked at *how* medieval Europeans created stained glass and incorporated it into their greatest churches. But *why* did they undertake such time-consuming and costly decoration? Suger, the scholarly twelfth-century abbot of Saint-Denis outside Paris who rebuilt his basilica in the Gothic style, spoke of the spiritual force of his new glass windows:

> When…the loveliness of the many-colored gems has called me away from external cares…then it seems to me that I see myself dwelling in some strange region of the universe which neither exists entirely in the slime of the earth nor entirely in the purity of heaven; and that, by the grace of God, I can be transported from this inferior to that higher world.*

In the Greek philosophers, the Bible, and the Church Fathers, light always represents one way of imagining the unimaginable reality of God. For Suger and his contemporaries, the luminous effect of stained glass suggested the very presence of God. Earthquakes, fires, and wars have destroyed most of the glass that was installed in the Middle Ages. Today's visitor to Europe views more or less valid nineteenth-century reconstructions, except at Canterbury in England and Chartres in France, where almost all of the original glass survives. Usually medieval churches were laid out on an east-west axis. The western façade was normally pierced by tall "lancet" windows and by a single "rose" window. These windows typically portrayed scenes from the life of Christ and/or the Virgin Mary. The northern aisle windows usually contained Old Testament scenes, the southern windows New Testament scenes.

Stained glass played a key role, alongside sculpture, preaching, and churchyard dramas, in communicating the faith to ordinary people. Seldom has a teaching tool been so beautiful. Scholars also speak of stained glass as "painting with glass." Indeed, the art form most like stained glass is painting, especially the painting of illuminations on the pages of manuscripts.

QUESTIONS

1. How was stained glass made and assembled into windows?

2. What kinds of subjects were depicted on stained glass windows?

3. Who was the audience for stained glass windows?

---

*Suger, *De rebus in administratione sua gestis*, ed. E. Panofsky, 2d ed. (Princeton, N.J.: Princeton University Press, 1979), pp. 63–65.

SECTION SUMMARY

- Vernacular literature spread quickly and widely in high medieval Europe.

- Vernacular literature produced *chansons de geste*, romances, lays, sagas, and poetry.

- The High Middle Ages saw the full flowering of Romanesque architecture and then its eclipse by the Gothic style.

The thirteenth century was the most mature period for French Gothic architecture and also the time when Gothic spread most widely throughout Europe. Its popularity may be attributed to the superiority of French masons and stonecutters and also to the tremendous prestige of French culture. By 1300, distinctive Gothic traditions shaped the urban landscape in almost all parts of Europe from Iceland to Poland.

CHAPTER SUMMARY

Comparisons between the Europe of 900 and the Europe of 1300 are instructive both as reminders of what had happened and as suggestions of what was to come. In 900, Carolingian Europe was being attacked on every side. By 1300, Europe was vastly larger than in Carolingian times; not only was its geography greater, but it also had expanded in economic, political, military, and cultural terms.

FOCUS QUESTIONS

- Into what principal social groups were the people of high medieval Europe organized?

- Why did some spiritual movements result in heresy, while others ended in new religious orders?

- What signs do you find of an expanding intellectual climate in high medieval Europe?

- What were the hallmarks of vernacular culture?

At least among the elite, society was divided into "those who pray," "those who fight," and "those who work." Constant waves of monastic reform modeled good spiritual behavior, and monks thought of themselves as society's natural leaders. Bishops embraced reform, too, but as they were often nobles, their views were more flexible than those held by monks. They also saw themselves as leaders. Warrior-nobles *were* the governing class, marked by chivalry, their distinctive ethos that emphasized prowess, courage, loyalty, and generosity. Peasants did much of the "work" in medieval society and generally found the conditions of their lives improving. Townspeople enjoyed expanding opportunities but always suffered under the prejudices of landholding elites. In religious life, urban occupations, and rural pursuits, women experienced some improvements in their conditions of life but always faced legal and social prejudices. The condition of Europe's Jews grew progressively dangerous.

The High Middle Ages saw the birth of powerful religious movements. Some men and women who opposed the wealth and immorality of some clerics, and who wished to preach and teach, veered off into heresy. The Mendicants—Franciscans and Dominicans, chiefly—led holy and blameless lives, worked among the poor or preached against heretics, and always had the approval of the papacy. Several religious movements were especially popular among women and constituted the first exclusively women's movements in the history of Christianity.

Latin studies in literature, law, theology, and philosophy remained important. Europe's expansion brought scholars into increasing contact with ancient Greek, Jewish, and Arab thought, which spurred new research and opened new questions. The increasing prominence of logic drove theology and philosophy to the center of the curriculum and led to the production of majestic summas, compendiums of knowledge in various fields. Formed as guilds of either masters or students, universities were among the most original and durable medieval achievements.

Vernacular literature, literature in "native" languages, spread quickly and widely in high medieval Europe, achieving visibility and prominence everywhere. Vernacular literature was written in many genres: *chansons de geste*, romances, lays, sagas, and poetry. The High Middle Ages saw the full flowering of Romanesque architecture and then its eclipse by Gothic. Magnificent cathedrals are testimony to the prosperity and pride of high medieval Europe.

KEY TERMS

Cluny (p. 260)
Francis of Assisi (p. 268)
Dominic de Guzman (p. 269)
canon law (p. 272)

Bernard of Clairvaux (p. 274)
Hildegard of Bingen (p. 274)
Thomas Aquinas (p. 275)

summa (p. 275)
chivalry (p. 279)
Romanesque (p. 281)
Gothic (p. 281)

 This icon will direct you to additional materials on the website: www .cengage.com/history/ noble/westciv6e.

NOTES

1. John Addington Symonds, *Wine, Women and Song: Medieval Latin Students' Songs* (reprint, New York: Cooper Square, 1966), p. 69.

2. From *Lyrics of the Troubadours and Trouvères,* translated by Frederick Goldin, copyright © 1973 by Frederick Goldin. Used by permission of Doubleday, a division of Random House, Inc

3. From lyrics by Castellozza in *The Women Troubadeurs* by Meg Bogin, (W.W. Norton, 1976). Copyright © 1976 by Magda Bogin. Reprinted by permission of Magda Bogin.

 See our interactive eBook for map and primary source activities.

11

The Crisis of the Western Christian Church

War and the Struggle Over Political Power, 1300–1450

Crisis in Economy and Society

The Consolidation of Political Power, 1450–1500

A Time of Judgment
On this cover for a fifteenth-century government account book, symbols of death—arrows, a scythe, and a horse—carry the angel of death from place to place. (Bildarchiv Preussischer Kulturbesitz/Art Resource, NY)

Crisis and Recovery in Late Medieval Europe, 1300–1500

I n the fourteenth century, Europeans sang an old Franciscan hymn, "Day of Wrath, Day of Burning." Its verses described the fear and disorder that would accompany the end of the world and God's judgment of the saved and the damned. That hymn could well have been in the mind of the painter of the facing illustration. When countless Europeans, such as these poor souls beneath the winged angel of death, fell victim to epidemic disease, many people thought they knew why. The illustrator seems to believe it was God's judgment against sinners, including these gamblers sickened by the angel's plague-tipped arrows. The flood, fire, and pestilence that ravaged late medieval Europe were thought to be premonitions of the breakdown of the world and a time of judgment.

The late Middle Ages (ca. 1300–1500) are often described as a period of continued crisis and decline that put an end to the growth and expansion of the previous three centuries. In truth, however, the years of crisis in the fourteenth and early fifteenth centuries gave way to a dramatic economic, social, and political recovery in the fifteenth century. The cultural and intellectual changes that accompanied the crisis and recovery are the focus of Chapter 12, "The Renaissance."

Military, political, religious, economic, and social crises burdened Europe in the fourteenth and early fifteenth centuries. Between 1337 and 1453, France and England fought a war that touched most of the states of western Europe. The Hundred Years' War, as it has come to be known, was fought primarily over English claims to traditionally French lands. Aristocrats in many parts of Europe challenged the hereditary rights of their rulers. In the towns of Germany and Italy, patrician classes moved to reduce the influence of artisans and laborers in government, instituting oligarchies or even aristocratic lordships in place of more democratic governments.

Questions of power and representation also affected the Christian church as ecclesiastical claims to authority came under attack. Secular governments challenged church jurisdictions. Disputed papal elections led to the so-called Great Schism, a split between rival centers of control in Rome and Avignon (a city in what is now the south of France). In the aftermath of the crisis, the papacy was forced to redefine its place in both the religious life and the political life of Europe.

A series of economic and demographic shocks worsened these political and religious difficulties. Part of the problem was structural: The population of Europe had grown too large to be supported by the resources available. Famine and the return of the plague in 1348 sent the economy into long-term decline. In almost every aspect of political, religious,

FOCUS QUESTIONS

- How did the Great Schism change the church and the papacy?

- What forces limited the political power of rulers in England, France, and Italy?

- How were economic and social structures changed by plague and economic crisis?

- How did the political makeup of Europe in 1500 differ from that in 1300?

 This icon will direct you to additional materials on the website: www .cengage.com/history/ noble/westciv6e.

 See our interactive eBook for map and primary source activities.

and social life, then, the fourteenth and early fifteenth centuries marked a pause in the growth and consolidation that had characterized the earlier medieval period.

Yet, out of the crises, a number of significant changes emerged. By 1500, the European population and economy were again expanding. England and France emerged strengthened by military and political conflicts, and the consolidation of the Spanish kingdoms, the Ottoman Empire, and the states of eastern Europe altered the political and social makeup of Europe. None of the transformations could have been predicted in 1300, as Europe entered a religious, political, and social whirlwind.

THE CRISIS OF THE WESTERN CHRISTIAN CHURCH

How did the Great Schism change the church and the papacy?

Early in the fourteenth century, the king of France attempted to kidnap the pope. His act initiated a series of crises that challenged traditional ideas about church government and the role of the church in the various countries of Europe. First, the popes and their entourages abandoned their traditional residences in central Italy and moved to Avignon, an imperial enclave in the south of modern France. Then, in the wake of a disputed election, two and later three rivals claimed the papal throne. Simultaneously, the church hierarchy faced challenges from radical reformers who wished to change it. At various times, all the European powers became entangled in the problems of the church. In the wake of the crisis, the papacy realized that it needed a stronger, independent base. Papal recovery in the fifteenth century was predicated on political autonomy in central Italy.

The Babylonian Captivity, 1309–1377

The Christian church was in turmoil as a result of an attack on Pope Boniface VIII (r. 1294–1303) by King Philip IV (r. 1285–1314) of France. The king attempted to kidnap Boniface, intending to try him for heresy because of the pope's challenges to the king's authority within his own kingdom. The outstanding issues revolved around the powers of the pope and the responsibilities of the clergy to political leaders. It was, in fact, largely because of tensions with the northern kingdoms that the French archbishop of Bordeaux (bor-DOE) was elected Pope Clement V (r. 1305–1314). Clement chose to remain north of the Alps in order to seek an end to warfare between France and England and to protect, to the extent possible, the wealthy religious order of the Knights of the Temple, or Templars (see page 261), which Philip was in the process of suppressing. After the death of Boniface, it was clear that the governments of Europe had no intention of recognizing papal political authority as absolute.

Clement's pontificate marked the beginning of the so-called Babylonian Captivity, a period from 1309 to 1378, when popes resided almost continuously outside of Italy. In 1309, Clement moved the papal court to Avignon, on the Rhône River in a region that was still part of the Holy Roman Empire—the name that, by the fourteenth century, was given to the medieval empire whose origin reached back to Charlemagne.

The papacy and its new residence in Avignon became a major religious, diplomatic, and commercial center. The size of the court changed as dramatically as its venue: Although the thirteenth-century papal administration required only two hundred or so officials, the bureaucracy in Avignon grew to about six hundred. It was not just the pope's immediate circle that expanded the population of Avignon. Artists, writers, lawyers, and merchants from across Europe were drawn to the new center of administration and hub of patronage. Papal administrators intervened actively in local ecclesiastical affairs, and the pope's revenues from annates (generally a portion of the first year's revenues from an ecclesiastical office granted by papal letter), court fees, and provisioning charges continued to grow.

Not everyone approved of this situation. It was the Italian poet and philosopher Francesco Petrarch (1304–1374) who first referred to the Avignon move as a **Babylonian Captivity of the Papacy**.

Babylonian Captivity of the Papacy Term used to describe the period from 1309 to 1378 when popes resided outside of Italy, relating the pontificate's move to the period when the tribes of Israel lived in exile.

Recalling the account in the Hebrew Bible of the exile of the Israelites and New Testament images of Babylon as the center of sin and immorality, he complained of

> [an] unholy Babylon, Hell on Earth, a sink of iniquity, the cesspool of the world. There is neither faith, nor charity, nor religion. . . . [1]

Two of the most vigorous critics were Saint Catherine of Siena (1347–1380) and Saint Bridget of Sweden (1303–1373). They were part of a remarkable flowering of religious feeling among women who were strong moral critics within their communities. Unlike others, Catherine and Bridget left their homes and neighborhoods and led the call for religious reform and a return of the papacy to Rome.

The Great Schism, 1378–1417

In 1377, Pope Gregory XI (r. 1370–1378) bowed to critics' pressure and did return to Rome. He was shocked by what he found: churches and palaces in ruin and the city violent and dangerous. By the end of 1377, he had resolved to retreat to Avignon, but he died before he could flee Rome. During a tumultuous election, the Roman populace entered the Vatican Palace and threatened to break into the conclave itself, demanding that there be an Italian pope. The subsequent election of the archbishop of Bari, Urban VI (r. 1378–1389), was soon challenged by dissidents who then elected a French cardinal who took the name Clement VII (r. 1378–1394). The church now had two popes.

After some hesitation, Western Christians divided into two camps, initiating the **Great Schism** (SKIZ-em), a period of almost forty years during which no one knew for sure who was the true pope. This was a deadly serious issue for all. The true pope had the right to appoint church officials, decide important moral and legal issues, and allow or forbid taxation of the clergy by the state.

The crisis gave impetus to new discussions about church government: Should the pope be considered the sole head of the church? Debates within the church followed lines of thought already expressed in the towns and kingdoms of Europe. Representative bodies—the English Parliament, the French Estates General, the Swedish Riksdag (RIX-dog)—already claimed the right to act for the realm, and in the city-states of Italy, ultimate authority was thought to reside in the body of citizens. Canon lawyers and theologians similarly argued that authority resided in the whole church, which had the right and duty to come together in council to correct and reform the church hierarchy. Even the most conservative of these **conciliarists** agreed that the "universal church" had the right to respond in periods of heresy or schism. More radical conciliarists argued that the pope as bishop of Rome was merely the first among equals in the church hierarchy and that he, like any other bishop, could be corrected by a gathering of his peers—that is, by an ecumenical council.

The rival popes resisted international pressure to end the schism. In exasperation, the cardinals, the main ecclesiastical supporters of the rival popes, called a general council in Pisa, which deposed both popes and elected a new one. Since the council lacked the power to force the rivals to accept deposition, the result was that three men now claimed to be the rightful successor of Saint Peter. Conciliarists, by themselves, could not mend the split in the church.

Resolution finally came when the Holy Roman emperor Sigismund (r. 1411–1437) forced the diplomatically isolated third papal claimant, John XXIII (r. 1410–1415), to call a general council of the church. The council, which met from 1414 to 1418 in the German imperial city of Constance, could never have succeeded without Sigismund's support. At one point, he forced the council to remain in session even after Pope John had fled the city in an attempt to end deliberations.

CHRONOLOGY

1303	Pope Boniface VIII attacked at Anagni and dies
1305	Election of Pope Clement V
1309	Clement V moves papal court to Avignon; beginning of Babylonian Captivity
1337	Beginning of Hundred Years' War between England and France
1348–1351	Black Death
1356	German emperor issues Golden Bull
1378	Great Schism
1381	English Rising
1397	Union of Kalmar unites Denmark, Norway, and Sweden
1410	Battle of Tannenberg
1414–1418	Council of Constance
1415	Battle of Agincourt
1420	Treaty of Troyes
1431	Execution of Joan of Arc
1438	Pragmatic Sanction of Bourges
1453	End of the Hundred Years' War Ottoman Turks conquer Constantinople
1469	Marriage of Ferdinand and Isabella unites kingdoms of Aragon and Castile
1480	Ivan III ends Tatar overlordship of Moscow
1485	Tudor dynasty established in England
1492	Spanish conquest of Granada Jews expelled from Spanish lands Columbus commissioned to discover new lands
1494	Charles VIII invades Italy

Great Schism The period from 1378 to 1417 when there were two and eventually three claimants to the papal throne.

conciliarists People who argued that the pope was merely "the first among equals" and that therefore a council of church leaders could correct or discipline a pope.

Gregory XI Returns to Rome   This highly stylized painting conveys the hopes of European Christians when Gregory XI returned from Avignon in 1377. Saint Catherine of Siena, who had pleaded for the pope's return, is seen in the foreground.   (Scala/Art Resource, NY)

Heresy and the Council of Constance, 1414–1418

Sigismund hoped that a council could help him heal deep religious and civil divisions in Bohemia, the most important part of his family's traditional lands (see **MAP 11.3**). Far from healing religious division, however, the actions of the council exacerbated tensions in central Europe and created a climate of religious distrust that poisoned relations for more than a century. Bohemia and its capital, Prague, were Czech-speaking. Prague was also the seat of the Luxemburg dynasty of German emperors and the site of the first university in German or Slavic lands. Religious and theological questions quickly became entangled with the competing claims of Czech and German factions. The preaching and teaching of the Czech reformer **Jan Hus** (ca. 1370–1415) were at the center of the debate. As preacher in the Bethlehem Chapel in Prague from 1402 and eventually as rector of the university, Hus was the natural spokesman for the non-German townspeople in Prague and the Czech faction at the university. His criticisms of the

Jan Hus   Czech reformer who attacked clerical privileges and advocated church reform. He was executed as a heretic at the Council of Constance in 1415.

church hierarchy, which in Prague was primarily German, fanned into flames the smoldering embers of Czech national feeling. It was Sigismund's hope that a council might clarify the orthodoxy of Hus's teachings and heal the rift within the church of Bohemia.

The council's response to the theological crisis was based on the church's experience with heresy over the previous forty years, primarily the teachings of John Wyclif (1329–1384). In the 1370s, Wyclif, an Oxford theologian and parish priest, began to criticize in increasingly angry terms the state of the clergy and the abuses of the church hierarchy. By 1387, his ideas had been declared heretical and his followers were hunted out. Wyclif believed that the church could be at once a divine institution and an earthly gathering of individuals. Thus, in his opinion, individual Christians need not unquestioningly obey the pronouncements of the church hierarchy. Final authority lay only in the Scriptures, insisted Wyclif, who sponsored the first translations of the Bible into English. He gathered about himself followers called "Lollards," who emphasized Bible reading and popular piety; some even supported public preaching by women. According to one disciple, "Every true man and woman being in charity is a priest."[2]

Wyclif's influence continued on the Continent, especially in the circle of Jan Hus and the Czech reformers. By 1403, the German majority in the university had condemned Hus's teaching as Wycliffite, thus initiating almost a decade of struggle between Czechs and Germans, Hussites and Catholics. This was the impasse that Sigismund hoped the **Council of Constance** could settle. Accordingly, he offered a suspicious Hus a safe conduct pass to attend the council. The council, however, revoked the pledge of safe conduct and ordered Hus to recant his beliefs. He refused and the council condemned him as a heretic and burned him at the stake on July 6, 1415.

Far from ending Sigismund's problems with the Bohemians, the actions of the council provided the Czechs with a martyr and hero. The execution of Hus provoked a firestorm of revolution in Prague. Czech forces roundly defeated an imperial army sent in to restore order. The Hussite movement gathered strength and spread throughout Bohemia. Moderate Hussites continued Hus's campaign against clerical abuses and claimed the right to receive both the bread and the wine during the sacrament of Communion. Radical Hussites argued that the true church was the community of spiritual men and women; they had no use for ecclesiastical hierarchy of any kind. The German emperors were unable to defeat a united Hussite movement. In 1433, a new church council and moderate Hussites negotiated an agreement that allowed the Hussites to continue some of their practices, including receiving both bread and wine at Communion, while returning to the church. Radical Hussites refused the compromise, and the war dragged on until 1436. Bohemia remained a center of religious dissent, and the memory of Hus's execution at a church council would have a chilling effect on discussions of church reform during the Reformation in the sixteenth century.

Council of Constance
General council of the church convened by the Holy Roman emperor to deal with schism and church reform. It elected Pope Martin V to end the Great Schism.

The Execution of Jan Hus
Stripped of the signs of ecclesiastical office, Jan Hus was forced to wear a paper hat indicating he was a heresiarch, the leader of heretics. This and similar images were meant to show the legitimacy of his execution, but in Bohemia he was revered as a martyred saint. (The Art Archive/University Library Prague/Gianni Dagli Orti/Picture Desk)

The Reunion and Reform of the Papacy, 1415–1513

To most of the delegates at the Council of Constance, the reunion and reform of the papacy were more important than the issue of heresy. And as we will see, attempts to deal with reform and reunion seemed in the eyes of the popes to threaten the political independence and the moral leadership of the papacy itself. This too would remain a problem well into the sixteenth century.

The council deposed two claimants and forced the third to resign. Then, in 1417, the council elected a Roman nobleman as Pope Martin V (r. 1417–1431).

The council justified its actions in what was perhaps its most important decree, *Haec sancta synodus* ("This sacred synod"): "This sacred synod of Constance ... declares ... that it has its power immediately from Christ, and that all men, of every rank and position, including even the pope himself are bound to obey it in those matters that pertain to the faith."[3] Popes could no longer expect to remain unchallenged if they made claims of absolute dominion, and ecclesiastical rights and jurisdictions increasingly were matters for negotiation.

Reform was more difficult. Both the cardinals and the popes viewed any reforms to the present system as potential threats to their ability to function. The council, however, recognized the need for further reforms. A second reform council met at Basel from 1431 to 1449, but with modest results. The council again tried to reduce papal power, but this time, it received little support from European governments.

Because of the continuing conciliarist threat, the papacy needed the support of the secular rulers of Europe. Thus, the papacy was forced to accept compromises on the issues of reform, on ecclesiastical jurisdictions and immunities, and on papal revenues. Various governments argued that it was they, and not the pope, who should be responsible for ecclesiastical institutions and jurisdictions within their territories.

Lay rulers wanted church officials in their territories to belong to local families. They wanted ecclesiastical institutions to be subject to local laws and administration. By the 1470s, it was clear that they wanted to have local prelates named as cardinal-protectors. These were not churchmen who could serve the church administration in Rome; rather they functioned as mediators between local governments and the papacy.

The reunited papacy had to accept claims it would have staunchly opposed a century earlier. One of the most important of these was the Pragmatic Sanction of Bourges of 1438. The papacy was unable to protest when the French clergy, at the urging of the king, abolished papal rights to annates, limited appeals to the papal court, and reduced papal rights to appoint clergy within France without the approval of the local clergy or the Crown. Similar concessions diminished church authority throughout Europe.

With reduced revenues from legal fees, annates, and appointments, the popes of the fifteenth century were forced to derive more and more of their revenue and influence from the Papal States. By 1430, the Papal States accounted for about half of the annual income of the papacy. Papal interests increasingly centered on protecting the papacy's influence as a secular ruler of a large territory in central Italy. Further, it saw political independence as essential to its continued moral leadership. Thus, the papacy had to deal with many of the same jurisdictional, diplomatic, and military challenges that faced other medieval governments.

SECTION SUMMARY

- A political crisis forced the papacy to abandon central Italy and move to the south of France.

- A disputed papal election left two claimants—one French, the other Italian—and no clear way to resolve the issue.

- The religious beliefs of John Wyclif and Jan Hus challenged the basis of papal authority.

- In addition to resolving the disputed election, conciliarists claimed authority to correct and reform the papacy.

- By 1450, the papacy was reunited but weakened in relation to the European kingdoms.

WAR AND THE STRUGGLE OVER POLITICAL POWER, 1300–1450

What forces limited the political power of rulers in England, France, and Italy?

A lawyer who served King Philip IV of France (r. 1285–1314) observed that "everything within the limits of his kingdom belongs to the lord king, especially protection, high justice and dominion."[4] Royal officials in England and France generally believed that "liberties"—that is, individual rights to local jurisdictions—originated with the king. These ideas were the result of several centuries of centralization of political power in royal hands. At almost the same time, however, an English noble challenged royal claims on his lands, saying, "Here, my lords, is my warrant," as he brandished a rusty long sword. "My ancestors came with William the Bastard [that is, William the Conqueror, in 1066] and conquered their lands with the sword, and by the sword I will defend them against anyone who tries to usurp them."[5] The views of the royal lawyer and the feisty earl exemplify the central tension over power in the late Middle Ages. The struggle over political power was played out in the context of the **Hundred Years' War**, which affected not just England and France but also most of western Europe, especially Italy, as mercenary soldiers traveled south during temporary lulls in the fighting. In England and France, the crisis led to strengthened monarchies. In Italy, however, local and regional entities exercised many of those liberties the old Englishman wanted to protect with his sword.

The Hundred Years' War, 1337–1453

In the twelfth and thirteenth centuries, centralization of royal power in England and France had proceeded almost without interruption. In the fourteenth century, matters changed in both countries. Questions of the nature of royal power, common responsibility, and hereditary rights to rule challenged the power of the English and French monarchs. In both countries, competition began largely over dynastic issues, but by the mid-fifteenth century, resolution of the wars led to governments with a more distinctly national tone to them.

ENGLAND

In England, fears arising from the growing power of the English crown and the weakness of a gullible king brought issues to a head during the reign of Edward II (r. 1307–1327). By the early fourteenth century, resident justices of the peace (JPs) were replacing the expensive and inefficient system of traveling justices. In theory, the JPs were royal officials doing the king's bidding, but this was often not the case in reality. These unpaid local officials were modestly well-to-do gentry, who were often clients of local magnates. When the king was not vigilant, justices were prone to use their offices to carry out local vendettas and feuds and to protect the interests of the wealthy and powerful.

The barons, the titled lords of England, were interested in controlling more than just local justices. Fearing that Edward II would continue many of the centralizing policies of his father, the barons passed reform ordinances in 1311, limiting the king's right to wage war, leave the realm, grant lands or castles, or appoint chief justices and chancellors without the approval of Parliament, which they dominated. Special taxes or subsidies were to be paid to the public Exchequer rather than into the king's private treasury. Some of these ordinances were later voided, but the tradition of parliamentary consent remained a key principle of English constitutional history.

The baronial influence grew because Edward II was a weak and naive king, easily influenced by court favorites. After a humiliating defeat at the hands of the Scots at the Battle of Bannockburn (1314), his position steadily deteriorated until he was deposed in 1327 by a coalition of barons led by his wife, Queen Isabella. After a short regency, their son, Edward III (r. 1327–1377), assumed the throne. He was a cautious king, ever aware of the violence and rebelliousness of the baronage.

FRANCE

French kings seemed significantly more powerful in the early fourteenth century. A complex succession crisis, however, made clear the limits of French kingship. In 1328, the direct Capetian line, which had sired the kings of France since the election of Hugh Capet in 987, finally died out. The last Capetians did produce daughters, but by the fourteenth century, many argued that according to custom the French crown should pass through the male line only. Thus, the French nobility selected as king Philip of Valois (Philip VI; r. 1328–1350), a cousin of the last king through the male line (Charles IV; r. 1322–1328). He was chosen in preference to the daughters of the last Capetian kings and, more significantly, in preference to King Edward III of England, whose mother, Isabella, was the daughter of King Philip IV (r. 1285–1314).

Controversy over succession was just one of the disputes between the French and English. An even longer-standing issue was the status of lands within France that belonged to the English kings. In 1340, climaxing a century of tensions over English possessions in France, Edward III of England formally claimed the title "King of France," and the Hundred Years' War was on.

The war was marked by quick English raids and only occasional pitched battles. With a population of about 16 million, France was far richer and more populous than England. On at least one occasion, the French managed to field an army of over 50,000; the English mustered only 32,000

Hundred Years' War
Series of conflicts, 1337–1453, fought over English claims within the French monarchy. It ended with the nearly complete expulsion of the English from French lands.

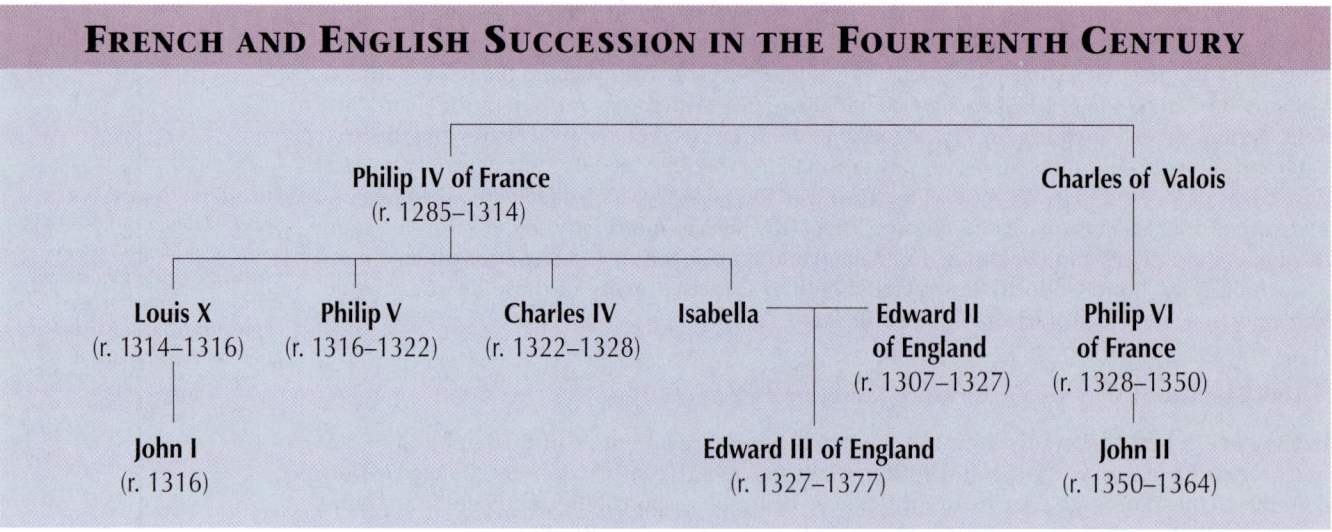

FRENCH AND ENGLISH SUCCESSION IN THE FOURTEENTH CENTURY

at most. These armies were easily the largest ever assembled by a medieval European kingdom. In almost every engagement, the English were outnumbered. Their strategy, therefore, was to avoid pitched battles except on the most advantageous terms. Edward III engaged in extremely destructive raids, hoping to lure the French into ill-considered attacks. The English stole what they could, destroyed what they could not steal, and captured enemy knights to hold for ransom.

STAGES OF THE WAR The war can be divided into four stages. The first stage (1337–1360) was characterized by a rapid series of English assaults and victories. The few pitched battles, including Crécy (1346) and Poitiers (1356), show how Edward's strategy worked (see **MAP 11.1**). In these cases, the English gathered their forces in careful defensive positions and took advantage of an individualistic French chivalric ethos according to which, in the words of one knight, "who does the most is worth the most." The key to the English defensive position was the use of longbowmen and cannon. Arrows from the longbow had more penetrating power than a bolt from a crossbow, and the longbow could be fired much more rapidly. By 1300, Europeans had forged cannon for use in siege warfare and to protect defensive positions. Although there is a debate over how effective they were, when used in combination with the longbow, they effectively disrupted and scattered advancing troops.

In the second stage of the war (1360–1396), French forces responded more cautiously to the English tactics and slowly regained much of the territory they had lost. However, during this stage, the disruptions and expenses of war placed a huge burden on both French and English society. First, in the wake of the French defeat at Poitiers in 1356, France was rocked by a series of urban and rural revolts and protests. Later, in 1381, the English faced a similar series of protests over taxes and the costs of war. Finally, because of stress over the war and general noble dissatisfaction, Richard II was forced to abdicate the English throne. Parliament then elected as king Henry IV (r. 1399–1413), the first ruler from the House of Lancaster. Richard died in prison under mysterious circumstances in 1400.

A fateful shift occurred in the third stage of the war (1396–1422). King Charles VI (r. 1380–1422) of France suffered bouts of insanity throughout his long reign, which made effective French government almost impossible. The English king Henry V (r. 1413–1422) renewed his family's claim to the French throne.

The Battle at Agincourt The English victory at Agincourt marked the high point of English influence in France. Once again English archers defeated a larger, mounted force. (The Granger Collection, New York)

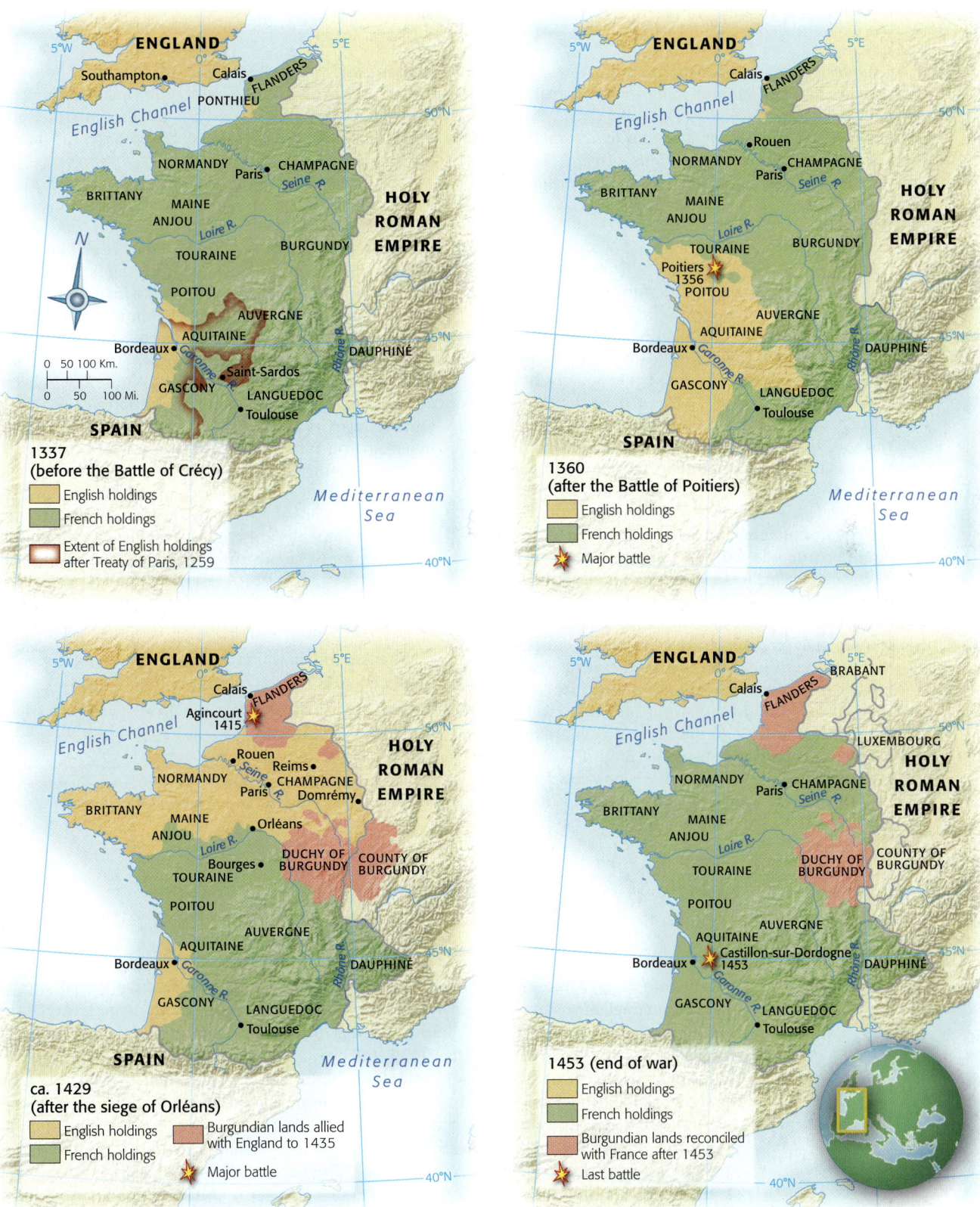

🌐 **MAP 11.1—England and France in the Hundred Years' War**
The succession of maps suggests both why hit-and-run tactics worked for the English early in the war and why the English were ultimately unable to defeat the French and take control of all of France.

The Inquisition of Joan of Arc

An important question at the trial of Joan of Arc was whether her acts had any authoritative value: Did the voices she heard originate with God or the Devil? The judges wanted to demonstrate to their own satisfaction that Joan was one of "the sowers of deceitful inventions" of which the Gospels warned. They fully expected that external signs could reveal hidden truths. The following memorandum is a summation of the commission's case against the maid.

You said that your king received a sign by which he knew you were sent from God, that it was St. Michael, in the company of a host of angels. ... You have said that you are certain of future and contingent events that you recognized men you had never seen, through the voices of St. Catherine and St. Margaret. ... Regarding this article, the clergy find superstition, divination, ... and vain boasting.

You said that you wore and still wear man's dress at God's command and to His good pleasure, for you had instruction from God to wear this dress, and so you put on a short tunic, jerkin, and hose with many points. You even wear your hair cut above the ears, without keeping about you anything to denote your sex, save what nature has given you. ... The clergy declare that you blaspheme against God, despising Him and His sacraments, that you transgress divine law, Holy Scripture and the canons of the Church, ... that you are given to idolatry and worship of yourself and your clothes, according to the customs of the heathen.

You have declared that you know well that God loves certain living persons better than you, and that you learned this by revelation from St. Catherine and St. Margaret; also that those saints speak French, not English, as they are not on the side of the English. And since you knew that your voices were for your king, you began to dislike the Burgundians. ... Such matters the clergy pronounce to be a rash and presumptuous assertion, a superstitious divination, a blasphemy uttered against St. Catherine and St. Margaret, and a transgression of the commandment to love our neighbors. ...

You declared that to those whom you call St. Michael, St. Catherine and St. Margaret, you did reverence, bending the knee ... vowing them your virginity ... now touching these matters, the clergy affirm. ... You are an idolatress, an invoker of demons, an apostate from the faith, a maker of rash statements, a swearer of an unlawful oath.

And you have said ... that you know that all the deeds of which you have been accused in your trial were wrought according to the command of God and that it was impossible for you to do otherwise. ... Wherefore the clergy declare you to be schismatic, an unbeliever in the unity and authority of the Church, apostate and obstinately erring from the faith. ... [The inquisitor admonished her,] "You have believed in apparitions lightly, instead of turning to God in devout prayer to grant you certainty; and you have not consulted prelates or learned ecclesiastics to enlighten yourself: although, considering your condition and the simplicity of your knowledge, you ought to have done so."

QUESTIONS

1. What are the signs that indicated to the judges that Joan was a heretic?
2. Why do the judges believe that Joan's "voices" are false?

Source: "The Inquisition of Joan of Arc" from *The Trial of Jeanne d'Arc*, trans. W.P. Barrett, 1932. Reprinted by permission of Gotham House.

At Agincourt in 1415, the English (led by Henry himself) again enticed a larger French army into attacking an English position fortified by longbows and cannon. By the terms of the Treaty of Troyes (1420), Charles VI's son (the future Charles VII) was declared illegitimate and disinherited; Henry married Catherine, the daughter of Charles VI, and he was declared the legitimate heir to the French throne. A final English victory seemed assured, but both Charles VI and Henry V died in 1422, leaving Henry's infant son, Henry VI (r. 1422–1461), to inherit both thrones.

The kings' deaths ushered in the final stage of the Hundred Years' War (1422–1453), the French reconquest. In 1428, military and political power seemed firmly in the hands of the English and the great aristocrats. Yet, in a stunning series of events, the French were able to reverse the situation.

JOAN OF ARC In 1429, with the aid of the mysterious **Joan of Arc** (d. 1431), the French king, Charles VII, was able to raise the English siege of Orléans (or-lay-OHN) and begin the reconquest of the north of France. Joan was the daughter of prosperous peasants from an area of Burgundy that had suffered under the English and their Burgundian allies. Her "voices" told her to go to the king and assist him in driving out the English. Like many late medieval mystics, she reported regular visions of divine revelation. Even politically or militarily important female leaders depended initially on religious charisma. One of the tests that supported Joan's claim to divine direction was her identification of Charles, who had disguised himself among his courtiers. Dressed as a man, she was Charles's most famed and feared military leader. With Joan's aid, the king was crowned in the cathedral at Reims, the traditional site of French coronations. Joan was captured during an audacious attack on Paris itself and eventually fell into English hands. Because of her "unnatural dress" and her claim to divine guidance, she was condemned and burned as a heretic in 1431. (See the feature, "The Written Record: The Inquisition of Joan of Arc.") A heretic only to the English and their supporters, Joan almost instantly became a symbol of French resistance. Pope Calixtus III reversed the condemnation in 1456, and Joan was canonized in 1920. The heretic became Saint Joan, patron of France.

Despite Joan's capture, the French advance continued. By 1450, the English had lost all their major centers except Calais (ca-LAY). In 1453, the French armies captured the fortress of Castillon-sur-Dordogne (kasti-YON sir dor-DON-ya) in what was to be the last battle of the war (see **Map 11.1**). There was no treaty, only a cessation of hostilities.

The war touched almost every aspect of life in western Europe: political, religious, economic, and social. It ranged beyond the borders of France, as Scotland, Castile, Aragon, and German principalities were, at various times, drawn into the struggle. French and English support for rival popes prevented early settlement of the Great Schism in the papacy (see page 291). Further, the war caused a general rise in the level of violence in society. As Henry V casually observed, "War without fire is as bland as sausages without mustard."[6] Because of the highly profitable lightning raids, this war was never bland. During periods of truce, many soldiers simply ranged through France, pillaging small towns and ravaging the countryside. Others went in search of work as mercenaries, especially in Germany, Poland, and Italy. Truces in France did not necessarily mean peace in Europe.

Italy

Compared with France and England, fourteenth- and fifteenth-century Italy was a land of cities. In northern Europe, a town of over 20,000 or 30,000 people was unusual; only Paris and London boasted more than 100,000 people in the fourteenth century. Yet, at one time or another, in the late Middle Ages, Milan, Venice, Florence, and Naples all had populations near or exceeding 100,000, and countless other Italian towns boasted populations of well over 30,000. Unlike northern European states with their kings or emperors, however, the Italian peninsula lacked a unifying force. The centers of power were in Italy's flourishing cities. Political life revolved around the twin issues of who should dominate city governments and how cities could learn to coexist peacefully.

By the late thirteenth century, political power in most Italian towns was divided among three major groups. First was the old urban nobility that could trace its wealth back to grants of property and rights from kings, emperors, and bishops in the tenth and eleventh centuries. Second was the merchant families who had grown wealthy in the twelfth and thirteenth centuries, as Italians led the European economic expansion into the Mediterranean. Third, challenging these entrenched urban groups were the modest artisans and merchants who had organized trade, neighborhood, or militia groups and referred to themselves as the *popolo*, or "people." Townspeople gathered together in factions based on wealth, family, profession, neighborhood, and even systems of clientage that reached back into the villages from which many of them had come. "War and hatred have so multiplied among the Italians," observed one Florentine, "that in every town there is a division and enmity between two parties of citizens."

Riven with factions, townspeople often would turn control of their government over to a *signor* (sin-YOUR), a "lord" or "tyrant," often a local noble with a private army. Once firmly in power, the tyrant often allowed the government to continue to function as it had, requiring only that he control all major political appointments. The process might appear democratic, but it represented a profound shift in power. In the case of Milan, the noble Viscontis (vis-KON-tees) used support from the emperor Henry VII (r. 1308–1313) to drive their opponents out of the city. Eventually granting Milan and its territories as a duchy, the Viscontis, and later their Sforza successors, made marriage alliances with the French crown and created a splendid court culture. In a series of wars between the 1370s and 1450s, the dukes of Milan expanded their political control throughout most of Lombardy, Liguria, and, temporarily, Tuscany. The Viscontis maintained control of the city and much of the region of Lombardy until the last scion of the family died in 1447.

Joan of Arc Charismatic peasant who heard voices telling her to assist the French crown in its war against England. She was captured and eventually executed as a heretic.

City-States

THE REPUBLICS The great republics of Venice and Florence escaped domination by signori, but only by undertaking significant constitutional change. In both republics, political life had been disrupted by the arrival of immigrants and by the demands of recently enriched merchants and speculators for a voice in government. In 1297, reacting to increased competition for influence, the Venetian government began a series of reforms that would come to be known as the "Closing of the Grand Council." This enlarged the council to about eleven hundred members from those families eligible for public office, but its eventual effect was to freeze out subsequent arrivals from ever rising to elite status. The Venetian patriciate became a closed urban nobility. Political, factional, and economic tensions were hidden beneath a veneer of serenity as Venetians developed a myth of public-spirited patricians who governed in the interests of all the people, leaving others free to enrich themselves in trade and manufacture.

In Florence, the arguments over citizenship and the right of civic participation disrupted public life. Violent wealthy families, immigrants, and artisans of modest background were cut off from civic participation. A series of reforms, culminating in the Ordinances of Justice of 1293 to 1295, restricted political participation in Florence to members in good standing of certain merchant and artisan guilds. Members of violence-prone families were defined as *Magnate* (literally, "the powerful") and disqualified from holding public office. In spite of the reforms, political power remained concentrated in the hands of the great families, whose wealth was based primarily on banking and mercantile investments. These families used their political influence and economic power to dominate Florentine life.

There were short-lived attempts to reform the system and extend the rights of political participation to include the more modest artisans and laborers. The most dramatic was in 1378, when the Ciompi (CHOMP-ee), unskilled workers in Florence's woolen industry, led a popular revolution hoping to expand participation in government and limit the authority of the guild masters over semiskilled artisans and day laborers. They created new guilds to represent the laborers who had no voice in government. Barely six weeks after the Ciompi insurrection, however, wealthy conservatives began a reaction suppressing, exiling, or executing the leaders of the movement and eventually suppressing the new guilds. Political and economic power was now even more firmly in the grip of influential patricians.

Following a crisis in 1434, brought on by war and high taxes, virtual control of Florentine politics fell into the hands of Cosimo de' Medici (day-MAY-di-chi), the wealthiest banker in the city. From 1434 to 1494, Cosimo, his son Piero, his grandson Lorenzo, and Lorenzo's son dominated the government in Florence. Although the Medicis were always careful to pay homage to Florentine republican traditions, their control was virtually as complete as that of the lords of towns such as Ferrara and Milan.

Indeed, by the middle of the fifteenth century, little differentiated the republics—Florence and Venice—from cities, such as Milan and Mantua, where lords held sway. Although Florentines maintained that they intervened to protect Florentine and Tuscan "liberty" when the Viscontis of Milan threatened Tuscany and central Italy, their interests went beyond simple defense. Relations among the great cities of Milan, Venice, Florence, Rome, and Naples were stabilized by the Peace of Lodi and the creation of the Italian League in 1454. In response to endemic warfare in Italy and the looming threat of the Ottoman Turks in the eastern Mediterranean (see pages 312–314), the five powers agreed to the creation of spheres of influence that would prevent any one of them from expanding at the expense of the others.

The Journey of the Magi The story of the journey of the Magi to Bethlehem to find the baby Jesus seemed a perfect image of the power and wisdom of rulers. This painting (a detail) of the Magi was commissioned for the private chapel of Cosimo de' Medici, the de facto ruler of Florence. (Palazzo Medici Riccardi, Florence/Scala/Art Resource, NY)

The limits of these territorial states became clear when King Charles VIII of France invaded Italy in 1494 to assert his hereditary claim to the kingdom of Naples. The French invasion touched off a devastating series of wars called the Habsburg-Valois Wars (1496–1559). French claims were challenged by the Habsburg emperors and also by the Spanish, who themselves made claims on southern Italy and much of Lombardy. The cost of prolonged warfare kept almost all governments in a state of crisis.

In Florence, the wars destroyed the old Medici-dominated regime and brought in a new republican government. Anti-Medici efforts were initially led by the popular Dominican preacher Girolamo Savonarola (1452–1498). In the constitutional debates after 1494, Savonarola argued that true political reform required a sweeping purge of the evils of society. Gangs of youth flocked to his cause, attacking prostitutes and homosexuals. Many of his followers held "bonfires of vanities," burning wigs, silks, and other luxuries. In 1498, when his followers had lost influence in the government, Savonarola was arrested, tortured, and executed.

In spite of republican reforms, new fortresses, and a citizen militia, the Florentine government was unable to defend itself from papal and imperial armies. In 1512, the Habsburg emperor restored Medici control of Florence. The Medicis later became dukes and then grand dukes of Tuscany. The grand duchy of Tuscany remained an independent, integrated, and well-governed state until the French Revolution of 1789. Venice also managed to maintain its republican form of government and its territorial state until the French Revolution, but like the grand dukes of Tuscany, the governors of Venice were no longer able to act independently of the larger European powers.

The Habsburg-Valois Wars ended with the Treaty of Cateau-Cambrésis (kah-toe kam-bray-SEE) in 1559, which left the Spanish kings in control of Milan, Naples, Sardinia, and Sicily. Thus, the Spanish dominated Italy, but without the centralizing control typical of England and France. Venice, Tuscany, the Papal States, and even lesser republics and principalities retained significant influence, as Italy remained a land of regional governments.

SECTION SUMMARY

- The Hundred Years' War was fought over English dynastic claims within the French kingdom.
- The costs of war contributed to social and political unrest in both countries.
- As a result of the war, the English lost all their significant possessions within the French kingdom.
- Italy was a land of populous, independent cities and regional states.
- By the fifteenth century, most Italian governments were dominated by merchant oligarchies or by lords.

CRISIS IN ECONOMY AND SOCIETY

How were economic and social structures changed by plague and economic crisis?

After nearly three centuries of dramatic growth, Europe, in 1300, was seriously overpopulated, with estimates ranging from about 80 million to as high as 100 million. In some parts of Europe, population would not be this dense again until the late eighteenth century. Opportunities dwindled because of overpopulation, famine, war, and epidemic, which also brought changes in trade and commerce. As the population began to decline, this trend, along with deflation and transformed patterns of consumption, affected agriculture, which was still the foundation of the European economy. Recovery from all these crises altered the structure and dynamics of families, the organization of work, and the culture in many parts of Europe. As a result of the crises, there had been a relative shift in economic and demographic vitality from Italy to England, France, and central Europe.

Famine and Declining Births

People in many parts of Europe were living on the edge of disaster in 1300. Given the low level of agricultural technology and the limited amount of land available for cultivation, it became increasingly difficult for the towns and countryside to feed and support the expanding population.

Growing numbers of people competed for land to farm and for jobs. Farm sizes declined throughout Europe, as parents tended to divide their land among their children. Rents for farmland increased, as landlords found that they could play one land-hungry farmer against another. Competition for jobs kept urban wages low, and when taxes were added to high rents and low wages, many peasants and artisans found it difficult to marry and raise families. Thus, because of reduced opportunities brought on by overpopulation, poor townspeople and peasants tended to marry late and have smaller families.

More dramatic than this crisis of births were the deadly famines that occurred in years of bad harvests. The great famine of 1315 to 1322 marks a turning point in the economic history of Europe. Wet and cold weather repeatedly ruined crops in much of northern Europe. Food stocks were quickly exhausted, and mass starvation followed. At Ypres, in Flanders, 2,800 people (about 10 percent of the population) died in just six months and shortages continued. Seven other severe famines were reported in the south of France or Italy during the fourteenth century.

If Europe's problem had merely been one of famine brought on by overpopulation, rapid recovery should have been possible. However, the difficulties of overpopulation were exacerbated by war and plague. As noted previously, the devastation of cities and the countryside was a common tactic in the Hundred Years' War. It was also typical of the local wars in parts of Spain, Germany, and especially Italy. The destruction of trees and vineyards and the theft of livestock made it difficult for rural populations to survive. Then, in 1348, the **Black Death** or "the great Mortality," as contemporaries called it, struck Europe.

Black Death An epidemic, possibly of bubonic plague, that wiped out one-third or more of Europe's population between 1348 and 1351. It initiated almost three centuries of epidemics.

The Black Death

Today there is no consensus as to what caused the Black Death. In the early twentieth century, after the bacillus that causes bubonic plague was identified by French and Japanese physicians in Hong Kong, it was assumed that bubonic plague was the cause. Subsequently, there have been controversial claims that DNA fragments of bubonic plague have been found in mass graves. Yet, bubonic plague usually travels slowly and infects a relatively small portion of a given population. By contrast, the Black Death seemed to race across Europe, wiping out entire families and infecting whole cities. Because of this evidence, some historical epidemiologists have speculated that the cause may actually have been anthrax or even a "hemorrhagic plague" similar to the Ebola virus.

THE SPREAD OF THE DISEASE

Although the historical identification of the Black Death remains controversial, contemporaries had little doubt about the source of the disease. Genoese traders, they believed, contracted the plague in Caffa, on the Black Sea coast. Infected sailors carried the disease south into Egypt and west into Sicily, then on to Genoa and Venice. From there, it followed established trade routes first into central Italy; later to the south of France, the Low Countries, and England; and finally, through the North and Baltic Seas, into Germany and the Slavic lands to the east (see **MAP 11.2**).

Mortality rates varied, but generally 60 percent or more of those infected died. In the initial infestation of 1348 to 1351, 25 to 35 percent of Europe's population may have died. In some of Europe's larger cities, the death rate may have been as high as 60 percent. In Florence, for example, the population probably declined from about 90,000 to about 50,000 or even less. The shock and disruption were immense. Governments in some towns simply ceased to function at the height of the epidemic. Chroniclers reported that no one could be found to care for the sick or bury the dead. Although abandonment of the sick was probably more a fear than a reality, the epidemic nonetheless significantly disrupted daily life.

Just as areas were rebounding from the initial outbreak of the plague, it returned between 1360 and 1363, and then, for three centuries thereafter, almost no generation could avoid it. It has been calculated that in central Italy, where the best records are available, the plague returned on average every eleven years between 1350 and 1400. Less is known about the plague in Muslim lands and in the eastern Mediterranean, but the situation seems to have been similar to the European experience. Because the plague tended to carry off the young, the almost generational return of the disease accounts for the depressed population levels found in many parts of Europe until the late fifteenth century and in western Asia until the late seventeenth or eighteenth century.

Lacking an understanding of either contagion or infection, fourteenth-century doctors depended on traditional theories inherited from the Greeks, especially the work of Galen (GAY-len), to treat the plague. In Galenic medicine, good health depended on the proper balance of bodily and environmental forces; it could be upset by corrupt air, the movement of planets, and even violent

🌐 **MAP 11.2—The Progress of the Black Death**

The Black Death did not advance evenly across Europe; rather, as is clear from the dates at which it struck various regions, it followed the main lines of trade and communication.

shifts in emotions. Yet, in the fifteenth and sixteenth centuries, as the rhythms of the infestations became clearer, towns and, later, territorial governments perceived the contagious nature of the disease. Officials instituted increasingly effective quarantines and embargoes to restrict the movement of goods and people from areas where the plague was raging. Some argue that it was the eventual extension of these efforts throughout Europe that led to the gradual reduction and then disappearance of the plague from western Europe by the early eighteenth century.

Alongside medical theory, however, another class of explanations developed. Taking a lead from miracle stories in which Jesus linked illness and sin, many Christians considered the Black Death a signal of the Last Judgment, or at least a sign of the severe judgment of God on a sinful world. Given that view, a traditional, and logical, religious response was to urge various moral reforms and penitential acts, such as charitable gifts, special prayers, and holy processions. (See the feature, "The Visual Record: A Painting of the Plague.") Many Muslim theologians also concluded that "the plague is part of Allah's punishment." Women were often thought to be a source of moral pollution and hence one of the causes of God's wrath. In Muslim Egypt, women were ordered off the streets; in Christian Europe prostitutes were driven out of towns.

A movement of penitents called "flagellants" arose in Hungary and spread quickly into Germany and across France and the Low Countries. In an imitation of Christ's life and sufferings, they sought to atone in their own bodies for the sins of the world. Following an ancient Christian tradition, they ritually beat (flagellated) themselves between the shoulders with metal-tipped whips. Through their

SOCIAL AND CULTURAL RESPONSES

processions and sufferings, these pilgrims hoped to bring about a moral and religious transformation of society. The arrival of flagellants was often an occasion for an end of feuds and political violence within a community. But their arrival, just as often, was an occasion for political and even religious unrest. Authorities recognized the flagellants and the leaders of the religious riots as dangerous and drove them from towns.

In a quest for a purer, truly Christian society, the flagellants brought suspicion on all those who were not Christian or who were otherwise suspect. Some parts of Europe witnessed murderous attacks on outsiders, especially lepers and Jews, who were suspected of spreading the contagion in an attempt to bring down Latin Christendom. These attacks probably have more to do with tensions and fears already existing in parts of Europe than with the provocations of the flagellants. Like many other anti-Semitic myths, the rumors of wells poisoned by lepers and Jews seemed to arise in the south of France and spread in their most virulent forms to German towns along the Rhine. In Strasbourg attacks on Jews preceded the arrival of the plague. Except in a few districts, officials opposed attacks on Jews, lepers, and heretics. Doctors and churchmen often observed that Jews were unlikely culprits, since the plague claimed Jewish as well as Christian victims. Despite official rejection of popular rumors and fears, from the mid-fourteenth century, life became more difficult for the Jews of Christian Europe.

It was a commonplace among contemporary chroniclers that "so many did die that everyone thought it was the end of the world." Yet it was the very young, the elderly, and the poor—those least likely to pay taxes, own shops, or produce children—who were the most common victims. And even in towns, such as Florence, where mortality rates were extraordinarily high, recovery from the initial epidemic was rapid. Government offices were closed at most for only a few weeks; markets reopened as soon as the death rate began to decline; and within two years, tax receipts were back at preplague levels. Yet plague, fear of plague, and social and economic disruption caused by epidemic disease became a regular feature of European life. Thus, famine, warfare, plague, and population decline fueled the economic and social transformations of the late Middle Ages.

Trade and Agriculture

In the aftermath of plague, the economy of Europe changed in a number of profound ways. Disruptions brought on by population decline were accompanied by changes in the basic structure of economic life. In particular, Italy's domination of the European economy was challenged by the growth of trade and manufacturing in many other parts of Europe. Further, by 1500, the relative power of Italian bankers declined as they came to face competition from equally astute northern bankers.

Saint Roch Cured by an Angel Saint Roch is often shown with an exposed plague bubo. The image offered Christians comfort since he was cured because of his faith and charity. It offers modern historians evidence that bubonic plague was responsible for at least some of the mortality. (Courtesy, Bayerisches Nationalmuseum)

Discussions of the economy must begin with Italy because it was the key point of contact between Europe and the international economy. In 1300, Italian merchants sold woolens produced in Flanders and Italy to Arab traders in North Africa, who sold them along the African coast and as far south as the Niger Delta. The Italians used the gold that they collected in payment to buy spices and raw materials in Byzantium, Egypt, and even China. They resold these highly prized goods in the cities and at regional fairs of northern Europe. Italian traders also sold spices, silks, and other luxuries throughout Europe, from England to Poland.

Because of their expertise in moving bullion and goods and their ready sources of capital, Italian merchants, such as the Ricciardis of Lucca who flourished in England, were ideal bankers and financial advisers to the popes and European rulers, who appreciated sources of ready capital. In times of war, rulers tended to trade the rights to various revenues to Italian bankers, who had cash at hand. Merchants from Cremona, Genoa, Florence, and Siena forged commercial agreements with the kings of France, Aragon, and Castile, and with the papacy. The most powerful bank in fifteenth-century Europe was the Medici bank of Florence. Founded in 1397 by Giovanni de' Medici (1360–1429), the bank grew quickly because of its role as papal banker. Medici agents transferred papal revenues from all parts of Europe to Rome and managed papal alum mines, which provided an essential mineral to the growing cloth industry.

The dramatic career of the Frenchman Jacques Coeur (1395?–1456) demonstrates that by the mid-fifteenth century, Italian merchants were not the only Europeans who understood international trade. After making a fortune trading in southern France, Coeur managed the French royal mint and became the financial adviser of King Charles VII (r. 1422–1461). He put the French monarchy back on a solid financial footing after the Hundred Years' War, in the process, becoming the wealthiest individual in France.

By 1500, Italians faced increased competition from local merchants throughout Europe. From as early as the late thirteenth century, trade along the North and Baltic Seas in northern Europe was dominated by the **Hanseatic League**, an association of over a hundred trading cities centered on the German city of Lübeck. By the late fourteenth and early fifteenth centuries, the Hansa towns controlled grain shipments from eastern Europe to England and Scandinavia. The league's domination waned in the second half of the fifteenth century, however, as Dutch, English, and even southern German merchants gained shares of the wool, grain, and fur trades.

In contrast to the Hanseatic League of towns, merchants in southern Germany adopted Italian techniques of trade, manufacture, and finance to expand their influence throughout central Europe. German merchants regularly bought spices in the markets of Venice and distributed them in central and eastern Europe. By the fifteenth century, the townspeople of southern Germany also produced linen and cotton cloth, which found ready markets in central and eastern Europe.

The Fugger (FOO-ger) family of Augsburg in southern Germany was the most prosperous of the German commercial families. Jacob Fugger (1459–1525) was a dominant figure in the spice trade and also participated in a number of unusually large loans to a succession of German princes. Jacob Fugger's wealth increased fourfold between 1470 and 1500. The Fuggers were indispensable allies of the German emperors. Jacob himself ensured the election of Charles V as Holy Roman emperor in 1519, making a series of loans that allowed Charles to buy the influence that he needed to win election.

As wealthy as the great merchants were, in most parts of Europe, prosperity was still tied to agriculture and the production of food grains. In northern and western Europe, foodstuffs were produced on the manorial estates of great churchmen and nobles. These estates were worked by a combination of farmers paying rents, serfs who owed a variety of labor services, and day laborers who were hired during planting and harvesting. In the face of a decimated population, landlords and employers found themselves competing for the reduced number of laborers who had survived the plague.

Cloth manufacture, not agriculture, was the part of the European economy that changed most dramatically in the late Middle Ages. First in Flanders, then later in England, Germany, and the rest of Europe, production shifted from urban workshops to the countryside. Industries in rural areas tended to be free of controls on quality or techniques. Rural production, whether in Flanders, England, or Lombardy, became the most dynamic part of the industry.

Rural cloth production was least expensive because it could be done as occasional or part-time labor by farmers, or by their wives or children, during slack times of the day or season.

ITALIAN AND NORTHERN MERCHANTS

NEW TRADING PATTERNS

Hanseatic League   An association of over a hundred German trading towns, which dominated trade in the North Sea and Baltic Sea regions during the fourteenth and fifteenth centuries.

THE RURAL ECONOMY

A Painting of the Plague

Writers who survived the coming of pestilential disease in 1348 described a world of terror in which things seemed changed forever. Look at this painting, St. Sebastian Interceding for the Plague-Stricken, created by the Flemish artist Josse Lieferinxe between 1497 and 1499. One dying man seems to be falling terrified to the ground, while a female bystander in the background screams in alarm. Images of Christ, Saint Sebastian (pierced by arrows), a devil, and a priest seem to indicate that something terrifying and undreamed-of is happening. But what exactly was the terror, and what had changed?

The art of the later Middle Ages is an extremely valuable source for understanding social and religious values. As you look at St. Sebastian Interceding for the Plague-Stricken, the first step is to understand what men and women in the fourteenth and fifteenth centuries thought about death. After 1400 European Christians often depicted the universality of death in paintings showing the Dance of Death. The motif varies, but typically Death grasps the hands of men and women, rich and poor, noble and peasant, and leads them away. Deathbed scenes were another popular motif. In the late Middle Ages most people believed that at death the good and evil acts committed by an individual were tallied in the Book of Life and the person was either granted eternal life, first in Purgatory and then Paradise, or consigned to eternal suffering in Hell. Judgment scenes often depict the Virgin Mary or another saint pleading before God or contending with the Devil or demons over the souls of the dying.

It was essential for people to prepare for a good death. Individuals studied the artes moriendi, or "arts of dying." A lingering, painful illness was often interpreted as an opportunity for penitential suffering that would benefit the soul. At the point of death, the dying person could confess and receive absolution for sins and the last sacraments of the church. From that moment on, he or she needed to maintain a calm faith, free from fear. Salvation and eternal life depended on avoiding further sin, especially the questioning of God's forgiveness and mercy. Death was a public event. Clergy, family, religious societies, even neighbors helped the dying person to avoid losing faith at the end. The person might pray, "Virgin Mary, Mother of God, I have placed my hope in you. Free my soul from care, and from Hell, and bitter death."*

The concept of a good death is critical to understanding the European response to the plague. To be sure, individuals rarely look forward to death, then or now. Numerous writers and chroniclers lamented the suddenness of death and the lack of priests to hear confessions. Individuals who were healthy in the morning might be dead by nightfall. The suddenness, the lack of time to prepare for a good death, heightened the dread that accompanied the onset of the illness.

Medieval Christians turned to saints to represent them before God at the point of death and to stop the onslaught of the plague. Three patron saints were especially popular. The Virgin Mary was often shown using her cloak to shelter towns and individuals from arrows carrying pestilence. Saint Roch, himself a victim of the plague, was thought to intercede and protect those who prayed in his name. And Saint Sebastian, an early Christian who as part of his elaborate martyrdom survived being shot with arrows (later understood as symbols of death caused by the plague), was thought to be an especially effective patron during epidemics. In times of plague, people went on pilgrimages to local shrines dedicated to these or local saints, carried images of the saints in processions, and built churches and chapels in honor of the saints in thanks for deliverance from the plague.

With these issues in mind, what do we see in Lieferinxe's painting? The painting portrays an outbreak of the plague. We note first the body of the dead person, carefully shrouded.

Because production was likely to be finished in the countryside (beyond guild supervision), the merchant was free to move the cloth to wherever it could be sold most easily and profitably; guild masters had no control over price or quality.

Two other developments also changed the woolen trade of the fifteenth century: the rise of Spain as an exporter of unprocessed wool and the emergence of England, long recognized as a source of prime wool, as a significant producer of finished cloth. Spain was an ideal region for the pasturing of livestock. By the fifteenth century, highly prized Spanish wool from merino sheep was regularly exported to Italy, Flanders, and England. By 1500, over three million sheep grazed in Castile alone, and revenues from duties on wool formed the backbone of royal finance.

In England, in contrast, economic transformation was tied to cloth production. During the fifteenth century, England reduced its export of its high-quality raw wool and began instead to export its own finished cloth. In 1350, the English exported just over 5,000 bolts of cloth. By the 1470s, exports had risen to 63,000 bolts, and they doubled again by the 1520s. The growth of cloth exports contributed enormously to the expansion of London. During the fourteenth and fifteenth centuries, English commerce became increasingly controlled by London merchant-adventurers. Soon after 1500, over 80 percent of the cloth for export passed through the hands

Ideally the dead, like the corpse here, were taken to a church by friends and relatives and given a Christian burial. This was an important part of the ritual meant to ease the suffering of the soul in Purgatory. But chroniclers often reported that so many died, and died so quickly, that no one could be found to bury them properly. In many towns the dead were gathered on carts and hauled to gaping common graves outside the towns. We can see one such cart leaving the castle in the background. In a series of images, then, Lieferinxe shows what mattered most to people. In the foreground is the shrouded body attended by a priest and other clerics bearing a cross. This person experienced a good death. In contrast, the man who has fallen behind the body is suffering a bad death, one that caught him unaware. He is the object of the concern and grief of those near him. In the sky just above the castle walls, a white-robed angel and a horned, ax-wielding demon contend over the souls of the dead and dying. At the top of the painting Christ listens to the prayers of Saint Sebastian. The painting thus portrays the impact and horror of plague and also the way Christians were expected to respond to it.

Returning to our original question, we can conclude that the terror of epidemic plague was not entirely like a modern panic. Medieval people saw the Black Death, its ghastly devastation, and its only possible solution or meaning in terms of traditional religious values: The true terror was to be caught unaware.

QUESTIONS

1. What is a good death?
2. What responses to epidemic diseases can you find in this image?
3. Which parts of the image illustrate panic and which do not?

Lieferinxe: St. Sebastian Interceding for the Plague-Stricken (Collection of The Walters Art Museum. Photo © The Walters Art Museum, Baltimore)

*Quoted in Philippe Ariès, *The Hour of Our Death* (New York: Knopf, 1981), p. 108.

---

of the Londoners. This development, coupled with the rise of London as a center of administration and consumption, laid the foundation for the economic and demographic growth that would make London the largest and most prosperous city in western Europe by the eighteenth century.

The new structures of agriculture, manufacture, and trade in the fifteenth century challenged customs and institutions by admitting new entrepreneurs into the marketplace. However, Europe was still a conservative society in which social and political influence was more prized than economic wealth. Patricians in many European towns acted to dampen competition and preserve traditional values. Great banking families, such as the Medicis of Florence, tended to avoid competition and concentrations of capital. They did not try to drive their competitors out of business because the leaders of rival banks were their political and social peers. In northern Europe, governments in towns, such as Leiden, restricted the concentration of resources in the hands of the town's leading cloth merchants. Their aim was to ensure full employment for the town's laborers, political power for the guild masters, and social stability in the town.

In the wake of plague, the patricians' role, literally as "city fathers," was challenged by artisans and laborers. As wages rose because of population decline, workers demanded more voice in public life. Famed revolts, like the English Rising of 1381 (see page 296) or the Ciompi Revolt in

PATTERNS OF ECONOMIC LIFE

Street Life in Medieval Towns In a world dependent on natural lighting, shops were entirely open to the street. It made social and economic life much more public than it is in the modern world. (Bibliothèque nationale de France)

Italy (see page 300) are only the tip of the iceberg. Numerous other rebellions are recorded across Europe in the second half of the fourteenth century. Laborers attempted to use demand for labor to social and political advantage.

Full employment was not just for men. Although men had controlled the guilds and most crafts in the thirteenth and early fourteenth centuries, women's guilds existed in several European cities, including Paris and Cologne. In Italy, some women could be found among the more prosperous crafts. Women often practiced their trades in the context of the family. In Cologne, for instance, women produced the linen yarn and silk cloths that their husbands sold throughout Europe. Speaking of the silkmakers of Cologne, a report noted that "the women are much more knowledgeable about the trade than are the men." Unlike southern Europe, where women had no public roles, some northern towns apparently allowed women's guilds to protect their members' activities as artisans and even peddlers. Because they often worked before marriage, townswomen in northern Europe tended to marry at a later age than did women in Italy. Many women earned their own marriage dowries. Since they had their own sources of income and often managed the shop of a deceased husband, women could be surprisingly independent. They were consequently under less pressure to remarry at the death of a spouse. Although their economic circumstances varied considerably, up to a quarter of the households in northern towns such as Bern and Zurich were headed by women. Many of them were widows, but many others, perhaps a third, were women who had never married.

If plague and population decline created new opportunities for women, the fifteenth century brought new restrictions to women's lives. In England, brewing ale had been a highly profitable

Women at Work
Although guild records tend to ignore the contributions of women, many women worked in their husbands' shops. In this miniature a woman is selling jewelry. Widows often managed the shops they inherited. (Bibliothèque nationale de France)

part-time activity that women often combined with the running of a household. Ale was usually produced in small batches for household use and whatever went unconsumed would be sold. The introduction of beer changed matters. Because hops were added as a preservative during brewing, beer was easier to produce, store, and transport in large batches. Beer brewing became a lucrative full-time trade, reducing the demand for the alewife's product and providing work for men as brewers. At the same time, the rights of women to work in urban crafts and industries were reduced. Wealthy fathers became less inclined to allow wives and daughters to work outside the home. Guilds banned the use of female laborers in many trades and severely limited the rights of widows to supervise their spouses' shops.

Despite the narrowing of economic opportunities for women, the overall economic prospects of peasants and laborers improved. Lower rents and increased wages in the wake of the plague meant a higher standard of living for small farmers and laborers. Before the plague struck in 1348, most poor Europeans had subsisted on bread or grain-based gruel, consuming meat, fish, and cheese only a few times a week. A well-off peasant in England had lived on a daily ration of about two pounds of bread and a cup or two of oatmeal porridge washed down with three or four pints of ale. Poorer peasants generally drank water except on very special occasions. After the plague, laborers were more prosperous. Adults in parts of Germany may have consumed nearly a liter of wine, a third of a pound of meat, and a pound or more of bread each day. Elsewhere, people could substitute an equivalent portion of beer, ale, or cider for the wine. Hard times for landlords were good times for peasants and day laborers.

Landlords in England responded to the shortage of labor by converting their lands to grazing in order to produce wool for the growing textile market. In parts of Italy, landlords invested in canals, irrigation, and new crops in order to increase profits. In eastern Germany and Poland, landlords were able to take advantage of political and social unrest to force tenants into semi-free servile status. This so-called second serfdom created an impoverished workforce whose primary economic activity was in the lord's fields, establishing commercial grain farming. Increasingly in the second half of the century, grains cultivated in Poland and Prussia found their way to markets in England and the Low Countries. Europe east of the Elbe River became a major producer of grain, but at a heavy social cost.

The loss of perhaps a third of the urban population to the plague had serious consequences in the towns of Europe. Because of lower birthrates and higher death rates, late medieval towns needed a constant influx of immigrants to expand or even to maintain their populations. These immigrants did not find life in the cities easy, however. Citizenship in most towns was restricted to masters in the most important guilds, and local governments were in their hands, if not under their thumbs. In many towns, citizens constructed a system of taxation that worked to their own economic advantage and fell heavily on artisans and peasants living in territories controlled by the towns. Unskilled laborers and members of craft guilds depended for their economic well-being on personal relationships with powerful citizens who controlled the government and the markets. Peace and order in towns and in the countryside required a delicate balance of the interests of the well-to-do and the more humble. When that balance was shattered by war, plague, and economic depression, the result was often a popular revolt, such as the Ciompi insurrection of 1378 in Florence and the Rising of 1381 in England.

SECTION SUMMARY

- The Black Death may have killed one-third or more of Europe's population.

- In response to the epidemics many groups attacked outsiders, lepers, and Jews.

- Italy's medieval bankers and merchants dominated trade between Europe, North Africa, and the eastern Mediterranean.

- By the late fifteenth century, north European merchants challenged Italian economic leadership.

- Cloth production, arranged by a putting-out system, was Europe's most important industry.

- By the end of the fifteenth century, women found it increasingly difficult to maintain a significant role in Europe's craft industries.

THE CONSOLIDATION OF POLITICAL POWER, 1450–1500

How did the political makeup of Europe in 1500 differ from that in 1300?

By 1500, it seemed that the French royal lawyer's claim that all within the kingdom belonged to the king was finally accepted. With the exception of Italy and Germany, strong central governments recovered from the crises of war and civil unrest that wracked the fourteenth and fifteenth centuries. The Hundred Years' War and the resulting disorganization in France and England seemed to strike at the heart of the monarchies. However, through the foundation of standing armies and the careful consolidation of power in the royal court, both countries seemed stronger and more able to defend themselves in the second half of the century. And as the Italians learned in the wars following the French invasion of 1494, small regional powers were no match for the mighty monarchies.

France, England, and Scandinavia

In France, recovery from a century of war was based on a consolidation of the monarchy's power. A key to French military successes had been the creation of a paid professional army, which replaced the feudal host and mercenary companies of the fourteenth century. Charles VII created Europe's first standing army, a cavalry of about eight thousand nobles under the direct control of royal commanders. Charles also expanded his judicial claims. He and his son, Louis XI (r. 1461–1483), created new provincial *parlements*, or law courts, at Toulouse, Grenoble, Bordeaux, and Dijon. They also required that local laws and customs be registered and approved by the parlements.

A second key to maintaining royal influence was the rise of the French court as a political and financial center. Through careful appointments and judicious offers of annuities and honors, Charles VII and Louis XI drew the nobility to the royal court and made the nobles dependent on it. "The court," complained a frustrated noble, "is an assembly of people who, under the pretense of acting for the good of all, come together to diddle each other; for there's scarcely anyone who isn't engaged in buying and selling and exchanging … and sometimes for their money we sell them our ... humanity."[7] By 1500, France had fully recovered from the crisis of war and was once again a strong and influential state.

The fate of the English monarchy was quite different. Henry VI (r. 1422–1461) turned out to be weak-willed, immature, and prone to bouts of insanity—inherited, perhaps, from his French grandfather, Charles VI (see pages 296–298). The infirmity of Henry VI and the loss of virtually all French territories in 1453 led to factional battles known as the Wars of the Roses—the red rose symbolized Henry's House of Lancaster, the white the rival House of York. Edward of York eventually deposed Henry and claimed the Crown for himself as Edward IV (r. 1461–1483). He faced little opposition because few alternatives existed. English public life was again thrown into confusion, however, at Edward's death. The late king's brother, Richard, duke of Gloucester, claimed the protectorship over the 13-year-old king, Edward V (r. April–June 1483), and his younger brother. Richard seized the boys, who were placed in the Tower of London and never seen again. He proclaimed himself king and was crowned Richard III (r. 1483–1485). He withstood early challenges to his authority but in 1485 was killed in the Battle of Bosworth Field, near Coventry, by Henry Tudor, a leader of the Lancastrian faction. Henry married Elizabeth, the surviving child of Edward IV. Symbolically at least, the struggle between the rival claimants to the Crown appeared over.

Henry VII (r. 1485–1509), like Edward IV who preceded him, recognized the importance of avoiding war and taxation. Following Edward's example, Henry controlled local affairs through the traditional system of royal patronage. He also imitated Edward in emphasizing the dignity of the royal office. Henry solidified ties with Scotland and Spain by marrying his daughter, Margaret Tudor, to James IV of Scotland and his sons, Arthur and (after Arthur's death) Henry, to Catherine of Aragon, daughter of the Spanish rulers Ferdinand and Isabella. The English monarchy of the late fifteenth century departed little from previous governments. The success of Henry VII was based on several factors: the absence of powerful opponents; lower taxation thanks to twenty-five years of peace; and the desire, shared by ruler and ruled alike, for an orderly realm built on the assured succession of a single dynasty.

Public authority varied greatly across Scandinavia. In Norway, Denmark, and Sweden the power of the king was always mediated by the influence of the council, made up of the country's leading landowners. Power was based on ownership or control of lands and rents. All the Scandinavian countries were home to a significant class of free peasants, and they were traditionally represented in the popular assemblies that had the right to elect kings, authorize taxes, and make laws. Scandinavians spoke similar Germanic languages and were linked by close social and economic ties. Thus, it is not surprising that the crowns of the three kingdoms were joined during periods of crisis. In 1397, the dowager queen Margaret of Denmark was able to unite the Scandinavian crowns by the Union of Kalmar, which would nominally endure until 1523.

Eastern Europe and Russia

Two phenomena had an especially profound effect on the governments of eastern Europe. One was the emergence of a newly important ruling dynasty. The other was the decline of Mongol, or Tatar, influence in the region. Since the thirteenth century, much of eastern Europe had been forced to acknowledge Tatar dominion and pay annual tribute. Now, the Tatar subjugation was challenged and finally ended.

As in much of Europe, political power was segmented and based on personal relationships between family members, communities, clients, and friends. Life in the East was further complicated by the mix of languages, cultures, and religions. Native Catholic and Orthodox Christian populations were further diversified in the fourteenth century by the arrival of Muslims in the Balkans and Ashkenazi Jews throughout most of the region. Escaping growing persecution in their traditional homelands in France and western Germany, the Ashkenazim migrated to Poland, Lithuania, and Ruthenian lands (parts of modern Russia), where they lived under their own leaders and followed their own laws.

This mix of cultures and religions played a role in the growth of new states. Under the pretext of converting their pagan neighbors to Christianity, the mostly German Teutonic knights sought to expand eastward against the kingdom of Poland and the Lithuanian state. They were

POLAND AND LITHUANIA

thwarted, however, by a profound dynastic shift. In 1386, Grand Duke Jagiello (yahg-YELL-loh) of Lithuania, who reigned from 1377 to 1434, converted to Catholic Christianity and married Hedwig, the daughter and heir of King Louis of Poland (r. 1370–1382). The resulting dynastic union created a state with a population of perhaps six million that reached from the Baltic nearly to the Black Sea. Polish-Lithuanian power slowed and finally halted the German advance to the east. The descendants of Jagiello, called Jagiellonians, had no hereditary right to rule Poland, and the Lithuanians opposed any Polish administrative influence in their lands. Yet, because of Jagiellonian power, the Poles continued to select them as kings. At various times, Jagiellonians also sat on the thrones of Bohemia and Hungary.

Poland and Lithuania remained more closely tied to western Europe than to the Russian East. They tended to be Catholic rather than Orthodox Christians. They wrote in a Roman rather than a Cyrillic script, and their political institutions resembled those of western Europe. Polish nobles managed to win a number of important concessions, the most significant being freedom from arbitrary arrest and confinement. This civil right was secured in Poland well before the more famous English right of habeas corpus. It was during this period, and under the influence of the Polish kings, that Cracow emerged as the economic and cultural center of Poland. Cracow University was founded in 1364, in response to the foundation of Prague University by the emperor Charles IV in 1348. After the dynastic union of Poland and Lithuania, Polish language and culture increasingly influenced the Lithuanian nobility. This union laid the foundation for the great Polish-Lithuanian commonwealth of the early modern period.

THE RISE OF MOSCOW

Lithuania had never been conquered by the Tatars, and its expansion contributed to the decline of Tatar power. The rise of Moscow, however, owed much to the continuing Tatar domination. Since the Mongol invasions in the thirteenth century, various towns and principalities of Kievan Rus had been part of a Tatar sphere of influence. This primarily meant homage and payment of an annual tribute.

A key to the emergence of Moscow occurred when Ivan I (r. 1328–1341), Prince of Moscow, was named Grand Prince and collector of tribute from the other Russian princes. It was not for nothing that he was called "the Moneybag." It was during this same period that the head of the Russian Orthodox Church was persuaded to make his home in Moscow, and in 1367, the princes began to rebuild the Kremlin walls in stone.

The decisive change for Moscow, however, was the reign of Ivan III (r. 1462–1505). By 1478, Ivan III, called "Ivan the Great," had seized the famed trading center of Novgorod. Two years later, he was powerful enough to renounce Mongol overlordship and refuse further payments of tribute. After his marriage to an émigré Byzantine princess living in Rome, Ivan began to call himself "Tsar" (Russian for "Caesar"), implying that in the wake of the Muslim conquest of Constantinople, Moscow had become the new Rome.

The Ottoman Empire

The most profound political and cultural transformation of the late Middle Ages took place in the Balkans with the conquest of Constantinople (1453) and the emergence of the Ottoman Turks as a major European power (see **MAP 11.3**). They solidified a fragmented and unstable area and from their base spread their influence throughout the Mediterranean and Europe.

The eastern Mediterranean region was a politically tumultuous area in the fourteenth century, when the Ottoman Turks were first invited into the Balkans by the hard-pressed Byzantine emperor. In the 1420s, as the Turks and the Hungarians fought for influence in Serbia, the Serbian king moved easily from alliance with one to alliance with the other. Elites often retained their political and economic influence by changing religion.

An Ottoman victory over a Christian crusading army at Varna, on the Black Sea coast, in 1444 changed the dynamics and virtually sealed the fate of Constantinople. It was only a matter of time before the Turks took the city. When Mehmed (MEH-met) II (r. 1451–1481) finally turned his attention to Constantinople in 1453, the siege of the city lasted only fifty-three days. The destruction of the last vestiges of the Roman imperial tradition that reached back to the emperor Augustus sent shock waves through Christian Europe and brought forth calls for new crusades to liberate the East from the evils of Islam. It also stirred anti-Christian feelings among the Turks. The rise of the Ottoman Turks transformed eastern Europe and led to a profound clash between Christian and Muslim civilizations.

🌐 **MAP 11.3—Turkey and Eastern Europe**

With the conquest of Constantinople, Syria, and Palestine, the Ottoman Turks controlled the eastern Mediterranean and dominated Europe below the Danube River. The Holy Roman emperors, rulers of Italy, and kings of Spain had to be concerned about potential invasions by land or by sea.

After the fall of Constantinople, the Turks worked to consolidate their new territories. Through alliance and conquest, Ottoman hegemony extended through Syria and Palestine, and by 1517, to Egypt. Even the Muslim powers of North Africa were nominally under Turkish control. In short order, they expanded to the west and north, seizing Croatia, Bosnia, Dalmatia, Albania, eastern Hungary, Moldavia, Bulgaria, and Greece. Turkish strength was based on a number of factors. The first was the loyalty and efficiency of the sultan's crack troops, the Janissaries. These troops were young boys forcibly taken from the subject Christian populations, trained in the Turkish language and customs, and converted to Islam. Although they functioned as special protectors of the Christian community from which they were drawn, they were separated from it by their new faith. Because the Turkish population viewed them as outsiders, they were particularly loyal to the sultan.

The situation of the Janissaries underlines a secondary explanation for Ottoman strength: the unusually tolerant attitudes of Mehmed, who saw himself not only as the greatest of the *ghazi* (crusading warriors who were considered the "instruments of Allah"), but also as emperor, heir to Byzantine and ancient imperial traditions. Immediately after the conquest of Constantinople, he repopulated the city with Greeks, Armenians, Jews, and Muslims. Mehmed especially welcomed Sephardic Jews from Spain and Portugal to parts of his empire. Thessalonica (Salonika), for example, was second only to Amsterdam as a Sephardic Jewish center until the community was destroyed in World War II. Religious groups in the cities lived in separate districts centered on a church or synagogue, and each religious community retained the right to select its own leaders. (See the feature, "The Global Record: A Disputation.") Mehmed made Constantinople the capital of the new Ottoman Empire, and by building mosques, hospitals, hostels, and bridges, he breathed new life into the city, which he referred to as Istanbul—that is, "the city." In the

The Siege of Constantinople   The siege of Constantinople by the Turks required the attackers to isolate the city both by sea and by land. This miniature from the fifteenth century shows the Turkish camps, as well as the movements of Turkish boats, completing the isolation of the city.
(Bibliothèque nationale de France)

fifty years following the conquest, the population of the city grew an extraordinary 500 percent, from about 40,000 to over 200,000, making it the largest city in Europe, as it had been in Late Antiquity.

At a time when Christian Europe seemed less and less willing to tolerate non-Christian minorities, the Ottoman Empire's liberal attitude toward outsiders seemed striking. Muslims and non-Muslims belonged to the same trade associations and traveled throughout the empire. Mehmed had no qualms about making trade agreements with the Italian powers in an attempt to consolidate his control. In Serbia, Bulgaria, Macedonia, and Albania, he left in place previous social and political institutions, requiring only loyalty to his empire.

The Union of Crowns in Spain

While expanding across the Mediterranean, the Turks came in contact with the other new state of the fifteenth century, the newly unified kingdom of Spain. As in Poland-Lithuania, the Spanish monarchy was only a dynastic union. In 1469, Ferdinand, heir to the kingdom of Aragon and Catalonia, married Isabella, daughter of the king of Castile. Five years later, Isabella became queen of Castile, and in 1479, Ferdinand took control of the kingdom of Aragon. This union of Crowns eventually would lead to the creation of a united Spain, but true integration was still a distant dream in 1469.

CASTILE AND ARAGON   The permanence of the union was remarkable because the two kingdoms were so different. Castile was a much larger and more populous state. It had taken the lead in the Reconquista, the fight begun in the eleventh century to reclaim Iberia from Muslim rule. As a result, economic power within Castile was divided among the groups most responsible for the Reconquista: military orders and nobles. The military orders of Calatrava, Santiago, and Alcantara were militias formed by men who had taken a religious vow similar to that taken by a monk, with an added commitment to fight against the enemies of Christianity. In the course of the Reconquista, the military orders assumed control of vast districts. Lay nobles who aided in the Reconquista also held large tracts of land and proudly guarded their independence.

Castile's power stemmed from its agrarian wealth. During the Reconquista, Castilians took control of large regions and turned them into ranges for grazing merino sheep, producers of the prized merino wool exported to the markets of Flanders and Italy (see page 306). To maximize the profits from wool production, the kings authorized the creation of the Mesta, a brotherhood of sheep producers. The pastoral economy grew to the point that, by the early sixteenth century, Castilians owned over three million sheep.

Economic power in Castile lay with the nobility, but political power rested with the monarch. Because the nobility was largely exempt from taxation, nobles ignored the Cortes (cor-TEZ), the popular assembly, which could do little more than approve royal demands. The towns of Castile were important only as fortresses and staging points for militias, rather than as centers of trade and commerce.

The kingdom of Aragon was dramatically different. The center of the kingdom was Barcelona, an important trading center in the Mediterranean. In the fourteenth and fifteenth centuries, the kings of Aragon concentrated their efforts on expanding their influence in the

THE GLOBAL RECORD

A Disputation

Konstantin Mihailovic, a Serb by birth, was captured by the Turks during the conquest of Constantinople in 1453. He later served with the Turks until he returned to the Christian forces in 1463. His description of a typical Turkish disputation, or debate, taking place in the presence of the sultan or another dignitary is an interesting example of how the Muslim, Jewish, and Christian peoples of the Balkans tried to understand one another.

The masters and scribes have among themselves this custom: they arrange their deliberations before the highest lord after the emperor. … And then they begin to argue one against the other, speaking mostly about the prophets. Some [of these Turkish scribes] recognize Our Lord Jesus Christ as a prophet, and others as an archprophet, alongside God the Creator of Heaven and earth. And also the Lord, from the time when the Mohammedan faith began, created eight hundred camels, like invisible spirits, which go around every night and gather evil *Busromane* [i.e., the Muslim, or the Chosen People of God] from our [Muslim] graves and carry them to *kaur* graves [the Kaury are "the Confused People," i.e., the Christians]; and then gather good kaury and carry them to our graves. And now the good kaury will stand with our Busroman council and the evil Busromane will stand with the kaur council on Judgment Day before God. For [a pious one] says … , "The Christians have a faith but have no works." Therefore Mohammed will lead the Busromane to Paradise and Jesus will order the Christians to hell. Moses will sorrow for the Jews that they have not been obedient to him. … He [one of the scribes] spoke in this way: "Elias and Enoch are both in body and soul in paradise; but before Judgment Day they must die. But Jesus both in body and in soul is in heaven. He is the only one who will not die a death but will be alive forever and ever. Mohammed both in body and soul was in heaven, but remained with us on earth." And then the masters began to dispute, one in one way and one in another, and there were many words among them. And having raised a cry one against another, they began to throw books at one another. [Then the official in charge of the disputation] … told them to cease this disputation and he ordered that food be brought them according to their custom and they gave them water to drink, since they do not drink wine. And then, having eaten their fill, they gave thanks to God, praying for the souls of the living and the dead and for those who fight against the kaury or Christians.

QUESTIONS

1. Like many people, the scribes in the debate are aware that good and evil behavior is not the special preserve of one people. How do they explain that individuals will be punished or rewarded for their deeds?

2. Christian theologians traditionally considered Muslims to be heretics who could not be saved. How do these debaters evaluate Christians?

Source: Konstantin Mihailovic, *Memoirs of a Janissary*, translated by Benjamin Stolz. Copyright © 1975. Reprinted by permission of Michigan Slavic Publications.

Mediterranean, especially south of France and Italy. By the middle of the fifteenth century, the Aragonese empire included the kingdom of Naples, Sicily, the Balearic (ba-LEER-ik) Islands, and Sardinia.

The power of the Aragonese king, in sharp contrast to the Castilian monarchy, was limited because the Crown was not unified. The ruler was king in Aragon and Navarre but only count in Catalonia. Aragon, Catalonia, and Valencia each maintained its own Cortes. In each area, the traditional nobility and the towns had a great deal more influence than did their counterparts in Castile. The power of the Cortes is clear in the coronation oath taken by the Aragonese nobility: "We who are as good as you and together are more powerful than you, make you our king and lord, provided that you observe our laws and liberties, and if not, not."[8] The distinction between Aragon and Castile could not be stronger.

Initially, the union of the crowns of Aragon and Castile did little to unify the two monarchies. Nobles fought over disputed boundaries, and Castilian nobles felt exploited by Aragonese merchants. Trade duties and internal boundaries continued to be disputed. The two realms even lacked a treaty to allow for the extradition of criminals from one kingdom to the other. Castilians never accepted Ferdinand as more than their queen's consort. After the death of Isabella in 1504, he ruled in Castile only as regent for his infant grandson, Charles I (r. 1516–1556). "Spain" would not emerge in an institutional sense until the late sixteenth century.

Nonetheless, the reign of Isabella and Ferdinand marked a profound change in politics and society in the Iberian kingdoms and in Europe in general. Ferdinand and Isabella married their daughter Joanna to Philip of Habsburg in 1496 to draw the Holy Roman Empire into the Italian wars brought on by the French invasion (see page 301). The marriage of their daughter Catherine of Aragon to Prince Arthur of England in 1501 was designed to obtain yet another ally against the

French. Those two marriages would have momentous consequences for European history in the sixteenth century.

1492: MUSLIMS AND JEWS The reign of Ferdinand and Isabella is especially memorable because of the events of 1492. In January of that year, a crusading army conquered Granada, the last Muslim stronghold in Iberia. In March, Ferdinand and Isabella ordered the Jews of Castile and Aragon to convert or leave the kingdom within four months. In April, Isabella issued her commission authorizing Christopher Columbus "to discover and acquire islands and mainland in the Ocean Sea" (see pages 362–364).

The conquest of Granada and the expulsion of the Jews represented a radical shift in the Spanish mentality. Until the beginning of the fifteenth century, Spain maintained a level of religious tolerance unusual in Christendom. In the fourteenth century, perhaps 2 percent of the population of Iberia was Jewish, and the Muslim population may have been as high as 50 percent. The various groups were inextricably mixed. The statutes of the Jewish community in Barcelona were written in Catalan, a Spanish dialect, rather than in Hebrew. *Maranos*, Jewish converts to Christianity, and *moriscos*, Muslim converts, mixed continuously with Christians and with members of their former religions. It was difficult at times to know which religion these converts, or *conversos*, actually practiced. One surprised northern visitor to Spain remarked that one noble's circle was filled with "Christians, Moors, and Jews and he lets them live in peace in their faith."

This tolerant mingling of Christians, Muslims, and Jews had periodically occasioned violence. All three communities, in fact, preferred clear boundaries between the groups. In 1391, however, a series of violent attacks had long-lasting and unfortunate effects on Iberian society. An attack on the Jews of Seville led to murders, forced conversions, and suppression of synagogues throughout Spain. In the wake of the assault, large portions of the urban Jewish population either converted to Christianity or moved into villages away from the large commercial cities. The Jewish population in Castile may have declined by a fourth. Although the anti-Jewish feelings were expressed in religious terms, the underlying cause was anger over the economic prominence of some Jewish or converso families. After 1391, anti-Jewish feeling increasingly became racial. As one rebel said, "The converso remains a Jew and therefore should be barred from public office."[9]

Hostility and suspicion toward Jews grew throughout the fifteenth century, until Ferdinand and Isabella concluded that the only safe course was to order all Jews to accept baptism. Jews who would not convert would have to leave the kingdom within four months. The order was signed on March 31, 1492, and published in late April, after an unsuccessful attempt by converso and Jewish leaders to dissuade the monarchs from implementing it.

Many Jews could not dispose of their possessions in the four months allowed and so chose to convert and remain. But it is estimated that about ten thousand Jews left Aragon and that even more left Castile. Many moved to Portugal and then to North Africa. Some went east to Istanbul or north to the Low Countries. A number of others moved to the colonies being established in the New World in the vain hope of avoiding the Inquisition, which was already underway when the expulsion order was issued (see below). In 1504, the expulsion order was extended to include all Muslims.

The economic and social costs of the expulsion were profound. Not every Muslim or Jew was wealthy and cultured, but the exiles did include many doctors, bankers, and merchants. Spanish culture, long open to influences from Muslim and

Alfonso de Espina's Fortress of Faith (1474) The diatribe against heretics, Muslims, and Jews fanned religious tensions in Spain. In this image from the book, Jews, Muslims, heretics, and demons are depicted as related threats to Christianity. Blindfolded Jews (blind to Christian Truth), Muslim warriors, and the Devil himself are seen assaulting the fortress of faith. (© Topham/The Image Works)

Jewish sources, became narrower and less willing to accept new ideas. After the expulsion, a chasm of distrust opened between the "Old Christians" and the "New Christians"—that is, those newly converted. As early as the first decades of the fifteenth century, some religious orders had refused to accept "New Christians." They required that their members demonstrate *limpieza de sangre*, a purity of blood. By 1500, the same tests of blood purity became prerequisites for holding most religious and public offices. Thus, by the end of the fifteenth century, the Iberian kingdoms had created more powerful, unified governments, but at a terrible cost to the only portion of Christendom that had ever practiced religious tolerance.

Complaints that led to the expulsion arose from a variety of sources. The fact that many of the most important financiers and courtiers were Jews or conversos bred jealousies and tensions among the communities. All three religious communities favored distinct dress and identifying behaviors. Old Christians seemed concerned that many of the conversos might reconvert to Judaism, and the fear of reconversion, or "judaizing," led many to advocate the institution of the **Spanish Inquisition**.

Inquisitions were well known in many parts of Europe, but the Spanish Inquisition was unique because in 1478, Pope Sixtus IV placed the grand inquisitor under the direct control of the monarchs. Like most Christian rulers, Ferdinand and Isabella believed that uniform Christian orthodoxy was the only firm basis for a strong kingdom. Inquisitors attacked those aspects of converso tradition that seemed to make the conversos less than fully Christian. They were concerned that many conversos and maranos had converted falsely and were secretly continuing to follow Jewish or Muslim rituals—a fear that some recent scholars have argued was unfounded.

Because its administration, finances, and appointments were in Spanish, not papal, hands, the Spanish Inquisition quickly became an important instrument for the expansion of state power. Many inquisitors used their offices to attack wealthy or politically important converso families not just to drive them from public life but also to fill the royal treasury, which was where the estates of those judged guilty wound up. "This inquisition is as much to take the conversos' estates as to exalt the faith," concluded one despairing conversa woman.[10]

> **Spanish Inquisition**
> A church court under monarchical control established in 1478 to look for "false Christians" among the newly converted Muslims and Jews.

The Limits of Consolidation: Germany

The issue of central versus local control played a key role in German affairs as well. The Holy Roman Empire of the late Middle Ages was dramatically different from the empire of the early thirteenth century. Emperors generally were unable to claim lands and preside over jurisdictions outside Germany, and within Germany, power shifted eastward. Imperial power had previously rested on lands and castles in southwestern Germany. These strongholds melted away, as emperors willingly pawned and sold traditional crown lands in order to build up the holdings of their own families. Emperor Henry VII (r. 1308–1313) and his grandson, Charles IV (r. 1347–1378), for example, liquidated imperial lands west of the Rhine in order to secure the House of Luxemburg's claims to the crown of Bohemia and other lands in the east. The Habsburgs in Austria, the Wittelsbachs in Bavaria, and a host of lesser families staked out power bases in separate parts of the empire. As a result, Germany unraveled into a loose collection of territories. More seriously, the power of each emperor depended almost entirely on the wealth and power of his dynastic lands.

The power of regional authorities in the empire was further cemented by the so-called **Golden Bull** of 1356, the most important constitutional document of late medieval German history. In it, Charles IV declared that henceforth the archbishops of Cologne, Mainz, and Trier, plus the secular rulers of Bohemia, the Rhenish Palatinate, Saxony, and Brandenburg, would be the seven electors responsible for the choice of a new emperor. He further established that the rulers of these seven principalities should have full jurisdictional rights within their territories. The Golden Bull acknowledged the power of regional princes, but it did nothing to solve the inherent weakness of an electoral monarchy. Between 1273 and 1519, Germany elected fourteen emperors from six different dynasties, and only once, in 1378, did a son follow his father. The contrast between Germany and the monarchies of Iberia, France, and England is striking. By 1350, Germany had no hereditary monarchy, no common legal system, no common coinage, and no representative assembly. Political power rested in the hands of the territorial princes.

> **Golden Bull** Edict of Holy Roman Emperor Charles IV establishing the method of electing a new emperor. It acknowledged the political autonomy of Germany's seven regional princes.

SECTION SUMMARY

- By the end of the fifteenth century, both England and France had stronger, more centralized governments.

- By the fifteenth century a strong Polish-Lithuanian state had emerged to halt German expansion to the east.

- The rise of Moscow marked the end of Tatar domination in eastern Europe.

- Ottoman Turks established a strong empire that came to dominate the eastern Mediterranean and the Balkans.

- The union of the Aragonese and Castilian crowns created a Spanish monarchy intent on enforcing political unity and religious uniformity.

- In German lands, regional powers emerged to challenge and limit the power of the empire.

Territorial integration was least effective in what is now Switzerland, where a league of towns, provincial knights, and peasant villages successfully resisted a territorial prince. The Swiss Confederation began modestly enough in 1291, as a voluntary association to promote regional peace. By 1410, the confederation had conquered most of the traditionally Habsburg lands in the Swiss areas. Though still citizens of the Holy Roman Empire, the Swiss maintained an independence similar to that of the princes. Their expansion culminated with the Battle of Nancy in Lorraine in 1477, when the Swiss infantry defeated a Burgundian army and killed Charles the Bold, the duke of Burgundy. From then on "turning Swiss" was a common threat made by German towns and individuals who hoped to slow territorial centralization.

CHAPTER SUMMARY

The Europe of 1500 was profoundly different from the Europe of two centuries earlier. The religious, political, and economic crises of the fourteenth and early fifteenth centuries seemed about to destroy the progress of the previous centuries. But the recovery of the second half of the fifteenth century was nearly as dramatic as the preceding disasters.

FOCUS QUESTIONS

- How did the Great Schism change the church and the papacy?
- What forces limited the political power of rulers in England, France, and Italy?
- How were economic and social structures changed by plague and economic crisis?
- How did the political makeup of Europe in 1500 differ from that in 1300?

In the aftermath of schism and conciliar reform, the church also was transformed. Because of conciliar challenges to papal authority, popes had to deal much more carefully with the governments of Europe. They found themselves vulnerable to pressures from the other European powers. Recognizing that, in the end, popes could count on support only from those areas they controlled politically, the papacy became an Italian regional power.

The Hundred Years' War between England and France was a continuation of a long struggle between two royal houses. The English won dramatic battles, but they could not control the territory. As a result, by the end the English lost all their significant possessions in France. The result contributed to the eventual centralization and growth of royal power in the two kingdoms.

The economy had grown more complex in the wake of the epidemic disease and dramatic population decline. Changes included the relative decline of the Italian economy as new patterns of trade and banking and new manufacturing techniques spread throughout Europe. Commerce and manufacture were now more firmly rooted in northern Europe. Italian merchants and bankers faced stiff competition from local counterparts throughout Europe.

Recovery was equally dramatic for the governments of Europe. After the Hundred Years' War and challenges from aristocrats, townsmen, and peasants, governments grew stronger as kings, princes, and town patricians used royal courts and patronage to extend their control. Military advances in the fifteenth century, such as the institution of standing armies, gave the advantage to larger governments. This was as true in Hungary as it was in France. Yet recovery among the traditional Western powers was largely overshadowed by the emergence of the tsars in Moscow and the rise of the Ottoman and Spanish Empires. These three emergent powers upset the political and diplomatic balance in Europe and would dominate politics and diplomacy in the next century.

KEY TERMS

Babylonian Captivity of the Papacy (p. 290)

Great Schism (p. 291)

conciliarists (p. 291)

Jan Hus (p. 292)

Council of Constance (p. 293)

Hundred Years' War (p. 295)

Joan of Arc (p. 299)

Black Death (p. 302)

Hanseatic League (p. 305)

Spanish Inquisition (p. 317)

Golden Bull (p. 317)

 This icon will direct you to additional materials on the website: www .cengage.com/history/ noble/westciv6e.

NOTES

1. Quoted in Guillaume Mollat, *The Popes at Avignon, 1305–1378* (London: Thomas Nelson, 1963), p. 112.

2. Quoted in Mary Aston, *Lollards and Reformers: Images and Literacy in Late Medieval Religion* (Ronceverte, W.V.: Hambledon, 1984), p. 60.

3. Quoted in Francis Oakley, *The Western Church in the Later Middle Ages* (Ithaca, N.Y.: Cornell University Press, 1979), pp. 65–66.

4. Quoted in Charles T. Wood, *Joan of Arc and Richard III* (New York: Oxford University Press, 1988), pp. 56–57.

5. Quoted in Michael T. Clanchy, "Law, Government, and Society in Medieval England," *History* 59 (1974): 75.

6. A. Buchon, *Choix des Chroniques* (Paris, 1875), p. 565, as quoted in John Gillingham and J. C. Holt, eds., *War and Government in the Middle Ages* (Totowa, N.J.: Barnes & Noble, 1984), p. 85.

7. Quoted in Peter Shervey Lewis, *Later Medieval France: The Polity* (New York: Macmillan, 1968), p. 15.

8. Quoted in Angus MacKay, *Spain in the Middle Ages: From Frontier to Empire, 1000–1500* (London: Macmillan, 1977), p. 105.

9. Quoted in Angus MacKay, "Popular Movements and Pogroms in Fifteenth-Century Spain," *Past & Present* 55 (1972): 52.

10. Haim Beinart, ed., *Records of the Trials of the Spanish Inquisition in Ciudad Real*, vol. 1 (Jerusalem: Israel Academy of Sciences and Humanities, 1974), p. 391, trans. Duane Osheim.

See our interactive eBook for map and primary source activities.

12

Raphael: School of Athens (detail)
Raphael created this classical setting by using the technique of linear
perspective. (Scala/Art Resource, NY)

The Renaissance

The painting on the left, *School of Athens* by Raphael (1483–1520), was commissioned for the Stanze (STAN-zay), the papal apartments in the Vatican. At the center, Plato and Aristotle advance through a church-like hall, surrounded by the great thinkers and writers of the ancient world. But Raphael portrayed more than just ancient wisdom. The figure of Plato is, in fact, a portrait of Leonardo da Vinci. A brooding Michelangelo leans on a marble block in the foreground. In a companion painting on the opposite wall, Raphael depicted a gathering of the greatest scholars of Christendom. In this way, he brought together Christian and classical, writers and artists, and captured the entire cultural reform plan of the **Renaissance**.

The revival these paintings celebrate was a response to the religious, social, economic, and political crises discussed in the previous chapter. Italians, and later Europeans, generally found themselves drawn to imitate Roman literature, ethics, and politics. The wisdom of antiquity seemed to offer an opportunity to perfect the theological ideas about moral and political life current in the earlier Middle Ages. Further, Renaissance writers were convinced that all knowledge, pagan and Christian, ancient and modern, could be combined into a single, uniform view of the world.

Renaissance Italians wrote of themselves and their contemporaries as having "revived" arts, "rescued" painting, and "rediscovered" classical authors. They even coined the phrases "Dark Ages" and "Middle Ages" to describe the period that separated the Roman Empire from their own times. They believed that their society saw a new age, a rebirth of culture. And, to this day, we use the French word for "rebirth," *renaissance*, to describe the period of intense creativity and change that began in Italy in the fourteenth century and then extended to all of Europe.

This view comes to us primarily from the work of the nineteenth-century Swiss historian Jacob Burckhardt. In his book, *The Civilization of the Renaissance in Italy* (1860), he argued that Italians were the first individuals to recognize the state as a moral structure free from the restraints of religious or philosophical traditions. Burckhardt believed that people are entirely free. Their success or failure depends on personal qualities of creative brilliance, rather than on family status, religion, or guild membership. Burckhardt thought he saw, in Renaissance Italy, the first signs of the romantic individualism and nationalism that characterized the modern world.

In fact, as brilliant as Renaissance writers and artists were, they do not represent a radical shift from the ideas or values of medieval culture. As we have seen, there were no "Dark Ages." Although the culture of Renaissance Europe was in many aspects new and innovative, it had close ties both to the ideas of the High Middle Ages and to traditional Christian values.

How, then, should we characterize the Renaissance in Europe? The Renaissance was an important cultural movement that aimed to reform and renew by imitating what the

FOCUS QUESTIONS

- How did Italians use classical values to deal with cultural and political issues?
- What was "new" about Renaissance art?
- In what ways did humanism outside Italy differ from Italian humanism?
- How did European rulers use Renaissance art and culture?

This icon will direct you to additional materials on the website: www .cengage.com/history/ noble/westciv6e.

See our interactive eBook for map and primary source activities.

Renaissance A word that has come to define any period of intense creativity. In this case, it refers specifically to a cultural movement based on imitating classical culture.

reformers believed were classical and early Christian traditions in art, education, religion, and political life. Italians, and then other Europeans, came to believe that the social and moral values, as well as the literature, of classical Greece and Rome offered the best formula for changing their own society for the better. This enthusiasm for a past culture became the vehicle for changes in literature, education, and art that established cultural standards that were to hold for the next five hundred years.

HUMANISM AND CULTURE IN ITALY, 1300–1500

How did Italians use classical values to deal with cultural and political issues?

Italians turned to models from classical antiquity in their attempts to deal with current issues of cultural, political, and educational reform. A group of scholars, who came to be known as humanists, began to argue the superiority of the literature, history, and politics of the past. As humanists discovered more about ancient culture, they were able to understand more clearly the historical context in which Roman and Greek writers and thinkers lived. And by the early sixteenth century, their debates on learning, civic duty, and the classical legacy had led them to a new vision of the past and a new appreciation of the nature of politics.

The Emergence of Humanism

humanism Western European literary and cultural movement, which emphasized the superiority of Greek and Roman literature and especially its values of personal and public morality.

Humanism initially held greater appeal in Italy than elsewhere in Europe because the culture in central and northern Italy was significantly more secular and more urban than the culture of much of the rest of Europe. Members of the clergy were less likely to dominate government and education in Italy. Quite the reverse: Boards dominated by laymen had built and were administering the great urban churches of Italy. Religious hospitals and charities were often reorganized and centralized under government control. Italy was the most urbanized region of Europe. Even the powerful Italian aristocracy tended to live at least part of the year in towns and conform to urban social and legal practices.

Differences between Italy and northern Europe are also apparent in the structure of local education. In northern Europe, education was organized to provide clergy for local churches. In the towns of Italy, education was much more likely to be supervised by town governments to provide training in accounting, arithmetic, and the composition of business letters. Public grammar masters taught these basics, and numerous private masters and individual tutors were prepared to teach all subjects. Giovanni Villani, a fourteenth-century merchant and historian, described Florence in 1338 as a city of nearly 100,000 people, in which perhaps as many as 10,000 young girls and boys were completing elementary education and 1,000 were continuing their studies to prepare for careers in commerce. Compared with education in the towns of northern Europe, education in Villani's Florence seems broad-based and practical.

Logic and Scholastic philosophy (see page 275) dominated university education in northern Europe in the fourteenth and fifteenth centuries but had less influence in Italy, where education focused on the practical issues of town life rather than on theological speculation. Educated Italians of this period were interested in the *studia humanitatis*, which we now call humanism. By *humanism*, Italians meant rhetoric and literature—the arts of persuasion. Poetry, history, letter writing, and oratory, based on standardized forms and aesthetic values, consciously borrowed from ancient Greece and Rome were the center of intellectual life. In general, fourteenth-century Italians were suspicious of ideological or moral programs based on philosophical arguments or religious assumptions about human nature.

By 1300, it was usual for towns to celebrate the feast days of their patron saints as major political, as well as religious, festivals. And town governments often supervised the construction and expansion of cathedrals, churches, and hospitals as signs of their wealth and prestige.

Literature of the early fourteenth century tended to emphasize the culture of towns. The most famous and most innovative work of the fourteenth century, *The Decameron* by Giovanni Boccaccio (1313–1375), pondered moral and ethical issues, but in the lively context of Italian town life. Boccaccio (bo-KAH-cho) hoped the colorful and irreverent descriptions of contemporary

Italians, which make his *Decameron* a classic of European literature, would also lead individuals to understand both the essence of human nature and the folly of human desires. The plot involves a group of privileged young people who abandon friends and family during the plague of 1348 to go into the country. There, on successive days, they mixed feasting, dancing, and song with one hundred tales of love, intrigue, and gaiety. With its mix of traditional and contemporary images, Boccaccio's book spawned numerous imitators in Italy and elsewhere.

Like Boccaccio, the majority of educated Italians in the early fourteenth century were not particularly captivated by thoughts of ancient Rome. Italian historians chose to write the histories of their hometowns. Most, including Giovanni Villani of Florence, were convinced that their towns could rival ancient Rome. Theirs was a practical world in which most intellectuals were men trained in notarial arts—the everyday skills of oratory, letter writing, and the recording of legal documents.

Petrarch and Early Humanism

The first Italians who looked back consciously to the literary and historical examples of ancient Rome were a group of northern Italian lawyers and notaries who imitated Roman authors. These practical men found Roman history and literature more stimulating and useful than medieval philosophy. Writers, such as Albertino Mussato of Padua (1262–1329), adopted classical styles in their poetry and histories. Mussato used his play *The Ecerinis* (1315) to tell of the fall of Can Grande della Scala, the tyrannical ruler of Verona (d. 1329), and to warn his neighbors of the dangers of tyranny. From its earliest, the classical revival in Italy was tied to issues of moral and political reform.

This largely emotional fascination for the ancient world was transformed into a literary movement for reform by **Francesco Petrarch** (1304–1374), who popularized the idea of mixing classical moral and literary ideas with the concerns of the fourteenth century. Petrarch was the son of an exiled Florentine notary living at the papal court in Avignon. Repelled by the urban violence and wars he had experienced on his return to Italy, Petrarch was highly critical of his contemporaries: "I never liked this age," he once confessed. He criticized the papacy in Avignon, calling it the "Babylonian Captivity" (see pages 290–291); he supported an attempt to resurrect a republican government in Rome; and he believed that imitation of the actions, values, and culture of the ancient Romans was the only way to reform his sorry world.

Petrarch believed that an age of darkness—he coined the expression "Dark Ages"—separated the Roman world from his own time and that the separation could be overcome only through a study and reconstruction of classical values: "Once the darkness has been broken, our descendants will perhaps be able to return to the pure, pristine radiance."[1] Petrarch's program, and, in many respects, the entire Renaissance, involved, first of all, a reconstruction of classical culture; then, a careful study and imitation of the classical heritage; and finally, a series of moral and cultural changes that went beyond the mere copying of ancient values and styles.

Petrarch labored throughout his life to reconstruct the history and literature of Rome. He learned to read and write classical Latin. In the 1330s, he discovered a number of classical works, including orations and letters by Cicero, the great philosopher, statesman, and opponent of Julius Caesar (see pages 134–135). Cicero's letters to his friend Atticus were filled with gossip, questions about politics in Rome, and complaints about his forced withdrawal from public life. They create the portrait of an individual who was much more complex than the austere philosopher of medieval legend.

Petrarch's humanism was not worldly or secular; he was and remained a committed Christian. He recognized the tension between the Christian present and pagan antiquity. He wrote a dialogue,

CHRONOLOGY

1304–1314	Giotto paints Arena Chapel in Padua
1345	Petrarch discovers Cicero's letters to Atticus
1348–1350	Boccaccio, *The Decameron*
1393–1400	Chaucer, *The Canterbury Tales*
1401	Ghiberti wins competition to cast baptistery doors, Florence
1405	Christine de Pizan, *The Book of the City of the Ladies*
1427	Unveiling of Masaccio's *Trinity*
1434	Van Eyck, *The Arnolfini Wedding*
1440	Valla, *On the Donation of Constantine*
1440s	Vitterino establishes Villa Giocosa in Mantua
1450s	Gutenberg begins printing with movable metal type
1460	Gonzaga invites Mantegna to Mantua
1475	Pope Sixtus IV orders construction of Sistine Chapel
1494	Dürer begins first trip to Venice
1501	Michelangelo, *David*
1511	Erasmus, *The Praise of Folly*
1513	Machiavelli, *The Prince*
1516	More, *Utopia*
1528	Castiglione, *The Book of the Courtier*

Francesco Petrarch

Influential poet, biographer, and humanist who strongly advocated imitation of the literary and moral values of the leading Greek and Roman writers.

Petrarch Responds to His Critics

Many traditional philosophers and theologians criticized humanists as "pagans" because of their lack of interest in logic and theology and their love of non-Christian writers. In this letter defending humanistic studies, Petrarch explains the value of Cicero's work to Christians.

[Cicero] points out the miraculously coherent structure and disposition of the body, sense and limbs, and finally reason and sedulous activity.... And all this he does merely to lead us to this conclusion: whatever we behold with our eyes or perceive with our intellect is made by God for the well-being of man and governed by divine providence and counsel.... [In response to his critics who argued for the superiority of philosophy he adds:] I have read all of Aristotle's moral books. Some of them I have also heard commented on.... Sometimes I have become more learned through them when I went home, but not better, not so good as I ought to be; and I often complained to myself, occasionally to others too, that by no facts was the promise fulfilled which the philosopher makes at the beginning of the first book of his *Ethics*, namely, that "we learn this part of philosophy not with the purpose of gaining knowledge but of becoming better." I see virtue, and all that is peculiar to vice as well as to virtue, egregiously defined and distinguished by him and treated with penetrating insight. When I learn all this, I know a little bit more than I knew before, but mind and will remain the same as they were, and I myself remain the same.... However, what is the use of knowing what virtue is if it is not loved when known? What is the use of knowing sin if it is not abhorred when it is known? However,

everyone who has become thoroughly familiar with our Latin authors knows that they stamp and drive deep into the heart the sharpest and most ardent stings of speech by which those who stick to the ground [are] lifted up to the highest thoughts and to honest desire....

Cicero, read with a pious and modest attitude, ... was profitable to everybody, so far as eloquence is concerned, to many others as regards living. This was especially true in [Saint] Augustine's case.... I confess, I admire Cicero as much or even more than all whoever wrote a line in any nation. ... If to admire Cicero means to be a Ciceronian, I am a Ciceronian. I admire him so much that I wonder at people who do not admire him.... However, when we come to think or speak of religion, that is, of supreme truth and true happiness, and of eternal salvation, then I am certainly not a Ciceronian, or a Platonist, but a Christian. I even feel sure that Cicero himself would have been a Christian if he had been able to see Christ and to comprehend His doctrine.

QUESTIONS

1. Why is Cicero a valuable author to study?
2. Why does Petrarch believe Cicero is superior to Aristotle?
3. Does it seem that Petrarch sees any limits to the moral value of Cicero?

Source: From *The Renaissance Philosophy of Man,* ed. Ernst Cassirer, Paul Oskar Kristeller and John H. Randall, pp. 86, 103–04, 114–115. Reprinted by permission of the publisher, the University of Chicago Press.

The Secret, reflecting his own ambivalence. Did his devotion to reading and imitating classical authors involve a rejection of traditional Christian values? "My wishes fluctuate and my desires conflict, and in their struggle they tear me apart," he confessed.[2] Yet, he prized the beauty and moral value of ancient learning. He wrote *The Lives of Illustrious Men*, biographies of men from antiquity whose thoughts and actions he deemed worthy of emulation. To spread humanistic values, he issued collections of his poems, written in Italian, and his letters, written in classically inspired Latin. He believed that study and memorization of the writings of classical authors could lead to the internalization of the ideas and values expressed in those works, just as a honeybee drinks nectar to create honey. He argued that ancient moralists were superior to Scholastic philosophers, whose work ended with the determination of truth, or correct responses. "The true moral philosophers and useful teachers of the virtues," he concluded, "are those whose first and last intention is to make hearer and reader good, those who do not merely teach what virtue and vice are but sow into our hearts love of the best ... and hatred of the worst."[3] (See the feature, "The Written Record: Petrarch Responds to His Critics.")

civic humanism
An ideology, popular with the political leaders of Florence, that emphasized Rome's classical republican virtues of duty and public service.

Humanistic Studies

Petrarch's program of humanistic studies became especially popular with the wealthy oligarchy who dominated political life in Florence. The Florentine chancellor Coluccio Salutati (1331–1406), and a generation of young intellectuals who formed his circle, evolved an ideology of civic humanism.

Civic humanists wrote letters, orations, and histories praising their city's classical virtues and history. In the process, they gave a practical and public meaning to the Petrarchan program. Civic humanists argued, as had Cicero, that there was a moral and ethical value intrinsic to public life. In a letter to a friend, Salutati wrote that public life is "something holy and holier than idleness in [religious] solitude." To another he added, "The active life you flee is to be followed both as an exercise in virtue and because of the necessity of brotherly love."[4]

More than Petrarch himself, civic humanists desired to create and inspire men of virtue who could take the lead in government and protect their fellow citizens from lawlessness and tyranny. In the early years of the fifteenth century, civic humanists applauded Florence for remaining a republic of free citizens. Florence remained free of a lord, unlike Milan whose government was dominated by the Viscontis (see page 345). In his *Panegyric on the City of Florence* (ca. 1405), Leonardo Bruni (ca. 1370–1444) recalled the history of the Roman Republic and suggested that Florence could re-create the best qualities of the Roman state. To civic humanists, the study of Rome and its virtues was the key to the continued prosperity of Florence and similar Italian republics.

One of Petrarch's most enthusiastic followers was Guarino of Verona (1374–1460), who became the leading advocate of educational reform in Renaissance Italy. After spending five years in Constantinople learning Greek and collecting classical manuscripts, he became the most successful teacher and translator of Greek literature in Italy. Greek studies had been advanced by Manuel Chrysoloras (1350–1415), who, after his arrival from Constantinople in 1397, taught Greek for three years in Florence. Chrysoloras was later joined by other Greek intellectuals, especially after the fall of Constantinople to the Turks in 1453. Guarino built on this interest in Greek culture.

EDUCATIONAL REFORM

Guarino emphasized careful study of grammar and memorization of large bodies of classical history and poetry. He was convinced that through a profound understanding of Greek and Latin literature and a careful imitation of the style of the great authors, a person could come to exhibit the moral and ethical values for which Cicero, Seneca, and Plutarch were justly famous. Although it is unclear whether Guarino's style of education produced such results, it did provide a thorough training in literature and oratory. In an age that admired the ability to speak and write persuasively, the new style of humanistic education pioneered by Guarino spread quickly throughout Europe. The elegy spoken at Guarino's funeral sums up Italian views of humanistic education, as well as the contribution of Guarino himself: "No one was considered noble, as leading a blameless life, unless he had followed Guarino's courses."

Guarino's example was widely followed. One of his early students, Vittorino da Feltre (1378–1446), was appointed tutor at the Gonzaga court of Mantua. Like Guarino, he emphasized close literary study and careful imitation of classical authors. But the school he founded, the Villa Giocosa (jo-KO-sa), was innovative because he advocated games and exercises, as well as formal study. In addition, Vittorino required that bright young boys from poor families be included among the seventy affluent students normally resident in his school. Vittorino was so renowned that noblemen from across Italy sent their sons to be educated at the Villa Giocosa.

Since Italians viewed humanistic education as a preparation for public life, it was not necessary for laborers, women, or others without political power. Leonardo Bruni of Florence once composed a curriculum for a young woman to follow. He emphasized literature and moral philosophy, but, he cautioned, there was no reason to study rhetoric: "For why should the subtleties of … rhetorical conundrums consume the powers of a woman, who never sees the forum? … The contests of the forum, like those of warfare and battle, are the sphere of men."[5] To what extent did women participate in the cultural and artistic movements of the fourteenth and fifteenth centuries? Many assumed that women were intellectually and morally weaker than men. And Bruni saw a limited value to humanistic education for women, but his views were not unopposed.

THE LIMITS OF HUMANISM

During the fifteenth century, many women did learn to read and even to write. Religious women and wives of merchants read educational and spiritual literature. Some women needed to write in order to manage the economic and political interests of their families. Alessandra Macinghi-Strozzi (ma-CHIN-ghee STROT-zi) of Florence (1407–1471), for example, wrote numerous letters to her sons in exile, describing her efforts to find spouses for her children and to influence the government to end their banishments. Her letters, in fact, demonstrate the subtle, indirect power women used to influence politics.

Private Reading   Robert Campin's painting of Saint Barbara of 1438 shows a typical Flemish interior with a woman reading. It was not unusual for well-to-do women to read even if they could not write.   (Museo de Prado/Institut Amatller d'Art Hispanic)

Women acted with care because many men were suspicious of literate women. Just how suspicious is evident in the career of Isotta Nogarola of Verona (b. 1418), one of a number of fifteenth- and sixteenth-century Italian women whose literary abilities equaled those of male humanists. Isotta quickly became known as a gifted writer, but men's response to her work was mixed. One anonymous critic suggested that it was unnatural for a woman to have such scholarly interests and accused her of equally unnatural sexual interests. Guarino of Verona himself wrote warning her that if she was truly to be educated, she must put off female sensibilities and find "a man within the woman."[6]

The problem for humanistically educated women was that, as Bruni observed, society provided no acceptable public role for them. A noblewoman, such as Isabella d'Este (DES-tay) (see page 345), wife of the duke of Mantua, might gather humanists and painters around her at court, but it was not generally believed that women themselves could create literary works of true merit. When women tried, they were usually rebuffed and urged to reject the values of civic humanism and to hold instead to traditional Christian virtues of rejection of the world. In other words, a woman who had literary or cultural interests was expected to enter a convent. That was a friend's advice to Isotta Nogarola. It was wrong, he said, "that a virgin should consider marriage, or even think about that liberty of lascivious morals."[7] Throughout the fifteenth and early sixteenth centuries, some women in Italy and elsewhere in Europe learned classical languages and philosophy, but they became rarer as time passed. The virtues of humanism were public virtues, and Europeans of the Renaissance remained uncomfortable with the idea that women might act directly and publicly.

The Transformation of Humanism

The fascination with education based on ancient authorities was heightened by the discovery in 1416, in the Monastery of Saint Gall in Switzerland, of a complete manuscript of Quintilian's *Institutes of Oratory*, a first-century treatise on the proper education for a young Roman patrician. The document was found by Poggio Bracciolini (PO-joe bra-cho-LEE-nee) (1380–1459), who had been part of the humanist circle in Florence. The discovery was hardly accidental. Like Petrarch, the humanists of the fifteenth century scoured Europe for ancient texts to read and study. In searching out the knowledge of the past, these fifteenth-century humanists made a series of discoveries that changed their understanding of language, philosophy, and religion. Their desire to imitate led to a profound transformation of knowledge.

A Florentine antiquary, Niccolò Niccoli (1364–1437), coordinated and paid for much of this pursuit of "lost" manuscripts. A wealthy bachelor, Niccolò spent the fortune he had inherited from his father by acquiring ancient statuary, reliefs, and, most of all, books. When he died, his collection of more than eight hundred volumes of Latin and Greek texts became the foundation of the humanist library housed in the Monastery of San Marco in Florence. Niccolò had specified that all his books "should be accessible to everyone," and humanists from across Italy and the rest of Europe came to Florence to study his literary treasures. Niccolò's library prompted Pope Nicholas V (r. 1447–1455) to begin the collection that is now the Apostolic Library of the Vatican in Rome. The Vatican library became a lending library, serving the humanist community in Rome. Similar collections were assembled in Venice, Milan, and Urbino. The Greek and Latin sources preserved in these libraries allowed humanists to study classical languages in a way not possible before.

The career of Lorenzo Valla (1407–1457) illustrates the transformation that took place in the fifteenth century, as humanism swept Europe. Valla was born near Rome and received a traditional human-istic education in Greek and Latin studies. He spent the rest of his life at universities and courts lecturing on philosophy and literature. Valla's studies had led him to understand that languages change with time—that they, too, have a life and a history. In 1440, he published a work called *On the Falsely Believed and Forged Donation of Constantine*.

The donation purported to record the gift by the emperor Constantine (r. 311–337) of juris-diction over Rome and the western half of the empire to the pope when the imperial capital was moved to Constantinople (see pages 170–172). In the High and late Middle Ages, the papacy used the document to defend its right to political dominion in central Italy. The donation had long been criticized by legal theorists, who argued that Constantine had no right to make it. Valla went further and attacked the legitimacy of the document itself. Because of its language and form, he argued, it could not have been written at the time of Constantine: Valla was correct; the *Donation* was an eighth-century forgery.

> Through his [the writer's] babbling, he reveals his most impudent forgery himself.... Where he deals with the gifts he says "a diadem … made of pure gold and precious jew-els." The ignoramus did not know that the diadem was [like a turban and] made of cloth, probably silk. … He thinks it had to be made of gold, since nowadays kings usually wear a circle of gold set with jewels.[8]

Valla later turned his attention to the New Testament. Jerome (331–420) had put together the Vulgate edition of the Bible in an attempt to create a single accepted Latin version of the Hebrew Bible and the New Testament (see page 193). In 1444, Valla completed his *Annotations on the New Testament*. In this work, he used his training in classical languages to correct Jerome's stan-dard Latin text and to show numerous instances of mistranslations. His annotations on the New

LORENZO VALLA AND HISTORICAL PERSPECTIVE

On the Falsely Believed and Forged Donation of Constantine This work demonstrated that an important papal claim to political rule of central Italy was based on an eighth-century forgery.

The Donation of Constantine Pope Julius II commissioned Raphael to include this painting of Constantine's purported gift in the Stanze, the papal apartments in the Vatican. The classical and imperial images were meant to emphasize that the Church was the heir to Roman imperial authority. (Scala/Art Resource, NY)

Testament were of critical importance to humanists outside Italy and were highly influential during the Protestant Reformation.

RENAISSANCE PHILOSOPHY

Like Valla, many other humanists anticipated that literary studies would lead eventually to philosophy. In 1456, a young Florentine began studying Greek with just such a change in mind. Supported by the Medici rulers of Florence, Marsilio Ficino (1433–1499) began a daunting project: to translate the works of Plato into Latin and to interpret Plato in light of Christian doctrine and tradition.

Ficino believed that Platonism, like Christianity, demonstrated the dignity of humanity. He wrote that everything in creation was connected along a continuum ranging from the lowliest matter to the person of God. The human soul was located at the midpoint of this hierarchy and was a bridge between the material world and God. True wisdom, and especially experience of the divine, could be gained only through contemplation and love. According to Ficino, logic and scientific observation did not lead to true understanding. Humans, he observed, know logically only what they can define in human language; individuals can, however, love things, such as God, that they are not fully able to comprehend.

Ficino's belief in the dignity of man was shared by Giovanni Pico della Mirandola (mi-RAHN-do-la) (1463–1494), who proposed to debate, with other philosophers, nine hundred theses dealing with the nature of man, the origins of knowledge, and the uses of philosophy. Pico extended Ficino's idea of the hierarchy of being, arguing that humans surpassed even the angels in dignity. Angels held a fixed position in the hierarchy, just below God. In contrast, humans could move either up or down in the hierarchy, depending on the extent to which they embraced spiritual or worldly interests. Pico further believed that he had proved that all philosophies contain at least some truth. He was one of the first humanists to learn Hebrew and to argue that divine wisdom could be found in Jewish as well as Christian and pagan mystical literature.

THE UNITY OF KNOWLEDGE

Pico's ideas were shared by other humanists, who contended that an original, unified, divine illumination—a "Pristine Theology," they called it—preceded even Plato and Aristotle. These humanists found theological truth in what they believed was ancient Egyptian, Greek, and Jewish magic. Ficino himself popularized the *Corpus Hermeticum* (the Hermetic collection), an amalgam of magical texts of the first century A.D. that was thought mistakenly to be the work of an Egyptian magician, Hermes Trismegistos. Humanists assumed Hermes wrote during the age of Moses and Pythagoras. Like many mystical writings of the first and second centuries, Hermetic texts explained how the mind could influence and be influenced by the material and celestial worlds.

Along with exploring Hermetic magic, many humanists of the fifteenth and sixteenth centuries investigated astrology and alchemy. All three systems posit the existence of a direct, reciprocal connection between the cosmos and the natural world. In the late medieval and Renaissance world, astrological and alchemical theories seemed reasonable. By the late fifteenth century, many humanists assumed that personality was profoundly affected by the stars and that the heavens were not silent regarding human affairs. It was not by accident that, for a century or more after 1500, astrologers were official or unofficial members of most European courts.

Interest in alchemy was equally widespread, though more controversial. Alchemists believed that everything was made of a primary material and that, therefore, it was possible to transmute one substance into another. The most popular variation, and the one most exploited by hucksters and frauds, was the belief that base metals could be turned into gold. The hopes of most alchemists, however, were more profound. They were convinced that they could unlock the secrets of the entire cosmos. On a personal and religious, as well as on a material level, practitioners hoped to make the impure pure. The interest in understanding and manipulating nature that lay at the heart of Hermetic magic, astrology, and alchemy was an important stimulus to scientific investigations and, ultimately, to the rise of modern scientific thought.

Humanism and Political Thought

The humanists' plan to rediscover classical sources meshed well with their political interests. Petrarch and the civic humanists believed that rulers, whether in a republic or a principality, should exhibit all the classical and Christian virtues of faith, hope, love, prudence, temperance, fortitude, and justice. A virtuous ruler would be loved as well as obeyed. The civic humanists viewed governments and laws as essentially unchanging and static. They believed that when change does occur, it most likely happens by chance—that is, because of fortune (the Roman goddess Fortuna). Humanists believed that the only protection against chance is true virtue, for the virtuous would never be dominated by fortune. Thus, beginning with Petrarch, humanists advised rulers to love their subjects, to be generous with their possessions, and to maintain the rule of law. Humanistic tracts of the fourteenth and fifteenth centuries were full of classical and Christian examples of virtuous actions by moral rulers.

The French invasions of Italy in 1494 (see page 301), and the warfare that followed, called into question many of the humanists' assumptions about the lessons and virtues of classical civilization. Francesco Guicciardini (gwih-char-DEE-nee) (1483–1540), a Florentine patrician who had served in papal armies, suggested that, contrary to humanistic hopes, history held no clear lessons. Unless the causes of separate events were identical down to the smallest detail, he said, the results could be radically different. An even more thorough critique was offered by Guicciardini's friend and fellow Florentine, **Niccolò Machiavelli** (1469–1527). In a series of writings, Machiavelli developed what he believed was a new science of politics. He wrote *Discourses on Livy*, a treatise on military organization, a history of Florence, and even a Renaissance play titled *The Mandrake Root*. He is best remembered, however, for *The Prince* (1513), a small tract numbering fewer than a hundred pages.

Machiavelli felt that his contemporaries paid too little heed to the lessons to be learned from history. Thus, in his discourses on Livy he comments on Roman government, the role of religion, and the nature of political virtue, emphasizing the sophisticated Roman analysis of political and military situations. A shortcoming more serious than ignorance of history, Machiavelli believed, was his contemporaries' ignorance of the true motivations for people's actions. His play, *The Mandrake Root*, is a comedy about the ruses used to seduce a young woman. In truth, however, none of the characters is fooled. All of them, from the wife to her husband, realize what is happening but use the seduction to their own advantage. In the play, Machiavelli implicitly challenges the humanistic assumption that educated individuals will naturally choose virtue over vice. He explicitly criticizes these same assumptions in *The Prince*. Machiavelli holds the contrary view: that individuals are much more likely to respond to fear and that power rather than morality makes for good government.

Machiavelli's use of the Italian word *virtù* led him to be vilified as amoral. Machiavelli deliberately chose a word that meant both "manliness" or "ability" and "virtue as a moral quality." Earlier humanists had restricted *virtù* to the second meaning, using the word to refer to upright qualities such as prudence, generosity, and bravery. Machiavelli tried to show that, in some situations, these "virtues" could have violent, even evil, consequences. If, for example, a prince was so magnanimous in giving away his wealth that he was forced to raise taxes, his subjects might come to hate him. Conversely, a prince who, through cruelty to the enemies of his state, brought peace and stability to his subjects might be obeyed and perhaps even loved. A virtuous ruler must be mindful of the goals to be achieved—that is what Machiavelli really meant by the phrase often translated as "the ends justify the means."

Like Guicciardini, Machiavelli rejected earlier humanistic assumptions that one needed merely to imitate the great leaders of the past. Governing is a process that requires different skills at different times, he warned: "The man who adapts his course of action to the nature of the times will succeed and, likewise, the man who sets his course of action out of tune with the times will come to grief."[9] The abilities that enable a prince to gain power may not be the abilities that will allow him to maintain it.

With the writings of Machiavelli, humanistic ideas of intellectual, moral, and political reform came to maturation. Petrarch and the early humanists believed fully in the powers of classical wisdom to transform society. Machiavelli and his contemporaries admitted the importance of classical wisdom, but also recognized the ambiguity of any simplistic application of classical learning to contemporary life.

Niccolò Machiavelli
A government functionary and political theorist in Florence, whose most famous work, *The Prince*, emphasized that the successful ruler must anticipate and adapt to change.

SECTION SUMMARY

- The culture of Italy was more urban and less clerical than the rest of Europe.

- Francesco Petrarch popularized cultural movements that attempted to use Roman learning to change moral values and public behavior in Europe.

- Because women lacked a role in public life, their relationship to the humanistic movement was limited.

- By the end of the fifteenth century, humanists had developed a sense of historical change.

- Political crisis in Italy led Machiavelli to challenge the assumptions about morality and public life.

PAINTING AND THE ARTS, 1250–1550

What was "new" about Renaissance art?

Townspeople and artists in Renaissance Italy shared the humanists' perception of the importance of classical antiquity. Filippo Villani (d. 1405), a wealthy Florentine from an important business family, wrote that artists had recently "reawakened a lifeless and almost extinct art." In the middle of the fifteenth century, the sculptor Lorenzo Ghiberti concluded that, with the rise of Christianity, "not only statues and paintings [were destroyed], but the books and commentaries and handbooks and rules on which men relied for their training." Italian writers and painters themselves believed that the recovery of past literary and artistic practices was essential if society was to recover from the "barbarism" that they believed characterized the recent past.

The Renaissance of the arts is traditionally divided into three periods. In the early Renaissance, artists imitated nature; in the middle period, they rediscovered classical ideas of proportion; in the High Renaissance, artists were "superior to nature but also to the artists of the ancient world," according to the artist and architect Giorgio Vasari (1511–1574), who wrote a famous history of the eminent artists of his day.

Early Renaissance Art

The first stirrings of the new styles can be found in the late thirteenth century. The greatest innovator of that era was Giotto di Bondone of Florence (ca. 1266–1337). Although Giotto's background was modest, his fellow citizens, popes, and patrons throughout Italy quickly recognized his skill. He

Giotto's Naturalism
Later painters praised the naturalistic emotion of Giotto's painting. In this detail from the Arena Chapel, Giotto portrays the kiss of Judas, one of the most dramatic moments in Christian history. (Scala/Art Resource, NY)

traveled as far south as Rome and as far north as Padua, painting churches and chapels. According to later artists and commentators, Giotto broke with the prevailing stiff, highly symbolic style and introduced lifelike portrayals of living persons. He produced paintings of dramatic situations, showing events located in specific times and places. The frescoes of the Arena Chapel in Padua (1304–1314), for example, recount episodes in the life of Christ. In a series of scenes leading from Christ's birth to his crucifixion, Giotto situates his actors in towns and countryside in what appears to be actual space. Even Michelangelo, the master of the High Renaissance, studied Giotto's painting. Giotto was in such demand throughout Italy that his native Florence gave him a public appointment, so that he would be required by law to remain in the city.

Early in the fifteenth century, Florentine artists devised new ways to represent nature that surpassed even the innovations of Giotto. The revolutionary nature of these artistic developments is evident from the careers of Lorenzo Ghiberti (gi-BER-tee) (1378–1455), Filippo Brunelleschi (broon-eh-LES-key) (1377–1446), and Masaccio (1401–ca. 1428). Their sculpture, architecture, and painting began an ongoing series of experiments with the representation of space through **linear perspective**. Perspective is a system for representing three-dimensional objects on a two-dimensional plane. It is based on two observations: (1) as parallel lines recede into the distance, they seem to converge; and (2) a geometric relationship regulates the relative sizes of objects at various distances from the viewer. Painters of the Renaissance literally found themselves looking at their world from a new perspective.

In 1401, Ghiberti won a commission to design door panels for the baptistery of San Giovanni in Florence. He was to spend much of the rest of his life working on two sets of bronze doors on which were recorded the stories of the New Testament (the north doors) and the Old Testament (the east doors). Ghiberti used the new techniques of linear perspective to create a sense of space into which he placed his classically inspired figures. Later, in the sixteenth century, Michelangelo remarked that the east doors were worthy to be the "Doors of Paradise," and so they have been known ever since.

In the competition for the baptistery commission, Ghiberti had beaten the young Filippo Brunelleschi, who, as a result, gave up sculpture for architecture and later left Florence to study in Rome. While in Rome, he is said to have visited and measured surviving examples of classical architecture—the artistic equivalent of humanistic literary research. According to Vasari, he was capable of "visualizing Rome as it was before the fall." Brunelleschi's debt to Rome is evident in his masterpiece, Florence's foundling hospital. Built as a combination of hemispheres and cubes and resembling a Greek stoa or an arcaded Roman basilica, the long, low structure is an example of how profoundly different Renaissance architecture was from the towering Gothic of the Middle Ages. But his experience in Rome was also critical to his famous plan for constructing a dome over the Cathedral of Santa Maria del Fiore in Florence. The Florentines were replacing their old cathedral with a vast new one. But until Brunelleschi, no one had been able to design a dome to cover the 180-foot space created by the vast new nave. He designed mutually supporting internal and external domes that were stronger and lighter than a single dome would have been.

In the first decade of the fifteenth century, many commentators believed that painting would never be as innovative as either sculpture or architecture. They knew of no classical models that had survived for imitation. Yet, the possibilities in painting became apparent in 1427 with the unveiling of Masaccio's *Trinity* in the Florentine Church of Santa Maria Novella. Masaccio (ma-SAH-cho) built on revolutionary experiments in linear perspective to create a painting in which a flat wall seems to become a recessed chapel. The space created is filled with the images of Christ crucified, the Father, and the Holy Spirit.

The Doors of Paradise   Ghiberti worked on panels for the baptistery from 1401 to 1453. In his representations of scenes from the Old Testament, he combined a love of ancient statuary with the new Florentine interest in linear perspective.   (Baptistery of San Giovanni, Florence/ Scala/Art Resource, NY)

linear perspective
A revolutionary technique developed by early-fifteenth-century Florentine painters for representing three-dimensional objects on a two-dimensional plane.

In the middle years of the fifteenth century, artists came to terms with the innovations of the earlier period. In the second half of the fifteenth century, however, artists such as the Florentine Sandro Botticelli (bot-ti-CHEL-ee) (1445–1510) added a profound understanding of classical symbolism to the technical innovations of Masaccio and Brunelleschi. Botticelli's famous *Primavera* (*Spring*, 1478), painted for a member of the Medici family, is filled with Neo-Platonic symbolism concerning truth, beauty, and the virtues of humanity.

High Renaissance Art

The high point in the development of Renaissance art came at the beginning of the sixteenth century. Artists in Venice learned perspective from the Florentines and added their own tradition of subtle coloring in oils. The works of Italian artists were admired well beyond the borders of Italy. Even Sultan Mehmed II of Constantinople valued Italian painters. (See the feature, "The Global Record: Gentile Bellini Travels to Meet the Turkish Sultan.") Italian painters, goldsmiths, and architects continued to work in the Ottoman Empire through the sixteenth century.

The work of two Florentines, **Leonardo da Vinci** (1452–1519) and **Michelangelo Buonarroti** (1475–1564), best exemplifies the sophisticated heights that art achieved early in the sixteenth century. Leonardo, the bastard son of a notary, was raised in the village of Vinci outside of Florence. Cut off from the humanistic milieu of the city, he desired, above all else, to prove that his artistry was the equal of his formally schooled social superiors. In his notebooks, he confessed, "I am fully conscious that, not being a literary man, certain presumptuous persons will think they may reasonably blame me, alleging that I am not a man of letters."[10] But he defended his lack of classical education by arguing that all the best writing, like the best painting and invention, is based on the close observation of nature. Close observation and scientific analysis made Leonardo's work uniquely creative in all these fields. Leonardo is famous for his plans, sometimes prophetic, for bridges, fortresses, submarines, and airships. In painting, he developed chiaroscuro, a technique for using light and dark in pictorial representation, and showed aerial perspective. He painted horizons as muted, shaded zones rather than with sharp lines. It was Leonardo's analytical observation that had the greatest influence on his contemporaries.

Michelangelo, however, was widely hailed as the capstone of Renaissance art. In the words of a contemporary, "He alone has triumphed over ancient artists, modern artists and over Nature itself." In his career, we can follow the rise of Renaissance artists from the ranks of mere craftsmen to honored creators, courtiers who were the equals of the humanists—in fact, Michelangelo shared Petrarch's concern for reform and renewal in Italian society. We can also discern the synthesis of the artistic and intellectual transformations of the Renaissance with a profound religious sensitivity.

The importance of Michelangelo's contribution is obvious in two of his most important works: the statue *David* in Florence and his commissions in the **Sistine Chapel** of the Vatican in Rome. From his youth, Michelangelo had studied and imitated antique sculpture, to the point that some of his creations were thought by many actually to be antiquities. He used his understanding of classical art in *David* (1501). Florentines recalled David's defeat of the giant Goliath, saving Israel from almost certain conquest by the Philistines. *David* thus became a symbol of the youthful Florentine republic struggling to maintain its freedom against great odds. As Vasari noted, "Just as David had protected his people and governed them justly, so whoever ruled Florence should vigorously defend the city and govern it with justice."[11]

Michelangelo was a committed republican and Florentine, but he spent much of his life working in Rome on a series of papal commissions. In 1508, he was called by Pope Julius II (r. 1503–1513) to work on the ceiling of the Sistine Chapel. Michelangelo spent four years decorating the ceiling with hundreds of figures and with nine scenes from the Book of

Leonardo da Vinci A famous painter, engineer, and scientist who rejected arguments and ideas based on imitation of the ancients. Rather, he advocated careful study of the natural world.

Sistine Chapel The chapel at the Vatican Palace, containing Michelangelo's magnificent paintings of the Creation and Last Judgment; it captures the cultural, religious, and ideological program of the papacy.

The Pietà Michelangelo sculpted three versions of Mary holding the crucified Jesus. This late, unfinished work reveals Michelangelo's desire to show the suffering of Christ. (Scala/Art Resource, NY)

Gentile Bellini Travels to Meet the Turkish Sultan

Giovanni and Gentile Bellini were two of the leading Renaissance artists in Venice. Their fame spread throughout the Mediterranean and resulted in this unusual cultural meeting in 1479. A portrait of the emperor Mehmed II by Gentile now hangs in the National Gallery in London.

Some portraits having been taken to Turkey to the Grand Turk [the sultan] by an ambassador, that emperor was so struck with astonishment that, although the Mohammedan laws prohibit pictures, he accepted them with great goodwill, praising the work without end, and what is more, requesting that the master himself be sent to him. But the Senate, considering that Giovanni could ill support the hardships, resolved to send Gentile his brother, and he was conveyed safely in their galleys to Constantinople, where being presented to Mehmed [II], he was received with much kindness as an unusual visitor. He presented a beautiful picture to the prince, who admired it much, and could not persuade himself to believe that a mortal man had in him so much of the divinity as to be able to express the things of nature in such a lively manner. Gentile painted the Emperor Mehmed himself from life so well that it was considered a miracle, and the emperor, having seen many specimens of his art, asked Gentile if he had the courage to paint himself; and Gentile having answered "Yes," before many days were over he finished a lifelike portrait by means of a mirror, and brought it to the monarch, whose astonishment was so great that he would have it a divine spirit dwelt in him. And had not this art been forbidden by the law of the Turks, the emperor would never have let him go. But either from fear that people would murmur, or from some other cause, he sent for him one day, and having thanked him, and given him great praise, he bade him to ask whatever he would and it should be granted him without fail. Gentile modestly asked for nothing more than that he would graciously give him a letter of recommendation to the Senate and Lords of Venice. His request was granted in as fervent words as possible, and then, loaded with gifts and honors, and with the dignity of a cavalier, he was sent away. Among the other gifts was a chain of gold of two hundred and fifty crowns weight, worked in the Turkish manner. So, leaving Constantinople, he came safely to Venice, where he was received by his brother Giovanni and the whole city with joy, every one rejoicing in the honors which Mehmed had paid him. When the Doge and Lords [of Venice] saw the letters of the emperor, they ordered that a provision of two hundred crowns a year should be paid him all the rest of his life.

QUESTIONS

1. What seems to be the role of Renaissance art and artists in Venetian and Turkish diplomacy?

2. What does Bellini's trip to Constantinople suggest about relations between the Turks and Christians?

Source: *Stories of the Italian Renaissance from Vasari*, arranged and translated by E. L. Seeley (London and New York, 1908), pp. 135–137.

Genesis, including the famous *Creation of Adam*. In the late 1530s, at the request of Pope Clement VII (r. 1523–1534), he completed *The Last Judgment*, which covers the wall above the altar. In that painting, the techniques of perspective and the conscious recognition of debts to classical culture recede into the background as the artist surrounds Christ in judgment with saints and sinners. In the hollow, hanging skin of flayed Saint Bartholomew we can detect a psychological self-portrait of an artist increasingly concerned with his own spiritual failings.

Michelangelo's self-portrait reminds us that the intellectual content of the artist's work is one of its most enduring traits. He was a Platonist who believed that the form and beauty of a statue are contained, buried, in the stone itself. The artist's job is to peel away excess material and reveal the beauty within. As he noted in one of his poems, sculpting is a process not unlike religious salvation:

> *Just as by carving … we set*
> *Into hard mountain rock*
> *A living figure*
> *Which grows most where the stone is most removed;*
> *In like manner, some good works …*
> *Are concealed by the excess of my very flesh.*[12]

Renaissance Art in the North

In the early fifteenth century, while Brunelleschi and Masaccio were revolutionizing the ways in which Italian artists viewed their world, artists north of the Alps, especially in Flanders, were making equally striking advances in the ways they painted and sculpted. Artistic innovation in northern Europe began with changes tied closely to the world of northern courts; only later did artists take up the styles of the Italian Renaissance. Northerners took Italian Renaissance art and fit it to a new environment.

Northern art of the late fourteenth and fifteenth centuries changed in two significant ways. In sculpture, the long, austere, unbroken vertical lines typical of Gothic sculpture gave way to a much more complex and emotional style. In painting, Flemish artists moved from ornate, vividly colored paintings to experiments with ways to create a sense of depth. Artists strove to paint and sculpt works that more faithfully represented reality. The sculptures of Claus Sluter (1350–1406), carved for a family chapel of the Burgundian dukes at Champmol, captured a lifelike drama unlike the previous Gothic sculpture. Court painters, such as Jan van Eyck (ca. 1390–1441), in miniatures, portraits, and altar paintings, also moved away from a highly formalized style to a careful representation of specific places. In van Eyck's portrait of the Italian banker and courtier Giovanni Arnolfini and his bride, the image of the painter is reflected in a small mirror behind the couple, and above the mirror is written, "Jan van Eyck was here, 1434." Whereas Italians of the early fifteenth century tried to re-create space through linear perspective, the Flemish used aerial perspective, softening colors and tones to give the illusion of depth.

The influence of Renaissance styles in the north of Europe dates from the reign of the French king Francis I (r. 1515–1547), when Italian artists in significant numbers traveled north. Francis invited Italian artists to his court—most notably Leonardo da Vinci, who spent his last years in France. The most influential of the Italian style creations in France was doubtless Francis's château Fontainebleau, whose decorations contained mythologies, histories, and allegories of the kind found in the Italian courts. Throughout the sixteenth century, Italianate buildings and paintings sprang up throughout Europe.

Perhaps the most famous artist who traveled to Italy, learned Italian techniques, and then transformed them to suit the environment of northern Europe was Albrecht Dürer of Nuremberg (1471–1528). Son of a well-known goldsmith, Dürer became a painter and toured France and Flanders, learning the techniques popular in northern Europe. Then, in 1494, he left Nuremberg on the first of two trips to Italy, during which he sketched Italian landscapes and studied the work of Italian artists, especially in Venice. What he learned in Italy, combined with the friendship of some of Germany's leading humanists, formed the basis of Dürer's works, which blended northern humanistic interests with the Italian techniques of composition and linear perspective. Dürer worked in charcoal, watercolors, and paints, but his influence was most widely spread through his numerous woodcuts covering classical and contemporary themes. His woodcut, *Whore of Babylon*, prepared in the context of the debate over the reform of the church, is based on sketches of Venetian prostitutes completed during his first visit to Italy.

Numerous other artists and engravers traveled south to admire and learn from the great works of Italian artists. The engravings they produced and distributed back home made the southern innovations available to those who would never set foot in Italy. In fact, some now lost or destroyed creations are known only through the copies engraved by northern artists eager to absorb Italian techniques.

Van Eyck: The Arnolfini Wedding   Careful observation of people and places was typical of the new art of both northern and southern Europe. Van Eyck seems to have re-created this scene to the smallest detail. His own image appears in the mirror on the wall.   (The National Gallery, London/Art Resource, NY)

Art and Patronage

The variety and vitality of art in the Renaissance depended, in large measure, on the economic prosperity of Europe's cities and towns. Because of banking, international trade, and even service as mercenaries, Italians, and particularly Florentines, had money to spend on arts and luxuries. Thus, the Italians of the Renaissance, whether as public or private patrons, could afford to use consumption of art as a form of competition for social and political status.

It was not just the elite who could afford art. Surprisingly, modest families bought small religious paintings, painted storage chests, and decorative arts. Moralists advised families to buy small paintings of the Virgin Mary or the baby Jesus. Families also bought small paintings of saints considered special to their town or family. Wealthy and modest families alike bought brightly decorated terra-cotta pitchers, platters, and plates. Decorative arts were a critical social marker for families at all levels. (See the feature, "The Visual Record: Renaissance Marriage Chests.") Thus, the market for art steadily increased in the fourteenth and fifteenth centuries, as did the number of shops and studios in which artists could be trained.

Artists in the modern world are accustomed to standing outside society as critics of conventional ideas. In the late Middle Ages and Renaissance, artists were not alienated commentators. In 1300, most art was religious in subject, and public display was its purpose. Throughout Europe, art fulfilled a devotional function. Painted crucifixes, altarpieces, and banners were often endowed as devotional or penitential objects. The Arena Chapel in Padua, with its frescoes by Giotto, was funded by a merchant anxious to pay for some of his sins.

In the late Middle Ages and Renaissance, numerous paintings and statues throughout Italy (and much of the rest of Europe) were revered for their miraculous powers. During plague, drought, and times of war people had recourse to the sacred power of the saints represented in these works of art. (See the feature, "The Visual Record: A Painting of the Plague" in Chapter 11, pages 306–307.) The construction of the great churches of the period was often a community project that lasted for decades, even centuries. The city council of Siena, for example, voted to rebuild its Gothic Cathedral of Saint Mary, saying that the Blessed Virgin "was, is and will be in the future the head of this city" and that through veneration of her "Siena may be protected from harm." Accordingly, although the subject of art was clearly and primarily religious, the message was bound up in civic values.

Portrait of a Black Man   Albrecht Dürer sketched this portrait in the early sixteenth century, most likely in a commercial center such as Venice or Nuremberg. By that time, it was common to show one of the three Magi as black, but such depictions, unlike Dürer's drawing here, were rarely based on portrait studies.   (Graphische Sammlung, Albertina, Vienna)

ART AND THE COMMUNE

The first burst of artistic creativity in the fourteenth century was paid for by public institutions. Communal governments built and decorated city halls to house government functionaries and to promote civic pride. Most towns placed a remarkable emphasis on the beauty of the work. Civic officials often named special commissions to consult with a variety of artists and architects before approving building projects. Governments, with an eye to the appearance of public areas, legislated the width of streets, height limits, and even the styles of dwelling façades.

Public art in Florence was often organized and supported by various guild organizations. Guild membership was a prerequisite for citizenship, so guildsmen set the tone in politics, as well as in the commercial life of the city. Most major guilds commissioned sculpture for the Chapel of Or San Michele. This was a famous shrine in the grain market (its painting of the Virgin Mary was popularly thought to have wonder-working powers). The room above the chapel eventually became the seat of the Guelf Party, the city's most powerful political organization. Guilds took responsibility for building and maintaining other structures in the city as well. Guildsmen took pride in creating a beautiful environment that would reflect not only on the city and its patron saint, but also on the power and influence of the guild itself.

INDIVIDUAL PATRONS

The princes who ruled outside the republics of Italy often had similarly precise messages that they wished to communicate. Renaissance popes embarked on a quite specific ideological program in the late fifteenth century to assert their dual roles as spiritual leaders of Christendom and temporal lords of a central Italian state (see pages 346–347). Rulers, such as the Este dukes of

Men and Women Playing Cards   This fresco painted in the early fifteenth century in Milan is typical of the art used to decorate the homes of the wealthy. It depicts one of the pastimes of noble families. (Scala/Art Resource, NY)

Ferrara and the Sforza dukes of Milan, constructed castles within their cities or hunting lodges and villas in the countryside and adorned them with pictures of the hunt or murals of knights in combat—scenes that emphasized their noble virtues and their natural right to rule.

By the mid-fifteenth century, patrons of artworks in Florence and most other regions of Italy were more and more likely to be wealthy individuals. Many of the patrons who commissioned and oversaw artists were women. Women paid for the construction of convents and chapels. In many cases, their patronage can simply be understood as an extension of their families, but in many other cases, it was not. One woman who had lived for years as a concubine of a merchant in Florence used her dead lover's bequest to commission a painting titled *Christ and the Adulteress*, making clear that even women in her situation could hope for God's mercy.

Republics, in which all families were in principle equal, initially distrusted the pride and ambition implied by elaborate city palaces and rural villas. By the middle of the fifteenth century, however, such reserve was found in none but the most conservative republics, such as Venice and Lucca. Palaces, gardens, and villas became the settings in which the wealthy could entertain their peers, receive clients, and debate the political issues of the day. The public rooms of these palaces were decorated with portraits, gem collections, rare books, ceramics, and statuary. Many villas and palaces included private chapels. In the Medici palace in Florence, for example, the chapel is the setting for a painting of the Magi (the three wise men who came to worship the infant Jesus), in which the artist, Benozzo Gozzoli (1420–1498), used members of the Medici family as models for the portraits of the Magi and their entourage (see the painting on page 300). The Magi, known to be wise and virtuous rulers, were an apt symbol for the family that had come to dominate the city.

Artists at princely courts were expected to work for the glory of their lord. Often the genre of choice was the portrait. One of the most successful portraitists of the sixteenth century was Sofonisba Anguissola (1532–1625). Anguissola won renown as a prodigy because she was female and from a patrician family; one of her paintings was sent to Michelangelo, who forwarded it to the Medici in Florence. Since women would never be allowed to study anatomy, Anguissola concentrated her talents on portraits and detailed paintings of domestic life. Later, she was called to the Spanish court, where the king, queen, and their daughter sat for her. She continued to paint after her marriage and return to Italy. Even in her nineties, she welcomed painters from all parts of Europe to visit and discuss techniques of portraiture.

SECTION SUMMARY

- Renaissance painters were especially prized for their ability to depict particular events in realistic, natural seeming settings.
- Beginning with Brunelleschi, artists consciously searched for ancient models for their work.
- Northern artists were keenly aware of Italian art, but they contributed a realism based on contrasts of dramatic colors.
- The work of Michelangelo shows the combination of artistic skill with humanistic moral and philosophical values.

THE SPREAD OF THE RENAISSANCE, 1350–1536

In what ways did humanism outside Italy differ from Italian humanism?

By 1500, the Renaissance had spread from Italy to the rest of Europe. Well beyond the borders of the old Roman Empire, in Prague and Cracow, for example, one could find a renewed interest in classical ideas about art and literature. As information about the past and its relevance to contemporary life spread, however, the message was transformed in several important ways. Outside Italy, Rome and its history played a much less pivotal role. Humanists elsewhere in the West were interested more in religious than in political reform, and they responded to a number of important local interests. Yet, the Renaissance notion of renewal based on a deep understanding and imitation of the past remained at the center of the movement. The nature of the transformation will be clearer if we begin by considering the nature of vernacular literatures before the emergence of Renaissance humanism.

Vernacular Literatures

The humanistic movement was not simply a continuation of practical and literary movements. The extent of its innovation will be clearer if we look briefly at the vernacular literatures (that is, written in native languages, rather than Latin) of the fourteenth and fifteenth centuries.

As in Italy, fourteenth-century writers elsewhere were not immediately drawn to classical sources. Boccaccio's work, for example, influenced another vernacular writer, Geoffrey Chaucer (ca. 1343–1400), the son of a London burgher, who served as a diplomat, courtier, and member of Parliament. Chaucer's most famous work, *The Canterbury Tales*, consists of stories told by a group of thirty pilgrims who left the London suburbs on a pilgrimage to the shrine of Saint Thomas Becket at Canterbury Cathedral. The narrators and the stories themselves describe a variety of moral and social types, creating an acute, sometimes comic, portrait of English life. The Wife of Bath is typical of Chaucer's pilgrims: "She was a worthy woman all her life, husbands at the churchdoor she had five." After describing her own marriages she observes that marriage is a proper way to achieve moral perfection, but it can be so only, she asserts, if the woman is master!

Although Chaucer's characters present an ironic view of the good and evil that characterize society, Chaucer's contemporary, William Langland (ca. 1330–1400), took a decidedly more serious view of the ills of English life. Whereas Boccaccio and Chaucer all told realistic tales about life as it truly seemed to be, Langland used the traditional allegorical language (that is, symbolic language in which a place or person represents an idea) of medieval Europe. In *Piers Plowman*, Langland writes of people caught between the "Valley of Death" and the "Tower of Truth." He describes the seven deadly sins that threaten all of society and follows with an exhortation to do

Renaissance Marriage Chests

The image here shows a marriage procession, including a servant carrying a large chest, or cassone. The picture is self-referential, since it was painted on the front of just such a cassone. We know that the painter of this image was Lo Scheggia (lo-SKED-ja) (1406–1486), the younger brother of Masaccio, and that he was recording a popular story of a marriage between the Bardi and Buondelmonte families of Florence. Lo Scheggia's work exhibits many of the characteristics we associate with Renaissance style. But historians often want to evaluate more than just painting technique. Historians of material culture are interested in the objects themselves and in the meanings that contemporaries gave to the possession and exhibition of them. To understand this, we need to know when and where cassoni were produced, why individuals prized them, and what the study of this image from a cassone can tell us about life in Renaissance Italy.

These highly practical chests were used by all but the poorest members of society. In houses that lacked closets, cabinets, and other kinds of storage space, everything was kept in wooden chests. Larger chests were used to store clothing, bedding, jewelry, and even weapons. Smaller chests were used for money, account books, and documents. Many of these chests had secret compartments where, for example, a businessman might keep his most sensitive papers. The most important chests made up the furnishings of the master of the house's bedroom. In a Renaissance palace the master's bedroom was also the room where he met with important allies and family members and conducted his most private business.

Cassoni took on new meaning between the late fourteenth and early sixteenth centuries. During that time, it was common for a groom to commission a matched set of chests: one for himself and the second to hold the fine clothes and jewelry that were part of his wife's dowry. These chests were decorated inside and out with scenes from classical mythology, medieval romances, and other popular stories. Classical Roman figures, such as Lucretia, who sacrificed her life to maintain her virtue, were common subjects. Some chests celebrated the virtues of chastity or fortitude—virtues thought to be essential in a proper wife. Thus, cassoni came to represent the taste, wealth, and social status of the families involved.

With these thoughts in mind, let us look closely at Lo Scheggia's cassone painting. The first thing we should notice is the procession at the left of the picture. We see a man accompanying a woman dressed in black into a house. The two are followed by others leading a horse (a sign of nobility) and carrying bedclothes and the chest. The procession testifies to the very public completion of the marriage process, which often stretched over months, if not years. It began with an engagement, followed by a promise of marriage, then a symbolic exchange of rings and physical consummation of the marriage, usually at the bride's home. The marriage was finalized by a procession to the groom's home. This procession celebrated publicly the alliance between the two families, as well as their standing in the community. Everyone noted carefully what and how much was carried in the procession, which was an indication of the size of the bride's dowry. The decoration of the marriage chest(s) in some way reflected the families involved.

What does the cassone image by Lo Scheggia indicate? The bride is the key to the story. Typically, a wealthy bride wore bright new clothes and jewelry, but this bride is dressed in black. The image tells a story not unlike that of Romeo and Juliet. The families of the bride and groom, Lionora de' Bardi and Ippolito Buondelmonte, had been

---

better. Both Chaucer and Langland expected that their audiences would immediately recognize commonly held ideas and values.

Despite the persistence of old forms of literature, new vernacular styles arose, although they still dealt with traditional values and ideas. Letters like those of the Paston family in England or Alessandra Macinghi-Strozzi in Italy described day-to-day affairs of business, politics, and family life. Letters dictated and sent by Saint Catherine of Siena and Angela of Foligno offered advice to the troubled. Small books of moral or spiritual writings were especially popular among women readers in the fourteenth and fifteenth centuries, among them *The Mirror for Simple Souls* by Marguerite of Porete (d. 1310). Though Marguerite was ultimately executed as a heretic, her work continued to circulate anonymously. Her frank descriptions of love, including God's love for humans, inspired many other writers in the fourteenth and fifteenth centuries. Less erotic, but equally riveting, was the memoir of Margery Kempe, an alewife from England, who left her husband and family, dressed in white (symbolic of virginity), and joined other pilgrims on trips to Spain, Italy, and Jerusalem.

One of the most unusual of the new vernacular writers was Christine de Pizan (1369–1430), the daughter of an Italian physician at the court of Charles V of France. When the deaths of her father and husband left her with responsibility for her children and little money, she turned to writing. From 1389 until her death, she lived and wrote at the French court. She is perhaps best known for *The Book of the City of the Ladies* (1405). In it, she added her own voice to what is known

Lo Scheggia: The Bardi-Buondelmonte Wedding (Alberto Bruschi di Grassina Collection, Florence/Bridgeman Art Library International)

enemies for generations. Despite this fact, the two were in love. We can read the tale of their love in three scenes from right to left. In the first scene on the right, Ippolito is caught in Lionora's house. He refuses to declare his love for her because he wants to protect her reputation. In the middle scene, Lionora, dressed as a widow, interrupts Ippolito's trial and declares her love for him. By dressing as a widow, she symbolically declares that they have already made their wedding vows and are, in fact, married. The authorities accept her declaration, and in the final scene on the left, the marriage is made public. Ippolito leads Lionora in a marriage procession, complete with wedding chest, to their new home. According to tradition, their marriage ended the feud between the two families.

We do not know who commissioned this chest. Nonetheless, we can now step back and speculate a bit about what Florentines might have noticed when they viewed the procession in which this cassone was carried through the streets of Florence. The image of the wedding couple and the servants carrying expensive dowry items, as well as the chest itself, testifies to the importance of the families involved. In a community such as Florence, where certain families were at the center of politics and public life, this image no doubt reminded those watching the procession of the power of prominent families and the critical role of marriage alliances in maintaining civic peace.

QUESTIONS

1. Look carefully at the image. Can you identify what seems most significant in the procession of the bride and groom?

2. How would this particular image influence the meaning that observers might give to the procession of the bride and groom?

as the *querelle des femmes*, the "argument over women." Christine wrote to counter the prevalent opinions of women as inherently inferior to men and incapable of learning or moral judgments. She argued that the problem was education: "If it were customary to send daughters to school like sons, and if they were then taught the natural sciences, they would learn as thoroughly and understand the subtleties of all the arts and sciences as well as sons." Christine described, in her book, an ideal city of ladies in which prudence, justice, and reason would protect women from ignorant male critics.

All these vernacular writings built on popular tales and sayings as well as on traditional moral and religious writings. Unlike the early humanists, the vernacular writers saw little need for new cultural and intellectual models.

The Impact of Printing

The spread of humanism beyond Italy was aided greatly by the invention of printing. In the fifteenth century, the desire to own and to read complete texts of classical works was widespread, but the number of copies was severely limited. Manuscripts required time and money to hand-copy, collate, and check each new copy. Poggio Bracciolini's letters are filled with complaints about the time and expense of reproducing the classical manuscripts he had discovered. One copy he had commissioned was so inaccurate and illegible as to be nearly unusable. Traveling to repositories and libraries was often easier than creating a personal library. It was rarely possible for someone who read a manuscript once to obtain a complete copy to compare with other works.

The invention of printing with movable lead type changed things dramatically. Although block printing had long been known in China, it was only in the late fourteenth century that it became a popular way to produce playing cards and small woodcuts in Europe. In China, an entire page would be carved on a single wooden block. **Johann Gutenberg** developed molds by which single letters or individual words could be cast in metal. Metal fonts could produce many more copies before they had to be recast. And further, they could be reused to print different pages. Between 180 and 200 copies of the so-called Gutenberg Bible were printed in 1452 and 1453. It was followed shortly by editions of the Psalms. By 1470, German printing techniques had spread to Italy, the Low Countries, France, and England. It has been estimated that, by 1500, a thousand presses were operating in 265 towns (see **Map 12.1**). The output of the early presses was extremely varied, ranging from small devotional books and other popular and profitable literature to complete editions of classical authors and their humanistic and theological texts.

Johann Gutenberg
German inventor of movable metal type. His innovations led to the publication of the first printed book in Europe, the Gutenberg Bible, in the 1450s.

🌐 Map 12.1—The Spread of Printing

Printing technology moved rapidly along major trade routes to the most populous and prosperous areas of Europe. The technology was rapidly adopted in peripheral areas as well as in highly literate centers such as the Low Countries, the Rhine Valley, and northern Italy.

Printing allowed for a dramatic expansion of libraries. Early humanists had to strive to create a library of several hundred volumes. The Venetian printer Aldus Manutius (1450–1515) himself printed and distributed over 120,000 volumes!

Printing allowed for the creation of agreed-upon standard editions of works in law, theology, philosophy, and science. Scholars in different parts of the European world could feel fairly confident that they and their colleagues were analyzing identical texts. Similarly, producing accurate medical and herbal diagrams, maps, and even reproductions of art and architecture was easier. Multiple copies of texts also made possible the study of rare and esoteric literary, philosophical, and scientific works. An unexpected result of the print revolution was the rise of the printshop as a center of culture and communication. The printers Aldus Manutius in Venice and Johannes Froben (d. 1527) in Basel were humanists. Both invited humanists to work in their shops editing their texts and correcting the proofs before printing. Printshops became a natural gathering place for clerics and laymen. Thus, they were natural sources of humanist ideas and later, in the sixteenth century, of Protestant religious programs.

Humanism Outside Italy

As the influence of the humanist movement extended beyond Italy, the interests of the humanists changed. Although a strong religious strain infused Italian humanism, public life lay at the center of Italian programs of education and reform. Outside Italy, however, moral and religious reform formed the heart of the movement. Northern humanists wanted to renew Christian life and reinvigorate the church. Critics of the church complained that the clergy were wealthy and ignorant and that the laity were uneducated and superstitious. To amend those failings, northern humanists were involved in building educational institutions, in unearthing and publishing texts by Church Fathers, and in chronicling local customs and history. The works of the two best-known humanists, Thomas More and Desiderius Erasmus, present a sharp critique of contemporary behavior and, in the case of Erasmus, a call to a new sense of piety. The religious views of Erasmus were so influential that northern humanism has generally come to be known as "Christian humanism."

The intellectual environment into which humanism spread from Italy had changed significantly since the thirteenth century. The universities of Paris and Oxford retained the status they had acquired earlier but found themselves competing with a host of new foundations. Like Paris, almost all had theological faculties dominated by scholastically trained theologians. Nevertheless, the new foundations often had chairs of rhetoric, or "eloquence," which left considerable scope for those who advocated humanistic learning. These new universities, from Cracow (1367) to Uppsala in Sweden (1477), also reflected the increased national feeling in various regions of Europe. The earliest university in the lands of the German Empire, the Charles University in Prague (1348), was founded at the request of Emperor Charles IV, whose court was in Prague. The foundation of a new university at Poszony (1465) by Johannes Vitéz was part of a cultural flowering of the Hungarian court at Buda. A supporter of King Matthias Corvinus, Vitéz corresponded with Italian humanists, collected manuscripts, and tried to recruit humanist teachers to come to Buda. The universities in Vienna (1365), Aix (1409), Louvain (1425), and numerous other cities owed their foundations to the pride and ambition of local leaders.

HUMANISM AND UNIVERSITIES

The humanists associated with the new universities were often educated in Italy, but they brought a new perspective to their work. Humanists in Sweden wrote histories of the Goths, celebrating the contributions of Germans to European culture. Polish humanists wrote similarly, in one case trying to define where in eastern Europe one could draw the line between Europe and Asia.

Humanists on faculties of law at French universities used humanistic techniques of historical and linguistic study. Italian-trained French lawyers introduced what came to be called the "Gallican style" of jurisprudence. Because legal ideas, like language, changed over time, they argued that Roman law had to be studied as a historically created system and not as an abstract and unchanging structure. Humanists, like Guillaume Budé (1468–1540), moved from the study of law to considerations of Roman coinage, religion, and economic life in order to better understand the formation of Roman law. The desire to understand the law led other humanist-legists to add the study of society in ancient Gaul to their work on Rome, and then to examine the law of other societies as well.

HUMANISM
AND RELIGION

The new universities often became centers of linguistic studies. Humanistic interest in language inspired the foundation of "trilingual" colleges in Spain, France, and the Low Countries to foster serious study of Hebrew, Greek, and Latin. Like Italian humanists, other humanists believed that knowledge of languages would allow students to understand more clearly the truths of Christianity. Typical of this movement was the archbishop of Toledo, Francisco Jiménez de Cisneros (1436–1517), who founded the University of Alcalá in 1508 with chairs of Latin, Greek, and Hebrew. He began the publication of a vast new edition of the Bible, called the "Polyglot ('many tongued') Bible" (1522) because it had parallel columns in Latin, Greek, and, where appropriate, Hebrew. Unlike Valla, Jiménez intended his translations not to challenge the Vulgate but merely to clarify its meaning. The university and the Bible were part of an effort to complete the conversion of Muslims and Jews and to reform religious practices among the old Christians.

To these humanists, the discovery and publication of early Christian authors seemed critical to any reform within the church. Jacques Lefèvre d'Étaples (le-FEV-ra du-TAHP-le) (1455–1536) of France was one of the most famous and influential of these humanistic editors of early Christian texts. After 1500, he concentrated on editing the texts of the early Church Fathers. The true spirit of Christianity, he believed, would be most clear in the works and lives of those who had lived closest to the age of the apostles. Christian humanists, inspired by Lefèvre, became key players in the later Reformation movements in France.

Tensions between the humanists and the advocates of Scholastic methods broke out over the cultural and linguistic studies that formed the heart of the humanist program. Taking to heart the humanistic belief that all philosophies and religions, not just Christianity, contained universal moral and spiritual truths, Johannes Reuchlin (RYE-klin) (1455–1522) of Württemberg embarked on a study of the Jewish Cabala. Johannes Pfefferkorn, a Dominican priest and recent convert from Judaism, attacked Reuchlin's use of Jewish traditions in the study of Christian theology. Sides were quickly drawn. The theological faculties of the German universities generally supported Pfefferkorn. The humanists supported Reuchlin. In his own defense, Reuchlin issued *The Letters of Illustrious Men*, a volume of correspondence he had received in support of his position. This work gave rise to one of the great satires of the Renaissance, *The Letters of Obscure Men* (1516), written by anonymous authors and purporting to be letters from various narrow-minded Scholastics in defense of Pfefferkorn. Although the debate arose over the validity of Hebraic studies for Christian theology, and not over humanistic ideas of reform or wisdom, it indicates the division between the humanists and much of the Scholastic community. Many people initially misunderstood the early controversies of the Protestant Reformation as a continuation of the conflicts between humanists and Scholastic theologians over the uses of Hebrew learning.

Humanists as Critics

Thomas More　Well-known humanist and chancellor of England under Henry VIII. His best-known work, *Utopia*, describes a fictional land of peace and harmony that has outlawed private property.

Desiderius Erasmus
Prominent Dutch humanist who is best known for his satire *The Praise of Folly*.

The careers of two humanists in particular exemplify the strength—and the limits—of the humanistic movement outside Italy: Sir **Thomas More** (1478–1535) of London and **Desiderius Erasmus** (1466–1536) of Rotterdam. Their careers developed along very different paths. More was educated at St. Anthony's School in London and became a lawyer. He translated Lucan and wrote a humanistic history of Richard III while pursuing his public career. Erasmus, on the other hand, was born the illegitimate son of a priest in the Low Countries. Forced by relatives into a monastery, he disliked the conservative piety and authoritarian discipline of traditional monastic life. Once allowed out of the monastery to serve as an episcopal secretary, he never returned. He made his way as an author and editor.

THOMAS MORE

More is most famous for his work *Utopia* (1516), the description of an ideal society located on the island of Utopia (literally, "nowhere") in the newly explored oceans. This powerful and contradictory work is written in two parts. Book I is a debate over the moral value of public service between Morus, a well-intentioned but practical politician, and Hythloday, a widely traveled idealist. Morus tries to make the bureaucrat's argument about working for change from within the system. Hythloday rejects the argument out of hand. Thomas More himself seems to have been unsure, at that time, about the virtues of public service. He was of two minds, and the debate between Morus and Hythloday reflects his indecision. As part of his critique of injustice and immoral governments in Europe, Hythloday describes in Book II the commonwealth of Utopia, in which there is no private property but strict equality of possessions, and, as a result, harmony, tolerance, and little or no violence.

Since the publication of *Utopia*, debates have raged about whether More, or anyone, could ever really hope to live in such a society. Some scholars have questioned how seriously More took this work—he seems to have written the initial sections merely to amuse friends. Yet, whatever More's intentions, Utopia's society of equality, cooperation, and acceptance continues to inspire social commentators.

Ironically, More, like his creation Morus, soon found himself trying to work for justice within precisely the sort of autocratic court that Hythloday criticized. Not long after the completion of *Utopia*, More entered the service of King Henry VIII (r. 1509–1547), eventually serving as chancellor of England. As a staunch Catholic and royal official, More never acted on utopian principles of peace and toleration. He was, in fact, responsible for the persecution of English Protestants in the years before the king's break with Rome (see pages 395–396). He implied that society could be reformed, yet, in the period after 1521, his humanism and his vision of utopian justice and tolerance had no influence on his own public life.

Unlike More, who was drawn to the power of king and pope, Erasmus always avoided working for authorities. Often called the "Prince of Humanists," he was easily the best-known humanist of the early sixteenth century. He lived and taught in France, England, Italy, and Switzerland. Of all the humanists, it was Erasmus who most benefited from the printing revolution. The printer Aldus Manutius invited him to live and work in Venice, and he spent the last productive years of his life at Johannes Froben's press in Basel.

DESIDERIUS ERASMUS

Over a long career, Erasmus brought out repeated editions of works designed to educate Christians. His *Adages*, first published in 1500, was a collection of proverbs from Greek and Roman sources. The work was immensely popular, and Erasmus repeatedly issued expanded editions. He tried to present Greek and Roman wisdom that would illuminate everyday problems. *The Colloquies* was a collection of popular stories. Designed as primers for students, they presented moral lessons, even as they taught good language. His ironic *The Praise of Folly* (1511) was dedicated to Thomas More. An oration by Folly in praise of folly, it is satire of a type unknown since antiquity. Folly's catalog of vices includes everyone from the ignoramus to the scholar. But more seriously, Erasmus believed, as Saint Paul had said, that Christians must be "fools for Christ." In effect, human existence is folly. Erasmus's *Folly* first made an observation that Shakespeare would refine and make famous: "Now the whole life of mortal men, what is it but a sort of play in which … [each person] plays his own part until the director gives him his cue to leave the stage."[13]

Erasmus's greatest contributions to European intellectual life were his edition of and commentaries on the New Testament. His was a critical edition of the Greek text and a Latin translation independent of the fourth-century Latin Vulgate of Jerome. Unlike Jiménez, Erasmus corrected parts of the Vulgate. He rejected the authority of tradition, saying, "The sin of corruption is greater, and the need for careful revision by scholars is greater also, where the source of corruption was ignorance."[14] What was revolutionary in his edition was his commentary, which emphasized the literal and historical recounting of human experiences. Erasmus's Bible was the basis of later vernacular translations of Scripture during the Reformation.

Underlying Erasmus's scholarly output was what he called his "Philosophy of Christ." Erasmus was convinced that the true essence of Christianity was to be found in the life and actions of Christ. Reasonable, self-reliant, truly Christian people did not need superstitious rituals or magic. In his *Colloquies*, he tells of a terrified priest who, during a shipwreck, promised everything to the Virgin Mary if only she would save him from drowning. But, Erasmus observed, it would have been more practical to start swimming!

Erasmus believed that a humanistic combination of classical and Christian wisdom could wipe away violence, superstition, and ignorance. Yet, his philosophy of Christ, based on faith in the goodness and educability of the individual, was swamped in the 1520s and 1530s by the sectarian claims of both Protestants and Catholics. Although Erasmus's New Testament was influential in the Reformation, his calls for reforms based on tolerance and reason were not.

SECTION SUMMARY

- Vernacular literatures of northern Europe emphasized religious and moral themes drawn from daily life.

- The development of printing using movable type made books more widely available. Humanists in northern Europe were more closely linked to university life and less tied to ideas of Roman public life.

- Thomas More and Desiderius Erasmus used their humanistic learning to develop a sophisticated critique of contemporary life.

POLITICS AND RENAISSANCE CULTURE

How did European rulers use Renaissance art and culture?

The educational reforms of the humanists and the innovations in the arts between 1300 and 1550 provided an opportunity for rulers and popes alike to use culture to define and celebrate their authority. Art, literature, and politics merged in the brilliant life of the Renaissance Italian courts, both secular and papal. To understand fully the Renaissance and its importance in the history of Europe, we need to examine the uses of culture by governments, specifically investigating the transformation of European ideas about service at court. We will take as a model the politics and cultural life at one noble court: the court of the Gonzaga family of Mantua. Then, we will see how the Renaissance papacy melded the secular and religious aspects of art, culture, and politics in its glittering court in Rome. Finally, we will discuss the development of the idea of the Renaissance gentleman and courtier made famous by Baldassare Castiglione (ka-stee-lee-OH-nay), who was reared at the Gonzaga court.

The Elaboration of the Court

The courts of northern Italy recruited artists and humanists inspired by classical civilization, and they closely imitated many of the values and new styles that were developing in the courts of northern Europe, such as the court of Burgundy. Throughout Europe, attendance at court became increasingly important to members of the nobility as a source of revenue and influence. Kings and the great territorial lords were equally interested in drawing people to their courts as a way to influence and control the noble and the powerful.

Rulers in most parts of Europe instituted monarchical orders of knighthood to reward allies and followers. The most famous in the English-speaking world was the Order of the Garter, founded in 1349 by King Edward III. The orders were but one of the innovations in the organization of the court during the fourteenth and fifteenth centuries. The numbers of cooks, servants, huntsmen, musicians, and artists employed at court jumped dramatically in the late Middle Ages. In this expansion, the papal court was a model for the rest of Europe. The popes at Avignon, in the fourteenth century, already had households of nearly six hundred persons. If all the bureaucrats, merchants, local officials, and visitors who continually swarmed around the elaborate papal court were also counted, the number grew even larger.

Courts were becoming theaters built around a series of widely understood signs and images that the ruler could manipulate. Culture was meant to reflect the reputation of the ruler. On important political or personal occasions, rulers organized jousts or tournaments around themes drawn from mythology. The dukes of Milan indicated the relative status of courtiers by inviting them to participate in particular hunts or jousts. They similarly organized their courtiers during feasts or elaborate entries into the towns and cities of their realms.

The late fourteenth and fifteenth centuries were periods of growth in the political and bureaucratic power of European rulers. The increasingly elaborate and sumptuous courts were one of the tools that rulers used to create a unified culture and ideology. At the court of the Gonzagas in Mantua, one of the most widely known of the fifteenth-century courts, the manipulation of Renaissance culture for political purposes was most complete.

The Court of Mantua

The city of Mantua, with perhaps 25,000 inhabitants in 1500, was small compared with Milan or Venice—the two cities with which it was most commonly allied. Located in a rich farming region near the Po River, Mantua did not have a large merchant or manufacturing class. Most Mantuans were involved in agriculture and regional trade in foodstuffs. The town had been a typical medieval Italian city-state until its government was overthrown by the noble Bonacolsi family in the thirteenth century. The Bonacolsis, in turn, were ousted in a palace coup in 1328 by their former comrades, the Gonzagas, who ruled the city until 1627.

The Gonzagas faced problems typical of many of the ruling families in northern Italy. The state they were creating was relatively small, their right to rule was not very widely recognized, and their control over the area was weak. The first step for the Gonzagas was to construct fortresses and fortified towns that could withstand foreign enemies. The second step was to gain recognition of their right to rule. In 1329, they were named imperial vicars, or representatives in the region. Later, in 1432, they bought the title "marquis" from the emperor Sigismund for the relatively low price of £12,000—equivalent to a year's pay for their courtiers. By 1500, they had exchanged that title for the more prestigious "duke."

Presiding over a strategic area between the Milanese and Venetian states, the Gonzagas maintained themselves through astute diplomatic connections with other Italian and European courts and through service as well-paid mercenaries in the Italian wars of the fifteenth and sixteenth centuries.

The family's reputation was enhanced by Gianfrancesco (jan-fran-CHES-ko) (d. 1444) and Lodovico, who brought the Renaissance and the new court style to Mantua. By 1500, as many as eight hundred or more nobles, cooks, maids, and horsemen may have gathered in the court. Critics called them idlers, "who have no other function but to cater to the tastes of the Duke." It was under the tutelage of the Gonzagas that Vittorino da Feltre created his educational experiment in Villa Giocosa, which drew noble pupils from throughout Italy. It would be hard to overestimate the value for the Gonzagas of a school that attracted sons of the dukes of Urbino, Ferrara, and Milan and of numerous lesser nobles. The family also called many artists to Mantua. Lodovico invited Antonio Pisano, called Pisanello (ca. 1415–1456), probably the most famous court artist of the fifteenth century. Pisanello created a series of frescoes on Arthurian themes for the Gonzaga palace. In these frescoes, Lodovico is portrayed as a hero of King Arthur's Round Table.

The Gonzagas are best known for their patronage of art with classical themes. The Florentine writer and architect Leon Battista Alberti (1404–1472) redesigned the façade of the Church of Sant'Andrea for the Gonzagas, in the form of a Roman triumphal arch. The church, which long had been associated with the family, became a monument to the Gonzaga court, just as the Arch of Constantine in Rome had celebrated imperial power a thousand years earlier. In the 1460s, Lodovico summoned Andrea Mantegna (1441–1506) to his court. Trained in Padua and Venice, Mantegna was, at that time, the leading painter in northern Italy. His masterwork is the *Camera degli Sposi* (literally, "the room of the spouses"), completed in 1474. It features family portraits of Lodovico Gonzaga and his family, framed in imitations of Roman imperial portrait medallions. One scene shows Lodovico welcoming his son, a newly appointed cardinal, back from Rome. Lodovico even included the portrait of the Holy Roman emperor who had never been to Mantua but was related to Lodovico's wife, Barbara of Brandenburg. As Mantegna finished the work, diplomats and rulers throughout Italy carefully monitored it—proof to all of the new status of the Gonzagas.

The Gonzaga court, like most others, was both public and private. On the one hand, finances for the city, appointments to public offices, and important political decisions were made by the men who dominated the court. On the other hand, as the prince's domestic setting, it was a place where women were expected to be seen and could exert their influence. Women were thus actively involved in creating the ideology of the court. Through the patronage of classical paintings, often with moral and political messages, wives of princes helped make the court better known and more widely accepted throughout Italy and Europe.

The arrival at court of Isabella d'Este (1494–1539), as the wife of Francesco Gonzaga, marked the high point of the Renaissance in Mantua. Isabella had received a classical education at Ferrara and maintained an interest in art, architecture, and music all her life. Isabella was also an accomplished musician, playing a variety of string and keyboard instruments. She and others of the Gonzaga family recruited Flemish and Italian musicians to their court. By the end of the sixteenth century, Mantua was one of the most important musical centers of Europe. As a patron of the arts, she knew what she wanted. Isabella used the general interest in the cultural life of Mantua as a way to increase contacts with the Italian and European powers. She used these informal cultural connections to further the family's political and diplomatic goals.

In the fourteenth century, Petrarch had complained that however enjoyable feasting in Mantua might be, the place was dusty, plagued by mosquitoes, and overrun with frogs. By the end of the fifteenth century, the Gonzagas had transformed their city and secured a prominent place for themselves on the Italian, and the European, stage.

The Renaissance Papacy

The issues of power and how it is displayed had religious as well as secular dimensions. After its fourteenth- and fifteenth-century struggles over jurisdiction, the papacy found itself reduced, in many respects, to the status of an Italian Renaissance court. But popes still needed to defend their primacy within the church from conciliarists, who had argued that all Christians, including the pope, were bound to obey the commands of general councils. The ideological focus of the revived papacy was Rome.

THE TRANSFORMATION OF ROME

The first step in the creation of a new Rome was taken by Pope Nicholas V (r. 1446–1455), a cleric who had spent many years in the cultural environment of Renaissance Florence. Hoping to restore Rome and its church to their former glory, Nicholas and his successors patronized the arts, established a lively court culture, and sponsored numerous building projects. Nicholas was an avid collector of ancient manuscripts that seemed to demonstrate the intellectual and religious primacy of Rome. He invited numerous artists and intellectuals to the papal court, including Leon Battista Alberti. He based his treatise, *On Architecture* (1452), on his research in topography and reading done in Rome. This was the most important work on architecture produced during the Renaissance. It was probably under Alberti's influence that Nicholas embarked on a series of ambitious urban renewal projects in Rome, which included bridges, roads, and a rebuilt Saint Peter's Basilica.

The transformation of Rome had an ideological purpose. As one orator proclaimed, "Illuminated by the light of faith and Christian truth, [Rome] is destined to be the firmament of religion . . . , the secure haven for Christians."[15] Thus, the papal response to critics was to note that Rome and its government were central to political and religious life in Christendom. By reviving

Giving of the Keys to Saint Peter   Pietro Perugino's painting of Saint Peter receiving from Christ the keys to "bind and loose" on earth and in heaven illustrates the basis of papal claims to authority within the Christian church. This is the central message of the decorative plan of the Sistine Chapel. (Scala/Art Resource, NY)

the style and organization of classical antiquity, the church sought to link papal Rome to a magnificent imperial tradition, reaching back to Augustus and even to Alexander the Great. To papal supporters, only one authority could rule the church. Early tradition and the continuity of the city itself, they assumed, demonstrated papal primacy.

One particular monument in Rome captures most vividly the cultural, religious, and ideological program of the papacy: the Sistine Chapel in the Vatican Palace. The chapel is best known for the decoration of the ceiling by the Florentine artist Michelangelo (see pages 332–333) and for the striking images in his painting of the Last Judgment. The chapel, however, was commissioned by Pope Sixtus IV in 1475. It was to be an audience chamber in which an enthroned pope could meet the representatives of other states. In addition, it was expected that the college of cardinals would gather in the chapel for the election of new popes.

THE SISTINE CHAPEL

The decorations done before Michelangelo painted the ceiling reflect the intellectual and ideological values that Sixtus hoped to transmit to the ambassadors and churchmen who entered the chapel. Along the lower sidewalls are portraits of earlier popes, a feature typical of early Roman churches. More ideologically significant, however, are two cycles of paintings of the lives of Moses and Christ, drawing parallels between them. To execute the scenes, Sixtus called to Rome some of the greatest artists of the late fifteenth century: Sandro Botticelli, Domenico Ghirlandaio, Luca Signorelli, and Pietro Perugino. The works illustrate the continuity of the Old Testament and New Testament and emphasize the importance of obedience to the authority of God. The meaning is most obvious in Perugino's painting of Saint Peter receiving the keys to the Kingdom of Heaven from Christ. The allusion is to Matthew 16:18: "Thou art Peter and upon this rock I shall build my church." The keys are the symbol of the claim of the pope, as successor to Saint Peter, to have the power to bind and loose sinners and their punishments. Directly across from Perugino's painting is Botticelli's *The Judgment of Corah*, which portrays the story of the opponent who challenged the leadership of Moses and Aaron while the Israelites wandered in the wilderness. Corah and his supporters, according to Numbers 16:33, fell live into Hell. Various popes recalled the fate of Corah and the rebels. The pope was bound to oppose the council, Pope Eugenius argued, "to save the people entrusted to his care, lest together with those who hold the power of the council above that of the papacy they suffer a punishment even more dire than that which befell Corah."[16] The meaning of the painting and the entire chapel could not be clearer.

The effects of Renaissance revival were profound. Rome grew from a modest population of about 17,000 in 1400 to 35,000 in 1450. By 1517, the city had a population of over 85,000, five times its population at the end of the Great Schism. The papal program was a success. Rome was transformed from a provincial town to a major European capital, perhaps the most important artistic and cultural center of the sixteenth century. Visitors to the Sistine Chapel, like visitors to the papal city itself, were expected to leave with a profound sense of the antiquity of the papal office and of the continuity of papal exercise of religious authority. Because the building and decorating were being completed as the Protestant Reformation was beginning in Germany, some historians have criticized the expense of the political and cultural program undertaken by the Renaissance popes. But to contemporaries on the scene, the work was a logical and necessary attempt to strengthen the church's standing in Christendom.

Castiglione and the European Gentleman

Renaissance ideas did not just spread in intellectual circles. They also were part of the transformation of the medieval knight into the early modern "gentleman." In 1528, Baldassare Castiglione (1478–1529) published *The Book of the Courtier*. The work, which describes the ideal behavior of a courtier, was based on Castiglione's own distinguished career serving in Italian courts. Set at the court of Urbino, the book chronicles a series of fictional discussions over the course of four nights in March 1507. Among the participants are the duchess of Urbino, Elizabeth Gonzaga; Emilia Pia, her lady-in-waiting; and a group of humanists, men of action, and courtiers. In four evenings, members of the circle try to describe the perfect gentleman of court. In the process, they debate the nature of nobility, humor, women, and love.

Castiglione describes, in many respects, a typical gathering at court, and the discourses reflect contemporary views of relations between men and women. The wives of princes were

Federigo da Montefeltro's Studiolo The duchy of Urbino was a showpiece of Renaissance court life and was the eventual locale for Castiglione's *Book of the Courtier.* It owed much of its fame to Duke Federigo da Montefeltro. Federigo's study is decorated with an expensive inlaid wooden design. Its illusion of great space and the expense of its construction were meant to celebrate Federigo's wealth and power. (Scala/Art Resource, NY)

expected to be organizers of life at court but also paragons of domestic virtues. Women were expected to manage the household and even the financial interests if her husband was away. Noble and elite women also played an important, but indirect, role in political and diplomatic negotiations. Women communicated informally ideas and information that could not be passed in public dispatches. But even powerful women had to be careful about public appearances. In Castiglione's book, for example, the women organize the discussion, and the men discuss. Although the women direct and influence the talk by jokes and short interventions, they cannot afford to dominate the debate. As Emilia Pia explains, "[women] must be more circumspect, and more careful not to give occasion for evil being said of them ... for a woman has not so many ways of defending herself against false calumnies as a man has."[17] Thus, in debate, as in politics and diplomacy, the influence of women was most effective when it was indirect.

The topics of such discussions were not randomly chosen. Castiglione explains that he wished "to describe the form of courtiership most appropriate for a gentleman living at the courts of princes." Castiglione's popularity was based on his deliberate joining of humanistic ideas and traditional chivalric values. Although his topic is the court with all its trappings, he tells his readers that his models for the discussion were Latin and Greek dialogues, especially those of Cicero and Plato. As a Platonist, he believed that all truly noble gentlemen have an inborn quality of "grace." It has to be brought out, however, just as Michelangelo freed his figures from stone.

What struck Castiglione's readers most was his advice about behavior. Francesco Guicciardini of Florence once remarked, "When I was young, I used to scoff at knowing how to play, dance, and sing, and other such frivolities. ... I have nevertheless seen from experience that these ornaments and accomplishments lend dignity and reputation even to men of good rank."[18] Guicciardini's comment underlines the value that readers found in Castiglione's work. Grace may be inbred, but it must be brought to the attention of those who control the court. Courtiers should, first of all, study the military arts. They have to fight, but only on occasions when their prowess will be noticed. Castiglione adds practical advice about how to dress, talk, and participate in music and dancing: Never leap about wildly when dancing as peasants might, but dance only with an air of dignity and decorum. Castiglione further urges the courtier to be careful in dress: the French are "overdressed"; the Italians too quickly adopt the most recent and colorful styles. Bowing to the political, as well as social realities of Spanish domination of Italy, Castiglione advises black or dark colors, which "reflect the sobriety of the Spaniards, since external appearances often bear witness to what is within."

According to Castiglione, the courtier must take pains "to earn that universal regard which everyone covets." Too much imitation and obvious study, however, lead to affectation. Castiglione counsels courtiers to carry themselves with a certain diffidence or unstudied naturalness (*sprezzatura*) covering their artifice. Accomplished courtiers should exhibit "that graceful and nonchalant spontaneity (as it is often called) ... so that those who are watching them imagine that they couldn't and wouldn't even know how to make a mistake." Thus, Castiglione's courtier must walk a fine line between clearly imitated and apparently natural grace.

Castiglione's book was an immediate success and widely followed even by those who claimed to have rejected it. By 1561, it was available in Spanish, French, and English translations. The reasons are not difficult to guess. It was critical for the courtier "to win for himself the mind and favour of the prince," and even those who disliked music, dancing, and light conversation learned Castiglione's arts "to open the way to the favour of princes." Many of the courtly arts that Castiglione preached had been traditional for centuries. Yet, Castiglione's humanistic explanations and emphasis on form, control, and fashion had never seemed so essential as they did to the cultured gentlemen of the courts of the Renaissance and early modern Europe.

SECTION SUMMARY

- Rulers found Renaissance art and culture to be convenient vehicles to explain or justify political power.
- The Gonzaga rulers of Mantua followed a conscious policy of recruiting famous artists to work at their court.
- The papacy used art and culture to explain and justify their predominance in Rome and the Christian church.
- Castiglione's dialogue on behavior at court became a European bestseller because of its explanation of how to succeed at court.

CHAPTER SUMMARY

The Renaissance was a broad cultural movement that began in Italy in response to a series of crises in the early fourteenth century. It was a cultural and ideological movement based on the assumption that study and imitation of the past was the best method for reform and innovation in the future. The impulse for change arose from the belief, shared by thinkers from Petrarch to Machiavelli, that a great deal could be learned from study of the Roman past. This was the basis for humanistic innovations in language, history, and politics. Even revolutionary thinkers, such as Lorenzo Valla and Niccolò Machiavelli, began with the study of classical literature and history.

The same transformation is evident among the artists. Early in the fifteenth century, Florentines who experimented with perspective were intent on recovering lost Roman knowledge, and Michelangelo was praised not only for mastering, but also for surpassing, Roman norms. Similar trends were evident in northern Europe, where artists like Albrecht Dürer combined their understanding of Italian art with northern ideas. Throughout Europe, art was an important component of religious and political culture.

FOCUS QUESTIONS

- How did Italians use classical values to deal with cultural and political issues?
- What was "new" about Renaissance art?
- In what ways did humanism outside Italy differ from Italian humanism?
- How did European rulers use Renaissance art and culture?

Humanistic studies outside of Italy were less tied to public life. Moral and spiritual issues were more important. Yet, the same movement from imitation to transformation is evident. Erasmus and More valued humanistic learning from Italy, but in *The Praise of Folly* and *Utopia*, the use of past ideas and models was neither simple nor direct. Both authors, however, shared with Italian humanists the idea that humanistic values could lead to a transformation of individuals and society as a whole.

The integration of art, literature, and public life was most evident in the ways that governments used art. The Gonzaga court and the papacy clearly recognized the value of artistic and literary works as vehicles for explaining and justifying power and influence. The beauty of Mantegna's painting and the power of Michelangelo's frescoes do not obscure their messages about power and authority.

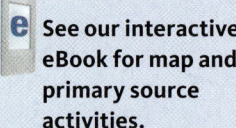 This icon will direct you to additional materials on the website: www .cengage.com/history/ noble/westciv6e.

KEY TERMS

Renaissance   (p. 321)

humanism   (p. 322)

Francesco Petrarch (p. 323)

civic humanism (p. 324)

On the Falsely Believed and Forged Donation of Constantine   (p. 327)

Niccolò Machiavelli (p. 329)

linear perspective   (p. 331)

Leonardo da Vinci   (p. 332)

Sistine Chapel   (p. 332)

Johann Gutenberg   (p. 340)

Thomas More   (p. 342)

Desiderius Erasmus   (p. 342)

See our interactive eBook for map and primary source activities.

NOTES

1. Quoted in J. B. Trapp, ed., *Background to the English Renaissance* (London: Gray-Mills Publishing, 1974), p. 11.

2. Quoted in N. Mann, *Petrarch* (Oxford: Oxford University Press), p. 67.

3. Petrarch, "On His Own Ignorance and That of Many Others," in *The Renaissance Philosophy of Man*, ed. Ernst Cassirer, Paul Oskar Kristeller, and John H. Randall (Chicago: University of Chicago Press, 1948), p. 105.

4. Quoted in Benjamin G. Kohl and Ronald G. Witt, *The Earthly Republic* (Philadelphia: University of Pennsylvania Press, 1978), p. 11.

5. Quoted in M. L. King, *Women of the Renaissance* (Chicago: University of Chicago Press, 1991), p. 194.

6. Quoted ibid., p. 222.

7. Quoted ibid., p. 198.

8. K. R. Bartlett, *The Civilization of the Italian Renaissance* (Lexington, Mass.: D. C. Heath, 1992), p. 314.

9. Quoted ibid., p. 160.

10. Quoted in *The Notebooks of Leonardo da Vinci*, ed. J. P. Richter, vol. 1 (New York: Dover, 1883 and 1970), p. 14.

11. Giorgio Vasari, *The Lives of the Artists*, trans. George Bull (Baltimore: Penguin, 1965), p. 338.

12. Julia Bondanella and Mark Musa, eds., *The Italian Renaissance Reader* (New York: Meridian Books, 1987), p. 377.

13. Quoted in A. Rabil, Jr., *Renaissance Humanism: Foundations, Forms, and Legacy*, vol. 2 (Philadelphia: University of Pennsylvania Press, 1988), p. 236.

14. Quoted ibid., p. 229.

15. Raffaele Brandolini, quoted in Charles L. Stinger, *The Renaissance in Rome* (Bloomington: Indiana University Press, 1985), p. 156.

16. Quoted in Leopold D. Ettlinger, *The Sistine Chapel Before Michelangelo* (Oxford: Oxford University Press, 1965), p. 105.

17. Quoted in R. M. San Juan, "The Court Lady's Dilemma: Isabella d'Este and Art Collecting in the Renaissance," *Oxford Art Journal* 14 (1991): 71.

18. Quoted in R. W. Hanning and D. Rosand, eds., *Castiglione: The Ideal and the Real in Renaissance Cultur*e (New Haven, Conn.: Yale University Press, 1983), p. 17.

13

Hernán Cortés Cortés—here shown with Doña Marina—is greeted by local leaders during the march to Tenochtitlán. (Trans. no. V/C 31[2]. Courtesy Department of Library Sciences, American Museum of Natural History)

European Overseas Expansion to 1600

Hernán Cortés's (kor-TEZ) march in 1519 through the Valley of Mexico toward Tenochtitlán (teh-NOCK-tit-lan), the Aztec capital, was recorded not only in Spaniards' journals, but also by local witnesses. In the native portrayal shown here, an elegantly garbed Mexica leader brings food and supplies to Cortés. Behind the adventurer are his own Spanish soldiers and his native allies. Many native peoples saw the Spanish as their defenders against the Aztecs, their harsh, recently arrived overlords. The woman standing next to Cortés is Malintzin, who later adopted the Spanish name Doña Marina. She was an Aztec noblewoman, traded by her stepfather to the Maya, and eventually given to Cortés. As a translator and interpreter, she was an essential ally during the conquest of Mexico.

The image, with its baskets of bread, meats, and fodder, is part of a pictograph telling the story of Cortés in the Nahuatl (na-HWAT-luh) language of the Mexica peoples. The arrival of the Spanish began a cultural exchange between the Spanish and the peoples of the Americas that was more complex than anyone initially imagined. The picture captures the contradictory aspects of European contact with Asia and the Americas. Europeans called it discovery, but they were encountering sophisticated, fully functioning political and cultural worlds. Doña Marina's presence also reminds us of a more general truth—that without allies, pilots, and interpreters among the native peoples, Europeans would have been lost both in the New World and in the Old.

Cortés's meeting with the Mexica peoples was part of a program of European overseas expansion that began in the last decade of the fifteenth century and would eventually carry Europeans to every part of the world. It would change how Europeans thought of themselves and how they understood their own connections to the rest of the world. Their expansion unified the "Old World" continents of Asia, Africa, and Europe with a "New World"—the Americas and the islands of the Pacific.

Those who focus on the transfer of European religion and culture view exploration and settlement as marking the creation of a new world with new values. However, the descendants of the native peoples who greeted the newly arriving Europeans—the Amerindians and the Aborigines, Maori, and Polynesians of the Pacific islands—remind us that the outsiders invaded another world. Their arrival brought modern warfare and epidemic diseases that virtually destroyed indigenous cultures.

Spain sent its explorers west because the Portuguese already controlled the eastern routes to Asia around the African coast and because certain technological innovations made long open-sea voyages possible. Thus, the story includes national competition, the development of navigational techniques, and strategic choices.

FOCUS QUESTIONS

- What did Europeans know about the wider world in the Middle Ages?
- How did the Portuguese exploit their new connection to the East?
- Why did the Spanish choose to sail west in their attempt to find Asia?
- How did the Spanish conquer and control the new world they entered?
- What changes did European expansion bring to the Old World and the New?

This icon will direct you to additional materials on the website: www.cengage.com/history/noble/westciv6e.

See our interactive eBook for map and primary source activities.

Finally, the Europeans overthrew the great empires of the Aztecs and the Inca, but the transfer of European culture was never as complete as the Europeans thought or expected. As our image suggests, the language and customs of the conquered peoples, blanketed by European language and law, survived, though the lands colonized by the Europeans would never again be as they had been before their encounter with the Old World.

THE EUROPEAN BACKGROUND, 1250–1492

What did Europeans know about the wider world in the Middle Ages?

By 1400, Europeans already had a long history of connections with Africa and Asia. They regularly traded with Arabs in North Africa, traveled through the Muslim lands on the eastern edge of the Mediterranean, and eventually reached India, China, and beyond. After 1400, however, Europeans developed the desire and the ability to travel overseas to distant lands in Africa and Asia. Three critical factors behind the exploratory voyages of the fifteenth and early sixteenth centuries were technology, curiosity and interest, and geographic knowledge. A series of technological innovations made sailing far out into the ocean less risky and more predictable than it had been. The writings of classical geographers, myths and traditional tales, and merchants' accounts of their travels fueled popular interest in the East and made ocean routes to the East seem safe and reasonable alternatives to overland travel.

Early Exploration and Cultural Interactions

Medieval Europeans knew there were lands to their west. Irish monks and Norse settlers traveled there. Indeed, by the late ninth century, Norse sailors, primarily Norwegians, had constructed boats combining oars and sails with strong-keeled hulls, which they used to travel to Iceland, Greenland, and eventually Vinland—the coast of Labrador and Newfoundland. The Norse traveled in families. A woman named Gudridr gave birth to a son in North America before returning to Iceland and eventually going on a pilgrimage to Rome. Although the settlements in North America and Greenland ultimately failed, the Norse were followed by English, French, and Spanish fishermen who regularly visited the rich fishing grounds off North America.

CONTACTS THROUGH TRADE The Greeks and Romans had cultivated contacts with the civilizations of Asia and Africa, and despite the nation-building focus of the Middle Ages, interest in the lands beyond Christendom had never been lost. In the thirteenth and fourteenth centuries, European economic and cultural contacts with these lands greatly increased. The rising volume of trade between Europe and North Africa brought with it information about the wealthy African kingdoms of the Niger Delta. The Mongols, in the thirteenth century, allowed European merchants and missionaries to travel along trade routes extending all the way to China, opening regions formerly closed to them by hostile Muslim governments.

Trade in the Mediterranean also kept Christians and Muslims, Europeans and North Africans, in close contact. Europeans sold textiles to Arab traders, who carried them across the Sahara to Timbuktu, where they were sold for gold bullion to residents of the ancient African kingdoms of Ghana and Mali, located just above the Niger River. European chroniclers recorded the pilgrimage to Mecca of Mansa Musa, the fabulously wealthy fourteenth-century emperor of Mali. Italian merchants tried unsuccessfully to trade directly with these African kingdoms, but Arab merchants prevented any permanent contact.

Europeans enjoyed more successful trade connections farther east. The discovery in London of a brass shard inscribed with a Japanese character attests to the breadth of connections in the early fourteenth century. Since the Roman period, the Mediterranean had been connected to Asia by the Silk Road, in reality, a network of roads that carried people, ideas, and commerce. In the Middle Ages, European access to the Silk Road had been restricted by local rulers. After the rise of the Mongols, Italian merchants regularly traveled east through Constantinople and on to India and China. By the fourteenth century, they knew how long travel to China might take and the probable expenses along the way. European intellectuals also maintained an interest in the lands beyond Christendom. They had read the late classical and early medieval authors who described Africa, the Indies, and China.

The work of the greatest of the classical geographers, Ptolemy (TOL-eh-mee) of Alexandria (ca. A.D. 127–145), was known only indirectly until the early fifteenth century, but medieval thinkers read avidly and speculated endlessly about the information contained in the works of authors from Late Antiquity. For instance, one author reported that snakes in Calabria, in isolated southern Italy, sucked milk from cows and that men in the right circumstances became wolves—the earliest mention of werewolves. By the twelfth century, fictitious reports circulated widely in the West of a wealthy Christian country in the East or possibly in Africa. Chroniclers, at that time, talked of Prester John, who some thought was a wealthy and powerful descendant of the Magi, the wise men from the East who Scripture says visited the baby Jesus. The legend of the kingdom of Prester John probably reflects some knowledge of the Christian groups living near the shrine of Saint Thomas in India or the Christian kingdom of Ethiopia. In the fifteenth century, European Christians looked to Prester John for aid against the rising Turkish empire.

GEOGRAPHIC KNOWLEDGE

CHRONOLOGY

ca. 1400	Portuguese reach Azores
1444	Prince Henry "the Navigator" discovers Cape Verde Islands
1487	Dias becomes first European to sail around Cape of Good Hope
1492	Columbus reaches New World
1494	Treaty of Tordesillas
1497	Da Gama sails to India around Cape of Good Hope
	Cabot sights Newfoundland
1501	Vespucci concludes Columbus discovered a new continent
1507	Waldseemüller issues the first map showing "America"
1510	Portuguese capture Goa
1513	Balboa becomes first European to see Pacific Ocean
1519–1522	Magellan's expedition sails around the world
1519–1523	Cortés conquers the Aztecs, destroys Tenochtitlán
1533	Pizarro conquers Cuzco, the Inca capital
1534	Cartier discovers St. Lawrence River
1542	Charles V issues "New Laws"
1545	Spanish discover Potosí silver mines

Tales of geographic marvels are epitomized by *The Travels of Sir John Mandeville,* a book probably written in France, but purporting to be the observations of a knight from St. Albans, just north of London. Mandeville says that he left England in 1322 or 1323 and traveled to Constantinople, Jerusalem, Egypt, India, China, Persia, and Turkey. Sir John describes the islands of wonders, inhabited by dog-headed humans, one-eyed giants, headless men, and hermaphrodites. Less fantastically, Mandeville reports that the world could be, and in fact had been, circumnavigated.

More reliable information became available in the thirteenth century, largely because of the arrival of the Mongols. Jenghiz Khan (JEN-gus KAHN) and his descendants created an empire that reached from eastern Hungary to China (see page 252). This pax Mongolica, or area of Mongol-enforced peace, was a region in which striking racial and cultural differences were tolerated. In the 1240s and 1250s, a series of papal representatives traveled to the Mongol capital at Karakorum near Lake Baikal in Siberia. The letters of these papal ambassadors, who worked extensively to gain converts and allies for a crusade against the Turks, were widely read and greatly increased accurate knowledge about Asia. Other missionaries and diplomats journeyed to the Mongol court, and some continued farther east to India and China. By the early fourteenth century, the church had established a bishop in Beijing.

Italian merchants followed closely on the heels of the churchmen and diplomats. The pax Mongolica offered the chance to trade directly in Asia and the adventure of visiting lands known only from travel literature. In 1262, Niccolo and Maffeo Polo embarked from Venice on their first trip to China. On a later journey, they took Niccolo's son, Marco (1255–1324). In all, they spent twenty-four years in China. Marco dictated an account of his travels to a Pisan as they both languished as prisoners of war in a Genoese jail in 1298. It is difficult to know how much of the text represents Marco's own observations and how much is chivalric invention by the Pisan. Some modern commentators have even speculated that Marco himself never traveled to China. His contemporaries, however, had no doubts. The book was an immediate success even among Venetians, who could have exposed any fraud. Christopher Columbus himself owned and extensively annotated a copy of Marco Polo's *Travels,* which combines a merchant's observations of ports, markets, and trade with an administrator's eye for people and organizations.

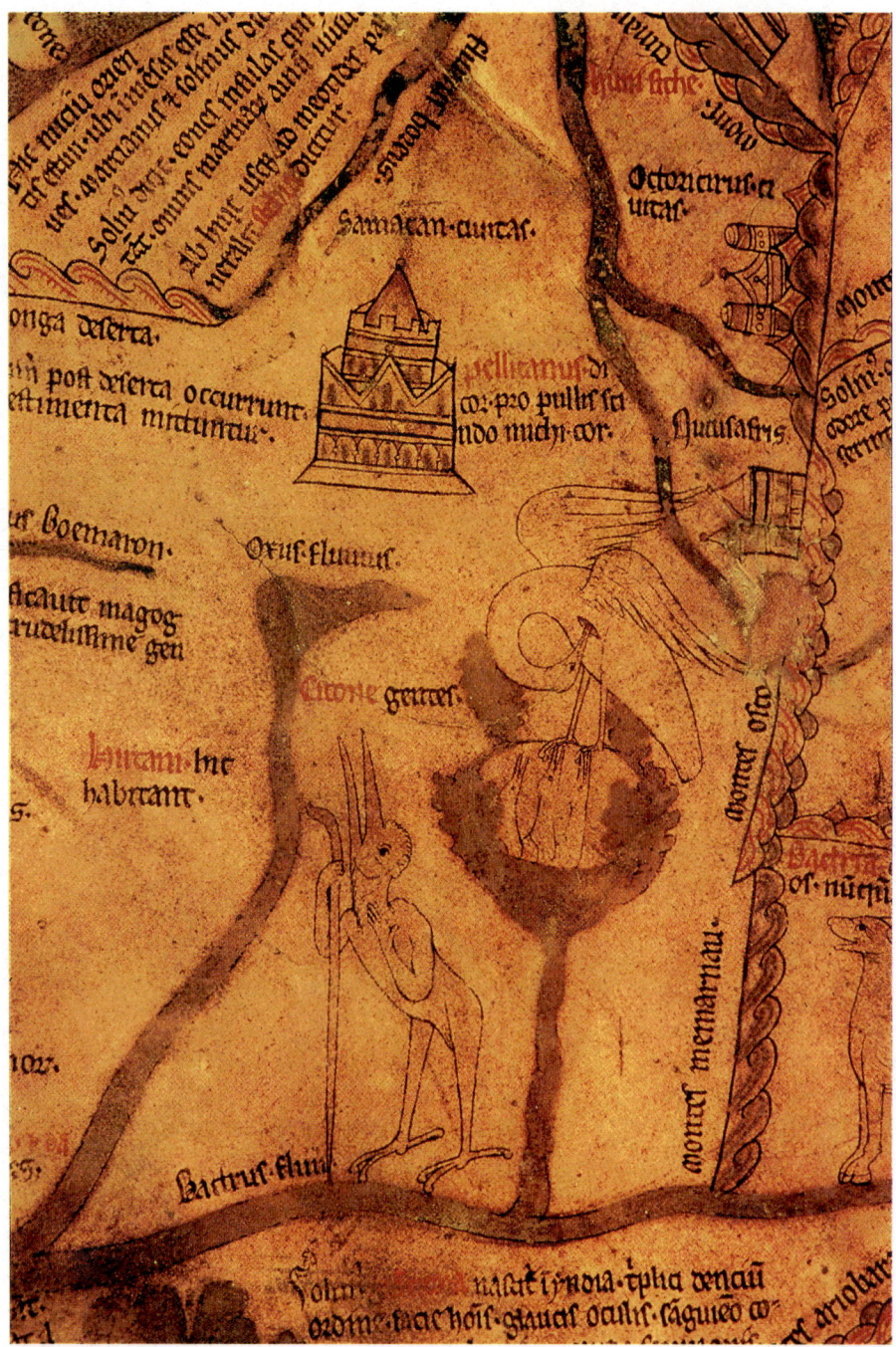

Hereford Mappa Mundi   Like other medieval illustrations of Eastern lands, this thirteenth-century map combines known fact with myth. The top section locates the city of Samarcand (modern-day Samarkand, Uzbekistan). At the bottom, next to a mythical bird-person, a pelican feeds its young with its own blood.   (The Dean and Chapter of Hereford and the Hereford Mappa Mundi Trust)

By 1300, a modest community of Italians had settled in China. By the late thirteenth and fourteenth centuries, Italian traders were traveling directly to the East in search of Asian silks, spices, pearls, and ivory. They, and other European merchants, could consult the *Handbook for Merchants* (1340), compiled by the Florentine Francesco Pegalotti (pey-gah-LOW-tee), which described the best roads, the most hospitable stopping points, and the appropriate freight animals for a trip to the East. Fragmentary reports of Europeans in the Spice Islands (also known as the Moluccas), Japan, and India indicate that many Europeans other than merchants traveled simply for the adventure of visiting new lands.

Navigational Innovations

The invention of several navigational aids in the fourteenth and fifteenth centuries made sailing in open waters easier and more predictable. Especially important was the fly compass, consisting of a magnetic needle attached to a paper disk (or "fly"). The simple compass had been invented in China and was known in Europe by the late twelfth century, but because it was not initially marked off in degrees, it was only a rudimentary aid to navigation. By 1500, astrolabes and other devices enabling sailors to use the positions of the sun and stars to assist in navigation had also become available. An astrolabe allowed sailors to measure the altitude of the polestar in the sky and thereby calculate the latitude, or distance north or south of the equator, at which their ship was sailing. Still, until the general adoption of charts marked with degrees of latitude, most navigators sailed by relying on the compass, experience, and instinct.

The most common Mediterranean ship of the late Middle Ages was a galley powered by a combination of sails and oars. Such a vessel was able to travel quickly and easily along the coast, but it was ill-suited for sailing the open seas. Throughout the Mediterranean, shipbuilders experimented with new designs, and during the fifteenth century, the Portuguese and Spanish perfected the caravel and adapted the European full-rigged ships. Large, square sails efficiently caught the wind and propelled these ships forward, and smaller triangular sails (lateens) allowed them to tack diagonally across a headwind, virtually sailing into the wind.

By the 1490s, the Portuguese and Spanish had developed the ships and techniques that would make long open-sea voyages possible. What remained was for Europeans, especially the Portuguese and Spanish, to conclude that such voyages were both necessary and profitable.

The Revolution in Geography

Sea routes to Asia seemed more important by the end of the fourteenth century. With the conversion of the Mongols to Islam, the breakdown of Mongol unity, and the subsequent rise of the Ottoman Turks, the highly integrated and unusually open trade network fell apart. The caravan routes across southern Russia, Persia, and Afghanistan were abruptly closed to Europeans. Western merchants once again became dependent on Muslim middlemen.

The reports of travelers, however, continued to circulate long after the trade routes shut down, contributing to a veritable revolution in geographic knowledge in the decades before the Portuguese and Spanish voyages.

In 1375, Abraham Cresques (KRESK), a Jewish mathematician from the Mediterranean island of Majorca, produced what has come to be known as the *Catalan World Atlas.* He combined the traditional medieval *mappa mundi* (world map) with a Mediterranean *portolan.* The mappa mundi often followed the O-T form—that is, a circle divided into three parts representing Europe, Africa, and Asia, the lands of the descendants of Noah. Jerusalem—the heart of Christendom—was always at the center of the map. What the map lacked in accuracy, it made up in symbolism. The portolan, in contrast, was entirely practical. Sailors valued it because of its accurate outline of coasts, complete with sailing instructions and reasonable portrayals of ports, islands, and shallows along with general compass readings. The *Catalan World Atlas* largely holds to the portolan tradition but has more correct representations of the lands surrounding the Mediterranean.

In the fifteenth century, following Ptolemy's suggestions, mapmakers began to divide their maps into squares, marking lines of longitude and latitude. This format made it possible to show, with some precision, the contours of various lands and the relationships between landmasses. Numerous maps of the world were produced in this period. The culmination of this cartography was a globe constructed for the city of Nuremberg in 1492, the very year Columbus set sail. From these increasingly accurate maps, it has become possible to document the first exploration of the Azores, the Cape Verde Islands, and the western coast of Africa.

After his voyages, Columbus observed that maps had been of no use to him. True enough. But without the accumulation of knowledge by travelers and the mingling of that knowledge with classical ideas about geography, it is doubtful whether Columbus or the Portuguese seaman Vasco da Gama would have undertaken—or could have found governments willing to support—the voyages that so dramatically changed the relations between Europe and the rest of the world.

SECTION SUMMARY

- Throughout the Middle Ages, Europe had indirect trade connections with Asia and Africa.

- In the fourteenth century, Italian merchants traveled widely in central and eastern Asia.

- Technological advances in ship design and navigation made it possible to sail far into the Atlantic.

- Restrictions on land routes between Europe and Asia made sailing to Asia a practical economic venture.

PORTUGUESE VOYAGES OF EXPLORATION, 1350–1515

How did the Portuguese exploit their new connection to the East?

Portugal, a tiny country on the edge of Europe, for a short time led the European overseas expansion. Portuguese sailors were the first Europeans to perfect the complex techniques of using the winds and currents of the South Atlantic, especially along the western coast of Africa (see **MAP 13.1**). As the Portuguese moved down the African coast, and later, as they tried to compete commercially in Asia, they adapted traditional Mediterranean cultural and commercial attitudes to fit the new environment in which they found themselves. In some areas, the Portuguese created networks of isolated naval and trading stations to control the movement of goods. In other areas, they attempted to create substantial colonies, inhabited by Portuguese settlers. In still other areas, they used slaves to produce commercial products for the international market. Spain and the other European states would use these same strategies in Asia and the New World as they expanded their economic and political interests overseas.

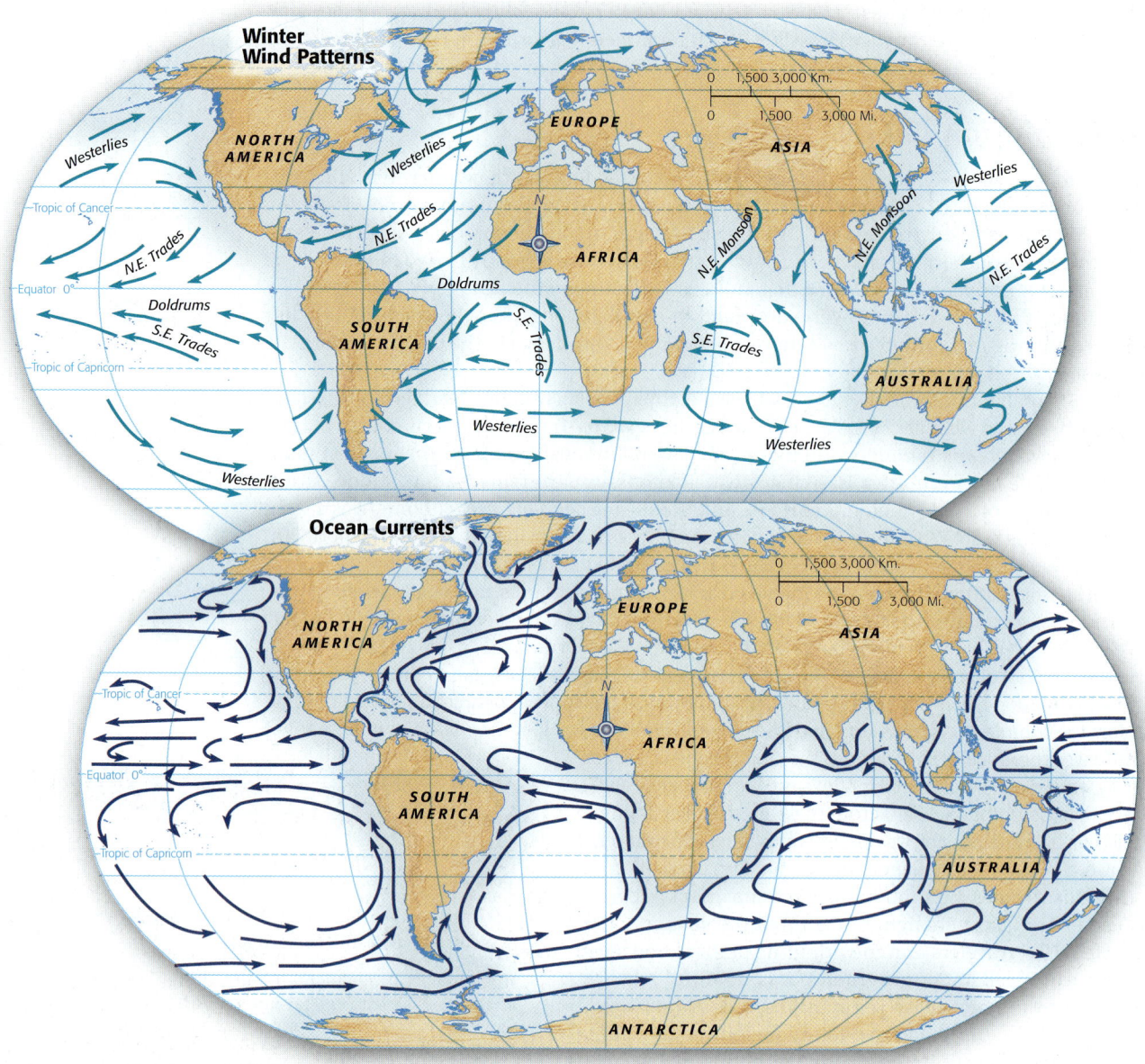

🌐 **MAP 13.1—Winds and Currents**

Winds and ocean currents move in giant clockwise and counterclockwise circles that limit the directions in which ships can sail efficiently. It was impossible, for example, for the explorers to sail directly south along the entire western coast of Africa.

The Early Voyages

Portugal, like other late medieval European states, hoped that exploration and expansion would lead to "gold and Christians." The search for Christians was accelerated in the fifteenth century by the growing power of the Ottoman Turks. Europeans increasingly desired an alliance with the mythical Christian kingdoms of the East to open a second front against the militant Turks. Further, rediscovering the "lost" Christians and the hope of reclaiming Jerusalem fed Christian expectations that they were living in the last days before Christ's return.

For the Portuguese, facing the Atlantic and insulated from a direct Turkish threat, the lure of gold was always mixed with their religious motives. The nearest source of gold was well known to late medieval Christians: the African kingdoms of the Niger Delta. The problem for European traders and their governments was that overland contacts with this wealthy region remained controlled by the Muslim merchants of North Africa. The Portuguese and Spanish hoped to break the monopoly by taking control of the North African coast or by means of a flanking movement along the western coast of Africa.

Actual exploration of the Atlantic had begun long before Europeans recognized the extent of the Turkish threat. By 1350, the Madeiras and the Canaries, groups of islands off the western coast of Africa, regularly were included on European maps. By about 1365, Portuguese, Spanish, and probably French sailors were visiting the Canary Islands. By 1400, the Azores (AY-zorz), a chain of islands one-third of the way across the Atlantic, were known and, from early in the fifteenth century, were routine ports of call for Portuguese ships (see **MAP 13.2**). These voyages were no mean feat, calling for sophisticated ocean sailing out of sight of land for weeks at a time.

In the second decade of the fifteenth century, the Portuguese expansion began in earnest with the capture of the Muslim port of Ceuta (say-OO-tuh) on the coast of Morocco. From then on, the Portuguese moved steadily down the western coast of Africa. They were led by **Prince Henry "the Navigator"** (1394–1460), the younger son of King John I (r. 1385–1433). Legend has it that Prince Henry founded a school for the study of geography and navigation at Sagres, on the southwestern coast of Portugal. Whether he did or not, contemporaries agreed that Prince Henry was intent on reaching the "River of Gold"—that is, the Gold Coast of Africa and the Niger Delta. To accomplish this, he sponsored a series of expeditions down the African coast, reaching Senegal and the Cape Verde Islands by 1444. The Portuguese quickly established trading stations in the region and soon were exporting gold and slaves to Lisbon.

The islands off the coast of Africa were uninhabited, except for the Canaries, which the Portuguese tried unsuccessfully to keep from the Spanish. Thus, the Portuguese could not merely plant trading communities within a larger population. As a result, by the early 1440s, the Portuguese were bringing sheep, seed, and peasants to these hitherto unoccupied islands, and the Crown was granting extensive lordships to encourage reluctant nobles to relocate to the Azores. The islanders survived largely by exporting sheep and grain to Iberia.

A significant transformation occurred on Madeira in the 1440s, when the Portuguese introduced sugar cane to the island. A great many workers were needed to cut the cane, and expensive mills and lengthy processing were required to extract and produce sugar. On Madeira, most of the work was done by Portuguese peasants. However, when the Portuguese extended sugar cultivation

Prince Henry "the Navigator" The prince who directed Portuguese exploration and colonization along the west coast of Africa.

🌐 **MAP 13.2—World Exploration, 1492–1535**
The voyages of Columbus, da Gama, and Magellan charted the major sea-lanes that became essential for communication, trade, and warfare for the next three hundred years.

to the newly discovered and colonized Cape Verde Islands in the 1460s, they found that Portuguese peasants would not work voluntarily in the sultry equatorial climate. Soon, the Portuguese introduced slave-based farming to maximize production and profits.

Slaves, imported from the Black Sea areas, had been used in agriculture since the introduction of sugar cultivation into the Mediterranean in the thirteenth century. The Portuguese had been trading in slaves along the western coast of Africa since the 1440s—the date from which black slaves appear in Lisbon. African slaves, along with slaves from northern and eastern Europe, could be found in Italy and throughout the Mediterranean in the fifteenth century, most often as domestics or laborers in small enterprises. Not since Roman times, however, had slave-based industries developed on the scale of the Portuguese sugar plantations. Sugar production in the New World eventually would be modeled on a plantation system begun by the Portuguese on their island colonies in the Atlantic.

The Search for a Sea Route to Asia

Until the middle of the fifteenth century, the Niger Delta remained the focus of Portuguese interest. Only after securing control of the western coast of Africa did the Portuguese look seriously at sailing around Africa and discovering a sea route to Asia.

The fifteenth-century sailors who first tried to sail down the coast of Africa faced enormous difficulties. Water and wind currents tend to move in clockwise and counterclockwise circles, against which it is difficult for a sail-powered ship to make progress (see **MAP 13.1**). Winds near the equator generally blow from the east; farther north and south, the westerlies prevail. Some zones, in certain seasons, are pockets of stillness—called doldrums—with few breezes to propel ships. A navigator had to find winds and currents moving in the direction he wished to travel. Sailing directly from port to port was virtually impossible.

Knowledge of winds and currents allowed Bartholomeu Dias (1450?–1500) to explore the coast of southern Africa in 1487. He followed the traditional Portuguese routes until southeasterly winds forced him to sail south and west, almost to the Brazilian and Argentine coasts. Then, he was able to ride the westerlies well past the southern tip of Africa, where he turned north. On his return, he sighted what he called the "Cape of Storms," later renamed the "Cape of Good Hope" by the Portuguese king. Dias had perfected the techniques for searching out currents in the Southern Hemisphere and opened the way to India.

Vasco da Gama Pioneering Portuguese trader, whose voyage to East Africa and India began the four-hundred-year presence of the Portuguese in the Indian Ocean.

A decade after Dias's return from the Cape of Good Hope, **Vasco da Gama** (1460?–1524) set sail on a voyage that would take him to Calicut on the western coast of India (see **MAP 13.2**). Using the information gathered from countless navigators, travelers, and even spies sent into East Africa, da Gama set sail in 1497, with four square-rigged, armed caravels and over 170 men. He had been provided with maps and reports that indicated what he might expect to find along the eastern coast of Africa. He also carried textiles and metal utensils, merchandise of the type usually traded along the western coast of Africa. This was a trading mission and, in no sense, a voyage of discovery.

Da Gama followed established routes beyond the Cape of Good Hope and into the Indian Ocean. He traveled up the coast until he reached Malindi in Mozambique, where he secured an Arab pilot who taught him the route to Calicut. Although the goods the Portuguese traders presented were not appropriate for the sophisticated Asian market, da Gama did manage to collect a cargo of Indian spices, which he brought back to Portugal, arriving in 1499. From that pioneering voyage until the Portuguese lost their last colonies in the twentieth century (Goa, 1961; Mozambique, 1975), Portugal remained a presence in the Indian Ocean.

The Portuguese in Asia

Muslims predominated in the Indian Ocean, but in fact, a mixture of ethnic and religious groups—including Muslims, Hindus, Chinese, Jains, and Nestorian Christians—participated in the movement of cottons, silks, and spices throughout the region. There were numerous small traders, as well as prosperous long-distance merchants with connections reaching into central Asia, Africa, and China.

Less than a century before Vasco da Gama's arrival, the Chinese seaman Zheng He (JUNG HUH) made a series of voyages into the Indian Ocean. In 1405, he led a huge armada of 317 ships and over 27,000 sailors on an expedition designed to expand the trade and political influence of Ming China. He would make six subsequent trips before a new emperor, intent on concentrating his resources on China's internal development, ended the ventures. With the retreat of the Chinese, trade returned to its previous patterns.

The hodgepodge of trade reflected the political situation. Vasco da Gama's arrival coincided with the rise of the Moguls, Muslim descendants of Jenghiz Khan. By 1530, they had gained control of most of northern India, and during the sixteenth century, their influence increased in the south. The wealth and security of the Moguls depended on landed power. They generally left traders and trading ports to themselves. Throughout the sixteenth century, the Moguls remained tolerant of India's religious, cultural, and economic diversity. Neither Muslim nor Hindu powers initially considered the Portuguese an unusual threat.

Asians may not have worried much about the Portuguese because, at first, there were so few of them. Vasco da Gama arrived with only three ships. And the subsequent fleet of Pedro Alvares Cabral carried only fifteen hundred men. In the 1630s, after more than a century of emigration, probably no more than ten thousand Portuguese were scattered from modern Indonesia to the east coast of Africa. In addition to government officials, Portuguese settlers were likely to be petty traders, local merchants, and poorly paid mercenaries.

Portuguese in India   This watercolor by a Portuguese traveler shows the varied peoples and customs and the great wealth to be found in India. Europeans were fascinated by all that seemed different from their own world.   (Biblioteca Casanatense, Rome. Photo: Humberto Nicoletti Serra)

The Portuguese faced a number of problems as they attempted to compete in Eastern markets. There were very few of them and the trade goods they brought with them had little value in sophisticated, highly developed Asian markets. In most cases, they bought spices, textiles, and dyes with gold and silver brought from mines in central Europe and the New World. They could not profit from the India trade by competing with the indigenous traders. In response, they created a seaborne **trading-post empire**—an empire based on control of trade rather than on colonization. It was, in fact, a model that fit well with their crusading experience in North Africa and their desire to push back Muslim control.

Despite disadvantages, Portugal's commercial empire succeeded, thanks especially to fortified, strategically placed naval bases. As early as Vasco da Gama's second expedition in 1502, the Portuguese bombarded Calicut and defeated an Arab fleet off the coast of India. This encounter set the stage for Portugal's most important imperial strategist, Alfonso d'Albuquerque (1453–1515), governor-general of Portuguese colonies in India. He convinced the monarchy that the key to dominance in the region was the creation of fortified naval bases commanding the Bay of Bengal and thereby controlling access to the coveted Spice Islands. (See the feature, "The Written Record: Albuquerque Defends the Portuguese Empire.") By 1600, the Portuguese had built a network of naval bases that reached from Mozambique and Mombasa on the east coast of Africa to Goa on the west coast of India and the island of Macao off southeastern China (see **Map 13.2**).

The Portuguese established a royal trading firm, the Casa da India, to manage the booming market in cinnamon, ginger, cloves, mace, and a variety of peppers. Although their control was far from total, the Portuguese did become significant exporters of spices to Europe. More significant was the creation of the Portuguese Estado da India, or India office, to oversee Portuguese naval forces, administer ports, and regulate maritime trade. Under the Portuguese system, all merchants were expected to acquire export licenses and to ship products through Portuguese ports. Though a vigorous and highly profitable local trade remained out of Portuguese control, Asians still often found it more convenient to cooperate than to resist, and most agreed to pay for export licenses and trade through Portuguese ports. They even found it expedient to ship in European-style vessels and to use Portuguese as the language of commerce.

trading-post empire
A system developed by the Portuguese to allow them to use fortified naval bases to dominate commerce in the Indian Ocean.

SECTION SUMMARY

- The Portuguese were especially interested in trade with the West African kingdoms along the Gold Coast.

- The Portuguese developed complex navigational techniques that allowed them to sail around the tip of Africa and into the Indian Ocean.

- Before the arrival of the Portuguese, the Muslim Mogul Empire left seaborne trade under the control of various ethnic and religious groups.

- The Portuguese established a trading-post empire that allowed them to dominate trade in the Indian Ocean.

Albuquerque Defends the Portuguese Empire

In this letter of 1512, to the king of Portugal, Alfonso d'Albuquerque, the governor-general of Portugal's colonies in India, informs the king of conditions in the East, explains his strategy, and defends himself against his critics.

The first time the Muslims entered Goa, we killed one of their captains. They were greatly grieved by the [Portuguese] capture of Goa and there is great fear of Your Highness among them. You must reduce the power of [the Muslim] rulers, take their coastal territories from them and build good fortresses in their principal places. Otherwise you will not be able to set India on the right path and you will always have to have a large body of troops there to keep it pacified. Any alliance which you may agree with one or other Indian king or lord must be secured, Sire, because otherwise you may be certain that, the moment your back is turned, they will at once become your enemies.

What I am describing has now become quite usual among them. In India there is not the same punctiliousness as in Portugal about keeping truth, friendship and trust, for nobody here has any of these qualities. Therefore, Sire, put your faith in good fortresses and order them to be built; gain control over India in time and do not place any confidence in the friendship of the kings and lords of this region because you did not arrive here with a just cause to gain domination of their trade with blandishments and peace treaties. Do not let anybody in Portugal make you think that this is a very hard thing to achieve and that, once achieved, it will place you under great obligation. I tell you this, Sire, because I am still in India and I would like people to sell their property and take part in this enterprise that is so much to your advantage, so great, so lucrative and so valuable. . . .

In a place where there is merchandise to be had and the Muslim traders will not let us have precious stones or spices by fair dealing, and we want to take these foods by force, then we must fight the Muslims for them. If, on the other hand, they see us with a large body of troops, they do us honor, and no thought of deceit or trickery enters their heads. They exchange their goods for ours without fighting and they will abandon the delusion that they will expel us from India.

QUESTIONS

1. Why does Albuquerque believe that fortresses are essential to a Portuguese presence in India?
2. What Portuguese reaction does Albuquerque fear?

Source: T. F. Earle and J. Villiers, eds., *Albuquerque: Caesar of the East,* p. 109. Copyright © 1990 by Aris and Phillips. Reprinted by permission of the publisher.

SPANISH VOYAGES OF EXPLORATION, 1492–1522

Why did the Spanish choose to sail west in their attempt to find Asia?

Spanish overseas expansion seems a logical continuation of the centuries-long Reconquista (see pages 249–250). In 1492, just before Columbus set sail, Castile was finally able to conquer the last Muslim kingdom of Granada and unify all of Iberia, with the exception of Portugal, under a single monarchy. Initially, in 1479, the Spanish kingdoms had agreed to leave the exploration and colonization of the African coast to the Portuguese, yet, they watched nervously as the Portuguese expanded their African contacts. Portuguese successes led Castilians to concentrate their efforts on what came to be called the "Enterprise of the Indies"—that is, the conquest and settlement of Central and South America.

The sailing and exploring necessary to compete with the Portuguese produced critical information about ocean winds and currents and facilitated later voyages. They also established the basic approaches that the Spanish would follow in their exploration, conquest, and colonization of the lands where they dropped anchor.

The Role of Columbus

The story of the enterprise begins with Christopher Columbus (1451–1506), a brilliant seaman, courtier, and self-promoter who has become a symbol of European expansion. Columbus, however, was not a bold pioneer who fearlessly did what no others could conceive of doing. He benefited from long-standing interests in the world beyond European shores.

Columbus was born into a modest family in Genoa and spent his early years in travel and in the service of the Castilian and Portuguese crowns. His vision seems to have been thoroughly traditional and medieval. He knew the medieval geographic speculations inherited from Arab, and ultimately Classical Greek, sources. Medieval seafarers did not fear a flat earth; rather, the concern was whether a ship could cover the vast distances necessary to sail west to Asia. Studying information in *Imago Mundi* (*Image of the World,* 1410), by the French philosopher Pierre d'Ailly (die-YEE) (1350–1420), Columbus convinced himself that the distance between Europe and Asia was much less than it actually is. D'Ailly's estimate put the east coast of Asia within easy reach of the western edge of Europe. "This sea is navigable in a few days if the wind is favorable," d'Ailly concluded.

Columbus's own study convinced him that the distance from the west coast of Europe to the east coast of Asia was about 5,000 miles, instead of the actual 12,000. Columbus's reading of traditional sources put Japan in the approximate location of the Virgin Islands. (It is not surprising that Columbus remained convinced that the Bahamas were islands just off the coast of Asia.) When Amerindians told him of Cuba, he concluded that it "must be Japan according to the indications that these people give of its size and wealth."[1]

On the basis of first-century descriptions, Columbus assured Spanish authorities that King Solomon's mines were only a short distance west of his newly discovered islands. In addition to finding the gold of Solomon, Columbus expected that by sailing farther west he could fulfill a series of medieval prophecies that would lead to the conversion of the whole world to Christianity. This conversion, he believed, would shortly precede the Second Coming of Christ. In Columbus's own view, then, his voyages were epochal not because they were ushering in a newer, more secular world, but because they signaled the fulfillment of Christian history.

Columbus's enthusiasm for the venture was only partially shared by the Spanish monarchs, Ferdinand and Isabella. Vasco da Gama had been well supplied with a flotilla of large ships and a crew of over 170 men, but Columbus sailed in 1492 with three small vessels and a crew of 90. Da Gama carried extra supplies and materials for trade and letters for the rulers he knew he would meet. Columbus had nothing similar in his sea chest. His commission did authorize him as "Admiral of Spain" to take possession of all he should find, but royal expectations do not seem to have been great.

Yet, on October 12, about ten days later than he had expected, Columbus reached landfall on what he assumed were small islands in the Japanese chain. He had actually landed in the Bahamas. Because Columbus announced to the world that he had arrived in the Indies, the indigenous peoples have since been called "Indians" and the islands are called the "West Indies."

Columbus reported to the Spanish monarchs that the inhabitants on the islands were friendly and open to the new arrivals. He described a primitive, naked people eager, he believed, to learn of Christianity and European ways. Indeed, the Tainos, or Arawaks, whom he had mis-identified, did live simple, uncomplicated lives. The islands easily produced sweet potatoes, maize, beans, and squash, which, along with fish, provided an abundant diet. Initially, these people shared their food and knowledge with the newcomers, who they seem to have thought were sky-visitors.

The Spanish, for their part, praised the Tainos. The visitors generally believed that they had discovered a compliant, virtuous people who, if converted, would be exemplars of Christian virtues to Europeans. Columbus himself observed:

> They are very gentle and do not know what evil is; nor do they kill others, nor steal; and they are without weapons. They say very quickly any prayer that we tell them to say, and they make the sign of the cross, †. So your Highnesses ought to resolve to make them Christians.[2]

The Spanish authorities changed their opinion quickly. The settlers Columbus left at his fortress set an unfortunate example. They seized food stocks, kidnapped women, and embarked on a frenzied search for gold. Those who did not kill one another were killed by enraged Tainos.

During succeeding voyages, Columbus struggled to make his discoveries the financial windfall he had promised the monarchs. He was utterly unable to administer this vast new land. He quickly lost control of the colonists and was forced to allow the vicious exploitation of the island population. He and other Spanish settlers claimed larger and larger portions of the land and required the Indians to work it. Islands that easily supported a population of perhaps a million natives could not support those indigenous peoples and the Spanish newcomers and still provide exports to Spain. Scholars have estimated that the native population of the islands may have fallen to little more than thirty thousand by 1520, largely because of diseases (see pages 375–376). By the middle of the sixteenth century, the native population had virtually disappeared.

Columbus remained convinced that he would find vast fortunes just over the horizon. However, he found neither the great quantities of gold he promised nor a sea passage to Asia. With the islands in revolt and his explorations seemingly going nowhere, the Spanish monarchs stripped Columbus of his titles and commands. Once, he was returned to Spain in chains. Even after his final transatlantic trip, he continued to insist that he had finally found either the Ganges (GAN-jeez) River of India or one of the rivers that according to the Hebrew Bible flow out of the earthly paradise. Although Columbus died in 1506, rich and honored for his discoveries, he never did gain all the power and wealth he had expected. He remained frustrated and embittered by the Crown's refusal to support one more voyage, during which he expected to find the mainland of Asia.

In 1501, after sailing along the coast of Brazil, the Florentine geographer Amerigo Vespucci (1451–1512) drew the obvious conclusion from the information collected by Columbus's explorations. He argued that Columbus had discovered a new continent unknown to the classical world. These claims were accepted by the German mapmaker Martin Waldseemüller (vald-SAY-mill-er), who, in 1507, honored Amerigo's claim by publishing the first map showing "America."

Columbus's Successors

Columbus's explorations set off a debate over which nations had the right to be involved in trade and expansion. Portuguese claims were based on a papal bull of 1481, issued by Pope Sixtus IV (r. 1471–1484), that granted Portugal rights to all lands south of the Canaries and west of Africa. After Columbus's return, the Spaniards lobbied one of Sixtus's successors, Alexander VI (r. 1492–1503), whose family, the Borgias, was from the kingdom of Aragon. In a series of bulls, Pope Alexander allowed the Spanish to claim all lands lying 400 miles or more west of the Azores. Finally, in the **Treaty of Tordesillas** (tor-day-SEE-yas) (1494), Spain and Portugal agreed that the line of demarcation between their two areas should be drawn 1,480 miles west of the Azores. The treaty was signed just six years before Pedro Alvares Cabral (1467–1520) discovered the coast of Brazil. Thus, the Spanish unwittingly granted the Portuguese rights to Brazil.

Adventurers and explorers worried little about the legal niceties of exploration. Even as Columbus lay dying in 1506, others, some without royal permission, sailed up and down the eastern coasts of North and South America. Amerigo Vespucci traveled on Spanish vessels as far as Argentina, while Spanish explorers sailed among the islands of the Caribbean and along the coast of the Yucatán Peninsula. Vasco Nuñez de Balboa (1475–1519) crossed the Isthmus of Panama in 1513 and found the Pacific Ocean exactly where the natives living in the region said it would be.

The most important of the explorations that Columbus inspired was the voyage undertaken by **Ferdinand Magellan** in 1519 (see **Map 13.2**). Although his motives are unclear, Magellan (1480?–1521) may have planned to complete Columbus's dream of sailing to the Indies. By the 1510s, mariners and others understood that the Americas were a new and hitherto unknown land, but they did not know what lay beyond them or what distance separated the Americas from the Spice Islands of Asia. After sailing along the well-known coastal regions of South America, Magellan continued south, charting currents and looking for a passage into the Pacific. Late in 1520, he beat his way through the dangerous straits (now the Strait of Magellan) separating Tierra del Fuego (ti-AIR-ah del foo-WAY-go) from the mainland. These turbulent waters marked the boundary of the Atlantic and Pacific Oceans. It took almost four months to travel from the straits to the Philippines. The crew suffered greatly from scurvy and a shortage of water and, at times, had to eat the rats aboard ship to survive. One crew member reported, "We ate biscuit, which was no longer biscuit, but powder of biscuit swarming with worms, for they had eaten the good."[3]

Treaty of Tordesillas
A treaty negotiated between Spain and Portugal dividing the newly explored lands in the New World and the Old. All New World lands except Brazil were given to the Spanish.

FERDINAND MAGELLAN

Ferdinand Magellan
The Spanish explorer who established the routes by which ships could sail around the world.

Nevertheless, Magellan managed to reach the Philippines by March 1521. A month later, he was killed by natives.

Spanish survivors, in two remaining ships, continued west, reaching the Moluccas, or Spice Islands, where they traded merchandise that they had carried along for a small cargo of cloves. A single surviving ship continued around Africa and back to Spain, landing with a crew of 15 at Cádiz in September 1522, after a voyage of three years and the loss of four ships and 245 men. Magellan completed and confirmed the knowledge of wind and ocean currents that European sailors had been accumulating. One of his sailors wrote of him, "More accurately than any man in the world did he understand sea charts and navigation."[4] The way was now open for the vast expansion of Europeans and European culture into all parts of the world.

Although the pope seemingly divided the non-European world between the Spanish and the Portuguese, Spanish adventurers were not the only ones to follow in Columbus's wake. The French and the English never accepted the pope's right to determine rights of exploration. They did, however, concentrate their explorations farther north. Building on a tradition of fishing off the coast of Newfoundland, English sailors under the command of John Cabot (1450?–1499?) sighted Newfoundland in 1497, and later voyages explored the coast as far south as New England. Cabot initiated an intense period of English venturing that would lead to an unsuccessful attempt to found a colony on Roanoke Island in 1587 and eventually to a permanent settlement at Jamestown in 1607. French expeditions followed Cabot to the north. In 1534, Jacques Cartier (kar-ti-YAY) (1491–1557) received a royal commission to look for a northern passage to the East. He was the first European to sail up the St. Lawrence River and began the process of exploration and trading that would lead to a permanent presence in Canada beginning in the early seventeenth century. But British and French settlements in the New World came later. The sixteenth century belonged to the Spanish.

ENGLISH AND FRENCH EXPLORERS

SECTION SUMMARY

- Columbus was a brilliant seaman whose exploration was based on geographic knowledge accumulated in the previous centuries.

- The frenzied Spanish search for wealth destroyed the economies of the island peoples.

- Magellan's voyage around the world completed the geographic knowledge necessary for commerce connecting Europe, Asia, and the New World.

- It was only with the writings of Amerigo Vespucci that most Europeans accepted the idea that Columbus had sailed to a previously unknown continent.

SPAIN'S COLONIAL EMPIRE, 1492–1600

How did the Spanish conquer and control the new world they entered?

Spanish penetration of the New World was a far cry from the model of the Portuguese in Asia. The Spaniards established no complex network of trade and commerce, and no strong states opposed their interests. A trading-post empire could not have worked in the New World. To succeed, the Spaniards needed to colonize and reorganize the lands they had found.

Between 1492 and 1600, almost 200,000 Spaniards immigrated to the New World. "New Spain," as they called these newly claimed lands, was neither the old society transported across the ocean nor an Amerindian society with a thin veneer of Spanish and European culture. To understand the history of New Spain, it is essential to grasp what it replaced, and how: The Spaniards overthrew two major civilizations and created new institutions in the wake of conquest. The whole story is not conquest and extermination—many of the Spanish attempted to secure fair treatment for the indigenous peoples who were now part of the Spanish Empire.

The Americas Before the European Invasion

The Spaniards, and later their European peers, entered a world vastly different from their own. It was a world formed by two momentous events—one geological, the other anthropological. The first was the creation of the continents of North and South America. The Americas, along with Africa and the Eurasian landmass, were once part of a single supercontinent. The breakup of this supercontinent left the Americas, Africa, and Eurasia free to evolve in dramatically different ways. The continental breakup occurred millions of years ago, long before the appearance of human beings and many other forms of mammalian life.

The second momentous event was the peopling of the Americas. Some migrants may have come over the seas. Most, though, arrived thanks to a temporary rejoining of the Americas to the Eurasian landmass by land and ice bridges that allowed Asians to cross over what is now the Bering Strait to the Americas in the period between 40,000 and 15,000 B.C. Their timing had a great impact. They arrived in the Americas long before the beginnings of the Neolithic agricultural revolution, which involved the domestication of numerous plants and animals. The agricultural revolution in the Americas occurred around 3000 B.C., perhaps six thousand years after similar developments in the Old World. The peoples of the Americas created complex societies, but those societies lacked large domesticated meat or pack animals (the llama was the largest), iron, other hard metals, and the wheel.

Nonetheless, by the time of Columbus's arrival, relatively populous societies were living throughout North and South America. Population estimates for the two continents range from 30 million to 100 million—50 million seems the most commonly accepted figure. North America saw the development of complex Mound Builder societies in the East and along the Mississippi River and pueblo societies in the deserts of the American Southwest. In Central and South America, there may have been 350 tribal or clan groups concentrated around fifteen or more cultural centers. But the greatest powers in the Amerindian world were the **Aztecs** in central and coastal Mexico and the **Inca** in the mountains of Peru.

Aztecs People who dominated the Valley of Mexico from the fourteenth to the sixteenth centuries and whose empire was destroyed by Cortés.

Inca A mountain empire that flourished in Peru. It was conquered for Spain by Pizarro.

THE AZTECS

When the collection of tribes, now known as the "Aztec" (or Mexica) peoples, appeared in central Mexico in the early fourteenth century, they found an already flourishing civilization concentrated around the cities and towns dotting the Valley of Mexico. The Aztecs conquered and united the many Nahuatl-speaking groups living in the valley, forming a confederation centered in Tenochtitlán, a city of perhaps 200,000 people built on an island in Lake Texcoco (see **MAP 13.3**). In early-sixteenth-century Europe, only London, Constantinople, and Naples would have been as large as the Aztec capital. It literally rose out of the water of Lake Texcoco. Only Venice could have equaled the sight. The whole valley supported an unusually high population of about a million. Using canals along the edge of the lake and other canals in Tenochtitlán itself, merchants easily moved food, textiles, gold and silver ornaments, jewels, and ceremonial feathered capes into the city markets. Spaniards later estimated that fifty thousand or more people shopped in the city on market days.

Tenochtitlán The Aztec capital was built on an island. Its central temples and markets were connected to the rest of the city and the suburbs on the lakeshore by numerous canals. The city and its surrounding market gardens seemed to the Spanish to be floating on water. (The Newberry Library, Chicago)

Religion was integral to the Aztecs' understanding of their empire. They believed that the world was finite and that they lived in the last of five empires. It was only regular human sacrifice to Huitzilopochtli (wheat-zeel-oh-POSHT-lee) that allowed the world to continue: The hearts of victims were necessary to sustain their god, to ensure that the sun would rise each morning. Thus, life for the Aztecs required a relentless parade of death.

Tenochtitlán was the center of an imperial culture based on tribute. Towns and villages under Aztec control owed ongoing allotments of food and precious metals to the Aztecs. To emphasize that Aztec power and dominance were complete, the Aztecs not only collected vast quantities of maize, beans, squash, and textiles, but demanded payment in everything down to centipedes and snakes. The most chilling tribute, however, was in humans for sacrifice. When the wars of expansion that had provided prisoners came to an end, the Aztecs and their neighbors fought "flower wars"—highly ritualized battles to provide prisoners to be sacrificed. Five thousand victims

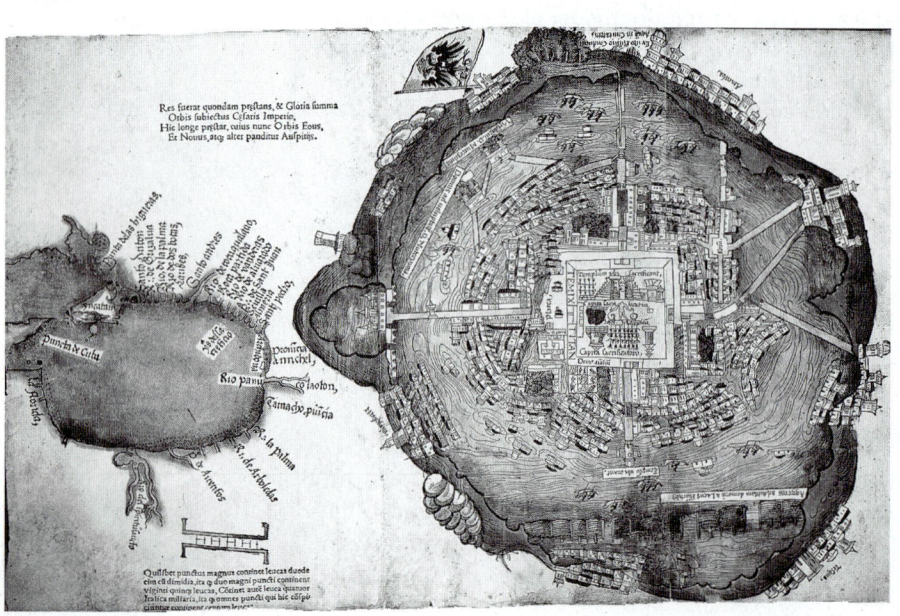

🌐 **MAP 13.3—Mexico and Central America**

The Valley of Mexico was a populous region of scattered towns, most of which were part of the Aztec Empire. As Cortés marched inland from Vera Cruz toward the valley, he passed through lands that for generations had been in an almost constant state of war with the Aztecs.

were sacrificed at the coronation of Moctezuma II (r. 1502–1520) in 1502. Even more, reportedly twenty thousand, were sacrificed at the dedication of the great temple of Huitzilopochtli in Tenochtitlán.

Aztec society maintained a perpetual state of war with the peoples beyond the mountains that ringed the Valley of Mexico—especially the people along the Caribbean coast. Given this constant state of war, plus the heavy burdens in tribute placed on the near by subject cities, it is no wonder that the Aztecs were obsessed by the contingencies of life. At the end of each calendar cycle of fifty-two years, all fires in the empire were extinguished until fire-priests ascertained that the world would continue. And the Aztec world did continue until August 1523 (see page 369).

THE INCA

The other great Amerindian empire of the fifteenth century, the empire of the Inca, was also of recent origin. During the fifteenth century, the Inca formed efficient armies and expanded their control beyond the central highlands of Peru. Fifteen thousand miles of roads and a sophisticated administrative system allowed the Inca to create a state that extended from modern-day Ecuador to Chile (see **MAP 13.4**). As they expanded, they demanded political control and tribute, but seem to have been tolerant of local traditions and language. The Inca perfected systems of irrigation and bridge-building, initiated by earlier inhabitants of the region. The empire, centered on the city of Cuzco high in the mountains of Peru, was able to sustain a population that may have reached 10 million by the end of the fifteenth century.

Human sacrifice, though not unknown to the Inca people, was not an essential part of their religious life. Their state was unsettled, however, by increasingly harsh tax exactions. Under the Inca system, the title Sapa Inca, or "Emperor," was inherited by the eldest son of the ruler's principal wife. The ruler's wealth, however, was retained by the rest of his family, who maintained the court as if the ruler still lived. Thus, each new ruler needed money to finance the creation of an entirely new court, and taxes were not only high but continuously climbing.

Both great Amerindian empires, despite their brilliance, rested on uneasy conquests. Subject groups would be willing allies for any invader.

Hernán Cortés The Spanish commander who conquered the Aztec Empire with a tiny force of Spaniards, reinforced by numerous Indian allies.

Doña Marina An enslaved Mexica noblewoman who served as translator and guide for Cortés.

The Spanish Conquests

Hernán Cortés (1485–1546) was ambitious to make something of himself in the New World. Of a poor but aristocratic background, from the Extremadura region of southwestern Spain, he had gone to the West Indies in 1504 to seek his fortune in the service of the governor of Cuba. The governor gave him a commission to lead an expeditionary force to investigate reports of a wealthy and prosperous mainland Indian civilization. From the beginning, Spanish authorities seem to have distrusted Cortés's aims. In fact, he departed hastily from Cuba to evade formal notification that the governor had revoked his commission because of insubordination.

Cortés landed in Mexico at the site of the city he would name Vera Cruz ("True Cross") early in 1519, with a tiny command of five hundred men, sixteen horses, eleven ships, and a few pieces of artillery. Aided by a devastating outbreak of smallpox and Amerindian peoples happy to shake off Aztec control, Cortés and his troops managed to destroy the network of city-states dominated by the Aztecs of Tenochtitlán in two years and lay claim to the Valley of Mexico for the king of Spain. The manner in which Cortés explained and justified his mission can serve as a model against which to measure the adventures of other sixteenth-century Europeans in the Americas.

Cortés, like Machiavelli (see page 329), believed in the power of truly able leaders (men of *virtù*) to overcome chance through bold acts. Even so, an attempt to capture a city of 200,000 with an army of 500 appears more foolhardy than bold. Cortés seems to have attempted it simply because he found himself with very little choice. With his commission revoked by the governor of Cuba, Cortés arrived on the mainland as a rebel against both the governor of Cuba and the king of Spain. He burned his ships in Vera Cruz harbor, making clear to all his men that there was no turning back. Much of what he did and said concerning the great Aztec Empire was an attempt to justify his initial act of insubordination and win back royal support. He quickly found allies among native groups who, for their own reasons, wished to see the Aztec Empire destroyed. The allied forces moved toward Tenochtitlán.

Cortés was greatly aided by fortune in the form of Malintzin, a Mexica woman who, after her conversion to Christianity, called herself **Doña Marina** (ca. 1501–1550). Malintzin was Cortés's interpreter and, later, his mistress. Without her, one of Cortés's followers recalled, "we could not have understood the language of New Spain and Mexico." Her story illustrates many of the complex interactions at play in sixteenth-century Mexico. Born a noble Aztec, she was sold by her stepfather and mother, ending up in the hands of the Maya. They gave her, along with twenty other women, to Cortés. Knowing both the Maya and Mexica languages, and quickly learning Spanish, she was the one person who could mediate between Spaniard and native. After bearing Cortés

⊕ MAP 13.4—The Inca Empire
The Inca Empire was accessible from Spanish strongholds in Mexico only by sea. Spanish exploration and domination brought the destruction of Inca mountain citadels and the transfer of administrative power to the new Spanish city of Lima on the coast.

a son, she finished her life in Spain as the wife of a Spanish gentleman. Like many of the natives, who felt no affection for the Aztecs of Tenochtitlán, she did not find it difficult to aid the Spaniards.

Despite the help of Malintzin and Spaniards who had previously lived with the natives, the meeting of Aztecs and Spaniards demonstrated the breadth of the chasm separating the Old World and the New. At first, the Aztec king Moctezuma was unconcerned about the coming of the Spaniards. Later, he seems to have attempted to buy them off. And finally, he and his successors fought desperately to drive them out of Tenochtitlán. The Aztecs' indecision was caused in large part by the fact that in neither words nor gestures did the two groups speak the same language. Hearing that the Spaniards were on the march, Moctezuma sent ambassadors bearing gold, silver, and other costly gifts, which they presented in a most humble fashion to the Spaniards. To a modern ear, the gifts sound like (and have often been interpreted to be) desperate attempts to buy off the invaders. To Cortés, or any European or Asian resident of the Old World, such gifts were a sign of submission. But to Moctezuma, and most Amerindians, the giving of gifts with great humility by otherwise powerful and proud people could be a show of status, power, and wealth. Seen in that light, Moctezuma's lavish gifts and apparent humility were probably meant to demonstrate the superiority of his civilization, and Cortés's acceptance of the gifts indicated to the Aztecs, at least, a recognition of Spanish inferior status.

Spaniards later explained that the Aztecs believed that Quetzalcoatl, the serpent-god symbolically conquered by Huitzilopochtli, had traveled to the east, promising one day to return and reclaim his lands, thus ending Aztec rule. The Spaniards believed that Moctezuma's ambivalence toward them was rooted in his belief in that myth.

Aztec Warrior   This watercolor, by a Mexican artist who was trained in European painting, depicts a pre-Aztec ruler. The dress and the stone-edged sword would have been typical of the Aztecs, too.   (Bibliothèque nationale de France)

The story does not hold up in light of the evidence, the myth of the return of Quetzalcoatl was first recorded in Spanish, not Mexica, sources long after the conquest. In truth, neither Cortés nor historians can satisfactorily explain, in Western terms, Moctezuma's initial response to the Spaniards. Cortés took the Aztec leader captive in 1521 and began what would be a two-year battle to take control of the capital and its empire. Although weakened by the arrival of smallpox and other virulent Old World diseases, the Aztecs continued to fight, even as more and more of the subject peoples joined the Spanish besiegers. The Spaniards cut off food and water to Tenochtitlán, but still the Aztecs fought.

Different understandings of the rules of war, different traditions of diplomacy, and different cultures prevented the Aztecs and Cortés from reaching any understanding. Warfare in pre-conquest America was highly ritualized. Armies captured enemies either to enslave them or to sacrifice them in one of the temples. The Spaniards, to Aztec eyes, killed indiscriminately and needlessly on the battlefield. Cortés later complained of the Aztecs' refusal to negotiate: "We showed them more signs of peace than have ever been shown to a vanquished people." It was a conflict that neither side could resolve in any other way; thus, by August 1523, Cortés and his allies had destroyed completely the garden city of Tenochtitlán.

LATER CONQUESTS

Cortés's recurring insubordination was an unfortunate model. His own lieutenants later rebelled against his control and attempted to create their own governments as they searched for riches and El Dorado, a mythical city of gold. Later adventurers marched throughout the North American Southwest and Central and South America, following rumors of hidden riches. Using private armies and torturing native peoples, veterans of Cortés's army and newly arrived speculators hoped to find wealth that would allow them to live like nobles on their return to Spain.

Francisco Pizarro (1470–1541) was the most successful of the private adventurers. Poor and illegitimate at birth, he arrived in the Americas ambitious for riches and power. After serving in Balboa's army, participating in several slaving expeditions, and helping to found Panama City, Pizarro was prosperous but still not wealthy. Rumors of Inca wealth filtered through to Central America. Pizarro and two partners resolved in 1530 to lead an expedition down the west coast of South America in search of the Inca capital. Benefiting from disorganization, caused by a smallpox epidemic and ensuing civil war, Pizarro was able to find local sympathizers.

Like Cortés, he used numerous Indian allies in his most important battles. Aided by Amerindians, eager to throw off Inca domination, he captured and executed the Sapa Inca and conquered the capital of Cuzco by 1533. He later built a new capital on the coast at Lima (see **MAP 13.4**), from which he worked to extend his control over all of the old Inca Empire. Pizarro and his Spanish partners seized vast amounts of gold and silver from the Inca. The Spanish eventually found silver mines at Potosí (po-to-SEE), which would be a critical source of revenue for the Spanish monarchy. Resistance to Spanish rule continued into the 1570s, when the last of the independent Inca strongholds was finally destroyed.

Colonial Organization

The Spanish crown needed to create a colonial government that could control the actions of its headstrong adventurers and create an orderly economy. Although the Spaniards proclaimed that they would "give to those strange lands the form of our own [land]," the resulting political and economic organization of the new Spanish possessions was a curious mixture of old and new.

The head of the administration was the monarchy. As early as the reigns of Ferdinand and Isabella, Spanish monarchs had tried to curb the excesses of the explorers and conquerors who traveled in their name. Isabella initially opposed the enslavement of Amerindians and any slave trade in the new lands. Further, the monarchs promoted a broad-based debate about the rights of Amerindians and the nature of religious conversion. It was royal policy that native rights, even the right not to become Christian, were to be protected. Mexicans had to accept missionaries, but they did not have to convert. Royal control, however, was limited by the sheer distance between the court and the new provinces. On average, it took the Spanish fleet two years to complete a round-trip voyage. It could easily take two years for a royal response to a question to arrive at its destination. Things moved so slowly that as one viceroy ruefully noted, "If death came from Madrid, we should all live to a very old age." Given the difficulties of communication, the powers of local administrators had to be very broad.

Council of the Indies
An administrative body established in 1524 to oversee commerce and administration in Spain's colonial possessions.

By 1535, Spanish colonial administration was firmly established in the form it would retain for the next two hundred years. The king created the **Council of the Indies**, located at court, eventually in Madrid, which saw to all legal and administrative issues pertaining to the new possessions. The new territories themselves were eventually divided into the viceroyalty of New Spain (primarily Central America and part of Venezuela) and the viceroyalty of Peru.

In New Spain, royal administrators created Indian municipalities, or districts, in which Spaniards had no formal right to live or work. Government in these municipalities remained largely in the hands of pre-conquest native elites. Throughout the sixteenth century, official documents in these communities continued to be written in Nahuatl, the Aztec language. These native communities were, however, fragile. Colonists and local administrators often interfered in the hope of gaining control. (See the feature, "The Global Record: An Inca Nobleman Defends His Civilization.")

encomienda   A royal protectorship granted with the obligation to protect and Christianize the people. Instead, natives became virtual slaves.

The Colonial Economy

The problem that most plagued the government was the conquerors' desire for laborers to work on the lands and in the mines that they had seized. From Columbus's first visit, the Spanish adopted a system of forced labor developed in Spain. A colonist called an *encomendero* (en-co-men-DARE-o) was offered a grant, or *encomienda* (en-co-mi-EN-da), of a certain number

An Inca Nobleman Defends His Civilization

Felipe Guaman Poma was born into a noble Inca family with a long history of service first to the Inca kings and later to the Spanish administrators. Although Guaman Poma became a Christian and adapted to Spanish rule, he appealed to the king of Spain in 1613 to intervene on behalf of the Indian peoples. In this section he describes the evils he has seen and suggests how the king could remedy them.

The aforementioned priests . . . do not act like the blessed priests of Saint Peter. . . . Rather, they give themselves over to greed for silver, clothing, and things of the world. . . . [They] ask for Indians to carry to market their wine, peppers, coca, and maize. Some have Indians bring mountain wine and coca down from the high plains to the hot lowlands. Being highland people, they die from fever and chills. . . . [They] have thread spun and woven, oppressing the widows and unmarried women, making them work without pay. . . . And in this [dealing with the priests] the Indian women become notorious whores. . . . [The priests] clamor to involve themselves too much in judicial matters. . . . As a result they enter into disputes and initiate petitions and are bad examples for the pueblo [i.e., village]. . . . They treat them so imperiously and thereby destroy the Indians of this kingdom.

The ancient [Andean] priests . . . acted devoutly and gave good example, as with the virgins and nuns of the temples. And so the rest [of the Indians] submitted to their justice and law. They were Christians in everything but their idolatry.

Because of such damage and so many complaints lodged against them, these fathers and pastors should be appointed on an interim basis—for a year at a time if he is good; and if he is not, may he not remain a single day. He should be at least fifty years old because a child's or a young man's follies are not good. . . . They should be proven and tested for academic preparation as well as for humility, charity, love and fear of God and justice, and for knowledge of the Quechua [or] Aymara languages of the Indians, needed to reach them, confess them, and preach the Gospel and sermons [to them].

They should be examined by the reverend fathers . . . who are great scholars and preachers in the world. Those [who pass the examinations] should be sent to Your Lordship and to the head viceroy for appointment as interim pastors, posting a guaranteed bond. With this they will lose their arrogance; they will obey your lordship.

In the time of the conquest of a province there was only one priest in charge of instruction; . . . he demanded no silver and only enough to eat. Thus these first ones were exemplary saints. They . . . did not pretend to be a bishop or a magistrate. Thus [the people] converted to God giving themselves over to peace and to the royal Crown.

QUESTIONS

1. What are the complaints about the behavior of Christian priests? What do these complaints imply about the place of a priest in a village?

2. What role does Guaman Poma expect priests to play in a village?

3. What are the benefits Guaman Poma expects villagers to receive from Spanish administrators?

Source: Kenneth Mills and William B. Taylor, eds., *Colonial Latin America: A Documentary History.* Copyright 2002 by Scholarly Resources, Inc. Reprinted by permission of Scholarly Resources, Inc.

of people or tribes who were required to work under his direction. The Spanish government expected that the encomendero was to be a protector of the conquered peoples, someone who would Christianize and civilize them. In theory, Indians who voluntarily agreed to listen to missionaries or to convert to Christianity could not be put under the control of an encomendero. If natives refused to hear the missionaries, however, the Spaniards believed they had the right of conquest. In many areas, encomenderos allowed life to continue as it had, simply collecting traditional payments that the pre-conquest elites had claimed. In other cases, where the subject peoples were forced into mining districts, the conditions were brutal. The treatment of native peoples was "more unjust and cruel," one reformer concluded, "than Pharaoh's oppression of the Jews."

The pressures exerted by the encomenderos were worsened by the precipitous fall in the indigenous population. Old World diseases, such as smallpox and measles, swept through peoples with no previous exposure to them (see pages 375–376). In central Mexico, where we know most about population changes, the pre-conquest population was at least 10 million to 12 million and may have been twice that. By the mid-sixteenth century, the native population may have declined to just over 6 million, and it probably plunged to less than 1 million early in the seventeenth century, before beginning to grow again.

A large population was essential to the Spanish and the Portuguese. The Caribbean islands and Brazil were ideal for the production of sugar—a commercial crop in great demand

Guaxtepec Map This detail from a map from 1580 shows the mixture of Spanish and Mexica that represents the ideal impact of Charles V's New Laws. The map shows a native village, but with a monastery at the center. The map is explained with Spanish captions and Nahuatl pictographic symbols. (Relación Geográfica map of Guaxtepec, Nettie Lee Benson Latin American Collection, the University of Texas Libraries)

throughout Europe. At first, plantations and mines were worked by Amerindians, but when their numbers shrank, the Spanish and Portuguese imported large numbers of slaves from Africa.

Africans had participated in the initial stages of the conquest. (See the feature, "The Visual Record: The Mulattos of Esmeraldas.") Some had lived in Spain and become Christian; indeed, Amerindians called them "black whitemen." Most Africans, however, were enslaved laborers. African slaves were in Cuba by 1518; they labored in the mines of Honduras by the 1540s. After the 1560s, the Portuguese began mass importations of African slaves into Brazil to work on the sugar plantations. It has been estimated that 62,500 slaves were brought into Spanish America and 50,000 into Brazil during the sixteenth century. By 1810, when the movement to abolish the slave trade began to gather momentum, almost 10 million Africans had been involuntarily transported to the New World to work the fields and mines on which the colonial economy depended.

The conquerors had hoped to find vast quantities of wealth that they could take back to the Old World. In the viceroyalty of Mexico, the search for El Dorado remained largely unsuccessful. The discovery, in 1545, of the silver mines at Potosí in Peru, however, fulfilled the Spaniards' wildest dreams. Between 1550 and 1650, the Spanish probably sent back to Spain 181 tons of gold and 16,000 tons of silver, one-fifth of which was paid directly into the royal treasury.

The flood of silver and gold did have a significant impact on the Continent. The treasure represents one-quarter of the income of King Philip II of Spain in the 1560s and made him the richest monarch in Europe. The New World bonanza funded Spanish opposition to the Protestant Reformation and Spain's attempts to influence the politics of most of its neighbors. And the Spanish coins, the *reales* (re-AL-es) and *reales a ocho* (re-AL-es a O-cho) (the "pieces of eight" prized by English pirates), became the common coin of European traders and even Muslim and Hindu traders in the Indian Ocean. In a world with limited commercial credit, the Spanish treasure was critical for a truly integrated system of world trade.

The Debate Over Indian Rights

To most conquerors, the ruthless pursuit of wealth and power needs little justification, but the more thoughtful among the Spaniards were uneasy. "Tell me," demanded Friar Antonio Montesinos (mon-teh-SEE-nos) in 1511, "by what right or justice do you hold these Indians in such cruel and horrible slavery? By what right do you wage such detestable wars on these people who lived idly and peacefully in their own lands?"[5]

Initially, the conquerors claimed the right to wage a just war of conquest if Amerindians refused to allow missionaries to live and work among them. Later, on the basis of reports of human sacrifice and cannibalism, written by Columbus and other early explorers, Europeans concluded that the inhabitants of the New World rejected basic natural laws. Juan Gines de Sepulveda (HWAN HE-nays de se-PUL-ve-da), chaplain of King Charles I of Spain, argued that the idolatry and cannibalism of the Indians made them, in Aristotle's terms, natural slaves—"barbarous and inhuman peoples abhorring all civil life, customs and virtue." People lacking "civil life" and "virtue" clearly could not be allowed self-government. Other writers commented that nakedness and cannibalism were both signs of the lack of "civility" among the Amerindians. Sepulveda implied that Indians were merely "humanlike," not necessarily human.

Franciscan and Dominican missionaries were especially vocal opponents of views such as Sepulveda's. Missionaries initially argued that Indians were innocents and ideal subjects for conversion to the simple piety of Christ and his first apostles. In their eyes, Indians were like children who could be converted and led by example and, where necessary, by stern discipline. The simple faith of the newly Christian native peoples was to be an example, the missionaries believed, for the lax believers of old Europe. These mendicants saw themselves as advocates for Indians; they desired to protect the natives from the depredations of the Spanish conquerors and the corruptions of European civilization.

The most eloquent defender of Indian rights was **Bartolomé de Las Casas** (1474–1566), a former encomendero who became a Dominican missionary and eventually bishop of Chiapas in southern Mexico. Las Casas passionately condemned the violence and brutality of the Spanish conquests. In a famous debate with Sepulveda, Las Casas rejected the "humanlike" argument. "All races of the world are men," he declared. All are evolving along a historical continuum. It was wrong, he added, to dismiss any culture or society as outside or beyond natural law. Like all other peoples, Indians had reason. That being the case, even the most brutal could be civilized and Christianized, but by conversion, not coercion.

In the view of Las Casas, the argument for natural slavery was indefensible.

King Charles accepted Las Casas's criticisms of the colonial administration. In 1542, he issued "New Laws," aimed at ending the virtual independence of the most adventurous encomenderos. He further abolished Indian slavery and greatly restricted the transfer of encomiendas. We should have no illusion, however, that these measures reflected a modern acceptance of cultural pluralism. The very mendicants who protected the Indians assumed that Westernization and Christianization would quickly follow mercy. When it did not, as during revolts in the 1560s, the mendicants themselves sometimes reacted with a puzzled sense of anger, frustration, and betrayal.

Bartolomé de Las Casas A former encomendero and the first bishop of Chiapas who passionately defended Indian rights and urged the passage of laws abolishing Indian slavery.

SECTION SUMMARY

- Before the arrival of the Spanish, the Aztecs and Inca were large empires that dominated surrounding tribes and clans.

- Cortés found ready allies among the peoples dominated by the two empires.

- The conquest of Mexico set off a Spanish expansion, barely under the control of the Crown.

- The Crown eventually attempted to protect Amerindians by restricting encomiendas, outlawing Indian slavery, and forming Indian-controlled communities.

The Mulattos of Esmeraldas

This painting, which is entitled *Los Mulatos de Esmeraldas*, is the earliest known signed colonial portrait, dating back to 1599. It was commissioned by Juan del Barrio de Sepúlveda, judge of the Audiencia of Quito. He sent it to the Spanish king in Madrid, where the painting still resides. The artist who painted this very European-styled painting was an Amerindian named Andrés Sánchez Galque who had trained with a Spanish Dominican. The resulting work is a striking mix of native and Spanish cultures and leads a historian to ask, "What does this image suggest about colonial Latin America?"

It demonstrates, first of all, how quickly even isolated areas became integrated into a complex international culture. In the center of the painting stands Don Francisco de Arobe, the head of one of two important Afro-Indian clans that dominated the region since the middle of the sixteenth century. He is flanked by his two sons, Don Petro (on his right) and Don Domingo (on his left). Don Francisco is of mixed ancestry—his father was African, his mother an enslaved Nicaraguan. The parents had escaped into the wild region of Esmeraldas, an isolated coastal area northwest of Quito (see **Map 13.2**). It was an area that the Spanish imagined was filled with gold and perhaps, as its name seemed to imply, emeralds. It was also an area that various missionaries and private adventurers attempted to control in the name of the Crown. They were convinced that had they subdued Esmeraldas, their reward would have been treasure and political power.

In the half-century before this portrait was painted, the mulatto groups had variously negotiated with, helped, and avoided the Spanish. Clan leaders regularly promised to become Christian, to give food to the explorers, and to help in the search for gold and other treasures. Throughout the sixteenth century, they regularly and successfully resisted incorporation into the empire. The leader of one clan had offered allegiance to the Spanish if they would name him governor "over your subjects and vassals and natives." And

so, it is no doubt significant that the Spanish named Don Francisco governor. It was, in fact, his peaceful submission to the Audiencia that occasioned this surprising work. All this makes the portrait fascinating, but ambiguous. Are the three, as some have suggested, "trophies, stuffed and mounted on a wall of blue" or perhaps crafty diplomats who preferred "Renaissance dissimulation to . . . rebellion?"*

The three figures have struck a pose typical in Renaissance portraits. Don Francisco looks directly at the viewer, while his sons look only at him. The three are wearing Spanish cloaks and ruffled collars, over what is probably a South American poncho, but the design of the material suggests it is European or Asian in origin. What is most striking is the gold jewelry—earrings and noseplugs. These very likely were scavenged from burial mounds left in the region by earlier native peoples. Spanish visitors to Esmeraldas often commented on the gold jewelry of the mulattos. The mulatto clans often used promises of gold to mesmerize the adventurers who came. The three also are wearing shell necklaces—a tradition among coastal peoples reaching back perhaps a millennium. And finally, they are carrying spears, probably a combination of local wood and imported steel tips.

But how to interpret the image? The first thing a historian must do is acknowledge that we cannot know for sure the thoughts of the painter, the patron, or the three who posed. But we can line up the visual evidence that might lead us to a tentative conclusion. First, notice the interesting mix of dress. The three men doubtless would not have worn so many layers of clothing at home, along the steamy seacoast. Are the Spanish additions indications that Don Barrio, the judge of the Audiencia in Quito, dressed them to look more subdued, Spanish, and civilized? All three are addressed as "don," an honorific title that indicates both Christian conversion and elevated social status. But if that is the case, why are there no crosses, no signs of deference? They continue wear their coastal shells and their gold

THE COLUMBIAN EXCHANGE

What changes did European expansion bring to the Old World and the New?

Columbian Exchange
A term used to describe the blending of cultures between the Old World and the New. Columbus, and others who followed, brought plants, animals, and diseases that transformed North and South America.

The conquerors, adventurers, and traders who completed the expansion, begun by the voyages of Christopher Columbus and Vasco da Gama, profoundly altered the Old World and the New. A system of world trade had been in place before 1492, but now, as the Spanish proclaimed, Europe, and especially Spain, were at the center of economic and political life. As the Spanish and other Europeans moved throughout the world, they carried with them religions, ideas, people, plants, animals, and diseases—forever uniting the Old World and the New. This blending of cultures is known as the **Columbian Exchange**.

The Mulattos of Esmeraldas (Institut Amatller d'Art Hispanic)

jewelry taken from sites still unknown to the Spanish. Their hats are in their hands, perhaps a sign of respect or submission, but their eyes are not downcast or submissive. Don Francisco looks directly at the viewer and all three hold their spears. They may now be Spanish subjects, but Don Francisco does have the look of a governor.

In the end, it may be that Don Francisco and Judge Barrio would not have agreed on what the painting signified. But the ambiguity of the portrait does demonstrate to subsequent historians the extent to which understanding the Spanish role in Latin America requires more than simply ideas of conquest, domination, or rebellion. Identities may have been transformed, but persons like Don Francisco seem to be more than just obedient subjects.

QUESTIONS

1. Look at the portrait and try to identify those items that seem native or Spanish.

2. Can you find indications of either submission or independence in the portraits?

---

* The first conclusion is from Kenneth Mills and William B. Taylor, eds., *Colonial Latin America: A Documentary History* (Wilmington, Del.: SR Books, 2002), p. 160; the second from Kris Lane, *Quito, 1599* (Albuquerque: University of New Mexico Press, 2002), p. 33.

Disease

Columbus, and those who followed him, brought not only people to the New World, but also numerous Old World diseases. "Virgin-soil" epidemics—that is, epidemics of previously unknown diseases—are invariably fierce. Although the New World may have passed syphilis to Spain, from which it quickly spread throughout the Old World, diseases transferred from the Old World to the New were much more virulent than syphilis. Smallpox spread from Cuba to Mexico as early as 1519. It was soon followed by diphtheria, measles, trachoma, whooping cough, chickenpox, bubonic plague, malaria, typhoid fever, cholera, yellow fever, scarlet fever, amoebic dysentery, influenza, and some varieties of tuberculosis. Disease served as the silent ally of the conquerors. At critical points during the conquest of Tenochtitlán, smallpox was raging in the Aztec population. The disease later moved along traditional trade networks, often arriving in parts of North and South America decades before the Old World adventurers appeared. An

Images of the New World A mix of fact and fiction characterized many early images of the New World. The text below this illustration claims that these natives share everything, even wives; that they are cannibals; and that they have no government. The woodcut seems to justify Spanish domination. (Spencer Collection, New York Public Library/Art Resource, NY)

epidemic shortly before Pizarro's expedition to Peru carried off the Sapa Inca and may have contributed to the unrest and civil war that worked to the advantage of the invaders.

Lacking sources, historians cannot trace accurately the movement of epidemic diseases or their effects on New World populations, yet many archaeologists and historians remain convinced that Old World diseases moved north from Mexico and ravaged and disrupted Amerindian populations in eastern North America long before the arrival of European immigrants. In most of the New World, 90 percent or more of the native population was destroyed by wave after wave of previously unknown afflictions. Explorers and colonists did not enter an empty land but rather an *emptied* one.

It was at least partially because of disease that both the Spanish and the Portuguese needed to import large numbers of African slaves to work their plantations and mines. With the settlement of southeastern North America, commercial agriculture was extended to include the production of tobacco and later cotton. As a result of the needs of plantation economies and the labor shortages caused by epidemics, African slaves were brought in by the thousands, then hundreds of thousands. In the Caribbean and along the coasts of Central and South America, the Africans created an African Caribbean or African American culture that amalgamated African, European, and American civilizations.

Plants and Animals

The impact of Old World peoples on native populations was immediately evident to all parties. However, scholars have recently argued that the importation of plants and animals had an even more profound effect than the arrival of Europeans. The changes that began in 1492 created "Neo-Europes" in what are now Canada, the United States, Mexico, Argentina, Australia, and New Zealand. The flora and fauna of the Old World, accustomed to a relatively harsh, competitive environment, found ideal conditions in the new lands. Like the rabbits that overran the Canary Islands and eventually Australia, Old World plants and animals multiplied, driving out many New World species.

The most important meat and dairy animals in the New World today—cattle, sheep, goats, and pigs—are imports from the Old World. Sailors initially brought pigs or goats aboard ship because they were easily transportable sources of protein. When let loose on the Caribbean islands, they quickly took over. The spread of horses through what is now Mexico, Brazil, Argentina, the United States, and Canada was equally dramatic. To the list of domesticated animals can be added donkeys, dogs, cats, and chickens. The changes these animals brought were profound. Cattle, pigs, and chickens quickly became staples of the New World diet. Horses enabled Amerindians and Europeans to travel across and settle the vast plains of both North and South America.

Gardening in Spanish Mexico This closed Spanish-style garden is a mix of the old and the new. Workers use both a Spanish hoe and an indigenous spade to cultivate new plants introduced by the Spanish. (Biblioteca Nacional, Madrid/Institut Amatller d'Art Hispanic)

The flora of the New World was equally changed. Even contemporaries noted how Old World plants flourished in the New. By 1555, European clover was widely distributed in Mexico—Aztecs called it "Castilian grass." Other Old World grasses, as well as weeds such as dandelions, quickly followed. Domesticated plants, including apples, peaches, and artichokes, spread rapidly and naturally in the hospitable new environment. The Old World also provided new and widely grown small grains such as oats, barley, and wheat. Early in the twentieth century, it was estimated that only one-quarter of the grasses found on the broad prairies of the Argentine pampas were native before the arrival of Columbus.

The exchange went both ways. Crops from the New World also had an effect on the Old. By the seventeenth century, maize (or American corn), potatoes, sweet potatoes, and many varieties of beans had significantly altered the diets of Europe and Asia. New crops supported the dramatic population growth that invigorated Italy, Ireland, and Scandinavia. With the addition of the tomato in the nineteenth century, much of the modern European diet became dependent on New World foods. The new plants and new animals, as well as the social and political changes initiated by the Europeans, pulled the Old World and the New more closely together.

Culture

One reason for the accommodation between the Old World and the New was that the Europeans and Amerindians tended to interpret conquest and cultural transformation in the same way. The peoples living in the Valley of Mexico believed that their conquest was fated by the gods and that their new masters would bring in new gods. The Spaniards' beliefs were strikingly similar, based on the revelation of divine will and the omnipotence of the Christian God. Cortés, by whitewashing former Aztec temples and converting native priests into white-clad Christian priests, was in a way fulfilling the Aztecs' expectations about the nature of conquest.

Acculturation was also facilitated by the Spanish tendency to place churches and shrines at the sites of former Aztec temples. The shrine of the Virgin of Guadalupe (gwa-da-LOO-peh) (on the northern edge of modern Mexico City), for example, was located on the site of the temple of the goddess Tonantzin (to-NAN-tzin), an Aztec fertility-goddess of childbirth and midwives. The shrine of Guadalupe is a perfect example of the complex mixture of cultures. The shrine initially appealed to *creoles*—people of mixed Spanish and Mexican descent. In the seventeenth century and after, it came to symbolize the connection of poor Mexicans to Christianity and was a religious rallying point for resisting state injustices.

The colonists tended to view their domination of the New World as a divine vindication of their own culture and civilization. During the sixteenth century, they set about remaking the world they had found. In the century after the conquest of Mexico, Spaniards founded 190 new cities in the Americas. Lima, Bogota, and many others were proudly modeled on and compared with the cities of Spain. In 1573, King Philip II (r. 1556–1598) established ordinances requiring all new cities to be laid out on a uniform grid with a main plaza, market, and religious center. In these cities, religious orders founded colleges for basic education, much like the universities they had organized in the Old World. In 1551, a century before English colonists founded Harvard University in Massachusetts, the Crown authorized the first universities in the New World. The universities in Mexico City and Lima mirrored the great Spanish university in Salamanca, teaching law and theology to the colonial elites. Colonists attempted to re-create in all essentials the society of Spain.

The experience of the Spanish and Portuguese in the sixteenth century seemed confirmed by the later experiences of the French and English in the seventeenth century. In seventeenth-century New England, the English Puritan John Winthrop concluded, "For the natives, they are nearly all dead of smallpox, so as the Lord hath cleared our title to what we possess."[6] A seventeenth-century French observer came to a similar conclusion: "Touching these savages, there is a thing that I cannot omit to remark to you, it is that it appears visibly that God wishes that they yield their place to new peoples."[7] Political philosophers believed that in the absence of evidence that the indigenous peoples were improving the land, the rights to that land passed to those who would make the best use of it. Thus, colonists believed that they had divine and legal sanction to take and to remake these new lands in a European image.

SECTION SUMMARY

- Old World diseases, introduced into the New World, destroyed perhaps 90 percent of the indigenous population.

- Thousands of enslaved Africans were brought to the New World to replace the lost population.

- Old World plants and animals transformed the economy of the New World.

- The cult of the Virgin of Guadalupe shows how religious practices of the Old World were influenced by New World religious practices.

CHAPTER SUMMARY

As we have seen, there was never a time when Europeans were unaware of or unconcerned about the outside world. In addition to traditional geographical knowledge, reaching back to the classical world, Europeans had valuable trade contacts via Muslim traders with both Africa and Asia. Further, in the thirteenth century, Italian merchants and adventurers began making regular trips through central Asia to China and even to Japan.

Yet, the expansion begun by the Portuguese along the coast of Africa and then on to India began a fateful transformation of European economic, political, and cultural influence. The Portuguese voyages were almost never adventures of discovery. By rumor and careful reading, explorers had ideas about what they would find. Nonetheless, they were faced with challenges that led them to adapt their Mediterranean and European ways of organization. The Portuguese developed a trading-post system to control trade in Asia.

Portuguese control of the African coast seemed to foreclose Spanish connections to Asian markets. Yet, based on a misunderstanding of classical texts, Columbus convinced the Spanish that the shortest route to Asia involved sailing west. Although Columbus never acknowledged it, by early in the sixteenth century, the Spanish knew that he had found a world unknown to the Old World.

In the wake of savage conquest and exploitation by adventurers, the Spanish developed a system of law and administration that transformed the world they had found. In the New World, even as the Spanish conquered peoples and changed

FOCUS QUESTIONS

- What did Europeans know about the wider world in the Middle Ages?

- How did the Portuguese exploit their new connection to the East?

- Why did the Spanish choose to sail west in their attempt to find Asia?

- How did the Spanish conquer and control the new world they entered?

- What changes did European expansion bring to the Old World and the New?

their languages, governments, and religions, many aspects of Amerindian culture survived in the local Indian municipalities.

The meeting of the Old World and the New brought unexpected changes to both. The old empires of the Americas were replaced by a Spanish colonial government. They brought with them foods, livestock, religion, and traditional European culture. They also brought diseases that decimated populations and transformed economies.

Modern historians have made us very aware of what was lost during the violent and tragic conquests that were part of European expansion. It is impossible to say whether the economic and technical benefits of the amalgamation of the Old World and the New outweigh the costs. Even those who celebrate the transformation of the New World would probably agree with the conclusions of a Native American in the Pacific Northwest: "I am not sorry the missionaries came. But I wish they had known how to let their news change people's lives from the inside, without imposing their culture over our ways."[8]

KEY TERMS

Prince Henry "the Navigator" (p. 359)

Vasco da Gama (p. 360)

trading-post empire (p. 361)

Treaty of Tordesillas (p. 364)

Ferdinand Magellan (p. 364)

Aztecs (p. 366)

Inca (p. 366)

Hernán Cortés (p. 368)

Doña Marina (p. 368)

Council of the Indies (p. 370)

encomienda (p. 370)

Bartolomé de Las Casas (p. 373)

Columbian Exchange (p. 374)

 This icon will direct you to additional materials on the website: www.cengage.com/history/noble/westciv6e.

 See our interactive eBook for map and primary source activities.

NOTES

1. Quoted in William D. Phillips, Jr., and Carla Rahn Phillips, *The Worlds of Christopher Columbus* (Cambridge: Cambridge University Press, 1992), p. 163.

2. Quoted ibid., p. 166.

3. Quoted in J. H. Parry, ed., *The European Reconnaissance: Selected Documents* (New York: Harper & Row, 1968), p. 242.

4. Quoted in Alfred W. Crosby, *Ecological Imperialism: The Biological Expansion of Europe, 900–1900* (Cambridge: Cambridge University Press, 1986), p. 125.

5. Quoted in Mark A. Burkholder and Lyman L. Johnson, *Colonial Latin America* (Oxford: Oxford University Press, 1990), p. 29.

6. Quoted in Crosby, p. 208.

7. Quoted ibid., p. 215.

8. Quoted in Maria Parker Pascua, "Ozette: A Makah Village in 1491," *National Geographic* (October 1991), p. 53.

14

CHAPTER OUTLINE

El Greco: The Burial of the Count de Orgaz   This traditional chapel painting shows the close connection between the earthly and celestial realms in traditional Catholic Christianity.   (Institut Amatller d'Art Hispanic)

The Age of the Reformation

El Greco's *The Burial of the Count de Orgaz* encapsulates the hopes and contradictions of the age of the Reformation. El Greco ("the Greek") first learned to paint on the island of Crete, then studied and worked in Venice and Rome before settling in Spain. This painting expresses the medieval Christian understanding of a good death. We see a saintly knight surrounded by clergy and witnesses as his soul (in the form of a cloud-wrapped body) is commended to Christ. But El Greco (1541–1614) painted during a period of social, political, and religious turmoil, when medieval assumptions about the unity of the Christian world and the nature of salvation were being challenged by religious reformers and their political supporters.

If we look more closely at the painting, we can see what Catholic Christians wished to emphasize. The two figures are Saint Stephen, the first Christian martyr, and Saint Augustine, perhaps the most important of the early Church Fathers. They represent the continuity of the Christian tradition. But just as important is the heavenly hierarchy of saints and angels reaching from the count upward to Christ. At the very top are Saint John and Saint Mary, who are interceding with Christ for the count's soul. The hierarchy of saints and intercessors so vividly painted by El Greco represents one of the clearest differences between the two contending visions of Christian life and society. Most reformers rejected the idea that salvation depended on the intervention of others, no matter how saintly. Salvation was a simpler process. The hierarchy of saints and angels depicted by El Greco seemed unnecessary.

The crisis of the Reformation began with a challenge to the religious authority of the papacy. Debates over the power and status of the church that raged during this period, however, did not occur in a political vacuum. Support for the old church was an issue of state that profoundly affected the exercise of political authority in the Holy Roman Empire. In England and Scandinavia, by contrast, monarchs viewed the church as a threat to strong royal government, and reformers soon found themselves with royal patrons. Elsewhere, especially in eastern Europe, no strong central governments existed to enforce religious unity, and so a variety of Christian traditions coexisted.

By the second half of the sixteenth century, political and religious leaders concentrated their energies on a process of theological definition and institutionalization that led to the formation of the major Christian religious denominations we know today. They created Roman Catholic, Anglican, Reformed (Calvinist), and Lutheran churches as clearly defined confessions, with formally prescribed religious beliefs and practices.

An important aspect of the reform movement was the emphasis on individual belief and religious participation. Far from freeing the individual, however, the Christian churches of the late sixteenth century all emphasized correct doctrine and orderliness in personal

FOCUS QUESTIONS

- Why did the reformers feel it was necessary to establish entirely new churches outside the Roman Catholic Church?

- What political factors limited Charles V's ability to respond to the religious crisis?

- Why did the English monarchs take the lead in efforts to reform the English church?

- How did ideas of church reform influence social and political developments in the rest of Europe?

- How did Catholic and Protestant Christians differ from each other by the end of the Reformation?

This icon will direct you to additional materials on the website: www.cengage.com/history/noble/westciv6e.

See our interactive eBook for map and primary source activities.

behavior. Although early Protestants rejected a system that they accused of oppressing the individual, the institutions that replaced the old church developed their own traditions of control. The increased moral discipline advocated by churches accompanied and even fostered the expansion of state power that would characterize the late sixteenth and seventeenth centuries.

THE REFORMATION MOVEMENTS, CA. 1517–1545

Why did the reformers feel it was necessary to establish entirely new churches outside the Roman Catholic Church?

Martin Luther   German theologian and religious reformer who began the Protestant Reformation in 1517 by questioning, and finally discarding, Catholic teaching about penance and salvation.

In 1517, **Martin Luther**, a little-known professor of theology in eastern Germany, launched a protest against practices in the late medieval church. Luther's criticisms struck a responsive chord with many of his contemporaries and led to calls for reform across much of Europe. All the reformers, even the most radical, shared with Luther a sense that the essential sacramental and priestly powers claimed by the late medieval church were illegitimate. These reformers initially had no intention of forming a new church; they simply wanted to return Christianity to what they believed was its earlier, purer form. Although their various protests resulted in the creation of separate and well-defined religious traditions, the differences among the reformers became clear only in the second half of the sixteenth century. Thus, it is appropriate to speak of "Reformation movements" rather than a unified Protestant Reformation.

The Late Medieval Context

In the flourishing religious life of the late Middle Ages, questions of an individual's salvation and personal relationship to God and to the Christian community remained at the heart of religious practice and theological speculation. Christians believed in a holy covenant in which God would save those who, by means of the church's sacraments and through penitential and charitable acts, were partners in their own salvation. Foremost among the penitential acts was the feeding of "Christ's Poor," especially on important feast days. The pious constructed and supported hospices for travelers and hospitals for the sick. Christians went on pilgrimages to shrines, such as the tomb of Saint Thomas Becket in Canterbury or the Church of Saint James of Compostela in Spain. They also endowed chapels, called chantry chapels, where prayers would be offered for their own souls. To moralists, work itself was, in some sense, a penitential and ennobling act.

POPULAR RELIGION   The most common religious practice of the late Middle Ages was participation in religious brotherhoods. Urban brotherhoods were usually organized around a craft guild or neighborhood; rural brotherhoods were more likely to include an entire village or parish. Members vowed to attend monthly meetings, to participate in processions on feast days, and to maintain peaceful and charitable relations with fellow members.

The most typical religious feast was that of *Corpus Christi* (the "Body of Christ"). The feast celebrated and venerated the sacrament of the mass and the ritual by which the bread offered to the laity became the actual body of Christ. Corpus Christi was popular with the church hierarchy because it emphasized the role of the priest in the central ritual of Christianity. The laity, however, equated Corpus Christi with the body of citizens who made up the civic community. Thus, religious identity seemed to be at the very heart of social identity. The most revered saint in the late Middle Ages, however, was the Virgin Mary, the mother of Jesus. The most popular new pilgrimage shrines in the north of Europe were dedicated to the Virgin. It was she, townspeople believed, who protected them from invasion, plague, and natural disasters. In such a society, it was impossible to distinguish between religion and society, church and state.

WOMEN AND RELIGION   Women played a prominent role in late medieval religious life. Holy women who claimed any sort of moral standing often did so because of visions or prophetic gifts, such as knowledge of future events or discernment of the status of souls in Purgatory. The Italian Blessed Angela of Foligno (fo-LIN-yo) (ca. 1248–1309) had several visions and became the object of a large circle of devoted followers. She was typical of a number of late medieval religious women who, on the death of a spouse, turned to religion. They tended to gather "families" around them, people whom they described as their spiritual "fathers" or "children." They offered moral counsel and boldly warned businessmen and politicians of the dangers of lying and sharp dealings.

In the late Middle Ages, religious houses for women probably outnumbered those for men. For unmarried or unmarriageable (because of poverty or disabilities) daughters, convents provided an economical, safe, and controlled environment. Moralists denounced the dumping of women in convents: "They give [unmarriageable daughters] to a convent, as if they were the scum and vomit of the world," Saint Bernardino of Siena (1380–1444) complained. The general public, however, believed that well-run communities of religious women promoted the spiritual and physical health of the general community. In a society in which women were not allowed to control their own property and, except among the nobility, lacked a visible role in political and intellectual life, a religious vocation may have had a compelling appeal. At the least, it permitted women to define their own religious and social relationships. Well-to-do or aristocratic parents also appreciated the fact that the traditional gift that accompanied a daughter entering a religious house was much smaller than a dowry.

Some women declined to join convents, which required vows of chastity and obedience to a Rule and close male supervision. They could be found among the many pilgrims who visited local shrines, the great churches of Rome, or even the holy city of Jerusalem. Many other women chose to live as anchoresses, or recluses, in closed cells beside churches and hospitals or in rooms in private homes. Men and women traveled from all parts of England seeking the counsel of the Blessed Julian of Norwich (d. after 1413), who lived in a tiny cell built into the wall of a parish church. The most controversial group of religious women was the Beguines, who lived in communities without taking formal vows and often with minimal connections to the local church hierarchy. By the early fifteenth century, Beguines were suspect because clerics believed that these independent women rejected traditional religious cloistering and the moral leadership of male clergy; consequently, it was thought, they were particularly susceptible to heresy.

A more conservative movement for renewal in the church was the Brothers and Sisters of the Common Life, founded by the Dutchman Geert Groote (HIRT HROW-ta) (1340–1384). A popular preacher and reformer, Groote gathered male and female followers into quasi-monastic communities at Deventer in the Low Countries. Members followed a strict, conservative spirituality that has come to be known as the *devotio moderna*, or "modern devotion." Although they called themselves "modern," their piety was traditional. They advocated the contrary ideals of fourteenth-century religious life: broader participation by the laity and strict control by clerical authorities.

Religious life in the late medieval period was broadly based and vigorous. Theologians, laypeople, and popular preachers could take heart that they were furthering their own salvation and that of their neighbors. Thus, the Reformation of the sixteenth century involved more than simple moral reform.

CHRONOLOGY

1513–1517	Fifth Lateran Council meets to consider reform of the Catholic Church
1517	Luther makes public his "Ninety-five Theses"
1518	Zwingli is appointed people's priest of Zurich
1520	Pope Leo X condemns Luther's teachings
1521	Luther appears at the Diet of Worms
1524–1525	Peasant revolts in Germany
1527	Imperial troops sack Rome
1530	Melanchthon composes the Augsburg Confession summarizing Lutheran belief
1534	Calvin flees Paris Loyola founds the Society of Jesus
1535	Anabaptist community of Münster is destroyed
1536	Calvin arrives in Geneva and publishes *Institutes of the Christian Religion*
1545–1563	Council of Trent meets to reform Catholic Church
1555	Emperor Charles V accepts the Peace of Augsburg
1559	Parliament passes Elizabethan Act of Supremacy and Act of Uniformity

Martin Luther and the New Theology

Martin Luther (1483–1546) eventually challenged many of the assumptions of late medieval Christians. He seemed to burst onto the scene in 1517, when he objected to the way in which papal indulgences—that is, the remission of penalties owed for sins—were being bought and sold in the archbishopric of Magdeburg. Luther's father, a miner from the small town of Mansfeld,

Crowning with Thorns Late medieval Christians meditated on Christ's sufferings and preferred images like this one, painted by Jörg Breu, that shows a tortured Christ living in their own time.
(Courtesy, Augustiner Chorherrenstift, Herzogenburg. Photo: Fotostudio Wurst Erich)

had hoped that his son would take a degree in law and become a wealthy and prestigious lawyer. Luther chose instead to enter a monastery and eventually become a priest.

JUSTIFICATION BY FAITH

Luther recalled having been troubled throughout his life by a sense of his own sinfulness and unworthiness. According to late medieval theology, the life of a Christian was a continuing cycle of sin, confession, contrition, and penance. Luther came to believe that the church's requirement that believers achieve salvation by means of confession, contrition, and penance made too great a demand on the faithful. Instead, Luther said, citing the New Testament, salvation (or justification) was God's gift to the faithful. Luther's belief is known as **justification by faith**. Acts of charity were important products resulting from God's love, but in Luther's opinion, they were not necessary for salvation. In Luther's theology, the acts of piety so typical of the medieval church were quite unnecessary for salvation because Christ's sacrifice had brought justification once and for all. Justification came entirely from God and was independent of human works.

justification by faith
Luther's doctrine that Christians can be saved only by grace, a free gift of God and independent of any penitential or charitable acts.

Luther also attacked the place of the priesthood in the sacramental life of the church and, by extension, the power and authority a church might claim in public life. Priests, in Luther's view, were not mediators between God and individual Christians. John Wyclif and Jan Hus (see page 293) had argued against the spiritual authority of unworthy priests. Luther, however, challenged the role of all clergy, and of the institutional church itself, in the attainment of salvation. Thus, he argued for a "priesthood of all believers."

CONTROVERSY OVER INDULGENCES

In the years before 1517, Luther's views on salvation and his reservations about the traditional ways of teaching theology attracted little interest outside his own university. Matters changed, however, when he questioned the sale of indulgences, rewards for pilgrimages or for noteworthy acts of charity or sacrifice. The papacy frequently authorized the sale of indulgences to pay various expenses. Unscrupulous priests often left the impression that purchase of an indulgence freed a soul from Purgatory. After getting no response to his initial complaints, Luther posted his "Ninety-five Theses" on the door of the Wittenberg Castle church, the usual way to announce topics for theological debates. His text created a firestorm, when it was quickly translated and printed throughout German-speaking lands. His charges against the sale of indulgences encapsulated German feelings about unworthy priests and economic abuses by the clergy. Luther was acclaimed as the spokesman of the German people. (See the feature, "The Written Record: Martin Luther's Address to the Christian Nobility of the German Nation.")

Responding to the crisis in Germany, Pope Leo X (r. 1513–1521) condemned Luther's teachings in 1520 and gave him sixty days to recant. Luther refused to do so and publicly burned the papal letter. In 1521, Emperor **Charles V** called an imperial diet, or parliament, at Worms to deal with the religious crisis. Charles demanded that Luther submit to papal authority. Luther, however, countered that religious decisions must be based on personal experience and conscience informed by a study of Scripture. Luther's refusal became a ringing statement conscience, when a later editor added the famous, "Here I stand. I can do no other, may God help me."

The emperor and his allies stayed firmly in the papal camp, and the excommunicated Luther was placed under an imperial ban—that is, declared an outlaw. As Luther left the Diet of Worms, friendly princes took him to Wartburg Castle in Saxony, where they could protect him. During a year of isolation at Wartburg, Luther used Erasmus's edition of the Greek New Testament as the basis of a translation of the New Testament into German, which became an influential literary as well as religious work.

Charles V Holy Roman emperor and King Charles I of Spain. His empire included Spain, Italy, the Low Countries, Germany, and the New World.

The Reformation of the Communities

Luther challenged the authority of the clerical hierarchy and called on laypeople to take responsibility for their own salvation. His ideas spread rapidly in the towns and countryside of Germany because he and his followers took advantage of the new technology of printing. (See the feature, "The Visual Record: A Reformation Woodcut.") Perhaps 300,000 copies of his early tracts were published in the first years of the protest. Luther's claim that the Scriptures must be the basis of all life and his appeal to the judgment of the laity made sense to the men and women in towns and villages, where councils of local people were accustomed to making decisions based on ideas of the common good.

The impact of Luther's ideas quickly became evident. If the active intercession of the clergy was not necessary for the salvation of individuals, then, according to Luther's followers, there was no reason for the clergy to remain unmarried and celibate, nor for men and women to cloister themselves in monasteries and convents. Because Luther's followers believed that penitential acts were not prerequisites for salvation, they tended to set aside the veneration of saints and give up pilgrimages to the shrines and holy places all over Europe.

Many historians have referred to the spread of these reform ideas as the "Reformation of the Common Man." Where Luther's own reform was individual and doctrinal, the reformation in towns and villages was led by the people and contained a strong communal sense. The message seems to have spread especially quickly among artisan and mercantile groups, which put pressure on town governments to press for reform. Agitation was often riotous. One resident of Augsburg exposed himself during a church service to protest what he believed was an evil and idolatrous service. Women on both sides of the reform stepped away from traditional ideas about male and female roles. One reformer demanded to be judged "not according to the standards of a woman, but according to the standards of one . . . filled with the Holy Sprit."[1] Women, like Katherine Zell of Strasbourg, who married a former priest dedicated their lives to the social and moral work of community reform. They became strong moral voices in the turbulent struggles in their communities. Other women wrote tracts advocating reform or defending the old order, and still others used shovels and rakes to defend religious values.

The process of reform in Zurich is instructive. **Huldrych Zwingli** (SVING-lee) (1484–1531), son of a rural official, received a university education and became a typical late medieval country priest, right down to his publicly acknowledged mistress. Yet, after experiences as a military chaplain and an acquaintance with the humanist writings of Erasmus, Zwingli began to preach

Huldrych Zwingli Town preacher of Zurich and leading reformer in Switzerland and southwest Germany. He emphasized the role of the godly community in the process of individual salvation.

Martin Luther's Address to the Christian Nobility of the German Nation

Luther wrote this tract to the rulers of Germany to explain the nature of his conflict with the church over ecclesiastical authority. In this excerpt, he outlines his disagreements with the system of clerical status and immunities that had grown throughout the Middle Ages.

The Romanists have very cleverly built three walls around themselves. In the first place, when pressed by the temporal power, they have made decrees and declared that the temporal power had no jurisdiction over them, but that on the contrary, the spiritual power is above the temporal. In the second place, when the attempt is made to reprove them with the Scriptures, they raise the objection that only the Pope may interpret the Scriptures. In the third place if threatened with a council, their story is that no one may summon a council but the Pope.

Let us begin by attacking the first wall. It is pure invention that the Pope, bishops, priests, and monks are called the spiritual estate while princes, lords, craftsmen, and peasants are the temporal estate. This is indeed a piece of deceit and hypocrisy: all Christians are truly of the spiritual estate. The Pope or bishop anoints, shaves heads, ordains, consecrates, and prescribes garb different from that of the laity, but he can never make a man into a Christian or into a spiritual man by so doing. He might well make a man into a hypocrite or a humbug and a blockhead, but never a Christian or a spiritual man. Therefore a priest in Christendom is nothing else but an officeholder. As long as he holds his office, he takes precedence; where he is deposed, he is a peasant or a townsman like anybody else.

The second wall is still more loosely built and less substantial. The Romanists want to be the only masters of Holy Scripture, although they never learn a thing from the Bible their life long. Besides, if we are all priests, and all have one faith, one gospel, one sacrament, why should we not also have the power to test and judge what is right or wrong in matters of faith?

The third wall falls of itself, when the first two are down. When the Pope acts contrary to the Scriptures, it is our duty to stand by the Scriptures and to reprove him and to constrain him, according to the word of Christ. The Romanists have no basis in Scripture for their claim that the Pope alone has the right to call or to confirm a council. This is just their own ruling, and it is only valid so long as it is not harmful to Christendom or contrary to the laws of God.

QUESTIONS

1. What are the ideas that Luther claims the papacy uses to protect itself from criticism?
2. Under what conditions does Luther allow that church authorities may make rules?

Source: Martin Luther, "Three Treatises," in *The American Edition of Luther's Works* (Philadelphia: Fortress Press, 1970), pp. 10–22. Copyright © 1943 Muhlenberg Press. Used by permission of Augsburg Fortress.

strongly biblical sermons. In 1522, he defended a group of laymen in Zurich, who protested by breaking the required Lenten fast. Later in the same year, he requested episcopal permission to marry. Early in 1523, he led a group of reformers in a public debate over the nature of the church. The city council declared in favor of the reformers, and Zurich became in effect a Protestant city.

Unlike Luther, Zwingli believed that reform should be a communal movement—that town governments should take the lead in bringing reform to the community. Zwingli explained that the moral regeneration of individuals was an essential part of God's salvation. In the years following 1523, the reformers restructured church services, abolishing the mass. They also removed religious images from churches and suppressed monastic institutions.

The reform message spread from towns into the countryside, but often with effects that the reformers did not expect or desire. Luther thought his message was a spiritual and theological one. Many peasants and modest artisans, however, believed that Luther's message of biblical freedom carried material, as well as theological, meaning.

In many parts of Germany, landlords and local governments had increased their claims for rents and services from villagers and peasants. Their tenants and subjects, however, argued that new tithes and taxes not only upset tradition, but violated the Word of God. Their demands that landlords and magistrates give up human ordinances and follow "Godly Law" soon turned violent. Peasants, miners, and villagers in 1524 and 1525 participated in a series of uprisings that began on the borderlands between Switzerland and Germany and spread throughout southwestern Germany, upper Austria, and even northern Italy. Bands of peasants and villagers, perhaps a total of 300,000 in the empire, revolted against their seigneurial lords or even their territorial overlords.

Luther initially counseled landlords and princes to redress the just grievances. As reports of riots and increased violence continued to reach Wittenberg, however, Luther condemned the rebels as "mad dogs" and urged that they be suppressed. Territorial princes and large cities quickly raised armies to meet the threat. The peasants were defeated and destroyed in a series of battles in April 1525. A townsman of Zurich noted the result, "Many came to a great hatred of the preachers, where before they would have bitten off their feet for the Gospel."[2]

John Calvin and the Reformed Tradition

The revolts of 1524 and 1525 demonstrated the mixed messages traveling under the rubric "true" or "biblical" religion. In the 1530s, the theological arguments of the reformers began to take on a greater clarity, mostly because of the Franco-Swiss reformer **John Calvin** (1509–1564). Calvin received a humanistic education in Paris and became a lawyer before coming under the influence of reform-minded thinkers in France. In 1534, he fled from Paris, as royal pressures against reformers increased. He arrived in Geneva in 1536, where he would remain, except for a short exile, until the end of his life.

The heart of Calvin's appeal lay in his formal theological writings. In 1536, he published the first of many editions of the *Institutes of the Christian Religion*, which was to become the summa of Reformed theology. Here he outlined his understanding of how only some were predestined to salvation. And, he added, there were ways to tell who was and who was not to be saved.

Like Luther, Calvin viewed salvation as a mysterious gift from God. Yet, Calvin differed from Luther in a crucial aspect. Salvation was by grace, but it was part of progressive sanctification. This was a critical difference, for Luther did not believe that human behavior could be transformed. We are, he said, "simultaneously justified and sinners." By contrast, Calvin believed that there could be no salvation "if we do not also live a holy life." Thus, the religious behavior of the individual and the community was evidence of justification. As a result, Calvin believed that it was the church's duty to promote moral progress. Public officials were to be "vicars of God." They had the power to lead and correct both the faithful and the unregenerate sinners who lived in Christian communities. In his years in Geneva, Calvin tried to create a "Christian Commonwealth," but Geneva was far from a theocracy.

Elders—the true leaders of the Genevan church—were selected from the patriciate who dominated the civil government of the city. Thus, it makes as much sense to speak of a church

John Calvin A Franco-Swiss theologian whose *Institutes of the Christian Religion* was the key text of Reformed theology. He stressed the absolute power of God.

Iconoclasm Calvinists believed that Christians had to live in communities in which "true religion" was practiced. Iconoclasts (image smashers) cleansed churches of all paintings and statuary that might lead people back to the worship of idols—that is, the medieval cult of saints. This illustration shows just how organized iconoclasm really was. (Calvinists destroying statues in the Catholic Churches, 1566 (engraving), Flemish School, (16th century)/Private Collection/The Bridgeman Art Library)

A Reformation Woodcut

Erhard Schön's 1533 woodcut, "There Is No Greater Treasure Here on Earth Than an Obedient Wife Who Desires Honor," and other broadsheets like it, informed and amused Europeans of all walks of life in the late fifteenth and sixteenth centuries. Schön's image of a henpecked husband and his wife followed by others would have been instantly recognizable to most people. Accompanying texts clarified the message implied in the woodcut itself. But how may we, centuries later, "read" this message? How does the modern historian analyze Schön's broadsheet to investigate popular ideas about social roles, religion, and politics? What do this and similar broadsheets tell us about popular responses to the social and religious tumults of the sixteenth century?

Look at the simple and clear lines of the woodcut. They give a clue about the popularity of broadsheets. They were cheap and easy to produce and were printed on inexpensive paper. Artists would sketch an image that an artisan would later carve onto a block. A printer could produce a thousand or more copies from a single block. Even famous artists, such as Albrecht Dürer (see pages 334–335), sold highly profitable prints on religious, political, and cultural themes.

Almost anyone could afford broadsheets. Laborers and modest merchants decorated their houses with pictures on popular themes. In the middle of the fifteenth century, before the Reformation, most images were of saints. It was widely believed, for example, that anyone who looked at an image of Saint Christopher would not die on that day.

During the political and religious unrest of the sixteenth century, artists increasingly produced images that referred to the debates over religion. Schön himself made his living in Nuremberg producing and selling woodcuts. He and other artists in the city were closely tuned to the attitudes of the local population. One popular image was titled "The Roman Clergy's Procession into Hell."

Schön's "Obedient Wife" reflects a fear shared by both Protestants and Catholics: the rebellious nature of women. Evidence suggests that women in the late fifteenth and sixteenth centuries may have been marrying at a later age and thus were likely to be more independent-minded than their younger sisters. The ranks of single women were swollen by widows and by former nuns who had left convents and liberated themselves from male supervision. Thus, it was not difficult for men in the sixteenth century to spot women who seemed dangerously free from male control.

Let us turn again to the woodcut, to see what worried villagers and townspeople and how Schön depicted their fears. Notice the henpecked husband. He is harnessed to a cart carrying laundry. Both the harness and the laundry were popular images associated with women's duties. During popular festivals, German villagers often harnessed unmarried women to a plow to signify that they were shirking their duty by not marrying and raising children. Doing the laundry was popularly thought to be the first household chore that a powerful wife would force on her weak-kneed husband. Countless other images show women, whip in hand, supervising foolish husbands as they pound diapers with a laundry flail. "Woe is me," says the poor man, all this because "I took a wife." As if the message were not clear enough, look at what the woman carries in her left hand: his purse, his sword, and his pants. (The question "Who wears the pants in the family?" was as familiar then as it is now.) But the woman responds that he is in this position not because of marriage but because he has been carousing: "If you will not work to support me, then you must wash, spin, and draw the cart."*

The figures following the cart are commenting on the situation. The young journeyman is asking the maiden at his side, "What do you say about this?" She responds coyly, "I have no desire for such power." The woman dressed as a fool counsels the young man never to marry and thus to avoid anxiety and suffering. But an old man, identified as "the wise man," closes the procession and ends the debate. "Do not listen to this foolish woman," he counsels. "God determines how your life together will be, so stay with her in love and suffering and always be patient."

If we think about this woodcut's images and text, we can understand the contrary hopes and fears in sixteenth-century Germany. Like the young woman, the Christian wife was expected to eschew power either inside or outside the home. Martin Luther concluded that "the

governed by the town as a town dominated by the church. The elders actively intervened in education, charity, and attempts to regulate prostitution. Consistories, or church courts, made up of preachers and community elders who enforced moral and religious values, became one of the most important characteristics of Reformed (Calvinist) communities.

Reformed churchmen reacted promptly and harshly to events that seemed to threaten their vision of the Christian community. The most famous episode involved the capture, trial, and execution of Michael Servetus (1511–1553), a Spanish physician and radical theologian who rejected traditional doctrines such as the Trinity and specifically criticized many of Calvin's teachings in the *Institutes*. After corresponding with Servetus for a time, Calvin remarked that

"There Is No Greater Treasure Here on Earth Than an Obedient Wife Who Desires Honor,"
Erhard Schön (Schlossmuseum, Gotha)

husband is the head of the wife even as Christ is head of the Church. Therefore as the Church is subject to Christ, so let wives be subject to their husbands in everything" (Ephesians 5:23–24). Authority was to be in the hands of husbands and fathers. But if the good wife was required to avoid power, the good husband was expected to follow Luther's precepts for the Christian family. As the wise old man observes, the husband must be a loving and forgiving master.

Schön's woodcut and others similar to it should remind you of the "argument over women" discussed in Chapter 12 (see 338–339). The words of the wise man and the young maid bring to mind Christine de Pizan's *Book of the City of the Ladies* when they urge love and understanding, but their hopefulness is undercut by the power and immediacy of the image. As the broadsheet clearly demonstrates, suspicion of women characterized even the most simple literature of Reformation Europe.

QUESTIONS

1. What conclusion might a viewer draw about women from thinking about the three women pictured in this woodcut?

2. How does the image of the godly marriage differ in this woodcut and the picture of the holy household (see page 405)?

---

*Keith Moxey, *Peasants, Warriors and Wives: Popular Imagery in the Reformation* (Chicago: University of Chicago Press, 1989), pp. 108–109; includes a translation of portions of the text in the broadsheet.

if Servetus were in Geneva, "I would not suffer him to get out alive." After living in various parts of Europe, Servetus eventually did come anonymously to Geneva. He was recognized and arrested. Calvin was as good as his word. After a public debate and trial, Servetus was burned at the stake for blaspheming the Trinity and the Christian religion. Calvin's condemnation of Servetus was all too typical of Christians in the sixteenth century. Lutherans, Calvinists, and Catholics all believed that protection of true religion required harsh measures against the ignorant, the immoral, and the unorthodox. All too few would have agreed with the humanist reformer Sebastian Castellio that "To burn a heretic is not to defend a doctrine, but to burn a man."[3]

The Radical Reform of the Anabaptists

Anabaptists Radical reformers in Germany and Switzerland who emphasized that baptism should only be of adults and that Christians should separate themselves into communities of the "truly redeemed."

Michael Servetus was but one of a number who felt Luther, Zwingli, and Calvin had not gone far enough. Called **Anabaptists** (or "rebaptizers" because of their rejection of infant baptism) or simply "radicals," they tended to take biblical commands more literally than the mainline reformers. More interested in behavior and community standards than in learned theological arguments, they believed that only adults should be baptized, and then, only after confession of sin. In their view, Christians should live apart in communities of the truly redeemed. Thus, civil oaths or public office were a compromise with "the Abomination," that is, unreformed civil society.

Radicals, such as the revolutionaries who took control of the northern German city of Münster, rejected infant baptism, adopted polygamy, and proclaimed a new "Kingdom of Righteousness." The reformers of Münster instituted the new kingdom in the city by rebaptizing those who joined their cause and expelling those who opposed them. They abolished private property rights and instituted new laws concerning morality and behavior. Leadership in the city eventually passed to a tailor, Jan of Leiden (d. 1535), who proclaimed himself the new messiah and lord of the world. After a sixteen-month siege, the bishop of Münster and his allies recaptured the city in 1535. Besieging forces massacred men, women, and children. Jan of Leiden was captured and executed by mutilation with red-hot tongs.

In the wake of the siege of Münster, leaders, such as Menno Simons (1495–1561), who founded the Mennonites, and Jakob Hutter (d. 1536), who founded the Hutterian Brethren, or Hutterites, rejected their predecessors' violent attempts to establish truly holy cities. To varying degrees, they also rejected connections with civil society, military service, and even civil courts. They did, however, believe that their own communities were exclusively of the elect. They tended to close themselves off from outsiders and enforce a strict discipline over their members. The elders of these communities were empowered to excommunicate or "shun" those who violated the groups' precepts. Anabaptist communities have proved unusually durable. Hutterite and Mennonite communities continue to exist in western Europe, North America, and parts of the former Soviet Union.

Like Luther, all of the early reformers appealed to the authority of the Bible in their attacks on church tradition. Yet, in the villages and towns of Germany and Switzerland, many radicals were prepared to move far beyond the positions Luther had advocated. When they did so, Luther found himself in the odd position of appealing for vigorous action by the very imperial authorities whose previous inaction had allowed his own protest to survive.

SECTION SUMMARY

- Women played an important role in popular religious observance in the Middle Ages.

- Luther's religious ideas challenged the late medieval church's understanding of sin and salvation rather than immoral behavior.

- The key to Luther's theology was his emphasis on the role of grace and biblical authority.

- Calvin's religious reforms centered on the role of the Reformed community in enforcing religious discipline.

- Radical reformers and Anabaptists formed small, tightly controlled communities suspicious of the outside world.

THE EMPIRE OF CHARLES V (R. 1519–1556)

What political factors limited Charles V's ability to respond to the religious crisis?

Luther believed that secular authorities should be neutral in religious matters. In his eyes, the success of the early Reformation was simply God's will:

[W]hile I slept or drank Wittenberg beer with my friends, the Word [of God] so greatly weakened the Papacy that no prince or emperor ever inflicted such losses on it.[4]

Luther's belief in the Word of God was absolute, yet, he must have known, even as he drank his beer, that the Holy Roman emperor could have crushed the reform movements if he had been able to enforce imperial decrees. But attempts to resolve religious conflict became entangled with the need to hold together the family lands of the Habsburg emperor. The eventual religious settlement required a constitutional compromise that preserved the virtual autonomy of the great princes of Germany. Charles had dreamed of using his imperial office to restore and maintain the political and religious unity of Europe. The realities of sixteenth-century Europe, however, made nobles afraid of the emperor, even when he tried to preserve the unity of the church.

Imperial Challenges

Emperor Charles V (r. 1519–1556) was the beneficiary of a series of marriages that, in the words of his courtiers, seemed to re-create the empire of Charlemagne. From his father, Philip of Habsburg, he inherited claims to Austria, the imperial crown, and Burgundian lands that included the Low Countries and the county of Burgundy. Through his mother, Joanna, the daughter of Ferdinand and Isabella of Spain, Charles became heir to the kingdoms of Castile, Aragon, Sicily, Naples, and Spanish America (see **Map 14.1**). By 1506, he was duke in the Burgundian lands; in 1516, he became king of Aragon and Castile; and in 1519, he was elected Holy Roman emperor. Every government in Europe had to deal with one part or another of Charles's empire. His chancellor enthused, "[God] has set you on the way towards a world monarchy, towards the gathering of all Christendom under a single shepherd."

Charles seems sincerely to have desired such a world monarchy, but he faced challenges in each of the areas under his control. Between 1517 and 1522, when religious reform was making dramatic advances in Germany, many of the most important towns of Spain were in open rebellion against the Crown. In Castile, for example, grandees, townspeople, and peasants had many complaints. But most of all, they objected that too many of his officials were foreigners whom he had brought with him from his home in Flanders. Protests festered in the towns and villages of Castile and finally broke out into a revolt called the *Comunero* (townsmen's or citizens') movement. Charles's forces eventually took control of the situation, and by 1522, he had crushed the Comuneros. However, in the critical years between 1522 and 1530, he was careful to spend much of his time in his Spanish kingdoms.

🌐 **Map 14.1—The Global Empire of Charles V.**
Religious and political change were profoundly affected by the complexity of the empire of Charles V. German calls for reform had to be understood in the context of an immense empire.

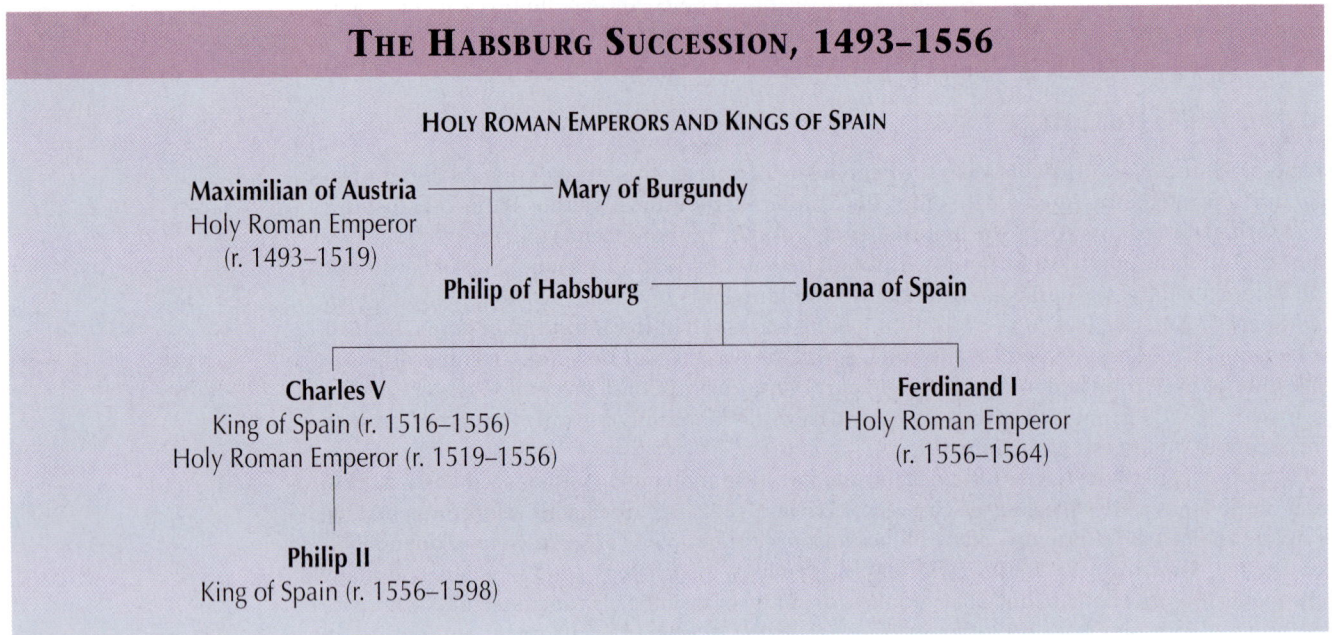

THE HABSBURG SUCCESSION, 1493–1556

HOLY ROMAN EMPERORS AND KINGS OF SPAIN

Maximilian of Austria ——— **Mary of Burgundy**
Holy Roman Emperor
(r. 1493–1519)

Philip of Habsburg ——— **Joanna of Spain**

Charles V
King of Spain (r. 1516–1556)
Holy Roman Emperor (r. 1519–1556)

Ferdinand I
Holy Roman Emperor
(r. 1556–1564)

Philip II
King of Spain (r. 1556–1598)

Charles's claims in Italy, as well as in the Pyrenees and the Low Countries, brought him into direct conflict with the Valois kings of France. In the critical 1520s, the Habsburgs and the Valois fought a series of wars (see page 301). Charles dramatically defeated the French at Pavia in northern Italy in 1525, sacked and occupied Rome in 1527, and became the dominant power in Italian politics. The Habsburg-Valois Wars, however, dragged on until, in exhaustion, the French king Henry II (r. 1547–1559) and the Spanish king Philip II (r. 1556–1598) signed the Treaty of Cateau-Cambrésis in 1559.

Charles was not the only ruler to claim the title "emperor" and a tradition of authority reaching back to the Roman Empire. After the conquest of Constantinople in 1453, the sultan of the Ottoman Turks often referred to himself as "the Emperor." After consolidating control of Constantinople and the Balkans, Turkish armies under the command of the emperor Suleiman (r. 1520–1566), known as "the Magnificent," resumed their expansion to the north and west. After capturing Belgrade, Turkish forces soundly defeated a Hungarian army at the Battle of Mohács in 1526. Charles appealed for unity within Christendom against the threat. Even Martin Luther agreed that Christians should unite during invasion.

Suleiman's army besieged Vienna in 1529 before being forced to retreat. The Turks also deployed a navy in the Mediterranean and, with French encouragement, began a series of raids along the coasts of Italy and Spain. The Turkish fleet remained a threat throughout the sixteenth century. The reign of Suleiman marked the permanent entry of Turkey into the European military and diplomatic system. Turkish pressure was yet another reason Charles was unable to deal with German Protestants in a direct and uncompromising way. (See the feature, "The Global Record: Duels Among Europeans and Turks.")

German Politics

The political configuration of Germany had an ongoing influence on the course of religious reform. In 1500, Germany was much less centralized than France or England. Indeed, the empire lacked a unified legal system, and the emperor himself had only one vote on the imperial council. In many respects, political centralization and innovation were characteristics of individual territories, not of the empire as a whole. The power of the emperor depended on his relations with the towns and princes of Germany.

In the first years after Luther issued his "Ninety-five Theses," he was defended by the elector Frederick of Saxony, who held a key vote in Charles's quest for election as Holy Roman emperor. As long as Frederick protected Luther, imperial officials had to proceed against the reformer with caution. When Luther was outlawed by the imperial Diet of Worms in 1521, Frederick and many

The Capture of Belgrade, 1521   During the sixteenth century, Ottoman Turks dominated the Balkans militarily and were a significant force in European diplomacy. They were masters of coordinated attacks combining artillery and infantry.   (Österreichische Nationalbibliothek)

other princes and towns refused to enforce the edict against him and his followers unless their own grievances against the emperor and their complaints about the church were taken up at the same time. At the Diet of Speyer in 1526, delegates passed a resolution empowering princes and towns to settle religious matters in their territories as they saw it. In effect, this resolution legitimated the reform in territories where authorities chose to follow the new teachings and presaged the final religious settlement in Germany.

German authorities took advantage of the emperor's relative powerlessness and made choices reflecting a complex of religious, political, and diplomatic issues. Some rulers acted in ways that were even more consciously cynical and self-serving. The grand master of the religious order of the Teutonic Knights, Albrecht von Hohenzollern (1490–1568), who controlled the duchy of Prussia, renounced his monastic vows and secularized the order's estates (that is, he transferred them from church to private ownership), which then became East Prussia, hereditary lands of the Hohenzollern family. In other territories, rulers managed to claim the properties of suppressed religious orders. In the autonomous towns, many decisions about religion were often made with one eye on the choices made by neighbors and competitors.

Some rulers found their personal reservations about Luther reinforced by their fears of popular unrest. Luther's call for decisions based on personal conscience seemed to the dukes of Bavaria, for example, to repudiate princely authority and even to provoke anarchy. In the confused and fluid situation of the 1520s and 1530s, imperial interests were never the primary issue.

The Religious Settlement

With the fading of the Turkish threat on Vienna in 1529, Charles V renewed his pressure on the German principalities at a meeting of the imperial diet at Augsburg in 1530. It was for this diet that Philipp Melanchthon (1497–1560), Luther's closest adviser, prepared the **Augsburg Confession**, which would become the basic statement of the Lutheran faith. Melanchthon hoped that the document would form the basis of compromise with Catholic powers, but that possibility was rejected out of hand by the imperial party. Charles aimed to end the reform movement and enforce bans on Luther's teachings.

Augsburg Confession
Document, written by Philipp Melanchthon, that became the most widely accepted statement of the Lutheran faith.

Duels Among Europeans and Turks

Augier Ghislain de Busbecq (1522–1592), a Flemish diplomat in the service of Ferdinand I of Austria (who became Emperor Ferdinand I after the abdication of Charles V), was twice sent to Constantinople as ambassador. Understanding the Turks and their interests was critical for the Germans as attacks by the Turks in eastern Europe prevented the empire from either suppressing the German Protestants or pressing German claims against the French. The following selection is part of a letter written from Constantinople in 1560. In it Busbecq discusses violence among the Turks. He contrasts Turkish political and individual control with the Europeans' desire for a violent defense of personal honor. Duels were an increasing problem in sixteenth-century Europe.

The mention I made a while ago of matters in the confines of Hungary, gives me occasion to tell you, what the Turks think of duels, which among Christians are accounted a singular badge of personal valor. There was one Arstambey, a sanjack [district official], who lived on the frontier of Hungary, who was very much famed as a robust person [Arsta signifies a lion in Turkish]. He was an expert with the bow; no man brandished his sword with more strength; none was more terrible to his enemy. Not far from his district there also dwelt one Ulybey, also a sanjack, who was jealous of the same praise. And this jealousy (initiated perhaps by other occasions) at length occasioned hatred and many bloody combats between them. It happened thus, Ulybey was called to Constantinople, upon what occasion I know not. When he arrived there, the Pashas [governors] had asked many questions of him in the Divan [court] concerning other matters. At last they demanded how it was that he and Arstambey came to fall out. To put his own cause in the best light, he said that once Arstambey had laid an ambush and wounded him treacherously. Which he said Arstambey need not have done, if he would have shown himself worthy of the name he bears because Ulybey often challenged him to fight hand to hand and never refused to meet him on the field. The Pashas, taking great offense, replied, "How dare you challenge a fellow soldier to a duel? What? Was there no Christian to fight with? Do both of you eat your emperor's bread? And yet, you attempt to take one another's life? What precedent did you have for this? Don't you know that whichever of you had died, the emperor would have lost a subject?" Whereupon, by their command, he was carried off to prison where he lay pining for many months. And at last, with difficulty, he was released, but with the loss of his reputation.

It is quite different among us Christians. Our people will draw their swords many times against each other before they ever come in sight of a public enemy, and unfortunately, they count it a brave and honorable thing to do. What should one do in such a case? Vice has usurped the seat of virtue and that which is worthy of punishment is counted noble and glorious.

QUESTIONS

1. How did Turkish officials understand the significance of private violence?

2. What most distinguishes the Turkish empire from Christendom?

Source: *The Four Epistles of A.G. Busbequius Concerning His Embassy to Turkey* (London: J. Taylor & J. Wyat, 1694), pp. 196–198.

Religious reform and political resistance to imperial power, however, remained closely connected. In the religious Peace of Augsburg of 1555, the emperor formally acknowledged the principle that sovereign princes could choose the religion to be practiced in their territories—*cuius regio, eius religio* ("whose territory, his religion"). There were limits, however: Leaders had only two choices—remain under papal authority or adopt the Augsburg Confession outlined by Melanchthon. Reformed churches associated with Zwingli or Calvin were not legally recognized (see **MAP 14.2**).

Shortly after the settlement, Charles abdicated his Spanish and imperial titles. Exhausted by years of political and religious struggle, he ceded the imperial crown to his brother, Ferdinand (r. 1556–1564). He transferred his possessions in the Low Countries, Spain, Italy, and the New World to his son, Philip II (r. 1556–1598). Charles had believed his courtiers when they had compared his empire to that of the ancient Romans. He had accepted that his duty as emperor was to unite Christendom under one law and one church. But in no part of his empire did he ever command the authority that would have allowed him to unite his lands politically, let alone to reestablish religious unity. Following his abdication, Charles retired to a monastery in Spain, where he died in 1558.

SECTION SUMMARY

- Charles V united under his personal rule Germany, the Low Countries, Spain, most of Italy, and Latin America.

- Political control in the area of Charles's empire was just weak enough that Charles was never able to act effectively against Luther and his allies.

- Throughout the sixteenth century, the Ottoman Turks were a major threat to the western European powers.

- The religious Peace of Augsburg (1555) recognized the political and religious autonomy of the independent princes and towns.

🌐 **MAP 14.2—Catholics and Protestants in 1555**
At the time of the Peace of Augsburg, Christendom in western Europe was divided into three major groups. Lutheran influence was largely confined to parts of Germany and Scandinavia, while Calvinist influence was strong in Switzerland, Scotland, the Low Countries, and parts of France. Most of the West remained within the Roman Catholic Church.

THE ENGLISH REFORMATION, 1520–1603

Why did the English monarchs take the lead in efforts to reform the English church?

The Reformation in England is often called a monarchical Reformation. In contrast with Germany, where reform occurred in spite of imperial opposition, in England, the Crown instituted the reform. As in Germany, however, institutional change in the church followed from both secular issues and reform ideas. In England, an initially hostile monarch began to tolerate reform when he perceived the papacy as an unbiblical, tyrannical force blocking essential state policy. And by the middle of the sixteenth century, it was royal interest in compromise that brought a settlement that left England a curious hybrid of reformed and traditional religious practices.

Henry VIII and the Monarchical Reformation

England had close economic ties to Germany. Reformers from Wittenberg and other Protestant towns influenced English merchants from London who traded and traveled on the Continent. One reformer, William Tyndale (ca. 1494–1536), served as a bridge between the Continent and England. He had a humanistic education in classical languages and began working on an English translation of the Bible in the 1520s. Forced by the church hierarchy to flee London, he visited Luther in Wittenberg, before settling in Antwerp, where he completed his English New Testament. By 1526, copies of his translation and his religious tracts flooded England. By the 1520s, Lutheran influence was noticeable in London and Cambridge. There is still debate about just how strong this early influence was. To some extent, the ground may have been prepared for the reformers by the few surviving Lollards (see page 293), who tended to be literate and were an ideal market for Tyndale's English Bible and his numerous reformist tracts. But religious brotherhoods, lay piety, and traditional forms of penance remained an important part of religious life. If reform was to succeed, it required support from the king.

Henry VIII (r. 1509–1547) began his reign as a popular and powerful king. Handsome, athletic, and artistic, he seemed to be the ideal ruler. At first, he was quite hostile to Luther's reform ideas. He wrote *Defense of the Seven Sacraments*, which earned him the title "Defender of the Faith" from a grateful Pope Leo X. Throughout his life, Henry remained suspicious of many Protestant ideas, but he led the initial phase of the break with the papacy because of his political problems with the highly orthodox Holy Roman emperor Charles V. The first phase of the English Reformation was thus monarchical.

Henry VII had initiated closer relations with Spain when he married his eldest son, Arthur, Prince of Wales, to Ferdinand of Aragon's daughter, Catherine. After Arthur's death, the future Henry VIII was married to his brother's widow in 1509. **Henry VIII** later tried to further the Anglo-imperial alliance when he arranged a treaty by which the emperor Charles V, who was Catherine of Aragon's nephew, agreed to marry Henry's daughter, Mary Tudor. But by the late 1520s, the Anglo-imperial alliance fell apart when Charles, responding to Spanish pressures, renounced the proposed marriage and instead married a Portuguese princess.

Henry VIII King of England who broke with the church over the issue of his divorce. In the end, Henry claimed that, as king, he was the head of the Church in England.

DIVORCE

Henry's relations with Charles were further hampered by what the English called "the King's Great Matter"—that is, his determination to divorce Catherine. Recalling the unrest of the Wars of the Roses (see page 311), Henry believed that he needed a son to ensure that the Tudors could maintain control of the English crown. By 1527, Henry and Catherine had a daughter, Mary, but no living sons. Henry became convinced that he remained without a male heir because, by biblical standards, he had committed incest by marrying his brother's widow. As Leviticus 20:21 says, "If a man takes his brother's wife, it is impurity; they shall remain childless." Henry desired an annulment. Unfortunately for him, Leo X's successor, Pope Clement VII (r. 1523–1534), was a virtual prisoner of imperial troops who had recently sacked Rome and taken control of most of Italy. As long as Charles supported Catherine of Aragon and his forces occupied Rome, a papal annulment was out of the question.

The king's advisers quickly divided into two camps. Sir Thomas More, humanist writer (see pages 342–343), royal chancellor and staunch Catholic, urged the king to continue his policy of negotiation with the papacy and his efforts to destroy the growing Protestant party. Until his resignation in 1532, More led royal authorities in a vigorous campaign against the dissemination of the newly translated Tyndale Bible and against the spread of Protestant ideas. More was opposed and eventually ousted by a radical party of Protestants led by Thomas Cranmer (1489–1556) and Thomas Cromwell (1485?–1540), who saw in the king's desire for a divorce an effective wedge to pry Henry out of the papal camp. Cromwell, who eventually replaced More as chancellor, advised the king that the marriage problem could be solved by the English clergy without papal interference.

MONARCHICAL REFORMATION

Act of Supremacy Act of the English Parliament, during the Protestant Reformation, that finalized the break with the Catholic Church by declaring the king to be head of the Church of England. Henry VIII required a public oath supporting the act, which Sir Thomas More refused to take; More was then executed for treason.

Between 1532 and 1535, Henry and Parliament took a number of steps that effectively left the king in control of the church in England. In 1533, Parliament ruled that appeals of cases concerning wills, marriages, and ecclesiastical grants had to be heard in England. In May, an English court annulled the king's marriage to Catherine. Four months later, Henry's new queen, Anne Boleyn, gave birth to a daughter, Elizabeth.

After the split, the king began to seize church properties. Parliamentary action culminated in the passage of the **Act of Supremacy** in 1534, which declared the king to be "the Protector and only Supreme Head of the Church and the Clergy of England." Henry meant to enforce his control by requiring a public oath supporting the act. Sir Thomas More refused to take the oath and was arrested, tried, and executed for treason.

Cromwell and Cranmer had hoped to use "the King's Great Matter" as a way to begin a Lutheran-style reform of the church. But, Henry remained suspicious of religious change. Between 1534 and Henry's death in 1547, neither the Protestant nor the Catholic party was able

Reform of the Old Church   This woodcut shows the Protestant understanding of the reforms of Edward VI, the removal of Catholic paraphernalia, and Edward's patronage of the Bible and Holy Communion.   (Courtesy, Brown University Library)

to gain the upper hand at court or at Canterbury. Substantive changes in the English church would be made by Henry's children.

Reform and Counter-Reform Under Edward and Mary

Prince Edward, Henry's only surviving son in 1547, was born to Henry's third wife, Jane Seymour. He was only 10 years old when his father died. By chance, Edward Seymour, who was Prince Edward's uncle, and the Protestant faction were in favor at the time of Henry's death. Seymour was named duke of Somerset and Lord Protector of the young King Edward VI (r. 1547–1553). Under Somerset, the Protestants were able to make significant changes in religious life in England. Edward completed the "dissolution of the monasteries"—the process of confiscating properties belonging to chapels and shrines—that his father had begun. In an act of great symbolic meaning, priests were legally allowed to marry. Finally, Archbishop Cranmer introduced the first edition of the English *Book of Common Prayer* in 1549. The publication updated some late medieval English prayers and combined them with liturgical and theological ideas taken from Luther, Zwingli, and Calvin. In its beautifully expressive English, it provided the laity with a primer on how to combine English religious traditions with reform theology. If Edward had not died of tuberculosis in 1553, England's reform would have looked very much like the movement in Switzerland and southern Germany.

Protestant reformers attempted to prevent Mary Tudor (r. 1553–1558), Henry's Catholic daughter, from claiming the throne, but Mary and the Catholic party quickly took control of the court and the church. Mary immediately declared previous reform decrees to be void. Cardinal Reginald Pole (1500–1558), who had advocated reform within the Catholic Church, became the center of the Catholic restoration party in Mary's England. Pole rooted out Protestants within the church. More than eight hundred gentlemen, clerics, and students fled England for Protestant havens on the Continent. Some officials, including Cranmer, chose to remain and paid with their lives. In all, three hundred Protestants, mostly artisans and laborers, were tried and executed by church courts, earning the queen her nickname, "Bloody Mary."

The policies of the queen brought about an abrupt change in official policy. Many parishes quickly and easily returned to traditional Roman religious practices. Statues were removed from hiding and restored to places of honor in churches and chapels. In many others, there was an uneasy amalgam of traditional and reformed. Although conclusive evidence is lacking, the queen's initial successes may indicate that the Reformation was not broadly supported by the people. In fact, a Catholic reform led by Mary might have succeeded had the queen not died after little more than six years on the throne. At her death, the issue of the reform in England was far from certain.

SECTION SUMMARY

- England's Reformation was monarchical because it was shaped and directed by the cultural and political needs and attitudes of the monarchs.

- Cranmer's *Book of Common Prayer* organized and introduced into England the ideas of the continental Reformation.

- Queen Mary might have succeeded in restoring much of traditional church practice had she not died after just a short reign.

FRANCE, SCANDINAVIA, AND EASTERN EUROPE, 1523–1560

How did ideas of church reform influence social and political developments in the rest of Europe?

In England and in the empire of Charles V, the success of the new religious reforms depended greatly on the political situation. It would be naive to conclude, as Luther claimed, that "the Word did everything." Yet, this complex religious reform movement cannot be reduced to the politics of kings and princes. The issues will be clearer if we survey politics and reform in the rest of Europe, noting whether and to what extent the new ideas took root (see **Map 14.2**). In France, for example, the widespread, popular support of the old religion limited the options of the country's political leaders. Similarly, in northern Europe, religious reform was an issue of both popular feeling and royal politics.

France

Luther's work, and later the ideas of the urban reformers of southwestern Germany and Switzerland, passed quickly into France. Geneva is in a French-speaking area, close to the French border. Perhaps because of France's proximity to the Calvinists in French-speaking Switzerland or because of the clarity and power of Calvin's *Institutes*, French Protestants, known as Huguenots, were tied more closely to the Calvinists of Geneva than to the Lutherans of Germany.

At the height of the Reformation's popularity, Protestants probably represented no more than 10 percent of the total population of France. Protestants seem to have comprised a diverse mix that included two of the three most important noble families at court: the Bourbon and Montmorency families. Clerics interested in moral reform and artisans who worked at new trades, such as the printing industry, also made up a significant portion of the converts. Perhaps reflecting the numerous printers and merchants in their numbers, Protestants tended to be of higher than average literacy. They were particularly well represented in towns and probably constituted a majority in the southern and western towns of La Rochelle, Montpellier, and Nîmes. Paris was the one part of the realm in which they had little influence, and this may have been their undoing.

The conservative theologians of the Sorbonne in Paris were some of Luther's earliest opponents. They complained that many masters at the University of Paris were "Lutheran." But as in Germany, there was no clear understanding of who or what a Lutheran was. The Sorbonne theologians were also suspicious of a number of "pre-reformers," including the humanistic editor Jacques Lefèvre d'Étaples (1455–1536; see page 342), who, late in life, had come to an understanding of justification quite like Luther's. Others were clerics intent on religious reform within the traditional structures. Unlike Luther and the French Protestants, these pre-reformers did not challenge the priests' relationship to the sacraments. They were interested in the piety and behavior of churchmen. They never challenged the role of the clergy in salvation. King Francis's own sister, Margaret of Angoulême (1492–1549), gathered a group of religious persons, including several reformers, at her court. However, Margaret herself urged that theology be left to scholars; she believed that the laity should stick to simple pieties. Like Margaret, most French Christians had no clear sense that Protestant teachings required a complete break with medieval Christian traditions.

Like other monarchs, Francis I (r. 1515–1547) largely interpreted religious issues in the context of royal interests. Primarily engaged in the seemingly intractable wars with the Habsburgs, Francis generally ignored religious questions. He was not initially opposed to what seemed to be moral reform within the church. His own view was that the king's duty was to preserve order and prevent scandal, and at first, carrying out that duty meant protecting reformers whom the conservative militants persecuted. The king feared disorder more than he feared religious reform.

On October 18, 1534, however, Francis's attitude changed when he and all Paris awoke to find the city littered with anti-Catholic placards containing, in the words of the writers, "true articles on the horrible, great and insufferable abuses of the Papal Mass." The "Affair of the Placards" changed Francis's ideas about the sources of disorder. Opposition to traditional religious practices became more difficult and more dangerous. John Calvin himself was forced to leave Paris, and eventually

The Great Cauldron   In dramatic images, this French woodcut shows the Protestant expectation that the Bible carried down by the Holy Spirit will overturn the whole cauldron of false images and errors that supported the old church.   (Bibliothèque nationale de France)

France, because he feared persecution. Between 1534 and 1560, some ten thousand Protestants fled France, many joining Calvin in Geneva.

By the middle of the sixteenth century, it was clear that neither Protestant nor Catholic factions would be able to control religious and political life in France. Francis I died in 1547, and the stage was set for a series of destructive factional struggles over religion and political power that would continue for the rest of the century (see Chapter 15).

Scandinavia

All of Scandinavia became Lutheran. Initial influences drifted north from Germany, carried by Hanseatic merchants and students who had studied at the universities of northern Germany. Yet, the reform in Sweden and Denmark, even more than in England, was monarchical. In both Scandinavian kingdoms, the kings began with an attack on the temporal rights and properties of the church. Changes in liturgy and practice came later, as reformers gained royal protection.

In Sweden, the establishment of a strong monarch required concern for religious reform. Gustav Vasa, a leading noble, was able to secure the loyalty of most of the Swedes and in 1523, he was elected king of Sweden. Gustav's motto was "All power is of God." Like Henry VIII of

and renewal could counter the malaise he perceived. Other reforming bishops could be found throughout Catholic Europe.

THE ROLE OF MUSIC AND MYSTICISM

New religious foundations sprang up to renew the church. Members of the new orders set out to change the church through example. The Florentine Filippo Neri (1515–1595) founded the Oratorian order, so named because of the monks' habit of leading the laity in prayer services. Filippo was joined in his work by Giovanni Palestrina (ca. 1525–1594), who composed music for the modest, but moving, prayer gatherings in Rome. Palestrina's music combined medieval plainchants with newer styles of polyphony, creating complex harmonies without obscuring the words and meaning of the text. The popularity of the Oratorians and their services can be measured in part by the fact that oratories, small chapels modeled on those favored by Filippo, remain to this day important centers of musical life in the city of Rome.

The Catholic reform of the sixteenth century, however, was better known for its mystical theology than for its music. In Italy and France, but especially in Spain, a profusion of reformers chose to reform the church through austere prayer and contemplative devotions. Teresa of Avila (1515–1582), who belonged to a wealthy converso family (see page 317), led a movement to reform the lax practices within the religious houses of Spain. Famed for her rigorous religious life, her trances, and her raptures, Teresa animated a movement to reform the order of Carmelite nuns in Spain. Because of her writings about her mystical experiences, she was named a "Doctor of the Church," a title reserved for the greatest of the church's theologians.

JESUITS

Society of Jesus (Jesuits) Religious group founded in 1534 by Ignatius Loyola; they were famed for their role in the Catholic Counter-Reformation.

Ignatius Loyola A Spanish nobleman and founder of the Society of Jesus. Loyola's order vowed absolute authority to the papacy.

The most important of the new religious orders was the **Society of Jesus**, or Jesuits, founded in 1534 by **Ignatius Loyola** (1491–1556). He initially meant to organize a missionary order directed at converting the Muslims. The structure of his order reflected his military experience. It had a well-defined chain of command, leading to the general of the order and then to the pope. To educate and discipline the members, Loyola composed *Spiritual Exercises*, emphasizing the importance of obedience. He encouraged his followers to understand their own attitudes, beliefs, and even lives as less important than the papacy and the Roman church. If the church commands it, he concluded, "I will believe that the white object I see is black." He prohibited Jesuits from holding any ecclesiastical office that might compromise their autonomy. After papal approval of the order in 1540, the Jesuits directed their activities primarily to education in Catholic areas and reconversion of Protestants.

Throughout Europe, Jesuits gained fame for their work as educators of the laity and as spiritual advisers to the political leaders of Catholic Europe. In the late sixteenth and early seventeenth centuries, they were responsible for a number of famous conversions, including that of Christina (1626–1689), the Lutheran queen of Sweden, who abdicated her throne in 1654 and spent the rest of her life in Rome. Jesuits were especially successful in bringing many parts of the Holy Roman Empire back into communion with the papacy. They have rightly been called the vanguard of the Catholic reform movement.

CATHOLIC REFORM

Index of Prohibited Books A list of books banned by the Roman Catholic Church because of moral or doctrinal error. It was thought that this would inhibit the spread of Protestant ideas.

Catholic reformers were convinced that one of the reasons for the success of the Protestants was that faithful Christians had no clear guide to orthodox teachings. The first Catholic response to the reformers was to try to separate ideas they held to be correct from those they held to be incorrect. Successive popes made public lists of books and ideas that they considered to be in error. The lists were combined into the *Index of Prohibited Books* in 1559. The climate of suspicion was such that the works of humanists, such as Erasmus, were prohibited alongside the works of Protestants, such as Martin Luther. In times of religious tensions, the *Index* could be vigorously enforced. In Italy, for example, no editions of the Holy Bible in Italian translation were published in the late sixteenth and seventeenth centuries. In general, however, the *Index* could not prevent the circulation of books and ideas. It was finally suppressed in 1966.

COUNCIL OF TRENT

During the first half of the sixteenth century, Catholics joined Protestants in calls for an ecumenical council that all believed would solve the problems dogging the Christian church. But in the unsettled political and diplomatic atmosphere that lasted into the 1540s, it was impossible to find any agreement about where or when a universal council should meet. Finally, in 1545, at a time when the hostilities between the Valois and Habsburgs had cooled, Pope Paul III (r. 1534–1549) was able to convene an ecumenical council in the city of Trent, a German imperial city located on the Italian side of the Alps.

The **Council of Trent** marked and defined Roman Catholicism for the next four hundred years. Reformers within the Catholic Church hoped that it would be possible to create a broadly based reform party within the church and that the council would define theological positions acceptable to the Protestants, making reunion possible.

The Council of Trent sat in three sessions between 1545 and 1563. The initial debates were clearly meant to mark the boundaries between Protestant heresy and the orthodox positions of the Catholic Church. In response to the Protestant emphasis on Scripture alone, the council affirmed that Scripture has to be interpreted in the context of Church tradition. Delegates rejected the humanists' work on the text of the Bible, declaring that the Latin Vulgate edition compiled by Jerome in the late fourth century was the authorized text. In response to the widely held Protestant belief that salvation came through faith alone, the council declared that good works were not merely the outcome of faith but prerequisites to salvation. The council rejected Protestant positions on the sacraments, the giving of wine to the laity during Holy Communion, the marriage of clergy, and the granting of indulgences.

To assume that the council's decrees were merely negative, however, is to ignore the many ways in which the decrees of the council were an essential part of the creation of the Roman Catholic Church that would function for the next four centuries. The delegates at Trent generally felt that the real cause behind the Protestant movement was the lack of leadership and supervision within the church. Many of the acts of the council dealt with that issue.

First, the council affirmed apostolic succession—the idea that the authority of a bishop is transmitted through a succession of bishops, ultimately leading back through the popes to Saint Peter. Thus, the council underlined the ultimate authority of the pope in administrative, as well as theological, matters. The council ordered that local bishops should reside in their dioceses; that they should establish seminaries to see to the education of parish clergy; and that, through regular visitation and supervision, they should make certain that the laity participated in the sacramental life of the church. In the final sessions of the council, the nature of the Roman Catholic Church was summed up in the Creed of Pius IV, which, like the Lutheran Augsburg Confession, expressed the basic position of the church.

A Mystical Reformer Saint Teresa of Avila came from a converso family. She believed that renewal within the Christian church would come through mysticism, prayer, and a return to traditional religious practices. She founded a reformed Carmelite order of nuns to further religious renewal in Spain. (Institut Amatller d'Art Hispanic)

Council of Trent An ecumenical council of the Roman Catholic Church called to both respond to the Protestant challenge and institute reforms in the Catholic Church. Its decrees established the basic tenets of Roman Catholicism for the next four hundred years.

Confessionalization

The labors of the Jesuits and the deliberations of the Council of Trent at midcentury proved that reconciliation between the Protestant reformers and the Catholic Church was not possible. Signs of the separation include the flight of important Protestant religious leaders from Italy in the late 1540s and the wholesale migration of Protestant communities from Modena, Lucca, and other Italian towns to France, England, and Switzerland. These actions signify the beginnings of the theological, political, and social separation of "Protestant" and "Catholic" in European society. Further, the states of Europe saw themselves as the enforcers of religious uniformity within their territories. It is from this time forward that denominational differences become clearer.

The theological separation was marked in a number of concrete and symbolic ways. Churches in which both bread and wine were distributed to the laity during the sacrament of Holy Communion passed from Catholic to Protestant. Churches in which the altar was moved forward to face the congregation but the statuary was retained were likely to be Lutheran. Churches in which statues were destroyed and all other forms of art were removed were likely to be Reformed (Calvinist), for Calvin had advised that "only those things are to be sculpted or painted which the eye is capable of seeing; let not God's majesty, which is far above the perception of the eyes, be debased through unseemly representations."[5] Even matters such as singing differentiated the churches. Although the Calvinist tradition tended to believe that music, like art, drew the Christian away from consideration of the Word, Luther believed that "next to the Word of God, music deserves the highest praise." Lutherans emphasized congregational singing and the use of music within the worship service. Countless pastors in the sixteenth and seventeenth centuries followed Luther in composing hymns and even theoretical tracts on music. This tradition would reach its zenith in the church music of Johann Sebastian Bach (1685–1750), most of whose choral works were composed to be part of the normal worship service.

Music had played an important role in Catholic services since well before the Reformation. It was really architecture that distinguished Catholic churches from Protestant churches in the late sixteenth and seventeenth centuries. In Rome, the great religious orders built new churches in the baroque style (see page 437). Baroque artists and architects absorbed all the classical lessons of the Renaissance and then went beyond them, sometimes deliberately violating them. Baroque art celebrates the supernatural, the ways in which God is not bound by the laws of nature. Whereas Renaissance art was meant to depict nature, baroque paintings and sculpture seem to defy gravity. The work celebrates the supernatural power and splendor of the papacy. This drama and power are clear in the construction of the Jesuit Church of the Gesù (jeh-ZOO) in Rome and, even more so, in Gianlorenzo Bernini's (1598–1680) throne of Saint Peter, made for Saint Peter's Basilica in the Vatican. The construction of baroque churches, first in Spain and Italy, but especially in the Catholic parts of Germany, created yet another boundary between an austere Protestantism and a visual and mystical Catholicism.

The Regulation of Religious Life

Because of the continuing religious confusion and political disorder brought on by the reforms, churchmen, like state officials, were intent on maintaining religious order within their territories by requiring what they understood to be the practice of true Christianity. In an ironic twist, both Protestant and Catholic authorities followed much the same program. In both camps, regulation of religion became a governmental concern. Religious regulation and state power grew at the same time. This true religion was much less a public and communal religion than medieval Christianity had been. In the age of confessionalization, theologians—both Protestant and Catholic—became preoccupied with the moral status and interior life of individuals. Sexual sins and gluttony now seemed more dangerous than economic sins, such as avarice and usury. Even penance was understood less as a "restitution" that would reintegrate the individual into the Christian community, than as a process of coming to true contrition for one's sins.

All of the major religious groups in the late sixteenth century emphasized education, right doctrine, and social control. In Catholic areas, it was hoped that a renewed emphasis on private confession by the laity would lead to a proper understanding of doctrine. During this period, Charles Borromeo, archbishop of Milan (1538–1584), introduced the private confessional box, which isolated priest and penitent from the prying ears of the community. This allowed confessors the time and opportunity to instruct individual consciences with care. As early as the 1520s, some Lutheran princes had begun visitations to ensure that the laity understood basic doctrine.

Churchmen in both Protestant and Catholic areas used catechisms—handbooks containing instruction for the laity. The first and most famous was by Luther himself. Luther's *Small Catechism* includes the Lord's Prayer, Ten Commandments, and Apostles' Creed, along with simple, clear explanations of what they mean. More than Catholic rulers, Protestant rulers used church courts to enforce discipline within the community. Churchmen began to criticize semi-religious popular celebrations, such as May Day, harvest feasts, and the Feast of Fools, whose origins lay in popular myths and practices that preceded Christianity. Such observances were now scorned for encouraging superstition and mocking the social and political order with, for example, parodies of ignorant clergy and foolish magistrates.

Religious authorities were also concerned by what seemed to be out-of-control mysticism and dangerous religious practices, especially among women. The impact of the Reformation on the status of women has often been debated. The Protestant position is that the Reformation freed women from the cloistered control of traditional convents. Further, the Protestant attack on state-controlled prostitution reduced one of the basest forms of exploitation. To the realists who argued that young, unmarried men would always need sexual outlets, Luther replied that

The Holy Household   One of the most popular ideas among Protestants was that true religion should be taught and preserved in the Christian family, presided over by the father. The detail in this painting shows not only the interior of a Flemish home, but also the role of the father and the symbolic importance of meals eaten together.   (The Shakespeare Birthplace Trust)

one cannot merely substitute one evil practice for another. Critics of the Reformation counter that a convent was one of very few organizations that a woman could administer and direct. Women who took religious vows, Catholics point out, could engage in intellectual and religious pursuits similar to those enjoyed by men. The destruction of religious houses for women, Catholics argue, destroyed one of the few alternatives that women had to life in an authoritarian, patriarchal society.

In fact, in the late sixteenth and early seventeenth centuries, both Protestant and Catholic authorities viewed with suspicion any signs of religious independence by women. In the first years of the Reformation, some women did leave convents, eager to participate in the reform of the church. They wrote tracts concerning the morality of the clergy. And, for a time, women served as deacons in some Reformed (Calvinist) churches. Yet, like the female witches discussed in Chapter 15, these religious women seemed somehow dangerous. Lutheran and Calvinist theologians argued that a woman's religious vocation should be in the Christian care and education of her family. And even the most famous of the sixteenth- and seventeenth-century female Catholic mystics were greeted with distrust and some hostility. Religious women in Catholic convents were required to subordinate their mysticism to the guidance they received from male spiritual advisers. Calvinist theologians exhibited similar suspicions toward the theological and spiritual insights of Protestant women. For the laity, in general, and for women, in particular, the late Reformation brought increased control by religious authorities.

SECTION SUMMARY

- Catholic reform emphasizing moral reform and renewed piety had begun before Luther's protests.

- The Council of Trent defined Catholic doctrine for the next four hundred years.

- During the second half of the sixteenth century, Protestant and Catholic churches became more clearly differentiated by architecture and ritual.

- Both traditions emphasized personal discipline and self-control, which became an important part of the early modern state.

CHAPTER SUMMARY

During the age of the Reformation, Europe experienced a number of profound shocks. The medieval assumption of a unified Christendom in the West was shattered. No longer could Europeans assume that, at heart, they held similar views of the world and the place of individuals in it. Charles V had begun his reign with hopes for one law, one faith, and one empire. He ended it by dividing his empire and retiring to a monastery.

The Protestant challenge did not simply attack the institutional structure or the moral lapses as previous heretical movements had done. The early Protestant reformers rejected the penitential system that was at the heart of the medieval church. Peasants and artisans argued that Luther's message of Christian freedom liberated them from both economic and spiritual oppression. Both Protestant and peasant claimed all authority must rest on Holy Scripture. They rejected the traditions of the late Middle Ages.

Emperor Charles V was opposed to Luther and wanted to maintain the unity of the church and of his empire. But he faced almost continuous problems in one part or another of his empire. Both the French and the Turks did all they could to reduce his power. Consequently, even after years of struggle, he was forced, in the religious Peace of Augsburg, to accept the principle that the towns and regional principalities had the right to accept either traditional Catholic worship or the new Lutheran reform.

In England, on the other hand, the monarchy was powerful enough that Henry VIII was able to shift religious debate and declare himself the head of the Church in England. But Henry's children were alternately Protestant, Catholic, and Protestant again. The result in England was a church that maintained certain aspects of traditional Catholic Christianity, even as it allowed a married clergy and accepted other Protestant reforms.

Monarchies and republics throughout Europe came to view religious institutions and religious choices as matters of state. In Scandinavia, monarchs seemed to have favored the Lutherans as a way to weaken the power of the Catholic clergy. While in France, Francis I was willing to allow some Protestant protests, until it seemed that religious unrest threatened public order. At that point, he began to suppress Protestant worship, acknowledging the fact that France had largely remained Catholic. Much of the rest of eastern Europe followed no clear pattern. When faced with theological challenges and cries for moral reform, governments reacted in ways that offered religious change and bolstered the claims of secular authorities.

By the second half of the sixteenth century, Protestants and Catholics had largely adopted patterns that made clear which religion was favored. Calvinist churches were spare; Catholic churches, ornate; and Lutheran churches, filled with varieties of music.

As a part of their reform movements, both Protestant and Catholic governments redoubled their efforts to regulate religion and moral life. In Catholic countries, the church hierarchy extended its control over the religious life of the laity. Thus, both Reformation and Counter-Reformation brought about a significant strengthening of religious and secular authorities.

FOCUS QUESTIONS

- Why did the reformers feel it was necessary to establish entirely new churches outside the Roman Catholic Church?

- What political factors limited Charles V's ability to respond to the religious crisis?

- Why did the English monarchs take the lead in efforts to reform the English church?

- How did ideas of church reform influence social and political developments in the rest of Europe?

- How did Catholic and Protestant Christians differ from each other by the end of the Reformation?

 This icon will direct you to additional materials on the website: www .cengage.com/history/ noble/westciv6e.

KEY TERMS

NOTES

1. Quoted in Merry Wiesner-Hanks, "Women and Religious Change," in *The Cambrdige History of Christianity, volume 6 Reform and Expansion 1500–1660* (Cambridge: Cambridge University Press, 2007), p467.

2. Quoted in Robert W. Scribner, *The German Reformation* (London: Macmillan, 1986), p. 32.

3. Quoted in Carter Lindberg, *The European Reformations* (New York: Blackwell Publishers, 1996), p. 269.

4. Quoted in Euan Cameron, *The European Reformation* (Oxford: Clarendon Press, 1991), pp. 106–107.

5. Quoted in Lindberg, p. 375.

e See our interactive eBook for map and primary source activities.

15

The Saint Bartholomew's Day Massacre (The Art Archive/Musée des Beaux Arts Lausanne/Gianni Dagli Orti/Picture Desk)

Europe in the Age of Religious Wars, 1560–1648

Three well-dressed gentlemen stand over a mutilated body; one of them holds up the severed head. Elsewhere, sword-wielding men engage in indiscriminate slaughter, even of babies. Corpses are piled up in the background. This painting memorializes the grisly events of August 24, 1572. A band of Catholic noblemen, accompanied by the personal guard of the king of France, had hunted down a hundred Protestant nobles, asleep in their lodgings in and around the royal palace, and murdered them in cold blood. The king and his counselors had planned the murders as a preemptive strike because they feared that other Protestant nobles were gathering an army outside Paris. But the calculated attack became a massacre when ordinary Parisians, overwhelmingly Catholic and believing they were acting in the king's name, turned on their neighbors. About three thousand Protestants were slain in Paris over the next three days.

This massacre came to be called the Saint Bartholomew's Day Massacre for the Catholic saint on whose feast day it fell. Though horrible in its scope, the slaughter was not unusual in the deadly combination of religious and political antagonisms it reflected. Religious conflicts were, by definition, intractable political conflicts, since virtually every religious group felt that all others were heretics who could not be tolerated and must be eliminated. Rulers of all faiths looked to divine authority and religious institutions to uphold their power.

In the decades after 1560, existing political tensions led to instability and violence, especially when newly reinforced by religious differences. Royal governments continued to consolidate authority, but resistance to royal power by provinces, nobles, or towns accustomed to independence now might have a religious sanction. Warfare over these issues had consumed the Holy Roman Empire in the first half of the sixteenth century. The conflict now spilled over into France and the Netherlands and threatened to erupt in England. In the early seventeenth century, the Holy Roman Empire once again was wracked by a war simultaneously religious and political in origin. Regardless of its roots, warfare itself had become more destructive than ever before thanks to innovations in military technology and campaign tactics. Tensions everywhere were also worsened by economic changes, especially soaring prices and unemployment. The political and religious struggles of the era took place against a background of increasing want, and economic distress was often expressed in both political and religious terms.

FOCUS QUESTIONS

- What circumstances permitted Spain's ambitious policies and to what degree were they successful?
- What conditions led to civil war in France? How did religious and political conflict develop differently in England?
- Why did war erupt again within the Holy Roman Empire and what was the significance of the conflict?
- What caused the economic stresses of these decades and how did ordinary people cope with them?
- In what ways do the literature and art of this period reflect the political, social, and religious conflicts of the age?

This icon will direct you to additional materials on the website: www.cengage.com/history/noble/westciv6e.

See our interactive eBook for map and primary source activities.

A period of tension, even extraordinary violence, in political and social life, the era of the late sixteenth and early seventeenth centuries was also distinguished by great creativity in some areas of cultural and intellectual life. The plays of Shakespeare, for example, mirrored the passions, but also reflected on the dilemmas of the day and helped to analyze Europeans' circumstances with a new degree of sophistication.

IMPERIAL SPAIN AND THE LIMITS OF ROYAL POWER

What circumstances permitted Spain's ambitious policies and to what degree were they successful?

Philip II King of Spain (r. 1556–1598), son of Charles V who ruled Spain at the height of its influence.

To contemporary observers, no political fact of the late sixteenth century was more obvious than the ascendancy of Spain. Philip II (r. 1556–1598) ruled Spanish conquests in the New World, as well as wealthy territories in Europe, including the Netherlands and parts of Italy. Yet imperial Spain did not escape the political, social, and religious turmoil of the era. Explosive combinations of religious dissent and political disaffection led to revolt against Spain in the Netherlands. This conflict revealed the endemic tensions of sixteenth-century political life: nobles, towns, and provinces trying to safeguard remnants of medieval autonomy against efforts at greater centralization—with the added complications of economic strain and religious division. The revolt also demonstrated the material limits of royal power, since even with treasure from American conquests pouring in, Philip could, at times, barely afford to keep armies in the field. As American silver dwindled in the seventeenth century, Philip's successors faced severe financial and political strains, even in their Spanish domains.

The Revolt of the Netherlands

Philip's power stemmed in part from the far-flung territories he inherited from his father, the Habsburg king of Spain and Holy Roman emperor Charles V: Spain, the Low Countries (the Netherlands), the duchy of Milan, the kingdom of Naples, the conquered lands in the Americas, and the Philippine Islands in Asia. (Control of Charles's Austrian lands had passed to his brother, Ferdinand, Philip's uncle; see **Map 15.1**.) Treasure fleets bearing silver from the New World began to reach Spain regularly during Philip's reign. Spain was now the engine powering a trading economy unlike any that had existed in Europe before. To supply its colonies, Spain needed timber and other shipbuilding materials from the hinterlands of the Baltic Sea. Grain from the Baltic fed the urban populations of Spain (where wool was the principal cash crop) and the Netherlands, while the Netherlands, in turn, was a source of finished goods, such as cloth. The major exchange point for all of these goods was the city of Antwerp in the Netherlands, the leading trading center of all of Europe by 1550.

The Netherlands were the jewel among Philip's European possessions. These seventeen provinces (constituting mostly the modern nations of Belgium and the Netherlands) had been centers of trade and manufacture since the twelfth century. In the fourteenth and fifteenth centuries, they had enjoyed political importance and a period of cultural innovation under the control of the dukes of Burgundy. Like his father, Philip was, technically, the ruler of each province separately—that is, he was count of Flanders, duke of Brabant, and so forth. (See **Map 15.2**.) By Philip's reign, a sort of federal system of government had evolved to accommodate the various centers of power. Each province had an assembly (Estates) in which representatives of leading nobility and towns authorized taxation, but each also acknowledged a central administration in Brussels that represented Philip. Heading the council of state in Brussels was a governor-general, Philip's half sister, Margaret of Parma.

BACKGROUND TO THE REVOLT Philip's clumsy efforts to adjust this distribution of power in his favor pushed his subjects in the Netherlands into revolt. Born and raised in Spain, Philip had little real familiarity with the densely populated, linguistically diverse Netherlands, and he never visited there after 1559. Early in his reign, tensions in the Netherlands arose over taxation and Spanish insistence on maintaining tight control. Bad harvests and disruptions of trade, caused by wars in the Baltic region in the 1560s, depressed the Netherlands' economy and made it difficult for the provinces to pay the taxes Spain demanded. When the Peace of Cateau-Cambrésis (kahtoe kam-bray-SEE) of 1559 brought an end to the long struggle between the Habsburgs and the Valois (val-WAH) kings of France, the people of the Netherlands had reason to hope for lower taxes and reduced levels of Spanish control, yet neither was forthcoming. Indeed, Philip named to the council of state in Brussels officials who were Spaniards themselves or had close ties to the Spanish court, bypassing local nobles who had fought for Philip and his father before 1559.

Philip only added to the discontent by unleashing an invigorated repression of heresy. Unlike his father, Philip directed the hunt for heretics, not just at lower-class dissenters, but also at well-to-do Calvinists—followers of the French Protestant religious reformer John Calvin—whose numbers were considerable. Punishment for heresy now included confiscation of family property along with execution of the individual. By 1565, town councils in the Netherlands routinely refused to enforce Philip's religious policies, believing that their prosperity—as well as their personal security—depended on restraint in the prosecution of heresy. Leading nobles also stopped enforcing the policies on their estates.

Encouraged by greater tolerance, Protestants began to hold open-air meetings and attract new converts in many towns. In a series of actions called the "iconoclastic fury," Calvinist townsfolk around the provinces stripped Catholic churches of the relics and statues they believed idolatrous. At the same time, reflecting the economic strain of these years, some townsfolk rioted to protest the price of bread. One prominent nobleman warned Philip, "All trade has come to a standstill, so that there are 100,000 men begging for their bread who used to earn it…which is [important] since poverty can force people to do things which otherwise they would never think of doing."[1]

CHRONOLOGY

1556–1598	Reign of Philip II
1558–1603	Reign of Elizabeth I
1559	Act of Supremacy (England)
1562–1598	Religious wars in France
1565	Netherlands city councils and nobility ignore Philip II's law against heresy
1566	Calvinist "iconoclastic fury" begins in the Netherlands
1567	Duke of Alba arrives in the Netherlands
1571	Defeat of Turkish navy at Lepanto
1576	Sack of Antwerp
1579	Union of Utrecht
1588	Defeat of Spanish Armada
1589–1610	Reign of Henry IV
1598	Edict of Nantes (France)
1609	Truce between Spain and the Netherlands declared
1618–1648	Thirty Years' War
1620	Catholic victory at Battle of White Mountain
1621	Truce between Spain and the Netherlands expires; war between Spain and the Netherlands begins
1629	Peace of Alais
1631	Swedes under Gustav Adolf defeat imperial forces
1635	Peace of Prague
1640–1653	"Long Parliament" in session in England
1648	Peace of Westphalia

THE PROVINCES REVOLT

In early 1567, armed Calvinist insurgents seized two towns in the southern Netherlands in hopes of stirring a general revolt that would secure freedom of worship. Margaret of Parma quelled the uprisings by rallying city governments and loyal nobles, now fearful for their own property and power. But by then, far away in Spain, a decision had been made to send in the Spanish duke of Alba with an army of ten thousand men.

When Alba arrived in August 1567, he repeated every mistake of Spanish policy that had triggered rebellion in the first place. He billeted troops in friendly cities, established new courts to try rebels, arrested thousands of people, executed about a thousand rebels (including Catholics as well as prominent Protestants), and imposed heavy taxes to support his army.

Margaret of Parma resigned in disgust and left the Netherlands. Protestants from rebellious towns escaped into exile, where they were joined by nobles who had been declared traitors for resisting Alba's policies. The most important of these was William of Nassau (NAS-saw), prince of Orange (1533–1584), whose lands outside the Netherlands, in France and the Holy Roman Empire, lay beyond Spanish reach and so could be used to finance continued warfare against Spain. A significant community with military capability began to grow in exile.

In 1572, ships of exiled Calvinist privateers, known as the "Sea Beggars," began preying on Spanish shipping and coastal fortresses from bases in the northern provinces. These provinces,

🌐 **MAP 15.1—The Spanish Habsburgs and Europe, ca. 1556**

Philip II's control of territories in northern Italy permitted the overland access of Spanish troops to the Netherlands and heightened the Spanish threat to France. Lands bordering the western Mediterranean made the sea a natural sphere of Spanish influence as well. Habsburg lands in central Europe were controlled after 1556 by Charles V's brother Ferdinand and his descendants.

increasingly Calvinist, became the center of opposition to the Spanish, who concentrated their efforts against rebellion in the wealthier southern provinces. Occasionally, the French and English lent aid to the rebels.

The war in the Netherlands was a showcase for the new and costly technology of warfare in this period. Many towns were (or came to be, as a consequence of the revolt) equipped with "bastions," newly designed walled defenses that could resist artillery fire; such cities could not be taken by storm. Where bastions had been built, military campaigns consisted of grueling sieges, skirmishes in surrounding areas for control of supplies, and occasional pitched battles between besiegers and forces attempting to break the siege. Vast numbers of men were required, both for effective besieging forces and for garrisoning the many fortresses that controlled the countryside and defended access to major towns.

In an attempt to supply the Netherlands with veteran troops and materiel from Spain and Spanish territories in Italy, the Spanish developed the "Spanish Road," an innovative string of supply depots where provisions could be gathered in advance of troops marching to the Netherlands (see **MAP 15.1**). Maintaining its large armies, however, taxed Spain's resources

The City of Antwerp   Antwerp, in the southern Netherlands, was the point of sale for Portuguese spices brought around Africa from India; the selling and transshipping center for Baltic goods, including timber, fur, and grain; and the source for manufactured goods such as cloth.   (Musées royaux des Beaux-Arts de Belgique)

to the breaking point. Even with American silver at hand, Philip could, at times, barely afford to keep armies in the field. Inevitably, large numbers of troops also exhausted the countryside, and both soldiers and civilians suffered great privations. On occasion, Spanish troops reacted violently to difficult conditions and to delayed pay (American treasure dwindled badly between 1572 and 1578). In 1576, they sacked the hitherto loyal city of Antwerp and massacred about eight thousand people. Bitterly remembered as the "Spanish Fury," the massacre prompted leaders in the southern provinces to raise their own armies to protect themselves against the Spanish. Late in 1576, they concluded an alliance with William of Orange and the northern rebels.

The alliance between northern and southern provinces did not last. The provinces were increasingly divided by religion, and their differences were skillfully exploited by Philip's new commander, Margaret of Parma's son Alexander Farnese (far-NAY-zee), duke of Parma. With silver from America filling the king's coffers again, Parma wooed the Catholic elites of the southern provinces back into loyalty to Philip, in return for promises to respect their provincial liberties and safeguard their property from troops.

FORMATION OF THE
UNITED PROVINCES

In 1579, the northern provinces united in a defensive alliance, the Union of Utrecht (OO-trekt), against the increasingly unified south. Parma's forces could not push beyond the natural barrier of rivers that bisect the Low Countries (see **MAP 15.2**), particularly as Spain diverted money to conflicts with England in 1588 and France after 1589. In 1609, a truce was finally concluded between Spain and the northern provinces. This truce did not formally recognize the "United Provinces" as an independent entity, though in fact they were. The modern

🌐 **MAP 15.2—The Netherlands, 1559–1609**

The seventeen provinces of the Netherlands were strikingly diverse politically, economically, and culturally.

United Provinces as of 1609

Spanish Netherlands

Truce line, 1609

Boundary of the Holy Roman Empire

nations of Belgium (the southern Spanish provinces) and the Netherlands are the distant result of this truce.

The independent **United Provinces** (usually called, simply, the Netherlands) was a fragile state, an accident of warfare at first. But commercial prosperity began to emerge as its greatest strength. Much of the economic activity of Antwerp had shifted north to Amsterdam in the province of Holland because of fighting in the south and a naval blockade of Antwerp by rebel ships. Philip's policies had created a new enemy nation and had enriched it at his expense.

In addition, the revolt of the Netherlands lured Spain into wider war, particularly against England. Spain and England had a common foe in France and common economic interests, and Philip had married Mary Tudor, the Catholic queen of England (r. 1553–1558). Even after Mary's death and the accession of her Protestant half sister, Queen Elizabeth (r. 1558–1603), Spanish-English relations remained cordial. Relations started to sour, however, when Elizabeth began tolerating the use of English ports by the rebel Sea Beggars and authorizing attacks by English privateers on Spanish treasure fleets. In response, Spain supported Catholic resistance to Elizabeth within England, including plots to replace her on the throne with her Catholic cousin, Mary, Queen of Scots. Greater Spanish success in the Netherlands, raids by the Spanish and English on each other's shipping, and Elizabeth's execution of Mary in 1587 prompted Philip to order an invasion of England. A fleet (*armada*) of Spanish warships sailed in 1588.

"The enterprise of England," as the plan was called in Spain, represented an astounding logistical effort. The **Armada** was supposed to clear the English Channel of English ships in order to permit an invading force—troops under Parma in the Netherlands—to cross on barges. The sheer number of ships required —about 130—meant that some, inevitably, were slower supply ships, or vessels designed for the more protected waters of the Mediterranean. The English also had the advantage in arms, since they had better long-range artillery and better-trained gunners. Spain's Armada was defeated by the English and by bad weather that dispersed much of the fleet. The invasion failed and fewer than half of the 130-ship Armada ever made it back to Spain.

United Provinces The seven northern provinces of the Low Countries that successfully revolted against Spanish rule in the late sixteenth century and became the modern nation of the Netherlands.

Armada Massive fleet of Spanish warships sent against England by Philip II but defeated by the English navy and bad weather in 1588. The tactics used by the English helped set the future course of naval warfare.

Successes at Home and Around the Mediterranean

Despite his overseas empire and his preoccupation with the Netherlands, many of Philip's interests still centered on the Mediterranean. In his kingdoms of Spain and their Mediterranean sphere of interest, Philip made his power felt more effectively, though not without effort.

Philip's father, Charles V, had tried to secure the western Mediterranean against the Ottoman Turks and their client states along the African coast, but it was under Philip that the Turkish challenge in the western Mediterranean receded. The Spanish allied temporarily with the papacy and Venice—both were concerned with Turkish naval power in the Mediterranean—and their combined navies inflicted a massive defeat on the Turkish navy at Lepanto, off the coast of Greece, in October 1571 (see **MAP 15.1**). The Turks remained the leading power in the eastern Mediterranean,

Le Maſſacre fait a Vaſsy le premier iour de Mars. 1562.

A. La grange ou l'on preſchoit ou eſtoyent enuiron 1200 perſonnes.
B. Monſieur de Guiſe qui commandoit.
C. Le Miniſtre dedans la Chaire priant Dieu.
D. Le Miniſtre ſe cuydant ſauuer eſt bleſſé en pluſieurs lieux

& euſt eſté tué ſi l'eſpee ne fuſt rompue en deux.
E. Le Cardinal de Guyſe appuyé ſur 1; cimentiere de la paroiſſe.
F. Le toict que les gens du preſche rompent pour eux ſauuer.
G. Pluſieurs qui ſe iettans ſur la muraille de la ville ſe ſauuent

aux champs.
H. Pluſieurs qui ſe cuydans ſauuer ſur le toict ſont harquebouſés.
I. Le trone des poures arraché,
k. Les trompettes qui ſonnerent par deux diuerſes fois,

Massacre at Vassy This contemporary engraving by two Protestant artists depicts the Duke of Guise (*center left*) and his men coldly butchering Huguenot worshipers at Vassy. In a Catholic version of the event, the Protestants were killed by gunfire after pelting Guise's men with rocks when they tried to disperse the worshipers. (HIP/Art Resource, NY)

members of leading noble families—including the Bourbons, princes of royal blood—had converted to Protestantism and worshiped openly in their rooms in the palace. In 1561, Catherine convened a national religious council to reconcile the two faiths. When it failed, she chose provisional religious toleration as the only practical course and issued a limited edict of toleration of Huguenots (HEW-guh-nots) in the name of the king in January 1562.

The edict solved nothing. Ignoring its restrictions, Protestants armed themselves, while townspeople of both faiths insulted and attacked one another at worship sites and religious festivals. In March 1562, the armed retainers of a Catholic duke killed a few dozen Protestants gathered in worship at Vassy (vah-SEE), near one of the duke's estates. The killing, bringing the military power of the nobility to bear on the broader problem of religious division, sparked the first of six civil wars.

DECADES OF CIVIL WAR In some ways, the initial conflict in 1562 was decisive. The Protestant army lost the principal pitched battle of the war in December. This defeat reduced the appeal of the Protestant movement to nobles. The limited rights granted by the peace edict in 1563 made it difficult for Protestants in towns—where the vast majority of them lived—to worship. But if the Huguenots were not powerful enough to win, neither were they weak enough to be decisively beaten.

The turning point most obvious to contemporaries came a decade later. The Protestant faction, still represented at court by the Bourbon princes and their allies, pressed the king for war against Spain to aid Protestant rebels in the Netherlands. Opposed to another war against Spain and alarmed by rumors of Huguenot armies massing outside Paris, Charles IX (r. 1560–1574) and his mother authorized royal guards to murder the Protestant leaders on August 24, 1572—Saint Bartholomew's Day. These murders touched off a massacre of Protestants throughout Paris and, once news from Paris had spread, throughout the kingdom.

The Saint Bartholomew's Day Massacre revealed the degree to which religious differences had strained the fabric of community life. Neighbor murdered neighbor in an effort to rid the community of heretical pollution; bodies of the dead were mutilated. Gathered in the south of France, the remaining Huguenot forces vowed "never [to] trust those who have so often and so treacherously broken faith and the public peace."[3] Huguenot writers published tracts arguing that royal power was by nature limited and that rebellion was justified against tyrants who overstepped their legitimate authority.

Many Catholics also renounced reconciliation. Some noblemen formed a Catholic league to fight in place of the weakened monarchy. Charles's successor, his brother Henry III (r. 1574–1589), was forced to cooperate with first one of the warring parties and then another. In December 1588, he resorted to murdering two leaders of the ultra-Catholic faction; in turn, he was murdered by a priest in early 1589.

The new king was the Bourbon prince Henry of Navarre, who became Henry IV (r. 1589–1610). He was a Protestant, and he had to fight for his throne. He faced Catholic armies now subsidized by Philip II of Spain, an extremist Catholic city government in Paris, and subjects who were tired of war but mainly Catholic. Given these obstacles, the politically astute Henry agreed to convert to Catholicism.

After his conversion in 1593, many of Henry's subjects believed that only rallying to the monarchy could save France from chaos. In any case, nobles were increasingly inclined to cooperate with the Crown. Service to a successful king was honorable and a source of patronage; Henry was personally esteemed because he was a talented general and brave, gregarious, and charming. The nobility forced the citizens of Paris and other cities to accept Henry's authority. The civil war period thus proved to be an important phase in the accommodation of the nobility to the power of the state.

In April 1598, Henry granted toleration for the Huguenot minority in a royal edict proclaimed in the city of Nantes (NAHNT). The **Edict of Nantes** was primarily a repetition of provisions from the most generous edicts that had ended the various civil wars. Nobles were allowed to practice the Protestant faith on their estates; townspeople were granted more limited rights to worship in selected towns in each region. Protestants were also guaranteed rights of self-defense—specifically, the right to maintain garrisons in about two hundred towns. About half of these garrisons would be paid for by the Crown.

The problem was that the Edict of Nantes, like any royal edict, could be revoked by the king at any time. Moreover, the provision allowing Protestants to keep garrisoned towns reflected concessions to Protestant aristocrats, who could support their followers by paid garrison duty. It also reflected the assumption that living peacefully amid religious diversity might prove to be impossible. Thus, although Henry IV ended the French religious wars, he had not solved the problem of religious and political division within France.

Edict of Nantes 1598 edict of Henry IV, granting France's Protestants (Huguenots) the right to practice their faith and maintain defensive garrisons.

The Consolidation of Royal Authority in France, 1598–1643

During Henry IV's reign, France began to recover from the long years of civil war. Population and productivity began to grow; the Crown increased royal revenue by nibbling away at traditional local self-government and control of taxation.

Yet, Henry's regime was stable only in comparison with the preceding years of civil war. The power of the great nobility had not been definitively broken. Also, the king had agreed to a measure, known as the *paulette* (named for the functionary who first administered it), that allowed royal officeholders to own their offices and to pass on those offices to their heirs in return for the payment of an annual fee. The paulette was primarily a device to raise revenue after decades of civil war, but it also helped cement the loyalty of royal bureaucrats at a critical time, particularly that of the royal judges of the supreme law court, the Parlement of Paris, who had recently agreed to register the Edict of Nantes only under duress. However, the paulette made royal officeholders largely immune from royal control, since their posts were now in effect property, like the landed property of the traditional nobility.

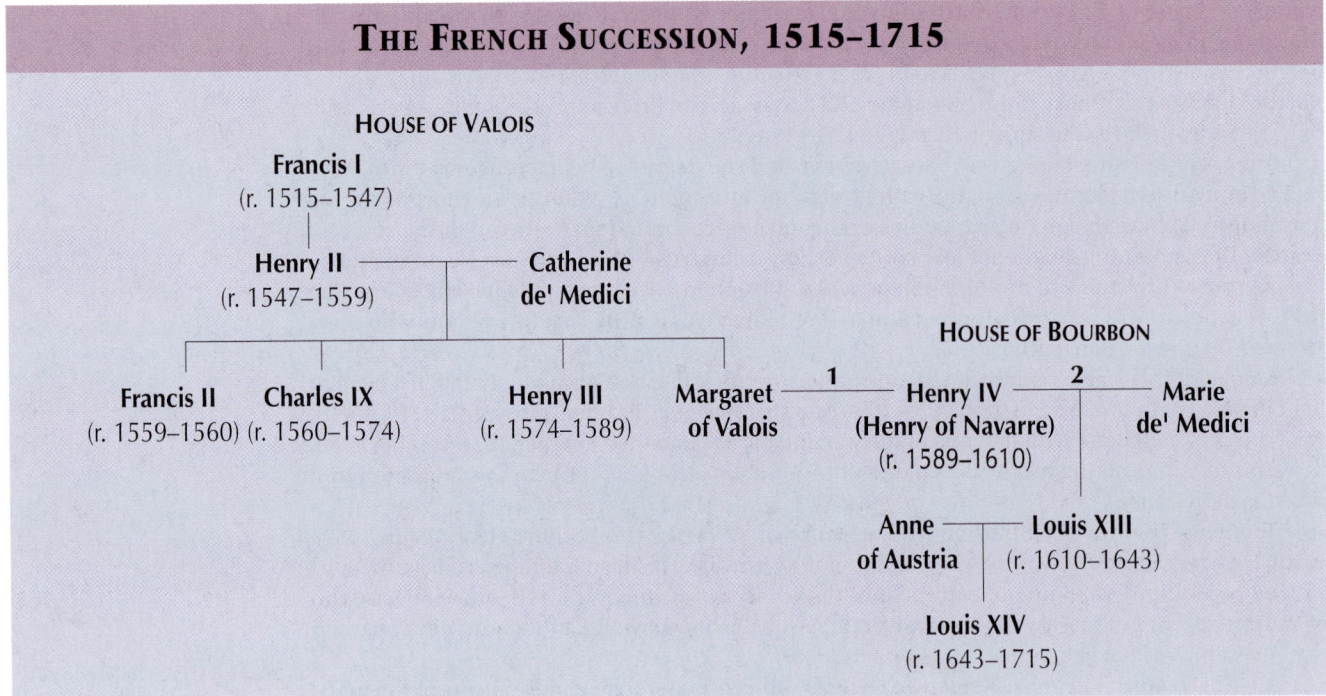

THE FRENCH SUCCESSION, 1515–1715

HOUSE OF VALOIS

Francis I
(r. 1515–1547)

Henry II ———— **Catherine**
(r. 1547–1559)   **de' Medici**

HOUSE OF BOURBON

Francis II   **Charles IX**   **Henry III**   **Margaret** 1 **Henry IV** 2 **Marie**
(r. 1559–1560) (r. 1560–1574)   (r. 1574–1589)   **of Valois**   **(Henry of Navarre)**   **de' Medici**
                                                                    (r. 1589–1610)

Anne ——— **Louis XIII**
of Austria   (r. 1610–1643)

Louis XIV
(r. 1643–1715)

In 1610, a fanatical Catholic assassinated Henry IV. Henry's death brought his 9-year-old son, Louis XIII (r. 1610–1643), to the throne with Louis's mother, Marie de' Medici, initially serving as regent. Within four years, Louis faced a major rebellion by his Huguenot subjects in southwestern France. Huguenots felt that Louis's policies, including his recent marriage to a Spanish princess, meant that royal support for toleration was wavering. The war persisted, on and off, for eight years, as the French royal troops, like the Spanish in the Netherlands, had difficulty breaching the defenses of even small fortress towns held by the Protestants. The main Huguenot stronghold was the well-fortified port city of La Rochelle, which had grown wealthy from European and overseas trade. Not until the king took the city, after a siege lasting more than a year, did the Protestants accept a peace on royal terms.

The Peace of Alais (ah-LAY) (1629) reaffirmed the policy of religious toleration but rescinded the Protestants' military and political privileges. It was a political triumph for the Crown because it deprived French Protestants of the means for further rebellion, while reinforcing their dependence on the Crown for religious toleration. Most of the remaining great noble leaders began to convert to Catholicism.

The Peace of Alais was also a personal triumph for the king's leading minister, who crafted the treaty and had directed the bloody siege that made it possible. Armand-Jean du Plessis (1585–1642), Cardinal Richelieu (RISH-el-yiuh), came from a provincial noble family and rose in the service of the queen mother. He was admired and feared for his skill in the political game of seeking and bestowing patronage—a crucial skill in an age when elites received offices and honors through carefully cultivated relationships at court. He and the king—whose sensitive temperament Richelieu handled adeptly—formed a lasting partnership that had a decisive impact, not only on French policy, but also on the entire shape of the French state.

Richelieu favored an aggressive foreign policy to counter what he believed still to be the greatest external threat to the French crown: the Spanish Habsburgs. After war resumed between the Netherlands and Spain in 1621 (see page 428), Richelieu attacked Spanish possessions in Italy, superintended large-scale fighting against Spain in the Netherlands itself, and subsidized Swedish and German Protestant armies fighting the Habsburgs in Germany.

Richelieu's policies were opposed by many French people, who saw taxes double, then triple, in just a few years. Many courtiers and provincial elites favored keeping the peace with Spain, a fellow Catholic state, and objected to alliances with German Protestants. They were also alarmed by the revolts that accompanied the peasants' distress. Their own status was also directly threatened by Richelieu's monopoly of royal patronage and by his creation of new offices, which undermined their power. In 1632, for example, Richelieu created the office of *intendant*. Intendants had wide powers for defense and administration in the provinces that overrode the established bureaucracy.

By 1640, Richelieu's ambitious foreign policy seemed to be bearing fruit. The French had won territory along their northern and eastern borders by their successes against Habsburg forces. But when Richelieu and Louis XIII died within five months of each other, in December 1642 and May 1643, Louis XIII was succeeded by his 5-year-old son, and the warrior-nobility, as well as royal bureaucrats, would waste little time before challenging the Crown's new authority.

Precarious Stability in England: The Reign of Elizabeth I, 1558–1603

England experienced no civil wars during the second half of the sixteenth century, but religious dissent challenged the stability of the monarchy. In **Elizabeth I** (r. 1558–1603), England—in stark contrast to France—possessed an able and long-lived ruler. Elizabeth was well educated in the humanistic tradition and was already an adroit politician at the age of 25, when she acceded to the throne at the death of her Catholic half sister, Mary Tudor (r. 1553–1558).

Elizabeth faced the urgent problem of effecting a religious settlement. Her father, Henry VIII (r. 1509–1547), had broken away from the Catholic Church for political reasons but had retained many Catholic doctrines and practices. A Calvinist-inspired Protestantism had been prescribed for the Church of England by the advisers of Henry's successor, Elizabeth's young half brother, Edward VI (r. 1547–1553). True Catholicism, such as her half sister Mary had tried to reimpose, was out of the question. The Roman church had never recognized Henry VIII's self-made divorce from Mary's mother and thus regarded Elizabeth as a bastard with no right to the throne.

Elizabeth reimposed royal control over the church and made limited concessions to accommodate the beliefs of a wide range of her subjects. In 1559, Parliament passed a new Act of Supremacy, which restored the monarch as head of the Church of England. Elizabeth dealt with opposition to the act by arresting bishops and lords whose votes would have blocked its passage by Parliament. The official prayer book, in use in Edward's day, was revised to include elements of both traditional and radical Protestant interpretations of Communion. But church liturgy, clerical vestments, and, above all, the hierarchical structure of the clergy closely resembled Catholic practices. The Act of Uniformity, also passed in 1559, required all worship to be conducted according to the new prayer book. Although uniformity was required in worship, Elizabeth was careful, in her words, not to "shine beacons into her subjects' souls."

Catholicism continued to be practiced, especially by otherwise loyal nobility and gentry in the north of England, who worshiped privately on their estates. But priests returning from exile beginning in the 1570s, most newly imbued with the proselytizing zeal of the Counter-Reformation (the Catholic response to the Protestant Reformation), practiced it more visibly and were zealously prosecuted for their boldness. In the last twenty years of Elizabeth's reign, approximately 180 Catholics were executed for treason, two-thirds of them priests. (By 1585, being a Catholic priest in itself was a crime.)

In the long run, the greater threat to the English crown came from the most radical Protestants in the realm, known (by their enemies initially) as **Puritans**. Puritanism was a broad movement for reform of church practice along familiar Protestant lines: an emphasis on Bible reading, preaching, and private scrutiny of conscience; a de-emphasis on institutional ritual and clerical authority. Most Puritans had accepted Elizabeth's religious compromise because they had no choice, but grew increasingly alienated by her insistence on clerical authority and her refusal to change any elements of the original religious settlement. A significant Presbyterian underground movement began to form among them. Presbyterians wanted to dismantle the episcopacy—the hierarchy of priests and bishops—and to govern the church instead with councils, called "presbyteries," that included lay members of the congregation. Laws were passed late in the queen's reign to enable the Crown to prosecute

Elizabeth I   Able and long-lived ruler who firmly established Protestantism in England and defended the nation against the Spanish Armada, but who bequeathed financial, religious, and political problems to her successors.

Puritans   Radical Protestants in late-sixteenth- and seventeenth-century England who became a majority in Parliament during the reign of Charles I and led opposition to the king.

more easily, and even to force into exile, anyone who attended "nonconformist" (non-Anglican) services.

The greatest challenge Elizabeth faced from Puritans came in Parliament, where they were well represented by many literate gentry. Parliament met only when called by the monarch. In theory, members could merely voice opinions and complaints; they could not initiate legislation and prescribe policy. However, only Parliament could vote taxes. Further, since it had in effect helped constitute royal authority by means of the two Acts of Supremacy, Parliament's merely advisory role had been expanded by the monarchy itself. During Elizabeth's reign, Puritans capitalized on Parliament's enlarged scope, using meetings to press for further religious reform. In 1586, they went so far as to introduce bills calling for an end to the episcopacy and the Anglican prayer book. Elizabeth had to resort to imprisoning one Puritan leader to end debate on the issue and on Parliament's right to address it.

Also during Elizabeth's reign, efforts at English expansion in the New World began, in the form of unsuccessful attempts at colonization and successful raids on Spanish possessions. However, the main focus of her foreign policy remained Europe itself. Elizabeth, like all her forebears, felt her interests tightly linked to the independence of the Netherlands, whose towns were a major outlet for English wool. Philip II's aggressive policy in the Netherlands increasingly alarmed her, especially in view of France's weakness. She began to send small sums of money to the rebels and allowed their ships access to southern English ports, from which they could raid Spanish-held towns on the Netherlands' coast. In 1585, in the wake of the duke of Parma's successes against the rebellions, she committed troops to help the rebels.

Her decision was a reaction, not only to the threat of a single continental power dominating the Netherlands, but also to the threat of Catholicism. From 1579 to 1583, the Spanish had helped the Irish fight English domination and were involved in several plots to replace Elizabeth with her Catholic cousin, Mary, Queen of Scots. These threats occurred as the return of Catholic exiles to England peaked. The victory over the Spanish Armada in 1588 was quite rightly celebrated, for it ended any Catholic threat to Elizabeth's rule.

The success against the Armada has tended to overshadow other aspects of Elizabeth's foreign policy, particularly with regard to Ireland. Since the twelfth century, an Anglo-Irish state, dominated by transplanted English families, had been loosely supervised from England, but most of

Elizabeth I: The Armada Portrait Both serene and resolute, Elizabeth is flanked by "before" and "after" glimpses of the Spanish fleet; her hand rests on the globe in a gesture of dominion that also memorializes the circumnavigation of the globe by her famous captain, Sir Francis Drake, some years before. (Elizabeth I, Armada Portrait, c. 1588 (oil on panel), Gower, George (1540–96) (attr. to)/ Woburn Abbey, Bedfordshire, UK/The Bridgeman Art Library)

Ireland remained under the control of Gaelic chieftains. Just as Charles V and Philip II attempted to tighten their governing mechanisms in the Netherlands, so did Henry VIII's minister, Thomas Cromwell, streamline control of outlying areas such as Wales and Anglo-Ireland. Cromwell proposed that the whole of Ireland be brought under English control, partly by the established mechanism of feudal ties: The Irish chieftains were to pay homage as vassals to the king of England.

Under Elizabeth, this legalistic approach gave way to virtual conquest. Elizabeth's governor, Sir Henry Sidney, appointed in 1565, inaugurated a policy whereby Gaelic lords, by means of various technicalities, could be entirely dispossessed of their lands. Any Englishman capable of raising a private force could help enforce these dispossessions and settle his conquered lands as he saw fit. This policy provoked stiff Irish resistance, which was viewed as rebellion and provided the rationale for further military action, more confiscations of lands, and more new English settlers. Eventually the Irish, with Spanish assistance, mounted a major rebellion, consciously Catholic and aimed against the "heretic" queen. The rebellion gave the English an excuse for brutal suppression and massive transfers of lands to English control. The political domination of the Irish was complete with the defeat, in 1601, of the Gaelic chieftain Hugh O'Neill, lord of Tyrone, who had controlled most of the northern quarter of the island. Although the English were unable to impose Protestantism on the conquered Irish, to Elizabeth and her English subjects, the conquests in Ireland seemed as significant as the victory over the Spanish Armada.

The English enjoyed relative peace at home during Elizabeth's reign. However, her reign ended on a note of strain. The foreign involvements, particularly in Ireland, had been very expensive. Taxation granted by Parliament more than doubled during her reign, and local taxes further burdened the people. Price inflation related to government spending, social problems caused by returned unemployed soldiers, and a series of bad harvests heightened popular resentment against taxation. Despite her achievements, therefore, Elizabeth passed two problems on to her successors: unresolved religious tensions and financial instability. Elizabeth's successors would also find in Parliament an increasing focus of opposition to their policies.

Rising Tensions in England, 1603–1642

In 1603, Queen Elizabeth died, and James VI of Scotland, the Protestant son of Mary, Queen of Scots, ascended to the English throne as James I (r. 1603–1625). Tensions between Anglicans and Puritans were briefly quieted under James because of a plot, in 1605, by Catholic dissenters. The Gunpowder Plot, as it was called, was a conspiracy to blow up the palace housing both king and Parliament at Westminster. Protestants of all stripes again focused on their common enemy, Catholics—though only temporarily.

JAMES I

Financial problems were James's most pressing concern. Court life became more elaborate and an increasing drain on the monarchy's resources. James's extravagance was partly to blame, but so were pressures for patronage from courtiers. To the debts left from the Irish conflicts and wars with Spain, James added new expenses to defend the claims of his daughter and her husband, a German prince, to rule Bohemia (see page 427).

To raise revenue without Parliament's consent, James relied on sources of income that the Crown had enjoyed since medieval times: customs duties, wardship (the right to manage and liberally borrow from the estates of minor nobles), and the sale of monopolies, which conveyed the right to be sole agent for a particular kind of goods. James's increase of the number of monopolies for sale was widely resented. Merchants objected to the arbitrary restriction of production and trade; common people found that they could no longer afford certain ordinary goods, such as soap, under monopoly prices. Criticism of the court escalated, particularly by the nobility, as James indulged in extreme favoritism of certain courtiers. He even created a new noble title—baronet—which he sold to socially ambitious commoners.

When James summoned Parliament to ask for funds in 1621, Parliament used the occasion to protest court corruption and the king's financial measures. The members revived the medieval procedure of impeachment and removed two royal ministers from office. In 1624, still faced with expensive commitments to Protestants abroad, James again called Parliament, which voted new taxes but also openly debated the wisdom of the king's foreign policy.

CHARLES I

Tensions between Crown and Parliament increased under James's son, Charles I (r. 1625–1649). Charles's foreign policy caused both financial strain and political opposition. Charles declared war on Spain and supported the Huguenot rebels in France. Many merchants opposed this

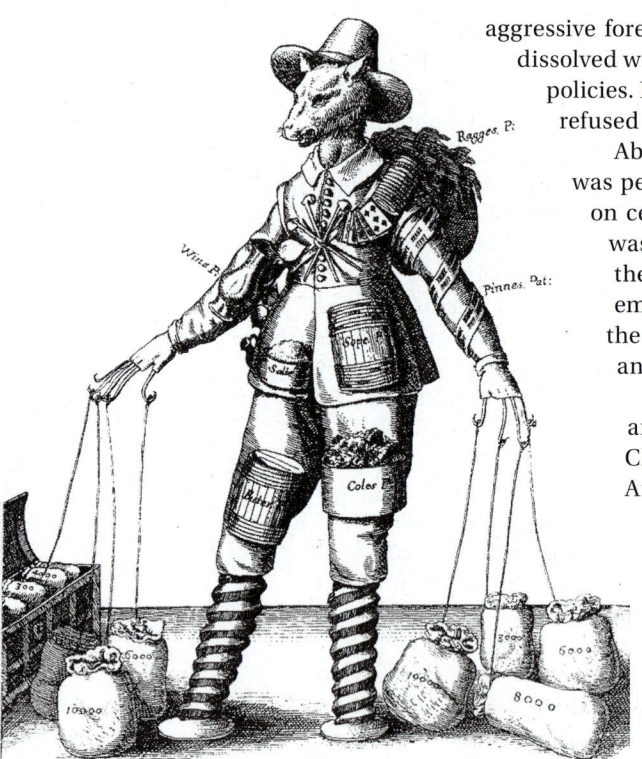

Criticism of Monopolies   Holders of royally granted monopolies were bitterly resented by English consumers and tradespeople alike, as this contemporary print reveals. The greedy beast pictured here controls even ordinary commodities such as pins, soap, and butter.   (Courtesy of the Trustees of the British Museum)

aggressive foreign policy because it disrupted trade. In 1626, Parliament was dissolved without granting any monies, in order to stifle its objections to his policies. Instead, Charles levied a forced loan and imprisoned gentry who refused to lend money to the government.

Above all, Charles's religious policies caused controversy. Charles was personally inclined toward "high church" practices: an emphasis on ceremony and sacrament reminiscent of Catholic ritual. He also was a believer in Arminianism, a school of thought that rejected the Calvinist notion that God's grace cannot be earned, and hence emphasized the importance of the sacraments and the authority of the clergy. Charles's views put him on a collision course with gentry and aristocrats who leaned toward Puritanism.

Charles's views were supported by William Laud (1573–1645), archbishop of Canterbury from 1633, and thus leader of the Church of England. He tried to impose changes in worship, spread Arminian ideas, and censor opposing views. He also challenged the redistribution of church property, which had occurred in the Reformation of the sixteenth century, and thereby alienated the gentry on economic as well as religious grounds.

Charles's style of rule worsened religious, political, and economic tensions. Cold and intensely private, he lacked the charm and the political skills to disarm his opponents. His court was ruled by formal protocol, and access to the king was highly restricted—a serious problem in an age when proximity to the monarch was a guarantee of political power.

Revenue and religion dominated debate in the Parliament of 1628–1629, which Charles had called, once again, to get funds for his foreign wars. Parliament presented the king with a document called the Petition of Right, which protested his financial policies, as well as arbitrary imprisonment. (Seventeen members of Parliament had been imprisoned for refusing loans to the Crown.) Though couched conservatively as a restatement of customary practice, the petition, in fact, claimed a tradition of expanded parliamentary participation in government. Charles dissolved Parliament in March 1629, having decided that the money he might extract was not worth the risk.

For eleven years, Charles ruled without Parliament. When he was forced to summon it again in 1640, the kingdom was in crisis. Royal finances were in desperate straits, even though Charles had pressed collection of revenues far beyond traditional bounds.

1640: THE KINGDOM IN CRISIS

The immediate crisis and the reason for Charles's desperate need for money was a rebellion in Scotland. Like Philip II in the Netherlands, Charles tried to rule in Scotland through a small council of men who did not represent local elites. Worse, he also tried to force his "high church" practices on the Scots. The Scottish church had been more dramatically reshaped during the Reformation and now was largely Presbyterian in structure. The result of Charles's policies was riots and rebellion. Unable to suppress the revolt in a first campaign in 1639, Charles was forced to summon Parliament for funds to raise a more effective army.

But the Parliament that assembled in the spring of 1640 provided no help. Instead, members questioned the war with the Scots and other royal policies. Charles's political skills were far too limited for him to reestablish a workable relationship with Parliament under the circumstances. Charles dissolved this body, which is now known as the "Short Parliament," after just three weeks. Even more stinging than Charles's dissolution of the Parliament was the lack of respect he had shown the members: A number of them were harassed or arrested. Mistrust, fomented by the eleven years in which Charles had ruled without Parliament, thus increased.

Another humiliating defeat at the hands of the Scots, later in 1640, made summoning another Parliament imperative. Members of the "Long Parliament" (it sat from 1640 to 1653) took full advantage of the king's predicament. Charles was forced to agree not to dissolve or adjourn Parliament without the members' consent and to summon Parliament at least every three years. Parliament abolished many of the traditional revenues he had abused and impeached and removed from office his leading ministers, including Archbishop Laud. The royal commander deemed responsible for the Scottish fiasco, Thomas Wentworth, earl of Strafford, was executed without trial in May 1641.

The execution of Strafford shocked many aristocrats in the House of Lords (the upper house of Parliament), as well as some moderate members of the House of Commons. Meanwhile, Parliament began debating the perennially thorny religious question. A bare majority of members favored abolition of Anglican bishops as a first step in thoroughgoing religious reform. Working people in London, kept updated on the issues by the regular publication of parliamentary debates, demonstrated in support of that move. Moderate members of Parliament, in contrast, favored checking the king's power, but not upsetting the Elizabethan religious compromise.

An event that unified public and parliamentary opinion at a crucial time—a revolt against English rule in Ireland in October 1641—temporarily eclipsed these divisions over religious policy but did not diminish suspicion of the king. Fearing that Charles would use Irish soldiers against his English subjects, Parliament demanded that it control the army to put down the rebellion. In November, the Puritan majority introduced a document known as the "Grand Remonstrance," an appeal to the people and a long catalog of parliamentary grievances against the king. It passed by a narrow margin, further inflaming public opinion in London against Charles. The king's remaining support in Parliament eroded in January 1642, when he tried to arrest five members on charges of treason. The five escaped, and the stage was set for wider violence. The king withdrew from London, unsure he could defend himself there, and began to raise an army. In mid-1642, the kingdom stood at the brink of civil war.

SECTION SUMMARY

- France suffered through more than thirty years of civil war after 1562, caused by religious conflict, weak rulers, and powerful nobility.

- The French religious wars ended in the 1590s, when war-weary elites rallied behind the talented king Henry IV; Henry decreed religious toleration in the Edict of Nantes.

- After Henry, religious and political conflict broke out again, but the king's minister, Cardinal Richelieu, successfully reinforced royal authority.

- Elizabeth I of England weathered religious and political tensions at home and challenges from abroad during her long reign.

- James I and Charles I struggled with limited financial resources, unpopular policies, and religious division.

- Parliamentary resistance to Charles's authority and policies led England to a political crisis in 1640.

THE HOLY ROMAN EMPIRE AND THE THIRTY YEARS' WAR

Why did war erupt again within the Holy Roman Empire and what was the significance of the conflict?

The Holy Roman Empire enjoyed a period of comparative quiet after the Peace of Augsburg halted religious and political wars in 1555. The 1555 agreement had permitted rulers of the various states within the empire to impose either Catholicism or Lutheranism in their lands. By the early seventeenth century, however, fresh causes of instability brought about renewed fighting. One factor was the rise of Calvinism, for which no provision had been necessary in 1555. Also destabilizing was the attempt by the Austrian Habsburgs to reverse the successes of Protestantism, both in their own lands and in the empire at large, and to solidify their control of their own diverse territories. The result was a devastating conflict known as the **Thirty Years' War** (1618–1648).

Like conflicts elsewhere in Europe, the Thirty Years' War reflected religious tensions, regionalism versus centralizing forces, and dynastic and strategic rivalries between rulers. As a result of the war, the empire was eclipsed as a political unit by the regional powers that composed it.

Thirty Years' War Destructive war (1618–1648) involving most European countries but fought in Germany, resulting from religious tensions, regionalism versus centralizing forces, and dynastic and strategic rivalries between rulers.

Fragile Peace in the Holy Roman Empire, 1556–1618

The Austrian Habsburgs ruled over a diverse group of territories in the Holy Roman Empire, as well as northwestern Hungary. On his abdication in 1556, Emperor Charles V granted the Habsburg lands in the Holy Roman Empire to his brother, Ferdinand (see the chart on page 415), who was duly crowned emperor when Charles died in 1558.

MAP 15.3—Europe During the Thirty Years' War, 1618–1648
The Thirty Years' War was fought largely within the borders of the Holy Roman Empire. It was the result of conflicts within the empire as well as the meddling of neighbors for their own strategic advantages.

Though largely contiguous, Ferdinand's territories comprised independent duchies and kingdoms. In addition to the Habsburgs' ancestral lands (separate territories more or less equivalent to modern Austria in extent), Ferdinand also ruled the non-German lands of Bohemia (the core of the modern Czech Republic) and Hungary (see **MAP 15.3**). Both kingdoms bestowed their crowns by election and had chosen Ferdinand, the first Habsburg to rule them, in separate elections in the 1520s and 1530s. Most of Hungary was now under Ottoman control, but the kingdom of Bohemia, with its rich capital, Prague, was a wealthy center of population and culture.

Unlike the Netherlands, each of these linguistically and culturally diverse lands was still governed by its own distinct institutions. Moreover, unlike their Spanish cousins, the Austrian Habsburgs made no attempt to impose religious uniformity in the late sixteenth century. Ferdinand was Catholic but tolerant of reform efforts within the church. Both he and his son, Maximilian II (r. 1564–1576), believed that an eventual reunion of the Catholic and Protestant faiths might be possible. During his reign, Maximilian worked to keep religious peace in the empire as a whole and granted limited rights of worship to Protestant subjects in the Habsburgs' own lands. Catholicism and many varieties of Protestantism flourished side by side in Maximilian's domains, particularly in Hungary and, especially, Bohemia, which had experienced a religious reform movement under Jan Hus in the fifteenth century.

Maximilian's son, Rudolf II (r. 1576–1612), shared the religious style of his father and grand-father. He patronized education and the arts and sponsored the work of scientists. Yet, Rudolf was a weak leader politically and was challenged by his brother and ambitious cousins for control both of Habsburg lands and of the empire itself. Meanwhile, the resurgence of Catholicism in the wake of the Council of Trent (1545–1563) had begun to shift the religious balance. Members of the Jesuit order arrived in Habsburg lands in the reign of Maximilian. Tough-minded and well trained, they established Catholic schools and became confessors and preachers to the upper classes. Self-confident Catholicism emerged as a potent form of cultural identity among the German-speaking ruling classes, and thus, as a religious impetus to further political consolidation of all the Habsburg territories.

Resurgent Catholicism spread in the empire as a whole, too, and many Catholic princes believed they might now eliminate Protestantism, as their ancestors had failed to do. Like the English under Elizabeth, Habsburg subjects and peoples in the empire had enjoyed a period of calm in political and religious matters. Now, as in England, the stage was set for conflict of both kinds.

The Thirty Years' War, 1618–1648

The Thirty Years' War was touched off in 1618 by a revolt against Habsburg rule in the kingdom of Bohemia. Rudolf II had made Bohemia's bustling capital, Prague, his imperial capital. Its powerful Protestant community had wrested formal recognition of its right to worship from Rudolf and his younger brother, Matthias (r. 1612–1619).

Matthias was quickly succeeded by his cousin Ferdinand II (r. 1619–1637), who did not honor these agreements. Educated by the Jesuits, Ferdinand sincerely believed that reimposing Catholicism was his Christian duty; he once stated that he would "sooner beg than rule over heretics."[4] He would not tolerate the political independence of nobles and towns in Bohemia or the religious pluralism that independence defended. As Philip II had done in the Netherlands, Ferdinand appointed a council to govern in his name, which enforced unpopular policies, such as denying the right to build Protestant churches and barring non-Catholics from serving in government.

On May 23, 1618, delegates to a Protestant assembly that had unsuccessfully petitioned Ferdinand to honor his predecessors' earlier guarantees marched to the palace in Prague where his officials met. After a confrontation over their demands, the delegates "tried" the officials on the spot for treason and, literally, threw them out of the palace window. The incident became known as the "Defenestration of Prague" (from the Latin *fenestra*, or "window"). (The officials survived because they fell into a pile of garbage in the moat.) The rebels set up their own government.

This upstart Bohemian government officially deposed Ferdinand and elected a new Bohemian king in 1619: Frederick, the Protestant elector of the Palatinate. His election had implications for the Holy Roman Empire as a whole because his territories in west-central Germany, called the Lower and Upper Palatinate, conveyed the right to be one of the seven electors who chose the emperor.

The revolt in Bohemia set off a wider war because foreign rulers also felt their interests to be involved. The English king, James I, supported Frederick because Frederick was married to his daughter. Spain's supply routes north from Italy to the Netherlands passed next to Frederick's lands in western Germany. France's first interest was its rivalry with Spain; thus, France kept its

The Defenestration of Prague This contemporary print memorializes the events of May 23, 1618. Bohemian Protestants "tried" two imperial officials for violating agreements that safeguarded their religious liberties. The two officials and their secretary were thrown out of the windows of Prague castle. (Corbis)

eye on the border principalities that were strategically important to Spain and wanted to keep Protestant, as well as Catholic, princes within the empire strong enough to thwart Austrian Habsburg ambitions. Thus, from the outset, the war was a conflict not only over the Habsburgs' power in their own lands, but also over the balance of religious and political power in the empire and in Europe (see **MAP 15.3**).

Ferdinand secured aid from Catholic princes, including his cousin, King Philip III (r. 1598–1621) of Spain, by promising them Frederick's lands in the Palatinate. By the fall of 1620, a Catholic army faced Bohemian rebels who had received little support as yet from fellow Protestants. The Battle of White Mountain, in November, was a complete Catholic victory.

Despite the rout, fighting did not end, but instead became more widespread. The 1609 truce between Spain and the Netherlands expired in 1621, and the nearby Lower Palatinate, now in Spanish hands, offered a staging point for Spanish forces and thus threatened the peace in that corner of the empire. Claiming to be a Protestant champion, the Protestant king of Denmark, Christian IV (r. 1588–1648), who was also duke of Holstein in northern Germany, entered the fight. He wanted to gain greater control over German Baltic seaports and to defend his northern German territories against any Catholic aggressors. Christian received little help from fellow Protestants, however. The Dutch were busy with Spain, the English were wary of fighting after Frederick's defeat, and Denmark's rival, the Swedes, were not interested in helping Danish ambitions in the Baltic.

Just as Protestant powers did not always support each other, neither did Catholic ones. When imperial forces defeated Denmark's armies in 1626, Catholic princes became alarmed at the possibility of greater imperial power in northern Germany. Led by the duke of Bavaria, they arranged a truce that resulted in Denmark's withdrawal from the fighting on relatively generous terms.

The Danish king's rival, Gustav Adolf, king of Sweden (r. 1611–1632), hoping to gain territory along the Baltic seacoast, now assumed the role of Protestant leader. Gustav Adolf was an innovative commander and his campaigns were capped by a victory over an imperial army at Breitenfeld, in Saxony, in 1631. However, the tide turned in favor of Ferdinand's forces when Gustav Adolf was killed in battle the following year; further imperial victories led to the Peace of Prague (1635), a general peace treaty favorable to Catholics.

The Peace of Prague brought only a temporary peace, however, because Ferdinand died shortly afterwards and French involvement increased now that other anti-Habsburg forces had been eclipsed. France seized imperial territory along its own eastern border and subsidized continued war within the empire by channeling monies to Protestant princes and mercenaries there. The fighting dragged on. By the end of the Thirty Years' War, order had disintegrated so completely in the wake of the marauding armies that both Catholic and Protestant rulers willingly allied with any power necessary, even religious enemies, to safeguard their states.

A comprehensive peace treaty became possible when France withdrew its sponsorship of the fighting in order to concentrate on its conflict with Spain, namely, the continued rivalry with the Spanish Habsburgs for control of territory along France's eastern and northern borders and in Italy. The French wanted only a workable balance of power in the empire, which had been achieved with a convincing defeat of imperial forces in 1645. Negotiations for peace began among war-weary states of the empire in 1643 and resulted in a group of agreements known as the **Peace of Westphalia** (west-FAIL-yuh) in 1648.

Peace of Westphalia
Treaty that ended the Thirty Years' War in 1648. The principalities within the Holy Roman Empire were recognized as virtually autonomous, severely weakening the power of the emperor.

The Effects of the War

The Thirty Years' War ruined the economy and decimated the population in many parts of the empire and had long-term political consequences for the empire as a whole. One reason for the war's devastation was a novel application of firepower to warfare that increased both the size of armies and their deadly force in battle. This was the use of volley fire, the arrangement of foot soldiers in parallel lines so that one line of men could fire while another reloaded. This tactic, pioneered in the Netherlands around the turn of the century, was refined by Gustav Adolf of Sweden. He amassed large numbers of troops and increased the rate of fire so that a virtually continuous barrage was maintained. He also used maneuverable field artillery to protect the massed infantry from cavalry charges.

Following Gustav Adolf's lead, armies of all the major states adopted these new offensive tactics. But defensive expertise—as in holding fortresses—also remained important, and pitched battles still tended to be part of sieges. The costs in resources and human life of this kind of warfare reached unheard-of dimensions. Compounding these effects of battle was the behavior of troops hired by enterprising mercenary generals, for whom loyalty to the princes who paid them took a back seat to personal advancement. They were contracted to provide and supply troops and thus were more willing than the princes would have been to allow armies to live "economically" on plunder. European states could field large armies but had not yet evolved the mechanisms fully to fund, and thus control, them. Popular printed literature and court drama both condemned the horrors of the war.

Where fighting had been concentrated, as in parts of Saxony, between one-third and one-half of the inhabitants of rural villages and major towns may have disappeared. Many starved, were caught in the fighting, or were killed by marauding soldiers. Some people migrated to other regions or joined the armies simply in order to survive.

The Peace of Westphalia was one of the most important outcomes of the war. The various individual treaties composing the Peace effectively put an end to religious war in the empire. Calvinism was recognized as a tolerated religion. The requirement that all subjects must follow their ruler's faith was retained, but some leeway was allowed for those who now found themselves under new rulers.

In political matters, the treaties reflected Swedish successes by granting them territory on the Baltic coast. France gained the important towns of Metz, Toul, and Verdun on its eastern border. Spain formally recognized the independence of the Netherlands. The son of Frederick, Protestant king of Bohemia, received back the smaller of the two Palatine territories that his father had held. The Upper Palatinate—as well as

The Horrors of War   The painter of this scene of soldiers plundering a farm in the Thirty Years' War was himself a veteran of Spanish campaigns in the Netherlands. The scene he depicts was commonplace in this era of poorly-supplied troops: soldiers loot a household, killing peasants who refused to hand over their own stores of food   (Soldiers Plundering a Farm during the Thirty Years' War, 1620 (oil on wood), Vrancx, Sebastian (1573–1647)/Deutsches Historisches Museum, Berlin, Germany/©DHM/The Bridgeman Art Library)

- The Holy Roman Empire was relatively peaceful until destabilized by the spread of Calvinism and the ambition of the Austrian Habsburgs to extend their political and religious control within the empire.

- The Thirty Years' War started in Bohemia (modern Czech Republic) when local leaders challenged Habsburg policies.

- The Bohemian revolt led to a wider war because many rulers, inside and outside Germany, had a stake in the balance of religious and political power there.

- Large armies of mercenaries caused widespread devastation in certain areas of Germany.

- The Peace of Westphalia established a new balance of power between states within the Holy Roman Empire, but the empire itself declined as a political entity.

the right to be a new elector of the emperor—was given to the Catholic duke of Bavaria.

The most important political outcome of the peace, however, was a new balance of power in the empire. Most of the major Catholic and Protestant rulers extended their territories at the expense of smaller principalities and cities. The principalities within the empire were acknowledged, in the peace, to be virtually autonomous, both from the emperor and from one another. In addition, the constitution of the empire was changed to make it very difficult for one prince or a group of princes to disrupt the peace in their own interests. As a result, the agreements at Westphalia were the beginning of one hundred years of peace within the Holy Roman Empire.

Another outcome was that the Habsburgs, though weakened as emperors, were strengthened as rulers of their own hereditary lands on the eastern fringes of the empire. They moved their capital back to Vienna from Prague, and the government of their hereditary lands gained in importance as administration of the empire waned.

ECONOMIC CHANGE AND SOCIAL TENSIONS

What caused the economic stresses of these decades and how did ordinary people cope with them?

Religious strife disrupted the everyday lives of whole communities in the late sixteenth and early seventeenth centuries. Wars devastated many areas of western Europe and contributed to severe economic decline in parts of the Low Countries (the Netherlands), France, and the Holy Roman Empire. But other factors, most notably a steady rise in prices, also played a role in the dramatic economic and social changes of the century after 1550. Economic changes altered power relations in cities, in the countryside, and in the relationship of both to central governments. Ordinary people managed their economic difficulties in a variety of ways: they sought new sources of work; they protested against burdensome taxes; sometimes they found scapegoats for their distress among their neighbors.

Economic Transformation and Social Change

The most obvious economic change was an unrelenting rise in prices. Sixteenth-century observers attributed rising prices to the inflationary effects of the influx of silver from Spanish territories in the New World. Historians now believe that European causes may also have helped trigger this **price revolution**. Steady population growth caused a relative shortage of goods, particularly food, and the result was higher prices. Between 1550 and 1600, with local variations, the price of grain may have risen between 50 and 100 percent, and sometimes more, in cities throughout Europe. Wages did not keep pace with prices; historians estimate that wages lost between one-tenth and one-fourth of their value by the end of the century.

Wealth in the countryside was also becoming more stratified. Population growth caused many peasant farms to be subdivided for numerous children, creating tiny plots that could not support the families who lived on them. Countless peasants lost what lands they had to wealthy investors who lent them money to rent more land or to buy seed and tools and then reclaimed the land when the peasants failed to repay. Land rents rose because of high demand and some peasants were unable to rent land at all. To survive, they sought work as day laborers for rich landlords or more prosperous farmers. Many found their way to cities, where they swelled the ranks of the poor. In eastern Europe, peasants faced other dilemmas, for their lands had a different relationship to the wider European economy. The more densely urbanized western Europe, whose wealth controlled the patterns of trade, sought bulk goods, particularly grain, from eastern Germany,

price revolution Steady rise in prices in the sixteenth and seventeenth centuries, resulting from population growth and the importation of precious metals from Spain's New World territories.

Poland, and Lithuania. Thus, there was an economic incentive for landowners in eastern Europe to bind peasants to the land, just as the desire of their rulers for greater cooperation had granted the landlords more power. Serfdom now spread in eastern Europe, while precisely the opposite condition—a more mobile labor force—grew in the West.

The growth of markets around Europe and in Spanish possessions overseas, as well as population growth within Europe, had a marked effect on patterns of production and the lives of artisans. Production of cloth on a large scale for export, for example, now required large amounts of capital—much more than a typical guild craftsman could amass. Cloth production was increasingly controlled by new investor-producers with access to distant markets. These entrepreneurs bought up large amounts of wool and hired it out to be cleaned, spun into thread, and woven into cloth by wage laborers in urban workshops or by pieceworkers in their homes. Thousands of poor women and men in the countryside around towns supported their families in this way. In towns, guilds still regulated most trades but, as their share of production declined, they could not accommodate the numbers of artisans who sought to join them. Fewer and fewer apprentices and journeymen could expect to become master artisans. The masters began to treat apprentices virtually as wage laborers, at times, letting them go during slow periods.

Another consequence of the circumstances guild members faced was the effort to reduce competition at the expense of the artisans' own mothers, sisters, and daughters. Increasingly, widows were forbidden to continue their husbands' enterprises, though they headed from 10 to 15 percent of households in many trades. Women had traditionally practiced many trades, but rarely followed the formal progress from apprenticeship to master status, since they usually combined work of this kind with household production. Outright exclusion of women from guilds occurred as early as the thirteenth century, but now began regularly to appear in guild statutes. Town governments also restricted women's participation even in work they had long dominated, such as selling in markets. Working women thus began to have difficulty supporting themselves if single or widowed and difficulty supporting their children.

Profits from expanding production and trade and from higher land values made more capital available to wealthy urban or landholding families to invest in the countryside, by buying land outright on which to live like **gentry** or by making loans to desperate peasants. Enterprising landholders raised rents on farming and grazing land wherever they could, or they converted land to the production of wool, grain, and other cash crops destined for distant markets.

As a result, a stratum of wealthy, educated, and socially ambitious "new gentry," as these families were called in England, began to grow. Many of the men of these families were royal officeholders. Many bought titles of nobility or were granted nobility as a benefit of their offices. They often lent money to royal governments. The monumental expense of wars made becoming a lender to government, as well as to individuals, an attractive way to live off personal capital.

No one would have confused these up-and-coming gentry with warrior-aristocrats from old families, but the social distinctions between them are less important (to us) than what they had in common: legal privilege, the security of landownership, and a cooperative relationship with the monarchy. Monarchs deliberately favored the new gentry as counterweights to independent aristocrats.

City governments also changed character. Town councils became dominated by small numbers of privileged families, now more likely to live from landed wealth, like gentry, than from trade or manufacture. By the beginning of the seventeenth century, traditional guild control of government had been eliminated in many places. The long medieval tradition of towns serving as independent corporate bodies had come to an end.

gentry Class of wealthy, educated, and socially ambitious families in western Europe, especially England, whose political and economic power was greatly enhanced during the sixteenth century.

Coping with Poverty and Violence

The common people of Europe did not submit passively to either the economic difficulties or the religious and political crises of their day. Whatever their religion, common people took the initiative in attacking members of other faiths to rid their communities of them. Heretics were considered to be spiritual pollution that might provoke God's wrath, and ordinary citizens believed that it was up to them to eliminate heretics if the state failed to do so.

Ordinary people fought in wars not only from conviction, but also from the need for self-defense and from economic choice. It was ordinary people who defended the walls of towns, dug siege works, and manned artillery batteries. Although nobles remained military leaders, armies consisted mostly of infantry made up of common people, not mounted knights. Women were part of armies, too. Much of the day-to-day work of finding food and firewood, cleaning guns, and repairing clothing was done by women looking after their husbands and lovers among the troops. Landless farm hands, day laborers, and out-of-work artisans joined armies because having work was attractive enough to outweigh the dangers of military life. Desertion was common; nothing more than the rumor that a soldier's home village was threatened might prompt a man to abandon his post. Battle-hardened troops could threaten their commanders, not only with desertion, but with mutiny. Occasionally, mutinies were brutally suppressed; more often, they were successful and troops received some of their back wages.

The devastation of religious war led to both peasant rebellions and urban uprisings. Peasants and townspeople rebelled because of high taxes and food shortages. Elites participated too; former soldiers, prosperous farmers, or even noble landlords whose economic fortunes were tied to peasant profits led some rural revolts. Rebels sometimes seized property—for example, they might distribute looted bread among themselves—and occasionally killed officials. Their protests rarely generated lasting political change and were usually brutally quashed.

Governments at all levels tried to cope with the increasing problem of poverty by changing the administration and scale of poor relief. In both Catholic and Protestant Europe, caring for the poor became more institutionalized and systematic, and more removed from religious impulses. Governments established public almshouses and poorhouses to dispense food or to care for orphans or the destitute in towns throughout Catholic and Protestant Europe. At first, these institutions reflected an optimistic vision of an ideal Christian community caring for its neediest members. But by 1600, the distribution of food was accompanied by attempts to distinguish "deserving" from "undeserving" poor, by an insistence that the poor work for their ration of food, and even by an effort to force the poor to live apart, in poorhouses.

A Beggar is Whipped Through the Streets   In this sixteenth-century woodcut, probably made in England, a poor man is tied up and led through the streets of a town while being whipped on his bare back. The gallows in the distance, just outside the city gates, imply that the poor were now thought of as dangerous outlaws.   ("A beggar is tied and whipped through the streets," c.1567 (woodcut) (b/w photo), English School, (16th century)/Private Collection/The Bridgeman Art Library)

These efforts were not uniformly successful. Although begging was outlawed by Catholic and Protestant city governments alike, it was never thoroughly suppressed. Catholic religious orders often resisted efforts at regulating their charitable work, even when they were imposed by Catholic governments. Nonetheless, the trend was clear. From viewing poverty as a fact of life and a lesson in Christian humility, European elites began to see it as a social problem and poor people as needing to be controlled.

The Hunt for Witches

Between approximately 1550 and 1650, Europe saw a dramatic increase in the persecution of women and men for witchcraft. Approximately one hundred thousand people were tried and about sixty thousand executed. The surge in witch-hunting was closely linked to communities' religious concerns and also to the social tensions that resulted from economic difficulties.

Certain types of witchcraft had long existed in Europe. So-called black magic of various kinds—one peasant casting a spell on another peasant's cow—had been common since the Middle Ages. The practice now seemed dangerous, especially to elites, who linked black magic to Devil worship. Catholic leaders and legal scholars began to advance such theories in the fifteenth century, and by the late sixteenth century, both Catholic and Protestant elites viewed a witch not only as someone who might cast harmful spells, but also as a heretic.

The impetus for most individual accusations of witchcraft came from within the communities where the "witch" lived— that is, from common people. Usually targeted were solitary or unpopular people whose difficult relationships with fellow villagers made them seem likely sources of evil. Often, such a person had practiced black magic (or had been suspected of doing so) for years, and the villagers took action only when faced with a community crisis, such as an epidemic.

Because they were often prompted by village disasters, individual accusations of witchcraft increased in this period in response to the crises that beset many communities. In addition, isolated accusations often started localized frenzies of active hunting for other witches. These more widespread hunts were driven, in part, by the anxieties of local elites about disorder and heresy and were facilitated by contemporary legal procedures that they applied. These procedures permitted lax rules of evidence and the use of torture to extract confessions. Torture or the threat of torture led most accused witches to "confess" and to name accomplices or other "witches." In this way, a single initial accusation could lead to dozens of prosecutions. In regions where procedures for appealing convictions were fragile or nonexistent, witch-hunts could expand with alarming speed and dozens of "witches" might be identified and executed before the whirlwind subsided. Aggressive hunts were common, for example, in the small principalities and imperial cities of the Holy Roman Empire, which were largely independent of higher political and judicial authority. (See the box, "The Written Record: A City Official Worries About Witch-Hunting.")

The majority of accused witches were women. Lacking legal, social, and political resources, women may have been more likely than men to use black magic for self-protection or advancement. Women's work often made them vulnerable to charges of witchcraft, since families' food supplies and routine medicines passed through women's hands. The deaths of young children or of domestic animals, such as a milk cow, were among the most common triggers for witchcraft accusation. The increase in poverty during the late sixteenth and early seventeenth centuries made poor women frequent targets of witch-hunts.

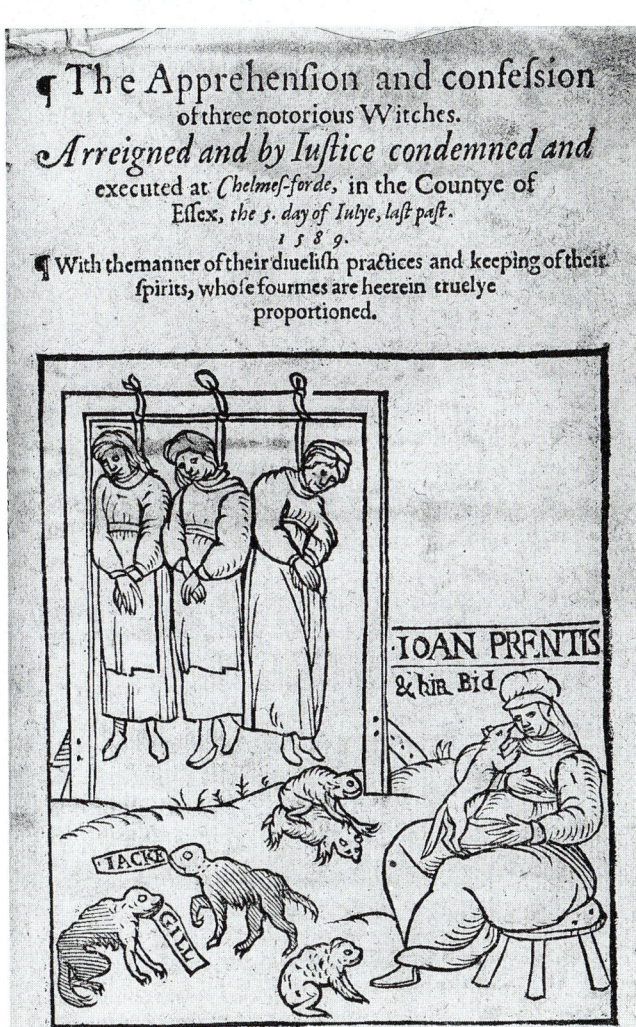

Publicizing Witch Trials Printed pamphlets, such as this one describing the execution of three women in Essex, England, spread the news of local "outbreaks" of witchcraft. One of the women, Joan Prentis, is also depicted surrounded by her animal familiars. The ferret in Joan's lap, the pamphlet relates, was the Devil himself in animal form. (Lambeth Palace Library)

A City Official Worries About Witch-Hunting

In this letter written to a friend in 1629, the chancellor to the prince-bishop of the German city of Würzburg describes the witch-hunt in his community.

As to the affair of the witches, which Your Grace thinks brought to an end before this, it has started up afresh, and no words can do justice to it. Ah, the woe and misery of it—there are still four hundred in the city, high and low, of every rank and sex, nay, even clerics, so strongly accused that they may be arrested at any hour. It is true that, of the people of my Gracious Prince here, some out of all the offices and faculties must be executed: clerics, elected councilors and doctors, city officials, court assessors several of whom Your Grace knows. There are law students to be arrested. The Prince-Bishop has over forty students who are soon to be pastors; among them thirteen or fourteen are said to be witches. A few days ago a Dean was arrested; two others who were summoned have fled.

The notary of our Church consistory, a very learned man, was yesterday arrested and put to the torture. In a word, a third part of the city is surely involved. The richest, most attractive, most prominent of the clergy are already executed. A week ago a maiden of nineteen was executed, of whom it is everywhere said that she was the fairest in the whole city, and was held by everybody a girl of singular modesty and purity. She will be followed by seven or eight others of the best and most attractive persons. . . . And thus many are put to death for renouncing God and being at the witch-dances, against whom nobody has ever else spoken a word.

To conclude this wretched matter, there are children of three or four years, to the number of three hundred, who are said to have had intercourse with the Devil. I have seen put to death children of seven, promising students of ten, twelve, fourteen and fifteen of the nobles—but I cannot and must not write more of this misery. There are persons of yet higher rank, whom you know, and would marvel to hear of, nay, would scarcely believe it; let justice be done. . . .

P.S. Though there are many wonderful and terrible things happening it is beyond doubt that, at a place called the Fraw-Rengberg, the Devil in person, with eight thousand of his followers, held an assembly and celebrated mass before them all, administering to his audience (that is, the witches) turnip-rinds and pairings in place of the Holy Eucharist. There took place not only foul but most horrible and hideous blasphemies, whereof I shudder to write. It is also true that they all vowed not to be enrolled in the Book of Life, but all agreed to be inscribed by a notary who is well known to me and my colleagues. We hope, too, that the book in which they are enrolled will yet be found, and there is no little search being made for it.

QUESTIONS

1. Which townspeople are victims of the witch-hunt?

2. Does the document reveal why the hunt is continuing? Who is in charge?

3. What is the author's attitude toward the events he describes? Does the chancellor believe that witchcraft exists?

Source: Alan C. Kors and Edward Peters, eds., *Witchcraft in Europe, 1100–1700: A Documentary History* (Philadelphia: University of Pennsylvania, 1972), pp. 251–252. Reprinted by permission of the University of Pennsylvania Press.

Both Christian dogma and humanistic writing portrayed women as morally weaker than men and thus more susceptible to the Devil's enticements. Writings on witchcraft described Devil worship in sexual terms, and the prosecution of witches had a voyeuristic, sexual dimension. The bodies of accused witches were searched for the "Devil's mark"—a blemish thought to be Satan's imprint. In some regions, women accounted for 80 percent of those prosecuted and executed. A dynamic of gender stereotyping was not always at work, however; in other regions, prosecutions were more evenly divided between men and women, and occasionally, men made up the majority of those accused.

The widespread witch-hunts virtually ended by the late seventeenth century, in part, because the intellectual energies of elites shifted from religious to scientific thought. The practice of witchcraft continued among common folk, although accusations of one neighbor by another never again reached the level of these crisis-ridden decades.

SECTION SUMMARY

- A price revolution caused a decline in the value of wages in the sixteenth century.

- Elites, particularly new gentry families, could grow rich by controlling increasingly scarce and valuable land.

- Economic hardship led common people to seek jobs in cities, join armies, and protest taxation.

- Persecutions for witchcraft dramatically increased between 1550 and 1650, reflecting both common people's search for scapegoats for their hard lives and elites' anxiety about controlling common people's religion.

WRITING, DRAMA, AND ART IN AN AGE OF UPHEAVAL

In what ways do the literature and art of this period reflect the political, social, and religious conflicts of the age?

Both imaginative literature and speculative writing, such as political theory, bear the stamp of their times. In the late sixteenth and early seventeenth centuries, political speculation concerned questions of the legitimacy of rulers and of the relationship of political power to divine authority—urgent problems in an age when religious division threatened the very foundations of states. Authors and rulers alike often relied on still-prevalent oral modes of communication to convey their ideas. Indeed, some of the greatest literature and some of the most effective political statements of the period were presented as drama and not conveyed in print. Nevertheless, literacy continued to spread and led to greater opportunities for knowledge and reflection. The medium of print became increasingly important to political life. In the visual arts, the dramatic impulse combined with religious purposes to create works that conveyed both power and emotion.

Literacy and Literature

Traditional oral culture changed slowly under the impact of the spread of printing, education, and literacy. Works of literature from the late sixteenth and early seventeenth centuries incorporate material from traditional folktales and reflect the coexistence of oral and literate culture. In *Don Quixote* (key-HO-tay), by Spain's Miguel de Cervantes (sair-VAHN-tayz) (1547–1616), the title character and his companion, Sancho Panza, have a long discussion about oral and literate traditions. The squire Panza speaks in the style that was customary in oral culture—a rather roundabout and repetitive style, which enabled the speaker and listener to remember what was said. Much of the richness of *Don Quixote* is due to the interweaving of prose styles and topical concerns from throughout Cervantes' culture—from the oral world of peasants to the refined world of court life. Yet, what enabled Cervantes to create this rich portrayal was his own highly developed literacy and the awareness of language that literacy made possible.

Much literature in this period stressed the value of education—particularly, by means of the humanist recovery of ancient wisdom, a new vision of what it meant to be a cultivated and disciplined man of the world. The French author Michel de Montaigne (1533–1592) was the epitome of the reflective gentleman. Montaigne (mon-TEN-yuh) was a judge in the parlement (law court) of Bordeaux. In 1570, he resigned from the court and retired to his small château, where he wrote his *Essais* (from which we derive the word *essays*), a collection of short reflections that were revolutionary in both form and content. Montaigne invented writing in the form of a sketch, an "attempt" (the literal meaning of *essai*) that enabled him to combine self-reflection with formal analysis.

Owing to the spread of printing, Montaigne had a virtually unparalleled opportunity to compare different events, values, and cultures through reading a wide variety of printed texts. His reflections range from the destructiveness of the French civil wars to the consequences of European exploration of the New World. Toward all of these events, Montaigne was able to achieve an analytic detachment remarkable for his day. For example, he noted ironically that Europeans labeled New World peoples "savages," yet, they committed seemingly endless and wanton violence against those "savages" and one another. (See the box "The Global Record: Montaigne Discusses Barbarity in the New World and the Old.") Montaigne's essays also reveal self-reflection—a distancing from himself. This distancing was also the result of literacy and leisure, which enabled him to enjoy long periods of solitude and reflection in the company of other solitary, book-bound voices. Montaigne's works mark the beginning of what we know as the "invention" of private life, in which an individual is defined more by internal character and personality traits than by social role.

The Great Age of Theater

The works of the great English poet and playwright William Shakespeare (1564–1616) are still compelling to us because of the profundity of the questions asked about love, honor, and political legitimacy; he asked these questions in terms appropriate to his own own day. One of his favorite

Montaigne Discusses Barbarity in the New World and the Old

In one of his most famous essays, the French jurist and essayist Michel de Montaigne (1533–1592) ironically compares the customs of Native Americans with the customs of his own society. Information about Native Americans came from published reports of European voyages and from news of individual Native Americans who had journeyed (usually forcibly) to Europe. Europeans' encounters with peoples in the New World gave Montaigne a vantage point from which to criticize his own society.

They have their wars with [other] nations, to which they go quite naked, with no other arms than bows or wooden spears. . . . It is astonishing that firmness they show in their combats, which never end but in slaughter and bloodshed; for, as to routs and terror, they know nothing of either.

Each man brings back as his trophy the head of the enemy he has killed. . . . After they have treated their prisoner well for a long time with all the hospitality they can think of . . . they kill him with their swords. This done, they roast him and eat him in common and send some pieces to their absent friends.

I am not sorry that we notice the barbarous horror of such acts, but am heartily sorry that . . . we should be so blind to our own. I think there is more barbarity . . . in tearing by tortures and the rack a body still full of feeling, in roasting a man bit by bit, having him bitten and mangled by dogs (as we have not only read but seen within fresh memory . . . among neighbors and fellow citizens, and what is worse, on the pretext of piety and religion).

Three of these men (were brought to France) . . . and [someone] wanted to know what they had found most amazing. . . . They said that in the first place they thought it very strange that so many grown men, bearded, strong and armed who were around the king . . . should submit to obey a child [the young French king]. . . . Second (they have a way in their language of speaking of men as halves of one another), they had noticed that there were among us men full and gorged with all sorts of good things, and that their other halves were beggars at their doors, emaciated with hunger and poverty; and they thought it strange that these needy halves could endure such injustice.

QUESTIONS

1. What practices in the two cultures is Montaigne commenting on in this excerpt?

2. In what ways does he find Native American culture admirable by comparison to his own? What aspects of his own culture is he criticizing?

3. How are contemporary events and conditions in France reflected in Montaigne's remarks?

Source: Donald M. Frame, trans., *The Complete Essays of Montaigne* (Stanford, Calif.: Stanford University Press, 1948), pp. 153, 155–159. Reprinted by permission of the publisher.

themes—evident in *Hamlet* and *Macbeth*—is the legitimacy of rulers. He also explored the contradictions in values between the growing commercial world he saw around him and the older, seemingly more stable world of feudal society. Subtle political commentary distinguishes Shakespeare's later writings near and shortly after the death of Elizabeth in 1603, when political and economic problems were becoming increasingly troublesome. In *Coriolanus*, he portrays commoners as poor but not ignorant; they are in fact fully rational and capable of analyzing their situation—perhaps more capable, Shakespeare hints, than their ruler. The play is safely set in ancient Rome, but the social and political tensions it depicts clearly applied to the Elizabethan present.

Shakespeare's extraordinary career was possible because his life coincided with the rise of professional theater. In the capitals of England and Spain, professional theaters first opened in the 1570s. Some drama was produced at court or in aristocratic households, but most public theaters drew large and very mixed audiences, including the poorest city dwellers. Playwrights, including Shakespeare, often wrote in teams, under great pressure to keep acting companies supplied with material. The best-known dramatist in Spain, Lope de Vega (LOW-pah day VAY-guh) (1562–1635), wrote more than fifteen hundred works on a wide range of topics. Although religious themes remained popular in Spanish theater, as an echo of medieval drama, most plays in England and Spain treated secular subjects and, as in *Coriolanus*, disguised political commentary.

Over time, theater became increasingly restricted to aristocratic circles. In England, Puritan criticism of the "immorality" of public performance drove actors and playwrights to seek royal patronage. The first professional theater to open in Paris, in 1629, quickly became dependent on Cardinal Richelieu's patronage. Inevitably, as court patronage grew in importance, the wide range of subjects treated in plays began to narrow to those of aristocratic concern, such as family honor and martial glory. These themes are depicted in the works of the Spaniard Pedro Calderón (kall-day-ROHN) (1600–1681), who wrote for his enthusiastic patron, Philip IV, and of the Frenchman Pierre Corneille (kore-NAY) (1606–1684), whose great tragedy of aristocratic life, *Le Cid*, was one of the early successes of the seventeenth-century French theater.

Drama's significance as an art form is reflected in its impact on the development of music: The opera, which weds drama to music, was invented in Italy in the early seventeenth century. The first great work in this genre is generally acknowledged to be *Orfeo* (*Orpheus*, 1607) by Claudio Monteverdi (mon-tay-VAIR-dee) (1567–1643). Opera, like drama, reflected the influence of humanism in its secular themes and in its emulation of Greek drama, which had used both words and music. The practice of music itself changed under the dramatic impulse. Monteverdi was the first master of a new musical style known as "monody," which emphasizes the progression of chords. Monodic music is inherently dramatic, creating a sense of forward movement, expectation, and resolution.

Drama, Art, and Political Thought

Whether produced on a public stage or at court or in a less formal setting, drama was a favored method of communication in this era because people responded to and made extensive use of the spoken word. Dramatic gesture and storytelling to get a message across were commonplace and were important components of politics.

What we might call "street drama" was a common event. When aristocratic governors entered major towns, such as when Margaret of Parma entered Brussels, an ostentatious formal "entry" was often staged. The dignitary would ride through the main gate, usually beneath a canopy made of luxurious cloth. Costumed townspeople staged brief symbolic dramas, such as of the story of David and Goliath, on the streets; the event might end with an elaborate banquet. A remnant of these proceedings survives today in the ceremony of giving distinguished visitors "the keys to the city," which, in the sixteenth century, really were functional.

Royalty made artful use of ceremony. Royal entries into towns took on an added weight, as did royal funerals and other such occasions. These dramas reinforced political and constitutional assumptions in the minds of witnesses and participants and, over time, there were revealing changes in the representations of royal power. In France, for example, the ritual entry of the king into Paris had originally stressed the participation of the leading guilds, judges, and administrators, symbolizing their active role in governing the city and the kingdom. But in the last half of the sixteenth century, the procession began to glorify the king alone.

Speculation about and celebration of power, as well as dramatic emotion, also occurred in the visual arts—most notably in painting and architecture, in the style now known as **baroque**. Baroque (ba-ROKE) style was a new kind of visual language that could project power and grandeur and simultaneously engage viewers' senses. (See the feature "The Visual Record: Baroque Art.")

The very fact that rulers experimented with self-representation suggests that questions about the nature and extent of royal power were far from settled. Queen Elizabeth I had the particular burden of assuming the throne in a period of great instability. Hence, she paid a great deal of attention to the image of herself that she conveyed in words and authorized to be fashioned in painting. Elizabeth styled herself variously as mother to her people and as a warrior-queen (drawing on ancient myths of Amazon women). More formal speculation about constitutional matters also resulted from the tumult

baroque Style of European art and architecture popular from the late sixteenth to early eighteenth centuries. Baroque art modified Renaissance techniques, adding dynamism and emotional energy, which resulted in works that were both impressively grand and emotionally engaging.

An Image of Royalty This dramatic painting of Charles I on horseback was one of several likenesses of the king painted by the baroque artist Anthony Van Dyck. This painting was originally hung at the end of a long gallery in one of the royal palaces, next to similarly triumphal images of Roman emperors. (The Royal Collection © 2003, Her Majesty Queen Elizabeth II)

Baroque Art

If today, you were to walk through the cathedral in the Belgian city of Antwerp and notice this painting, titled *The Raising of the Cross*, it might not strike you as remarkable. The crucifixion of Jesus is a frequent subject of religious painting, after all. But let us look at the image more carefully. First of all, this is a portrayal not of Jesus on the cross, but rather of the raising of the cross. In other words, it captures a moment of action, not its aftermath. The frame of the painting is filled with action as well. The figures on the left and at the center support the cross and push it up. At the bottom right, we see figures straining at ropes as they pull the cross upright. Our eye is drawn to the movement in the painting, partly by the use of light, which floods the figure of Jesus. We also note the unexpected diagonal position of the crucified figure, and we survey the image in order to make sense of it.

This is a dynamic painting, and simultaneously, an emotionally engaging one. We encounter Jesus not as a static, perhaps already dying, figure on the cross, but at the very moment of his crucifixion. There is also a striking similarity between the figure of Jesus and those of the men who are working hard to accomplish his crucifixion: They are all men, whose muscled bodies are more alike than not. The human pathos of the moment is brought to life.

The image you see before you is one of three panels in a triptych, or three-paneled altarpiece. The left-hand panel depicts Saint John, the Virgin Mary, and others witnessing Jesus' crucifixion. The panel on the right shows a Roman officer watching over his soldiers as they crucify two thieves. Whereas most triptychs of the period contained three unrelated images, here the panels combine to form a single story of the crucifixion.

This altarpiece was executed in 1610 by the influential painter Peter Paul Rubens (1577–1640), a native of Antwerp, in the southern Netherlands. Rubens was one of the great masters of what came to be called the baroque style. Baroque techniques were pioneered in the late sixteenth century in Italy, first in church design, and spread slowly, with many regional variations, especially throughout Catholic Europe, during the seventeenth century. The origin of the term *baroque* has been debated; it may have come from the Portuguese *barroco*, used to describe irregularly shaped pearls. The term, as applied to the arts, was initially derogatory, denoting distortion, illogic, and irregularity. Baroque painting was distinguished by the dramatic use of color and shading and by the dynamic energy of figures.

Baroque artists based their work on Renaissance achievements in representing the human form in a convincing three-dimensional space. But with the strong use of light, movement, and more robust and realistic human figures, these artists enhanced the drama and emotional impact of what they depicted.

Like baroque artists, baroque architects modified the precision, symmetry, and orderliness of Renaissance architecture to produce a sense of greater dynamism in space. Baroque churches, for example, were impressively grand and monumental, yet emotionally engaging at the same time. Façades and interiors were both massive and, through the clever use of architectural and decorative components, suggestive of movement. A good example of this is the work of Gianlorenzo Bernini (bare-NEE-nee) (1598–1680), who designed the portico outside Saint Peter's Basilica in Rome, as well as the highly ornate bronze canopy over the altar inside the basilica. Dramatic illusion in the interior of buildings—such as painting a chapel ceiling with figures receding as if ascending to heaven—was a common device in baroque architecture. One of the primary purposes of baroque architecture and art was to create simultaneously a display of power and an invitation to sensory experience. Baroque art encouraged piety that was not only emotionally involved, and thus satisfying, but also awe-inspired. In this way, it reflected the aims of the Counter-Reformation church, whose leaders were among its most important patrons.

Peter Paul Rubens's early training in Italy shaped him as an artist and established his secondary career as a diplomat. Throughout his life, he undertook diplomatic missions for the Habsburg viceroys in the Spanish Netherlands, gaining artistic commissions wherever he went. Rubens's subject matter varied widely, including church design and decoration, portraiture, and landscape painting, reflecting the fact that baroque art also had important secular applications. Indeed, magnificent baroque palaces symbolized the wealth and power of the elites (see the photos on pages 450 and 458).

Rulers began to employ artists as portrait painters, such as Rubens's pupil Anthony Van Dyck (1599–1641), whose painting of Charles I of England appears on page 435. Because portraits have become so common, we cannot fully appreciate how arresting this image would have been in its day. Like Rubens's *Raising of the Cross*, Van Dyck's image of Charles was an innovative rendering of familiar elements.

of the sixteenth and seventeenth centuries. As we have seen, the Protestant faction in France advanced arguments for the limitation of royal power. Alternative theories enhancing royal authority were offered, principally in support of the Catholic position, though also simply to buttress the beleaguered monarchy itself. The most famous of these appeared in *The Six Books of the Republic* (1576), by the legal scholar Jean Bodin (bo-DAHN) (1530–1596). Bodin was a Catholic, but offered a fundamentally secular perspective on the purposes and source of power within a

Rubens: The Raising of the Cross

(*Onze Lieve Vrouwkwerk, Antwerp Cathedral, Belgium/ Peter Willi/Bridgeman Art Library*)

The image of a ruler on horseback was well known, but it had never been exploited as fully by English monarchs as it had been by rulers on the Continent. This large portrait of the king was designed to be hung at the end of a long palace corridor so that, from a distance, a courtier would have the illusion of actually seeing the king riding proudly through a triumphal arch.* Compare this portrait with the much more stilted one of Elizabeth I on page 422. It is striking how effective the technical and stylistic innovations of baroque art and architecture were in expressing secular, as well as spiritual, power.

QUESTIONS

1. How does baroque art involve the viewer by appealing to senses and emotions?

2. Why was baroque painting effective for conveying political messages, as in Van Dyck's portrait of Charles I?

---

* This discussion draws on the work of Roy Strong, *Van Dyck: Charles I on Horseback* (New York: Viking, 1972), pp. 20–25.

state. His special contribution was a vision of a truly sovereign monarch. Bodin offered a theoretical understanding that is essential to states today and is the ground on which people can claim rights and protection from the state—namely, that there is a final sovereign authority. For Bodin, that authority was the king. Contract theory, devised by French Protestants to legitimize resistance to the monarchy, was abandoned when Henry IV granted toleration to the Huguenots in 1598. In England, theoretical justification of resistance to Charles I was initially limited to

SECTION SUMMARY

- Literacy and access to printed books enabled new levels of self-consciousness and self-reflection, as in the work of Montaigne.

- The rise of professional theater began in the 1570s; drama was a favored means of communication by writers as well as political leaders.

- Shakespeare and other writers and artists reflected on many of the current concerns about legitimate authority, religion, and human life in this period.

- Baroque art appealed to viewers' emotions, but also expressed power and grandeur.

- Political theorist Bodin developed the notion of sovereign authority within the state.

invoking tradition and precedent. Contract theory, as well as other sweeping claims regarding subjects' rights, would be more fully developed later in the century.

Bodin's theory of sovereignty, however, was immediately echoed in other theoretical works, most notably, that of Hugo Grotius (GROW-shus) (1583–1645). A Dutch jurist and diplomat, Grotius developed the first principles of modern international law. He accepted the existence of sovereign states that owed no loyalty to higher authority (such as the papacy) and thus needed new principles to govern their interactions. His major work, *De Jure Belli ac Pacis* (*On the Law of War and Peace*, 1625), was written in response to the turmoil of the Thirty Years' War. Grotius argued that relations between states could be based on respect for treaties voluntarily reached between them. In perhaps his boldest move, he argued that war must be justified, and he developed criteria to distinguish just wars from unjust ones.

CHAPTER SUMMARY

The late sixteenth and early seventeenth centuries were an era of intense struggle over political and religious authority. Rulers everywhere, through a variety of means, tried to buttress and expand their power. They were resisted by traditional centers of power, such as independent-minded nobles and wealthy townspeople. But they were also resisted by the novel challenge of religious dissent, which empowered even common people both to claim a greater right to question authority and to risk more in their attempts to oppose it.

The most powerful monarch of the day, the king of Spain, could not defeat a religious and political rebellion in the prosperous Netherlands, even with the resources of treasure from the New World. France was torn apart by decades of civil war before the Crown was able to impose a workable peace and reassert royal authority. In England, political and religiously inspired challenges to royal authority were contained by Elizabeth I, but not as effectively addressed by her successors. Meanwhile, the various states of the Holy Roman Empire were engulfed in a thirty-year war that also had political and religious roots and which became one of the most bitter and complex conflicts of the period.

War itself became more destructive, owing to new technologies and increasing resources devoted to it. Ordinary people also coped with the price revolution, which caused their wages to lose value and many to lose their land. The difficult economic circumstances of these decades meant that working people, desperate for secure livelihood, rioted or took up arms out of economic, as well as religious, concerns.

Yet, however grim the circumstances people faced, the technology of print and the spread of literacy helped spur speculative and creative works by providing the means for reflection and the audiences to receive and appreciate it. Ironically, the increased importance and grandeur of court life, though a cause of political strain, resulted in a new wave of patronage for art, literature, and drama. Other works, such as Shakespeare's plays, both reflect and reflect on the conflicts in the society of the day. Baroque art expressed both the religious passions of the era and the claims to authority by rulers.

FOCUS QUESTIONS

- What circumstances permitted Spain's ambitious policies and to what degree were they successful?

- What conditions led to civil war in France? How did religious and political conflict develop differently in England?

- Why did war erupt again within the Holy Roman Empire and what was the significance of the conflict?

- What caused the economic stresses of these decades and how did ordinary people cope with them?

- In what ways do the literature and art of this period reflect the political, social, and religious conflicts of the age?

KEY TERMS

Philip II (p. 410)

United Provinces (p. 414)

Armada (p. 414)

Huguenots (p. 417)

Edict of Nantes (p. 419)

Elizabeth I (p. 421)

Puritans (p. 421)

Thirty Years' War (p. 425)

Peace of Westphalia (p. 429)

price revolution (p. 430)

gentry (p. 431)

baroque (p. 437)

 This icon will direct you to additional materials on the website: www .cengage.com/history/ noble/westciv6e.

e **See our interactive eBook for map and primary source activities.**

NOTES

1. Geoffrey Parker, *The Dutch Revolt* (London: Penguin, 1985), p. 288, n. 5.

2. Quoted in A. W. Lovett, *Early Habsburg Spain, 1517–1598* (Oxford: Oxford University Press, 1986), p. 212.

3. Quoted in R. J. Knecht, *The French Wars of Religion, 1559–1598* (London: Longman, 1989), p. 109.

4. Quoted in Jean Berenger, *A History of the Habsburg Empire, 1273–1700*, trans. C. A. Simpson (London and New York: Longman, 1990), p. 239.

16

CHAPTER OUTLINE

France in the Age of Absolutism

The English Civil War and Its Aftermath

New Powers in Central and Eastern Europe

The Expansion of Overseas Trade and Settlement

Louis XIV in Roman Armor
(Scala/Art Resource, NY)

Europe in the Age of Louis XIV, ca. 1640–1715

The portrait of King Louis XIV of France as a triumphant warrior, to the left, was one of hundreds of such images of the king that decorated his palace at Versailles and other sites around his kingdom—where they made his subjects aware of his presence, regardless of whether he was in residence. In this painting, the contemporary artist Charles Le Brun depicts Louis as a Roman warrior, and his power is represented by a mixture of other symbols—Christian and pagan, ancient and contemporary. An angel crowns him with a victor's laurel wreath and carries a banner bearing the image of the sun. In his hand, Louis holds a marshal's baton—a symbol of military command—covered with the royal emblem of the fleur-de-lys (flur-duh-LEE). In the background, behind the "Roman" troops following Louis, is an idealized city.

These trappings symbolized the significant expansion of royal power during Louis's reign. He faced down the challenges of warrior-nobles, suppressed religious dissent, and tapped the nation's wealth to wage a series of wars of conquest. A period of cultural brilliance early in his reign and the spectacle of an elaborate court life crowned his achievements. In his prime, his regime was supported by a consensus of elites; such harmony was made possible by the lack of institutional brakes on royal authority. However, as his attention to symbolism suggests, Louis's power was not unchallenged. By the end of the Sun King's reign, the glow was fading: France was struggling under economic distress brought on by the many wars fought for his glory and had missed opportunities for commercial success abroad. Elites throughout France who had once accepted, even welcomed, his rule became critics, and common people outright rebels.

In England, by contrast, the Crown faced successful rebellion by subjects claiming religious authority and political legitimacy for their causes. Resistance to the expansion of royal authority, led by Parliament, resulted in the execution of the king and the establishment of a short-lived republic, the Commonwealth. Although the monarchy was restored, it became permanently weaker after the civil war. After the Thirty Years' War, vigorous rulers in central and eastern Europe undertook a program of territorial expansion and state building that led to the dominance in the region of Austria, Brandenburg-Prussia, and Russia. The power of these states derived, in part, from the economic relationship of their lands to the wider European economy. In all the major states of continental Europe, princely governments were able to monopolize military power for the first time, in return for economic and political concessions to noble landholders.

The seventeenth century also witnessed a dynamic phase of European expansion overseas, following on the successes of the Portuguese and the Spanish in the

FOCUS QUESTIONS

- How did Louis XIV successfully expand royal power in France and what were some of the achievements of his reign?

- What were the long-term consequences of the English civil war?

- Which states began to dominate central and eastern Europe and why were they successful?

- How and why did Europe's overseas trade and colonization expand in the seventeenth century and what effects did this expansion have on Europe itself?

This icon will direct you to additional materials on the website: www.cengage.com/history/noble/westciv6e.

See our interactive eBook for map and primary source activities.

fifteenth and sixteenth centuries. The Dutch created the most successful trading empire. Eager migrants settled in the Americas in ever-increasing numbers, while forced migrants—enslaved Africans—were transported by the thousands to work on the profitable plantations of European colonizers. Aristocrats, merchants, and peasants back in Europe jockeyed to take advantage of—or to mitigate the effects of—the local political and economic impact of Europe's expansion.

FRANCE IN THE AGE OF ABSOLUTISM

How did Louis XIV successfully expand royal power in France and what were some of the achievements of his reign?

Absolutism Extraordinary concentration of power and symbolic authority in royal hands, achieved particularly by the king of France (Louis XIV) in the seventeenth century.

Louis XIV Longest-reigning ruler in European history, he imposed "absolute" rule in France and his reign witnessed a great flowering of French culture.

Absolutism is a term often used to describe the extraordinary concentration of power in royal hands achieved by the kings of France, most notably **Louis XIV** (r. 1643–1715), in the seventeenth century. Louis continued the expansion of state power begun by his father's minister, Cardinal Richelieu (see page 421). The extension of royal power, under Louis as well as his predecessor, was accelerated by his desire to sustain an expensive and aggressive foreign policy. The policy itself was partly traditional—fighting the perpetual enemy, the Habsburgs, and seeking military glory—and partly new—expanding the borders of France. Louis XIV's successes in these undertakings made him both envied and emulated by other rulers: The French court became a model of culture and refinement. But increased royal authority was not accepted without protest: Common French people as well as elites dug in their heels over the cost of Louis's policies to them.

The Last Challenge to Absolutism: The Fronde, 1648–1653

Louis inherited the throne at the age of five in 1643. His mother, Anne of Austria (1601–1666), acted as regent, together with her chief minister and personal friend, Cardinal Jules Mazarin (mah-zah-RAHN) (1602–1661). They immediately faced revolts against the concentration of power in royal hands and the exorbitant taxation that had prevailed under Louis's father. The most serious revolt began in 1648, led by the Parlement (par-luh-MAWNH) of Paris and the other sovereign law courts in the capital.

The source of the Parlement's leverage over the monarchy was its traditional right to register laws and edicts, which amounted to judicial review. Now, the Parlement attempted to extend this power by debating and even initiating government policy. The sovereign courts sitting together drew up a reform program abolishing most of the machinery of government established under Richelieu and calling for consent to future taxation. The citizens of Paris rose to defend the courts when royal troops were sent against them in October.

Civil war waxed and waned around France from 1648 to 1653. Fighting was led by great aristocrats in the name of the parlements and other law courts. At the same time, further reform proposals were offered. For example, middling nobles in the region around Paris worked on their own reform program and made preparations for a meeting of the Estates General—a representative assembly—to enact it.

These revolts begun in 1648 were derided with the name "Fronde," which was a popular children's game. However, the Fronde (FRAWND) was not child's play; it constituted a serious challenge to the legacy of royal government as it had developed under Richelieu. It ended without a noteworthy impact on the growth of royal power for several reasons. First, Mazarin made strategic concessions to individual aristocrats, who were always eager to trade their loyalty for the fruits of royal service. Meanwhile, the Parlement of Paris accepted a return to royal authority when the civil war caused starvation as well as threatened its control of reform.

Moreover, the Parlement of Paris was a law court, not a representative assembly. Its legitimacy derived from its role as upholder of royal law, and it could not, over time, challenge the king on the pretext of upholding royal tradition in his name. Parlementaires saw the Estates General as a rival institution and helped quash the proposed meeting of representatives. They especially wanted to avoid reform that included abolition of the paulette, a fee guaranteeing the hereditary right to royal office (see page 420).

Unlike England, France had no single institutional focus for resistance to royal power. A strong-willed and able ruler, as Louis XIV proved to be, could counter challenges to royal power, particularly when he satisfied the ambitions of aristocrats and those bureaucrats who profited from the expansion of royal power.

France Under Louis XIV, 1661–1715

Louis XIV fully assumed control of government in 1661, at a propitious moment. The Peace of the Pyrenees in 1659 had ended, in France's favor, the wars with Spain that had dragged on since the end of the Thirty Years' War. As part of the peace agreement, Louis married a Spanish princess, Maria Theresa. In the first ten years of his active reign, Louis achieved a degree of control over the mechanisms of government unparalleled in the history of monarchy in France or anywhere else in Europe. Louis was an extremely vigorous and diligent king. He put in hours a day at a desk, while sustaining the ceremonial life of the court, with its elaborate hunts, balls, and other public events.

GOVERNMENT REFORMS

Louis did not invent any new bureaucratic devices, but rather used existing ranks of officials in new ways that increased government efficiency and further centralized control. He radically reduced the number of men in his High Council, the advisory body closest to the king, to include only three or four great ministers of state affairs. This intimate group, with Louis's active participation, handled all policymaking. The ministers of state, war, and finance were chosen exclusively from nonnoble men of bourgeois origin, whose training and experience fitted them for such positions. Jean-Baptiste Colbert (coal-BEAR) (1619–1683), perhaps the greatest of them, served as minister of finance and supervised most domestic policy from 1665 until his death. He was from a merchant family and had served for years under Mazarin.

Several dozen other officials, picked from the ranks of up-and-coming lawyers and administrators, drew up laws and regulations and passed them to the intendants for execution at the provincial level. Sometimes these officials at the center were sent to the provinces on short-term supervisory missions. The effect of this system was to bypass many entrenched provincial bureaucrats, particularly those known as tax farmers. Tax farmers were freelance businessmen who bid for the right to collect taxes in a region in return for a negotiated fee they paid to the Crown. The Crown, in short, did not control its own tax revenues. The money Louis's regime saved by the more efficient collection of taxes (revenues almost doubled in some areas) enabled the government to streamline the bureaucracy: Dozens of the offices created over the years to bring cash in were bought back by the Crown from their owners.

The system still relied on the bonds of patronage and personal service—political bonds borrowed from aristocratic life. Officials rose through the ranks by means of service to the great, and family connection and personal loyalty still were essential. Of the seventeen different men who were part of Louis XIV's High Council during his reign, five were members of the Colbert family, for example.

CHRONOLOGY

1602	Dutch East India Company formed
1607	Jamestown colony founded in Virginia
1608	Champlain founds Quebec City
1613	Michael becomes first Romanov tsar in Russia
1620	Pilgrims settle at Plymouth (Massachusetts)
1642–1648	Civil war in England
1643	Louis XIV becomes king of France
1648–1653	Fronde revolts in France
1649	Execution of Charles I
1649–1660	English Commonwealth
1659	Peace of the Pyrenees
1660	Monarchy restored in England
1661	Louis XIV assumes full control of government
1672–1678	Dutch War
1682	Peter the Great becomes tsar of Russia
1685	Edict of Nantes revoked
1688	Glorious Revolution
1699	Treaty of Carlowitz
1700–1721	Great Northern War
1701–1714	War of the Spanish Succession
1713	Peace of Utrecht
1715	Death of Louis XIV

ECONOMIC DEVELOPMENT

Colbert and the other ministers began to develop the kind of planned government policymaking that we now take for granted. Partly by means of their itinerant supervisory officials, they tried to formulate policy based on carefully collected information. How many men of military age were available? How abundant was this year's harvest? Answers to such questions enabled not only the formulation of economic policy, but also the deliberate management of production and services to achieve certain goals—above all, the recruitment and supply of the king's vast armies.

Colbert actively encouraged France's economic development in other ways. He reduced the internal tolls and customs barriers, which were relics of medieval landholders' rights. He encouraged industry with state subsidies and protective tariffs. He set up state-sponsored trading companies—the two most important being the East India Company and the West India Company, established in 1664.

mercantilism Economic policy pursued by western European states in the seventeenth and eighteenth centuries that stressed self-sufficiency in manufactured goods, tight government control of trade, and the absolute value of bullion.

Mercantilism is the term historians use to describe the theory behind Colbert's efforts. This economic theory stressed self-sufficiency in manufactured goods, tight control of trade to foster the domestic economy, and the absolute value of bullion. Both capital for development—in the form of hard currency, known as bullion—and the amount of world trade were presumed to be limited in quantity. Therefore, state intervention in the form of protectionist policies was believed necessary to guarantee a favorable balance of payments.

This static model of national wealth did not wholly fit the facts of growing international trade in the seventeenth century. Nevertheless, mercantilist philosophy was helpful to France. France became self-sufficient in the all-important production of woolen cloth, and French industry expanded notably in other sectors. Colbert's greatest success was the systematic expansion of the navy and merchant marine. By the end of Louis XIV's reign, the French navy was virtually the equal of the English navy.

RELIGIOUS LIFE

Beginning in 1673, Louis tried to bring the religious life of the realm more fully under royal control. He claimed some of the church revenues and powers of ecclesiastical appointment within France that the pope still exercised. Partly to bolster his position with the pope, he also began to attack the Huguenot community in France. First, he offered financial rewards for conversion to Catholicism. Then, he took more drastic steps, such as destroying Protestant churches and quartering troops in Huguenots' homes to force them to convert. In 1685, he revoked the Edict of Nantes. A hundred thousand Protestant subjects—including some six hundred army and navy officers—refused even nominal conversion to Catholicism and chose to emigrate.

Meanwhile, Louis faced resistance to his claims against the pope from within the ranks of French Catholics. These laypeople and clerics represented a movement within French Catholicism known as Jansenism, after Cornelius Jansen, a professor of theology whose writings inspired it. Jansenists practiced an austere style of Catholic religiosity that was akin to some Protestant doctrine in its notions about human will and sinfulness. Louis was wary of any challenge to either the institutional or symbolic unity of his regime and was particularly suspicious of Jansenism because its adherents included many of his political enemies, particularly among families of parlement officials. Late in Louis's reign, another pope obligingly declared many Jansenist doctrines to be heretical as part of a compromise agreement with Louis on matters of church governance and finance.

Despite these successes, the power of the Crown was still greatly limited by modern standards. The "divine right" of kingship, a notion formulated by Louis's chief apologist, Bishop Jacques Bossuet (BOS-soo-way) (1627–1704), did not mean unlimited power to rule; rather, it meant that hereditary monarchy was the divinely ordained form of government, best suited to human needs. *Absolutism* was not iron-fisted control of the realm, but rather the successful focusing of energy, loyalties, and symbolic authority in the Crown. The government functioned well in the opening decades of Louis's reign because his role as the focal point of power and loyalty was both logical, after the preceding years of unrest, and skillfully exploited. Much of the glue holding together the absolutist state lay in informal mechanisms, such as patronage and court life, as well as in the traditional hunt for military glory—all of which Louis amply supplied.

The Life of the Court

An observer comparing the lives of prominent noble families in the mid-sixteenth and mid-seventeenth centuries would have noticed striking differences. By the second half of the seventeenth century, most sovereigns or territorial princes had the power to crush revolts. The nobility relinquished its former independence but retained economic and social supremacy and, as a consequence, considerable political clout. Nobles also developed new ways to symbolize their privilege by means of cultural refinement. This process was particularly dramatic in France.

One sign of Louis's success in marshaling the loyalty of the aristocracy was the brilliant court life that his regime sustained. No longer able to wield independent political power, aristocrats lived at court whenever they could. There, they competed for patronage and prestige—for commands in the royal army and for honorific positions at court itself. A favored courtier might, for example, participate in the elaborate daily *lever* (LEV-ay) (arising) of the king; he might be allowed to hand the king his shirt—a demeaning task, yet a coveted one for the access to the king that it guaranteed. Courtiers now defended their honor with private duels, not warfare, and relied on precise etiquette and clever conversation to mark their political and social distinctiveness. (See the feature, "The Visual Record: Table Manners.")

Noblewomen and noblemen alike began to reflect on their new roles in letters, memoirs, and the first novels. A prominent theme of these works is the increasing need for a truly private life of affection and trust, with which to counterbalance the public façade necessary to an aspiring courtier. The most influential early French novel was *The Princess of Cleves* by Marie-Madeleine Pioche de la Vergne (1634–1693), best known by her title, Madame de Lafayette. Mme. de Lafayette's novel treats the particular difficulties faced by aristocratic women who, without military careers to bring glory and provide distraction, were more vulnerable than men to gossip and slander at court and more trapped by their arranged marriages.

Louis XIV's court is usually associated with the palace he built at Versailles (vare-SIGH), southwest of Paris. Some of the greatest talent of the day worked on the design and construction of Versailles from 1670 through the 1680s. It became a masterpiece of luxurious, but restrained, baroque style—a model for royal and aristocratic palaces throughout Europe for the next one hundred years.

Before Louis's court, in his later years, withdrew to Versailles, it traveled among the king's other châteaux around the kingdom, and in this itinerant period, court life was actually at its most creative. These early years of Louis's personal reign were the heyday of French drama. The comedian Jean-Baptiste Poquelin, known as Molière (mole-YARE) (1622–1673), impressed the young Louis with his productions in the late 1650s and was rewarded with the use of a theater in the main royal palace in Paris. Like Shakespeare earlier in the century, Molière explored the social and political tensions of his day. He satirized the pretensions of the aristocracy and the social climbing of the bourgeoisie. Some of his plays were banned, but most were not only tolerated, but extremely popular with the elite audiences they mocked. Their popularity is testimony to the confidence of Louis's regime in its early days.

Also popular at court were the tragedies of Jean Racine (rah-SEEN) (1639–1699), who was to the French theater what Shakespeare was to the English: the master of poetic language. His plays focus on the emotional and psychological lives of the characters and stress the unpredictable, usually unhappy, role of fate, even among royalty. The pessimism in Racine foreshadowed the less successful second half of Louis's reign.

The Burdens of War and the Limits of Power

Louis XIV started wars that dominated the attention of most European states in the second half of the seventeenth century. His wars sprang from traditional causes: the importance of the glory and dynastic aggrandizement of the king and the preoccupation of the aristocracy with military life. But if Louis's wars had familiar motives, they were far more demanding on state resources than any previous wars.

The new offensive tactics developed during the Thirty Years' War (see page 429) changed the character of armies in ways that demanded more resources for training. A higher proportion of soldiers became gunners, and their effectiveness lay in how well they operated as a unit. Armies began to train seriously off the field of battle because drill and discipline were vital to success. France's victories in the second half of the seventeenth century are partly traceable to the regime's attention to these tasks, as well as to recruitment and supply, which together constituted another phase of the "military revolution." The numbers of men on the battlefield increased somewhat as training increased the effectiveness of large numbers of infantry, but the total numbers of men in arms supported by the state at any time increased dramatically once the organization to support them was in place. Late in the century, France kept more than 300,000 men in arms when at war (which was most of the time).

Table Manners

If you were to sit down in a fancy restaurant, order a juicy steak, and then eat it with your bare hands, other diners would undoubtedly stare, shocked by your bad manners. It has not always been the case that table manners meant very much—were able to signal social status, for example. In fact, table manners did not always exist at all in the sense that we know them. How did they evolve? How did they come to have the importance that they do? And why should historians pay any attention to them?

Imagine that you have been invited to dinner at a noble estate in the year 1500. As you sit down, you notice that there are no knives, forks, and spoons at your place, and no napkins either. A servant (a young girl from a neighboring village) sets a roast of meat in front of you and your fellow diners.

Table Manners of the Upper Class in the Seventeenth Century
(Courtesy of the Trustees of the British Museum)

In 1667, Louis invoked rather dubious dynastic claims to demand from Spain lands in the Spanish Netherlands and the large independent county on France's eastern border called the Franche-Comté (FRAWNSH–con-TAY) (see **MAP 16.1**). After a brief conflict, the French obtained only some towns in the Spanish Netherlands.

Louis's focus then shifted to a new enemy, the Dutch. The Dutch had been allied with France since the beginning of their existence as provinces in rebellion against Spain. But the French now turned against them because of Dutch dominance of seaborne trade in the growing international economy. At first, the French tried to offset the Dutch advantage with tariff barriers against Dutch goods. But confidence in the French army led Louis's generals to urge action against the vulnerable Dutch lands. "It is impossible that his Majesty should tolerate any longer the insolence and arrogance of that nation," rationalized the usually pragmatic Colbert in 1670.[1]

The lords and ladies on either side of you hack off pieces of meat with the knives that they always carry with them, and then, they eat the meat with their fingers. Hunks of bread on the table in front of them catch the dripping juices.

One hundred fifty years later, in 1650, dinner is a much more "civilized" meal. Notice the well-to-do women dining in this engraving by the French artist Abraham Bosse (1602–1676). The table setting, with tablecloths, napkins, plates, and silverware, is recognizable to us. The lady at the extreme right holds up her fork and napkin in a somewhat forced and obvious gesture. These diners have the utensils that we take for granted, but the artist does not take them for granted: They are intended to be noticed by Bosse's elite audience.

In the seventeenth century, aristocrats and gentry signaled their political and social privilege with behavior that distinguished them from the lower classes in ways their more powerful ancestors had found unnecessary. Historians have called this the invention of civility. As we have seen, proper courtesy to one's superiors at court was considered essential. Rituals of honor and deference were increasingly taking the place of armed conflict as the routine behavior of the upper classes. Also essential, however, were certain standards of physical privacy and delicacy. Something as seemingly trivial as the use of a fork became charged with symbolic significance. As the actual power of the aristocrats was circumscribed by the state, they found new expressions of status. Since the sixteenth century, new kinds of manners had been touted in handbooks, reflecting changes that already had occurred at Italian courts. During the seventeenth century, these practices became more widespread and opened up a gulf between upper- and lower-class behavior.

Some of the new behaviors concerned bodily privacy and discretion. A nobleman now used a handkerchief instead of his fingers or coat sleeve, and he did not urinate in public. The new "rules" about eating are particularly interesting. Why did eating with a fork seem refined and desirable to aristocrats trying to buttress their own self-images? As any 3-year-old knows, eating with a fork is remarkably inefficient.

Using a fork kept you at a distance—literal and symbolic—from the animal you were eating. Napkins wiped away all trace of bloody juices from your lips. Interestingly, as diners began to use utensils, other eating arrangements changed in parallel ways. Sideboards had been in use for a long time, but pieces of meat were now discreetly carved on the sideboard and presented to diners in individual portions. The carcass was brought to the sideboard cut into roasts instead of unmistakably whole, and it was often decorated—as it is today—to further disguise it.

The new aristocrat was increasingly separated from the world of brute physical force, both in daily life and on the battlefield. In warfare, brute force was no longer adequate. Training, discipline, and tactical knowledge were more important and heightened the significance of rank, which separated officers from the vast numbers of common soldiers. Aristocrats now lived in a privileged world where violence—except for an occasional duel—was no longer a fact of life. Their new behavior codes signaled their new invulnerability to others. Above all, they worked to transform a loss—of the independence that had gone hand in hand with a more violent life—into a gain: a privileged immunity to violence.

Specific manners became important, then, because they were symbols of power. The symbolic distance between the powerful and the humble was reinforced by other changes in habits and behavior. A sixteenth-century warrior customarily traveled on horseback and often went from place to place within a city on foot, attended by his retinue. A seventeenth-century aristocrat was more likely to travel in a horse-drawn carriage. The presence of special commodities from abroad—such as sugar—in the seventeenth century created further possibilities for signaling status.

It is interesting to note that other personal habits still diverged dramatically from what we would consider acceptable today. Notice the large, stately bed in the same room as the dining table in Bosse's engraving. Interior space was still undifferentiated by our standards, and it was common for eating, talking, sleeping, and estate management all to go on in a single room. The grand bed is in the picture because, like the fork, it is a mark of status. Like virtually everything else, what is "proper" varies with historical circumstance.

QUESTIONS

1. Why did elites become interested in table manners in the seventeenth century?

2. How did manners function as effective symbols of power?

The Dutch War began in 1672, with Louis personally leading one of the largest armies ever fielded in Europe—perhaps 120,000 men. The English had also fought the Dutch over trade in the 1650s and now Louis secretly paid the English king, Charles II, to join an alliance against the Dutch.

At first, the French were spectacularly successful, but the Dutch opened dikes and flooded the countryside, and the land war became a soggy stalemate. At the same time, the Dutch beat combined English and French forces at sea and gathered allies who felt threatened by Louis's aggression. The French soon faced German and Austrian forces along their frontier, and by 1674, the English had joined the alliance against France as well. A negotiated peace in 1678 gave France further territory areas in the Spanish Netherlands, as well as control of the Franche-Comté, but it was an illusion of victory only.

Ensconced at Versailles since 1682, Louis seemed to be at the height of his powers. Yet, the Dutch War had in fact cost him more than he had gained. Reforms in government and finance ended under the pressure of paying for war, and old habits of borrowing money and selling offices were revived.

Versailles Palace, The Hall of Mirrors This ornate gallery, more than 75 yards long, connects the two wings of the palace. Seventeen huge windows and opposing walled mirrors flood the gallery with light. In addition to these dramatic effects, the designers included many thematic details, such as miniature fleur-de-lys entwined with suns to symbolize the union of France and Louis, in the gilded work near the ceiling. (Réunion des musées nationaux/Art Resource, NY)

Other government obligations, such as encouraging overseas trade, were neglected. Colbert's death in 1683 dramatically symbolized the end of an era of innovation in the French regime.

THE NINE YEARS' WAR

A new war, now known as the Nine Years' War, or King William's War, was touched off late in 1688 by a French invasion of Germany to claim an inheritance there. In his ongoing dispute with the pope, Louis also seized the papal territory of Avignon (ah-veen-YOHN) in southern France. Boldest of all, he helped the exiled Catholic claimant to the English crown, James II, mount an invasion to reclaim his throne (see page 455). Louis's unforgiving Dutch opponent, William of Orange, king of England from 1689 to 1702, led an alliance of all the major powers—Spain, the Netherlands, England, Austria, and the major German states—against the French. As with the Dutch War, the Nine Years' War was costly and, on most fronts, inconclusive. This time, though, there was no illusion of victory for Louis. In the Treaty of Ryswick (1697), Louis gave up most of the territories he had claimed or seized, as well as his contentious claim to papal revenues. The terrible burden of war taxes, combined with crop failures in 1693 and 1694, caused widespread starvation in the countryside. French courtiers began to criticize Louis openly.

THE WAR OF THE SPANISH SUCCESSION

The final and most devastating war of Louis's reign, called the War of the Spanish Succession, broke out in 1701. It was a straightforward dynastic clash between France and its perennial enemy, the Habsburgs. Both Louis and Habsburg Holy Roman emperor Leopold I (r. 1657–1705) hoped to claim, for their heirs, the throne of Spain, left open at the death in 1700 of the last Spanish Habsburg, Charles II. Charles II bequeathed the throne to Louis's grandson, Philip of Anjou, by reason of Louis's marriage to the Spanish princess Maria Theresa and Philip had quickly entered Spain to claim his new kingdom. War was made inevitable when, in an act of sheer belligerence, Louis

🌐 **MAP 16.1—Territorial Gains of Louis XIV, 1667–1715**
Louis's wars, though enormously expensive for France, produced only modest gains of territory along France's eastern and northern frontiers.

renounced one of the conditions of Charles's will: Philip's accession to the throne of Spain, Louis insisted, did not prevent his becoming king of France as well. The Dutch and English responded to the prospect of so great a disruption of the balance of power in Europe by allying with the emperor against France. The Dutch and English also wanted to defend their colonial interests, since the French had already begun to profit from new trading opportunities with the Spanish colonies.

Again, the French fought a major war on several fronts on land and at sea. Again, the people of France felt the cost in crushing taxes that multiplied the effects of harvest failures. Major revolts inside France forced Louis to divert troops from the war. For a time, it seemed that the French would be soundly defeated, but they were saved by the superior organization of their forces and by dynastic accident: Unexpected deaths in the Habsburg family meant that the Austrian claimant to the Spanish throne suddenly was poised to inherit rule of Austria and the empire as well. The English, more afraid of a revival of unified Habsburg control of Spain and Austria than of French domination of Spain, quickly called for peace negotiations.

The Peace of Utrecht in 1713 helped to set the agenda of European politics for the eighteenth century. Philip of Anjou was recognized as Philip V, the first Bourbon king of Spain, but on the condition that the Spanish and French crowns would never be worn by the same monarch. To maintain the balance of power against French interests, the Spanish Netherlands and Spanish territories in Italy were ceded by a second treaty in 1714 to Austria, which for many decades would be France's major continental rival. The Peace of Utrecht also marked the beginning of England's dominance of overseas trade and colonization. The French gave to England certain lands in Canada and the Caribbean and renounced any privileged relationship with Spanish colonies. England was allowed to control the highly profitable slave trade with Spanish colonies.

SECTION SUMMARY

- The Fronde were revolts against royal power early in Louis XIV's reign.

- Louis successfully rebuilt royal power using control of taxation, a reformed bureaucracy, and traditional political bonds, such as aristocratic patronage.

- The power Louis wielded has been labeled "absolutism" because there were no formal institutional limits on his authority.

- Court life in Louis's reign sponsored artistic creativity and encouraged a new emphasis on cultural refinement in the aristocracy.

- Louis started a series of costly wars from which the French state gained little.

Louis XIV had added small pieces of territory along France's eastern border (see **MAP 16.1**), and a Bourbon ruled in Spain. But the costs in human life and resources were great for the slim results achieved. The army and navy had swallowed up capital that might have fueled investment and trade; strategic opportunities overseas were lost, never to be regained. Louis's government had been innovative in its early years, but remained constrained by traditional ways of imagining the interest of the state.

THE ENGLISH CIVIL WAR AND ITS AFTERMATH

What were the long-term consequences of the English civil war?

Parliament English legislative institution, which used control over monies to bargain with the Crown over foreign and domestic policies, leading to civil war and the deposition of Charles I.

In England, unlike in France, a representative institution—**Parliament**—became an effective, permanent brake on royal authority. The process by which Parliament gained a secure role in governing the kingdom was neither easy nor peaceful, however. As we saw in Chapter 15, conflicts between the English crown and its subjects, culminating in the Crown-Parliament conflict, concerned control over taxation and the direction of religious reform. Beginning in 1642, England was beset by civil war between royal and parliamentary forces. The king was eventually defeated and executed, and for a time, the monarchy was abolished altogether. It was restored in 1660, but Parliament retained a crucial role in governing the kingdom—a role that was confirmed when, in 1688, it again deposed a monarch and established limits on future monarchs' power.

Civil War, 1642–1649

Fighting broke out between the armies of Charles I and parliamentary armies in the late summer of 1642. The Long Parliament (see page 424) continued to represent a broad coalition of critics and opponents of the monarchy, ranging from aristocrats, concerned primarily with abuses of royal prerogative, to radical Puritans, eager for thorough religious reform and determined to defeat the king. Fighting was halfhearted initially, and the tide of war at first favored Charles.

In 1643, however, the scope of the war broadened. Charles made peace with Irish rebels and brought Irish troops to England to bolster his armies. Parliament, in turn, received military aid from the Scots in exchange for promises that Presbyterianism would become the religion of England. Meanwhile, **Oliver Cromwell** (1599–1658), a Puritan member of the Long Parliament and a cavalry officer, helped reorganize parliamentary forces. The eleven-hundred-man cavalry, trained by Cromwell and known as the "Ironsides" and supported by parliamentary and Scottish infantry, defeated the king's troops at Marston Moor in July 1644. The victory made Cromwell famous.

Oliver Cromwell English Puritan general, during the English civil war, who governed as Lord Protector during the interregnum from 1653 to 1658.

Shortly afterward, Parliament further improved its forces by creating the New Model Army, rigorously trained like Cromwell's Ironsides. Sitting members of Parliament were barred from commanding troops; hence, upper-class control of the army was reduced. This army played a decisive role not only in the war, but also in the political settlement that followed the fighting.

The New Model Army won a convincing victory over royal forces at Naseby in 1645. In the spring of 1646, Charles surrendered to a Scottish army in the north. In January 1647, Parliament paid the Scots for their services in the war and took the king into custody. In the negotiations that followed, Charles tried to play his opponents off against one another, and, as he had hoped, divisions among them widened.

Most members of Parliament were Presbyterians, Puritan gentry who favored a strongly unified and state-controlled church along Calvinist lines. They wanted peace with the king in return for acceptance of the new church structure and parliamentary control of standing militias for a specified period. They did not favor wider political changes, such as extending the right to vote to ordinary people. These men were increasingly alarmed by the appearance of multiple religious sects and by the actual religious freedom that many ordinary people were claiming for themselves. With the weakening of royal authority and the disruption of civil war, censorship was relaxed, and public preaching by ordinary men, and even women, who felt divinely inspired was becoming commonplace.

Above all, Presbyterian gentry in Parliament feared more radical groups in the army and in London who had supported them up to this point, but who favored more sweeping political and religious change. Most officers of the New Model Army, such as Cromwell, were Independents, Puritans who, unlike the Presbyterians, favored a decentralized church, a degree of religious toleration, and a wider sharing of political power among men of property, not just among the very wealthy gentry. In London, a well-organized artisans' movement known as the "Levellers" went even further; Levellers favored universal manhood suffrage, equality under the law, better access to education, and decentralized churches—in short, the separation of political power from wealth and virtual freedom of religion. Many of the rank and file of the army were deeply influenced by Leveller ideas.

In May 1647, the majority in Parliament voted to offer terms to the king and to disband the New Model Army—without first paying most of the soldiers' back wages. This move provoked the first direct intervention by the army in politics. Representatives of the soldiers were chosen to present grievances to Parliament; when this failed, the army seized the king and, in August, occupied Westminster, Parliament's meeting place. Independent and Leveller elements in the army debated the direction of possible reform to be imposed on Parliament. One Leveller argued for universal manhood suffrage: "Every man that is to live under a government ought first by his own consent to put himself under that government; and I do think that the poorest man in England is not at all bound . . . to that government that he hath not had a voice to put himself under."[2]

In November, however, their common enemy Charles escaped from his captors and raised a new army with his former enemies, the Scots, who were also alarmed by the growing radicalism in England. Civil war began again early in 1648. Although it ended quickly with a victory by Cromwell and the New Model Army in August, the renewed war further hardened political divisions and enhanced the power of the army. The king was widely blamed for the renewed bloodshed, and the army did not trust him to keep any agreement he might now sign. When Parliament, still dominated by Presbyterians, once again voted to negotiate with the king, army troops, led by Colonel Thomas Pride, prevented members who favored Presbyterianism or negotiating with the king from attending sessions. The "Rump" Parliament that remained after "Pride's Purge" voted to try the king. A hasty trial followed and, on January 30, 1649, Charles I was executed for "treason, tyranny and bloodshed" against his people.

The Interregnum, 1649–1660

A Commonwealth—a republic—was declared. Executive power resided in a council of state. The House of Lords was abolished and legislative power resided in the one-chamber Rump Parliament. Declaring a republic proved far easier than running one, however. The execution of the king shocked most English and Scots and alienated many elites from the new regime. The legitimacy of the Commonwealth government would always be in question.

The tasks of making and implementing policy were hindered by the narrow political base on which the government now rested. Excluded were the majority of the reformist Presbyterian or Anglican gentry who had been purged from Parliament. Also excluded were the more radical Levellers; Leveller leaders in London were arrested when they published tracts critical of the new government. Within a few years, many disillusioned Levellers would join a new religious movement called the Society of Friends, or Quakers, which espoused complete religious autonomy. Quakers declined all oaths or service to the state, and they refused to acknowledge social rank.

Above all, the new government was vulnerable to the power of the army, which had created it. In 1649 and 1650, Cromwell led punitive expeditions to Ireland and Scotland, partly for sheer revenge and partly to put down resistance to Commonwealth authority. In Ireland, where Cromwell's forces were particularly ruthless, the English dispossessed more Irish landholders, which

Popular Preaching in England   Many women took advantage of the collapse of royal authority to preach in public—a radical activity for women at the time. This print satirizes the Quakers, a religious movement that attracted many women.   (Mary Evans Picture Library)

served to pay off the army's wages. Meanwhile, Parliament could not agree on systematic reforms, particularly the one reform Independents in the army insisted on: more broadly based elections for a new Parliament. Fresh from his victories, Cromwell led his armies to London and dissolved Parliament in the spring of 1652.

In 1653, a cadre of army officers drew up the "Instrument of Government," England's first—and still, today, only—written constitution. It provided for an executive, the Lord Protector, and a Parliament to be based on somewhat wider male suffrage. Cromwell was the natural choice for Lord Protector. Cromwell was an extremely able leader who was not averse to compromise, either in politics or religion. He believed in a state church, but, unlike his Presbyterian opponents, one that allowed for local control, including choice of minister, by individual congregations. He also believed in toleration for Catholics and Jews, as long as no one disturbed the peace.

As Lord Protector, Cromwell oversaw impressive reforms in law that reflected his belief in the limits of governing authority. For example, contrary to the practice of his day, he opposed capital punishment for petty crimes. The government of the Protectorate, however, accomplished little, given Parliament's internal divisions. The population at large still harbored royalist sympathizers; after a royalist uprising in 1655, Cromwell divided England into military districts and vested governing authority in army generals.

After Cromwell died of a sudden illness in September 1658, the Protectorate could not survive the strains over policy and the challenges to its legitimacy. In February 1660, the decisive action of one army general enabled all the surviving members of the Long Parliament to rejoin the Rump. The Parliament summarily dissolved itself and called for new elections. The newly elected Parliament recalled Charles II, son of Charles I, from exile abroad and restored the monarchy. The chaos and radicalism of the late civil war and "interregnum"—the period between reigns, as the years from 1649 to 1660 came to be called—now spawned a conservative reaction.

The Restoration, 1660–1685

Charles II (r. 1660–1685) claimed his throne at the age of 30. He had learned from his years of uncertain exile and from the fate of his father. He did not seek retribution, but rather offered a general pardon to all but a few rebels (mostly those who had signed his father's death warrant), and he suggested to Parliament a relatively tolerant religious settlement that would include Anglicans as well as Presbyterians.

That the reestablished royal government was not more tolerant than it turned out to be was not Charles's doing, initially, but Parliament's. During the 1660s, the "Cavalier" Parliament, named for royalists in the civil war, passed harsh laws aimed at religious dissenters. Anglican orthodoxy was reimposed, including the reestablishment of bishops and the Anglican Book of Common Prayer. All officeholders and clergy were required to swear oaths of obedience to the king and to the established church. As a result, hundreds of non-Anglican Protestants were forced out of office. Holding nonconformist religious services became illegal, and Parliament passed a "five-mile" act to prevent dissenting ministers even from traveling near their former churches. Property laws were tightened and the criminal codes made more severe.

The king's behavior, however, began to mimic prerevolutionary royalist positions. Charles II began to flirt with Catholicism, and his brother and heir, James, openly converted. Charles promulgated a declaration of tolerance that would have included Catholics, as well as nonconformist Protestants, but Parliament would not accept it. In 1678, Charles's secret treaties with the French became known (see page 449), and rumors of a Catholic plot to murder Charles and reimpose Catholicism became widespread. No firm evidence of the "Popish Plot" was ever unearthed, although thirty-five people were executed for alleged participation. Parliament passed the Test Act, which barred all but Anglicans from public office. As a result, the Catholic James was forced to resign as Lord High Admiral.

When Parliament then moved to exclude James from succession to the throne, Charles dissolved it. A subsequent Parliament, worried by the possibility of a new civil war, backed down. But the legacy of the previous civil war and interregnum was a potent one. After two decades of religious pluralism and broadly based political activity, it was impossible to reimpose religious conformity or to silence all dissent, even with harsh new laws on the books. It was also impossible to silence Parliament. Though reluctant to press too far, Parliament tried to assert its policies against the desires of the king.

However, by the end of his reign, Charles was financially independent of Parliament, thanks to increased revenue from overseas trade and secret subsidies from France, his recent ally against the Dutch. If he had been followed by an able successor, Parliament might have lost a good measure of its confidence and independence. But his brother James's reign and its aftermath further enhanced Parliament's power.

The Glorious Revolution, 1688

When James II (r. 1685–1689) succeeded Charles, Parliament was wary but initially cooperative. For example, it granted James customs duties for life, as well as funds to suppress a rebellion by one of Charles's illegitimate sons. James did not try to impose Catholicism on England as some had feared, but he did try to achieve toleration for Catholics in two declarations of indulgence in 1687 and 1688. However admirable his goal—toleration—he had essentially changed the law of the realm without Parliament's consent. He further undermined his position with heavy-handed tactics. When several leading Anglican bishops refused to read the declarations from their pulpits, he had them imprisoned and tried for seditious libel. However, a sympathetic jury acquitted them.

James also failed because of the coincidence of other events. In 1685, at the outset of James's reign, Louis XIV of France had revoked the Edict of Nantes. The possibility that subjects and monarchs in France and, by extension, elsewhere could be of different faiths seemed increasingly unlikely. Popular fears of James's Catholicism were thus heightened early in his reign, and his later declarations of tolerance, though they benefited Protestant dissenters too, were viewed with suspicion. Then, in 1688, the king's second wife, who was Catholic, gave birth to a son. The birth raised the specter of a Catholic succession.

In June 1688, to put pressure on James, leading members of Parliament invited William of Orange, husband of James's Protestant daughter, Mary, to come to England. William mounted an invasion that became a rout and James sought protection in France. William called Parliament, which declared James to have abdicated and offered the throne jointly to William and Mary. With French support, James invaded the British Isles in 1690, but was defeated by William at the Battle of Boyne, in Ireland, that year.

The substitution of William (r. 1689–1702) and Mary (r. 1689–1694) for James, known as the **Glorious Revolution**, was engineered by Parliament and confirmed its power. Parliament presented the new sovereigns with a Declaration of Rights upon their accession and, later that year, with a Bill of Rights that defended freedom of speech, called for frequent Parliaments, and required all future monarchs to be Protestant (see the feature, "The Written Record: The English Bill of Rights"). Parliament's role in the political process was ensured by its power of the purse, since William sought funds for his ambitious military efforts, particularly the Netherlands' ongoing wars with France.

The issues that had faced the English since the beginning of the century were common to all European states: religious division and elite power, fiscal strains and resistance to taxation.

Glorious Revolution
Bloodless English revolution in 1688 in which Parliament replaced the Catholic King James II with William (of Orange) and his wife, Mary (James's Protestant daughter), and imposed, on the new rulers, a Bill of Rights that confirmed Parliament's power.

SECTION SUMMARY

- In England, unlike in France, a representative institution controlled taxation and could effectively challenge royal policies.

- A civil war between Charles I and parliamentary forces ended with the defeat and execution of the king in 1649.

- Several groups, including wealthy gentry and ordinary townspeople, had allied to support Parliament, but they did not agree on a program of political and religious reform.

- The government of the interregnum did not last after the death of the Lord Protector, Oliver Cromwell, because too few of the original supporters of Parliament believed it legitimate or approved of its policies.

- The Crown was restored under Charles II but began to conflict again with Parliament over political and religious policy under his successor James II.

- The role of Parliament in English government was confirmed when William and Mary accepted the Crown under conditions stated in the Bill of Rights.

The English Bill of Rights

After King William and Queen Mary accepted the throne, they signed this Bill of Rights presented to them by Parliament in 1689. They therefore accepted not only the limits of royal power enshrined in the document but also the fact that Parliament could legislate how the monarchy was to function.

Whereas the Lords Spiritual and Temporal and Commons assembled at Westminster, lawfully, fully and freely representing all the estates of the people of this realm, did upon the thirteenth of February … present unto their Majesties, then called and known by the names and style of William and Mary, prince and princess of Orange, being present in their proper persons, a certain declaration in writing made by the said Lords and Commons in the words following, viz.:

Whereas the late King James the Second, by the assistance of diverse evil counselors, judges and ministers employed by him, did endeavor to subvert and extirpate the Protestant religion and the laws and liberties of this kingdom;

By assuming and exercising a power of dispensing with and suspending of laws and the execution of laws without consent of Parliament; …

By levying money for and to the use of the Crown by pretense of prerogative for other time and in other manner than the same was granted by Parliament;

By raising and keeping a standing army within this kingdom in time of peace without consent of Parliament, and quartering soldiers contrary to law;

By causing several good subjects being Protestants to be disarmed at the same time when papists were both armed and employed contrary to law;

By violating the freedom of election of members to serve in Parliament;

By prosecutions in the Court of King's Bench for matters and causes cognizable only in Parliament, and by diverse other arbitrary and illegal courses; …

And excessive bail hath been required of persons committed in criminal cases to elude the benefit of the laws made for the liberty of the subjects;

And excessive fines have been imposed;

And illegal and cruel punishments inflicted; …

All which are utterly and directly contrary to the known laws and statutes and freedom of this realm;

And whereas the said late King James the Second having abdicated the government and the throne being thereby vacant, his Highness the prince of Orange (whom it hath pleased Almighty God to make the glorious instrument of delivering this kingdom from popery and arbitrary power) did … cause letters to be written to the Lords Spiritual and Temporal being Protestants, and other letters to the several counties, cities, universities, boroughs and cinque ports,

Yet, the cataclysmic events in England—the interregnum, the Commonwealth, the Restoration, the Glorious Revolution—had set it apart from other states. A representative institution had become a partner of the monarchy.

NEW POWERS IN CENTRAL AND EASTERN EUROPE

Which states began to dominate central and eastern Europe and why were they successful?

By the end of the seventeenth century, three states dominated central and eastern Europe: Austria, Brandenburg-Prussia, and Russia. After the Thirty Years' War, the Habsburgs' dominance in the splintering empire waned, and they focused on expanding and consolidating their power in their hereditary possessions, centered in what became modern Austria. Brandenburg-Prussia, in northeastern Germany, emerged from obscurity to rival the Habsburg state. The rulers of Brandenburg-Prussia had gained lands in the Peace of Westphalia, and astute management transformed their relatively small and scattered holdings into one of the most powerful states in Europe. Russia's new stature in eastern Europe resulted in part from the weakness of its greatest rival, Poland, and the determination of one leader, Peter the Great, to assume a major role in European affairs. Sweden controlled valuable Baltic territory through much of the century, but eventually was also eclipsed by Russia as a force in the region.

The internal political development of states was dramatically shaped by their relationship to the wider European economy: They were sources of grain and raw materials for the more densely urbanized West. The development of and the competition among states in central and eastern Europe were closely linked to developments in western Europe.

for the choosing of such persons to represent them as were of right to be sent to Parliament. . . .

And thereupon the said Lords Spiritual and Temporal and Commons, pursuant to their respective letters and elections, being now assembled in a full and free representative of this nation, taking into their most serious consideration the best means for attaining the ends aforesaid, do in the first place (as their ancestors in like case have usually done) for the vindicating and asserting their ancient rights and liberties declare;

That the pretended power of suspending of laws or the execution of laws by regal authority without consent of Parliament is illegal;

That the pretended power of dispensing with laws or the execution of laws by regal authority, as it hath been assumed and exercised of late, is illegal; . . .

That levying money for or to the use of the Crown by pretense of prerogative, without grant of Parliament, for longer time, or in other manner than the same is or shall be granted, is illegal;

That it is the right of the Subjects to petition the king, and all commitments and prosecutions for such petitioning are illegal;

That the raising or keeping a standing army within the kingdom in time of peace, unless it be with consent of Parliament, is against law;

That the subjects which are Protestants may have arms for their defense suitable to their conditions and as allowed by law;

That election of members of Parliament ought to be free;

That the freedom of speech and debates or proceedings in Parliament ought not to be impeached or questioned in any court or place out of Parliament;

That excessive bail ought not to be required, nor excessive fines imposed nor cruel and unusual punishments inflicted; . . .

And that for redress of all grievances, and for the amending, strengthening and preserving of the laws, Parliaments ought to be held frequently.

QUESTIONS

1. How, specifically, does this document limit royal power?
2. What rights were the creators of this document most concerned to protect, in your view?
3. Would any of the rights protected here have been useful to common English people?

Source: *The Statutes: Revised Edition*, vol. 1 (London: Eyre and Spottiswoode, 1871), pp. 10–12.

The Consolidation of Austria

The Thirty Years' War (see pages 427–430) weakened the Habsburgs as emperors but strengthened them in their own lands. The main Habsburg lands in 1648 were a collection of principalities comprising modern Austria, the kingdom of Hungary (largely in Turkish hands), and the kingdom of Bohemia (see **MAP 16.2**). In 1714, Austria acquired the Spanish Netherlands (modern Belgium), which were renamed the Austrian Netherlands. Although language and ethnic differences prevented an absolutist state along French lines, Leopold I (r. 1657–1705) made political and institutional changes that enabled the Habsburg state to become one of the most powerful in Europe through the eighteenth century.

Much of the coherence that already existed in Leopold's lands had been achieved by his predecessors after the Thirty Years' War. The lands of rebels in Bohemia had been confiscated and redistributed among loyal, mostly Austrian, families. In return for political and military support for the emperor, these families were given the right to exploit their newly acquired land and the peasants who worked it. The desire to recover population and productivity after the destruction of the Thirty Years' War gave landlords further incentive to curtail peasants' autonomy, particularly in devastated Bohemia. Austrian landlords throughout the Habsburg domains provided grain and timber for the export market and foodstuffs for the Austrian armies, while elite families provided the army with officers. This political-economic arrangement provoked numerous serious peasant revolts, but the peasants were not able to force changes in a system that suited both the elites and the central authority.

Although Leopold had lost much influence within the empire itself, an imperial government including a war ministry, financial bureaucracy, and the like still functioned in his capital, Vienna. Leopold worked to extricate the government of his own lands from the apparatus of imperial institutions, which were staffed largely by Germans more loyal to imperial, than to Habsburg, interests.

Baroque Splendor in Austria   The Belvedere Palace (whose name means "beautiful view") was built near Vienna as the summer residence of the great aristocratic general Prince Eugene of Savoy, who had successfully led Habsburg armies against the Turks and had reaped many rewards from Leopold and his successors. The palace shares many features in common with Louis XIV's palace of Versailles.   (Erich Lessing/Art Resource, NY)

In addition, Leopold used the Catholic Church as an institutional and ideological support for his state. Leopold's personal ambition was to reestablish devout Catholicism throughout his territories. Acceptance of Catholicism became the litmus test of loyalty to the Habsburg regime, and Protestantism vanished among elites. Leopold encouraged the work of Jesuit teachers and members of other Catholic religious orders. These men and women helped staff his government and administered religious life down to the most local levels.

Leopold's most dramatic success, as a Habsburg and a religious leader, was his reconquest of the kingdom of Hungary from the Ottoman Empire. Since the mid-sixteenth century, the Habsburgs had controlled only a narrow strip of the kingdom. Preoccupied with fighting France, Leopold did not himself choose to begin a reconquest. His centralizing policies, however, alienated nobles and townspeople in the portion of Hungary he did control, as did his repression of Protestantism, which had flourished in Hungary. Hungarian nobles began a revolt, aided by the Turks, aiming for a reunited Hungary under Ottoman protection.

The Habsburgs won, instead, in part because they received help from the Venetians, the Russians, and especially the Poles, whose lands in Ukraine were threatened by the Turks. The Turks overreached their supply lines to besiege Vienna in 1683. When the siege failed, Habsburg armies slowly pressed east and south, recovering Buda, the capital of Hungary, in 1686 and Belgrade (modern Serbia) in 1688. The **Treaty of Carlowitz** ended the fighting in 1699, after the first conference where European allies jointly dictated terms to a weakening Ottoman Empire. Austria's allies had also gained at the Ottomans' expense: The Poles recovered the threatened Ukraine, and the Russians gained a vital foothold on the Black Sea.

Leopold gave control of reclaimed lands to loyal Austrian officers but could not fully break the traditions of Hungarian separatism. Hungary's great aristocrats—whether they had defended the Habsburgs against Turkish encroachment or guarded the frontier for Turkish overlords—retained their independence. The peasantry, as elsewhere, suffered a decline in status as a result of the Crown's efforts to ensure the loyalty of elites. In the long run, Hungarian independence weakened the Habsburg state, but in the short run, Leopold's victory over the Turks and the recovery of Hungary were momentous events, confirming the Habsburgs as the preeminent power in central Europe.

The Rise of Brandenburg-Prussia

Several German states, in addition to Austria, gained territory and stature after the Thirty Years' War. By the end of the seventeenth century, the strongest was **Brandenburg-Prussia**, a conglomeration of small territories held, by dynastic accident, by the Hohenzollern family. The two principal territories were electoral Brandenburg, in northeastern Germany, with its capital, Berlin, and the duchy of Prussia, a fief of the Polish crown along the Baltic coast east of Poland proper (see **Map 16.2**). In addition, the Hohenzollerns ruled a handful of small principalities near the Netherlands. These unpromising lands became a powerful state, primarily because of the work of Frederick William, known as "the Great Elector" (r. 1640–1688).

Frederick William used the occasion of a war to effect a permanent change in the structure of government. He took advantage of a war between Poland and its rivals, Sweden and Russia (described in the next section), to win independence for the duchy of Prussia from Polish overlordship. When his involvement in the war ended in 1657, he kept intact the general war commissariat, a combined civilian and military body that had efficiently directed the war effort, bypassing traditional councils and representative bodies. He also used the standing army to force the payment of high taxes. Most significantly, he established a positive relationship with the Junkers (YUNG-kurz), hereditary landholders, which ensured him both revenue and loyalty. The Junkers surrendered their accustomed political independence in return for greater economic and social power over the peasants who worked their lands. The freedom to control their estates led many nobles to invest in profitable agriculture for the export market. The peasants were serfs who received no benefits from the increased productivity of the land.

Frederick William further enhanced his state's power by sponsoring industry. These industries did not have to fear competition from urban producers because the towns had been frozen out of the political process and saddled with heavy taxes. Though an oppressive place for many Germans, Brandenburg-Prussia attracted many skilled refugees, such as Huguenot artisans fleeing Louis XIV's France.

Other German states, such as Bavaria and Saxony, had vibrant towns, largely free peasantries, and weaker aristocracies but were relative nonentities in international affairs. Power on the European stage depended on military force. Whether in a large state like France or in a small one like Brandenburg-Prussia, that power usually came at the expense of the people.

Competition Around the Baltic

The rivers and port cities of the Baltic coast were conduits for the growing trade between the Baltic hinterland and the rest of Europe. Trade in grain, timber, furs, iron, and copper was vital to the entire European economy and caused intense competition, especially between Poland-Lithuania and Sweden, to control the coast and inland regions. In 1600, a large portion of the Baltic hinterland lay under the control of Poland-Lithuania, a vast state at the height of its power, but one that would prove an exception to the pattern of expanding royal power in the seventeenth century.

Poland and Lithuania had been jointly governed since a marriage united their ruling families in the late Middle Ages. Even so, the two states retained distinct traditions. Like some of the Habsburgs' territories, Poland-Lithuania was a multiethnic state, particularly the huge duchy of Lithuania, which included Ruthenia (modern Belarus and Ukraine). Poles spoke Polish, a Slavic language, and were primarily Catholic, although there were also large minorities of Protestants,

Treaty of Carlowitz
Treaty imposed by the European allies on the Ottoman Empire, by which the Austrians, Venetians, Russians, and Poles gained territory at the Turks' expense.

Brandenburg-Prussia
Group of German territories ruled by the Hohenzollern family that became one of Europe's most powerful states in the seventeenth century.

MAP 16.2—New Powers in Central and Eastern Europe, to 1725

The balance of power in central and eastern Europe shifted with the strengthening of Austria, the rise of Brandenburg-Prussia, and the expansion of Russia at the expense of Poland and Sweden.

Map Legend

- French Bourbon lands
- Spanish Bourbon lands
- Austrian Habsburg lands
- Prussian lands
- Great Britain
- Boundary of the Holy Roman Empire
- Russian Empire
- Russian gains, by 1725
- Ottoman Empire, 1722

Map Labels

RUSSIAN EMPIRE

Moscow

St. Petersburg

INGRIA

ESTONIA

LIVONIA

Riga

Smolensk

BELARUS

Minsk

FINLAND

KINGDOM OF SWEDEN

SWEDEN

NORWAY

Oslo

KINGDOM OF DENMARK

DENMARK

Baltic Sea

North Sea

LITHUANIA

POLAND-LITHUANIA

Warsaw

PRUSSIA

Königsberg

Gdansk

Vistula R.

BRANDENBURG

Berlin

Elbe R.

SAXONY

SILESIA

Oder R.

BOHEMIA

HANOVER

UNITED NETHERLANDS

Utrecht

Rhine R.

PALATINATE

Strasbourg

LORRAINE

Danube R.

BAVARIA

AUSTRIA

Vienna

HOLY ROMAN EMPIRE

SWITZERLAND

ALPS

SAVOY

MILAN

MODENA

GENOA

Po R.

TUSCANY

PAPAL STATES

Rome

Corsica (Genoa)

Sardinia (Austria)

KINGDOM OF NAPLES

Naples

Sicily (Savoy)

CROATIA

SLAVONIA

BOSNIA

HERZEGOVINA

MONTENEGRO

SERBIA

Belgrade

REPUBLIC OF VENICE

Adriatic Sea

HUNGARY

Buda

Pest

TRANSYLVANIA

CARPATHIAN MTS.

MOLDAVIA MTS.

WALLACHIA

Danube R.

BULGARIA

ALBANIA

GREECE

OTTOMAN EMPIRE

Constantinople

Aegean Sea

ANATOLIA

ARMENIA

KURDISTAN

Black Sea

CRIMEA

COSSACKS

UKRAINE

Kiev

Poltava

Dnieper R.

Dniester R.

DON COSSACKS

Don R.

Mediterranean Sea

Minorca (Gr. Br.)

Balearic Is.

Marseilles

FRANCE

Paris

Seine R.

Loire R.

Toulouse

Garonne R.

Rhône R.

CATALONIA

SPAIN

Madrid

Ebro R.

Duero R.

Tagus R.

GIBRALTAR (Gr. Br.)

PORTUGAL

Lisbon

GREAT BRITAIN

SCOTLAND

Edinburgh

ENGLAND

London

Thames R.

IRELAND

Dublin

ATLANTIC OCEAN

300 Mi.

300 Km.

150

Riga

Rhine R.

Orthodox Christians, and Jews in Poland. Lithuanians, whose language was only distantly related to the Slavic languages, were mostly Catholic as well, although Orthodox Christianity predominated among the Ruthenians, who spoke a Slavic language related to both Russian and Polish.

The state commanded considerable resources, including the ports of Gdansk and Riga on the Baltic and grain-producing lands in the interior. However, Poland-Lithuania had internal weaknesses. It was a republic of the nobility, with a weak elected king at its head. The great nobles, whose fortunes increased with the grain trade, ran the affairs of state through the national parliament, the Sejm (SAME). They drastically limited the ability of the Crown to tax and to grant new titles of nobility, as was the practice throughout Europe. These limitations meant that the king could not reward the loyalty of wealthy gentry or the small numbers of urban elites, so that they might be a counterweight to noble power. Limited funds also meant that the Polish crown would be hard put to defend its vast territories when challenged by its rivals.

Strains began to mount within Poland-Lithuania in the late sixteenth century. The spread of the Counter-Reformation, encouraged by the Crown, created tensions with both Protestant and Orthodox subjects in the diverse kingdom. As the power of landholding nobles grew with Poland's expanding grain exports, impoverished peasants were bound to the land, and lesser gentry, particularly in Lithuania, were shut out of political power. In Ukraine, communities of **Cossacks**, nomadic farmer-warriors, grew as Polish and Lithuanian peasants fled harsh conditions to join them. The Cossacks had long been tolerated because they served as a military buffer against the Ottoman Turks to the south, but now Polish landlords wanted to reincorporate the Cossacks into the profitable political-economic system they controlled.

In 1648, the Polish crown faced revolt and invasion that it could not fully counter. The Cossacks led a major uprising, which included Ukrainian gentry as well as peasants. In 1654, the Cossacks tried to assure their autonomy by transferring their allegiance to Moscow. They became part of a Russian invasion of Poland-Lithuania that, by the next year, had engulfed much of the eastern half of the dual state. At the same time, Poland's perennial rival, Sweden, seized central Poland in a military campaign marked by extreme brutality. Many Polish and Lithuanian aristocrats continued to act like independent warlords and cooperated with the invaders to preserve their own local power.

Operating with slim resources, Polish royal armies eventually managed to recover much territory—most important, the western half of Ukraine (see **Map 16.2**). But the invasions and subsequent fighting were disastrous. The population of Poland declined by as much as 40 percent, and vital urban economies were in ruins. The Catholic identity of the Polish heartland had been a rallying point for resistance to the Protestant Swedes and the Orthodox Russians, but the religious tolerance that had distinguished the diverse Polish kingdom and had been mandated in its constitution was now abandoned. In addition, much of its recovery of Lithuanian territory was only nominal.

The elective Polish crown passed in 1674 to the military hero Jan Sobieski (so-BYESS-key) (r. 1674–1696), known as "Vanquisher of the Turks" for his role in raising the siege of Vienna in 1683. Given Poland's internal weakness, however, Sobieski's victories, in the long run, helped the Ottomans' other foes—Austria and Russia—more than they helped the Poles. After his death, Poland would be vulnerable to the political ambitions of its more powerful neighbors. The next elected king, Augustus II of Saxony (r. 1697–1704, 1709–1733), dragged Poland back into war, from which Russia would emerge the clear winner in the power struggle in eastern Europe.

The Swedes, meanwhile, successfully vied with the Poles for control of the lucrative Baltic coast. Swedish efforts to control Baltic territory had begun in the sixteenth century, first to counter the power of its perennial rival, Denmark, in the western Baltic. Sweden then competed with Poland to control Livonia (modern Latvia) and its major port city, Riga. By 1617, under Gustav Adolf, the Swedes gained the lands to the north of Livonia surrounding the Gulf of Finland (the most direct outlet for Russian goods), and in 1621, they displaced the Poles in Livonia itself. Swedish intervention in the Thirty Years' War (see page 428) had been part of this campaign to secure Baltic territory. And the Treaty of Westphalia (1648, see page 429) confirmed Sweden's gains on the Baltic.

The port cities held by Sweden were profitable but simply served to pay for the costly wars necessary to seize and defend them. Indeed, Sweden did not have the resources to hold Baltic territory over the long term, and it gained little from its aggression against Poland in the 1650s. Owing to its earlier gains, Sweden managed to reign supreme on the Baltic coast until the end of the century, when it was supplanted by the powerful Russian state.

Cossacks Russian term meaning "free men" originally applied to people of central Asian origin in the hinterland of the Black Sea. After 1500, many peasants escaping serfdom in Poland-Lithuania and Russia fled and became "Cossacks."

Russia Under Peter the Great

The Russian state grew dramatically in the sixteenth century, under Ivan IV (r. 1533–1584), the first Russian ruler to routinely use the title "Tsar" (Russian for "Caesar"). Ivan's use of the title reflected his imperial intentions. He expanded the territory under Moscow's control south to the Caspian Sea and east into Siberia. Within his expanding empire, Ivan ruled as an autocrat. The need to gather tribute money for Mongol overlords in medieval times had concentrated many resources in the hands of Muscovite princes. Ivan was able to bypass noble participation and create ranks of officials loyal only to him.

Ivan came to be called "the Terrible," from a Russian word meaning "awe-inspiring." Although a period of disputed succession to the throne, known as the "Time of Troubles," followed Ivan's death in 1584, the foundations of the large and cohesive state he had built survived until a new dynasty of rulers was established in the seventeenth century.

The Romanovs, an aristocratic family related to Ivan's, became the new ruling dynasty in 1613. Michael (r. 1613–1645) was named tsar by an assembly of aristocrats, gentry, and commoners who were more alarmed by the civil wars and recent Polish invasions than by a return to strong tsarist rule. Michael was succeeded by his son, Alexis (r. 1645–1676), who presided over the extension of Russian control to eastern Ukraine in 1654, following the wars in Poland, and developed an interest in cultivating relationships with the West.

Peter the Great   Energetic and tyrannical Russian tsar who forcibly westernized Russian state and society and made Russia into a great power.

A complete shift of the balance of power in eastern Europe and the Baltic, in Russia's favor, was achieved by Alexis's son, Peter I (r. 1682–1725), "the Great." **Peter the Great** accomplished this by military successes against his enemies and by forcibly reorienting Russian government and society toward involvement with the rest of Europe.

Peter was almost literally larger than life. Nearly 7 feet tall, he towered over most of his contemporaries and had physical and mental energy to match his size. He set himself to learning trades and studied soldiering by rising through the ranks of the military like a common soldier. He traveled abroad to learn as much as he could about western European economies and governments. He wanted the revenue, manufacturing output, technology and trade, and, above all, up-to-date army and navy that other rulers enjoyed.

Immediately on his accession to power, Peter initiated a bold series of changes in Russian society. His travels had taught him that European monarchs coexisted with a privileged, but educated, aristocracy and that a brilliant court life symbolized and reinforced their authority.

Peter the Great   This portrait by a Dutch artist captures the tsar's "westernizing" mission by showing Peter in military dress according to European fashions of the day.
(Bildarchiv Preussischer Kulturbesitz/Art Resource, NY)

So, he set out to refashion Russian society in what amounted to an enforced cultural revolution. He provoked a direct confrontation with Russia's traditional aristocracy over everything from education to matters of dress. He elevated numerous new families to the ranks of gentry and created an official ranking system for the nobility to encourage and reward service to his government.

Peter's effort to reorient his nation culturally, economically, and politically toward Europe was most obvious in the construction of the city of St. Petersburg on the Gulf of Finland, which provided access to the Baltic Sea (see **MAP 16.2**). In stark contrast to Moscow, dominated by the medieval fortress of the Kremlin, St. Petersburg was a modern European city with wide avenues and palaces designed for a sophisticated court life.

Although Peter was highly intelligent, practical, and determined to create a more productive and better governed society, he was also cruel and authoritarian. Peasants already bore the brunt of taxation, but their tax burden worsened when they were assessed arbitrarily by head and not by output of the land. The building of St. Petersburg cost staggering sums in both money and workers' lives. Peter's entire reform system was carried out tyrannically; resistance was brutally suppressed. Victims included his own son, who died after torture while awaiting execution for questioning his father's policies. Peter faced rebellions by elites, as well as common people, against the exactions and the cultural changes of his regime.

A major reason for the high cost of Peter's government to the Russian people was his ambition for territorial gain—hence, his emphasis on an improved, and costly, army and navy. He recruited experienced foreign technicians and created the Russian navy from scratch. At first, ships were built in the south to contest Turkish control of the Black Sea. Later, they were built in the north to secure and defend the Baltic. Peter also modernized the Russian army by employing tactics, training, and discipline he had observed in the West. He introduced military conscription and built munitions plants. By 1709, Russia was able to manufacture most of the up-to-date firearms its army needed.

Russia waged war virtually throughout Peter's reign. He struck at the Ottomans and their client state in the Crimea. Peter was most successful against his northern competitor, Sweden, for control of the weakened Polish state and the Baltic Sea. The conflicts between Sweden and Russia, known as the Great Northern War, raged from 1700 to 1709 and, in a less intense phase, lasted until 1721. By the Treaty of Nystadt in 1721, Russia gained its present-day territory in the Gulf of Finland near St. Petersburg, plus Livonia and Estonia. These acquisitions gave Russia a secure window on the Baltic and, in combination with its gains of Lithuanian territory earlier in the century, made Russia the preeminent Baltic power, at Sweden's and Poland's expense.

SECTION SUMMARY

- After the Thirty Years' War, Austria, Brandenburg-Prussia, and Russia became the dominant states in central and eastern Europe.

- Central and eastern Europe provided raw materials for the wider European economy, which enhanced elites' power over peasants, increased revenues to states, and caused wars between states over these resources.

- The Austrian Habsburgs consolidated their power in their territories within the Holy Roman Empire and reconquered Hungary from the Ottoman Turks.

- Although composed of a collection of small principalities, Brandenburg-Prussia became a powerful state.

- Poland-Lithuania declined in the seventeenth century because the elective monarchy could not defend itself against independent aristocrats, rebellious Cossacks, or powerful neighboring states.

- Russia was forcibly modernized by Peter the Great and became the most powerful state in eastern Europe under his reign, eclipsing Sweden in control of Baltic territories.

THE EXPANSION OF OVERSEAS TRADE AND SETTLEMENT

How and why did Europe's overseas trade and colonization expand in the seventeenth century and what effects did this expansion have on Europe itself?

By the beginning of the seventeenth century, competition from the Dutch, French, and English was disrupting the Spanish and Portuguese trading empires in the New World and in Asia. During the seventeenth century, the Dutch not only became masters of the spice trade, but broadened the market to include many other commodities. In the Americas, a new trading system linking Europe, Africa, and the New World came into being with the expansion of tobacco and, later, sugar production. French and English colonists began settling in North America in increasing numbers. Overseas trade also had a crucial impact on life within Europe: on patterns of production and consumption, on social stratification, and on the distribution of wealth.

The Growth of Trading Empires: The Success of the Dutch

By the end of the sixteenth century, the Dutch and the English were making incursions into the Portuguese-controlled spice trade with areas of India, Ceylon, and the East Indies. Spain had annexed Portugal in 1580, but the drain on Spain's resources, from its wars with the Dutch and French, prevented Spain from adequately defending its enlarged trading empire in Asia. The Dutch and, to a lesser degree, the English rapidly supplanted Portuguese control of this lucrative trade (see **Map 16.3**).

The Dutch were particularly well placed to dominate overseas trade. They already dominated seaborne trade within Europe, including the most important long-distance trade, which linked Spain and Portugal—with their wine and salt, as well as spices, hides, and gold from abroad—with the Baltic seacoast, where these products were sold for grain and timber produced in Germany, Poland-Lithuania, and Scandinavia. The geographic position of the Netherlands and the fact that the Dutch consumed more Baltic grain than any other area, because of their large urban population, help to explain their dominance of this trade. In addition, the Dutch had improved the design of their merchant ships to maximize their profits. By 1600, they had

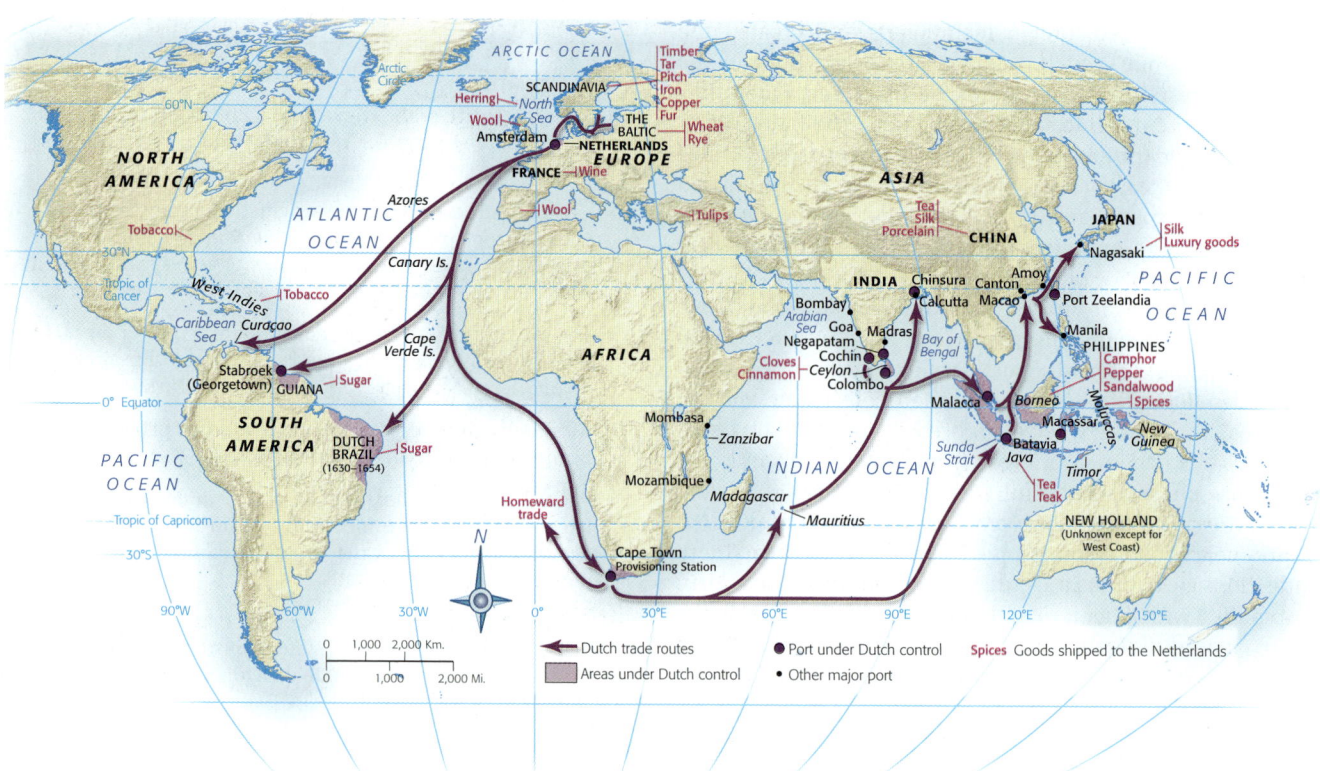

🌐 **Map 16.3—Dutch Commerce in the Seventeenth Century**
The Dutch supplanted Portuguese control of trade with Asia and dominated seaborne trade within Europe.

developed the *fluitschip* (flyship), a cheaply built vessel with a long, flat hull and simple rigging, that carried goods economically.

The Dutch succeeded in Asia because of institutional, as well as technological, innovations. In 1602, the **Dutch East India Company** was formed. The company combined government management of trade, typical of the period, with both public and private investment. In the past, groups of investors had funded single voyages or small numbers of ships on a one-time basis. The formation of the Dutch East India Company created a permanent pool of capital to sustain trade. After 1612, investments in the company were negotiable as stock. These greater assets allowed proprietors to spread the risks and delays of longer voyages among larger numbers of investors. In addition, more money was available for warehouses, docks, and ships. The English East India Company, founded in 1607, also supported trade, but more modestly. It had one-tenth the capital of the Dutch company and did not use the same system of permanent capital held as stock by investors until 1657. The Bank of Amsterdam, founded in 1609, became the depository for the bullion that flowed into the Netherlands with the flood of trade. The bank established currency exchange rates and issued paper money and instruments of credit to facilitate commerce.

A dramatic expansion of trade with Asia resulted from the Dutch innovations, so much so that by 1650, the European market for spices was glutted, and traders' profits had begun to fall. To control the supply of spices, the Dutch seized some of the areas where they were produced. The Dutch and English also responded to the oversupply of spices by diversifying their trade. The proportion of spices in cargoes from the East fell from about 70 percent at mid-century to just over 20 percent by the century's end. New consumer goods, such as tea, coffee, and silk and cotton fabrics, took their place. Eventually, the Dutch and the English, alert for fresh opportunities, entered the local carrying trade among Asian states. This enabled them to make profits even without purchasing goods, and it slowed the drain of hard currency from Europe—currency in increasingly short supply, as silver mines in the Americas were depleted.

Dutch East India Company   Commercially innovative Dutch company, formed in 1602, that combined government management of trade with both public and private investment.

The "Golden Age" of the Netherlands

The prosperity occasioned by the Dutch trading empire created social and political conditions within the Netherlands unique among European states. The concentration of trade and shipping sustained a healthy merchant oligarchy and also a prosperous artisanal sector. Disparities of wealth were smaller here than anywhere else in Europe. The shipbuilding and fishing trades, among others, supported large numbers of workers with a high standard of living for the age.

The Netherlands appeared to contemporaries to be an astonishing exception to the normal structures of politics. Political decentralization in the Netherlands persisted. The Estates General (representative assembly) for the Netherlands as a whole had no independent powers of taxation. Each of the seven provinces retained considerable autonomy. Wealthy merchants in the Estates of the province of Holland, in fact, constituted the government for the entire nation for long periods because of Holland's economic dominance. The head of government was the executive secretary, known as the pensionary, of Holland's Estates.

Holland's only competition in the running of affairs came from the House of Orange, aristocratic leaders of the revolt against Spain (see pages 410–413). They exercised what control they had by means of the office of *stadtholder* (STAHT-hole-der)—a kind of military governorship—to which they were elected in individual provinces. Their principal interest, traditional military glory and dynastic power, accounted for some of their influence, since they led the Netherlands' defense against Spanish attacks until the Peace of Westphalia in 1648 and against French aggression after 1672. Their power also came from their status as the only counterweight within the Netherlands to the dominance of Amsterdam's (in Holland) mercantile interests. Small towns, dependent on land-based trade or rural areas dominated by farmers and gentry, looked to the stadtholders of the Orange family to defend their interests.

As elsewhere, religion was a source of political conflict. The stadtholders and the leading families of Holland, known as regents, vied for control of the state church. Regents of Holland generally favored a less rigid and austere form of Calvinism than did the stadtholders. Their view reflected the needs of the diverse urban communities of Holland, where thousands of Jews, as well as Catholics and various Protestants, lived. Dutch commercial dominance involved the Netherlands in costly wars throughout the second half of the century. Between 1657 and 1660, the Dutch fought the Swedes to safeguard the sea-lanes and port cities of the Baltic. The most costly conflicts came from the rivalry of England and France. Under Cromwell, the English attempted to close their ports to the Dutch carrying trade. In 1672, the English, under Charles II, allied with the French, hoping that together they could destroy Dutch commercial power and even divide the Netherlands' territory between them. The Dutch navy, rebuilt since Cromwell's challenge, soon forced England out of the alliance.

But there were long-term consequences of these wars for the Dutch state. As a result of the land war with France, the Estates in Holland lost control of policy to William of Nassau (d. 1702), prince of Orange, after 1672. William drew the Netherlands into his family's long-standing close relationship with England. Like previous members of his family, William had married into the English royal family: His wife was Mary, daughter of James II. After William and Mary assumed the English throne, Dutch commerce actually suffered more when allied with England than in its previous rivalry. William used Dutch resources for the land war against Louis XIV and reserved, for the English navy, the fight at sea. By the end of the century, Dutch maritime strength was being eclipsed by English sea power.

The Growth of Atlantic Commerce

In the seventeenth century, the Dutch, the English, and the French joined the Spanish as colonial and commercial powers in the Americas. The Spanish colonial empire, in theory a trading system closed to outsiders, was in fact vulnerable to other European traders. Spanish treasure fleets were themselves a glittering attraction. In 1628, for example, a Dutch captain seized the entire fleet. But by then, Spain's goals and those of its competitors had begun to shift. The limits of an economy based on the extraction, rather than the production, of wealth became clear with the declining output of the Spanish silver mines during the 1620s. In response, the Spanish and their Dutch, French, and English competitors expanded the production of cash crops: tobacco, dyestuffs, and, above all, sugar.

Vermeer: The Letter
This is a later work by one of the great artists of the Dutch "Golden Age." Dutch art was distinguished by common, rather than heroic, subjects–here, a merchant-class woman writes a letter. The masterful use of lighting and perspective in paintings such as this one would not be equaled until the age of photography. (Bridgeman-Giraudon/Art Resource, NY)

plantation system
Agricultural system, first developed by the Portuguese, in which forced labor produced cash crops on large estates owned by absentee landlords.

The European demand for tobacco and sugar, both addictive substances, grew steadily in the seventeenth century. The **plantation system**—the use of forced labor to produce cash crops on vast tracts of land—had been developed on Mediterranean islands in the Middle Ages by European entrepreneurs, using slaves procured in Black Sea ports by Venetian and Genoese traders. Sugar production by this system had been established on Atlantic islands, such as the Cape Verde Islands, using African labor, and then in the Americas, by the Spanish and Portuguese. Sugar production in the New World grew from about 20,000 tons a year in 1600 to about 200,000 tons by 1770.

In the 1620s, while the Dutch were exploiting Portuguese weakness in the Eastern spice trade, they were also seizing sugar regions in Brazil and replacing Portuguese slave traders in African ports. The Portuguese were able to retake most of their Brazilian territory in the 1650s. But the Dutch, because they monopolized the carrying trade, were able to become the official supplier of slaves to Spanish plantations in the New World and the chief supplier of slaves, as well as other goods, to most other regions. (See the feature, "The Global Record: Journal of a Dutch Slave Ship.") The Dutch made handsome profits dealing in human cargo until the end of the seventeenth century, when they were supplanted by the British.

The Dutch introduced sugar cultivation to the French and English after learning it themselves in Brazil. Sugar plantations began to supplant tobacco cultivation, as well as subsistence farming, on the Caribbean islands the English and French controlled. Beginning in the late sixteenth century, English and French seamen had seized islands in the Caribbean to use as provisioning stations and staging points for raids against or commerce with Spanish colonies. Some island outposts had expanded into colonies and attracted European settlers—some, as in North America, coming as indentured servants—to work the land. Sugar cultivation drastically transformed the character of these island settlements because it demanded huge outlays of capital

Sugar Manufacture in Caribbean Colonies Production of sugar required large capital outlays, in part because the raw cane had to be processed quickly, on-site, to avoid spoilage. This scene depicts enslaved workers operating a small sugar mill on the island of Barbados in the seventeenth century. In the background, a press crushes the cane; in the foreground, the juice from the cane is boiled down until sugar begins to crystallize. (Mary Evans Picture Library)

and continual supplies of unskilled labor. Large plantations, owned by wealthy, often absentee landlords and dependent on slave labor, replaced smaller-scale independent farms. The most profitable sugar colonies were, for the French, the islands of Martinique and Guadeloupe and, for the English, Barbados and Jamaica.

Early Colonies in North America

Aware of the overwhelming Spanish advantage in the New World, and still hoping for treasures, such as the Spanish had found, the English, French, and Dutch were also eager to explore and settle North America. From the early sixteenth century on, French, Dutch, English, and Portuguese seamen had fished and traded off Newfoundland. By 1630, small French and Scottish settlements in Acadia (near modern Nova Scotia) and on the St. Lawrence River and English settlements in Newfoundland were established to systematically exploit the timber, fish, and fur of the North Atlantic coasts.

In England, rising unemployment and religious discontent created a large pool of potential colonists, some of whom were initially attracted to early farming and trading settlements in the Caribbean. The first of the English settlements to endure, in what was to become the United States, was established at Jamestown, named for James I, in Virginia in 1607. ("Virginia," named for Elizabeth I, the "Virgin Queen," was an extremely vague designation for the Atlantic coast of North America and its hinterland.)

ENGLISH SETTLEMENTS

The Crown encouraged colonization, but a private company, similar to those that financed long-distance trade, was established to organize the enterprise. The directors of the Virginia Company were London businessmen. Investors and would-be colonists purchased shares. Shareholders among the colonists could participate in a colonial assembly, although the governor appointed by the company was the final authority.

The colonists arrived in Virginia with ambitious and optimistic instructions: to open mines, establish profitable agriculture, and search for sea routes to Asia. But at first, the colonists struggled even to survive in the unfamiliar environment. "Though there be fish in the seas … and beasts in the woods … they are so wild and we so weak and ignorant, we cannot trouble them much," wrote Captain John Smith from Virginia to the directors in London.[3] The native peoples in Virginia, unlike those in Spanish-held territories, were not organized in urbanized, rigidly

Journal of a Dutch Slave Ship

These excerpts from a journal kept by the captain of the Dutch ship St. Jan record a 1659 slave-trading voyage that began in Africa and ended on Curaçao, a Dutch island colony in the Caribbean.

The 8th [of March]. We arrived with our ship on Saturday before Arda [in modern Benin] to take onboard the surgeon's mate, and tamarinds as refreshment for the slaves. We set sail the next day to continue our voyage to Rio Reael.

The 22nd [of May]. We weighed anchor again and sailed out of the Rio Reael. . . . We acquired there in trade two hundred and nineteen slaves, men and women, boys as well as girls; and we set our course for [islands in the Gulf of Biafra] in order to seek food for the slaves, because nothing was to be had in Rio Reael.

The 26th ditto. On Monday we arrived [on the islands]. We spent seven days there looking but barely obtained enough for the slaves' daily consumption; therefore we decided to sail [up a nearby river] to see whether any food could be found there.

The 29th [of June]. On Sunday we decided to continue our voyage because there was also little food [up the river mouth] for the slaves because of the heavy rain which we had daily and because many slaves were suffering from dysentery caused by the bad food supplied to us at [St. George del Mina, a Dutch fort established to serve the slave trade]. . . .

The 11th [of August]. We lay sixteen days at Cape Lopez [modern Gabon] in order to take on water and firewood. Among the water barrels some forty were taken apart to be repaired because our cooper died . . . [and] we had no one who could repair them.

The 24th [of September]. On Friday we arrived at the island of Tobago [in the Caribbean] where we took on water and also bought some bread for our crew because for three weeks they have had no rations.

The 1st of November. We lost our ship on the reef [east of Curaçao] and our crew fled in the boat immediately. There was no chance to save the slaves because we had to abandon the ship on account of heavy surf.

The 4th ditto. We arrived with the boat at . . . Curaçao. The [governor] dispatched two sloops to retrieve the slaves from the shipwreck. One of the sloops was taken by a pirate together with eighty-four slaves.

QUESTIONS

1. Note the dates in the captain's journal. How much time was devoted to trade and provisioning in Africa? How much time to the transatlantic journey?

2. Note the details the captain includes. What do these details reveal about how the voyage was planned? For whom is he recording these details, and why?

3. A companion document reveals that 110 of the 219 captive men, women, and children died during the voyage across the Atlantic. Does knowing this information change how you interpret this document? What happened to the captives who survived the journey?

Source: Charles T. Gehring and J. A. Schiltkamp, eds., *New Netherlands Documents*, vol. 17 (Interlaken, N.Y.: Heart of the Lakes Publishing, 1987), pp. 128–131. Used by permission from the *New Netherlands Project*, The New York State Library.

hierarchical societies that, after conquest, could provide the invaders with a labor force. In fact, most of the native population was quickly wiped out by European diseases. The introduction of tobacco as a cash crop a few years later saved the colonists economically—although the Virginia Company had already gone bankrupt and the Crown had assumed control of the colony. With the cultivation of tobacco, the Virginia colony, like the Caribbean islands, became dependent on forced, eventually slave, labor.

Among the Virginia colonists were impoverished men and women who came as servants, indentured to those who had paid their passage—that is, they were bound by contract to pay off their debts by several years of labor. Colonies established to the north, in what was called "New England," also drew people from the margins of English society. Early settlers there were religious dissidents. The first to arrive were the Pilgrims, who arrived at Plymouth (modern Massachusetts) in 1620. They were a community of religious Separatists who had originally immigrated to the Netherlands from England for freedom of conscience.

Following the Pilgrims, came Puritans, escaping escalating persecution under Charles I. The first, in 1629, settled under the auspices of another royally chartered company, the Massachusetts Bay Company. Among their number were many prosperous Puritan merchants and landholders. Independence from investors in London allowed them an unprecedented degree of self-government once the Massachusetts Bay colony was established.

Nevertheless, the colonies in North America were disappointments to England because they generated much less wealth than expected. Shipping timber back to Europe proved too expensive, although New England forests did supply some of the Caribbean colonists' needs. The fur trade became less lucrative, as English settlement pushed the Native Americans, who did most of the trapping, west and as French trappers to the north encroached on the trade. Certain colonists profited enormously from the tobacco economy, but the mother country did so only moderately because the demand in Europe for tobacco never matched the demand for sugar. The English settlements did continue to attract more migrants than other colonizers' outposts. By 1640, Massachusetts had some fourteen thousand European inhabitants. Through most of the next century, the growth of colonial populations in North America would result in an English advantage over the French in control of New World territory.

FRENCH SETTLEMENTS

The French began their settlement of North America at the same time as the English, in the same push to compensate for their mutual weakness in comparison to the Spanish (see **MAP 16.4**). The French efforts, however, had very different results, owing partly to the sites of their settlements, but mostly to the relationship between the mother country and the colonies. The French hold on territory was always tenuous because of the scant number of colonists who could be lured from home. There seems to have been less economic impetus for colonization from France than from England. After the French crown took over the colonies, the religious impetus also evaporated, since only Catholics were allowed to settle in New France. Moreover, the Crown forced a hierarchical political organization on the French colonies. A royal governor directed the colony, and large tracts of land were set aside for privileged investors. Thus, North America offered little to tempt French people of modest means who were seeking a better life.

The first successful French colony was established in Acadia in 1605. This settlement was an exception among the French efforts because it was founded by Huguenots, not by Catholics. A few years later, the explorer Samuel de Champlain (1567?–1635) navigated the St. Lawrence River and founded Quebec City (1608). He convinced the royal government, emerging from its preoccupations with religious wars at home, to promote the development of the colony. French explorers went on to establish Montreal, farther up the St. Lawrence (1642), and to explore the Great Lakes and the Mississippi River basin (see **MAP 16.4**).

Such investment as the French crown was able to attract went into profitable trade, mainly in furs, and not into the difficult business of colonization. French trappers and traders who ventured into wilderness areas were renowned for their hardiness and adaptability, but they did not bring their families and establish settled, European-style towns. Quebec remained more of a trading station, dependent on shipments of food from France, than a growing urban community. Much of the energy of French colonization was expended by men and women of religious orders—the "Black Robes"—bringing their zeal to new frontiers. By the middle of the seventeenth century, all of New France had only about three thousand European inhabitants.

The seeming weakness of the French colonial effort in North America was not much noticed at the time. French and English fishermen, trappers, and traders competed intensely, and the French often reaped the greater share of profits, owing to their closer ties with Native American trading systems. Outright battles occasionally erupted between English and French settlements. But for both England and France, indeed for all colonial powers, the major profits and strategic interests in the New World lay to the south, in the sugar-producing Caribbean. For example, in 1674, the Dutch gave up their trading center, New Amsterdam (modern-day New York City) to the English in return for recognition of the Dutch claims to sugar-producing Guiana (modern Suriname) in South America.

The growth of the plantation system meant that, by far, the largest group of migrants to European-held territories in the Americas was forced migrants: African men and women sold

🌐 **MAP 16.4—The English and French in North America, ca. 1700**

By 1700, a veritable ring of French-claimed territory encircled the coastal colonies of England. English-claimed areas, however, were more densely settled and more economically viable.

into slavery and shipped, like other cargo, across the Atlantic to work on Caribbean islands, in South America and southern North America. A conservative estimate is that approximately 1.35 million Africans were forcibly transported as slave labor to the New World during the seventeenth century.

The Impact of Trade and Warfare Within Europe

Within Europe, the economic impact of overseas trade was profound. Merchants and investors in a few of Europe's largest cities reaped great profits. Mediterranean ports, such as Venice, once the heart of European trade, did not share in the bonanza from the new trade with Asia or the Americas. Atlantic ports, such as Seville, through which most Spanish commerce with the New World flowed, and, above all, Amsterdam began to flourish. The population of Amsterdam increased from about 30,000 to 200,000 in the course of the seventeenth century.

All capital cities, however, not just seaports, grew substantially during the 1600s. Increasing numbers of government officials, courtiers and their hangers-on, and people involved in trade lived and worked in capital cities. These cities also grew indirectly from the demand such people generated for workers, such as carters and domestic servants, and products, ranging from fashionable clothing to exotic foodstuffs. For the first time, large numbers of country people found work in cities. Perhaps as much as one-fifth of the population of England passed through London at one time or another, creating the mobile, volatile community so active in the English civil war and its aftermath.

But social stratification intensified despite the expanding economy. Poverty increased in cities, even in vibrant Amsterdam, because cities attracted people fleeing rural unemployment with few skills and fewer resources. As growing central governments heaped tax burdens on peasants, many rural people were caught in a cycle of debt; the only escape was to abandon farming and flock to cities. Patterns of consumption reflected the economic gulf between city dwellers; most people could not afford to buy the spices or sugar that generated such profits.

Peasant rebellions occurred throughout the century as a result of depressed economic conditions and the heavy taxation that accompanied expanded royal power and extensive warfare. Some small-scale revolts involved direct action, such as seizing the tax collector's grain or stopping the movement of grain to the great cities. Urban demand often caused severe food shortages in rural areas in western Europe, despite the booming trade in grain with eastern Europe via the Baltic.

The scale of popular revolts, especially against taxation, meant that thousands of troops sometimes had to be diverted from a state's foreign wars. As a matter of routine, soldiers accompanied tax officials and enforced collection all over Europe. As the ambitions of rulers grew, so too did the resistance of ordinary people to the exactions of the state.

SECTION SUMMARY

- The Dutch innovations in ship design and forms of investment helped them dominate overseas trade.

- The wealth from trade supported a higher standard of living, wider political participation, and more religious tolerance in the Netherlands than elsewhere in Europe.

- The Dutch, the English, and the French expanded their trade and colonization in the Americas, following Spain and Portugal's earlier successes.

- Most European profits from trade and settlement in the Americas came from plantation agriculture, using slave labor, established on Caribbean islands.

- Overseas trade, together with more centralized governments, resulted in the spectacular growth of coastal and capital cities, wider divisions between rich and poor, and increased peasant rebellions.

CHAPTER SUMMARY

Following the most powerful monarchy in Europe, France, most states had moved from internal division—with independent provinces and aristocrats going their own way—to greater coherence. In France, Louis XIV's brand of government, which has been labeled "absolutism," arose from successful use of traditional political mechanisms, such as patronage, plus the defeat of any institutional brakes on his authority. Court life in Louis's reign sponsored artistic creativity and encouraged a new emphasis on cultural refinement in the aristocracy. In the military realm, however, Louis started a series of costly wars from which the French state gained little.

In England, a civil war over the very issue of parliamentary participation in government led to the temporary abolition of the monarchy itself. The Crown was restored under Charles

II, but conflicts arose again over political and religious policy under his successor James II. The year 1688 marked the "Glorious Revolution," in which Parliament helped bring William and Mary to the throne. Parliament's power was ensured by the Declaration of Rights and Bill of Rights, which have lasting significance today.

States, troubled by religious and political turmoil or on the political margins early in the century, evolved into secure and dynamic centers of power: the Netherlands, the Habsburg domains, Brandenburg-Prussia, and Russia. This stability was both cause and consequence of rulers' desires to make war on an ever larger scale. The Austrian Habsburgs reconquered Hungary from the Ottoman Turks, while the power of Poland-Lithuania declined in the seventeenth century because it was unable to defend itself against independent aristocrats, rebellious Cossacks, or powerful neighboring states. Russia was forcibly modernized by Peter the Great and became the most powerful state in eastern Europe, eclipsing Sweden in control of Baltic territories. By the end of the century, only those states able to field massive armies were competitive on the European stage. The Netherlands, a stark exception to the pattern of centralized royal control, began more closely to resemble other states under the pressure of warfare by century's end.

At the beginning of the century, overseas trade and colonization had been the near monopoly of Spain and Portugal. At the end of the century, the English, French, and Dutch had supplanted them in controlling trade with Asia and were reaping many profits in the Americas, especially from the extension of plantation agriculture. The Dutch were a successful trading empire because of their innovations in ship design and forms of investment. With their wealth from trade, they supported a higher standard of living, wider political participation, and more religious tolerance. Beneath all these developments lay significant economic, social, and cultural shifts. One effect of the increased wealth generated by overseas trade and the increased power of governments to tax their subjects was a widening gulf between rich and poor. New styles of behavior and patterns of consumption highlighted differences between social classes.

FOCUS QUESTIONS

- How did Louis XIV successfully expand royal power in France and what were some of the achievements of his reign?

- What were the long-term consequences of the English civil war?

- Which states began to dominate central and eastern Europe and why were they successful?

- How and why did Europe's overseas trade and colonization expand in the seventeenth century and what effects did this expansion have on Europe itself?

KEY TERMS

absolutism (p.444)

Louis XIV (p. 444)

mercantilism (p. 446)

Parliament (p. 452)

Oliver Cromwell   (p. 452)

Glorious Revolution   (p. 455)

Treaty of Carlowitz   (p. 459)

Brandenburg-Prussia (p.459)

Cossacks   (p. 461)

Peter the Great   (p. 462)

Dutch East India Company (p. 464)

plantation system   (p. 466)

 This icon will direct you to additional materials on the website: www .cengage.com/history/ noble/westciv6e.

e See our interactive eBook for map and primary source activities.

NOTES

1. Quoted in D. H. Pennington, *Europe in the Seventeenth Century*, 2d ed. (London: Longman, 1989), p. 508.

2. G. E. Aylmer, ed., *The Levellers in the English Revolution* (Ithaca, N.Y.: Cornell University Press, 1975), pp. 100–101.

3. Philip A. Barbour, ed., *The Complete Works of Captain John Smith (1580–1631)*, vol. 2 (Chapel Hill: University of North Carolina Press, 1986), p. 189.

17

Descartes and Queen Christina
René Descartes (*second from the right*) instructs Queen Christina of Sweden and her
courtiers.　(Réunion des musées nationaux/Art Resource, NY)

A Revolution in Worldview

The year is 1649. Queen Christina of Sweden welcomes us with her gaze and her gesture to witness a science lesson at her court. Her instructor, the French philosopher René Descartes, clutches a compass and points to an astronomical drawing. The young queen, 23 years old at the time, was already well known as a patron of artists and scholars. Christina had invited Descartes to her court because of his achievements in physics and philosophy. This painting depicts the fact that during Christina's lifetime, new theories in the field of astronomy revolutionized the sciences and required new definitions of matter to explain them. Descartes earned fame both for his new theories about matter and for his systematic approach to using human reason to understand the universe. This painting celebrates both Descartes's work and Christina's sponsorship of it.

The revolution within the sciences had been initiated in the sixteenth century by the astronomical calculations and hypotheses of Nicholas Copernicus, who theorized that the earth moves around the sun. The work of the Italian mathematician and astronomer Galileo Galilei, as well as others, added evidence to support this hypothesis. Their work overturned principles of physics and philosophy that had held sway since ancient times. Later generations of scientists and philosophers, beginning with Descartes, labored to construct new principles to explain the way nature behaves. The readiness of scientists, their patrons, and educated laypeople to push Copernicus's hypothesis to these conclusions came from several sources: their exposure to the intellectual innovations of Renaissance thought, the intellectual challenges and material opportunities represented by the discovery of the New World, and the challenge to authority embodied in the Reformation. They advanced and discussed scientific theories in print for the first time. Also, the new science offered prestige and technological advances to the rulers, such as Christina, who sponsored it.

By the end of the seventeenth century, a vision of an infinite but orderly cosmos appealing to human reason had, among educated Europeans, largely replaced the medieval vision of a closed universe centered on the earth and suffused with Christian purpose. Religion became an increasingly subordinate ally of science as confidence in an open-ended, experimental approach to knowledge came to be as strongly held as religious conviction. It is because of this larger shift in worldview, not simply because of particular scientific discoveries, that the seventeenth century can be called the era of the Scientific Revolution.

Because religious significance had been attached to previous scientific explanations and religious authority had defended them, the new astronomy automatically led to an enduring debate about the compatibility of science and religion. But the revolution in worldview was not confined to astronomy or even to science generally. As philosophers gained confidence in human reason and the intelligibility of the world, they turned to new speculation about human affairs. They began to challenge traditional justifications for the hierarchical nature of society and the sanctity of authority, just as energetically as Copernicus and his followers had overthrown old views about the cosmos.

FOCUS QUESTIONS

- How did the Copernican theory challenge traditional views of the universe?

- How and why did new theories about astronomy lead to a broader Scientific Revolution?

- How did the new scientific worldview lead people to challenge traditional notions of society, the state, and religion?

This icon will direct you to additional materials on the website: www.cengage.com/history/noble/westciv6e.

See our interactive eBook for map and primary source activities.

THE REVOLUTION IN ASTRONOMY, 1543–1632

How did the Copernican theory challenge traditional views of the universe?

The origins of the seventeenth-century revolution in worldview lie, for the most part, in developments in astronomy. Because of astronomy's role in the explanations of the world and human life that had been devised by ancient and medieval scientists and philosophers, any advances in astronomy were bound to have widespread intellectual repercussions. By the early part of the seventeenth century, fundamental astronomical beliefs had been successfully challenged. The consequence was the undermining of both the material (physics) and the philosophical (metaphysics) explanations of the world that had been standing for centuries.

The Inherited Worldview

Most ancient and medieval astronomers accepted the perspective on the universe that unaided human senses support—namely, that the earth is fixed at the center of the universe and the celestial bodies, such as the sun and the planets, rotate around it. The regular movements of heavenly bodies and the obvious importance of the sun for life on earth made astronomy a vital undertaking for both scientific and religious purposes in many ancient societies. Astronomers in ancient Greece carefully observed the heavens and learned to calculate and to predict the seemingly circular motion of the stars and the sun about the earth. The orbits of the planets were more difficult to explain, for the planets seemed to travel both east and west across the sky at various times and with no regularity that could be mathematically understood. Indeed, the word *planet* comes from a Greek word meaning "wanderer."

We now know that all the planets simultaneously orbit the sun at different speeds in paths that are at different distances from the sun. The relative positions of the planets constantly change; sometimes other planets are "ahead" of the earth and sometimes "behind." In the second century A.D., the Greek astronomer Ptolemy (TAHL-eh-mee) attempted to explain the planets' occasional "backward" motion by attributing it to "epicycles"—small circular orbits within the larger orbit. Ptolemy's mathematical explanations of the imagined epicycles were extremely complex, but neither Ptolemy nor medieval mathematicians and astronomers were ever able fully to account for planetary motion.

Ancient physics, most notably the work of the Greek philosopher Aristotle (384–322 B.C.), explained the fact that some objects (such as cannonballs) fall to earth but others (stars and planets) seem weightless relative to earth because of their composition: Different kinds of matter have different inherent tendencies and properties. In this view, all earthbound matter (like cannonballs) falls because it is naturally attracted to earth—heaviness being a property of earthbound things.

In the Christian era, the Aristotelian explanation of the universe was infused with Christian meaning and purpose. The heavens were said to be made of different, pure matter because they were the abode of the angels. Both the earth and the humans who inhabited it were changeable and corruptible. Yet, God had given human beings a unique and special place in the universe, which was thought to be a closed world with the stationary earth at the center. Revolving around the earth in circular orbits were the sun, moon, stars, and planets. The motion of all lesser bodies was caused by the rotation of all the stars together in the vast crystal-like sphere in which they were embedded.

A few ancient astronomers theorized that the earth moved about the sun. Some medieval philosophers also adopted this heliocentric thesis (*helios* is the Greek word for "sun"), but it remained a minority view because it seemed to contradict both common sense and observed data. The sun and stars *appeared* to move around the earth with great regularity. Moreover, how could objects fall to earth if the earth was moving beneath them? Also, astronomers detected no difference in angles from which observers on earth viewed the stars at different times. Such differences would exist, they thought, if the earth changed positions by moving around the sun. It was inconceivable that the universe could be so large and the stars so distant that the earth's movement would produce no measurable change in the earth's position with respect to the stars.

Several conditions of intellectual life in the sixteenth century encouraged new work in astronomy and led to the revision of the earth-centered worldview. The most important was the work of Renaissance humanists in recovering and interpreting ancient texts. Now able to work with new Greek versions of Ptolemy, mathematicians and astronomers noted that his explanations for the motion of the planets were imperfect and not simply inadequately transmitted, as they had long believed. Also, the discovery of the New World dramatically undercut the assumption that ancient knowledge was superior. The existence of the Americas specifically undermined Ptolemy's authority once again, for it disproved many of the assertions in his *Geography*, which had just been recovered in Europe the previous century.

The desire to explain heavenly movements better was still loaded with religious significance in the sixteenth century and was heightened by the immediate need for reform of the Julian calendar (named for Julius Caesar). Ancient observations of the movement of the sun, though remarkably accurate, could not measure the precise length of the solar year. By the sixteenth century, the cumulative error of this calendar had resulted in a change of ten days: The spring equinox fell on March 11 instead of March 21. An accurate and uniform system of dating was necessary for all rulers and their tax collectors and record keepers. And because the calculation of the date of Easter was at stake, a reliable calendar was the particular project of the church.

Impetus for new and better astronomical observations and calculations arose from other features of the intellectual and political landscape as well. Increasingly, as the century went on, princely courts became important sources of patronage for and sites of scientific activity. Rulers, eager to buttress their own power by symbolically linking it to dominion over nature, sponsored investigations of the world, as Ferdinand and Isabella had so successfully done, and displayed the marvels of nature at their courts. Sponsorship of science also yielded practical benefits: better mapping of the ruler's domains and better technology for mining, gunnery, and navigation.

Finally, schools of thought fashionable at the time, encouraged by the humanists' critique of tradition, hinted at the possibilities of alternative physical and metaphysical systems. The ancient doctrine of Hermeticism (named for the mythical originator of the ideas, Hermes Trismegistos), revived since the Renaissance, claimed that matter is universally imbued with divine (or magical) spirit. Drawing on Hermeticism was Paracelsianism, named for the Swiss physician Philippus von Hohenheim (1493–1541), who called himself Paracelsus (literally "beyond Celsus," an acclaimed Roman physician whose works had just been recovered). Paracelsus (pair-uh-SEL-sus) scoffed at the notion that ancient authorities were the final word on the workings of nature. Paracelsus offered an alternative to accepted medical theory, put forth by the ancient physician Galen (ca. 131–201), who was as revered as Aristotle. Galen (GAY- len) believed that an imbalance of bodily "humors" caused illness. Paracelsus substituted a theory of chemical imbalance that anticipated our modern understanding of pathology. He was wildly popular wherever he taught because he successfully treated many illnesses and lectured openly to laymen.

Neo-Platonism, another school of thought, had a more systematic and far-reaching impact. Neo-Platonism was a revival, primarily in Italian humanist circles, of certain aspects of Plato's thought. It contributed directly to innovation in science because it emphasized the abstract nature of true knowledge and thus encouraged mathematical investigation. This provided a spur to astronomical studies, which, since ancient times, had been concerned more with mathematical analysis of heavenly movements than with physical explanations for them. Also, like Hermeticism and Paracelsianism, Neo-Platonism had a mystical dimension that encouraged creative speculation about the nature of matter and the organization of the universe. Neo-Platonists were particularly fascinated by the sun as a symbol of the one divine mind or soul at the heart of all creation.

CHRONOLOGY

1543	Copernicus, *De Revolutionibus Orbium Caelestium* Vesalius, *On the Fabric of the Human Body*
1576	Construction of Brahe's observatory begins
1603	Accadèmia dei Lincei founded in Rome
1609	Kepler's third law of motion
1610	Galileo, *The Starry Messenger*
1620	Bacon, *Novum Organum*
1628	Harvey, *On the Motion of the Heart*
1632	Galileo, *Dialogue on the Two Chief Systems of the World*
1633	Galileo condemned and sentenced to house arrest
1637	Descartes, *Discourse on Method*
1651	Hobbes, *Leviathan*
1660	Boyle, *New Experiments Physico-Mechanical* Royal Society of London founded
1666	Académie Royale des Sciences founded in France
1686	Fontenelle, *Conversations on the Plurality of Worlds*
1687	Newton, *Principia (Mathematical Principles of Natural Philosophy)*
1690	Locke, *Two Treatises of Government and Essay on Human Understanding*
1702	Bayle, *Historical and Critical Dictionary*

Tycho Brahe's Observatory Brahe gathered the best talent, including German instrument makers and Italian architects, to build his state-of-the-art observatory near Copenhagen. Brahe named the complex Uraniborg, for Urania, the muse of astronomy. (General View of the Observatory of Uraniborg, constructed c. 1584 by Tycho Brahe (1546–1601) on the island of Hven, Denmark from 'Le Theatre du Monde' or 'Nouvel Atlas', published in Amsterdam, 1645 (coloured engraving) by Willem Blaeu (1571–1638) and Joan (1596–1673)/Private Collection/Archives Charmet/The Bridgeman Art Library)

Kepler's contribution to the new astronomy, like that of Copernicus, was fundamentally mathematical. In it, we can see the stamp of the Neo-Platonic conviction about the purity of mathematical explanation. Kepler spent ten years working to apply Brahe's data to the most intricate of all the celestial movements—the motion of the planet Mars—as a key to explaining all planetary motion. Mars is close to the earth, but its orbital path is farther from the sun. This combination produces dramatic and puzzling variations in the apparent movement of Mars to an earthly observer.

The result of Kepler's work was laws of planetary motion that, in the main, are still in use. First, Kepler eliminated the need for epicycles by correctly asserting that planets follow elliptical, and not circular, orbits. Elliptical orbits could account, both mathematically and visually, for the motion of the planets when combined with Kepler's second law, which describes the *rate* of a planet's motion around its orbital path. Kepler noted that the speed of a planet in its orbit slows proportionally as the planet's distance from the sun increases. A third law demonstrates that the distance of each planet from the sun and the time it takes each planet to orbit the sun are in a constant ratio.

Kepler's work was a breakthrough because it mathematically confirmed the Copernican heliocentric hypothesis. In so doing, the work directly challenged the ancient worldview, in which heavenly bodies constantly moved in circular orbits around a stationary earth. Kepler's laws invited speculation about the properties of heavenly and terrestrial bodies alike. In fact, a new physics would be required to explain the novel motion that Kepler had posited. Kepler himself, in Neo-Platonic fashion, attributed planetary motion to the sun: "[The sun] is a fountain of light, rich in fruitful heat, most fair, limpid and pure … called king of the planets for his motion, heart of the world for his power … Who would hesitate to confer the votes of the celestial motions on him who has been administering all other movements and changes by the benefit of the light which is entirely his possession?"[1]

Galileo Galilei Italian physicist and astronomer who provided evidence supporting the heliocentric theory and helped develop the science of mechanics.

Galileo and the Triumph of Copernicanism

Galileo Galilei holds a preeminent position in the development of astronomy because, first, he provided compelling new evidence to support Copernican theory and, second, he contributed to the development of a new physics—or, more precisely, mechanics—that could account for the movements of bodies in new terms. In short, he began to close the gap between the new astronomy and new explanations for the behavior of matter. Just as important, his efforts to publicize his findings and his condemnation by the church spurred popular debate about Copernican ideas in literate society and helped to determine the course science would take.

Galileo's career also illustrates, in dramatic fashion, the dependence of scientists on and their vulnerability to patronage relationships. Born to a minor Florentine noble family, Galileo began studying medicine at the nearby University of Pisa at the age of 17, but became intrigued by problems of mechanics and mathematics. He began studying those disciplines at Pisa under the tutelage of a Florentine court mathematician and became a lecturer in mathematics there in 1589, at age 25, after publishing promising work in mechanics. Three years later, well-connected fellow mathematicians helped him secure a more prestigious professorship at the University of Padua, where Copernicus had once studied. Galileo skillfully cultivated the learned Venetian aristocrats (Venice ruled Padua at this time) who controlled academic appointments and secured renewals and salary raises over the next eighteen years.

During his years at Pisa and Padua, Galileo pursued his revolutionary work in mechanics, although he did not publish the results of his experiments until much later. Galileo's principal contribution to mechanics lay in his working out of an early theory of inertia. As a result of a number of experiments with falling bodies (balls rolling on carefully constructed inclines—not free-falling objects that, according to myth, he dropped from the Leaning Tower of Pisa), Galileo ventured a new view of what is "natural" to objects. Galileo's view was that uniform motion is as natural as a state of rest. In the ancient and medieval universe, all motion needed a cause, and all motion could be explained in terms of purpose. "I hold," Galileo countered, "that there exists nothing in external bodies … but size, shape, quantity and motion."[2] Galileo retained the old assumption that motion was somehow naturally circular. Nevertheless, his theory was a crucial step in explaining motion according to new principles and in fashioning a worldview that accepted a mechanical universe devoid of metaphysical purpose.

The results of this work were, for the most part, not published until the end of his life. In the meantime, Galileo became famous for his astronomical observations, which he began in 1609 and which he parlayed into a position back at the Florentine court. Early that year, Galileo learned of the invention of a primitive telescope (which could magnify distant objects only three times) and quickly improved on it to make the first astronomically useful instrument. In *Sidereus Nuncius (The Starry Messenger,* 1610), he described his scrutiny of the heavens with his telescope in lay language. He documented sighting previously undetectable stars, as well as moons orbiting the planet Jupiter. In another blow to ancient descriptions of the universe, he noted craters and other "imperfections" on the surface of the moon. Three years later, he published his solar observations in *Letters on Sunspots.* Sunspots are regions of relatively cool gaseous material that appear as dark spots on the sun's surface. For Galileo, sunspots and craters on the moon proved that the heavens are not perfect and changeless, but rather are like the supposedly "corrupt" and changeable earth. His telescopic observations also provided further support for Copernican heliocentrism. Indeed, Galileo's own acceptance of Copernicanism can be dated to this point because magnification revealed that each heavenly body rotates on its axis: Sunspots, for example, can be tracked across the visible surface of the sun as the sun rotates.

Galileo had already been approached by various Italian princes and in turn sought to woo their support with gifts of some of his earlier inventions, such as a military compass. He aimed his *Starry Messenger* at the Medici dukes of Florence, naming Jupiter's moons the "Medicean Stars" and publishing the work to coincide with the accession of the young Cosimo II, whom he had tutored as a youth. In 1610, he returned in triumph to his native Tuscany as court philosopher to the grand duke. Soon, however, his own fame and the increasing acceptance of Copernicanism aroused opposition. In 1615, Galileo was denounced to the Inquisition by a Florentine friar. Galileo defended himself to his patrons and to the wider scientific community by arguing, in print, that the new science did not challenge religion. (See the feature, "The Written Record: Galileo Asserts Science and Religion Are Compatible.") After an investigation, the geokinetic theory (that the earth moves) was declared heretical, but Galileo himself was allowed to continue to use Copernican theory, but only as a theory. Indeed, a number of the most fervent practitioners of the new science continued to be clergymen who followed Galileo's work with interest. A new pope, elected in 1623, was a Tuscan aristocrat and an old friend of Galileo. Galileo dedicated his work on comets, *The Assayer* (1624), to Urban VIII in honor of his election.

Galileo Asserts Science and Religion are Compatible

After Galileo Galilei's work on sunspots was released, many learned followers grew anxious about the implications of the new science. In the letter excerpted here, published in 1615 and widely circulated, Galileo reassures the mother of Cosimo II, the dowager grand duchess of Tuscany, that the new science does not contradict Christianity. The Catholic Church would eventually condemn Galileo for his beliefs, arguing that it was wrong to contradict established knowledge about the heavens. Although the church's actions constrained the development of science in some (predominantly Catholic) regions, throughout Europe investigators continued to find ways to make the new science fully compatible with their faiths.

Some years ago, as Your Serene Highness well knows, I discovered in the heavens many things that had not been seen there before our own age. The novelty of these things, as well as some consequences which followed from them . . . stirred up against me no small number of professors—as if I had placed these things in the sky with my own hands in order to upset nature and overturn the sciences . . . [These professors] go about invoking the Bible, which they would have minister to their deceitful purposes. Contrary to the sense of the Bible and the intention of the holy Fathers, if I am not mistaken, they would extend such authorities until even in purely physical matters—where faith is not involved—they would have us altogether abandon reason and the evidence of our own senses in favor of some biblical passage, though under the surface meaning of its words this passage may contain a different sense. . . .

I think that in discussions of physical problems we ought to begin not from the authority of scriptural passages, but from sense experience and necessary demonstrations. . . . I should judge that the authority of the Bible was designed to persuade men of those articles and propositions which, surpassing all human reasoning, could not be made credible by science, or by any means other than through the very mouth of the Holy Spirit. . . .

But I do not feel obliged to believe that the same God who has endowed us with senses, reason and intellect has intended to forgo their use and by some other means to give us knowledge which we can attain by them. He would not require us to deny sense and reason in physical matters which are set before our eyes and minds by direct experience or necessary demonstrations. This must be especially true in those sciences of which but the faintest trace . . . is to be found in the Bible. Of astronomy, for instance, so little is found that none of the planets except Venus are so much as mentioned. . . .

Now, if the Holy Spirit has purposely neglected to teach us propositions of this sort as irrelevant to the highest goal (that is, to our salvation), how can anyone affirm that it is obligatory to take sides on them, and that one belief is required by faith, while another side is erroneous? . . . I would assert here something that was heard from [a respected cleric]: . . . "the intention of the Holy Ghost is to teach us how to go to heaven, not how heaven goes." . . . [And] in St. Augustine we read: "If anyone shall set the authority of Holy Writ against clear and manifest reason, . . . he opposes to the truth not the meaning of the Bible, which is beyond his comprehension, but rather his own interpretation. . . . "

Moreover, we are unable to affirm that all interpreters of the Bible speak with divine inspiration, for if that were so there would exist no differences between them about the sense of a given passage. Hence [it would be wise] not to permit anyone to usurp scriptural texts and force them in some way to maintain any physical conclusion to be true, when at some future time the senses . . . may show the contrary. Who indeed will set bounds to human ingenuity? Who will assert that everything in the universe capable of being perceived is already discovered and known?

QUESTIONS

1. How does Galileo justify pursuing scientific investigation against certain claims of faith?

2. Do you think that Galileo's arguments would have been reassuring to the grand duchess? Why or why not?

3. Why might the arguments have further angered those church officials already hostile toward Galileo's work?

Source: *Discoveries and Opinions of Galileo*, by Galileo Galilei, translated by Stillman Drake, copyright © 1957 by Stillman Drake. Used by permission of Doubleday, a division of Random House, Inc.

Now in his 60s, Galileo began to work on a book that summarized his life's work—*Dialogue on the Two Chief Systems of the World* (1632), structured as a conversation among three characters debating the merits of Copernican theory. Given the work's sensitive subject matter, Galileo obtained explicit permission from the pope to write it and cleared some portions with censors before publication. The work was the most important single source in its day for the popularization of Copernican theory, but it led to renewed concerns in Rome. Galileo had clearly overstepped the bounds of discussing Copernicanism in theory only and appeared to advocate it. Simplicio, the character representing the old worldview, was, as his name suggests, an example of ignorance, not wisdom.

Moreover, the larger political context affecting Galileo's patrons and friends had changed. The pope was being threatened by the Spanish and Austrian Habsburg rulers for his tepid support in the Thirty Years' War, in which Catholic forces were now losing to Protestant armies (see page 428). He could no longer be indulgent towards his friend, Galileo. Galileo was forced to stand trial for heresy in Rome in 1633. When, in a kind of plea-bargain arrangement, he pled guilty to a lesser charge of inadvertently advocating Copernicanism, Pope Urban intervened to insist on a weightier penalty. Galileo's book was banned, he was forced to formally renounce his "error," and he was sentenced to house arrest. Galileo lived confined and guarded, continuing his investigations of mechanics, until his death eight years later.

SECTION SUMMARY

- The Scientific Revolution began in 1543 with the publication of Copernicus's mathematical calculations supporting the heliocentric theory.

- Tycho Brahe and Johannes Kepler confirmed Copernicus's hypothesis with new data and more thorough mathematical explanations of the motions of planets.

- Galileo's observations with his telescope provided new evidence to support Copernican theory; his experiments in mechanics contributed to new explanations for the behavior of matter.

- Galileo's advocacy of Copernicanism led to his condemnation by the church.

THE SCIENTIFIC REVOLUTION EXPANDS, CA. 1600–1700

How and why did new theories about astronomy lead to a broader Scientific Revolution?

Galileo's work found such a willing audience in part because Galileo, like Kepler and Brahe, was not working alone. Dozens of other scientists were examining old problems from the fresh perspective offered by the breakthroughs in astronomy. Some analyzed the nature of matter, now that it appeared that all matter in the universe was somehow the same, despite its varying appearances. Many of these thinkers addressed the metaphysical issues that their investigations inevitably raised. They began the complex intellectual and psychological journey toward a new worldview, one that accepted the existence of an infinitely large universe of undifferentiated matter with no obvious place in it for humans.

The Uses of the New Science

No less a man than **Francis Bacon** (1561–1626), lord chancellor of England during the reign of James I, wrote a utopian essay extolling the benefits of science for a peaceful society and for human happiness. In *New Atlantis*, published one year after his death, Bacon argued that science would produce "things of use and practice for man's life."[3] In *New Atlantis* and *Novum Organum* (1620), Bacon reveals his faith in science by advocating patient, systematic observation and experimentation to accumulate knowledge about the world. He argues that the proper method of investigation "derives axioms from … particulars, rising by gradual and unbroken ascent, so that it arrives at the most general axioms of all. This is the true way but untried."[4]

Bacon did not undertake experiments himself, although his widely read works were influential in encouraging both the **empirical method** (relying on observation and experimentation) and inductive reasoning (deriving general principles from particular facts). Given the early date of his writings, it might seem difficult to account for his confidence in the benefits of science. Bacon was a visionary, but his writings reflect the widespread interest in science within his elite milieu, an interest actively encouraged by the state. In another of his writings, he argues that a successful state should concentrate on effective "rule in religion *and nature*, as well as civil administration."[5]

Bacon's pronouncements reflect the fact that an interest in exploring nature's secrets and exercising "dominion over nature" had become an indispensable part of princely rule. Princely courts were the main sources of financial support for science and the primary sites of scientific work during Bacon's lifetime. Part of the impetus for this development had come from the civic humanism of the Italian Renaissance, which had celebrated the state and service to it and had provided models both for educated rulers and for cultivated courtiers. Attention to science and to its benefits for the state also reflects the scope, and pragmatism, of princely resources and ambitions: the desire of rulers for technical expertise in armaments, fortification, construction, navigation, and mapmaking. (See the feature, "The Visual Record: Modern Maps.")

Francis Bacon England's lord chancellor during the reign of James I and author of influential works encouraging the empirical scientific method and inductive reasoning.

empirical method Philosophical view developed by Bacon and Locke, which holds that all knowledge is based on observation and experimentation and that general principles should be derived from particular facts.

The lure of the New World and the drive for overseas trade and exploration especially encouraged princely support of scientific investigation. A renowned patron of geographic investigation, from mapmaking to navigation, was Henry, prince of Wales (d. 1612), eldest son of James I. Prince Henry patronized technical experts such as gunners and seamen, as well as those with broader and more theoretical expertise. One geographer at his court worked on the vital problem of calculating longitude, sketched the moon after reading and emulating Galileo's work with the telescope, and, in the spirit of empiricism associated with Bacon, compiled information about the new territory Virginia, including the first dictionary of any Native American language.

Science was an ideological, as well as a practical, tool for power. Most courts housed collections of marvels, specimens of exotic plants and animals, and mechanical contrivances. These collections demonstrated the ruler's interest in investigation of the world—in other words, his or her status as an educated individual. Collections and the work of court experts also enhanced the ruler's reputation as a patron and person of power. Galileo was playing off such expectations when he named his newly discovered moons of Jupiter "Medicean Stars." Like all patronage relationships, the status was shared by both partners; indeed, the attention of a patron was a guarantee of the researcher's scientific credibility.

By the beginning of the seventeenth century, private salons and academies where investigators might meet on their own were another significant milieu of scientific investigation. These, too, had their roots in the humanist culture of Italy, where circles of scholars without university affiliations had formed. Though also dependent on private resources, these associations were an important alternative to princely patronage, since a ruler's funds might wax and wane according to his or her other commitments. Private organizations could avoid the stark distinctions of rank that were inevitable at courts, yet mimicked courts in the blend of scholars and educated courtiers they included. This more collegial, but still privileged, environment also fostered a sense of legitimacy for the science pursued there: Legitimacy came from the recognition of fellow members and, in many cases, from publication of work by the society itself.

The earliest academy dedicated to scientific study was the *Accadèmia Segreta* (Secret Academy), founded in Naples in the 1540s. The members pursued experiments together in order, in the words of one member, "to make a true anatomy of the things and operations of nature itself."[6] During the remainder of the sixteenth century and on into the seventeenth, such academies sprang up in many cities. The most celebrated was the *Accadèmia dei Lincei* (ack-uh-DAY-mee-uh day-ee lin-CHAY-ee), founded in Rome by an aristocrat in 1603. Its most famous member, Galileo, joined in 1611. The name "Lincei," from *lynx*, was chosen because of the legendary keen sight of that animal, an appropriate mascot for "searchers of secrets." Galileo's fame and the importance of his discoveries forced all such learned societies to take a stand for or against Copernicanism. Throughout the seventeenth century, the investigation of nature would continue in increasingly sophisticated institutional settings.

Scientific Thought in France

René Descartes French philosopher and mathematician who emphasized skepticism and deductive reasoning in his most influential treatise, *Discourse on Method*. He offered the first alternative physical explanation of matter after the Copernican revolution.

Philosophers, mathematicians, and educated elites thus engaged in lively debate and practical investigation throughout Europe in the first half of the seventeenth century. In France, the great questions about cosmic order were being posed, ironically, at a time of political disorder. The years following the religious wars saw the murder of Henry IV, another regency, and further civil war in the 1620s (see pages 419–420). In this environment, questions about order in the universe and the possibilities of human knowledge took on particular urgency. It is not surprising that a Frenchman, **René Descartes** (1596–1650), created the first fully articulated alternative worldview.

DESCARTES AND A NEW WORLDVIEW

Descartes (day-KART) developed and refined his thinking in dialogue with a circle of other French thinkers. His work became more influential among philosophers and laypeople than the work of some of his equally talented contemporaries because of its thoroughness and rigor, grounded in Descartes's mathematical expertise, and because of his graceful, readable French. His system was fully presented in his *Discours de la méthode* (*Discourse on Method*, 1637). Descartes described some of his intellectual crises in his later work, *Meditations* (1641).

Descartes accepted Galileo's conclusion that the heavens and the earth are made of the same elements. He drew on ancient atomic models (that had not, then, been generally accepted) to create a new theory about the nature of matter. His theory that all matter is made up of identical bits, which he named "corpuscles," is a forerunner of modern atomic and quantum theories. Descartes believed that all the different appearances and behaviors of matter (for example, why stone is always hard and water is always wet) could be explained solely by the size, shape,

A Collection of Naturalia　Collections of exotic specimens, such as this display in Naples, symbolized the ruler's authority by suggesting his or her power over nature.　(From *Hevelius*, *Machinae coelestis*. By permission of the Houghton Library, Harvard University)

and motion of these "corpuscles." Descartes's was an extremely mechanistic explanation of the universe. It nevertheless permitted new, more specific observations and hypotheses and greater understanding of inertia. For example, because he reimagined the universe as being filled with "corpuscles" free to move in any direction, "natural" motion no longer seemed either circular (Galileo's idea) or toward the center of the earth (Aristotle's idea). The new understanding of motion would be crucial to Isaac Newton's work later in the century.

In his works, Descartes tries to resolve the crisis of confidence that the new discoveries about the universe had produced. The collapse of the old explanations about the world made Descartes and other investigators doubt not only what they knew, but also their capacity to know anything at all. Their physical senses—which denied that the earth moved, for example—had been proved untrustworthy. Descartes's solution was to reenvision the human rational capacity, the mind, as completely distinct from the world—that is, as distinct from the human body and its unreliable sense perceptions. In a leap of faith, Descartes presumed that God would not have given humans a mind if that mind consistently misled them. For Descartes, God became the guarantor of human reasoning capacity, and humans were distinguished by that capacity. This is the significance of his famous claim "I think, therefore I am."

Descartes thus achieved a resolution of the terrifying doubt about the world—a resolution that exalted the role of the human knower. The Cartesian universe was one of mechanical motion, not purpose or mystical meaning, and the Cartesian human being was preeminently a mind that could apprehend that universe. In what came to be known as "Cartesian dualism," Descartes proposed that the human mind is detached from the world and yet, at the same time, can objectively analyze the world.

Modern Maps

Modern mapping was developed during the Scientific Revolution. Like most of the changes associated with the Scientific Revolution, changes in mapping were the result of several influences: innovations in Renaissance art, knowledge gleaned from voyages of exploration, the impact of new astronomical discoveries, the interest and support of princely patrons, and the spread of new ideas by means of print. All of these factors enabled Europeans of this era to have a literally new view of their world. Yet, as in the work of Copernicus, developments in mapping also depended on the continued use of data accumulated in previous centuries. In the examples shown here, we can see the dramatic progress in mapmaking over the course of the sixteenth and seventeenth centuries.

Consider the brightly colored map of western Europe and North Africa reproduced here. It is a reproduction from a 1584 atlas of printed sea charts made by a Dutchman, Lucas Waghenauer. To our eye, the map may look decorative, even quaint. Sailing ships and sea monsters, not drawn to scale, populate the oceans. Most of the major states, such as England and France, are adorned with a crest identifying their ruling dynasties.

Because some of its features appear decorative to us, we may not realize the considerable innovation that the map represented in its day. First, it is an example of the revolutionary method of depicting space achieved in the Renaissance. The discovery of linear perspective by Renaissance artists enabled them to create the illusion of three-dimensional space in their paintings and to likewise depict territory, on a map, as imagined from the perspective of a distanced observer. In addition, the landforms appear in relatively accurate relationship to one another because mapmakers, following the newly recovered *Geography* by Ptolemy, used increasingly accurate projections of the globe to represent landforms on a two-dimensional map.*

The projection used for this map was particularly useful because compass bearings could be represented as straight lines. The many straight lines that crisscross this map are called "rhumb" lines; they represent compass headings that could be used to navigate between two points. Compass bearings between points on coastlines appeared on hand-drawn medieval sea charts (after the invention of the compass in about 1250). So, this sixteenth-century map combines medieval knowledge with new knowledge of geography and of how to depict landforms accurately. In addition, the information in this map was all the more useful because it was published, along with many other sea charts, in book form.

Europe and North Africa, 1584 (The Art Archive/John Webb/Picture Desk)

Now, let us look at the apparently simpler map of the coastline of France, made about one hundred years later, in 1693. We immediately note that virtually all the decorative elements are gone. There are no sea monsters and no ships to sail the abundant seas. The map is a line drawing; it is not even colored. The simplified style of the map by itself testifies to further progress in mapmaking, and to the ability of users to absorb information from maps. To make sense of this map, the viewer would need to be familiar with the representation of France from other maps since, for example, the land borders are not sketched in.

Indeed, the map conveys abundant information, all of which reflects scientific advancement over the intervening 100 years. The figure of a compass marks the Paris meridian, advertising that the site of the city has been precisely determined by means of its longitude. A horizontal line

Descartes's ambitious view of human reason emphasizes deductive reasoning (a process of reasoning in which the conclusion follows necessarily from the stated premises), a natural consequence of his philosophical rejection of sense data. The limits of deductive reasoning for scientific investigation would be realized and much of Cartesian physics rejected by the end of the century. Nevertheless, Descartes's assumption about the objectivity of the observer would become an enduring part of scientific practice. In Descartes's day, the most radical aspect of his thought was the reduction of God to the role of guarantor of knowledge. Many fellow scientists

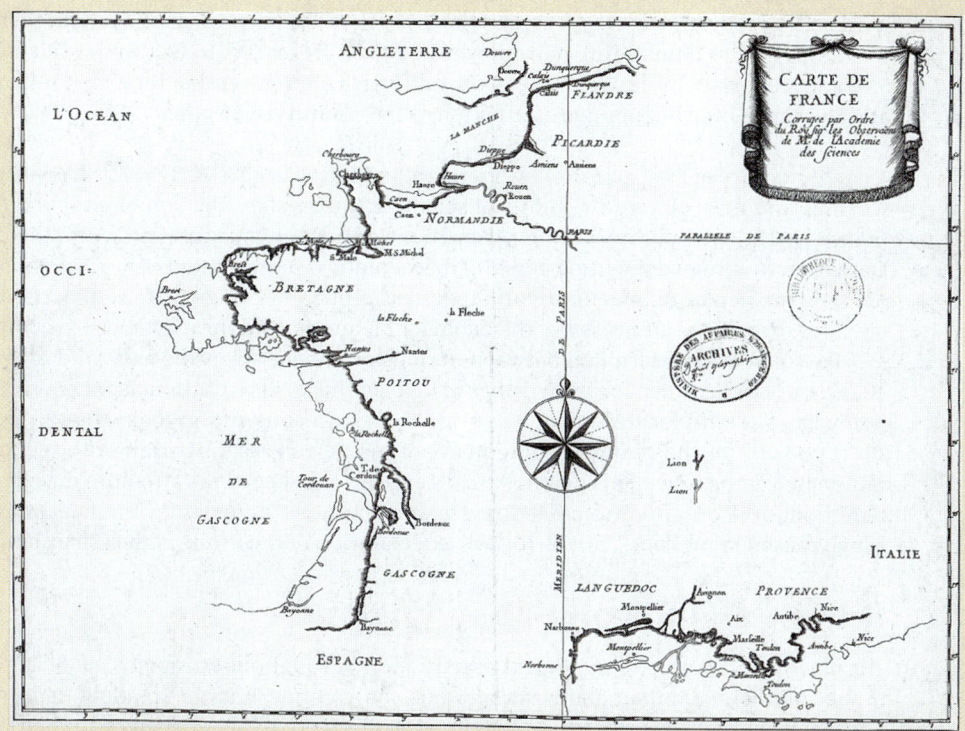

The French Coastline, 1693 (Bibliothèque nationale de France)

marks its latitude. More accurate calculation of longitude had been made possible by the work of Johannes Kepler and Galileo Galilei, whose mapping of heavenly bodies provided known points in the night sky from which to calculate the longitude of the observer's position on earth. Calculation of latitude had always been easier, since it involved only determining the angle of the sun above the horizon, but it also became more precise by use of better instrumentation in the seventeenth century. (Note: Above and to the right of the compass symbol are modern circular and oval stamps identifying the archive where the map is housed; these marks would not have appeared when the map was originally published.)

After 1650, French cartographers, among others, systematically collected astronomical observations from around the world so they could map all known lands more precisely. In addition to claiming the correct coordinates for Paris, this map also dramatically corrects earlier maps of the coastline of France. The map superimposes a corrected view (the darker line) of the coastline over an older rendering (the fainter line, mostly outside of the darker line). Thus, this map not only provides information, but also boldly demonstrates the progress of mapmaking itself.

The legend of the map calls attention to this progress. It reads, "Map of France, corrected by order of the King by the observations of Messieurs of the Academy of Sciences." The map thus also documented royal patronage of scientific work. It is interesting, however, that the king is mentioned discreetly, in what is coming to be a standardized label on the map. The information in the map stands alone, without royal crests or decorations, because the public that viewed the map by now accepted and expected updated knowledge about the world.

QUESTIONS

1. What different types of information does the first map supply? Identify as many as you can.

2. What would have appeared most impressive about the second map, to a contemporary?

---

*This discussion of the evolution of mapmaking and of these examples draws on the work of Norman J. W. Thrower, *Maps and Civilization* (Chicago: University of Chicago Press, 1996). chaps. 5 and 6.

and interested laypeople were fearful of Descartes's system because it seemed to encourage "atheism." In fact, Descartes's faith had been necessary for the construction of his new world system—but the system did work without God.

Descartes would have been surprised and offended by charges of atheism, but he knew that his work would antagonize the church. He moved to the Netherlands to study in 1628, and his *Discourse* was first published there. His long residence in the Netherlands led him to advocate religious toleration late in his life. In 1649, at the urging of an influential friend with contacts at the Swedish court, Descartes accepted the invitation of Queen Christina to visit there. Christina was an eager but demanding patron, who required Descartes to lecture on scientific topics at 5:00 a.m. each day. The long hours of work and harsh winter weather took their toll on his health, and Descartes died of pneumonia after only a few months in Sweden.

PASCAL AND THE LIMITS OF SCIENTIFIC KNOWLEDGE

A contemporary of Descartes, fellow Frenchman Blaise Pascal (1623–1662), drew attention in his writings and in his life to the limits of scientific knowledge. The son of a royal official, Pascal (pahss-KAHL) was perhaps the most brilliant mind of his generation. A mathematician like Descartes, he stressed the importance of mathematical representations of phenomena, built one of the first calculating machines, and invented probability theory. He also carried out experiments to investigate air pressure, the behavior of liquids, and the existence of vacuums.

Pascal's career alternated between periods of intense scientific work and religious retreat. Today, he is well known for his writings justifying the austere Catholicism known as Jansenism (see page 446) and for his explorations of the human soul and psyche. His *Pensées* (*Thoughts*, 1657) consists of the published fragments of his defense of Christian faith, which remained unfinished at the time of his death. Pascal's appeal for generations after him may lie in his attention to matters of faith and of feeling. His most famous statement, "The heart has its reasons which reason knows not," can be read as a declaration of the limits of the Cartesian worldview.

Science and Revolution in England

The new science had adherents and practitioners throughout Europe by 1650. Dutch scientists in the commercial milieu of the Netherlands, for example, had the freedom to pursue practical and experimental interests. The Dutch investigator Christiaan Huygens (HI-ghenz) (1629–1695) worked on a variety of problems, including air pressure and optics. In 1657, he invented and patented the pendulum clock, the first device to measure accurately small units of time, essential for a variety of measurements.

England proved a unique environment for the development of science in the middle of the century. In a society torn by civil war, differing positions on science became part and parcel of disputes over Puritanism, church hierarchy, and royal power. Scientific, along with political and religious, debate was generally encouraged by the collapse of censorship, beginning in the 1640s.

During the 1640s, natural philosophers with Puritan leanings were encouraged in their investigations by dreams that science, of the practical Baconian sort, could be the means by which the perfection of life on earth could be brought about and the end of history—the reign of the saints preceding the return of Christ—could be accelerated. Their concerns ranged from improved production of gunpowder (for the armies fighting against Charles I) to surveying and mapmaking. Perhaps the best-known member of this group was Robert Boyle (1627–1691). In his career, we can trace the evolution of English science through the second half of the seventeenth century.

Boyle and his colleagues were theoretically eclectic, drawing on Cartesian mechanics and even Paracelsian chemical theories. They attacked the English university system, still under the sway of Aristotelianism, and proposed widespread reform of education. They were forced to moderate many of their positions, however, as the English civil wars proceeded. Radical groups, such as the Levellers, used Hermeticism and the related Paracelsianism as part of their political and religious tenets. The Levellers and other radical groups drew on the Hermetic notion that matter is imbued with divine spirit; they believed that each person was capable of divine knowledge and a godly life without the coercive hierarchy of church and royal officials.

Boyle and his colleagues responded to these challenges. They gained institutional power when they accepted positions at Oxford and Cambridge. They formed the core of the Royal Society of London, which they persuaded Charles II to recognize and charter on his accession to the throne in 1660. They worked out a theoretical position that combined the orderliness of mechanism, a continued divine presence in the world, and a Baconian belief in scientific progress. This unwieldy set of notions was attractive to the educated elite of the day, who wanted the certainties of science, but did not want to give up certain authoritarian aspects of the old Christian worldview.

Their most creative contribution, both to their own cause and to the advancement of science, was their refinement of experimental philosophy and practice. In 1660, Boyle published *New Experiments Physico-Mechanical*. The work describes the results of his experiments with an air pump he had designed, and it lays out general rules for experimental procedure. Descartes had accounted for motion by postulating that "corpuscles" of matter interact, thereby eliminating the possibility of a vacuum in nature. Recent experiments on air pressure suggested otherwise, however, and Boyle tried to confirm their findings with his air pump.

Boyle's efforts to demonstrate that a vacuum could exist—by evacuating a sealed chamber with his pump—were not successes by modern standards because his experiments could not readily be duplicated. Boyle tied the validity of experimental results to the agreement of witnesses to the experiment—a problematic solution, since only investigators sympathetic to his hypothesis and convinced of his credibility usually witnessed the results. In response to a Cambridge scholar who criticized his interpretation of one experiment, Boyle replied that he could not understand his critic's objections, "the experiment having been tried both before our whole society [the Royal Society of London], and very critically, by its royal founder, his majesty himself."[7] In other words, rather than debate differing interpretations, Boyle appealed to the authority and prestige of the participants. In English science of the mid-seventeenth century, therefore, we have a further example of the fact that new truths, new procedures for determining truth, and new criteria for practitioners were all being established simultaneously.

The Achievement of Isaac Newton

The Copernican revolution reached its high point with the work of the Englishman **Isaac Newton** (1643–1727), born one year almost to the day after Galileo died. Newton completed the new explanation for motion in the heavens and on earth that Copernicus's work had required and that Kepler, Galileo, and others had sought.

After a difficult childhood and an indifferent education, Newton entered Cambridge University as a student in 1661. Copernicanism and Cartesianism were being hotly debated, though not yet officially studied. Newton made use of Descartes's work in mathematics to develop his skill on his own, and by 1669, he had invented calculus. (He did not publish his work at the time, and another mathematician, Gottfried von Leibniz [LIBE-nits], later independently developed calculus and vied with Newton for credit.)

Newton won a fellowship at Cambridge in 1667 and became a professor of mathematics in 1669, at the recommendation of a retiring professor with whom he had shared his work on calculus. With less demanding teaching assignments, he was able to devote much of the next decade to work on optics—an important area of study for testing Descartes's corpuscular theory of matter.

In the 1680s, Newton experienced a period of self-imposed isolation from other scientists after a particularly heated exchange with one colleague, provoked by Newton's difficult temperament. During this decade, he returned to the study of alternative theories about matter. As a student at Cambridge, he had been strongly influenced by the work of a group of Neo-Platonists who were critical of Cartesian theory that posited God as a cause of all matter and motion but removed God, or any other unknown or unknowable force, as an explanation for the behavior of matter. The Neo-Platonists' concerns were both religious and scientific. As Newton says in some of his early writing, while a student, "However we cast about we find almost no other reason for atheism than this [Cartesian] notion of bodies having . . . a complete, absolute and independent reality."[9]

Newton now read treatises in alchemy and Hermetic tracts and began to imagine explanations for the behavior of matter (such as for bits of cloth fluttered from a distance by static electricity) that Cartesian corpuscular theory could not readily explain. Precisely what the forces were that caused such behavior, he was not sure, but his eclectic mind and his religious convictions enabled him to accept their existence.

It was this leap that allowed him to propose the existence of gravity—a mysterious force that accounts for the movements of heavenly bodies in the vacuum of space. Others had speculated about the existence of gravity; indeed, the concept of inertia worked out by Galileo, Descartes, and others suggested the need for the concept of gravity. Otherwise, if a planet

Isaac Newton English physicist, mathematician, and natural philosopher. His mathematical computation of the laws of gravity and planetary motion, which he combined with a fully developed theory of inertia, completed the explanation for motion initiated by Nicholas Copernicus.

Isaac Newton Pictured here about fifteen years after the publication of *Principia*, Newton was also one of the developers of calculus. The cumbersome mathematics he still relied on, however, has led one scholar to ponder: "What manner of man he was who could use as a weapon what we can scarcely lift as a burden."[8] (By courtesy of the National Portrait Gallery, London)

were "pushed" (say, in Kepler's view, by the "motive force" of the sun), it would continue along that course forever unless "pulled back" by something else.

Newton's extraordinary contribution to a new mechanistic understanding of the universe was the mathematical computation of the laws of gravity and planetary motion, which he combined with a fully developed concept of inertia. In 1687, Newton published *Philosophia Naturalis Principia Mathematica* (*Mathematical Principles of Natural Philosophy;* usually called *Principia*). In this mathematical treatise—so intricate that it was baffling to laypeople, even those able to read Latin—Newton laid out his **laws of motion** and expressed them as mathematical theorems that can be used to test future observations of moving bodies. Then he demonstrated that these laws also apply to the solar system, confirming the data already gathered about the planets and even predicting the existence of an, as yet, unseen planet. His supreme achievement was his law of gravitation, with which he could predict the discovery of the invisible planet. This law states that every body, indeed every bit of matter, in the universe exerts over every other body an attractive force proportional to the product of their masses and inversely proportional to the square of the distance between them. Newton not only accounted for motion, but definitively united heaven and earth in a single scheme and created a convincing picture of an orderly nature.

laws of motion The laws of gravity, planetary motion, and inertia first laid out in the seventeenth century by Isaac Newton.

Neither Newton nor anyone else claimed that his theorems resolved all questions about motion and matter. Exactly what gravity is and how it operates were not clear, as they still are not. Newton's laws of motion are taught today because they still adequately account for most problems of motion. The fact that so fundamental a principle as gravity remains unexplained in no way diminishes Newton's achievement but is clear evidence of the nature of scientific understanding: Science provides explanatory schemas that account for many—but not all—observed phenomena. No schema explains everything, and each schema contains open doorways that lead both to further discoveries and to blind alleys. Newton, for example, assumed that the forces that accounted for gravity would mysteriously work on metals so that, as alchemists predicted, they might "quickly pass into gold."[10]

After the publication of *Principia*, Newton was more of a celebrated public figure than a practicing scientist. He helped lead resistance to James II's Catholicizing policies in the university, and he became the familiar of many other leading minds of his day, such as John Locke (see page 495). Newton became the president of the Royal Academy of Sciences in 1703 and was knighted in 1705, the first scientist to be so distinguished. By the end of his life, universities in England were dominated by men who acclaimed and built on his work. The transformation of the institutional structure of science in England was complete.

Developments In Chemistry, Biology, and Medicine

The innovations in astronomy that led to the new mechanistic view of the behavior of matter did not automatically spill over to other branches of science. In astronomy, innovation came after the ancient and medieval inheritance had been fully assimilated and its errors disclosed. Other branches of science followed their own paths, though all were strongly influenced by the **mechanistic worldview**.

mechanistic worldview Seventeenth-century philosophical view that saw the world as a machine that functions in strict obedience to physical laws, without purpose or will.

In chemistry, the mechanistic assumption that all matter was composed of small, equivalent parts was crucial to understanding the properties and behaviors of compounds (combinations of elements). But knowledge of these small units of matter was not yet precise enough to be of much use in advancing chemistry conceptually. Nevertheless, the flawed conceptual schema did not hold back all chemical discovery and development. Lack of understanding of gases, and of the specific elements in their makeup, for example, did not prevent the improvement of gunpowder. Indeed, unlike the innovations in astronomy, conceptual breakthroughs in chemistry and biology owed a great deal to the results of plodding experiment and the slow accumulation of data.

A conceptual leap forward was made in biology in the sixteenth and seventeenth centuries as a result of practical knowledge, because biological knowledge was mostly a by-product of the practice of medicine. The recent discovery of *On Anatomical Procedures*, a treatise by the ancient physician Galen, encouraged dissection and other research. Andreas Vesalius (1514–1564), in particular, made important advances by following Galen's example. Born in Brussels, Vesalius (vuh-SAY-lee-us) studied at the nearby University of Louvain and then at Padua, where he was appointed professor of surgery. He ended his career as physician to Emperor Charles V and his son, Philip II of Spain. In his teaching at Padua, Vesalius acted on the newly recovered Galenic teachings by doing dissections himself rather than giving the work to technicians. In 1543, he

Vesalius on Human Anatomy The meticulous illustrations in Vesalius's work helped ensure its success. The medium of print was essential for accurate reproduction of scientific drawings. Note also the way the human body, in this drawing of musculature, is depicted as dominating the landscape. (Terri Torretto/Dover Publications)

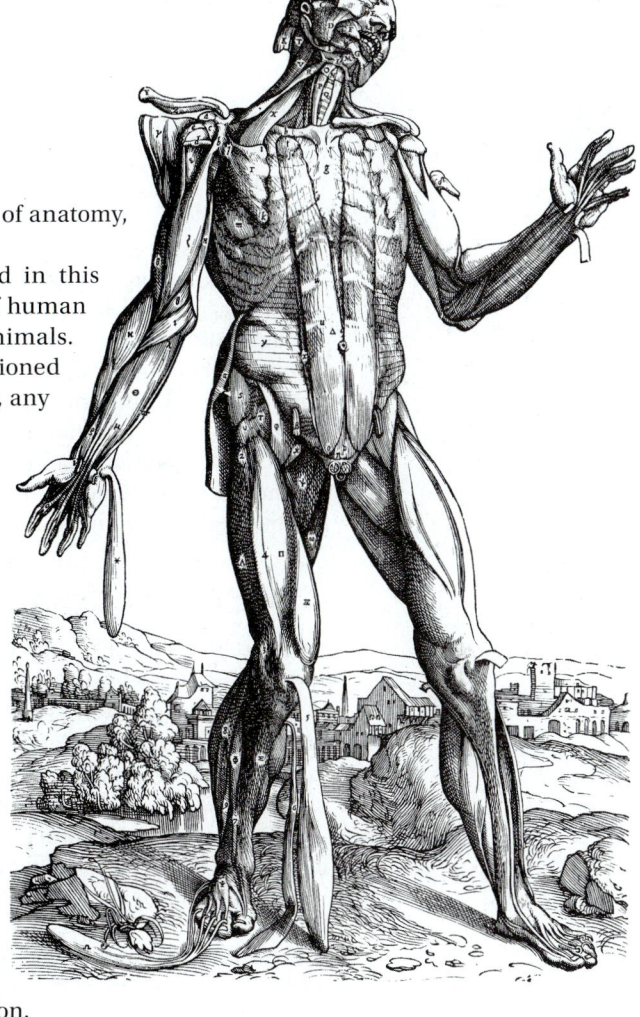

published versions of his lectures as an illustrated compendium of anatomy, *De Humani Corporis Fabrica* (*On the Fabric of the Human Body*).

The results of his dissections of human corpses, revealed in this work, demonstrated a number of errors in Galen's knowledge of human anatomy, much of which had been derived from dissection of animals. Neither Vesalius nor his immediate successors, however, questioned overall Galenic theory about the functioning of the human body, any more than Copernicus had utterly rejected Aristotelian physics.

The slow movement from new observation to changed explanation is clearly illustrated in the career of the Englishman William Harvey (1578–1657). Much like Vesalius, Harvey was educated first in his own land and then at Padua, where he benefited from the tradition of anatomical research. Also like Vesalius, he had a career as a physician, first in London and later at the courts of James I and Charles I.

Harvey postulated the circulation of the blood—postulated rather than discovered, because owing to the technology of the day, he could not observe the tiny capillaries where the movement of arterial blood into the veins occurs. After conducting vivisectional experiments on animals that revealed the actual functioning of the heart and lungs, he reasoned that circulation of the blood must occur. He carefully described his experiments and his conclusions in *Exercitatio Anatomica de Motu Cordis et Sanguinis in Animalibus* (1628), usually shortened to *De Motu Cordis* (*On the Motion of the Heart*).

Harvey's work challenged Galenic anatomy and, like Copernicus's discoveries, created new burdens of explanation. According to Galenic theory, the heart and lungs helped each other to function. The heart sent nourishment to the lungs through the pulmonary artery, and the lungs provided raw material for the "vital spirit," which the heart gave to the blood to sustain life. The lungs also helped the heart sustain its "heat." This heat was understood to be an innate property of organs, just as "heaviness," in traditional physics, had been considered an innate property of earthbound objects.

From his observations, Harvey came to think of the heart in mechanistic terms: as a pump to circulate the blood. But he adjusted, rather than abandoned, Galenic theories concerning "heat" and "vital spirit." The lungs had been thought to "ventilate" the heart by providing air to maintain "heat," just as a bellows blows air on a fire. In light of his discovery of the pulmonary transit (that all of the blood is pumped through the lungs and back through the heart), Harvey suggested instead that the lungs carried out some of these functions for the blood, helping it to concoct the "vital spirit." Only in this sense did he think of the heart as a machine, circulating this life-giving material throughout the body.

Harvey's explanation of bodily functions, in light of his new knowledge, did not constitute a rupture with Galenic tradition. But by the end of his life, Harvey's own adjustments of Galenic theory were suggesting new conceptual possibilities. His work inspired additional research in physiology, chemistry, and physics. Robert Boyle's efforts to understand vacuums can be traced in part to questions Harvey raised about the function of the lungs and the properties of air.

SECTION SUMMARY

- Interest in the new science spread in the seventeenth century as many scholars accepted Copernican theory and as rulers realized the possible advantages of scientific advances.

- René Descartes built on the work of Galileo to formulate a new theory about the nature of matter.

- Descartes believed that humans could understand nature by using reason, not by trusting sensory data.

- English scientists, such as Robert Boyle, began to use experimental methods.

- Isaac Newton developed new laws of motion, still in use today, that explain the behavior of matter on earth and in space with a single set of mathematical principles.

- Advances in the life sciences included new anatomical discoveries by Andreas Vesalius and work by William Harvey on the circulation of the blood.

THE NEW SCIENCE IN CONTEXT: SOCIETY, POLITICS, AND RELIGION

How did the new scientific worldview lead people to challenge traditional notions of society, the state, and religion?

Scientists wrestled with questions about God and human capacity every bit as intently as they attempted to find new explanations for the behavior of matter and the motion of the heavens. Eventually, the profound implications of the new scientific worldview would affect thought and behavior throughout society. Once people no longer thought of the universe in hierarchical terms, they could question the hierarchical organization of society. Once people questioned the authority of traditional knowledge about the universe, the way was clear for them to begin to question traditional views of the state, the social order, and even the divine order. Such profound changes of perspective took hold very gradually, however. The advances in science did lead to revolutionary cultural change, but until the end of the seventeenth century, traditional institutions and ideologies limited its extent.

The Beginnings of Scientific Professionalism

Institutions both old and new supported the new science developing in the sixteenth and seventeenth centuries. Some universities were the setting for scientific breakthroughs, but court patronage, a well-established institution, also sponsored scientific activity. The development of the Accadèmia dei Lincei, to which Galileo belonged, and of other academies was a step toward modern professional societies of scholars, although these new organizations depended on patronage.

In England and France, royally sponsored scientific societies were founded in the third quarter of the century, reflecting rulers' keen interest in science. The Royal Society of London, though charted by the king in 1660, received no money. It remained an informal institution sponsoring amateur scientific interests, as well as specialized independent research. The Académie Royale des Sciences in France, established in 1666 by Jean-Baptiste Colbert, Louis XIV's minister of finance (see page 445), sponsored research but also supported chosen scientists with pensions. These associations were extensions to science of traditional kinds of royal recognition and patronage. Thus, the French Académie was well funded but tightly controlled by the government of Louis XIV, while the Royal Society of London received little of Charles II's scarce resources or precious political capital. Like the earlier academies, these royally sponsored societies published their fellows' work; in England, the *Philosophical Transactions of the Royal Society* began in 1665.

The practice of seventeenth-century science took place in so many diverse institutions—academies, universities, royal courts—that neither *science* nor *scientist* was rigorously defined. Science, as a discipline, was not yet detached from broad metaphysical questions. Boyle, Newton, Pascal, and Descartes all concerned themselves with questions of religion, and all thought of themselves not as scientists but, like their medieval forebears, as natural philosophers. These natural philosophers were still members of an elite who met in aristocratic salons to discuss literature, politics, or science with equal ease and interest. Nevertheless, the beginnings of a narrowing of the practice of science to a tightly defined, truly professional community are evident in these institutions.

Women Scientists and Institutional Constraints

The importance of court life and patronage to the new science had, at first, enabled women to be actively involved in the development of science. Women ran important salons in France; aristocratic women everywhere were indispensable sources of patronage for scientists; and women themselves were scientists, combining, as did men, science with other pursuits. Noblewomen and daughters of gentry families had access to education in their homes, and a number of such women were active scientists—astronomers, mathematicians, and botanists. The astronomer Maria Cunitz (KOO-nits) (1610–1664), from Silesia (a Habsburg-controlled province, now in modern Poland), learned six languages with the encouragement of her father, a physician. Later, she published a useful simplification of some of Kepler's mathematical calculations. Women from some artisanal families also received useful training at home. Such was the case of the German entomologist Maria Sibylla Merian (1647–1717). Merian learned the techniques of illustration in the workshop of her father, an artist in Frankfurt. She later used her artistic training and her refined powers of observation to study and record the features and behaviors of insects and plants in the New World.

Margaret Cavendish, duchess of Newcastle (1623–1673), wrote several major philosophical works, including *Grounds of Natural Philosophy* (1668). She was a Cartesian but was influenced by Neo-Platonism. She believed matter to have "intelligence" and thus disagreed with Descartes's views on matter, but she criticized fellow English philosophers on the grounds that, like Descartes, she distrusted sensory knowledge as a guide to philosophy.

Margaret Cavendish was aware of the degree to which her participation in scientific life depended on informal networks and on the resources available to her because of her aristocratic status. Women scientists from more modest backgrounds, without Cavendish's resources, had to fight for the right to employment, as public institutions gained importance as settings for the pursuit of science. The German astronomer Maria Winkelman (VINK-el-mahn) (1670–1720), for example, tried to succeed her late husband in an official position in the Berlin Academy of Sciences in 1710, after working as his unofficial partner during his tenure as astronomer to the academy. The academy withheld an official position from Winkelman after her husband's death, however, despite her experience and accomplishments (she had discovered a new comet, for example, in 1702). The secretary of the academy stated: "That she be kept on in an offcial capacity to work on the calendar or to continue with observations simply will not do. Already during her husband's lifetime the society was burdened with ridicule because its calendar was prepared by a woman. If she were now to be kept on in such a capacity, mouths would gape even wider."[11] Winkelman worked in

Astronomers Elisabetha and Johannes Hevelius　The Heveliuses were one of many collaborating couples among the scientists of the seventeenth century. Women were usually denied pensions and support for their research when they worked alone, however.　(Houghton Library)

private observatories but was able to return to the Berlin Academy only as the unofficial assistant to her own son, whose training she herself had supervised. As the new science gained in prestige, women scientists often found themselves marginalized. While women were routinely accepted as members of Italian academies, they were excluded from formal membership in the academies in London and Paris, although they could use the academies' facilities and received prizes from the societies for their work.

The New Science, the State, and the Church

The new natural philosophy had implications for traditional notions about the state. The new worldview that all matter, whether in the heavens or on earth, was identical and answerable to discernible natural laws gradually undermined political systems resting on a belief in the inherent inequality of persons and on royal prerogative. By the middle of the eighteenth century, a fully formed alternative political philosophy would argue for more "rational" government in keeping with the rational, natural order of things. But the change came slowly, and while it was coming, traditional rulers found much to admire and utilize in the new science.

Technological possibilities of the new science were very attractive to governments. Experiments with vacuum pumps had important applications in the mining industry, for example. Governments also sponsored pure, and not only applied, scientific research. A French naval expedition to Cayenne, in French Guiana, led to refinements of the pendulum clock but had, as its main purpose, progressive observations of the sun to permit the calculation of the earth's distance from the sun. Members of the elite saw the opportunity not only for practical advances, but also for prestige and, most important, confirmation of the orderliness of nature. It is hard to overestimate the psychological impact and intellectual power of this fundamental tenet of the new science—namely, that nature is an inanimate machine that reflects God's design not through its purposes, but simply by its orderliness. Thus, in the short run, the new science supported a vision of order that was very pleasing even to an absolute monarch, such as Louis XIV.

As we have seen, scientists themselves flourished in close relationships with princes and actively sought their patronage. Christiaan Huygens left the Netherlands to accept the patronage of Louis XIV and produced, in France, some of his most important work in optics and mechanics. Huygens had learned from his father, secretary to the princes of Orange in the Netherlands, that a princely court not only offered steady support, but also opened doors to other royal academies and salons. Huygens published some of his early research through the Royal Society in London, thanks to contacts his father had established. When Galileo left his position at Padua for the Medici court in Florence, he wrote to a friend, "It is not possible to receive a salary from a Republic [Venice] ... without serving the public, because to get something from the public one must satisfy it and not just one particular person; ... no one can exempt me from the burden while leaving me the income; and in sum I cannot hope for such a benefit from anyone but an absolute prince."[12]

Scientists and scientific thought also remained closely tied to religion in both practical and institutional ways during the seventeenth century. Both religion and the Catholic Church, as an institution, were involved with scientific advancement from the time of Copernicus. Copernicus himself was a cleric, as were many philosophers and scientists after him. This is not surprising, for most research in the sciences to this point had occurred within universities sponsored and staffed by members of religious orders, who had the education, time, and resources necessary for scientific investigation. Some of Descartes's closest collaborators were clerics, as were certain of Galileo's aristocratic patrons and his own protégés. Moreover, religious and metaphysical concerns were central to the work of virtually every scientist. The entire Cartesian process of reasoning about the world, for example, was grounded in Descartes's certainty about God. Copernicus, Kepler, Newton, and others believed they perceived God's purpose in the mathematical regularity of nature.

The notion that religion was the opponent of science in this era is a result of Galileo's trial and represents a distortion even of that event. It is true that the new astronomy and mechanics challenged traditional interpretations of Scripture, as well as the fundamentals of physics and metaphysics that were taught in universities. Thus, in its sponsorship of universities, the church was literally invested in the old view, even though individual churchmen investigated and taught Copernican ideas. The rigid response of the church hierarchy to Galileo is partially explained by the aftermath of the Protestant Reformation, which, in the minds of many churchmen—including Galileo's accusers and some of his judges—had demonstrated the need for a firm response to any challenge to the church's authority. Galileo seemed particularly threatening because he was well known, wrote for a wide audience, and, like the Protestants, presumed to interpret the Scriptures. Galileo may well have escaped punishment entirely had it not been for the political predicament faced by the pope at the time of his trial, however.

The condemnation of Galileo shocked many clerics, including the three who had voted for leniency at his trial. Clerics who were also scientists continued to study and teach the new science where and when they could. Copernicanism was taught by Catholic missionaries abroad. (See the feature, "The Global Record: Jesuits and Astronomy in China.") To be sure, Galileo's trial did have a chilling effect on scientific investigation in many Catholic regions of Europe. Investigators could and did continue their research, but many could publish results only by smuggling manuscripts to Protestant lands. After the middle of the seventeenth century, many of the most important empirical and theoretical innovations in science occurred in Protestant regions. However, Protestant leaders had also not been receptive to Copernican ideas at first because the ideas seemed to defy scriptural authority as well as common sense. In 1549, one of Martin Luther's associates wrote: "The eyes are witnesses that the heavens revolve in the space of twenty four hours. But certain men, either from love of novelty or to make a display of ingenuity, have concluded that the earth moves.... Now it is want of honesty and decency to assert such notions.... It is part of a good mind to accept the truth as revealed by God and to acquiesce in it."[13]

Protestant thinkers were also as troubled as Catholics by the metaphysical dilemmas that the new theories seemed to raise. In 1611, one year after Galileo's *Starry Messenger* appeared,

Science and Royal Power   This painting memorializes the founding of the French Académie des Sciences and the building of the royal observatory in Paris. Louis himself is at the center of the painting, reflecting the symbolic importance of royal power in the sponsorship of science.   (Erich lessing/Art Resource, NY)

the English poet John Donne (1573–1631) reflected on the confusion that now reigned in human affairs, with the heavenly hierarchy dismantled:

> *[The] new Philosophy calls all in doubt,*
> *The Element of fire is quite put out,*
> *The Sun is lost, and th'earth, and no man's wit*
> *Can well direct him where to look for it*
> *… … … …*
> *Tis all in pieces, all coherence gone;*
> *All just supply, and all Relation:*
> *Prince, Subject, Father, Son, are things forgot,*
> *For every man alone thinks he hath got*
> *To be a Phoenix, and that then can be*
> *None of that kinde, of which he is, but he.*[14]

The challenge of accounting, in religious terms, for the ideas of Copernicus and Descartes became more urgent for Protestants as the ideas acquired an anti-Catholic status after the trial of Galileo in 1633 and as they became common scientific currency by about 1640. As we have seen, Newton was able to develop his theories on motion and gravity in part because of a religious certainty about divine force that could account for the motion of bodies in a vacuum. In short, religion did not merely remain in the scientists' toolbox of explanations; it remained a

Jesuits and Astronomy in China

The Italian Matteo Ricci (1552–1610) was one of the first Jesuit missionaries to establish himself at the imperial court in China. Ricci's willingness to learn the Chinese language and his own scientific knowledge was crucial to his acceptance at the Chinese court. Jesuit missionaries who followed Ricci in the seventeenth century found their scientific expertise equally valued, and several openly taught Copernican theory in the East. Chinese interest in European knowledge was itself new. In previous centuries, Europeans had eagerly borrowed from China, including knowledge of papermaking and printing.

The Chinese have not only made considerable progress in moral philosophy but in astronomy and in many branches of mathematics as well. At one time they were quite proficient in arithmetic and geometry, but in the study and teaching of these branches of learning they labored with more or less confusion. They divide the heavens into constellations in a manner somewhat different from that which we employ. Their count of the stars outnumbers the calculations of our astronomers by fully four hundred, because they include in it many of the fainter stars which are not always visible. And yet with all this, the Chinese astronomers take no pains whatever to reduce the phenomena of celestial bodies to the discipline of mathematics. Much of their time is spent in determining the moment of eclipses and the mass of the planets and the stars, but here, too, their deductions are spoiled by innumerable errors. Finally they center their whole attention on that phase of astronomy which our scientists term astrology, which may be accounted for by the fact that they believe that everything happening on this terrestrial globe of ours depends upon the stars.

Some knowledge of the science of mathematics was given to the Chinese by the Saracens [Mongols], who penetrated into their country from the West, but very little of this knowledge was based upon definite mathematical proofs. What the Saracens left them, for the most part, consisted of certain tables of rules by which the Chinese regulated their calendar and to which they reduced their calculations of planets and the movements of the heavenly bodies in general. The founder of the family which at present regulates the study of astrology prohibited anyone from indulging in the study of this science unless he were chosen for it by hereditary right. The prohibition was founded upon fear, lest he who should acquire a knowledge of the stars might become capable of disrupting the order of the empire and seek an opportunity to do so.

QUESTIONS

1. In what ways is Ricci both appreciative and critical of Chinese science?

2. What do Ricci's comments about Chinese science reveal about his own assumptions concerning astronomy and mathematics and how to study them appropriately?

Source: Louis J. Gallagher, trans., *China in the Sixteenth Century: The Journals of Matthew Ricci: 1583–1610* (New York: Random House, 1953), pp. 30–31. Copyright 1942, 1953 and renewed 1970 by Louis J. Gallagher, S.J. Used by permission of Random House, Inc.

---

fundamental building block of scientific thought and central to most scientists' lives, whether they were Catholic or Protestant.

The New Science and Political Thought at the End of the Seventeenth Century

Thomas Hobbes English philosopher who argued in *Leviathan* that people are made up of mechanistic appetites and so need a strong ruler to govern them. However, he also envisioned citizens as potentially equal and constrained neither by morality nor by natural obedience to authority.

Traditional institutions and ideologies checked the potential effects of the new science for a time, but by the middle of the seventeenth century, political theory was beginning to reflect the impact of the mechanistic worldview. Political philosophers began to doubt that either the world or human society was an organic whole in which each part was distinguished in nature and function from the rest. Thomas Hobbes, John Locke, and others reimagined the bonds that link citizens to one another and to their rulers.

THOMAS HOBBES Because of the political turmoil in England, **Thomas Hobbes** (1588–1679) spent much of his productive life on the Continent. After the beginnings of the parliamentary rebellion, he joined a group of royalist émigrés in France. He met Galileo and lived for extended periods in Paris, in contact with the circle of French thinkers that included Descartes. Like Descartes, he theorized about the nature and behavior of matter and published a treatise on his views in 1655.

Hobbes is best known today for *Leviathan* (1651), his treatise on political philosophy. In *Leviathan*, Hobbes applies to the world of human beings his largely Cartesian view of nature as composed of "self-motivated," atom-like bits of matter. Hobbes viewed people as mechanistically as he viewed the rest of nature. In his view, people are made up of appetites of various sorts—the same kind of innate forces that drive all matter. The ideal political system, he concluded, is one in which a strong ruler controls the disorder that inevitably arises from the clash of people's desires. Unlike medieval philosophers, Hobbes did not draw analogies between the state and the human body (the king as head, judges and magistrates as arms, and so forth). Instead, he compared the state to a machine that "ran" by means of laws and was kept in good working order by a skilled technician—the ruler.

Hobbes's pessimism about human behavior and his insistence on the need for restraint imposed from above reflect, as does the work of Descartes, a concern for order in the wake of upheaval—in Hobbes's case, civil war in his native England. This concern was one reason he was welcomed into the community of French philosophers, who were naturally comfortable with royalty as a powerful guarantor of order. But Hobbes's work, like theirs, was a radical departure because it envisioned citizens as potentially equal and constrained neither by morality nor by natural obedience to authority.

Another Englishman, **John Locke** (1632–1704), offered an entirely different vision of natural equality among people and, consequently, of social order. Locke's major works, *Essay on Human Understanding* (1690) and *Two Treatises of Government* (1690), reflect the experimentalism of Robert Boyle, the systematizing rationality of Descartes, and other strands of the new scientific thought. In his *Essay*, Locke provides a view of human knowledge more pragmatic and utilitarian than the rigorous mathematical model of certainty used by many other philosophers. He argues that human knowledge is largely the product of experience. He agrees with Descartes that reason orders and explains human experience, but unlike Descartes, he doubts that human reason has unlimited potential to comprehend the universe. Locke, however, offered a more optimistic vision of the possible uses of reason. Whereas Descartes was interested in mentally ordering and understanding the world, Locke was interested in actually functioning *in* the world.

Locke's treatises on government reflect his notion of knowledge based on experience, as well as his particular experiences as a member of elite circles following the Restoration in England. Trained in medicine, he served as personal physician and general political assistant to one of the members of Parliament most opposed to Charles II's pretensions to absolutist government. When James II acceded to the throne in 1685, Locke remained in the Netherlands, where he had fled to avoid prosecution for treason. He became an adviser to William of Orange and returned to England with William and Mary in 1688. Locke's view of the principles of good government came to reflect the pro-parliamentary stance of his political milieu.

Unlike Hobbes, Locke argued that people are capable of self-restraint and mutual respect in their pursuit of self-interest. The state arises, he believed, from a contract that individuals freely enter into to protect themselves, their property, and their happiness from possible aggression by others. They can invest the executive and legislative authority to carry out this protection in monarchy or any other governing institution, though Locke believed that the English Parliament was the best available model. Because sovereignty resides with the people who enter into the contract, rebellion against the abuse of power is justified. At the core of Locke's schema is thus a revolutionary vision of political society based on human rights.

Locke's experience as an English gentleman is apparent in his emphasis on private property, which he considered a fundamental human right. Nature, he believed, cannot benefit humankind unless it is worked by human hands, as on a farm, for example. Private ownership of property guarantees its productivity and entitles the owner to participate in Locke's imagined contract. Indeed, Locke's political vision is unequivocal, and unbending, on the nature of property. Locke even found a justification for slavery. He also did not consider women to be independent beings in the same way as men. The family, he felt, is a separate domain from the state, not bound by the same contractual obligations. Locke and many other seventeenth-century thinkers were unable to imagine a new physical or political reality without invoking a notion of gender as a "natural" principle of order and hierarchy. Margaret Cavendish, among others, disputed the validity of such arbitrary distinctions in capacities and rights between men and women; nevertheless, men frequently used them. Locke's use of gender as an arbitrary organizing principle gave his bold new vision of rights for certain men a claim to being "natural." The use of gender-specific vocabulary to describe nature itself had the effect of making the new objective attitude toward the world seem "natural." Works by seventeenth-century scientists are filled with references to nature as a woman who must be "conquered," "subdued," or "penetrated."

JOHN LOCKE

John Locke English philosopher who asserted that the state arises from a contract that individuals freely endorse. Therefore, because sovereignty resides with the people, rebellion against abuse of power is justified—a revolutionary vision of a political society based on human rights.

18

Café Society in the Eighteenth Century
(G. Dagli Orti/The Art Archive)

Europe on the Threshold of Modernity, ca. 1715–1789

Drinks are set before these gentlemen on their table, but this is more than just a social gathering. The men are absorbed in intense conversation. One man raises his hand, perhaps to emphasize his point, while another listens with a skeptical smirk. Several others eagerly follow their conversation. Other animated discussions go on at nearby tables. The setting depicted here was altogether new in the eighteenth century, when this picture was made, and a caption that originally accompanied the illustration reveals its importance: "Establishment of the new philosophy: our cradle was the café."

Cafés—coffeehouses—were as revolutionary in their day as the Internet is in our own. They were one of the principal places where educated people could debate the "new philosophy"—what we now call Enlightenment philosophy—and could explore its implications for social and political life. Men gathered in clubs and cafés; women directed private gatherings known as salons. Both men and women read more widely than ever before.

What the new science did to physics, the Enlightenment did to politics. The Enlightenment transferred into political and social thought the intellectual revolution that had already occurred in the physical sciences. Hence, it constituted a revolution in political philosophy, but it was also much more. The era witnessed the emergence of an informed body of public opinion, critical of the prevailing political system. The relationship between governments and the governed had begun to change: Subjects of monarchs were becoming citizens of nations.

The notion that human beings, using their rational faculties, could not only understand nature but might also transform their societies was appealing to rulers as well, in part for the traditional reason—strengthening state power. Frederick the Great of Prussia, Catherine the Great of Russia, and other monarchs self-consciously tried to use Enlightenment precepts to guide their efforts at governing. They had mixed success because powerful interests opposed their efforts at reform and because, ultimately, their own hereditary and autocratic power was incompatible with Enlightenment ideals.

Profound changes in economic and social life accompanied this revolution in intellectual and political spheres. The increasing economic and strategic importance of overseas colonies made them important focal points of international conflict. Economic growth spurred population growth, which in turn stimulated industry and trade. As the century closed, Europe was on the threshold of truly revolutionary changes in politics and production that had their roots in the intellectual, economic, and social ferment of eighteenth-century life.

FOCUS QUESTIONS

- What were the most important ideas in Enlightenment thought, and what were some of the intellectual, social, and political conditions that favored its development?

- To what extent did the activities of rulers, particularly "enlightened despots," reflect Enlightenment ideals, and to what extent did they reflect traditional concerns of state power?

- How and why did trade and production increase in the eighteenth century?

- How did warfare and its consequences change in the eighteenth century?

 This icon will direct you to additional materials on the website: www.cengage.com/history/noble/westciv6e.

See our interactive eBook for map and primary source activities.

THE ENLIGHTENMENT

What were the most important ideas in Enlightenment thought, and what were some of the intellectual, social, and political conditions that favored its development?

The Enlightenment was an intellectual movement that brought to political and social questions the confidence in the intelligibility of natural law that Newton and other scientists had recently achieved. Following Descartes and Locke, Enlightenment thinkers believed that human beings could discern and work in concert with the laws of nature for the betterment of human life. Above all, Enlightenment thought gave people the confidence to question tradition. A belief grew that society must be grounded on rational foundations to be determined by humans, not arbitrary foundations determined by tradition and justified by religious authority.

Enlightenment thought was debated in increasingly widespread publications, such as newspapers. There were new opportunities for exchanging views in literary societies, salons, and cafés. These new means of sharing information ensured that informed public opinion would become a new force in political and cultural life. Given this broad base, Enlightenment thinking was certain to challenge the very foundations of social and political order.

Voltaire: The Quintessential Philosophe

philosophes French term referring to thinkers and critics of the Enlightenment era, including Voltaire and Rousseau.

Voltaire French writer, critic, and reformer who embodied the spirit of eighteenth-century rationalism: its confidence, its increasingly practical bent, its wit and sophistication.

In France, Enlightenment thinkers were known as **philosophes** (fee-low-ZOHFS), a term meaning not a formal philosopher but rather a thinker and critic. The most famous of the philosophes was **Voltaire** (1694-1778). A prolific writer, critic, and reformer, Voltaire embodied the spirit of eighteenth-century rationalism: its confidence, its increasingly practical bent, its wit and sophistication. He was widely admired throughout Europe, including by several rulers. Born François-Marie Arouet to a middle-class family, he took the pen name Voltaire in 1718, after one of his early plays was a critical success. Like many philosophes, Voltaire moved in courtly circles but was often on its margins. His mockery of the regent for the young French king earned him a year's imprisonment in 1717, and an exchange of insults with a leading courtier some years later led to enforced exile in Great Britain for two years.

After returning from Britain, Voltaire published his first major philosophical work. *Lettres philosophiques (Philosophical Letters*, 1734) revealed the influence of his British sojourn and helped to popularize Isaac Newton's achievements in mathematics and science. To confidence in the laws governing nature, Voltaire added cautious confidence in humans' attempts to discern truth. From the Englishman Locke's work, he was persuaded to value education. These elements gave Voltaire's philosophy both its passionate conviction and its sensible practicality.

Voltaire portrayed Great Britain as a more rational society than France. The British government had a more workable set of institutions; the economy was less crippled by the remnants of feudal privilege, and education was not in the hands of the church. He was particularly impressed with the relative religious and intellectual toleration evident across the Channel. Voltaire was one of many French thinkers who singled out the Catholic Church as the archenemy of progressive thought. Philosophes constantly collided with the church's negative views of human nature and resented its control over most education and its influence in political life. Typical of Voltaire's criticism of the church is his stinging satire of the clerics who had condemned Galileo: "I desire that there be engraved on the door of your holy office: Here seven cardinals assisted by minor brethren had the master of thought of Italy thrown into prison at the age of seventy, made him fast on bread and water, because he instructed the human race."

After the publication of his audacious *Letters*, Voltaire was again forced into exile from Paris, and he lived for some years in the country home of a woman with whom he shared a remarkable intellectual and emotional relationship: Emilie, marquise du Châtelet (shot-uh-LAY) (1706–1749). Châtelet was a mathematician and a scientist. She prepared a French translation of Newton's *Principia*, while Voltaire worked on his own writing projects, which included a commentary on Newton's work. Because of Châtelet's influence, Voltaire became more knowledgeable about the sciences and more serious in his efforts to apply scientific rationality to human affairs. He was devastated by her sudden death in 1749.

Shortly afterward he accepted the invitation of the king of Prussia, Frederick II, to visit Berlin. His stay was stormy and brief because of disagreements with other court philosophers. He then lived for a time in Geneva, Switzerland, until his criticisms of the city's moral codes forced yet another exile on him. He spent most of the last twenty years of his life at his estates on the Franco-Swiss border, where he could be relatively free from interference by any government. These were productive years. He produced his best-known satirical novelette, *Candide*, in 1758. It criticized aristocratic privilege and the power of the church as well as the naiveté of philosophers who took "natural law" to mean that the world was already operating as it should.

In contrast, Voltaire believed that only by struggle could the accumulated habits of centuries be overturned. This belief led to his political activities. He became involved in several celebrated legal cases in which individuals were pitted against the authority of the church, which was still backed by the authority of the state. Voltaire's pursuit of justice in these cases was relentless. In addition to writing plays, novelettes, and essays, he published a stream of political tracts to champion specific causes and to argue for reform. He also worked close to home, initiating agricultural reform on his estates and working to improve the status of peasants in the vicinity.

Voltaire died in Paris in May 1778, after a triumphal welcome for the staging of one of his plays. By then, he was no longer leader of the Enlightenment in strictly intellectual terms. Thinkers and writers more radical than he had become prominent during his long life. They dismissed some of his beliefs, such as the notion that a monarch could introduce reform. But Voltaire had provided a crucial stimulus to French thought with his *Philosophical Letters* and through the example of his own prolific writing and political involvement. Until the end of his life, Voltaire remained a bridge between the increasingly diverse body of Enlightenment thought and the literate elite audience.

CHRONOLOGY	
1715–1774	Reign of Louis XV in France
1722–1742	Walpole first British "prime minister"
1734	Voltaire, *Philosophical Letters*
1740–1748	War of the Austrian Succession
1740–1780	Reign of Maria Theresa of Austria
1740–1786	Reign of Frederick the Great of Prussia
1746	Battle of Culloden
1748	Montesquieu, *The Spirit of the Laws* Hume, *An Enquiry Concerning Human Understanding*
1751–1765	Diderot, *Encyclopedia*
1756–1763	Seven Years' War
1758	Voltaire, *Candide*
1762	Rousseau, *The Social Contract*
1762–1796	Reign of Catherine the Great of Russia
1772	First partition of Poland
1776	Smith, *The Wealth of Nations*
1780–1790	Reign of Joseph II of Austria
1792	Wollstonecraft, *A Vindication of the Rights of Woman*

The Variety of Enlightenment Thought

A variety of thinkers contributed to the development of Enlightenment ideas. There were differences among philosophes about major issues. For example, though there was virtual unanimity in criticism of the Catholic Church, there was no unanimity about the existence or nature of God. Voltaire was a theist who believed in a creator of the universe, but not a specifically Christian God. Some philosophes were outright atheists, arguing that a universe operating according to discoverable laws needs no divine presence to explain or justify its existence. In spite of—and partly because of—their disagreements, a number of the philosophes remain among the most important political thinkers in modern times.

MONTESQUIEU

Charles de Secondat (1689–1755), baron of Montesquieu (mawn-tess-KYUH), a French judge and legal philosopher, combined the belief that human institutions must be rational with Locke's assumption of human educability. Montesquieu's treatise, *De L'Esprit des lois (The Spirit of the Laws*, 1748), published in twenty-two printings within two years, argued that laws were not meant to be arbitrary rules but derived naturally from human society: The more evolved a society was, the more liberal were its laws. This notion that progress is possible within society and government deflated Europeans' pretensions with regard to other societies, for a variety of laws could be equally "rational" given different conditions. Montesquieu is perhaps best known to Americans as the advocate of the separation of legislative, executive, and judicial powers that became enshrined in the U.S. Constitution later in the century. To Montesquieu, this scheme seemed to parallel in human government the balance of forces observable in nature; moreover, the arrangement seemed best to guarantee liberty.

Voltaire Visits Frederick the Great of Prussia Voltaire leans forward, at left, to discuss a point of philosophy with Frederick. Skill at witty conversation enabled philosophes such as Voltaire to advance fundamental criticisms of society even to elite audiences. (Bildarchiv Preussischer Kulturbesitz/Art Resource, NY)

ECONOMIC THOUGHT AND THE SCOTTISH ENLIGHTENMENT

Adam Smith Scottish economist who developed the doctrine of "laissez-faire" in his treatise, *The Wealth of Nations* (1776).

Enlightenment philosophers also investigated the "laws" of economic life. For example, French thinkers, known as *physiocrats*, proposed ending "artificial" control over land in order to free productive capacity and permit the flow of crops to market. Their target was traditional forms of land tenure, including collective control of village lands by peasants and traditional rights over land and labor by landlords. The freeing of restrictions on manufacture and trade, as well as agriculture, was proposed by the Scotsman **Adam Smith** in his treatise, *An Inquiry into the Nature and Causes of the Wealth of Nations* (1776).

Smith (1723–1790) was a professor at the University of Glasgow. Scottish universities did not require specialization in subject matter and were open to ideas from abroad, enabling Smith's and others' unique contributions to Enlightenment thought.

Smith is best known in modern times as the originator of "laissez-faire" economics. *Laissez-faire* (LESS-ay-fair), or "let it run on its own," assumes that an economy will regulate itself, without interference by government and, of more concern to Smith, without the monopolies and other economic privileges common in his day. But this schema was not merely a rigid application of natural law to economics. His ideas grew out of an optimistic view of human nature and rationality that was heavily indebted to Locke. Humans, Smith believed, have drives and passions that they can direct and govern by means of reason and inherent mutual sympathy. Thus, Smith suggested, in seeking their own achievement and well-being, people are often "led by an invisible hand" simultaneously to benefit society as a whole. Smith's countryman and friend David Hume (1711–1776) investigated economics, politics, and religion but is best known today for his radical critique of the human capacity for knowing. He was the archskeptic, taking Locke's view of the limitations on human reason to the point of doubting the efficacy of any sensory data. His major exposition of these views, *An Enquiry Concerning Human Understanding* (1748), led to important innovations later in the century in the work of the German philosopher Immanuel Kant. At the time, though, Hume's arguments were almost contrary to the prevailing spirit that embraced empirical knowledge. Hume himself separated this work from his other writings on moral, political, and economic philosophy, which were more in tune with contemporary views.

THE ENCYCLOPEDIA

Mainstream confidence in empirical knowledge and in the intelligibility of the world is evident in the multiauthored *Encyclopédie (Encyclopedia)*. This seventeen-volume compendium of knowledge, criticism, and philosophy was assembled by leading philosophes in France and published there between 1751 and 1765. The volumes were designed to contain state-of-the-art knowledge about arts, sciences, technology, and philosophy. The guiding philosophy of the project, set forth by its chief editor, Denis Diderot (DEED-uh-row) (1713–1784), was a belief in the advancement of human happiness through the advancement of knowledge. The *Encyclopedia* was revolutionary in that it not only intrigued and inspired intellectuals, but also assisted thousands of government officials and professionals.

The encyclopedia project illustrates the political context of Enlightenment thought as well as its philosophical premises. The Catholic Church placed the work on the *Index of Prohibited Books*, and the French government might have barred its publication but for the fact that the official who would have made the decision was himself drawn to Enlightenment thinking. Many other officials, however, worked to suppress it. Thus, like Voltaire, the contributors to the *Encyclopedia* were admired by certain segments of the elite and persecuted by others in their official functions.

GENDER INEQUALITIES

The *Encyclopedia* reflects the complexities and limitations of Enlightenment thought on another issue: the position of women. One might expect that challenging accepted knowledge and traditional power arrangements would lead to arguments for the equality of women with men, and thus, for extending women's rights. Indeed, some contributors to the *Encyclopedia* blamed women's inequality with men not on inherent gender differences, but rather on laws and customs that had excluded women from education. However, other contributors blamed women, and not society, for their plight, or they argued that women had talents that fit them only for the domestic sphere.

Both positions were represented in Enlightenment thought as a whole. The assumption of the natural equality of all people provided a powerful ground for arguing the equality of women with men. Some thinkers, such as Mary Astell (1666–1731), challenged Locke's separation of family life from the public world of free, contractual relationships. "If absolute authority be not necessary in a state," she reasoned, "how comes it to be so in a family?" Most such thinkers advocated increased education for women, if only to make them fit to raise enlightened children. By 1800, the most radical thinkers were advocating full citizenship rights for women and equal rights to property, along with enhanced education.

The best-known proponent of those views was an Englishwoman, Mary Wollstonecraft (1759–1797), who wrote *A Vindication of the Rights of Woman* (1792). She assumed that most elite women would devote themselves to domestic duties, but she argued that without the responsibilities of citizenship, the leavening of education, and economic independence, women could be neither fully formed individuals nor worthy of their duties. "[F]or how can a being be generous who has nothing of its own? Or virtuous, who is not free?" she asked.[1] Working women, she concluded, needed political and economic rights simply to survive.

ROUSSEAU

A notion of women's limited capacities was one element in the deeply influential writings of **Jean-Jacques Rousseau** (1712–1778). Like Locke, Rousseau (roo-SO) could conceive of the free individual only as male, and he grounded both his criticism of the old order and his novel political ideas in an arbitrary division of gender roles. Rousseau's view of women was linked to a critique of the artificiality of elite, cosmopolitan society in which Enlightenment thought was then flourishing, and in which aristocratic women were fully involved. Rousseau believed in the educability of men but was as concerned with issues of character and emotional life as with cognitive knowledge. Society—particularly artificial courtly society—was corrupting, he believed. The

Jean-Jacques Rousseau
French philosophe who imagined an egalitarian society governed by the "general will" in *The Social Contract* and was a sharp critic of aristocratic society.

Rousseau Discusses the Benefits of Submitting to the General Will

In this excerpt from his Social Contract, Rousseau describes the relationship of individuals to the general will. Notice the wider-ranging benefits Rousseau believes men will enjoy in society as he envisions it. Rousseau is clearly interested in intellectual, moral, and emotional well-being.

I assume that men reach a point where the obstacles to their preservation in a state of nature prove greater than the strength that each man has to preserve himself in that state. Beyond this point, the primitive condition cannot endure, for then the human race will perish if it does not change its mode of existence …

"How to find a form of association which will defend the person and goods of each member with the collective force of all, and under which each individual, while uniting himself with the others, obeys no one but himself, and remains as free as before." This is the fundamental problem to which the social contract holds the solution. …

The passing from the state of nature to the civil society produces a remarkable change in man; it puts justice as a rule of conduct in the place of instinct, and gives his actions the moral quality they previously lacked. … And although in civil society man surrenders some of the advantages that belong to the state of nature, he gains in return far greater ones; his faculties are so exercised and developed, his mind is so enlarged, his sentiments so ennobled, and his whole spirit so elevated that … he should constantly bless the happy hour that lifted him for ever from the state of nature and from a stupid, limited animal made a creature of intelligence and a man. …

For every individual as a man may have a private will contrary to, or different from, the general will that he has as a citizen. His private interest may speak with a very different voice from that of the public interest; his absolute and naturally independent existence may make him regard what he owes to the common cause as a gratuitous contribution, the loss of which would be less painful for others than the payment is onerous for him; and fancying that the artificial person which constitutes the state is a mere fictitious entity (since it is not a man), he might seek to enjoy the rights of a citizen without doing the duties of a subject. The growth of this kind of injustice would bring about the ruin of the body politic.

Hence, in order that the social pact shall not be an empty formula, it is tacitly implied in that commitment—which alone can give force to all others—that whoever refuses to obey the general will shall be constrained to do so by the whole body, which means nothing other than that he shall be forced to be free; for this is the necessary condition which, by giving each citizen to the nation, secures him against all personal dependence, it is the condition which shapes both the design and the working of the political machine, and which alone bestows justice on civil contracts—without it, such contracts would be absurd, tyrannical and liable to the grossest abuse.

QUESTIONS

1. What benefits will citizens find in society as Rousseau envisions it?

2. In what ways is Rousseau concerned with freedom?

Source: Jean-Jacques Rousseau, *The Social Contract*, translated by Maurice Cranston. Reprinted by permission of PFD on behalf of The Estate of Maurice Cranston. Copyright © 1968 by Maurice Cranston.

---

worthy citizen had to cultivate virtue and sensibility, not manners or refinement as courtiers do. Rousseau believed women should be the guarantors of the "natural" virtues of children and nurturers of the emotional life and character of men.

Rousseau's emphasis on the education and virtue of citizens was the underpinning of his larger political vision, set forth in *Du Contrat social* (*The Social Contract*, 1762). He imagined an egalitarian republic—possible particularly in small states, such as his native Geneva—in which men would consent to be governed because the government would determine and act in accordance with the "general will" of the citizens. The "general will" was not majority opinion, but rather what each citizen *would* want if he were fully informed and were acting in accordance with his highest nature. The "general will" became apparent whenever the citizens met as a body and made collective decisions, and it could be imposed on all inhabitants. (See the feature, "The Written Record: Rousseau Discusses the Benefits of Submitting to the General Will.") This was a breathtaking vision of direct democracy—but one with ominous possibilities, for Rousseau rejected the institutional checks on state authority proposed by Locke and Montesquieu.

Rousseau's work reflects, to an extreme degree, a central tension in Enlightenment thought: It was part of elite culture as well as its principal critic. The son of a humble family, Rousseau always sensed himself an outcast in the sophisticated world of Parisian salons. However, he depended on the patronage of several aristocratic women, even as he criticized the influence of such women. His own personal life did not match his prescriptions for others. He completely neglected to give his four children the education that he argued was vital; indeed, he abandoned them all to an orphanage. He was nevertheless profoundly important as a critic of an elite society still dominated by status and privilege.

The Growth of Public Opinion

It is impossible to appreciate the significance of the Enlightenment without understanding the degree to which it was a part of public life. Most of the philosophes came from modest backgrounds. They influenced the privileged elite of their day because of the social and political environment in which their ideas were elaborated. Indeed, one of the most important features of the Enlightenment was the creation of an informed body of public opinion that stood apart from court society.

THE READING PUBLIC

Increased literacy and access to books and other printed materials are an important part of the story. Perhaps more important, the kinds of reading that people favored began to change. We know from inventories made of people's belongings at the time of their deaths (required for inheritance laws) that books in the homes of ordinary people were no longer just traditional works such as devotional literature. Ordinary people now read secular and contemporary philosophical works. As the availability of such works increased, reading itself evolved from a reverential encounter with old ideas to a critical encounter with new ideas. Solitary reading for reflection and pleasure became more widespread.

New kinds of reading material were available. Regularly published periodicals in Great Britain, France, and Italy served as important means for the spread of enlightened opinion in the form of reviews, essays, and published correspondence. Some of these journals had been in existence since the second half of the seventeenth century, when they had begun as a means to circulate the new scientific work. Now subscribers included Americans anxious to keep up with intellectual life in Europe. In addition to newsletters and journals, newspapers, which were regularly published even in small cities throughout western and central Europe, circulated ideas. Newspapers were uniquely responsive to their readers. They began to carry advertisements, which both produced revenue for papers and widened readers' exposure to their own communities. Even more important was the inauguration of letters to the editor. Newspapers thus became venues for the often rapid exchange of news and opinions.

Habits of reading and responding to written material changed not only because of this increased and changing reading matter, but also because of changes in the social environment. In the eighteenth century, forerunners of the modern lending libraries made their debut. In Paris, for a fee, one could join a *salle de lecture* (sahl duh lek-TOOR) (literally, a "reading room") where the latest works were available to any member. Booksellers, whose numbers increased dramatically, found ways to meet readers' demands for inexpensive access to reading matter. One might pay for the right to read a book in the bookshop itself. Newspapers were available in such shops and in cafés. In short, new sites encouraged people to see themselves not just as readers, but as members of a reading public.

THE SALONS

Among the most famous and most important of these venues were the Parisian **salons**, regular gatherings in private homes, where Voltaire and others read their works-in-progress aloud and discussed them. Several Parisian women—mostly wealthy, but of modest social status—invited courtiers, bureaucrats, and intellectuals to meet in their homes at regular times each week. The *salonnières* (sal-on-YAIR) (salon leaders) themselves read widely in order to facilitate the exchange of ideas among their guests. This mediating function was crucial to the success of the salons. Manners and polite conversation had been a defining feature of aristocratic life since the seventeenth century, but they had largely been means of displaying status and safeguarding honor. The leadership of the salonnières and the protected environment they provided away from court life enabled a further evolution of "polite society" to occur: Anyone with appropriate manners could participate in conversation as an equal. The assumption of equality in turn enabled conversation to turn away from maintaining the status quo to questioning it.

salons Regular gatherings in eighteenth-century Parisian private homes, where Voltaire and other philosophes read and discussed their works; the exchange of ideas was facilitated by female *salonnières* (salon leaders).

The influence of salons was extended by the wide correspondence networks the salonnières maintained. Perhaps the most famous salonnière in her day, Marie-Thérèse Geoffrin (zhoh-FRAN) (1699–1777) corresponded with Catherine the Great, the reform-minded empress of Russia, as well as with philosophes outside Paris and with interested would-be members of her circle. The

The Growth of the Book Trade   Book ownership dramatically increased in the eighteenth century, and a wide range of secular works—from racy novelettes to philosophical tracts—was available in print. In this rendering of a bookshop, shipments of books have arrived from around Europe. Notice the artist's optimism in the great variety of persons, from the peasant with a scythe to a white-robed cleric, who are drawn to the shop by "Minerva" (the Roman goddess of wisdom).   (Musée des Beaux-Arts de Dijon)

ambassador of Naples regularly attended her salon while in Paris and exchanged weekly letters with her when home in Italy. He reflected on the importance of salon leaders such as Geoffrin when he wrote from Naples lamenting, "[Our gatherings here] are getting farther away from the character and tone of those of France, despite all [our] efforts. … There is no way to make Naples resemble Paris unless we find a woman to guide us, organize us, *Geoffrinise* us."[2]

Various clubs, local academies, and learned and secret societies, such as Masonic lodges, copied some features of the salons of Paris. Hardly any town was without a private society that functioned both as a forum for political and philosophical discussion and as an elite social club. Here mingled doctors, lawyers, and local officials—some of whom enjoyed the fruits of the political system in offices and patronage. In Scotland, universities were flourishing centers of Enlightenment thought, but political clubs in Glasgow and Edinburgh also were centers of debate.

Ideas circulated beyond the membership of salons and clubs, in turn, by means of print. Newsletters reporting the goings-on at salons in Paris were produced by some participants. The exchange and spread of Enlightenment ideas, regardless of the method used, encouraged a type of far-reaching political debate that had never before existed, except possibly in seventeenth-century England. The greatest impact of the Enlightenment, particularly in France, was not the creation of any specific program for political or social change. Rather, its supreme legacy was an informed body of public opinion that could generate change.

The Arts in the Age of Reason

The Enlightenment reverberated throughout all aspects of cultural life. Just as the market for books and the reading public expanded, so did the audience for works of art in the growing leisured urban circles of Paris and other great cities. The modern cultured public—a public of concertgoers and art gallery enthusiasts—began to make its first appearance and constituted another arena in which public opinion was shaped. Courts around Europe continued to sponsor composers, musicians, and painters by providing both patronage and audiences. Yet some performances began to take place in theaters and halls outside the courts in venues more accessible to the public. And, beginning in 1737, one section of the Louvre (LOO-vruh) palace in Paris was devoted annually to public exhibitions of painting and sculpture (though by royally sponsored and approved artists). In both France and Britain, public discussion of art began to occur in published reviews and criticisms: The role of art critic was born. Works of art were also sold by public means, such as auctions. As works became more available, demand grew and production increased.

The Moralizing Message of Neoclassical Art   The French painter Jacques-Louis David portrays the mourning of the Trojan hero Hector by his wife, Andromache. This kind of art tried to depict and encourage virtuous feelings. David was well known for depicting his subjects with simple gestures—such as the extended arm of Andromache here—that were intended to portray sincere emotion.   (Private Collection/The Stapleton Collection/Bridgeman Art Library International)

In subject matter and style, these various art forms exhibited great variety. A favorite theme of painters was an exploration of private life and emotion sometimes called the "cult of sensibility." Frequently, these works depicted private scenes of upper-class life, especially moments of intimate conversation or flirtation.

The cult of sensibility was also nurtured by increased literacy, greater access to books, and the need to retreat from the elaborate artifice of court life. The novel became an increasingly important genre for exploring social problems and human relationships. Daniel Defoe, in *Robinson Crusoe* (1717), used realism for purposes of social commentary, while the novels of Samuel Richardson (1689–1761)—*Pamela* (1740) and *Clarissa* (1747–1748)—explored personal psychology and passion. The cult of sensibility was not mere entertainment; it also carried the political and philosophical message, echoing Rousseau's work, that honest emotion was a "natural" virtue and that courtly manners, by contrast, were both irrational and degrading. The enormous popularity of Rousseau's own novels, *La Nouvelle Héloïse* (1761) and *Emile* (1762), for example, came from the fact that their intense emotional appeal was simultaneously felt to be uplifting.

A revival of classical subjects and styles after the middle of the century evoked what were thought to be the pure and timeless values of classical heroes. This revival revealed the influence of Enlightenment thought because the artists assumed the educability of their audience by means of example. Classical revival architecture illustrated a belief in order, symmetry, and proportion. Americans are familiar with its evocations because it became the architecture of their public buildings, but even churches were built in this style in eighteenth-century Europe. The classical movement in music reflected both the cult of sensibility and the classicizing styles in the visual arts. Embodied in the works of Austrians Franz Josef Haydn (1732–1809) and Wolfgang Amadeus Mozart (1756–1791), this movement saw the clarification of musical structures, such as the modern sonata and symphony, and enabled melody to take center stage.

Another trend in art and literature was a fascination with nature and with the seemingly "natural" in human culture—less "developed" or more historically distant societies. One of the most popular printed works in the middle of the century was the alleged translation of the poems of Ossian (AHSH-un), a third-century Scots Highland poet. Early English, German, Norse, and other folktales were also "discovered" (in some cases invented) and published, some in several editions during the century. Folk life, other cultures, and untamed nature itself thus began to be celebrated at the very time they were being more definitively conquered. (See the feature, "The Visual Record: Gardens.") Ossian, for example, was celebrated just as the Scottish Highlands were being pillaged and pacified by the English after the clans' support for a rival claimant to the English throne. Once purged of any threat, the exotic image of another culture (even the folk culture of one's own society) could be a spur to the imagination. The remote became romantic and offered a sense of distance from which to measure one's own sophistication and superiority.

SECTION SUMMARY

- The "Enlightenment" was an intellectual movement that brought confidence in human reason and the workings of natural law from the sciences into political and social thought.

- A wide range of thinkers, known as philosophes, contributed to Enlightenment thought; opinions about religion, the limits of human reason, the equality of the sexes, and other issues were energetically debated.

- Enlightenment ideas were spread by publications, such as newspapers, and were discussed in cafés and salons; an informed body of public opinion independent of government and the court was created for the first time.

- Art became more accessible to the public; works of art became more thematically varied than before, though many explored "natural" emotion.

EUROPEAN STATES IN THE AGE OF ENLIGHTENMENT

To what extent did the activities of rulers, particularly "enlightened despots," reflect Enlightenment ideals, and to what extent did they reflect traditional concerns of state power?

Mindful of the lessons to be learned from the civil war in England, and eager to repeat the achievements of Louis XIV, European rulers in the eighteenth century continued their efforts to govern with greater effectiveness. Some, like the rulers of Prussia and Russia, were encouraged in their efforts by Enlightenment ideas that stressed the need for reforms in law, economy, and government. Like Voltaire, they believed that monarchs could be agents for change. The changes were uneven, however, and at times, owed as much to traditional efforts at better government as to "enlightened" opinion. However limited their "enlightened" policies, monarchs were changing their views of themselves and their public images from self-aggrandizing absolutist to diligent servant of the state. The state was increasingly seen as separate from the ruler, with dramatic consequences for the future.

France During the Enlightenment

It is one of the seeming paradoxes of the era of the Enlightenment that critical thought about society and politics flourished in France, an autocratic state. Yet France was blessed with a well-educated elite, a tradition of scientific inquiry, and a legacy of cultured court life that, since the early days of Louis XIV, had become the model for all Europe (see pages 446–447). French was the international intellectual language, and France was the most fertile center of cultural life. Both Adam Smith and David Hume, for example, spent portions of their careers in Paris and were welcomed into Parisian salons. In fact, the French capital was an environment that encouraged debate precisely because of the juxtaposition of the vibrant new intellectual climate with the institutional rigidities of its political system. In France, patronage and privilege were the sole avenues to power, a system that excluded many talented and eager members of the elite.

The French state continued to embody fundamental contradictions. As under Louis XIV, the Crown sponsored scientific research, subsidized commerce and exploration, and tried to rationalize the royal administration. Royal administrators tried to chip away at the traditional privileges that hampered effective government—such as the exemption most nobles enjoyed from taxation. However, the Crown also continued to claim the right to govern autocratically, and the king was supported both ideologically and institutionally by the Catholic Church. A merchant in the bustling port of Bordeaux might be glad of the royal navy's protection of the colonies, and of the Crown's efforts to build better roads for trade within France. However, with his fellow Masons, he would fume when church officials publicly burned the works of Rousseau and resent his exclusion from any formal voice in politics.

The problems facing the French government were made worse by two circumstances: first, the strength of the elites' defense of their privileges, and second, mounting government debt from foreign wars. Fiscal reform was increasingly urgent, yet entrenched elites stood in the way of change. Louis XIV was followed on the throne by his 5-year-old great-grandson, Louis XV (r. 1715–1774). During the regency early in his reign, the supreme law courts, the parlements, reclaimed the right to object to royal edicts and thus to exercise some control over the enactment of law. Throughout Louis XV's reign, his administration often locked horns with the parlements, particularly as royal ministers tried various schemes to cope with financial crises.

The power of the parlements came not only from their routine role in government, but also from the fact that parlementaires were all legally noble and owned their offices, just as a great nobleman owned his country estate. In addition, the parlements were the only institutions that could legitimately check royal power. As such, they were often supported in their opposition to royal policies by the weight of public opinion. On the one hand, enlightened opinion believed in the rationality of doing away with privileges, such as the ownership of offices. On the other hand, the role of consultative bodies and the separation of powers touted by Montesquieu, himself a parlementaire, were much prized. And even our Bordeaux merchant, who had little in common with privileged officeholders, might nevertheless see the parlementaires' resistance as his best protection from royal tyranny. The parlementaires, however, usually used their power for protecting the status quo.

A further check on reform was the character of the king himself. Louis XV displayed none of the kingly qualities of his great-grandfather. He was neither pleasant nor affable, and he was lazy. He did not give the "rationality" of royal government a good name. By the end of his reign, he was roundly despised. By the late 1760s, the weight of government debt from foreign wars finally forced the king into action. He threw his support behind the reforming schemes of his chancellor, Nicolas de Maupeou (mo-POO), who dissolved the parlements early in 1771 and created new law courts whose judges would not enjoy independent power.

The Crown lost control of reform when Louis died soon after, in 1774. His 20-year-old grandson, Louis XVI, well-meaning but insecure, allowed the complete restoration of the parlements. Further reform efforts, sponsored by the king and several talented ministers, came to nothing because of parlementary opposition. Not surprisingly, from about the middle of the century,

Gardens

What is a garden? Like most of the art forms that we see habitually, the garden is difficult to analyze or even to think of as an art form. Like the buildings they surround, however, gardens have much to tell us about human habits and values. Let us examine these eighteenth-century gardens for evidence of contemporaries' attitudes toward nature and their relationship with it.

Look at the two English-style gardens illustrated here. The first is next to the Governor's Mansion in Williamsburg, the capital of the English colony of Virginia. Construction of this garden began at the end of the seventeenth century; the photograph shows the restored gardens that tourists may visit today. The second garden, from the private estate of West Wycombe in England, looks very different—much more like a natural landscape. The engraving reproduced here dates from the 1770s. The two gardens represent distinct epochs in the development of the garden, hence the differences between them. However, each of these gardens in its own way celebrates human domination of nature.

This symbolic domination of nature is more obvious to us in the Williamsburg garden. The lawns and hedges are trimmed in precise geometrical shapes and are laid out, with the walkways, in straight lines. This "palace garden" was a small English variant of the classical garden developed in France—most spectacularly at the Versailles Palace—and then imitated throughout Europe during the seventeenth century. The garden at Versailles is so vast that at many points, all of nature visible to the eye is nature disciplined by humans.

We can think of such gardens as pieces of architecture, because that is how they were originally conceived. The design originated in the enclosed courtyard gardens of the homes of classical antiquity. The straight lines and square shapes of these gardens mimic the buildings they are attached to. In fact, these seventeenth- and eighteenth-century gardens were usually laid out as an extension of the buildings themselves. Notice the wide staircase that descends from the central axis of the Governor's Mansion into the central walkway of the garden. Other architectural details, such as the benches positioned at the ends of various walkways, add to the sense of the garden as an exterior room. The garden symbolizes the taming of nature into a pleasing vision of order and regularity.

However, the later eighteenth-century garden represents even greater confidence in the human relationship with nature, although it does not appear to do so at first glance. The extensive garden at first seems to be nature itself

Governor's Mansion and Formal Gardens at Williamsburg, Virginia   (© Robert Llewellyn)

Landscape Garden at West Wycombe, England (Courtesy of the Trustees of the British Museum)

plus a few added details, such as the statuary, and a few improvements, such as the grass kept trim by the workers in the foreground. Our familiarity with such landscapes—in our own suburban yards—keeps us from immediately perceiving how contrived such a landscape is. Nature, however, does not intersperse dense stands of trees or clumps of shrubbery with green expanses of lawns. Nor does nature conveniently leave portions of a hillside bare of trees to provide a view of the water from a palatial house on the hill (to the left). Note also that the waterfall cascading over rocks and statuary flows from an artificial lake, neatly bordered by a path.

This kind of garden reflects Enlightenment optimism about humans' ability to understand and work with nature. Such gardens were asymmetrical: Paths were usually curved, and lakes and ponds were irregularly shaped, as they would be in nature. Trees and shrubs were allowed to maintain their natural form. Nevertheless, this landscaping conveys a powerful message of confidence and order. Humans cannot bend or distort nature to their own ends, but they can live in harmony with it as they manage it and enjoy its beneficence. People were freed from regarding nature as hostile and needing to be fought. In this garden, one lives with nature but improves on it. The workers cutting the grass do not detract from the engraving but rather make the scene more compelling.

This brand of landscape gardening appeared in the English colonies across the Atlantic by the end of the eighteenth century. One of the best examples is at Monticello, Thomas Jefferson's Virginia estate, first designed in the 1770s and constructed and improved over the remainder of Jefferson's life (1743–1826). If you tour Monticello, you will notice a curving garden path bordered by flowers in season, with mature trees scattered here and there. Jefferson planned every inch of this largely random-looking outdoor space, just as he planned the regimented fruit and vegetable garden that borders it. The older, classical style of the Williamsburg garden is partly explained by its earlier date and also because this more aggressively controlling style lasted longer in the American colonies than in Europe, perhaps because "nature" seemed more wild and more formidable in the New World.

QUESTIONS

1. How do the two gardens depicted here reflect two different visions of human power over nature?

2. What explains the evolution of styles, over the eighteenth century, in this art form?

there had been calls to revive the Estates General, the representative assembly last convened in 1614. By the time an Estates General was finally called in the wake of further financial problems in 1788, the enlightened elites' habit of carrying on political debate and criticism outside the actual corridors of power, as well as their accumulated mistrust of the Crown, had created a volatile situation.

Monarchy and Parliament in Great Britain

After the deaths of William (d. 1702) and Mary (d. 1694), the British crown passed to Mary's sister, Anne (r. 1702–1714), and then to a collateral line descended from Elizabeth Stuart (d. 1662), sister of the beheaded Charles I. Elizabeth had married Frederick, elector of the Palatinate (and had reigned with him briefly in Bohemia at the start of the Thirty Years' War; see page 427), and her descendants were Germans, now electors of Hanover. The new British sovereign in 1714, George I (r. 1714–1727), was both a foreigner and a man of mediocre abilities. Moreover, his claim to the throne was immediately contested by Catholic descendants of James II (see page 455), who attempted to depose him in 1715 and later his son, George II (r. 1727–1760), in 1745.

The 1745 uprising was the more serious threat. The son of the rival Stuart claimant to the throne, Charles (known in legend as Bonnie Prince Charlie), landed on the west coast of Scotland, with French assistance. He led his forces south into England. Most of the British army and George II himself were on the Continent, fighting in the War of the Austrian Succession (see page 522). Scotland had been formally united with England in 1707 (hence, the term *Great Britain* after that time), and Charles had found some support among Scots dissatisfied with the economic and political results of that union.

But the vast majority of Britons, Scottish or English, did not want the civil war that Charles's challenge inevitably meant, especially on behalf of a Catholic claimant who relied on support from Britain's great rival, France. Charles's army, made up mostly of poor Highland clansmen, was destroyed at the Battle of Culloden (cull-UH-dun) in April 1746 by British army units, hastily returned from abroad. Charles fled back to France, and the British government used the failed uprising as justification for the brutal and forceful integration of the still-remote Scottish Highlands into the British state.

Despite this serious challenge to the new dynasty and the harsh response it occasioned, the British state, overall, enjoyed a period of relative stability as well as innovation in the eighteenth century. The civil war of the seventeenth century had reaffirmed both the need for a strong monarchy and the role of Parliament in defending elite interests. The power of Parliament had recently been reinforced by the Act of Settlement, by which the German Protestant heir to Queen Anne had been chosen in 1701. By excluding the Catholic Stuarts from the throne and establishing the line of succession, this document reasserted that Parliament determined the legitimacy of the monarchy. In fact, the act claimed greater parliamentary authority over foreign and domestic policy in the aftermath of William's constant involvement in war (see page 450).

In the eighteenth century, cooperation between monarchy and Parliament evolved further as Parliament became a more sophisticated and secure institution. Political parties—that is, distinct groups within the elite favoring certain foreign and domestic policies—came into existence. Two groups, the Whigs and the Tories, had begun to form during the reign of Charles II (d. 1685). The Whigs (named derisively by their opponents with a Scottish term for horse thieves) had resisted Charles's pro-French policies and his efforts to tolerate Catholicism. They had wholly opposed his brother and successor, James II. Initially, the Whigs favored an aggressive foreign policy against continental opponents, particularly France. The Tories (whose name was also a taunt, referring to Irish cattle rustlers) leaned toward a conservative view of their own role, favoring isolationism in foreign affairs and deference toward monarchical authority. Whigs generally represented the interests of the great aristocrats or wealthy merchants or gentry. Tories more often represented the interests of provincial gentry and the traditional concerns of landholding and local administration.

The Whigs were the dominant influence in government through most of the century to 1770. William and Mary, as well as Queen Anne, favored Whig religious and foreign policies. The loyalty of many Tories was called into question by their support for a Stuart, not Hanoverian, succession at Anne's death in 1714. The long Whig dominance of government was also ensured by the talents of Robert Walpole, a member of Parliament who functioned virtually as a prime minister from 1722 to 1742.

Walpole (1676–1745) was from a minor gentry family and was brought into government in 1714 with other Whig ministers in George I's new regime. An extremely talented politician, he took advantage of the mistakes of other ministers over the years and, in 1722, became both the first lord of the treasury and chancellor of the exchequer. No post or title of "prime minister" yet existed, but the great contribution of Walpole's tenure was to create that office in fact, if not officially. He chose to maintain peace abroad when and where he could and thus presided over a period of recovery and relative prosperity.

Initially, Walpole was helped in his role as go-between for king and Parliament by George I's own limitations. The king rarely attended meetings of his own council of ministers and was hampered by his limited command of English. Gradually, the Privy Council of the king became something resembling a modern cabinet dominated by a prime minister. By the end of the century, the notions of "loyal opposition" to the Crown within Parliament and parliamentary responsibility for policy had taken root.

In some respects, the maturation of political life in Parliament resembled the lively political debates in the salons of Paris. In both cases, political life was being legitimized on a new basis. In England, however, that legitimation was enshrined in a legislative institution, which made it especially effective and resilient. Parliament was not yet in any sense representative of the British population, however. Because of strict property qualifications, only about 200,000 adult men could vote. In addition, representation was very uneven and heavily favored traditional landed wealth. Some constituencies with only a few dozen voters sent members to Parliament. Many of these "pocket boroughs" were under the control of (in the pockets of) powerful local families who could intimidate the local electorate, particularly in the absence of secret ballots.

Political Satire in England   This gruesome image, showing England being disemboweled by members of the government, criticizes the government's acceptance of a treaty with France. Satirical images such as this one were increasingly part of the lively and more open political life in eighteenth-century England.   (Courtesy of the Trustees of the British Museum)

Movements for reform of representation in Parliament began in the late 1760s as professionals, such as doctors and lawyers, with movable (as opposed to landed) property and merchants in booming but underrepresented cities began to demand the vote. As the burden of taxation grew—the result of the recently concluded Seven Years' War (discussed later in this chapter)—these groups felt increasingly deprived of representation. Indeed, many felt kinship with the American colonists who opposed increased taxation by the British government on these same grounds and revolted in 1775.

However, the reform movement faltered over the issue of religion. In 1780, a tentative effort by Parliament to extend some civil rights to British Catholics provoked rioting in London (known as the Gordon Riots, after one of the leaders). The riots lasted for eight days and claimed three hundred lives. Pressure for parliamentary reform had been building, but this specter of a popular movement out of control temporarily ended the drive for reform by disenfranchised elites.

"Enlightened" Monarchy

Arbitrary monarchical power might seem antithetical to Enlightenment thought. After all, the Enlightenment stressed the reasonableness of human beings and their capacity to discern and act in accord with natural law. Yet, monarchy seemed an ideal instrument of reform to Voltaire and to many of his contemporaries. The work of curtailing the influence of the church, reforming legal codes, and eliminating barriers to economic activity might be done more efficiently by a powerful monarch than by other available means. Historians have labeled a number of rulers of this era "enlightened despots" because of the arbitrary nature of their power, yet the enlightened or reformist uses to which they put it.

SCANDINAVIA

In Denmark, in 1784, a reform-minded group of nobles, led by the young crown prince Frederick (governing on behalf of his mentally ill father), began to apply Enlightenment remedies to the kingdom's economic problems. This move was a bold departure from the past because, in Denmark, the Crown had governed without significant challenge from the landholding nobility since the mid-seventeenth century and the nobility enjoyed ironclad domination of the peasantry. The reformers encouraged freer trade and sought, above all, to improve agriculture by elevating the status of the peasantry. With improved legal status and with land reform, which enabled some peasants to own the land they worked for the first time, agricultural productivity in Denmark rose dramatically. These reforms constitute some of the clearest achievements of any of the "enlightened" rulers.

In contrast to Denmark, Sweden had a relatively unbroken tradition of noble involvement in government, stemming in part from its marginal economy and the consequent stake of the nobility in the Crown's aggressive foreign policy. Since Sweden's eclipse as a major power after the Great Northern War (see page 462), factions of the Swedish parliament, the Diet, had fought over the reins of government, somewhat like the emerging political parties in Britain. Ironically, it was in Sweden, and not Denmark, that an "enlightened despot" emerged. King Gustav III (r. 1771–1796) staged a coup to regain control of policy from the Diet and began an ambitious program of reform of the government. Restrictions on trade in grain and other economic controls were liberalized, the legal system was rationalized, the death penalty was strictly limited, and legal torture was abolished.

Despite his achievements, Gustav III suffered the consequences of advancing reform by autocratic means in a kingdom with a strong tradition of representative government. Gustav eventually tried to deflect the criticisms of the nobility by reviving grandiose—but completely unrealistic—schemes for the reconquest of Baltic territory. In 1796, he was mortally wounded by an assassin hired by disgruntled nobles.

PRUSSIA

"**Enlightened despotism**" aptly describes the rule of Frederick II of Prussia (r. 1740–1786), known as **Frederick the Great**. Much of the time, Frederick resided in his imperial electorate of Brandenburg, near its capital, Berlin. His scattered states, which he extended by seizing new lands, are referred to as Prussia rather than Brandenburg-Prussia because members of his family were now kings of Prussia thanks to their ambitions and the weakness of the Polish state, of which Prussia had once been a dependent duchy. In many ways, the Prussian state *was* its military victories, for Frederick's bold moves and the policies of his father, grandfather, and great-grandfather committed the state's resources to a military presence of dramatic proportions. Prussia was on the European stage at all only because of that driving commitment.

The institutions that constituted the state and linked the various provinces under one administration were dominated by the needs of the military. Frederick II's father, Frederick William (r. 1713–1740), had added an efficient provincial recruiting system to the state's central institutions, which he also further consolidated. But in many other respects, the Prussian state was in its infancy. There was no tradition of political participation—even by elites—and little chance of cultivating any. Nor was there any political or social room for maneuver at the lower part of the social scale. The rulers of Prussia had long ago given in to the aristocracy's demand for tighter control over peasant labor on their own lands in return for their support of the monarchy. The rulers relied on the nobles for local administration and army commands. Thus, the kinds of social, judicial, or political reforms that Frederick could hope to carry out without undermining his own power were starkly limited.

Frederick tried to modernize agricultural methods and simultaneously to improve the condition of the peasants, but he met stiff resistance from the noble landholders. He did succeed in abolishing serfdom in some regions. He tried to stimulate the economy by sponsoring state industries and trading monopolies, but too few resources and too little initiative from the tightly controlled merchant communities stymied his plans. Simplifying and codifying the inherited jumble of local laws was a goal of every ruler. A law code published in 1794, after Frederick's death, was partly the product of his efforts.

Frederick's views of the role of Enlightenment thought reflect the limitations of his situation. One doesn't have to lead a frontal assault on prejudices consecrated by time, he believed; instead, one must be tolerant of superstition because it will always have a hold on the masses. Perhaps his most distinctive "enlightened" characteristic was the seriousness with which he took his task as ruler. He was energetic and disciplined to a fault. In his book, *Anti-Machiavel* (1741), he argued that a ruler has a moral obligation to work for the betterment of the state. He styled himself as

Enlightened despotism
Term for the reform-oriented rule of eighteenth-century monarchs. Enlightened despots applied Enlightenment remedies to economic problems and encouraged education and legal reform, but did not dismantle elites' privileges or share their own power.

Frederick the Great
Autocratic king of Prussia who transformed the country into a major military power and also sponsored "enlightened" reforms.

the "first servant" or steward of the state. However superficial this claim may appear, Frederick compares favorably with Louis XV of France, who, having a far more wealthy and flexible society to work with, did much less.

The Habsburg ruler **Maria Theresa** of Austria (r. 1740–1780) was guided more by traditional concerns for effective rule and compassion for her subjects than by Enlightenment ideas. After surviving the near dismemberment of Austrian territories in the War of the Austrian Succession (see page 522), she embarked on an energetic program of reform to improve the administration of her territories. "Austria," it must be remembered, is a term of convenience; the state was a very medieval-looking hodgepodge that included present-day Austria, the kingdoms of Bohemia and Hungary, the Austrian Netherlands, and lands in northern Italy. Among her more successful reforms were improved assessment and collection of taxes to tap the wealth of her subjects more effectively and thus better defend all her domains. She improved her subjects' access to justice and limited the exploitation of serfs by landlords. She made primary schooling universal and compulsory, in order to better train peasants for the army. Although the policy was far from fully implemented at the time of her death, hers was the first European state with so ambitious an education policy. Maria Theresa accomplished all of this without being particularly "enlightened" personally. She was a devout Catholic who cherished orthodoxy in religious matters. She did not welcome Enlightenment philosophy to her court and feared freedom of the press.

Many of the ministers and bureaucrats who implemented Maria Theresa's reforms were themselves well versed in "enlightened" ideas. The diverse character of the Habsburg lands meant that some members of the governing elite came from the Netherlands and from Italy, where sympathy for the Enlightenment was well rooted by comparison with the relatively poorer and more rural society of the Austrian hinterland. Moreover, the language of the Habsburg court was French (Maria Theresa spoke it fluently); thus, no amount of local censorship—which, in any case, Maria Theresa relaxed—could prevent the governing class from reading and absorbing Enlightenment philosophy in its original language.

Maria Theresa was followed on the throne by her two sons, Joseph II (r. 1780–1790) and Leopold II (r. 1790–1792), each of whom counted himself a follower of the Enlightenment. After his mother's death, Joseph II carried out bold initiatives that she had not attempted, including freedom of the press, significant freedom of religion, and the abolition of serfdom in Habsburg lands.

Like Frederick the Great, Joseph regarded himself as a servant of the state. Also like Frederick, he was limited in his reform program by the economic and social rigidities of the society he ruled; he could not directly assault the privileges of great landholders, on whose wealth the state depended. His despotic methods—he imposed reforms autocratically—antagonized many of these powerful subjects. His more able brother, Leopold, spent much of his two-year reign dexterously saving reforms enacted by his mother and, especially, his brother in the face of mounting opposition.

Perhaps the most powerful ruler with a claim to the title "enlightened despot" was Catherine, empress of Russia (r. 1762–1796). **Catherine the Great**, as she came to be called, was the true heir of Peter the Great in her abilities, policies, and ambitions. Her determination and political acumen were evident soon after she was brought to the Russian court from her native Germany in 1745. After enduring brutal treatment by her husband, Tsar Peter III, Catherine engineered a coup in which he was killed, and then ruled alone for more than thirty years.

Like any successful ruler of her age, Catherine counted territorial aggrandizement among her chief achievements: she expanded Russian territory at the expense of the Ottoman Empire and Poland-Lithuania.

Nevertheless, Catherine counted herself a sincere follower of the Enlightenment. Like Frederick, she attempted to take an active role in the European intellectual community; she corresponded with Voltaire over the course of many years and acted as patron to the encyclopedist Diderot. One of Catherine's boldest political moves was the secularization of church lands. Although Peter the Great had extended government control of the Russian Orthodox Church, he had not touched church lands. Catherine also licensed private publishing houses; the number of books published in Russia tripled during her reign. This enriched cultural life was one of the principal causes of the flowering of Russian literature that began in the early nineteenth century.

The stamp of the Enlightenment on Catherine's policies is also clearly visible in her attempts at legal reform. In 1767, she convened a legislative commission and provided it with a guiding

AUSTRIA

Maria Theresa Habsburg archduchess of Austria and queen of Hungary and Bohemia who reformed and centralized the administration of her Austrian and Bohemian lands.

RUSSIA

Catherine the Great Empress of Russia who, through an astute policy of wars and alliances, expanded her country's borders. An "enlightened despot," she advanced the westernizing reforms begun by Peter the Great.

Catherine the Great as a young woman This portrait of Catherine was painted when she first came to the Russian court from her native Germany in 1745. Catherine wears formal court dress and the portrait introduces her as a "Grand Duchess," a Russian title reserved for the royal family. (Portrait of Grand Duchess Yekatrina Alexeyevna, later Catherine II, c.1745, Grooth, Georg Christoph (1716-49)/Hermitage, St. Petersburg, Russia/The Bridgeman Art Library)

document, the *Instruction*, which she had written herself. The commission was remarkable because it included representatives of all classes, including peasants. Catherine hoped for a general codification of law as well as reforms, such as the abolition of torture and capital punishment—reforms that made the *Instruction* radical enough to be banned from publication in other countries. She did not propose changing the legal status of serfs, however, and class conflict made the commission unworkable in the end. Most legal reforms were eventually accomplished piecemeal and favored the interests of landed gentry.

Like the Austrian rulers, Catherine undertook far-reaching administrative reform to create more effective local units of government but, again, political imperatives were fundamental, and reforms in local government strengthened the hand of the gentry. The legal subjection of peasants in serfdom was also extended as a matter of state policy to help win the allegiance of landholders in newly acquired areas. In Russia, as in Prussia and Austria, oppression of the peasantry continued because the monarch wanted to ensure the allegiance of the elites who lived from the peasants' labor. Catherine particularly valued the cooperation of elites because the expanding Russian state was incorporating new peoples, such as the Tatars in the Crimea, and attempting to manage its relationships with border peoples such as the Cossacks. Catherine's reign witnessed one of the most massive and best-organized peasant rebellions of the century. Occurring in 1773, the rebellion expressed the grievances of the thousands of peasants who joined its ranks and called for the abolition of serfdom. The revolt took its name, however, from its Cossack leader, Emelian Pugachev (poo-guh-CHOFF) (d. 1775), and reflected also the Cossacks' resistance to centralized control. The dramatic dilemmas faced by Catherine illustrate both the promise and the costs of state formation throughout Europe. State consolidation permitted the imposition of internal peace, coordinated economic policy, and reform of justice, but it came at the price of greater—in some cases much greater—control and coercion of the population.

SECTION SUMMARY

- In France, the royal government tried unsuccessfully to eliminate the privileges of nobility, which limited state revenue and kept most people shut out of the political process.

- The Parliament in England was securely established as a part of government; political parties, representing differing interests among the elite, began to develop.

- "Enlightened despots," such as Frederick the Great in Prussia, ruled autocratically but used their power for some reforms in law, education, and public welfare.

THE WIDENING WORLD OF TRADE AND PRODUCTION

How and why did trade and production increase in the eighteenth century?

The importance of international trade and colonial possessions to the states of western Europe grew enormously in the eighteenth century (see **MAP 18.2**). Between 1715 and 1785, Britain's trade with North America rose from 19 to 34 percent of its total trade, and its trade with Asia and Africa rose from 7 to 19 percent of the total. By the end of the century, more than half of all British trade was carried on outside Europe; for France, the figure was more than a third. Plantation agriculture based on slave labor in European colonies created profits and products that drove much of this trade. Equally profound changes were occurring in the European countryside. Population, production, and consumption were beginning to grow beyond the bounds that all preceding generations had lived within and taken for granted.

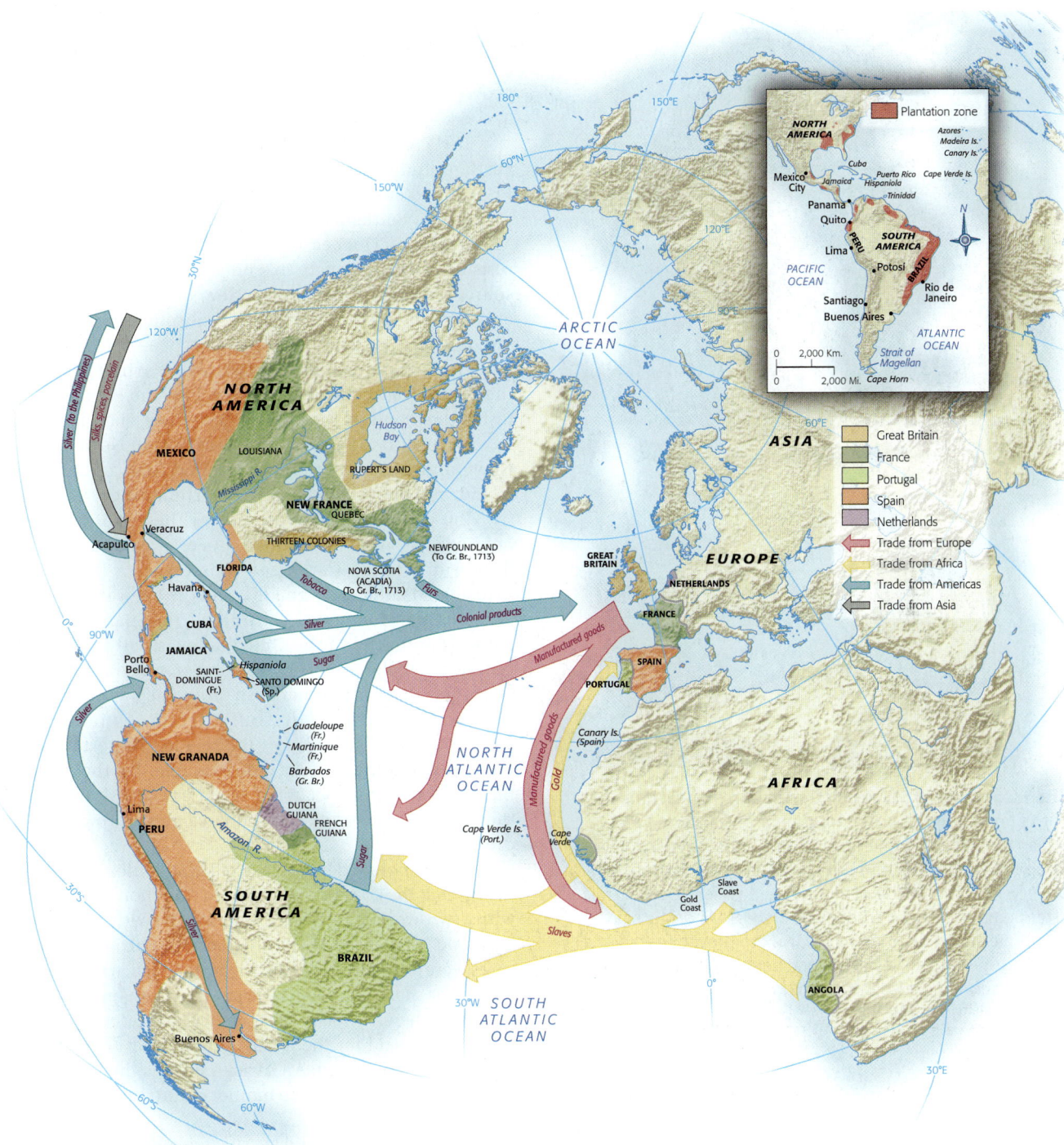

🌐 Map 18.1—The Atlantic Economy, ca. 1750

The triangle trade linked Europe, Africa, and European colonies in the Americas. The most important component of this trade for Europe was the plantation agriculture of the Caribbean islands, which depended on enslaved Africans for labor.

The Atlantic World: Expanding Commerce and the Slave Trade

European commercial and colonial energies were concentrated in the Atlantic world in the eighteenth century because the profits were greatest there. The colonial population of British North America grew from about 250,000 in 1700 to about 1.7 million by 1760. The densely settled New England colonies provided a market for manufactured goods from the mother country, although

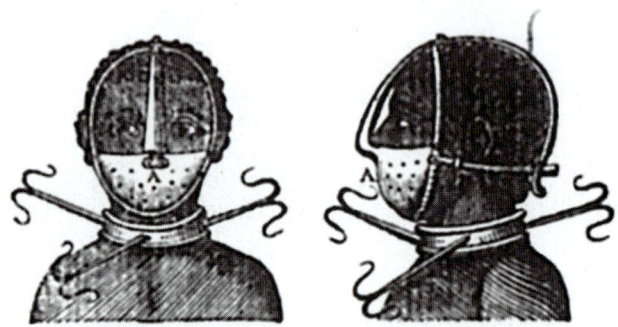

The Treatment of Slaves on Caribbean Plantations
These images of the brutal treatment of slaves on West Indian plantations come from a report published in England designed to convince the British public of the horrors of slavery. At top, a husband and wife are violently separated after being sold to different slave owners. At bottom, a mouthpiece and neck guard are used to prevent escape. The treatment of slaves described here is also documented in other surviving accounts from the eighteenth century. (New York Public Library/Art Resource, NY)

they produced little by way of raw materials or bulk goods on which traders could make a profit. The colonies of Maryland and Virginia produced tobacco, the Carolinas rice and indigo (a dyestuff). England re-exported all three throughout Europe at considerable profit.

The French in New France, only 56,000 in 1740, were vastly outnumbered by British colonists. Nevertheless, the French had successfully expanded their control of territory in Canada. Settlements sprang up between the outposts of Montreal and Quebec on the St. Lawrence River. Despite resistance, the French extended their fur trapping—the source of most of the profits New France generated—west and north along the Great Lakes, consolidating their hold by building forts at strategic points. They penetrated as far as the modern Canadian province of Manitoba, where they cut into the British trade run out of Hudson Bay. The French also contested the mouth of the St. Lawrence River and the Gulf of St. Lawrence with the British. The British held Nova Scotia and Newfoundland, the French controlled parts of Cape Breton Island, and both states fished the surrounding waters.

The commercial importance of these North American holdings, as well as those in Asia, was dwarfed by the European states' Caribbean possessions, however. The British held Jamaica, Barbados, and the Leeward Islands; the French, Guadeloupe and Martinique; the Spanish, Cuba and Santo Domingo; and the Dutch, a few small islands. Sugar, produced on plantations by slave labor, was the major source of profits, along with other cash crops such as coffee, indigo, and cochineal (another dyestuff). The concentration of shipping to this region indicates the region's importance in the European trading system. For example, by the 1760s, the British China trade occupied seven or eight ships a year. In the 1730s, British trade with Jamaica alone drew three hundred ships.

The economic dependence of the colonies on slave labor meant that the colonies were tied to their home countries not with a two-way commercial exchange, but with a three-way, or "triangle," trade (see **Map 18.1**). Certain European manufactures were shipped to ports in western Africa, where they were traded for slaves. Captive Africans were transported to South America, the Caribbean, or North America, where planters bought and paid for them with profits from their sugar and tobacco plantations. (See the feature, "The Global Record: An African Recalls the Horrors of the Slave Ship.") Sugar and tobacco were then shipped back to the mother country to be re-exported at great profit throughout Europe.

This plantation economy in the Caribbean was vulnerable to slave revolts, as well as to competition among the Europeans. Often, wars over control of the islands significantly disrupted production and lessened profits for the European planters on the islands and for their trading partners back in Europe. The growing demands by Europeans for sugar and other products kept the plantation system expanding, despite these challenges, throughout the eighteenth century. The **slave trade** grew dramatically as a result. Approximately five times as many Africans— perhaps as many as seven million people—were forcibly transported to the Americas as slaves in the eighteenth century as in the seventeenth.

The slave trade became an increasingly specialized form of oceangoing commerce (for example, slave traders throughout Europe adopted a standardized ship design) and, at the same time, one increasingly linked to the rest of European commerce by complex trade and financial ties. In England, London merchants who imported Asian goods, exported European manufactures, or distributed Caribbean sugar could provide credit for slave traders based in the northern city of Liverpool to fund their journeys to Africa and then the Americas.

slave trade Europeans' trade with Africa in which involuntary laborers were shipped to the Americas to be sold to owners of, especially, sugar plantations. The trade reached its peak in the eighteenth century, when approximately seven million Africans were shipped across the Atlantic.

An African Recalls the Horrors of the Slave Ship

Olaudah Equiano (ca. 1750–1797) was an Ibo from the Niger region of West Africa. He first experienced slavery as a boy when kidnapped from his village by other Africans, but nothing prepared him for the brutality of the Europeans who bought and shipped him to Barbados, in the British West Indies. His narration of the horrors of the "Middle Passage" between Africa and the Americas may represent a composite story of others' experiences as well as his own. Nevertheless, his account remains one of the few written records by an African survivor of a slave ship.

The first object which saluted my eyes when I arrived on the [African] coast was the sea and a slave ship, which was then riding at anchor, and waiting for its cargo. ... When I was carried on board I was immediately handled, and tossed up, to see if I were sound, by some of the crew. ... When I looked around the ship ... and saw ... a multitude of black people of every description chained together, every one of their countenances expressing dejection and sorrow, I no longer doubted of my fate. ...

I was not long suffered to indulge my grief; I was soon put down under the decks, and there I received such a salutation in the nostrils as I had never experienced in my life; so that with the loathsomeness of the stench ... I became so sick and low that I was not able to eat. ... I now wished for the last friend, death, to relieve me; but soon, to my grief, two of the white men offered me eatables; and, on my refusing to eat, one of them held me fast by the hands and laid me across, I think, the windlass, and tied my feet while the other flogged me severely.

One day, when we had a smooth sea and a moderate wind, two of my wearied countrymen, who were chained together ... , preferring death to such a life of misery, somehow made through the nettings and jumped into the sea; immediately another dejected fellow who [was ill and so not in irons] followed their example; and I believe many more would very soon have done the same, if they had not been prevented by the ship's crew who were instantly alarmed. Those of us that were the most active were in a minute put down under the deck; and there was such a noise and confusion amongst the people of the ship as I have never heard before, to stop her, and get the boat to go after the slaves. However, two of the wretches were drowned, but they got the other and afterwards flogged him unmercifully for thus attempting to prefer death to slavery. In this manner we continued to undergo more hardships than I can now relate; hardships which are inseparable from this accursed trade.

QUESTIONS

1. What particular horrors of the Middle Passage seem to stand out in Equiano's mind? What is the significance of these vignettes?

2. What clues in this excerpt reveal the audience Equiano had in mind for his narrative?

Source: *The Interesting Narrative of the Life of Olaudah Equiano, or Gustavus Vassa, the African* (London, 1793); reprinted in David Northrup, ed., *The Atlantic Slave Trade* (Boston: Houghton Mifflin, 2002), pp. 68–70.

MORE FOOD AND MORE PEOPLE

Throughout European history, there had been a delicate balance between available food and numbers of people to feed. Population growth had accompanied increases in the amount of land under cultivation. From time to time, however, population growth surpassed the ability of the land to produce food, and people became malnourished and prey to disease. In 1348, the epidemic known as the Black Death struck just such a vulnerable population in decline. After this catastrophic decline in the fourteenth century, the European population experienced a prolonged recovery, and in the eighteenth century, the limits that had previously been reached began to be exceeded for the first time.

The cause was not a decline in infant mortality, which remained as high as ever. Even Queen Anne of England outlived every one of the seventeen children she bore (and all but one of them died in infancy). Instead, population growth occurred because of a decline in the death rate for adults and a simultaneous increase in the birthrate in some areas, owing to earlier marriages. Adults began to live longer partly because of a decline in the incidence of plague. However, the primary reason adults were living longer was that more and different kinds of food began to be produced. Adults were better nourished and thus better able to resist disease. The increase in the food supply also meant that more new families could be started.

Food production increased because new crops were introduced and agricultural methods changed. The cumulative effect of these changes was so dramatic that historians have called them an **agricultural revolution**. In the past, peasants safeguarded the fertility of the land by alternately cultivating some portions while letting others lie fallow or using them as pasture. Manure provided fertilizer, but during the winter, livestock could not be kept alive in large numbers. Limited food for livestock meant limited fertilizer, which in turn meant limited production of food for both humans and animals.

agricultural revolution
Dramatic increase in food production from the sixteenth to eighteenth centuries, brought about by changes in agricultural practices and cultivation of new crops. The agricultural revolution allowed the population of Europe to expand beyond historic limits.

Gérard Dou: The Vegetable Seller　　The specialization of agriculture meant that a more varied diet was available to increasing numbers of Europeans. (Musée des Beaux-Arts, Nimes/Giraudon/Art Resource, NY)

The new crops now being planted included fodder, such as clover, legumes, and turnips, that did not deplete the soil and could be fed to livestock over the winter. The greater availability of animal manure in turn boosted grain production. In addition, the nutrient-dense potato was introduced from the Americas in the sixteenth century. It could feed more people per acre than could grain. In certain areas, farming families produced potatoes to feed themselves, while they grew grain to be sold and shipped elsewhere.

More food being produced meant more food available for purchase. The opportunity to buy food freed up land and labor. A family that could purchase food might decide to convert its farm to specialized use, such as raising dairy cattle, which meant, in turn, that several families might be supported by a piece of land that had previously supported only one. Over a generation or two, a number of children might share the inheritance of what had previously been a single farm, yet each could make a living from his or her share, and population could grow as it had not done before.

Farmers had known about and experimented with many of the crops used for fodder for centuries. However, widespread planting of these crops and other changes were long in coming and happened in scattered areas because a farmer had to have control over land in order to make changes. In the traditional open-field system, peasants had split up all the land in the community so that each family might have a piece of each field. Dramatic change was unlikely when an entire community had to act together. Only prosperous farmers had spare capital to invest in new crops and few were inclined to take risks with the production of food and to trust the workings of the market. The bad condition of roads was reason enough not to rely on distant markets.

Yet, where both decent roads and growing urban markets existed, some farmers—even entire villages working together—were willing to produce for urban populations. Booming capital cities, such as London and Amsterdam, and trading centers, such as Glasgow and Bordeaux, demanded not only grain, but also specialized produce, such as dairy products and fruits and vegetables. Urbanization and improved transportation networks also encouraged agriculture because human waste produced by city dwellers—known as "night soil"—could be collected and distributed in the surrounding agricultural regions as fertilizer. By the late eighteenth century, pockets of intensive, diversified agriculture existed in England, northern France, the Rhineland in Germany, the Po Valley in Italy, and Catalonia in Spain.

In some areas, changes in agriculture were accompanied by a shift in power in the countryside. Where the traditional authority of the village to regulate agriculture was weak, peasants were vulnerable to wealthy landlords who wanted to reap the profits of producing for the new markets. In England, a combination of weak village structure and high demand from urban centers created a climate that encouraged landlords to treat land speculatively. They raised the rents that farmers paid for land and changed cultivation patterns on the land that they controlled directly. They appropriated the village common lands, a process known as "enclosure," and used them for cash crops such as sheep (raised for their wool) or beef cattle.

As a result, although the agricultural revolution increased the food supply to sustain more people in Europe, it did not create general prosperity. Many rural people were driven off the land or made destitute by the loss of the resources of common lands. Charitable institutions run by cities, churches, and central governments expanded to care for them—often in poorhouses where people received food and shelter but were forced to work and to live isolated against their will. Peasants in eastern Europe produced grain for export to the growing urban centers in western Europe, but usually by traditional methods. In both eastern and western Europe, the power and profits of landlords were a major force in structuring the rural economy.

The Growth of Industry

Agricultural changes led to further changes in economic and social life. As more food was grown with less labor, that labor was freed to take on other productive work. If enough people could be kept employed making useful commodities, the nonagricultural population could continue to grow. If population grew, more and more consumers would be born, and the demand for more goods would help continue the cycle of population growth, changes in production, and economic expansion. This is precisely what happened in the eighteenth century: A combination of forces increased the numbers of people who worked at producing a few key materials and products (see **Map 18.2**).

Especially significant was the expansion of the putting-out system. Also known as cottage industry, putting out involved the production of thread and cloth by spinners and weavers working in their own homes, usually in a farming village. An entrepreneur bought the raw materials and "put them out" to be finished by these workers. The putting-out system expanded in the eighteenth century, as the agricultural economy was transformed. All agricultural work was seasonal, demanding intensive effort and many hands at certain times but not others. The labor demands of the new crops meant that an even larger number of people periodically needed work away from the fields to make ends meet.

🌐 **Map 18.2—Population and Production in Eighteenth-Century Europe**
The growth of cottage industry helped to support a growing population. With changes in agriculture, more land-poor workers were available in the countryside to accept work as spinners, knitters, and weavers.

SECTION SUMMARY

- The involvement of European states in international trade and overseas colonization grew markedly in the eighteenth century.

- Approximately seven million Africans were forcibly transported to work on plantations producing cash crops in the Americas.

- The introduction of new crops and changes in cultivation led to increases in food production and what has been called the "agricultural revolution."

- Changes in agriculture enabled the European population to grow beyond previous limits.

- Industrial production, especially of cloth, increased because more people were available for the work, markets for the products expanded, and new technologies arose to meet the demand.

Overseas trade also stimulated production by increasing both the demand in Europe's colonies for cloth and other finished products and the demand at home for manufactured items, such as nails to build the ships that carried the trade. The production of cloth expanded, particularly, because heightened demand led to changes in the way cloth was made. Wool was increasingly combined with other fibers to make less expensive fabrics. By the end of the century, wholly cotton fabrics were being made cheaply in Europe from cotton grown in America by slave labor.

The invention of machines to spin thread, also in the late eighteenth century, markedly increased the rate of production. Cloth production became a spur to a transformed industrial economy because cheaper kinds of cloth could be made for mass consumption. The regions of England, France, and the Low Countries where the new technologies were introduced stood, by the end of the century, on the verge of a massive industrial transformation that would have unprecedented social consequences.

THE WIDENING WORLD OF WARFARE

How did warfare and its consequences change in the eighteenth century?

In the eighteenth century, a new constellation of states emerged to dominate politics in Europe. Alongside the traditional powers of England, France, and Austria were Prussia in central Europe and Russia to the east (see **MAP 18.3**); these five states would dominate European politics until the twentieth century. Common to all these states was their ability to field effective armies and, especially in the case of Britain, navies. Eighteenth-century rulers launched most wars to satisfy traditional territorial ambitions. Now, however, the increasing significance of overseas trade and colonization also made international expansion an important source of conflict, particularly between England and France. As warfare widened in scope, governments increasingly focused on recruiting and maintaining large navies and armies, with increasingly serious effects on ordinary people.

The Pattern of War Within Europe

Wars between European states in the eighteenth century still reflected a dynastic, rather than wholly strategic, view of territory. Although rational and defensible "national" borders were important, collecting isolated bits of territory was also still the norm. The wars between European powers thus became extremely complex strategically. France, for example, might choose to strike a blow against Austria by invading an Italian state in order to use the conquered Italian territory as a bargaining chip in eventual negotiations. Wars were carried out with complex systems of alliances and were followed by the adjustments of many borders and the changing control of small, scattered territories. Rulers of lesser states in Germany and Italy, particularly, remained important as allies and as potential rivals of the Great Powers.

Major wars during the mid-eighteenth century decided the balance of power in German-speaking Europe for the next hundred years. Prussia emerged as the equal of Austria in the region. The first of these wars, now known as the War of the Austrian Succession, began after the death of the Habsburg emperor Charles VI in 1740. Charles died without a male heir, and his daughter, Maria Theresa, succeeded him. Charles had worked to shore up his daughter's position as his heir by means of a treaty of sorts called the Pragmatic Sanction, which he had persuaded allies and potential opponents to accept. Nevertheless, when Charles VI died, rival heiresses and their husbands challenged Maria Theresa for control of her various lands. They were supported by France, the Habsburgs' perennial rival. Worst of all, Prussia, Austria's rival to the north, seized

🌐 MAP 18.3—The Partition of Poland and the Expansion of Russia

Catherine the Great acquired present-day Lithuania, Belarus, and Ukraine, which had once constituted the duchy of Lithuania, part of the multiethnic Polish kingdom.

the wealthy Bohemian province of Silesia (sigh-LEE-zhuh). Austrian lands were threatened with dismemberment.

Though her father had not left his armies or his treasury well equipped to fight a war, Maria Theresa proved a more tenacious opponent than anyone had anticipated. She was helped by Great Britain, which saw the possibility of gains against its colonial rival, France. Fighting eventually spread throughout Habsburg territories, including the Netherlands and in Italy, as well as abroad to British and French colonies. In a preliminary peace signed in 1745, Frederick the Great of Prussia was confirmed in possession of Silesia, but the throne of the Holy Roman Empire was returned to the Habsburgs—given to Maria Theresa's husband, Francis (Franz) I (r. 1745–1765). A final treaty in 1748 ended all the fighting that had continued since 1745, mostly by France and Britain overseas. The Austrian state had survived dismemberment, and Maria Theresa now embarked on the administrative and military reforms necessary to make her state less vulnerable in the future. Prussia, because of the annexation of Silesia and the psychological imprint of victory, emerged as a power of virtually equal rank to the Habsburgs.

The unprecedented threat that Austria now felt from Prussia led to a revolution in alliances across Europe. To isolate Prussia, Maria Theresa agreed to an alliance with France, the Habsburgs' long-standing enemy. Sweden and Russia, with territory to gain at Prussia's expense, joined as well.

Frederick the Great initiated the land phase of what came to be known as the Seven Years' War in 1756, hoping to prevent consolidation of the new alliances. Instead, he found that he had started a war against overwhelming odds. What saved him in part was limited English aid. The English, engaged with France in the overseas conflict that Americans call the French and Indian War, wanted France to be heavily committed on the Continent. Prussia managed to emerge intact—though strained economically and demographically. Prussia and Austria were confirmed as the two states of European rank in German-speaking Europe. Yet, their narrow escapes from being reduced to second-class status reveal how fragile even successful states could be and how dependent on successful armies.

Later in the century, Prussia further expanded its territory by working in concert with Russian expansion. In 1768, Catherine the Great initiated a war against the Ottoman Turks, from which Russia gained much of the Crimean coast. She also continued her predecessors' efforts to dominate the weakened Poland. She was aided in this goal by Frederick the Great, who proposed the deliberate partitioning of Poland to satisfy his own territorial ambitions as well as those of his competitors, Russia and Austria. In 1772, portions of Poland were gobbled up in the first of three successive "grabs" of territory (see **MAP 18.3**). Warsaw eventually landed in Prussian hands, but Catherine gained all of Belarus, Ukraine, and modern Lithuania—which had constituted the duchy of Lithuania.

Great Britain and France: Wars Overseas

The expansion of European trade and settlement abroad in the eighteenth century led to wars between major powers, particularly the British and the French, which were fought primarily overseas. The growth and the proximity of French and British settlements in North America ensured conflict (see **MAP 18.4**). The Caribbean and the coasts of Central and South America were strategic flashpoints as well. At the beginning of the eighteenth century, several substantial islands remained unclaimed by any power. The British were making incursions along the coastline of Central America claimed by Spain and were trying to break into the monopoly of trade between Spain and its vast possessions in the region. Public opinion in both Britain and France became increasingly sensitive to colonial issues.

During the century, England became the dominant naval power in Europe. Its navy protected its far-flung trading networks, its merchant fleet, and the coast of England itself. Within Europe, England's strategic interest lay in promoting a variety of powers there, none of which (or no combination of which) posed too great a threat to England or to its widespread trading system. A second, dynastic consideration in continental affairs was the electorate of Hanover, the large principality in western Germany that was the native territory of the Hanoverian kings of England. Early in the century especially, the interests of this German territory were a significant factor in British foreign policy. Unable to field a large army, given their maritime interests, the British sought protection for Hanover in alliances and subsidies for allies' armies on the Continent and paid for these ventures with the profits on trade. France, on the other hand, was inevitably more committed to affairs on the Continent than were the British. The French were able to hold their own successfully in both arenas during the 1740s, but by 1763, though preeminent on the Continent, they had lost many of their colonial possessions to the English. Conflict between England and France in colonial regions played out in three major phases. The first two coincided with the major land wars in Europe: the War of the Austrian Succession (1740–1748) and the **Seven Years' War** (1756–1763). The third phase coincided with the rebellion of British colonies in North America—the American Revolution—beginning in the 1770s.

In the 1740s, France was heavily involved in the War of the Austrian Succession, while Britain vied with Spain for certain Caribbean territories. Both France and England also tested each other's strength in scattered colonial fighting, which produced a few well-balanced gains and losses. Their conquests were traded back when peace was made in 1748.

Tension was renewed almost immediately at many of the strategic points in North America. The French and British navies harassed each other's merchant shipping in the Gulf of St. Lawrence. The French reinforced their encirclement of British colonies with more forts along the Great Lakes and the Ohio River. When British troops (at one point led by the colonial commander George Washington) attempted to strike at these forts beginning in 1754, open fighting between the French and the English began.

Seven Years' War The first major war between European nations (Britain and France) started and fought largely in their overseas empires.

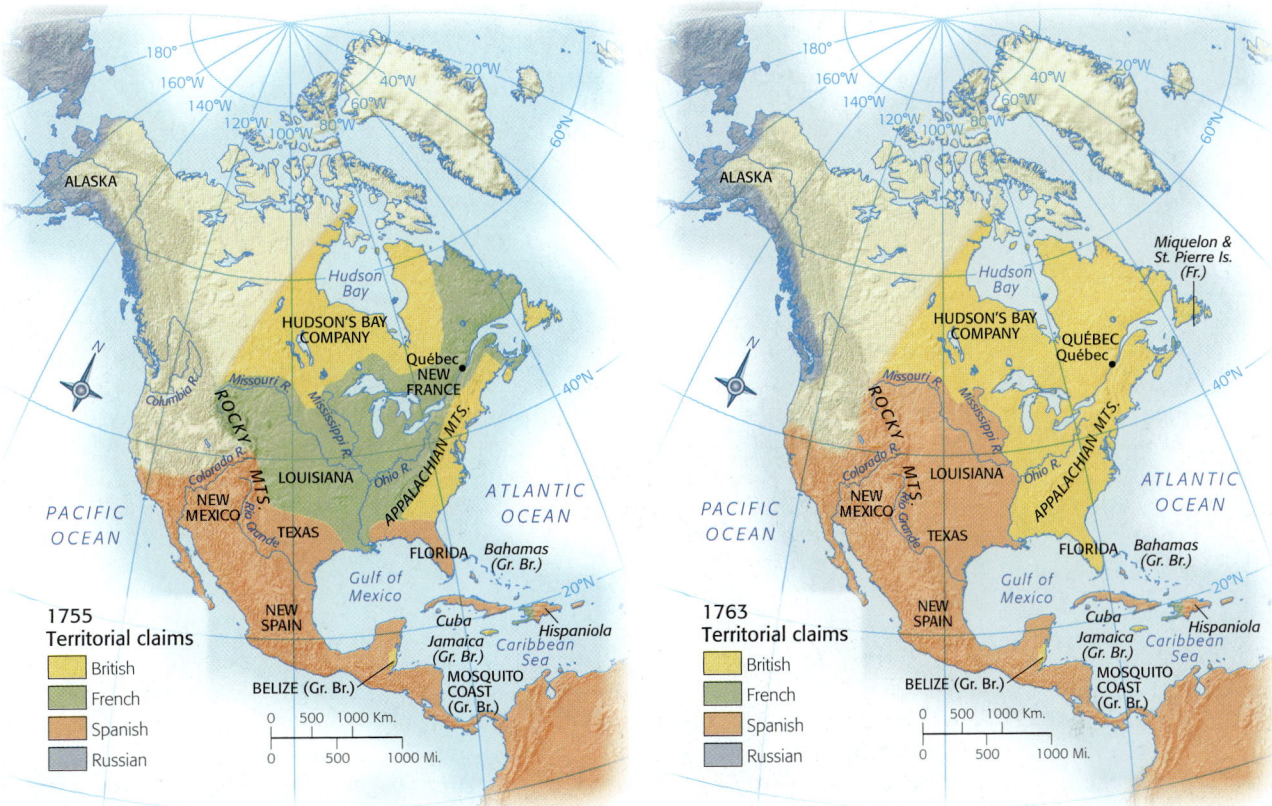

🌐 **MAP 18.4—British Gains in North America**

The British colonies on the Atlantic coast were effective staging posts for the armies that ousted the French from North America by 1763. However, taxes imposed on the colonies to pay the costs of the Seven Years' War helped spark revolt—the American Revolution—a decade later.

In India, meanwhile, both the French and the British attempted to strengthen their commercial footholds by making military and political alliances with local Indian rulers. The disintegration of the Mogul Empire heightened competition among regional Indian rulers and sparked a new level of ambition on the part of the European powers to gain territorial footholds for the purposes of trade. A British attack on a French convoy provoked a declaration of war by France in May 1756, three months before fighting in the Seven Years' War broke out in Europe. For the first time, a major war between European nations had started in their empires, signifying a profound change in the relation of these nations to the world.

The French had already committed themselves to an alliance with Austria and were increasingly involved on the Continent after Frederick II initiated war there in August 1756. Slowly, the drain of sustaining war both on the Continent and abroad began to tell, and Britain scored major victories against French forces. The cost of involvement on so many fronts meant that French troops were short of money and supplies. They were vulnerable to both supply and personnel shortages—especially in North America—because they were weaker than the British at sea and because New France remained sparsely settled and dependent on the mother country for food.

The French lost a number of fortresses on the Mississippi and Ohio Rivers and on the Great Lakes, and then, they also lost the interior of Canada with the fall of Quebec and of Montreal in 1759 and 1760, respectively (see **MAP 18.4**). In the Caribbean, the British seized the French island of Guadeloupe, a vital sugar-producer. Superior resources in India enabled the British to take several French outposts there, including Pondicherry (pon-dih-CHAIR-ee), the most important. By the terms of the Peace of Paris in 1763, France regained Guadeloupe, the most profitable of its American

The Death of General Wolfe at Quebec General Wolfe commanded British troops that in 1759 defeated the French at Quebec in Canada. Wolfe's death at the battle was memorialized ten years later by American-born artist Benjamin West. This image became widely popular after West sold cheap engraved versions. Notice West's sympathetic treatment of the Native American earnestly focused, like his British allies, on the death of the commander. (Private Collection/Phillips, Fine Art Auctioneers, New York, USA/The Bridgeman Art Library)

colonies, although Britain gained control of several smaller, previously neutral Caribbean islands to add to its own sugar-producing colonies of Jamaica and Barbados. In India, France retained many of its trading stations but lost its political and military clout. British power in India was dramatically enhanced not only by French losses, but also by victories over Indian rulers who had allied with the French. In the interior, Britain now controlled lands that had never before been under the control of any European power. British political rule in India, as opposed to merely a mercantile presence, began at this time. The British also held Canada. They emerged from the Seven Years' War as the preeminent world power among European states. The dramatic gains led some Britons to speak of the "British Empire" overseas.

The Costs of Warfare

In the eighteenth century, weapons and tactics became increasingly refined and armies more expensive to train and maintain. More reliable muskets were introduced. A bayonet that could slip over a musket barrel without blocking the muzzle was invented. Coordinated use of bayonets required even more careful drill of troops than did volley fire alone to ensure disciplined action in the face of enemy fire and charges. Artillery and cavalry forces also were subjected to greater standardization of training and discipline in action. Increased discipline of forces meant that commanders could exercise meaningful control over a battle for the first time. But such battles were not necessarily decisive, especially when waged against a comparable force. Indeed, training now was so costly that commanders were at times ironically reluctant to hazard their fine troops in battle at all.

In addition, wars could still be won or lost not on the battlefield, but on the supply line. Incentive still existed to bleed civilian populations and exploit the countryside. Moreover, when supply lines were disrupted and soldiers not equipped or fed, the armies of a major power could be vulnerable to smaller, less disciplined armies of minor states. Finally, even supplies, training, and sophisticated tactics could not guarantee success. Not until 1746, at Culloden, could the British army decisively defeat the fierce charge and hand-to-hand fighting of Highland clansmen by holding its position and using disciplined volley fire and bayonet tactics. Warfare became increasingly professional but was still an uncertain business with unpredictable results, despite its staggering cost.

One sure result of the new equipment, discipline, and high costs was that war became an ever greater burden on a state's resources and administration. It became increasingly difficult for small states, such as Sweden, to compete with the forces that others could mount. Small and relatively poor states, such as Prussia, that were able to support large forces did so by means of an extraordinary bending of civil society to the economic and social needs of the army. In Prussia, twice as many people were in the armed forces, proportionally, as in other states, and a staggering 80 percent of its meager state revenue went to sustain the army.

Warfare on this scale also represented an increased burden on common people. Most states introduced some form of conscription in the eighteenth century. Although the very poor often volunteered for army service to improve their lives, conscription of peasants (throughout Europe but particularly in Prussia and Russia) imposed a significant burden on peasant communities and a sacrifice of productive members to the state. Governments everywhere supplemented volunteers and conscripts with mercenaries and even criminals, as necessary, to fill the ranks without tapping the wealthier elements of the community. Men were sometimes taken out of poorhouses and forced to become soldiers. Thus, common soldiers were increasingly seen not as members of society, but as its rejects. Said Frederick II, "useful hardworking people should [not be conscripted but rather] be guarded as the apple of one's eye," and a French war minister agreed that armies had to consist of the "scum of people and of all those for whom society has no use."[3] Brutality became an accepted tool for governments to use to manage such groups of men, and the army increasingly became an instrument of social control used to contain individuals who otherwise might disrupt their own communities.

On the high seas, governments used their navies to suppress piracy. Piracy had been a way of life for hundreds of Europeans and colonial settlers since the sixteenth century. Indentured servants fleeing their obligations, runaway slaves, out-of-work laborers, and adventurers could take up the pirating life, which at least offered autonomy and a chance of some comforts. From the earliest days of exploration, European rulers had authorized men known as privateers to commit acts of war against specific enemies. The Crown took little risk and was spared the cost of arming the ships but shared in the plunder. True piracy—outright robbery on the high seas—was illegal, but in practice, the difference between piracy and privateering was negligible. As governments and merchants grew to prefer regular trade over the irregular profits of plunder, and as national navies developed in the late seventeenth century, a concerted effort to eliminate piracy began.

Because life on the seas was an increasingly vital part of European economic life in the eighteenth century, sea life began to resemble life on land in the amount of compulsion it entailed. Sailors in port were always vulnerable to forcible enlistment in the navy by impressment gangs, particularly during wartime. A drowsy sailor sleeping off a rowdy night could wake up to find himself aboard a navy ship. Press gangs operated throughout England and not just in major ports, for authorities were as interested in controlling "vagrancy" as in staffing the navy.

Like soldiers in the growing eighteenth-century armies, sailors in the merchant marine, as well as the navy, could be subjected to brutal discipline and appalling conditions. Merchant seamen attempted to improve their lot by trying to regulate their relationship with ships' captains. Contracts for pay on merchant ships became more regularized, and seamen often negotiated their terms very carefully, including, for example, details about how rations were to be allotted. Sailors might even take bold collective action aboard ship. The modern term for a work stoppage, *strike*, comes from the sailing expression "to strike sail," meaning to loosen the sails so that they cannot fill with wind. Its use dates from the eighteenth century, from "strikes" of sailors protesting unfair shipboard conditions.

The Idle Apprentice Is Sent to Sea, 1747. In one of a series of moralizing engravings by William Hogarth, the lazy apprentice is sent away to a life at sea. The experienced seamen in the boat introduce him to some of its terrors: one of them dangles a cat-o'nine tails (used for flogging), while another points out the distant gallows, where pirates and mutineers meet their fate. (*The Idle 'Prentice Turned Away and Sent to Sea*, plate V of 'Industry and Idleness', published 1833 (engraving), Hogarth, William (1697-1764)/Guildhall Library, City of London/The Bridgeman Art Library)

SECTION SUMMARY

- Prussia fought two major wars and emerged as the equal of Austria in German-speaking Europe.

- Russia expanded to the south and partitioned Poland together with Austria and Prussia.

- Britain and France fought over colonial possessions around the world; Britain won many of France's colonies by the end of the Seven Years' War in 1763.

- States recruited soldiers and equipped and trained their armies better than ever before, making war more costly and more demanding on their populations.

- Soldiers, sailors, and peasants found new ways to resist the burdens of forced labor, brutal conditions, and heavy taxation.

Seafaring men were an unusually large and somewhat self-conscious community of wage workers. But economic and political protests by ordinary people also showed interesting parallel changes. Peasant revolts—directly or indirectly a reaction to the costs of armies—had, in the past, ranged from small-scale practical actions against local tax collectors to massive uprisings that only a state's own army could suppress, such as the Pugachev rebellion. Peasant revolts continued to follow these patterns in the eighteenth century but in certain cases, peasants, like sailors, began to confront authority in new ways. They increasingly marshaled legal devices to maintain control over their land and to thwart landlords' efforts to enclose fields and cultivate cash crops. This change, though subtle, was important because it represented an effort to bring permanent structural change to the system and was not simply a temporary redress of grievances. In part, this trend toward "enlightened" revolt reflects increased access to information and the circulation of ideas about reform.

CHAPTER SUMMARY

The Enlightenment was an intellectual movement that applied to political and social thought the confidence in the intelligibility of natural law that Newton and other scientists had recently achieved. Prominent thinkers, called "philosophes," included influential individuals, such as Voltaire and Rousseau. But the Enlightenment was also a more general movement and one of its features was the growth of an informed body of public opinion outside the realm of government. The revolutionary potential of Enlightenment thought came from belief in its rationality and from the fact that it was both critical of its society and fashionable for educated elites to practice.

European rulers in the eighteenth century continued their efforts to govern with greater effectiveness; some self-consciously borrowed Enlightenment ideas to guide their policies, though they remained unwilling to share governing power. In France, although it was the center of the Enlightenment, the Crown failed to eliminate the privileges of nobility and could not adequately tap the wealth of the kingdom. In England, Parliament's role in government was securely established in this century, and new elites wanted to be represented in it.

Though some rulers were inspired by precepts of the Enlightenment, all were guided by traditional concerns of dynastic aggrandizement and strategic advantage. After dramatic expansion of trade, colonization, and the plantation system, conflict over colonial possessions became increasingly important, particularly between England and France. Partly as a result of growing commerce, the European economy was expanding, the population was growing beyond previous limits, and the system of production was being restructured.

FOCUS QUESTIONS

- What were the most important ideas in Enlightenment thought, and what were some of the intellectual, social, and political conditions that favored its development?

- To what extent did the activities of rulers, particularly "enlightened despots," reflect Enlightenment ideals, and to what extent did they reflect traditional concerns of state power?

- How and why did trade and production increase in the eighteenth century?

- How did warfare and its consequences change in the eighteenth century?

KEY TERMS

philosophes (p. 500)

Voltaire (p. 500)

Adam Smith (p. 502)

Jean-Jacques Rousseau (p. 503)

salons (p. 505)

Enlightened despotism (p. 514)

Frederick the Great (p. 514)

Maria Theresa (p. 515)

Catherine the Great (p. 515)

slave trade (p. 518)

agricultural revolution (p. 519)

Seven Years' War (p. 524)

 This icon will direct you to additional materials on the website: www .cengage.com/history/ noble/westciv6e.

NOTES

1. Moira Ferguson, ed., *First Feminists: British Women Writers, 1578–1799* (Bloomington: Indiana University Press, 1985), p. 426.

2. Quoted in Dena Goodman, *The Republic of Letters: A Cultural History of the French Enlightenment* (Ithaca, N.Y.: Cornell University Press, 1994), p. 89.

3. Quoted in M. S. Anderson, *Europe in the Eighteenth Century, 1713–1783*, 3d ed. (London: Longman, 1987), pp. 218–219.

See our interactive eBook for map and primary source activities.

19

A French Citizen Army
The National Guard of Paris leaves to join the army, September 1792
(detail).   (Photos12.com-ARJ)

An Age of Revolution, 1789–1815

These militiamen marching off to defend France against the invader in September 1792 appear to be heroes already. Adoring women in the crowd hand them laurel wreaths as they pass; the men march by, resolute and triumphant. Symbols of the ongoing revolution stand out as well: the prominent tricolor flag, the tricolor cockade in each man's hat. In fact, that September, France's citizen armies, for the first time, defeated the army of a foreign monarch poised to breach its borders and snuff out its revolution. The painting celebrates this triumph about to happen and thereby inspires confidence in the Revolution and pride in its citizen-soldiers.

Today the French Revolution is considered the beginning of modern European, as well as modern French, history. The most powerful monarch in Europe was forced to accept constitutional limits to his power by subjects convinced of their rights. Eventually, the king was overthrown and executed, and the monarchy abolished. Events in France reverberated throughout Europe because the overthrow of one absolute monarchy threatened fellow royals elsewhere. Revolutionary fervor on the part of ordinary soldiers enabled France's armies unexpectedly to best many of their opponents. By the late 1790s, the armies of France would be led in outright conquest of other European states by one of the most talented generals in European history: Napoleon Bonaparte. He brought to the continental European nations that his armies eventually conquered a mixture of imperial aggression and revolutionary change. Europe was transformed both by the shifting balance of power and by the spread of revolutionary ideas.

Understanding the French Revolution means understanding not only its origins, but also its complicated course of events and their significance. Challenging the king's power was not new, but overthrowing the king was revolutionary. A new understanding of the people became irresistible; they were the nation and, as citizens, had the right to representation in government. Louis XVI was transformed from the divinely appointed father of his people to an enemy of the people, worthy only of execution. Central to the Revolution was the complex process by which public opinion was shaped and, in turn, shaped events. Change was driven in part by the power of symbols—flags, rallying cries, inspiring art—to challenge an old political order and legitimize a new one.

FOCUS QUESTIONS

- What factors led to revolution in France in 1789?
- Why did several phases of revolutionary change occur after 1789 and what were the characteristics of each phase?
- What impact did the Revolution and Napoleonic rule have on France, the rest of Europe, and the wider world?

This icon will direct you to additional materials on the website: www .cengage.com/history/ noble/westciv6e.

See our interactive eBook for map and primary source activities.

THE ORIGINS OF REVOLUTION, 1775–1789

What factors led to revolution in France in 1789?

"I am a citizen of the world," wrote John Paul Jones, captain in the fledgling U.S. Navy, in 1778. He was writing to a Scottish aristocrat, apologizing for raiding the lord's estate while marauding along the British coast during the American Revolution. Jones (1747–1792), born a Scotsman himself, was one of the thousands of cosmopolitan Europeans who were familiar with European cultures on both sides of the Atlantic. As a sailor, Jones literally knew his way around the Atlantic world, but he was a "citizen of the world" in another sense as well. The Scotsman replied to Jones, surprised by the raid, since he was sympathetic to the American colonists; he was a man of "liberal sentiments" like Jones himself.[1] Both Jones and the Scottish lord felt they belonged to an international society of gentlemen who recognized certain Enlightenment principles regarding just and rational government.

The Atlantic world of the late eighteenth century was united both by practical links of commerce and shared ideals about liberty. The strategic interests of the great European powers were also always in play, however. Thus, when the American colonists actively resisted British rule and then in 1776 declared their independence from Britain, the consequences were wide-ranging: British trading interests were challenged, French appetites for gains at British expense were whetted, and illusive notions about liberty seemed more plausible. The victory of the American colonies in 1783, followed by the creation of the U.S. Constitution in 1787, further heightened the appeal of liberal ideas elsewhere. Attempts at liberal reform were mounted in several states, including Ireland, the Netherlands, and Poland. However, the American Revolution had the most direct impact on later events in France because the French had been directly involved in the American effort.

Revolutionary Movements in Europe

While the British government faced the revolt of the American colonies, it also confronted trouble closer to home. Many Britons had divided loyalties, and many who did favor armed force to subdue the American rebellion were convinced that the war was being mismanaged; they demanded reform of the ministerial government. The American rebellion also had ripple effects in other parts of Europe.

A reform movement sprang up in Ireland in 1779. The reformers demanded greater autonomy from Britain. Like the Americans, Irish elites—mostly of English or Scottish origin—felt like disadvantaged junior partners in the British Empire. They objected to policies that favored British imperial interests over those of the Irish ruling class: for example, the exclusion of Irish ports from overseas commerce in favor of English and Scottish ones and the grant of political rights to Irish Catholics so that they might fight in Britain's overseas armies.

The reformers expressed their opposition to British policies not only in parliamentary debates, but also in military defiance. Following the example of the American rebels, they set up a system of local voluntary militia to resist British troops if necessary. The Volunteer Movement was neutralized when greater parliamentary autonomy for Ireland was granted in 1782, following the repeal of many restrictions on Irish commerce. Unlike the Americans, the Irish elites faced an internal challenge to their own authority—the Catholic population whom they had for centuries dominated—which forced them to reach an accommodation with the British government.

Meanwhile, a political crisis with constitutional overtones was also brewing in the Netherlands. The United Provinces (the Netherlands) was governed by a narrow oligarchy of old merchant families, particularly in Amsterdam, and a military governor, the "stadtholder," from the princely House of Orange. The interests of the merchants and of the stadtholder frequently conflicted. Tensions between them deepened during the American Revolution, as merchants favored trade with the colonists and the prince favored maintaining an English alliance.

The conflict changed character when the representatives of the various cities, calling themselves the Dutch "Patriot" Party, defended their positions not merely on the grounds of their traditional political influence within the Netherlands, but also with wider claims to American-style liberty. The Patriots, in turn, were quickly challenged by newly wealthy traders and professionals, long disenfranchised by their closed merchant oligarchy, who demanded liberty too. These challengers briefly took over the Patriot movement. Just as many Irish rebels accepted the concessions of 1782, the Patriot oligarchs in the Netherlands did nothing to resist an invasion in 1787 that restored the power of the stadtholder, the prince of Orange, because it also ended the challenge to their own control of urban government.

Both the Irish volunteers and the Dutch Patriots, though members of very limited movements, echoed the American rebels in practical and ideological ways. Both were influenced by the economic and political consequences of Britain's relationship with its colonies. Both were inspired by the success of the American rebels and their thoroughgoing claims for political self-determination.

Desire for political reform flared in Poland as well during this period. Government reform was accepted as a necessity by Polish leaders after the first partition of Poland in 1772 had left the remnant state without some of its wealthiest territories (see **MAP 18.3** on page 523). Beginning in 1788, however, reforming gentry in the *Sejm* (representative assembly) went further; they established a commission to write a constitution, following the American example. The resulting document, known as the May 3 (1791) Constitution, was the first codified constitution in Europe; it was read and admired by George Washington.

Poles thus established a constitutional monarchy in which representatives of major towns, as well as gentry and nobility, could sit as deputies. The *liberum veto*, or individual veto power, which had allowed great nobles to obstruct royal authority, was abolished. However, Catherine the Great, empress of Russia, would not tolerate a constitutional government operating so close to her own autocratic regime; she ordered an invasion of Poland in 1792. The unsuccessful defense of Poland was led by, among others, a Polish veteran of the American Revolution, Tadeusz Kosciuszko (tah-DAY-oosh kos-USE-ko) (1746–1817). The second, more extensive partition of Poland followed, to be answered in turn in 1794 by a widespread insurrection against Russian rule, spearheaded by Kosciuszko. The uprising was mercilessly suppressed by an alliance of Russian and Prussian troops. Unlike the U.S. Constitution, from which they drew inspiration, the Poles' constitutional experiment was doomed by the power of its neighbors.

The American Revolution and the Kingdom of France

As Britain's greatest commercial and political rival, France naturally was drawn into Britain's struggle with its North American colonies. In the Seven Years' War (1756–1763), the French had lost many of their colonial settlements and trading outposts to the English (see page 526). Stung by this outcome, certain French courtiers and ministers pressed for an aggressive colonial policy that would regain for France some of the riches in trade that Britain now threatened to monopolize. The American Revolution seemed to offer the perfect opportunity. The French extended covert aid to the Americans from the very beginning of the conflict in 1775. After the first major defeat of British troops by the Americans—at the Battle of Saratoga in 1777—France formally recognized the independent United States and committed troops, as well as funds, to the American cause. John Paul Jones's famous ship, the *Bonhomme Richard* (bon-OHM ree-SHARD), was purchased and outfitted by the French government, as were many other American naval vessels. French support was decisive. In 1781, the French fleet kept reinforcements from reaching the British force besieged by George Washington at Yorktown. The American victory at Yorktown effectively ended the war; the colonies' independence was formally recognized by the Treaty of Paris in 1783.

The consequences for France of its American alliance were momentous. Aid for the Americans saddled France with a debt of about 1 billion *livres* (pounds), which represented as much as one-quarter of the total debt that the French government was trying to service. A less tangible impact of the American Revolution came from the direct participation of about nine thousand French soldiers, sailors, and aristocrats. The best known is the Marquis de Lafayette, who became an aide to George Washington and helped command American troops. For many

CHRONOLOGY

1775–1783	American Revolutionary War
1779–1782	Irish Volunteer Movement
1788	U.S. Constitution ratified; Reform movement begins in Poland; "Patriot" movement ends in the Netherlands
1789	French Estates General meets at Versailles (May); Third Estate declares itself the National Assembly (June); Storming of the Bastille (July)
1791	Polish constitution French king Louis XVI captured attempting to flee (June) Slave revolt begins in Saint Domingue
1792	France declares war on Austria; revolutionary wars begin (April); Louis XVI arrested; France declared a republic (August–September)
1793	Louis XVI guillotined
1793–1794	Reign of Terror in France
1799	Napoleon seizes power in France
1801	Concordat with pope
1804	Napoleon crowned emperor Napoleonic Civil Code Independence of Haiti (Saint Domingue) declared
1805	Battle of Trafalgar; Battle of Austerlitz
1806	Dissolution of Holy Roman Empire
1812	French invasion of Russia
1814	Napoleon abdicates and is exiled French monarchy restored
1815	Hundred Days (February–June) Battle of Waterloo

humble men, the war was simply employment. For others, it was a quest of sorts. For them, the promise of the Enlightenment—belief in human rationality, natural rights, and universal laws by which society should be organized—was brought to life in America.

Exposure to the American conflict occurred at the French court, too. Beginning in 1775, a permanent American mission to Versailles lobbied hard for aid. The chief emissary of the Americans was Benjamin Franklin (1706–1790), a philosophe by French standards whose writings and scientific experiments were already known to European elites. His talents—among them, a skillful exploitation of a simple, Quaker-like demeanor—succeeded in promoting the idealization of America at the French court.

The U.S. Constitution, the various state constitutions, and the debates surrounding their ratification were all published in Paris and much discussed in salons and at court, where lively debate about reform of French institutions had been going on for decades. America became the prototype of the rational republic—the embodiment of Enlightenment philosophy. It was hailed as the place where the irrationalities of inherited privilege did not prevail. A British observer, Arthur Young (1741–1820), believed that "the American revolution has laid the foundation of another in France, if [the French] government does not take care of itself."[2]

By the mid-1780s, there was no longer a question of whether the French regime would experience reform but rather a question of what form the reform would take. The royal government was almost bankrupt. A significant minority of the politically active elite was convinced that France's system of government was irrational. Nevertheless, a dissatisfied elite and a financial crisis—even fanned by a successful revolt elsewhere—do not necessarily lead to revolution. Why did the French government—the *Ancien Régime* (ahn-SYEN ray-ZHEEM) or "Old Regime," as it became known after the Revolution—not "take care of itself"?

The Crisis of the Old Regime

The Old Regime was brought to the point of crisis in the late 1780s by three factors: (1) heavy debts that dwarfed an antiquated system for collecting revenue; (2) institutional constraints on the monarchy that defended privileged interests; and (3) public opinion that envisioned thoroughgoing reform and pushed the monarchy in that direction. Another factor was the ineptitude of the king, Louis XVI (r. 1774–1793).

Louis came to the throne in 1774, a year before the American Revolution began. He was a kind, well-meaning man better suited to be a petty bureaucrat than a king. The queen, the Austrian Marie Antoinette (1755–1793), was regarded with suspicion by the many who despised the "unnatural" alliance with Austria the marriage had sealed. She, too, was politically inept, unable to negotiate the complexities of court life, and widely rumored to be selfishly wasteful of royal resources despite the realm's financial crises.

The fiscal crisis of the monarchy had been a long time in the making and was an outgrowth of the system by which the greatest wealth was protected by traditional privileges. At the top of the social and political pyramid were the nobles, a legal grouping that included warriors and royal officials. In France, nobility conferred exemption from much taxation. Thus, the royal government could not directly tax its wealthiest subjects.

This situation existed throughout much of Europe, a legacy of the power of the nobility in medieval times. Unique to France, however, was the strength of the institutions that defended this system. Of particular importance were the royal law courts, the parlements (par-luh-MAWHN), which claimed a right of judicial review over royal edicts. All the parlementaires—well-educated lawyers and judges—were technically noble and loudly defended the traditional privileges of all nobles. Louis XV (d. 1774), near the end of his life, had successfully undermined the power of the parlements by a bold series of moves. Louis XVI, immediately after coming to the throne, buckled under pressure and restored the parlements to full strength.

Deficit financing had been a way of life for the monarchy for centuries. After early efforts at reform, Louis XIV (d. 1715) had reverted to common fund-raising expedients, such as selling offices, which only added to the weight of privileged investment in the old order. England had established a national bank to free its government from the problem, but the comparable French effort early in the century had been undercapitalized and had failed. Late in the 1780s, under Louis XVI, one-fourth of the annual operating expenses of the government was borrowed, and half of all government expenditure went to paying interest on its debt. Short-term economic crises, such as disastrous harvests, added to the cumulative problem of government finance.

The Common People Crushed by Privilege In this contemporary cartoon, a nobleman in military dress and a clergyman crush a commoner under the rock of burdensome taxes and forced labor *(corvées)*. The victim's situation reflects that of the peasantry, but his stylish clothes would allow affluent townspeople to identify with him. (Musée Carnavalet, Paris/Giraudon/Art Resource, NY)

The king employed able finance ministers who tried to institute fundamental reforms, such as replacing the tangle of taxes with a simpler system in which all would pay and eliminating local tariffs, which were stifling commerce. The parlements and many courtiers and aristocrats, as well as ordinary people, resisted these policies. Peasants and townsfolk did not trust the "free market" (free from traditional trade controls) for grain; most feared that speculators would buy up the grain supply and people would starve. Trying to implement such reforms in times of grain shortage almost guaranteed their failure. Moreover, many supported the parlements simply because they were the only institution capable of standing up to the monarchy. But not all members of the elite joined the parlements in opposing reform. The imprint of "enlightened" public opinion was apparent in the thinking of some courtiers and thousands of educated commoners who believed that the government and the economy had to change. They openly debated the nature and extent of reform at court, in salons, cafes, and other gathering places.

In 1787, the king called an "Assembly of Notables"—an ad hoc group of elites—to support him in facing down the parlements and proceeding with some changes. But he found little support. Some notables, even men sympathetic to reform, either did not support particular proposals or were reluctant to allow the monarchy free rein. Others, reflecting the influence of the American Revolution, maintained that a "constitutional" body such as the Estates General, which had not been called since 1614, needed to make these decisions.

Ironically, nobles and clergy who were opposed to reform supported the call for the Estates General too, confident they could control its deliberations. The three Estates met and voted separately by "order"—clergy (First Estate), nobles (Second Estate), and commoners (**Third Estate**). The combined votes of the clergy and nobles would presumably nullify whatever the Third Estate might propose.

The Estates General

In 1788, mounting pressure from common people, as well as courtiers, led Louis to summon the Estates General. On Louis's orders, deputies were to be elected by local assemblies, which were chosen in turn by wide male suffrage. Louis mistakenly assumed he had widespread support in the provinces and wished to tap it by means of this grassroots voting. Louis also agreed

Third Estate In France, the common people, as distinct from the clergy (First Estate) and nobles (Second Estate), in the representative body the Estates General.

that the Third Estate should have twice as many deputies as the other two Estates, but he did not authorize voting by head rather than by order, which would have brought about the dominance of the Third Estate. Nevertheless, the king hoped that the specter of drastic proposals put forth by the Third Estate would frighten the aristocrats and clergy into accepting some of his reforms.

Louis's situation was precarious when the Estates General convened in May 1789. Already a groundswell of sentiment confirmed the legitimacy of the Estates General and the authority of the Third Estate to enact change. Political pamphlets circulated arguing that the Third Estate deserved enhanced power because it carried the mandate of the people. The most important of these was *What Is the Third Estate?* (1789) by Joseph Emmanuel Sieyès (1748–1836), a church official from the diocese of Chartres. The sympathies of Abbé Sieyès (say-EZ), as he was known, were with the Third Estate: His career had stalled because he was not noble. Sieyès argued that the Third Estate represented the nation because it did not reflect special privilege.

Among the deputies of the first two Estates—clergy and nobility—were men, such as the Marquis de Lafayette (1757–1834), who were sympathetic to reform. In the Third Estate, a large majority of deputies reflected the most radical political thought possible for men of their standing. Most were lawyers and other professionals who were functionaries in the government but, like Sieyès, of low social rank. They frequented provincial academies, salons, and political societies. They were convinced of the validity of their viewpoints and determined on reform, and they had little stake in the system as it was. When this group convened and met with resistance from the First and Second Estates, and from Louis himself, it seized the reins of government and a revolution began.

1789: A Revolution Begins

As soon as the three Estates convened at the royal palace at Versailles, conflicts surfaced. The ineptness of the Crown was immediately clear. On the first day of the meetings in May, Louis and his ministers failed to introduce a program of reforms for the deputies to consider. This failure raised doubt about the monarchy's commitment to reform. More important, it allowed the political initiative to pass to the Third Estate. The deputies challenged the Crown's insistence that the three Estates meet and vote separately. Deputies to the Third Estate refused to be certified (that is, to have their credentials officially recognized) as members of only the Third Estate rather than as members of the Estates General as a whole.

For six weeks, the Estates General was unable to meet officially, and the king did nothing to break the impasse. During this interlude, the determination of the deputies of the Third Estate strengthened. More and more deputies were won over to the notion that the three Estates must begin in the most systematic way: France must have a written constitution.

THE NATIONAL ASSEMBLY

By the middle of June, more than thirty reformist members of the clergy were sitting jointly with the Third Estate, which had invited all deputies from all three Estates to meet and be certified together. On June 17, the Third Estate simply declared itself the **National Assembly** of France. At first, the king did nothing, but when the deputies arrived to meet on the morning of June 20, they discovered they had been locked out of the hall. Undaunted, they assembled instead in a nearby indoor tennis court and produced the document that has come to be known as the **Tennis Court Oath**. It was a collective pledge to meet until a written constitution had been achieved. Only one deputy refused to support it. Sure of their mandate, the deputies had assumed the reins of government.

The king continued to handle the situation with both ill-timed self-assertion and feeble attempts at compromise. As more and more deputies from the First and Second Estates joined the National Assembly, Louis "ordered" the remaining loyal deputies to join it, too. Simultaneously, however, he ordered troops to come to Paris. He feared disorder in the wake of the recent disturbances throughout France and believed that any challenge to the legitimacy of arbitrary monarchical authority would be disastrous.

The king's call for troops aroused Parisians' suspicions. Some assumed a plot was afoot to starve Paris and destroy the National Assembly. With a population of about 600,000, Paris was one of the largest cities in Europe and it was the political nerve center of the nation—the site of the publishing industry, salons, and the homes of parlementaires and royal ministers. It was also

National Assembly
Legislative body formed in France in June 1789, when members of the Third Estate in the Estates General, joined by some deputies from the clergy, declared themselves the representatives of the nation.

Tennis Court Oath
Pledge signed by all but one deputy of the National Assembly in France on June 20, 1789, to meet until a constitution was drafted.

The Tennis Court Oath   It was raining on June 20, 1789, when the deputies found themselves barred from their meeting hall and sought shelter in the royal tennis court. Their defiance created one of the turning points of the Revolution; the significance was recognized several years later by the creator of this painting.   (Réunion des Musées Nationaux/Art Resource, NY)

a working city, with thousands of laborers of all trades plus thousands more—perhaps one-tenth of the inhabitants—jobless recent immigrants from the countryside. The city was both extremely volatile and extremely important to the stability of royal power.

It took little—news of the dismissal of a reformist finance minister—for Paris to erupt in demonstrations and looting. Crowds besieged City Hall and the royal armory, where they seized thousands of weapons. A popular militia formed as citizens armed themselves. Armed crowds attacked other sites of royal authority, including the huge fortified prison, the Bastille, on the morning of July 14. The Bastille now held only a handful of petty criminals, but it still remained a potent symbol of royal power and, the crowd assumed, held large supplies of arms. The garrison commander at first mounted a hesitant defense, then decided to surrender after citizens managed to secure cannons and drag them to face the prison. Most of the garrison were allowed to go free, although the commander and several officers were murdered by the crowd.

THE STORMING OF THE BASTILLE

The citizens' victory was a great embarrassment to royal authority. The king immediately had to embrace the popular movement. He came to Paris and, in front of crowds at City Hall, donned the red and blue cockade worn by the militia and ordinary folk as a badge of resolve and defiance. This symbolic action signaled the reversal of the Old Regime—politics would now be based on new principles.

Encouraged by events in Paris, inhabitants of cities and towns around France staged similar uprisings. In many areas, the machinery of royal government completely broke down. City councils, officials, and even parlementaires were thrown out of office. Popular militias took control of the streets. A simultaneous wave of uprisings shook the countryside. Most of them

Women's March on Versailles, October 1789   Parisian marketwomen marched the 12 miles to the king's palace at Versailles, some provisioning themselves with tools or weapons as they left the capital.   (Réunion des Musées Nationaux/Art Resource, NY)

were the result of food shortages, but their timing added momentum to the more strictly political protests in cities.

TOWARD CONSTITUTIONAL GOVERNMENT

These events forced the members of the National Assembly to work energetically on the constitution and to pass legislation to satisfy popular protests against economic and political privileges. On August 4, the Assembly abolished the remnants of powers that landlords had enjoyed since the Middle Ages, including the right to force peasants to labor on the lord's land and the bondage of serfdom itself. Although largely symbolic, because serfdom and forced labor had been eliminated in much of France, these changes were hailed as the "end of feudalism." A blow was also struck at established religion by eliminating the tithe, the forced payment of one-tenth of a person's income to the church. At the end of August, the Assembly issued the **Declaration of the Rights of Man and the Citizen**. It was a bold assertion of the foundations of a newly conceived government, closely modeled on portions of the U.S. Constitution. Its preamble declared "that [since] the ignorance, neglect or contempt of the rights of man are the sole cause of public calamities and the corruption of governments," the deputies were "determined to set forth in a solemn declaration the natural, inalienable and sacred rights of man."[3]

Declaration of the Rights of Man and the Citizen
Document issued by the National Assembly of France in August 1789. Modeled on the U.S. Constitution, it asserted "the natural, inalienable and sacred rights of man."

In September, the deputies debated the king's role in a new constitutional government. Monarchists favored a government rather like England's, with a two-house legislature, including an upper house representing the hereditary aristocracy and a royal right to veto legislation. More radical deputies favored a single legislative chamber and no veto power for the king. The Assembly compromised: The king was given a three-year suspensive veto—the power to suspend legislation for the sitting of two legislatures. This was still a formidable amount of power but a drastic curtailment of his formerly absolute sovereignty.

THE WOMEN'S MARCH TO VERSAILLES

Again Louis resorted to troops. This time he called them directly to Versailles, where the Assembly sat. News of the troops' arrival provoked outrage, which heightened with the threat of another grain shortage. Early on the morning of October 5, women in the Paris street markets saw the empty grocers' stalls and took immediate collective action. "We want bread!" they shouted at the steps of City Hall. Because they were responsible for procuring their families' food, women often led protests over bread shortages. This protest, however, went far beyond the ordinary. A crowd of thousands gathered and decided to walk all the way to Versailles, accompanied by the popular militia (now called the "National Guard"), to petition the king directly for sustenance.

At Versailles, a joint delegation of the women and deputies from the National Assembly was dispatched to see the king. Some of the women fell at the feet of the king with their tales of hardship, certain that the "father of the people" would alleviate their suffering. He did order stored grain supplies distributed in Paris, and he agreed to accept the constitutional role that the Assembly had voted for him. The king also agreed to return to Paris to reassure the people and was escorted back to the capital by both popular militia and bread protesters. Already, dramatic change had occurred as a result of a complex dynamic among the three Estates, the Crown, and the people of Paris. The king was still assumed to be the fatherly guardian of his people's well-being, but his powers were now limited and his authority badly shaken. The Assembly had begun to govern in the name of the "nation," and so far, it had the support of the people.

SECTION SUMMARY

- Inspired by events in America, elites in Ireland, the Netherlands, and Poland pushed for greater political liberty.

- France's support for the American colonies against Great Britain increased French government debt and exposed French soldiers and courtiers to revolutionary ideas.

- By the late 1780s, French royal government was in crisis owing to bankruptcy, institutions that impeded reform, and agitation for reform within elite society.

- The French Revolution began in 1789 when the Estates General convened, and commoners in the Third Estate claimed a mandate to write a constitution and enact major changes in law.

- French citizens, led by the Parisians, formed popular militias, attacked royal fortresses, and marched to Versailles to confront the king.

THE PHASES OF THE REVOLUTION, 1789–1799

Why did several phases of revolutionary change occur after 1789 and what were the characteristics of each phase?

The French Revolution was a complicated affair. It was a series of changes, in a sense, a series of revolutions, driven not by one group of people but by several groups. Even among elites convinced of the need for reform, the range of opinion was wide. The people of Paris continued to be an important force for change. Country people also became active, primarily in resisting changes forced on them by the central government.

All of the wrangling within France was complicated by foreign reaction to events there. Defending the revolution against foreign enemies soon became a routine burden for the fragile revolutionary governments. In addition, they had to cope with the continuing problems that had precipitated the Revolution in the first place, including the government's chronic indebtedness and frequent grain shortages. Finally, the Revolution itself was an issue in that, once the traditional arrangements of royal government had been altered, momentum for further change was unleashed.

The First Phase Completed, 1789–1791

At the end of 1789, Paris was in ferment, but for a time, forward progress blunted the threat of disastrous divisions between king and Assembly and between either of them and the people of Paris. The capital continued to be the center of lively political debate. Salons continued to meet; academies and private societies proliferated. Deputies to the Assembly joined existing societies or helped to found new ones. Several would be important throughout the Revolution—particularly the Jacobin (JACK-oh-bin) Club, named for the monastic order whose buildings the members used as a meeting hall.

These clubs represented the gamut of revolutionary opinion. Some, in which ordinary Parisians were well represented, focused on economic policies that would directly benefit common people. Women were active in a few of the more radical groups. Monarchists dominated other clubs. At first, similar to the salons and debating societies of the Enlightenment era, the clubs quickly became sources of political pressure on the government. A bevy of popular newspapers also contributed to the vigorous political life in the capital.

The broad front of revolutionary consensus began to break apart as the Assembly made decisions about the constitution and about policies to address France's still-desperate financial situation. The largest portion of the untapped wealth of the nation lay with the Catholic Church, an obvious target of anticlerical reformers. The deputies made sweeping changes: They kept church buildings intact and retained the clergy as salaried officials of the state. They abolished all monasteries, though they pensioned the monks and nuns to permit them to continue as nurses and teachers where possible. Boldest of all, the Assembly seized most of the vast lands of the church and declared them national property *(biens nationaux)* to be sold for revenue for the state.

However, revenue was needed faster than the property could be inventoried and sold, so government bonds *(assignats* [ah-see-NYAH]) were issued against the eventual sale of church lands. Unfortunately, in the cash-strapped economy, the bonds were treated like money, their value became inflated, and the government never realized the hoped-for profits. A greater problem was the political divisiveness generated by the restructuring of the church. Many members of the lower clergy, living as they did near ordinary citizens, were among the most reform-minded of the deputies. These clergy were willing to go along with many changes, but the required oath of loyalty to the state made a mockery of clerical independence.

De Christianate

The Civil Constitution of the Clergy, as these measures were called, was passed by the Assembly in July 1790 because the clerical deputies opposing it were outvoted. More than half of the churchmen did take the oath of loyalty. Those who refused, concentrated among the higher clergy, were in theory thrown out of their offices. A year later (April 1791), the pope declared that clergy who had taken the oath were suspended from their offices. Antirevolutionary sentiment grew among thousands of French people, particularly in outlying regions, to whom the church was still vital as a source of charity and a center of community life.

Meanwhile, the Assembly proceeded with administrative and judicial reform. The deputies abolished the medieval provinces as administrative districts and replaced them with uniform *départements* (departments). They declared that local officials would be elected—a revolutionary dispersal of power that had previously belonged to the king.

As work on the constitution drew to a close in the spring of 1791, the king decided that he had had enough. Royal authority, as he knew it, had been virtually dismantled and Louis himself was now a virtual prisoner in the Tuileries (TWEE-lair-ee) Palace in central Paris. The king and his family attempted to flee France. On June 20, 1791, they set out in disguise. However, the party was stopped—and recognized—in the town of Varennes (vah-REN) near the eastern border of the kingdom.

Louis and his family were returned to Paris under lightly disguised house arrest. It was discovered that he had left behind a document that condemned the constitution and revealed his intention was to invade France with Austrian troops, if necessary. He and the queen had sent money abroad ahead of themselves. Thus, in July 1791, just as the Assembly was completing its proposal for a constitutional monarchy, the monarch himself could no longer be trusted.

Editorials and street protests against the monarchy increased. In one incident, known as the Massacre of the Champ (Field) de Mars (SHOM duh MARSS), government troops led by Lafayette fired on citizens at an antimonarchy demonstration that certain Parisian clubs had organized; about fifty men and women died. This inflammatory incident heightened tensions between moderate reformers satisfied with the constitutional monarchy, such as Lafayette, and outspoken republicans who wanted to eliminate the monarchy altogether.

Nevertheless, on September 14, the king formally swore to uphold the constitution. He had no choice. The event became an occasion for celebration, but suspicion of the monarchy continued. Also, the tension between the interests of common Parisians and the provisions of the new constitution could not be glossed over. Though a liberal document for its day, the constitution reflected the views of the elite deputies who had created it. The right to vote, based on a minimal property qualification, was given to about half of all adult men. However, these men only chose electors, for whom the property qualifications were higher. The electors in turn chose deputies to national bodies as well as local officials. Although, in theory, any eligible voter could be an elected deputy or official, in fact, few ordinary citizens would become deputies or local administrators. A new Declaration of Rights accompanied the constitution; it reflected a fear of the masses that had not existed when the Declaration of the Rights of Man and the Citizen was first promulgated in 1789. Freedom of the press and freedom of assembly, for example, were not fully guaranteed.

Educated women had joined some of the Parisian clubs and had attempted to influence the Assembly to consider women's rights, but the constitution granted neither political rights nor legal equality to women. Nor had the Assembly passed laws beneficial to women, such as the legalization of divorce. A Declaration of the Rights of Woman was drafted by a woman named Olympe de Gouges (oh-LAMP duh GOOZH) to draw attention to the treatment of women in the new constitution.

In any case, very soon after the constitution was implemented, the fragility of the new system became clear. The National Assembly declared that its members could not serve in the first assembly to be elected under the constitution. Thus, the members of the newly elected Legislative Assembly, which began to meet in October 1791, lacked any of the cohesiveness that would have come from collective experience. Also, unlike the previous National Assembly, they did not represent a broad range of opinion but were mostly republicans.

In fact, the Legislative Assembly was dominated by republican members of the Jacobin Club. They were known as Girondins (zhih-ron-DEHN), after the region in southwestern France from which many of the club's leaders came. The policies of these new deputies and continued pressure from the ordinary citizens of Paris would cause the constitutional monarchy to collapse in less than a year.

The Second Phase and Foreign War, 1791–1793

An additional pressure on the new regime soon appeared: a threat of foreign invasion and a war to respond to the threat. Aristocratic émigrés, including the king's brothers, had taken refuge in nearby German states and were planning to invade France. The emperor and other German rulers did little actively to aid the plotters. Austria and Prussia, however, in the Declaration of Pillnitz of August 1791, declared, as a concession to the émigrés, that they would intervene if necessary to support the monarchy in France.

CHRONOLOGY	
The French Revolution	
May 5, 1789	Estates General meets in Versailles
June 17, 1789	Third Estate declares itself the National Assembly
June 20, 1789	Tennis Court Oath
July 14, 1789	Storming of the Bastille
August 27, 1789	Declaration of the Rights of Man and the Citizen
October 5–6, 1789	Women's march on Versailles Louis XVI returns to Paris
July 1790	Civil Constitution of the Clergy
June 1791	Louis XVI captured attempting to flee
August 1791	Declaration of Pillnitz
September 1791	New constitution implemented
October 1791	Legislative Assembly begins to meet
April 1792	France declares war on Austria
August 10, 1792	Storming of the Tuileries; Louis XVI arrested
September 21, 1792	National Convention declares France a republic
January 21, 1793	Louis XVI guillotined
May 1793	First Law of the Maximum
July 1793	Terror inaugurated
July 1794	Robespierre guillotined; Terror ends
October 1795	Directory established
November 1799	Napoleon seizes power

The threat of invasion, when coupled with distrust of the royal family, seemed more real to the revolutionaries in Paris than it may actually have been. But many deputies hoped for war. They assumed that the outcome would be a French defeat, which would lead to a popular uprising that would rid them, at last, of the monarchy. In April 1792, under pressure from the Assembly, Louis XVI declared war against Austria. From this point on, foreign war would be an ongoing factor in the Revolution.

At first, the war was indeed a disaster for France. The army had not been reorganized into an effective fighting force after the loss of many aristocratic officers and the addition of newly self-aware citizens. On one occasion, troops insisted on putting an officer's command to a vote. Early defeats further emboldened critics of the monarchy. Under the direction of the Girondins, the Legislative Assembly began to press for the deportation of priests who had been leading demonstrations against the government. The Assembly abolished the personal guard of the king and summoned provincial National Guardsmen to Paris.

The king's resistance to these measures, as well as fears of acute grain shortages owing to a poor harvest and the needs of the armies, created further unrest. Crowds staged boisterous marches near the royal palace, physically confronted the king, and forced him to don the "liberty cap," a symbol of republicanism. The king's authority and prestige were now thoroughly undermined.

Louis XVI in 1792 The king, though a kindly man, had neither the character nor the convictions necessary to refashion royal authority symbolically as the Revolution proceeded. When Parisian crowds forced him to wear the "liberty cap," the monarchy was close to collapse. (Metropolitan Museum of Art, The Elisha Whittelsey Collection, The Elisha Whittelsey Fund, 1962 [62.520.333]. Image © The Metropolitan Museum of Art)

sans-culottes Ordinary citizens of revolutionary Paris, whose derisive nickname referred to their inability to afford fashionable knee pants ("culottes").

By July 1792, tensions had become acute. The grain shortage was severe; Austrian and Prussian troops, committed to saving the royal family, were threatening to invade; and, most important, Parisian citizens were better organized and more determined than ever before. In each of the forty-eight "sections"—administrative wards—of Paris, a miniature popular assembly thrashed out all the events and issues of the day, just as deputies in the nationwide Legislative Assembly did. Derisively called **sans-culottes** (sahn-koo-LOT) ("without knee pants") because they could not afford elite fashions, the ordinary Parisians in the section assemblies included shopkeepers, artisans, and laborers. Their political organization enhanced their influence with the Assembly, the clubs, and Parisian newspapers. By late July, most sections of the city had approved a petition calling for the exile of the king, the election of new city officials, the exemption of the poor from taxation, and other radical measures.

In August, the sans-culottes took matters into their own hands. On the night of August 9, after careful preparations, representatives of the section assemblies constituted themselves as a new city government with the aim of "saving the state." The next day, August 10, they assaulted the Tuileries Palace, where the royal family was living. Hundreds of royal guards and citizens died in the bloody confrontation. The king and his family were imprisoned in one of the fortified towers in the city, under guard of the popularly controlled city government.

With the storming of the Tuileries Palace, the second major phase of the Revolution began: the establishment of republican government in place of the monarchy. By their intimidating numbers, the people of Paris now controlled the Legislative Assembly. Some deputies fled. Those who remained agreed under pressure to dissolve the Assembly and make way for another body to be elected by universal manhood suffrage. On September 20, that assembly, known as the National Convention, began to meet. The next day, the Convention declared the end of the monarchy and set to work crafting a constitution for the new republic.

Coincidentally, that same September day, French forces won their first genuine victory over the allied Austrian and Prussian invasion forces. Though not a decisive battle, it was a profound psychological victory. A citizen army had defeated the professional force of a ruling prince. The victory bolstered the republican government and encouraged it to put more energy into the wars. Indeed, maintaining armies in the field became a weighty factor in the delicate equilibrium of revolutionary government. The new republican regime let it be known that its armies were not merely for self-defense but for the liberation of all peoples in the "name of the French Nation."

Meanwhile, the Convention faced the divisive issue of what to do with the king. Some of the king's correspondence, discovered after the storming of the Tuileries, provided the pretext for charges of treason. The Convention held a trial for him, which lasted from December 11, 1792, to January 15, 1793. He was found guilty of treason by an overwhelming vote (683 to 39); the republican government would not compromise with monarchy. Less lopsided was the sentence: Louis was condemned to death by a narrow majority, 387 to 334.

The consequences for the king were immediate. On January 21, 1793, Louis mounted the scaffold in a public square near the Tuileries and was beheaded. The execution split the ranks of the Convention and soon resulted in the breakdown of the institution itself.

The Faltering Republic and the Terror, 1793–1794

In February 1793, the republic was at war with virtually every state in Europe; the only exceptions were the Scandinavian kingdoms and Russia. Moreover, the regime faced widespread counterrevolutionary uprisings within France. Vigilance against internal and external enemies became a top priority. The Convention established an executive body, the Committee of Public Safety. In theory, this executive council was answerable to the Convention as a whole. But as the months passed, it acted with greater and greater autonomy not only to govern, but also to eliminate enemies. The broadly based republican government represented by the Convention began to disintegrate.

In June 1793, pushed by the Parisian sections, a group of extreme **Jacobins** purged the Girondin deputies from the Convention, arresting many of them. The Girondins were republicans who favored an activist government in the people's behalf, but they were less radical than their fellow Jacobins who now moved against them, less insistent on central control of the Revolution, and less willing to share power with the citizens of Paris. After the purge, the Convention still met, but most authority lay with the Committee of Public Safety.

Now, new uprisings against the regime began as revolts by Girondin sympathizers added to counterrevolutionary revolts by peasants and aristocrats. As resistance to the government mounted and the foreign threat continued, a dramatic event in Paris led the Committee of Public Safety officially to adopt a policy of political repression. A well-known figure of the Revolution, Jean Paul Marat (1743–1793), publisher of a radical newspaper very popular with ordinary Parisians, was murdered on July 13 by Charlotte Corday (1768–1793), an aristocratic woman. Shortly afterward, a longtime member of the Jacobin Club, **Maximilien Robespierre** (ROBES-pee-air) (1758–1794), joined the Committee and called for "Terror"—the systematic repression of internal enemies. He was not alone in his views. Members of the section assemblies of Paris led demonstrations to pressure the government into making Terror the order of the day.

Since the previous autumn, the guillotine had been at work against identified enemies of the regime, but now a more systematic apparatus of Terror was put in place. A Law of Suspects allowed citizens to be arrested simply on vague suspicion of counterrevolutionary sympathies. Revolutionary tribunals and an oversight committee made arbitrary arrests and rendered summary judgments. In October, a steady stream of executions began, beginning with the queen, imprisoned since the storming of the Tuileries the year before. The imprisoned Girondin deputies followed, and then the beheadings continued relentlessly. Paris witnessed about 2,600 executions from 1793 to 1794.

Around France, the verdicts of revolutionary tribunals led to approximately 14,000 executions. Another 10,000 to 12,000 people died in prison. Ten thousand or more were killed, usually by summary execution, after the defeat of counterrevolutionary uprisings. The aim of **the Terror** was not merely to crush active resistance; it was also to silence simple dissent. The victims in Paris included not only aristocrats and former deputies, but also sans-culottes. The radical Jacobins wanted to seize control of the Revolution from the Parisian citizens who had lifted them to power.

ROBESPIERRE AND THE COMMITTEE FOR PUBLIC SAFETY

Jacobins In revolutionary France, a republican political club named for a monastic order.

A Victim of the Terror Manon Phlipon (1754–1793), known as Madame Roland, led an influential Parisian salon and was married to an important Girondin deputy. She was arrested and guillotined with other Girondins in 1793. Her last words on the scaffold were: "Oh Liberty, what crimes are committed in thy name!" (Portrait of a Woman, c.1787 (oil on canvas), Labille-Guiard, Adelaide (c.1749-1803)/Musee des Beaux-Arts, Quimper, France/The Bridgeman Art Library)

Robespierre Justifies Terror Against Enemies of the Revolution

In this excerpt from a speech before the National Convention in December 1793, Robespierre justifies the revolutionary government's need to act in a vigorous manner in order to defend itself from challenges within and without.

The defenders of the Republic must adopt Caesar's maxim, for they believe that "nothing has been done so long as anything remains to be done." Enough dangers still face us to engage all our efforts. It has not fully extended the valor of our Republican soldiers to conquer a few Englishmen and a few traitors. A task no less important, and one more difficult, now awaits us: to sustain an energy sufficient to defeat the constant intrigues of all the enemies of our freedom and to bring to a triumphant realization the principles that must be the cornerstone of public welfare. ... Revolution is the war waged by liberty against its enemies; a constitution is that which crowns the edifice of freedom once victory has been won and the nation is at peace. The revolutionary government has to summon extraordinary activity to its aid precisely because it is at war. It is subjected to less binding and less uniform regulations, because the circumstances in which it finds itself are tempestuous and shifting, above all because it is compelled to deploy, swiftly and incessantly, new resources to meet new and pressing dangers. The principal concern of a constitutional government is civil liberty; that of a revolutionary government, public liberty. [A] revolutionary government is obliged to defend the state itself against the factions that assail it from every quarter. To good citizens revolutionary government owes the full protection of the state; to the enemies of the people it owes only death. ...

Is a revolutionary government the less just and the less legitimate because it must be more vigorous in its actions and freer in its movement than ordinary government? No! For it rests on the most sacred of all laws, the safety of the people, and on necessity, which is the most indisputable of all rights. It also has its rules, all based on justice and on public order. It has nothing in common with anarchy or disorder; on the contrary, its purpose is to repress them and to establish and consolidate the rule of law. It has nothing in common with arbitrary rule; it is public interest which governs it and not the whims of private individuals.

QUESTIONS

1. How does Robespierre describe the differences between constitutional and revolutionary government?
2. How does Robespierre defend the legitimacy of revolutionary government?

Source: "Robespierre Justifies the Terror" from *Robespierre,* edited by George Rudé, 1967, 1995, pp. 58–63

Maximilien Robespierre French lawyer and revolutionary leader, influential member of the Committee of Public Safety (1793–1794); advocated Terror to suppress internal dissent.

the Terror Systematic repression of internal enemies undertaken by French revolutionary government from 1793 to 1794. Approximately fourteen thousand people were executed, including aristocrats, Girondins, and sans-culottes.

Robespierre embodied all the contradictions of the policy of Terror. He was an austere, almost prim man who lived very modestly—a model, of sorts, of the virtuous, disinterested citizen. His unbending loyalty to his political principles earned him the nickname "the Incorruptible." The policies followed by the government during the year of his greatest influence, from July 1793 to July 1794, included generous and humane policies to benefit ordinary citizens as well as the atrocities of official Terror. (See the feature, "The Written Record: Robespierre Justifies Terror Against Enemies of the Revolution.") In May 1793, the Convention had instituted the Law of the Maximum, which controlled the price of grain so that city people could afford their staple food— bread. In September, the Committee extended the law to apply to other necessary commodities. Extensive plans were made for a system of free and universal primary education. Slavery in the French colonies was abolished in February 1794. Divorce, first legalized in 1792, was made easier for women to obtain. In addition, the government of the Committee of Public Safety was effective in providing direction for the nation at a critical time. In August 1793, it instituted the first mass conscription of citizens into the army *(levée en masse* [leh-VAY ohn MAHSS]), and a consistently effective popular army came into existence. In the autumn of 1793, this army won impressive victories.

SOCIAL REFORMS IN THE NAME OF REASON

In the name of "reason," traditional rituals and rhythms of life were changed. One reform of long-term significance was the introduction of the metric system of weights and measures. Although people continued to use the old, familiar measures for a very long time, the change was eventually accomplished, leading the way for standardization throughout Europe. Equally "rational," but not as successful, was the elimination of the traditional calendar;

weeks and months were replaced by uniform thirty-day months and *decadi* (ten-day weeks with one day of rest), and all saints' days and Christian holidays were eliminated. The years had already been changed—Year I had been declared with the founding of the republic in the autumn of 1792.

Churches were rededicated as "temples of reason." Robespierre believed that outright atheism left people with no basis for personal or national morality; he promoted a cult of the Supreme Being. New public festivals were solemn civic ceremonies intended to ritualize and legitimize the new political order. But the French people generally resented the elimination of the traditional calendar and the attacks on the church. In the countryside, massive peasant uprisings protested the loss of poor relief, community life, and familiar ritual.

Divorce law and economic regulation were a boon, especially to urban women, but women's participation in section assemblies and in all organized political activity—which had been energetic and widespread—was banned in October 1793. The particular target of the regime was the **Society of Revolutionary Republican Women**, a powerful club representing the interests of female sans-culottes. By banning women from political life, the regime helped to ground its legitimacy, since the seemingly "natural" exclusion of women might make the new system of government appear part of the "natural" order. (See the feature, "The Visual Record: Political Symbols.") Outlawing women's clubs and barring women from section assemblies also eliminated one source of popular power, from which the regime was now trying to distance itself.

Society of Revolutionary Republican Women   In revolutionary Paris, a powerful political club that represented the interests of female sans-culottes.

THE END OF THE TERROR

The main policy differences between the Committee and members of the Convention concerned economic matters: how far to go to assist the poor, the unemployed, and the landless. Several of the moderate critics of Robespierre and his allies were guillotined for disagreeing about policy and for doubting the continuing need for the Terror itself. Their deaths helped precipitate the end of the Terror by causing Robespierre's power base to shrink so much that it had no further legitimacy. Also, French armies had soundly defeated Austrian troops on June 26, so there was no longer any need for the emergency status that the Terror had thrived on.

Deputies to the Convention finally dared to move against Robespierre in July 1794. In late July, the Convention voted to arrest Robespierre, the head of the revolutionary tribunal in Paris, and their closest associates and allies in the city government. On July 28 and 29, Robespierre and the others—about a hundred in all—were guillotined, and the Terror ended.

The Thermidorian Reaction and the Directory, 1794–1799

After Robespierre's death, the Convention reclaimed the executive powers that the Committee of Public Safety had seized. It dismantled the apparatus of the Terror, repealed the Law of Suspects, and forced the revolutionary tribunals to adopt ordinary legal procedures. The Convention also passed into law reforms, such as expanded public education, that had been proposed the year before but not enacted. This post-Terror phase of the Revolution is called the "Thermidorian Reaction" because it began in the revolutionary month of Thermidor (July 19–August 17).

Lacking the weapons of the Terror, the Convention was unable to enforce controls on the supply and price of bread. Thus, economic difficulties and a hard winter produced famine by the spring of 1795. The people of Paris tried to retain influence with the new government. In May, crowds marched on the Convention chanting "Bread and the Constitution of '93," referring to the republican constitution drafted by the Convention but never implemented because of the Terror. The demonstrations were met with force and were dispersed.

Members of the Convention remained fearful of a renewed, popularly supported Terror, on the one hand, and royalist uprisings on the other. Counterrevolutionary uprisings had erupted in the fall of 1794, and landings on French territory by émigré forces occurred the following spring. The Convention drafted a new constitution that limited popular participation in government, as had the first constitution of 1791. The new plan allowed fairly widespread (but not universal) male suffrage, but only for electors, who would choose deputies for the two houses of the legislature. The property qualifications for being an elector were very high, so all but elite citizens were effectively disenfranchised. The Convention also decreed that

Political Symbols

During the French Revolution, thousands of illustrations in support of various revolutionary (or counterrevolutionary) ideas were reproduced on posters, on handbills, and in pamphlets. Some satirized their subjects, such as Marie Antoinette, or celebrated revolutionary milestones, such as the fall of the Bastille. The etching here of the woman armed with a pike, dating from 1792, falls into this category. Other pictures, such as the representation from 1795 of Liberty as a young woman wearing the liberty cap, symbolized or reinforced various revolutionary ideals.*

Political images like these are an invaluable though problematic source for historians. Let us examine these two images of women and consider how French people during the Revolution might have responded to them. To understand what they meant to contemporaries, we must know something about the other images that these would have been compared to. We must also view the images in the context of the events of the Revolution itself. Immediately, then, we are presented with an interpretive agenda. How ordinary and acceptable was this image of an armed woman? If women were not citizens coequal with men, how could a woman be a symbol of liberty? What, in short, do these political images reveal about the spectrum of political life in their society?

The woman holding the pike stares determinedly at the viewer. Many details confirm what the original caption announced: This is a French woman who has become free. In her hat she wears one of the symbols of revolutionary nationhood: the tricolor cockade. The badge around her waist celebrates a defining moment for the revolutionary nation: the fall of the Bastille. Her pike itself is inscribed with the words "Liberty or death."

The woman appears to be serving not merely as a symbol of free women. She comes close to being the generic image of a free citizen, willing and able to fight for liberty—an astonishing symbolic possibility in a time when women were not yet treated equally under the law or granted the same political rights as the men of their class. Other images prevalent at the time echo this possibility. Many contemporary representations of the women's march on Versailles in 1789 show women carrying arms, active in advancing the Revolution. By the time this image was created (most likely in 1792), many other demonstrations and violent confrontations by ordinary people had

An Armed Citizen, ca. 1792   (Bibliothèque nationale de France)

Directory French revolutionary government from 1795 to 1799, consisting of an executive council of five men chosen by the upper house of the legislature.

two-thirds of its members must serve in the new legislature, regardless of the outcome of elections. Although this maneuver enhanced the stability of the new regime, it undermined the credibility of the new vote.

The government under the new constitution, beginning in the fall of 1795, was called the **Directory**, for the executive council of five men chosen by the upper house of the new legislature. To avoid the concentration of authority that had produced the Terror, the members of the Convention had tried to enshrine separation of powers in the new system.

resulted in the creation of dozens of popular prints and engravings that showed women acting in the same ways as men.

Repeatedly during 1792, women proposed to the revolutionary government that they be granted the right to bear arms. Their request was denied, but it was not dismissed out of hand. There was debate, and the issue was in effect tabled. Nevertheless, women's actions in the Revolution had created at least the possibility of envisaging citizenship with a female face.

The image of Liberty from 1795 does not reflect the actions of women but rather represents their exclusion from political participation. It is one of a number of images of Liberty that portray this ideal as a passive, innocent woman, here garbed in ancient dress, surrounded by a glow that in the past had been reserved for saints. Liberty here is envisaged as a pure and lofty goal, symbolized as a pure young woman.

Late in 1793, during the Terror, women were excluded from formal participation in politics with the disbanding of women's organizations. Nor did they gain political rights under the Directory, which reestablished some of the limited gains of the first phase of the Revolution. The justification offered for their exclusion in 1793 was borrowed from Jean-Jacques Rousseau: it is contrary to nature for women to be in public life (see page 503). Women "belong" in the private world of the family, where they will nurture male citizens. Women embody ideal qualities such as patience and self-sacrifice; they are not fully formed beings capable of action in their own right.

Such notions made it easy to use images of women to embody ideals for public purposes. A woman could represent liberty precisely because actual women were not able to be political players.

The two images shown here thus demonstrate that political symbols can have varying relationships to "reality." The pike-bearing citizen is the more "real." Her image reflects the way of thinking about politics that became possible for the first time because of their actions. The other woman reflects not the attributes of actual women, but an ideal type spawned by the use of arbitrary gender distinctions to legitimize political power. In these images, we can see modern political life taking shape: the sophistication of its symbolic language, the importance of abstract ideas, such as liberty and nationhood—as well as the grounding of much political life in rigid distinctions between public and private, male and female.

Liberty as a Young Woman, ca. 1795 (S. P. Avery Collection, Miriam and Ira D. Wallach Division of Arts, Prints, and Photographs, The New York Public Library, Astor, Lenox, and Tilden Foundations/Art Resource, NY)

QUESTIONS

1. What circumstances explain the 1792 image of a woman as an armed citizen?

2. How would an idealized image of a young woman be useful as a symbol of liberty?

* This discussion draws on the work of Joan Landes, "Representing the Body Politic: The Paradox of Gender in the Graphic Politics of the French Revolution," and Darlene Gay Levy and Harriet B. Applewhite, "Women and Militant Citizenship in Revolutionary Paris," in Sara E. Melzer and Leslie W. Rabine, eds., *Rebel Daughters: Women and the French Revolution* (New York: Oxford University Press, 1992), pp. 15–37, 79–101.

However, the governments under the Directory were never free from outside plots or from their own extra-constitutional maneuvering. The most spectacular challenge was an attempted coup by the "Conspiracy of Equals," a group of extreme Jacobins who wanted to restore popular government and aggressive economic and social policy on behalf of the common people. The conspiracy ended with arrests and executions in 1797. When elections in 1797 and 1798 returned many royalist, as well as Jacobin deputies, the Directory itself abrogated the constitution: many "undesirable" deputies were arrested, exiled, or denied seats.

SECTION SUMMARY

- The phases of the French Revolution were shaped by elites' desires for change, demands of common people, and the need to defend France against foreign monarchs.

- Between 1789 and 1791, the National Assembly wrote a constitution, seized and sold church property, ended traditional obligations of peasants, and reorganized local government.

- In 1791, the constitution was implemented and a Legislative Assembly elected.

- In 1792, Parisian citizens overthrew the monarchy; the Convention, elected by universal manhood suffrage, governed the republic.

- Control of the government passed to the Committee of Public Safety, which defended France from foreign invasion and gave economic assistance to common people, but also implemented a policy of official Terror in which thousands of French people were killed.

- After the Terror, suffrage was again restricted, but the government of the Directory could not bring stability.

The armies of the republic did enjoy some spectacular successes during these years, for the first time carrying the fighting—and the effects of the Revolution—onto foreign soil. French armies conquered the Dutch in 1795. In 1796–1797, French armies led by the young general **Napoleon Bonaparte** seized control of northern Italy from the Austrians. Both regions were transformed into "sister" republics, governed by local revolutionaries but under French protection. By 1799, however, conditions had once again reached a crisis point. The demands of the war effort, together with rising prices and the continued decline in the value of the assignats, brought the government again to the brink of bankruptcy. The government also seemed to be losing control of the French countryside; there were continued royalist uprisings, local political vendettas between moderates and Jacobins, and outright banditry.

Members of the Directory had often turned to sympathetic army commanders to suppress dissent and to carry out purges of the legislature. They now invited General Bonaparte to help them form a government that they could more strictly control. Two members of the Directory plotted with Napoleon and his brother, Lucien Bonaparte, to seize power on November 9, 1799.

THE NAPOLEONIC ERA AND THE LEGACY OF REVOLUTION, 1799–1815

What impact did the Revolution and Napoleonic rule have on France, the rest of Europe, and the wider world?

Napoleon Bonaparte
French general who took part in a coup in 1799 against the Directory, Napoleon consolidated power as first consul and ruled as emperor from 1804 to 1815.

Talented, charming, and ruthless, Napoleon Bonaparte (1769–1821) was the kind of person who gives rise to myths. His audacity, determination, and personal magnetism enabled him to profit from the political instability in France and to establish himself in power. Once in power, he temporarily stabilized the political scene by fixing in law the more conservative gains of the Revolution. He also used his power and his abilities as a general to continue wars of conquest against France's neighbors, which helped deflect political tensions at home.

Napoleon's troops exported the Revolution as they conquered most of Europe. In most states that came under French control, law codes were reformed, governing elites were opened to talent, and public works were upgraded. Yet French conquest also meant domination, pure and simple, and involvement in France's rivalry with Britain. The Napoleonic era left Europe an ambiguous legacy—war and its enormous costs, yet also revolution and its impetus to positive change.

Napoleon: From Soldier to Emperor, 1799–1804

Napoleon was from Corsica, a Mediterranean island that had passed from Genoese to French control in the eighteenth century. The second son of a large gentry family, he was educated at military academies in France, and he married the politically well-connected widow Joséphine de Beauharnais (Bow-are-NAY) (1763–1814), whose aristocratic husband had been a victim of the Terror.

Napoleon steered a careful course through the political turmoil of the Revolution. By 1799, his military victories had won him much praise and fame. He had demonstrated his ruthlessness in 1795, when he ordered troops guarding the Convention to fire on a Parisian crowd. He had capped his successful Italian campaign of 1796–1797 with an invasion of Egypt in an attempt to strike at British influence and trade connections in the eastern Mediterranean. The Egyptian campaign failed in its goals, but individual victories during the campaign ensured Napoleon's military reputation.

Napoleon's partners in the new government after the November 1799 coup soon learned of his great political skill and ambition. In theory, the new system was a streamlined version of the Directory: Napoleon was to be first among equals in a three-man executive—"First Consul," according to borrowed Roman terminology. But Napoleon quickly asserted his primacy among them and began not only to dominate executive functions, but also to bypass the authority of the regime's various legislative bodies.

His increasingly authoritarian rule was successful in part because he included, among his advisors and ministers, men of many political stripes—Jacobins, reforming liberals, even former Old Regime bureaucrats. He welcomed many exiles back to France, including all but the most ardent royalists. He thus stabilized his regime by healing some of the rifts among ruling elites. Napoleon combined toleration with ruthlessness, however. Between 1800 and 1804, he imprisoned, executed, or exiled dozens of individuals for alleged Jacobin agitation or royalist sympathies, including a prince of the royal family, whom he had kidnapped and coldly murdered.

Under Napoleon's regime, any semblance of free political life ended. Legislative bodies lost all initiative in the governing process, becoming rubber stamps for the consuls' policies. There were no meaningful elections. Voters chose only candidates for a kind of pool of potential legislators, from which occasional replacements were chosen by members of the Senate, an advisory body entirely appointed by Napoleon himself. Political clubs were banned; the vibrant press of the revolutionary years wilted under heavy censorship. Napoleon also further centralized the administrative system, set up by the first wave of revolutionaries in 1789, by establishing the office of prefect to govern the départements. All prefects and their subordinates were appointed by Napoleon, thus extending the range of his power and undermining local government.

Certain administrative changes that enhanced central control, such as for tax collection, had more positive effects. Napoleon oversaw the establishment of the Bank of France, modeled on the Bank of England. The bank provided capital for investment and helped stabilize French currency. Perhaps the most important achievement early in his regime was the Concordat of 1801. This treaty with the pope solved the problem of church-state relations that for years had provoked counterrevolutionary rebellions. The agreement allowed for the resumption of Catholic worship and the continued support of the clergy by the state, but also accepted the more dramatic changes accomplished by the Revolution. Church lands that had been sold were guaranteed to their new owners. Although Catholicism was recognized as the "religion of the majority of Frenchmen," Protestant churches also were allowed, and their clergy were paid. Later, Napoleon granted new rights to Jews as well.

The law code that Napoleon established in 1804 was much like his accommodation with the church in its limited acceptance of revolutionary gains. His **Civil Code** (also known as the *code napoléon*, or Napoleonic Code) honored the revolutionary legacy in its guarantee of equality before the law and its requirement for the taxation of all social classes; it also enshrined modern forms of property ownership and civil contracts. Neither the code nor Napoleon's political regime fostered individual rights, especially for women. Divorce was no longer permitted except in rare instances. Women lost all property rights when they married, and they generally faced legal domination by fathers and husbands.

Napoleon was careful to avoid heavy-handed displays of power. He cleverly sought ratification of each stage of his assumption of power through national plebiscites (referendums in which all eligible voters could vote for or against proposals)—one plebiscite (pleb-ih-SIGHT) for a new constitution in 1800 and another when he claimed consulship for life in 1802. He approached his final political coup—declaring himself emperor—with similar dexterity. Long before he claimed the imperial title, Napoleon had begun to sponsor an active court life appropriate to imperial pretensions. The empire

Napoleon Crossing the Alps   This stirring portrait by the great neoclassical painter Jacques-Louis David memorializes Napoleon's 1796 crossing of the Alps before his victorious Italian campaign, as a general under the Directory. In part because it was executed in 1801–1802, the painting depicts the moment heroically rather than realistically. (In truth, Napoleon wisely crossed the Alps on a sure-footed mule, not a stallion.) Napoleon, as First Consul, wanted images of himself that would justify his increasingly ambitious claims to power.   (Réunion des Musées Nationaux/Art Resource, NY)

Civil Code   Law code established under Napoleon in 1804 that included limited acceptance of revolutionary gains, such as a guarantee of equality before the law and taxation of all social classes.

was proclaimed in May 1804 with the approval of the Senate; it was also endorsed by another plebiscite. Napoleon rewarded members of his family and political favorites with noble titles that allowed no legal privilege but carried significant prestige. Old nobles were allowed to use their titles on this basis. Many members of the elite, whatever their origins, tolerated Napoleon's claims to power because he safeguarded fundamental revolutionary gains yet reconfirmed their status.

Conquering Europe, 1805–1810

Napoleon maintained relatively peaceful relations with other nations, while he consolidated power within France, but war soon resumed against political and economic enemies—principally Britain, Austria, and Russia. Tensions with the British quickly reescalated when Britain resumed aggression against French shipping in 1803, and Napoleon countered by seizing Hanover, the ancestral German home of the English king. England was at war at sea with Spain and the Netherlands, client states that Napoleon had forced to support him. Napoleon began to gather a large force on the northern coast of France; his objective was to invade England.

The British fleet, commanded by Horatio Nelson (1758–1805), intercepted a combined French and Spanish fleet that was to have been the invasion force and inflicted a devastating defeat off Cape Trafalgar in southern Spain (see **Map 19.1**) on October 21, 1805. The victory ensured British mastery of the seas and, in the long run, contributed to Napoleon's demise. In the short run, the defeat at Trafalgar paled for the French beside Napoleon's impressive victories on land. Napoleon abandoned the plans to invade England and, in August, marched his army east through Germany to confront the great continental powers, Austria and Russia.

In December 1805, Napoleon's army routed a combined Austrian and Russian force near Austerlitz (AW-stir-lits), north of Vienna (see **Map 19.1**). The Battle of Austerlitz was his most spectacular victory. Austria sued for peace. In further battles in 1806, French forces defeated Prussian, as well as Russian, armies once again. Prussia was virtually dismembered, but Napoleon tried to remake Russia into a contented ally. His hold on central Europe would not be secure with a

🌐 **Map 19.1—Napoleonic Europe, ca. 1810**
France dominated continental Europe after Napoleon's victories.

hostile Russia, nor would the anti-British economic system that he envisioned—the Continental System (see page 552)—be workable without Russian participation.

French forces were still trying to prevail in Spain, which had been a client state since its defeat by revolutionary armies in 1795 but was resisting outright rule by a French-imposed king, one of Napoleon's brothers. In 1808, however, Napoleon turned his attention to fully subduing Austria. After another loss to French forces in 1809, Austria, like Russia, accepted French political and economic hegemony in a sort of alliance. Thus, by 1810, Napoleon had transformed most of Europe into allied or dependent states (see **MAP 19.1**). The only exceptions were Britain and the parts of Spain and Portugal that continued, with British help, to resist France.

The states least affected by French hegemony were its reluctant allies: Austria, Russia, and the Scandinavian countries. At the other extreme were territories that had been incorporated into France. These included the Austrian Netherlands, territory along the Rhineland, and sections of Italy that bordered France. These regions were occupied by French troops and were treated as though they were départements of France itself.

In most other areas, some form of French-controlled government was in place, usually headed by a member of Napoleon's family. In both northern Italy and the Netherlands, where "sister" republics had been established after French conquests under the Directory, Napoleon imposed monarchies. Rulers were also installed in the kingdom of Naples and in Spain. Western German states of the Holy Roman Empire that had allied with Napoleon against Austria were organized into the Confederation of the Rhine, with Napoleon as its "Protector." Two further states were created, largely out of the defeated Prussia's territory: the kingdom of Westphalia in western Germany and the Grand Duchy of Warsaw in the east (see **MAP 19.1**).

Napoleon's domination of these various regions had complex, and at times contradictory, consequences. On the one hand, Napoleonic armies essentially exported the French Revolution, in that French domination brought with it the Napoleonic Civil Code, and with it political and economic reform like that of the early phases of the Revolution. Equality before the law was decreed following the French example. This meant the end of noble exemption from taxation in the areas where it existed. The complex snarl of medieval taxes and tolls was replaced with straightforward property taxes that were universally applied. As a consequence, tax revenues rose dramatically—by 50 percent in the kingdom of Italy, for example. Serfdom and forced labor also were abolished, as they had been in France in August 1789.

"And It Cannot Be Changed"   This horrifying scene of an execution of rebels against French rule in Spain was one of a series of etchings by Madrid artist Francisco Goya. In the 1810 series, titled "The Disasters of War," Goya was severely critical of French actions, as well as of barbarities committed by the British-backed Spaniards.   (Foto Marburg/Art Resource, NY)

In most Catholic regions, the church was subjected to the terms of the Concordat of 1801. The tithe (forced contributions to support the church) was abolished, church property seized and sold, and monasteries closed. Although Catholicism remained the state-supported religion in these areas, Protestantism was tolerated, and Jews were granted rights of citizenship. Secular education, at least for males, was encouraged.

On the other hand, Napoleon would allow in the empire only those aspects of France's revolutionary legacy that he tolerated in France itself. Just as he had suppressed any meaningful participatory government in France, so too did he suppress it in conquered regions. This came as a blow in states such as the Netherlands, which had experienced its own democratizing "Patriot" movement and which had enjoyed republican self-government after invasion by France during the Revolution itself. Throughout Napoleon's empire, many of the benefits of streamlined administration and taxation were offset by the drain of continual warfare. Deficits rose three- and fourfold, despite increased revenues. And throughout Europe, Napoleon gave away land to reward his greatest generals and ministers, thereby exempting those lands from taxation and control by his own bureaucracy.

If true self-government was not allowed, a broad segment of the elite in all regions was nevertheless won over to cooperation with Napoleon by being welcomed into his bureaucracy or into the large multinational army, called the *Grande Armée* (grawnd are-MAY). Their loyalty was cemented when they bought confiscated church lands.

The impact of Napoleon's Continental System was equally mixed. Under this system, the Continent was in theory closed to all British shipping and goods. The effects were uneven, and smuggling to evade controls on British goods became a major enterprise. Regions heavily involved in trade with Britain or its colonies suffered in the new system, as did overseas trade in general when Britain gained dominance of the seas after Trafalgar. However, the closing of the Continent to British trade, combined with increases in demand to supply Napoleon's armies, spurred the development of continental industries, at least in the short run.

Defeat and Abdication, 1812–1815

Whatever its achievements, Napoleon's empire was ultimately fragile because of the hostility of Austria and Russia, as well as the power of Britain. Russia was a particularly weak link in the chain of alliances and subject states because Russian landowners and merchants objected when their vital trade in timber for the British navy was interrupted and when supplies of luxury goods, brought in British ships, began to dwindle. A century of close alliances with German ruling houses made alliance with a French ruler an extremely difficult political option for Tsar Alexander I.

It was Napoleon, however, who ended the alliance by provoking a breach with Russia. He suddenly backed away from an arrangement to marry one of Alexander's sisters and accepted an Austrian princess instead. (He had divorced Joséphine because their marriage had not produced an heir.) Also, he seized lands in Germany belonging to a member of Alexander's family. When Alexander threatened rupture of the alliance if the lands were not returned, Napoleon mounted an invasion. Advisers warned him about the magnitude of the task he seemed so eager to undertake—particularly about winter fighting in Russia—but their alarms went unheard.

Napoleon's previous military successes had stemmed from a combination of strategic innovations and pure audacity. Napoleon divided his forces into independent corps. Each corps included infantry, cavalry, and artillery. Organized in these workable units, his armies could travel quickly by several separate routes and converge in massive force to face the enemy. Leadership on the battlefield came from a loyal and talented officer corps that had grown up since army commands had been thrown open to nonaristocrats during the Revolution. The final ingredient for success was the high morale of French troops. Since the first victory of the revolutionary armies in September 1792, citizen-soldiers had proved their worth. Complicated troop movements and bravery on the battlefield were possible when troops felt they were fighting for their *nation*, not merely their ruling dynasty. Napoleon's reputation as a winning general added a further measure of self-confidence.

The campaign against Russia began in June 1812. It was a spectacular failure. Napoleon had gathered a force of about 700,000 men—about half from France and half from allied states—a force twice as large as Russia's. But the strategy of quickly moving independent corps and assembling massive forces could not be implemented. Bold victories had often enabled Napoleon's troops to live off the countryside while they waited for supplies to catch up to the front line. But when the enemy attacked supply lines, the distances traveled were very great, the countryside was impoverished, or battles were not decisive, Napoleon's ambitious strategies proved futile. In varying degrees, these conditions prevailed in Russia.

By the time the French faced the Russians in the principal battle of the Russian campaign—at Borodino (bore-uh-DEE-no), west of Moscow (see **Map 19.1**)—the Grande Armée had been on the march for two and a half months and was already less than half its original strength. After the indecisive but bloody battle, the French occupied and pillaged Moscow but found scarcely enough food and supplies to sustain them. When Napoleon finally retreated from Moscow late in October, the fate of the French forces was all but sealed. As they retreated, the soldiers who had not died in battle died of exposure or starvation or were picked off by Russian peasants as they scavenged for food or fuel. Of the original 700,000 troops of the Grand Armée, fewer than 100,000 made it out of Russia.

Napoleon left his army before it was fully out of Russia to counter a coup attempt in Paris. The collapse of his reign had begun, spurred by a coincidental defeat in Spain. In Spain, a rebel Cortes (national representative assembly) had continued to meet in territory that the French did not control, and British troops supported resistance to the French. In 1812, as Napoleon was advancing against Russia, the collapse of French control accelerated. By the time Napoleon reached Paris at the turn of the new year, an Anglo-Spanish force led by the duke of Wellington was poised to invade France.

Napoleon lost his last chance to stave off a coalition of all major powers against him when he refused an Austrian offer of peace for the return of conquered Austrian territories. With Britain willing to subsidize the allied armies, Tsar Alexander determined to destroy Napoleon, and the Austrians now anxious to share the spoils, Napoleon's empire collapsed. The allies invaded France and forced Napoleon to abdicate on April 6, 1814.

Napoleon was exiled to the island of Elba, off France's Mediterranean coast. He was installed as the island's ruler and was given an income drawn on the French treasury. Meanwhile, however, the restored French king was having his own troubles. Louis XVIII (r. 1814–1824) was the brother of the executed Louis XVI (he took the number eighteen out of respect for Louis XVI's son, who had died in prison in 1795). The new monarch had been out of the country and out of touch with its circumstances since the beginning of the Revolution. In addition to the delicate task of establishing his own legitimacy, he faced enormous practical problems, including pensioning off thousands of soldiers now unemployed and still loyal to Napoleon.

Napoleon, bored and almost penniless in his island kingdom (the promised French pension never materialized), took advantage of the circumstances and returned surreptitiously to France on February 26, 1815. His small band of attendants was joined by the soldiers sent by the king to halt his progress. Louis XVIII abandoned Paris to the returned emperor. Napoleon's triumphant return lasted only one hundred days, however. Though some soldiers welcomed his return, many members of the elite were reluctant to throw in their lot with Napoleon again, and many ordinary French citizens were disenchanted, especially since the defeat in Russia, with the high costs, in conscription and taxation, of his armies. In any case, Napoleon's reappearance galvanized the divided allies, who had been haggling over a peace settlement, into unity. Napoleon tried to strike decisively against the allies, but he lost against English and Prussian troops in his first major battle, at Waterloo (in modern Belgium; see **Map 19.1**) on June 18, 1815. When Napoleon arrived in Paris after the defeat, he discovered the government in the hands of an ad hoc committee that included the Marquis de Lafayette. Under pressure, he abdicated once again. This time, he was exiled to the tiny, remote island of St. Helena in the South Atlantic, where he died in 1821.

The Legacy of Revolution for France and the World

The process of change in France between 1789 and 1815 was so complex that it is easy to overlook the overall impact of the Revolution. Superficially, the changes seemed to come full circle—with first Louis XVI on the throne, then Napoleon as emperor, and then Louis XVIII on the throne. Even though the monarchy was restored, however, the Revolution had discredited absolute monarchy in theory and practice.

Louis XVIII had to recognize the right of "the people," however narrowly defined, to participate in government and to enjoy due process of law. Another critical legacy of the Revolution and the Napoleonic era was a centralized political system of départements rather than a patchwork of provinces. For the first time, a single code of law applied to all French people. Most officials—from département administrators to city mayors—were appointed by the central government until the late twentieth century. This centralization had a positive side: the government sponsored national

FRANCE

scientific societies, a national library and archives, and a system of teachers' colleges and universities. Particularly under Napoleon, canal- and road-building projects improved transport systems.

Napoleon's legacy, like that of the Revolution itself, was mixed. His self-serving reconciliation of aristocratic pretensions with the opening of careers to men of talent ensured the long-term success of revolutionary principles from which the elite as a whole profited. His reconciliation of the state with the Catholic Church helped to stabilize his regime and cemented some revolutionary gains. The restored monarchy could not renege on these gains. Yet, whatever his achievements, Napoleon's overthrow of constitutional principles worsened the problem of political instability. His brief return to power in 1815 reflects the degree to which his power had always been rooted in military adventurism and in the loyalty of soldiers and officers. Similarly, the swiftness of his collapse suggests that the empire under Napoleon was not an enduring solution to the political instability of the late 1790s; indeed, it was no more secure than any of the other revolutionary governments.

Although Louis XVIII acknowledged the principle of constitutionalism at the end of the Revolution, his regime rested on fragile footing. Indeed, the fragility of new political systems was one of the most profound legacies of the Revolution. There was division over policies, but even greater division over legitimacy—that is, the acceptance by a significant portion of the politically active citizenry of a particular government's right to rule. Before the Revolution started, notions about political legitimacy had undergone a significant shift. The deputies who declared themselves to be the National Assembly in June 1789 already believed that they had a right to do so. In their view, they represented "the nation," and their voice had legitimacy for that reason. These deputies brought to Versailles not only their individual convictions that "reason" should be applied to the political system, but also their experience in social settings where those ideas were well received. In their salons, clubs, and literary societies, they had experienced the familiarity, trust, and sense of community that are essential to effective political action. The deputies' attempt to transplant their sense of community into national politics, however, was not wholly successful, in part because of their naïve refusal to stand for election under the new constitution. The king also actively undermined the system because he disagreed with it in principle. The British parliamentary system, by comparison, though representative only of a tiny elite, had a long history as a workable institution for lords, wealthy commoners, and rulers. This shared experience was an important counterweight to differences over fundamental issues, so that Parliament as an institution both survived political crises and helped resolve them. In France, politics was established on new principles, yet still lacking were the practical means to achieve the promise inherent in those principles.

EUROPE AND ITS COLONIES

France's conquests in Europe were the least enduring of the changes of the revolutionary era. Nevertheless, French domination of Europe had certain lasting effects: Elites were exposed to modern bureaucratic management, and equality under the law transformed social and political relationships. The breakdown of ancient political divisions provided important practical grounding for later cooperation among elites in nationalist movements. In Napoleon's kingdom of Italy, for example, a tax collector from Florence for the first time worked side by side with one from Milan.

The most important legacy of the French Revolution in Europe was the very success of the Revolution. The most powerful absolute monarchy in Europe had succumbed to the demands of its people for dramatic social and political reforms. Throughout Europe in the nineteenth century, ruling dynasties faced revolutionary movements that demanded constitutional government and resorted to force to achieve it.

The most important legacy of the revolutionary wars, however, was the change in warfare itself, made possible by the citizen armies of the French. Citizen-soldiers, who identified closely with their nation, even when conscripts, proved able to maneuver and attack on the battlefield in ways that the brutishly disciplined poor conscripts in royal armies would not. In response, other states tried to build competing armies; the mass national armies that fought the world wars of the twentieth century were the result.

European colonial possessions changed hands during the revolutionary wars. The British took advantage of Napoleon's preoccupation with continental affairs by seizing French colonies and the colonies of the French-dominated Dutch. In 1806, they seized the Dutch colony of Cape Town in southern Africa—crucial for support of trade around Africa—as well as French bases along the African coast. In 1811, they grabbed the island of Java (modern Indonesia).

Indeed, one clear legacy of the Revolution was the expansion of British trade and colonial control, made possible by Britain's sea power. Britain's maritime supremacy and seizure of French possessions expanded British trading networks overseas—though in some cases only temporarily—and closer to home, particularly in the Mediterranean. As long as the British had

Napoleon's Letter to Toussaint-Louverture

In November 1801, Napoleon sent this letter to the governor of the colony of Saint Domingue, Toussaint-Louverture. Toussaint, a former slave, had commanded an army, composed largely of ex-slaves, which had restored order in Saint Domingue following a complicated civil war. As he mentions in the letter, Napoleon had dispatched a force to reestablish French control of the formerly profitable colony. Although Toussaint was captured and later died in a French prison, Napoleon's forces were not successful in reestablishing French control.

To Citizen General Toussaint Louverture, commander in chief of the armies of Saint-Domingue, Peace with England and with other powers in Europe [now] enables France to pay attention to its colony of Saint-Domingue. We are sending General Leclerc, our brother-in-law, to serve as captain general and governor of the colony. He is accompanied by forces suitable to make the sovereignty of France respected. In these circumstances, it pleases us to hope that you will demonstrate to us and to all of France the sincerity of the sentiments that you have continually expressed in your letters to us. We hold you in very high esteem and it pleases us to acknowledge the great service you have rendered to the French people. … Called by your talents and by the force of circumstance to command, you have ended civil war. … The constitution you have made contains many good things but also things which are contrary to the dignity and the sovereignty of the French people, of which the people of Saint-Domingue form only a part. The circumstances in which you found yourself, surrounded on all sides by enemies, perhaps made some provisions of the constitution necessary and legitimate. But, happily, now that things have changed you will be able to render homage to the sovereignty of the Nation of which you are one of the most illustrious citizens. … Any contrary conduct … would lead you to lose the many rights you have earned to the recognition and the benefits of the Republic [and] would bring you to the edge of a precipice which, in swallowing you up, would contribute to the misery of the brave blacks, whose courage we admire and whose rebellion we would be sorry to have to punish.

Help the new captain general with your counsel, your influence and your talents. What could you want? The freedom of blacks? You know that in every country we have entered we have given liberty to the people who did not have it. Do you want respect, honors and fortune? … Given the services you have rendered and our esteem for you, you cannot be in doubt that respect, honors and fortune await you.

Make known to the peoples of Saint-Domingue that our concerns for their well-being were often impotent because of the demands of war that we faced. But now, peace and the force of our government will assure them prosperity and liberty. Tell them that if liberty is to them the most important right, that it cannot be enjoyed without the title of "French citizen" and that all acts contrary to the nation, and contrary to the obedience they owe its government and to its representative, the captain general, will be crimes against the national sovereignty. … And you, General, consider that if you are the first man of color to have arrived at such a pinnacle of power … you are also, before God and before us, responsible for their good conduct. …

QUESTIONS

1. What, in your opinion, was Napoleon trying to accomplish with this letter?

2. How would Toussaint-Louverture have interpreted Napoleon's words?

Source: Paul Rossier, ed., *Lettres du Général Leclerc* (Paris: Société de l'Histoire des Colonies Françaises, 1937). Translated by Kristen B. Neuschel.

---

been involved in trade with India, the Mediterranean had been important for economic and strategic reasons because it lay at the end of the land route for trade from the Indian Ocean. Especially after Napoleon's aggression in Egypt in the 1790s, the British redoubled their efforts to control strategic outposts in the Mediterranean.

The British economy would expand dramatically in the nineteenth century as industrial production soared. The roots for growth were laid in this period in the countryside of Britain, where changes in agriculture and in production were occurring. These roots were also laid in Britain's overseas possessions as tighter control of foreign sources of raw materials, notably raw Indian cotton, meant rising fortunes back in Britain. In regions of India, the East India Company was increasing its political domination, and hence, its economic stranglehold on Indian commodities. The export of Indian cotton rose significantly during the revolutionary period as part of an expanding trading system that included China, the source of tea.

On the most productive of the French-controlled Caribbean islands, Saint Domingue (SAHN dome-ANGUE), the French Revolution inspired a successful rebellion by the enslaved plantation workers.

The National Assembly in Paris had delayed abolishing slavery in French colonies, despite the moral appeal of such a move, because of pressure from the white planters and out of fear

François Dominique Toussaint-Louverture
Former slave who governed the island of Saint Domingue (Haiti) as an independent state after the slave revolt of 1791.

REVOLUTION IN THE ATLANTIC WORLD

20

CHAPTER OUTLINE

Preconditions for Industrialization

New Modes of Production

Social, Cultural, and Environmental Impacts

Responses to Industrialization

George Robertson: Nat-Y-Glo Iron Works

(National Museums & Galleries of Wales)

The Industrial Transformation of Europe, 1750–1850

As the French Revolution gave way to the fires of war in continental Europe, across the Channel, fires belched flame and smoke from England's factory chimneys, lighting the night sky and blocking the day's sun. The painting on the left depicts Shropshire, England, in 1788, a region previously renowned for its natural beauty. Industrial activity had already transformed its landscape beyond recognition. Abraham Darby (1676–1717) and his descendants built one of the largest and most important concentrations of ironworks in Shropshire because it contained the ideal combination of coal and iron deposits. In the 1830s, the French socialist Louis Blanqui (blahn-KEE) (see page 600) suggested that just as France had recently experienced a political revolution, so Britain was undergoing an "industrial revolution." Eventually, that expression entered the general vocabulary to describe the advances in production that occurred first in England and then dominated most of western Europe by the end of the nineteenth century. Although mechanization transformed Europe, it did so unevenly. In many areas, the changes were gradual, suggesting the term *revolution* was not always appropriate. Great Britain offered a model of economic change because it was the first to industrialize; each nation subsequently took its own path and pace in a continuous process of economic transformation.

Industrial development left its mark on just about every sphere of human activity. Scientific and rational methods altered production processes, removing them from the home—where entire families had often participated—to less personal workshops and factories. Significant numbers of workers left farming to enter mining and manufacturing, and major portions of the population moved from rural to urban environments. Machines replaced or supplemented manual labor.[1]

Mechanical production often meant that skilled artisans lost not only their livelihood, but their craft identity as well; it also drew women and children out of the home and into factories. New modes of production offered unprecedented opportunities for manufacturers, merchants, and entrepreneurs to create and amass wealth at levels previously unimaginable. Mechanization also caused pollution and environmental destruction. Miners in search of coal, iron ore, and other minerals cut deep gashes into the earth. The rapid growth of cities resulted in crowded slums, poor sanitation, filth, and visible poverty.

Industrialization simultaneously created unprecedented advancement and opportunity as well as unprecedented hardships and social problems. The social gap between the rich and the working poor increased. The latter, with a growing sense of solidarity, struggled to protect and advance their interests.

FOCUS QUESTIONS

- What factors allowed Europe to industrialize before the rest of the world?
- Which inventions appear to have been the most important in launching industrialization?
- What impact did industrialization have on the environment and on social classes?
- What did workers gain and lose as a result of industrialization, and how did they respond?

 **This icon will direct you to additional materials on the website: www .cengage.com/history/ noble/westciv6e**

 See our interactive eBook for map and primary source activities.

industrialization A system of mass production of goods in which specialization, mechanization, and new sources of mineral energy made manufacturing efficient and profitable.

PRECONDITIONS FOR INDUSTRIALIZATION

What factors allowed Europe to industrialize before the rest of the world?

Industrialization—the substitution of human and animal power by mineral power—required a massive shift of labor and capital resources from agriculture to manufacturing and services. Europe was endowed with a unique combination of conditions—geographic, cultural, economic, demographic—that made this shift and its timing possible. Industrialization did not simply consist of mechanization. It consisted of, and required, simultaneous growth in commerce, population, and agricultural production. Capital accumulation for investment in industry required an entrepreneurial spirit and government support for banking and trading. As farmers applied new scientific methods to food production, less expensive and more abundant food caused the population to grow. This growth created a higher demand for manufactured goods. More efficient food production reduced the need for agricultural labor, allowing or forcing migration to urban manufacturing centers.

Why Europe?

A unique set of circumstances in Europe favored its potential for rapid economic development. Centralized state power and highly developed legal systems protected merchant trade and facilitated the accumulation of wealth for further investment. Such security was nonexistent in other parts of the world, such as the Ottoman Empire, where corruption hampered the development of a commercial spirit. Europe's greater cultural, political, and social diversity also favored its economic development. Challenges to dominant religious and political powers that had come from the Reformation, Counter-Reformation, and the Enlightenment promoted innovation. Toleration for such freedom was a rarity in Asia, where large territories tended to be dominated by a single ruler and faith. International competition among European states drove them to try to outdo one another. Governments actively encouraged industries and commerce to enrich their countries and make them more powerful than their neighbors. None of these factors alone explains why industrialization occurred, but their combination facilitated the process as well as its timing.[2] Finally, it is important to emphasize that industrialization radically transformed power relationships between the West and nonindustrial Africa, Asia, and South America. By 1900, the West had economically and militarily overwhelmed the other parts of the world. (See the feature, "The Global Record: Alexis de Tocqueville's Thoughts on Colonization.")

Transformations Accompanying Industrialization

A number of other transformations favored economic innovation in Europe. In the agricultural sector, farmers learned to rotate crops rather than leaving a portion of their land fallow when soil became depleted. In addition, they began using fertilizers, and introduced new crops from the Americas—such as the potato and maize—which not only flourished in poor soil, but replenished the soil with nitrogen. New, more efficient plows enabled farmers to cultivate more land with less labor. Most important, the new crops and the more efficient cultivation of traditional ones increased the capacity to feed a growing population and freed many people to migrate to urban industries. Until these changes began occurring in the eighteenth century, food production required the work of 80 percent of the European population.

Population growth also helped promote industrialization. The population of Europe increased dramatically throughout the industrial era, doubling between 1750 and 1850. This growth was partly due to a lowering of the death rate. Infant mortality had been very high from illness and disease, such as gastrointestinal disorders, smallpox, diphtheria, and tuberculosis. Although none of these diseases had been medically conquered, slow improvement in sanitation and food intake after 1750 enabled children to better resist them. New employment opportunities led to earlier marriages and thus higher fertility. This growing population supplied the labor force for the new industries and provided the large surge in consumers of various industrial goods.

In the countryside, industrialization was foreshadowed by a form of production that had developed beginning in the seventeenth century—the **putting-out system**, or cottage industry. During the winter, and at other slack times, peasants took in handwork such as spinning, weaving, or dyeing. Often they were marginal agriculturists, frequently women, who, on a part-time basis, could augment the family income. Entrepreneurs discovered that some individuals were better than others at specific tasks. Rather than have one household process the wool through all the steps of production until it was a finished piece, the entrepreneur would buy wool produced by one family, then take it to another to spin, a third to dye, a fourth to weave, and so on. This system of production allowed merchants to ignore guild restrictions and accumulate greater wealth, which later became a basis for investment in full-scale industrialization.

Transportation improved significantly in the eighteenth century, particularly in response to expanding markets for agricultural and manufactured products. Better roads were built; new coaches and carriages could travel faster and carry heavier loads. Government and private companies built canals linking rivers to each other or to lakes. Road- and canal-building hastened and cheapened transportation, which facilitated the movement of raw materials to factories and finished goods to local and distant markets.

Britain's Lead in Industrial Innovation

Britain was the first to industrialize for many reasons. It was the first European country to have a standard currency, tax, and tariff system. Although Britain was by no means an egalitarian society, it accommodated some movement between the classes. Ideas and experiments were readily communicated among entrepreneurs, workers, and scientists.

In addition, England had gained an increasing share of international trade since the seventeenth century. This trade provided capital for investment in industrial plants. The world trade network also ensured that Britain had a market beyond its borders; high demand from foreign markets made mass manufacture feasible. The international trade network also enabled Britain to import raw materials for its industry, the most important of which was cotton.

Earlier than its competitors, Britain had a national banking system that could finance industries in areas where private funding fell short. In addition to numerous London banks, six hundred provincial banks serviced the economy by 1810. Banking could flourish because Britons had wide experience in trade, had accumulated considerable wealth, and found a constant demand for credit.

Britain's geography also favored industrial development. It was rich in coal and iron, whose deposits were in close proximity to one another—an important advantage because coal was used to process iron (see **Map 20.1**). A relatively narrow island, Britain had easy access to water, which was by far the cheapest means of transportation. Compared with the Continent, it had few toll roads, so moving goods was relatively easy and inexpensive.

British workers were generally more skilled and earned higher wages than their continental counterparts. As food prices fell, they also had more discretionary income to spend on manufactured goods. But because labor was more costly than on the Continent, British business owners had an incentive to find labor-saving devices and reduce the number of workers needed for production.

CHRONOLOGY

1712	Newcomen invents steam-operated water pump
1733	Kay invents flying shuttle
1750–1800	Three million Africans are brought to the Americas as slaves
1753	First steam engine in the Americas
1760s	Hargreaves invents spinning jenny
1765	Watt improves steam engine with separate condenser
1769	Arkwright patents water frame for spinning
1785	Cartwright patents power loom
1793	Whitney invents cotton gin
1804	Jacquard invents automatic loom
1811–1812	Luddites organize
1825	Börsig builds first steam engine in Germany
1831, 1834	Workers' uprising in Lyon
1832	Cholera epidemic
1834	Creation of German customs union, the Zollverein
1844	Workers' uprising in Silesia
1851	Majority of Britain's population becomes urban

putting-out system
Sometimes called "cottage industry," the production in country homes of items like thread and cloth by spinners and weavers for an entrepreneur who furnished raw materials and sold the finished product.

Alexis de Tocqueville's Thoughts on Colonization

The French military conquest of Algeria, beginning in 1830, provides an example of how economic modernization gave Europeans a sense of superiority and changed their relationship with the rest of the world. Charles X, king of France, sent the French military to the town of Algiers in response to a perceived insult from the dey (Algerian governor). Alexis de Tocqueville (1805–1859), member of the French parliament and author of the famous Democracy in America, *like many Europeans, thought that industrial progress not only enabled but legitimized the military and economic takeover of undeveloped regions inhabited by people of color. He also argued that white settlement would facilitate military conquest. In the first excerpt below, Tocqueville shares his awe at the vibrancy of urban culture in Algiers, and he describes how the French have begun to tear down and rebuild sections of the town. In the second excerpt, he observes how the effort to force European civilization on Muslims had unfortunate consequences.*

From "Notes on the Voyage to Algeria in 1841"

First appearance of [Algiers]: I have never seen anything like it. Prodigious mix of races and costumes, Arab, Kabyle, Moor, Negro, Mahonais, … French. Each of these races, tossed together in a space much too tight to contain them, speaks its language, wears its attire, displays different mores … The entire lower town seems in a state of destruction and reconstruction. On all sides, one sees nothing but recent ruins, buildings going up; one hears nothing but the noise of the hammer. It is Cincinnati transported onto the soil of Africa.

The French are substituting broad arcaded streets for the Moors' tortuous little alleys. This is a necessity of our civilization. But they are also substituting their architecture for that of the Moors, and this is wrong; for the latter is very appropriate to the needs of the country, and besides, it is charming. …

From "First Report on Algeria," 1847

The indigenous towns were invaded, turned upside down, and sacked by our administration even more than by our arms. … In the vicinity of Algiers itself, the very fertile areas were torn from the hands of the Arabs and given to Europeans who, not being able or not wanting to cultivate them themselves, rented them to these same indigenous people, who thus became the mere farmers of the domains that had belonged to their fathers. Elsewhere, tribes or factions of tribes that were not hostile to us, or even more who had fought with us and sometimes without us, were pushed off their territory. We accepted conditions we did not fulfill, we promised indemnities we did not pay, thus allowing our honor to suffer even more than the interests of these indigenous peoples. …

Muslim society in Africa was not uncivilized; it was merely a backward and imperfect civilization. There existed within it a large number of pious foundations, whose object was to provide for the needs of charity or for public instruction. We laid our hands on these revenues everywhere, partly diverting them from their former uses; we reduced the charitable establishments and let the schools decay, we disbanded seminaries. Around us knowledge has been extinguished, and recruitment of men of religion and men of law has ceased; that is to say, we have made Muslim society much more miserable, more disordered, more ignorant, and more barbarous than it had been before knowing us. …

It is not along the road of our European civilization that they must, for the present, be pushed, but in the direction proper to them; we must demand of them things that suit their ways, and not those contrary to them. Individual property, industry, and sedentary dwelling [as opposed to nomadic lifestyle] are in no way contrary to the religion of Muhammad. Arabs know or have known these things elsewhere; they are known and appreciated by some in Algeria itself. Why do we despair of making them familiar to a greater number? … Islam is not absolutely impenetrable to enlightenment.

… If our arms have decimated certain tribes, there are others whom our commerce has enriched and strengthened considerably, and who feel and understand this. Everywhere the prices that the indigenous people can get for their wares and their labor have increased greatly by our presence. In addition, our agriculturalists gladly make use of indigenous manpower. The European needs the Arab to make his lands valuable; the Arab needs the European to obtain a high salary.

QUESTIONS

1. How does Tocqueville react to Algerian culture? Why does he compare Algiers with Cincinnati? How are the French attempting to remake Algeria in their own image?

2. What are Tocqueville's assumptions about economic modernization in Algeria and its appropriateness for indigenous culture?

Source: de Tocqueville, Alexis. Edited and translated by Jennifer Pitts. *Writings on Empire and Slavery.* pp. 36, 140, 142, 145. © 2000 Jennifer Pitts. Reprinted with permission of The Johns Hopkins University Press.

First Railroad, from Manchester to Liverpool, England The engineer George Stephenson (1781–1848) first built engines that could pull coal at mines; in 1821, he constructed the first "locomotive" for public transportation. Four years later, the first regular railroad line, connecting Manchester with Liverpool, was erected. (Private Collection/The Stapleton Collection/Bridgeman Art Library)

The population of Great Britain increased by 8 percent in each decade from 1750 to 1800, partly as a result of industrial growth. This swelling population, in turn, expanded the market for goods. The most rapid population growth occurred in the countryside, causing a steady movement of people from rural to urban areas. The presence of this workforce was another contributing factor in Britain's readiness for change.

Britain was far more open to dissent than were other European countries at the time. A large proportion of British entrepreneurs was Quaker or belonged to one of the dissenting (non-Anglican) religious groups. Perhaps **dissenters** were accustomed to questioning authority and treading new paths. They were also well educated and, as a result of common religious bonds, inclined to provide mutual aid, including financial support.

Plentiful harvests in the years 1715 to 1750 also favored Britain and influenced the timing of industrial change. Farmers with good earnings could afford to order the new manufactured iron plows, and demand for industrial goods generally rose with population growth, improvements to the transportation system, and the growing availability of capital for investment. Thus, each change triggered more change; the cumulative effect was staggering.

SECTION SUMMARY

- Europe, and especially Great Britain, was endowed with rich iron and coal deposits, one of the most important factors that gave them the lead in industrialization.

- Improvements in agricultural production during the eighteenth century contributed to population growth, which in turn created a surplus labor force available for industrial production in urban areas and as well as a market for mass-produced goods.

- Toleration of religious diversity and dissent, especially in Great Britain, helped inspire innovation and an entrepreneurial spirit.

- The expansion of overseas trade from the seventeenth century onward created new sources of raw materials for manufacture, such as cotton.

- Merchants brought raw materials to the countryside for processing, leading to the development of cottage industry (the putting-out system), the division of labor, and specialization of tasks—all precursors of and steps toward industrialization.

- Centralized governments supported national banks and encouraged commerce, which in turn led to improved transportation.

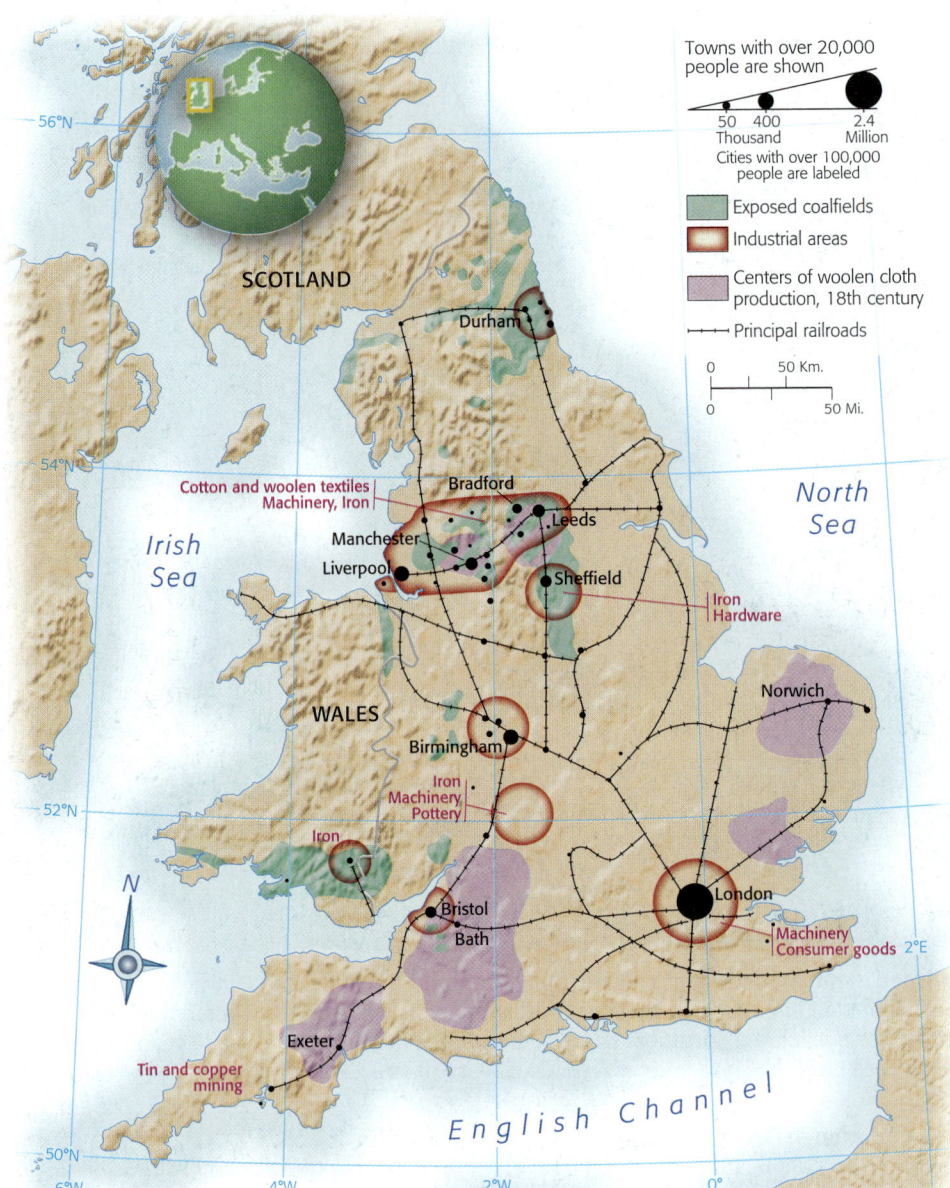

🌐 **Map 20.1—The Industrial Transformation in England, ca. 1850**
Industry developed in the areas rich in coal and iron fields. Important cities sprang up nearby and were soon linked by a growing rail network.

NEW MODES OF PRODUCTION

Which inventions appear to have been the most important in launching industrialization?

dissenters In England, a person belonging to a sect other than the Church of England.

mass production System in which great numbers of people work in centralized factories to mechanically produce large quantities of goods. The steam engine led to mass-produced textiles.

Several important technological advances powered European industry, and breakthroughs in one field often led to breakthroughs in others. Major technological innovations first transformed textiles and iron. At first limited to the British Isles, industry spread to the Continent, a development that occurred unevenly in various regions and at different times.

Mass Production

A series of inventions in the eighteenth century led to the **mass production** of textiles. One of the earliest was the flying shuttle (a shuttle carries the thread back and forth on a loom),

British Cotton Manufacture Machines simultaneously performed various functions. The carding machine (*front left*) separated cotton fibers, readying them for spinning. The roving machine (*front right*) wound the cotton onto spools. The drawing machine (*rear left*) wove patterns into the cloth. Rich in machines, this factory needed relatively few employees; most were women and children. (The Granger Collection, New York)

introduced in Britain in 1733 by John Kay (1704–1764). Kay's flying shuttle accelerated the weaving process to such an extent that it increased the demand for thread. James Hargreaves (1720–1778) met this need in the 1760s with his invention of the spinning jenny, a device that spun thread from wool or cotton. Improvements in spinning thread, such as the mule of Samuel Crompton (1753–1827), made the spinning jenny increasingly efficient, and by 1812, one jenny could produce as much yarn as two hundred hand spinners. In 1769, Richard Arkwright (1732–1792) patented the water frame, a machine capable of simultaneously spinning multiple threads. The frame was originally powered by waterfall, but in the 1780s, Arkwright began operating it with a steam engine. This mode of production created a glut of thread for hand weavers, which then led to the development of the power loom by Richard Cartwright in 1785. These innovations in turn increased the demand for raw cotton, inspiring American Eli Whitney (1765–1825) to invent the cotton gin, which sped up the removal of seeds from raw cotton. These innovations mechanized cotton manufacturing, moving most production from the home to factories. The industry's output increased 130-fold between 1770 and 1841.

The cotton manufacturing industry in Great Britain initiated an important departure from traditional production. For the first time in history, a staple industry was based on a natural resource that was not domestically produced—Britain's imports of cotton, mostly from the U.S. South, multiplied fivefold after 1790. Manufactured cotton became so cheap that it competed effectively with all handmade textiles. Comfortable and easy to wash, the popularity of cotton may have improved public health as well, for it enabled people to own several changes of clothing and keep them clean. Everyone was eager to buy British cottons. The enormous growth in the demand for raw cotton had a collateral impact: By making cotton production

A French Woman Goes to Work

The new cotton mills presented several obstacles to women workers. They had to negotiate the machinery while wearing the petticoats and aprons that custom required. Such dress could catch in the machinery, causing broken limbs and loss of a job, if not of life. At work and on their way to and from the British mills or at the less mechanized garment workshops of France, women had to pass dangerous places, where some experienced sexual harassment. Suzanne Voilquin (ca. 1801–ca. 1876) went to work to help her family after her mother had died. She took a job not at a mill or a factory, as was common in England, but as an embroiderer in a small workshop in Paris. In this selection, she writes of her experiences as a young woman from about 1823 to 1825.

We had to be at our looms at seven o'clock sharp and, even before setting out on the long race to get there on time, we had to carry out all our little household duties as quickly as we could. If certain details made us late, Mrs. Martin [her employer] would accept no excuses and offer no reprieve. We had to pay in kind, that is to say, make good those few minutes at the end of the day's work. When our days were prolonged in this way, I had a horrible fear of meeting on my return one of those contemptible men who makes a game of accosting young working women and frightening them with disgraceful remarks. When this happened, my nerves were always on edge and I lacked all physical courage. It was quite otherwise with … Adrienne [her younger sister]. She would say to me, … "Dear Sister, aren't I here?" (She was barely fifteen.) "If the occasion arises, why then you'll see that *a person's worth is not measured in years!*" And indeed, one evening, she gave me positive proof. Around nine o'clock … we were stopped by the vulgar words and filthy gestures of some poor wretch. As always, I stood there trembling and unable to speak before this reviler. Adrienne, on the contrary, experienced a moment of sublime energy. She managed to find such a tone of resolve, while brandishing an enormous key before his eyes, that he backed away, and, when we reached the corner of the main street, we were delivered from his insolent remarks.

Mrs. Martin seemed satisfied with our work, and we were accepted as regular employees. And so, at the end of the first week, we were very proud to deposit on our father's mantelpiece the eighteen francs we earned as wages. It was the same each week, for he had made himself the provisioner of our little group.

That cruel year was brought to an end by an accident that nearly caused my sister the loss of her right hand. My father's wail when he thought his child had been maimed for life was heart-rending. He cried!

… Around this time, my father wanted to marry us off. … The widower whom my father begged me to marry was fairly well established but neither handsome nor pleasant nor witty. Moreover, he came with a son twelve or thirteen years old, a charming Parisian street urchin who had been very badly raised. As a result, my mind, my senses, my whole being rebelled against the thought of such a match.

QUESTIONS

1. What is Suzanne Voilquin's attitude toward work? What hardships does she face?
2. What does this excerpt tell you about family relations? Why does Suzanne's father want to "marry her off"?

Source: From Mark Traugott, ed. and trans., *The French Worker: Autobiographies from the Early Industrial Era*, Copyright © 1993 The Regents of the University of California. Reprinted by permission of The University of California Press.

more profitable, it also made slave labor in the U.S. South more attractive. Between 1750 and 1800, approximately three million Africans were forcibly transported to the New World. The slave economy in the Americas influenced Britain's economy in several ways. Slave-produced sugar in the West Indies and cotton in the American South shifted Britain's trade patterns from Asia to the Atlantic. The cotton trade, and later, other products, linked the economies of various nations and peoples. No longer, as in preindustrial trade, were all goods locally made, nor did the consumers have personal contact with the producers of goods they purchased. Increasingly, specialization became the norm. The results were high production and low prices for finished textile products. Hand sewing and needlework, usually done by young women, completed the garment-making process. (See the feature, "The Written Record: A French Woman Goes to Work.")

New Energy Sources and Their Impacts

Before the age of industrialization, humans, animals, wind, and water provided the power sources for production. Humans and animals were limited in their capacities to drive the large mills needed to grind grain or cut wood. Wind was unreliable because it was not constant. Water-driven mills depended on the seasons—streams dried up in the summer and froze in the winter. And water mills could be placed only where a strong current of water flowed. Clearly, the infant industries needed a power source that was constant and not confined to riverbanks. In the eighteenth and nineteenth centuries, two new sources of energy fueled industrial production: coal and steam.

Coal, long in use for heating households, for the first time came to be used for metal processing. Traditionally, smelters used charcoal to extract iron from ore. Eventually, however, the source of charcoal—wood—became depleted in Britain. Abraham Darby's invention of coke (refined coal) smelting in 1708 allowed coal to substitute for charcoal in the process of refining metals. Although coal was plentiful, the increased demand for it depleted the surface seams in mines, and it became necessary to go farther underground. But as pits deepened, they reached pools of ground water, and drainage became a critical obstacle to coal mining. In 1709, Thomas Newcomen (1663–1729) patented a **steam engine** that, within a few years, was able to pump water from the pit bottom to the surface of the mine shaft. James Watt (1736–1819) improved it, and by developing a separate condenser, Watt devised an engine that could power a variety of machines. Thus, steam engines could also operate textile mills that had previously been powered by water or wind.

steam engine The steam engine provided mechanized power for manufacturing and made factories and mass production possible.

The steam engine, initially used to meet the increased demand for coal, by the late 1700s, also powered the blast furnaces in the coke smelting process, as well as driving the forge hammers that shaped iron. Iron output increased dramatically by 1800. The greater supply of iron and the use of steam stimulated other changes. Wooden machines, which wore out rapidly, were replaced by relatively cheap and durable iron machines. The steam engine made it practical to organize work in a factory. Locating a manufacturing plant where it was most convenient eliminated the expense of transporting raw materials to be worked on at a natural but fixed power source, such as a waterfall. The central factory also reinforced work discipline. These **factories** were large, austere edifices, sometimes inspired by military architecture and therefore resembling barracks. With the introduction of blast furnaces and other heat-producing manufacturing methods, the tall factory chimney became a common sight on the industrial landscape.

factories Centralized workplaces where a number of people cooperate to mass-produce goods. The steam engine as a central power source in factories led to huge productivity increases.

The steam engine powered a dramatic growth in production. It increased the mechanical power of machinery used to forge iron and to produce equipment for spinning and weaving. Assisted by machines, workers were enormously more productive than when they depended solely on hand-operated tools. In the year 1700, spinning 100 pounds of cotton took 50,000 worker-hours; by 1825 it took only 135—a 370-fold increase in productivity capacity per worker.

Improvements in manufacturing methods and techniques increased the production of a large variety of goods, usually at lower prices. Industrial change started with cotton, but breakthroughs in the use of iron and coal continued and sustained these changes.

Inventors and Entrepreneurs

Inventions triggered the industrial age, and the continued flow of new ones sustained it. Rather than cling to traditional methods, many **entrepreneurs** persistently challenged tradition and attempted to find new ways of improving production. In this age of invention, innovation was prized as never before. The early inventors and industrialists came from various backgrounds. Jean Marie Jacquard, for example, whose invention is illustrated below, was a craftsman. Other inventors came from the merchant class, since the possession of capital was a distinct advantage in launching an industrial enterprise.

entrepreneurs People who assume the risks of organizing and investing in new business ventures, inventions, and innovations.

Entrepreneurs took the financial risk of investing in new types of enterprises. Most industrialists ran a single plant by themselves or with a partner, but even in the early stages, some ran several plants. Some enterprises were vertically integrated, controlling production at many stages. The Peels in Britain owned operations ranging from spinning to printing and even banking. The entrepreneurs' dynamism and boldness fostered the growth of the British industrial system, making that small nation the workshop of the world.

The Spread of Industry to the Continent

As the first to industrialize, Britain not only gained an economic edge over the Continent, but it offered a model for economic change. Visitors, such as German engineer August Börsig

The Jacquard Loom   Joseph-Marie Jacquard (1752–1834) invented this loom in 1804, and it was widely adopted in both France and England. While it was not "industrial" in the sense that its source of power was the human energy of a skilled craftsman, it nonetheless embodied a significant modern advancement. The pasteboard punch cards controlled the action of the loom to create complex designs automatically, making it possible for amateur weavers to produce highly prized fabrics. The punch card was an important precursor to computing hardware and programming. The looms' cards were interchangeable. They could also be stolen—an early instance of software piracy. (Loom designed by Joseph Marie Jacquard (1752-1834) 2nd half of 19th century (engraving) (b/w photo), French School, (19th century)/Private Collection/Archives Charmet/The Bridgeman Art Library)

(BEUR-sick), came to Britain, studied local methods of production, and returned home to set up blast furnaces and spinning works inspired by British design. Some visitors even resorted to industrial espionage, smuggling blueprints of machines out of Britain. Despite a British law that forbade local artisans to emigrate, some did leave, including entrepreneurs who helped set up industrial plants in France and Belgium. By the 1820s, British technicians were all over Europe.

The Börsig Ironworks in the 1840s   August Börsig (1804–1854), an artisan and engineer, founded these ironworks in Berlin after studying steam engines in Britain. He built the first German steam engine in 1825 and the first locomotive in 1842. The factory expanded to meet the needs of the burgeoning German rail system. By the time of Börsig's death, his factory had built five hundred locomotives.   (Preussischer Kulturbesitz Bildarchiv/Art Resource, NY)

Even though engineers and entrepreneurs wished to emulate British methods, no other country could replicate the British pattern of industrialization, and the various paths taken toward modernization demonstrate how the "revolutionary" nature of these changes was contingent upon a precise combination of factors. Wars and revolutions of the late eighteenth century had not only slowed economic growth in France, but they cut off the flow of information and new techniques coming from Britain. France also lacked the rapid population growth that had made possible, if not necessitated, economic change in Britain. Moreover, revolutionary and Napoleonic legislation had relieved French peasants of some of the misery that drove their British counterparts to leave the land for urban industry. The Napoleonic Code of 1804 abolished **primogeniture**, so that when a peasant died, all of his children, at least in principle, enjoyed equal inheritance, which enabled many to remain on the land.

Because French labor was still quite cheap, many goods could be manufactured inexpensively by hand; thus, the incentive to invest in laborsaving devices was absent. French entrepreneurs who did seek to emulate British accomplishments faced serious cultural and geographical challenges. France had traditionally produced high quality luxury goods that were not well disposed to the methods of mass production; it also had fewer iron and coal deposits that, unlike in Britain, were geographically dispersed (see **Map 20.2**). Soon, however, French manufacturers found themselves facing British competition; they were the first to feel the negative effects of being industrial latecomers.

The situation in Germany was quite different from that of both Britain and France. The Napoleonic invasions caused considerable destruction, but they also brought some positive

primogeniture   A legal inheritance system that provided the firstborn, usually the firstborn son, the right to inherit all the family land and farm.

🌐 MAP 20.2—Continental Industrialization, ca. 1850

Industry was still sparse on the Continent, but important regions had developed near major coal deposits in Liège, the Ruhr, and Silesia.

economic, social, and administrative benefits. Restrictive guilds declined. The French occupiers suppressed many tariffs and taxes that had hindered trade between German states; they also reduced the number of separate states, established a single unified legal system, and introduced a single standard of measurement based on the metric system. These changes remained intact after Napoleon's defeat in 1815.

Government in the German states played an important role in the adoption of improved methods of manufacturing. Eager for industrial development, the Prussian state sent an official to Britain to observe the puddling process (the method by which iron is freed of carbon) and bring that expertise back home. The Prussian government promoted industrial growth by investing in a transportation network to carry raw materials for processing and finished goods to their markets. To spur both trade and industrial growth, Prussia took the lead in creating a customs union, the *Zollverein* (TZOLL-fair-eyn), which abolished tariffs among its members. By 1834, a market embracing eighteen German states with a population of 23 million had been created. German industrial growth accelerated dramatically in the 1850s. Massive expenditures on railways created a large demand for metal, which pressured German manufacturers to enlarge their plant capacities and increase efficiency. The German states were not yet politically unified, but the German middle classes saw economic growth as the means by which their country could win a prominent place among Europe's nation-states.

■ **FIGURE 20.1—The Increase in Gross National Product per Capita in Principal European Countries, 1830–1913**

The countries that industrialized rapidly—such as the United Kingdom in particular, and also Belgium, France, and Germany—experienced dramatic increases in per capita income during the nineteenth century. Other countries, such as Greece and Portugal, economically trailed the industrial leaders, and per capita income there remained essentially flat.

(Source: From Norman J. G. Pounds, *An Historical Geography of Europe, 1800–1914.* Cambridge University Press, 1985. Used by permission of the publisher.)

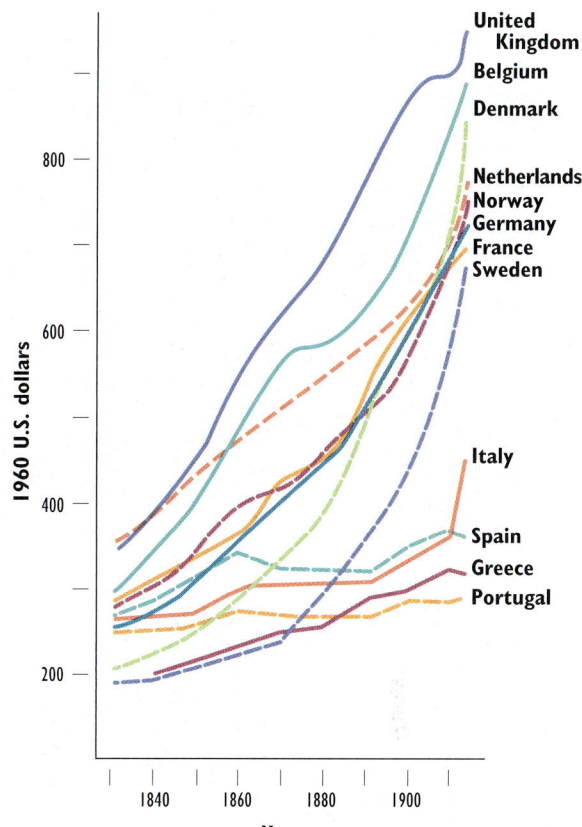

Germany successfully emulated Britain and overtook France's rate of economic growth. Toward the end of the nineteenth century, Germany pioneered in the electrical engineering and chemical industries. If France experienced the disadvantages of being a latecomer to industrialization, Germany reaped the benefits of that status. The Germans were able to avoid costly and inefficient early experimentation and adopted the latest, proven methods; moreover, Germany entered fields that Britain had neglected.

Elsewhere in Europe, economic progress remained slow, even by the end of the nineteenth century. As long as Russia retained serfdom (until 1861), it would lack the mobile labor force needed for industrial growth. And until late in the century, the ruling Russian aristocracy hesitated to adopt an economic system in which wealth was not based on labor-intensive agriculture. With the exception of its only important industrial center in Bohemia, Austria remained heavily agrarian (see **MAP 20.2**).

The impoverished southern Mediterranean countries experienced little economic growth. With mostly poor soil, their agriculture yielded only a meager surplus. Spain, lacking coal and access to other energy sources, could not easily diversify its economic base. Some industry emerged in Catalonia, especially around Barcelona, but it was limited in scope and did not have much impact on the rest of the country. The Italian peninsula was still industrially underdeveloped in the middle of the nineteenth century. There were modest advances, but growth was too slow to have a measurable positive impact on the Italian economy. In 1871, 61 percent of Italy's population was still agrarian.

Although by midcentury only a few European nations had experienced industrialization to any great extent, many more would do so by the end of the century, pressured by vigorous competition from their more advanced neighbors (see **FIGURE 20.1**). Economic modernization had political and international implications as well, for industrialized nations had the backing of military might and superiority. Compared with the rest of the world, the European continent in the nineteenth century had acquired a distinct material culture that was increasingly based on machine manufacture or was in the process of becoming so. The possession of "skillful industry," one Victorian writer exulted, was "ever a proof of superior civilization." Although only some regions of Europe were industrialized, many Europeans came to view themselves as obviously "superior," while deeming all other races inferior. (See the feature, "The Global Record: Alexis de Tocqueville's Thoughts on Colonization.")

SECTION SUMMARY

- The influx of raw cotton into Britain, innovations that sped up the processes of spinning and weaving, as well as the mechanical removal of cotton seeds, led the revolution in textile production.

- The introduction of the blast furnace and steam engine doubled iron production at the end of the eighteenth century, leading to the production of less expensive and more durable machines, such as those used for textiles. Steam-driven machines led to the centralization of production into factories.

- The innovations that came with industrial production also depended upon entrepreneurs who were hungry for profits and willing to take investment risks.

- The pace of industrialization varied among nations and changed the nature of competition among them; the material culture produced by machine manufacture led Europeans to view themselves as a superior civilization with the military capability for colonial conquest.

SOCIAL, CULTURAL, AND ENVIRONMENTAL IMPACTS

What impact did industrialization have on the environment and on social classes?

Industry transformed people's lives, individually and collectively. It altered how they made a livelihood, where and how they lived, even how they thought of themselves. Because industry required new specialized skills, the range of occupations that people adopted expanded dramatically.

Industrialization also transformed the way society functioned. Until the eighteenth century, power and influence derived from hereditary privilege, which meant aristocratic birth and possession of land. From the late eighteenth century on, however, an emerging social class, whose wealth was self-made and whose influence was based on economic contributions to society, began to challenge the aristocracy. Industrialization also caused extraordinary growth of cities and dramatically altered the natural environment. Europeans faced not only new urban social problems, but also the dangerous pollution of their air and water.

Urbanization and Its Discontents

A sociologist at the end of the nineteenth century observed, "The most remarkable social phenomenon of the present century is the concentration of population in cities."[3] The number and size of cities grew as never before. The major impetus for urban growth was the concentration of industry in cities and the resulting need of large numbers of urban workers and their families for goods and services (see **MAP 20.3**).

Industrialization was not the only catalyst. Increased commercial, administrative, and other service functions drew people to cities, even in countries that had not yet witnessed much industrialization, such as France, Holland, Italy, and Switzerland. Urban growth in some places was explosive. In the entire eighteenth century, London grew by only 200,000; but in the first half of the nineteenth century, it grew by 1.4 million, more than doubling its size. Census figures show that by 1851, Britain was the first country to have as many people living in cities as in the countryside. For Germany, that date was 1891, and for France, it was not until 1931. In addition to industry, **urbanization** transformed cities and the way they grew. Large concentrations of people provided convenient markets for goods, services, and a labor pool. But they also encouraged a more intense social and cultural engagement, which could support, for example, scientific societies and laboratories where engineers and scientists could share new ideas.

Larger cities attracted migrants from great distances, including from beyond the nation's borders. The Irish arrived in large numbers to work in the factories of Lancashire, in northwestern England; Belgians came for mine work in northern France; and Poles sought employment in the Ruhr Valley of western Germany. Industrial activity stimulated the growth of world trade and shipping across the seas, taking merchant sailors far from home. Many large cities were marked by diverse populations, which included people with different native languages, religions, and national origins and, increasingly, of different races. Africans and Asians inhabited port cities, such as Amsterdam, Marseille, and Liverpool.

A multitude of ills accompanied urban growth and caused mortality rates to rise dramatically in some locations. In mid-nineteenth century France and Britain, annual death rates averaged about 22 per thousand, but in some industrial cities, it rose to 39.2, with infants dying at especially high rates. Social inequality in the face of death was startling. Including the high child mortality rate, the average age at death among upper-class Liverpool families in 1842 was 35; for members of laborers' families, it was 15. In 1800, boys living in urban slums were on average 8 inches shorter than the sons of rich urban dwellers.

The early stages of industrialization created severe conditions for the poor, especially in rapidly growing cities, where they lived in urban slums. The squalor of St. Giles—London's most notorious slum—had such shock value that it became a tourist attraction. (See the feature, "The Visual Record: St. Giles.") Housing shortages in many cities forced large numbers of people to cram into small areas. To accommodate the influx of workers, houses were built back to back on small lots and had insufficient lighting and ventilation. The dizzying pace of

urbanization Term related to the growth of cities, largely connected to the industrialization of the late eighteenth and nineteenth centuries.

MAP 20.3—Cities Reaching Population Level of 100,000 by 1750, 1800, and 1850

In 1750, the largest cities owed their existence primarily to commerce, but industrialization caused populations to concentrate more in cities. England, the leading industrial nation, contained many of the largest cities.

(Source: Data from Tertius Chandler, *Four Thousand Years of Urban Growth: An Historical Census* [Lewistown, N.Y.: St. David's University Press, 1987], pp. 22–24.)

Map legend:
- 100,000 in 1750
- Reached 100,000 by 1800
- Reached 100,000 by 1850

urban growth made it impossible for cities to provide basic sanitary facilities. The causes of many diseases, such as typhus, cholera, and tuberculosis, were unknown; the dirt, dampness, and darkness of crowded tenements and polluted streets created the conditions that fostered disease.

In manufacturing towns, factory chimneys spewed soot, and everything was covered with dirt and grime. Smoke was a major ingredient of the famous London fog, which not only reduced visibility, but posed serious health risks. Refuse, including the rotting corpses of dogs and horses, littered city streets. In 1858, the stench from sewage and other rot in London was so putrid that the British House of Commons was forced to suspend its sessions.

It is not surprising that cholera, a highly infectious disease transmitted through contaminated water, swept London and other European urban centers. In the 1830s, one of the first epidemics of modern times struck Europe, killing 100,000 in France, 50,000 in Britain, and 238,000 in Russia. Typhoid fever, also an acute infectious disease, struck mostly the poor but did not spare the privileged. Queen Victoria of Great Britain nearly died of it; her husband, Prince Albert, did.

Social Class and Family Life

A French countess, using the pen name Daniel Stern, wrote in the 1830s and 1840s about the emergence of "a class apart, as if it were a nation within the nation," working in factories and mines, called "by a new name: the industrial **proletariat**."[7] Originally used to designate the poorest propertyless wretches in Roman society, the term *proletariat* became synonymous with the

proletariat Karl Marx's term for the new class of industrial workers who owned none of the means of production and were dependent on factory owners for their livelihoods.

St. Giles

This woodcut first appeared in the *Illustrated London News* in the early 1840s, and then in Thomas Beames's, *The Rookeries of London* (1852). It is difficult to overestimate the power of such imagery, particularly in the press. Such visual portrayals did not necessarily exaggerate slum conditions, but they did help create and disseminate distinct impressions about the poor. Note the implied promiscuousness of the disheveled couple, and the indifferent attitude of the mother (who might be single), with her arm draped lackadaisically over her nursing infant.

Surrounded by the well-to-do neighborhoods of Oxford Street, Regent Street, Trafalgar Square, and the Strand, St. Giles had once been a village outside London,

inhabited by wealthy people. But London's rapid expansion swallowed it; by 1740, dwellings to accommodate the poor—called "rookeries"—were built in courtyards and alleys between the original streets, and the wealthier population moved out. The rapid degeneration of neighborhoods, such as St. Giles, in fast-growing urban centers of Britain, France, and Germany took local authorities by surprise. Overcrowding worsened the already poor sanitary conditions. A single privy in a courtyard was likely to serve dozens, sometimes even a few hundred, tenants. Waste from the privy might contaminate nearby wells, or drain through open sewers to a nearby river, which was likely to be the local source of drinking water—and a breeding ground for cholera. Some

St. Giles   (From Thomas Beames, The Rookeries of London. Photo: Harvard Imaging Service)

class of workers developing in the burgeoning factories. What distinguished this growing class throughout the nineteenth century was that it was relatively unskilled and totally dependent on the factory owners for its livelihood. Even lowly apprentices of earlier eras never occupied such a precarious status because guild rules and traditions protected them from arbitrariness. The guild system also made it possible for apprentices to become journeymen and then master artisans, owning their own tools and working on their own time and on their own premises. Improvement in status and owning the means of production would never be a possibility for the new proletariat.

tenants lacked toilets and relieved themselves in the streets. The practice of storing human waste in heaps alongside houses for sale as manure also contributed to the pervasive stench and the spread of bacteria. Water in the cities was scarce and filthy. Only the rich had piped water. The poor had to supply themselves from public fountains or wells and were often obliged to carry water a considerable distance.

Social Reformers and medical experts who visited St. Giles and other urban slums in European cities tended to focus repeatedly on the dangers of promiscuity, disease, crime, and moral contagion, often employing the same words and metaphors to describe what they had seen or what others had written. They especially decried what they perceived to be the immoral conditions in which families lived. Physician James Philips Kay, for example, who practiced medicine in Manchester, England, wrote in 1832 of how "A whole family is often accommodated on a single bed, and sometimes a heap of filthy straw and a covering of old sacking hide them in one undistinguished heap, debased alike by penury, want of economy and dissolute habits. Frequently, the inspectors found [that] ... more than one family lived in a damp cellar, containing only one room, in whose pestilential atmosphere from twelve to sixteen persons were crowded. To these fertile sources of disease were sometimes added the keeping of pigs and other animals in the house, with other nuisances of the most revolting character."[4] Inspectors often dwelled on the mixture of sexes across generations sharing beds, implying incest and animal-like behavior.

In his *Condition of the Working Class in England* (1845), Friedrich Engels described St. Giles as a place where "no human being" would wish to live: broken windows, crumbling walls, stinking piles of garbage and filth that "surpassed description." He might have been referring to the printed image of St. Giles when he emphasized how overcrowding produced "brutal indifference" and "unfeeling isolation," where humankind dissolved into "monads, of which each one has a separate essence, and a separate purpose, the world of atoms. . . . "[5] Indeed, with the possible exception of the little girl (whose back is to the viewer) and the middle-class woman (on the right, in the back) toward whom she might be approaching for a handout, there is not a single mutual gaze among those portrayed in this print—each individual is looking outward or downward. Note as well that the middle-class woman's gaze is disapproving, not sympathetic. Middle-class women often ventured into slums for charitable works—one of the few excuses respectable women had to be in public. But the charity was limited by morals; providers wanted to be certain that only the "worthy" poor received it.

Beames, who included the same print in his book, seems to draw his description of St. Giles from the image as much as from his own visit there:

> ... squalid children, haggard men, with long uncombed hair, in rags, most of them smoking, many speaking Irish; women without shoes or stockings—a babe perhaps at the breast, with a single garment, confined to the waist by a bit of string; wolfish looking dogs; decayed vegetables strewing the pavement; low public houses; linen hanging across the street to dry; the population stagnant in the midst of activity; lounging about in remnants of shooting jackets, leaning on the window frames, blocking up the courts and alleys; with young boys gathered round them, looking exhausted as though they had not been to bed. Never was there so little connection between masses of living beings and their means of livelihood.[6]

Engels and Beames both expressed deep concern about how the working class became mixed with "prostitutes, thieves, and criminals." Indeed, a closer look at the couple in the print suggests the woman is a prostitute, and the figure lying prone is probably drunk. Not only are the numerous children subject to terrible influences, but so are honest laborers. Beames feared that because workers could not live on their low wages, criminal temptations would spread like a "plague." But the contagion of crime was not the only threat. If the working poor ever united to challenge social injustice, they might foment violent revolution.

QUESTIONS

1. Study more closely the details in the wood block. What do you think are the intentions of the artist?

2. Do you think this wood block is an accurate representation of St. Giles's entire population?

3. What were the dangers, real or perceived, of ignoring the plight of the poor in neighborhoods like St. Giles?

As industry advanced and spread, more and more people depended on it for a livelihood. In the putting-out system, during an agricultural downturn, a cottager could spend more time on hand labor; when demand for piecework slacked off, the cottager could devote more time to cultivating the land. But people living in industrial cities had no such backup: Any downturn in the economy translated into layoffs or job losses. In addition, the introduction of new industries often devastated laborers in older forms of production. The mechanization of cotton production reduced the earning power of weavers. Cheap cotton production also drove down workers' wages in other textiles with higher production costs, such as linen, because of competition.

Children Toiling in Mines Able to crawl in narrow mine shafts, many children were employed underground. In this woodcut, a woman joins a child in his labor. Often, whole families worked together and were paid a fixed price for the amount of coal extracted. (Rischgitz/Hulton Archive/Getty Images)

Most factory work was dirty and laborious and took place in grim plants with heavy, noisy machinery. Sixteen-hour workdays were common. Child labor was widespread. With no safety provisions, the workers were prone to accidents and exposed to dangerous substances or circumstances. Mercury, used in hat manufacturing, gradually poisoned the hatmakers and often led to dementia, hence, the term *mad hatters*. Lead, used in paints and pottery, also had a devastating impact on workers' health.

Young girls especially suffered poor health from heavy labor. In 1842, 18-year-old Ann Eggley testified to a parliamentary commission that she had been a mineworker since the age of 7 and hauled carriages loaded with ore weighing 800 pounds for twelve hours a day. Isabel Wilson, another mineworker, testified that she had given birth to ten children and had suffered five miscarriages. These women—overworked, exhausted, and vulnerable to disease—faced premature death.

Did industrialization improve the workers' lot? Until the mid-nineteenth century, information about workers' standard of living, measured by income and expenses, is incomplete. Generally, incomes were so low that workers usually spent between two-thirds and three-fourths of their budget on food. The best evidence comes from Britain, where an average family of five needed at least 21 shillings a week to fend off poverty. Skilled workers might earn as much as 30 shillings a week, but most were unskilled and earned substantially less. All workers faced the insecurity of illness or old age resulting in lost wages or unemployment. Women and children usually had to pitch in. Even when women were the main breadwinners, they almost never received wages sufficient to meet the needs of their own subsistence, let alone those of an entire family. Regardless of what work they performed, women always earned a fraction of men's wages. Employers based women's wages on the assumption that they supplemented the income of a husband or father.

From the beginning, industrialization increased society's wealth, but historians continue to debate whether and at what point it benefited workers. "Optimist" historians argue that some of the new wealth trickled down to the lower levels of society. "Pessimist" historians say that a downward flow did not necessarily occur. Statistics suggest that by the 1840s, workers' lives in Britain did improve. Their real income rose by 40 percent between 1800 and 1850 because of relatively low prices of many basic goods. As the cost of cloth declined, the dress of working-class people noticeably improved. Nonetheless, the general trend in real wages meant little when workers faced frequent cycles of unemployment or underemployment, when they lived in crowded, unsanitary conditions, or when a major economic downturn, such as occurred in the 1840s, made their situation even more precarious.

Industrialization also had dramatic impacts on the character of family and household among both the middle and working classes. Industrial capitalism gave rise to a new middle class or **bourgeoisie**, whose wealth derived from the capitalistic activities of trade, finance, and manufacturing. Previously, the wives and daughters of small shopkeepers readily performed tasks, such as bookkeeping or serving customers, because the businesses were in or near the home. But as small businesses became public companies with venues outside the home, women ceased participating. Family life came to reflect these new economic realities, justified and reinforced by a new set of cultural values. In more than any other social class, new family values based on gender distinctions became just as important a signifier of class identity as wealth itself. Catherine Hall notes that "A man's dignity lay in his occupation; a woman's gentility was destroyed if she had one."[8] The nineteenth-century world of market capitalism made wealth—rather than aristocratic bloodlines—the sign of success and power. Conspicuous consumption on homes, home furnishings, and clothing offered visible proof of success.

> **bourgeoisie** another word for the middle class, commonly associated with the rise of capitalism, industrialization, and the accumulation of wealth.

With business affairs removed from the home and enough wealth that women's employment was not required, motherhood and women's devotion to it became more idealized in the middle class than it ever had been in the past. Women developed a "cult of domesticity" in which they devoted themselves to their children and to home décor—or supervised servants who did—as men became preoccupied with work and with male sociability. While bourgeois men and women did not always live up to these ideals, they did generally embrace them as a prescription appropriate for family life in the new industrial world. These ideals also became a basis for judgment of those who did not live up to them—the lower classes and errant women of all classes.

Industrialization transformed working-class life in ways very different from the middle classes. Many families could not afford to keep women and children at home as production became mechanized and left the household. The textile industries especially employed children and women in the lowliest positions, where they tended machines, tied broken threads, and performed menial tasks. Factory work often undermined the ability of working women to take care of their children. As farmers or cottagers, they had been able to work and supervise children simultaneously. When women had to leave the home to work, it was not uncommon for an older child, sometimes only 5 or 6 years of age, to be entrusted with the care of infants and toddlers. Urban and rural women sometimes resorted to more dangerous methods of child-care. Many mothers sent their children to wet nurses in the countryside, where—if they survived—they stayed for up to two years. The mortality of these babies was high, as they were often neglected. In France and Italy, the poorest of mothers—especially single mothers—abandoned their infants at foundling homes, which in turn sent them out to be wet nursed. In many cases, baby-farming was no more than a camouflaged form of infanticide. Mothers who kept their children, but were obliged to leave them unwatched at home during factory hours, sometimes pacified them with mixtures of opium, readily available from the local apothecary.

Women's work patterns, however, were sporadic; many only worked before their children were born, or after they grew older. Overall, relatively few women were in the wage market—by 1850, only about a quarter in both Britain and France. Of that quarter, few worked in factories; far more were in agriculture, crafts industries (which still flourished despite poor working conditions), and domestic service.

The textile industry employed children once they were over the age of 5 or 6. Their size and agility made them useful for certain jobs, such as reaching under machines to pick up loose cotton and replacing bobbins. Elizabeth Bentley began work as a doffer (bobbin replacer) in 1815 at the age of 6. At the age of 23, she testified before a parliamentary commission that she normally worked from 6:00 A.M. to 7:00 P.M., but for six months, worked sixteen-hour days, beginning at 5:00 A.M. She told the commission that children were strapped if they arrived late. She had only forty minutes at noon to eat, but said "I had not much to eat, and the little I had I could not eat it, my appetite was so poor. ... " The commission noted that she was "considerably deformed ... in consequence of this labor."[9] Child labor certainly did not start with the industrial transformation;

Unionization Membership Certificate Pictured here is an elaborate certificate for membership in the Amalgamated Society of Engineers. Note the wide array of symbolism and allegory on which it draws, with images of classical antiquity, Greek mythology, and the modern material culture of the nineteenth century. (Eileen Tweedy/The Art Archive/Picture Desk)

conditions brought on by competition from machine-made cotton fabrics, attacked the homes of the wealthy. In 1855, in Barcelona, the government tried to dissolve unions, and fifty thousand workers went on strike, carrying placards that warned "Association or Death."

Economic problems were not the only concern of laboring people. Some employers compelled workers to conform to severe discipline even outside the workplace. In some cases, they were forbidden to read certain newspapers, compelled to attend religious services, and could marry only with the employer's permission. Workers resented the intrusiveness into their private lives and resisted these attempts at control. Unions provided a means to resist unreasonable regulation and secure decent wages and working conditions by organizing strikes and supporting members during work stoppages.

Although there were early attempts in Britain to organize unions on a national basis, most were centered on a single craft or a single industry. Because labor unions originated in the crafts tradition, the earliest members were skilled craftsmen who organized to protect their livelihoods from the challenge that industrialization posed. These craftsmen were usually literate and longtime residents of their communities. They provided the labor movement with much of its leadership and organization. Skilled craft workers also played a strong role in developing a sense of class-consciousness. The language and institutions that they had developed over decades, and sometimes over centuries, became the common heritage of workers in general.

Workers increasingly understood the powerful potential of organized labor. As a French workers' paper declared in 1847, "If workers came together and organized . . . nothing would be able to stop them." But unionization nonetheless faced formidable obstacles throughout the nineteenth century. Unions were illegal in Britain until 1825, in Prussia until 1859, and in France until the 1860s. Even where they were legal, authorities often used press censorship and armed force against strikers. Moreover, population growth made it difficult for workers to withhold labor lest they be replaced by others only too willing to take their places.

The working classes were, moreover, never a monolithic group. They consisted of people with varying skills, responsibilities, and incomes. Artisans, more highly paid and respected by employers, often looked upon unskilled workers with contempt. Most often work was segregated by sex, making it more difficult for women and men to share a common cause. Even when they worked side by side in the industrial workplace, male and female laborers usually felt little common identity. Men worried that women were undermining their earning power by accepting lower wages. They often excluded women from their unions. Men sometimes even went on strike to force employers to discharge women. Nor was there solidarity across nationalities. Foreign workers were not well informed about local conditions, or so desperate for work they were willing to overlook them. British workers were hostile toward the Irish, the French toward the Belgian and Italian immigrants. The hostility often led to anti-immigrant riots. Many forces fostered dissension among the working classes in the nineteenth century, undermining the potential effectiveness of unions.

Political action offered another means to seek justice. In the 1830s and 1840s, British and French workers agitated for the right to vote as a way to put themselves on equal footing with the privileged and to win better conditions. Their anger over their failure to win political representation strengthened working-class solidarity against the upper classes. Politically organized workers played a major role in the revolutions that would rock Europe in 1848 (see pages 607–612). They showed that their organizations were legitimate representatives of the people and that the government needed to concern itself with the workers' lot. In general, advocates of the lower classes upheld the ideal of a moral economy—one in which all who labored received a just wage and every person was assured a minimum level of well-being.

By the mid-nineteenth century, as noted in the "Visual Record" illustration of St. Giles on pages 574–575, the middle classes had developed a clear fear of workers and viewed them as a single class that threatened society. It was not unusual for members of the elite to refer to workers as "the swinish multitude" or, as the title of a popular English book put it, *The Great Unwashed* (1868). In France, reference was alternately made to "the dangerous classes" and "the laboring classes." Not just workers, but even the privileged, seemed to see relations between the groups as a form of class war.

SECTION SUMMARY

- As guilds declined (or were prohibited), new worker solidarities based on religion, language, a sense of social justice, and shared experiences provided the foundation for the emergence of trade unions.

- Workers at times resorted to violence in their effort to preserve more traditional modes of production and protect their right to work.

- Friendly societies and unions sought to provide health, accident, unemployment, and funeral benefits.

- Professional unionization faced the obstacles of government repression as well as the diversity of the labor force itself: skilled workers versus the unskilled; men versus women; nationals versus foreigners.

21

CHAPTER OUTLINE

Restoration and Reaction, 1814–1830

Ideological Confrontations

The Quest for Reform, 1830–1848

The Revolutions of 1848

Barricades in Vienna, Austria, May 1848

(Historisches Museum (Museen der Stadt Wien) Vienna/Gianni Dagli Orti/The Art Archive/Picture Desk)

Restoration, Reform, and Revolution, 1814–1848

In 1848, Europe experienced a revolutionary wave, unprecedented in over a half century since the heady days of the French Revolution. Workers, artisans, and even members of the middle classes poured into the streets to challenge authoritarian rulers and the militaries that tried to repress rebellion. As illustrated in the painting at the left, they built street barricades to defend themselves and to trap and attack military troops. Barricades, long a part of urban insurrectionary history, had almost become an art form. Revolutionaries systematically tore the paving stones from streets and beams from the façades of houses. To build the barricade, they confiscated passing omnibuses, carriages, and carts to pile rubble, along with empty barrels and casks. The barricades they built sometimes rose as high as nine feet.

In addition to its material reality, this painting represents the spirit present at the barricades, as well as in the revolutions as a whole. Its mixture of social classes and genders shows the inclusive camaraderie in conquering the streets, as even fraternizing soldiers listen attentively to the speaker atop the rubble. The neatly piled shovels and signs of meal preparation suggest a systematic order in the midst of a chaos that is only apparent. The figure hung in effigy reminds the viewer of the seriousness of the event. Scenes such as this burst forth in major cities throughout western and eastern Europe.

The revolutions of 1848 had their ideological origins in the irrepressible forces unleashed in the Revolution of 1789. With the end of the Napoleonic Wars in 1815, the victorious Great Powers—Austria, Great Britain, Prussia, and Russia—tried to reestablish as much of the old European state system as possible. The international arrangements they carved out at the Congress of Vienna were soon shaken by outbreaks of nationalist fervor. Nationalists aimed either to create larger political units, as in Italy and Germany, or to win independence from foreign rule, as in Greece. In addition to nationalism, which had in part been sparked by Napoleonic reforms, other new ideologies, such as romanticism, liberalism, and socialism, born of the Enlightenment and French Revolution, prevented a complete restoration of the old order. (An ideology is a structured, organized set of ideas that reflects a group's thinking about life or society.) The ideologies that helped promote revolution continued to shape development in the second half of the century, as well as throughout the twentieth.

As revolution swept through Europe, a similar pattern took place: After the first exhilarating moments of emancipation from authoritarian monarchies, conflict, disappointment, and failure allowed the forces of reaction and repression to take control. Revolutionaries did not win all their goals, and in many cases, the forces of order crushed them. Yet by midcentury, major intellectual, social, and political changes had occurred.

FOCUS QUESTIONS

- What were the goals of the Restoration, and the sources of resistance to it?
- What major ideologies developed in the first half of the nineteenth century?
- How did the restorations that followed the Napoleonic era give way to reform?
- What were the main causes of the revolutions of 1848, and what roles did nationalism, liberalism, and socialism play in inciting and sustaining revolution?

This icon will direct you to additional materials on the website: www.cengage.com/history/noble/westciv6e.

See our interactive eBook for map and primary source activities.

RESTORATION AND REACTION, 1814–1830

What were the goals of the Restoration, and the sources of resistance to it?

By the end of the French Revolution and Napoleonic wars, the ruling elite believed that the upheavals of the previous twenty-five years had proved that human beings could not rely on reason, on man-made constitutions, or on laws to govern themselves. They therefore sought to restore the order of the past by redrawing territorial boundaries to establish a balance of power among the Great Powers, and reinstating the traditional foundations of hierarchy that would assure stability: religion, monarchy, and aristocracy. But members of the middle and working classes, especially in cities, resisted the effort to turn the clock back.

The Congress of Vienna, 1814–1815

Congress of Vienna
Conference called by the Great Powers after Napoleon's defeat. They sought long-term stability as they drew new territorial boundaries and restored some of the rulers who had been overthrown.

The defeat of Napoleon put an end to French dominance in Europe. In September 1814, the victorious Great Powers—Austria, Great Britain, Prussia, and Russia—convened an international conference, the **Congress of Vienna**, to negotiate the terms of peace. The victors sought to draw territorial boundaries advantageous to themselves and to provide long-term stability on the European continent. Having faced a powerful France, which had mobilized popular forces with revolutionary principles, the victors decided to erect an international system that would remove such threats. Following principles of "legitimacy and compensation," they redrew the map of Europe (see **MAP 21.1**). Rulers who had been overthrown were restored to their thrones. The eldest surviving brother of Louis XVI of France became King Louis XVIII. In Spain, Ferdinand VII was restored to the throne from which Napoleon had toppled him and his father. The restoration, however, was not as complete as its proponents claimed. After the French Revolution, certain new realities had to be recognized. For example, Napoleon had consolidated the German and Italian states; the process was acknowledged in the former with the creation of a loose German Confederation. In Italy, the number of independent states had shrunk to nine. Also, unlike earlier French kings, Louis XVIII could not rule as an absolute monarch after a generation without one.

Negotiations at the Congress of Vienna strengthened the territories bordering France, enlarged Prussia and created the kingdom of Piedmont-Sardinia, joined Belgium to Holland, and provided the victors with spoils and compensation for territories bartered away. Austria received Venetia and Lombardy in northern Italy to strengthen its position and to redress the loss of Belgium (to the Netherlands) and parts of Poland (to Russia). Prussia was allowed to annex part of Saxony, Posen, and the port city of Danzig in return for giving up parts of Poland. England acquired a number of colonies and naval out posts. Thus, with one hand, these conservative statesmen swore their loyalty to the prerevolutionary past, and with the other, they redrew national boundaries with no consideration for the inhabitants whose territories changed.

The leading personality at the Congress of Vienna was the Austrian foreign minister, Prince Clemens von Metternich (MEH-ter-nick) (1773–1859). An aristocrat in exile from the Rhineland, which had been annexed by revolutionary France, he had gone into the service of the Habsburg Empire and risen to become its highest official. Personal charm, tact, and representation of a state that, for the time being, was satisfied with its territories made Metternich seem a disinterested statesman and enabled him to wield enormous influence on the congress's proceedings.

Because it was Napoleon's belligerent imperialism that had brought the powers together in Vienna, France was at first treated as an enemy at the conference. By the end, however, France was included as one of the five Great Powers jointly known as the "Concert of Europe." The Concert continued to function for nearly forty years, meeting and resolving international crises and preventing any major European war from breaking out. Underlying the states' cooperation was the principle of a common European destiny.

Restored Monarchs in Western Europe

The most dramatic restoration of the older order occurred in France. The restored Bourbons turned the clock back, not to 1789 but closer to 1791, when the country had briefly enjoyed a constitutional monarchy. Moreover, it maintained the Napoleonic Code with its provisions of legal equality.

The Bourbon constitution provided for a parliament with an elected lower house, the Chamber of Deputies, and an appointed upper house, the Chamber of Peers. Although suffrage to the Chamber of Deputies was limited to a small elite of men with landed property—only 100,000 voters, about 0.2 percent of the population—this constitution was a concession to representative government that had not existed in the Old Regime (see page 534). Louis XVIII (r. 1814–1824) stands out among European rulers because he realized that it would be necessary to compromise on the principles of popular sovereignty proclaimed by the French Revolution.

Compared with the rest of Europe, Great Britain enjoyed considerable constitutional guarantees and a parliamentary regime. Social unrest beset Britain as it faced serious economic dislocation with the arrival of peace in 1815. The sudden drop in government expenditures, the return into the economy of several hundred thousand war veterans, financial disarray, and plummeting prices caused disruption for the poor and the middle classes. They were especially incensed over the clear economic advantages that the landed classes, who dominated Parliament, had secured for themselves. In 1815, the Parliament passed legislation—known as the **Corn Laws**—that imposed high tariffs on various forms of imported grain. These laws shielded landowning grain producers from international competition and allowed them to reap huge profits at the expense of consumers.

All these issues caused various forms of protest. Workers and the urban middle classes found their government retrograde and repressive. Traumatized by the French Revolution, the ruling class clung to the past, certain that advocates for change were Jacobins in disguise wishing to foment revolution.

In August 1819, sixty thousand people gathered in St. Peter's Fields in Manchester to demand universal suffrage for men and women alike, an annual Parliament, and other democratic reforms. The crowd was peaceful and unarmed, yet mounted soldiers charged, killing eleven and wounding four hundred. The use of military force against the peaceful demonstrators as if they were the French at Waterloo shocked and outraged the British public, and they branded the confrontation "the Peterloo Massacre." Parliament responded by passing the so-called Six Acts, which outlawed freedom of assembly and effectively imposed censorship. Through much of the 1820s, Britain appeared resistant to reform.

CHRONOLOGY

1808	Beethoven, *Pastoral* Symphony
1814–1815	Congress of Vienna
1819	Peterloo Massacre
	Carlsbad Decrees
1821	Spanish revolt
	Greek Revolution
1821–1825	Spanish colonies in the Americas win independence
1823	Monroe Doctrine
1824	Owen establishes New Harmony
1825	Decembrists in Russia
1830	July Revolution in France
	Ottoman Empire recognizes Serbian autonomy
1832	Great Reform Bill in Britain
1833	Abolition of slavery in British colonies
1834	Turner, *Fire at Sea*
1838	"People's charter" in Great Britain
1839	Anti-Corn Law League
1845–1848	Hungry '40s
1848	Marx and Engels, *Communist Manifesto*
	Revolutions of 1848

Corn Laws Laws passed by the British Parliament in 1815 that placed tariffs on imported foreign grains to protect domestic grain producers from international competition.

Eastern Europe

Having seen the turmoil unleashed by the French Revolution and having suffered at the hands of Napoleon's Grande Armée, the states of central and eastern Europe were particularly committed to maintaining absolute government. The Austrian Empire's far-flung territories seemed to its Habsburg rulers to require a firm hand (see **MAP 21.1**); they could countenance no challenge or threat to their imperial power in the wake of French revolutionary rhetoric about liberty. Nor, in this multinational empire, could rulers tolerate a sense of national identity provoked by the Napoleonic wars. The emperor, Francis I (r. 1792–1835), clung to his motto, "Rule and change nothing." Prince Metternich, Francis's chief minister and key figure in the "Concert of Europe" from 1815, viewed the French Revolution of 1789 as a disaster and believed his task was to hold the line against the threat of revolution. Quick to interpret protests or the desire for change as a threat to the fundamental order, Metternich established a network of secret police and informers to spy on the imperial subjects and keep them in check.

🌐 **MAP 21.1—Europe in 1815**

Intent on regaining the security and stability of prerevolutionary years, the Great Powers redrew the map of Europe at the Congress of Vienna.

In most of the German states, the political order was similarly authoritarian and inflexible. The states of Baden, Württemberg, and Bavaria had granted their subjects constitutions, although effective power remained in the hands of the ruling houses. Prussia was ruled by an alliance of the king and the *Junkers* (YUNG-kurz), the landowning aristocrats who staffed the officer corps and the bureaucracy. Their administrative efficiency earned widespread admiration in Europe. But throughout the German states, the urban middle classes, intellectuals, journalists, university professors, and students were frustrated with the existing system. They were disappointed by the lack of free institutions and the failure of the patriotic wars against Napoleon to create a united Germany. University students formed *Burschenschaften* (BOOR-shen-shaft-en), or brotherhoods, whose slogan was "Honor, Liberty, Fatherland." Metternich reacted swiftly in July 1819 with the Carlsbad Decrees; these decrees established close supervision over the universities, censorship of the press, and dissolution of the youth groups. Wholesale persecution of people who advocated representative government or nationalistic ideas followed. The Prussian king dismissed his more enlightened officials.

Italy, by the end of Napoleon's reign, consisted of nine political states; the consolidation of states and the influence of Napoleonic rule had begun to inspire among some Italians a notion of national identity. At the same time, Austria exercised considerable power over Italy through its possession, from the Congress of Vienna, of its northern territories, Lombardy and Venetia. Austria also had dynastic ties to several ruling houses in the central part of the peninsula, and had political alliances with the papacy. The only ruling house free of Austrian ties—and hence, eventually looked to by nationalists as a possible rallying point for the independence of the peninsula—was the Savoy dynasty of Piedmont-Sardinia. But it was in Austria's interest to maintain disunity.

By far the most autocratic of the European states was tsarist Russia. Alexander I (r. 1801–1825) was an enigmatic character who puzzled his contemporaries. His domestic policy vacillated between liberalism and reaction; his foreign policy wavered between brutal power politics and apparently selfless idealism. When the Congress of Vienna gave additional Polish lands to the tsar, establishing the kingdom of Poland, he demonstrated his liberalism to the world (and curried favor with his new subjects) by granting Poland a liberal constitution. But he offered no such constitution to his own people. Within a few years, moreover, he violated the same Polish constitution he had approved, by refusing

Metternich   A consummate statesman and aristocrat, the Austrian prince Metternich tried to quell revolution at home and abroad. Some called his era the Metternichean age. (Réunion des Musées Nationaux/Art Resource, NY)

"Peterloo" Massacre   In August 1819 at St. Peter's Fields in Manchester, England, a crowd demanding parliamentary reform was charged by government troops, leading to bloodshed.   (The National Archives, Public Record Office)

to call the Diet into session. His planned efforts to abolish serfdom between 1803 and 1812 also failed. As much as he desired freedom for serfs, he was unwilling to impose the necessary policies toward that end because they would be detrimental to the interests and privileges of the landed gentry.

Toward the end of his rule, Alexander became increasingly authoritarian and repressive, probably in response to growing opposition. Myriad groups—Russian military officers who had served in western Europe, Russian Freemasons who had corresponded with Masonic lodges in western Europe, and Russian intellectuals who read Western liberal political tracts—had warmed to the ideals of individual freedom and constitutionalism. These groups formed secret societies with varying agendas. Some envisioned Russia as a republic, others as a constitutional monarchy, but all shared a commitment to the abolition of serfdom and the establishment of a freer society.

Alexander died in December 1825, without designating which of his brothers would succeed him. Taking advantage of the confusion, the military conspirators declared in favor of the older brother, Constantine, in the belief that he favored a constitutional government. The younger brother, Nicholas, claimed to be the legal heir. The St. Petersburg garrison, whose officers believed that the military could bring about change on its own, rallied to the conspirators' cause.

The "Decembrist uprising," as it is known, quickly failed. The military revolt in the Russian capital was badly coordinated with uprisings planned in the countryside, and Nicholas moved quickly to crush the rebellion. He had the leaders, called the **Decembrists**, executed, sent to Siberia, or exiled. In spite of its tragic end, throughout the nineteenth century, the Decembrist uprising served as an inspiration to Russians resisting tsarist oppression.

Decembrists Group of Russian military officers, later viewed as martyrs, who led the unsuccessful December 1825 rebellion seeking to install a constitutional monarchy.

Spain and Its Colonies

Spain, under the Napoleonic occupation, had in 1812 elected a national parliament, the Cortes. It issued a democratic constitution that provided for universal manhood suffrage and a unicameral legislature with control over government policy. Supporters and admirers of the constitution in Spain were known as "friends of liberty," and the term *liberal* was coined. But in 1814, Ferdinand VII (r. 1808, 1814–1833), the Bourbon king of Spain whom Napoleon had ousted, returned to power. Though he promised to respect the liberal 1812 constitution, Ferdinand believed in the divine right of kings and was hostile to the new order. With support from the aristocracy and from segments of the general population still loyal to the call of throne and altar, Ferdinand had liberals arrested or driven into exile.

Ferdinand's plan to restore Spain to its earlier prominence included a reassertion of control over its American colonies. The Spanish dominions had grown restless in the eighteenth century, for they had witnessed the advent of an independent United States and the French occupation of Spain itself. Spain's emboldened colonies had refused to recognize the Napoleonic regime in Madrid and became increasingly self-reliant. Their attitude did not change when French control of Spain ended. Ferdinand refused to compromise with the overseas territories. Instead, he gathered an army to subdue them. Some liberal junior officers, declaring the army's loyalty to the constitution of 1812, won support from the rank and file, who balked at going overseas. This military mutiny coincided with a sympathetic provincial uprising to produce the "revolution of 1820," the first major assault on the European order established in 1815 at the Congress of Vienna. Ferdinand appealed to the European powers for help. France intervened on his behalf and crushed the uprising.

Ferdinand restored his reactionary regime but could not regain Spain's American colonies. The British, sympathetic to the cause of Latin American independence and eager for commercial access to the region, opposed reconquest, and their naval dominance of the seas kept Spain in its place. By 1825, all of Spain's colonies on the mainland in Central and South America had won their freedom.

SECTION SUMMARY

- At the Congress of Vienna (1814–1815), Austria, Great Britain, Prussia, and Russia, having defeated Napoleon, redrew territorial boundaries for their own advantage and restored previous rulers to create stability.

- Western Europe had constitutional monarchies, though they faced a variety of social and political discontents.

- Eastern Europe remained committed to absolutist monarchies that took measures to repress any protest or revival of revolutionary thinking.

- Spain returned to absolute monarchy, exiling liberals, but lost its American colonies.

IDEOLOGICAL CONFRONTATIONS

What major ideologies developed in the first half of the nineteenth century?

The conservative order established in 1815 was inspired by the desire of rulers to return to the past. But the appeal of Enlightenment ideals never faded completely, nor did the promises of revolutionary reform. Those who challenged the restored order did so through a number of ideologies responding to the economic and political turmoil of the era.

Conservatism

The architects of the restoration justified their policies with doctrines based on the ideology of **conservatism**, emphasizing the need to preserve the existing order of monarchies, aristocracy, and an established church. As a coherent movement, conservatism sprang up during and after the French Revolution to resist the forces of change. Before the American and French Revolutions, the existing political institutions appeared to be permanent. When the old order faced serious challenges in the late eighteenth and early nineteenth centuries, conservatism emerged as an ideology justifying traditional authority.

Edmund Burke (1729–1797), a British statesman and political theorist, launched one of the first intellectual assaults on the French Revolution. The revolutionary National Assembly had asserted that ancient prerogatives were superseded by the rights of man and principles of human equality based on appeals to natural law. In *Reflections on the Revolution in France* (1790), Burke countered that such claims were abstract and dangerous and that the belief in human equality undermined the social order. Government should be anchored in tradition, he argued. The very longevity of Old Regime institutions proved their usefulness, and they should be preserved. Burke's writings were widely read and influential on the Continent.

Reaction against the French Revolution also inspired a moral and religious conservatism. One of the most popular authors of this new morality was Hannah More (1745–1833), who saw piety as a rampart against rebellion. In a series of pamphlets titled *Cheap Repository Tracts*, she advocated the acceptance of the existing order and the solace of religious faith. Costing but a penny, the moral tracts were often handed out by the rich together with alms or food to the poor. More was the first writer in history to sell over a million copies; within three years, her sales doubled. Conservative values thus spread to a very large audience in both Britain and the United States, where one of her works appeared in thirty editions.

A more extreme version of conservatism was the counterrevolutionary or "ultraroyalist" ideology. Unlike Burke, who was willing to tolerate some change, counterrevolutionaries wanted to restore society to its prerevolutionary condition. The most extreme counterrevolutionaries were those who personally experienced the revolutionary upheavals. Count Joseph de Maistre (MESS-treh) (1753–1821), a nobleman whose estates were occupied by the invading French, described monarchy as a God-given form of government in his *Considerations on France* (1796). Any attempt to abolish or even limit it was a violation of divine law. According to de Maistre and his fellow reactionaries, only the authority of church and state could prevent human beings from falling into evil ways. De Maistre advocated stern government control, including the generous use of the death penalty, to keep people loyal to throne and altar.

Conservative ideas were not limited to intellectual circles; at times they had mass appeal, even for the peasantry. Especially in bourgeois and aristocratic circles, conservatism extended to private life, and placed priority on family stability, with a strict separation of gender roles and a strong sense of patriarchy, in which the husband and father held exclusive authority. Conservatism was also influenced by **romanticism**, with its glorification of the past, taste for pageantry, and belief in the organic unity of society.

Romanticism

The romantic movement emerged in the 1760s as a rebellion against the rationalist values of the Enlightenment, and persisted until the 1840s. Primarily an expression of the arts, it included writers, painters, and composers. In contrast to the philosophes and their emphasis on reason (see

conservatism Ideology underlying the order established in Europe in 1815, which afterward emphasized support for the existing order of monarchy, aristocracy, and an established church.

romanticism Cultural movement, prevalent from the 1760s to 1840s, that rebelled against rationalism and its Enlightenment values and prized sentiment.

Lord Byron in Albanian Costume The British romantic poet had himself painted in exotic garb. Romantics were attracted to what were believed to be the mysteries of the East, representing a truer, more authentic existence. (National Portrait Gallery, London)

Chapter 18), the romantics praised emotion and feeling. German writer Johann Wolfgang von Goethe (GOE-teh) (1749–1832), who declared, "Feeling is everything," offers a famous and influential example of this movement. His *Sorrows of Young Werther* (1774), the most widely read book of the era—Napoleon had a copy by his bedside—depicted the passions of the hero, who, depressed over unrequited love, kills himself. Many young men dressed in "Werther clothes"—tight black pants, long blue jacket, and buff yellow leather vest—which typified the clothing of tradesmen and provided a visual protest by young intellectuals against the frivolous dress of the upper classes. In some cases, they emulated the tragic hero by committing suicide.

Goethe and other writers exalted mythical figures as embodiments of human energy, passion, and heroism. In the dramatic poem, *Faust*, Goethe retold the legend of a man who sells his soul to the Devil in exchange for worldly success. In the poetic drama, *Prometheus Unbound*, the English romantic poet Percy Bysshe Shelley (1792–1822) took up a similar theme in celebrating Prometheus, who, according to Greek mythology, stole fire from the gods and gave it to human beings. In much the same spirit, many romantics lionized Napoleon for his military feats and ability to overthrow kings and states.

Many romantics drew their inspiration from nature. In contrast to the Enlightenment, whose philosophers and scientists had studied nature for the principles it could impart, the romantics worshiped its inherent beauty and formidable power. The German composer Ludwig van Beethoven (1770–1827) wrote his *Pastoral* Symphony in praise of idyllic nature, depicting the passions one might feel in contemplating its loveliness and serenity. The English poets William Wordsworth (1770–1850) and Samuel Taylor Coleridge (1772–1834) treated untamed wilderness as a particular subject of wonder. Fellow Englishman Joseph Mallord William Turner (1775–1851) displayed the raw passions of the sea. Before painting *Snowstorm: Steamboat off a Harbour's Mouth* (1842), Turner is said to have tied himself to a ship's mast and braved a snowstorm for four hours.

Disillusionment with the French Revolution inspired many romantics to rediscover religion as an authentic source of emotion, a sensibility in accord with the revival of popular religion in regions throughout Europe. For example, the German states experienced a revival of pietism, which stressed the personal relationship between the individual and God, unimpeded by theological formalities or religious authorities. The influence of pietism, with its emphasis on spirituality and emotion, spread throughout central Europe in schools and churches.

In England, religious emotion expressed itself in Methodism. Founded in the 1730s by the English preacher John Wesley (1703–1791), this popular movement emphasized salvation by a faith made active in one's life, a method of living. Appealing especially to the poor and desperate, Methodism, by the 1790s, had gained seventy thousand members; within a generation its flock quadrupled.

Romantics also celebrated the medieval past; artists painted images of Gothic ruins and buildings, while architects replicated its style in both private and public buildings. Writers, such as Sir Walter Scott (1771–1832) in Scotland and Victor Hugo (U-go) (1802–1885), recaptured chivalry and the age of faith in such popular works as *Ivanhoe* (1819) and *The Hunchback of Notre Dame* (1831). Exotic places also had great appeal to romantics. Recently conquered Algeria in North Africa provided scenes for French painters. Senegal, in West Africa, which the French recovered from the British in 1815, offered the setting for Théodore Géricault's powerful *Raft of the "Medusa."* (See the feature, "The Visual Record: *Raft of the 'Medusa.'"*)

Romantics challenged the cultural order in a number of ways. Appeals to emotion and sentiment were congenial to audiences without elite educations, especially as a new interest developed in folklore and rustic life. Viennese-born Franz Schubert (1797–1828) composed over 600 songs that echo the simplicity of folk tunes, and Frédéric Chopin (1810–1849) composed works influenced by the peasant music of his native Poland. The performance of romantic music in masses, symphonies, operas, choral groups, and even gatherings among friends in private homes grew considerably in the first half of the nineteenth century. Its popularity helped support musicians, not just in their performances, but in providing private music lessons, especially at the piano, whose presence became increasingly common in middle-class homes.

Romantic culture also found expression in relations between the sexes. The influential French writer Amandine-Aurore Dupin (1804–1876), better known by her pen name, George Sand (SAN), spoke for the emancipation of women from the oppressive supervision of their husbands, fathers, and brothers. In her personal life, Sand practiced the freedom she preached, dressing like a man, smoking cigars, and openly pursuing affairs with a number of well-known artists. But her many literary works also expressed her hopes for spiritual and political renewal, bearing the romantic era's utopian aspirations.

After the French Revolution, nobles and monarchs ceased sponsoring art on a grand scale and were expected to conduct their lives soberly. Cut off from royal patronage, artists had to depend on members of the new middle classes to buy paintings and books and attend plays and musical performances. Forced to live marginally, they cultivated the image of the artist as unconventional. In their lifestyles and their work, they deliberately rejected the norms of society. The romantic period gave rise to the notion of the starving genius, alienated from society and loyal only to his all-consuming art. Born of conservative reaction against the Enlightenment and French Revolution, romanticism also embodied the modern notions of liberty and appealed to an emerging sense of national identity. Romantics of many stripes declared their determination to overthrow the smug present and create a new world. Victor Hugo called for "no more rules, no more models" to constrain the human imagination. Romantic painters and musicians consciously turned their backs on the classical tradition in both subject matter and style. The English poet George Gordon, Lord Byron (1788–1824), declared war on kings, on established religion, and on the international order. A nationalist as well as a romantic, he died while fighting for the independence of Greece.

Nationalism

The ideology of nationalism emerged in, and partly shaped, this era. **Nationalism** is the belief that people derive their identity from their nation and owe it their primary loyalty. A list of criteria for nationhood is likely to include a common language, religion, and political authority, as well as common traditions and shared historical experiences.

In an era that saw the undermining of traditional religious values, nationalism offered a new locus of faith. To people who experienced the social turmoil brought about by the erosion of the old order, nationalism held out the promise of a new community. Nationalism became an ideal espoused as strongly as, and often in conjunction with, religion. The Italian nationalist Giuseppe Mazzini (mat-SEE-nee) (1805–1872) declared that nationalism was "a faith and mission" ordained by God. The Polish romantic poet and nationalist Adam Mickiewicz (MISS-kyev-ich) (1798–1855) compared perpetually carved-up Poland to the crucified Christ. The religious-like fervor of nationalism helps explain its widespread appeal.

The earliest manifestation of nationalism was cultural, originating in Rousseau's concept of the "general will" constituting the sovereign nation, greater than the sum of its parts. Johann Gottfried Herder (1744–1833), Rousseau's German disciple, elaborated on his mentor's ideas, declaring that every people has a "national spirit." To explore the unique nature of this spirit, intellectuals all over Europe began collecting local folk poems, songs, and tales, a trend also inspired by romanticism. In an effort to document the spirit of the German people, the Grimm brothers, Jacob (1785–1863) and Wilhelm (1786–1859), compiled fairy tales and published them between 1812 and 1818; among the better known are "Little Red Riding Hood" and "Snow White."

Political nationalism was born in the era of the French Revolution. French aristocrats resisted taxation by claiming that they embodied the rights of "the nation" and could not be taxed without its consent, which in turn gave the concept a currency that spread across all social classes. When revolutionary France was attacked by neighboring countries, which were ruled by kings and dukes, the Legislative Assembly called on the French people to rise and save the nation. The kingdom of France had become a nation of citizens who had a stake in its destiny. German and Italian intellectuals, in reaction to the French threat, developed a nationalist spirit. German philosopher Johann Gottlieb Fichte (FISH-te) (1762–1814), in a series of *Addresses to the German Nation* after the Prussian defeat at Jena, called on all Germans to stand firm against Napoleon. Germans, he claimed, were endowed with a special genius that had to be safeguarded

nationalism Belief that people derive their identity from their nation and owe it their primary loyalty. The criteria for nationhood typically included a common language, religion, and political authority, as well as common traditions and shared historical experiences.

Raft of the "Medusa"

In September 1816, the French were shocked at the news of the disaster that had befallen the government ship Méduse (Medusa) as it headed for Senegal in West Africa the previous July. Including the ship's crew, 400 passengers had boarded the vessel.

The captain of the ship was a nobleman, Duroys de Chaumareys (du-RWAH duh sho-mah-RAY), whom the restoration government had appointed solely on the basis of his family and political connections. Inexperienced as a seaman, the captain clumsily ran his ship aground on the Mauritanian coast, off West Africa, on July 2. The *Medusa* had only 6 lifeboats, capable of carrying a total of 250 people. For the rest of the passengers, a raft was rigged with planks, beams, and ropes. The captain and his officers forcibly took over the lifeboats, abandoning 150 passengers to the less secure raft. With no navigational tools and insufficient food and water, the passengers of the raft were left to the mercy of stormy seas and a brutal sun. Anger at officers for having abandoned them led seamen on the raft to murder some of their superiors. By the third day, driven by thirst and hunger, some passengers ate their dead companions—killed by exposure or drowned by huge waves. On the sixth day, the strongest among the survivors, fearing that their rations were dwindling, banded together and murdered the weaker ones. On the thirteenth day, the French frigate *Argus* spotted the raft and rescued 15 survivors. Five died soon after, leaving only 10 survivors out of the raft's original 150 passengers.

Although the government tried to suppress information about the event, the French press exposed the incompetence and cowardice of Captain de Chaumareys—reflecting the bad judgment of the Bourbon regime that had appointed him on the basis of his family status rather than experience. The selfish act of the captain and his fellow officers further suggested the narrow class interest of the restoration government, which favored aristocracy at the cost of the common people.

The French painter Théodore Géricault (1791–1824) befriended the ship's surgeon, Henri Savigny, one of the lucky ten who survived. Savigny provided Géricault (jair-ih-KO) with a direct eyewitness account of the event. The painter shared Savigny's sense of outrage against the government for having appointed the incompetent captain and for having treated the survivors callously. (At one point, the government arrested Savigny for publicizing the tragedy.) The light prison sentence imposed on the captain was another source of grievance.

The 1819 French government salon exposition of art was intended to be larger and more glorious than any previous one. Among its paintings was Géricault's huge canvas—the largest in that year's exposition—measuring 16 feet high by 24 feet wide and innocently titled "Scene of Shipwreck." The regime had wanted to gain glory for itself by exhibiting this impressive artwork without exposing the true subject. But the stratagem failed; everyone recognized the painting to be the *Raft of the "Medusa"* and an attack on the Bourbon regime.

The painting reproduced here depicts the moment the survivors spotted the frigate *Argus*, barely visible on the horizon. Notice the figure of an African standing at the fore of the raft, waving a red and white cloth to attract the ship's attention. The hope he symbolizes represents an attack on the slave trade, in which France was still engaged. The artist implicitly criticized the restoration regime for sanctioning commerce in humans. Just as the *Argus* is coming to the rescue of the shipwrecked, the painting appears to suggest, so Africans will see the day when their enslavement will be ended.

Historians often regard the *Raft of the "Medusa"* as the most important painting of French romanticism, and it includes nearly all the major themes of the movement. By locating the scene off the coast of Africa, Géricault incorporated an element of exoticism. Nature—cruel and unforgiving—is central to the scene, reflected in the turbulent sea, dark clouds, and imperiled raft. The canvas includes an extraordinary range of passions. Observe, for example, the inconsolable grief of the figure at the bottom left, a father cradling the dead body of his son. Other figures express despair and terror, and still others limitless hope. The painting evokes the dark passions lurking in the human heart. Although it does not show the scenes of insanity, murder, and cannibalism that the survivors had witnessed, they undoubtedly came to the minds of the viewers, who were familiar with the tragic events. The painting is a powerful

for the well-being of all humankind. Similarly, in reaction to French incursions, Italian writer Vittorio Alfieri (1749–1803) insisted that Italians, as the descendants and heirs of ancient Rome, should be the ones to lead the peoples of Europe.

For the most part, however, after the French Revolution and the Napoleonic era, early-nineteenth-century nationalism was generous and cosmopolitan in its outlook. Many nationalists in the 1830s and 1840s were committed to the ideal of a "Europe of free peoples." Victor Hugo even envisioned a "European republic" with its own parliament.

It is important to remember, however, that although many intellectuals found nationalism attractive, in the first half of the nineteenth century most people felt stronger local and regional affinities than national identities. Only after several decades of propaganda by nationalists and governments did Europeans begin to imagine themselves as part of a national rather than local community, and only then could they think of dying for their nations.

Géricault: Raft of the "Medusa"   (Erich Lessing/Art Resource, NY)

indictment of Enlightenment faith in humans as creatures of reason and balance.

Romantic artists wanted to engage the passions of those viewing, reading, or hearing their works. The *Raft of the "Medusa"* purposely stages the events in the foreground in order to pull viewers into the picture and make them participants in the drama. They thus share in the alternating feelings of terror and hope that swept the raft.

The fate of the painting and the artist followed a romantic script. When Géricault started the painting, he intended it as an indictment of the restoration government. He poured energy into it in an effort to take his mind off a disastrous love affair. As his work proceeded, he came to see the painting as an allegory of larger human passions and concerns. Yet when it was displayed, much to his disappointment, the painting was understood mainly in political terms. Disillusioned by this reaction, Géricault thereafter painted no major works.

He grew sickly, rarely bestirred himself, and died of bone tuberculosis in 1824 at age 33. He illustrates the romantics' view of a heroic life—the genius who performs a major feat and then dies young, before realizing his potential. To the romantics, human intent and effort often appeared thwarted by larger forces. This painting, originally meant to criticize the regime, was purchased after Géricault's death by the restoration government and hung in France's national museum, the Louvre.

QUESTIONS

1. What elements in the subject matter and style of this painting typify romanticism?

2. Why was this painting seen as a brutal critique of the French restoration government? What had been the artist's intent?

Liberalism

Liberalism was a direct descendant of the Enlightenment's critique of eighteenth-century absolutism. It is important not to confuse its original meaning with left-wing connotations "liberalism" has come to represent in the twenty-first century. Nineteenth-century liberals, like modern western "conservatives," believed that individual freedom was best safeguarded by reducing government powers to a minimum. They wanted to impose constitutional limits on government, to establish the rule of law, to sweep away all restrictions on individual enterprise—specifically, state regulation of the economy—and to ensure a voice in government for men of property and education. Liberalism was influenced by romanticism, with its emphasis on individual freedom and the imperative of the human personality to develop to its full potential. Liberalism was also affected by

liberalism Nineteenth-century economic and political theory that called for reducing government powers to a minimum. Liberals sought to eliminate state regulation of the economy and ensure a voice in government for men of property and education.

nationalism, especially in multinational autocratic states, such as Austria, Russia, and the Ottoman Empire, in which free institutions could be established only if political independence were wrested from, respectively, Vienna, St. Petersburg, and Constantinople. (Nationalism challenged the established order in the first half of the century, but in the second half, conservatives were to use nationalism as a means to stabilize their rule.)

ECONOMIC LIBERALISM

Liberalism was both an economic and a political theory. In 1776, Adam Smith (1723–1790), the influential Scottish economist, published *An Inquiry into the Nature and Causes of the Wealth of Nations*. Smith advocated freeing national economies from the fetters of the state. Under the mercantilist system, prevalent throughout Europe until about 1800, the state regulated the prices and conditions of manufacture. Smith argued for letting the free forces of the marketplace shape economic decisions. He believed that economics was subject to basic unalterable laws of human behavior that could be discerned and applied in the same fashion as natural laws. Chief among them, in Smith's view, was the compatibility of economic self-interest and the general good. He argued that entrepreneurs who lower prices sell more products, thus increasing their own profits *and* providing the community with affordable wares. In this way, an individual's drive for profit benefits society as a whole. The economy is driven as if "by an invisible hand." This competitive drive for profits, Smith predicted, would expand the "wealth of nations." In France, advocates of nonintervention by government in the economy were called supporters of **laissez-faire** (meaning "to leave alone, to let run on its own").

laissez-faire French term meaning "to leave alone," to advocate freeing national economies from the fetters of the state and allowing supply and demand to shape the marketplace.

Smith and his disciples formed what came to be known as the school of classical economy, emphasizing the importance of laissez-faire. Smith had been relatively optimistic about the capacities of the free market. He warned, however, that the market tended to form monopolies, and he suggested that government intervene to prevent this occurrence. He also thought marketplace could not provide for all human needs; the government needed to supply education, road systems, and an equitable system of justice.

Those who followed Smith, and who witnessed the negative results of industrial capitalism, developed gloomier views. In 1798, Thomas Malthus (1766–1834) published *An Essay on the Principle of Population*, which suggested that the rate of population growth was much higher than the rate of food production. Unless people had fewer children, they would suffer starvation. By their failure to exercise sexual restraint, the poor, Malthus declared, "are themselves the cause of their own poverty." The laws of economics suggested to Malthus that factory owners could not improve their workers' lot by increasing wages or providing charity because higher living standards would lead to more births, which in turn would depress wages and bring greater misery. He therefore advocated abstinence (birth control was considered sinful and unnatural) and thought couples should marry only when they could afford to raise children. Malthus himself had twelve.

David Ricardo (1772–1823) made his fortune in the stock market, retired young, and wrote on economics; his best-known work was *Principles of Political Economy* (1817). Ricardo argued that the only way capitalists could make profits in a competitive market would be to pay the lowest wages possible. Like Malthus's theory of population, Ricardo's "iron law of wages" provided scientific justification for the exploitation of workers.

POLITICAL LIBERALISM

Political liberalism also represented the belief that government should refrain from regulating human affairs in order to preserve freedom. But eventually some proponents of laissez-faire changed their attitudes about the role of the government when they witnessed the alarming results of industrialization and rapid urban growth. Around midcentury, some liberals called on the state to intervene in areas of concern that would have been unthinkable a half century earlier. Jeremy Bentham (1748–1832) argued that the purpose of government is to provide "the greatest happiness of the greatest number" and that governments should be judged on that basis. Bentham and his disciples believed that the test of government is its usefulness; thus, his theory is known as **utilitarianism**.

utilitarianism Political theory of Jeremy Bentham, who argued that the purpose of government is to provide "the greatest happiness of the greatest number" and that the test of government is its usefulness.

John Stuart Mill (1806–1873), a disciple of Bentham and the leading British economic and political thinker at midcentury, initially voiced strong support for laissez-faire economics in his *Principles of Political Economy* (1848). In subsequent editions, however, he noted that the free market could not address every human need, and he argued that the state had an obligation to relieve human misery.

In his essay, *On Liberty* (1859), one of the fundamental documents of nineteenth-century liberalism, Mill argued for the free circulation of ideas—even false ideas. For in the free marketplace of ideas, false ideas will be defeated, and truth vindicated, in open debate. Mill also asserted that all members of society should have equal access to freedom. Influenced by his wife, Harriet Taylor Mill (1807–1856), he wrote in *On the Subjection of Women* (1861) that women should be permitted to vote and should have access to equal educational opportunities and the professions. Such equality not only would be just, but also would have the advantage of "doubling the mass of mental faculties available for the higher service of humanity." Mill, the foremost male proponent of women's rights in his generation, helped win a broader audience for the principle of equality between the sexes.

Despite Mill's influence, many liberals, especially in the early nineteenth century, feared the masses and therefore vigorously opposed democracy. They feared that the common people, uneducated and supposedly gullible, would easily be swayed by demagogues who might become despotic or who, in a desire to curry favor with the poor, might attack the privileges of the wealthy. The French liberal Benjamin Constant denounced democracy as "the vulgarization of despotism"; the vote, he declared, should be reserved for the affluent and educated. When less fortunate Frenchmen denounced the property requirements that prevented them from voting, the liberal statesman François Guizot (1787–1874) smugly replied, "Get rich."

Guizot's comment reflects attitudes associated with the bourgeoisie, a social class that came of age in the nineteenth century. The word *bourgeois* derives from *burgers*, a term that referred to a group of people who gained wealth and civic identity from urban occupations beginning in the twelfth and thirteenth centuries. This class fully developed in the nineteenth century. If unsympathetic to extending suffrage to the lower classes, the *bourgeoisie* championed liberalism because it justified its own right to participate in governance. Economic liberalism was also attractive to merchants and manufacturers, who wished to gather wealth without state interference. The basic tenets of liberalism—the belief in the sanctity of human rights, of the freedoms of speech and of association, and of the rule of law and equality before the law—eventually became widely accepted, even among conservatives and socialists who originally opposed them.

Socialism

A fundamental element in the pursuit of happiness, according to liberals, was the ability to accumulate property. Socialists, on the other hand, believed that the "social" ownership of property, unlike private ownership, would benefit society as a whole. The notion that human happiness can best be ensured by the common ownership of property had been suggested in earlier times by individuals as different as the Greek philosopher Plato (427?–347 B.C.) and Sir Thomas More (1478–1535), the English author *of Utopia*. In the 1820s, troubled by the harsh condition of the working classes, thinkers in Britain and France began to espouse new theories to address the social ills produced by industrial capitalism. During the first half of the nineteenth century, most workers were still artisans, even in industrializing England, where manufacturing was increasingly large scale. Only in a later era would **socialism** address the issues raised by industry.

socialism Nineteenth-century economic and social doctrine and political movement that advocated the "social" or state ownership of property in order to create a more just system.

EARLY SOCIALIST THINKERS

During the French Revolution, Gracchus Babeuf (GRAH-kus bah-BOEF) (1760–1797), a minor civil servant, participated in the Conspiracy of Equals (see page 547). He believed political equality was meaningless without economic equality. Babeuf advocated revolution to bring about a "communist" society—a society in which all property would be owned in common and private property would be abolished. Work would be provided for everyone; medical services and education would be free to all. Upon the discovery of his plot, Babeuf was guillotined, but his theories and his example of conspiratorial revolutionary action would influence later socialists.

Several other important French thinkers made contributions to European socialism. Henri de Saint-Simon (saen-see-MON) (1760–1825), a French aristocrat, emphasized the need "to ameliorate as promptly and as quickly as possible the moral and physical existence of the most numerous class," and believed the state should ensure the welfare of the masses. He argued, furthermore, that technical experts, rather than an elite derived from birth, should govern the state and formulate economic policies.

Another vital contribution to socialist thought came from thinkers who tried to imagine an ideal world. They were later derisively dismissed as builders of utopias, fantasy worlds (the Greek word *utopia* means "no place"). Their schemes varied, but they shared the view that property should be owned in common and used for the common good. They also believed that society should rest on principles of cooperation rather than on competitive individualism.

Karl Marx　Through his writings and agitation, Marx transformed the socialism of his day and created an ideology that gave new direction to the course of events in the nineteenth and twentieth centuries.　(Bettmann/Corbis)

One of the earliest and most notable utopians was mill owner Robert Owen (1771–1859). Beginning in 1800, he ran a prosperous cotton mill in New Lanark, Scotland. He also provided generously for his workers, guaranteeing them jobs and their children a decent education. In his writings, Owen suggested the establishment of self-governing communities owning the means of production. Essentials would be distributed to all members according to their needs. His ideas for the new society also included equal rights for women. Owen received little support from fellow manufacturers and political leaders, and his own attempt in 1824 to establish an ideal society in the United States at New Harmony, Indiana, ended in failure after four years.

Another influential contributor to early socialist theory was the Frenchman Charles Fourier (foor-YAY) (1772–1837). A clerk and salesman, Fourier wrote in great detail about his vision of the ideal future society. It would consist of cooperative organizations called "phalansteries," each with sixteen hundred inhabitants who would live in harmony with nature and with one another. Everyone would be assured gainful employment, which would be made enjoyable by rotating jobs. Because cooperative communes often faced the issue of who would carry out the distasteful tasks, everyone would share the pleasant *and* unpleasant work.

Fourier had an important female following because of his belief in the equality of the sexes, and some of these women tried to put his ideas into action. In Belgium, the activist Zoé Gatti de Gamond (1806–1854) cofounded a phalanstery for women. She believed that if women could be assured of economic well-being, other rights would follow. Also inspired by Fourier, Flora Tristan (1801–1844) was an effective advocate for workers' rights. Her book, *Union Ouvrière (Workers' Union)*, suggested that all workers should contribute funds to establish a "Workers' Palace" in every town, where the sick and disabled would have shelter, and the workers' children could receive a free education. Crossing France on foot, she spread the word of workers' solidarity and self-help.

Socialism encompassed a variety of approaches. The French journalist Louis Blanc (BLAHN) (1811–1882) thought that by securing the vote, the common people could win control over the state and require it to serve their needs. Once in control of the state by the ballot, they in turn would establish "social workshops" in which the workers would be responsible for production and for supervision of business matters. Society should be established according to the maxim, "Let each produce according to his aptitudes and strength; let each consume according to his need." Blanc's contemporary Louis Blanqui (1805–1882) suggested a more violent mode of action. He advocated seizure of the state by a small, dedicated band of men who would establish equality for all through communism. His ideas strengthened the notion of class warfare.

MARXISM

Karl Marx (1818–1883) was the most important socialist of the nineteenth century. The son of a lawyer, he grew up in the Rhineland, an industrializing area of western Germany that was particularly open to political ideas and agitation. After his education in philosophy at the University of Berlin, he edited a newspaper that spoke out for freedom and democracy in Germany. Marx's radical journalism caused him to be exiled from the Rhineland. After living briefly in Paris, then Brussels, he settled in London in 1849. There he lived for the rest of his life, dedicated to establishing his ideas on what he viewed as scientific bases.

Along with many of his contemporaries, Marx believed that human history has a direction and a goal. In his mind, it was the abolition of capitalism, the victory of the proletariat, the disappearance of the state, and the ultimate liberation of all humankind. He insisted that material conditions, rather than ideas, govern the world. According to him, the process of history was grounded on the notion of "dialectical materialism," in which the inequality of conditions existing in any economic order—such as feudalism or capitalism—would inevitably engender opposition that would create a new order based on a new set of economic relationships, which would, in turn, create opposition. The dialectical process would continue until economic equality and freedom were established.

Marx grouped human beings into classes based on their relationship to the means of production. The prevailing economic system in western Europe in his time was industrial capitalism. Capitalists constituted a class because they owned the means of production. Workers—the proletariat—were a separate class because they did not own any of the means of production, nor would they ever be able to because the "iron law of wages" would keep them perpetually impoverished. Because these two classes had different relationships to the means of production, they had different—in fact, antagonistic—interests and were destined (Marx believed) to engage in a class struggle.

Some of Marx's contemporaries lamented the increasing hostility between workers and capitalists. Marx, however, saw the conflict as necessary to advance human history, and he sought to validate his thesis by studying the past. In the Middle Ages, he pointed out, the feudal class dominated society but eventually lost the struggle to the commercial classes. Now, in turn, the capitalists were destined to be defeated by the rising proletariat. Thus, industrial capitalism, he argued, was a necessary, if painful, economic stage through which humankind had to traverse on its way to liberation.

In his study of history and economics, Marx found not only justification for, but irrefutable proof of, the "scientific" basis of his ideas. Capitalism was itself creating the forces that would supplant it. The large industrial plants necessitated an ever greater workforce with a growing sense of class interest. The inherently competitive nature of capitalism would inevitably drive an increasing number of enterprises out of business, and a form of monopoly capitalism would emerge, abusive of both consumers and workers. Ever more savage competition would force businesses to fail, creating widespread unemployment. Angered and frustrated by their lot, workers would overthrow the system that had abused them for so long: "The knell of private property has sounded. The expropriators will be expropriated." Workers would take power and, to solidify their rule, would temporarily exercise the "dictatorship of the proletariat." Once that had taken place, the state would wither away. With the coming to power of the proletariat, the history of class war would end and the ideal society would prevail. In the absences of classes and struggles between them, history would end.

Marx's study of economics and history proved to him that the coming of socialism was not only desirable, but inevitable. The laws of history dictated that capitalism, having created the rising proletariat, would collapse. By labeling his brand of socialism as scientific, Marx gave it the aura it needed to become the faith of millions of people. To declare ideas scientific in the nineteenth century, when science was held in such high esteem, was to ensure their popularity.

In 1848, Marx and Friedrich Engels (1820–1895) published the *Communist Manifesto*. A pamphlet written for the Communist League, a group of Germans living in exile, the Manifesto made an appeal to the working classes of the world. The league deliberately called itself "Communist" rather than "Socialist." Communism was a revolutionary program, bent on changing property relations by violence; socialism was associated with more peaceful means of transformation. The pamphlet laid out Marx's basic ideas. "The history of all hitherto existing society," he said, "is the history of class struggles." In this pamphlet, Marx and Engels called on the proletariat to rise—"You have nothing to lose but your chains"—and create a society that would end human exploitation. The idea of an international workers' movement contrasted with the dominant currents of capitalism and nationalism.

A number of political and polemical works flowed from Marx's pen, but most of them remained unpublished during his lifetime. The first volume of his major work, *Capital*, was published in 1867; subsequent volumes appeared posthumously. **Marxism**, the body of Marx's thought, is complex and sometimes contradictory, but certain basic concepts resound throughout and were embraced by Marx's followers.

Marxism The "scientific socialism" of Karl Marx and Friedrich Engels, which stated that the working class inevitably would rebel against the capitalist owners and build a communist society.

SECTION SUMMARY

- From 1815 to 1848, conservatism provided the ideological foundations for restored monarchies and social hierarchy; the ideologies of romanticism, nationalism, liberalism, and socialism challenged that order.

- Romanticism was based on feeling and passion rather than on reason; it inspired the arts, but also revived religion and challenged the existing political order through its influence on nationalism.

- Nationalism—the identification with one's nation based on shared language, culture, political authority, and historical past—began to emerge in the first half of the nineteenth century.

- The economic and political theory of liberalism originated with and justified middle-class interests and stressed individual freedoms.

- Socialist ideologies—"utopian" and "scientific"—emerged in response to the harsh conditions of the working classes and offered an alternative to capitalism.

THE QUEST FOR REFORM, 1830–1848

How did the restorations that followed the Napoleonic era give way to reform?

The new ideologies challenged the existing order, and by the 1830s, in western Europe, revolution and the threat of revolution helped dismantle the most reactionary features of the restored regimes. But in central and eastern Europe, from the German states to Russia and to most of the Ottoman Empire, the political systems established in 1815 would persist virtually unchanged until midcentury.

Revolution of 1830 and the July Monarchy in France

While the restored Bourbon monarch, Louis XVIII, had understood the need to incorporate some principles of popular sovereignty into his regime, his ultra-reactionary brother and successor, Charles X (r. 1824–1830), tried to reestablish an Old Regime type monarchy whose rule would be unrestricted by a constitution. He promoted the revival of Catholicism and its influence in education. The death penalty was even authorized as punishment for any desecration of the churches or religious icons. He also tried to suppress any opposition with strict press censorship.

More general disenchantment came with an economic downturn in 1827, marked by poor harvests and increased unemployment in the cities. Discontent brought to Parliament a liberal majority that refused to accept the reactionary ministers the king appointed. On July 26, 1830, after the humiliating defeat of his party at the polls, the king issued a set of decrees suspending freedom of the press, dissolving the Chamber of Deputies, and stiffening property qualifications for voters in subsequent elections. The king appeared to be engineering a coup against the existing political system.

The first to protest were the Parisian journalists and typesetters, directly threatened by the censorship laws. On July 28, others joined the protest and began erecting barricades across many streets. After killing several hundred protesters, the king's forces lost control of the city. This **July Revolution** drove the king into exile.

July Revolution Uprising in Paris in July 1830 that forced King Charles X to abdicate and signaled a victory for constitutional reform over an absolute monarchy.

Alarmed by the crowds' clamor for a republic, the liberal opposition—consisting of some of the leading newspaper editors and sympathetic deputies—quickly drafted the duke of Orléans, Louis Philippe (r. 1830–1848), known for his liberal opinions, to occupy the throne.

As a result of the 1830 revolution in Paris, a more liberal regime was installed in France. Louis Philippe proclaimed himself "King of the French" (rather than of France), thus acknowledging that he reigned at people's behest. Freedom of the press was reinstated. Suffrage was extended to 200,000 men, twice as many voters as before. The July Monarchy, named after the month in which it was established by revolution, justified itself by celebrating the great Revolution of 1789. On the site where the Bastille had been razed in 1789, the government erected a large column with the names of the victims of the July 1830 revolution, thus suggesting continuity between those who had fought tyranny in 1789 and 1830.

Identification with the Revolution appeared to legitimize the regime but also had the potential to subvert it. Fearful that the cult of revolution would encourage violence against the new monarchy, the regime censored artistic production, promoting only works that extolled the period from 1789 to 1791, when the revolutionaries had attempted to found a constitutional monarchy. Now that the revolution of 1830 had established a constitutional monarchy, the regime was suggesting, any further uprisings were illegitimate. If the July Monarchy turned out not to be as liberal as its founders had hoped, foreign visitors coming from more authoritarian societies were nonetheless impressed by France's apparently liberal institutions. (See the feature, "The Global Record: A Moroccan Describes French Freedom of the Press.") Many French liberals, however, saw the regime as a travesty of the hopes and promises it had represented on coming to power in 1830.

British Reforms

The major political problem facing Britain in the early nineteenth century was the composition of Parliament, which failed to reflect the dramatic population shifts that had occurred since the seventeenth century. Industrialization had transformed mere villages into major cities—Manchester, Birmingham, Leeds, Sheffield—but those cities had no representation in Parliament. Localities whose population had declined, however, were still represented. In districts known as "pocket boroughs," single individuals owned the right to a seat in Parliament. In districts known as "rotten boroughs," a handful of voters elected a representative. As exemplified in the causes and consequences of the "Peterloo Massacre" (see page 589), Parliament continued to represent only the interests of the traditional landed elite at the expense of the urban middle and working classes.

News of the July 1830 revolution in Paris made conservatives fear the same fate as Charles X and encouraged British liberals to push for reform. The government introduced a reform bill to abolish or reduce representation for sparsely populated areas, and grant seats for the populous and unrepresented cities. The bill also proposed lowering property qualifications for the vote, which would extend the franchise to some middle-class men. Following a prolonged, bitter political battle between the government and middle classes on one side and the aristocracy on the other, the House of Lords finally passed what came to be known as the **Great Reform Bill** of 1832.

The reform bill enfranchised only the upper layers of the male middle class, or one in seven adult men. Nonetheless, it demonstrated the willingness of the political leaders to acknowledge the increasing economic importance of manufacturing. Parliament became a more representative forum whose makeup better reflected the shift of economic power from agricultural landowners to the industrial and commercial classes. The bill passed as a result of nationwide agitation, evidence that Britain's political system could respond to grievances and bring about reform peacefully.

A series of colonial reforms also showed the British Parliament's willingness to adapt to changing circumstances. Opposition to slavery had been voiced since the 1780s. (See the feature, "The Written Record: A Plea to Abolish Slavery in the British Colonies.") Slavery, the very opposite of human freedom, was an affront to liberal principles. Moreover, its persistence threatened the empire—in 1831, sixty thousand slaves rebelled in the British colony of Jamaica. Parliament heeded the call for change and in 1833 abolished slavery throughout the British Empire.

The antislavery campaign led to the extension of British power into Africa. Britain used its navy—the largest in the world—to suppress the traffic in humans and hinder its colonial rivals from benefiting from the slave trade. Needing bases for these patrols, the British established a number of minor settlements in West Africa, and thereby became the predominant European power along the coast. These possessions foreshadowed the increasing European intrusion into African affairs.

In addition, the British began to review the imperial administration of their white settler colonies. In response to an 1837 Canadian uprising opposing British rule, self-government for Canada was promulgated in 1839 and 1841. Eventually, all the British colonies with a majority of white settlers were given similar rights of self-rule. The idea of self-government for nonwhites in the colonies was not yet imagined.

Parliament's reforming zeal, and most particularly the Reform Bill of 1832, set off a movement among those who had not been granted the right to vote. **Chartism** sought political democracy as a means for social change. In 1838, political radicals with working-class support drew up a "people's charter," a petition calling for universal male suffrage, electoral districts with equal population, salaries and the abolition of property qualifications for members of Parliament, the secret ballot, and annual general elections. The Chartists hoped that giving workers the vote would end the dominance of the much smaller upper classes in Parliament and ensure an improvement in the workers' lot.

Chartism won wide support among men and women in the working classes, sparking demonstrations and petition drives of unprecedented size—millions signed the petition. Women participated to a larger extent than in any other political movement of the day, founding over a hundred female Chartist chapters. Some Chartists, especially female members, asked for women's voting rights, but this demand failed to gain overall adherence from the membership. Winning mass support during particularly hard economic years, Chartism lost followers during a temporary economic upswing. The movement also fell under the sway of advocates of violence, who scared off many artisans and potential middle-class supporters. Chartism failed as a political movement; yet it drew public attention to an integrated democratic program whose main provisions (except for yearly elections) would be adopted piecemeal over the next half century.

In 1839, urban businessmen founded the Anti-Corn Law League for the purpose of abolishing the tariffs on foreign grain imports that kept food prices so high. The Corn Laws were

Great Reform Bill British law that broadened the franchise and provided parliamentary seats for new urban areas that had not previously been represented.

Chartism Nineteenth-century British political movement calling for universal male suffrage, electoral districts with equal population, salaries and the abolition of property qualifications for members of Parliament, the secret ballot, and annual general elections.

A Moroccan Describes French Freedom of the Press

In 1845–1846, a Moroccan diplomatic mission visited Paris. The ambassador's secretary, Muhammad as-Saffar (d. 1881), wrote an account of the visit. Impressed by many aspects of French society, he praises France's press in the following passage. The "Sultan" as-Saffar refers to is King Louis Philippe. To this Moroccan observer, the extent to which the French enjoyed constitutional government was striking.

The people of Paris, like all the French indeed, like all of [Europe] are eager to know the latest news and events that are taking place in other parts [of the world]. For this purpose they have the gazette. [In] these papers … they write all the news that has reached them that day about events in their own country and in other lands both near and far.

This is the way it is done. The owner of a newspaper dispatches his people to collect everything they see or hear in the way of important events or unusual happenings. Among the places where they collect the news are the two Chambers, the Great and the Small, where they come together to make their laws. When the members of the Chamber meet to deliberate, the men of the gazette sit nearby and write down everything that is said, for all debating and ratifying of laws is matter for the gazette and is known to everyone. No one can prevent them from doing this. …

… [I]f someone has an idea about a subject but he is not a member of the press, he may write about it in the gazette and make it known to others, so that the leaders of opinion learn about it. If the idea is worthy they may follow it, and if its author was out of favor it may bring him recognition.

No person in France is prohibited from expressing his opinion or from writing it and printing it, on condition that he does not violate the law. …

In the newspapers they write rejoinders to the men of the two Chambers about the laws they are making. If their Sultan demands gifts from the notables or goes against the law in any way, they write about that too, saying that he is a tyrant and in the wrong. He cannot confront them or cause them harm. Also, if someone behaves out of the ordinary, they write about that too, making it common knowledge among people of every rank. If his deeds were admirable, they praise and delight in him, lauding his example; but if he behaved badly, they revile him to discourage the like.

Moreover, if someone is being oppressed by another, they write about that too, so that everyone will know the story from both sides just as it happened, until it is decided in court. One can also read in it what their courts have decided.

QUESTIONS

1. Based on the diplomat's reaction to the French system, what can you deduce about freedom of the press and the expression of public opinion in Morocco?

2. Do you think this observer has a positive opinion of the French press? Why or why not?

Source: *Disorienting Encounters: Travels of a Moroccan Scholar in France in 1845–1846. The Voyage of Muhammad as-Saffar*, edited and translated by Susan Gilson Miller, © 1992 by the Regents of the University of California. Reprinted by permission of the publisher, the University of California Press.

unpopular with manufacturers, who knew that low food prices would allow them to pay low wages. It was also unpopular with workers, who wanted bread at a price they could afford. The anti-Corn Law movement proved more effective than Chartism because the middle classes supported it. Alarmed by the threat of famine after the poor harvest of 1845, Parliament repealed the Corn Laws in 1846.

The repeal of the Corn Laws was a milestone in British history, demonstrating the extent to which organized groups could bring about economic improvements. A popular, mass organization had been able to shape public policy—a far cry from the days of Peterloo, when the government had not only ignored the public but attacked it with bayonets fixed.

The Absolutist States of Central and Eastern Europe

In contrast to many parts of western Europe, which saw important political changes in the 1830s, the absolutist states in central and eastern Europe were able to preserve themselves essentially unchanged until 1848—and in some cases even beyond.

The king of Prussia had repeatedly promised a constitution, but none had materialized. A representative Diet would not meet there until 1847. Renewed nationalist agitation swept the German states in the 1840s. A mass outpouring of patriotic sentiment erupted in response to possible French ambitions on the Rhine during a diplomatic crisis in 1840. Two patriotic songs were penned: "The Watch on the Rhine" and *"Deutschland, Deutschland über alles"* ("Germany, Germany Above All"); the latter became Germany's national anthem half a century later. German

A Plea to Abolish Slavery in the British Colonies

Among the causes that British reformers embraced was the abolition of slavery. The slave trade had been abolished in 1807; one more step was left—ending in the colonies the institution of slavery itself. In this petition to Parliament in 1823, the Society for the Mitigation and Gradual Abolition of Slavery Throughout the British Dominions explains the harsh and degrading nature of the institution. Trading in slaves had been abolished as immoral and unnatural; here the petitioners remind Parliament that holding slaves is no less abhorrent. Under the pressure of this type of agitation, Parliament in 1833 abolished slavery in the British Empire.

In the colonies of Great Britain there are at this moment upwards of 800,000 human beings in a state of degrading personal slavery.

These unhappy persons, whether young or old, male or female, are the absolute property of their master, who may sell or transfer them at his pleasure, and who may also regulate according to his discretion (within certain limits) the measure of their labour, their food, and their punishment.

Many of the slaves are (and all may be) branded like cattle, by means of a hot iron, on the shoulder or other conspicuous part of the body, with the initials of their master's name; and thus bear about them in indelible characters the proof of their debased and servile state. . . .

It can hardly be alleged that any man can have a right to obtain his fellow creatures in a state so miserable and degrading as has been described. And the absence of such right will be still more apparent, if we consider how these slaves were originally obtained.

They, or their parents, were the victims of the Slave Trade. They were obtained, not by lawful means, or under any colourable pretext, but by the most undisguised rapine, and the most atrocious fraud. Torn from their homes and from every dear relation in life, barbarously manacled, driven like herds of cattle to the sea-shore, crowded into the potential holds of slave ships, they were transported to our colonies and there sold in bondage. . . .

The Government and Legislature of this country have on various occasions, and in the most solemn and unequivocal terms denounced the Slave Trade as immoral, inhuman, and unjust; but the legal perpetuation of that state of slavery, which has been produced by it, is surely, in its principle, no less immoral, inhuman and unjust, than the trade itself. . . .

QUESTIONS

1. Why would the British Parliament abolish the slave trade but allow slavery to continue in its colonies?

2. Why did it take ten years from the time of this petition for slavery to be abolished? What changes occurred in the British Parliament that might explain the timing of abolition?

Source: Reprinted in *Circular Letters of the Society for the Mitigation and Gradual Abolition of Slavery Throughout the British Dominions* (April 1823).

---

rulers, who in the past had been reluctant to support the national idea, now attempted to co-opt it. Cologne's unfinished cathedral, for example, became a symbol of German enthusiasm; from all over Germany donations poured in to finish it. These events suggested a broadening base for nationhood, which potentially could replace the existing system of a fragmented Germany. But with minor exceptions, the system established in 1815 prevailed until 1848.

Many Italian governments—notably the papacy, the kingdom of Naples, and the central Italian duchies—also successfully resisted aspirations for freer institutions and a unified Italy with repressive policies, knowing that they could count on Austrian assistance to squelch any uprising. Indeed, Metternich did crush rebellions, which generated hatred of Austria among Italian liberals and nationalists.

Having come to the throne by virtue of repressing the Decembrist uprising of 1825, Russia's Tsar Nicholas I (r. 1825–1855) was obsessed with the danger of revolution and determined to suppress all challenges to his authority. The declared goal of his rule was to uphold "orthodoxy, autocracy, and nationality." Nicholas created a stern, centralized bureaucracy to control all facets of Russian life. He originated the modern Russian secret police, called the "Third Section"; a state within the state, it was above the law. Believing in the divine right of monarchs, Nicholas refused to accept limits to his imperial powers. The tsar supported the primacy of the Russian Orthodox Church within Russian society; the church in turn upheld the powers of the state. Nicholas also used nationalism to strengthen the state by exalting the country's past and by trying to "Russify" non-Russian peoples. After a nationalist rebellion in 1831 in Poland attempted to shake loose Russian control, Nicholas abrogated the kingdom's constitution and tried to impose the Russian language on its Polish subjects.

Russia's single most overwhelming problem was serfdom. Economically, serfdom had little to recommend it; free labor was far more efficient. Moreover, the serfs' dissatisfaction with their lot threatened public safety. Nicholas's thirty-year reign was checkered with over six hundred peasant uprisings, half of them put down by the military. Nicholas understood that serfdom had to be abolished for Russia's own good, but also he believed emancipation would only sow further disorder. Except for a few minor reforms, he did nothing.

Ottoman Empire and Greek Independence

Although less directly affected by the events of 1789–1815, the Ottoman Empire was not immune to the forces of change unleashed by revolutions and reform in the West. In its sheer mass, the Ottoman Empire continued to be a world empire. It extended over three continents. In Africa, it ran across the whole North African coast. In Europe, it stretched from Dalmatia (on the Adriatic coast) to Constantinople. In Asia, it extended from Mesopotamia (present-day Iraq) to Anatolia (present-day Turkey) (see **MAP 24.3**, p. 688). But it was an empire in decline, seriously challenged by foreign threats and by nationalist movements from within—and its decline would ultimately have consequences for the European and world order.

The Ottoman bureaucracy, once the mainstay of the government, had fallen into decay. In the past, officials had been recruited and advanced by merit; now lacking funds, Constantinople sold government offices. Tax collectors ruthlessly squeezed the peasantry. By the eighteenth century, the Janissaries, formerly an elite military force, had become an undisciplined band that menaced the peoples of the Ottoman Empire—especially those located at great distances from the capital. The reform-minded Sultan Selim III (r. 1789–1807) sought to curb the army, but rebellious Janissaries killed him. They then forced the new ruler, Mahmud II (r. 1808–1839), to retract most of the previous improvements.

The ideas of nationalism and liberty that triggered changes in western Europe also stirred the peoples of the Balkans. Most of the Ottoman Empire was inhabited by Muslims, but in the Balkans, Christians were in the majority. Ottoman officials usually treated religious minorities, such as Jews and Orthodox Christians, with tolerance. But the Christian subject peoples found in their religion a means of collectively resisting a harsh and at times capricious rule. Some Christian peoples in the Balkans looked back nostalgically to earlier eras—the Greeks to their great Classical civilization or the Serbs to their era of self-rule.

The Serbs were the first people to revolt successfully against Ottoman rule. A poor, mountainous region, Serbia suffered greatly from the rapaciousness of the Janissaries, and revolted in 1804. By 1815, the Ottomans had to recognize one of its leaders, Milosh Obrenovich (r. 1815–1839), as governor and allow the formation of a national assembly. In 1830, under pressure from Russia, which took an interest in fellow Slavs and members of the Orthodox faith, Constantinople recognized Milosh as hereditary ruler over an autonomous Serbia.

The Greeks' struggle led to complete independence from Ottoman rule. As merchants and seafarers, Greeks traveled widely throughout the Mediterranean world and beyond. They had encountered the ideas of the French Revolution and, in the 1790s, were affected by the nationalism spreading in Europe. Adamantios Koraïs (KOOR-ay-iss) (1748–1833), an educator living in revolutionary Paris, created a new, more elegant Greek and edited Greek classics to connect his fellow countrymen with their ancient and illustrious past. Greek cultural nationalism found an echo among some intellectuals, a group of whom conspired to restore Greek independence by political means.

A parallel movement developed among Greek peasants, who were hostile to the Ottoman Turks for having accumulated vast landholdings at their expense. Greek peasants joined an anti-Turkish revolt that began in 1821 and lasted several years.

Mehemet Ali   Painted by the famed British artist Sir David Wilkie, this portrait depicts the Egyptian leader at the height of his powers. Mehemet challenged the Ottoman Empire, winning for Egypt virtual independence and bringing Syria under his control.   (Tate Gallery, London/Art Resource, NY)

By 1827, the Ottomans, aided by their vassal Mehemet Ali (1769–1849) of Egypt, controlled most of the Balkan peninsula. The rest of Europe, excited by the idea of an independent Greece restored to its past greatness, widely supported the Greek movement for freedom. The Great Powers intervened in 1827, sending their navies to intercept supplies intended for the Ottoman forces. Their victory ensured the independence of Greece, which was ratified by an international agreement in 1830. But in sanctioning the Greek nationalist insurrection, the allies of the Concert of Europe contradicted their own stated principles of opposing any challenge to the established order.

Losing influence in the Balkans, the Ottoman Empire also faced challenges elsewhere. Mehemet Ali, nominally subordinate to Constantinople, actually ruled Egypt as if it were independent. He wrested Syria away in 1831 and threatened to march against his overlord, the sultan. Britain and Russia, concerned that an Ottoman collapse would upset the region's balance of power, intervened on the empire's behalf. Constantinople won back Syria, but in 1841 had to acknowledge Mehemet Ali as the hereditary ruler of Egypt. The survival of the Ottoman Empire was beginning to depend on the goodwill—and self-interest—of the Great Powers.

SECTION SUMMARY

- In July 1830, the French responded to reactionary measures taken by their king with revolution, ushering in the more liberal July Monarchy; these events inspired serious opposition to other regimes.

- British liberals responded to France's July Revolution by redrawing the voting districts to reflect the growth of cities, widening the franchise to include the middle classes, and loosening colonial rule over white settler populations.

- Having suffered more directly from Napoleonic invasions, rulers in the Austrian Empire, the German states, and Russia remained determined to preserve absolute political power from 1815 to 1848; they effectively repressed agitation for liberal reform and aspirations for national unification.

- National movements from within and foreign threats from without challenged the religiously diverse Ottoman Empire, already in decay because of its corrupt bureaucracy; Serbs and Greeks successfully revolted against Ottoman rule.

THE REVOLUTIONS OF 1848

What were the main causes of the revolutions of 1848, and what roles did nationalism, liberalism, and socialism play in inciting and sustaining revolution?

From France in the west to Poland in the east, at least fifty separate revolts and uprisings shook the Continent in 1848, the most extensive outbreak of popular violence in nineteenth-century Europe (see **MAP 21.2**). The revolt had an impact far beyond Europe's borders. The revolutions inspired Brazilians to rise up against their government. In Bogota, Colombia, church bells rang, and in New York public demonstrations enthusiastically greeted the announcement of a republic in France. And as a result of the Parisian revolution, slaves in French colonies were finally emancipated.

The revolutions of 1848 also brought women into the political arena, creating new opportunities to criticize their legal status. In France, feminist clubs and newspapers proliferated as they never had before. In central, eastern, and southeastern Europe, revolution gave women political experience that promoted an emancipatory consciousness among them. The revolutions produced a long list of eloquent feminists throughout Europe who made various demands through their newspapers, magazines, and in their political participation. But just as had happened in the French Revolution of 1789, revolutionary governments eventually excluded women from politics, censored their newspapers, and disbanded their clubs.

Roots of Rebellion

The widespread outbreak of discontent occurred for many reasons, some of which stemmed from the pressure that population growth put on available resources. In the countryside, increased restrictions in access to land frustrated peasants. Although in the past many had enjoyed free access to village commons, these were coming increasingly under private control, or the peasants faced competition for their use. Also, the poor once had relatively free access to forests to forage for firewood, but restrictions on this right also now led to frequent conflicts.

🌐 **Map 21.2—Major Uprisings and Reforms, 1848–1849**

In no other year had as many revolts broken out simultaneously. In many cases, the revolutions led to reforms and new constitutions.

In the urban environment, a crisis erupted in the handicrafts industry, which dominated city economies. Urban artisans were being undercut by the putting-out system or cottage industry, in which capitalists had goods produced in the countryside by cottagers—part-time artisans who supported themselves as well through agriculture and were thus willing to work for lower wages. Crises in the crafts hurt the journeymen who wanted to be masters; they had to serve far longer apprenticeships and in many cases could never expect promotion. Where the guild system still existed, it was in decline, unable to protect the economic interests of artisans anxious about their futures.

These developing concerns came to a crisis point as a result of the economic depression of 1845–1846. In 1845, a crop disaster destroyed the basic food of the poor in northern Europe. The Irish suffered the most catastrophically from this blight: One million starved to death between 1844 and 1851. As the price of food doubled from its 1840 level, an industrial downturn accompanied these agricultural disasters, creating massive unemployment. Municipal and national governments seemed unable to deal with the crowding, disease, and unsanitary conditions that were worsening already high tensions in the cities, the sites of national governments. New liberal, socialist, and nationalist ideologies had created hope for change, as well as a vision for what it should be. The insurrections seeking to overthrow existing regimes disoriented the established political and administrative elites, and they found they could not count on their traditional sources of support.

In February, 1848, a revolution in Paris overthrew the king. News of Louis Philippe's fall triggered a ripple effect, spreading turbulence to over fifty localities in Europe. In France, the revolution was for political and social rights, particularly the rights to vote and to work. In several other countries, another issue was added to the combustible situation—nationalism. Once revolution in the German states broke out, the demands arose for national unification. National unity also became a goal throughout the Italian peninsula; northern Italians also desired independence from the Habsburg Empire. The cry for national independence went out in other Habsburg lands: The Hungarians, Poles, and Czechs all wanted to be masters of their own destinies and free from Vienna's control.

Liberals: From Success to Defeat

The revolutions of 1848 went through two basic stages: unity in the shared goal of regime change, followed by disagreement about what should replace the toppled regimes. In the first stage, liberal demands for more political freedoms, such as the right to vote, joined with popular demands for social and economic justice. In France, the victors declared a republic, which provided basic constitutional freedoms and granted universal male suffrage (the first European regime to do so). The provisional government attempted to solve the problem of widespread unemployment by creating jobs through a system of "national workshops." Inspired by the example of Paris, crowds in Vienna demonstrated and petitioned the emperor. Having lost control over the capital, Metternich resigned and fled to England. On March 15, 1848, the Austrian imperial court, faced with continued agitation by students and workers, announced its willingness to issue a constitution. Even more important was Austria's decision to abolish serfdom.

The news from Paris also acted as a catalyst for change in the German states, where dukes and princes dismissed their cabinets and instituted constitutions. Prussia was initially conspicuous for being untouched by the revolutionary wave. But when news of Metternich's fall in Vienna reached Berlin on March 16, middle-class liberals and artisans demonstrated for reforms. King Friedrich Wilhelm IV (r. 1840–1861) surprised his subjects on March 21 by announcing support for a united, free, constitutional Germany. He appointed as chief minister a liberal Rhenish businessman, who in a ceremonial march through Berlin symbolically walked ahead of the king. Representative government was introduced, and suffrage was extended, though it was still restricted to men of property from the liberal professions and the business classes. As in Austria, the German countryside was appeased by reducing some of the feudal arrangements that still existed in many areas.

The second stage of the revolution marked a breakdown in the unity that had initially formed against the old regimes. With the enemy defeated or compliant, the middle classes, peasants, and workers no longer had a common goal. In France, the peasants, who at least had not opposed the revolution, by April 1848, were hostile to the new republic. They decried the additional taxes that had to be levied to pay for the national workshops supporting unemployed urban workers. Armed with the vote, the peasants elected conservative landowners, lawyers, and notaries—a group nearly identical to the pre-1848 deputies. In June, the new parliament terminated the costly national workshops that had employed thousands of workers. The latter, in despair, revolted. The government carried out a bloody repression, killing 3,000 and arresting 15,000.

The propertied classes, feeling menaced by the poor, looked to authority for security. Of the several candidates for president in 1848, Louis Napoleon (1808–1873), a nephew of Napoleon Bonaparte, appealed to the largest cross section of the population. The middle class was attracted by the promise of authority and order. Peasants, disillusioned by the tax policies of the republic, remained loyal to the memory of Napoleonic glory. Workers, embittered by the government's repression of the June uprisings, were impressed by Louis Napoleon's vaguely socialistic program. Louis Napoleon was elected president. Three years later, he dissolved the National Assembly by force and established a personal dictatorship. In 1852, he declared himself Emperor Napoleon III.

In Austria and Germany, the middle classes became wary of the lower classes; the class conflict in Paris intensified their concern. Once the peasants had won their freedom from feudal dues in Germany and from serfdom in the Austrian Empire, they were no longer interested in what was occurring in the capital. Thus, the alliance in favor of change disappeared, and it could not even serve as a bulwark against counter-revolution. In Austria, the reactionary forces around the court, led by General Windischgrätz, reconquered Vienna in October 1848 for the emperor and

King Friedrich Wilhelm IV Announcing His Devotion to German Unity   This print, distributed by the thousands, shows the grateful people—well-dressed middle-class citizens and humble artisans united in their purpose—acclaiming the king *(center)* on horseback. The black, red, and gold flags, the symbol of German unity since the Napoleonic Wars, are prominently displayed.   (Germanisches\National Museum Nuremberg)

suspended the liberals' constitution. In December, the king of Prussia, who had appeared to bow to liberal opinion, regained his courage and dismissed the elected assembly. Most of the liberal forces were spent and overcome by the end of the year.

The Nationalist Impulse

The revolutions did not break out because of nationalism, but once they erupted, the nationalist cause helped shape the outcome in several regions. Faced with internal turmoil, Prussia and Austria—whose rulers opposed German unification, lest it undermine their power—could not prevent the question of a united Germany from coming to the fore. In March 1848, a self-appointed national committee invited five hundred prominent German liberals to convene in Frankfurt to begin the process of unifying the German states into a single nation. In addition to fulfilling a long-standing liberal dream, a united Germany would consolidate the liberal victory over absolutism. The gathering called for suffrage based on property qualifications, thus excluding most Germans from the political process and alienating them from the evolving new order. The first all-German elected legislature met in May 1848 in Frankfurt to pursue unification. It faced the thorny issue of which regions should be included and which excluded in this new Germany. The most ambitious plan envisioned a *Grossdeutschland* (GROSE-doyt-shlant), or large Germany, consisting of all the members of the German Confederation, including the German-speaking parts of Austria and the German parts of Bohemia. Such a solution would include many non-Germans, including Poles, Czechs, and Danes. The proponents of *Kleindeutschland* (KLINE-doyt-shlant), or small Germany, which would exclude Austria and its possessions, saw their solution as a more likely scenario, although it would exclude many Germans. The proposal of a small Germany succeeded in the end, largely because the reassertion of Austrian imperial power in the fall of 1848 put the non-German areas under Vienna's control out of reach.

The Prussian reassertion of royal power, though partial, was a signal for other German rulers in late 1848 to dismiss their liberal ministers. The moment for liberalism and national unification to triumph had passed by the time the **Frankfurt Assembly** drew up a constitution in the spring of 1849. Having opted for the *Kleindeutsch* solution, the parliament offered the throne to Friedrich Wilhelm IV, king of Prussia. Although the king was not a liberal, he ruled the largest state within the designated empire. If power could promote and protect German unity, he possessed it in the form of the Prussian army. But Friedrich Wilhelm feared that accepting the throne would lead to war with Austria. Believing in the principle of monarchy, he also did not want an office offered by representatives of the people, and so he refused the offer. Lacking an alternative plan, most members of the Frankfurt Assembly went home. A rump parliament and a series of uprisings in favor of German unity were crushed by the Prussian army.

In Italy, too, nationalist aspirations emerged once a revolt, triggered by social and economic grievances, had broken out. In the years before 1848, nationalists and liberals hoped somehow to see their program of a united and free Italy implemented. News of the Paris uprising in February galvanized revolutions in Italy. Italians, under Austrian rule, forced the Austrians to evacuate their Italian possessions. Revolts and mass protests in several Italian states led rulers to grant, or at least promise, a constitution. The king of Piedmont, Charles Albert (r. 1831–1849), who hoped to play a major part in unifying Italy, did grant his people a constitution. In Austrian Italy, the middle classes, although eager to be free of foreign rule, feared radical elements among the laborers. They believed that annexation to nearby Piedmont would provide security from both Austria and the troublesome lower classes. The king of Piedmont decided to unite Italy under his throne if doing so would prevent the spread of radicalism to his kingdom. The persistent nationalist and revolutionary sentiment provoked Charles Albert to declare war on Austria, first in March 1848, and again a year later. Both times he was defeated, the second in only six days. Humiliated, the king resigned his throne to his son, Victor Emmanuel II (r. 1849–1878). The Austrians quickly reconquered their lost provinces and reinstated their puppet governments, dashing the dream of a united Italy.

In the multinational empire of the Habsburgs, nationalism manifested itself in the form of demands for national independence from foreign rule. With Austria's power temporarily weakened, as a result of revolution in Vienna, nationalist revolts broke out not only in Italy, but simultaneously in Hungary, the Czech lands, and Croatia. The Austrian emperor yielded in Hungary, giving it virtual independence. Constitutional government was established, but participation in the political process was limited to Magyars, who were the single largest ethnic group, constituting 40 percent of the population. The other nationalities in Hungary—Romanians,

Ballots, Not Bullets   This print from 1848 encourages the revolutionary on the barricades to put away his rifle and trust the democratic process. Pointing to the rifle, our French revolutionary announces, "This is for the external enemy." "As for the internal ones," he says, indicating the election urn, "this is how one fights them loyally." (Roger Viollet/Getty Images)

Frankfurt Assembly
Popularly elected national assembly that attempted to create a unified German state.

Constitutional Government in Denmark On March 21, 1848, fifteen thousand Danes, inspired by the example of Paris, marched on the palace to demand constitutional rights. Unlike the protests at the French capital, however, this event was peaceful and led to the establishment of a constitutional government. This painting honors the new parliament that came into being after the liberal constitution was adopted in 1849. (Photo, Statens Museum for Kunst, Copenhagen)

Slovaks, Croats, and Slovenes—preferred the more distant rule of Austrian Vienna to Magyar authority. The Czech lands also witnessed agitation, but there and elsewhere the tide favoring the nationalists turned. The revolt against the empire was not coordinated, and the various nationalisms were often in conflict with one another. Once the emperor reestablished his power in Vienna, he could move against his rebellious subjects. The Austrian Empire bombarded Prague into submission, and with Russian help, brought Hungary to heel, and then reestablished its authority in Italy. If the nationalist fires had been quenched, the dangers nationalism posed to the survival of the Habsburg Empire were also revealed.

Three major countries escaped the revolutionary wave that washed across Europe. In Great Britain, the government had proven capable of adjusting to some of the major popular demands, averting the need for revolution. In Russia, the repressive tsarist system prevented any defiance from escalating into an opposition mass movement. Spain was also spared. General Ramón Narváez (nar-VA-yes) (1799–1868) brutally ran the country from 1844 to 1851. When he was on his deathbed, the priest asked him whether he forgave his enemies. He answered, "I have no enemies. I have shot them all!"

SECTION SUMMARY

- Across the Continent, the roots for revolution lay in increasingly restricted resources among rural peasants and urban workers; the harvest failures and economic depression of 1845–1846 turned this situation into a crisis.

- The liberal impulse to revolution at first united middle classes, peasants, and workers in demands for political freedoms and economic justice.

- Once regimes gave into the challenge or were overturned, the goals of different social classes conflicted; the divisions between them opened the path to reaction and repression.

- Liberal revolution in eastern and central Europe inspired movements of national unification in the German states and in Italy, Hungary, the Czech lands, and Croatia, all at the expense of the Austrian Empire.

CHAPTER SUMMARY

In 1814 and 1815, after more than twenty-two years of war, the powers that finally defeated Napoleon—Great Britain, Austria, Prussia, and Russia—wanted to restore the prerevolutionary Old Regime to Europe. The Congress of Vienna sought to establish international stability by creating a balance of power. To that end, the Great Powers even brought the vanquished nation of France—with its Bourbon monarchy reinstated—into the Concert of Europe on equal footing.

In reaction to the revolutionary challenges of the late eighteenth century, new ideologies—conservatism, romanticism, nationalism, liberalism, and socialism—took root, and shaped the outlook, movements, and policies of the first half of the nineteenth century. While conservatism sought to stem the tides of change through repressive measures in both eastern and western Europe, the other ideologies called for and justified it. The severe economic downturn and the social displacements of the 1840s, along with perceptions of social injustice and profound desire for representative, if not democratic institutions, culminated in the Revolutions of 1848.

Most of the aspirations of the 1848 revolutions failed to be realized as authoritarian regimes regained the upper hand by 1851. Although counterrevolutionary forces temporarily defeated both the liberal and nationalistic impulses behind the revolutions of 1848, experiments born of these events suggested new modes of political organization that would later come to fruition.

FOCUS QUESTIONS

- What were the goals of the Restoration, and the sources of resistance to it?

- What major ideologies developed in the first half of the nineteenth century?

- How did the restorations that followed the Napoleonic era give way to reform?

- What were the main causes of the revolutions of 1848, and what roles did nationalism, liberalism, and socialism play in inciting and sustaining revolution?

KEY TERMS

Congress of Vienna (p. 588)

Corn Laws (p. 589)

Decembrists (p. 592)

conservatism (p. 593)

romanticism (p. 593)

nationalism (p. 595)

liberalism (p. 597)

laissez-faire (p. 598)

utilitarianism (p. 598)

socialism (p. 599)

Marxism (p. 601)

July Revolution (p. 602)

Great Reform Bill (p. 603)

Chartism (p. 603)

Frankfurt Assembly (p. 611)

 This icon will direct you to additional materials on the website: www .cengage.com/history/ noble/westciv6e.

See our interactive eBook for map and primary source activities.

22

CHAPTER OUTLINE

The Changing Nature of International Relations

Forging New Nation-States, 1850–1871

Fragile Empires

The Development of Western Democracies

Wilhelm I at Versailles
Wilhelm is proclaimed ruler of the German Empire, 1871. (akg-images)

Nationalism and Political Reform, 1850–1880

The ceremonial occasion depicted in the painting on the left is a monumental one for European and world history: The crowned heads of different German states, without the benefit of a parliament or popular vote, proclaim the unification of all their states under one nation. On the podium, standing just behind the newly declared kaiser, Wilhelm I, is Crown Prince Friedrich Wilhelm (later Kaiser Friedrich III). To the kaiser's left, with his arm upraised, is the grand duke of Baden. In the middle of the scene, resplendent in his white uniform, is Bismarck, the political architect of German unification. On the right nearby is Field Marshal Helmuth von Moltke (von molt-KEH), the military genius who provided the series of military victories allowing Prussia to unify Germany under its aegis. The location of this ceremony also has profound symbolism as well as irony: Four months after delivering a humiliating defeat to France, a unified Germany was proclaimed in the famed Hall of Mirrors in the grandiose palace of Versailles, the former seat of French kings and royal court.

Germany had become a united nation by war. In the generation after 1850, the contours of European politics changed—new states appeared on the map, and within their national borders a good number of states reformed their political institutions. To meet the demand for popular participation in government so forcefully expressed in 1848, every European state except the Ottoman and Russian Empires found it necessary to have a parliament. Rare before midcentury, such institutions became common thereafter. No longer was the demand for popular participation seen as a threat to the existing political and social order. In fact, popular participation, or the appearance of it, gave the existing order a legitimacy it had not enjoyed since before the French Revolution. Nationalism flourished during this period, emerging as a decisive force throughout the West.

These political transformations occurred in an era of unprecedented economic growth and prosperity. Industrial production expanded the economy; the discovery of gold in California in 1848 led to the expansion of credit (since currencies were backed by gold), which in turn led to the founding of new banks and mass investments in growing industries. The standard of living rose significantly in industrializing nations. Between 1850 and 1880, industrial production increased by 90 percent in Great Britain and by 50 percent in France. The middle classes expanded dramatically.

In the first half of the century, international relations had been dominated by the congress system, in which representatives of the major European states met periodically to refine and preserve the balance of power. This system collapsed in the second half of the

FOCUS QUESTIONS

- How did the Crimean War affect international relations?

- What respective processes led to the unifications of Italy and Germany into nation-states, and how did they differ?

- How did the Austrian, Ottoman, and Russian Empires deal with the challenges they faced?

- How did western European states create democracies?

 This icon will direct you to additional materials on the website: www .cengage.com/history/ noble/westciv6e.

See our interactive eBook for map and primary source activities.

Realpolitik   Style of governing based on practical and material factors, rather than on ethics or ideology, and that uses all means, including war, to expand the influence and power of a state.

century, as political leaders pursued the narrow nationalist interests of their respective states. Instead of negotiating with one another, a new generation of leaders employed brute military force—or the threat of its use—to resolve international conflicts. The new age was dominated not by ideals but by force, announced Bismarck, the main practitioner of what became known as **Realpolitik**, a policy in which war became a regular instrument of statecraft.

THE CHANGING NATURE OF INTERNATIONAL RELATIONS

How did the Crimean War affect international relations?

congress system   System of European international relations in the first half of the nineteenth century in which the major European states cooperated to preserve the balance of power.

Following the 1815 Congress of Vienna (see Chapter 21), European states attempted, through the **congress system**, to work out their differences by negotiation, avoiding situations in which one state triumphed at the cost of another. The Crimean War and the subsequent national realignments it caused raised mutual suspicions, leading nations to act in their own self-interests and to ignore the concerns of the other major players in the international system. This reorientation facilitated the emergence of nation-states at the expense of traditional empires.

Florence Nightingale   This photograph was taken in 1856, shortly after Nightingale returned to England from the Crimean War. Her privileged background provided the official connections that helped her nursing services succeed.   (Florence Nightingale, c.1860 (b/w photo), English Photographer, (19th century)/Florence Nightingale Museum, London, UK/The Bridgeman Art Library)

The Crimean War, 1854–1856

The Crimean War had many causes. Principally, however, it had to do with Russia claiming the right to protect Orthodox Christians within the predominantly Muslim Ottoman Empire. This claim led to war between Russia and the Ottoman Empire in 1853, resulting in a Russian victory. The defeat of the Ottoman Empire made it more vulnerable to further Russian incursions.

British and French statesmen had considerable interest in the conflict. Britain had long feared that the collapse of the Ottoman Empire would lead Russia to seek territorial gains in the Mediterranean. Such a move would challenge Britain's naval supremacy in that region. An explosion of public sentiment against Russia's aggressiveness also obliged the British government to consider military action. Meanwhile, the French emperor, Napoleon III, believed that successful war against Russia would provide the opportunity to redraw European borders. He hoped that a new order would lead to increased French power and influence. Napoleon also imagined that fighting side by side with Britain could lay the foundation for Anglo-French friendship. And so England and France rushed to defend the Ottoman Empire and declared war on Russia in March 1854.

All sides fought the war poorly, with woefully inadequate leadership. Five times more casualties resulted from disease than from enemy fire. Although the Russians had a standing army of a million men, their poor communications and supply systems prevented them from ever fielding more than a quarter of their forces. In Britain, the press and members of Parliament denounced their side's inadequate materiel and incompetent leadership. For the first time, the press played an active role in reporting war; the new technologies of the telegraph and photography brought to readers at home the gruesome realities of battle. One of the few heroic figures to emerge from this conflict was the English nurse Florence Nightingale (1820–1910), who organized a nursing service to care for the British sick and wounded. Later, her wartime experience allowed her to pioneer nursing as a professional calling. (See the feature, "The Written Record: Florence Nightingale in the Crimean War.")

After almost two years of fighting in the Balkans and the Crimean peninsula, Russia abandoned the key fortress of Sevastopol in September 1855. The conflict killed three-quarters of a million people—more than any European war between the end of the Napoleonic Wars and World War I. It was a particularly futile, senseless war whose most important consequence was political: It unleashed dramatic new changes in the international order that allowed for the emergence of the new nation-states.

The Congress of Paris, 1856

The former combatants met in Paris in February 1856 to work out a peace treaty. Their decisions—which pleased no one—shaped relations among European states for the next half century. Russian statesmen were especially discontented, as their country was forbidden to have a fleet in the Black Sea. Nor did French leaders feel that their nation had benefited, other than the prestige of holding the congress in Paris. The north Italian state of Piedmont (Kingdom of Sardinia), which had joined the allies, only gained a vague statement about the unsatisfactory nature of Italy's existing situation. Prussia was invited to attend the congress only as an afterthought and hence also felt slighted.

Although the war seemed to have sustained the integrity of the Ottoman Empire, the peace settlement weakened it indirectly by dictating reforms in the treatment of its Christian populations. These reforms impaired the empire's ability to repress the growing nationalist movements in the Balkans. British political leaders, galled by the heavy sacrifices of the war, moved toward isolationism in foreign policy. Austrian policymakers had hoped Britain and France would aid them in preserving the Habsburg Empire; instead, these powers, angry that Austria had not helped in the war, offered no assistance—a stance that would further weaken Habsburg imperial hegemony. At the time the peace treaty was signed, few people foresaw the enormous results that would flow from it.

By and large, the decisions reached in Paris would be disregarded or unilaterally revised as competition and rivalry between the major powers destabilized the international system. This new international climate also allowed new states to take shape without international sanction.

CHRONOLOGY

1851	Louis Napoleon's coup d'état
1854–1856	Crimean War
1860	Italy united under Piedmontese rule
1861	Great Reforms in Russia
1862	Bismarck appointed minister president of Prussia
1864	Austria and Prussia attack Denmark and occupy Schleswig-Holstein
1866	Austro-Prussian War
	Abolition of estate system in Sweden
1867	Second Reform Bill in England
	Austro-Hungarian compromise
1870	Franco-Prussian War
	Rome, joined to Italy, becomes its capital
	Declaration of French Third Republic
1871	Unification of German Empire
	Paris Commune
1876	Bulgarian horrors
1878	Congress of Berlin

SECTION SUMMARY

- The Crimean War of 1854–1856 marked the end of the spirit of cooperation that had resulted from the Congress of Vienna in 1815.

- The Crimean War was caused by the Russian defeat of the Ottomans in 1853, British fear of Russian influence in the Mediterranean, and Napoleon III's desire to increase French influence.

- The 1856 Congress of Paris humiliated Russia and restricted its military access to the Black Sea. The postwar settlement dictated reforms in the treatment of Christians in the Ottoman Empire, which, in turn, impaired the Ottoman ability to repress nationalist movements in the Balkans.

Crimean War   This photograph shows the interior of the Sevastopol fortress after it had been battered into surrender. The Crimean War was the first conflict to be documented by photographers.   (The Art Archive/Picture Desk)

FORGING NEW NATION–STATES, 1850–1871

What respective processes led to the unifications of Italy and Germany into nation-states, and how did they differ?

In the aftermath of the Crimean War, both Italy and Germany became united as nation-states. These new states resulted in part from issues left unresolved in the Revolutions of 1848, and from the collapse of the congress system established in 1815. In both cases, national unification resulted from a series of wars. In Italy, the relatively liberal constitutional monarchy of Piedmont-Sardinia (Kingdom of Sardinia) initiated the unification process. Prussia, with a long tradition of militarism and authoritarianism, forged German unification. The resulting states reflected the stark differences between their respective goals and the means of realizing them.

Italian Unification, 1859–1870

The revolution of 1848 in Italy (see pages 609–611) had revealed an interest in national unification, but the attempt had failed. Idealists, such as Giuseppe Mazzini (see page 595), had preached that Italy would be unified not by its rulers but by its people, who would rise and establish a free republic. Instead, the deed was done by royalty, by war, and with the help of a foreign state. Although ideals were not absent from the process of unification, cynical manipulation and scheming also came into play.

risorgimento   Italian term, beginning in the late eighteenth century, for the political and cultural renewal of Italy. It later came to be associated with Italian unification.

Since the late eighteenth century, some Italians had been calling for a ***risorgimento*** (ree-sor-djee-MEN-toe), a political and cultural renewal of Italy. By the mid-nineteenth century,

Florence Nightingale in the Crimean War

Florence Nightingale used her influential family connections to win an appointment to the Crimean battlefield. Once there, she organized nursing for the wounded and was able to secure additional personnel and medical supplies for her hospital. Women were supposed to be sheltered from the harsh realities of the outside world, but as this letter indicates, Nightingale was not spared war in its cruelest aspects.

We have no room for corpses in the wards. The Surgeons pass on to the next, an excision of the shoulder-joint—beautifully performed and going on well—[cannon] ball lodged just in the head of the joint, and fracture starred all round. The next poor fellow has two stumps for arms—and the next has lost an arm and leg. As for the balls, they go in where they like, and do as much harm as they can in passing. That is the only rule they have. The next case has one eye put out, and paralysis of the iris of the other. He can neither see nor understand. But all who can walk come into us for Tobacco, but I tell them that we have not a bit to put into our own mouths. Not a sponge, nor a rag of linen, not anything have I left. Everything is gone to make slings and stump pillows and shirts. These poor fellows have not had a clean shirt nor been washed for two months before they came here, and the state in which they arrive from the transport is literally crawling. I hope in a few days we shall establish a little cleanliness. But we have not a basin nor a towel nor a bit of soap nor a broom—I have ordered 300 scrubbing brushes. But one half the Barrack is so sadly out of repair that it is impossible to use a drop of water on the stone floors, which are all laid upon rotten wood, and would give our men fever in no time. . . .

I am getting a screen now for the Amputations, for when one poor fellow, who is to be amputated tomorrow, sees his comrade today die under the knife it makes an impression—and diminishes his chance. But, anyway, among these exhausted frames the mortality of the operations is frightful.

QUESTIONS

1. How did Florence Nightingale's presence on the Crimean battlefield defy Victorian middle-class gender roles? How did it reaffirm them?

2. What does her description convey about the impact that modern technology had on warfare by 1854?

Source: Letter to Dr. William Bowman, November 14, 1854, in *"I Have Done My Duty": Florence Nightingale in the Crimean War, 1854–56*, ed. Sue M. Goldie, *1987*, pp. 37–38. Copyright © 1987. Reprinted by permission of University of Iowa Press.

---

the idea was actively supported by a small, elite group consisting of the educated middle class, urban property owners, and members of the professions. For merchants, industrialists, and professionals, a unified state would provide a larger stage on which to pursue their ambitions.

THE PLOT TO UNIFY ITALY

After the failed 1848 revolution, most Italian rulers resorted to repression. Only the northern Italian kingdom of Piedmont-Sardinia kept the liberal constitution adopted during the 1848 revolution, and it welcomed political refugees from other Italian states. Not only politically, but economically, it was a beacon to the rest of Italy, establishing modern banks and laying half the rail lines on the peninsula.

The statesman who was to catapult Piedmont into a position of leadership in the dramatic events leading to Italian unification was Count Camillo di Cavour (1810–1861). The son of a Piedmontese nobleman and high government official, Cavour was sympathetic to the aspirations of the middle class and saw in Britain and France models of what Italy ought to become: a liberal and economically advanced society.

Cavour was ambitious, hardworking, and driven to succeed. A well-known journalist and the editor of the newspaper *Risorgimento*, he joined the government in 1850. Two years later, King Victor Emmanuel appointed him prime minister. Cavour shared the enthusiasm of the middle classes for an Italian nation, but his vision did not include all of Italy—only its north and center—which then could dominate the rest of the peninsula in a loose federation. Unifying the north and center would first require ousting Austria from the northern provinces. The failures of 1848 had taught Cavour that this task would require foreign help, especially from France.

When the Crimean War broke out in 1854, Cavour supported the British and the French, hoping to advance his cause. He sent twenty thousand troops to the Crimea, one-tenth of whom died. This act gained him a seat at the Congress of Paris, where his presence boosted Piedmont's prestige—and where he and Napoleon III had an opportunity to meet and size up each other.

Because Austria had been France's traditional opponent, Napoleon III favored the cause of Italian liberation from its rule; destroying Austria's power in Italy might strengthen France. Thus, in July 1858, the French emperor and the Piedmontese prime minister met secretly to discuss how

MAP 22.1—The Unification of Italy, 1859–1870

Piedmontese leadership under Cavour in the north, and national-ist fervor inspired by Garibaldi in the south, united Italy.

Kingdom of Sardinia before 1859
To Kingdom of Sardinia, 1859
To Kingdom of Sardinia, 1860
To Kingdom of Italy, 1866, 1870
★ Major battle
▬ Boundary of Kingdom of Italy after unification

Italian unity could be achieved. They agreed that Piedmont would stir up trouble in one of Austria's Italian territories in an effort to goad the Austrians into war. According to the plan, France would join the war to help the Piedmontese expel Austria from the northern provinces of Lombardy and Venetia. In exchange, the French emperor demanded the Piedmontese provinces of Nice and Savoy, which bordered France.

War between Austria and Piedmont broke out in April 1859. By June, the combined Piedmontese and French forces had routed the Austrians at Magenta and Solferino (see **MAP 22.1**). So bloody were these battles that the color magenta was named after the deep red of the soaked battlefield. The horrors of this war also inspired the founding of the Red Cross.

Shocked by the bloodshed he had witnessed, Napoleon III decided to end the fighting instead of pressing on. He was further alarmed because Prussia had begun to mobilize its army to support Austria. His plan for Italy had meanwhile begun to unravel: Several central Italian states expressed a desire to be annexed to Piedmont, which would have resulted in an independent state much larger than Napoleon III had anticipated. These factors led him to betray Cavour; he made an agreement with the Austrians, which gave Lombardy to Piedmont, but allowed Venetia to remain within the Austrian Empire.

UNIFICATION ACHIEVED, 1860

Napoleon's betrayal outraged Cavour, but unexpected events in the south also changed his vision of national unification. The centuries-old misgovernment of the Kingdom of the Two Sicilies (Naples and Sicily) led to an uprising on the island of Sicily in April 1860. The revolutionary firebrand Giuseppe Garibaldi (1807–1882) set sail for Sicily in May 1860 with but a thousand poorly armed, red-shirted followers to help the island overthrow its Bourbon ruler. Winning that struggle, Garibaldi's forces crossed to the mainland in August. Victory followed victory, and enthusiasm for Garibaldi grew. His army swelled to 57,000 men, and he won the entire kingdom of Naples.

Threatened by the advance of Garibaldi's power and fearing its reach into the Papal States, Cavour sent his army into the area in September 1860. Although Garibaldi was a republican, he was convinced that Italy could best achieve unity under the king of Piedmont-Sardinia, and he willingly submitted the southern part of Italy, which he controlled, to the king, Victor Emmanuel II (r. 1849–1878). Thus, by November 1860, Italy had been united under the Kingdom of Sardinia (see **Map 22.1**). The united territories affirmed their desire to be part of the new Italy through plebiscites based on universal male suffrage. The 1848 constitution of Piedmont became the constitution of the newly united Italy. Cavour lived to relish his handiwork for only a few months, as he died of an undiagnosed illness in May 1861. His last words were "Italy is made—all is safe."

Still to be joined to the new state were Austrian-held Venetia in the northeast and Rome and its environs, held by the pope with the support of a French garrison. But within a decade, a favorable international situation enabled the fledgling country to acquire both key areas. Upon its defeat in the Austro-Prussian War in 1866, Austria ceded Venetia to Italy. Four years later, the Franco-Prussian War forced the French to evacuate Rome, which they had occupied since 1849. Rome was joined to Italy and became its capital in 1870. With that event, unification was complete.

National unity had been achieved, but it was frail. The uprisings that Garibaldi had led in the south were motivated more by hatred of the Bourbons than by fervor for national unification. And once the union was achieved, the north behaved like a conquering state—sending its officials to the south, raising taxes, and imposing its laws. In 1861, civil war broke out and lasted five years; it produced more casualties than the entire effort of unification.

**THE PROBLEMS OF
A UNIFIED ITALY**

Garibaldi Leading His "Red Shirts" to Victory Over the Neapolitan Army, May 1860
Garibaldi's conquests in the south and Cavour's in the north opened the way for Italian unification.   (Scala/Art Resource, NY)

Other major divisions remained. In 1861, only 2.5 percent of the population spoke the national language, Florentine Italian. Economics also divided the country. The north was far more industrialized than the rural south. In the south, child mortality was higher, life expectancy was lower, and illiteracy was close to 90 percent. The Catholic Church remained hostile to the new Italian state. The popes, left to rule a tiny domain—a few square blocks around the papal palace known as the Vatican—considered themselves prisoners. They denounced anyone who participated in elections. Thus, many Italian Catholics refused to recognize the new state for decades, thwarting its legitimacy.

In the face of such divisions, Piedmont-Sardinia imposed strong central control, resolutely refusing a federal system of government, which many Italians in an earlier era had hoped for. This choice reflected fear that any other form of government might lead to a fate similar to that of the United States, whose federal system of government led to secessionism and the Civil War in early 1861. The constitution Piedmont-Sardinia imposed on unified Italy limited suffrage to men of property and education—less than 2 percent of the population. Further, as prime minister, Cavour created and manipulated parliamentary majorities in favor of his cabinet, reversing the logic behind the parliamentary system in which cabinets were supposed to represent, and answer to, freely elected legislative bodies. Nevertheless, the new unified Italy was a liberal state that guaranteed legal equality and freedom of association, and provided more freedom for its citizens than the Italian people had seen for centuries.

German Unification, 1850–1871

Like Italy, Germany had long been a collection of states. Since 1815, the thirty-eight German states had been loosely organized in the German Confederation. Like Piedmont-Sardinia in Italy, one German state, powerful Prussia, led the unification movement. And just as Italy had in Cavour a strong leader who imposed his will, so did German unification have a ruthless and cunning champion: **Otto von Bismarck**, minister president of Prussia. But whereas Cavour, for all his wiliness, was committed to establishing a liberal state, Bismarck was wedded to autocratic rule.

Otto von Bismarck
Nineteenth-century German statesman who, through a series of aggressive wars, united Germany. Germany became the dominant power in Europe under his administration.

The revolutionaries of 1848 had failed in their attempt to achieve German unification when the king of Prussia refused to accept a throne offered by the elected Frankfurt Assembly (see page 611). As the painting at the beginning of this chapter illustrates, German unification was ratified not by the ballot, as it was in Italy, but by the acclamation of the crowned heads of Germany. The nation was united by the use of military force and the imposition of Prussian absolutism over the whole country.

THE RISE OF BISMARCK

Austria under Metternich had always treated Prussia as a privileged junior partner. After Metternich's fall in 1848, however, rivalry erupted between the two German states. Each tried to manipulate, for its own benefit, the desire for national unity that had become manifest during the revolution of 1848.

In March 1850, representatives from a number of German states met to consider unification under Prussian sponsorship. Austria opposed such a union and, with Russian support, threatened war. Since the Prussian military was not strong enough to challenge Austria, Prussia agreed to abandon the plan for unification and to accept Austrian leadership in Germany. But a decade later, the new Prussian king, Wilhelm I (r. 1861–1888), was determined to strengthen Prussia by expanding the size and effectiveness of the army. The parliament, however, refused to approve funding for a military buildup. The conflict was not simply about the budget; it was an issue of who should govern the country—the king or the elected representatives. To get his way, the king appointed Count Otto von Bismarck as minister president.

Bismarck was a Junker, a Prussian aristocrat known for his reactionary views, who had opposed the liberal movement in 1848. As Prussian emissary to the German Confederation, he had challenged Austrian primacy. Devoted to his monarch, Bismarck sought to heighten Prussian power in Germany and throughout Europe through policies based on "Realpolitik," stressing pragmatic considerations at the expense of ethics and the law. He faced down the parliament, telling the Budget Commission in 1862, "The position of Prussia in Germany will be decided not by its liberalism but by its power … not through speeches and majority decisions are the great questions of the day decided—that was the mistake of 1848 and 1849—but by iron and blood."[1]

Bismarck tried to win over the liberals by suggesting that with military force at its disposal, Prussia could lead German unification. But the liberals continued to resist, and the parliament voted against the military reforms. Unfazed, Bismarck carried out the military measures anyway and ordered the collection of the necessary taxes. The citizens acquiesced and paid to upgrade their army. Prussia would not yield to parliamentarism as Britain had.

German liberals faced a dilemma: Which did they value more—the goal of nationhood or the principles of liberty? To oppose Bismarck effectively, German liberals knew they would have to ally themselves with the working classes, but they feared the workers and forestalled forming a unified front of opposition. Germany appeared embarked on an illiberal course.

Bismarck ingeniously exploited the weakness of the liberals and the growing desire for German unification, further strengthened by the Franco-Austrian War of 1859, during which Germans had feared that the French would attack across the Rhine River. Many came to believe that only a strong, united Germany could give its inhabitants security. Prussia had already led the important move toward economic unification with the *Zollverein*, a customs union that included most German states, but excluded Austria. Founded in 1834, the customs union had become more extensive with the passage of time; even states that were politically hostile to Prussia joined the union to protect their economic interests. Economic unity led to all-German professional and cultural associations that surpassed state boundaries; it was an indispensable stage in the process toward political unity. By 1860, the idea of a united Germany had gained a substantial appeal.

Having built up the military and established the supremacy of royal power in Prussia, Bismarck was ready to enlarge its role in Germany—and he believed that war against Austria was the only means to do so. Conflicts over the provinces of Schleswig (SHLES-vik) and Holstein (HOLL-shteyn) served as a pretext (see **Map 22.2**). In 1864, Prussia and Austria had successfully gone to war against Denmark to secure the independence of these two German-speaking provinces. Bismarck then used disputes over their joint administration as an excuse for war against Austria. Prussia attacked Austrian-administered Holstein in June 1866, launching the Austro-Prussian War. After a scant seven weeks, the newly reformed Prussian army won a decisive victory in the Battle of Sadowa (SAH-doe-wah). Prussia's industrial superiority had enabled it to equip its soldiers with the Dreyse needle guns, new breech-loading rifles with innovative pins capable of firing rounds at a faster rate than traditional guns. They also allowed troops to fire from a prone position, while the Austrians, with their muzzle loaders, had to stand up to shoot. With military victory, Prussia annexed its smaller neighbors, which had supported Austria. In Bismarck's scheme, this enlarged Prussia would dominate the newly formed North German Confederation, comprising all the states north of the Main (MINE) River. From now on, Austria was excluded from German affairs.

The triumph of Sadowa made Bismarck a popular hero. Elections held on the day of the battle returned a conservative pro-Bismarck majority to the Prussian parliament. The legislature, including a large number of liberals mesmerized by the military victory, voted to legalize retroactively the illegal taxes that had been levied since 1862 to upgrade the military. In making this compromise, liberals gave national unity higher priority than constitutional institutions, which they mistakenly thought could be secured later.

The unification of Germany, like that of Italy, was facilitated by a favorable international situation. The Crimean War had estranged Russia from Austria, once allies. Although it would have been opportune for France to intervene on the Austrian side in the Austro-Prussian War, the French emperor had been lulled into inaction by vague Prussian promises of support for French plans to annex Luxembourg. Once the war was won, Bismarck reneged on these promises. France was left with the problem of a strong, enlarged Prussia on its eastern border, which threatened France's position as a Great Power. British leaders likewise did not intervene in the unification process. Disillusioned by the results of the Crimean War, they were in an isolationist mood. Moreover, Britain's government was sympathetic to the rise of a fellow Protestant power.

Bismarck's design was almost complete. Only the southern German states remained outside the North German Confederation. He obliged them to sign a military treaty with Prussia and established a customs parliament for all the members of the Zollverein (the customs union), including the southern German states. The southern states, which were Catholic and sympathetic to Austria, were reluctant to see German unity advance any further. Only some dramatic event could remove their resistance.

French leaders were also determined to prevent German unity—French security had relied on a weak and divided Germany since the mid-seventeenth century.

Both Berlin and Paris anticipated war, which came soon enough, precipitated by a crisis over the Spanish succession. In 1868, a military coup had overthrown the Spanish queen Isabella, and the provisional government offered the throne to a Catholic member of the Hohenzollerns

Zollverein Customs union formed among states in the German Confederation beginning in 1834, creating an important step to later political unification of the German nation-state.

PRUSSIAN WARS AND GERMAN UNITY

THE FRANCO-PRUSSIAN WAR AND UNIFICATION, 1870–1871

🌐 **Map 22.2—The Unification of Germany, 1866–1871**

A series of military victories made it possible for Prussia to unite the German states under its domain.

(HO-en-tsoll-ernz), the reigning Prussian monarch's family. The French viewed this candidacy as an unacceptable expansion of Prussian power and influence. Fearing a two-front war with Prussia in the east and Spain in the south, they insisted that the Hohenzollerns refuse the proffered throne. As passions heated, Bismarck was elated at the prospect of war, but King Wilhelm was not. On July 12, 1870, Wilhelm engineered the withdrawal of the young prince's candidacy for the Spanish throne, removing the cause for war. Bismarck was bitterly disappointed.

Not content with this diplomatic victory, the French pushed their luck further. On July 13, the French ambassador met the king of Prussia at the resort spa of Ems and demanded guarantees that no Hohenzollern would ever again be a candidate for the Spanish throne. Unable to provide any more concessions without a serious loss of prestige, the Prussian king refused the French petition.

Wilhelm telegraphed an account of his meeting to Bismarck. The chancellor immediately seized the opportunity this message provided. He edited the message to make the exchange between king and ambassador seem more curt than it actually had been; then he released it to the press. As he hoped, the French interpreted what became known as the "Ems Dispatch" to be a deliberate snub to their ambassador, and overreacted. Napoleon III was deluged with emotional demands that he avenge the imagined slight to French national honor. On July 15, he declared war.

The Prussians led a well-planned campaign. An army of 384,000 Prussians was rushed by rail to confront a force of 270,000 Frenchmen. The French had the advantage of better rifles, but the Prussians were equipped with heavier cannon, which could pulverize French positions from a distance. Within a few weeks, Prussia won a decisive victory at Sedan (seh-DAEN), taking the French emperor prisoner on September 2. The French continued the struggle, despite difficult odds. Infuriated by the continuation of the war, the Prussians resorted to extreme measures. They took hostages and burned down whole villages, and then laid siege to Paris, starving and bombarding its beleaguered population.

Throughout Germany, the outbreak of the war aroused general enthusiasm for the Prussian cause. Exploiting this popular feeling, Bismarck called on leaders of the southern German states to accept the unification of Germany under the Prussian king. Reluctant princes, such as the king of Bavaria, were bought off with bribes. On January 18, 1871, the German princes met in the Hall of Mirrors at the palace of Versailles, symbol of past French greatness. There, they acclaimed the Prussian king as Kaiser Wilhelm I, German emperor.

In May 1871, the Treaty of Frankfurt established the peace terms (see **Map 22.1**). France was forced to give up the industrially rich provinces of Alsace and Lorraine and to pay Germany a heavy indemnity of five billion francs. These harsh terms embittered the French, leading many to desire revenge and establishing a formidable barrier to future Franco-German relations.

THE CHARACTER OF THE NEW GERMANY

German unity had been won through a series of wars—against Denmark in 1864, Austria in 1866, and France in 1870. The military had played a key role in forging German unity; victory in these wars had been due to the extraordinary leadership of Field Marshall Helmuth von Moltke and the Prussian general staff, the importance of which is represented in von Moltke's pride of place next to Bismarck in the opening illustration to this chapter. The military was established as a dominant force in the new nation. Italian unity had been sanctioned by plebiscites and a vote by an elected assembly accepting the popular verdict. The founding act of the new German state, as the illustration also shows, was the acclamation of the German emperor by German rulers on the soil of a defeated neighbor. Thus, the rulers placed themselves above elected assemblies and popular sanction.

On the surface, the constitution of the new Germany was remarkably democratic. It provided for an upper, appointed house, the *Bundesrat* (BOON-tes-raht), representing the individual German states, and a lower house, the *Reichstag* (RYSH-stak), which was elected by universal manhood suffrage. The latter might seem a surprising concession from Bismarck. But he knew the liberals lacked mass support and had confidence that he would be able to create majorities that could be manipulated for his purposes.

The authoritarianism of Prussia was projected onto all of Germany. The king of Prussia occupied the post of emperor, and the chancellor and other cabinet members were responsible only to him, and not to parliament. Only the emperor could make foreign policy and war, command the army, and interpret the constitution.

The emergence of a strong, united Germany shattered the European balance of power. In February 1871, the British political leader Benjamin Disraeli observed that the unification of Germany was a "greater political event than the French revolution of last century. … There is not a diplomatic tradition which has not been swept away. You have a new world. … The balance of power has been entirely destroyed."[2]

SECTION SUMMARY

- The reconfiguration of international relations after the Crimean War, in addition to persistent desires for national unification from 1848 among various groups, created opportunities for the unification of Italy and Germany into new nation-states. The strongest states in each achieved unification through conspiracy, war, and policies reflecting the new "Realpolitik" that characterized domestic and international relations.

- Italy's unification began with the Piedmont-Sardinian Prime Minister Cavour's plotting war against Austria with Napoleon III of France in order to free Lombardy and Venetia of Austrian rule. Giuseppe Garibaldi and his army advanced the process when rebellion against the Bourbon monarchy broke out in the south, and it was completed in 1870 as a by-product of the Franco-Prussian War.

- The Zollverein, a customs union that included most German states, but excluded Austria, helped advance support for national unification under Prussia. Prussia's reformed and expanded army, which Bismarck achieved without legislative approval, assured Prussian success in wars against Denmark (1864), Austria (1866), and France (1870), which finalized unification without Austria.

- Though Italian and German unifications each resulted from wars, the former had the benefit of plebiscites, while the latter did not, reflecting the more authoritarian character of the new German nation. Germany, henceforth, became the dominant power on the European continent, shattering the balance of power.

FRAGILE EMPIRES

How did the Austrian, Ottoman, and Russian Empires deal with the challenges they faced?

The three large empires of central and eastern Europe, battered by aggressive behavior from other European states and challenged by internal tensions, attempted to weather the endless crises they confronted. The Austrian, Ottoman, and Russian Empires labored to fortify their regimes with political reforms, but only Austria tried to accommodate democratic impulses by establishing a parliament. The Ottoman sultans and the Russian tsars clung tenaciously to their autocratic traditions.

The Dual Monarchy in Austria-Hungary

Emperor Franz Joseph (r. 1848–1916) had come to the Austrian throne as an 18-year-old in that year of crisis, 1848. He was a well-meaning monarch who took his duties seriously. His upbringing was German, he lived in German-speaking Vienna, and he headed an army and a bureaucracy that was mostly German. But Franz Joseph was markedly cosmopolitan. He spoke several of his subjects' languages and thought of himself as the emperor of all his peoples. A much-loved, regal figure, Franz Joseph provided a visible symbol of the state. He lacked imagination, however, and did little more than try to conserve a disintegrating empire coping with the modern forces of liberalism and nationalism.

After the war with Piedmont and France (see page 620), Austrian statesmen sensed the vulnerability of their empire. To give the government credibility, in February 1861, Franz Joseph issued what became known as the **February Patent**, which guaranteed civil liberties and provided for local self-government and a parliament elected by eligible males.

February Patent
Enactment issued in 1861 by the Austrian emperor Franz Joseph that established a constitutional monarchy in the old Austrian Empire.

The need to safeguard the remaining territories was clear. By 1866, the Austrian Habsburgs were no longer a German or an Italian power (Venetia had been handed over to a united Italy in return for assisting Prussia in defeating Austria). The strongest challenge to Habsburg rule came from Hungary, where the Magyars insisted on self-rule, a claim based on age-old rights and Vienna's initial acceptance of autonomy in 1848. Since Magyar cooperation was crucial for the well-being of the Habsburg Empire, the government entered into lengthy negotiations with Magyar leaders in 1867. The outcome was the **Compromise of 1867**. The agreement divided the Habsburg holdings into Austria in the west and Hungary in the east (see **MAP 22.3**). Each was independent, but they were linked by the person of the emperor of Austria, Franz Joseph, who was also king of Hungary. Hungary had full internal autonomy and participated jointly in imperial affairs—state finance, defense, and foreign relations. The new state created in 1867 was known as the dual monarchy of Austria-Hungary.

Compromise of 1867
Agreement that divided the Habsburg Empire into Austria in the west and Hungary in the east, a dual monarchy under Emperor Franz Joseph called Austria-Hungary.

The compromise confirmed Magyar dominance in Hungary. Although numerically a minority, the Magyars were nonetheless the largest of several ethnic groups; they controlled the Hungarian parliament, the army, the bureaucracy, and other state institutions. They opposed self-rule of other ethnic groups in the kingdom who spoke different languages: the Croats, Serbs, Slovaks, and Romanians. They also attempted a policy of Magyarization—teaching only Magyar in the schools, conducting all government business in Magyar, and giving access to government positions only to those fully assimilated in Magyar culture. This arrangement created frustrations and resistance among the various nationalities under their rule.

The terms of the compromise also gave the Hungarians a voice in imperial foreign policy. The Magyars feared that Slavic groups outside the empire, who planned to form independent states or had already done so, would inspire fellow Slavs in Austria-Hungary to revolt. To prevent that, the Hungarians favored an expansionist foreign policy in the Balkans, which the monarchy embraced (see **MAP 22.3**). Having lost its influence in Germany, Austria-Hungary saw the Balkans as an area in which it could assert itself—a policy that led to hostilities with other states.

The Ailing Ottoman Empire

At midcentury, the Ottoman Empire was still one of the largest European powers, but it faced unrest within its borders and threats from the expansionist designs of its neighbors. The ailing empire was commonly referred to as "the sick man of Europe." Over the next twenty-five years, the empire shed some of its territory and modernized its government, but nothing could save it from decline in the face of nationalist uprisings in its Balkan possessions.

🌐 **MAP 22.3—Austria-Hungary in 1878**

The Compromise of 1867 produced the dual monarchy of Austria-Hungary. A state of many languages and ethnicities, the Austro-Hungarian Empire occupied Bosnia in 1878, bringing more dissatisfied peoples under its rule. Tensions in the Balkans would lead to the outbreak of world war in 1914.

Map legend:

Ethnic majority
- Czechs
- Germans
- Hungarians
- Italians
- Poles
- Romanians
- Carpatho-Ukrainians (Ruthenians)
- Serbs & Croats
- Slovaks
- Slovenes

— Boundary of the Habsburg Monarchy
— Boundary of the Kingdom of Hungary

As early as the 1840s, the Ottoman Empire had begun various reform movements to bring more security to its subjects. Emulating Western institutions, the reforms introduced security of property, equity in taxation, and equality before the law regardless of religion. Government officials—who previously had been free to collect taxes arbitrarily, sending the required amount to the central government and keeping the rest—were given fixed salaries and subjected to regular inspections.

These reforms were strengthened after the Crimean War by further imperial edicts. Many young intellectuals were impatient with the pace of change, however, and critical of the sultan. Unable to freely express their opinions at home, some went into exile in Paris and London in the late 1860s. Their hosts called them the **Young Turks**, an expression that became synonymous with activists for change and improvement.

The failure to hold on to its empire caused further dissatisfaction with Ottoman rule among its people, and in the spring of 1876, rioters demanded and won the establishment of constitutional government. Within a year, however, the new sultan, Abdul Hamid II (r. 1876–1909), dismissed the constitutional government and reverted to personal rule. Part of the administration's problem was financial. The easy terms of foreign credit lured the sultan into taking out huge loans to finance extravagant projects. In spite of drought and famine, the authorities raised taxes to pay debts, fostering widespread discontent.

WESTERN-STYLE REFORM

Young Turks Young intellectuals who wanted to transform the Ottoman Empire into a more modern, Westernized state. The expression has subsequently come to designate any group of activists pushing for political change.

received some land, but its value was vastly overrated and its quantity insufficient for peasant families. To make ends meet, most freed peasants continued working for their former masters.

mir Russian peasant commune. After Tsar Alexander II freed the serfs in 1861, the mir determined land use and paid the government mortgages and taxes.

The local commune, or **mir**, handled the mortgage payments and taxes that the central government imposed on the peasants. The mir (MEER) determined how the land was to be used, and it paid collectively for the mortgages and taxes on the land. As a consequence, the commune needed peasants to remain on the land, and they could leave only with its permission. Freed from serfdom, the peasants still suffered many constraints. In fact, the emancipation declaration was accompanied by massive peasant uprisings that had to be put down by force.

The tsar and his advisers feared the large mass of uneducated peasants as a potential source of anarchy and rebellion. They depended on the mir to preserve control, even though the commune system had some inherent economic disadvantages. Since increased productivity benefited the commune as much as the individual peasant, there was little incentive for peasants to improve their land, and agricultural yields remained low.

GOVERNMENT REFORM

zemstvos Village or district assemblies created by Tsar Alexander II in 1864 as part of the Great Reform; they elected delegates to regional assemblies.

Between 1800 and 1850, the Russian population had increased from 36 million to 59 million, and administering this vast country had become increasingly difficult. Overcentralized, with a poorly trained civil service, the government was unable to cope effectively with the problems of its people. Emancipation of the serfs greatly exacerbated this situation, as suddenly 22 million illiterate peasants threatened to overwhelm existing institutions. To address these problems, an 1864 law created village or regional governments, or **zemstvos** (SEMST-vose), which gave Russians the authority and the opportunity to use initiative in local matters.

The zemstvos were largely controlled by the gentry and not particularly democratic. They were forbidden to debate political issues, and their decisions could be overridden or ignored by local officials appointed by the tsar. Some hoped that zemstvos could become the basis for self-government at the national level and looked for the creation of an all-Russian zemstvo, but the tsar firmly squelched such hopes. He jealously continued to insist and depend on an undivided and undiminished autocracy. Nonetheless, the zemstvos were a viable attempt to modernize an overburdened central government and created an important precedent for self-government.

The tsar also created an independent judiciary that ensured equality before the law, public jury trials, and uniform sentences. Russian political leaders recognized that growth in commerce and industry required public confidence in the judiciary and the rule of law. Businessmen would no longer fear arbitrary intervention by capricious officials and could develop enterprises in greater security.

In addition, censorship of the press was abolished. Under the previous tsar, Nicholas I, all ideas that did not conform to government policy were censored. Such censorship prevented the central government from being well informed about public opinion or about the effects of its policies on the country. Under Alexander, openness in the press was viewed as a remedy for corruption and misuse of power.

Reform also extended to the Russian army. Its structure and methods became more Western. Military service, previously limited to peasants, became the obligation of all Russian men, who submitted to a lottery. Those with an "unlucky" number entered the service. In an effort to make military service more attractive, the length of service was drastically cut and corporal punishment was abolished. Access to the officer corps was to be by merit rather than by social connection. The Ministry of War also improved the system of reserves, enabling Russia to mobilize a larger army with more modern weapons in case of war.

The Great Reforms represented considerable change for Russia. Nonetheless, Alexander remained wedded to the principles of autocracy. His aim in abolishing serfdom and introducing other reforms was to modernize and strengthen Russia and stabilize his divinely mandated rule. Like most Russians, Alexander believed that only the firm hand of autocracy could hold together a large, ethnically diverse country. The tsarist regime thus remained repressive, flexible only to the degree that its rulers had the will and wisdom to be.

SECTION SUMMARY

- Internal tensions and aggressive behavior of the European powers, as well as nationalist aspirations in the Balkan provinces, forced the Austrian, Ottoman, and Russian Empires to reform.

- Loss of the Italian territories and Magyar desire for self-rule in Hungary weakened Austrian rule. The Compromise of 1867 divided Habsburg territories into the dual monarchy of Austria-Hungary.

- The Ottoman Empire became weakened by nationalist uprisings in its Balkan possessions, making it prey to Western imperialistic ambitions. Territorial shifts, such as the transfer of Bosnia and Herzegovina to Austrian administration, created conditions for further instability and war in the Balkans.

- Russia undertook a series of reforms beginning in 1861: the abolition of serfdom, establishment of local governments, equality before the law, abolition of press censorship, and improvements in military service.

THE DEVELOPMENT OF WESTERN DEMOCRACIES

How did western European states create democracies?

In the generation after 1850, Britain, France, and several smaller states in northern Europe made major strides forward in creating democratic political systems and cultures. Although universal manhood suffrage had been instituted only in France, all these countries' governments were responsible to elected representatives of the voters.

Victorian Britain

The mid-nineteenth century was a period of exceptional wealth and security for Britain, as the population as a whole began to share in the economic benefits of industrialization. Britain enjoyed both social and political peace. The political system was not challenged as it had been in the generation after the Napoleonic Wars. A self-assured, even smug, elite—merchants, industrialists, and landowners—developed a political system reflecting liberal values.

Although suffrage was still restricted to propertied Christian men before the 1850s, the parliamentary system was firmly established, with government clearly responsible to the electorate. The importance of Parliament was symbolized by the new building in which it met, finished in 1850 and of unprecedented splendor and size. The form of government developed in its halls after midcentury aroused the curiosity and envy of much of the world. (See the feature, "The Global Record: A Japanese View of the British Parliament.")

In the twenty years after 1846, five different political parties vied for power. Depending on the issue, parties and factions coalesced to support particular policies. After 1867, however, a clear two-party system emerged: Liberal and Conservative (Tory), both with strong leadership. This development gave the electorate a distinct choice. The Conservatives were committed to preserving traditional institutions and practices, whereas the Liberals were more open to change.

Two strong-minded individuals headed these parties and dominated British political life for over a generation: William E. Gladstone (1809–1898), a Liberal, and Benjamin Disraeli (1804–1881), a Conservative. Both Gladstone and Disraeli were master debaters; Parliament and the press hung on their every word. Each was capable of making speeches lasting five hours or more and of conducting debates that kept the house in session until 4:00 A.M. The rivalry between the two men thrilled the nation and made politics a popular pastime.

The Conservatives' electoral base came from the landed classes, from Anglicans, and from England, rather than the rest of the United Kingdom (consisting of Scotland, Wales, and Ireland). The Liberals' base came from the middle classes, from Christian groups other than the Church of England, and from Scotland and Wales. In the House of Commons, both parties had a large number of members from the landed aristocracy, but cabinet members were increasingly chosen for political competence rather than family background. Aristocratic birth was no longer a requirement for reaching the pinnacle of power.

The competition for power between the Liberals and the Conservatives led to an extension of suffrage in 1867. The

Disraeli and Gladstone: Victorian Political Rivals   This 1868 cartoon from *Punch* magazine captures the politicians' personalities. Disraeli was known as vain and theatrical, while Gladstone was dour and moralistic.   (Mary Evans Picture Library)

A Japanese View of the British Parliament

In 1862, the Japanese government sent its first diplomatic mission to Europe. Accompanying the delegation was a young translator, Fukuzawa Yukichi (1835–1901). Intrigued by what he saw and eager to interest his fellow Japanese in the West, Fukuzawa published several books. In fact, all books about the West in Japan came to be known as "Fukuzawa-bon." Toward the end of his life, in his Autobiography, he described how, while in London, he had tried to understand the workings of the British Parliament.

Of political situations at that time, I tried to learn as much as I could from various persons that I met in London . . . though it was often difficult to understand things clearly as I was as yet unfamiliar with the history of Europe. . . . A perplexing institution was representative government. When I asked a gentleman what the "election law" was and what kind of an institution the Parliament really was, he simply replied with a smile, meaning I suppose that no intelligent person was expected to ask such questions. But these were the things most difficult of all for me to understand. In this connection, I learned that there were different political parties—the Liberal and the Conservative—who were always "fighting" against each other in the government.

For some time it was beyond my comprehension to understand what they were "fighting" for, and what was meant, anyway, by "fighting" in peace time. "This man and that man are 'enemies' in the House," they would tell me. But these "enemies" were to be seen at the same table, eating and drinking with each other. I felt as if I could not make much out of this. It took me a long time, with some tedious thinking, before I could gather a general notion of these separate mysterious facts. In some of the more complicated matters, I might achieve an understanding five or ten days after they were explained to me. But all in all, I learned much from this initial tour of Europe.

QUESTIONS

1. Why might the Japanese visitor have been puzzled by the use of the words *fighting* and *enemies* in this context?

2. Would Japanese readers have obtained a good idea of the British parliamentary system based on this report?

Source: *The Autobiography of Fukuzawa Yukichi*, trans. Eiizhi Kiyooka. Copyright 1948, 2007 by Columbia University Press. Reproduced with permission of Columbia University Press via Copyright Clearance Center.

Second Reform Bill

British legislation that extended suffrage to clerks, artisans, and other skilled workers by lowering property qualifications.

Second Reform Bill lowered property qualifications for the vote, thus extending it from 1.4 million to 2.5 million men out of a population of 22 million. The bill also equalized electoral districts, which gave new urban areas better representation. Although some in Parliament feared that these changes would lead to the masses capturing political power—"a leap into the dark," one member called it—in fact, no radical change ensued. Extending the vote to clerks, artisans, and other skilled workers made them feel more a part of society and thus bolstered the existing system rather than undermining it. John Stuart Mill, then a member of Parliament, along with his colleague and wife, Harriet Taylor Mill (1807–1856), championed the cause of women's suffrage; but he had few allies in Parliament, and that effort failed.

As the extension of voting rights increased the size of the electorate, parties became larger and stronger. Strong party systems meant alternation of power between the Liberals and the Conservatives. With an obvious majority and minority party, the monarch could no longer play favorites in choosing a prime minister. The leader of the majority party had to be asked to form a government. Thus, even though Queen Victoria (r. 1837–1901) detested Gladstone, she had to ask him to form governments when the Liberals won parliamentary elections. (See the feature, "The Visual Record: An Engraving of the British Royal Family.")

The creation of a broad-based electorate also meant that politicians had to make clear appeals to the public and its interests. In the past, oratory had been limited to the halls of Parliament, but after the electoral reforms, it occurred in the public arena as well. Public election campaigns increasingly had to appeal to the common man. The adoption of the secret ballot in 1872 protected lower-class voters from intimidation by their employers, landowners, or other social superiors. In 1874, the first two working-class members of Parliament were elected, sitting as Liberals.

France: From Empire to Republic

France took a more tumultuous path to parliamentary democracy than Britain. Revolutions and wars overthrew existing political systems and inaugurated new ones. Each time the French seemed to have democracy within reach, the opportunity slipped away.

The constitution of the Second French Republic (1848–1852) provided for a single four-year presidential term. Frustrated by this limitation of power, Louis Napoleon engineered a coup d'état in 1851 to extend his presidency to a ten-year term. The following year, he called for a plebiscite to confirm him as Napoleon III (r. 1852–1870), emperor of the French. Both of these moves were resisted in the countryside, particularly in the south, but massive repression defeated all opposition.

In the rest of the country, huge majorities of voters endorsed first the prolonged presidency and then the imperial title. Much of the populace genuinely supported Louis Napoleon in these two plebiscites. But prefects—local administrators appointed by the government—had helped produce the favorable majorities by manipulating elections. As emperor, Napoleon III made no claim to divine right and kept in place the apparatus of parliamentary government—including universal male suffrage. He could not, however, tolerate any opposition and used police force to repress it. He also suppressed freedom of assembly and regulated the press. In subsequent legislative elections, local prefects also assured that "official" candidates—those loyal to the regime—were elected to the legislature.

Napoleon III never enjoyed deep support, but his most vociferous opponents either fell silent or, like poet Victor Hugo, were driven into exile. Many republicans continued to harbor resentment because he had usurped the constitution of 1848. But economic growth in the 1850s and 1860s, some of which resulted from his own business-expanding policies, helped stabilize his regime. Most Frenchmen, including urban workers and peasants, generally enjoyed better living standards, and many of those who initially opposed him came to support him. With his power consolidated by 1859, Napoleon III began to relax his dictatorial rule, and a more liberal atmosphere prevailed in the 1860s. In an attempt to win over the opposition, Napoleon made some concessions, easing censorship and making his government more accountable to the parliament. But instead of winning him new support, liberalization allowed the expression of mounting opposition.

Republican candidates were elected to the legislature. Workers won limited rights to strike, and labor unions were virtually legalized. A number of issues—including opposition to policies of free trade, widespread hostility toward the influence of the Catholic Church, and the desire for more extensive freedom of expression and assembly—helped forge a republican alliance of the middle classes and workers. This alliance was strongest in the large cities and in some southern regions notorious for their opposition to central government control. Republicanism was better organized than in earlier years and had a more explicit program. Moreover, its proponents were now better prepared to take over the government, if the opportunity arose.

By 1869, the regime of Napoleon III, which declared itself a "liberal empire," had evolved into a constitutional monarchy, responsible to the parliament. In a plebiscite in May 1870, Frenchmen supported the liberal empire by a vote of five to one. It might have endured had Napoleon III not rashly declared war against Prussia two months later in a huff over the supposedly insulting Ems dispatch (see page 625). Rapid defeat at the hands of Bismarck brought down the empire. In September, at news of the emperor's capture, the republican opposition in the parliament declared a republic. It continued the war but had to sign an armistice in January 1871.

The leader of the new government was an old prime minister of Louis Philippe, Adolphe Thiers (tee-YAIR) (1797–1877). Before signing a definitive peace, the provisional government held elections. The liberals, known as republicans, since they favored a republic, were identified with continuing the war; the conservatives, mostly royalists, favored peace. Mainly because of their position on this issue, the royalists won a majority from a country discouraged by defeat.

The new regime had no time to establish itself before a workers' uprising in the spring of 1871 shook France, reminding the rest of Europe of revolutionary dangers. The uprising was called the **Paris Commune**—a name referring to the municipal government that harked back to 1792 to 1794, when the Paris crowds had dictated to the national government. The Commune insisted on its right to local rule. Radicals and conservatives greeted the Commune as a workers' revolt intended to establish a workers' government. Marx described it as the "bold champion of the emancipation of labor." Women took an active part, fighting on the barricades, pouring scalding water on soldiers, posting revolutionary broadsides. Louise Michel (1830–1905) was a schoolteacher who became famous for her leadership in active fighting and for her agitation for socialism and women's rights.

Although labor discontent played a role in the Paris Commune, other forces also contributed, notably the earlier Prussian siege of Paris during the Franco-Prussian War. Paris had become radicalized during the siege: The rich had evacuated the city, leaving a power vacuum quickly filled by the lower classes. Parisians suffered much because of the siege; angered that their economic needs went unmet and their courage against the Prussians unnoticed, they rose up against the new French government. The paramount issue of food sparked the massive women's participation in the uprising. The Commune, composed largely of artisans, now governed the city.

Paris Commune Parisian workers' uprising intended to establish a workers' government under home rule. It was violently suppressed by the army of the conservative French government.

An Engraving of the British Royal Family

This illustration of the British royal family might have been that of any upper-middle-class family. Queen Victoria is plainly dressed; her husband, Prince Albert, wears a dark business suit; the children are clothed in simple outfits. The simplicity conveyed by the family extends to the image of the rest of England, depicted as a quaint farm with a grouping of common people. Notice the crown hovering over this idyllic pastoral scene.

Illustrations of this type—appearing in a song book that would find its way into British homes—familiarized the British with their monarch. Surrounded by her husband and children, the queen focuses her gaze not on the viewer—a British subject—but on her children. It is her husband, the prince, who, protective of his family, gazes outward. In the past, representations of the monarchy had suggested power and intimidation. The aura of the close-knit, nuclear royal family suggested a reassuring serenity to British subjects. It also offered a model for the family and gender very much like those to which middle-class families aspired.

Victoria cultivated the image of herself as contented mother, but in reality, she resented much about motherhood. She complained of the extent to which her pregnancies interfered with her daily routines and prevented her from traveling and from being with her beloved Albert. She lamented, "I think our sex a most unenviable one." She described childbearing as an "annoyance" that made her feel "so pinned down—one's wings clipped." She also refused to romanticize birthing, seeing it as an animal-like act that reduced a woman to "a cow or a dog." For the births of her seventh and eighth children, she resorted to the uncommon practice of using chloroform to alleviate the pain of labor—the first public figure to do so openly. Even after their infancy, Victoria continued to describe her children as "an awful plague and anxiety" who showed no gratitude. But such views were expressed privately, and the public never suspected Victoria's ambivalence about motherhood.

Despite her complaints, the highly moral image of Victoria's family life contrasted with that of her predecessors. Her grandfather George III (r. 1760–1820) had been plagued with bouts of insanity. Her uncle George IV (r. 1820–1830) was a notorious philanderer. George IV and his brothers, the duke of Clarence (later to be William IV [r. 1830–1837]) and the duke of Kent (Victoria's father), were bigamists. They fathered a large brood of children out of wedlock and were implicated in numerous public scandals.

Public outrage at the excesses of Victoria's predecessors had produced a call to abolish the institution of monarchy. Given the disrepute into which the monarchy had fallen and the rise of republican sentiment, the crowning of a woman in 1837 may have substantially lessened antimonarchical sentiment. Victoria, as a young, seemingly frail woman coming to the throne at age 18, lent a certain gallantry to the royal household. Moreover, as a female monarch, she was seen as less of a threat to constitutional liberties.

The image of Victoria shown here intentionally contrasts her reign with those of her predecessors. The simple terms in which she and her family are depicted appealed to the growing middle class of the second half of the nineteenth century. The portrayal also fit the emerging democratic spirit—and electoral power—of the lower classes. Henceforth, monarchs would not be able to ignore public opinion. This image marks a historical departure in other ways. Victoria is surrounded by four of her children (eventually, she would have nine). Her royal predecessors had died without leaving any legitimate direct heirs, thus endangering the regular succession to the throne. This engraving sent the message that the royal line was assured. British people, wary of a female ruler, could find solace, not only from her husband's confident gaze outward, but in knowing that Victoria would be succeeded by one of her sons.

Unlike Victoria's uncles and father, who were wastrels and bankrupts, the queen and her husband lived frugally by royal standards and conducted an exemplary family life. Royal wealth increased under Prince Albert's careful administration. Instead of being subject to various debtors, the British royal house became one of the wealthiest and most prominent landowners in Great Britain. It is most telling that by the time of her death in 1901, Victoria had considerably strengthened the institution of monarchy, having restored confidence in and respect for it.

Under Victoria's rule, Britain completed the process of becoming a constitutional monarchy. The queen cultivated the image of being above politics and a symbol of national unity. Fellow monarchs in central and eastern Europe exercised greater power, but after World War I, they were all toppled. In Britain, monarchy in its constitutional form endured. Victoria established a pattern of public and private behavior by which members of subsequent generations of the British royal family were to be judged. This portrayal of the royal family also suggests the important role that visual imagery played in creating public support for state power in the nineteenth century.

In March 1871, the Commune declared itself free to carry out policies independent of the central government, temporarily located in Versailles. It sought free universal education, a fairer taxation system, a minimum wage, and disestablishment of the official Catholic Church. Finding these goals too radical, the conservative French government sent the army to suppress the Commune. It massacred 25,000 people, arrested 40,000, and deported several thousand more.

ILLUSTRATED BOOK OF BRITISH SONG.

THY CHOICEST GIFTS IN STORE. ON HER BE PLEASED TO POUR.

GOD SAVE THE QUEEN.

Illustration from the Illustrated Book of British Song (Visual Connection Archive)

QUESTIONS

1. Why did it make sense for the British royal family to have itself portrayed so simplistically? What values does this engraving communicate to British subjects?

2. How does this engraving exemplify the importance of visual imagery in conveying the meaning of monarchy to British subjects?

The crushing of the Paris Commune and some of its sister communes in southern France, which had also asserted local autonomy, signified the increasing power of centralized government. One mark of the emerging modern state was its capacity to squelch popular revolts that, in the past, had constituted serious threats. Western Europe would never again witness a popular uprising of this magnitude.

Despite its brutality, the suppression of the Commune reassured many Frenchmen. The question now at hand was what form the new government would take. The monarchist majority in the democratically elected parliament offered the throne to the Bourbon pretender. However, he insisted he would become king only if the *tricouleur*—the blue, white, and red flag of the Revolution, which long since had become a cherished national symbol—were discarded and replaced by the white flag of the house of Bourbon. This was unacceptable, so France remained a republic. The republic, as Thiers put it, "is the regime which divides us the least."

By 1875, the parliament had approved a set of basic laws that became the constitution of the Third Republic. Ironically, a monarchist parliament had created a liberal, democratic parliamentary regime. A century after the French Revolution, the republican system of government in France was firmly launched.

Scandinavia and the Low Countries

France and especially Britain served as models of parliamentary democracy for the smaller states in northern Europe. Denmark, Sweden, Norway, Holland, and Belgium recast their political institutions at midcentury. Several of the states were affected by the revolutions of 1848. That year, protesters in Denmark demanded enlarged political participation (see page 612), Sweden saw minor riots, and the king of the Netherlands (after 1830, Holland and the Netherlands refer to the same country) feared revolution in the neighboring German states would spill into his country. In Copenhagen, King Frederick VII (r. 1848–1863), who had no stomach for a confrontation, accepted a constitution providing for parliamentary government. "Now I can sleep as long as I like," he is reputed to have said.

Sweden's parliamentary system, in place since the Middle Ages, had representation by estates—noble, clergy, burgher, and peasant. The 11,000 nobles were given the same weight as the 2.5 million to 3 million peasants. After the riots of 1848, liberal aristocrats recognized that abolition of the estates system would best preserve their privileges, removing the major issue that had provoked popular resentments. In 1866, the estates were finally replaced by a parliament with two houses. The upper house was restricted to the wealthiest landowners and the lower house to men of property, providing the vote to 20 percent of adult men. Norway had been joined to Sweden in 1814 under the Swedish king, but it had a separate parliament and made its own laws. Swedish rule rankled the Norwegians, however, and in the 1850s, the Norwegian Liberal Party began to insist that the king should not have the final word in governance. Instead, they argued, the parliament, representative of the Norwegian people, should be supreme. In 1883, the principle that government officials are responsible to parliament won out. In 1905, Norway peacefully separated from Sweden and became an independent state.

In the Netherlands, as a result of the revolutions of 1848, the king recognized the need to strengthen support for his crown by acceding to liberals' demands for parliamentary government. By midcentury, government officials in the Netherlands were responsible to the parliament rather than to the king. A new constitution guaranteed the principles of freedom of speech, assembly, and religion.

Belgium had enjoyed a liberal constitution from the time it became an independent state after its revolution in 1830, but because no strong party system materialized, the king was able to appoint to government whomever he pleased. In the 1840s, the liberals organized, and the king, reluctantly, had to invite them to govern in 1848. The new government reduced property qualifications for voting, thus increasing the electorate.

Contrary to the conservative backlashes that rescinded reform following the revolutions of 1848 elsewhere, the sweeping reforms in northern European states became the basis for their evolution into full democracies. For full democracy to take hold, the electorate had to be broadened. These years witnessed much agitation for universal male suffrage. Property qualifications, wherever they were instituted, were questioned and resisted. For instance, in Sweden, the stipulation that a man had to earn 800 crowns a year to be a voter unleashed a pamphlet war: What if a man earned only 799 crowns? Did that make him less qualified? Although suffrage still remained limited in these countries, it was only a matter of time before democracy would be achieved.

SECTION SUMMARY

- By the late 1860s, a two-party system emerged in Britain: Conservative (Tory) and Liberal.

- The Second Reform Bill (1867) in Britain extended the vote and equalized voting districts, giving significantly more representation to urban areas.

- War and revolution continued to shape France's path to democracy. The French Second Republic, born of revolution, gave way to the authoritarian rule of Louis Napoleon, who became Napoleon III in 1852.

- The Franco-Prussian War of 1870–1871 ended the Second Empire of Napoleon III and gave birth to the French Third Republic.

- Denmark, Sweden, Norway, the Netherlands, and Belgium peacefully established governments responsible to parliaments rather than to their kings, providing the basis for their evolution toward full democracies.

CHAPTER SUMMARY

Liberal nationalists in the early nineteenth century had believed that Europe would be freer and more peaceful if each people had a separate nation, if the power between those nations could be balanced. The Crimean War proved them wrong. The Great Powers became rival states in pursuit of their own self-interests, largely at the expense of the Ottoman Empire. The post-war peace settlement impaired Ottoman efforts to repress nationalist movements in the Balkans.

The Crimean War and its aftermath also created an international climate that permitted the emergence of two newly unified nation-states, Italy and Germany. In the case of Italy, unification occurred through the leadership of Cavour in Piedmont-Sardinia (Kingdom of Sardinia). After waging war against Austria to acquire the northern provinces (with partial success), Cavour brought the revolutionary national movement of the south, led by Garibaldi, under the centralized control of Piedmont-Sardinia. Plebiscites and an elected assembly sanctioned Italian unification.

Germany, through a series of wars, became unified under the authoritarian, centralized control of Prussia. Bismarck annexed the northern German states after defeating Austria. After Prussia's victory in war against France, Bismarck was able to press the southern states into unity with the north. This process lent the German state, even with parliamentary rule, an authoritarian and militaristic character. The rulers of the various German states accepted unification by personal acclamation rather than through consent from the German people.

FOCUS QUESTIONS

- How did the Crimean War affect international relations?

- What respective processes led to the unifications of Italy and Germany into nation-states, and how did they differ?

- How did the Austrian, Ottoman, and Russian Empires deal with the challenges they faced?

- How did western European states create democracies?

The Austrian and Ottoman Empires faced the daunting challenges of nationalistic movements seeking to break away from their rule. In the effort to keep their empires intact, rulers offered various reforms from above, modeled on the West; but at the same time, they attempted to exert centralized rule to suppress breakaway movements. Austria compromised by establishing a dual monarchy with Hungary. But the empire then turned its aggressive ambitions toward the Balkans in order to exert control over Slavic people. These ambitions further challenged the Ottoman Empire, already weakened by defeat in war against Russia in 1853. The 1856 Congress of Paris and subsequent Balkan wars led to the creation of the independent and sovereign states of Romania and Bulgaria, formerly Ottoman provinces.

Russia, considering itself a protector of Slavic peoples, took advantage of the Ottoman Empire's weakness to wage war against it, further fueling Balkan nationalism and extending its influence there. In the face of its own domestic ills, Russia instituted major reforms on a Western model; nonetheless it remained autocratic, repressive, and inflexible.

Britain, France, and several northern European states became increasingly democratic, answerable to a growing electorate. Britain successfully and peacefully extended suffrage and maintained its monarchy. In France, the crushing of the Paris Commune spelled doom for those who wanted a nation of decentralized self-governing units. Indeed, strong, centralized governments increasingly became the norm. In other states, parliaments had only limited powers; but once they were in place, they gradually gained more power and expanded the electorate. Parliaments gave governments the appearance of legitimacy through the consent of their peoples. Hence, all European rulers, except those of the Ottoman and Russian Empires, found it necessary to have a parliament.

KEY TERMS

Realpolitik (p. 616)

congress system (p. 616)

risorgimento (p. 618)

Otto von Bismarck (p. 622)

Zollverein (p. 623)

February Patent (p. 626)

Compromise of 1867 (p. 626)

Young Turks (p. 627)

mir (p. 630)

zemstvos (p. 630)

Second Reform Bill (p. 632)

Paris Commune (p. 633)

This icon will direct you to additional materials on the website: www.cengage.com/history/noble/westciv6e.

NOTES

1. Quoted in Otto Pflanze, *Bismarck and the Development of Germany*, vol. 1 (Princeton, N.J.: Princeton University Press, 1990), p. 184.

2. Quoted in William Flavelle Monypenny and George Earle Buckle, *The Life of Benjamin Disraeli: Earl of Beaconsfield*, vol. 2 (London: John Murray, 1929), pp. 473–474.

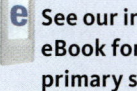 See our interactive eBook for map and primary source activities.

23

Felix Valloton: Le bon marché
(Snark/Art Resource, NY)

The Age of Optimism, 1850–1880

The Bon marché (the "good deal") was the first department store in Paris. Opening its doors in the 1850s, it served as a model for others in France and abroad. The store bought goods in mass quantities and thus could sell them at low prices. Constructed of glass and iron, the Bon marché represented the new, modern age. It combined under one roof a large range of products that previously had been available only in separate specialty shops—a time-saving convenience in an increasingly harried age. The store also had a large catalog sales department for customers too busy or distant to shop in person. Filled with toys, bed linens, furniture, crystal, and other items, the department store was a symbol of the new opulence of the middle classes.

FOCUS QUESTIONS

- What technological changes led to the expansion of the European economy after the mid-nineteenth century?

- How did the economic expansion affect the various social classes, and city versus rural areas, differently?

- What problems did urbanization create, and what were the solutions?

- What new scientific, intellectual, and cultural trends emerged in this period, and what impact did they have on systems of belief?

This new type of store would not have been possible in an earlier age. It represents a culmination of the various technological and social changes that the West experienced as industrialization advanced in the second half of the nineteenth century. Industrial innovation had lowered the price of glass and steel, so that these new, huge commercial emporiums could be built at reasonable cost. Railroads brought into the city large quantities of increasingly mass-produced goods, as well as out-of-town customers. In town, trams and omnibuses transported shoppers to the store. The penny press provided advertising for the department store, which in turn supported the emergence of this new medium. The expansion of the postal system facilitated catalog sales and the mailing of parcels to customers. And the higher incomes available to many people allowed them to purchase more than just the necessities. This era gave birth to the consumer society.

To a large extent, the growing middle classes, who were filled with optimism and convinced they were living in an age of progress, shaped prevailing attitudes in the second half of the nineteenth century. John Stuart Mill proclaimed that in his era "the general tendency is and will continue to be…one of improvement—a tendency towards a better and happier state." Across the Channel in France, the social thinker Auguste Comte (1798–1857) concurred, confidently stating, "Human development brings…an ever growing amelioration." The successful application of science and technology to social problems gave many men and women confidence in the human ability to improve the world. People controlled their environments to a degree never before possible. On farms, they increased the fertility of the soil; to the burgeoning cities, they brought greater order through urban planning and dazzling architecture. Scientists used new methods to study and combat disease. Public authorities founded schools, trained teachers, and reduced illiteracy. Transportation and communication rapidly improved.

Not all of society benefited from the fruits of progress. The new wealth was far from equally shared. Eastern and southern Europe changed little, and even in the western

This icon will direct you to additional materials on the website: www.cengage.com/history/noble/westciv6e.

 See our interactive eBook for map and primary source activities.

regions a large part of the population still lived in great misery. If some cities carried out ambitious programs of urban renewal, others continued to neglect slums. Public sanitation programs did not affect the majority of Europeans who lived in rural areas. Despite spectacular advances in science, much of the population maintained a traditional belief in divine intervention. Many intellectuals strongly denounced the materialism and smugness of the age, stressing the meanness and ignorance that lay just beneath the surface.

INDUSTRIAL GROWTH AND ACCELERATION

What technological changes led to the expansion of the European economy after the mid-nineteenth century?

Beginning in the 1850s, western Europe experienced an unprecedented level of economic expansion. Manufacturers created new products and harnessed new sources of energy. An enlarged banking system provided more abundant credit to fund this expansion. Scientific research improved methods of manufacture. A revolution in transportation speedily delivered goods and services to distant places. Technological innovation profoundly changed the daily lives of many Europeans.

The "Second Industrial Revolution"

second industrial revolution Interrelated economic changes after 1850 that included new sources of energy, new products, new methods of manufacture, and new materials, such as mass-produced steel, synthetic dyes, and aluminum.

The interrelated cluster of economic changes that began in the generation after 1850 is often called the **second industrial revolution**. It was characterized by a significant speedup in production and by the introduction of new materials, such as mass-produced steel, synthetic dyes, and aluminum. Manufacturers replaced the traditional steam engine with stronger steam-powered turbines or with machines powered by new forms of energy—petroleum and electricity.

The second half of the nineteenth century has often been called the "age of steel." In 1856, Sir Henry Bessemer (1813–1898) discovered a method that produced in twenty minutes the same amount of steel previously produced in twenty-four hours. In the next two decades, further advances in steel production yielded even more dramatic results. In Great Britain, for example, steel production increased fourfold, and by the 1880s, its price fell by 50 percent. Greater steel production made possible the expansion of the rail system, the creation of a steamship fleet, and an explosive growth in the building industry. Once a rare alloy used only for the finest swords and knives, steel became the material that defined the age.

Significant changes in the supply of credit further stimulated economic expansion. Discovery of gold in California and Australia led to the inflow of huge amounts of the precious metal to Europe, expanding the supply of money and credit. This led to the establishment of the modern banking system.

Each advance made possible additional changes. Increased wealth and credit financed industrial plant expansion and an ambitious infrastructure of roads, railroads, and steamships, which in turn boosted trade. Between 1850 and 1870, the value of world trade increased by 260 percent.

By the 1880s, important scientific discoveries fueled industrial improvements. Electricity came into wider use, replacing coal as a source of energy. Synthetic dyes revolutionized the textile industry, as did alkali in the manufacture of soap and glass. Dynamite, invented by the Swedish chemist Alfred Nobel (no-BELL) (1833–1896) in the 1860s, made it possible to level hills and blast tunnels through mountains, facilitating construction. Nobel's will established a prestigious prize in his name to honor significant contributions to science and peace.

Transportation and Communication

The rail system grew dramatically in the middle decades of the nineteenth century. By 1880, total European railroad mileage reached 102,000. In 1888, the Orient Express line opened, linking Constantinople to Vienna and thus to the rest of Europe. Speed also conquered distance. By midcentury, trains ran 50 miles per hour, ten times faster than when they were invented. The cost of rail transport steadily decreased, allowing for its greater use. Between 1850 and 1880, in Germany, the number of rail passengers increased tenfold and the volume of goods eightyfold. In France and Great Britain, the increases were nearly as impressive.

Ocean transportation was also revolutionized. In 1869, the French built the Suez Canal across Egyptian territory, linking the Mediterranean to the Red Sea and the Indian Ocean. The canal reduced, by 40 percent, the thirty-five-day journey between London and Bombay. More efficient carriers—such as the clipper ship and the steamship—were developed. By 1880, European shipping carried nearly three times the cargo it had thirty years earlier.

The optimism born of conquering vast distances was reflected in a popular novel by the French writer Jules Verne (DJOOL VAIRN) (1828-1905), *Around the World in Eighty Days* (1873). The hero, Phineas Fogg, travels by balloon, llama, and ostrich, as well as by the modern steam locomotive and steamship, to accomplish in eighty days a feat that, only thirty years earlier, would have taken at least eleven months. In 1889, the New York newspaper the *World,* in a publicity gambit to increase readership, sent its reporter Nellie Bly (1867-1922) on an around-the-world trip to see if she could beat fictional Phineas Fogg's record. Readers breathlessly kept up with reports of her progress. She circled the globe in 72 days, 6 hours, 11 minutes, and 14 seconds. Such was the impact of the steamship, the locomotive, the Suez Canal—and the newspaper.

Along with the new speed, advances in refrigeration changed food transport. Formerly, refrigeration could be achieved only with natural ice, cut from frozen ponds and lakes, but this changed in the 1870s with the introduction of mechanical ice-making machines. By the 1880s, dairy products and meat were being transported vast distances by rail and even across the seas by ship. Thanks to these advances, the surplus food of the Americas and Australia, rich in grasslands, could offer Europe a cheaper and far more varied diet.

Regular postal service was also a child of the new era of improved transportation. In 1840, Britain instituted a postage system based on standard rates. Replacing the earlier practice in which the recipient paid for the delivery of a letter, the British system enabled the sender to buy a stamp—priced at just one penny— and drop the letter into a mailbox. It was collected, transported speedily by the new railroads, and delivered. The efficiency and low cost of mail led to a huge increase in use.

The reformed postal service and transoceanic telegraphs revolutionized the exchange of information. The telegraph was invented in the early 1830s, and by the 1860s, telegraph wire had been laid on both the European and North American continents; the two continents were then connected via the transatlantic cable. By the 1870s, telegraph lines extended 650,000 miles, connecting twenty thousand towns and villages around the world.

The telegraph had many uses. Newspapers prided themselves on being "wired" and thus able to provide readers the latest news. Governments found the telegraph useful in collecting information and issuing orders to subordinates, better assuring imperial authority over distant

CHRONOLOGY

1813	Gas streetlamps in London
1820s	Omnibuses introduced in France
1830	Lyell founds the principles of modern geology
1831	Faraday discovers electromagnetic induction
1833	Telegraph invented
1840	Penny stamp introduced
1848	England adopts first national health legislation
1850s	Age of clipper ships
	Trams added to public transportation systems
1851	Crystal Palace
1852–1870	Rebuilding of Paris
1859	Darwin, *On the Origin of Species*
1863	Europe's first underground railroad, in London
1864	Pope Pius IX issues *Syllabus of Errors*
1865	Transoceanic telegraph cable installed
	Lister initiates antiseptic surgery
	University of Zurich admits women
1869	Opening of Suez Canal
	Mendeleev produces periodic table of elements
1874	Impressionist exhibition
1875	Bell invents telephone
	Electric lights in Paris
1881	Pasteur proposes germ theory of disease
1891	Pope Leo XIII issues *Rerum novarum*

French Board Game: Around the World in 80 Days   This French board game, based on Jules Verne's novel *Around the World in Eighty Days*, illustrates with a steam locomotive the new speed with which people could travel, suggesting as well the technological power to colonize exotic territories (see Chapter 24).   ('Le Voyage Autour du Monde', cover of a box for a game based on 'Around the World in 80 Days' by Jules Verne (1828–1905) (litho), French School, (19th century)/Private Collection/Archives Charmet/The Bridgeman Art Library)

territories. In the 1840s, it took ten weeks for a message and a reply to go from London to Bombay and back. Thirty years later, the exchange took four minutes.

The telegraph was also a tool of warfare. The first conflict in which it played a crucial role was the Crimean War. The British and French high commands in London and Paris were able to communicate with their officers in the Crimea, directing operations from afar. It was also the first war whose unfolding events were communicated immediately through the telegraph to newspapers at home. Charles Dickens described the telegraph as "of all our modern wonders the most wonderful." Even more than improved transportation, it transformed the world into an instant, global village. As the governor of New York said at a commemorative event, "Men speak to one another now, though separated by the width of the earth, with lightning's speed and as if standing face to face."

To the telegraph was added another instant form of communication. In 1875, the American Alexander Graham Bell (1847–1922) invented a machine capable of transmitting the human voice by electrical impulses; in 1879, the first telephones were installed in Germany; two years later, they appeared in France. At first a curiosity, used to listen to a musical or theatrical production at a distance, the phone entered the homes of the elite and became a new form of interpersonal communication.

SECTION SUMMARY

- After 1850, steam-powered turbines and new sources of energy, such as electricity, increased the pace and quantity of industrial production.

- New methods of steel production made possible the expansion of railroads, the construction of steamships, and explosive growth in the building industry.

- The Suez Canal helped revolutionize ocean transportation by cutting travel time to India and other parts of Asia nearly in half, while ships as well became more efficient.

- The telegraph, telephone, and standardized mail systems sped up communications and collapsed global distances of time and space.

The Suez Canal   Opened in 1869, the canal cut through one hundred miles of Egyptian desert to enable passage between the Mediterranean and the Red Seas. It reduced by half the voyage from Europe to India and the rest of Asia, and particularly benefited Britain. The Suez Canal exemplified the speeding up of transportation and communication in the second half of the nineteenth century.   (The Inauguration Procession of the Suez Canal at El-Guisr in 1865, from 'Voyage Pittoresque a travers l'Isthme de Suez' by Marius Fontane, engraved by Jules Didier (1831-c.80) 1869–70 (colour litho), Riou, Edouard (1833–1900)/Bibliotheque des Arts Decoratifs, Paris, France/Archives Charmet/The Bridgeman Art Library International)

SOCIAL IMPACTS OF ECONOMIC GROWTH

How did the economic expansion affect the various social classes, and city versus rural areas, differently?

Industrial advances transformed the traditional structure of European society. Fewer people worked the land; more worked in manufacturing and services. Because political power no longer depended as much upon landed property ownership and inherited titles, the aristocracy had to find new channels through which they could exercise social and political influence; to varying degrees, they had to share power with the middle classes. Generally, life for both industrial and farm workers improved in this period. However, great disparities persisted, and many people continued to suffer from profound deprivation.

The Adapting Aristocracy

Always a small, exclusive group, the European aristocracy in the nineteenth century represented less than 1 percent of the population. Many of noble birth were quite poor and economically indistinguishable from their nonnoble neighbors. Others owned vast estates and were fabulously wealthy.

Distinctions between aristocrats and members of the upper middle class became increasingly blurred. Noble families in financial straits often married their children to the offspring of wealthy merchants. And many nobles who previously had shunned manufacture participated in the new economy by becoming industrialists and bankers. Idle members of the nobility became rarer. Although many aristocrats still enjoyed a lavish lifestyle, others adopted the habits of successful business people.

The power of the aristocracy surprisingly persisted through much of the nineteenth century, despite the theories of egalitarianism sweeping Europe in the aftermath of the French Revolution and the rapidly changing social structure engendered by industrialization. In Prussia, some of the wealthiest industrialists came from the highest aristocracy. The heavily aristocratic officer corps played an important role in running the Prussian state and unified Germany. In France, about 20 to 25 percent of officers and many diplomats were aristocrats. In Britain, officers, diplomats, and high-ranking civil servants were usually of noble birth. In Austria and Russia, aristocratic origin continued to be the norm for government service.

The Expanding Middle Classes

bourgeois century
Characterization of the nineteenth century. Having expanded dramatically with industrialization, the bourgeoisie helped shape western European society.

Up to the eighteenth century, society had been divided into legally separate orders on the basis of birth. In the nineteenth century, it became more customary to classify people by their economic functions, whose variety grew as the industrial and services sectors expanded. The "middle class" included such people as wealthy manufacturers, country physicians, and bank tellers. Given this diversity, it has become common to use the plural and think of all these people as forming the "middle classes." Another term frequently used to describe them is the *bourgeoisie,* which usually refers to those with higher than average wealth.

The nineteenth century has often been described as the **bourgeois century**, because, especially in western Europe, the middle classes not only expanded numerically, but had an enormous social and cultural influence. Rapidly growing trade and manufacture meant more entrepreneurs and managers, while the increasingly complex society called for more engineers, lawyers, accountants, and bankers. New standards of comfort and health increased the demand for merchants and doctors, while urban renovations required architects and contractors, among other professionals.

The middle and lower levels of middle-class society grew most rapidly. In the 1870s, about 10 percent of urban working-class people reached lower-middle-class status by becoming storekeepers, lower civil servants, clerks, or salespeople. As industries matured, the increasing use of machinery and better industrial organization created a greater need for clerks and bureaucrats rather than laborers. Large import-export businesses, insurance companies, and department stores provided opportunities of this kind. So did the expansion of government services.

The social impact of job growth was great. The men and women staffing these new positions often came from modest backgrounds. For the son or daughter of peasants to become village postmaster, schoolteacher, or clerk in a major firm signified social ascension, however modest. Accessibility to its ranks was certainly one of the strengths of the bourgeoisie, an ever-growing group whose promise of social respectability and material comfort exercised a compelling force of attraction over the lower classes.

A widening subgroup of the middle classes consisted of professionals, those whose prestige rested on the claim of exclusive expertise in a particular field. In the early nineteenth century, requirements for exercising a profession, though they varied by country, became more stringent. Medical doctors, for instance, began requiring specialized education to distinguish themselves from herbalists, midwives, bonesetters, healers, and other competitors, and they insisted on their exclusive right to exercise their profession. Doctors controlled access to their ranks by establishing powerful professional associations.

Interior of a Danish Middle-Class Home   With its stuffed furniture, lace curtains and tablecloths, and gilt-edged framed paintings, this meticulously decorated living room contrasted sharply with the grimy exterior of the industrial city from which it provided a sheltered escape.   (National Museum of Denmark (Nationalmuseet))

Similarly, other professions, such as law, architecture, and engineering, encouraged **professionalization** through the adoption of common requirements and standards of expertise. By midcentury, either professional associations or the state itself accredited members of the professions. Women had limited access to these professions; typically their opportunities were confined to lower teaching positions. After the Crimean War, as a result of Florence Nightingale's efforts (see page 617), nursing became an increasingly popular profession for women. Even so, the dominant culture generally opposed middle-class women's salaried employment outside the home.

The growing role of the state in society led to bureaucratic expansion. Civil servants were increasingly subjected to educational requirements and had to pass civil service exams, sharply reducing the role that patronage played in the assignment of government positions.

Middle-Class Lifestyles

The standard of living among the middle classes varied considerably, ranging from the wealthy entrepreneur who bought a château, or built one, to the low-level clerk who dwelled in a modest apartment. All of them lived in new standards of comfort. Their homes increasingly had running water, upholstered furniture, and enough space to provide separate sleeping and living quarters. They owned several changes of clothing and consumed a varied diet that included meat and dairy products, sugar, coffee, and tea. They read books and subscribed to newspapers and journals. Having at least one servant was a requisite for anyone who wished to be counted among the middle classes in the mid-nineteenth century.

By 1900, servants were still common among bourgeois households, but their number was declining in proportion to the population as a whole. As service industries developed, the need for servants decreased. With the growth of cab services, for instance, a family could dispense with a coachman and groom. Toward the end of the century, domestics' wages rose as competing forms of employment vied for their service, and households below the upper layers of the bourgeoisie found it difficult to afford domestic help.

The need to escape the relentless stimulation of crowded cities gave rise to resort towns throughout Europe, devoted principally to the amusement of the well-off. Water cures—bathing in hot springs and drinking the mineral waters thought to have special attributes—became fashionable, as did gambling in resorts such as Baden-Baden in Germany and Vichy in France. For the first time, tourism became big business. Thomas Cook (1808–1892), an Englishman, organized tours to the Crystal Palace exhibition of 1851 in London, the largest world exposition, which highlighted industrial accomplishments. Discovering the large market for guided travel, Cook began running tours in England and on the Continent. Middle-class wealth and leisure time led to the construction of more hotels, restaurants, and cafés.

The middle classes, at least on the surface, sought to foster a set of values about proper conduct. They believed their successes were due not to birth, but to talent and effort. They wanted to be judged by their merits, and they expected their members to abide by strict moral principles. Their lives were supposed to be disciplined, especially with regard to sex and drink. The age was called "Victorian" because the middle classes in Britain saw in the queen, who reigned for two-thirds of the century, a reflection of their own values. (See the feature, "The Visual Record: An Engraving of the British Royal Family" on pages 634–635 in Chapter 22.) **Victorian morality**, widely preached but not always practiced, was often viewed as hypocritical by social critics. Yet as the middle classes came to dominate society, their values established social norms. Public drunkenness was discouraged, and anti-alcohol movements vigorously campaigned against drinking. Public festivals were regulated, making them more respectable and less rowdy.

In spite of their differences in education, wealth, and social standing, most of the bourgeoisie resembled one another in dress, habits of speech, and deportment. Bourgeois men dressed somberly, in dark colors, avoiding any outward signs of luxury. Their clothing fit closely and lacked decoration—a symbolic adjustment to the machine age, in which elaborate dress hampered activity. It also reflected a conscious attempt to emphasize achievement-oriented attitudes, and new standards for what constituted honorable manhood. Through dress and other fashionable tastes, middle classes distinguished themselves from what they viewed as a decadent and effeminate nobility.

Bourgeois conventions regarding women's dress were the opposite of men's, further reinforcing gender distinctions—women's clothing became the material symbol of male success.

professionalization
Standardization of requirements and regulation of expertise, especially in medicine, law, architecture, and engineering.

Victorian morality
Nineteenth-century ethos wherein the strict moral principles of the dominant middle class became the social norm. The middle classes saw in Queen Victoria a reflection of their own values.

The Crystal Palace Built in 1851, this building was the largest glass and steel structure of its time. Site of the first great international exposition, the Crystal Palace displayed the inventiveness and opulence of the age. (Courtesy of the Trustees of the British Museum)

Extravagant amounts of colorful fabrics used to fashion huge, beribboned hoop dresses reflected the newfound wealth of the middle classes and confirmed their view of women as ornaments whose lives were to be limited to the home and made easier by servants. The language and paraphernalia of idealized domesticity dominated this era. While the man was out in the secular world earning a living and advancing his career, the bourgeois woman was supposed to provide her family with an orderly, comfortable shelter from the storms of daily life. In 1861, London housewife Isabella Mary Mayson Beeton published *Mrs. Beeton's Book of Household Management*, which provided British middle-class women with advice on running their households. This book reflected middle-class values in fostering discipline, frugality, and cleanliness. The ideal woman decorated the rooms, changed the curtains with the seasons and styles, supervised the servants, kept the accounts, oversaw the children's homework and religious education, and involved herself in charitable works. In Britain, this book was outsold only by the Bible. In the decades around midcentury, the notion of two **separate spheres**—one male and public, the other female and private—reached its height.

In spite of the relatively passive role assigned to bourgeois women, many were very active. Some helped their husbands or fathers in the office, the business, or the writing of scientific treatises. Others achieved success on their own terms, running their own businesses, writing, painting, or teaching. Though advice books prescribed a world of separate spheres, in practice, the boundaries between them were not always rigid. In general, however, even bright and intellectually curious young girls most often could not receive as good an education as their brothers, nor, as a consequence, could they pursue as interesting a career.

Some liberals insisted that sexual difference should not constitute the basis for denying equal rights to women. Proponents of women's rights demanded equal access to education

separate spheres Notion of two distinct sets of roles—one male and public, the other female and private. While the man was out in the world advancing his career, the bourgeois woman was to run her home.

Ladies' Bicycling Fashion This new mode of transportation suggested possibilities for female emancipation. Free on her bicycle, the young woman is contrasted with the man, who rides only a tricycle. (From Karin Helm [ed.], Rosinen aus der Gartenlaube [Gutersloh: Signum Verlag, n.d.]. Reproduced with permission.)

and the professions. Slowly, secondary and university education was made available to young women. On the European continent, the University of Zurich was the first university to admit women, in 1865. Although British universities admitted women, they did not initially grant them degrees. In spite of discriminatory laws, harassment by male students, and initial obstruction by professional and accrediting groups, a few female doctors and lawyers practiced in England by the 1870s and on the Continent in the following decades.

Women more easily penetrated the lower levels of middle-class occupations. Expanding school systems, civil services, and businesses provided new employment opportunities for them. By the 1890s, women comprised two-thirds of primary school teachers in England and half the post office staff in France. Some new technologies created jobs that became heavily feminized, such as the positions of typist and telephone operator.

Improving Conditions among Workers and the Poor

The increased prosperity and greater productivity of the period gradually improved the conditions of both female and male workers in the generation after 1850. Their wages and standards of living rose, and they enjoyed more job security. In Britain, the earning power of the average worker rose by one-third between 1850 and 1875. For the first time, workers were able to put money aside to tide them over in hard times. They had greater access to leisure activities that previously had been limited to the upper classes. Expanded rail connections enabled workers to visit resort towns. New music and dance halls, popular theaters, and other forms of public entertainment sprang up to claim workers' increased spending money.

Nonetheless, conditions of poverty persisted among many workers throughout Europe and a vast gulf remained between them and the middle and upper classes. In the 1880s, in the northern French industrial city of Lille, the combined property of twenty thousand workers equaled the estate of one average industrialist. Life expectancies still varied dramatically according to income. In Bordeaux in 1853, the life expectancy of a male bourgeois was twenty years greater than that of a male laborer.

The disparity between rich and poor was especially striking in the case of domestics, one of the most common sources of employment for women. Servants led tiring and restricted lives under the close supervision of their employers. They worked

Telephone Operators in London New technologies opened up new employment opportunities for women. Telephone operators formed a completely feminized profession. (Jacques Boyer/Roger Viollet/Getty Images)

overly long hours and often worked six and a half days a week. Housed in either the basement or the attic, servants experienced extremes of cold, heat, and humidity. Sometimes they were subjected to physical or sexual abuse by the master of the house, his sons, or the head of the domestic staff. And yet, for impoverished rural women with little chance of finding better work, domestic service offered an option few could refuse. It provided free housing, food, and clothing and sometimes allowed a servant to save an annual sum that might reach one-third to one-half of a worker's yearly wages. These savings could serve as a dowry, enabling a young woman to marry advantageously.

Although some members of the working class managed to enter the lower levels of the middle classes, most remained mired in the same occupations as their grandparents. Poverty was still pervasive, and workers more commonly suffered from industrial and urban diseases, such as tuberculosis.

The difficult conditions imposed on industrial workers led to debates in several countries about the need for the state to protect them. The growing militancy of organized labor, fear of social upheaval, and the rising strength of socialist political parties motivated some governments to act. Moreover, viewing populations as a national resource, states grew increasingly concerned about infant mortality and declining birthrates. While some legislators rejected government intervention in the free operation of market forces, others argued that the laws of supply and demand exploited those who ought to have been protected—especially very young children and pregnant women.

Britain led the way with the Factory Acts, regulating child and female labor. The British workweek, typically 73 hours in the 1840s, was reduced to 56 hours in 1874. In newly unified Germany, the government wanted to impress workers with state benefits so they would abandon the growing Socialist Party and back the kaiser's authoritarian government. In the 1880s, it thus provided a comprehensive welfare plan that included health insurance and old-age pensions, and then reduced the work day to 11 hours. In France, the republican government also sought to defuse class war by passing a number of laws toward the end of the century. Particularly concerned about declining fertility, they regulated female factory labor, especially that of pregnant women. Most of this legislation only applied to large-scale industrial labor, and did not improve the situations among other working poor. And in eastern Europe, where industry was still in its infancy, workers remained unprotected by the law.

Apart from state initiatives, upper- and middle-class individuals, inspired by pity and religious teachings, also became concerned about conditions among workers and the poor. Women especially engaged in charity and social reform. As many as half a million English women involved themselves in charities or efforts to enact social legislation. In Sweden, by the 1880s, women had founded shelters for the destitute, old-age homes, a children's hospital, an asylum for the mentally handicapped, and various societies to promote female industry.

Government efforts to improve conditions through the regulation of public health also resulted in oppositional movements. In Great Britain, Josephine Grey Butler (1828–1906) waged a fierce battle against the harsh laws directed against prostitutes. The Contagious Diseases Acts (beginning in 1864) empowered the police to arrest any woman suspected of prostitution and to force her to be examined for venereal disease. Largely as a result of Butler's efforts, these acts were repealed in 1886. Annie Wood Besant (1847–1933) became an active social reformer on behalf of the poor. At a time when governments were becoming concerned about falling birthrates (resulting in limits on women's rights to work), she argued that poor women suffered from excessive childbearing and that their children died too often because of their poverty. With Charles Bradlaugh (1833–1891), Besant republished a pamphlet that contained information on birth control. British authorities called the publication pornographic and brought Besant and Bradlaugh to trial in 1877. After being found guilty, Bradlaugh and Besant won the case on appeal. In 1888, Besant turned her attention to protecting the health of young women workers, and in 1893, she went to India to establish schools for girls, educate widows, and agitate for Indian home rule.

The church also intervened in social issues. Pope Leo XIII (r. 1878–1903) reflected a trend of growing religious social consciousness and reinforced it among Catholics when in 1891, he issued his encyclical *Rerum novarum* (*Of New Things*), which defined Christians' moral responsibility for the poor. He declared, "Rich men and masters should remember this—that to exercise pressure for the sake of gain upon the indigent and the destitute and to make one's profit out of the need of another is condemned by all laws, human and divine." His message was taken up in France, Italy, and Spain among activists who became known as social Catholics. In England, Protestants founded the Salvation Army to assist the poor in 1878. Religious groups also hoped to win converts to their faith through the assistance they provided.

social Catholics Catholics in western Europe who believed that society bore responsibility for the well-being of the poor.

The Transformation of the Countryside

Before the nineteenth century, the countryside had hardly changed, but beginning at midcentury, it transformed radically. Especially in western Europe, an increasing number of people left the land. In 1850, 20 percent of the British people worked in agriculture; by 1881, they constituted only 11 percent of the population. The decrease in the number of agricultural workers led in many places to labor shortages and therefore higher wages for farmhands.

The food supply grew significantly as agricultural methods became more efficient. Not only was more land cultivated, but the yield per acre increased. In 1760, an agricultural worker in England could feed himself and one other person; by 1841, he could feed himself and 2.7 others. Food production on the continent similarly became more efficient, allowing greater access to better nutrition and consequently a drop in mortality rates; the population of Europe almost doubled between 1800 and 1880.

Higher yields were the result of an increased use of manure, augmented in the 1870s by saltpeter imported from Chile and, beginning in the 1880s, by chemical fertilizers manufactured in Europe. Innovations in tools also improved productivity. In the 1850s, steam-driven threshing machinery was introduced in some parts of western Europe. Organizational techniques borrowed from industrial labor, including specialization and regular schedules, also contributed to greater productivity on the land.

New and expanded technologies began to break through the insularity of rural life. Improved roads and dramatically expanded rail lines enabled farmers to extend their markets nationally and internationally. They also brought teachers into the villages, making school systems national. Local dialects, and in some cases, even distinct languages that peasants had spoken for generations, were replaced by a standardized national language. Local provincial costumes became less

Steam-Powered Thresher   This image shows the thresher being operated in the French countryside in 1860. Its loud noise and relentlessly rhythmic speed changed the pace and sensibility of rural labor, and sometimes prolonged the hours demanded of workers. It would be decades before this kind of technology became a common sight in Europe, but it was a harbinger of the change coming to the rural world.   (Bibliothèque nationale de France)

SECTION SUMMARY

- As landed wealth and hereditary titles declined in importance during the second half of the nineteenth century, the old aristocracy adapted by participating more in manufacturing, banking, and the professions.

- New technologies of the second industrial revolution and the expansion of commerce, government bureaucracy, and the professions dramatically increased the size and influence of the middle classes.

- The middle classes (bourgeoisie) developed their own moral code, including the notion of separate spheres for men and women; but many women defied their prescribed role and sought the right to higher education and entry into the professions.

- Standards of living generally rose among workers, but stark class disparities of wealth and living conditions persisted in many areas; legislation and private charity attempted to redress social ills, often in order to undermine the potential of worker militancy and socialist politics.

- New agricultural methods and technologies greatly increased agricultural production; modernization also created competition for agricultural and cottage industry products, forcing migration from the countryside.

common as styles fashionable in the cities spread to the countryside via mail-order catalogs. The farm girls who went to the cities to work as domestic servants returned to their villages with urban and middle-class ideals. The military draft brought the young men of the village into contact with urban folk and further spread urban values to the countryside.

Many rural regions, however, suffered from modernization. The growth of urban manufacturing caused rural cottage industry to decline, depriving agricultural workers of the supplementary income on which they previously relied during slack seasons. Railroads bringing goods made elsewhere wiped out some of the local markets on which cottage industries had depended. Grain brought by steamship from distant Canada and Argentina often undersold European wheat. The resultant crisis caused millions to emigrate; they left the land for towns and cities or even migrated across the seas to the Americas and Australia (see page 668).

These trends had a striking effect in the rural areas of western Europe. Eastern Europe, in contrast, was hardly touched by them. In Russia, agriculture remained backward; the average yield per acre in 1880 was one-quarter that in Great Britain. The land sheltered a large surplus population that was underemployed and contributed little to the rural economy. In the Balkans, most peasants were landless and heavily indebted.

URBAN PROBLEMS AND SOLUTIONS

What problems did urbanization create, and what were the solutions?

Epidemics, crowding, crime, and traffic jams were among the many problems that accompanied explosive urban growth in the nineteenth century. In the second half of the century, city governments more aggressively tackled these problems by developing public health measures and urban planning. They provided amenities, such as streetlights, public transportation, and water and sewer systems, and they established large, more efficient police forces. Cities gradually became safer and more pleasant places to live, although for a long time, city dwellers continued to suffer high mortality rates.

City Planning and Urban Renovation

Most of Europe's cities, originating in the Middle Ages as walled enclaves, had grown haphazardly into major industrial centers. Their narrow, crooked streets could not accommodate the increased trade and daily movement of goods and people, and traffic snarls were common. City officials began to recognize that broad, straight avenues would help relieve the congestion and also bring sunlight and fresh air into the narrow and perpetually dank lanes and alleys. (See the feature, "The Visual Record: The Modern City and Photography.")

The most extensive program of urban rebuilding took place in midcentury Paris. Over a period of eighteen years, Napoleon III and his aide Baron Georges Haussmann (1809–1891) transformed Paris from a dirty medieval city to a beautiful modern one (see **MAP 23.1**). Haussmann and his engineers carved broad, straight avenues through what had been overcrowded areas. They built visually elegant, if uniform, apartment houses on the new tree-lined avenues. Public monuments and buildings, such as the new opera house, enhanced the city. The urban renewal program drove tens of thousands of the poorest Parisians to the outskirts of the city, leading to greater social segregation than had previously existed. The boulevards created the environment

Pissarro: *L'avenue de l'Opéra, Sunlight, Winter Morning*   Camille Pissarro, one of the leading impressionists, portrayed the broad new Parisian avenue designed by Baron Haussmann. The avenue leads to the new opera in the background, also planned during the Second Empire. Note the active pedestrian as well as equestrian traffic.   (Erich Lessing/Art Resource, NY)

that nurtured the development of department stores, and street life became bourgeois. Boulevards also provided access for quick troop movements in the event of social upheaval, and made building barricades more difficult.

Haussmann's extensive work in Paris served as a model for other cities, and although none was rebuilt as extensively, many underwent significant improvements. The cities of Europe began to display an expansive grace and sense of order, supporting the belief of the middle classes that theirs was an age of progress.

The Introduction of Public Services

Beginning at midcentury, government at the central and local levels helped make cities more livable through sanitary reforms, public transportation, and lighting. Medical practitioners in the 1820s had observed that disease and higher mortality were related to dirt and lack of clean air, water, and sunshine. Since diseases spreading from the poorer quarters of town threatened the rich and powerful, there was a general interest in improving public health by clearing slums, broadening streets, and supplying clean air and water to the cities.

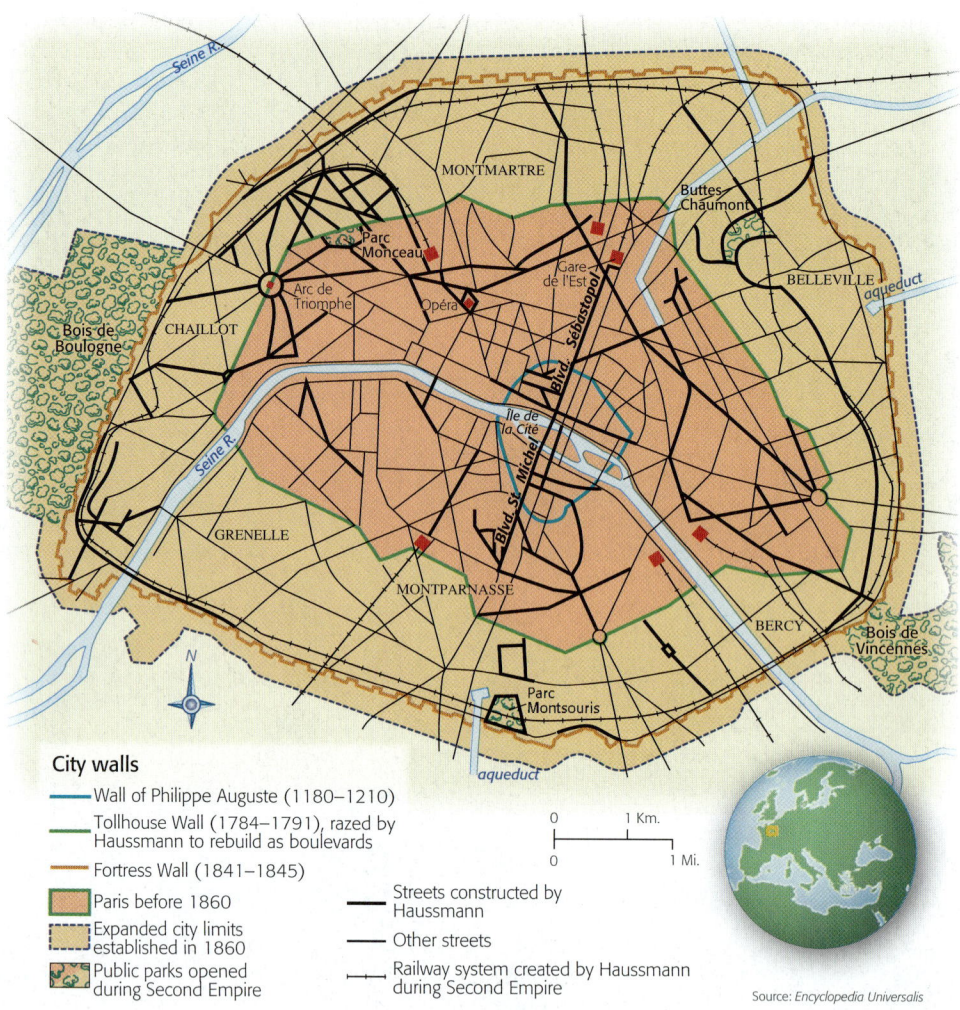

City walls

— Wall of Philippe Auguste (1180–1210)

— Tollhouse Wall (1784–1791), razed by Haussmann to rebuild as boulevards

— Fortress Wall (1841–1845)

▨ Paris before 1860

▨ Expanded city limits established in 1860

▨ Public parks opened during Second Empire

— Streets constructed by Haussmann

— Other streets

┼ Railway system created by Haussmann during Second Empire

0   1 Km.

0   1 Mi.

Source: Encyclopedia Universalis

🌐 **Map 23.1—Haussmann's Paris, 1850–1870**

During the reign of Napoleon III, Baron Georges Haussmann reshaped the city of Paris, replacing its narrow medieval streets with a system of broad avenues and public parks and encircling the city with a railway.

Reform began in England with the Public Health Bill of 1848. This legislation established national standards for urban sanitation and required cities to regulate the installation of sewers and the disposal of refuse. The 1875 Health Act mandated certain basic health standards for water and drainage. Armed with these laws, cities and towns took the initiative: Birmingham cleared 50 acres of slums in the 1870s, for example.

London also took the lead in supplying public water, a service later adopted by Paris and many other cities. Berlin had a municipal water system in 1850, but it would be several decades before clean water was available in every household. In Paris, which typically led France in innovations, 60 percent of the houses had running water in 1882. As running water in the home became a standard rather than a luxury, bathing became more common. The English upper classes had learned the habit of frequent bathing from their colonial experience in India; on the Continent, it did not become the custom until about the third quarter of the nineteenth century.

All these changes had a direct impact on the lives of city dwellers. Between the 1840s and 1880, London's death rate fell from 26 per thousand to 20 per thousand. During the same period, the rate in Paris declined from 29.3 per thousand to 23.7 per thousand. Improved water supplies sharply reduced the prevalence of waterborne diseases, such as cholera and typhoid.

With the provision of urban transportation, city dwellers no longer had to live within walking distance of their workplaces. In the 1850s, the French introduced the tram—a carriage drawn on a rail line by horses. It could pull larger loads of passengers faster than its predecessor, the horse-drawn omnibus. Because of the many rail stations in London and the difficulty of getting from one station to another in time to make a connection, the British built an underground railway in 1863, the predecessor of the subway system. Technological improvements made the bicycle a serious means of transportation. By the mid-1880s, nearly 100,000 bicycles were being pedaled around Great Britain; by 1900, France had 1 million bicycles.

Improvements in public transportation and urban renewal projects led workers to move out of the inner city and into the less dense and less expensive suburbs. This trend in turn led to a decrease in urban population density that eventually helped make the city a healthier place to live.

Gaslights also improved city life, making it easier and safer to be outside at night. (Prior to gaslights, city dwellers depended mainly on moonlight or, rarely, expensive and time-consuming oil lamps—which had to be lit one at a time.) In 1813, London was the first city to be illuminated by gas; Berlin followed in 1816. Electrical lights were introduced in Paris in 1875, although they were not common until the end of the century.

Cities also significantly expanded police forces to impose order, control criminal activity, and discourage behavior deemed undesirable, such as dumping garbage on the street, relieving oneself in public, and carousing late at night. In 1850, London was the best-policed city in Europe, with a 5,000-man force. Paris had around 3,000 police officers.

SECTION SUMMARY

- Rapid population growth occurred in cities that had originally been constructed in haphazard fashion; to cope with the problems of growth, city officials began programs of urban renovation.

- The most notable example of urban renewal was that of Haussmann in Paris, which became a model in cities elsewhere.

- Central and local governments introduced sanitary reforms to combat disease, such as installing sewers, regulating the disposal of refuse, and supplying public water.

- Improvement in public transportation allowed workers to leave the overcrowded conditions in urban centers, further contributing to improved health.

CULTURE IN AN AGE OF OPTIMISM

What new scientific, intellectual, and cultural trends emerged in this period, and what impact did they have on systems of belief?

The improving economic and material conditions of the second half of the nineteenth century buoyed European thinkers. Many believed that men and women were becoming more enlightened, and they expressed faith in humankind's ability to transform the world with a parade of scientific and technological breakthroughs. The world seemed knowable and perfectible, especially through expanded education. This faith advanced secularism, while it undermined the certainties of traditional religion. The arts reflected these new values, emphasizing realism and science—as well as an underlying foreboding about the dark side of this "age of optimism."

Educational and Cultural Opportunities

At the beginning of the nineteenth century, governments took little responsibility for providing education. Some upper-class children were educated with private tutors, and others attended elite schools. A few charity schools offered minimal education for the poor. In the second half of the nineteenth century, governments took direct action to establish free and mandatory primary education, largely as a result of extended voting rights. In England, the Second Reform Bill of 1867 reduced the tax-based voting qualification, extended suffrage to better-off workers, and prompted a movement to ensure that the new voters were educated. The English government provided significant subsidies for education, set educational standards, and established a national inspection system to enforce them. France joined England in establishing mandatory primary education in the 1880s for boys and girls. Other European countries did the same; by 1900, all but one percent of Germans met the standards of literacy.

The goal of public education was to instill love of country, discipline, and obedience to authority, as well as basic skills of reading, writing, and arithmetic. It also sought to instill discipline.

By insisting on punctuality and obliging students to carry out repetitive tasks, schools formed youth to fit into the emerging industrial society and the civic culture of nation-states. The obedience and respect for authority learned at school shaped the soldiers and factory workers of the future. And regardless of political inclination, each regime took advantage of its control of the educational system to inculcate the love of one's country and of its form of government.

Secondary education was, on the whole, available only to the privileged few in the upper middle classes, giving them access to the universities and the professions. A small fraction of the lower middle class attended universities; the children of workers and peasants were totally absent.

Other public institutions made culture available to the masses in new ways. Between 1840 and 1880, the number of large libraries in Europe increased from forty to five hundred. The French national public library, the *Bibliothèque nationale,* was established in Paris in the 1860s. This iron and glass building, radical for its time, was an impressive monument to the desire to make reading available to an expanded public. Beyond cities, traveling libraries allowed books to reach rural populations.

Museums and art galleries, which in the previous century had been open to only a select few, gradually became accessible to the general public, making their national cultural heritages available to the masses; even the poorer classes gained access to these temples of culture by the late nineteenth century. The dramatic rise in literacy and new sources of cultural enrichment resulted from, and contributed to, the processes of modernization; they exposed the masses to new, potentially transformative ideas, experiences, and modes of understanding the rapidly changing world.

Darwin and Evolution

By midcentury, most thinkers accepted the notion of the change and transformation of society—and, by analogy, of the natural environment. The French thinker Auguste Comte (oh-GOOST KONT) championed the notion that human development—human history—proceeded through distinct and irreversible stages. Human progress would lead inexorably upward to the final and highest stage of development, the "positive"—or scientific-stage. Widely read throughout Europe and Latin America, Comte's writings helped bolster faith in science—and scientific advances of the nineteenth century seemed to confirm his precepts. Comte's philosophy, known as **positivism**, dominated the era. Whereas the romantics had emphasized feeling, the positivists found truth in what could be measured and verified. They were confident that scientific methods would ensure the continued progress of humanity.

positivism Philosophy of the French thinker Auguste Comte who asserted that human history progressed through distinct and irreversible stages, leading to the final and highest stage of development, the positive—or scientific—stage.

Faith in science and progress helped create the intellectual environment for rethinking progress in the biological realm. While the concept of biological evolution was not new, Charles Darwin (1809–1882) was the first to offer a systematic explanation of the process. As the naturalist on an official British scientific expedition in the 1830s, he had visited the Galápagos Islands off the western coast of South America. There, he discovered species similar to but very different from those on the mainland. Could they be the results of separate creations? Or was it more likely that in varying environments they had adapted differently? Darwin proposed that closely related species compete for food and living space. In this struggle, those in each species that are better adapted to the environment have the advantage over the others and hence are more likely to survive. In the "struggle for existence," only the fittest endure. Those surviving, Darwin surmised, pass on the positive traits to their offspring. He called the mechanism that explained the evolution and development of new species "natural selection," a process that he proposed was imperceptible but continuous. Darwin's observations in the Galápagos Islands became the basis for *On the Origin of Species by Means of Natural Selection* (1859), the most important scientific work of the nineteenth century. (See the feature, "The Written Record: Darwin's Basic Laws of Evolution.")

Darwin's theory that evolution in nature was inevitable echoes the nineteenth-century conviction that the present represented an ever more developed stage of the past. Many viewed his work as confirmation that societies—like species—were preordained to evolve toward progressively higher stages. Darwin at first avoided the question of whether the laws of evolution applied to human beings as well. The notion of human evolution would throw into question humanity's uniqueness and its separation from the rest of creation by its possession (in the Christian view) of a soul. But Darwin finally did confront the issue in *The Descent of Man* (1871), in which he presented evidence that humanity, too, is subject to these natural laws. The recognition that human

Darwin's Basic Laws of Evolution

Writing in an age of vast transformations, Darwin could imagine the mutability of all nature, including species, over time. And like his contemporaries, he could imagine that evolution would lead to improvement, to increasing "perfection" of various species. A religious man who lost much of his faith as a result of his scientific investigations, Darwin was anxious to reassure Christians, hence his attempt to portray evolution as part of God's divine plan.

Nothing at first can appear more difficult to believe than that the more complex organs and instincts have been perfected, not by means superior to, though analogous with, human reason, but by the accumulation of innumerable slight variations, each good for the individual possessor. Nevertheless, this difficulty, though appearing to our imagination insuperably great, cannot be considered real if we admit the following propositions, namely, that all parts of the organisation and instincts offer, at least, individual differences—that there is a struggle for existence leading to the preservation of profitable deviations of structure or instinct and, lastly, that gradations in the state of perfection of each organ may have existed, each good of its kind. The truth of these propositions cannot, I think, be disputed....

As geology plainly proclaims that each land has undergone great physical changes, we might have expected to find that organic beings have varied under nature, in the same way as they have varied under domestication. And if there has been any variability under nature, it would be an unaccountable fact if natural selection had not come into play....

There is grandeur in this view of life, with its several powers, having been originally breathed by the Creator into a few forms or into one; and that, whilst this planet has gone cycling on according to the fixed law of gravity, from so simple a beginning endless forms most beautiful and most wonderful have been, and are being evolved.

QUESTIONS

1. What role does natural selection play in Darwin's theory, and what is the logic behind it?

2. How and why does Darwin attempt to reconcile his theory with religion?

Source: Charles Darwin, *On the Origin of Species by Means of Natural Selection*, 6th ed., vol. 2 (1872; repr., New York: Appleton, 1923), pp. 267–268, 279, 305–306.

---

beings are members of the animal kingdom, like other species, disturbed him, and the admission, he wrote, "is like confessing a murder." Nonetheless, for Darwin scientific evidence took precedence over all other considerations.

These assertions shocked Christians, many of whom denounced the new scientific findings. Some argued that science and faith belonged to two different worlds. Others claimed that there was no reason why God could not have created the world through natural forces. In the long run, however, **Darwinism** seemed to undermine the certainties of religious orthodoxies; many found religion incompatible with scientific discovery.

Some contemporaries took Darwin's theories beyond biology and applied them to human social development. Social Darwinists argued that human societies evolve in the same way as plants and animals. According to their logic, human societies—races, classes, nations—like species, were destined to compete for survival, and some would be condemned to fade away. And from these harsh laws, a better humanity would evolve. The British social theorist Herbert Spencer (1820-1903), who coined the expression "survival of the fittest," believed that society should be established in such a way that the strongest and most resourceful would survive. The weak, poor, and improvident were not worthy of survival, and if the state helped them survive—for instance, by providing welfare—it would only perpetuate the unfit. Poverty, according to Spencer and his followers, was a sign of biological inferiority; wealth was a sign of success in the struggle for survival. In Europe and the United States (where Spencer was extremely popular, selling hundreds of thousands of books), **Social Darwinism** justified callousness toward the poor at home and toward imperial conquest abroad. The European subjugation of Africans and Asians through colonization confirmed for Social Darwinists white racial superiority. People of color were seen as poorly endowed to compete in the race for survival (see Chapter 24). Darwin's theory was also used to justify inequality of the sexes, as men were thought to be more highly evolved than women.

Darwinism Influential theory of biological evolution, first put forth by Charles Darwin. He proposed that all forms of life continuously develop through natural selection, whereby those that are better adapted to the environment have the advantage and are more likely to survive and pass on their beneficial traits to their offspring.

Social Darwinism Theory of social evolution that states that human societies evolve in the same way as plants and animals, and that the weak, poor, and improvident are not worthy of survival.

Monkey Man Darwin's controversial theory of evolution made him a worldwide celebrity as well as an object of scorn. Caricatures of Darwin as a "monkey man" proliferated. This one is from an 1878 issue of the French satirical journal, *La Petite Lune*. (Library of Congress Prints and Photographs Division Washington, D.C. [LC-USZ62-88790])

Physics, Chemistry, and Medicine

Dramatic scientific advances in the nineteenth century confirmed the prevalent belief that human beings could understand and control nature. From the seventeenth century, scientists had studied nature through careful observation, seeking to develop theories by explaining its regularities. By the 1850s, major breakthroughs in physics established the field of electrical science. In chemistry, new elements were discovered almost every year. In 1869, Russian chemist Dmitri Mendeleev (men-del-LAY-ef) (1834–1907) developed the periodic table, which arranged the elements by their atomic weight. He left blank spaces for elements still unknown but that he was confident existed. Within ten years, three of these elements were discovered, affirming the belief that scientific knowledge not only can be experimentally tested, but also has predictive value. Such triumphs further enhanced science's prestige.

Once a practicing hobby among amateurs, science became increasingly specialized. In the nineteenth century, as the state and industry became more involved in promoting scientific research, the scientist became a professional employed by a university, a hospital, or some other institution. Scientific journals and meetings of scientific associations disseminated new discoveries and theories. Around midcentury, a number of important breakthroughs occurred in medicine. Before the development of anesthesia, surgical intervention was limited. With only alcohol to dull the patient's pain, even the swiftest surgeons could perform only modest surgical procedures. In the 1840s, however, the introduction of ether and then chloroform allowed people to undergo more extensive surgery. It also was used to relieve pain in more routine procedures and in childbirth; Queen Victoria asked for chloroform when in labor.

Increasingly, physicians applied the scientific experimental method to medicine, and as a result their concerns reached beyond the treatment of diseases to the discovery of their origins. Louis Pasteur (1822–1895) achieved notable breakthroughs when he discovered that microbes, small organisms invisible to the naked eye, cause various diseases. Pasteur found that heating milk to a certain temperature kills disease-carrying organisms. This process, called pasteurization, reduced the incidence of gastrointestinal illnesses that caused a high rate of infant deaths. Pasteur initiated other advances as well in the prevention of disease. Vaccination against smallpox had started in England in the eighteenth century, but Pasteur invented vaccines for other diseases and was able to explain the process by which the body, inoculated with a weak form of bacilli, developed antibodies that successfully overcame more serious infections. In England, the surgeon Joseph Lister (1827–1912) developed an effective disinfectant, carbolic acid, to kill the germs that cause gangrene and other infections in surgical patients. Lister's development of germ-free procedures transformed the science of surgery. By reducing the patient's risk, more ambitious surgery could be attempted. Eventually, midwives and doctors, by washing their hands and sterilizing their instruments, began to reduce the incidence of the puerperal, or "childbed," fever, a toxic infection that killed women after childbirth. The increasingly scientific base of medicine and its visible success in combating disease improved its reputation.

Birth of the Social Sciences

No field in the human sciences flourished as much in the nineteenth century as that of history. In an era undergoing vast transformations, many people became interested in change over time, particularly with regard to their own national histories. The father of modern historical writing is the German Leopold von Ranke (von RANG-kuh) (1795–1886). Departing from the tradition of earlier historians, who explained the past as the ongoing fulfillment of an overarching purpose— whether divine will, the human liberation, or some other goal—Ranke insisted that the role of the historian was to "show how things actually were." Like a scientist, the historian must be objective and dispassionate. Only by viewing humankind of all eras and environments on their own terms could historians arrive at a better understanding of humanity.

This perspective transformed the study of history into a discipline with recognizable common standards of evidence. Historians studied and interpreted original (or "primary") sources; they collected and published their findings; they founded professional organizations and published major journals.

Other social sciences also developed in this period. Anthropology, the comparative study of people in different societies, had been the subject of speculative literature for hundreds of years. Increased contacts with non-European societies in the nineteenth century—the effect of burgeoning trade, exploration, and missionary activities—stimulated anthropological curiosity. In 1844, the Society of Ethnology was founded in Paris, followed by the Anthropological Society (1859). London, Berlin, and Vienna quickly followed suit, establishing similar societies in the 1860s. Anthropologists speculated on the causes of perceived differences among human races, mainly attributing the variations to their physical structures. They offered apparent "scientific" backing to the era's racism, explaining that non-Europeans were condemned to an existence inferior to the white races.

The main anthropological theorist in Britain was Edward Tylor (1832–1917), the son of a brass manufacturer. Through his travels, Tylor came into contact with non-European peoples, who aroused his curiosity. Strongly influenced by the evolutionary doctrines of his day, Tylor believed that the various societies of humankind were subject to discoverable scientific laws. Tylor posited that if one could travel back in time, one would find humankind increasingly unsophisticated. So, too, the farther one traveled from Europe, the more primitive humankind became. Thus, according to his view, the contemporary African was at a level of development similar to that of Europeans in an earlier era.

Tylor was not technically a racist, since he argued that the conditions of non-Europeans resulted from their social and cultural institutions—not from their biology. Eventually, they would "evolve" and become akin to Europeans. Like racists, however, social evolutionists believed in European superiority. Anthropology gave "scientific" sanction to the idea of a single European people who shared either a similar biological structure or a common stage of social development, which distinguished them from non-Europeans.

The term *sociology* was coined by Auguste Comte. A number of ambitious thinkers, among them the English "social philosopher" Herbert Spencer (see page 655), considered the influence that social conditions exerted on individuals. In the 1840s, various social reformers published detailed statistical investigations that suggested relationships between, for instance, income, disease, and death rates. A few decades later, researchers spelled out the theoretical principles underlying sociology. Emile Durkheim (DIRK-hime) (1858–1917), among the first to do so, insisted that sociology was a verifiable science. His disciples, and the journal he founded, ensured the success of sociology as a professionalized discipline.

In the past, history, anthropology, and sociology were the purview of amateurs; now professional historians, anthropologists, and sociologists took over these fields, engaging in full-time research and teaching at universities or research institutes. Professionalization and specialization led to significant advances in several disciplines, but it also led to the fragmentation and compartmentalization of knowledge. People of broad learning and expertise became far less common.

The Challenge to Religion

Religion had assumed increased importance as a bulwark of order in the wake of the 1848 revolutions. In France, Napoleon III gave the Catholic Church new powers over education, and the bourgeoisie flocked to worship. In Spain, moderates who had been anticlerical (opposed to the clergy) began to support the church, and in 1851, they signed a concordat (an agreement with the papacy) declaring Roman Catholicism "the only religion of the Spanish nation." In Austria in 1855, the state surrendered powers it had acquired in the 1780s, returning to bishops full control over the clergy, the seminaries, and the administration of marriage laws.

In 1848, the papacy had been nearly overthrown by revolution, and in 1860, it lost most of its domains to Italy. Thus, Pope Pius IX became a sworn enemy of liberalism. In 1864, he issued the *Syllabus of Errors,* in which he condemned a long list of faults that included "progress," "liberalism," and "modern civilization." To establish full control over the clergy and believers, the Lateran Council in 1870 issued the controversial doctrine of papal infallibility, which declared that the pope, when speaking officially on matters of faith and morals, is incapable of error. This doctrine became a target of anticlerical opinion.

The political alliance the Catholic Church struck with reactionary forces meant that when new political groups came to power, they moved against the church. In Italy, since the church had discouraged national unification, conflict raged between the church and the new state. In Germany, Catholics had either held on to their regional loyalties or favored unification under Austrian auspices. When Protestant Prussia unified Germany, Chancellor Bismarck viewed the Catholics with suspicion as unpatriotic and launched a campaign against them, the *Kulturkampf* (KOOL-toor-kampf) ("cultural struggle"). Bismarck expelled the Jesuits and attempted to establish state control over the Catholic schools and appointment of bishops. Not satisfied, he seized church property and imprisoned or exiled eighteen hundred priests.

In France, the republicans, who finally won the upper hand over the monarchists in 1879, bitterly resented the church's support of the monarchist party. Strongly influenced by Comte's ideas of positivism, republicans believed that France would not be a free country until the power of the church was diminished and its nonscientific or antiscientific disposition was overcome. The republican regime reduced the role of the church in education as well as some other clerical privileges.

Greater tolerance, or perhaps indifference to religion in general, led to more acceptance of religious diversity. In 1854 and 1871, England opened university admission and teaching posts at all universities to non-Anglicans. In France, too, the position of religious minorities improved. Some of the highest officials of the Second Empire were Protestants, as were some early leaders of the Third Republic and some important business leaders and scientists.

Legal emancipation of Jews, started in France in 1791, subsequently spread to the rest of the Continent. The British allowed Jews to hold seats in the House of Commons in 1858, and in the House of Lords the following decade. In the 1860s, Germany and Austria-Hungary granted Jews the rights of citizenship. Although some Jews occupied high office in France and Italy, they had to convert to Christianity before they could aspire to such positions in Germany and Austria-Hungary. In other fields, such as banking and commerce, access was easier. Social discrimination continued, however—most of European society refused to accept Jews as social equals.

Because conditions for most people of western Europe improved with the expanding economy, Jews drew relatively less attention as they too took advantage of new opportunities. In other parts of the continent, Jews were not so fortunate. In eastern Europe, they incurred resentment when they moved into commerce, industry, and the professions. Outbreaks of violence against them, called *pogroms,* occurred in Bucharest, the capital of Romania, in 1866 and in the Russian seaport of Odessa in 1871. Although economic rivalries may have fueled anti-Semitism, they do not completely explain it. In most cases, anti-Jewish sentiment occurred in the areas of Europe least exposed to liberal ideas of human equality and human rights.

Culture in the Age of Material Change

Advances in technology and science became reflected in the arts, especially in the movement known as **modernism**, which rejected traditional forms of cultural expression and embraced new ones. Some artists optimistically believed they could more accurately portray reality by adopting scientific methods, objectively depicting their subjects. The materialism of the age, however, also disillusioned a minority of artists, who warned against its loss of values.

Photography had a direct impact on artistic perspectives. The inventions of the Frenchman Louis Daguerre (dah-GAIR) (1789–1851) made the camera relatively usable by the 1830s. The introduction of celluloid film and American George Eastman's (1854–1932) invention of the Kodak camera, which became mass-produced and affordable, gave wide public access to the practice of photography by the 1890s. Photographic services were in high demand; by the 1860s, thirty thousand people in Paris made a living from photography and allied fields. (See the feature, "The Visual Record: The Modern City and Photography.")

The ability of photography to depict a scene with exactitude had a significant impact on art. On the one hand, it encouraged many artists to be true to reality, to reproduce on the canvas a visual image akin to that of a photograph. On the other hand, some artists felt that such realism was no longer necessary in their sphere. However, the great majority of the public, which now had wide access to museum exhibitions, was accustomed to photographic accuracy and desired art that was representative and intelligible. Realistic works of art met this need, at least superficially.

modernism   A set of cultural tendencies and movements finding expression in new forms of art, architecture, and in attitudes and practices that rejected traditional forms of cultural expression.

Courbet: *The Stone Breakers* This realistic 1849 painting depicts the rough existence of manual laborers. The bleakness of the subject matter and the style in which it was carried out characterized much of the realist school of art. (The Stone Breakers, 1849 (oil on canvas) (destroyed in 1945), Courbet, Gustave (1819–77)/Galerie Neue Meister, Dresden, Germany/© Staatliche Kunstsammlungen Dresden/The Bridgeman Art Library)

Many artists discarded myths and symbols to portray the world as it actually was, or at least as it appeared to them—a world without illusions, everyday life in all its grimness. The realist painter Gustave Courbet (koor-BAY) (1819–1877) proclaimed himself "without ideals and without religion." His fellow Frenchman Jean-François Millet (mil-LAY) (1814–1875) held a similar opinion. Instead of romanticizing peasants in the manner of earlier artists, he painted the harsh physical conditions under which they labored. In England, the so-called pre-Raphaelites took as their model those painters prior to Raphael in Renaissance Italy, who had depicted the realistic simplicity of nature. In painting historical scenes, these artists meticulously researched the landscape, architecture, fauna, and costumes of their subjects.

Photography and science also helped inspire completely new approaches to painting that abandoned traditional standards and shocked artistic sensibilities. On April 15, 1874, six French artists—Edgar Degas (1834–1917), Claude Monet (1840–1926), Camille Pissarro (1830–1903), Auguste Renoir (1840–1919), Alfred Sisley (1839–1899), and Berthe Morisot (1841–1895)—opened an exhibition in Paris that a critic disparagingly called **impressionist**, after the title of one of Monet's paintings, *Impression: Sunrise*. The impressionists were influenced by new theories of physics that claimed images were transmitted to the brain as small light particles that the brain then reconstituted. The impressionists wanted their paintings to capture what things looked like before the brain "distorted" them. Many of these painters unconventionally left their studios to paint objects exactly as they looked outdoors when light hit them at a certain angle. Monet, for example, emphasized outdoor painting and the need for spontaneity—for reproducing subjects without preconceptions about how earlier artists had depicted them—and seeking to show exactly how the colors and shapes struck the eye. Monet was particularly interested in creating multiple paintings of the same scene—from different viewpoints, under different weather

impressionist Late-nineteenth-century style of painting pioneered by the French artists Degas, Monet, Pissarro, Renoir, Sisley, and Morisot.

A Chinese Official's Views of European Material Progress

Educated in European universities, Ku Hung-Ming rose to become a high official in the Chinese court. His essays were penned under the impact of the European military intervention in China during the Boxer Rebellion in 1900 (see page 673). Ku denounced European notions of superiority over Asia by arguing that material progress was not an appropriate measure of a civilization's value.

In order to estimate the value of a civilization, it seems to me, the question we must finally ask is not what great cities, what magnificent houses, what fine roads it has built and is able to build; what beautiful and comfortable furniture, what clever and useful implements, tools and instruments it has made and is able to make; no, not even what institutions, what arts and sciences it has invested: the question we must ask, in order to estimate the value of a civilization—is what type of humanity, what kind of men and women it has been able to produce. In fact, the man and woman—the type of human beings—which a civilization produces, it is this which shows the essence, the personality, so to speak, the soul of that civilization. Now if the men and women of a civilization show the essence, the personality and soul of that civilization, the language which the men and women in that civilization speak, shows the essence, the personality, the soul of the men and women of that civilization....

To Europeans, and especially to unthinking practical Englishmen, who are accustomed to take what modern political economists call "the standard of living" as the test of the moral culture of or civilization of a people, the actual life of the Chinese and of the people of the East at the present day, will no doubt appear very sordid and undesirable. But the standard of living by itself is not a proper test of the civilization of a people. The standard of living in America at the present day, is, I believe, much higher than it is in Germany. But although the son of an American millionaire, who regards the simple and comparatively low standard of living among the professors of a German University, may doubt the value of the education in such a University, yet no educated man, I believe, who has traveled in both countries, will admit that the Germans are a less civilized people than the Americans.

QUESTIONS

1. How does the Chinese official define civilization? How does his view differ from the European view?
2. What is Ku Hung-Ming's idea of a hierarchy of civilization?
3. According to the ideas in this reading, what is the connection between progress and civilization?

Source: Ku Hung-Ming, *The Spirit of the Chinese People,* 2d ed. (Beijing: Commercial Press, 1922), pp. 1, 144–145.

conditions, at different times of day—to underscore that no single "correct" depiction could possibly capture a subject.

The school of realism also influenced literature, especially the novel. Departing from romanticism, realist novels did not glorify life or infuse it with mythical elements; they portrayed instead the stark realities of daily existence. Charles Dickens (1812–1870), who came from a poor background and had personally experienced the inhumanity of the London underworld, wrote novels depicting the lot of the poor with humor and sympathy. The appalling social conditions he described helped educate his large middle-class audience on the state of the poor.

Another realist, the French novelist Gustave Flaubert (flo-BEAR) (1821–1880), consciously debunked the romanticism of his elders. His famous novel, *Madame Bovary,* depicts middle-class life—particularly that of the married woman—as bleak, boring, and meaningless. The heroine seeks to escape the narrow confines of provincial life by adulterous and disastrous affairs.

Two Russian novelists of the realist school—arguably the greatest and most influential of all time—exploded onto the literary scene in the 1870s. Leo Tolstoy's (1828–1910) *War and Peace,* rather than portraying battle as heroic, showed individuals trapped by forces beyond their control. Small and insignificant events, as well as major ones, governed human destiny. Feodor Dostoyevsky (1821–1881) realistically portrayed the psychological dimensions of his characters in novels, such as *Crime and Punishment* (1866), *The Idiot* (1868), and *The Brothers Karamazov* (1879–1880).

The naturalist school of literature, a successor to realism, reflected positivist philosophy and grounded its methods in the natural sciences. Emile Zola (1840–1902), a Frenchman, belonged to this school. The writer, he declared, should record and represent human behavior scientifically. He described his own work as similar to "the analysis that surgeons make on cadavers."

The Modern City and Photography

This photo of Piccadilly Square in Manchester documents the modernization of the nineteenth-century city and, at the same time, conveys the sense of immediacy that photography provided as a new means of representation.

Taken in the 1880s, this photo* shows evidence of the great progress that had taken place in photography since its invention half a century earlier. In 1839, Louis Daguerre publicized the method of fixing an image on silvered copperplate. At first, the cameras and equipment were so cumbersome that photography was confined to studios. Thus, the only images were portraits of people and the occasional still life. As the camera became simpler, photographers could leave the studio and take pictures outdoors. The introduction of the dry plate method in the 1870s made film far more sensitive to light, reducing exposure time to a fraction of a second. Now a photograph could capture movement without reducing it to a blur, as in this bustling city scene.

Originally, photography had been regarded as a more exact, and less expensive, form of illustration and so was influenced by the conventions of painting. Because of the slowness of taking pictures and the obvious presence of the photographer with bulky equipment, most early photographs, even outdoor shots, were staged. But soon thereafter, thanks to technical innovations, photographers could capture a scene even without the cooperation of the subject. None of the subjects in this photo has eye contact with the camera. In fact, they seem unaware of the photographer as they go about their daily business.

This photo also conveys important visual information about the emerging modern city. A vibrant textile city, Manchester had a population that more than doubled to 600,000 inhabitants between 1830 and 1900. Piccadilly was its commercial center. As the photo here shows, it had been built as a large open square intended for the easy movement of pedestrians and wagons. City planners of the nineteenth century created squares and broad, straight avenues feeding into them, such as suggested here. Replacing old slums and narrow alleys, broad avenues eased the flow of traffic and admitted fresh air and sunlight. The square contained fancy stores with dwellings situated on the upper floors behind the elegantly crafted façades.

Piccadilly, the commercial center of Manchester, had warehouses and offices where buyers purchased textiles that they would in turn sell to retail consumers. As seen in this photo, Piccadilly Square, as a commercial center, required public transportation to move people quickly on the broad new avenues. Notice the rails for the horse-drawn tramway that had been introduced as early as the 1820s. They were the first means of mass transportation within the city. Trams on rails reduced friction and allowed a horse to pull a far greater load. In this case, the tram, located in the center of the photo, is a double-decker.

The large modern city required ease of communication at night as well as in the daytime. Street lighting not only provided that convenience, but also made the streets more secure by making potential crime more visible. Streetlamps became the norm in large cities, especially in the better neighborhoods. The elegant gaslights viewable in the photo of Piccadilly Square were replaced a few years later by electric lamps that were cheaper to operate and allowed for the spread of city lighting.

An industrial town, Manchester was not a particularly pleasant city to live in. Visitors complained of its grime, pollution, and foul smells. Many members of the commercial classes lived in wealthy suburbs and commuted by tram to work in the center. Sometime after this picture was taken, the horse-drawn tram was replaced by the electric tram, which could transport more people faster than its predecessor. Its lower cost also meant that it was accessible to most workers. With the advent of the electric tram, workers also began to move to the suburbs, making the center less crowded.

If the modern photograph was different from a painting, photography still adhered to some of the traditions of painting—notably composition. The photographer composed this image by making choices, for example, as to what to put in the foreground. Our eye centers on the harried merchant crossing the well-ordered street with its backdrop of amenities.

Compare this photograph with Camille Pissarro's *L'avenue de l'Opéra, Sunlight, Winter Morning* on page 651. Paris, known as the "city of light," was very different from Manchester, though like that industrial city, the new boulevards resulting from "Hausmannization" allowed for a larger and speedier flow of traffic and commerce. Pissarro also conveys in this painting the bustle—and perhaps alienation—some felt in modern life. Note the predominance of solitary figures in both the painting and the photograph. Wide boulevards meant that pedestrians did not "run into each other" and socialize as readily as they had on narrow streets. Indeed, Pissarro and other impressionist painters disdained the modernization of cities and turned instead to the suburbs and rural landscapes, leaving the

Zola's Rougon-Macquart (roo-ZHON-mah-KAR) series, which includes the novels *Nana* (1880) and *Germinal* (1885), describes the experience of a family over several generations. He emphasizes the impact environment and heredity had on his characters' lives of degradation and vice, in which they seem to be locked in a Darwinian struggle for survival: Some are doomed by the laws of biology to succeed, others to succumb.

Piccadilly Square, Manchester, ca. 1886 (Topham Picturepoint/The Image Works)

documentation of urban change to photographers. Pissarro thought Paris had become "ill" from all of its changes.

The chemical and optical breakthroughs that made the camera such an effective new tool were implemented by inventors in cities, such as London, Paris, and Berlin. Photographers in turn took pictures of some of the great technical feats of their era, such as the Eiffel Tower. The modern aspects of the city, such as the scene in this photo, were frequent subjects for the photographer's lens. Before the end of the century, photographs such as this were commonly used on postcards. The producers and consumers of postcards were more fascinated by the reality of representation rather than the beauty of particular sites, as postcards geared toward tourism would later embrace.

QUESTIONS

1. How did modernization—urbanization, commercialization, the design of cities, and modern means of transportation—change people's sensual experience and perceptions?

2. In its replication of "reality," how did photography both record and create our understanding of the past? How did it both replicate traditional art and create new ways of seeing?

*The advice of Thomas Prasch in the choice of this photo is gratefully acknowledged.

Although this era generally celebrated material progress, a number of intellectuals reacted against it. They were alarmed by the prospect of the popular masses achieving political power through winning the vote and by mass production and consumption. They denounced the smug and the self-satisfied, who saw happiness in acquisition and consumption. Some condemned the age in severe terms. Dostoyevsky railed against the materialism and egotism of the West,

SECTION SUMMARY

- Darwin's theory of evolution reinforced the belief among some of the inevitability of human progress; others found the placement of human beings in the same category as animal species profoundly disturbing.

- Social Darwinists applied Darwin's theories to human society in order to justify social and gender inequality, racial hierarchies, and "survival of the fittest."

- The application of the scientific method (experimentation) transformed fields, such as physics (especially electrical science), chemistry, and medicine.

- The scientific method also transformed the study of human society, professionalizing the fields of history, anthropology, and sociology.

- Scientific discoveries and theories undermined religious belief among some people; others, however, reacted to the harshness of the material world by embracing religion more fervently.

- Science and technology infused the arts with a new emphasis on realism and on the importance of visual representations.

branding its civilization as driven by "trade, shipping, markets, factories." In Britain—the nation that seemed to embody progress—the historian Thomas Carlyle (1795–1881) berated his age as one not of progress but of selfishness. He saw parliamentarianism as a sham, and he called for a strong leader to save the nation from endless debates and compromises. Unlike most of his contemporaries, who saw in material plenty a sign of progress, Carlyle saw the era as one of decline, bereft of spiritual values.

In France, republicans saw in the ostentation of the Second Empire a sign of depravity and decline. The 1870–1871 defeat in war and the insurrection of the Paris Commune contributed to the mood of pessimism among many intellectuals. Flaubert detested his own age, seeing it as petty and mean. The characters in Zola's Rougon-Macquart novels slide steadily downward as each generation's mental faculties, social positions, and morals degenerate. Some people abroad also were unimpressed with developments in Europe. (See the feature, "The Global Record: A Chinese Official's Views of European Material Progress.")

Not all were optimistic in this age of optimism. If many people celebrated what they viewed as an age of progress, others claimed that under the outer trappings of material comfort lay a frightening ignorance of aesthetic, moral, and spiritual values.

CHAPTER SUMMARY

During the second half of the nineteenth century, the cluster of technological innovations known as the second industrial revolution—mass-produced steel, synthetic dyes, new forms of energy, and the speedup in production—created for many Westerners an era of unprecedented material plenty. The expansion of railroads, advances in shipping, the standardization of postal service, and the inventions of the telegraph and telephone collapsed distances of time and space, and brought Europe further into a global economy.

Economic changes transformed the class structure of many European countries: the middle classes expanded, and their values and tastes defined the second half of the century. Conditions for the lower classes generally improved, but many rural and urban laborers still lived in poverty. To address problems of urban growth and threats of social upheaval, local governments took measures to improve public health and provide advice and material assistance. The need to shape a loyal citizenry inspired national governments to provide free and compulsory primary education.

Intellectual and cultural currents reflected material changes and the confidence they inspired. Scientific methods were applied to the study of human behavior. Novelists and painters, like scientists, aimed to dissect the world around them, adopting realism in the arts. Some intellectuals, however, were repulsed by the crass self-satisfaction of the bourgeoisie, and they despised their age's worship of industry and materialism.

FOCUS QUESTIONS

- What technological changes led to the expansion of the European economy after the mid-nineteenth century?

- How did the economic expansion affect the various social classes, and city versus rural areas, differently?

- What problems did urbanization create, and what were the solutions?

- What new scientific, intellectual, and cultural trends emerged in this period, and what impact did they have on systems of belief?

KEY TERMS

second industrial
    revolution   (p. 640)
bourgeois century   (p. 644)
professionalization   (p. 645)

Victorian morality   (p. 645)
separate spheres   (p. 646)
social Catholics   (p. 649)
positivism   (p. 654)

Darwinism   (p. 655)
Social Darwinism   (p. 655)
modernism   (p. 659)
impressionist   (p. 660)

 This icon will direct
you to additional
materials on the
website: www
.cengage.com/history/
noble/westciv6e.

See our interactive
eBook for map and
primary source
activities.

24

The "Unsinkable" Titanic
The *Titanic* proudly announces its maiden voyage.   (Christie's Images/CORBIS)

Imperialism and Escalating Tensions, 1880–1914

In April 1912, the *Titanic*, the largest and most technologically advanced passenger ship ever built, sailed from England for New York. Its owners, the White Star Line, boasted that this majestic vessel testified to "the progress of mankind" and would "rank high in the achievements of the twentieth century." Though hailed as "virtually unsinkable," on the night of April 12, the *Titanic* struck an iceberg south of Newfoundland and rapidly sank. More than 1,500 of the 2,100 people aboard perished in the icy North Atlantic waters. The overconfident captain had not taken warnings of icebergs in the ship's path seriously enough.

Two years later, European society was hit by a major disaster—the outbreak of a world war. That such a disaster would end the era that contemporaries called the *belle époque* (BELL eh-POK)—"beautiful epoch"—was as unimaginable as the *Titanic*'s fate. The economy had been booming, and more nations seemed to be adapting to democracy and extending suffrage. Yet hand in hand with these trends of apparent progress appeared troubling tendencies. Forces beneath the surface threatened European social stability, which is why, in 1914, a lone assassin's bullet could set off a series of reactions that brought a whole era to a tragic close.

In the decades prior to 1914, governing became more complex as nations grew larger. The population of Europe jumped from 330 million in 1880 to 460 million by the outbreak of war. A larger population coupled with extended suffrage made reaching political consensus more difficult. The example of democracy in some countries led to discontent in the autocracies that failed to move toward freer institutions. Where freer institutions did exist, those excluded from them—women, ethnic minorities, and the poor—became ever more resentful.

Intellectuals no longer felt certain that the world was knowable, stable, or subject to mastery by rational human beings. Some jettisoned rationality and instead glorified emotion, irrationality, and in some cases violence. The works of painters and writers seemed to anticipate the impending destruction of world order.

The anxieties and tensions that beset many Europeans took a variety of forms. Ethnic minorities became targets of hatred. European states embarked on a race for empire throughout the world, forcibly subjecting non-Europeans to white domination. European states felt increasingly insecure, worried that they would be subject to attack. They established standing armies, shifted alliances, drafted war plans, and, in the end, went to war.

FOCUS QUESTIONS

- What were the main motivations for European imperialism?

- In what ways did the worldview of intellectuals living in the belle époque differ from that of a generation earlier?

- What factors made parliamentary rule in Great Britain, France, and Italy dysfunctional?

- What various crises weakened autocratic rule in Germany, Russia, and the Ottoman Empire?

- What responsibility did each of the Great Powers have for the outbreak of war in 1914?

 This icon will direct you to additional materials on the website: www.cengage.com/history/noble/westciv6e.

 See our interactive eBook for map and primary source activities.

THE NEW IMPERIALISM AND THE SPREAD OF EUROPE'S INFLUENCE

What were the main motivations for European imperialism?

Part of Europe's self-confidence during the period from the 1880s to 1914 derived from the unchallenged sway it held over the rest of the globe. The age of empire building that started in Europe in the sixteenth century seemed to have ended by 1750. Then, in the 1880s, European states launched a new era of expansionism, conquering an unprecedented amount of territory. In only twenty-five years, Europeans subjugated 500 million people—one-half of the world's non-European population.

European expansion also marked the globe in a massive movement of people. Between 1870 and 1914, 55 million Europeans moved overseas, mainly to Australia, the United States, Canada, and Argentina. Scandinavians, Italians, Germans, Britons, Portuguese, and other groups each left a cultural and economic imprint on their adopted land, introducing new customs, tastes, and farming techniques. This phenomenal expansion of overseas migrations added to Europe's global influence.

But the more dramatic impact of European influence in this era assumed the form of ambitious conquest. The term the **new imperialism** differentiates this phase of European expansion from the earlier stage of empire building, which had focused on the Americas. Nineteenth-century imperialism centered on Africa and Asia. Unlike the earlier period, the new imperialism occurred in an age of mass participation in politics, accompanied by expressions of popular enthusiasm.

new imperialism Era of European overseas expansion launched in the 1880s. Europeans subjugated 500 million people in Africa and Asia.

Petersen: *Emigrants Preparing to Depart* Edward Petersen's 1890 painting depicts Danish emigrants preparing to leave their homeland. Between 1860 and 1914, 300,000 people emigrated from the small country of Denmark, most of them to the United States. (Courtesy of the Aarhus Kunstmuseum. Reproduced with permission of Thomas, Poul, and Ole Hein Pedersen, Aarhus.)

Economic and Social Motives

The desire for huge markets and the hope for profit—much of it illusory—stirred an interest in empire. Colonies, it was believed, would provide eager buyers for European goods that would stimulate production at home. Yet colonies did not represent large markets for the metropolitan countries. France's colonies represented only 12 percent of its foreign trade, and Germany's even less. Great Britain's trade with its colonies represented a considerable one-third of its foreign trade, but most of that was with the white settlement colonies, such as Canada and Australia, not with those acquired in the era of the new imperialism.

Lack of profitability, however, mattered little to many proponents of empire. Some of them, known as social imperialists, argued that possession of an empire could resolve social as well as economic issues. An empire could offer an outlet for a variety of domestic frustrations. German and Italian imperialists often argued that their nations needed colonies in which to resettle their multiplying poor. Once the overseas territories were acquired, however, few Europeans found them attractive for settlement.

Nationalistic Motives

To a large extent, the desire to assert national power triggered empire building, particularly in the last third of the nineteenth century when the new nation-states of Italy and Germany had emerged. The latter in particular, in its rapid industrialization, became a daunting source of economic competition. Territorial expansion became a new means to compete effectively on the world stage.

The British Empire, with India as its crown jewel, constituted the largest, most powerful, and apparently wealthiest of all the European domains. Although the real source of Britain's wealth and power was the country's industrial economy, many people believed that its success came from its vast empire. The British example thus stimulated other nations to carve out empires. Their activities in turn triggered British anxieties. Britain and France unleashed a scramble for Africa and Asia; in Asia, Britain also competed with Russia.

France, defeated by Prussia in 1870, found in its colonies proof that it was still a Great Power. Germany and Italy, which formed their national identities relatively late, cast a jealous eye on the British and French empires and decided that if they were to be counted as Great Powers, they too would need overseas colonies. Belgium's King Leopold II (r. 1876–1909) spun out various plans to acquire colonies to compensate for his nation's small size. In the race for colonies, worldwide strategic concerns stimulated expansion. Because the Suez Canal ensured the route to India, the British established a protectorate over Egypt in 1882. Then, fearing a rival power might threaten their position by encroaching on the Nile, in the next decade, they extended their control all the way south to Uganda (see **Map 24.1**). Russia, fearing a British takeover in central Asia, expanded toward Afghanistan, while the British movement northwestward to Afghanistan had a similar motivation—to prevent Russia from encroaching on India. The "great game" played by Russia and Britain in central Asia ended only in 1907, with the signing of the Anglo-Russian Entente.

The desire to control the often-turbulent frontiers of newly acquired areas drove much of this expansion. Once those frontiers had been brought under control, there were, of course, new frontiers that had to be subdued. As a Russian foreign minister said of such an incentive for expansion, "The chief difficulty is to know where to stop." The imperial powers rarely did.

CHRONOLOGY

1873	Three Emperors' League
1882	Britain seizes Egypt
	Triple Alliance of Germany, Italy, and Austria-Hungary
1884	Three Emperors' League renewed
1890	Kaiser Wilhelm II dismisses Bismarck as chancellor
1894	Franco-Russian Alliance
	Beginning of the Dreyfus affair
1900	King of Italy assassinated
1903	Emmeline Pankhurst founds the Women's Social and Political Union
1904	Anglo-French Entente
1905	Einstein proposes theory of relativity
	Revolution in Russia
1907	Anglo-Russian Entente
1908	Young Turk rebellion in Ottoman Empire
1911	Italy colonizes Libya
	Second Moroccan crisis
June 28, 1914	Assassination of Archduke Franz Ferdinand
August 4, 1914	With the entry of Britain, Europe is at war

🌐 MAP 24.1—Africa in 1914

European powers in the late nineteenth century conquered most of Africa. Only Liberia and Ethiopia were left unoccupied at the start of World War I.

Other Ideological Motives

In addition to the search for profit and nationalistic pride, Europeans developed other strong rationalizations for imperialism. The remarkable technological and scientific advances of the nineteenth century made many imperialists believe it was Europe's duty to modernize Africa and Asia. Railroads, telegraphs, hospitals, and schools would open colonial peoples—if necessary, by brute force—to beneficent European influences.

The dramatic disparity between European material culture and that of colonial peoples in Africa and Asia offered Europeans apparent proof of their own innate superiority. They viewed Africans and Asians as primitive, inferior peoples, still in their evolutionary "infancy." Influenced by Darwin's theory of evolution (see pages 654–657), many imperialists argued that human groups competed in the struggle for survival in the same way that different species competed in nature. Dubbed "Social Darwinists," these thinkers believed that the most basic struggle occurred between the races. They also believed in a predetermined outcome: The white race, already superior, was destined to succeed, and the nonwhites to succumb.

Many Europeans paternalistically believed they had a duty to "civilize" the people they deemed inferior. The British bard of imperialism, Rudyard Kipling (1865–1936), celebrated this view in his poem "White Man's Burden" (1899):

> *Take up the White Man's burden—*
> *Send forth the best ye breed—*
> *Go bind your sons to exile*
> *To serve your captives' need.*

Each nation was certain that providence had chosen it for a colonial mission. The French Prime Minister Jules Ferry (feh-REE) declared it the duty of his country "to civilize the inferior races." Although European states rivaled each other in colonial acquisitions, they also believed they shared a common mission and a common destiny that distinguished them from the ascribed savagery and backwardness of non-Europeans. Their success at empire building reinforced those views.

Colonial acquisitions triggered public support for further expansion of the empire, much of which was expressed by the founding of various colonial societies. One million people joined the British Primrose League, which lobbied for empire as well as other patriotic goals. Though

Dutch Colonial Officials in the Dutch East Indies   In this club in an outpost of empire (in present-day Indonesia), the comforts of European bourgeois life were lovingly recreated. Absent from this photo are the countless Indonesian servants who were part of the colonial officials' lives. (Royal Tropical Institute)

more limited in size, Germany, France, and Italy had similar organizations. Colonial societies generally drew their membership from the professional middle classes—civil servants, professors, and journalists—who were quite open to nationalist arguments. These societies produced a steady stream of propaganda favoring empire building.

Much of the literature celebrating empire building employed masculine terms to describe it. Primarily a male venture, conquest alone required "virility." But writers also contrasted the colonizer's manliness with the supposed effeminacy of the colonized peoples, as well as with the domestic passivity of European wives, sisters, or mothers. If European women did venture overseas, they went as helpmates to male colonial officials or as missionaries. Believing that they would have a positive influence on the world, women missionaries, either as members of a religious order or joining their husbands, went to the colonies to spread Western religions and European values. A few women heroically explored distant lands; the Englishwoman Mary Kingsley (1862–1900) made two exploration trips into Africa. Her popular books focused British interest on overseas territories, but they in no way shook the established view that empire was a man's enterprise.

Conquest, Administration, and Westernization

Industrialization gave Europeans the means to conquer overseas territories. Their rapid-fire weapons, steam-driven gunboats, and oceangoing vessels demonstrably assured their power overseas. Telegraphic communications tied the whole world into a single network, allowing Europeans to gather information and coordinate military and political decision making. Such advantages made Europeans virtually invincible in a colonial conflict. One remarkable exception was the 1896 Italian defeat in Adowa at the hands of an Ethiopian force, which was not only superior in numbers, but better armed.

Conquest was often brutal. In September 1898, British-led forces slaughtered 20,000 Sudanese at the Battle of Omdurman. From 1904 to 1908, an uprising in southwest Africa against German rule led to the killing of an estimated 60,000 of the Herero people. The German general, who had expressly given an order to exterminate the whole population, was awarded a medal by Kaiser Wilhelm II.

Colonial governments could be brutally insensitive to the needs of the indigenous peoples. (See the feature, "The Global Record: Chief Montshiwa Petitions Queen Victoria.") To save administrative costs in the 1890s, France put large tracts of land in the French Congo under the control of private rubber companies, which systematically and savagely coerced the local people to collect the sap of the rubber trees. When the scandal broke in Paris, the concessionary companies were abolished, and the French state reestablished its control. The most notorious example of exploitation, terror, and mass killings occurred in the Belgian Congo. Leopold II of Belgium had acquired it as a personal empire. It was his private domain, and he was accountable to no one for his actions there. To his shame, Leopold mercilessly exploited the Congo, and to expedite the collection of rubber, instituted the systematic torture and killing of its people. An international chorus of condemnation finally forced the king to surrender his empire and put it under the administration of the Belgian government, which abolished some of the worst features of Leopold's rule.

Imperialism also spread Western technologies, institutions, and values. By 1914, Great Britain had built 40,000 miles of rail lines in India—nearly twice as much as in Britain. In India and Egypt, the British erected hydraulic systems that irrigated previously arid lands. Colonials built cities, often modeled on the European grid system. In some cases, they were graced with large, tree-lined avenues, and some neighborhoods were equipped with running water and modern sanitation. Schools,

IN THE RUBBER COILS.

SCENE—*The Congo "Free" State.*

Rubber Coils in Belgian Congo The Belgians colonized the Congo hoping to exploit its resources. This critical cartoon, published in the British satirical magazine *Punch* in 1906, shows a Congolese ensnared in the rubber coils of the Belgian king Leopold in the guise of a serpent. Rubber was the major cash crop, introduced by the Belgians to generate profits. (Punch Cartoon Library & Archive)

patterned after those in Europe, taught the imperial language and spread Western ideas and scientific knowledge—though only to a small percentage of the local population.

The European empire builders created political units that had never existed before. In many parts of Africa, they ignored tribal and indigenous differences, which had serious repercussions in the postcolonial world. Although there had been many efforts in the past to join the whole Indian subcontinent under a single authority, the British were the first to accomplish this feat (see **Map 24.2**). Through a common administration, rail network, and trade, Britain gave Indians the sense of a common condition, leading in 1885 to the founding of the India Congress Party. The Congress Party platform included the demand for constitutional government, representative assemblies, and the rule of law—concepts all based on Western theory and practice. Though initially demanding reforms within the British colonial system, the Congress Party eventually became India's major nationalist group.

In contact with Europeans, native intellectuals in colonized societies adopted a European ideology—nationalism. Indians, having studied in British schools or visited Britain, were most likely to be nationalists. They founded a movement, known as "Young India," harking back to "Young Italy" and other European nationalist movements founded during the mid-1800s (see page 595–596). Similarly, in French Algeria before World War I, a "Young Algerians" movement sprang up.

It was to be several decades before nationalism successfully challenged the European empires. In the meantime, overseas achievements confirmed Europeans' sense of themselves as agents of progress and builders of a new and better world. Europeans arrogantly believed that they knew what was best for other people, and when necessary, readily used force to implement their ideas.

The ties of empire also marked European cultures. Scenes from the colonial world often became the subjects of European art, such as Paul Gauguin's paintings of Tahiti and advertising posters for products as different as soap and whiskey. (See the feature, "The Visual Record: Imagining Empire.") A growing number of people from the colonies also came to live in European cities. By 1900, some former colonial subjects, despite various forms of discrimination, had become full participants in the lives of their host countries; two Indians won election to the British Parliament in the 1890s.

Unanticipated Consequences: Rebellion and Colonial War

The new imperialism encountered resistance from indigenous populations and caused war between colonizers. Two important examples, one of rebellion in China, the other of war in South Africa, exemplify the high material and moral costs Europe's compulsion for conquest entailed.

A prolonged decline in the effective rule of the Chinese government (the Qing dynasty), which was exacerbated by defeat in a war with Japan in 1895, opened the way to further economic incursions from western powers. By 1900, France, Britain, Russia, Germany, the United States, and Japan had exacted territorial and trading concessions from China, including rights to build railroads and control ports. The influx of Europeans included missionaries who sought to convert the Chinese to Christianity. Chinese peasants deeply resented both the economic disruptions and the contempt westerners showed for their ancient civilization. A secret society, "Righteous and Harmonious Fists" (called "Boxers" by westerners) staged a series of violent attacks in 1900–1901 against missionaries, engineers, Chinese Christians, diplomats, and merchants. They killed more than 200 westerners. In an unusual moment of cooperation, the Great Powers sent a combined expedition of 20,000 troops to crush the rebellion; they then demanded a huge indemnity from the Chinese government.

A much larger conflict unfolded in South Africa between Dutch settlers (called Afrikaners or Boers) and the British. The Boers and British had been competing with one another for African territory for nearly one hundred years. Tensions grew worse with the discovery of gold and diamonds, and the subsequent influx of 10,000 British and other foreigners to the Dutch state of Transvaal. In a series of disputes over the rights of the new arrivals, as well as over the competition for gold, the British decided to incorporate the Boer states into a federation under British control. In 1899, they goaded the Boers into war, thinking their victory would be swift.

The outnumbered Boers proved to be far more skilled in their sharpshooting and guerilla tactics than the 400,000 British troops; indeed, this war revealed to the British how physically unfit their soldiers were, many of whom had been drawn from the ranks of the poor and suffered from ailments, such as rickets. Both sides demonstrated cruelty, but the British employed methods that earned international condemnation. They adopted a "scorched earth" policy,

MAP 24.2—Asia in 1914

China, Siam (Thailand), and a portion of Persia were the only parts of Asia still independent after the Great Powers, including the United States and Japan, subjugated the continent to alien rule.

Territories held by Western powers

- Great Britain
- France
- Netherlands
- United States
- Russian Empire

- Japan and its territories
- Independent Asian states
- Ottoman Empire
- Major railroads

PACIFIC OCEAN

INDIAN OCEAN

Equator 0°

Tropic of Cancer

RUSSIAN EMPIRE

SIBERIA

Sea of Okhotsk

Sakhalin

Karafuto (1905)

JAPANESE EMPIRE

Sea of Japan (East Sea)

Vladivostok (1860, 1910)

KOREA (1905, 1910)

Lüshun (Port Arthur) (Japan 1905)

Weihai (Gr. Br. 1898)

Jiaozhou (Ger. 1898)

Ryuku Is. (Jap.)

East China Sea

Shanghai (Gr. Br. 1842)

Nanjing

Formosa (1895)

Fuzhou

Xiamen (Gr. Br. 1842)

Guangzhou (Gr. Br. 1842)

Macao (Port. 1557)

Hong Kong (France 1898)

Zhanjiang

Hainan

South China Sea

Philippine Is. (U.S. 1898)

Manila

BRITISH NORTH BORNEO (1888)

SARAWAK (1888)

Borneo

DUTCH EAST INDIES

New Guinea

Timor (Portugal 1859)

Celebes

Java (1619)

Batavia (Neth.)

Sumatra

Singapore (Gr. Br. 1819)

MALAY STATES (1874, 1909)

Saigon

FRENCH INDOCHINA (1859, 1907)

Haiphong

Hanoi

SIAM

Bangkok

Kunming

Chongqing

CHINA

Wuhan

Tianjin

Beijing

Shenyang (Mukden)

Harbin

MANCHURIA

JEHOL

Khabarovsk (1858)

Chita

AMUR DISTRICT (1858)

Amur R.

Lake Baikal

Irkutsk

OUTER MONGOLIA (Russian influence, 1912)

INNER MONGOLIA

SINKIANG

Huang He R.

Yangzi R.

TIBET

HIMALAYA MTS.

BHUTAN

NEPAL

BURMA (1852, 1885)

Rangoon

Calcutta

Bay of Bengal

Andaman Is. (Gr. Br.)

Yanaon (Fr.)

Madras

Pondicherry (Fr.)

Karikal (Fr.)

Ceylon

Ganges R.

Delhi

KASHMIR (1846)

PUNJAB

INDIA

Indus R.

Goa (Port.)

Bombay

Diu (Port.)

Karachi

BALUCHISTAN (1885)

AFGHANISTAN

BRITISH SPHERE (1907)

Kushka

Merv (1884)

Samarkand (1868)

Tashkent (1864)

Andizhan (1871)

Bukhara

Kazalinsk

Aral Sea

Lake Balkash

Trans-Siberian Railway

Omsk

Orenburg

Samara

Moscow

St. Petersburg

Helsinki

Riga

Warsaw

Brest-Litovsk

Kiev

Dnieper R.

Volga R.

RUSSIAN SPHERE (1907)

IRAN

Tehran

Baku

Ashkhabad (1881)

Krasnovodsk

Caspian Sea

Persian Gulf

OMAN (1891)

HADRAMAUT (1888)

WEST ADEN (1903)

KUWAIT (1899)

Baghdad

ARABIA

Medina

Red Sea

OTTOMAN EMPIRE

Damascus

Beirut

Angora

Kars (1878)

Batum (1878)

Constantinople

Black Sea

Mediterranean Sea

Danube R.

Nile R.

AFRICA

Arabian Sea

N

0   500   1,000 Mi.

0   500   1,000 Km.

Chief Montshiwa Petitions Queen Victoria

In 1885, Bechuanaland, in southern Africa, became a British protectorate. The Bechuana leaders saw British protection as a means to prevent takeover by the Boers, Dutch-speaking white settlers who were aggressively expanding in South Africa. The British were cavalier about their responsibilities, however, and a few years later allowed the British South Africa Company, a particularly exploitive enterprise, to take control of Bechuanaland. In protest, Chief Montshiwa (1815–1896), a major chief of the Baralong people, petitioned Queen Victoria for redress. His petition was supported by missionary lobbying, and most of Bechuanaland was saved from the clutches of the company.

Mafeking, 16 August 1895

To the Queen of England and Her Ministers:

We send greetings and pray that you are all living nicely. You will know us; we are not strangers. We have been your children since 1885.

Your Government has been good, and under it we have received much blessing, prosperity, and peace....

We Baralong are very astonished because we hear that the Queen's Government wants to give away our country in the Protectorate to the Chartered Company; we mean the B[ritish] S[outh] A[frica] Company.

Our land there is a good land, our fathers lived in it and buried in it, and we keep all our cattle in it. What will we do if you give our land away? My people are increasing very fast and are filling the land.

We keep all the laws of the great Queen; we have fought for her; we have always been the friends of her people; we are not idle; we build houses; we plough many gardens; we sow....

Why are you tired of ruling us? Why do you want to throw us away? We do not fight against your laws. We keep them and are living nicely.

Our words are No: No. The Queen's Government must not give my people's land in the Protectorate to the Chartered Company....

Peace to you all, we greet you;
Please send a good word back.
I am etc,
Montshiwa

QUESTIONS

1. What are Chief Montshiwa's grievances?
2. Why did the missionaries lend their support to the chief?
3. How does Montshiwa view the relationship between his people and the queen?

Source: S. M. Molema, *Montshiwa, 1815–1896* (Cape Town: G. Struik, 1966), pp. 181–182.

---

a military strategy that involves destruction of anything that supports the enemy. They thus burned homesteads and crops, and poisoned wells. The policy also included amassing Boer and African women, children, and workers in "concentration camps"—the first time this term was used.

The war ended with an armistice in 1902 and a toll of about 75,000 deaths, more than one-third of which occurred among Boer women and children confined in the concentration camps. Their deaths resulted from food deprivation and subjection to unhygienic conditions that fostered the spread of deadly diseases. Black Africans, many of whom also died for the same reasons in separate concentration camps, suffered famine from the massive destruction of their farmlands. Because Boers were of European descent, news of the concentration camps turned international public opinion against the British.

The Boxer Rebellion and the Boer War illustrate the degree to which pursuit of trading rights and natural resources readily resulted in violence, with permanent consequences for Europeans, indigenous cultures, and settler populations. Although the Boxers failed, peasant opposition to the corrupt Chinese government grew as a result of their rebellion, as did a movement for national independence, causing the Qing dynasty to fall in 1911. In addition to tarnishing Britain's reputation, the Boer War resulted in institutionalized racism. Joining the British Union of South Africa, Boers continued their long-term oppression of Africans by establishing Apartheid, the official policy of white supremacy and separation of blacks and whites that lasted until 1994.

SECTION SUMMARY

- Although the quest for commercial profit helped motivate imperialism, the colonies did not become large markets of the colonizing powers.

- Growing nationalism, rivalry among the Great Powers, and the need to protect the frontiers of already acquired colonies also generated empire building.

- Technological superiority, strong public support, notions of racial and cultural superiority, and a "civilizing mission" justified colonial conquest in the minds of Europeans.

- Industrialization produced powerful weaponry that made colonial conquest possible; European powers brought Western technologies, methods of administration and education, and ideologies, such as nationalism, to the colonized.

- The Boxer Rebellion and the Boer War exemplify the high costs and unintended consequences of imperialism, effecting permanent changes for European, indigenous, and settler populations.

FROM OPTIMISM TO ANXIETY: POLITICS AND CULTURE

In what ways did the worldview of intellectuals living in the belle époque differ from that of a generation earlier?

Most of the beliefs and institutions that had seemed so solid in the "age of optimism" came under attack in the next generation. Forces hostile to liberalism became increasingly vocal. In the arts and philosophy, doubt and relativism replaced the earlier confidence associated with positivism.

The Erosion of the Liberal Consensus

In 1850, liberals assumed that with the passage of time more and more people would be won over to their worldview. But the course of events in the late nineteenth century gave way to ideas and movements—some new, some rooted in the past—that chipped away at the liberal consensus. Prominent among these were socialism, anarchism, a new political right, racism, and anti-Semitism.

Liberals themselves retreated from some of their basic tenets in the face of changing circumstances. For example, a free market economy had always been one of their fundamental principles. But under the pressure of economic competition, liberals supported tariffs at home and created closed markets in their empires. To ensure workers' safety, they passed legislation requiring employers to improve working conditions. In some countries, liberals advocated income taxes and instituted welfare programs. These reforms were intended to strengthen the state by winning support from the masses and by fostering the growth of a healthy population through limited aid to mothers and children.

Historically, liberals had typically stood for an expansion of civil liberties, yet they saw nothing wrong or inconsistent in continuing to deny women both the vote and free access to education and professional advancement. In the face of labor agitation, many of them ceased supporting civil liberties for workers and favored instead the violent crushing of strikes.

In the effort to address real-life problems of the day, however, liberals encountered a paradox at the heart of their ideology: Creating rights for one group (such as workers or women) infringed on those of others (such as employers or men). Whatever action liberals took seemed to reveal a willingness to breach fundamental principles.

The Growth of Socialism and Anarchism

Among the groups challenging the power and liberal ideology of the middle classes were the socialist parties, both Marxist and non-Marxist, whose goal was to win the support of workers by espousing their causes. Socialists varied in their notions of how their goals should be achieved. Some favored pursuing objectives gradually and peacefully; others were dedicated to a violent overthrow of capitalist society.

SOCIALISM   British socialists founded the Fabian Society in 1884, named after the Roman general noted for winning by avoiding open, pitched battles. The Fabians criticized the capitalist system as inefficient, wasteful, and unjust. They believed that by gradual, democratic means, Parliament could transfer factories and land from the private sector to the state, which would manage them for the benefit of society as a whole. More efficient and more just, socialism would come into being not through class war but through enlightened ideas. This gradualist approach became the hallmark of British socialism; it shaped the ideology of the Labour Party that would gain electoral success in the 1920s.

In Germany, various strands of socialism came together when a single united party was formed in 1875. But within a few years, a debate that generally divided socialism broke up the German party: Could socialism come about by gradual democratic means, or, as Marx had contended, would it require a violent revolution? The German socialist leader Eduard Bernstein (1850–1932), who had visited England and had soaked up the influence of the Fabians, argued for gradualism in a book with the telling English title *Evolutionary Socialism* (1898). Marx had been wrong, said Bernstein, to suggest that capitalism necessarily led to the increasing wretchedness of the working class. The capitalist economy had in fact expanded and been able to provide for steadily improved conditions. Rather than having to seize power by some cataclysmic act,

Jean Jaurès An ideological moderate, the French socialist leader Jean Jaurès (zhaw-REZ) (1859–1914) was one of France's greatest orators. Much of his socialism was based on ethical notions about social justice, rather than on Marxist doctrine. Here Jaurès addresses a social gathering in 1913. On the eve of World War I, he was assassinated for his efforts to prevent war. (Branger/Roger Viollet/Getty Images)

workers could win more political power through piecemeal democratic action, and achieve their goals through legislation. Since he argued for a revision of Marxist theory, Bernstein was labeled a "revisionist." Opposing him in this great debate was the party theoretician, Karl Kautsky (KOUT-skee) (1854–1938). Kautsky insisted that nothing short of a revolution would institute socialism.

Despite internal divisions, European socialists achieved some success in making their movement international. In 1864, Marx helped found the International Workers' Association, known as the First International. The more robust **Second International** succeeded it in 1889. The International met yearly and debated issues of concern to socialists, including deteriorating relations among the Great Powers. As early as 1893, the International urged European states to resolve their conflicts by mandatory arbitration. In 1907, sensing impending war, the International called on workers to strike and refuse military service in case of international conflict.

Another movement that sought to liberate the downtrodden was anarchism, which proclaimed that humans could be free only when the state had been abolished. According to anarchist theory, in a stateless society, people would naturally join together in communes and share the fruits of their labor. Some anarchists believed they could achieve their goal through education. Others hoped to speed up the process by making direct attacks on existing authority.

The Russian nobleman Michael Bakunin (bah-KOO-neen) (1814–1876), frustrated at the authoritarianism of his homeland, became a lifelong anarchist. He challenged tsarism at home and participated in the 1848 revolutions throughout Europe. He viewed all governments as repressive and declared unilateral war on them, stating, "The passion for destruction is also a creative passion." His ideas were particularly influential in Italy, Spain, and parts of France, especially among the artisan classes.

Many anarchists of this period wanted to bring about the new society by "propaganda of the deed" aimed at dissolving the state. They formed secret terrorist organizations that assassinated heads of state or those close to them. Between 1894 and 1901, anarchists killed a president of France, a prime minister of Spain, an empress of Austria, a king of Italy, and a president of the United States. These murders fixed the popular image of anarchism as a violence-prone ideology.

Without accepting the anarchists' methods, some labor activists shared their hostility toward parliamentary institutions. They argued that only a purely working-class movement, such as unionization, could achieve workers' goals. According to this line of thought, known as "syndicalism" (after the French word for unions), workers would amass their power in unions and, at the right moment, carry out a general strike, crippling capitalist society and bringing it down.

ANARCHISM

Second International
International socialist organization founded in 1889 that met yearly to debate issues of broad concern. It called for workers to strike and refuse military service.

The New Right, Racism, and Anti-Semitism

Beginning in the 1880s, a "new right" emerged among conservatives, the traditional opponents of liberalism. The new right distinguished itself with populist and demagogic tactics, particularly with regard to nationalism—a sentiment that had made traditional conservatives support war. Alienated by democracy and social egalitarianism, many in this new right rejected doctrines of human equality and embraced racist ideologies.

Many Europeans believed that human races differed not only physiologically, but in their endowed intelligence and other qualities (see page 658). At midcentury, the Frenchman Arthur

Imagining Empire

In 1822, Joseph Huntley opened a small bakery in Reading, England. It was located near a coaching inn on the busy road between London and Bath. From a handbasket, he sold biscuits to hungry coach travelers passing through. In 1832, Huntley's son, an ironmonger, began producing tin boxes for the biscuits, which allowed them to "retain their freshness for years" and to travel worldwide without breaking. The bakery expanded rapidly. George Palmer joined the business in 1841; five years later, they purchased a former silk factory of 5,000 square feet that occupied more than half an acre. From this point on, Huntley & Palmers mass-produced their biscuits. By 1898, Huntley & Palmers was the largest biscuit manufacturer in the world, employing more than 5,000 men and women in a cluster of factory buildings comprising a "small city" unto itself on 24 acres.*

The image depicted here, a trade card advertising the Huntley & Palmers product, portrays a British hunting party in India around the turn of the nineteenth century. This card and the story behind the company it represents illustrate several themes inherent to nineteenth-century Western civilization: Industrial capitalism, the modernization in transportation, global commerce, and most poignantly, the interaction between imperialism and advertising.

The expansion of Huntley & Palmers in the second half of the century could not have occurred without the "second industrial revolution" (see pages 640–642). Improved modes of transportation, improved metal production for packaging, the building of the Suez Canal, and the expansion of empire brought Huntley & Palmers biscuits to ever greater distances. Export to the British colonies began in the 1840s. By 1874, the company could boast that "seldom a ship sails from England that does not bear within [its] ribs a Reading biscuit." By the end of the nineteenth century, Huntley & Palmers had sales representatives in China, Japan, India, South Africa, and North and South America. Ten percent of all its exports went to Britain's most important colony, India. Foreign companies produced biscuits under the Huntley & Palmers license in India, France, New Zealand, and Australia. The company increasingly relied on raw materials imported from overseas—eggs came from Ireland, coconuts came from Barbados and the West Indies, and cocoa came from West Africa.

An important reason for Huntley & Palmers' success lay in advertising—whose aesthetics had changed dramatically with new technologies of print and color. In addition to newspaper advertisements, handbills and multi-colored posters placarded urban surfaces. Particularly pervasive were trade cards, usually 4 x 6 inches in size, such as the one presented here. Huntley & Palmers produced hundreds of these trade cards, with vibrantly colored images on the front and a description of their latest products on the back. They showed not only how the biscuits could be found all over the world, but how they were transported, such as by camel, hot air balloon, elephant, and ship. Retailers distributed the cards, which were so appealing that they became collectors' items.

The card shown here depicts a tiger hunt in India, to which only those who had power and authority—royalty and senior imperial officials—were given the honor of attending. Members of the hunting party sit atop the crates in which 10-pound tins of Huntley & Palmers' biscuits have been shipped, transported by a British-built railroad, and then carried on elephants. Retaining their civilized British custom, the hunters take their tea break after killing tigers, whose carcasses hang from the elephants. The Indians function not only as their guides, but also as servants to them, performing functions women would perform at home. The relationship the colonizer had to native men was one that effeminized the latter. The scene also suggests the successful and safe insertion of British civilization into an exotic, adventurous, and potentially dangerous context.

In addition to cards, images such as this were placed on the biscuit tins themselves and on calendars, on posters, and in catalogs. Advertisements that included colonial themes conveyed the message that biscuits could bring a "taste of home" to British who found themselves anywhere on the globe; their images made imperialism seem safe, adventurous, and appealing.

Advertising also targeted the colonies. One image from 1902, for example, depicts an Indian market located in a narrow shadowy street where two upper-class British ladies negotiate with a turbaned figure. Once again, the portrayal suggests potential danger lurking in the shadows; but a tin of Huntley & Palmers biscuits is displayed on the stall, with more stacked in the background, bringing a sense of safety and familiarity to an otherwise strange scene. This 1902 image was used for trade cards, as well as for pocket calendars that were placed inside the tins as a promotional gift.

Similar images on the tins made them into collectable objects that are of great value today. One of the most elaborate is an "Arabian Nights" tin from 1888 featuring the adventures of Ali Baba and his encounter with the

---

anti-Semitism
Centuries-old prejudice against and demonization of Jews that became virulent in the 1880s with the emergence of the ultranationalist and racist ideologies and political movements.

de Gobineau (1816–1882) published his *Essay on the Inequality of Human Races*, declaring that race "dominates all other problems and is the key to it." Biologists and early anthropologists made similar statements, which gave racism a "scientific" aura. Race came to be the principle explanation for social, cultural, and ethnic differences among human groups.

The pseudo-scientific concepts of race helped fuel **anti-Semitism**. For centuries, Jews had been the object of suspicion and bigotry. Originally, the basis of the prejudice was religious. As early as the Middle Ages, however, the argument emerged that "Jewish blood" was different. And with the popularization of racist thinking in the nineteenth century, Jews were

Trade Card Advertising Huntley & Palmers Biscuits (Robert Opie Collection)

forty thieves. Stories such as these—and the distribution of images depicting such figures in exotic dress—influenced European perceptions of the Muslim world.

Huntley & Palmers iconography turned ordinary objects—trade cards, tins, calendars—into vehicles that carried multiple messages about imperial domination into the homes of ordinary people in Europe and around the globe. The images showed that Huntley & Palmers biscuits could accompany civilized British men (and occasionally women) into sites of potential danger. The biscuit represented all that was civilized about the British—from its mass production and distribution, to its ability to preserve the habit of tea time—and it offered symbolic proof of British capacity to tame nature and establish order over the "uncivilized." For consumers at home and abroad, Huntley & Palmers represented the success of British imperial dominance.

Huntley & Palmers became so associated with the export business that in 1953 a cartoon depicted their tins of biscuits arriving by spaceship to curious aliens on the planet Mars. So dependent was the company for its success on the British Empire, post-World War II decolonization was one of the factors that caused its closure in 1972.

QUESTIONS

1. What role did the British Empire play in the success of companies such as Huntley & Palmers? What role, in turn, did such a company play in the British experience of empire?

2. How did advertising contribute to the shaping of national, ethnic, and gender identities, and to the way Europeans imagined Empire?

*Most of the historical information on Huntley & Palmers comes from "The Huntley & Palmers Collection" on the Reading Museum website, at http://www.huntleyandpalmers.org.uk.

commonly viewed as a separate, inferior race, unworthy of the same rights as the majority of the population.

Historically, Christians had relegated Jews to marginal positions. In the Middle Ages, when land was the basis of wealth and prestige, Jews were prohibited from owning land, and thus confined to urban trades, among which was money-lending. They incurred high risks by lending money: They often were not paid back and faced unsympathetic courts when they tried to collect their debts. To counteract these risks, Jewish moneylenders charged high interest rates that earned them their unpopular reputation as usurers.

The emancipation of the Jews, which began in France with the Revolution and spread to Germany and Austria by the 1860s, provided them with unprecedented opportunities. Some members of society found it hard to adjust to the prominence that some Jews gained. Because their increased social standing and success were concurrent with the wrenching social transformations brought by industrialization and urbanization, anti-Semites pointed to the Jews as perpetrators of these unsettling changes. They became the targets for resentment toward the rich, even though most Jews were of modest means.

Anti-Semitic political movements emerged in the 1880s. Depicting Jews as dangerous and wicked, they called for their exclusion from the political arena and from certain professions. In some cases, proponents suggested that Jews be expelled from the state. In Berlin, the emperor's chaplain, Adolf Stöcker (SHTOE-kur) (1835–1909), founded an anti-Semitic party, hoping to make political inroads among the working-class supporters of socialism. In France, Edouard Drumont (1844–1917) published one of the bestsellers of the second half of the nineteenth century, *Jewish France*, in which he blamed all the nation's misfortunes on the Jews. Anti-Semitism in eastern Europe was more deadly. In Russia, organized *pogroms*, or mass attacks, killed two thousand Jews in the 1880s and one thousand in 1905, frightening two million into exile, mostly to the United States.

In the face of growing hostility, some Jews speculated that they would be safe only in their own nation. The Austrian Jewish journalist Theodore Herzl (HER-tsl) (1860–1904), outraged by the Dreyfus affair in France, in which a Jewish officer was imprisoned on trumped-up charges of treason (see pages 684–685), founded the Zionist movement. He advocated establishing a Jewish state in the Jews' ancient homeland of Palestine. At first, the Zionist movement won a following only in eastern Europe, where the Jews were particularly ill-treated—but by 1948, **Zionism** culminated in the creation of the state of Israel.

Irrationality and Uncertainty

In contrast to the confidence in reason and science that had prevailed at midcentury, a sense of irrationality and uncertainty characterized the era starting in the 1880s. The positivism of the earlier era had emphasized the surface reality of "progress" but had ignored the emotional and intuitive aspects of life. By the 1890s, a neo-romantic mood, emphasizing emotion and feeling, stirred major intellectual movements.

PHILOSOPHY

The work of the German philosopher Friedrich Nietzsche (FREED-reesh NEET-sheh) (1844–1900) vividly expressed the tension between reason and emotion. He proclaimed that rationality had led humankind into a meaningless abyss. Reason would not resolve human problems, nor would any preconceived ideas. "God is dead," Nietzsche announced. With no God, humankind was free of all outside constraints, free to overthrow all conventions. Nietzsche admonished his readers to challenge existing institutions and accepted truths, and to create new ones.

The French philosopher Henri Bergson (BERK-sohn) (1859–1940) argued that science—and indeed life—must be interpreted not rationally, but intuitively. "Science," Bergson declared, "can teach us nothing of the truth; it can only serve as a rule of action." Only a reliance on human feeling could provide access to the meaningful truths, such as those of religion, literature, and art.

SOCIAL SCIENCES

Various disciplines of knowledge subscribed to the notion that human beings are often irrational, governed by deep-seated instinctive forces. The Austro-Hungarian **Sigmund Freud** (1856–1939) believed that unconscious feelings and emotions motivated human behavior. He founded psychoanalysis, a method of treating psychic disorders by exploring the unconscious. While earlier physicians had described ailments as physical in origin, Freud saw their roots as psychological, the result of unresolved inner conflicts. He stressed that irrational forces played a significant role in human behavior.

The social theorist Gaetano Mosca (1858–1941) pessimistically argued that the desire to dominate is a basic part of human nature. His book, *Elements of Political Science* (1891), posited that in all societies—even democratic ones—an elite minority rules over the majority. Beneath slogans touting the public good lies selfish ambition, and the thirst for power is never slaked—a poor prognosis for socialist ideals.

ARTS

In the arts, the idea of being **avant-garde**—French for "forefront"—took hold among creative people. Breaking the taboos of society and the conventions of one's craft were, for them, signs of artistic creativity.

Zionism Nationalist Jewish movement beginning in the late nineteenth century. In face of anti-Semitism, Zionism advocated establishing a Jewish state in the Jews' ancient homeland of Palestine.

Sigmund Freud Austrian founder of psychoanalysis, a method of treating psychic disorders by exploring the unconscious, based on the belief that people are motivated by unconscious feelings and drives.

avant-garde French for "forefront," the term refers to early-twentieth-century artists who inspired unconventional techniques, considered themselves precursors of new styles, and called for the rejection of existing forms of expression.

Munch: *The Scream* Painted in 1893, this work reflects the fear and horror that some intellectuals experienced at the end of the nineteenth century. (© 2008 The Munch Museum/The Munch-Ellingsen Group/Artist's Rights Society (ARS), NY. Erich Lessing/Art Resource, NY)

In protest against the mass culture of their day, artists focused on images that were unique. Unlike earlier art, which had a clear message, the art of this era did not. Many artists no longer believed their role was to portray or spread ideals. Rather, they tended to be introspective and even self-absorbed. The public at large found it difficult to decipher the meaning of the new art, but a number of patrons supported the avant-garde artists' talent and insight.

Unlike the realists who preceded them, artists in the 1890s surrendered to neo-romanticism, trying to investigate and express inner forces. As the French painter Paul Gauguin (1848–1903) noted, the purpose of painting is to communicate not how things look, but the emotions they convey. The Russian Wassily Kandinsky (vass-IH-lee kan-DIN-skee) (1866–1944) asked viewers of his art to "look at the picture as a graphic representation of a mood and not as a representation of objects." Artists appeared to be examining the hidden anxieties of society. The Norwegian painter Edvard Munch (MOONGK) (1863–1944) emphasized scenes of violence, fear, and sheer horror.

RELIGION AND SCIENCE

The era of uncertainty undermined both religious belief and confidence in science. Although large numbers of people still held traditional religious beliefs, indifference to organized religion spread. In urban areas of western Europe, church attendance declined, while various forms and practices of mysticism—such as séances—became more widespread. Some people were attracted to Eastern religions, such as Buddhism and Hinduism, perhaps reflecting a loss of faith in Western culture itself.

Scientists of this period questioned long-held commonsense beliefs. During the last week of the century, the German physicist Max Planck (1858–1947) suggested that light and other kinds of electromagnetic radiation, such as radio waves, which had always been considered continuous trains of waves, actually consist of individual packages of well-defined energy, which he called "quanta." In 1905, Albert Einstein (1879–1955) proposed the theory of relativity, which required a drastic change in fundamental ideas about space and time. To the three dimensions of space—length, breadth, and width—was added a complicating fourth dimension, that of time. The new ideas were not easily grasped. The old concept of a fixed cause tied to a fixed effect became unhinged, because even though things happen predictably, they also happen randomly.

SECTION SUMMARY

- The liberal ideology of the early nineteenth century could not address economic and social practicalities by the century's end. Civil and political liberties, some concluded, could not apply to everyone.

- Two strands of socialism emerged by the end of the nineteenth century: one that advocated violent revolution, and another—revisionism—that argued change could come through gradual, democratic means. The latter became more dominant.

- A "new right" of the late nineteenth century embraced nationalism and rejected democracy and the notion of human equality. It also adopted racist and anti-Semitic ideologies.

- By the 1890s, a neo-romantic mood emphasized the validity of feeling and emotion, while irrationality and uncertainty permeated philosophy, the social sciences, the arts, religion, and science itself.

VULNERABLE DEMOCRACIES

What factors made parliamentary rule in Great Britain, France, and Italy dysfunctional?

By the end of the nineteenth century, most of Europe's political systems floundered in crisis. The major powers with democratic institutions—Great Britain, France, and Italy—confronted volatile public opinion and had difficulty winning a broad consensus for their policies. They struggled with new challenges emerging from an expanded electorate; the latter expressed frustration over government failures to meet its competing and contradictory demands. Turning away from the democratic precept of resolving differences through the ballot and legislation, many people—both in government and out—were willing to resort to extraparliamentary means, including violence, to see their interests prevail.

Great Britain

In Great Britain, the Reform Bill of 1884 extended the vote to two of every three adult men, doubling suffrage to five million. To win votes from this enlarged electorate, some politicians made demagogic promises, which—to the exasperation of their constituents—they often later broke. Representing a population with more diverse interests and values, members of Parliament found compromise more difficult than in the past when they represented a much narrower set of interests.

The problem of Ireland persisted. The Irish seethed under British rule. In 1886, Prime Minister William Gladstone (GLAD-sten) proposed autonomy, or "home rule," for Ireland. But many opposed this plan. If Ireland, a predominantly Catholic country, ruled itself, the local Protestant majority in Ulster (the northeast part of the island) would be overwhelmed by Catholic control. In addition, the Conservative Party in England opposed changing the existing relationship with Ireland. With considerable political maneuvering, the Liberals finally pushed a home-rule bill through the House of Commons in 1911, but it was obstructed in the House of Lords and was not slated to go into effect until September 1914.

Passage of the home-rule bill did not resolve the Irish problem. Many segments of British society showed they were willing to resort to extralegal and even violent means. Fearing Catholic domination, Protestants in northern Ireland armed themselves in their determination to resist home rule. Catholic groups also took up arms, insisting on the unity of the island. The Conservative Party in Britain called on Ulster Protestants to revolt, and British officers said they would not take military action against them. The behavior of the Conservatives and the army indicated a breakdown of order and authority—a disregard for tradition by two of its major bulwarks. Only the outbreak of world war in 1914 delayed a showdown over Ireland, and then by only a few years.

Irish home rule was not the only issue that eroded civility in the British Parliament. Liberals, who dominated the House of Commons from 1906, committed themselves to an impressive array of social reforms, such as old-age pensions. To finance such measures, the feisty chancellor of the exchequer, David Lloyd George (1863–1945), proposed raising income taxes and death duties and levying a tax on landed wealth. A bill with these measures easily passed the House of Commons in 1909 but was stymied in the upper chamber. Motivated by economic self-interest and personal spite against the Liberals, a majority in the House of Lords voted against the bill. Lloyd George expressed his outrage that a handful of magnates in the upper chamber—sitting there not by election, but by hereditary right—could thwart the will of the people. A major constitutional crisis ensued.

In 1911, the government sponsored a bill to limit the legislative power in the House of Lords to a suspensive veto—meaning that any bill defeated there would simply be suspended for a predetermined period, such as two years. The House of Lords initially refused to pass the bill, but finally conceded when the king threatened to appoint four hundred new lords.

During the debate over the bill, Conservatives resorted to brawling and refused to let the prime minister speak. It was the first time in British parliamentary history that such a breach of conduct had occurred. The British Parliament, considered the model for supporters of free institutions, had shown itself unable to resolve issues in a civil manner.

Violence also broke out in another unexpected place: the women's suffrage movement. Most liberal males, when speaking of the need to extend human liberty, had excluded women because they thought public affairs an inappropriate arena for them. In 1903, Emmeline Pankhurst

A Suffragist Attempts to Chain Herself to the Gates of Buckingham Palace, London, 1914 In their effort to win the vote, women resorted to civil disobedience, and police often violently intervened. (Popperfoto/Classicstock.com/Getty Images)

(1858–1928) and her two daughters founded the Women's Social and Political Union, whose goal was immediate suffrage.

Angered and frustrated by their lack of progress, the **suffragists** (often referred to by contemporaries as "suffragettes"), led by the Pankhursts, began a more militant program of protest in 1906. They disrupted the proceedings in Parliament, broke windows at the prime minister's residence, slashed canvases at the National Gallery, burned down empty houses, dropped acid into mailboxes, and threw bombs. They even threatened the lives of the prime minister and the king. In 1913, Emily Wilding Davidson sacrificed her life to the cause of female suffrage when, before thousands of spectators at the Derby, she threw herself in front of the king's horse. These acts of violence and tragedy drew condemnation, but they also brought worldwide attention to the cause.

But these acts also incurred severe punishment. Imprisoned suffragists often engaged in hunger strikes, which provoked the authorities to force-feed them—an extremely painful and humiliating procedure that amounts to torture. Female protesters also incurred physical attacks in public. (See the feature, "The Written Record: Pankhurst Testifies on Women's Rights.") That women would resort to violence, and that men inside and outside government would retaliate in kind, demonstrated how widespread the cult of force had become.

suffragists Activists who, beginning in the late nineteenth century, organized to win the vote for women and adopted increasingly violent tactics. Also called "suffragettes."

France

The Third Republic, founded in 1870 after France's humiliating military defeat by Prussia, also struggled with an ongoing series of crises. Enemies of the Republic, on both the political left and right, continually called for the abolition of democracy.

Pankhurst Testifies on Women's Rights

In 1908, the suffragists, led by Emmeline Pankhurst, issued a handbill calling on the people of London to "rush" Parliament and win the vote for women. The legal authorities interpreted their action as a violation of the peace, and several suffragists, including Pankhurst, were put on trial. They put up a spirited defense, in which Pankhurst movingly explained her motives for leading the suffragist cause.

I want you to realise how we women feel; because we are women, because we are not men, we need some legitimate influence to bear upon our law-makers. Now, we have tried every way. We have presented larger petitions than were ever presented for any other reform, we have succeeded in holding greater public meetings than men have ever had for any reform, in spite of the difficulty which women have in throwing off their natural diffidence, that desire to escape publicity which we have inherited from generations of our fore-mothers; we have broken through that. We have faced hostile mobs at street corners, because we were told that we could not have that representation for our taxes which men have won unless we converted the whole of the country to our side. Because we have done this, we have been misrepresented, we have been ridiculed, we have had contempt poured upon us. The ignorant mob at the street corner has been incited to offer us violence, which we have faced unarmed and unprotected by the safeguards which Cabinet Ministers have. We know that we need the protection of the vote even more than men have needed it....

We believe that if we get the vote it will mean better conditions for our unfortunate sisters. We know what the condition of the woman worker is...and we have been driven to the conclusion that only through legislation can any improvement be effected, and that that legislation can never be effected until we have the same power as men have to bring pressure to bear upon our representatives and upon Governments to give us the necessary legislation....

I should never be here if I had the same kind of power that the very meanest and commonest of men have—the same power that the wife-beater has, the same power that the drunkard has. I should never be here if I had that power, and I speak for all the women who have come before you and other magistrates....

If you had power to send us to prison, not for six months, but for six years, for sixteen years, or for the whole of our lives, the Government must not think that they can stop this agitation. It will go on....

We are here not because we are law-breakers; we are here in our efforts to become lawmakers.

QUESTIONS

1. What is the logic behind Pankhurst's comment that women need the "protection of the vote" even more than men? What is her main argument here for why women should get the vote?

2. Do you think women were justified in breaking laws in order to obtain their goal? Why or why not? How did their behavior compare with that of men, both within and outside of the British Parliament?

Source: F. W. Pethick Lawrence, ed., *The Trial of the Suffragette Leaders* (London: The Women's Press, 1909), pp. 21–24.

This situation resulted in part from the French government's lack of strong leadership. The need to build coalitions among the several parties in the parliament rewarded those politicians who had moderate, but often mediocre, programs. Supporters of the republic actually found lackluster leadership appealing. They continued to fear that a strong leader might—as Louis Napoleon had in 1851—exploit his support to make himself dictator.

The regime lurched from one crisis to another. The most notorious was the Dreyfus affair. In October 1894, Captain Alfred Dreyfus (1859–1935) of the French army was arrested and charged with passing military secrets to the German embassy. Dreyfus (DRY-fooss) seems to have attracted suspicion because he was the only Jewish officer on the general staff. The evidence was flimsy—a handwritten letter that some thought Dreyfus had penned, although other experts testified that the handwriting was not his.

This letter, and materials that later turned out to be forged, led the French army to court-martial Dreyfus and sentence him to life imprisonment on Devil's Island off the coast of South America. By March 1896, the general staff had evidence that another officer, Major Esterhazy, was actually the spy. But to reopen the case would be to admit the army had made an error, and the general staff refused to do this.

By late 1897, when the apparent miscarriage of justice became widely known, French society split over "the affair." The political left argued for reopening the case. The army and its supporters—right-wing politicians, royalists, and zealous Catholics—argued that the decision should stand. They believed the army, as a bulwark against internal and foreign threats, should be above the law, and the fate of a single man—guilty or innocent—was immaterial. From the outset, Dreyfus was the target of virulent anti-Semitism.

The affair unleashed a swirl of controversy and rioting, which led the government to order a retrial in 1899. But the court again found Dreyfus guilty—this time with "extenuating circumstances" and the recommendation that he be pardoned. Finally, in 1906, Dreyfus was fully exonerated.

The strong encouragement many Catholics gave to those who supported the original verdict confirmed the republicans' belief that the church was a menace to the regime. The politicians who backed Dreyfus—anticlericals—were voted into the parliament. In 1905, they passed a law separating church and state, thus ending the privileged position the Catholic Church had enjoyed. Violent language and physical confrontations on both sides accompanied this division. Catholics trying to prevent state officials from entering churches to take required inventories sometimes resorted to force, using weapons or, in one case, a bear chained to the church. Armed soldiers broke down church doors and dragged priests away.

Labor problems also triggered repeated confrontations with the government. Increased labor militancy produced long, drawn-out strikes, which in 1904 alone led to the loss of four million workdays. Rural workers agitated as well, particularly in the Midi, the south of France. This region suffered from a crisis in the wine industry caused by a disease that attacked the vines, competition from cheap foreign wines, and fraud. The region witnessed increased rural proletarianization as landholdings became concentrated in fewer hands. Rural militancy led to a revolt in 1907. Troops were sent in; they killed dozens and won for the Radical regime the title "government of assassins."

Italy

Italy, the third major power in Europe to adopt parliamentary government, also had grave problems. Although unification took place in 1860, genuine national unity proved elusive. As in the past, the south especially challenged the central government. Assertive regionalism, crime, and poverty made this area resistant to most government programs.

The parliamentary system established in 1860 was far from democratic. Property qualifications limited suffrage to less than 3 percent of the population. Between 1870 and 1890, the Italian government introduced some important reforms, but the relatively low standard of living failed to improve. In the fifty years after unification, the population increased from 25 million to 35 million, and the country had limited resources to deal with such growth. In the south, a few wealthy landowners held large private estates, while the majority of the peasants were landless and forced to work for minimum wages. In the north, industrialization had started, but the region was not rich in coal or iron. To be competitive, industry paid very low wages, and the workers lived in abject misery.

Conditions on the land and in the factories led to widespread protests. In 1893, a Sicilian labor movement won the adherence of 300,000 members, who seized land and attacked government offices. The government responded with massive force and declared martial law. As unrest spread throughout the peninsula in 1896, the government placed half of the provinces under military rule. A cycle of violence and repression gripped the nation. In this turbulent atmosphere, an anarchist killed King Umberto I on July 29, 1900.

After the turn of the century, a new prime minister, Giovanni Giolitti (jo-VAH-nee jo-LEE-tee) (1842–1928), tried to end the upheaval. He used government force more sparingly and showed a spirit of cooperation toward the workers. Seeking to divert

SÉANCE ORAGEUSE A LA CHAMBRE ITALIENNE

Riots in Italian Parliament Party strife and conflicts between individuals in the Italian parliament were so severe that often they degenerated into fisticuffs. This illustration catches a particularly violent moment of a parliamentary debate. (Roger-Viollet/The Image Works)

SECTION SUMMARY

- Democratic governments in western Europe experienced crises that led to forceful repression. The British resorted to violence or uncivil behavior over the issues of Irish home rule, a constitutional crisis over social reform, and women's suffrage.

- Democracy in the French republic was threatened by the nation-splitting Dreyfus affair, the role of the Catholic Church, and labor militancy.

- Regionalism, poverty, social strife, violence, and unrepresentative government challenged Italy's efforts at parliamentary democracy.

attention from domestic ills and appeal to nationalist fervor, Giolitti launched an attack on Libya in 1911, wresting it from the ailing Ottoman Empire. This arid territory was bereft of economic promise, but imperialists championed the conquest as a test of national virility and the foundation of national greatness.

The government also resorted to force for its domestic problems when, in June 1914, a national strike led to rioting. Workers seized power in several municipalities, and in northern Italy, they proclaimed an independent republic. It took 100,000 government troops ten days to restore order. The workers' brazen defiance led some nationalist right-wing extremists to form groups of "volunteers for the defense of order," anticipating the vigilante thugs who were to make up the early bands of Italian fascism.

AUTOCRACIES IN CRISIS

What various crises weakened autocratic rule in Germany, Russia, and the Ottoman Empire?

Four major autocracies dominated central and eastern Europe: Germany, Austria-Hungary, the Ottoman Empire, and Russia. If the democracies encountered difficulties in these years, the autocracies faced even more vehement opposition. As the demands for more democracy grew louder, protesters resorted to violence and governments in turn used force to maintain themselves.

The severity of autocratic rule varied from state to state, ranging from the absolutism of the Ottoman Empire to the semiparliamentary regime of Germany; but in all of the states, the ruler had the final political say. Resistance to the autocracies included broad popular challenges to the German imperial system, discontent among ethnic minorities in the nearly ungovernable empire of Austria-Hungary, and revolution and war in the Russian and Ottoman Empires.

Germany

Although Germany had a parliament, the government was answerable to the kaiser, not the people's electoral representatives. To rule effectively, Chancellor Otto von Bismarck quelled opposition through manipulation and intrigue. He used an attempt to assassinate the emperor as the excuse to ban the Socialist Party in 1879. He also persecuted Catholics and their institutions in order to strengthen Protestant Prussia. These measures, however, did not prevent the growth of the Socialist and Catholic Center Parties.

Bismarck's tenure in office depended on the goodwill of the emperor, Wilhelm I, who died in 1888. He was succeeded by his son, Friedrich, who ruled only a few months, and then by his grandson, Wilhelm II (r. 1888–1918). The young Kaiser Wilhelm was ill fit to govern. He could not bear any limitation to his power, announcing, "There is only one ruler in the Reich and I am he. I tolerate no other." Intimidated by Bismarck and dismayed by his domestic and foreign policies, the kaiser dismissed him.

Wilhelm II was determined to make Germany a world power whose foreign policy would have a global impact. He

Wilhelm II The German emperor liked to be viewed in a heroic and military posture. A restless individual, Wilhelm changed uniforms eight times daily and traveled ceaselessly among his seventy-five castles and palaces. (Landesarchiv Berlin)

wanted Germany to have colonies, a navy, and major influence among the Great Powers. This policy, **Weltpolitik**—"world politics"—greatly troubled Germany's neighbors. The kaiser's bombastic threats and the prospect of a new, assertive power in central Europe made them wary. Within Germany, however, Weltpolitik won support.

Although the nationalist appeals impressed many Germans, others challenged the emperor's autocratic style and increasingly viewed his behavior as irresponsible. In the elections of 1912, one-third of all Germans voted for Socialist Party candidates. Thus, the largest single party in the Reichstag challenged both the capitalist system and autocracy. Labor militancy also reached new heights. In 1912, one million workers—a record number—went on strike. Increasingly, Germans pressed for a government accountable to the people's elected representatives.

Weltpolitik Meaning "world politics," the term describes the policy pursued, with nationalistic appeals and bombastic threats, by Kaiser Wilhelm II to make Germany a world power.

Austria-Hungary

A series of crises also wracked the neighboring Austro-Hungarian Empire. In an age of intense nationalism, a multinational empire was an anomaly, as the emperor Franz Joseph (r. 1848–1916) himself acknowledged. Despite the Compromise of 1867 (see page 626) that regulated the relationship between Austria and Hungary, conflict grew, particularly over control of their joint army. Hungary increasingly saw its interests as separate from Austria's and probably would have broken loose from the dual monarchy had world war not occurred.

In the Hungarian half of the empire, the Magyar rule faced growing challenges. Other nationalities opposed Magyarization—the imposition of the Magyar language and institutions—and insisted on the right to use their own languages in their schools and administrations. The Hungarian government censored and imprisoned nationalist leaders. The Austrian half of the empire was equally strife-ridden.

These conflicts had no easy solutions. Hoping to dilute the influence of nationalist middle-class intellectuals, the Habsburg government introduced universal male suffrage in 1907. The result backfired. The extended suffrage produced a parliament that included thirty ethnically based political parties, making a workable majority nearly impossible to achieve.

The virulence of debate based on nationality and class divisions grew to unprecedented extremes. Within the parliament, deputies threw inkwells at each other, rang sleigh bells, and sounded bugles. Parliament ceased to be relevant. By 1914, the emperor had dissolved it and several regional assemblies, and ruled Austria by decree. Emperor Franz Joseph feared that the empire would not survive him.

Ottoman Empire

The Ottoman Empire suffered the most advanced case of dissolution prior to 1914, undermined by both secessionist movements within its borders and aggression from other European powers. Sultan Abdul Hamid II (r. 1876–1909) ruled the country as a despot and authorized mass carnage against those who contested his rule, earning him the title "the Great Assassin."

Young, Western-educated Turks—the so-called Young Turks—disgusted at one-man rule and the continuing loss of territory and influence, overthrew Abdul Hamid in July 1908. They set up a government responsible to an elected parliament. The Young Turks hoped to stem the loss of territory by establishing firmer central control, but their efforts had the opposite effect. The various nationalities of the empire resented the imposition of Turkish education and administration. Renewed agitation broke out in Macedonia, in Albania, and among the Armenians. The government carried out severely repressive measures to end the unrest, massacring thousands of Armenians.

To foreign powers, the moment seemed propitious to plunder the weakened empire. In 1911, Italy occupied Libya, an Ottoman province. Greece, Bulgaria, and Serbia formed the Balkan League and waged a successful war against the empire in 1912. Albania became independent, and Macedonia was partitioned among members of the League. This war stripped the empire of most of its European possessions (see **Map 24.3**).

Russia

The Great Reforms of the 1860s, intended to resolve Russia's problems, instead unleashed new forces because they coincided with major social changes. Tsarist rule became even more difficult.

MAP 24.3—The Ottoman Empire

The Ottoman Empire once included much of southeastern Europe, western Asia, and North Africa. Secessionist movements and European aggression caused it to lose most of its European, Caucasus, and North African territories. By 1914, it was restricted largely to parts of western Asia.

The needs of a modernizing country led to an increase in the number of universities. The newly educated Russian youths almost instantly began an ardent, sustained critique of autocracy. In the absence of a sizable middle class upholding liberal, advanced ideas, university students and graduates, who came to be known as the *intelligentsia*, saw it as their mission to transform Russia.

In the 1870s, university youths by the thousands organized a populist movement, hoping to bring change to the countryside. These young idealists, both men and women, intended to educate the peasants and make them more politically aware. But instead, they encountered peasant suspicion and government repression. Large numbers of populists were arrested and put on trial. Disaffected by such results, radicals formed the People's Will, which sought to hasten revolution by murdering public officials.

In response, the regime intensified repression. But it also sought to broaden its public support. In 1881, Tsar Alexander II decided to create an advisory committee that some thought would eventually lead to a parliamentary form of government. Just before the tsar signed the decree establishing this committee, the People's Will assassinated him. The son who succeeded him, Tsar Alexander III (r. 1881–1894), blamed the assassination on his father's leniency, and so decided to make the government even more autocratic, weakening his father's reforms and reducing local self-rule.

When Alexander's son, Nicholas II (r. 1894–1917), succeeded to the throne in 1894, he too was determined to maintain autocratic rule. However, he lacked the methodical, consistent temperament such a pledge required, as well as a coherent policy for his troubled country.

Serious problems had accumulated that threatened the stability of the regime. Conditions worsened in the countryside as explosive population growth increased pressure on the land.

Despite the abolition of serfdom, the peasants were not free to move around. Agriculture remained inefficient, far inferior to that of western Europe. Between 1861 and 1914, the peasant population grew by 50 percent, but it acquired only 10 percent more land. In 1891, famine broke out in twenty provinces, killing a quarter of a million people.

Although Russia remained largely agrarian, there were pockets of industrial growth. Some factories and mining concerns had as many as six thousand employees. When workers grew incensed at their condition and insistent on winning the same rights and protection as workers in western Europe, they engaged in massive strikes that crippled industry.

Political dissatisfaction with the autocracy grew among all social classes—the slowly expanding middle classes and aristocrats demanded the right to political participation. Various revolutionary groups committed to socialism flourished. Socialist Revolutionaries, heirs to the People's Will, emerged as a political force in the 1890s. They believed that the peasants would bring socialism to Russia.

In 1898, the Russian Social Democratic Party was founded. A Marxist party, it promoted the industrial working class as the harbinger of socialism. In 1903, that party split into the Menshevik and Bolshevik factions. The Mensheviks insisted that Russia had to go through the stages of history Marx had outlined—to witness the full development of capitalism and its subsequent collapse before the socialists could come to power. The **Bolsheviks**, a minority group, were led by Vladimir Ilich Lenin (1870–1924), a zealous revolutionary and Marxist. Rather than wait for historical forces to undermine capitalism, he insisted that a revolutionary cadre could seize power on behalf of the working class. Lenin favored a small, disciplined, conspiratorial party, like the People's Will, while the Mensheviks favored a more open, democratic party.

In February 1904, war broke out between Russia and Japan in a dispute over control of northern Korea. In the face of Russian military ineptitude, popular opposition to tsarism grew. An economic slowdown heightened social tensions.

Beginning in January 1905, a series of demonstrations, strikes, and other acts of collective violence erupted. Together they were dubbed "the revolution of 1905." On a Sunday of that month, 400,000 workers gathered in front of the tsar's St. Petersburg palace. Rather than hear their demands, officials ordered soldiers to fire on them, resulting in 150 deaths and hundreds more wounded. "Bloody Sunday" inflamed the populace, who now viewed the tsar as a murderer of his people. Unrest spread to most of the country. The regime's prestige deteriorated further with reports of increasing losses in the war with Japan. By September 1905, Russia had to sue for peace and admit defeat. Challenged in the capital, where independent workers' councils called *soviets*

Bolsheviks Faction of the Russian Socialist Democratic Party led by Marxist Vladimir Ilich Lenin (1870–1924), who insisted that an exclusive revolutionary cadre could seize power on behalf of the working class.

Workers' Demonstration in Moscow, 1905 In 1905, workers as well as peasants protested against the Russian autocracy. To bring the revolution under control, Nicholas II was obliged to grant several concessions.
(Novosti/Sovfoto)

SECTION SUMMARY

- In Germany after 1890, Wilhelm II's aggressive foreign policy menaced other European powers, while his autocratic governing style created widespread opposition to his rule.

- Parliamentary rule in Austria-Hungary failed because of ongoing conflicts between the two monarchies, as well as between the multiple nationalities within each.

- The Ottoman Empire continued to suffer from both secessionist movements within its borders and aggression from other European powers; by 1912, the empire had lost most of its European possessions.

- In Russia, the emergence of revolutionary socialist groups, deteriorating conditions of peasants, worker discontent, and defeat in war with Japan fueled opposition to tsarist rule. The revolution of 1905 and subsequent reforms failed to stem the regime's problems.

had sprung up, the government also lost control over the countryside, the site of widespread peasant uprisings.

Fearing for his regime, Nicholas hoped to disarm the opposition by meeting some of its demands. He granted major constitutional and civil liberties, including freedom of religion, speech, assembly, and association. The tsar also established an elective assembly, the Duma, with restricted male suffrage and limited political power. It quickly became an arena for criticizing autocracy. Nicholas responded by suspending the Duma and changing its electoral base and rules of operation. This blatant breach of his promise to establish constitutionalism and parliamentarianism even disillusioned many conservatives.

Although the government reduced the peasants' financial obligations, weakened the power of the commune, or *mir* (see page 630), and extended local self-rule to the peasants, these changes did little to alleviate rural poverty. Labor unrest also mounted. In 1912, 725,000 industrial workers went on strike; that number doubled in the first half of 1914. On the eve of the outbreak of the First World War, workers were building barricades.

THE COMING WAR

What responsibility did each of the Great Powers have for the outbreak of war in 1914?

Instability and upheaval characterized international relations in the years between 1880 and 1914. But the outbreak of war was by no means inevitable. Common sense dictated against it, and some intelligent people predicted that in the new modern era, war would become so destructive that it would be unthinkable. Finally, no European state wanted a war, although the Great Powers carried on policies that brought them to its brink.

Power Alignments

Triple Alliance Military alliance established in 1882 among Germany, Austria-Hungary, and Italy to counter the Franco-Russian Alliance (later the Triple Entente).

Germany enjoyed an unchallenged position in the international order of the 1870s and 1880s. It was united in an alliance with the two other eastern conservative states—Russia and Austria-Hungary—in the Three Emperors' League, formed in 1873 and renewed by treaty in 1884. It also formed part of the **Triple Alliance** with Austria and Italy. France stood alone, without allies. Britain, with little interest in continental affairs, appeared to be enjoying a "splendid isolation."

However, Germany's alliance system was not free from problems. Two of its allies, Austria-Hungary and Russia, were at loggerheads over control of the Balkans. How could Germany be the friend of both? Wary of apparent German preference for Austria, Bismarck signed the Reinsurance Treaty in 1887, assuring Russia that Germany would not honor its alliance with Austria if the latter attacked Russia. After Bismarck's resignation in 1890, Kaiser Wilhelm allowed the Reinsurance Treaty to lapse. Alarmed, the Russians turned to France and, in January 1894, signed the Franco-Russian Alliance, by which each side pledged to help the other should Germany attack either of them.

The Great Powers on the Continent were now divided into two alliances, the Triple Alliance and the Franco-Russian Alliance. Britain formally belonged to neither, but if it favored any side, it would be the German-led alliance because of colonial rivalries with France over Africa and with Russia over Asia.

In the 1890s, Germany lost British goodwill. Launching his Weltpolitik, Wilhelm II built up the German navy. An island nation dependent on international trade for its economic survival, Britain had developed a navy second to none—and it saw the German naval buildup as a threat to its security.

In the face of a mounting German menace, France and Britain decided to reconcile their differences. In 1904, they signed an understanding, or *entente*, resolving their rivalries in Egypt. In 1907, Great Britain and Russia regulated their competition for influence in Persia (present-day Iran) with the Anglo-Russian Entente. Europe was now loosely divided into a new configuration of two groups: the Triple Alliance of Germany, Austria-Hungary, and Italy, and the **Triple Entente** of Great Britain, France, and Russia.

Triple Entente Military alliance between Great Britain, France, and Russia, completed in 1907, countering the Triple Alliance.

The Momentum Toward War

Only through a series of crises did these alignments solidify to the point where their members were willing to go to war to save them. In 1905, and again in 1911, France and Germany nearly went to war over their respective interests in Morocco; both instances left Germany with the appearance of unreasonable aggressiveness. Meanwhile, the unstable situation in the Balkans sharpened tensions between Austria and Russia.

The heightened international tensions forced the European states to increase their arms expenditures, which in turn increased their sense of insecurity. In 1906, Britain launched a new class of ships—the *Dreadnought*. Powered by steam turbines, it was the fastest ship afloat; heavily armored, it could not be sunk easily, and its 12-inch guns made it a menace on the seas. The British had thought the Germans incapable of building equivalent ships. But they did, wiping out British supremacy. Britain felt less secure than at any time since the Napoleonic Wars, and it continued an expensive and feverish naval race with Germany.

Meanwhile, the growing war-making capacity of Russia created great anxieties within Germany. The Japanese defeat of the tsarist empire in 1905 had revealed the Russian military to be inferior—a lumbering giant, slow to mobilize and maneuver. As a result, Germany had not been particularly afraid of its eastern neighbor. But stung by its humiliation in 1905, Russia quickly rebuilt its army and planned an extensive rail network in the west, which would, in the event of war, be used for military purposes. Germany now felt encircled by a hostile Russia to the east and an equally unfriendly France to the west, and by 1912, some military officers and government officials began thinking about a preventive war. If war was inevitable, many Germans argued, it should occur before Russia became even stronger.

Many political leaders viewed the escalating arms race as a form of madness. Between 1904 and 1913, French and Russian arms expenditures increased by 80 percent, those of Germany by 120 percent, those of Austria-Hungary by 50 percent, and those of Italy by 100 percent. British foreign secretary Sir Edward Grey (1862–1933) warned that if the arms race continued, "it will submerge civilization."

But most Europeans did not fear warfare. The Western powers had not experienced a major conflict since the Crimean War (1854–1856). Most policymakers believed that the next war would be short. The wars that had so dramatically changed the borders of European states in the second half of the nineteenth century, notably the Austro-Prussian War of 1866 and the Franco-Prussian War of 1870, had been decided within a few weeks. Because few imagined that the next war would be either long or brutal, Europe's leaders did not make a major effort to prevent it.

The territorial rivalry between Austria and Russia triggered international disaster. For decades enmity had been growing between the two empires over control of the Balkans (see **MAP 24.4**). In 1903, following a bloody military coup that killed the king and queen of Serbia, a pro-Russian party took control of the Serbian government. In 1908, Austria shocked Russia by annexing the province of Bosnia (which it had

🌐 **MAP 24.4—The Balkans in 1914**

By 1914, the Ottoman Empire was much diminished, containing virtually no European territory. Political boundaries did not follow nationality lines. Serbia was committed to unite all Serbs at the expense of the Austro-Hungarian Empire.

The Shot Heard Round the World   The young Serb nationalist Gavril Princip shoots Franz Ferdinand, the heir to the Austro-Hungarian throne, and his consort. The assassination led to the outbreak of World War I. (Three Lions/Hulton Archive/Getty Images)

administered since the Congress of Berlin in 1878; see page 728). Austria's action thwarted Serbia's ambition of annexing Bosnia, which had many Serb inhabitants. Still weakened from the 1905 war with Japan, Russia had to accept diplomatic defeat and abandoned its ally, Serbia. But Russia was determined not to cave in again.

Undeterred, Serbia spread anti-Austrian propaganda and sought to unify under its banner Slavs living in the Balkans—including those under Austrian rule. As a result, many Austrian officials were convinced that the survival of the Austro-Hungarian Empire required the destruction of Serbia. On June 28, 1914, the heir to the Habsburg throne, Archduke Franz Ferdinand, visited Sarajevo in Austrian-ruled Bosnia. A young Bosnian-Serb nationalist hostile to Austrian rule, who had been trained and armed by a Serb terrorist group called the Black Hand, assassinated the archduke and his wife.

The assassination of the heir to the throne provided Austria with an ideal pretext for military action. The German kaiser, fearing that failure to support Vienna would lead to Austrian collapse and a Germany bereft of any allies, urged Austria to attack Serbia. On July 23, Austria issued an ultimatum to Serbia, deliberately worded in such a way as to be unacceptable. When Serbia refused the ultimatum, Austria declared war on July 28.

Perceived self-interest motivated each state's behavior in the ensuing crisis. Russia's status as a Great Power required that it not allow its client state, Serbia, to be humiliated, much less obliterated. In the past, the French government had acted as a brake on Russian ambitions in the Balkans. On the eve of the war in 1914, France counseled restraint, but it did not withhold its promise of aid to Russia, its only ally on the Continent. Since 1911, France had increasingly feared isolation in the face of what it perceived as growing German aggression. To remain a Great Power, France needed to preserve its friendship with Russia and help that country maintain its own Great Power status.

Germany could not allow Austria, its only ally, to be destroyed. Its leaders may also have seen the crisis as a propitious moment to begin a war that they believed was going to occur anyway. The Germans no doubt thought it expedient to strike before the Entente powers, especially Russia, became stronger. After declaring war on Russia, Germany then invaded France through Belgium to prevent it from coming to Russia's aid. The British, concerned for their ally France and outraged by the violation of Belgian neutrality (to which all the Great Powers had been signatories since 1839), on August 4, declared war on Germany. Europe was at war. Eventually, so would be much of the world.

SECTION SUMMARY

- By 1907, Europe was loosely divided into the Triple Alliance of Germany, Austria-Hungary, and Italy and the Triple Entente of Great Britain, France, and Russia.

- Mounting crises solidified the alliances: France and Germany came into conflict over Morocco; all the countries, but especially Britain and Germany, engaged in an arms race; rivalry over the Balkans between Russia and Austria intensified when the latter annexed Bosnia.

- Anti-Austrian sentiments in Serbia led to the assassination of the Austrian archduke Franz Ferdinand, provoking Austria to declare war on Serbia; the system of alliances then brought all of the Great Powers into war.

CHAPTER SUMMARY

In the decades prior to 1914, Europe appeared to dominate the globe. With the intention of acquiring new sources of wealth, trade, and the trappings of international power and prestige, Europeans forcibly conquered most of Africa and much of Asia. They also conceived of their mission as one that brought civilization to inferior peoples. They introduced both technology and Western education to the colonized subjects. The scramble to build empires reflected growing competition among the Great Powers, but it also produced anxiety and tensions over them.

Between 1880 and 1914, many intellectuals abandoned the optimism of the generation that preceded them and saw in materialism and democracy the evidence of decline and decadence. They suggested that a hidden, irrational dimension of life lurked beneath the tranquil surface. Among the new nationalist right, fear of mass society gave way to racist and anti-Semitic ideologies.

In Western democracies, improved conditions also led to rising expectations. People grew more demanding, insisting in sometimes violent ways on their political and economic rights. Although mass movements, such as socialism and women's suffrage, generally used peaceful means in their campaigns to change society, some of their members advocated and employed violence. Anarchism appeared to stalk Europe. States readily used brutality in efforts to quell various protest movements, even resorting to martial law.

In central and eastern Europe, similar problems emerged. Extremist opposition to autocratic rule joined with the conflicts between national and ethnic groups to destabilize regimes. Everywhere in Europe, domestic ills raised the stakes in competition for overseas empire; at the same time, the traditional empires of Austria-Hungary and Turkey were threatened with dissolution.

Every European power had some responsibility for feeding the international tensions that led to the outbreak of war in 1914. France and Germany clashed over Morocco; Austria and Russia competed for influence over the Balkans; Britain and Germany raced each other to build warships. The Weltpolitik of Wilhelm II menaced France and Britain. Among European thinkers and leaders, force had become widely accepted as the means to an end; all the powers (except Britain) built up large standing armies with millions of men and lethal modern equipment. As rising tensions tightened the alliance system, Europe divided into two armed camps. Some leaders—notably those of Austria-Hungary and Germany—favored war over negotiation in July 1914.

FOCUS QUESTIONS

- What were the main motivations for European imperialism?

- In what ways did the worldview of intellectuals living in the belle époque differ from that of a generation earlier?

- What factors made parliamentary rule in Great Britain, France, and Italy dysfunctional?

- What various crises weakened autocratic rule in Germany, Russia, and the Ottoman Empire?

- What responsibility did each of the Great Powers have for the outbreak of war in 1914?

KEY TERMS

new imperialism (p. 668)

Second International (p. 677)

anti-Semitism (p. 678)

Zionism (p. 680)

Sigmund Freud (p. 680)

avant-garde (p. 680)

suffragists (p. 683)

Weltpolitik (p. 687)

Bolsheviks (p. 689)

Triple Alliance (p. 690)

Triple Entente (p. 691)

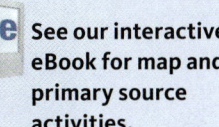 This icon will direct you to additional materials on the website: www.cengage.com/history/noble/westciv6e.

See our interactive eBook for map and primary source activities.

25

Passchendaele, Belgium, 1917
(The Art Archive/Picture Desk)

War and Revolution, 1914–1919

Mud. It was not what soldiers had in mind when they headed off to war in August 1914 amid visions of glory, gallantry—and quick victory. But after heavy rain and constant shelling, mud was a fact of life for those fighting on the western front—Belgium and northern France—during the fall of 1917. The mud was so pervasive, in fact, that soldiers literally drowned in it. These Canadian troops are holding the line on November 14, 1917, at the end of the Battle of Passchendaele (PAH-shun-dale), a British-led assault that began late in July. That assault pushed the Germans back a mere 5 miles—at the cost of 300,000 lives. There was no end to the war in sight.

Some had thought a major war impossible in rational, civilized Europe. Others had devoutly wished for war—precisely to break out of the stifling bourgeois conventions of rational, civilized Europe. When war actually began early in August 1914, the European mood was generally enthusiastic, even festive. No one was prepared for what this war would bring, including the hellish scenes of mud, smoke, artillery craters, blasted trees, decaying bodies, and ruined buildings that came to frame the daily experience of those on the western front. A far wider and more destructive war would follow within a generation, but it was World War I, known to contemporaries as "the Great War," that shattered the old European order, with its comfortable assumptions of superiority, rationality, and progress. After this war, neither Westerners nor non-Westerners could still believe in the privileged place of Western civilization in quite the same way.

The war that began in August was supposed to be over by Christmas. The British government promised "business as usual." But the fighting bogged down in a stalemate during the fall of 1914, then continued for four more years. By the time it ended, in November 1918, the war had strained the whole fabric of life, affecting everything from economic organization to literary vocabulary, from journalistic techniques to the role of women.

Partly because the war grew to become the first "world war," it proved the beginning of the end of European hegemony. The intervention of the United States in 1917 affected the military balance and seemed to give the war more idealistic and democratic purposes. The geographic reach of the war was itself unprecedented, especially after the intervention of the Ottoman Empire spread the fighting to the Middle East. Because of European colonial networks, the war also involved many other non-Europeans in combat or support roles. Although the old colonialism continued into the postwar era, the war nourished the forces that would later overthrow it.

Because of all the strains it entailed, the war had many unintended consequences. Revolutions dramatically changed the political landscape first in Russia, then in Germany.

FOCUS QUESTIONS

- How and why had the course of the war by 1917 defied the expectations that had surrounded the beginning of fighting in August 1914?

- Why did this prove a total war, making necessary new forms of socioeconomic coordination and even systematic propaganda?

- Why did the first revolution in Russia pave the way for a second, spearheaded by the Bolsheviks?

- Why did Germany and its allies end up losing the war even after forcing Russia to make a separate peace by early 1918?

- What factors shaped the peace settlement that the victors imposed on Germany and its allies in 1919–1920?

 This icon will direct you to additional materials on the website: www .cengage.com/history/ noble/westciv6e.

 See our interactive ebook for map and primary source activities.

The Habsburg and Ottoman Empires collapsed. So when the victors met early in 1919 to shape the peace, they confronted a situation that could not have been foreseen in 1914. Their effort to determine the contours of the postwar world, and thus the immediate meaning of the war, left much unresolved.

THE UNFORESEEN STALEMATE, 1914–1917

How and why had the course of the war by 1917 defied the expectations that had surrounded the beginning of fighting in August 1914?

When the war began in August 1914, enthusiasm and high morale, based on expectations of quick victory, marked both sides. But fighting on the crucial western front led to a stalemate by the end of 1914, and the brutal encounters of 1916 made it clear that this was not the sort of war most had expected. By early 1917, the difficulties of the war experience brought to the surface underlying questions about what all the fighting was for—and whether it was worth the price.

August 1914: The Domestic and Military Setting

Although some, including Helmuth von Moltke (MOLT-kuh), chief of the German general staff, worried that this would prove a long, destructive war testing the very fabric of Western civilization, the outbreak of fighting early in August produced a wave of euphoria and a remarkable degree of domestic unity. To many, war came almost as a relief; the issues that had produced intermittent crisis for the past decade would at last find definitive solution. Especially to educated young people, the war promised an escape from the stifling bourgeois world and the prospect of societal renewal.

An unexpected display of patriotism from the socialist left reinforced the sense of domestic unity and high morale. Forgetting their customary rhetoric about international proletarian solidarity, socialist parties rallied to their respective national war efforts almost everywhere in Europe. To socialists and workers, national defense against a more backward aggressor seemed essential to the eventual creation of socialism. When, on August 4, the German Socialist Party delegation in the Reichstag voted with the other parties to give the government the budgetary authority to wage war, it was clear that the Second International had failed in its long-standing commitment to keep the workers of Europe from slaughtering each other.

In France, the government had planned, as a precaution, to arrest roughly one thousand trade union and socialist leaders in the event of war, but no such arrests were necessary. The order of the day was **Sacred Union**, which meant that French leaders from across the political spectrum agreed to cooperate for the duration of the war. Rather than seek to sabotage the war, Socialist leaders joined the new government of national defense. Germany enjoyed a comparable "Fortress Truce," including an agreement to suspend labor conflict during the war, although no Socialist was invited to join the war cabinet.

Sacred Union   An agreement between leaders of different French political groups to cooperate during World War I.

On the eve of war, the forces of the Triple Entente outnumbered those of Germany and Austria-Hungary. Russia had an army of over 1 million men, the largest in Europe, and France had 700,000. Britain, which did not introduce conscription until 1916, had about 250,000. Germany led the Central Powers with 850,000; Austria-Hungary contributed 450,000. Though outnumbered, the Central Powers had potential advantages in equipment, coordination, and speed over their more dispersed adversaries. The outcome was hardly a foregone conclusion in August 1914.

After the fighting began, a second group of nations intervened one by one, expanding the war's scope and complicating the strategic alternatives. In November 1914, the Ottoman Empire, fearful of Russia, joined the Central Powers, thereby extending the war along the Russo-Turkish border and on to the Middle East. For Arabs disaffected with Ottoman Turkish rule, the war presented an opportunity to take up arms—with the active support of Britain and France. Italy, after dickering with both sides, committed itself to the Entente in the Treaty of London of April 1915. This secret agreement specified the territories Italy would receive—primarily the Italian-speaking areas still within Austria-Hungary—in the event of Entente victory. In September 1915, Bulgaria entered the war on the side of the Central Powers, seeking territorial advantages at the expense of Serbia, which had defeated Bulgaria in the Second Balkan War in 1913. Finally, in August 1916, Romania intervened on the side of the Entente, hoping to gain Transylvania, then part of Hungary.

Thus, the war was fought on a variety of fronts (see **Map 25.1**). This fact, combined with uncertainties about the role of sea power, led to ongoing debate among military decision makers about strategic priorities. Some expected that Britain and Germany would quickly be drawn into a decisive naval battle. But though Britain promptly instituted an effective naval blockade on imports to Germany, the great showdown on the seas never materialized. Despite the naval rivalry of the prewar years, World War I proved fundamentally a land war.

Germany faced not only the long-anticipated two-front war against Russia in the east and France and Britain in the west; it also had to look to the southeast, given the precarious situation of its ally Austria-Hungary, which was fighting Serbia and Russia, then also Italy and Romania as well. On the eastern front, Germany was largely successful, forcing first Russia, then Romania, to seek a separate peace by mid-1918. But it was the western front that proved decisive.

Into the Nightmare, 1914–1916

With the lessons of the wars of German unification in mind, both sides had planned for a short war based on rapid offensives. According to the Schlieffen (SHLEE-fyn) Plan, drafted in 1905, Germany would concentrate first on France, devoting but one-eighth of its forces to containing the Russians, who would need longer to mobilize. After taking just six weeks to defeat France, Germany would focus on Russia. French strategy, crafted by commander-in-chief Joseph Joffre (JOFF-ruh), similarly relied on rapid offensives. The boys would be home by Christmas—or so it was thought.

Although German troops encountered more opposition than expected from the formerly neutral Belgians, they moved swiftly through Belgium into northern France during August. By the first week of September, they had reached the Marne River, threatening Paris and forcing the French government to retreat south. But French and British troops counter-attacked, forcing the Germans to fall back and begin digging in along the Aisne (ENN) River. By holding off the German offensive at this first Battle of the Marne, the Entente had undercut the Schlieffen Plan—and with it, it turned out, any chance of a speedy victory by either side.

During the rest of the fall of 1914, each side tried—unsuccessfully—to outflank the other. When, by the end of November, active fighting ceased for the winter, a military front of about 300 miles had been established, all the way from Switzerland to the coast of the North Sea in Belgium (see **Map 25.1**). This line failed to shift more than 10 miles in either direction over the next three years. The result of the first six weeks of fighting on the western front was not a gallant victory but a grim and unforeseen stalemate.

Virtually from the start, the war took a fiercely destructive turn. In northern France in September 1914, the Germans fired on the famed Gothic cathedral at Reims (RAANZ), severely damaging its roof and nave, because they believed—apparently correctly—that the French were using one of its towers as an observation post. If such a catastrophe could happen to one of the great monuments in Europe, what else might this war bring?

CHRONOLOGY

August 1914	Fighting begins
September 1914	French forces hold off the German assault at the Marne
August–September 1914	German victories repel Russian invasion on eastern front
May 1915	Italy declares war on Austria-Hungary
February–December 1916	Battle of Verdun
July–November 1916	Battle of the Somme
January 1917	Germans resume unrestricted submarine warfare
March 1917	First Russian revolution: fall of the tsar
April 1917	U.S. declaration of war
July 1917	German Reichstag war aims resolution
November 1917	Second Russian revolution: the Bolsheviks take power
March 1918	Treaty of Brest-Litovsk between Germany and Russia
March–July 1918	Germany's last western offensive
June 1918	Initial outbreak of the "Spanish flu"
July 1918	Second Battle of the Marne
November 1918	Armistice: fighting ends
January 1919	Paris Peace Conference convenes
June 1919	Victors impose Treaty of Versailles on Germany

● **Map 25.1—The War in Europe, 1914–1918**

Although World War I included engagements in East Asia and the Middle East, it was essentially a European conflict, encompassing fighting on a number of fronts. On the western front, in northern France and Belgium, trench warfare developed and the best-known battles of the war were fought. Notable sites include Verdun, Passchendaele, and the Marne and Somme Rivers.

No Trenches in Sight
Spirits were high early in August 1914, as soldiers like these in Paris marched off to war. None foresaw what fighting this war would be like. None grasped the long-term impact the war would have. (Women bidding farewell to the troops, 1914 (b/w photo), Moreau, Jacques (b.1887)/Archives Larousse, Paris, France/Giraudon/ The Bridgeman Art Library)

The two sides were forced to settle into a war of attrition relying on an elaborate network of defensive trenches. Although separated by as much as 5 miles in some places, enemy trenches were sometimes within shouting distance, so there was occasionally banter back and forth, even attempts to entertain the other side. But the trenches quickly became almost unimaginably gruesome—filthy, ridden with rats and lice, noisy and smoky from artillery fire, and foul-smelling, partly from the odor of decaying bodies.

As defensive instruments, however, the trenches proved quite effective. Each side quickly learned to take advantage of barbed wire, mines, and especially machine guns to defend its positions. A mass of barbed wire, 3 to 5 feet high and 30 yards wide, guarded a typical trench. The machine gun had been developed before the war as an offensive weapon; few foresaw the decided advantage it would give the defense. But with machine guns, soldiers could defend trenches even against massive assaults—and inflict heavy casualties on the attackers.

Despite the advantages of defensive trenches, neither side could give up the vision of a decisive offensive. Thus, the troops were periodically called on to go "over the top" and then across "no man's land" to assault the dug-in enemy. Again and again, however, such offensives proved futile, producing incredibly heavy casualties.

For the soldiers on the western front, the war became a nightmarish experience in a hellish landscape. Bombardment by new, heavier forms of artillery scarred the terrain with craters, which became muddy, turning the landscape into a near swamp. Beginning early in 1915, tear gas, chlorine gas, and finally mustard gas found use on both sides. Although the development of gas masks significantly reduced the impact of this menacing new chemical warfare, the threat of poison gas added another nightmarish element to the experience of those who fought the war.

The notions of patriotism, comradeship, duty, and glory that had been prevalent in 1914 gradually dissolved as soldiers experienced the horrors of this war. A French soldier, questioning his own reactions after battle in 1916, responded with sarcasm and irony: "What sublime emotion inspires you at the moment of assault? I thought of nothing other than dragging my feet out of the mud encasing them. What did you feel after surviving the attack? I grumbled because I would have to remain several days more without *pinard* [wine]. Is not one's first act to kneel down and thank God? No. One relieves oneself."[1]

Trench Warfare Grim though they were, the trenches proved effective for defensive purposes. Here a British soldier guards a trench at Ovillers, on the Somme, in July 1916. (The Art Archive/Picture Desk)

Although the Germans had been denied their quick victory in the west, by the end of 1914, they occupied much of Belgium and almost one-tenth of France, including major industrial areas and mines producing most of France's coal and iron. On the eastern front, as well, the Germans won some substantial advantages in 1914—but not a decisive victory.

The first season of fighting suggested that the pattern in the east would not be trench warfare, but rapid movement across a vast but thinly held front. When hostilities began in August, the Russians mustered more quickly than anticipated, confronting an outnumbered German force in a menacing, if reckless, invasion of East Prussia. But by mid-September, German forces under General Paul von Hindenburg (1847–1934) and his chief of staff, General Erich Ludendorff (1865–1937), repelled the Russian advance, taking a huge number of prisoners and seriously demoralizing the Russians.

As a result of this victory, Hindenburg and Ludendorff emerged as heroes, and they would play major roles in German public life thereafter. Hindenburg became chief of staff of the entire German army in August 1916, but the able and energetic Ludendorff proved the key figure as this duo gradually assumed undisputed control of the whole German war effort, both military and domestic.

Seeking a Breakthrough, 1915–1917

After the campaigns of 1915 proved inconclusive, German leaders decided to concentrate in 1916 on a massive offensive against the French fortress at Verdun, intending to inflict a definitive defeat on France. To assault the fortress, the Germans gathered 1,220 pieces of artillery for attack along an 8-mile front. Included were thirteen "Big Bertha" siege guns, weapons so large that nine tractors were required to position each of them; a crane was necessary to insert the shell, which weighed over a ton. The level of heavy artillery firepower that the Germans applied at Verdun was unprecedented in the history of warfare.

German forces attacked on February 21, taking the outer defenses of the fortress, and appeared poised for victory. The tide turned, however, when General Philippe Pétain (puh-TANH) (1856–1951) assumed control of the French defense. Pétain had the patience and skill necessary to organize supply networks for a long siege. Furthermore, he proved able, through considerate treatment, to inspire affection and confidence among his men. By mid-July, the French army had repelled the German offensive, although only in December did the French retake the outer defenses of the fortress. The French had held in what would prove the war's longest, most trying battle—one that killed over 700,000 people.

To relieve pressure on Verdun, the British led a major attack at the Somme River on July 1, 1916. On that day alone, the British suffered almost 60,000 casualties, including 21,000 killed. Fighting continued into the fall, but the offensive proved futile in the end. One-third of those involved, or over 1 million soldiers, ended up dead, missing, or wounded.

Dominated by the devastating battles at Verdun and the Somme, the campaigns of 1916 finally extinguished the high spirits of the summer of 1914. Both sides suffered huge losses— apparently for nothing. By the end of 1916, the front had shifted only a few miles from its location at the beginning of the year.

In light of the frustrating outcome so far, the French turned to new military leadership, replacing Joffre as commander-in-chief with Robert Nivelle (nuh-VELL), who promptly sought to prove himself with a new offensive early in 1917. Persisting even as it became clear that this effort had no chance of success, Nivelle provoked increasing resistance among French soldiers, some of whom were refusing to follow orders by the end of April.

With the French war effort in danger of collapse, the French government replaced Nivelle with General Pétain, the hero of the defense of Verdun. Pétain reestablished discipline by adopting a conciliatory approach—improving food and rest, visiting the troops in the field, offering encouragement, even dealing relatively mercifully with the resisters themselves. To be sure, many of the soldiers who had participated in this near mutiny were court-martialed, and over 3,400 were convicted. But of the 554 sentenced to death, only 49 were actually executed.

After the failure of the Nivelle offensive, the initiative fell to the British under General Douglas Haig, who was convinced, despite skepticism in the British cabinet, that Nivelle's offensive had failed simply because of tactical mistakes. Beginning near Ypres (EE-pray) in Belgium on July 31, 1917, and continuing until November, the British attacked. As before, the effort yielded only minimal territorial gains—about 50 square miles—at a horrifying cost, including 300,000 British and Canadian casualties. Known as the Battle of Passchendaele, the British offensive of 1917 ranks with the Battles of Verdun and the Somme as the bloodiest of the war.

1917 as a Turning Point

Meanwhile, the Germans decided to concentrate on the eastern front in 1917 in an effort to knock Russia out of the war. This intensified German military pressure helped spark revolution in Russia, and in December 1917, Russia's new revolutionary regime asked for a separate peace (see page 710). The defeat of Russia freed the Germans at last to concentrate on the west, but by this time, France and Britain had a new ally.

On April 6, 1917, the United States entered the war on the side of the Entente, in response to Germany's controversial use of submarines. Germany did not have enough surface ships to respond to Britain's naval blockade, whether by attacking the British fleet directly or by mounting a comparable blockade of the British Isles. So the Germans decided to use submarines to interfere with shipping to Britain. Submarines, however, were too vulnerable to be able to surface and confiscate goods, so the Germans had to settle for sinking suspect ships with torpedoes. In February 1915, they declared the waters around the British Isles a war zone and served notice that they would torpedo not only enemy ships, but also neutral ships carrying goods to Britain.

The German response was harsh, but so was the **British blockade**, which violated earlier international agreements about the rights of neutral shipping and the scope of wartime block-ades. The British had agreed that only military goods, such as munitions and certain raw materi-als, not such everyday goods as food and clothing, were subject to confiscation. Yet, in blockading Germany, the British refused to make this distinction, prompting the sarcastic German quip that Britannia not only rules the waves but waives the rules.[2]

In May 1915, a German sub torpedoed the *Lusitania*, a British passenger liner, killing almost 1,200 people and producing widespread indignation. Partly because 128 of those killed were Americans, U.S. president Woodrow Wilson issued a severe warning, which con-tributed to the German decision in September 1915 to pull back from unrestricted submarine

British blockade Britain's naval blockade of Germany during World War I; it seriously impeded the German war effort.

SECTION SUMMARY

- Although the war was fought on a variety of fronts and even expanded beyond Europe, the fighting on the western front, in a relatively small chunk of Belgium and northern France, proved decisive.

- At the outset, each side expected a short war of rapid offensives, but the struggle on the western front produced a stalemate, based on defensive trench warfare, by the end of 1914.

- The defensive trenches proved difficult to attack, especially because of barbed wire and the machine gun.

- Massive assaults during 1916–1917 failed to produce the intended breakthrough for either side, though they resulted in horrifying numbers of casualties.

- Though the United States declared war in 1917, in response to Germany's resumption of unrestricted submarine warfare, it was not equipped to make an immediate difference on European battlefields.

warfare. But as German suffering under the British blockade increased, pressure mounted on Berlin to put the subs back into action.

The issue provoked bitter debate. Chancellor Theobald von Bethmann-Hollweg (BETT-mahn-HOHL-veg) (1856–1921) and the civilian authorities opposed resumption, fearing it would provoke the United States to enter the war. But Ludendorff and the military finally prevailed, arguing that even if the United States did intervene, U.S. troops could not get to Europe in time to have a major impact. Germany announced it would resume unrestricted submarine warfare on January 31, 1917, and the United States responded with a declaration of war on April 6.

Many on both sides doubted that U.S. intervention would make a pivotal difference; most assumed—correctly—that it would take at least a year for the American presence to materialize in force. Still, the entry of the United States gave the Entente at least the promise of more fighting power. And the United States seemed capable of renewing the sense of purpose on the Entente side, showing that the war had a meaning that could justify the unexpected costs and sacrifice.

THE EXPERIENCE OF TOTAL WAR

Why did this prove a total war, making necessary new forms of socioeconomic coordination and even systematic propaganda?

As the war dragged on, the distinction between the military and civilian spheres blurred. Suffering increased on the home front, and unprecedented governmental mobilization of society proved necessary to wage war on the scale required. Because it became "total" in this way, the war decisively altered not only the old political and diplomatic order, but also culture, society, and the patterns of everyday life.

Hardship on the Home Front

The war meant food shortages, and thus malnutrition, for ordinary people in the belligerent countries, although Britain and France, with their more favorable geographic positions, suffered considerably less than others. Germany was especially vulnerable, and the British naval blockade exacerbated an already dire situation. With military needs taking priority, the Germans encountered shortages of the chemical fertilizers, farm machinery, and draft animals necessary for agricultural production. The government began rationing bread, meat, and fats during 1915. The increasing scarcity of food produced sharp increases in diseases, such as rickets and tuberculosis, and in infant and childhood mortality rates.

The need to pay for the war produced economic dislocations as well. Government borrowing covered some of the cost for the short term, but to underwrite the rest, governments all over Europe found it more palatable to inflate the currency, by printing more money, than to raise taxes. The notion that the enemy would be made to pay once victory had been won seemed to justify this decision. But this way of financing the war meant rising prices and severe erosion of purchasing power for ordinary people all over Europe.

In France and Germany, the labor truces of 1914 gave way to increasing strike activity during 1916. With an especially severe winter in 1916–1917 adding to the misery, there were serious instances of domestic disorder, including strikes and food riots, in many parts of Europe during 1917. The revolution that overthrew the tsarist autocracy in Russia that same year began with comparable protests over wartime food shortages.

The strains of war even fanned the flames in Ireland, where an uneasy truce over the home-rule controversy accompanied the British decision for war in 1914. Partly because of German efforts to stir up domestic trouble for Britain, unrest built up again in Ireland, culminating in the Easter

Rebellion in Dublin in 1916. The brutality with which British forces crushed the uprising intensified demands for full independence—precisely what Britain would be forced to yield to the Irish republic shortly after the war.

Moreover, new technologies made civilians more vulnerable to wartime violence. Although bombing from aircraft began with an immediate military aim—to destroy industrial targets or to provide tactical support for other military units—it quickly became clear that night bombing, especially, might demoralize civilian populations. In 1915, German airplanes began bombing English cities, provoking British retaliation against cities in western Germany. These raids had little effect on the course of the war, but they showed that new technologies could make warfare more destructive, even for civilians.

Domestic Mobilization

Once it became clear that the war would not be over quickly, leaders on both sides realized that the outcome would not be determined on the battlefield alone. Victory required mobilizing all of the nation's resources and energies. So World War I became a **total war**, involving the entire society.

> **total war**   The concept, first associated with World War I, that war requires the mobilization of all a nation's resources and energies.

The British naval blockade on Germany, which made no distinction between military and nonmilitary goods, was a stratagem characteristic of total war. The blockade would not affect Germany's immediate strength on the battlefield, but it could damage Germany's long-term war-making capacity. Thus, Germany seemed to need stringent economic coordination and control. By the end of 1916, the country had coordinated all aspects of economic life for the war effort. Under the supervision of the military, state agencies, big business, and the trade unions were brought into close collaboration. The new system included rationing, price controls, and compulsory labor arbitration, as well as a national service law enabling the military to channel workers into jobs deemed vital to the war effort.

The Germans did not hesitate to exploit the economy of occupied Belgium, requisitioning foodstuffs even to the point of causing starvation among the Belgians themselves. They forced sixty-two thousand Belgians to work in German factories under conditions of virtual slave labor. By the time this practice was stopped in February 1917, nearly a thousand Belgian workers had died in German labor camps.

The body coordinating Germany's war economy was the **Kriegsrohstoffabteilung (KRA)** (kreegs-roh-stoff-AHB-ty-loong), or "War Raw Materials Office." Led initially by the able Jewish industrialist Walther Rathenau (RAT-un-ow) (1867–1922), this agency came to symbolize the unprecedented coordination of the German economy. Recognizing that Germany lacked the raw materials for a long war, Rathenau devised an imaginative program that included the development of synthetic substitute products and the creation of new mixed (private and government) companies to allocate raw materials. The KRA's effort was remarkably successful—a model for later economic planning and coordination in Germany and elsewhere.

> **Kriegsrohstoffabteilung (KRA)**   The "War Raw Materials Office" that coordinated Germany's World War I economy.

Although Germany presented the most dramatic example, this sort of domestic coordination was evident everywhere. In Britain, the central figure was David Lloyd George (1863–1945), appointed to the newly created post of minister of munitions in 1915. During his year in office, ninety-five new factories opened, soon overcoming the shortage of guns and ammunition that had impeded the British war effort until then. His performance made Lloyd George seem the person who could organize Britain for victory. Succeeding Herbert Asquith as prime minister in December 1916, he would direct the British war effort to its victorious conclusion.

Accelerating Socioeconomic Change

Everywhere, the war effort quickened the long-term socioeconomic change associated with industrialization. Government orders for war materiel fueled industrial expansion. The needs of war spawned new technologies—advances in food processing and medical treatment, for example—that would carry over into peacetime.

With so many men needed for military service, women were called on to assume new economic roles—such as running farms in France, or working in the new munitions factories in Britain. During the course of the war, the number of women employed in Britain rose from 3.25 million to 5 million. In Italy, 200,000 women had war-related jobs by 1917. Women also played indispensable roles at the front, especially in nursing units.

The expanded opportunities of wartime intensified the debate over the sociopolitical role of women that the movement for women's suffrage had stimulated. The outbreak of war led some antiwar feminists to argue that women would be better able than men to prevent wars, which

ВСЕ ДЛЯ ВОЙНЫ!

ПОДПИСЫВАЙТЕСЬ НА 5½%

ВОЕННЫЙ ЗАЕМЪ.

Working Women and the War All over Europe, governments recruited women to work in munitions factories. This Russian government poster uses an image of working women to rally support for the war. The text reads, "Everything for the war effort! Subscribe to the war loans at 5½ percent." (Eileen Tweedy/The Art Archive/Picture Desk)

SECTION SUMMARY

- Partly because of the advent of new technologies, the war threatened civilian populations in unforeseen ways.

- The unexpected length of the war forced domestic mobilization, both to maintain civilian morale and to enhance the production necessary to sustain the military effort.

- Britain's naval blockade of Germany forced German leaders to adopt innovative, highly centralized forms of socioeconomic coordination, partly to spearhead the development of substitute products.

- Domestic mobilization accelerated socioeconomic change, especially by enhancing employment opportunities for women.

- Systematic attempts to discredit the enemy, by intellectuals as well as governments, made it harder to envision the scope for a lasting peace.

---

were essentially masculine undertakings. Women should have full access to public life, not because they could be expected to respond as men did, but because they had a distinctive—and valuable—role to play. At the same time, by giving women jobs and the opportunity to do many of the same things men did, the war undermined the stereotypes that had long justified restrictions on women's political roles and life choices.

For many women, doing a difficult job well, serving their country in this emergency situation, afforded a new sense of accomplishment, as well as a new taste of independence. Women were now much more likely to have their own residences and to go out on their own, eating in restaurants, even smoking and drinking. Yet, while many seized new opportunities and learned new skills, women frequently had to combine paid employment with housework and child rearing, and those who left home—to serve in nursing units, for example—often felt guilty about neglecting their traditional family roles.

Propaganda and the "Mobilization of Enthusiasm"

Because the domestic front was crucial to sustaining a long war of attrition, it became ever more important to shore up civilian morale as the war dragged on. The result was what the historian Elie Halévy called the "mobilization of enthusiasm"—the manipulation of collective passions by governments on an unprecedented scale. Every country instituted extensive censorship, even of soldiers' letters from the front. Because of concerns about civilian morale, the French press carried no news of the Battle of Verdun, with its horrifying numbers of casualties. In addition, systematic propaganda included not only patriotic themes, but also attempts to discredit the enemy, even through outright falsification of the news.

At the outset of the war, the brutal behavior of the German armies in Belgium made it easy for the French and the British to demonize the Germans. Having expected to pass through neutral Belgium unopposed, the Germans were infuriated by the Belgian resistance they encountered. At Louvain, late in August 1914, they responded to alleged Belgian sniping by shooting a number of hostages and setting the town on fire, destroying the famous old university library. This episode led the *London Times* to characterize the Germans as "Huns," a reference to the central Asian tribe that began invading Europe in the fourth century. Stories about German soldiers eating Belgian babies began to circulate.

In October 1914, ninety-three German intellectuals, artists, and scientists signed a manifesto, addressed to "the world of culture," justifying Germany's conduct in Belgium and its larger purposes in the war. As passions heated up, major intellectuals on both sides began denigrating the culture of the enemy and claiming a monopoly of virtue for their own side.

As the war dragged on, some came to believe that real peace with an adversary so evil, so abnormally different, was simply not possible. There must be no compromise but rather total victory, no matter what the cost. At the same time, however, war-weariness produced a countervailing tendency to seek a "white peace," a peace without victory for either side. But in 1917, as Europeans began earnestly debating war aims, the Russian Revolution and the intervention of the United States seemed to change the war's meaning.

Devastation at Louvain   Unexpected destruction at the outset of the war fanned the flames of hatred and changed the stakes of the conflict. Located in the path of the first German advance, the Belgian city of Louvain was particularly hard-hit.   (The Art Archive/Imperial War Museum/Picture Desk)

THE TWO RUSSIAN REVOLUTIONS OF 1917

Why did the first revolution in Russia pave the way for a second, spearheaded by the Bolsheviks?

Strained by war, the old European order cracked first in Russia in 1917. Initially, the overthrow of the tsarist autocracy seemed to lay the foundations for parliamentary democracy. But by the end of the year, the Bolsheviks, the smallest and most extreme of Russia's major socialist parties, had taken power, an outcome that was hardly conceivable when the revolution began.

The Wartime Crisis of the Russian Autocracy

The Russian army performed better than many had expected; as late as June 1916, it mounted a successful offensive against Austria-Hungary. Russia had industrialized sufficiently by 1914 to sustain a modern war, at least for a while, and the country's war production increased significantly by 1916. But even early in 1915, perhaps a fourth of Russia's newly conscripted troops were sent to the front without weapons; they were told to pick up rifles and supplies from the dead. Moreover, Russia suffered from problems of leadership and organization that made it less prepared for a long war than the other belligerents.

In August 1915, Tsar Nicholas II (1868–1918) assumed personal command of the army, but his absence from the capital only accelerated the deterioration in government and deepened the divisions within the ruling clique. With the tsar away, the illiterate but charismatic Siberian "holy man" Grigori Rasputin (ca. 1872–1916) emerged as the key political power within the circle of the German-born Empress Alexandra (1872–1918). He won her confidence because of his alleged ability to control the bleeding of her hemophiliac son, Alexis, the heir to the throne. Led by Rasputin, those around the empress made a shambles of the state administration. Many educated Russians, appalled at what was happening, assumed—incorrectly—that pro-German elements at court were responsible for the eclipse of the tsar and the increasing governmental chaos. One Duma deputy asked of the government's performance, "Is this stupidity, or is it treason?"

Finally, late in December 1916, Rasputin was assassinated by aristocrats seeking to save the autocracy from these apparently pro-German influences. This act indicated how desperate the situation had become, but eliminating Rasputin made little difference.

By the end of 1916, the difficulties of war had combined with the strains of rapid wartime industrialization to produce a revolutionary situation in Russia. The country's urban population had mushroomed, and now, partly because of transport problems, the cities faced severe food shortages. Strikes and demonstrations spread from Petrograd (the former St. Petersburg—a name abandoned as too German at the start of the war) to other cities during the first two months of 1917. In March, renewed demonstrations in Petrograd, spearheaded by women protesting the lack of bread and coal, led to revolution.

The March Revolution and the Fate of the Provisional Government

At first, the agitation that began in Petrograd on March 8, 1917, appeared to be just another bread riot. Even when it turned into a wave of strikes, the revolutionary parties (see page 689) expected it to be crushed by government troops. But when they were called out to help the police break up the demonstrations, the soldiers generally avoided firing at the strikers. Within days, they were sharing weapons and ammunition with the workers; the government's troops were joining what was now becoming a revolution.

Petrograd Soviet The *soviet* (council) of leaders of strike committees and army regiments elected in March 1917, when Petrograd's workers protested in response to severe wartime shortages.

Late in the afternoon of March 12, leaders of the strike committees, delegates elected by factory workers, and representatives of the socialist parties formed a *soviet*, or council, following the example of the revolution of 1905, when such soviets had first appeared. Regiments of the Petrograd garrison also began electing representatives, soon to be admitted to the **Petrograd Soviet**, which officially became the Council of Workers' and Soldiers' Deputies. This soviet was now the ruling power in the Russian capital. It had been elected and was genuinely representative—though of a limited constituency of workers and soldiers. Following the lead of Petrograd, Russians elsewhere promptly began forming soviets, so that over 350 local units were represented when the first All-Russian Council of Soviets met in Petrograd in April. The overwhelming majority of their representatives were Mensheviks and Socialist Revolutionaries; about one-sixth were Bolsheviks.

provisional government The body that ruled Russia from March to November 1917, in the wake of the revolution that overthrew the tsarist regime.

On March 14, a committee of the Duma, recognizing that the tsar's authority had been lost for good, persuaded Nicholas to abdicate, then formed a new **provisional government**. This government was to be strictly temporary, paving the way for an elected constituent assembly, which would write a constitution and establish new governmental institutions.

Considering the strains that had produced the revolution of 1905 after the Russo-Japanese War, it was hardly surprising that the autocratic system would shatter now, in light of this far more trying war and the resulting governmental disarray. Russia had apparently experienced, at last, the bourgeois political revolution necessary to develop a Western-style parliamentary democracy. Even from an orthodox Marxist perspective, the immediate priority was to help consolidate the new democratic order, which would then provide the framework for the longer-term pursuit of socialism.

Although the fall of the tsarist government produced widespread relief, Russia's new leaders faced difficult questions about priorities. Should they focus their efforts on revitalizing the Russian war effort? Or, given the widespread war-weariness in the country, should they focus on domestic political reform? For now, the Petrograd Soviet was prepared to give the provisional government a chance to govern. But the soviet was a potential rival for power if the new government failed to address Russia's immediate problems.

The provisional government took important steps toward democracy, establishing universal suffrage, civil liberties, autonomy for ethnic minorities, and labor legislation, including provision for an eight-hour workday. But the government failed in two key areas, fostering discontents that the Bolsheviks soon exploited. First, it persisted in fighting the war. Second, it dragged its feet on agrarian reform.

The provisional government's determination to renew the war effort stemmed from concern about Russia's obligations to its allies, its national honor and position among the great powers. The long-standing goal of Russian diplomacy—an outlet to the Mediterranean Sea through the Dardanelles—seemed within reach if Russia could continue the war and contribute to an Entente victory.

Although the March revolution began in the cities, the peasantry soon moved into action as well, seizing land, sometimes burning the houses of their landlords. By midsummer, a full-scale peasant war seemed to be developing in the countryside, and calls for agrarian reform became increasingly urgent. Partly from expediency, partly from genuine concern for social justice, the provisional government promised a major redistribution of land. But it insisted that the reform be carried out legally—not by the present provisional government, but by a duly elected constituent assembly.

Calling elections would thus seem to have been the first priority. The new political leaders kept delaying, however, waiting for the situation to cool off. But playing for time was a luxury they could ill afford. As unrest grew in the countryside, the authority of the provisional government diminished and the soviets gained in stature. But what role were the soviets to play?

The Bolsheviks Come to Power

In the immediate aftermath of the March revolution, the Bolsheviks had not seemed to

Lenin as Leader   Although he was in exile during much of 1917, Lenin's leadership was crucial to the Bolshevik success in Russia. He is shown here addressing a May Day rally in Red Square, Moscow, on May 1, 1919. (ITAR-TASS/Sovfoto)

differ substantially from their rivals within the socialist movement, at least on matters of immediate concern—the war, land reform, and the character of the revolution itself. But the situation began to change in April when Lenin, assisted by the German military, returned from exile in Switzerland. The Germans assumed—correctly, it turned out—that the Bolsheviks would help undermine the Russian war effort. Largely through the force of Lenin's leadership, the Bolsheviks soon took the initiative within the still-developing revolution in Russia.

Born Vladimir Ilich Ulianov, **Vladimir Lenin** (1870–1924) came from a comfortable upper-middle-class family. He was university-educated and trained as a lawyer. But after an older brother was executed in 1887 for participating in a plot against the tsar's life, Lenin followed him into revolutionary activity. Arrested for the first time in 1895, he was confined to Siberia until 1900. He then lived in exile abroad for almost the entire period before his return to Russia in 1917.

The Bolshevik Party was identified with Lenin from its beginning in 1903, when it emerged from the schism in Russian Marxist socialism. Because of his emphases, Bolshevism came to mean discipline, organization, and a special leadership role for a revolutionary vanguard. Lenin proved effective because he was a stern and somewhat forbidding figure, disciplined, fiercely intelligent, sometimes ruthless. As a Bolshevik colleague put it, Lenin was "the one indisputable leader … a man of iron will, inexhaustible energy, combining a fanatical faith in the movement, in the cause, with an equal faith in himself."[3]

Still, Lenin's reading of the situation when he returned to Petrograd in April astonished even many Bolsheviks. He argued that the revolution was about to pass from the present bourgeois-democratic stage to a socialist phase, involving proletarian dictatorship in the form of government by the soviets. So the Bolsheviks should begin actively opposing the provisional government, especially by denouncing the war as fundamentally imperialist and by demanding the distribution of land from the large estates to the peasants. This latter measure had long been

EARLY YEARS UNDER LENIN

Vladimir Lenin   Russian revolutionary and leader of the Bolsheviks since 1903, he masterminded the November 1917 revolution that overthrew the provisional government and led to a communist regime in Russia.

identified with the Socialist Revolutionaries; most Bolsheviks had envisioned collectivization and nationalization instead.

As Lenin saw it, the strains of war had made all of Europe ripe for revolution. A revolution in Russia would provide the spark to ignite a wider proletarian revolution, especially in Germany. He did not envision backward Russia seeking to create socialism on its own. Although some remained skeptical of Lenin's strategy, he promptly won over most of his fellow Bolsheviks. And thus, the Bolsheviks began actively seeking wider support by promising peace, land, and bread.

THE BOLSHEVIK REVOLUTION

In April 1917, moderate socialists still had majority support in the soviets, so the Bolsheviks sought to build support gradually, postponing any decisive test of strength. But events escaped the control of the Bolshevik leadership in mid-July when impatient workers, largely Bolshevik in sympathy, took to the streets of Petrograd on their own. The Petrograd Soviet refused to support the uprising, and the provisional government had no difficulty getting military units to put it down, killing two hundred in the process. Though the uprising had developed spontaneously, Bolshevik leaders felt compelled to offer public support, and this gave the government an excuse to crack down on the Bolshevik leadership. Lenin managed to escape to Finland, but a number of his colleagues were arrested and jailed.

With the Bolsheviks on the defensive, counterrevolutionary elements in the Russian military decided to seize the initiative with a march on Petrograd in September. To resist this attempted coup, the provisional government, now led by the young Socialist Revolutionary Alexander Kerensky (1881–1970), had to rely on anyone who could help, including the Bolsheviks. And thanks to Bolshevik propaganda, the soldiers under the command of the counterrevolutionaries refused to fight against the upholders of the revolution in Petrograd. Thus, the coup was thwarted. Within days, the Bolsheviks won their first clear-cut majority in the Petrograd Soviet, and then shortly gained majorities in most of the other soviets as well.

During the fall of 1917, the situation became increasingly volatile, eluding control by anyone. People looted food from shops; peasants seized land, sometimes murdering their landlords. Desertions and the murder of officers increased within the Russian military.

With the Bolsheviks now the dominant power in the soviets, and with the government's control diminishing, Lenin, from his hideout in Finland, urged the Bolshevik central committee to prepare for armed insurrection. Although some found this step too risky, the majority accepted Lenin's argument that the provisional government would continue dragging its feet, inadvertently giving right-wing officers time for another coup.

Because Lenin remained in hiding, the task of organizing the seizure of power fell to Leon Trotsky (1870–1940), who skillfully modified Lenin's aggressive strategy. Lenin wanted the Bolsheviks to rise in their own name, in opposition to the provisional government, but Trotsky linked the insurrection to the cause of the soviets and played up its defensive character against the ongoing danger of a counterrevolutionary coup. With the political center at an impasse, the only alternative to such a coup seemed to be a Bolshevik initiative to preserve the Petrograd Soviet, by now the key institutional embodiment of the revolution and its promise. Trotsky's interpretation led people who wanted simply to defend the soviet to support the Bolshevik action.

During the night of November 9, armed Bolsheviks and regular army regiments occupied key points in Petrograd, including railroad stations, post offices, telephone exchanges, power stations, and the national bank. Able to muster only token resistance, the provisional government collapsed. Kerensky escaped and mounted a futile effort to rally troops at the front for a counterattack. In contrast to the March revolution, which had taken about a week, the Bolsheviks took over the capital, overthrowing the Kerensky government, literally overnight and almost without bloodshed.

But though the Bolsheviks enjoyed considerable support in the network of soviets, it was not clear that they could extend their control across the whole Russian Empire. Moreover, from their own perspective, the revolution's immediate prospects, and its potential wider impact, were bound up with the course of the war. Would the Bolshevik Revolution in Russia prove the spark for revolution elsewhere in war-weary Europe, as Lenin anticipated?

The Russian Revolution and the War

Having stood for peace throughout the revolution, the Bolsheviks promptly moved to get Russia out of the war, agreeing to an armistice with Germany in December 1917. They hoped that Russia's withdrawal would speed the collapse of the war effort on all sides and that this, in turn, would intensify the movement toward revolution elsewhere in Europe. The Russian Revolution was but a chapter in this larger story. As Lenin noted to Trotsky, "If it were necessary for us to go under to assure the success of the German revolution, we should have to do it. The German revolution is vastly more important than ours." Indeed, said Lenin to the Bolsheviks' party congress of March 1918, "It is an absolute truth that we will go under without the German revolution."[4]

After assuming control in November, the Bolsheviks published the tsarist government's secret agreements specifying how the spoils were to be divided in the event of a Russian victory. They hoped to inflame revolutionary sentiment elsewhere by demonstrating that the war had been, all along, an imperialist offensive on behalf of capitalist interests. This Bolshevik initiative added fuel to the controversy already developing in all the belligerent countries over the war's purpose and significance.

SECTION SUMMARY

- The strains of war led to a revolution that ended the tsarist order in Russia in March 1917.

- Although the soviet, or workers' and soldiers' council, was a major force in Petrograd, the first Russian revolution of 1917 was not intended to produce a socialist system.

- The provisional government proved ineffective because it dragged its feet on land reform and insisted on maintaining the war effort.

- Due partly to the leadership of Lenin and Trotsky, the Bolsheviks were able to seize the initiative and take power from the provisional government in November 1917.

- The Bolsheviks envisioned their takeover as a spark to revolution elsewhere in war-torn Europe.

THE NEW WAR AND THE ALLIED VICTORY, 1917–1918

Why did Germany and its allies end up losing the war even after forcing Russia to make a separate peace by early 1918?

Because the stakes of the war changed during 1917, the eventual outcome included consequences that Europeans could not have foreseen in 1914. German defeat brought revolution against the monarchy and the beginning of a new democracy. Austro-Hungarian defeat brought the collapse of the Habsburg monarchy and thus the opportunity for its national minorities to form nations of their own. As the old European order fell, grandiose new visions competed to shape the postwar world.

The Debate over War Aims

Allied war aims agreements, such as the Treaty of London that brought Italy into the war in 1915, had remained secret until the Bolsheviks published the tsarist documents. Products of old-style diplomacy, those agreements had been made by a restricted foreign policy elite; even members of the elected parliaments generally did not know their contents. The debate over war aims that developed in 1917 thus became a debate over decision making as well. Many assumed that a more democratic approach to foreign policy would minimize the chances of war, since the people would not agree to wars for dynastic or business interests. In addition, there were exhortations for all the parties in the present war to renounce annexations and settle for a white peace. It was time to call the whole thing off and bring the soldiers home.

Seeking to counter such sentiments, especially the Russian contention that the war was not worth continuing, the idealistic U.S. president, Woodrow Wilson (1856–1924), insisted on the great potential significance of an Allied victory. In his State of the Union speech of January 1918, and in several declarations thereafter, Wilson proposed **Fourteen Points** to guide the new international order. Notable among them were open diplomacy, free trade, reduced armaments, self-determination for nationalities, a league of nations, and a recasting of the colonial system to ensure equal rights for the indigenous populations.

Lenin and Wilson, then, offered radically different interpretations of the war, with radically different implications for present priorities. Yet, compared with the old diplomacy, they had something in common. Together, they seemed to represent a whole new approach to international relations—and the possibility of a more peaceful world. Thus, they found an eager audience among the war-weary peoples of Europe.

Despite the strains of the war, Sacred Union in France did not weaken substantially until April 1917, with General Nivelle's disastrous offensive. But then, as near mutiny began to develop within the army, rank-and-file pressures forced socialist leaders to demand clarification, and perhaps revision, of French war aims. Suddenly the French government was under pressure to

Fourteen Points
Proposals by U.S. president Woodrow Wilson to guide the new international order that would follow an Allied victory in World War I.

suggest that the war had idealistic and democratic purposes. Doubts about the government's goals were beginning to fuel active opposition to the war.

The same pressures were at work in Germany. Antiwar sentiment grew steadily within the Social Democratic Party (SPD) until the antiwar faction split off and formed the Independent Socialist Party (USPD) in April 1917. A large-scale debate over war aims, linked to considerations of domestic political reform, developed in the Reichstag by the summer of 1917. On July 19, a solid 60 percent majority passed a new war aims resolution, which affirmed that Germany's purposes were solely defensive, that Germany had no territorial ambitions. Germany, too, seemed open to a white peace.

But just as the dramatic events of 1917 interjected new pressures for moderation and peace, pressures in the opposite direction also mounted as the war dragged on. It seemed to some that this war was only the beginning of a new era of intense international competition. The current war convinced top German officials that Germany's geography and dependence on imports made it especially vulnerable. So Germany had to seize the present opportunity to conquer the means to fight the next war on a more favorable footing. Many German officials believed that Germany could achieve parity with Britain, and thus, the basis for security and peace, only if it maintained control of the Belgian coast. German expansion into Russian Poland and up the Baltic coast of Lithuania and Latvia seemed essential as well.

Treaty of Brest-Litovsk
Harsh peace terms that Germany imposed on Russia in March 1918.

When, in response to the Russian request for an armistice, Germany was able to dictate the peace terms, as specified in the **Treaty of Brest-Litovsk** of March 1918, it became clear how radically annexationist Germany's war aims had become. European Russia was to be largely dismembered, leaving Germany in direct or indirect control of 27 percent of Russia's European territory, 40 percent of its population, and 75 percent of its iron and coal. All the Reichstag parties except the Socialists accepted the terms of the treaty, which, in fact, produced a renewed determination to push on to victory.

France, less vulnerable geographically than Germany, tended to be more modest. But news of the terms the Germans had imposed at Brest-Litovsk inflamed the French, reinforcing their determination to fight on to an unqualified victory. Only thus could France secure the advantages necessary to ward off an ongoing German menace.

The Renewal of the French War Effort

Domestic division in France reached its peak during the fall of 1917. In November, with France's ability to continue fighting in doubt, President Raymond Poincaré (1860–1934) called on Georges Clemenceau (1841–1929) to lead a new government. The 76-year-old Clemenceau (klem-ahn-SOH) was known as a "hawk"; his appointment portended a stepped-up prosecution of the war. His message was simple as he appeared before the Chamber of Deputies on November 20, 1917: "If you ask me about my war aims, I reply: my aim is to be victorious." For the remainder of the war, France was under the virtual dictatorship of Clemenceau and his cabinet.

Clemenceau moved decisively on both the domestic and military fronts. By cracking down on the antiwar movement—imprisoning antiwar leaders, suppressing defeatist newspapers—he stiffened morale on the home front. Understanding that lack of coordination between French and British military leaders had hampered the Allied effort on the battlefield, Clemenceau persuaded the British to accept the French general Ferdinand Foch (FOHSH) (1851–1929) as the first supreme commander of all Allied forces in the west. In choosing Foch, known for his commitment to aggressive offensives, Clemenceau was pointedly bypassing Pétain, whom he found too passive, even defeatist. After some initial friction, Clemenceau let Foch have his way on the military level, and the two proved an effective leadership combination.

The German Gamble, 1918

As the military campaigns of 1918 began, Germany seemed in a relatively favorable position: Russia had been knocked out of the war, and American troops were yet to arrive. Moderates in Germany wanted to seize the opportunity to work out a compromise peace while there was still a chance. But military leaders persuaded Kaiser Wilhelm II that Germany could win a definitive victory on the western front if it struck quickly, before U.S. help became significant. Since Germany would be out of reserves by summer, the alternative to decisive victory in the west would be total German defeat.

The German gamble almost succeeded. From March to June 1918, German forces seized the initiative with four months of sustained and effective attacks. By May 30, they had again reached the Marne, where they had been held in 1914. Paris, only 37 miles away, had to be evacuated once more (see **MAP 25.1**). As late as mid-July, Ludendorff remained confident of victory, but by mid-August, it was becoming clear that Germany lacked the manpower to exploit the successes of the offensive.

The German advance had caused mutual suspicion between the French and the British at first, but under Foch's leadership, the Western allies eventually managed more effective coordination. And on June 4, over a year after the U.S. declaration of war, American troops went into action for the first time. As the Allied counterattack proceeded, 250,000 U.S. troops were arriving per month, considerably boosting Allied morale and battlefield strength.

By June 1918, Europe was experiencing the first outbreak of a virulent new influenza virus, promptly dubbed the "Spanish flu," though it had originated in South Africa. Because of their inferior diets, German soldiers proved far more susceptible to the disease than their adversaries, a fact that significantly affected Germany's combat performance during the crucial summer of 1918.

Germany lost the initiative for good during the second Battle of the Marne, which began on July 15 with yet another German attack. Foch launched a sustained counterattack on July 18, using tanks to good advantage, and maintained the momentum thereafter. By early August, the whole western front began to roll back. With astonishing suddenness, the outcome was no longer in doubt, although most expected the war to drag on into 1919. Few realized how desperate Germany's situation had become.

Meanwhile, Germany's allies began falling one by one. In the Balkans, an Allied offensive broke through the German-Bulgarian line in September, prompting the Bulgarians to ask for an armistice. The Turkish military effort collapsed in October. With the defeat of Russia in 1917, German troops joined the Austrians on the Italian front, breaking through the Italian line at Caporetto late in 1917 and almost inflicting a decisive defeat. But after retreating, the Italians managed to regroup and hold—and eventually to drive the Austrians back. The Italian victory at Vittorio Veneto forced Austria's unconditional surrender on November 3, 1918. But by this point, the armies of the Habsburg Empire were disintegrating along nationality lines.

Military Defeat and Political Change in Germany

By late September, it was clear to Ludendorff that his armies could not stop the Allied advance. On September 29, he informed the government that to avoid invasion, Germany would have to seek an immediate armistice. Hoping to secure favorable peace terms and to foist responsibility for the defeat onto the parliamentary politicians, Hindenburg and Ludendorff asked that a government based on greater popular support be formed. A leading moderate, Prince Max von Baden (BAH-dyn) (1867–1929), became chancellor, and he promptly replaced Ludendorff with General Wilhelm Groener (GREU-nur) (1867–1939), who seemed more democratic in orientation. By now it was clear that ending the war could not be separated from the push for political change in Germany, especially because it was widely assumed that a more democratic Germany could expect more favorable peace terms.

After securing a written request for an armistice from Hindenburg, Prince Max sent a peace note to President Wilson early in October, asking for an armistice based on Wilson's Fourteen Points. During the month that followed, Prince Max engineered a series of measures, passed by the Reichstag and approved by the emperor, that reformed the constitution, abolishing the three-class voting system in Prussia and making the chancellor responsible to the Reichstag. At last, Germany had a constitutional monarchy. Not completely satisfied, President Wilson encouraged speculation that Germany could expect better peace terms if Wilhelm II were to abdicate and Germany became a republic.

But a far more radical outcome seemed possible during late 1918 and early 1919. As negotiations for an armistice proceeded in October, the continuing war effort produced instances of mutiny in the navy and breaches of discipline in the army. By early November, workers' and soldiers' councils were being formed all over Germany, just as in Russia the year before. On November 7, antiwar socialists in Munich led an uprising of workers and soldiers that expelled the king of Bavaria and proclaimed a new Bavarian republic. Its provisional government promptly sought its own peace negotiations with the Allies. On November 9, thousands of workers took to the streets of Berlin to demand immediate peace, and the authorities could not muster enough military resources to move against them.

"stab in the back" myth
The notion, widely held among Germans after their unexpected loss in World War I, that political intrigue and revolution at home had sabotaged the German military effort.

The senior army leadership grew concerned that the collapse of government authority would undermine the ability of officers even to march their troops home. So Hindenburg and Groener persuaded the emperor to abdicate. Having lost the support of the army, Wilhelm II accepted the inevitable and left for exile in the Netherlands.

With the German right, including the military, in disarray, and with the centrist parties discredited by their support for what had become an annexationist war, the initiative passed to the socialists. They, at least, had been in the forefront of the movement for peace. But the socialists had divided in 1917, mostly over the question of response to the war. The mainstream of the SPD, by supporting the war for so long, had irrevocably alienated the party's leftist socialist wing. The most militant of these leftist socialists, led by Karl Liebknecht (1871–1919) and Rosa Luxemburg (1870–1919), envisioned using the workers' and soldiers' councils as the basis for a full-scale revolution, more or less on the Bolshevik model.

The SPD, on the other hand, clung to its reformist heritage and insisted on working within parliamentary institutions. Party leaders argued that a Bolshevik-style revolution was neither appropriate nor necessary under the circumstances. On November 9, just hours before the revolutionaries proclaimed a soviet-style republic, SPD moderates proclaimed a parliamentary republic, soon to be led by the moderate socialist Friedrich Ebert (A-bairt) (1871–1925).

Birth from military defeat was especially disabling for the new republic because the German people were so little prepared for defeat when it came. Vigorous censorship had kept the public in the dark about Germany's real situation, so the request for an armistice early in October came as a shock. At no time during the war had Germany been invaded from the west, and by mid-1918, the German army had seemed on the brink of victory. It appeared inconceivable that Germany had lost a military decision, plain and simple. Thus, the **"stab in the back" myth**, the notion that political intrigue and revolution at home had sabotaged the German military effort, developed to explain what otherwise seemed an inexplicable defeat. This notion would prove a heavy burden for Germany's new democracy to bear.

SECTION SUMMARY

- By 1917, the will to continue the war was flagging on both sides, as some began to question war aims and even to call for a "white peace."

- The idealism of U.S. president Wilson, with his Fourteen Points, suggested to Europeans that the war might indeed be worth fighting to a victorious conclusion.

- The harsh Treaty of Brest-Litovsk that Germany imposed on Russia reflected changes in German war aims.

- The leadership combination of Clemenceau and Foch was crucial to the renewal of the French war effort.

- Germany's gamble on one last massive offensive during the summer of 1918 almost succeeded, but, led by France, the Allies began forcing the Germans back, prompting Germany to ask for an armistice.

- German leaders decided to turn from Wilhelm II's imperial regime toward democracy, partly in an effort to secure more favorable peace terms.

THE OUTCOME AND THE IMPACT

What factors shaped the peace settlement that the victors imposed on Germany and its allies in 1919–1920?

After the armistice officially ended the fighting on November 11, 1918, it was up to the war's four victors—France, Britain, Italy, and the United States—to establish the terms of peace and, it was to be hoped, a new basis for order at the same time. But after all that had happened since August 1914, it was not clear what a restoration of peace and order would require. Revolution had undermined, or threatened to undermine, the old political order in much of Europe. And the involvement of non-Europeans in the war seemed to suggest that Europe would no longer dominate world affairs in quite the way it had.

The Costs of War

Raw casualty figures do not begin to convey the war's human toll, but they afford some sense of its magnitude. Estimates differ, but it is generally agreed that from 10 million to 13 million military men lost their lives, with another 20 million wounded. In addition, between 7 million and 10 million civilians died as a result of the war and its hardships. In the defeated countries especially, food shortages and malnutrition continued well after the end of the fighting. Thus, the Spanish flu that had affected the balance on the battlefield early in the summer of 1918 returned with particularly devastating results during the fall. The influenza pandemic killed perhaps 40 million people worldwide.

Germany suffered the highest number of military casualties, but France suffered the most in proportional terms. Two million Germans were killed, with another 4 million wounded. Military deaths per capita for France were roughly 15 percent higher than for Germany—and twice as severe as for Britain. Of 8 million Frenchmen mobilized, over 5 million were killed or wounded. Roughly 1.5 million French soldiers, or 10 percent of the active male population, were killed—and this in a country already concerned about demographic decline. The other belligerents suffered less, but still in great numbers. Among the military personnel killed were 2 million Russians, 500,000 Italians, and 114,000 Americans.

Economic costs were heavy as well. In addition to the privations suffered during the years of war, Europeans found themselves reeling from inflation and saddled with debt, especially to the United States, once the war was over. Although the immediate transition to a peacetime economy did not prove as difficult as many had feared, the war and its aftermath produced an economic disequilibrium that lingered, helping to produce a worldwide depression by the 1930s.

The Search for Peace in a Revolutionary Era

The war had begun because of the nationality problem in Austria-Hungary, and it led not simply to military defeat for Austria-Hungary, but to the breakup of the Habsburg system (see **Map 25.3**). In east-central Europe, the end of the war brought bright hopes for self-determination to peoples like the Czechs, Slovaks, Poles, Serbs, and Croats. Even before the peacemakers opened deliberations in January 1919, some of these ethnic groups had begun creating a new order on their own. For example, a popular movement of Czechs and Slovaks established a Czechoslovak republic on October 29, 1918, and a new Yugoslavia and an independent Hungary similarly emerged from indigenous movements. Czechoslovakia and Yugoslavia were made up of different ethnic groups that found cooperation advantageous now but that might well disagree in the future (see **Map 25.2**). Moreover, many of these countries lacked traditions of self-government, and they had reason to feud among themselves. With the Habsburg system no longer imposing one form of stability, a power vacuum seemed likely in this potentially volatile part of Europe.

The Bolshevik Revolution in Russia immeasurably complicated the situation. The unsettled conditions in Germany and the former Habsburg territories seemed to invite the spread of revolution—precisely according to Lenin's script. Shortly after taking power, Lenin and his party had begun calling themselves "communists," partly to jettison the provincial Russian term *bolshevik*, but especially to underline their departure from the old reformist socialism of the Second International. In adopting "communism," they wanted to make it clear that they stood for a revolutionary alternative, and they actively sought to inspire revolution elsewhere.

Outside Russia, the greatest communist success was in Hungary, where a communist regime under Béla Kun governed Budapest and other parts of the country from March to August 1919, when it was put down by Allied-sponsored

🌐 **Map 25.2—Ethnicity in East-Central Europe, 1919**
Ethnic diversity made it hard to create homogeneous nation-states in east-central Europe. The new states that emerged after World War I mixed ethnic groups, and ethnic tensions would contribute to future problems.

forces. At about the same time, communist republics lasted for months in the Slovak part of Czechoslovakia and in the important German state of Bavaria. Even in Italy, which had shared in the victory, socialists infatuated with the Bolshevik example claimed that the substantial labor unrest during 1919 and 1920 was the beginning of full-scale revolution.

Further complicating the postwar situation were the defeat and dissolution of the Turkish Ottoman Empire, which had controlled much of the Middle East in 1914. The Arab revolt against the Turks that developed in the Arabian peninsula in 1916 did not achieve its major military aims, though it caused some disruption to the Turkish war effort. Its success was due partly to the collaboration of a young British officer, T. E. Lawrence (1888–1935), who proved an effective military leader and an impassioned advocate of the Arab cause. The support that Britain had offered the Arabs suggested that independence, perhaps even a single Arab kingdom, might follow from a defeat of the Ottoman Empire.

But British policy toward the Arabs was uncertain and contradictory. Concerned about the Suez Canal, the British government sought to tighten its control in Egypt by declaring it a protectorate in 1914, triggering increased anti-British sentiment in the region. The secret Sykes-Picot Agreement of May 1916, named for the British and French diplomats who negotiated it, projected a division of the Ottoman territories of the Middle East into colonial spheres of influence. France would control Syria and Lebanon, while Britain would rule Palestine and Mesopotamia, or present-day Iraq (see **Map 25.4**).

Potentially complicating the situation in the region was Zionism, the movement to establish a Jewish state in Palestine. Led by Chaim Weizmann (1874–1952), a remarkable Russian-born British chemist, the Zionists reached an important milestone when British foreign secretary Arthur Balfour (1848–1930) cautiously announced, in the Balfour Declaration of November 1917, that the British government "looked with favor" on the prospect of a "Jewish home" in Palestine. At this point, Jews were only 10 percent of the population in Palestine. British leaders sympathetic to Zionism saw no conflict in simultaneously embracing the cause of the Arabs against the

An Arab in Paris   Prince Faisal *(foreground)* attended the Paris Peace Conference, where he lobbied for the creation of an independent Arab kingdom from part of the former Ottoman Turkish holdings in the Middle East. Among his supporters was the British officer T. E. Lawrence *(middle row, second from the right)*, on his way to legend as "Lawrence of Arabia." (Bettmann/Corbis)

Ottoman Turks. Indeed, Arabs and Jews, each seeking self-determination, could be expected to collaborate.

In the heat of war, the British established their policy for the former Ottoman territories without careful study. Thus, they made promises and agreements that were not entirely compatible. After the war, the victors' efforts to install a new order in the Middle East would create fresh conflicts.

The Peace Settlement

The peace conference took place in Paris, beginning in January 1919. Its labors led to separate treaties with each of the five defeated states. The first and most significant was the **Treaty of Versailles** with Germany, signed in the Hall of Mirrors of the Versailles Palace on June 28, 1919. Treaties were also worked out, in turn, with Austria, Bulgaria, Hungary, and finally, in August 1920, Turkey.

Treaty of Versailles
Peace treaty that the victors in World War I imposed on a defeated Germany in 1919.

This was to be a dictated, not a negotiated, peace. Germany and its allies were excluded, as was revolutionary Russia. The passions unleashed by the long war had dissolved the possibility of a more conciliatory outcome, a genuinely negotiated peace. However, spokesmen for many groups—from Slovaks and Croats to Arabs, Jews, and pan-Africanists—were in Paris as well, seeking a hearing for their respective causes. Both the Arab Prince Faisal (1885–1933), who would later become king of Iraq, and Colonel T. E. Lawrence were on hand to plead for an independent Arab kingdom. (See the feature, "The Global Record: Prince Faisal at the Peace Conference.") The African American leader W E. B. DuBois (doo-BOYS) (1868–1963), who took his Ph.D. at Harvard in 1895, led a major pan-African congress in Paris concurrently with the peace conference.

THE PARTICIPANTS

The fundamental challenge for the peacemakers was to reconcile the conflicting visions of the postwar world that had emerged by the end of the war. U.S. president Wilson represented the promise of a new order that could give this terrible war a lasting meaning. As he toured parts of Europe on his way to the conference, Wilson was greeted as a hero. Clemenceau, in contrast, was a hard-liner concerned with French security and dismissive of Wilsonian ideals. Since becoming prime minister in 1917, he had stressed that only permanent French military superiority over Germany, and not some utopian league of nations, could guarantee a lasting peace. The negotiations at Paris centered on this fundamental difference between Wilson and Clemenceau. Although Britain's Lloyd George took a hard line on certain issues, he also sought to mediate, helping engineer the somewhat awkward compromise that resulted. When, after the peace conference, he encountered criticism for the outcome, Lloyd George replied, "I think I did as well as might be expected, seated as I was between Jesus Christ and Napoleon Bonaparte."[5]

SHIFTING POWERS

In Article 231 of the final treaty, the peacemakers sought to establish a moral basis for their treatment of Germany by assigning responsibility for the war to Germany and its allies. The Germans were required to pay reparations to reimburse the victors for the costs of the war, although

The Victors and the Peace   In June 1919, the leaders of the major victorious powers exude confidence after signing the Treaty of Versailles with Germany. From the left are David Lloyd George of Britain, Georges Clemenceau of France, and Woodrow Wilson of the United States.   (Bettmann/Corbis)

the actual amount was not established until 1921. The determination to make the loser pay was one of the factors keeping both sides from seeking a compromise peace by 1917.

Germany was also forced to dismantle much of its military apparatus. The army was to be limited to a hundred thousand men, all volunteers. The treaty severely restricted the size of the German navy as well, and Germany was forbidden to manufacture or possess military aircraft, submarines, tanks, heavy artillery, or poison gas.

France took back Alsace and Lorraine, the provinces it had lost to Germany in 1871 (see **Map 25.3**). But for France, the crucial security provision of the peace settlement was the treatment of the adjacent Rhineland section of Germany itself. For fifteen years, Allied troops were to occupy the west bank of the Rhine River in Germany—the usual military occupation of a

🌐 **Map 25.3—Europe after the Peace Conference, 1920**
With Russia, Austria-Hungary, Germany, and Ottoman Turkey defeated, the peacemakers finalized major changes in the European map. France, Italy, and Denmark gained significant territory, while a number of new countries were established in the east-central part of the continent.

defeated adversary. But this would only be temporary. The long-term advantage for France was to be the permanent demilitarization of all German territory west of the Rhine and a strip of 50 kilometers along its east bank. Germany was to maintain no troops on this part of its own soil; in the event of hostilities, French forces would be able to march into Germany unopposed.

French interests also helped shape the settlement in east-central Europe. To ensure that Germany would again face potential enemies from both the east and the west, French leaders envisioned building a network of allies in east-central Europe. The first was the new Poland, created from Polish territories formerly in the German, Russian, and Austro-Hungarian Empires. That network might come to include Czechoslovakia, Yugoslavia, and Romania as well. These states would be weak enough to remain under French influence but, taken together, strong enough to replace Russia as a significant force against Germany.

Partly as a result of French priorities, Poland, Czechoslovakia, Yugoslavia, and Romania ended up as large as possible, either by combining ethnic groups or by incorporating minorities that, on ethnic grounds, belonged with neighboring states (see **MAP 25.2**). The new Czechoslovakia included not only Czechs and Slovaks, but also numerous Germans and Magyars. Indeed, Germans, mostly from the old Bohemia, made up 22 percent of the population of Czechoslovakia. By contrast, Austria, Hungary, and Bulgaria, as defeated powers, found themselves diminished (see **MAP 25.3**). What remained of Austria, the German part of the old Habsburg Empire, was prohibited from choosing to join Germany, an obvious violation of the Wilsonian principle of self-determination.

Desires to contain revolutionary Russia were also at work in the settlement in east-central Europe. A band of states in east-central Europe, led by France, could serve not only as a check to Germany, but also as a shield against the Russian threat. Romania's aggrandizement came partly at the expense of the Russian Empire, as did the creation of the new Poland. Finland, Latvia, Estonia, and Lithuania, all part of the Russian Empire for over a century, became independent states (see **MAP 25.3**).

The territorial settlement cost Germany almost 15 percent of its prewar territory, but German bitterness over the peace terms stemmed above all from a sense of betrayal. In requesting an armistice, German authorities had appealed to Wilson, who had not emphasized war guilt and reparations. He seemed to be saying that the whole prewar international system, not one side or the other, had been responsible for the current conflict. Yet, the peacemakers now placed the primary blame on Germany, so for Germans, the terms of the peace greatly intensified the sting of defeat.

Wilson had been forced to compromise with French interests in dealing with east-central Europe, but he achieved a potentially significant success in exchange—the establishment of a **League of Nations**, embodying the widespread hope for a new international order. (See the feature, "The Written Record: The Covenant of the League of Nations.") According to the League covenant worked out by April, disputes among member states were to be settled no longer by war, but by mechanisms established by the new assembly. Other members were to participate in sanctions, from economic blockade to military action, against a member that went to war in violation of League provisions.

How could Wilsonian hopes for a new international order be squared with the imperialist system, which seemed utterly at odds with the ideal of self-determination? Elites among the colonial peoples had tended to support the war efforts of their imperial rulers, but often in the hope of winning greater autonomy or even independence. The Indian leader Mohandas Gandhi (GAHN-dee) (1869–1948), who had been educated in the West and admitted to the English bar in 1889, even helped recruit Indians to fight on the British side. But his aim was to speed Indian independence, and he led demonstrations that embarrassed the British during the war. (See the feature, "The Global Record: Gandhi Advocates Nonviolence," on page 760 in Chapter 27.)

Colonial peoples participated directly in the war on both sides. In sub-Saharan Africa, for example, German-led Africans fought against Africans under British or French command. France brought colonial subjects from West and North Africa into frontline service during the war. But one result was an expansion of political consciousness that led more of those subject to imperialism to question the whole system.

The hope that support for the Western powers in wartime would eventually be rewarded led China and Siam (now Thailand) to associate with the Allied side in 1917, in an effort to enhance

A NEW INTERNATIONAL ORDER?

League of Nations An international organization established at the end of World War I without the membership of the United States. Though its covenant called for the peaceful settlement of disputes and for sanctions against a member that went to war in violation of League provisions, it failed to prevent the escalating violence that culminated in World War II.

Prince Faisal at the Peace Conference

With the war nearing its end in October 1918, British authorities, in line with provisions of the Sykes-Picot Agreement, permitted Faisal ibn-Husayn (1885–1933) to set up a provisional Arab state, with its capital at Damascus. As head of a delegation from this area to the Paris Peace Conference, Faisal claimed to speak for all Arab Asia, but some on the Arabian peninsula challenged his claim. In the memorandum of January 1919 that follows, he outlined the Arab position, mixing pride and assertiveness with a recognition that the Arabs would continue to need the support and help of Western powers. After the peace was concluded, Faisal found himself caught up in British and French rivalries as he was installed as king—first of Syria, then of Iraq (Mesopotamia). But his efforts were central to the eventual achievement of Arab independence in the Middle East.

We believe that our ideal of Arab unity in Asia is justified beyond need of argument. If argument is required, we would point to the general principles accepted by the Allies when the United States joined them, to our splendid past, to the tenacity with which our race has for 600 years resisted Turkish attempts to absorb us, and, in a lesser degree, to what we tried our best to do in this war as one of the Allies....

The various provinces of Arab Asia—Syria, Irak [sic], Jezireh, Hedjaz, Nejd, Yemen—are very different economically and socially, and it is impossible to constrain them into one frame of government.

We believe that Syria, an agricultural and industrial area thickly peopled with sedentary classes, is sufficiently advanced politically to manage her own internal affairs. We feel also that foreign technical advice and help will be a most valuable factor in our national growth. We are willing to pay for this help in cash; we cannot sacrifice for it any part of the freedom we have just won for ourselves by force of arms.

...The world wishes to exploit Mesopotamia rapidly, and we therefore believe that the system of government there will have to be buttressed by the men and material resources of a great foreign Power. We ask, however, that the Government be Arab, in principle and spirit, the selective rather than the elective principle being necessarily followed in the neglected districts, until time makes the broader basis possible....

In Palestine the enormous majority of the people are Arabs. The Jews are very close to the Arabs in blood, and there is no conflict of character between the two races. In principles we are absolutely at one. Nevertheless, the Arabs cannot risk assuming the responsibility of holding level the scales in the clash of races and religions that have, in this one province, so often involved the world in difficulties. They would wish for the effective super-position of a great trustee, so long as a representative local administration commended itself by actively promoting the material prosperity of the country....

In our opinion, if our independence be conceded and our local competence established, the natural influences of race, language, and interest will soon draw us together into one people; but for this the Great Powers will have to ensure us open internal frontiers, common railways and telegraphs, and uniform systems of education. To achieve this they must lay aside the thought of individual profits, and of their old jealousies. In a word, we ask you not to force your whole civilisation upon us, but to help us to pick out what serves us from your experience. In return we can offer you little but gratitude.

QUESTIONS

1. How does Prince Faisal assess the prospects for unity among the diverse Arab peoples of Asia?

2. What role does Prince Faisal envision for the Western powers in Arab Asia?

Source: Encounters: Prince Faisal at the Peace Conference from J.C. Hurewitz, *Diplomacy in the Near and Middle East: A Documentary Record: 1914–1956*. D. Van Nostrand, 1956; reprinted by Archive Editions, UK, 1987.

---

their international stature. Each was seeking to restore full sovereignty in the face of increasing Western influence. China sent 200,000 people to work in France to help ease France's wartime labor shortage.

At the peace conference, spokesmen for the non-Western world tended to be moderate in their demands. And prodded by Wilson, the peacemakers made some concessions. German colonies and Ottoman territories were not simply taken over by the victors, in the old-fashioned way, but were placed under the authority of the League. The League then assigned them as mandates to one of the victorious powers, which was to report to the League annually on conditions in the area in question. Classes of mandates varied, based on how prepared for sovereignty the area was judged to be. In devising this system, the Western powers formally recognized, for the first time, that non-Western peoples under Western control had rights of their own and, in principle, were progressing toward independence.

Still, the mandate approach to the colonial question was a halting departure at best. Although Britain granted considerable sovereignty to Iraq in 1932, the victorious powers generally operated

Map Legend:

- Ottoman Empire in 1914
- British protectorate in 1914
- Area controlled under mandates from the League of Nations, 1920
- British Mandate
- French Mandate
- International boundaries, 1923

0   150   300 Km.
0   150   300 Mi.

🌐 **Map 25.4—The European Peace Settlement and the Middle East**

In light of the peace settlement, the end of Ottoman rule in the Middle East meant new roles for European powers, not independence for the peoples of the region. As had been envisioned with the Sykes-Picot Agreement of 1916, the British and French dominated the Middle East, although the new League of Nations mandate system was a departure from the earlier imperialism.

The Covenant of the League of Nations

In its very first part, before treating defeated Germany, the Treaty of Versailles established a new "League of Nations," outlining its aims and procedures as well as the obligations of its members. With this bold experiment, the war's victors sought to organize international relations on a radically new basis. The League's overriding aim was to settle international disputes without resort to war. But the League was also to fulfill an international responsibility, newly recognized here, for the gradual departure from colonialism. Although it instilled great hope at first, the League's inability to prevent aggression and war became clear during the 1930s. Even so, its failure prompted a still more determined effort to order international affairs with the creation of the United Nations in the aftermath of World War II.

The High Contracting Parties,

In order to promote international co-operation and to achieve international peace and security by the acceptance of obligations not to resort to war, by the prescription of open, just and honourable relations between nations, by the firm establishment of the understandings of international law as the actual rule of conduct among Governments, and by the maintenance of justice and a scrupulous respect for all treaty obligations in the dealings of organised peoples with one another,

Agree to this Covenant of the League of Nations. . . .

Article 12.

The Members of the League agree that if there should arise between them any dispute likely to lead to a rupture, they will submit the matter either to arbitration or to inquiry by the Council, and they agree in no case to resort to war until three months after the award by the arbitrators or the report by the Council. . . .

Article 16.

Should any Member of the League resort to war in disregard of its covenants under Articles 12, 13, or 15, it shall *ipso facto* be deemed to have committed an act of war against all other Members of the League, which hereby undertake immediately to subject it to the severance of all trade or financial relations, the prohibition of all intercourse between their nations and the nationals of the covenant-breaking State, and the prevention of all financial, commercial, or personal intercourse between the nationals of the covenant-breaking State and the nationals of any other State, whether a Member of the League or not. . . .

Article 22.

To those colonies and territories which as a consequence of the late war have ceased to be under the sovereignty of the States which formerly governed them and which are inhabited by peoples not yet able to stand by themselves under the strenuous conditions of the modern world, there should be applied the principle that the well-being and development of such peoples form a sacred trust of civilisation and that securities for the performance of this trust should be embodied in this Covenant.

The best method of giving practical effect to this principle is that the tutelage of such peoples should be entrusted to advanced nations who by reason of their resources, their experience or their geographical position can best undertake this responsibility, and who are willing to accept it, and that this tutelage should be exercised by them as Mandatories on behalf of the League.

QUESTIONS

1. How did the League of Nations expect to minimize the resort to war?
2. On what grounds did the League assume responsibility for overseeing the development of the former colonies of the defeated German and Ottoman Empires?

Source: *The Treaties of Peace, 1919–1923*, vol. 1 (New York: The Carnegie Endowment for International Peace, 1924), pp. 10, 14, 17, 19.

as before, assimilating the new territories into their existing systems of colonial possessions. After the hopes for independence raised in the Arab world during the war, this outcome produced a sense of betrayal among Arab leaders (see **Map 25.4**).

The Chinese similarly felt betrayed. Despite China's contributions to the Allied war effort, the victors acquiesced in special rights for Japan in China, causing a renewed sense of humiliation among the Chinese and provoking a boycott of Japanese goods. Although Western leaders were allowing a non-Western power, Japan, access to the imperial club, they were hardly departing from imperialism. For Chinese, Arabs, and others, the West appeared hypocritical. Those whose political consciousness had been raised by the war came to believe not only that colonialism should end, but that the colonial peoples themselves would have to take the lead in ending it.

Would the principal victors have the resolve, and the capacity, to preserve the new order they had established at Paris? Debate over the American role promptly developed in the United States as President Wilson sought Senate ratification of the Versailles treaty, which entailed U.S. membership in the League of Nations, as well as commitments to France and Britain. Wilson's opponents worried that League membership would compromise U.S. sovereignty, but other nations managed to overcome such concerns and join the new organization. American reluctance stemmed especially from the isolationist backlash that was developing against the U.S. intervention in the European war. Late in 1919, at the height of the debate, Wilson suffered a disabling stroke. The Senate then refused to ratify the peace treaty, thereby keeping the United States out of the League of Nations.

American disengagement stemmed partly from doubts about the wisdom of the peace settlement that quickly developed in both Britain and the United States. During the peace conference, a member of the British delegation, the economist John Maynard Keynes (KAINZ) (1883–1946), resigned to write *The Economic Consequences of the Peace* (1920), which helped undermine confidence in the whole settlement. Keynes charged that the shortsighted, vindictive policy of the French, by crippling Germany with a punishing reparations burden, threatened the European economy and thus the long-term peace of Europe. For some, then, the challenge was not to enforce the Versailles treaty but to revise it. This lack of consensus about the legitimacy of the peace made it especially hard to anticipate the longer-term consequences of the war.

The Cultural Impact of the Great War

Coming after a century of relative peace and apparent progress, this long and brutal war ended up shaking Europe's social and cultural foundations. The number of casualties, the advent of terrifying new weapons, and the destruction of famous old monuments—all gave the war an apocalyptic aura that heightened its psychological impact.

The war touched virtually everyone, but it marked for life those who had experienced the nightmare of the trenches. At first, traditional notions of glory, heroism, and patriotic duty combined with images of fellowship and regeneration to enable the soldiers to make a certain sense of their wartime experience. But as the war dragged on, such sentiments gradually eroded, giving way, in many cases, to resignation and cynicism. (See the feature, "The Visual Record: Max Beckmann's *The Night*.") But others, such as the young German soldier and writer Ernst Jünger (1895–1998), lauded

Severini: Armoured Train   In this painting from 1915, the Italian futurist Gino Severini (1883–1966) conveys the hard, steel-like imagery and the sense of disciplined modern efficiency that became associated with war, making it attractive to some young Europeans. (© 2006 Artist's Rights Society (ARS), New York/ADAGP, Paris. Richard S. Zeisler Collection, New York/ The Bridgeman Art Library)

Max Beckmann's *The Night*

"One of the most disagreeable images which the art of our century has to show," wrote the noted art historian and critic John Russell in 1981 of the painting we see here.* Max Beckmann (1884–1950) painted *The Night* during 1918–1919, as Germany was suffering military defeat, experiencing political turmoil, and encountering extreme economic hardship. And surely this unprecedented and disturbing image reflects that difficult combination of circumstances. But what are the sources of the imagery we see here, and what does this painting tell us about the war's cultural impact?

The young Beckmann established himself as an innovative painter before the war, working partly within the idiom of German expressionism. Emerging as a formal movement in 1905, expressionism became the major German contribution to the avant-garde in the visual arts. Expressionists like Ernst Ludwig Kirchner, Ernst Haeckel, and Franz Marc used unnatural colors and deformed natural appearance to convey emotion and to provoke a psychological response in the viewer. In much of their work, they sought an appropriately innovative response to the uncanniness, even the menace, of modern life—and especially the modern urban world, at once enticing and threatening.

Like so many of the educated youth of his generation, Beckmann initially welcomed the war as a source of renewal. Indeed, he was especially fascinated with its potentially cataclysmic effects, in light of his quasi-Nietzschean faith in the scope for a more intense form of life through struggle and suffering. After volunteering for service in the fall of 1914, he was assigned to the German medical corps. Working in a field hospital on the western front in 1915, Beckmann still found something grandly apocalyptic in the death, the suffering, the wounded bodies. Indeed, he welcomed the chance to observe all that up close; it inspired notes and sketches to be used as material for his art. At the same time, he began to envision conveying his ideas through images recalling the scourging of Christ.

But Beckmann's beliefs were being shaken, and his drawings during 1915 depicted suffering, pain, and death with ever greater intensity. That summer, he suffered a nervous breakdown and was sent back to Germany to recuperate. In 1917, he was finally discharged from the army as unfit for further service.

Beckmann turned back to painting in an effort to convey his increasingly disillusioning experience of the war. Like many expressionist artists, he had been influenced by late Gothic German painting, and *The Night* uses certain formal elements from that earlier tradition. Note especially the color—pure but thin, even sour—and the space—shallow and confined, with the figures almost piled atop one another. Beckmann also adapted the religious themes of German Gothic—not, however, as a believer. Rather, he valued their familiarity, as images of suffering, combined with suggestions of cruelty and guilt. Such familiar images seemed to offer the means to create the new, utterly unfamiliar imagery that, Beckmann felt, was necessary to convey what human beings had come to feel as a result of the war and its aftermath.

Here is how Beckmann put it at the end of 1918, precisely as he was working on *The Night:*

> The stronger my determination grows to grasp the unutterable things of this world, the deeper and more powerful the emotion burning inside me about our existence, the tighter I keep my mouth shut and the harder I try to capture the terrible, thrilling monster of life's vitality and to confine it, to beat it down and to strangle it with crystal-clear, razor-sharp lines and planes. . . . We must be a part of all the misery which is coming. We have to surrender our heart and our nerves, we must abandon ourselves to the horrible cries of pain of a poor deluded people.[†]

On the immediate level, *The Night* conveys a scene of violence, torture, and suffering, for three of the figures have apparently broken into a family's home (complete with dog and phonograph) in order to torture, rape, and perhaps kidnap or murder. Yet, the complex interplay between the figures suggests that we cannot easily distinguish perpetrators from victims.

The suffering figure on the left seems to be Beckmann himself, in the pose of the suffering Christ, yet his bandaged torturer may suggest the wounded to whom Beckmann had earlier ministered on the battlefield. In performing his medical duties, he had become haunted with the ambiguity between causing and relieving suffering, especially, perhaps, because he had initially observed the suffering of the wounded with the combination of voyeuristic excitement and clinical detachment we noted earlier. His initial attitude had been symptomatic of the somewhat cavalier attitude with which so many of the educated of his generation had gone off to war.

Another of the torturers is patterned after a blind figure in a fourteenth-century Italian fresco—yet is also made to look like Lenin and/or a contemporary German worker. With bourgeois and proletarian seemingly both implicated in gratuitous violence, there seems no scope for political redemption. Yet neither is the family's home a safe refuge

the war as the catalyst for a welcome new era of steel, hardness, discipline, organization, and machine precision.

Beginning in the late 1920s, a wave of writings about the war appeared. Many were memoirs, such as *Goodbye to All That* by the English writer Robert Graves (1895–1985) and *Testament of Youth* by Vera Brittain (1893–1970), who had served as a British army nurse at the front. But the

Beckmann: The Night (© 2006 Artist's Rights Society (ARS), New York/VG Bild-Kunst, Bonn. Erich Lessing/Art Resource, NY)

from the violence of politics and war. We all seem to be at once perpetrators and victims, caught in a claustrophobic space, with no place to escape, and little if any scope for action. We are even a hell unto ourselves.

Through this combination of images suggesting suffering and guilt, but seemingly precluding any hope of redemption, "Beckmann achieves," as Reinhard Spieler has put it, "a form which transcends commentary on his own time: the corruption and cruelty of postwar society is raised to a general and timeless level of human experience, to eternal night, to humanity's hell on earth." [†]

The Night conveys not simply the disarray of a moment—the German experience of defeat and revolutionary violence—but a changed sensibility; in the wake of World War I, the world could never be the same. Although he was determined to avoid sentimentality or collective self-pity, Beckmann still thought that we might hope, through art, to come to terms with all that recent historical experience had revealed. But it had come to seem that

we could do so only through "one of the most disagreeable images" in modern art.

QUESTIONS

1. Why does Beckmann place this combination of interconnected figures in such a shallow, confined space?

2. What relationship between the private domestic sphere and the public political sphere does Beckmann seem to be depicting in *The Night?*

---

[*] John Russell, *The Meanings of Modern Art* (New York: Harper & Row, 1981), p. 95.

[†] Max Beckmann, "Creative Credo," in *Art in Theory, 1900–1990: An Anthology of Changing Ideas*, edited by Charles Harrison and Paul Wood (Oxford: Blackwell, 1993), pp. 267–268.

[‡] Reinhard Spieler, *Max Beckmann, 1884–1950: The Path to Myth* (Cologne: Taschen, 1995), p. 38.

most famous retrospective was the novel *All Quiet on the Western Front* (1929) by the German Erich Maria Remarque (1898–1970); it sold 2.5 million copies in twenty-five languages in its first eighteen months in print. Remarque provided a gripping portrait of the experience of ordinary soldiers on the western front, but his book also reflected the disillusionment that had come to surround the memory of the war by the late 1920s. Not only were many dead or maimed for

SECTION SUMMARY

- Although Germany suffered the highest number of wartime casualties, France's losses in proportional terms were 15 percent higher—and twice as high as Britain's.

- The breakup of the Habsburg and Ottoman Empires, together with the defeat of Russia and Germany, raised hopes for self-determination among formerly subject peoples, but also complicated the challenges of peacemaking.

- The peace settlement represented an awkward compromise between Wilson's idealistic principles and Clemenceau's hardheaded concern for long-term French interests.

- The harsh peace terms imposed on Germany not only inflamed German opinion, but also seemed counterproductive to many elsewhere, thereby compromising the moral force of the peace settlement.

- Britain and France divided the Arab parts of the former Ottoman Empire according to the secret Sykes-Picot Agreement of 1916.

life, but all the sacrifices seemed to have been largely in vain, a sentiment that fueled determination to avoid another war in the future.

What followed from the war, most fundamentally, was a new sense that Western civilization was neither as secure nor as superior as it had seemed. The celebrated French poet Paul Valéry (1871–1945), speaking at Oxford shortly after the war, observed that "we modern civilizations have learned to recognize that we are mortal like the others. We had heard … of whole worlds vanished, of empires foundered. … Elam, Nineveh, Babylon were vague and splendid names; the total ruin of these worlds, for us, meant as little as did their existence. But France, England, Russia … these names, too, are splendid. … And now we see that the abyss of history is deep enough to bury all the world. We feel that a civilization is as fragile as a life."[6] Valéry went on to warn that the coming transition to peace would be even more difficult and disorienting than the war itself. So traumatic might be the convulsion that Europe might lose its leadership and be shown up for what it was in fact—a small corner of the world, a mere cape on the Asiatic landmass. Astounding words for a European, yet even Valéry, for all his foresight, could not anticipate what Europe would experience in the decades to follow.

CHAPTER SUMMARY

The war that began in August 1914 was supposed to be over in a few months, but after the French held at the first Battle of the Marne in September, it bogged down in a stalemate on the western front, thanks partly to the unforeseen effectiveness of defensive trenches. The massive assaults of 1916–1917 yielded horrifying numbers of casualties—but not the intended breakthrough for either side.

FOCUS QUESTIONS

- How and why had the course of the war by 1917 defied the expectations that had surrounded the beginning of fighting in August 1914?

- Why did this prove a total war, making necessary new forms of socio economic coordination and even systematic propaganda?

- Why did the first revolution in Russia pave the way for a second, spearheaded by the Bolsheviks?

- Why did Germany and its allies end up losing the war even after forcing Russia to make a separate peace by early 1918?

- What factors shaped the peace settlement that the victors imposed on Germany and its allies in 1919–1920?

Because it was so much longer and more difficult than expected, this first "world war" proved a total war, calling forth new forms of socioeconomic coordination and even systematic propaganda. Partly as a result, the war accelerated processes, from economic coordination to technological development to women's suffrage, that many found progressive.

But the war also caused cracks in the old order, first and most dramatically in Russia, where war-weariness led to a revolution overthrowing the tsarist regime early in 1917. Although this was not a socialist revolution, it paved the way by the end of 1917 to a second revolution, spearheaded by the Bolsheviks, who represented the more extreme wing of Russian Marxism. Although their own tactical prowess was also a factor, they were able to seize the initiative especially because of the mistakes of the provisional government, which kept Russia in the war and balked at systematic land reform. In taking power, the Bolsheviks were seeking not simply to control Russia, but to spark the wider revolution they believed essential if a viable new socialist order was to be created.

Although war-weariness on both sides prompted calls for a white peace by 1917, the defection of revolutionary Russia and the intervention of the United States dramatically altered the lineup—and even the potential meaning of the war. In 1918, Germany mounted a last-ditch offensive in the west that came close to succeeding. But France had toughened under Georges Clemenceau, and by that point, a lack of food, provisions, and manpower was fatally weakening the German effort. U.S. intervention gave the anti-German coalition the long-term advantage in any case. Although it entailed far more sacrifice than anyone had expected at the outset, the war reached a definitive outcome with the defeat of Germany and its allies by November 1918.

Conflicting aspirations among the victors led to an awkward peace settlement. Whereas Woodrow Wilson envisioned a new era in world affairs, based on national self-determination and a new League of Nations, Clemenceau was concerned to cement French superiority on the European continent in the face of Germany's greater long-term demographic, economic, and military potential. Such security considerations even compromised the principle of self-determination at the peace conference. But the harshness of the Treaty of Versailles, which produced much resentment even outside Germany, led some observers to doubt the peace could last for long.

KEY TERMS

Sacred Union   (p. 696)

British blockade   (p. 701)

total war   (p. 703)

Kriegsrohstoffabteilung (KRA)   (p. 703)

Petrograd Soviet   (p. 706)

provisional government (p. 706)

Vladimir Lenin   (p. 707)

Fourteen Points   (p. 709)

Treaty of Brest-Litovsk (p. 710)

"stab in the back" myth (p. 712)

Treaty of Versailles   (p. 715)

League of Nations   (p. 717)

 This icon will direct you to additional materials on the website: www .cengage.com/history/ noble/westciv6e.

NOTES

1. The remarks of Raymond Joubert, as quoted in John Ellis, *Eye-Deep in Hell: Trench Warfare in World War I* (Baltimore: Johns Hopkins University Press, 1989), p. 104.

2. Brian Bond, *War and Society in Europe, 1870–1970* (New York: Oxford University Press, 1986), p. 114.

3. A. N. Potresov, quoted in Richard Pipes, *The Russian Revolution* (New York: Random House, Vintage, 1991), p. 348.

4. Both statements are quoted in Koppel S. Pinson, *Modern Germany: Its History and Civilization*, 2d ed. (New York: Macmillan, 1966), p. 337.

5. Quoted in Walter Arnstein, *Britain Yesterday and Today: 1830 to the Present*, 6th ed. (Lexington, Mass.: D. C. Heath, 1992), p. 266.

6. Paul Valéry, *Variety*, 1st series (New York: Harcourt, Brace, 1938), pp. 3–4.

See our interactive ebook for map and primary source activities.

CHAPTER OUTLINE

Kees van Dongen: Au cabaret nègre (detail)

(© Artist's Rights Society (ARS), New York. Au Cabaret Negre, 1925 (oil on canvas), Dongen, Kees van (1877–1968)/
Private Collection/© DACS/Photo © Christie's Images/The Bridgeman Art Library)

The Illusion of Stability, 1919–1930

In 1925, Josephine Baker (1906–1975), a black entertainer from St. Louis, moved from the chorus lines of New York to the music halls of Paris, where she quickly became a singing and dancing sensation. Also a favorite in Germany, she was the most famous of the African American entertainers who took the cultural capitals of Europe by storm during the 1920s. After the disillusioning experience of war, many Europeans found a valuable infusion of vitality in Baker's jazz music, exotic costumes, and "savage," uninhibited dancing (see the poster on page 741).

The European attraction to African Americans as primitive, vital, and sensual reflected a good deal of racial stereotyping, but there really *was* something fresh and uninhibited about American culture, especially its African American variant. And even as they played to those stereotypes, black performers like Baker had great fun ironically subverting them. Many realized they could enjoy opportunities in parts of Europe that were still denied them in the United States. Baker herself was a woman of great sophistication who became a French citizen in 1937, participated in progressive causes, and was decorated for her secret intelligence work in the anti-Nazi resistance during World War II.

The prominence of African Americans in European popular culture was part of a wider infatuation with things American as Europeans embraced the new during the 1920s. Lacking the cultural baggage of Europe, America seemed to offer revitalization and modernity at the same time. With so many old conventions shattered by the war, the ideal of being "modern" became widespread among Europeans, affecting everything from sex education to furniture design. "Modern" meant no-nonsense efficiency, mass production, and a vital popular culture, expressed in jazz, movies, sport, and even advertising. (See the feature, "The Visual Record: Advertising" on pages 742–743.)

But Europeans themselves had pioneered modernism in many areas of the arts and sciences, and innovation continued after the war. Paris held its own as an international cultural center, hosting a decorative arts exhibition in 1925 that produced art deco, the sleek, "modernistic" style that helped give the decade its distinctive flavor. And in the unsettled conditions of postwar Germany, Berlin emerged to rival Paris for cultural leadership during what Germans called "the Golden Twenties."

Still, there was something dizzying, even unnerving, about the eager embrace of the new during the 1920s. The war had accelerated the long-term modernization process toward large industries, cities, and bureaucracies, and toward mass politics, society, and culture. That process was positive, even liberating, in certain respects, but it was also disruptive and disturbing. Some Europeans viewed the vogue of black American entertainers as a symptom of decadence that would further undermine the best of European civilization.

FOCUS QUESTIONS

- How did the differing priorities of Britain and France affect international relations during the 1920s?

- In what ways did the advent of communism and fascism seem to expand the range of political possibilities after World War I?

- Why, and on what basis, did sexuality, gender roles, and the "new woman" provoke so much concern during the 1920s?

- What factors made the future of the new German democracy so uncertain during the 1920s?

- How did cultural and intellectual leaders differ over the place of "tradition" as they sought to suggest how to come to terms with the new situation of the 1920s?

This icon will direct you to additional materials on the website: www .cengage.com/history/ noble/westciv6e.

See our interactive eBook for map and primary source activities.

In this sense, the postwar sense of release and excitement combined with an anxious longing for stability, for a return to order. Even in embracing the new, many were seeking a new basis for order and security.

Although the immediate disruptions of wartime carried over to 1923, a more hopeful era of relative prosperity and international conciliation followed, continuing until 1929. But there was much that called into question the ideal of a "world safe for democracy" that had surrounded the end of the war. Revolutionary Russia remained an uncertain force, even as it began seeking to build socialism on its own. In Italy, the democracy that had emerged in the nineteenth century gave way to the first regime to call itself fascist, and some of the new democracies in east-central Europe did not survive the decade. The postwar efforts at economic restabilization, apparently successful for a while, masked growing strains in the international economy. In one sphere after another, postwar restabilization was fragile—and could quickly unravel.

THE WEST AND THE WORLD AFTER THE GREAT WAR

How did the differing priorities of Britain and France affect international relations during the 1920s?

The war and the peace had weakened—and to some extent discredited—the European powers, who now found themselves saddled with foreign debts and unbalanced economies. Though the United States pulled back from a direct political role in Europe in 1919, it became far more active in world affairs, helping to engineer major conferences on arms limitation and international economic relations during the 1920s. But in crucial respects, the shape of the postwar international order still depended on Europeans. And colonial concerns continued to affect the balance of power in Europe, where it fell to the two major victors in the war, France and Britain, to enforce the controversial peace settlement.

The Erosion of European Power

Emerging from the war as the principal power in East Asia was a non-Western country, Japan, whose claims to the German bases in the region and to special rights in China were formally recognized at the Paris Peace Conference. With the Washington treaty of 1922, Japan won naval parity with Britain and the United States in East Asia. The Western nations were recognizing Japan as a peer, a great power—even a threat. Aspects of the Washington agreements were intended to block Japanese expansion in East Asia. If a new international system was to emerge, it would not be centered in Europe to the extent the old one had been.

As the old Europe lost prestige, President Wilson's ideals of self-determination and democracy were greeted enthusiastically outside the West—in China, for example. At the same time, the Russian revolutionary model appealed to those in the colonial world seeking to understand the mainsprings of Western imperialism—and the means of overcoming it. To some Chinese intellectuals by the early 1920s, Leninism was attractive because it showed the scope for mass mobilization by a revolutionary vanguard.

By the 1920s, a generation of anticolonialist, nationalist intellectuals was emerging to lead the non-Western world. Some were more radical than others, but most agreed that the challenge was to learn from the West and to modernize, but without simply copying the West and losing distinctive cultural identities. It was imperative to sift through tradition, determining what needed to be changed and what was worth preserving. The pioneering Chinese nationalist Sun Yixien (Sun Yat-sen, 1866–1925) was typical in recognizing the need to adopt the science and technology of the West. But China, he insisted, could do so in its own way, without sacrificing its unique cultural and political traditions. (See the feature, "The Global Record: Sun Yixien on Chinese Nationalism.")

As the greatest imperial power, Britain was especially vulnerable to the growing anticolonial sentiment. The struggle to hang on to its empire drew British energies away from the problems of Europe after the peace settlement.

In light of the strong Indian support for the British war effort, the British government promised in 1917 to extend the scope for Indian involvement in the colonial administration in India. Growing expectations as the war was ending provoked episodes of violence against the British, whose troops retaliated brutally in April 1919, firing indiscriminately into an unarmed crowd. This Amritsar Massacre helped galvanize India's independence movement, even though the British, seeking conciliation in the aftermath, extended self-rule by entrusting certain government services to Indians. Another milestone was reached in 1921, when Mohandas Gandhi, the British-educated leader of the Indian independence movement, shed his European clothes in favor of simple Indian attire. But it was on the basis of Western egalitarianism, not some indigenous value, that Gandhi demanded political rights for the "untouchables," the lowest group in India's long-standing caste system. (See the feature, "The Global Record: Gandhi Advocates Nonviolence" on page 760 in Chapter 27.)

In Egypt, a full-scale anti-British insurrection broke out in 1919. After British troops suppressed the rebellion, British authorities offered to grant moderate concessions, as in India. But Egyptian nationalists demanded independence, which was finally granted in 1922. Egypt gradually evolved into a constitutional monarchy, with representative government and universal suffrage. But Britain retained a predominant influence in Egypt until the nationalist revolution of 1952 (see page 837–838).

At the same time, nationalism was growing among West Africans who had studied in England. In March 1919, Western-educated Africans in the Gold Coast asked the British governor to establish representative institutions so that Africans could at least be consulted about governmental affairs. The West African National Congress, formed in 1920, made similar demands. The British agreed to new constitutions for Nigeria in 1923 and the Gold Coast in 1925 that took significant steps in that direction. They also agreed to build more schools, though they tended to promote practical education, including African languages and agriculture, whereas African leaders wanted students to learn the Western classics that "made gentlemen." Such conflicting priorities indicate the complexities in the relationships between colonial rulers and the emerging elites among the colonized peoples.

CHRONOLOGY

March 1919	Founding of the Italian fascist movement
November 1920	Russian civil war ends
March 1921	New Economic Policy announced at Russian Communist Party congress
October 1922	Mussolini becomes Italian prime minister
January 1923	French-led occupation of the Ruhr
November 1923	Peak of inflation in Germany
January 1924	First Labour government in Britain
	Death of Lenin
August 1924	Acceptance of the Dawes Plan on German reparations
October 1925	Treaty of Locarno
May 1926	Pilsudski's coup d'état in Poland
	Beginning of general strike in Britain
May 1927	Lindbergh completes first transatlantic solo flight
January 1929	Stalin forces banishment of Trotsky from Soviet Union
April 1929	Soviets adopt first economic Five-Year Plan
August 1929	Acceptance of the Young Plan on German reparations
October 1929	Death of Stresemann

Enforcing the Versailles Settlement

It was up to France and Britain to make sure the new international order worked, but it was not clear that either had the will and resources to do so. Cooperation between them was essential, yet sometimes their differences—in geography, in values, and in perceptions—seemed to doom them to work at cross-purposes.

France was the dominant power on the European continent after World War I, and until well into the 1930s, it boasted the strongest army in the world. Yet even in the early 1920s, a sense of artificiality surrounded France's image of strength. Thus, the shrillness and the defensiveness that came to mark French thinking and French policy.

In light of Germany's larger population and stronger industrial base, France's long-term security seemed to require certain measures to tip the scales in its favor. By imposing German disarmament and the demilitarization of the Rhineland, the Versailles treaty gave France immediate military advantages. Yet how long could these measures be maintained, once the passions of war had died down and Germany no longer seemed such a threat? France had hoped for British help in enforcing the treaty, but Britain was pulling back from the Continent to concentrate on its empire, just as it had after other major European wars.

Reinforcing Imperialist Rule In response to episodes of anticolonialist violence in Amritsar, India, early in 1919, the British brutally cracked down, most notably in the massacre of April 1919. Here British authorities enforce a decree in the wake of the beating of a female British doctor on this road—forcing any Indian using the road to crawl along it. (Courtesy of the National Army Museum, London)

In particular, the British wanted to avoid getting dragged into the uncertain situation in east-central Europe, where its own national interests did not seem to be at stake. Yet the French, to replace their earlier link with Russia, promptly developed an alliance system with several of the new or expanded states of the region, including Poland, Czechoslovakia, Romania, and Yugoslavia. France's ties to east-central Europe made the British especially wary of binding agreements with the French.

At first, France felt confident enough to take strong steps even without British support. In response to German foot-dragging in paying reparations, Prime Minister Raymond Poincaré decided to get tough in January 1923. Declaring the Germans in default, he sent French troops at the head of an international force to occupy the Ruhr industrial area and force German compliance. But the move backfired. The Germans adopted a policy of passive resistance in response, and the costs of the occupation more than offset the increase in reparations that France received.

British leaders viewed French policy as unnecessarily vindictive and bellicose, and they increasingly saw the Versailles treaty as counterproductive. Instead, they placed great store in the League of Nations and in the international arms reduction effort gaining momentum by the later 1920s. From 1923 on, France gradually lost the advantages it had gained by defeating Germany, and self-confidence gave way to defensiveness and resignation.

The defensive mentality found physical embodiment in the **Maginot Line**, a system of fortifications on France's eastern border. Remembering the defensive warfare of World War I and determined to preclude the sort of invasion France had suffered in 1914, the military convinced

Maginot Line A 200-mile system of elaborate permanent fortifications on France's eastern border, named for war minister André Maginot and built primarily during the 1930s. It was a defense against German frontal assault; in 1940, the Germans invaded by flanking the line.

Sun Yixien on Chinese Nationalism

Sun Yixien (Sun Yat-sen), widely regarded as the father of modern China, founded the Guomindang (Kuomintang), the Chinese nationalist movement, in 1912. Educated by Western missionaries in China, he lived in the United States for extended periods and came to admire the West in important respects. But he insisted that China, to make the best use of what the West offered, had to reconnect with its own unique traditions. Variations on this argument would be heard for decades as the rest of the world sought to come to terms with the seemingly more advanced West. The following passages are from an influential series of lectures that Sun Yixien presented in China in the early 1920s.

What is the standing of our nation in the world? In comparison with other nations we have the greatest population and the oldest culture, of four thousand years' duration. We ought to be advancing in line with the nations of Europe and America. But the Chinese people have only family and clan groups; there is no national spirit. Consequently, in spite of four hundred million people gathered together in one China, we are in fact but a sheet of loose sand. We are the poorest and weakest state in the world, occupying the lowest position in international affairs; the rest of mankind is the carving knife and the serving dish, while we are the fish and the meat. Our position now is extremely perilous; if we do not earnestly promote nationalism and weld together our four hundred millions into a strong nation, we face a tragedy—the loss of our country and the destruction of our race. To ward off this danger, we must espouse nationalism and employ the national spirit to save the country. . . .

But even if we succeed in reviving our ancient morality, learning, and powers, we will still not be able, in this modern world, to advance China to a first place among the nations. . . . [W]e will still need to learn the strong points of Europe and America before we can progress at an equal rate with them. Unless we do study the best from foreign countries, we will go backward. With our own fine foundation of

knowledge and our age-long culture, with our own native intelligence besides, we should be able to acquire all the best things from abroad. The strongest point of the West is its science. . . .

As soon as we learn Western machinery we can use it anytime, anywhere; electric lights, for example, can be installed and used in any kind of Chinese house. But Western social customs and sentiments are different from ours in innumerable points; if, without regard to customs and popular feelings in China, we try to apply Western methods of social control as we would Western machinery—in a hard and fast way—we shall be making a serious mistake. . . .

. . . For the governmental machinery of the United States and France still has many defects, and does not satisfy the desires of the people nor give them a complete measure of happiness. So we in our proposed reconstruction must not think that if we imitate the West of today we shall reach the last stage of progress and be perfectly contented. . . .

Only in recent times has Western culture advanced beyond ours, and the passion for this new civilization has stimulated our revolution. Now that the revolution is a reality, we naturally desire to see China excel the West and build up the newest and most progressive state in the world. We certainly possess the qualifications necessary to reach this ideal, but we must not merely imitate the democratic systems of the West.

QUESTIONS

1. Why does Sun Yixien think China, despite its ancient and sophisticated culture, has fallen behind the West?

2. On what grounds does Sun Yixien consider it necessary for China to study Western culture, as opposed to relying on its own traditions?

Source: Sun Yixien on Chinese Nationalism from Sun Yat-sen, *San Min Chu I: The Three Principles of the People* (Taipei, Taiwan: China Cultural Service, 1953).

French political leaders to adopt a defensive strategy based on a line of forts. Construction began in 1929, and the Maginot (MAH-zhih-noh) system reached preliminary completion in 1935, when it extended along France's border with Germany from Switzerland to the border with Belgium.

This defensive system was not consistent with the other major strands of French policy, especially its alliances with states in east-central Europe. If France emphasized defense behind an impregnable system of forts, what good were French security guarantees to such new allies as Poland and Czechoslovakia?

Still, the situation remained fluid during the 1920s. In France, as in Britain, national elections in 1924 produced a victory for the moderate left, ending a period of conservative nationalist dominance since the war. In each country, international relations became a major issue in the elections, and the outcome heralded a more conciliatory tack, especially in relations with Germany.

SECTION SUMMARY

- Although the prewar European colonial system remained largely in place after the war, Wilsonian ideals of self-determination spurred anticolonial sentiment in the colonized world.

- On the basis of their study in the West, intellectuals from Europe's colonies sought to combine Western values with indigenous traditions as they began spearheading the anticolonial struggle.

- More vulnerable geographically, France was initially more determined than Britain to keep Germany limited by strictly enforcing the Versailles settlement.

- France's confident, even aggressive, posture gradually gave way to the defensiveness of the "Maginot mentality," evident in the decision to build a series of defensive fortifications.

COMMUNISM, FASCISM, AND THE NEW POLITICAL SPECTRUM

In what ways did the advent of communism and fascism seem to expand the range of political possibilities after World War I?

I n making their revolution in 1917, the Russian Bolsheviks had expected to spark wider revolution. Hopes—and fears—that the revolution would spread were palpable in the immediate postwar period. Although the Russian Communists initially enjoyed extraordinary prestige on the European left, some Marxists grew skeptical or hostile as the nature of Leninist communism became clearer. The Russian model eventually produced a damaging split in international socialism. By the end of the 1920s, revolution elsewhere was nowhere in sight, and it seemed that, for the foreseeable future, the communist regime in Russia would have to go it alone.

By then, a new and unexpected political movement had emerged in Italy, expanding the political spectrum in a different direction. This was the first **fascism**, which brought Benito Mussolini to power in 1922. Emerging directly from the war, Italian fascism was violent and antidemocratic—and thus disturbing to many. Stressing national solidarity and discipline, the fascists were hostile not only to liberal individualism and the parliamentary system, but also to Marxist socialism, with its emphasis on class struggle and the special role of the working class. Claiming to offer a modern alternative to both, Italian fascism quickly attracted the attention of those in other countries who were disillusioned with parliamentary politics and hostile to the Marxist left. The interplay of communism and fascism, as new political experiments, added to the uncertainties of the postwar world.

fascism A violent, antidemocratic movement founded by Benito Mussolini in Italy in 1919. The term is widely used to encompass Hitler's Nazi regime in Germany and other movements stressing disciplined national solidarity and hostile to liberal individualism, the parliamentary system, and Marxist socialism.

Changing Priorities in Communist Russia, 1918–1921

Even after leading the revolution that toppled the provisional government in November 1917, the Bolsheviks could not claim majority support in Russia. When the long-delayed elections to select a constituent assembly were held a few weeks after the revolution, the Socialist Revolutionaries won a clear majority, while the Bolsheviks ended up with fewer than one-quarter of the seats. But the Bolsheviks dispersed the assembly by force when it met in January 1918. And over the next three years, the Communists, as the Bolsheviks renamed themselves, gradually consolidated their power, establishing a centralized and nondemocratic regime. Power lay not with the soviets, nor with some coalition of socialist parties, but solely with the Communist Party.

CIVIL WAR During its first years, the new communist regime encountered a genuine emergency that especially seemed to require such a monopoly of power. During 1918 to 1920, in what became a brutal civil war, the communist "Reds" battled counterrevolutionary "Whites," people who had been dispossessed by the revolution or who had grown disillusioned with the Communist Party. Moreover, foreigners eager to topple the communist regime began to intervene militarily. At the same time, several of the non-Russian nationalities of the old Russian Empire sought to take advantage of the unsettled situation to free themselves from Russian and communist control. Appointed "People's Commissar for War" in April 1918, Leon Trotsky forged a loyal and disciplined Red Army in an effort to master the difficult situation.

A series of thrusts, involving troops from fourteen countries, at one time or another, struck at Russia from a variety of points along its huge border. However, the Whites and the foreign troops never managed a coordinated strategy. By the end of active fighting in November 1920, the communist regime had not only survived but regained most of the territory it had lost early in the civil war (see **MAP 26.1**).

The need to launch the new communist regime in this way, fighting counterrevolutionaries supported by foreign troops, inevitably affected Communists' perceptions and priorities. Separatist sentiment might continue to feed counterrevolutionary efforts, so the new regime exerted careful control over the non-Russian nationalities. Thus, when the Union of Soviet Socialist Republics (USSR) was organized in December 1922, it was only nominally a federation of autonomous republics; strong centralization from the communist regime's new capital in Moscow was the rule from the start.

🌐 **Map 26.1—Foreign Intervention and Civil War in Revolutionary Russia, 1918–1920**

By mid-1918, the new communist regime was under attack from many sides, by both foreign troops and anticommunist Russians. Bolshevik-held territory shrank during 1919, but over the next year, the Red Army managed to regain much of what had been lost and to secure the new communist state. Anton Denikin, Alexander Kolchak, and Nicholas Yudenich commanded the most significant counterrevolutionary forces.

(Source: Adapted from The Times Atlas of World History, 3d ed. Reprinted by permission of HarperCollins Publishers Ltd. © HarperCollins Publishers Ltd.)

Comintern An association founded in March 1919 by the Communists (formerly Bolsheviks) to translate their success in Russia into leadership of the international socialist movement.

In March 1919, while fighting the civil war, the Russian Communists founded the Third, or Communist, International—widely known as the **Comintern**—to make clear their break with the seemingly discredited strategies of the Second International. Through the Comintern, the Russian Communists expected to translate their success in Russia into leadership of the international socialist movement. However, many old-line Marxists refused to admit that the leadership of European socialism had passed to the Communist rulers of backward Russia. As early as 1919, the German Karl Kautsky (1854–1938), who had been the leading spokesman for orthodox Marxism after the death of Friedrich Engels in 1895, harshly criticized Leninist communism as a heretical departure that would lead to despotism and severely damage international socialism.

From its founding in March 1919 until the spring of 1920, the Comintern actively promoted the wider revolution that Lenin had envisioned. Seeking to win mass support, the organization accented leftist solidarity and reached out to the rank and file in the labor unions. By the spring of 1920, however, it seemed clear that further revolution was not imminent, so Comintern leaders began focusing on a more protracted revolutionary struggle.

The Russians felt that poor organization and planning had undermined the wider revolutionary possibility in Europe during 1919 and 1920. The Comintern would cut through all the revolutionary romanticism to show what the Leninist strategy, or communism, meant in fact. The Russians themselves would have to call the shots because what communism meant, above all, was tight organization and discipline.

By early 1921, the Comintern's aggressive claim to leadership had split the international socialist movement, for the Comintern attracted some, but not all, of the members of the existing socialist parties. Those who now called themselves "communists" accepted the Leninist model and affiliated with the Comintern. Those who retained the "socialist" label rejected Comintern leadership; they still claimed to be Marxists but declined to embrace the Bolshevik strategy for taking power.

Late in 1923, the Comintern finally concluded that revolution elsewhere could not be expected any time soon. The immediate enemy was not capitalism or the bourgeoisie, but the socialists, the Communists' rivals for working-class support. The Communists' incessant criticism of the socialists, whom they eventually dubbed "social fascists," demoralized and weakened the European left, especially in the face of the growing threat of fascism by the early 1930s. The schism on the left remained an essential fact of European political life for half a century.

From Lenin to Stalin, 1921–1929

To win the civil war, the communist regime had adopted a policy of "war communism," a rough-and-ready controlled economy in which food and supplies were commandeered for the Red Army. At the beginning of 1921, the economy was in crisis. Industrial production equaled only about one-fifth the 1913 total, workers in key factories went on strike, and peasants were resisting further requisitions of grain. In March 1921, sailors at the Kronstadt naval base near Petrograd mutinied, suffering considerable loss of life as governmental control was reestablished.

New Economic Policy (NEP) A Russian economic liberalization measure aimed at reviving an economy in crisis. The NEP restored considerable scope for private enterprise and allowed peasants to sell some of their harvest.

With the very survival of the revolution in question, Lenin replaced war communism with the **New Economic Policy (NEP)** in March 1921. Although transport, banking, heavy industry, and wholesale commerce remained under state control, the NEP restored considerable scope for private enterprise, especially in agriculture and the retail sector. The economy quickly began to revive, and by 1927, was producing at prewar levels.

But what about the longer term? If revolution elsewhere was not on the immediate horizon, could the Soviet Union—relatively backward economically and scarred by over a decade of upheaval—build a socialist order on its own? Certain measures were obvious: The new regime engineered rapid improvements in literacy, for example. But the Marxist understanding of historical progress required industrialization, and so debate focused on how to promote industrial development under Soviet conditions.

Debate about priorities became intertwined with questions about the leadership of the new regime. Lenin suffered the first of a series of strokes in May 1922 and then died in January 1924, setting off a struggle among his possible successors. Leon Trotsky, an effective organizer and powerful thinker, was by most measures Lenin's heir apparent. Although he favored tighter economic controls to speed industrial development, Trotsky insisted that the top priority should be spreading the revolution to other countries.

Rivals for the Soviet Leadership   In July 1926 in Moscow, Soviet leaders carry the coffin of Feliks Dzerzhinsky, the first head of the secret police. Among them are Trotsky *(with glasses, center left)*, Stalin *(right foreground)*, and Bukharin *(with mustache, at far right)*, rivals for the Soviet leadership after Lenin's death. The winner, Stalin, would eventually have his two competitors killed.   (David King Collection)

In contrast, Nikolai Bukharin (1888–1938) wanted to concentrate on the gradual development of the Soviet Union, based on a more open and conciliatory strategy. Rather than tightening controls to squeeze a surplus from agricultural producers, the government should promote purchasing power by allowing producers to profit. By the time of his death, Lenin had apparently begun thinking along the same lines. And he had come to have considerable misgivings about the man who would win this struggle to direct the fragile new Soviet regime, **Joseph Stalin** (1879–1953).

Stalin was born Josef Djugashvili into a lower-class family in Georgia, in the Caucasus region. As an ethnic Georgian, he did not learn to speak Russian until he was 11 years old. From the position of party secretary, which he had assumed in 1922, Stalin established his control within the Soviet system by 1929. Though he lacked Trotsky's charisma and knew little of economics, he was highly intelligent and proved a master of backstage political maneuvering. Stalin first outmaneuvered Trotsky and his allies, removing them from positions of power and forcing Trotsky himself into exile in 1929. Bitterly critical of Stalin to the end, Trotsky was finally murdered by Stalin's agents in Mexico in 1940. Stalin's victory over those like Bukharin was more gradual, but ultimately just as complete. And his victory proved decisive for the fate of Soviet communism.

By the later 1920s, those who believed in the communist experiment were growing disillusioned with the compromises of the NEP. It was time for the Soviet Union to push ahead to a new order, leaving capitalism behind altogether. Even if revolution was not imminent elsewhere, the Soviet Union could show the way by building "socialism in one country." Genuine enthusiasm greeted the regime's turn to centralized economic planning in 1927 and its subsequent adoption of the first Five-Year Plan early in 1929. Central planning led to a program of crash industrialization, favoring heavy industry, by the end of that year. But this new, more radical direction was not fully thought through, and it soon caused incredible suffering.

To buy the necessary plant and equipment, the state seemed to require better control of agricultural output than had been possible under the NEP. The key was to squeeze the agricultural surplus from the peasantry on terms more favorable to the government. By forcing peasants into large, state-controlled collective farms, government leaders could more readily extract the surplus, which would then be sold abroad, earning the money to finance factories, dams, and power plants.

During the 1920s, the possibility of building a new socialist society in the Soviet Union had attracted a number of modernist artists, who assumed that artistic innovation went hand in hand with radical socioeconomic transformation. But in 1929, Soviet officials began mobilizing the

Joseph Stalin   Soviet dictator who jettisoned the New Economic Policy and instituted a program of crash industrialization and agricultural collectivization. He concluded the Nazi-Soviet Pact in 1939 but joined the Allies after the German invasion of the Soviet Union in 1941.

Tatlin: Monument to the Third International   Vladimir Tatlin created this model for a monument to the Third International, or Comintern, during 1919 and 1920. He envisioned a revolving structure of glass and iron; it would be twice as tall as the later Empire State Building. Although the monument was never built, Tatlin's bold, dynamic form symbolizes the utopian aspirations of the early years of the communist experiment in Russia.   (David King Collection)

cultural realm to serve the grandiose task of building socialism in one country. No longer welcoming modernist experiment, they demanded "socialist realism," which portrayed the achievements of the ongoing Soviet revolution in an inspiring, heroic light. Modernism, in contrast, they denounced as decadent and counterrevolutionary.

In retrospect, it is clear that a Stalinist revolution within the Soviet regime had begun by 1930, but where it was to lead was by no means certain—not even to Stalin himself. Still, the Soviet Union was pulling back, going its own way by the end of the 1920s. For the foreseeable future, the presence of a revolutionary regime in the old Russia would apparently be less disruptive for the rest of Europe than it had first appeared.

The Crisis of Liberal Italy and the Creation of Fascism, 1919–1925

Fascism emerged directly from the Italian experience of World War I, which proved especially controversial because the Italians could have avoided it altogether. No one attacked Italy in 1914, and the country could have received significant territorial benefits just by remaining neutral. Yet it seemed to many, including leading intellectuals and educated young people, that Italy could not stand idly by in a European war, especially one involving Austria-Hungary, which still controlled significant Italian-speaking areas. Participation in this major war would be the test of Italy's maturity as a nation. In May 1915, Italy finally intervened on the side of the Triple Entente. The government's decision stemmed not from vague visions of renewal, but from the commitment of tangible territorial gains that France and Britain made to Italy with the secret Treaty of London.

Despite the near collapse of the Italian armies late in 1917, Italy lasted out the war and contributed to the victory over Austria-Hungary. Supporters of the war felt that this success could lead to a thoroughgoing renewal of Italian public life. Yet many Italians had been skeptical of claims for the war from the outset, and the fact that it proved so much more difficult than expected hardly won them over. To socialists, Catholics, and many left-leaning liberals, intervention itself had been a tragic mistake. Thus, despite Italy's participation in the victory, division over the war's significance immensely complicated the postwar Italian political situation.

Skepticism was only confirmed when Italy did not secure all the gains it sought at the Paris Peace Conference. To be sure, the country got most of what it had been promised in the Treaty of London, but appetites increased with the dissolution of the Austro-Hungarian Empire. Many Italians were outraged at what seemed a denigration of the Italian contribution by France, Britain, and the United States. The outcome fanned resentment not only of Italy's allies, but also of the country's political leaders, who seemed too weak to deliver on what they had pledged.

The leaders of Italy's parliamentary democracy also failed to renew the country's political system in light of the war experience. To be sure, in a spirit of democratic reform, Italy adopted proportional representation to replace the old system of small, single-member constituencies in 1919. The new system meant a greater premium on mass parties and party discipline at the expense of the one-to-one bargaining that had characterized the earlier *trasformismo*. But the new multiparty system quickly reached an impasse—partly because of the stance of the Italian Socialist Party.

ITALIAN SOCIALISM   In contrast to the French and German parties, the Italian Socialists had never supported the war, and they did not accept the notion that the war experience could yield political renewal in the aftermath. So rather than reaching out to idealistic but discontented war veterans, Socialist leaders talked of imitating the Bolshevik Revolution. And the Italian situation seemed at least potentially revolutionary during 1919 and 1920, when a wave of strikes culminated in a series of factory occupations. But despite their revolutionary rhetoric, Italy's Socialist leaders did not understand the practical aspects of Leninism and did not carry out the planning and organization that might have produced an Italian revolution.

The established parliamentary system was at an impasse, and the Socialist Party seemed at once too inflexible and too romantic to lead some sort of radical transformation. It was in this context that fascism emerged, claiming to offer a third way. It was bound to oppose the Socialists and the socialist working class because of conflict over the meaning of the war and the kind of transformation Italy needed. And this antisocialist posture made fascism open to exploitation by reactionary interests. By early 1921, landowners in northern and central Italy were footing the bill as bands of young fascists drove around the countryside in trucks, beating up workers and burning down socialist meeting halls. But fascist spokesmen claimed to offer something other than mere reaction—a new politics that all Italians, including the workers, would eventually find superior.

At the same time, important sectors of Italian industry, which had grown rapidly thanks to wartime government orders, looked with apprehension toward the more competitive international economy that loomed after the war. With its relative lack of capital and raw materials, Italy seemed to face an especially difficult situation. Nationalist thinkers and business spokesmen questioned the capacity of the parliamentary system to provide the vigorous leadership that Italy needed. Prone to short-term bickering and partisanship, ordinary politicians seemed to lack the vision to pursue Italy's international economic interests and the will to impose the necessary discipline on the domestic level. Thus, the government's response to the labor unrest of 1919 and 1920 was hesitant and weak.

Postwar Italy, then, witnessed widespread discontent with established forms of politics, but those discontented were socially disparate, and their aims were not entirely compatible. Some had been socialists before the war, others nationalists hostile to socialism. While some envisioned a more intense kind of mass politics, others thought the masses already had too much power. Still, these discontented groups agreed on the need for an alternative to both parliamentary politics and Marxist socialism. And all found the germs of that alternative in the Italian war experience.

Benito Mussolini The founder of fascism is shown with other fascist leaders in 1922, as he becomes prime minister of Italy. Standing at Mussolini's left (*with beard*) is Italo Balbo, later a pioneering aviator and fascist Italy's air force minister. (Bettmann/Corbis)

THE RISE OF MUSSOLINI

Benito Mussolini
Founder of the fascist movement and subsequently dictator within the Italian fascist regime.

The person who seemed able to translate these aspirations into a new political force was **Benito Mussolini** (1883–1945), who had been a prominent socialist journalist before the war. Indeed, he was so talented that he was made editor of the Socialist Party's national newspaper in 1912, when he was only 29 years old. At that point, many saw him as the fresh face needed to revitalize Italian socialism.

His concern with renewal made Mussolini an unorthodox socialist even before 1914, and he was prominent among those on the Italian left who began calling for Italian intervention after the war began. The Italian Socialist Party refused to follow his lead, but through his new newspaper, *Il popolo d'Italia (The People of Italy)*, Mussolini helped rally the disparate groups that advocated Italian participation in the war. He saw military service once Italy intervened, and after the war he seemed a credible spokesman for those who wanted to translate the war experience into a new form of politics. Amid growing political unrest, he founded the fascist movement in March 1919, taking the term *fascism* from the ancient Roman *fasces*, a bundle of rods surrounding an ax carried on state occasions as a symbol of power and unity.

But fascism found little success at first. Even as it gathered force in violent reaction against the socialist labor organizations by 1921, the movement's direction was uncertain. Although young fascist militants wanted to replace the established parliamentary system with a new political order, Mussolini seemed to be using fascism as his personal instrument to achieve power within the existing system. When his maneuvering finally won him the prime minister's post in October 1922, it was not at all clear that a change of regime, or a one-party dictatorship, would follow.

A crisis in 1924 forced Mussolini's hand. In June, the moderate socialist Giacomo Matteotti (mah-tay-OH-tee) rose in parliament to denounce the renewed fascist violence that had accompanied recent national elections. His murder by fascist thugs shortly thereafter produced a great public outcry, though the responsibility of Mussolini and his government was unclear. Many establishment figures who had tolerated Mussolini as the man who could keep order now deserted him as a result of the **Matteotti murder**.

Matteotti murder The 1924 killing by fascist thugs of Italian moderate socialist Giacomo Matteotti; the public outcry following the murder eventually led Mussolini to commit to a more radical direction, which included the creation of a new, fascist form of state.

Mussolini sought at first to be conciliatory, but more radical fascists saw the crisis as an opportunity to end the compromise with the old liberal order and to begin creating a whole new political system. The crisis came to a head on December 31, 1924, when thirty-three militants called on Mussolini to insist that the way out of the crisis was not to delimit the scope of fascism, but to expand it. Mussolini was not an ordinary prime minister, but *Il Duce* (eel DOO-chay), spearheading an ongoing fascist revolution.

A few days later, on January 3, 1925, Mussolini committed himself to this more radical course in a speech to the Chamber of Deputies. Defiantly claiming responsibility for all that had happened, including all the violence, he promised to accelerate the transformation that had begun, he claimed, with his agitation for intervention in 1914.[1] And now began the creation of a new fascist state, although the compromises continued and the direction was never as clear as committed fascists desired.

Innovation and Compromise in Fascist Italy, 1925–1930

Early in 1925, the fascist government began to undermine the existing democratic system by imprisoning or exiling opposition leaders and outlawing nonfascist parties and labor unions. But fascism was not seeking simply a monopoly of political power; the new fascist state was to be totalitarian, all-encompassing, limitless in its reach. Under the liberal system, the fascists charged, the state had been too weak to promote the national interest, and Italian society had been too fragmented to achieve its potential. So Mussolini's regime both expanded the state's sovereignty and mobilized society to create a deeper sense of national identity and shared purpose. New organizations—for youth, for women, for leisure-time activities—were to make possible new forms of public participation.

corporativism, corporative state The system established in fascist Italy beginning in 1926 that sought to involve people in public life not as citizens, but as producers, through their roles in the economy.

The centerpiece of the new fascist state was **corporativism**, which entailed mobilizing people as producers, through organization of the workplace. Groupings based on occupation, or economic function, were gradually to replace parliament as the basis for political participation and decision making. Beginning in 1926, corporativist institutions were established in stages until a Chamber of Fasces and Corporations at last replaced the old Chamber of Deputies in 1939.

Especially through this **corporative state**, the fascists claimed to be fulfilling their grandiose mission and providing the world with a third way, beyond both outmoded democracy and misguided communism. The practice of corporativism never lived up to such rhetoric, but the effort to devise new forms of political participation and decision making was central to fascism's self-understanding and its quest for legitimacy. And that effort attracted much attention abroad, especially with the Great Depression of the 1930s.

Despite the commitment to a new regime, however, fascism continued to compromise with preexisting elites and institutions. The accommodation was especially evident in the arrangements with the Catholic Church that Mussolini worked out in 1929, formally ending the dispute between the church and the Italian state that had festered since national unification in 1870. With the Lateran Pact, Mussolini restored a measure of sovereignty to the Vatican; with the Concordat, he gave the church significant roles in public education and marriage law.

This settlement of an old and thorny dispute afforded Mussolini a good deal of prestige among nonfascists at home and abroad. But compromise with the church displeased many committed fascists, who complained that giving this powerful, autonomous institution a role in Italian public life compromised fascism's totalitarian ideal. Such complaints led to a partial crackdown on Catholic youth organizations in 1931, as Mussolini continued trying to juggle traditionalist compromise and revolutionary pretension.

By the end of the 1920s, then, it remained unclear whether Italian fascism was a form of restoration or a form of revolution. It had restored order in Italy, overcoming the labor unrest of the immediate postwar years, but it was order on a new, antidemocratic basis. Yet the fascists still claimed to be implementing a revolution of their own. Fascism could be violent and disruptive, dictatorial and repressive, but Mussolini's regime seemed dynamic and innovative. Though its ultimate direction remained nebulous, fascism attracted those elsewhere who were discontented with liberal democracy and Marxist socialism. It thus fed the volatility and ideological polarization that marked the European political order after World War I.

> ## SECTION SUMMARY
>
> - The question of whether to affiliate with the new Communist International (Comintern), established by the Russian Communists in 1919, split Marxist socialist parties throughout the world.
>
> - The struggle for the Soviet leadership with the death of Lenin became intertwined with questions about communist priorities in the wake of the New Economic Policy adopted in 1921.
>
> - A Stalinist revolution within the Soviet communist experiment had begun by 1930, but where it would lead was not clear.
>
> - The fascist reaction against both liberalism and socialism reflected deep divisions in Italy over the significance of the Italian war effort.
>
> - Once Mussolini committed himself to a decisively postliberal direction, the fascists fastened upon corporativism as the basis for a new, specifically fascist form of state.

TOWARD MASS SOCIETY

Why, and on what basis, did sexuality, gender roles, and the "new woman" provoke so much concern during the 1920s?

After a few years of wild economic swings just after the war, Europe enjoyed renewed prosperity by the later 1920s. Common involvement in the war had blurred class lines and accelerated the trend toward what contemporaries began to call "mass society." As the new prosperity spread the fruits of industrialization more widely, ordinary people increasingly set the cultural tone, partly through new mass media, such as film and radio. To some, the advent of mass society portended a welcome revitalization of culture and a more authentic kind of democracy, whereas others saw only a debasement of cultural standards and a susceptibility to populist demagoguery.

Economic Readjustment and the New Prosperity

In their effort to return to normal, governments were quick to dismantle wartime planning and control mechanisms. But the needs of war had stimulated innovations that helped fuel the renewed economic growth of the 1920s. The civilian air industry, for example, developed rapidly during the decade by taking advantage of wartime work on aviation for military purposes. More generally, newer industries, such as chemicals, electricity, and advanced machinery, significantly altered patterns of life in the more industrialized parts of the West.

The automobile, a luxury plaything for the wealthy before the war, began to be mass produced in western Europe. In France, automobile production shot up dramatically, from 40,000 in 1920 to 254,000 in 1929.

But the heady pace masked problems that lay beneath the relative prosperity of the 1920s, even in victorious Britain and France. While new industries prospered, old ones declined in the face of new technologies and stronger foreign competition. The sectors responsible for Britain's earlier industrial preeminence—textiles, coal, shipbuilding, and iron and steel—now had trouble competing. Rather than investing in new technologies, companies in these industries demanded government protection and imposed lower wages and longer hours on their workers. At the same time, British labor unions resisted the mechanization necessary to make these older industries more competitive.

Whereas such structural decline in industry was clearest in Britain, inflation and its psychological impact were most prominent in Germany and France. By the summer of 1923, Germany's response to the French occupation of the Ruhr had transformed an already serious inflationary problem, stemming from wartime deficit spending, into one of the great hyperinflations in history. At its height in November, when it took 4.2 trillion marks to equal a dollar, Germans had to cart wheelbarrows of paper money to stores to buy ordinary grocery items. By the end of 1923, the government managed to stabilize prices through currency reform and drastically reduced government spending—a combination that won greater cooperation from the victors. But the rampant inflation, and the readjustment necessary to control it, had wiped out the savings of ordinary people while profiting speculators and those in debt, including some large industrialists. This inequity left scars that remained even as Germany enjoyed a measure of prosperity in the years that followed.

Inflation was less dramatic in France, but there, too, it deeply affected perceptions and priorities. For over a century, from the Napoleonic era to the outbreak of war in 1914, the value of the French franc had remained stable. But the war started France on an inflationary cycle that shattered the security of its many small savers—those, such as teachers and shopkeepers, who had been the backbone of the Third Republic. To repay war debts and rebuild war-damaged industries, the French government continued to run budget deficits, and thereby cause inflation, even after 1918. The franc was finally restabilized in 1928, though at only about one-fifth its prewar value.

On the international level, war debts and reparations strained the financial system, creating problems with the financing of trade. Still, during the course of the 1920s, experts made adjustments that seemed to be returning the international exchange system to equilibrium. Only in retrospect, after the international capitalist system fell into crisis late in 1929, did it become clear how potent those strains were—and how inadequate the efforts at readjustment.

Work, Leisure, and the New Popular Culture

The wartime spur to industrialization produced a large increase in the industrial labor force all over Europe, and a good deal of labor unrest accompanied the transition to peacetime. Some of that agitation challenged factory discipline and authority relationships. Seeking to reestablish authority on a new basis for the competitive postwar world, business advocates fostered a new cult of efficiency and productivity, partly by adapting Taylorism and Fordism, influential American ideas about mass production. On the basis of his "time-and-motion" studies of factory labor, Frederick W. Taylor (1856–1915) argued that breaking down assembly-line production into small, repetitive tasks was the key to maximizing worker efficiency. In contrast, Henry Ford (1863–1947) linked the gospel of mass production to mass consumption. In exchange for accepting the discipline of the assembly line, the workers should be paid enough to buy the products they produced—even automobiles. Sharing in the prosperity that mass production made possible, factory workers would be loyal to the companies that employed them. Not all Europeans, however, welcomed the new ideas from America. In the new cult of efficiency and mass production, some saw an unwelcome sameness and a lowering of cultural standards.

CHANGING ROLES FOR WOMEN In light of the major role women had played in the wartime labor force, the demand for women's suffrage proved irresistible in Britain, Germany, and much of Europe, though not yet in France

The Sensational Josephine Baker After moving from the United States to Paris in 1925, Baker quickly created a sensation as a cabaret dancer and singer. Her exotic costumes played on the European association of Africa with the wild and uninhibited. This poster advertises her appearance at the Folies-Bergère, a famed Parisian music hall. (The Granger Collection, NY)

or Italy. In Britain, where calls for women's suffrage had earlier met with controversy (see page 683), the right to vote was readily conceded in 1918, though at first only to women over 30. By now, women no longer seemed a threat to the political system. And in fact, British women, once they could vote, simply flowed into the existing parties, countering earlier hopes—and fears—that a specifically feminist political agenda would follow from women's suffrage.

Although there was much discussion of the "new woman," especially in Germany, the wider place of women in society was uncertain during the 1920s, as the new sense of openness clashed with the desire to return to normal. (See the feature, "The Visual Record: Advertising.") Female employment remained higher than before the war, but many women—willingly or not—returned home, yielding their jobs to the returning soldiers. The need to replace the men killed in the war lent renewed force to the traditional notion that women served society, and fulfilled themselves, by marrying and rearing families. More generally, some men found the emancipated "new woman" threatening, and after all the disruptions of war, male leaders sometimes assumed that the very stability of the political sphere depended on conventional gender roles. Still, the decade's innovative impulse brought into the public arena subjects—largely taboo before the war—that might portend changes in gender roles later on. The desire to be "modern" produced, for example, a more open, unsentimental, even scientific discussion of sexuality and reproduction.

The new "rationalization of sexuality" fed demands that governments provide access to sex counseling, birth control, and even abortion as they assumed ever greater responsibilities for promoting social health. This trend was especially prominent in Germany, although German innovators learned from experiments in the new Soviet Union and from the birth control movement that Margaret Sanger (1883–1966) was spearheading in the United States.

The more open and tolerant attitude toward sexuality affected popular entertainment—for example, Josephine Baker's dancing and costumes, which would have been unthinkable before the war. Another result was the emergence of a more visible gay subculture, prominent especially in the vibrant cabaret scene in Berlin during the 1920s.

PROSPERITY AND THE CULTURE OF LEISURE

Mass consumption followed from the mass production bound up with the new prosperity of the 1920s. As it became possible to mass-produce the products of the second industrial transformation, more people could afford automobiles; electrical gadgets, such as radios and phonographs; and clothing of synthetic fabrics, developed through innovations in chemistry.

With the eight-hour workday increasingly the norm, growing attention was devoted to leisure as a positive source of human fulfillment—for everyone, not just the wealthy. European beach resorts grew crowded as more people had the time, and the means, to take vacations. An explosion of interest in soccer among Europeans paralleled the expansion of professional baseball and college football in the United States. Huge stadiums were built across Europe.

The growth of leisure was linked to the development of mass media and mass culture. During the early 1920s, radio became a commercial venture, reaching a mass audience in Europe, as in the United States and Canada. Although movies had begun to emerge as vehicles of popular entertainment even before the war, they came into their own during the 1920s, when the names of film stars became household words for the first time.

Advertising

A sleek new automobile. A stylish "new woman" who'd adore a Christmas gift of jewelry. These images from the 1920s catch our eye even today, but why? The designs look "modern" somehow, and they convey particular messages about efficiency and the good life. What do such advertisements tell us about the changes at work in Western culture after World War I?

Advertising, in one form or another, is as old as civilization itself. But the advent of printing expanded possibilities, and the second industrial revolution led to a big boost in advertising by the 1890s, as ads for new products like bicycles and sewing machines appeared in newspapers and magazines. But it was during the 1920s that modern advertising came into its own. As mass consumption grew, advertising budgets expanded dramatically, and professional ad agencies emerged to study tastes and determine how to shape the desires of consumers. Moreover, the advent of commercial radio in 1920 opened a whole new set of possibilities, including the scope for musical jingles.

Mass consumption required advertising to show people what to want. And during the 1920s, ad agencies began offering images of the good life, seeking to define the popular sense of what it meant to be "modern." They often drew from the United States, which stood for efficiency and a fast-paced life of fun, pleasure, and consumerist abundance. So eager were the Germans to follow the U.S. lead in advertising that they adopted the term *sex appeal*, leaving it untranslated.

The new products featured in the print and broadcast media ran the gamut from automobiles to cosmetics, from rayon apparel to chewing gum. When the Wrigley Company of Chicago opened a factory in Germany in 1925, chewing gum quickly became associated with Americanization—and its use increased dramatically. But luxury goods were prominent as well, as in elegant ads such as the two shown here. Even for the many who could not afford expensive jewelry or the six-cylinder Opel, images of the good life stimulated the desire to buy less costly versions. Automobile consumption rose sharply during the 1920s, thanks also to the new techniques of mass production that Henry Ford had pioneered in the United States.

Although advertising served the economic interests of business by stimulating consumption, many began to view it as an art form as well. Far more attention was paid to its design, so the advertising "look" of the 1920s differed dramatically from anything seen before. As in the examples here, the new ads were often self-consciously modern, using simplified typefaces and stylized images suggesting the sleek efficiency and precision of the new machine age. The jewelry ad features an elegant contemporary typeface, and the German automobile ad of 1928 relies on crisp, bold forms and a clean, modern design.

The new prominence of advertising raised issues that were debated all over, but especially in Weimar Germany, where conditions remained unsettled even as a measure of prosperity returned by 1924. From cultural standards to gender roles, much was being called into question, and the wider implications of advertising were central to the "culture wars" of the period.

At an international advertising congress in Berlin in 1929, critics charged that advertising was furthering the debasement of standards already associated with mass culture and Americanization. Defenders countered that advertising was rejuvenating the mainstream culture, which had grown either stale and conventional or overblown and elitist. The fact that advertising served a commercial purpose need not mean cultural debasement. On the contrary, they argued, this new meshing of the best design with popular culture was healthy. In 1928, G. F. Hartlaub, a leading German art dealer, summed up a widespread view when he observed that advertising was a "truly social, collective, mass art, the only one we now have. It shapes the visual habits of that anonymous collectivity, the public. Little by little an artistic attitude is hammered into the mass soul by billboards."*

A particular advertising target was the "new woman," with her bobbed hair, short skirts, and freer lifestyle. But the image of women in advertisements was controversial, especially in Weimar Germany. Partly because of the simplification of female attire, images of the new woman in popular magazines provoked much concern about the "masculinization" of women by the mid-1920s. Some men found such images aggressive, even threatening.

Yet at the same time, advertising often assumed women to be master consumers—or perhaps merely mindless shoppers. In the holiday advertisement here, the woman is chic and liberated in one sense, but she is urged to drape herself with jewelry—to indulge in conventional ornamentation. This was also an age that claimed to value efficiency purified of ornament, as with the stripped-down typeface in the automobile ad. So though gender differentiation and women's

---

Exploiting the new fascination with air travel, the American Charles Lindbergh (1902–1974) captured the European imagination in 1927 with the first solo flight across the Atlantic. Lindbergh's feat epitomized the affirmative side of the decade—the sense that there were new worlds to conquer and that there still were heroes to admire, despite the ironies of the war and the ambiguities of the peace.

Car Ad, 1928: The Six-Cylinder Opel Hits the Jackpot
(From Bärbel Schrader and Jürgen Schebera, *The "Golden" Twenties: Art and Literature in the Weimar Republic* [New Haven: Yale University Press, 1990]. Reproduced with permission.)

Jewelry Ad, 1920s: "Wear jewelry—It makes you a winner. And it's the ideal Christmas gift."
(akg-images)

roles were very much at issue in advertising, the relationship between portrayals of the new woman and genuine liberation remained uncertain.

Despite tensions and contradictions, advertising helped bring new issues to center stage after World War I. Although the ads of the 1920s assumed a prosperity that proved fleeting, the cultural change proved enduring. Eye-catching images of the sleek, the chic, the new—all bathed in "sex appeal"—became the staples of twentieth-century advertising, bound up with the new culture of mass consumption.

QUESTIONS

1. What factors led to the upsurge in advertising during the 1920s?

2. What seems specifically modern about the images we see here?

---

*Quoted in John Willett, *Art and Politics in the Weimar Period: The New Sobriety, 1917-1933* (New York: Pantheon, 1978), p. 137. Translation modified slightly.

Society and Politics in the Victorious Democracies

France and Britain seemed the best positioned of the major European countries to take advantage of renewed peace and stability to confront the sociopolitical problems of the postwar era. And during the 1920s, each seemed to return to normal. But was normal good enough, in light of the rupture of the war and the challenges of the emerging mass society?

Innovation in Cinema This poster advertises Fritz Lang's 1926 film *Metropolis*, which explored the dehumanization and exploitation of the modern city. (Schulz-Neudamm, Metropolis, 1926. Lithograph, 83" × 36½". Gift of Universum-Film-Aktiengesellschaft. Photograph © 1997 The Museum of Modern Art, New York/Art Resource, NY)

FRANCE

Victory in the Great War seemed to belie France's prewar concerns about decadence and decline. In the immediate aftermath of the war, Clemenceau and other French leaders were confident in dealing with radical labor unrest and aggressive in translating the battlefield victory into a dominant position on the European continent. But the tremendous loss of French lives had produced a new fear—that France could not withstand another such challenge. The renewed confidence thus proved hollow.

Although some in prewar France had worried about falling behind rapidly industrializing Germany, victory seemed to have vindicated France's more cautious, balanced economy, with its blend of industry and agriculture. Thus, the prewar mistrust of rapid industrial development continued. Rather than foster a program of economic modernization that might have promoted genuine security, the French pulled back even from the measure of state responsibility for the economy that had developed during the war. Although government grants helped reconstruct almost eight thousand factories, most were simply rebuilt as they had been before the war. Moreover, the working class benefited little from the relative prosperity of the 1920s.

GREAT BRITAIN

Britain made certain adjustments after the war but missed the chance to make others. The government's handling of the Easter Rebellion in Ireland in 1916 (see pages 702–703) intensified anti-British feeling and fed further violence. But the British finally forged at least a provisional resolution. The first step was to partition Ireland, creating a separate Ulster, or Northern Ireland, from those counties with Protestant majorities. Ulster then remained under the British crown when an independent Republic of Ireland was established in the larger, majority-Catholic part of the island in 1922.

The British political system remained stable between the wars, although the Labour Party supplanted the Liberals to become the dominant alternative to the Conservatives by the early 1920s. The Labour Party even got a brief taste of power when Ramsay MacDonald (1866–1937) formed Britain's first Labour government in January 1924. The coming of Labour to power resulted in a significant expansion of the governmental elite to incorporate those, like MacDonald himself, with genuinely working-class backgrounds.

However, it was the Conservative leader, Stanley Baldwin (1867–1947), who set the tone for British politics between the wars in three stints as prime minister from 1923 to 1937. Although he was the wealthy son of a steel manufacturer, Baldwin deliberately departed from the old aristocratic style of British Conservative politics. More down-to-earth and pragmatic, he was the first British prime minister to use radio effectively, and he made an effort to foster good relations with workers. Yet Baldwin's era was one of growing social tension.

With exports declining, unemployment remained high in Britain throughout the interwar period, never falling below 10 percent. The coal industry, though still the country's largest employer, had become a particular trouble spot in the British economy. As coal exports declined, British mine owners became ever more aggressive in their dealings with labor, finally, in 1926, insisting on a longer workday and a wage cut of 13 percent to restore competitiveness. The result was a coal miners' strike in May that promptly turned into a general strike, involving almost all of organized labor—about four million workers—in the most notable display of trade-union solidarity Britain had ever seen. For nine days, the economy stood at a virtual standstill. But threats of arrest and a growing public backlash forced the union leadership to accept a compromise. The miners continued the strike on their own, but they finally returned to work six months later at considerably lower wages.

Although, for somewhat different reasons, Britain and France both failed during the 1920s to take advantage of what would soon seem, in retrospect, to have been a precious opportunity to adjust their economies and heal social wounds. The lost opportunity would mean still deeper social tensions once the relative prosperity of the decade had ended.

SECTION SUMMARY

- The inflation that resulted from the war and its aftermath had long-term psychological consequences, most dramatically in Germany, but also in France.

- Adapting influential American ideas about mass production, business leaders throughout much of Europe fostered a new cult of efficiency and productivity as they sought to adjust to the more competitive postwar world economy.

- Although there was much discussion of the "new woman," reflecting a new sense of openness after the war, women were pulled in traditional as well as modernizing directions during the 1920s.

- Mass production yielded mass consumption, the growth of leisure, and the popularity of new media like movies and radio.

- Victory bred a certain complacency in Britain and France, each of which failed to take advantage of what would seem, in retrospect, to have been a precious opportunity to adjust their economies and deepen their democracies.

THE TRIALS OF THE NEW DEMOCRACIES

What factors made the future of the new German democracy so uncertain during the 1920s?

The war was supposed to have paved the way for democracy, and new democracies emerged in Germany, Poland, and elsewhere in Europe. But almost everywhere they led tortured lives and soon gave way to more authoritarian forms of government. So the postwar decade did not see the extension of the political democracy that optimistic observers associated with the emerging mass society.

The most significant test took place in Germany, where a new democracy emerged from the republic proclaimed in November 1918. Elections in January 1919 produced a constituent assembly that convened in Weimar, a town associated with what seemed the most humane German cultural traditions. The assembly gave this new Weimar Republic, as it came to be called, a fully democratic constitution. But the Weimar democracy had great difficulty establishing its legitimacy, and it was suffering serious strains by 1930.

Democracy Aborted in East-Central Europe

New democracies were established in much of central and eastern Europe after the war, but except in Czechoslovakia and Finland, the practice of parliamentary government did not match the initial promise. Democracy seemed divisive and ineffective, so one country after another adopted a more authoritarian alternative during the 1920s and early 1930s.

In Poland, for example, the democratic constitution of 1921 established a cabinet responsible to a parliamentary majority, but the parliament fragmented into so many parties that instability proved endemic from the start. Poland had fourteen different ministries from November 1918 to May 1926, when Marshal Josef Pilsudski led a coup d'état that replaced parliamentary government with an authoritarian regime stressing national unity. This suppression of democracy came as a relief to many Poles—and was welcomed even by the trade unions. After Pilsudski's death in 1935, a group of colonels ruled Poland until the country was conquered by Nazi Germany in 1939.

Democracy proved hard to manage in east-central Europe partly because of the economic difficulties resulting from the breakup of the Habsburg system. New national borders meant new economic barriers that disrupted long-standing economic relationships. Industrial centers, such as Vienna and Budapest, found themselves cut off from their traditional markets and sources of raw materials. In what was now Poland, Silesians had long been oriented toward Germany, Galicians toward Vienna, and those in eastern Poland toward Russia. Thus, the new Polish nation-state was hardly a cohesive economic unit.

The countries of east-central Europe remained overwhelmingly agrarian, and this, too, proved unconducive to democracy. Land reform accompanied the transition to democracy, making small properties the norm in much of the region. But because these units were often too small to be efficient, agricultural output actually decreased after land was redistributed, most dramatically in Romania and Yugoslavia. When agricultural prices declined in the late 1920s, many peasants had no choice but to sell out to larger landowners. What had seemed a progressive reform thus failed to provide a stable agrarian smallholder base for democracy.

Germany's Cautious Revolution, 1919–1920

Meanwhile, in Germany, the Weimar Republic began under particularly difficult circumstances. Born of military defeat, it was promptly forced to take responsibility for the harsh Treaty of Versailles in 1919. During its first years, moreover, the regime encountered severe economic dislocation, culminating in the hyperinflation of 1923, as well as ideological polarization that threatened to tear the country apart.

Although Germany had strong military and authoritarian traditions, the initial threat to the new democracy came not from the right, disoriented and discredited, but from the left, stimulated by the Russian example. Even after Karl Liebknecht and Rosa Luxemburg were captured and murdered in Berlin in January 1919, a serious chance of further revolution persisted through May 1919, and communist revolutionary agitation continued to flare up until the end of 1923.

As it turned out, there was no further revolution, partly because the parallel between Germany and Russia carried only so far. The new German government had made peace, whereas the leaders of the provisional government in Russia had sought to continue the war. Furthermore, those who ended up controlling the councils that sprang up in Germany during the fall of 1918 favored political democracy, not communist revolution; therefore, they supported the provisional government.

Even so, the revolutionary minority constituted a credible threat. And the new government made repression of the extreme left a priority—even if it meant leaving in place some of the institutions and personnel of the old imperial system. In November 1918, at the birth of the new republic, the moderate socialist leader Friedrich Ebert had agreed with General Wilhelm Groener, the new army head, to preserve the old imperial officer corps to help prevent further revolution. But when the regular army, weakened by war and defeat, proved unable to control radical agitation in Berlin in December, it seemed the republic would have to take extraordinary measures to defend itself from the revolutionary left. With the support of Ebert and Groener, Gustav Noske, the minister of national defense, began to organize "Free Corps," volunteer paramilitary groups to be used against the revolutionaries.

During the first five months of 1919, the government unleashed the Free Corps to crush leftist movements all over Germany, often with wanton brutality. In relying on right-wing paramilitary groups, the republic's leaders were playing with fire, but the immediate threat at this point came from the left. In 1920, however, the government faced a right-wing coup attempt, the Kapp Putsch. The army declined to defend the republic, but the government managed to survive thanks largely to a general strike by leftist workers. The republic's early leaders had to juggle both extremes because, as one of them put it, the Weimar Republic was "a candle burning at both ends."

Though sporadic street fighting by paramilitary groups continued, the republic survived its traumatic birth and achieved an uneasy stability by 1924. But Germany's postwar revolution had remained confined to the political level. There was no program to break up the cartels, with their concentrations of economic power. Even on the level of government personnel, continuity was more striking than change. There was no effort to build a loyal republican army, and no attempt to purge the bureaucracy and the judiciary of antidemocratic elements from the old imperial order. When right-wing extremists assassinated prominent leaders, such as the Jewish industrialist Walther Rathenau in 1922, the courts often proved unwilling to prosecute those responsible.

In light of the republic's eventual failure, the willingness of its early leaders to leave intact so much from the old order has made them easy targets of criticism. It can be argued, however, that the course they followed—heading off the extreme left, reassuring the established elites, and playing for time—was the republic's best chance for success. The new regime might establish its legitimacy by inertia, much like the Third Republic in France, which had similarly been born of defeat. Even lacking the sentimental fervor that had earlier surrounded democratic ideals, Germans might gradually become "republicans of reason," recognizing that this regime could be a framework for prosperity and renewed German prominence in international affairs. In the event of an early crisis, however, a republic consolidating itself in this cautious way might well find fewer defenders than opponents.

The constituent assembly elections of January 1919 took place before the peace conference had produced the widely detested Treaty of Versailles. By the time of the first regular parliamentary elections, in June 1920, the new government had been forced to accept the treaty. The three moderate parties that led the government suffered a major defeat, together dropping from 76 to 47 percent of the seats. These were the parties most committed to democratic institutions, but they were never again to achieve a parliamentary majority.

The 1920 elections revealed the problems of polarization and lack of consensus that would bedevil, and eventually ruin, the Weimar Republic. Because the electorate found it difficult to agree, or even to compromise, Germany settled into a multiparty system that led to unstable coalition government. And the strength, or potential strength, of the extremes immeasurably complicated political life for those trying to make the new democracy work. On the left, the Communist Party constantly criticized the more moderate Socialist Party for supporting the republic. On the right, the Nationalist Party (DNVP) played on nationalist resentments and fears of the extreme left—but the result was similarly to dilute support for the new republic. To the right, even of the Nationalists, were Adolf Hitler's National Socialists, or Nazis, who were noisy and often violent, but who attracted little electoral support before 1930.

Gustav Stresemann
German statesman of the Weimar Republic, he secured a reduction of Germany's reparations payments and negotiated the Treaty of Locarno, paving the way for Germany's entry into the League of Nations in 1926.

Gustav Stresemann and the Scope for Gradual Consolidation

All was not necessarily lost for the republic when the three moderate, pro-Weimar parties were defeated in 1920. Germans who were unsupportive or hostile at first might be gradually won over. After the death of President Ebert in 1925, Paul von Hindenburg, the emperor's field marshal, was elected president. In principle, having a conservative military leader from the old order in this role could have proven advantageous, helping to persuade skeptics that the new regime was a worthy object of German patriotism. But when crisis came by 1930, Hindenburg was quick to give up on parliamentary government—with devastating results.

The individual who best exemplified the possibility of winning converts to the Weimar Republic was **Gustav Stresemann** (STRAY-zuh-mahn) (1878–1929), the leader of the German People's Party (DVP), a conservative party that did not support the republic at the outset. But the DVP was relatively flexible and offered at least the possibility of broadening the republic's base of support. As chancellor, and especially as foreign minister, Stresemann proved the republic's leading statesman.

Stresemann's background and instincts were not democratic, but by the end of 1920, Germany's postwar political volatility had convinced him that if the new republic should go under, the outcome would not be the conservative monarchy he preferred but the triumph of the extreme left. Moreover, it had become clear that the new democratic republic was not likely to

Hopes for Peace   Foreign ministers Aristide Briand *(left)* of France and Gustav Stresemann of Germany spearheaded the improved international relations that bred optimism during the late 1920s. *(Corbis)*

be revolutionary on the socioeconomic level. It made sense, then, to work actively to make the new regime succeed. From within this framework, Germany could pursue its international aims, negotiating modifications of the Versailles treaty and returning to great power status.

Stresemann became chancellor in August 1923, when inflation was raging out of control. Within months, his government managed to get the German economy functioning effectively again, partly because the French agreed that an international commission should review the reparations question, specifying realistic amounts based on Germany's ability to pay. New plans worked out under American leadership—the Dawes Plan of 1924 and finally the Young Plan of 1929—seemed to specify a reasonable and workable settlement.

Quite apart from the immediate economic issue, Stresemann understood that better relations with France had to be a priority if Germany was to rejoin the great powers. French foreign minister Aristide Briand (bree-AHN) (1862–1932) shared Stresemann's desire for improved relations, and together they engineered a new, more conciliatory spirit in international affairs. Its most substantial fruit was the **Treaty of Locarno** of 1925. France and Germany accepted the postwar border between the two countries, which meant that Germany gave up any claim to Alsace-Lorraine. France, for its part, renounced the sort of direct military intervention in Germany that it had attempted with the Ruhr invasion of 1923 and agreed to begin withdrawing troops from the Rhineland ahead of schedule. Germany freely accepted France's key advantage, the demilitarization of the Rhineland, and Britain and Italy now explicitly guaranteed the measure.

By accepting the status quo in the West, Stresemann was freeing Germany to concentrate on eastern Europe, where he envisioned gradual but substantial revision in the territorial settlement that had resulted from the war. Especially with the creation of Poland, that settlement had come partly at Germany's expense. Stresemann, then, was pursuing German interests, not subordinating them to some larger European vision. But he was willing to compromise and, for the most part, to play by the rules as he did so.

With the Locarno treaty, the victors accepted Germany as a diplomatic equal for the first time since the war. Germany's return to good graces culminated in its entry into the League of Nations in 1926. The new spirit of reconciliation was widely welcomed. Indeed, Stresemann and Briand were joint winners of the Nobel Peace Prize for 1926.

Still, those on the right continually exploited German resentments by criticizing Stresemann's compromises with Germany's former enemies. Even when successful, from Stresemann's own perspective, his negotiations often cost his party electoral support. The controversy that surrounded Stresemann, a German conservative pursuing conventional national interests, indicates how volatile the German political situation remained, even with the improved economic and diplomatic climate of the later 1920s. Still, Stresemann's diplomatic successes were considerable, and his death in October 1929, at the age of 51, was a severe blow to the republic.

Treaty of Locarno The 1925 treaty in which Germany, again recognized as a diplomatic equal, freely agreed with France, Britain, and Italy to accept key aspects of the Versailles peace settlement.

An Uncertain Balance Sheet

Although Weimar Germany was better off in 1929 than it had been in 1923, the political consensus remained weak, the political party system remained fragmented, and unstable coalition government remained the rule. The immediate threat from the extreme left had been overcome, but many conservatives continued to fear that the unstable Weimar democracy would eventually open the way to a socialist or communist regime.

The Weimar Republic epitomized the overall European situation during the 1920s. As long as prosperity and international cooperation continued, the new German democracy might endure, even come to thrive. But the new institutions in Germany, like the wider framework of prosperity and stability, were fragile indeed. At the first opportunity, antidemocratic elites, taking advantage of their access to President Hindenburg, would begin plotting to replace the Weimar Republic with a more authoritarian alternative.

SECTION SUMMARY

- Although new democracies were established in central and eastern Europe after the war, parliamentary government proved divisive and ineffective in much of the region, so one country after another adopted a more authoritarian alternative.

- Germany's democratic political revolution was not accompanied by major changes in socioeconomic relations—or even in the administrative structures inherited from Wilhelm II's government.

- Because of polarization and lack of consensus in the electorate, the Weimar Republic quickly fell into a multiparty system that led to unstable coalition government.

- A conservative monarchist by instinct, Gustav Stresemann rallied to the Weimar Republic because he found it the best framework for restoring Germany to prosperity and international influence—and for heading off leftist revolution.

- Although many Germans continued to resent the peace settlement, the Treaty of Locarno of 1925 seemed to suggest a hopeful new spirit of reconciliation between France and Germany

THE SEARCH FOR MEANING IN A DISORDERED WORLD

How did cultural and intellectual leaders differ over the place of "tradition" as they sought to suggest how to come to terms with the new situation of the 1920s?

For all its vitality, the new culture of the 1920s had something brittle about it. The forces that produced a sense of openness, liberation, and innovation were disruptive and disturbing at the same time. Perhaps the frenetic pace only masked a deeper sense that things had started to come apart and might well get worse. The era called forth some notable diagnoses and prescriptions, but, not surprisingly, they differed dramatically.

Anxiety, Alienation, and Disillusionment

Concern about the dangers of the emerging mass civilization was especially clear in *The Revolt of the Masses* (1930), by the influential Spanish thinker José Ortega y Gasset (1883–1955). In his view, contemporary experience had shown that ordinary people, incapable of creating standards, remained content with the least common denominator. Communism and fascism indicated the violent, intolerant, and ultimately barbaric quality of the new mass age. But Ortega found the same tendencies in American-style democracy. The fact that much of Europe seemed to be moving toward the mass politics and culture of the United States was a symptom of the deeper problem, not a solution.

Concern with cultural decline was part of a wider pessimism about the condition of the West, which stood in stark contrast to the belief in progress, and the attendant confidence in Western superiority, that had been essential to Western self-understanding before 1914. The German thinker Oswald Spengler (1880–1936) made concern with decline almost fashionable with his bestseller of the immediate postwar years, *The Decline of the West* (1918), which offered a cyclical theory purporting to explain how spirituality and creativity were giving way to a materialistic mass-based culture in the West.

To Sigmund Freud (1856–1939), the eruption of violence and hatred during and after the war indicated a deep, instinctual problem in the human makeup (see page 680). In his gloomy essay, *Civilization and Its Discontents* (1930), Freud suggested that the progress of civilization requires individuals to bottle up their aggressive instincts, which are directed inward as guilt, but which may erupt in violent outbursts. This notion raised questions not only about the scope for continued progress, but also about the plausibility of the Wilsonian ideals that had surrounded the end of the war. Perhaps, with civilization growing more complex, the Great War had been only the beginning of a new era of hatred and violence.

The sense that something incomprehensible, even nightmarish, haunted modern civilization, with its ever more complex bureaucracies, technologies, and cities, found vivid expression in the work of the Czech Jewish writer Franz Kafka (1883–1924), most notably in the novels *The Trial* and *The Castle*, published posthumously in the mid-1920s. In a world that claimed to be increasingly rational, Kafka's individual is the lonely, fragile plaything of forces utterly beyond reason, comprehension, and control. In such a world, the quest for law, or meaning, or God, is futile, ridiculous.

Especially in the unsettled conditions of Weimar Germany, the anxiety of the 1920s tended to take extreme forms, from irrational activism to a preoccupation with death. Suicides among students increased dramatically. Youthful alienation prompted the novelist Jakob Wassermann (1873–1934) to caution German young people in 1932 that not all action is good simply because it is action, that feeling is not always better than reason and discipline, and that youth is not in itself a badge of superiority.

Recasting the Tradition

Expressions of disillusionment revealed something about human experience in the unsettled new world, but they were sometimes morbid and self-indulgent. Other cultural leaders sought to be more positive; the challenge was not to give vent to new anxieties, but to find antidotes to them. One direction was to recast traditional categories—in the arts, in religion, in politics—to make them relevant to contemporary experience. Although not all were optimistic about human prospects, many found such a renewal of tradition to be the best hope for responding to the disarray of the postwar world.

Among artists, even those who had been prominent in the modernist avant-garde before the war now pulled back from headlong experimentation and sought to pull things back together, though on a new basis. In music, composers as different as Igor Stravinsky (1882–1971) and Paul Hindemith (1895–1963) adapted earlier styles, though sometimes in an ironic spirit, as they sought to weave new means of expression into familiar forms. The overall tendency toward neoclassicism during the period was an effort to give musical composition a renewed basis of order.

One of the most striking responses to the anxieties of this increasingly secular age was a wave of neo-orthodox religious thinking, most prominent in Protestants like the German-Swiss theologian Karl Barth (1886–1968). In his *Epistle to the Romans* (1919), Barth reacted against the liberal theology, the attempt to marry religious categories to secular progress, that had become prominent by the later nineteenth century. The war, especially, had seemed to shatter the liberal notion that the hand of God was at work in history, and Barth emphasized the radical cleft between God and our human, historical world, sunken in sin. Recalling the arguments of Augustine and Luther, he portrayed humanity as utterly lost, capable at best of a difficult relationship with God through faith, grace, and revelation.

With democracy faring poorly in parts of Europe, and with fascism and communism claiming to offer superior alternatives, some sought to make new sense of the liberal democratic tradition. In Italy, Benedetto Croce (CROH-chay) (1866–1952) agreed with critics that the old justifications, based on natural law or utilitarianism, were deeply inadequate, but he also became one of Europe's most influential antifascists. The most significant innovations in modern thought, he argued, show us why democratic values, institutions, and practices are precisely what we need. We human beings are free, creative agents of a history that we make as best we can, without quite understanding what will result from what we do. Humility, tolerance, and equal access to political participation are essential to the process whereby the world is endlessly remade.

The new political challenges also stimulated fresh thinking within the Marxist tradition. By showing that Marxism could encompass consciousness as well as economic relationships, the Hungarian Georg Lukács (LOO-kash) (1885–1971) invited a far more sophisticated Marxist analysis of capitalist culture than had been possible before. Lukács accented the progressive role of realistic fiction and attacked the disordered fictional world of Kafka, which seemed to abandon all hope for human understanding of the forces of history. Though more eclectic, the Institute for Social Research, founded in Frankfurt, Germany, in 1923, gave rise to an influential tradition of criticism of capitalist civilization in what came to be known as the Frankfurt School. These innovations helped give the Marxist tradition a new lease on life in the West, even as it was developing in unforeseen ways in the Soviet Union.

The Search for a New Tradition

While some intellectuals sought renewal from within the European tradition, others insisted that a more radical break was needed—but also that the elements for a viable new cultural tradition were available.

Reflecting on the situation of women writers in 1928, the British novelist Virginia Woolf (1882–1941) showed how women in the past had suffered from the absence of a tradition of writing by women. By the 1920s, women had made important strides, but Woolf suggested that further advance required a more self-conscious effort by women to develop their own tradition. Most basically, women needed greater financial independence so that they could have the time for scholarship, the leisure for cultivated conversation and travel, and the privacy of "a room of one's own." Woolf also envisioned a new sort of historical inquiry, focusing on how ordinary women lived their lives, that could show contemporary women where they came from—and thus deepen their sense of identity. (See the feature, "The Written Record: Tradition and Women: The Conditions of Independence.")

A very different effort to establish a new tradition developed in Paris, where the poet André Breton (1896–1966) spearheaded the surrealist movement in literature and the visual arts. **Surrealism** grew directly from Dada, an artistic movement that had emerged in neutral Zurich, Switzerland, and elsewhere during the war. Radically hostile to the war, Dada artists developed shocking, sometimes nihilistic forms to deal with a reality that now seemed senseless and out of control. Some made collages from gutter trash; others indulged in nonsense or relied on chance to guide their art. By the

surrealism   A literary and artistic movement that emerged in Paris in the early 1920s, it sought to explore the subconscious, which it believed to hold something liberating for human beings.

Tradition and Women: The Conditions of Independence

Speaking in 1928 about the situation of women writers, the British novelist Virginia Woolf raised questions that were relevant to all women seeking the opportunity to realize their potential. Indeed, her reflections about the value of difference and the need for particular traditions inspired those seeking equal opportunity for decades to come. And her question about why we know so little about women's lives in the past helped stimulate later historians to investigate the experiences of ordinary people.

Woman…pervades poetry from cover to cover; she is all but absent from history.…Occasionally an individual woman is mentioned, an Elizabeth, or a Mary; a queen or a great lady. But by no possible means could middle-class women with nothing but brains and character at their command have taken part in any one of the great movements which, brought together, constitute the historian's view of the past. … What one wants … is a mass of information; at what age did she marry; how many children had she as a rule; what was her house like; had she a room to herself; did she do the cooking; would she be likely to have a servant? All these facts lie somewhere, presumably, in parish registers and account books; the life of the average Elizabethan woman must be scattered about somewhere, could one collect it and make a book of it. It would be ambitious beyond my daring, I thought, looking about the shelves for books that were not there, to suggest to the students of those famous colleges that they should rewrite history, though I own that it often seems a little queer as it is, unreal, lop-sided. …

But whatever effect discouragement and criticism had upon their writing—and I believe they had a very great effect—that was unimportant compared with the other difficulty which faced them (I was still considering those early nineteenth-century novelists) when they came to set their thoughts on paper—that is that they had no tradition behind them, or one so short and partial that it was of little help. For we think back through our mothers if we are women. It is useless to go to the great men writers for help, however much one may go to them for pleasure. …

… Women have sat indoors all these millions of years, so that by this time the very walls are permeated by their creative force, which has, indeed, so overcharged the capacity of bricks and mortar that it must needs harness itself to pens and brushes and business and politics. But this creative power differs greatly from the creative power of men. And one must conclude that it would be a thousand pities if it were hindered or wasted, for it was won by centuries of the most drastic discipline, and there is nothing to take its place. It would be a thousand pities if women wrote like men, or lived like men, or looked like men.… Ought not education to bring out and fortify the differences rather than the similarities?

QUESTIONS

1. Why does Woolf find something "lop-sided" about the body of historical writing available in her own time, and how does she believe the problem might be overcome?

2. Why does Woolf suggest that education ought to nurture a distinctive female voice?

Source: Virginia Woolf, *A Room of One's Own* (San Diego: Harcourt Brace Jovanovich, Harvest/HBJ, 1989), pp 43–45, 76, 87–88.

---

early 1920s, however, the surrealists felt it was time to create a new and deeper basis of order after the willful disordering of Dada. Having learned from Freud about the subconscious, they sought to adapt Dada's novel techniques—especially the use of chance—to gain access to the subconscious mind, which they believed contains a deeper truth, without the overlay of logic, reason, and conscious control.

But other artists, seeking to embrace the modern industrial world in a more positive spirit, found surrealism merely escapist. Among them was Walter Gropius (1883–1969), a pioneering modernist architect and leader of an influential German art school, the **Bauhaus**, during the 1920s. Gropius held that it was possible to establish new forms of culture, even a new tradition, that could be affirmative and reassuring in the face of the postwar cultural disarray. Rather than putting up familiar neoclassical or neo-Gothic buildings, "feigning a culture that has long since disappeared," the West had to face up to the kind of civilization it had become—industrial, technological, efficient, urban, mass-based. If people chose carefully from among the elements of this new machine-based civilization, they could again have a culture that worked, an "integrated pattern for living."[2]

This "constructive," pro-modern impulse was particularly prominent in Germany, but it could be found all over—in the

SECTION SUMMARY

- The shock of the war produced a sense of disillusionment and even decline that took many forms in the culture of the 1920s.

- Some accented the scope for recasting traditions during the 1920s, but others insisted on the need to form new traditions if the era's challenges were to be met.

- The contrast between surrealism and the German Bauhaus suggested a wider disagreement over whether Western culture was excessively rational or not rational enough.

- Whereas some, like Ortega y Gasset, were at best ambivalent about the advent of modern mass society, others welcomed it and sought to devise cultural forms that seemed more appropriate to a mass machine age.

Bauhaus An influential German art school, founded in 1919, that sought to adopt contemporary materials to develop new forms of architecture, design, and urban planning in response to the cultural uncertainty that followed World War I.

modernists of the Russian Revolution, in the French painter Fernand Léger (leh-ZHAY) (1881–1955), in the Swiss architect Le Corbusier (luh cor-BOO-zee-ay) (1887–1965). Whereas many of their contemporaries were at best ambivalent about the masses, these artists sought to bring high art and mass society together in the interests of both. And they welcomed the new patterns of life that seemed to be emerging in the modern world of mass production and fast-paced cities.

The Bauhaus Building, Dessau The Bauhaus, an influential but controversial German art school, was established in Weimar in 1919 and then moved to Dessau in 1925. Walter Gropius, its founding director, spearheaded the design of its headquarters building. Constructed in 1925–1926, it immediately became a symbol of the Weimar modernism that some admired and others detested. (Vanni/Art Resource, NY)

CHAPTER SUMMARY

FOCUS QUESTIONS

- How did the differing priorities of Britain and France affect international relations during the 1920s?

- Why did Italy turn from parliamentary democracy to fascism even after sharing in the victory in World War I?

- Why, and on what basis, did sexuality, gender roles, and the "new woman" provoke so much concern during the 1920s?

- What factors made the future of the new German democracy so uncertain during the 1920s?

- How did cultural and intellectual leaders differ over the place of "tradition" as they sought to suggest how to come to terms with the new situation of the 1920s?

In the wake of the most destructive war in history, questions about the new international framework, established at the peace conference of 1919–1920, were bound to be central. Although they bore the major responsibility for enforcing the peace, France and Britain seemed to drift apart as the British, preoccupied with colonial concerns, distanced themselves from politics on the Continent. Whereas France was willing to intervene actively to enforce the Versailles treaty, Britain placed greater faith in reconciliation and the new League of Nations.

The threat of leftist revolution was a major factor in the emergence of fascism in Italy, although the fascists claimed to offer a "third way," a modern alternative to *both* Marxist socialism and liberal democracy. Once Mussolini committed himself to a decisively postliberal direction, the fascists fastened upon corporativism as the basis for a new fascist form of state. Corporativism, they claimed, offered a way of transcending the class divisions accented by Marxism while also involving people in public life in more constant and direct ways than democracy had made possible.

The war had seemingly enhanced opportunities for women, and a new sense of openness carried into the postwar period. During the 1920s, sexuality, reproductive choices, gender roles, and family life were open to discussion as never before in the West. But in light of demographic losses and the brutalizing effects of the war, women encountered considerable pressure to conform to traditional roles of mothering and nurturing. Although the image of the liberated "new woman" was central to the era, women themselves were sometimes torn between conflicting roles and expectations.

Germany's Weimar Republic provided the central test of the bright hopes for democracy that marked the beginning of the postwar era. Yet the new German democracy was launched under the difficult circumstances of defeat, harsh peace terms, and ongoing revolutionary unrest. Moreover, the limits of political consensus in Germany meant a fragmented electorate, a complicated multiparty system, and a reliance on unstable coalition governments. Although the improved economic and diplomatic situation by 1925 enhanced the prospects for democracy, the Weimar Republic remained fragile and vulnerable.

In light of the cultural disruptions of the war and its aftermath, many intellectuals insisted that certain traditions could be recast to provide the sense of direction that people needed. But there was wide disagreement over which traditions were relevant. Whereas some pointed to religion, others fastened upon Marxism. Still others found it essential to return to more accessible forms in the arts, turning from the avant-garde experiment that had marked the prewar period. At the same time, however, figures as disparate as Virginia Woolf, André Breton, and Walter Gropius insisted that the means were available to develop *new* traditions, more appropriate to the needs and possibilities of the postwar world.

KEY TERMS

Maginot Line   (p. 730)

fascism   (p. 732)

Comintern (Third, or Communist, International)   (p. 734)

New Economic Policy (NEP)   (p. 734)

Joseph Stalin   (p. 735)

Benito Mussolini   (p. 738)

Matteotti murder   (p. 738)

corporativism, corporative state   (p. 738)

Gustav Stresemann   (p. 747)

Treaty of Locarno   (p. 748)

surrealism   (p. 750)

Bauhaus   (p. 752)

 This icon will direct you to additional materials on the website: www .cengage.com/history/ noble/westciv6e.

See our interactive eBook for map and primary source activities.

NOTES

1. Benito Mussolini, speech to the Italian Chamber of Deputies, January 3, 1925, from Charles F. Delzell, ed., *Mediterranean Fascism, 1919–1945* (New York: Harper & Row, 1970), pp. 59–60.

2. Walter Gropius, *Scope of Total Architecture* (New York: Collier Books, 1962), pp. 15, 67.

¡No pasarán! ("They shall not pass")
Defending the republic during the Spanish civil war.   (Biblioteca Nacional, Madrid)

The Tortured Decade, 1930–1939

"They shall not pass," proclaimed the charismatic Spanish communist Dolores Ibarruri (ee-bah-RUHR-ee) (1895–1989), whose impassioned speeches and radio broadcasts helped inspire the heroic defense of Madrid during the civil war that gripped Spain, and captured the attention of the world, during the later 1930s. Known as *La Pasionaria*—the passion flower—Ibarruri became a living legend for her role in defending the Spanish republic against the antidemocratic Nationalists seeking to overthrow it. But the Republican side lost, and she spent thirty-eight years in exile before returning to Spain in 1977, after the end of the dictatorship that resulted from the Spanish civil war.

In her effort to rally the Republican side, Ibarruri stressed the political power of women, and women were prominent in the citizen militias defending Madrid and other Spanish cities. Women fought for the republic partly because it seemed to open new opportunities for them, especially as it became more radical by 1936. But just as some women welcomed the new direction, others became politically active on the opposing Nationalist side—to support the church, to combat divorce, and to defend a separate sphere for women as the guardians of private life and family values.

The ideological polarization that characterized the Spanish civil war reflected the expanding reach of politics in the 1930s, when economic depression and the challenge from new, antidemocratic governments immeasurably complicated the European situation. The measures used to realign the international economy after World War I had seemed effective for most of the 1920s, but by 1929, they were beginning to backfire, helping to trigger the Great Depression. During the early 1930s, the economic crisis intensified sociopolitical strains all over the Western world—and beyond, heightening anti-Western feeling. In Germany, the Depression helped undermine the Weimar Republic and opened the way for the new Nazi regime under Adolf Hitler, whose policies led through a series of diplomatic crises to a new European war.

German Nazism paralleled Italian fascism in its reliance on a single charismatic leader, its willingness to use violence, and its hostility to both parliamentary democracy and Marxist socialism. But Nazism emphasized racism and anti-Semitism in a way that Italian fascism did not, and it more radically transformed its society.

At the same time, Stalin's communist regime in the Soviet Union seemed to converge, in some ways, with these new fascist regimes—especially with German Nazism. So, though they expressed widely different aims, Stalinism and Nazism are sometimes lumped together as instances of "totalitarianism." Both apparently sought control over all aspects of society, partly through the use of secret police agencies. But on closer inspection, the forms of coercion and violence in the Soviet and German regimes by the later 1930s were quite

FOCUS QUESTIONS

- With what array of measures did governments respond to the Great Depression?

- Why did the Stalinist attempt to build "socialism in one country" lead to the "terror-famine" of 1932–1933 and the "great terror" of 1937–1938?

- Through what measures did the Nazi regime claim to be improving the quality of the German population?

- Why did the "popular front" strategy prove counterproductive in both France and Spain?

- Why did the other countries not stop Hitler's Germany before it was strong enough to start a new European war in 1939?

 This icon will direct you to additional materials on the website: www.cengage.com/history/noble/westciv6e.

 See our interactive eBook for map and primary source activities.

different, and the extent to which each can be understood as an instance of totalitarianism remains controversial.

Fascism, Nazism, and communism seemed able to sidestep—or surmount—the ills of the Depression, yet they stood opposed to the parliamentary democracy that had long seemed the direction of progressive political change. So the democratic movement appeared to lose its momentum in the face of the political and economic challenges of the 1930s. The defeat, by early 1939, of the democratic republic in Spain by the authoritarian Nationalists seemed to exemplify the political direction of the decade.

THE GREAT DEPRESSION

With what array of measures did governments respond to the Great Depression?

If any single event can be said to have triggered the world economic crisis of the early 1930s, it was the stock market crash of October 1929 in the United States. But that crash had such an impact only because the new international economic order after World War I was extremely fragile. By October 1929, in fact, production was already declining in all the major Western countries except France.

The economies of Germany and the states of east-central Europe remained particularly vulnerable after the war, and in the increasingly interdependent economic world, their weaknesses magnified problems that started elsewhere. The crash of the U.S. stock market led to a restriction of credit in central Europe, which triggered a more general contraction in production and trade. Facing cruel dilemmas, policymakers proved unable to master the situation for the first few years of the crisis.

Causes of the Depression

Certain economic sectors, especially coal mining and agriculture, were already suffering severe problems by the mid-1920s, well before the stock market crash. British coal exports fell partly because oil and hydroelectricity were rapidly developing as alternatives. Unemployment in Britain was never less than 10 percent, even in the best of times between the wars. In agriculture, high prices worldwide during the war produced oversupply, which, in turn, led to a sharp drop in prices once the war was over. During the later 1920s, bumper harvests of grain and rice in many parts of the world renewed the downward pressure on prices. The result of low agricultural prices was a diminished demand for industrial goods, which impeded growth in the world economy.

Throughout the 1920s, finance ministers and central bankers had difficulty juggling the economic imbalances created by the war, centering on war debts to the United States and German reparations obligations to France, Britain, and Belgium. The strains in the system finally caught up with policymakers by 1929, when an international restriction of credit forced an end to the international economic cooperation that had been attempted throughout the decade.

The shaky postwar economic system depended on U.S. bank loans to Germany, funneled partly by international agreements, but also drawn by high interest rates. By 1928, however, U.S. investors were rapidly withdrawing their capital from Germany in search of the higher returns to be made in the booming U.S. stock market. This shift tightened credit in Germany. Then, the crash of the overpriced U.S. market in October 1929 deepened the problem by forcing suddenly strapped American investors to pull still more of their funds out of Germany. This process continued over the next two years, weakening the major banks in Germany and the other countries of central Europe, which were closely tied to the German economy. In May 1931, the bankruptcy of Vienna's most powerful bank, the Credit-Anstalt, made it clear that a crisis of potentially catastrophic proportions was in progress.

Despite attempts at adjustment on the international level, fears of bank failure or currency devaluation led to runs on the banks and currencies of Germany and central Europe. To maintain the value of the domestic currency, and thereby to resist the withdrawal of capital, government policymakers raised interest rates. This measure was not sufficient to stem the capital hemorrhage, but by restricting credit still more, it further dampened domestic economic activity.

Finally, the Germans seemed to have no choice but to freeze foreign assets—that is, to cease allowing conversion of assets held in German marks to other currencies. In this atmosphere, investors seeking the safest place for their capital tried to cash in currency for gold—or for British pounds, which could then be converted to gold. Europe's flight to gold, however, soon put such pressure on the British currency that Britain was forced to devalue the pound and sever it from the gold standard in September 1931. This proved the definitive end of the worldwide system of economic exchange based on the gold standard that had gradually crystallized during the nineteenth century.

The absence of a single standard of exchange, combined with various currency restrictions, made foreign trade more difficult, thereby diminishing it further. So did the scramble for tariff protection that proved a widespread response to the developing crisis. Crucial was the U.S. Smoot-Hawley Tariff Act of June 1930, which raised taxes on imports by 50 to 100 percent, forcing other nations to take comparable steps. Even Britain, long a bastion of free trade, adopted a peacetime tariff for the first time in nearly a century with the Import Duties Act of 1932, which imposed a 10 percent tax on most imports.

The decline of trade spread depression throughout the world economic system. By 1933, most major European countries were able to export no more than two-thirds, and in some cases as little as one-third, of the amount they had sold in 1929. At the same time, losses from international bank failures contracted credit and purchasing power and furthered the downward spiral, until by 1932 the European economies had shrunk to a little over half their 1929 size. This was the astonishing outcome of the short-lived prosperity of the 1920s.

Consequences and Responses

The Depression was essentially a radical contraction in economic activity; with less being produced and sold, demand for labor declined sharply. In Germany, industrial production by early 1933 was only half what it had been in 1929, and roughly six million Germans, or one-third of the labor force, were unemployed. In Germany, as elsewhere, the decline in employment opportunities helped produce a backlash against the ideal of the "new woman," working outside the home, which had been a prominent aspect of the new freedom of the 1920s. Even those men and women who hung on to jobs suffered from growing insecurity.

During the first years of the Depression, central bankers everywhere sought to balance budgets in order to reassure investors and stabilize currencies. With economies contracting and tax revenues declining, the only way to balance the budget was to sharply reduce government spending. In addition, governments responded to the decline in exports by forcing wages down, seeking to enhance competitiveness abroad. But by cutting purchasing power at home, both these measures reinforced the slowdown in economic activity.

CHRONOLOGY

October 1929	U.S. stock market crash helps trigger Great Depression
December 1929	Forced collectivization in Soviet agriculture begins
June 1930	Smoot-Hawley Tariff Act (U.S.)
May 1931	Bankruptcy of Vienna's Credit-Anstalt
January 1933	Hitler becomes German chancellor
December 1934	Assassination of Kirov
March 1935	Hitler announces rearmament
October 1935	Italy invades Ethiopia
March 1936	Germany remilitarizes the Rhineland
May 1936	Blum becomes French popular front prime minister
July 1936	Spanish civil war begins
March 1938	Third Moscow show trial; Bukharin and others convicted and executed
	Anschluss: Germany absorbs Austria
September 1938	"Appeasement": Munich conference ends Sudetenland crisis
November 1938	Crystal Night pogrom
March 1939	Dismemberment of Czechoslovakia
May 1939	Pact of Steel binds fascist Italy and Nazi Germany
August 23, 1939	Nazi-Soviet Pact
September 1, 1939	Germany invades Poland
September 3, 1939	Britain and France declare war on Germany

Unemployment in Britain
The Depression hit Britain hard—and its effects continued to be felt throughout the 1930s. These unemployed shipyard workers from Jarrow, in northeastern England, are marching to London in 1936 to present a protest petition. (Hulton Archive/Getty Images)

Economic policymakers based their responses on the "classical" economic model that had developed from the ideas of Adam Smith in the eighteenth century (see page 598). According to this model, a benign "invisible hand" ensured that a free-market price for labor, for capital, and for goods and services would produce an ongoing tendency toward economic equilibrium. A downturn in the business cycle was a normal and necessary adjustment; government interference would only upset this self-adjusting mechanism.

By 1932, however, it was clear that the conventional response was not working, and governments began seeking more actively to stimulate the economy. Although the British economist John Maynard Keynes would outline the rationale for governmental intervention in technical economic terms in 1936, governments could only experiment, and strategies varied widely. (See the feature, "The Written Record: The Government's Role in Managing a Free-Market Economy.") In the United States, Franklin D. Roosevelt (1882–1945) defeated the incumbent president, Herbert Hoover, in 1932 with the promise of a New Deal—a commitment to increase government spending to restore purchasing power. In fascist Italy, a state agency created to infuse capital into failing companies proved a reasonably effective basis for collaboration between government and business. In Germany, economics minister Hjalmar Schacht mounted an energetic assault on the economic problem after Hitler came to power in 1933. Government measures sealed off the German mark from international fluctuations, stimulated public spending—partly on rearmament—and kept wages low. By 1935, Germany was back to full employment. This success added tremendously to Hitler's popularity.

High unemployment in Norway, Sweden, and Denmark helped Social Democrats win power in all three of these Scandinavian countries by the mid-1930s. The new left-leaning governments responded to the economic crisis not by a frontal assault on capitalism, but by pioneering the "welfare state," providing such benefits as health care, unemployment insurance, and family allowances. To pay for the new welfare safety net, the Scandinavian countries adopted a high level of progressive taxation and pared military expenditures to a minimum. The turn to a welfare state eased the immediate human costs of the Depression and helped restore production by stimulating demand. At the same time, the Scandinavian model attracted much admiration as a "third way" between free-market capitalism and the various dictatorial extremes.

In the other European democracies, the Depression proved more intractable. Although Britain saw some recovery by the mid-1930s, it was especially the rearmament of the later 1930s,

The Government's Role in Managing a Free-Market Economy

In 1936, at the height of the Depression, the British economist John Maynard Keynes published The General Theory of Employment, Interest and Money, *which proved the most influential work in economics of the twentieth century. While recognizing the advantages of a free-market economy, Keynes noted that capitalism seemed to entail a built-in tendency toward unemployment, dramatically evident in the Depression. Thus some people were attracted to socialist or statist alternatives, which might include, for example, the wholesale nationalization of industry. But Keynes insisted that a more active role for government in managing the capitalist economy could overcome the tendency toward unemployment while preserving a democratic framework and the advantages of a market economy. Government could manage the economy especially through the "socialization of investment"—absorbing money through taxation and spending it to stimulate the economy toward full employment.*

The outstanding faults of the economic society in which we live are its failure to provide for full employment and its arbitrary and inequitable distribution of wealth and incomes....

...I conceive, therefore, that a somewhat comprehensive socialisation of investment will prove the only means of securing an approximation to full employment; though this need not exclude all manner of compromises and of devices by which public authority will co-operate with private initiative. But beyond this no obvious case is made out for a system of State Socialism which would embrace most of the economic life of the community. It is not the ownership of the instruments of production which it is important for the State to assume. If the State is able to determine the aggregate amount of resources devoted to augmenting the instruments and the basic rate of reward to those who own them, it will have accomplished all that is necessary. Moreover, the necessary measures of socialisation can be introduced gradually and without a break in the general traditions of society....

...The central controls necessary to ensure full employment will, of course, involve a large extension of the traditional functions of government. Furthermore, the modern classical theory has itself called attention to various conditions in which the free play of economic forces may need to be curbed or guided. But there will still remain a wide field for the exercise of private initiative and responsibility. Within this field the traditional advantages of individualism will still hold good.

Let us stop for a moment to remind ourselves what these advantages are. They are partly advantages of efficiency—the advantages of decentralisation and of the play of self-interest....

Whilst, therefore, the enlargement of the functions of government, involved in the task of adjusting to one another the propensity to consume and inducement to invest, would seem to a nineteenth-century publicist or to a contemporary American financier to be a terrific encroachment on individualism, I defend it, on the contrary, both as the only practicable means of avoiding the destruction of existing economic forms in their entirety and as the condition of the successful functioning of individual initiative....

The authoritarian state systems of today seem to solve the problem of unemployment at the expense of efficiency and of freedom. It is certain that the world will not much longer tolerate the unemployment which, apart from brief intervals of excitement, is associated—and, in my opinion, inevitably associated—with present-day capitalistic individualism. But it may be possible by a right analysis of the problem to cure the disease whilst preserving efficiency and freedom.

QUESTIONS

1. Why does Keynes argue for a considerably expanded role for government in coordinating the capitalist economy?

2. In what sense is Keynes trying to save free-market capitalism in light of the Depression and the appeal of the alternatives emerging in Italy, Germany, and the Soviet Union?

Source: From John Maynard Keynes, *The General Theory of Employment, Interest and Money*, pp. 372, 378–381. Reprinted by permission of J. S. Dring.

financed by borrowing, or deficit spending, that got the British economy growing again. France, less dependent on international trade, experienced the consequences of the world crisis only gradually. But by the early 1930s, France, too, was suffering its effects, which lingered to the end of the decade, helping to poison the political atmosphere.

The Impact Beyond the West

The radical restriction of international trade meant a sharp decline in demand for the basic commodities that colonial and other regions exported to the industrialized West. Economic strains fed nationalist, anti-Western sentiments in colonial nations. The increase in misery among rural

Gandhi Advocates Nonviolence

Mohandas Gandhi, a successful English-educated lawyer, emerged as a major force in the movement for Indian independence just after World War I. Calling first for a strategy of noncooperation with the British colonial overlords, Gandhi gradually developed a philosophy of nonviolent civil disobedience, which won widespread sympathy for the cause of Indian independence. The following excerpts from articles published in 1935 and 1939—years notable for outbreaks of violence elsewhere—explain the significance of nonviolence to Gandhi's overall strategy.

Non-violence to be a creed has to be all-pervasive. I cannot be non-violent about one activity of mine and violent about others. That would be a policy, not a life force. That being so, I cannot be indifferent about the war that Italy is now waging against Abyssinia.... India has an unbroken tradition of non-violence from times immemorial. But at no time in her ancient history, as far as I know it, has it had complete nonviolence in action pervading the whole land. Nevertheless, it is my unshakeable belief that her destiny is to deliver the message of non-violence to mankind....

...India as a nation is not non-violent in the full sense of the term.... Her non-violence is that of the weak.... She lacks the ability to offer physical resistance. She has no consciousness of strength. She is conscious only of her weakness. If she were otherwise, there would be no communal problems, nor political. If she were non-violent in the consciousness of her strength, Englishmen would lose their role of distrustful conquerors. We may talk politically as we like and often legitimately blame the English rulers. But if we, as Indians, could but for a moment visualize ourselves as a strong people disdaining to strike, we should cease to fear Englishmen whether as soldiers, traders or administrators, and they to distrust us. Therefore if we became truly non-violent we should carry Englishmen with us in all we might do. In other words, we being millions would be the greatest moral force in the world, and Italy would listen to our friendly word....

...[W]hen society is deliberately constructed in accordance with the law of non-violence, its structure will be different in material particulars from what it is today. But I cannot say in advance what the government based wholly on non-violence will be like.

What is happening today is disregard of the law of non-violence and enthronement of violence as if it were an eternal law. The democracies, therefore, that we see at work in England, America and France are only so called, because they are no less based on violence than Nazi Germany, Fascist Italy or even Soviet Russia. The only difference is that the violence of the last three is much better organized than that of the three democratic powers. Nevertheless we see today a mad race for outdoing one another in the matter of armaments. And if and when the clash comes, as it is bound to come one day, the democracies win, they will do so only because they will have the backing of their peoples who imagine that they have a voice in their own government whereas in the other three cases the peoples might rebel against their own dictatorships.

Holding the view that without the recognition of non-violence on a national scale there is no such thing as a constitutional or democratic government, I devote my energy to the propagation of nonviolence as the law of our life—individual, social, political, national and international. I fancy that I have seen the light, though dimly. I write cautiously, for I do not profess to know the whole of the Law. If I know the successes of my experiments, I know also my failures. But the successes are enough to fill me with undying hope. I have often said that if one takes care of the means, the end will take care of itself. Non-violence is the means, the end for every nation is complete independence.

QUESTIONS

1. What is the difference between "strong" and "weak" nonviolence in Gandhi's thinking?
2. Why does Gandhi play down the difference between the democracies and the dictatorships of the West?

Source: From Raghavan Iyer, ed., *The Essential Writings of Mahatma Gandhi*, 1991, pp. 245–247, 262–263. Reprinted by permission of the Navajivan Trust.

villagers in India, for example, spread the movement for national independence from urban elites to the rural masses. In this context, Mohandas Gandhi, who had become known by 1920 for advocating noncooperation with the British, became the first leader to win a mass following throughout the Indian subcontinent (see pages 717 and 729). Encouraging villagers to boycott British goods, Gandhi accented simplicity, self-reliance, and an overall strategy of nonviolent civil disobedience based on Indian traditions. (See the feature, "The Global Record: Gandhi Advocates Nonviolence.")

In Japan, the strains of the Great Depression helped produce precisely the turn to imperialist violence that Gandhi sought to counter. Densely populated, yet lacking raw materials, Japan was particularly dependent on international trade and reacted strongly as increasing tariffs elsewhere cut sharply into Japanese exports. Led by young army officers who were already eager for a less subservient form of Westernization, Japan turned to aggressive imperialism. As justification, the Japanese began arguing that they were spearheading a wider struggle to free East Asia from Western imperialism. (See the feature, "The Global Record: Japan's 'Pan-Asian' Mission" on page 802 in Chapter 28.) Attacking in 1931, Japanese forces quickly reduced Manchuria to a puppet state, but the Japanese met stubborn resistance when they began seeking to extend this conquest to the rest of China in 1937.

Japanese pressure indirectly advanced the rise of the Chinese communist movement, led by Mao Zedong (Mao Tse-tung, 1893–1976). Securing a base in the Yanan district in 1936, Mao began seeking to apply Marxism-Leninism to China through land reform and other measures to link the Communist Party elite to the Chinese peasantry. Mao was notable among those adapting Western ideas to build an indigenous movement that would at once overcome Western imperialism and create an alternative to Western liberal capitalism.

SECTION SUMMARY

- The new international economic interdependence after World War I entailed strains that were difficult to understand at the time—and that eventually helped produce the Great Depression.

- The effort to respond to the economic downturn through the principles of classical economics only deepened the crisis.

- The new regimes of the extreme left and right won greater prestige in some circles because they seemed to be surviving the global economic crisis more successfully than the capitalist democracies.

- Gradually, the democratic governments began trying out more innovative, interventionist responses to the Depression.

- By restricting imports into the industrialized West, the Depression hurt the non-Western world and helped fuel anticolonialist sentiment.

THE STALINIST REVOLUTION IN THE SOVIET UNION

Why did the Stalinist attempt to build "socialism in one country" lead to the "terror-famine" of 1932–1933 and the "great terror" of 1937–1938?

Seeking to build "socialism in one country," Joseph Stalin led the Soviet Union during the 1930s through an astounding transformation that mixed achievement with brutality and terror in often tragic ways. The resulting governmental system, which gave Stalin unprecedented power, proved crucial to the outcome of the experiment that had begun with the Russian Revolution of 1917. But whether the fateful turn of the 1930s had been implicit in the Leninist revolutionary model, or whether it stemmed mostly from unforeseen circumstances and Stalin's idiosyncratic personality, has long been controversial.

Crash Industrialization and Forced Collectivization

Stalin's program of rapid industrialization based on forced **collectivization** in agriculture began in earnest at the beginning of 1930. It entailed an assault on the better-off peasants, or *kulaks*, who were often sent to labor camps in Siberia while their lands were taken over by the government. The remaining peasants were herded into new government-controlled collective farms. So unpopular was this measure that many peasants simply killed their livestock or smashed their farm implements rather than have them collectivized. By 1934, the number of cattle in the Soviet Union was barely half what it had been in 1928.

collectivization Soviet program under Stalin that reshaped agriculture by forcing peasants into government-controlled collective farms in order to better finance rapid industrialization.

Collectivization served, as intended, to squeeze from the peasantry the resources needed to finance industrialization, but it was carried out with extreme brutality. What was being squeezed was not merely a surplus—the state's extractions cut into subsistence. So while Soviet agricultural exports increased after 1930, large numbers of peasants starved to death. The great famine that developed during 1932–1933 resulted in between five million and six million deaths, over half of them in Ukraine. This "terror-famine" went unrecorded in the Soviet press, and the Soviets refused help from international relief agencies.

By 1937, almost all Soviet agriculture took place on collective farms—or on state farms set up in areas not previously under agriculture. However, restrictions on private plots and livestock ownership were eased slightly after 1933, and partly as a result, agriculture rebounded and living standards began to rise. By the late 1930s, moreover, significant increases in industrial output had established solid foundations in heavy industry, including the bases for military production.

Collectivization in Soviet Agriculture At the "New Life" collective farm, not far from Moscow, women stand for the morning roll call. The Soviet collectivization effort of the 1930s rested in important measure on the forced mobilization of peasant women. (Russian State Film & Photo Archive at Krasnogorsk (RGAKFD))

Soviet propaganda, including art in the official socialist realist style, glorified the achievements of the new Soviet industrial and agricultural workers. "Stakhanovism" (stah-KAH-nov-izm), named for a coal miner who had heroically exceeded his production quota in 1935, became the term for the prodigious economic achievements that the regime valued as it proclaimed the superiority of the communist system.

But whatever its successes, this forced development program created many inefficiencies and entailed tremendous human costs. The Soviet Union could probably have done at least as well, with much less suffering, through other strategies of industrial development. Moreover, Stalin's program departed from certain socialist principles—egalitarianism in wages, for example—that the regime had taken very seriously during the late 1920s. By 1931, bureaucratic managers, concerned simply with maximizing output, were openly favoring workers in certain industries. Collective bargaining and the right to strike had vanished from the workers' arsenal.

From Opposition to Terror, 1932–1938

Stalin's radical course, with its brutality and uncertain economic justification, quickly provoked opposition. During the summer of 1932, a group centered on M. N. Ryutin (ree-YOU-tin) circulated among party leaders a two-hundred-page tract calling for a retreat from Stalin's economic program and a return to democracy within the party. It advocated readmitting those who had been expelled—including Stalin's archenemy, Leon Trotsky. Moreover, the document strongly condemned Stalin personally, describing him as "the evil genius of the Russian Revolution, who, motivated by a personal desire for power and revenge, brought the Revolution to the verge of ruin."[1]

Stalin promptly had Ryutin and his associates ousted from the party, then arrested and imprisoned. But especially as the international situation grew menacing during the 1930s, Stalin became ever more preoccupied with the scope for further opposition. Both Germany and Japan exhibited expansionist aims that might threaten Soviet territories. Trotsky from exile might work with foreign agents and Soviet dissidents to sabotage the Soviet development effort.

In December 1934, the assassination of Sergei Kirov (KIH-roff), party leader of Leningrad (the former Petrograd), indicated the potential for violence. But whether Stalin was actually responsible for the assassination, or simply felt vulnerable because of it, has long been in dispute. In any case, the determination to root out "wreckers," those assumed to be sabotaging the grandiose Soviet experiment, led gradually to purges, **show trials**, and even a kind of terror, with several categories of citizens vulnerable to arrest by the secret police. By the time it wound down, early in 1939, this "great terror" had significantly changed the communist regime—and Soviet society. But though the bare facts are clear, what to make of them is not.

In the three Moscow show trials, held during a twenty-month period from 1936 to 1938, noted Bolsheviks, including Nikolai Bukharin and major functionaries such as Genrikh Yagoda, recently removed as chief of the secret police, confessed to a series of sensational trumped-up charges: that they had been behind the assassination of Kirov, that they would like to have killed Stalin, that they constituted an "anti-Soviet, Trotskyite center," spying for Germany and Japan and preparing to sabotage Soviet industry in the event of war. Almost all the accused, including Bukharin and others who had been central to the 1917 revolution, were convicted and executed. Soviet authorities did not dare risk public trial for the few who refused, even in the face of torture, to play their assigned roles and confess. Among them was Ryutin, who was shot in secret early in 1937.

During 1937, a purge wiped out much of the top ranks of the army, with half the entire officer corps shot or imprisoned in response to unfounded charges of spying and treason. The Communist Party underwent several purges, culminating in the great purge of 1937 and 1938. Of the roughly two thousand delegates to the 1934 congress of the Communist Party, over half were shot during the next few years.

Although heated controversy remains over the number of victims of the Stalinist revolution, the totals are staggering. According to one influential high-end estimate, 8.5 million of the approximately 160 million people in the Soviet Union were arrested during 1937 and 1938, and of these, perhaps 1 million were executed by shooting. Half of those belonging to the Communist Party—1.2 million people—were arrested; of these, 600,000 were executed, and most of the rest died in **gulag** labor camps. Altogether, the terror surrounding the several purges resulted in as many as 8 million deaths. Estimates of the death toll from all of Stalin's policies of the 1930s, including forced collectivization, range as high as 20 million.

Communism and Stalinism

What was going on in this bizarre and lethal combination of episodes? Obviously, Stalinism was one possible outcome of Leninist communism, but was it the logical, even the inevitable, outcome? Leninism had accented centralized authority and the scope for human will to force events, so it may have created a framework in which Stalinism was likely to emerge. Yet Stalin's personal idiosyncrasies and growing paranoia seem to have been crucial for the Soviet system to develop as it did. But though he ended up the regime's undisputed leader, Stalin was part of a wider dynamic.

It was long assumed that Stalin was pursuing a coordinated policy of terror to create a system of total control. Yet recent research has shown that he was often merely improvising, responding to a situation that had become chaotic, out of control, as the Communists tried to carry through a revolution in a backward country. No one had ever attempted this sort of forced industrialization based on a centrally planned economy. At once idealistic, inexperienced, and suspicious, the regime's leaders really believed that failures must be due to sabotage—that "wreckers" were seeking to undermine the heroic Soviet experiment. Moreover, though Stalin tended to blow them out of proportion, there were genuine threats to the Soviet regime and his own leadership by the mid-1930s.

Whereas the terror was long viewed as almost random, it is now clearer that those in the upper and middle reaches of the Soviet system were the most vulnerable. Top officials encouraged ordinary workers to provide information about plant managers and local party officials who seemed incompetent or corrupt. And whether to serve the revolution or to vent personal resentments, such workers often took the initiative in denouncing their superiors, thereby playing important roles in the dynamic that developed.

But what explains the "confessions" that invariably resulted from the bizarre show trials? The accused sometimes succumbed to torture, and to threats to their families. But some, at least, offered false confessions because they believed that in doing so, they were still serving the communist cause. All along, the revolution had required a willingness to compromise personal

show trials Trials staged for ideological and propaganda reasons in the USSR.

gulag Originally an acronym for "main camp administration," it refers to the network of forced labor camps for political prisoners in the Soviet Union. There were at least 476 camps in all.

scruples, including "bourgeois" concerns about personal honor and dignity. Even though false, these confessions could help the communist regime ward off the genuine dangers it faced. So in confessing, the accused would be serving the long-term cause, which they believed to be bigger than Stalin and the issues of the moment. What some could not see—or admit—was that the triumph of Stalinism was fatally compromising the original revolutionary vision.

Although much was unplanned and even out of control, Stalin's ultimate responsibility for the lethal dynamic of the later 1930s is undeniable. At the height of the terror, he personally approved lists for execution, and he took advantage of the chain of events to crush all actual or imagined opposition. By 1939, Stalin loyalists constituted the entire party leadership.

Even as some turned away in disillusionment or despair, others found the regime's ruthlessness in rooting out its apparent enemies evidence of its ongoing revolutionary purpose. And whereas Stalin was not a charismatic leader like Hitler or Mussolini, he was coming for many to embody the ongoing promise of the communist experiment.

HITLER AND NAZISM IN GERMANY

Through what measures did the Nazi regime claim to be improving the quality of the German population?

Adolf Hitler   German dictator whose aggressive foreign policy led to World War II and whose policies of anti-Semitism and racial purity led to the murder of millions.

Beset with problems from the start, the Weimar Republic lay gravely wounded by 1932. Various antidemocratic groups competed to replace it. The winner was the Nazi movement, led by **Adolf Hitler**, who became chancellor in January 1933. It was especially Hitler's new regime in Germany that made the 1930s so tortured, for Hitler not only radically transformed German society, but fundamentally altered the power balance in Europe.

Nazism took inspiration from Italian fascism, but Hitler's regime proved more dynamic—and more troubling—than Mussolini's. Nazism was not conventionally revolutionary, in the sense of mounting a frontal challenge to the existing socioeconomic order. Some of its themes were traditionalist and even anti-modernizing. But in the final analysis, Nazism was anything but conservative. Indeed, it constituted a direct assault on what had long been held as the best of Western civilization.

The Emergence of Nazism and the Crisis of the Weimar Republic

National Socialist German Workers' (Nazi) Party (NSDAP)   The political party that grew from the movement that German dictator Adolf Hitler made his vehicle to power.

The **National Socialist German Workers' (Nazi) Party (NSDAP)** emerged from the turbulent situation in Munich just after the war. A center of leftist agitation, the city also became a hotbed of the radical right, nurturing a number of new nationalist, militantly anticommunist political groups. One of them, a workers' party founded under the aegis of the right-wing Thule Society early in 1919, attracted the attention of Adolf Hitler, who soon gave it his personal stamp.

Adolf Hitler (1889–1945) had been born not German but Austrian, the son of a middling government official. By 1913, he had become a German nationalist hostile to the multinational Habsburg empire, and he emigrated to Germany to escape service in the Austrian army. He was not opposed to military service per se, however, and when war broke out in 1914, he immediately volunteered to serve in the German army.

Corporal Hitler experienced firsthand the fighting at the front and, as a courier, performed bravely and effectively. Indeed, he was in a field hospital being treated for gas poisoning when the war ended. Although his fellow soldiers considered him quirky and introverted, Hitler found the war experience crucial; it was during the war, he said later, that he "found himself."

Following his release from the hospital, Hitler worked for the army in routine surveillance of extremist groups in Munich. In this role, he joined the infant German Workers' Party late in 1919. When his first political speech at a rally in February 1920 proved a resounding success, Hitler began to believe he could play a special political role. From this point, he gradually developed the confidence to lead a new nationalist, anticommunist, and anti-Weimar movement.

But Hitler jumped the gun in November 1923 when, with Erich Ludendorff at his side, he led the Beer Hall Putsch in Munich, an abortive attempt to launch a march on Berlin to overthrow the republic. On trial after this effort failed, Hitler gained greater national visibility as he denounced the Versailles treaty and the Weimar government. Still, *Mein Kampf* (*My Battle*), the political tract that he wrote while in prison during 1924, sold poorly. To most, Hitler was simply a right-wing rabble-rouser whose views were not worth taking seriously.

His failure in 1923 convinced Hitler that he should exploit the existing political system, but not challenge it directly, in his quest for power on the national level. Yet Hitler did not view the NSDAP as just another political party, playing by the same rules as the others. Thus, most notably, the Nazi Party maintained a paramilitary arm, the *Sturmabteilung* (SA), which provoked a good deal of antileftist street violence. Still, the Nazis remained confined to the margins of national politics, even as late as 1928, when they attracted only 2.6 percent of the vote in elections to the Reichstag.

The onset of the economic depression by the end of 1929 produced problems that the Weimar democracy could not handle—and that radically changed the German political framework. The pivotal issue was unemployment insurance, which became a tremendous financial burden for the government as unemployment grew. The governing coalition fell apart over the issue in March 1930, and this proved to be the end of normal parliamentary government in Weimar Germany.

President Paul von Hindenburg called on Heinrich Brüning (1885–1970), an expert on economics from the Catholic Center Party, to become chancellor. Brüning was to spearhead a hard-nosed, deflationary economic program intended to stimulate exports by lowering prices. Like most middle-class Germans, Brüning feared inflation, disliked unemployment insurance, and believed that Germany could not afford public works projects to pump up demand—the obvious alternative to his deflationary policy. But when he presented his program to the Reichstag, he encountered opposition not only from those on the left, but also from conservatives, eager to undermine the republic altogether. As a result, Brüning could get no parliamentary majority. Rather than resigning or seeking a compromise, he invoked Article 48, the emergency provision of the Weimar constitution, which enabled him to govern under presidential decree.

When this expedient provoked strenuous protests, Brüning dissolved the Reichstag and scheduled new elections for September 1930. A more conciliatory tack might have enabled the chancellor to build a new parliamentary majority—and save parliamentary government. In any case, the outcome of the elections was disastrous—for Brüning, and ultimately for Germany as well. While two of the democratic, pro-Weimar parties lost heavily, the two extremes, the Communists and the Nazis, improved their totals considerably. Indeed, this was a major breakthrough for the Nazis, whose share of the vote jumped from 2.6 percent to 18.3 percent of the total.

Brüning continued to govern, still relying on President Hindenburg and Article 48 rather than majority support in the Reichstag. But his program of raising taxes and decreasing government spending failed to revive the economy. Meanwhile, the growth of the political extremes helped fuel an intensification of the political violence and street fighting that had bedeviled the Weimar Republic from the beginning.

By this point, conservatives close to Hindenburg sensed the chance to replace the fragmented parliamentary system with some form of authoritarian government. A new, tougher regime would not only attack the economic crisis, but also stiffen governmental resistance against the apparent threat from the left. In May 1932, those advisers finally persuaded Hindenburg to dump Brüning, and two of them, Franz von Papen (PAH-pin) (1878–1969) and General Kurt von Schleicher (SHLY-shur) (1882–1934), each got a chance to govern in the months that followed. But neither succeeded, partly because of the daring strategy Hitler adopted.

When, following the ouster of Brüning, new elections were held in July 1932, the Nazis won 37.3 percent of the vote and the Communists 14.3 percent. Together, the two extremes controlled a majority of the seats in the Reichstag. Hitler, as the leader of what was now the Reichstag's largest party, refused to join any coalition—unless he could lead it as chancellor. Meanwhile, the authoritarian conservatives around President Hindenburg wanted to take advantage of the Nazis' mass support for antidemocratic purposes.

Finally, in January 1933, with government at an impasse, Papen lined up a new coalition that he proposed to Hindenburg to replace Schleicher's government. Hitler would be chancellor, Papen himself vice chancellor, and Alfred Hugenberg (1865–1951), the leader of the Nationalist Party, finance minister. For months, Hindenburg had resisted giving Hitler a chance to govern, but he felt this combination might work to establish a parliamentary majority, to box out the left, and to contain Nazism. So Hindenburg named Hitler Germany's chancellor on January 30, 1933.

It became clear virtually at once that the outcome of the crisis was a dramatic change of regime, the triumph of Hitler and Nazism. But though the Nazis had always wanted to destroy the Weimar Republic, they were not directly responsible for overthrowing it. The rise of Nazism was more a symptom than a cause of the crisis of Weimar democracy.

In one sense, the Weimar Republic collapsed from within, largely because the German people disagreed fundamentally about priorities after the war—and then again with the onset of the Depression. Thus, the new democracy produced unstable government based on multiparty coalitions, and it fell into virtual paralysis when faced with the economic crisis by 1930. At the same time, however, those around Hindenburg were particularly quick to begin undercutting democratic government in 1930, as the economic crisis seemed to intensify the threat from the extreme left.

With unemployment growing during the first years of the 1930s, both the Nazis and the Communists gained electoral support, but the Germans voting for the Nazis were not simply those most threatened economically. Nor did the Nazi Party appeal primarily to the uneducated or socially marginal. Rather, the party served as a focus of opposition for those alienated from the Weimar Republic itself. Although the Nazis did relatively poorly among Catholics and industrial workers, they put together a broad, fairly diverse base of electoral support, ranging from artisans and small shopkeepers to university students and civil servants. But though Hitler was clearly anti-Weimar, anticommunist, and anti-Versailles, his positive program remained vague; those who voted for the Nazis were not clear what they might be getting. In light of economic depression and political impasse, however, it seemed time to try something new.

The Consolidation of Hitler's Power, 1933–1934

When Hitler became chancellor, it was not obvious that a change of regime was beginning. Like his predecessors, he could govern only with the president's approval, and governmental institutions like the army, the judiciary, and the diplomatic corps, though hardly bastions of democracy, were not in the hands of committed Nazis. But even though an element of caution and cultivated ambiguity remained, a revolution quickly began, creating a new regime, the Third Reich.

On February 23, just weeks after Hitler became chancellor, a fire engulfed the Reichstag building in Berlin. It was set by a young Dutch communist acting on his own, but it seemed to suggest that a communist uprising was imminent. This sense of emergency gave Hitler an excuse to restrict civil liberties and imprison leftist leaders, including the entire Communist parliamentary delegation. Even in this atmosphere of crisis, the Nazis could not win a majority in the Reichstag elections of March 5. But support from the Nationalists and the Catholic Center Party enabled the Nazis to win Reichstag approval for an enabling act granting Hitler the power to make laws on his own for the next four years, bypassing both the Reichstag and the president.

Although the Weimar Republic was never formally abolished, the laws that followed fundamentally altered government, politics, and public life in Germany. The other parties were either outlawed or persuaded to dissolve, so that in July 1933, the Nazi Party was declared the only legal party. When President Hindenburg died in August 1934, the offices of chancellor and president were merged, and Germany had just one leader, Adolf Hitler, holding unprecedented power. Members of the German armed forces now swore loyalty to him personally.

During this period of power consolidation, Hitler acted decisively but carefully, generally accenting normalization. To be sure, his methods occasionally gave conservatives pause, most notably when he had several hundred people murdered in the "blood purge" of June 30, 1934. But this purge was directed especially against the SA, led by Ernst Röhm (1887–1934), who had had pretensions of controlling the army. His removal seemed evidence that Hitler was taming the radical elements in his own movement. In fact, however, this purge led to the ascendancy of the *Schutzstaffel* (SS), the select Nazi elite, directed by Heinrich Himmler (1900–1945). Linked to the Gestapo, the secret political police, the SS became the institutional basis for the most troubling aspects of Nazism.

Schutzstaffel (SS)
Specially selected Nazi elite, entrusted with the most sensitive ideological tasks of the Nazi regime—and responsible for many of its worst atrocities.

Hitler and Children Adolf Hitler was often portrayed as the friend of children. This photograph accompanied a story for an elementary school reader that described how Hitler, told it was this young girl's birthday, picked her from a crowd of well-wishers to treat her "to cake and strawberries with thick, sweet cream." (Bayerische Staatsbibliothek Munchen/Fotoarchiv Hoffmann)

Hitler's Worldview and the Dynamics of Nazi Practice

In achieving the chancellorship and in expanding his power thereafter, Hitler proved an adept politician, but he was hardly a mere opportunist, seeking to amass power for its own sake. The central components of Hitler's thinking—geopolitics, biological racism, anti-Semitism, and Social Darwinism—were by no means specifically German. They could be found all over the Western world by the early twentieth century.

Geopolitics claimed to offer a scientific understanding of world power relationships based on geographical determinism. In his writings of the 1920s, Hitler warned that Germany faced imminent decline unless it confronted its geopolitical limitations. To remain fully sovereign in the emerging new era of global superpowers like the United States, Germany would have to act quickly to expand its territory. Otherwise, it would end up like Switzerland or the Netherlands.

For decades, German imperialists had argued about whether Germany was better advised to seek overseas colonies or to expand its reach in Europe. As Hitler saw it, Germany's failure to make a clear choice had led to its defeat in World War I. Now choice was imperative, and current geopolitical thinking suggested the direction for expansion. Far-flung empires relying on naval support were said to be in decline. The future lay with land-based states—unified, geographically contiguous, with the space necessary for self-sufficiency. By expanding eastward into Poland

and the Soviet Union, Germany could conquer the living space, or *Lebensraum*, necessary for agricultural-industrial balance—and ultimately for self-sufficiency.

Though limited and mechanistic, this geopolitical way of thinking is at least comprehensible, in light of the German vulnerabilities that had become evident during World War I. The other three strands of Hitler's worldview were much less plausible, though each had become prominent during the second half of the nineteenth century. Biological racism insisted that built-in racial characteristics determine what is most important about any individual. Anti-Semitism went beyond racism in claiming that Jews had played, and continued to play, a special and negative role in history. The fact that the Jews were dispersed and often landless indicated that they were different—and parasitical. Finally, Social Darwinism, especially in its German incarnation, accented the positive role of struggle—not among individuals, as in a prominent American strand, but among racial groups.

The dominant current of racist thinking found the "Aryans" to be healthy, creative, and superior. Originally the Sanskrit term for "noble," *Aryan* gradually came to indicate the ancient language assumed to have been the common source of the modern Indo-European languages. An Aryan was simply a speaker of one of those languages. By the late nineteenth century, however, the term had become supremely ill defined. In much racist thinking, Germanic peoples were somehow especially Aryan, but race mixing had produced impurity—and thus degeneration. Success in struggle with the other races was the ultimate measure of vitality, the only proof of racial superiority for the future.

Hitler brought these themes together by emphasizing that humanity is not special, but simply part of nature, subject to the same laws of struggle and selection as the other animal species. Humanitarian ideals were thus dangerous illusions. As he put it to a group of officer cadets in 1944:

> Nature is always teaching us…that she is governed by the principle of selection: that victory is to the strong and that the weak must go to the wall. She teaches us that what may seem cruel to us, because it affects us personally or because we have been brought up in ignorance of her laws, is nevertheless often essential if a higher way of life is to be attained. Nature…knows nothing of the notion of humanitarianism, which signifies that the weak must at all costs be protected and preserved even at the expense of the strong.
>
> Nature does not see in weakness any extenuating reasons … on the contrary, weakness calls for condemnation.[2]

To Hitler, the Jews were not simply another of the races involved in this endless struggle. Rather, as landless parasites, they embodied the principles—from humanitarianism to class struggle—that were antithetical to the healthy natural struggle among racial groups. "Jewishness" was bound up with the negative, critical intellect that dared suggest things ought to be not natural but just, even that it was up to human beings to change the world, to make it just. The Jews were the virus keeping the community from a healthy natural footing. Marxist communism, embodying divisive class struggle as well as utopian humanitarian ideals, was fundamentally Jewish.

The central features of Nazism in practice, from personal dictatorship to the extermination of the Jews, followed from Hitler's view of the world. First, the racial community must organize itself politically for this ceaseless struggle. Individuals are but instruments for the success of the racial community. Parliamentary democracy, reflecting short-term individual interests, fosters selfish materialism and division, thereby weakening that community. The political order must rest instead on a charismatic leader, united with the whole people through bonds of common blood.

Nazi Aims and German Society

To create a genuine racial community, or *Volksgemeinschaft*, it was necessary to unify society and instill Nazi values, thereby making the individual feel part of the whole—and ultimately an instrument to serve the whole. This entailed more or less forced participation in an array of Nazi groupings, from the Women's Organization to the Hitler Youth, from the Labor Front to the "Strength Through Joy" leisure-time organization. Common participation meant shared experiences, such as weekend hikes and a weekly one-dish meal. Even the most ordinary, once-private activities took on a public or political dimension. Moreover, the Nazis devised unprecedented ways to stage-manage public life, using rituals like the Hitler salute, symbols like the swastika, new media like radio and film, and carefully orchestrated party rallies—all in an effort to foster this sense of belonging. (See the feature, "The Visual Record: Film as Propaganda.")

The Nazi regime enjoyed considerable popular support, but even after Hitler was well entrenched in power, most Germans did not grasp the regime's deeper dynamic. Some welcomed the sense of unity, the feeling of belonging and participation, especially after what had seemed the alienation and divisiveness of the Weimar years. Moreover, Hitler himself was immensely popular, partly because of his personal charisma, partly because his apparently decisive leadership was a welcome departure from the near paralysis of the Weimar parliamentary system. But most important, before the coming of war in 1939, he seemed to go from success to success, surmounting the Depression and repudiating the major terms of the hated Versailles treaty.

Hitler's propaganda minister, Joseph Goebbels (1897–1945), played on these successes to create a "Hitler myth," which made Hitler seem at once a hero and a man of the people, even the embodiment of healthy German ideals against the excesses and corruption that could be attributed to the Nazi Party. This myth became central to the Nazi regime, but it merely provided a façade behind which the real Hitler could pursue partially hidden, longer-term aims. These aims were not publicized directly because the German people did not seem ready for them. In this sense, then, support for Hitler and his regime was broad but shallow during the 1930s.

Moreover, resistance increased as the regime became more intrusive. Youth gangs actively opposed the official Hitler Youth organization as it grew increasingly overbearing and militaristic by the late 1930s. But people resisted especially by minimizing their involvement with the regime, retreating into the private realm, in response to the Nazi attempt to make everything public.

Did such people feel constantly under threat of the Gestapo, the secret police? In principle, the Gestapo could interpret the will of the *Führer*, or leader, and decide whether any individual citizen was "guilty" or not. And the Gestapo was not concerned about due process; on occasion, it simply bypassed the regular court system. But the Gestapo did not terrorize Germans at random. Its victims were generally members of specific groups, people suspected of active opposition, or people who protected those the Gestapo had targeted.

Moreover, changes and contradictions in Nazi goals allowed considerable space for personal choice. During the struggle for power, the Nazis had emphasized the woman's role as wife and mother and deplored the ongoing emancipation of women. Once Hitler came to power, concerns about unemployment reinforced these views. Almost immediately, Hitler's government began offering interest-free loans to help couples set up housekeeping if the woman agreed to leave the labor force. Such efforts to increase the German birthrate reinforced the emphasis on child rearing in Nazi women's organizations. Nonetheless, the size of the family continued to decrease in Germany, as elsewhere in the industrialized world during the 1930s.

Beginning in 1936, when rapid rearmament began to produce labor shortages, the regime did an about-face and began seeking to attract women back to the workplace, especially into jobs central to military preparation. These efforts were not notably successful, and by 1940, the military was calling for the conscription of women into war industries.

Further, the Nazis valued the family only insofar as it was congruent with the "health" of the racial community. They were determined to promote that health by actually implementing radical eugenics measures that had been discussed, but not seriously implemented, during the Weimar years. The Nazi regime encouraged childbearing and large families on the part of those considered fit, while simultaneously discouraging those considered unfit from having children. In pursuit of these goals, the regime regulated marriage, essentially politicized the family, and compromised traditional family values again and again.

Just months after coming to power in 1933, Hitler brushed aside the objections of Vice Chancellor Franz von Papen, a Catholic, and engineered a law mandating the compulsory sterilization of persons suffering from certain allegedly hereditary diseases. Medical personnel sterilized some 400,000 people, the vast majority of them "Aryan" Germans, during the Nazi years.

Eugenics was essentially one of two prongs of the Nazis' radical population policy. The other sought ethnic homogeneity, especially through measures directed against Germany's small Jewish minority. Although the regime began immediately to single out the Jews, Nazi Jewish policy remained an improvised hodgepodge prior to World War II. Within weeks after Hitler became chancellor in 1933, new restrictions limited Jewish participation in the civil service, in the professions, and in German cultural life—and quickly drew censure from the League of Nations. The Nuremberg Laws, announced at a party rally in 1935, included prohibition of sexual relations and marriage between Jewish and non-Jewish Germans. Beginning in 1938, the Jews had to carry special identification cards and to add "Sarah" or "Israel" to their given names.

THE RESPONSE OF THE GERMAN PEOPLE

WOMEN, FAMILY, AND REPRODUCTION

NAZI POLICY TOWARD GERMAN JEWS

Film as Propaganda

One of the extraordinary pieces of evidence from the Nazi period is *Triumph of the Will,* a documentary film on the sixth Nazi Party rally, which took place from September 4 to 10, 1934, in the historic city of Nuremberg, by this time the official site for such party rallies. Directed by a talented young woman named Leni Riefenstahl (1902–2003), *Triumph of the Will* has long been recognized as one of the most compelling propaganda films ever made. What can we learn from this film about how the Nazis understood and used propaganda? What was the Nazi regime trying to convey in sponsoring the film, with the particular images it contained?

A sense of the scope for political propaganda was one of the defining features of the Nazi movement virtually from its inception. In his quest for power, Hitler allotted an especially significant role to his future propaganda minister, Joseph Goebbels. Both Hitler and Goebbels saw that new media and carefully orchestrated events might be used to shape the political views of masses of people.

The Nazi Party held the first of what would become annual conventions in Nuremberg in 1927. From the start, these meetings were rallies of the faithful, intended to give the Nazi movement a sense of cohesion and common purpose; but they increasingly became carefully staged propaganda spectacles, with banners and searchlights, parades and speeches. When, by 1934, the regime had completed the task of immediate power consolidation, it seemed time to seize the potential of the film medium to carry the spectacle beyond those present in Nuremberg. The intention to make a film thus influenced the staging of the 1934 rally. Film would transform the six-day event into a single potent work of art.

When Hitler came to power, Goebbels, as propaganda minister, assumed control of the German film industry, and he was particularly jealous of his prerogatives in this sphere. If there was to be a film of one of the Nuremberg rallies, he assumed that he would be in charge. So he objected strenuously when Hitler decided that Riefenstahl, who was not even a party member, should film the 1934 rally.

Already popular as an actress, Riefenstahl had established her own filmmaking company in 1931, before she turned 30. Her first film won the admiration of Hitler, who sought her out and eventually proposed that she direct the film of the party rally. Although she was an artist with no special interest in politics, Riefenstahl, like many Germans, believed at this point that Hitler might be able to revive Germany's fortunes. So despite considerable reluctance, she bowed to Hitler's persistence and agreed to do the film—though only after she was guaranteed final control over editing. Her relations with Goebbels remained strained, but Hitler continued to support her as she made *Triumph of the Will.*

Riefenstahl developed the 107-minute film by editing 61 hours of footage that covered everything from Hitler's arrival and motorcade to the closing parades and speeches. As depicted on film, the party rally does not convey an overt ideological message. We hear Hitler simply trumpeting German renewal, not attacking Jews or glorifying conquest. Most striking in Riefenstahl's portrayal are the unity and epic monumentality that Nazism had apparently brought to Germany thanks to Hitler's leadership.

The film opens as Hitler emerges from dramatic cloud formations to arrive by airplane, descending from the sky like a god. He appears throughout the film as an almost superhuman figure, even, as in the shot shown here, as inspired, possessed, uncanny. Above all, he is a creator who shapes reality by blending will and art, forging masses of anonymous individuals into one people, one racial community, ready for anything. Those individuals seem, from one perspective, to lose their individuality in a monolithic mass, as in the shot of the parade grounds. But their sense of involvement in grandiose purposes charges them emotionally, even gives them a kind of ecstasy. The symbols, the massed banners, the ritualistic show of conformity, all strengthened this sense of participation in the new people's community. But unity and community were not ends in themselves; the film exalted military values and depicted a disciplined society organized for war.

Triumph of the Will extended participation in the spectacle to those who were not actually present in Nuremberg. Because the film chiseled the sprawling event into a work of art, seeing the film was in some ways more effective than being there. The Nazis looked for every means possible to involve the whole society in ritualistic spectacles that could promote a sense of belonging and unity. In addition to film, they made effective use of radio, even subsidizing the purchase of radio sets, or "people's receivers." Such new media were to help ordinary Germans feel a more meaningful kind of belonging than Weimar democracy made possible. But this was only an emotional involvement, not the active participation of free citizens invited to make rational choices.

But though Hitler and other Nazi leaders claimed periodically to be seeking a definitive solution to Germany's "Jewish problem," the dominant objective during the 1930s was to force German Jews to emigrate. About 60,000 of Germany's 550,000 Jews left the country during 1933 and 1934, and perhaps 25 percent had gotten out by 1938. The fact that the regime stripped emigrating Jews of their assets made emigration more difficult. Potential host countries, concerned about unemployment during the Depression, were especially unwilling to take in substantial numbers of Jews if they were penniless.

As seen in *Triumph of the Will*, the Leader ...

Triumph of the Will had its premiere in March 1935, with Hitler in the audience. It won several prizes in Germany and abroad but enjoyed only mixed success with the German public, especially outside the large cities. For some, it was altogether too artistic, and the Nazi regime did not use it widely for overt propaganda purposes. Still, the Nazis commissioned no other film about Hitler, for *Triumph of the Will* captured the way he wanted to be seen. Indeed, Hitler praised the film as an "incomparable glorification of the power and beauty of our Movement."

QUESTIONS

1. Why did Hitler feel it so important to film a Nazi party rally—and even to plan the rally with the filming in mind?

2. What relationship between Hitler and the Nazi movement does *Triumph of the Will* convey?

... and the Disciplined, Tightly Knit Community of Followers (Both photos from the Museum of Modern Art/Film Stills Archive)

On November 9, 1938, using the assassination of a German diplomat in Paris as a pretext, the Nazis staged the ***Kristallnacht* (Crystal Night)** pogrom, during which almost all the synagogues in Germany and about seven thousand Jewish-owned stores were destroyed. Between 30,000 and 50,000 relatively prosperous Jews were arrested and forced to emigrate after their property was confiscated. Although the German public had generally acquiesced in the earlier restrictions on Jews, this pogrom, with its wanton violation of private property, shocked many Germans.

***Kristallnacht* (Crystal Night)** Organized Nazi assault on Jewish businesses and synagogues during the night of November 9–10, 1938, following the assassination of a German diplomat in Paris.

Concentration camps—supplementary detention centers—had become a feature of the Nazi regime virtually at once, but prior to 1938, they were used primarily to hold political prisoners. As part of the Crystal Night pogrom, about 35,000 Jews were rounded up and sent to the camps, but most were soon released as long as they could document their intention to emigrate. When World War II began in 1939, the total camp population was about 25,000. The systematic physical extermination of the Jews began only during World War II.

EUTHANASIA AND NAZI PREPARATION FOR WAR

euthanasia program
The Nazi program of systematically killing people deemed superfluous or threatening to Germany's racial health because of their physical or mental disabilities.

However, the killing of others deemed superfluous or threatening to the racial community began earlier, with the so-called **euthanasia program** initiated under volunteer medical teams in 1939. Its aim was to eliminate chronic mental patients, the incurably ill, and people with severe physical handicaps. Those subject to such treatment were overwhelmingly ethnic Germans, not Jews or foreigners. Although the regime did all it could to make it appear the victims had died naturally, a public outcry developed, especially among relatives and church leaders, by 1941, when the program was largely discontinued. But by then, it had claimed 100,000 lives and seems essentially to have achieved its initial objectives.

This "euthanasia" program was based on the sense, fundamental to radical Nazism, that war was the norm and readiness for war the essential societal imperative. In war, societies send individuals to their deaths and, on the battlefield, make difficult distinctions among the wounded, letting some die in order to save those most likely to survive and return to battle. Struggle necessitates selection, which requires overcoming humanitarian scruples—especially the notion that "weakness" calls for special protection. Thus, it was desirable to kill even ethnic Germans who were deemed unfit, as "life unworthy of life."

Preparation for war was the core of Nazism in practice. The conquest of living space in the east would make possible a more advantageous agricultural-industrial balance. The result would be not only the self-sufficiency necessary for sovereignty, but also the land-rootedness necessary for racial health. Such a war of conquest would strike not only the allegedly inferior Slavic peoples of the region, but also detested communism, centered in the Soviet Union.

The point of domestic reorganization was to marshal the community's energies and resources for war. Because German business interests generally seemed congruent with Nazi purposes, Nazi aims did not appear to require some revolutionary assault on business elites or the capitalist economy. But the Nazis had their own road to travel, and beginning in 1936, they proved quite prepared to bend the economy, and to coordinate big business, to serve their longer-term aims of war-making.

The Nazi drive toward war during the 1930s transformed international relations in Europe. The responses of the other European powers, as they sought to deal with Hitler, reflected the increasingly polarized political context of the period. Before considering the fortunes of Hitler's foreign policy, we must consider fascism as a wider phenomenon—and the efforts of the democracies, on the one hand, and the Soviet Union, on the other, to come to terms with it.

SECTION SUMMARY

- The Nazis did not directly overthrow the Weimar Republic but ended up the beneficiaries when it reached an impasse during 1930–1933.

- The central components of Hitler's thinking—geopolitics, biological racism, anti-Semitism, and Social Darwinism—were neither original with Hitler nor specifically German.

- Among ordinary Germans, support for Hitler and his regime was broad but shallow during the 1930s.

- A radical eugenics program, entailing forced sterilization and eventually the actual killing of those deemed unfit, was central to Nazi action on the domestic level during the 1930s.

- During the 1930s, the Nazis began stripping German Jews of citizenship rights as part of a haphazard effort to encourage—or force—Jews to emigrate.

FASCIST CHALLENGE AND ANTIFASCIST RESPONSE, 1934–1939

Why did the "popular front" strategy prove counterproductive in both France and Spain?

Communism, fascism, and Nazism all repudiated the parliamentary democracy that had been the West's political norm. Each seemed subject to violence and excess, yet each had features that some found attractive, especially in light of the difficult socioeconomic circumstances of the 1930s. But communists and adherents of the various forms of fascism were bitterly hostile to each other, and the very presence of these new political systems caused polarization all over Europe.

Beginning in 1934, communists sought to join with anyone who would work with them to defend the democratic framework against further fascist assaults. Without democracy, the very survival of communist parties was in doubt. This effort led to new antifascist coalition governments in Spain and France. In each case, however, the Depression restricted maneuvering room, and these governments ended up furthering the polarization they were seeking to avoid. By mid-1940, democracy had fallen in Spain, after a brutal civil war, and even in France, in the wake of military defeat.

European Fascism and the Popular Front Response

Although some across Europe who were disaffected with democracy and hostile to communism found genuine fascism attractive, the line between fascism and conservative authoritarianism blurred in the volatile political climate of the 1930s. To many, any retreat from democracy appeared a step toward fascism.

In east-central Europe, political distinctions became especially problematic. Movements like the Arrow Cross in Hungary and the Legion of the Archangel Michael in Romania modeled themselves on the Italian and German prototypes, but they never achieved political power. Those who controlled the antidemocratic governments in Hungary and Romania, as in Poland, Bulgaria, and Yugoslavia, were authoritarian traditionalists, not fascists. Still, many government leaders in the region welcomed the closer economic ties with Germany that Hitler's economics minister, Hjalmar Schacht, engineered. The difference between authoritarianism and fascism remained clearest in Austria, where Catholic conservatives undermined democracy during 1933 and 1934. They were actively hostile to the growing pro-Nazi agitation in Austria, partly because they wanted to keep Austria independent.

In France, various nationalist, anticommunist, and anti-Semitic leagues gathered momentum during the early 1930s. They covered a spectrum from monarchism to outspoken profascism, but together they constituted at least a potential threat to French democracy. In February 1934, right-wing demonstrations against the Chamber of Deputies provoked a bloody clash with police and forced a change of ministry. As it began to seem that even France might be vulnerable, those from the center and left of the political spectrum began to consider collaborating to resist fascism. The communists, especially, took the initiative by promoting **popular fronts** of all those seeking to preserve democracy.

This was a dramatic change in strategy for international communism. Even as Hitler was closing in on the German chancellorship in the early 1930s, German Communists, following Comintern policy, continued to attack their socialist rivals rather than seek a unified response to Nazism. But by 1934, the threat of fascism seemed so pressing that Communists began actively promoting electoral alliances and governing coalitions with socialists and even liberal democrats to resist its further spread. From 1934 until 1939, Communists everywhere consistently pursued this "popular front" strategy.

By the 1930s, however, it was becoming ever harder to know what was fascist, what was dangerous, and what might lead where. As fears intensified, perceptions became as important as realities. Popular front governments, intended to preserve democracy against what appeared to be fascism, could seem to conservatives to be leaning too far to the left. Ideological polarization made democracy extraordinarily difficult. The archetypal example proved to be Spain, where a tragedy of classical proportions was played out.

popular fronts A term for antifascist electoral alliances and governing coalitions that communists promoted from 1934 until 1939 to resist the further spread of fascism.

Ideological Confrontation At a major international exhibition in Paris in 1937, the new antidemocratic political regimes made bold propaganda statements. With a sculpture from fascist Italy's pavilion in the foreground, we look across the Seine River to a classic representation of the ideological warfare of the 1930s: the Soviet Pavilion, on the left, facing the German Pavilion, on the right. Crowning the Soviet building is the noted sculpture by Vera Muchina, *Worker and Collective Farmer.* (AP Photos)

From Democracy to Civil War in Spain, 1931–1939

Spain became a center of attention in the 1930s, when its promising new parliamentary democracy, launched in 1931, led to civil war in 1936 and the triumph of a repressive authoritarian regime in 1939. An earlier effort at constitutional monarchy had fizzled by 1923, when King Alfonso XIII (1886–1941) supported a new military dictatorship. But growing opposition led first to the resignation of the dictator in 1930 and then, in April 1931, to the end of the monarchy and the proclamation of a republic. The elections for a constituent assembly that followed in June produced a solid victory for a coalition of liberal democrats and Socialists, as well as much hope for substantial reform.

A significant agrarian reform law was passed in 1932, but partly because of the difficult economic context, the new government was slow to implement it. Feeling betrayed, Socialists and agricultural workers became increasingly radical, producing growing upheaval in the countryside. Radicalism on the left made it harder for the moderates to govern and, at the same time, stimulated conservatives to become more politically active.

A right-wing coalition known as the CEDA, led by José Maria Gil Robles (heel ROH-blayce) (1898–1980), grew in strength, becoming the largest party in parliament with the elections of November 1933. In light of its parliamentary strength, the CEDA had a plausible claim to a government role, but it was kept from participation in government until October 1934. It seemed to the left, in the ideologically charged atmosphere of the time, that the growing role of the CEDA was a prelude to fascism.

A strong Catholic from the traditional Spanish right, Gil Robles refused to endorse the democratic republic as a form of government, but he and the CEDA were willing to work within it. So the Spanish left may have been too quick to see the CEDA as fascist—and to react when the CEDA finally got its government role. However, Mussolini and Hitler had each come to power more or less legally, from within parliamentary institutions. The German left had been criticized for its passive response to the advent of Hitler; the Spanish left wanted to avoid the same mistake.

Thus, when the CEDA finally got a role in the government, the left responded during the fall of 1934 with quasi-revolutionary uprisings in Catalonia and Asturias, where a miners' commune was put down only after two weeks of heavy fighting. In the aftermath, the right-leaning government of 1935 began undoing some of the reforms of the left-leaning government of 1931–1933, though still legally, within the framework of the parliamentary republic.

In February 1936, a popular front coalition to ward off fascism won a narrow electoral victory, sufficient for an absolute majority in parliament. As would be true in France a few months later, electoral victory produced popular expectations that went well beyond the essentially defensive purposes of the popular front. Hoping to win back the leftist rank and file and head off what seemed a dangerous attempt at revolution, the new popular front government began to implement a progressive program, now including the land reform that had been promised but not implemented earlier. It was too late, however, to undercut the growing radicalization of the masses. A wave of land seizures began in March 1936, followed by the most extensive strike movement in Spanish history, which by June was becoming clearly revolutionary in character.

Finally, in mid-July, several army officers initiated a military uprising against the government. Soon led by General Francisco Franco (1892–1975), these Nationalist insurgents took control of substantial parts of Spain. But elsewhere they failed to overcome the resistance of the republican Loyalists, those determined to defend the republic. So the result was not the intended military takeover but a brutal civil war, with numerous atrocities committed by both sides (see **MAP 27.1**).

Foreign intervention by the end of 1936 intensified the war's ideological ramifications. Both Fascist Italy and Nazi Germany actively supported the Nationalist insurgency. On the Republican side, the Communists, initially a distinct minority on the Spanish left, gradually gained the ascendancy, partly because they were disciplined and effective, partly because Soviet assistance enhanced their prestige.

Republican Loyalists assumed that Franco and the Nationalists represented another instance of fascism. But though he used the trappings of fascism in seeking to gain popular support, Franco was a traditional military man whose leadership role did not rest on personal charisma. He was not a fascist, but an authoritarian emphasizing order and Spain's Catholic traditions.

Meanwhile, the republic's leaders had to fight a civil war while dealing with continuing revolution in their own ranks. Developing especially in Catalonia from the uprisings of 1936,

🌐 MAP 27.1—The Spanish Civil War, 1936–1939

The Nationalist insurgents quickly took over most of northern and eastern Spain in 1936
and then gradually expanded their territory. The fall of Madrid early in 1939 marked the end
of the fighting. The revolutionary effort of 1936 and 1937 within the Republican zone was
centered in Barcelona.

(Source: Adapted from *The Times Atlas of World History*, 3d ed. Reprinted by permission of HarperCollins Publishers Ltd.
© HarperCollins Publishers Ltd.)

that revolution was not communist but anarcho-syndicalist in orientation. The Communists,
true to popular front principles, insisted that this was no time for such "infantile leftist"
revolutionary experiments. What mattered, throughout the Republican zone, was the factory
discipline necessary to produce essential war materiel. As a consequence, the Communists,
under Stalin's orders, were instrumental in putting down the anarchist revolution in Catalonia
in June 1937.

Despite considerable heroism on the Loyalist side, however, this single-minded prosecution
of the civil war did not prove enough to defeat the military insurgency. The war ended with the
fall of Madrid to the Nationalists in March 1939. General Franco's authoritarian regime governed
Spain until his death in 1975.

In Spain, as in Weimar Germany, the lack of consensus in a new republic made parliamentary
democracy difficult, and the wider ideological framework magnified the difficulties. With the
political boiling point so low, the left and the right each saw the other in extreme terms and
assumed that extraordinary response to the other was necessary. Thus, the left tended to view
even conservatives operating within a parliamentary framework as "fascist," and both sides were
relatively quick to give up on a democratic republic that seemed to be tilting too far in the wrong
direction.

Picasso: *Guernica*　Created for the Spanish Pavilion at the 1937 Paris Exhibition, Pablo Picasso's painting conveys horror and outrage—his response to the German bombing of the Basque town of Guernica (gair-NEE-kah, in Spanish; GWAIR-nee-kah, as customarily rendered in English) on a crowded market day in 1937, during the Spanish civil war. Picasso's stark, elemental imagery came to symbolize the violence and suffering of the whole era.　(Pablo Picasso, *Guernica* [1937, May-early June]. Oil on canvas. Art Resource, NY. © 2002 Artists Rights Society [ARS], New York/ADAGP, Paris)

France in the Era of the Popular Front

In France, as in Spain, concern to arrest the spread of fascism led to a popular front coalition that governed the country from 1936 to 1938. Although it did not lead to civil war, the popular front was central to the French experience of the 1930s, producing polarization and resignation and undermining confidence in the Third Republic.

Beginning in 1934, the French Communists took the initiative in approaching first the Socialists, then the Radicals, to develop a popular front coalition. In reaching out to the Radicals, the Communists stressed French patriotism and made no demand for significant economic reforms. Stalin gave this effort a major push in 1935 when, in a stunning change in the communist line, he stressed the legitimacy of national defense and explicitly endorsed French rearmament.

In the elections of April and May 1936, the popular front won a sizable majority in the Chamber of Deputies, putting the Socialists' leader, Léon Blum (1872–1950), in line to become France's first Socialist prime minister. The Communists pledged full support of the new Blum government, but to avoid fanning fears, they did not participate directly. However, despite the popular front's moderate and essentially defensive aims, the situation quickly began to polarize after the elections.

Fearing that the new Blum government would be forced to devalue the French currency, and thereby diminish the value of assets denominated in francs, French investors immediately began moving their capital abroad. At the same time, the popular front victory produced a wave of enthusiasm among workers that escaped the control of popular front leaders and culminated in a spontaneous strike movement, the largest France had ever seen. By early June, it had spread to all major industries nationwide. Although the workers' demands—for collective bargaining, a forty-hour workweek, and paid vacations—were not extraordinary, the movement involved sit-down strikes as well as the normal walkouts, and thus seemed quasi-revolutionary in character. The major trade union confederation, the Communists, and most Socialists, including Blum himself, saw the strikes as a danger to the popular front, with its more modest aims of defending the republic, and eagerly pursued a settlement.

That settlement, the Matignon (mah-tin-YON) Agreement of June 8, 1936, was a major victory for the French working class. Having been genuinely frightened by the strikes and now reassured that the popular front government would at least uphold the law, French industrialists were willing to make significant concessions. So the workers got collective bargaining, elected shop stewards, and wage increases as a direct result of Matignon, then a forty-hour week and paid vacations in a reform package promptly passed by parliament.

In the enthusiasm of the summer of 1936, other reforms were enacted as well, but after that, the popular front was forced onto the defensive. Two problems undermined its energy and cohesion: the noncooperation of French business and the Spanish civil war. The cautious response of Blum, the Socialist prime minister, is striking in each case, but he faced a situation with little maneuvering room.

From the outset, Blum stressed that he had no mandate for revolution, and as France's first Socialist prime minister, he felt it essential to prove that a Socialist could govern responsibly. Thus, he did not respond energetically to the capital flight, even though it produced serious currency and budgetary difficulties.

In responding to the Spanish civil war, Blum had to decide whether the French government should help the beleaguered Spanish republic, at least by sending supplies. Although he initially favored such help, Blum changed his mind under pressure from three sides. The Conservative government of Stanley Baldwin in Britain was against it. So was the French right; some even suggested that French intervention would provoke a comparable civil war in France. Moreover, the Radicals in his own coalition were generally opposed to helping the Spanish republic, so intervention would jeopardize the cohesion of the popular front itself.

Rather than help supply the Spanish republic, Blum promoted a nonintervention agreement among the major powers, including Italy and Germany. Many Socialists and Communists disliked Blum's cautious policy, especially as it became clear that Mussolini and Hitler were violating their hands-off pledges. As Blum stuck to nonintervention, the moral force of the popular front dissolved.

In 1938, a new government under the Radical Edouard Daladier (dah-lah-dee-YAY) (1884–1970), still nominally a creature of the popular front, began dismantling some of the key gains of 1936, even attacking the forty-hour week. Citing productivity and national security concerns, Daladier adopted pro-business policies and succeeded in attracting capital back to France. But workers, watching the gains they had won in 1936 slip away, felt betrayed. At the same time, businessmen and conservatives began blaming the workers' gains—such as the five-day week—for slowing French rearmament. Although such charges were not entirely fair, they indicated how poisoned the atmosphere in France had become in the wake of the popular front.

As France began to face the possibility of a new war, the popular front was widely blamed for French weakness. When war came at last, resignation and division were prevalent, in contrast with the patriotic unity and high spirits of 1914. It was partly for that reason that France was so easily defeated by Germany in 1940. And when France fell, the democratic Third Republic fell with it.

SECTION SUMMARY

- In light of the ideological polarization of the 1930s, many people found it difficult to distinguish between conservative authoritarianism and fascism.
- In a dramatic change in their international strategy, the Communists in 1934 began promoting "popular fronts," which were to bring together all those seeking to preserve democracy against fascism.
- The wider ideological framework magnified the difficulties of parliamentary democracy in Spain, contributing to the polarization that led to civil war.
- Although he sometimes exploited the trappings of fascism, General Franco was not a fascist but an authoritarian Catholic traditionalist.
- Though intended simply to preserve democracy, the popular front experiment in France produced a backlash and was widely blamed for French weakness as war loomed by the end of the 1930s.

THE COMING OF WORLD WAR II, 1935–1939

Why did the other countries not stop Hitler's Germany before it was strong enough to start a new European war in 1939?

Despite the promising adjustments of the 1920s, many of the problems that accompanied the World War I peace settlement were still in place when Hitler came to power. And Hitler had consistently trumpeted his intention to overturn that settlement. What scope was there for peaceful revision? Could the threat of war stop Hitler? By the last years of the 1930s, these questions tortured the Western world as Hitler went from one success to another, raising the possibility of a new and more destructive war. The power balance rested on the responses not only of the Western democracies, but of fascist Italy and the Soviet Union as well.

The Reorientation of Fascist Italy

During its first decade in power, Benito Mussolini's fascist regime in Italy concentrated on domestic reconstruction, especially the effort to mobilize people through their roles as producers within a new corporative state (see pages 738–739). But though corporativist institutions were gradually constructed, with great rhetorical fanfare, they bogged down in bureaucratic meddling. Corporativism proved more the vehicle for regimentation than for a more direct kind of participation. Fascism seemed to have stalled, partly because of compromise with prefascist elites and institutions, and partly because of its own internal contradictions. But the change in the international situation after Hitler came to power offered Mussolini some welcome space for maneuver.

Though Italy, like Germany, remained dissatisfied with the territorial status quo, it was not obvious that fascist Italy and Nazi Germany had to end up in the same camp. For one thing, Italy was anxious to preserve an independent Austria as a buffer with Germany, whereas many Germans and Austrians favored the unification of the two countries. Such a greater Germany might then threaten the gains Italy had won at the peace conference at Austria's expense. When, in 1934, Germany seemed poised to absorb Austria, Mussolini helped force Hitler to back down. He even warned that Nazism, with its racist orientation, threatened the best of European civilization.

As it began to appear that France and Britain might have to work with the Soviet Union to check Hitler's Germany, French and British conservatives pushed for good relations with Mussolini's Italy to provide ideological balance. So Italy was well positioned to play off both sides as Hitler began shaking things up on the international level. In 1935, just after Hitler announced significant rearmament measures, unilaterally repudiating provisions of the Versailles treaty for the first time, Mussolini hosted a meeting with the French and British prime ministers at Stresa, in northern Italy. In an overt warning to Hitler's Germany, the three powers agreed to resist "any unilateral repudiation of treaties which may endanger the peace of Europe."

However, Mussolini was already preparing to extend Italy's possessions in East Africa to encompass Ethiopia (also called Abyssinia). He assumed that the French and British, who needed his support against Hitler, would not offer significant opposition. Ethiopia had become a League of Nations member in 1923—sponsored by Italy, but opposed by Britain and France because it still practiced slavery. After a border incident, Italian troops invaded in October 1935, prompting the League to announce sanctions against Italy.

These sanctions were applied haphazardly, largely because France and Britain wanted to avoid damaging their longer-term relations with Italy. In any case, the sanctions did not deter Mussolini, whose forces prevailed through the use of aircraft and poison gas by May 1936. But they did make Italy receptive to German overtures in the aftermath of its victory. And the victory made Mussolini more restless. Rather than seeking to play again the role of European balancer, he sent Italian troops and materiel to aid the Nationalists in the Spanish civil war, thereby further alienating democratic opinion elsewhere.

Rome-Berlin Axis
Alliance between Hitler's
Nazi Germany and Mussolini's
fascist Italy, which began
informally in 1936, then was
cemented by an open-ended
military alliance, the Pact of
Steel, in 1939.

Conservatives in Britain and France continued to push for accommodation with Italy, hoping to revive the "Stresa front" against Hitler. Some even defended Italian imperialism in East Africa. But Italy continued its drift toward Germany. Late in 1936, Mussolini spoke of a new **Rome-Berlin Axis** for the first time. During 1937 and 1938, he and Hitler exchanged visits. Finally, in May 1939, Italy joined Germany in an open-ended military alliance, the Pact of Steel, but Mussolini made it clear that Italy could not be ready for a major European war before 1943.

Partly to strengthen this developing relationship, fascist Italy adopted anti-Semitic racial laws, even though Italian fascism had not originally been anti-Semitic. Indeed, the party had attracted Jewish Italians to its membership in about the same proportion as non-Jews. Although the imperial venture in Ethiopia had been popular among the Italian people, the seeming subservience to Nazi Germany displeased even many fascists. Such opposition helped keep Mussolini from intervention when war broke out in September 1939.

Restoring German Sovereignty, 1935–1936

During his first years in power, through 1936, Hitler could be understood as merely restoring German sovereignty, revising a postwar settlement that had been misconceived in the first place. However uncouth and abrasive he might seem, it was hard to find a basis for opposing him. Yet with the beginning of rearmament in 1935, and especially with the **remilitarization of the Rhineland** in March 1936, Hitler fundamentally reversed the power balance established in France's favor at the peace conference.

France's special advantage had been the demilitarization of the entire German territory west of the Rhine River and a 50-kilometer strip on the east bank. The measure had been reaffirmed at Locarno in 1925, now with Germany's free agreement, and it was guaranteed by Britain and Italy. Yet, on a Saturday morning in March 1936, that advantage disappeared as German troops moved into the forbidden area. The French and British acquiesced, uncertain of what else to do. After all, Hitler was only restoring Germany to full sovereignty.

But Hitler was not likely to stop there. As a result of the war and the peace, three new countries—Austria, Czechoslovakia, and Poland—bordered Germany (see **Map 27.2**). In each, the peace settlement had left trouble spots involving the status of ethnic Germans; in each, the status quo was open to question.

remilitarization of the Rhineland The reoccupation of Germany's Rhineland territory by German troops in March 1936, in clear violation of the Treaty of Versailles.

🌐 **Map 27.2—The Expansion of Nazi Germany, 1936–1939**

Especially with the remilitarization of the Rhineland in 1936, Hitler's Germany began moving, step by step, to alter the European power balance. In September 1939, the Soviet Union also began annexing territory, capitalizing on its agreement with Germany the month before.

Austria, Czechoslovakia, and Appeasement

As early as 1934, Hitler had moved to encompass his homeland, Austria, but strenuous opposition from Italy led him to back down. The developing understanding with Mussolini by 1936 enabled Hitler to focus again on Austria—initiating the second, more radical phase of his prewar foreign policy. On a pretext in March 1938, German troops moved into Austria, which was promptly incorporated into Germany. This time, Mussolini was willing to acquiesce, and Hitler was genuinely grateful.

The Treaty of Versailles had explicitly prohibited this *Anschluss*, or unity of Austria with Germany, though that prohibition violated the principle of self-determination. It was widely believed in the West, no doubt correctly, that most Austrians favored unity with Germany now that the Habsburg Empire had broken up. The *Anschluss* could thus be justified as revising a misconceived aspect of the peace settlement.

Czechoslovakia presented quite a different situation. Although it had preserved democratic institutions, the country included restive minorities of Magyars, Ruthenians, Poles, and—concentrated especially in the Sudetenland, along the German and Austrian borders—about 3.25 million Germans. After having been part of the dominant nationality in the old Habsburg Empire, those Germans were frustrated with their minority status in the new Czechoslovakia. Worse, they seemed to suffer disproportionately from the Depression. Hitler's agents actively stirred up their resentments.

Leading the West's response, when Hitler began making an issue of Czechoslovakia, was Neville Chamberlain (1869–1940), who followed Stanley Baldwin as Britain's prime minister in May 1937. An intelligent, vigorous, and public-spirited man from the progressive wing of the Conservative Party, Chamberlain has long been derided as the architect of the **"appeasement"** of Hitler at the Munich conference of 1938, which settled the crisis over Czechoslovakia. Trumpeted as the key to peace, the Munich agreement proved but a step to the war that broke out less than a year later. Yet, though it failed, Chamberlain's policy of appeasement stemmed not from cowardice or mere drift, and certainly not from some unspoken pro-Nazi sentiment.

Rather than let events spin out of control, as seemed to have happened in 1914, Chamberlain sought to master the difficult international situation through creative bargaining. Surely, he felt, the excesses of Hitler's policy resulted from the mistakes of Versailles; redo the settlement on a more realistic basis, and Germany would behave responsibly. The key was to pinpoint the sources of Germany's frustrations and, as Chamberlain put it, "to remove the danger spots one by one."

Moreover, in Britain as elsewhere, there were some who saw Hitler's resurgent Germany as a bulwark against communism, which might spread into east-central Europe—especially in the event of another war. Indeed, the victor in another war might well be the revolutionary left. To prevent such an outcome was worth a few concessions to Hitler.

The Czechs, led by Eduard Beneš (BAY-naish) (1884–1948), made some attempt to liberalize their nationality policy. But by April 1938, they were becoming ever less sympathetic to Sudeten German demands for autonomy, especially as German bullying came to accompany them. Tensions between Czechoslovakia and Germany mounted, and by late September 1938, war appeared imminent, despite Chamberlain's efforts to mediate. Both the French and the British began mobilizing, with French troops manning the Maginot Line for the first time.

A 1924 treaty bound France to come to the aid of Czechoslovakia in the event of aggression. Moreover, the Soviet Union, according to a treaty of 1935, was bound to assist Czechoslovakia if the French did so. And throughout the crisis, the Soviets pushed for a strong stand in defense of Czechoslovakia against German aggression. For both ideological and military reasons, however, the British and French were reluctant to line up for

appeasement　The policy employed by Britain's prime minister, Neville Chamberlain, to defuse the 1938 crisis with Germany's Adolf Hitler. Chamberlain acquiesced to Hitler's demands to annex the Sudetenland portion of Czechoslovakia, but this proved merely a step toward the war that broke out less than a year later.

The Illusion of Peace　Neville Chamberlain, returning home to Britain from Munich to a hero's welcome, waves the peace declaration that was supposed to have brought "peace in our time." This was late September 1938. Less than a year later, Europe was again at war.　(Central Press/Hulton Archive/Getty Images)

war on the side of the Soviet Union. The value of the Soviet military was uncertain, at best, at a time when the Soviet officer corps had just been purged.

By September, Hitler seemed eager to smash the Czechs by force, but when Mussolini proposed a four-power conference, he was persuaded to talk again. At Munich late in September, Britain, France, Italy, and Germany settled the matter, with Czechoslovakia and the Soviet Union excluded. Determined not to risk war over what seemed Czech intransigence, the British ended up agreeing to what Hitler had wanted all along—not merely autonomy for the Sudeten Germans, but German annexation of the Sudetenland.

The Munich agreement specified that all Sudeten areas with German majorities be transferred to Germany. Plebiscites were to be held in areas with large German minorities, and Hitler pledged to respect the sovereignty of the now diminished Czechoslovak state. Chamberlain and his French counterpart, Edouard Daladier, each returned home to a hero's welcome, having transformed what had seemed certain war to, in Chamberlain's soon-to-be-notorious phrase, "peace in our time."

Rather than settle the nationality questions bedeviling Czechoslovakia, the Munich agreement only provoked further unrest. Poland and Hungary, eager to exploit the new weakness of Czechoslovakia, agitated successfully to annex disputed areas with large numbers of their respective nationalities. Then unrest stemming from Slovak separatism afforded a pretext for Germany to send troops into Prague in March 1939. The Slovak areas were spun off as a separate nation, while the Czech areas became the Protectorate of Bohemia and Moravia. Less than six months after the Munich conference, most of what had been Czechoslovakia had landed firmly within the Nazi orbit (see **MAP 27.2**). It was no longer possible to justify Hitler's actions as an effort to unite all Germans in one state.

Poland, the Nazi-Soviet Pact, and the Coming of War

With Poland, the German grievance was still more serious, for the new Polish state had been created partly at German expense. Especially galling to Germans was the Polish corridor, which cut off East Prussia from the bulk of Germany in order to give Poland access to the sea. The city of Danzig (now Gdansk, Poland), historically Polish, but part of Germany before World War I, was left a "free city," supervised by the League of Nations.

Disillusioned by Hitler's dismemberment of Czechoslovakia and angered by the Germans' menacing rhetoric regarding Poland, Chamberlain announced on March 31, 1939, that Britain and France would intervene militarily should Poland's independence be threatened. Chamberlain was not only abandoning the policy of appeasement; he was making a clear commitment to the Continent, of the sort that British governments had resisted since 1919. He could do so partly because Britain was rapidly rearming. By early 1940, in fact, Britain was spending nearly as large a share of its national income on the military as Germany was. But Chamberlain's assertive statement was not enough to deter Hitler, who seems to have been determined to settle the Polish question by force. In an effort to localize the conflict, however, Hitler continued to insist that German aims were limited and reasonable. Germany simply wanted Danzig and German transit across the corridor; it was the Polish stance that was rigid and unreasonable. Hitler apparently believed that Polish stubbornness would alienate the British and French, undercutting their support. And as the crisis developed by mid-1939, doubts were increasingly expressed, on all sides, that the British and French were really prepared to aid Poland militarily—that they had the will "to die for Danzig."

Although they had been lukewarm to Soviet proposals for a military alliance, Britain and France began to negotiate with the Soviet Union more seriously during the spring and summer of 1939. But reservations about the value of a Soviet alliance continued to gnaw at Western leaders. For one thing, Soviet troops could gain access to Germany only by moving through Poland or Romania. But each had territory gained at the expense of Russia in the postwar settlement, so the British and French, suspicious of Soviet designs, were reluctant to insist that Soviet troops be allowed to pass through either country.

Even as negotiations between the Soviet Union and the democracies continued, the Soviets came to their own agreement with Nazi Germany on August 23, 1939, in a pact that astonished the world. Each side had been denouncing the other, and although Hitler had explored the possibility of Soviet neutrality in May, serious negotiations began only that August, when the Soviets got the clear signal that a German invasion of Poland was inevitable. It now appeared that no Soviet

Nazi-Soviet Pact Surprise agreement between the Soviet Union and Nazi Germany in August 1939 that each would remain neutral if the other went to war against some other nation.

alliance with Britain and France could prevent war. Under these circumstances, a nonaggression pact with Germany seemed better to serve Soviet interests than a problematic war on the side of Britain and France. So the Soviets agreed with the Germans that each would remain neutral in the event that either became involved in a war with some other nation.

The Soviet flip-flop stemmed partly from disillusionment with the British and French response to the accelerating threat of Nazism. The democracies seemed no more trustworthy, and potentially no less hostile, than Nazi Germany. But the Soviets were playing their own double game. A secret protocol to the **Nazi-Soviet Pact** apportioned major areas of east-central Europe between the Soviet Union and Germany. As a result, the Soviets soon regained much of what they had lost after World War I, when Poland, Finland, and other states had been created or aggrandized with territories that had been part of the tsarist empire.

The Nazi-Soviet Pact seemed to give Hitler the free hand he wanted in Poland. With the dramatic change in alignment, the democracies were surely much less likely to intervene. But Chamberlain, again determined to avoid the hesitations of 1914, publicly reaffirmed the British guarantee to Poland on August 25. Britain would indeed intervene if Germany attacked. And after the German invasion of Poland on September 1, the British and French responded with declarations of war on September 3.

With each step on the path to war, Hitler had vacillated between apparent reasonableness and wanton aggressiveness. Even in invading Poland, he apparently still hoped to localize hostilities. But he was certainly willing to risk a more general European war, and the deepest thrust of his policy was toward an all-out war of conquest—first against Poland, but ultimately against the Soviet Union. War was essential to the Nazi vision, and only when the assault on Poland became a full-scale war did the underlying purposes of Nazism become clear.

SECTION SUMMARY

- In light of the ideological polarization of the period, even the efforts to check Hitler by Britain and France, the major European democracies, depended partly on their relations with fascist Italy and the Soviet Union.

- Germany's remilitarization of the Rhineland in March 1936 prompted no military response by France and Britain, even though Germany's move removed the trump card that France had won with the Versailles treaty.

- In "appeasing" Hitler, Neville Chamberlain was not simply caving in but was seeking, through creative diplomacy, to remove the present sources of international hostility.

- Disillusioned by Hitler's course after the Munich agreement of September 1938, Chamberlain announced in March 1939 that Britain and France would intervene militarily should Germany threaten Poland's independence.

- Although they came to terms with Hitler's Germany in 1939, partly from mistrust of Britain and France, the Soviets quickly pursued their own aggressive aims in north-central Europe.

CHAPTER SUMMARY

The Great Depression caught decision makers in the democracies unprepared. Reflecting conventional economic thinking, their initial response was to keep government budgets balanced. But this required cutting government spending on such measures as unemployment benefits, which not only added to the human misery, but also intensified the economic contraction. The further effort to protect domestic economies through higher tariffs also worsened the downturn by restricting global trade. Only after several years, and for quite disparate reasons, did governments begin increasing spending and thereby stimulating renewed economic growth.

Stalin sought to rekindle the Russian revolutionary experiment by attempting to build "socialism in one country." The essential prerequisite was rapid industrialization, to be financed by squeezing the peasantry through forced collectivization in agriculture. Both the collectivization itself and the ensuing extractions of agricultural produce were extremely brutal, culminating in the "terror-famine" of 1932–1933. Partly because of its brutality, and partly because its economic results were mixed at best, the Stalinist departure produced opposition even from within the Communist Party. Seeking to root out those who might be sabotaging the Soviet experiment, Communist leaders embarked on a series of purges and show trials, but their effort gradually spun out of control, producing the "great terror" of 1937–1938.

FOCUS QUESTIONS

- With what array of measures did governments respond to the Great Depression?

- Why did the Stalinist attempt to build "socialism in one country" lead to the "terror-famine" of 1932–1933 and the "great terror" of 1937–1938?

- Through what measures did the Nazi regime claim to be improving the quality of the German population?

- Why did the "popular front" strategy prove counterproductive in both France and Spain?

- Why did the other countries not stop Hitler's Germany before it was strong enough to start a new European war in 1939?

Population engineering, based on eugenics on the one hand, racism and anti-Semitism on the other, was central to the Nazis' domestic program. Determined to implement radical eugenics measures that had been discussed but not implemented under the Weimar Republic, the regime launched a program of forced sterilization in 1933. By the eve of World War II, German medical personnel were actually killing mental patients, the terminally ill, and others deemed unfit. Even as they sought to "improve" the "Aryan" population through such eugenics measures, the Nazis also sought ethnic homogeneity, especially by stripping German Jews of citizenship rights in an effort to force emigration.

Hitler's consolidation of power in Germany and the apparent threat of fascism in France in 1934 prompted leaders of the Comintern to make resistance to the spread of fascism their top priority. To that end, communists spearheaded the formation of "popular fronts" with socialists and others concerned to preserve democratic institutions. But though it produced electoral successes in 1936 in Spain and France, the strategy proved polarizing. Popular front victories produced radical pressures that popular front governments had trouble containing. Those pressures eventually produced a backlash from the right. Partly as a result, democracy was defeated in both Spain and France by 1940.

Hitler's aggressive foreign policy provided an unprecedented challenge to the European order, but the leading democracies, Britain and France, were slow to respond. Eagerness to avoid another war affected their reactions, as did the ideological polarization of the decade. Up to a point, Hitler's steps could seem legitimate, in terms of principles of national sovereignty and ethnic self-determination that had been compromised to Germany's disadvantage at the Paris Peace Conference. In 1939, when Hitler's further steps could no longer be justified in such terms, the democracies, led by Britain, at last began to stiffen. However, Hitler was determined to crush Poland. Although the Nazi-Soviet Pact seemed to make the intervention of Britain and France less likely, the Nazi leader was more than willing to risk another European war.

KEY TERMS

collectivization (p. 761)

show trials (p. 763)

gulag (p. 763)

Adolf Hitler (p. 764)

National Socialist German Workers' (Nazi) Party (NSDAP) (p. 764)

Schutzstaffel **(SS)** (p. 766)

Kristallnacht **(Crystal Night)** (p. 771)

"euthanasia" program (p. 772)

popular fronts (p. 773)

Rome-Berlin Axis (p. 778)

remilitarization of the Rhineland (p. 779)

appeasement (p. 780)

Nazi-Soviet Pact (p. 782)

 This icon will direct you to additional materials on the website: www .cengage.com/history/ noble/westciv6e

NOTES

1. Quoted in Robert Conquest, *The Great Terror: A Reassessment* (New York: Oxford University Press, 1990), p. 24.
2. Quoted in Helmut Krausnick et al., *Anatomy of the SS State* (New York: Walker, 1968), p. 13.

e See our interactive eBook for map and primary source activities.

28

Atomic Bombing of Nagasaki, August 9, 1945
When this photo was taken, from an observation plane 6 miles up, thirty-five
thousand people on the ground had already died.   (akg-images)

The Era of the Second World War, 1939–1949

"The effects could well be called unprecedented, magnificent, beautiful, stupendous and terrifying. No man-made phenomenon of such tremendous power had ever occurred before.....Thirty seconds after the explosion came first, the air blast pressing hard against the people and things, to be followed almost immediately by the strong, sustained, awesome roar which warned of doomsday and made us feel that we puny things were blasphemous to dare tamper with the forces heretofore reserved to The Almighty."[1]

So wrote Brigadier General Thomas F. Farrell, who had just witnessed the birth of the atomic age. On July 16, 1945, watching from a shelter 10,000 yards away, Farrell had seen the first explosion of an atomic bomb at a remote, top-secret U.S. government testing ground near Alamogordo, New Mexico. Such a weapon had been little more than a theoretical possibility when World War II began, and it required a remarkable concentration of effort, centered first in Britain, then in the United States, to make possible the awesome spectacle that confronted General Farrell. Exceeding most expectations, the test revealed a weapon of unprecedented power and destructiveness.

Within weeks, the United States dropped two other atomic bombs—first on Hiroshima, then on Nagasaki—to force the surrender of Japan in August 1945. Thus ended the Second World War, the conflict that had begun six long years earlier with the German invasion of Poland. At first, Germany enjoyed remarkable success, prompting Italy to intervene and encouraging Japanese aggressiveness as well. But Britain held on even after its ally, France, fell to Germany in 1940. Then the war changed character in 1941 when Germany attacked the Soviet Union and Japan attacked the United States.

Britain, the United States, and the Soviet Union quickly came together in a "Grand Alliance," which spearheaded the victorious struggle against the Axis powers—Germany, Italy, and Japan. In Europe, the Soviet victory in a brutal land war with Germany proved decisive. In East Asia and the Pacific, the Americans gradually prevailed against Japan. The American use of the atomic bomb to end the war was the final stage in an escalation of violence that made World War II the most destructive war in history.

The ironic outcome of the Second World War was a new cold war between two of the victors, the United States and the Soviet Union. Emerging from the war with far greater power and prestige, each assumed a world role that would have been hard to imagine just a few years earlier. By the end of the 1940s, these two superpowers had divided Europe into

FOCUS QUESTIONS

- What were the outcomes of the war as of late spring 1941, before the German invasion of the Soviet Union and the intervention of the United States?

- What was the place of the Holocaust in the Nazi effort to begin constructing a "new order" in eastern Europe?

- How did the Grand Alliance of Britain, the United States, and the Soviet Union come together against the Axis powers?

- How did the Allies manage to defeat Nazi Germany in World War II, after Germany's remarkable initial successes?

- What was the relationship between the Allied victory in World War II and the coming of the cold war?

 This icon will direct you to additional materials on the website: www .cengage.com/history/ noble/westciv6e.

See our interactive eBook for map and primary source activities.

competing spheres of influence. Indeed, the competition between the United States and the Soviet Union almost immediately became global in scope, creating a bipolar world. And the cold war between them was especially terrifying because, seeking military advantage, they raced to stockpile ever more destructive nuclear weapons. Thus, the threat of nuclear annihilation helped define the cold war era.

World War II led to the defeat of Italy, Germany, and Japan and, in this sense, resolved the conflicts that had caused it. But the experience of this particular war changed the world forever. Before finally meeting defeat, the Nazis were sufficiently successful to begin implementing their "new order" in Europe, especially in the territories they conquered to the east. As part of this effort, in what has become known as the Holocaust, they began systematically murdering Jews in extermination camps, eventually killing as many as 6 million. The most destructive of the camps was at Auschwitz (OWSH-vits), in what had been Poland. Often paired after the war, Auschwitz and Hiroshima came to stand for the incredible new forms of death and destruction that the war had spawned—and that continued to haunt the world long after it had ended, posing new questions about the meaning of Western civilization.

GERMAN MILITARY SUCCESSES, 1939–1941

What were the outcomes of the war as of late spring 1941, before the German invasion of the Soviet Union and the intervention of the United States?

Instead of the enthusiasm evident in 1914, the German invasion of Poland on September 1, 1939, produced a grim sense of foreboding, even in Germany. Well-publicized incidents, such as the German bombing of civilians during the Spanish civil war and the Italian use of poison gas in Ethiopia, suggested that the frightening new technologies introduced in World War I would now be used on a far greater scale. This would be a much uglier war, more directly involving civilians.

Still, as in 1914, there were hopes at first that this new war could be localized and brief. Poland fell quickly, and Hitler publicly offered peace to Britain and France, seriously thinking that might be the end of it. The British and French refused to call off the war, but from 1939 through 1941, the Nazis won victory after victory, establishing the foundation for their new order in Europe.

Initial Conquests and "Phony War"

The Polish army was large enough to have given the Germans a serious battle. But in adapting the technological innovations of World War I, Germany had developed a new military strategy based on rapid mobility. Soon popularly known as *Blitzkrieg*, or lightning war, this strategy employed swift, highly concentrated offensives based on mobile tanks covered with concentrated air support, including dive-bombers that struck just ahead of the tanks. In Poland, this strategy proved decisive. The French could offer only token help, and the last Polish unit surrendered on October 2, barely a month after the fighting had begun. The speed of the German victory stunned the world.

Meanwhile, the Soviets began cashing in on the pact they had made with Nazi Germany a few weeks before. It offered a precious opportunity to undo provisions of the World War I settlement that had significantly diminished the western territories of the former Russian Empire. On September 17, with the German victory in Poland assured, Stalin sent Soviet forces westward to share in the spoils. Soon, Poland was again divided between Germany and Russia, just as most of it had been before 1914. The Baltic states of Estonia, Latvia, and Lithuania soon fell as well.

When Finland proved less pliable, the Soviets invaded in November 1939. In the ensuing "Winter War," the Finns held out bravely, and the Soviets managed to prevail by March 1940 only by taking heavy casualties. The difficult course of the war in Finland seemed to confirm suspicions that Stalin's purge during the mid-1930s had substantially weakened the Soviet army. Still, by midsummer 1940, the Soviet Union had regained much of the territory lost to Russia during the upheavals that followed the revolution of 1917.

In the west, little happened during the strained winter of 1939–1940, known as the "Phony War." Then, on April 9, 1940, the Germans attacked Norway and Denmark in a surprise move to preempt a British and French scheme to cut off the shipment of Swedish iron ore to Germany. Denmark fell almost at once, while the staunch resistance in Norway was effectively broken by the end of April. The stage was set for the German assault on France.

The Fall of France, 1940

On May 10, 1940, Germany attacked France and the Low Countries. The Germans invaded France through the Ardennes Forest, above the northern end of the Maginot Line—terrain so difficult the French had discounted the possibility of an enemy strike there (see pages 730–731). As in 1914, northern France quickly became the focus of a major war, pitting French forces and their British allies against invading Germans. But this time, in startling contrast to World War I, the Battle of France was over in less than six weeks, a humiliating defeat for the French.

The problem for France was not lack of men and materiel, but strategy. Germany had only a slight numerical advantage in tanks but used mobile tanks and dive-bombers to mount rapid, highly concentrated offensives. Anticipating another long, defensive war, France had dispersed its tanks among infantry units along a broad front. Once the German tank column broke through the French lines, it quickly cut through northern France and moved toward the North Sea. France's poor showing convinced the British that rather than commit troops and planes to a hopeless battle in France, they should get out and regroup for a longer global war. Early in June, 200,000 British troops—as well as 130,000 French—escaped German encirclement and capture through a difficult evacuation at Dunkirk (see **Map 28.1**).

By mid-June, Germany had won a decisive victory. As the French military collapsed, the French cabinet resigned, to be replaced by a new government under Marshal Philippe Pétain, who had led the successful French defense of Verdun during World War I. Pétain's government first asked for an armistice and then engineered a change of regime. The French parliament voted by an overwhelming majority to give Pétain exceptional powers, including the power to draw up a new constitution. So ended the parliamentary democracy of the Third Republic, which seemed responsible for France's weakness. The republic gave way to the more authoritarian **Vichy** (VEE-shee) regime, named after the resort city to which the government retreated as the Germans moved into Paris. The end of the fighting in France

CHRONOLOGY

September 1, 1939	Germany invades Poland
November 1939–March 1940	Soviets wage "Winter War" against Finland
April 9, 1940	Germany attacks Denmark and Norway
May 10	Germany attacks the Netherlands, Belgium, and France
June 22, 1941	Germany attacks the Soviet Union
August	Churchill and Roosevelt agree to the Atlantic Charter
December 7, 1941	Japan attacks Pearl Harbor
August 1942–February 1943	Battle of Stalingrad
November 1942	Allied landings in North Africa
April–May 1943	Warsaw ghetto revolt
July	Soviet victory in Battle of Kursk-Orel
July	Allied landings in Sicily; fall of Mussolini; Italy asks for an armistice
November	Teheran conference
June 6, 1944	D-Day: Allied landings in Normandy
February 1945	Yalta conference
May 7–8, 1945	Germany surrenders
June 1945	Founding of the United Nations
July–August 1945	Potsdam conference
August 6, 1945	U.S. atomic bombing of Hiroshima
August 15, 1945	Japan announces surrender
March 1947	Truman Doctrine
August 1947	India and Pakistan achieve independence
May 1948	Foundation of the state of Israel
1949	Communist takeover in China
June 1948–May 1949	Berlin blockade and airlift
August 1949	First Soviet atomic bomb
September 1949	Founding of the Federal Republic in West Germany

MAP 28.1—World War II: European Theaters

Much of Europe saw fighting during World War II, although different fronts were important at different times. What proved decisive was the fighting that ensued in the vast expanse of the Soviet Union after the Germans invaded in June 1941.

Vichy France Authoritarian French government, headquartered in the town of Vichy, that followed the Third Republic after France's defeat by Nazi Germany in 1940. The government collaborated with the victorious Germans, who occupied Paris.

Charles de Gaulle The youngest general in the French army, he called on French forces to follow his lead and continue the fight against Nazi Germany after the fall of France in June 1940.

resulted in a kind of antidemocratic revolution, but one in which the French people, stunned by military defeat, at first acquiesced.

According to the armistice agreement, the French government was not only to cease hostilities, but also to collaborate with the victorious Germans. French resistance began immediately, however. In a radio broadcast from London on June 18, **Charles de Gaulle** (1890–1970), the youngest general in the French army, called on French forces to rally to him to continue the fight against Nazi Germany. The military forces stationed in the French colonies, as well as the French troops that had been evacuated at Dunkirk, could form the nucleus of a new French army. Under the present circumstances of military defeat and political change, de Gaulle's appeal seemed quixotic at best. Most French colonies went along with what seemed the legitimate French government at Vichy—to which de Gaulle was a traitor. Yet a new Free French force grew from de Gaulle's remarkable appeal, and its subsequent role in the war compensated, in some measure, for France's humiliating defeat in 1940.

Winston Churchill and the Battle of Britain

With the defeat of France, Hitler seems to have expected that Britain, now apparently vulnerable to German invasion, would come to terms. And certainly some prominent Britons questioned the wisdom of remaining at war. But the British war effort found a new and effective champion in **Winston Churchill** (1874–1965), who replaced Neville Chamberlain as prime minister on May 10, when the German invasion of western Europe began. Although Churchill had been prominent in British public life for years, his career to this point had not been noteworthy for either judgment or success. He was obstinate, difficult, something of a curmudgeon. Yet he rose to the wartime challenge, becoming one of the notable leaders of the modern era. In speeches to the House of Commons during the remainder of 1940, he inspired his nation with perhaps the most memorable words of the war. Though some found a negotiated settlement with Germany even more sensible in light of the outcome in France, Churchill's dogged promise of "blood, toil, tears, and sweat" helped rally the British people, so that later he could say, without exaggeration, that "this was their finest hour."

After the fall of France, Churchill's Britain promptly moved to full mobilization for a protracted war. Indeed, Britain developed the most thoroughly coordinated war economy of all the belligerents, producing more tanks, aircraft, and machine guns than Germany did between 1940 and 1942. The National Service Act of 1941 subjected men ages 18 to 50 and women ages 20 to 30 to military or civilian war service. The upper age limits were subsequently raised to meet the demand for labor. Almost 70 percent of the 3 million people added to the British workforce during the war were women.

Britain, then, intended to continue the fight even after France fell. Hitler weighed his options and decided to attack. In light of British naval superiority, he hoped to rely on aerial bombardment to knock the British out of the war without an actual invasion. The ensuing Battle of Britain culminated in the nightly bombing of London from September 7 through November 2, 1940, killing fifteen thousand people and destroying thousands of buildings. But the British held. Ordinary people holed up in cellars and subway stations, while the fighter planes of the Royal Air Force fought back effectively, inflicting heavy losses against German aircraft over Britain.

Although the bombing continued into 1941, the British had withstood the worst the Germans could deliver, and Hitler began looking to the east, his ultimate objective all along. In December 1940, he ordered preparations for Operation Barbarossa, the assault on the Soviet Union. Rather than continuing the attack on Britain directly, Germany would use submarines to cut off shipping—and thus the supplies the British needed for a long war. Once Germany had defeated the Soviet Union, it would enjoy the geopolitical basis for world power, while Britain, as an island nation relying on a dispersed empire, would eventually be forced to come to terms.

Winston Churchill
British prime minister during World War II, his courage and decisiveness made him widely seen as one of modern Britain's greatest leaders.

Italian Intervention and the Spread of the War

Lacking sufficient domestic support, and unready for a major war, Mussolini could only look on as the war began in 1939. But as the Battle of France neared its end, it seemed safe for Italy to intervene, sharing in the spoils of what appeared certain victory. Thus, in June 1940, Italy declared war, expecting to secure territorial advantages in the Mediterranean, starting with Corsica, Nice, and Tunisia, at the expense of France. Italy also hoped eventually to supplant Britain in the region—and even to take the Suez Canal.

Although Hitler and Mussolini got along reasonably well, their relationship was sensitive. When Hitler seemed to be proceeding without Italy during the first year of the war, Mussolini grew determined to show his independence. Finally, in October 1940, he ordered Italian forces to attack Greece. But the Greeks mounted a strong resistance, thanks partly to the help of British forces from North Africa.

Meanwhile, Germany had established its hegemony in much of east-central Europe without military force, often by exploiting grievances over the outcome of the Paris Peace Conference in 1919. In November 1940, Romania and Hungary joined the Axis camp, and Bulgaria followed a few months later. But in March 1941, just after Yugoslavia had similarly committed to the Axis, a coup overthrew the pro-Axis government in Yugoslavia, and the new Yugoslav government prepared to aid the Allies.

British Resistance   At the height of the German bombing of Britain in 1940, Winston Churchill and his wife, Clementine, survey the damage in London.   (J. A. Hampton/Topical Hulton Archive/Getty Images)

SECTION SUMMARY

- In implementing its innovative *Blitzkrieg* strategy, Germany employed rapid, highly concentrated offensives that combined tanks and airpower to great effect.

- After Poland fell quickly, Hitler offered peace to Britain and France, seriously thinking that this particular war might be over.

- Once German victory in Poland was assured, the Soviet Union began sharing the spoils and, by midsummer 1940, had regained much of the territory lost during the upheavals that followed the Russian Revolution.

- In dramatic contrast with World War I, France in 1940 fell to German invasion in less than six weeks.

- The defeat of France led to the end of the Third Republic and the advent of the authoritarian Vichy regime, which was obliged by the armistice agreement to collaborate with Nazi Germany.

- Inspired by Churchill's determined leadership, the British withstood the sustained German air assault during the second half of 1940 and finally forced Hitler to alter his overall strategy.

By this point, Hitler had decided it was expedient to push into the Balkans with German troops, both to reinforce the Italians and to consolidate Axis control of the area. As the war's geographic extent expanded, its stakes increased, yet the Germans continued to meet every challenge. By the end of May 1941, they had taken Yugoslavia and Greece (see **Map 28.1**).

At the same time, the war was spreading to North Africa and the Middle East because of European colonial ties. The native peoples of the area sought to take advantage of the conflict to pursue their own independence. Iraq and Syria became involved, as the Germans, operating from Syria, administered by Vichy France, aided anti-British Arab nationalists in Iraq. But most important proved to be North Africa, where Libya, an Italian colony since 1912, lay adjacent to Egypt, with its strong British presence.

Under General Erwin Rommel, the famous "Desert Fox," Axis forces won remarkable victories in North Africa from February to May 1941. But successful though they had been, the German forays into North Africa and the Balkans had delayed the crucial attack on the Soviet Union.

THE ASSAULT ON THE SOVIET UNION AND THE NAZI NEW ORDER

What was the place of the Holocaust in the Nazi effort to begin constructing a "new order" in eastern Europe?

German troops invaded the Soviet Union on June 22, 1941. Although the Germans enjoyed the expected successes for a while, the Soviets eventually prevailed, spearheading the Allied victory in Europe. Supplies from their new Allies—Britain and eventually the United States—aided the Soviet cause, but the surprising strength of the Soviet military effort proved the most important factor. In winning the war, the Soviets suffered incredible casualties, and after they gained the initiative, they proceeded with particular brutality as they forced the invading Germans back into Germany.

In part, at least, the Soviets were responding to the unprecedented form of warfare unleashed by the Nazis. While preparing for the attack on the Soviet Union, Hitler had made it clear to the Nazi leadership that this was to be no ordinary military engagement but a war of racial-ideological extermination. The Germans penetrated well into the Soviet Union, reaching the apex of their power late in 1942. German conquests by that point enabled Hitler to begin constructing the new, race-based European order he had dreamed of. As part of this process, the Nazis began systematically killing Jews, first by shooting, then by mass-gassing them in specially constructed death camps.

An Ambiguous Outcome, 1941–1942

In ordering preparations for Operation Barbarossa in December 1940, Hitler decided to risk attacking the Soviet Union before knocking Britain out of the war. Then he invaded the Balkans and North Africa in what may have been an unnecessary diversion. In retrospect, it is easy to pinpoint that combination as his fatal mistake. But in light of the Soviet purges of the 1930s and what seemed the poor performance of the Soviet army against Finland, Hitler had reason to believe the Soviet Union would crack relatively easily. Western military experts had come to similar conclusions, estimating that German forces would need but six weeks to take Moscow. And if Germany were to defeat the Soviet Union with another *Blitzkrieg*, it could gain control of the oil and other resources required for a longer war against Britain and, if necessary, the United States.

Attacking the Soviet Union on June 22, 1941, German forces achieved notable successes during the first month of fighting, partly because Stalin was so unprepared for this German betrayal. Ignoring warnings of an impending German assault, he had continued to live up to his end of the 1939 bargain with Hitler, even supplying the Germans with oil and grain. After the attack, Russia's defenses were at first totally disorganized, and by late November, German forces were within 20 miles of Moscow.

But the Germans were ill-equipped for Russian weather, and as an early and severe winter descended, the German offensive bogged down. In December, the Soviets mounted a formidable surprise counterattack near Moscow. The German *Blitzkrieg*, which had seemed a sure thing in July, had failed. Germany might still prevail, but a different strategy would be required.

The Germans, however, still had the advantage. Although German forces failed to take the key city of Leningrad in 1941, they cut it off by blockade and, until early 1944, kept it under siege with relentless bombing and shelling. During the summer

Forgive me, comrade . . . On June 23, 1941, the day after Nazi Germany attacked the Soviet Union, the *London Daily Mail* published this cartoon depicting Hitler's betrayal of his 1939 pact with Stalin. (Solo Syndication/Associated Newspapers)

of 1942, they mounted another offensive, moving more deeply into the Soviet Union than before, reaching Stalingrad in November. But this proved the deepest penetration of German forces—and the zenith of Nazi power in Europe.

Hitler's New Order

By the summer of 1942, Nazi Germany dominated the European continent as no power had before (see **MAP 28.2**). German military successes allowed the Nazi regime to begin building a new order in the territories under German domination. Satellite states in Slovakia and Croatia, and client governments in Romania and Hungary, owed their existence to Nazi Germany and readily adapted to the Nazi system. Elsewhere in the Nazi orbit, some countries proved eager collaborators; others did their best to resist; still others were given no opportunity to collaborate but were ruthlessly subjugated instead.

The Nazis' immediate aim was simply to exploit the conquered territories to serve the continuing war effort. Precisely as envisioned, access to the resources of so much of Europe made Germany considerably less vulnerable to naval blockade than during World War I. France proved a particularly valuable source of raw materials; by 1943, for example, 75 percent of French iron ore went to German factories.

But the deeper purposes of the war were also clear in the way the Nazis treated the territories under their control, especially in the difference between east and west. Western Europe experienced plenty of atrocities, but Nazi victory there still led to something like conventional military occupation. The Germans tried to enlist the cooperation of local authorities in countries like Denmark, the Netherlands, and France, though with mixed results. And whereas the Nazis exploited the economy of France, for example, it never became clear what role France might play in Europe after a Nazi victory. However, in Poland, and later in the conquered parts of the Soviet Union, there was no pretense of cooperation, and it was immediately clear what the Nazi order would entail.

After the conquest of Poland, the Germans annexed the western part of the country outright and promptly executed, jailed, or expelled members of the Polish elite—professionals, journalists, business leaders, and priests. The Nazis prohibited the Poles from entering the professions and restricted even their right to marry. All the Polish schools and most of the churches were simply closed.

In the rest of Poland, known as the General Government, Nazi policy was slightly less brutal at first. Most churches remained open, and Poles were allowed to practice the professions, but the Nazis closed most schools above the fourth grade, as well as libraries, theaters, and museums, as they sought to root out every expression of Polish culture. Some Poles in this area were forced into slave labor, but a final decision as to whether the Polish population was to be exterminated, enslaved, or shipped off to Siberia was postponed—to be made after the wider war had been won.

With the conquest of Poland, Nazi leaders proclaimed that a new era of monumental resettlement in eastern Europe had begun. Germans selected for their racial characteristics were now resettled in the part of Poland annexed to Germany. Most were ethnic Germans who had been living outside Germany. During the fall of 1942, Heinrich Himmler's *Schutzstaffel* (SS), the select Nazi elite, began to arrest and expel peasants from the rest of Poland to make way for further German resettlement. By 1943, perhaps 1 million Germans had been moved into what had been Poland.

After the assault on the Soviet Union, Hitler made it clear that eastern Europe as far as the Ural Mountains was to be opened for German settlement. War veterans were to be given priority, partly because the German settlers would have to be tough to resist the Slavs, who would be concentrated east of the Urals. Himmler told SS leaders that to prepare for German colonization, Germany would have to exterminate 30 million Slavs in the Soviet Union. After the invasion, the SS promptly began executing prisoners of war, as well as any Soviet leaders they could find. However, the Nazis expected that several generations would be required for the resettlement of European Russia.

The Holocaust

Conquest of the east also opened the way to a more radical solution to the "Jewish problem" than the Nazis had contemplated before. Under the cover of war, they began actually killing the Jews within their orbit. Thus began the process, and the experience, that has come to be known as the Holocaust.

When and why this radical policy was chosen remains controversial. Although prewar Nazi rhetoric occasionally suggested the possibility of such physical extermination, talk of a "final solution to the Jewish problem" seemed to mean forced emigration. Although the precise chain

MAP 28.2—The Nazi New Order in Europe, 1942

At the zenith of its power in 1942, Nazi Germany controlled much of Europe. Concerned most immediately with winning the war, the Nazis sought to coordinate the economies of their satellite states and conquered territories. But they also began establishing what was supposed to be an enduring new order in eastern Europe. The inset shows the locations of the major Nazi concentration camps and the six extermination camps the Nazis constructed in what had been Poland.

EXTERMINATION AND CONCENTRATION CAMPS

REICHSKOMMISSARIAT OSTLAND

REICHSKOMMISSARIAT UKRAINE

Treblinka
Sobibor
Majdanek
Belzec
Poniatowa
Chelmno
GOVERNMENT GENERAL OF POLAND
Auschwitz
HUNGARY
SLOVAKIA

GREATER GERMANY
Sachsenhausen
Mauthausen
PROTECTORATE OF BOHEMIA & MORAVIA

Berlin
Buchenwald
Dachau
ITALY

DENMARK
Bergen-Belsen

Baltic Sea

Poland before Sept. 1, 1939
Extermination camp
Concentration camp

Main map labels

SOVIET UNION
Stalingrad
Moscow
Leningrad
Helsinki
FINLAND
NORWAY
Oslo
SWEDEN
Stockholm
DENMARK
Copenhagen
NORTHERN IRELAND
IRELAND
UNITED KINGDOM
London
NETHERLANDS
Amsterdam
BELGIUM
Brussels
Paris
FRANCE
VICHY FRANCE
Vichy
SWITZERLAND
LUXEMBOURG
Bonn
Berlin
Prague
PROTECTORATE OF BOHEMIA & MORAVIA
GREATER GERMANY
Vienna
Warsaw
GOVERNMENT GENERAL OF POLAND
REICHSKOMMISSARIAT OSTLAND
REICHSKOMMISSARIAT UKRAINE
Kiev
SLOVAKIA
HUNGARY
Budapest
CROATIA
SERBIA
Belgrade
ROMANIA
Bucharest
BULGARIA
Sofia
MONTENEGRO
ALBANIA
GREECE
Athens
TURKEY
Istanbul
ITALY
Rome
Crete
Sicily
Sardinia
Corsica
Malta (Gr. Br.)
SPAIN
PORTUGAL
TUNISIA
Black Sea
Caspian Sea
North Sea
Baltic Sea
Mediterranean Sea
ATLANTIC OCEAN

Volga R.
Don R.
Dnieper R.
Dniester R.
Vistula R.
Elbe R.
Rhine R.
Danube R.
Po R.
Rhône R.
Seine R.
Loire R.
Ebro R.
Tagus R.

Legend

Greater Germany
Italy, including occupied and annexed territories
Satellite states of Germany, including annexed territory
Areas under direct German control in the east
Countries under German military occupation in the west
Vichy France, nominally sovereign
Area of German military operations in the east
Neutral and non-belligerent states
Opponents of Greater Germany
Boundary of Greater Germany

0   150   300 Mi.
0   150   300 Km.

of events that led to a more radical approach will no doubt remain uncertain, it was surely bound up with the fortunes of the war.

THE GHETTOS

The conquest of Poland, with a Jewish population of 3.3 million, gave the Nazis control over a far greater number of Jews than ever before. In 1940, as part of their effort to create a new order, the Nazis began confining Polish Jews to ghettos set up in Warsaw and five other cities. Although much brutality and many deaths accompanied this process, the Nazis had not yet adopted a policy of systematic killing. Indeed, at first, no one knew what the ultimate fate of these Jews was to be. At this point, Nazi authorities were concentrating on removing, or even killing, non-Jewish Poles to make way for German resettlement. The fate of the Jews would be decided later. However, as the Polish ghettos grew more crowded and difficult to manage, Nazi officials in Poland began pressing for a more immediate solution.

THE SS PLAN FOR ANNIHILATION

Accompanying the military forces invading the Soviet Union were specially trained SS units assigned to kill Communist Party officials and adult male Jews. But soon some began murdering Jewish women and children as well. By late November 1941, the Nazis had killed 136,000 Jews, most by shooting, in the invaded Soviet territories. But this mode of killing proved both inefficient and psychologically burdensome—even for these specially trained killers. By late summer 1941, their experience in the Soviet Union, combined with the problems in the Polish ghettos, led Nazi leaders to begin seeking a more systematic and impersonal method of mass extermination.

The most likely scenario is that Hitler settled on physical extermination of the Jews in the thrill of what seemed impending victory over the Soviet Union. At the end of July 1941, Reinhard Heydrich of the SS began developing a detailed plan, and by the fall, the Nazis were sending German and Austrian Jews to the ghettos in Poland and actively impeding further Jewish emigration from Europe.

Systematic killing of Jews began later that fall. The Nazis took advantage of the personnel and the methods—especially the use of poison gas—that had proven effective during the "euthanasia" campaign of 1939 through 1941 in Germany (see page 772). By March 1942, they had constructed several extermination camps with gas chambers and crematoria, intended to kill large numbers of Jews and dispose of their bodies as efficiently as possible. The first victims were the Polish Jews who had already been confined to ghettos. The Nazis brutally suppressed attempts at resistance, like the Warsaw ghetto uprising of April and May 1943.

NAZI DEATH CAMPS

During the war, the Nazis constructed six death camps, although not all were operating at peak capacity at the same time. All six were located in what had been Poland (see inset, **MAP 28.2**). Horrifying though they were, the concentration camps in Germany, such as Dachau, Buchenwald, and Bergen-Belsen, were not extermination camps, although many Jews died in them late in the war.

Auschwitz-Birkenau
The largest of Nazi Germany's six extermination camps, all of which were located in what had been Poland.

The largest of the six death camps was the **Auschwitz-Birkenau** complex, which became the principal extermination center in 1943. The Nazis shipped Jews from all over Europe to Auschwitz, which was killing about twelve thousand people a day at the height of its operation in 1944. Auschwitz was one of two extermination camps that included affiliated slave-labor factories, in which Jews considered most able to work were often literally worked to death. Among the companies profiting from the arrangement were two of Germany's best known, Krupp and IG Farben.

The Jews typically arrived at one of the camps crammed into cattle cars on special trains. SS medical doctors subjected new arrivals to "selection," picking some for labor assignments and sending the others, including most women and children, to the gas chambers. Camp personnel made every effort to deceive Jews who were about to be killed, to lead them to believe they were to be showered and deloused. Even in camps without forced-labor factories, Jews were compelled to do much of the dirty work of the extermination operation. But under the brutal conditions of the camps, those initially assigned to work inevitably weakened; most were then deemed unfit and put to death.

SECRECY SURROUNDING THE CAMPS

The Nazis took every precaution to hide what was going on in the death camps. The SS personnel involved were sworn to silence. Himmler insisted that if secrecy was to be maintained, the operation would have to be quick—and total, to include women and children, "so that no Jews will remain to take revenge on our sons and grandsons." Indeed, he constantly sought to accelerate the process, even though it required labor and transport facilities needed for the war effort.

Himmler and the other major SS officials, such as Rudolf Höss (HOESS), the commandant at Auschwitz, or Adolf Eichmann (IKE-mahn), who organized the transport of the Jews to the camps,

The End of the Warsaw Ghetto   In April 1943, the sixty thousand Jews remaining in the Warsaw ghetto revolted rather than face shipment to the extermination camps. Many died in the ensuing fighting; others perished as the Germans set fire to the ghetto. Almost all the rest were captured and sent to their deaths at Treblinka. Before it was put down in May, the uprising killed at least three hundred Germans.   (AP Photos)

were not simply sadists who enjoyed humiliating their victims. Rather, they took satisfaction in doing what they believed was their duty without flinching, without signs of weakness. Addressing a group of SS members in 1943, Himmler portrayed the extermination of the Jews as a difficult "historical task" that they, the Nazi elite, must do for their racial community: "Most of you know what it means to see a hundred corpses piled up, or five hundred, or a thousand. To have gone through this and—except for cases of human weakness—to have remained decent, that has made us tough. This is an unwritten, never to be written, page of glory in our history."[2]

However, as Himmler's casual reference to "cases of human weakness" suggests, a minority of camp guards and others failed to live up to this image and indulged in wanton cruelty toward their helpless victims. For some, the extermination process became the occasion to act out sadistic fantasies. But though this dimension is surely horrifying, the bureaucratic, factory-like nature of the extermination process has seemed still more troubling in some respects, for it raises questions about the nature of modern rationality itself. The mass killing of Jews required the expertise of scientists, doctors, and lawyers; it required the bureaucratic organization of the modern state—all to provide the most efficient means to a monstrous end.

Despite the overriding emphasis on secrecy, reports of the genocide reached the West almost immediately in 1942. At first, however, most tended to discount them as wartime propaganda of the sort that had circulated during World War I, when stories about Germans eating Belgian babies whipped up war fever. Skepticism about extermination reports was easier because there were a few concentration camps, like Theresienstadt (teh-REZ-eh-en-shtat) in the former Czechoslovakia, that housed Jews who had been selected for special treatment. These camps were not used for extermination and were not secret; the Red Cross was even allowed to inspect

Theresienstadt several times. Those outside, and the German people as well, were led to believe that all the Jews were being interned, for the duration of the war, in camps like these, much as Japanese Americans were being interned in camps in the western United States at the same time. But even as the evidence grew, President Roosevelt, citing military priorities, refused pleas from Jewish leaders in 1944 to bomb the rail line into Auschwitz. As he saw it, the way to save as many Jews as possible was to win the war as quickly as possible.

AN ARRAY OF VICTIMS   The Nazis' policy of actually murdering persons deemed undesirable or superfluous did not start with, and was not limited to, the Jews. First came the "euthanasia" program in Germany, and the war afforded the Nazis the chance to do away with an array of other "undesirables," including Poles, Sinti and Roma ("Gypsies"), communists, homosexuals, and vagrants. The Nazis also systematically killed perhaps 2 million Soviet prisoners of war. So the most radical and appalling aspect of Nazism did not stem from anti-Semitism alone. This must not be forgotten, but neither must the fact that the Jews constituted by far the largest group of victims—perhaps 5.7 to 6 million, almost two-thirds of the Jews in Europe. (See the feature, "The Visual Record: Holocaust Snapshots.")

Collaboration in Nazi Europe

In rounding up Jews for extermination, and in establishing their new order in Europe, the Nazis found willing collaborators among several of the countries within their orbit. Collaboration with the victorious Nazi regime seemed to some the best way to pursue their own nationalist agendas. Croatia, earlier part of Yugoslavia, was eager to round up Jews and Gypsies, as well as to attack Serbs, as part of its effort to establish itself as a nation-state. But national circumstances varied across Europe, and so did degrees of collaboration. In Denmark, Norway, and the Netherlands, the Nazis thought racial kinship would matter, but they never found sufficient support to make possible genuinely independent collaborationist governments. Denmark did especially well at resisting the German effort to round up Jews, as did Italy and Bulgaria.

Vichy France was somewhere in the middle, and thus, it has remained particularly controversial. When the Vichy regime was launched during the summer of 1940, Marshal Pétain, its 84-year-old chief of state, enjoyed widespread support. Pétain promised to maximize French sovereignty and shield his people from the worst aspects of Nazi occupation. At the same time, the Vichy government claimed to be implementing its own "national revolution," returning France to authority, discipline, and tradition after the shambles of the Third Republic. Vichy's revolution was anti-Semitic and hostile to the left, so it seemed compatible, up to a point, with Nazism. And at first, Germany seemed likely to win the war. Thus, Pétain's second-in-command, Pierre Laval (la-VAHL), was willing to collaborate actively with the Nazis. The Vichy regime ended up doing much of the Nazis' dirty work for them—rounding up workers for forced shipment to German factories, hunting down members of the anti-German resistance, and picking up Jews to be sent to the Nazi extermination camps.

After the war, Pétain, Laval, and others were found guilty of treason by the new French government. Because of his advanced age, Pétain was merely imprisoned, while Laval and others were executed. Despite the contributions of de Gaulle's Free French and the French resistance, the shame of Vichy collaboration continued to haunt France, deepening the humiliation of the defeat in 1940.

Toward the Soviet Triumph

The import of what happened elsewhere in Europe depended on the outcome of the main event, the German invasion of the Soviet Union. Although the German Sixth Army, numbering almost 300,000 men, reached Stalingrad by late 1942, the Germans could not achieve a knockout. The Soviets managed to defend the city in what was arguably the pivotal military engagement of World War II. While some Soviet troops fought street by street, house by house, others counterattacked, encircling the German force. Hitler refused a strategic retreat, but his doggedness backfired. By the end of January 1943, the Soviets had captured the remaining German troops, very few of whom survived to return to Germany. Perhaps 240,000 German soldiers died in the Battle of **Stalingrad** or as prisoners afterward. But the price to the Soviets for their victory was far greater: A million Soviet soldiers and civilians died at Stalingrad.

Although the Germans resumed the offensive on several fronts during the summer of 1943, the Soviets won the tank battle of Kursk-Orel in July, and from then on, Stalin's Red Army moved relentlessly westward, forcing the Germans to retreat. By February 1944, Soviet troops had pushed the Germans back to the Polish border, and the outcome of the war was no longer in doubt.

Stalingrad Decisive World War II battle in which Soviet forces launched repeated counterattacks on Germany's Sixth Army, stopping it from advancing farther and finally forcing it to surrender.

The Soviet victory was incredible, in light of the upheavals of the 1930s and the low esteem in which most held the Soviet military in 1941. Portraying the struggle as "**the Great Patriotic War**" for national defense, Stalin managed to rally the Soviet people against the Germans. Rather than emphasize communist themes, he recalled the heroic defenses mounted against invaders in tsarist times, including the resistance to Napoleon in 1812. But though the Soviets ultimately prevailed, the cost in death, destruction, and suffering was almost unimaginable. For example, by the time Soviet forces finally broke the siege of Leningrad in January 1944, a million people in the city had died, most from starvation, freezing, or disease. And the Soviets won on the battlefield partly by taking incredible numbers of casualties.

The invading Germans gained access to major areas of Soviet industry and oil supply, and by the end of 1941 the country's industrial output had been cut in half. Yet the Soviet Union was able to weather this blow and go on to triumph. Outside help contributed, but only 5 to 15 percent of Soviet supplies came from the West. Between 1939 and 1941, Soviet leaders had begun building a new industrial base east of the Urals. And when the Germans invaded in 1941, the plant and equipment of 1,500 enterprises were dismantled and shipped by rail for reassembly farther east, out of reach of German attack. Then, beginning in 1942, thousands of brand-new factories were constructed in eastern regions as well.

Moreover, the earlier purges of the armed forces proved to have done less long-term damage than outside observers had expected. If anything, the removal of so many in the top ranks made it easier for talented young officers like Georgi Zhukov (1896–1974), who would become the country's top military commander, to rise quickly into major leadership positions.

When the United States entered the war in December 1941, the Soviets were fighting for survival. They immediately began pressuring the United States and Britain to open another front in Europe, preferably by landing in northern France, where an Allied assault could be expected to have the greatest impact. But the Allies did not invade northern France and open a major second front until June 1944. By then, the Soviets had turned the tide in Europe on their own.

"the Great Patriotic War"
Term for World War II devised by Joseph Stalin to rally Soviet citizens against the German invasion.

SECTION SUMMARY

- Although the German invasion of the Soviet Union in 1941 failed to bring the expected quick victory, the Germans drove still further into the country in 1942—but then met defeat at the Battle of Stalingrad.

- Brutal though it was, Nazi policy in northern and western Europe approached something like conventional military occupation, whereas in the conquered territories of the east, first and most dramatically in the former Poland, the Nazis engaged in radical population engineering as they began constructing a race-based "new order."

- By the end of 1941, the Holocaust became a systematic program as the Nazis decided to kill Jews and others by adapting the methods developed through the "euthanasia" program.

- Although the Jews constituted by far the largest group of victims, the Nazis also killed an array of others, from homosexuals to Soviet prisoners of war.

- After defeating the Germans at Kursk-Orel in July 1943, the Soviets began steadily advancing toward Germany, thereby turning the tide in Europe well before the U.S.-British landing in northern France opened a major second front in June 1944.

Stalingrad, November 1942 From September 1942 until the German surrender early in February 1943, this city on the Volga River saw some of the heaviest fighting of World War II. The Soviet victory, in the face of incredible casualties, was arguably the turning point of the war in Europe. (Sovfoto/Eastfoto)

Holocaust Snapshots

What are we to make of these pictures? In one sense, they appear to be ordinary snapshots of the sort that became popular between the wars, as inexpensive cameras became common consumer items for the first time. But these photographs are hardly ordinary; they depict disturbing aspects of the Nazi effort to exterminate the Jews between 1941 and 1945. So we wonder, who took these pictures—and why? Why did these particular images seem worth preserving? What do such photographs tell us about the mentality that made possible the monstrous process that we have come to know as the Holocaust?

More than 50 percent of the victims of the Holocaust died in the six extermination camps, the camps with systematic gassing facilities. Almost a quarter died from such factors as malnutrition, disease, or exhaustion while in transit, in the ghettos, or in the labor or concentration camps. The rest—more than one quarter of the victims—were killed individually, mostly by shooting, up close.

These photos, and many others like them, were taken by members of Hamburg-based Reserve Battalion 101 of the "order police," made famous through the somewhat conflicting accounts of Christopher R. Browning and Daniel Jonah Goldhagen.[3] This local branch of the complex German police system was sent to assist in the removal of Jews from a remote section of Poland in July 1942. Only upon arriving in the village of Józefów did these ordinary policemen find that their first task was to shoot large numbers of defenseless Jews one by one. When given their collective charge, these men were offered a chance to pull back from the actual murder of Jews. But the vast majority did what they were told—why?

We know that the men of Battalion 101 had not been specially selected and trained for such a task. Indeed, they were unprepared and surprised when, upon arriving in Józefów, they learned what they were there to do. Browning suggests that many of the men felt that they had to be tough, following orders based on government policy, whatever it entailed. Moreover, they did not want to appear weak or leave the dirty work to their comrades. Others tried not to think about what they were doing or masked it through heavy drinking.

But photographs like these suggest a further step. Ordinary Germans took them not so that they could forget, obviously, but precisely to remember and commemorate their participation. Indeed, the very act of taking the photographs was essential to their dehumanization and humiliation of the Jews. Notice the photo on the left, taken during the liquidation of the ghetto at Lukow, Poland, probably in the fall of 1942. Three of the four police officers are looking directly at the camera. Some of the officers have stern facial expressions, as if they are trying to convey their toughness and power. Others, such as the officer at far left, smile broadly for the camera. The Jews, meanwhile, are humiliated by being forced to kneel and raise their hands above their heads.

In the other photograph, Jews are shown digging their own graves. Unlike the one taken at Lukow, no officers appear in this photo and no one is posing for the camera. Yet somehow even this image seemed worth preserving in a snapshot.

What did these Germans find so memorable about what they were doing? We may first assume that sheer anti-Semitism was the key, a notion that Goldhagen wholeheartedly supports. He argues that these photographs manifest a virulent anti-Semitism endemic in German society even before the rise of Nazism. But most experts deny that German anti-Semitism had been especially pronounced before Hitler came to power, so something more complex was surely at work in the minds of these policemen. Especially as the Nazi revolution yielded an apocalyptic war of race, ideology, and annihilation, the Nazi regime's ongoing campaign to demonize the Jews affected the responses to the Jews by ordinary Germans. The Jews came to seem not merely superfluous, but alien and threatening.

Thus, the key variable was not anti-Semitism but the momentum of the Nazi revolution itself. By 1942, a sense of the extraordinariness of the overall Nazi enterprise had produced an altered frame of mind in many reaches of German society. For example, a doctor involved in the earlier "euthanasia" program, Friedrich Mennecke, sought, in his letters to his wife, to chronicle for posterity this, "the greatest of times" in which he was privileged to participate.[4] In the same vein, historians Michael Burleigh and Wolfgang Wippermann found, as central to the Holocaust, "the group intoxication with violence and the prospect of going outside the limits of received moral norms."[5]

The ongoing Nazi revolution caught up even the members of Reserve Battalion 101 in essential roles. So those who took, and kept, and perhaps showed off these photographs were not merely ordinary human beings, or even ordinary Germans, but ordinary *Nazified* Germans. To some extent they, too, believed themselves to be involved in an enterprise that was grandiose, unprecedented, and of world-historical import. They did not merely follow orders, but came to experience the "extraordinary exhilaration" that Saul Friedländer found central to the overall extermination process.[6] Partly as a result, they sometimes fell into the gratuitous cruelty evident in many of the photographs they took. Most of these men would not have been capable of such cruelty under ordinary circumstances.

When the veterans of police Battalion 101 were put on trial in the 1960s, one of them, Erwin Graffman, noted that only after the fact had it occurred to him that the killing had been wrong.[7] When acting, he had believed in the essential rightness of the wider Nazi revolution. The participation of such people is not to be explained simply through

Lukow, Poland, July 1942 (Yad Vashem Film and Photo Archive)

Lomazy, Poland, August 1942 (Courtesy, ZstL, Ludwigsburg, Germany)

universal, ahistorical mechanisms, as if "we all could have done it." Those operating from within the framework of the Nazi revolution were especially likely to have treated the Jews as they did, not just killing them, but often humiliating them—and finding something memorable in the process.

Thus, for these perpetrators, the import of capturing the extraordinary enterprise through snapshots. But twenty years later, those who took them found it almost impossible to explain what had been their mindset at the time. As Browning noted, "it was a different time and place, as if they had been on another political planet, and the political values and vocabulary of the 1960s were useless in explaining the situation in which they had found themselves in 1942."[8] Yet these haunting images remain.

QUESTIONS

1. What, beyond sheer anti-Semitism, seems to have stimulated the policemen of Battalion 101 to preserve these scenes for posterity?

2. Does Erwin Graffman seem credible, or merely self-serving, when he says that, at the time these photographs were taken, he genuinely believed what he was doing was right?

A GLOBAL WAR, 1941–1944

How did the Grand Alliance of Britain, the United States, and the Soviet Union come together against the Axis powers?

World War II proved unprecedented in its level of violence, partly because it eclipsed even World War I in its geographical reach. The European colonial presence quickly drew the war to North Africa and the Middle East. But the war's early results in Europe also altered the power balance in East Asia and the Pacific, where the Russians and the Japanese had long been antagonists. During the 1930s, the United States had also become involved in friction with Japan. By 1941, President **Franklin Delano Roosevelt** was openly favoring the anti-Axis cause, though it took a surprise attack by the Japanese in December 1941 to bring the United States into the war.

Franklin Delano Roosevelt U.S. president who served from 1933 to 1945, through the Great Depression of the 1930s and most of World War II.

Japan and the Origins of the Pacific War

Lacking the raw materials essential for industry, Japan had been especially concerned about foreign trade and spheres of economic influence as it modernized after 1868. By the interwar period, the Japanese had become unusually reliant on exports of textiles and other products. During the Depression of the 1930s, when countries all over the world adopted protectionist policies, Japan suffered from increasing tariffs against its exports. This situation tilted the balance in Japanese ruling circles from free-trade proponents to those who favored a military-imperialist solution.

To gain economic hegemony by force, Japan could choose either of two directions. The northern strategy, concentrating on China, would risk Soviet opposition as well as strong local resistance. The southern strategy, focusing on southeast Asia and the East Indies, would encounter the imperial presence of Britain, France, the Netherlands, and the United States.

Japan opted for the northern strategy in 1931, when it took control of Manchuria, in northeastern China. But the Japanese attempt to conquer the rest of China, beginning in 1937, led only to an impasse by 1940. Japanese aggression in China drew the increasing hostility of the United States, a strong supporter of the Chinese nationalist leader Jiang Jieshi (Chiang Kaishek) (1887–1975), as well as the active opposition of the Soviet Union. Clashes with Soviet troops along the border between Mongolia and Manchuria led to significant defeats for the Japanese in 1938 and 1939.

By 1941, Germany's victories in Europe had seriously weakened Britain, France, and the Netherlands, the major European colonial powers in southeast Asia and the East Indies. The time seemed right for Japan to shift to a southern strategy. Rather than focus on China, the Japanese would seek control of southeast Asia, a region rich in such raw materials as oil, rubber, and tin—precisely what Japan lacked. To keep the Soviets at bay, Japan agreed to a neutrality pact with the Soviet Union in April 1941.

Japan had already joined with Nazi Germany and fascist Italy in an anticommunist agreement in 1936. In September 1940, the three agreed to a formal military alliance. For the Germans, alliance with Japan was useful to help discourage U.S. intervention in the European war. Japan, for its part, could expect the major share of the spoils of the European empires in Asia. However, diplomatic and military coordination between Germany and Japan remained minimal.

The United States began imposing embargoes on certain exports to Japan in 1938, in response to the Japanese aggression in China. After Japan had assumed control of Indochina, nominally held by Vichy France, by the summer of 1941, the United States imposed total sanctions, and the British and Dutch followed, forcing Japan to begin rapidly drawing down its oil reserves. Conquest of the oil fields of the Dutch East Indies now seemed a matter of life and death to the Japanese.

These economic sanctions heightened the determination of Japanese leaders to press forward aggressively now, when the country's likely enemies were weakened or distracted. But the Japanese did not expect a definitive victory over the United States in a long, drawn-out war. Rather, they anticipated, first, that their initial successes would enable them to grab the resources to sustain a longer war if necessary, and, second, that Germany would defeat Britain, leading the United States to accept a compromise peace allowing the Japanese what they wanted—a secure sphere of economic hegemony in southeast Asia.

🌐 **MAP 28.3—The War in East Asia and the Pacific**

After a series of conquests in 1941 and 1942, the Japanese were forced gradually to fall back before advancing U.S. forces. When the war abruptly ended in August 1945, however, the Japanese still controlled much of the territory they had conquered.

The Japanese finally provoked a showdown on December 7, 1941, with a surprise attack on Pearl Harbor, a U.S. naval base in Hawaii. The next day, Japanese forces seized Hong Kong and Malaya, both British colonies, and attacked Wake Island and the Philippines, both under U.S. control. The United States promptly declared war; in response, Hitler kept an earlier promise to Japan and declared war on the United States. World War II was now unprecedented in its geographic scope (see **MAP 28.3**).

Much like their German counterparts, Japanese forces got off to a remarkably good start. By the summer of 1942, Japan had taken Thailand, the Dutch East Indies, the Philippines, and the Malay Peninsula. Having won much of what they had been seeking, the Japanese began devising the Greater East Asia Co-Prosperity Sphere, their own "new order" in the conquered territories. (See the feature, "The Global Record: Japan's 'Pan-Asian' Mission.")

The United States in Europe and the Pacific

During the first years of the war in Europe, the United States did not have armed forces commensurate with its economic strength; in 1940, in fact, its army was smaller than Belgium's. But the United States could be a supplier in the short term and, if it chose to intervene, a major player

Japan's "Pan-Asian" Mission

With the coming of war against the Western powers in 1941, the Japanese could claim to be freeing Asians from Western imperialism and establishing a new economic order in East Asia and the Pacific. This selection from an essay titled "Our Present War and Its Cultural Significance," written just after the bombing of Pearl Harbor by the well-known author Nagayo Yoshio (1888–1961), accents Japan's anti-Western mission in the region. Yoshio understood, especially from his country's recent experience in China, that Asians might find Japanese hegemony just as oppressive as Western domination. Although it served Japan's own economic interests and was often applied brutally, Japanese "pan-Asianism" helped fuel the reaction against Western imperialism in Asia and the Pacific, with lasting results after the war.

Whenever Japan has faced a powerful enemy it has been the *yamato damashii* [Japanese national spirit] which provided the basis of our courage. Now that we can talk in retrospect of the Sino-Japanese War, I am afraid our national spirit has not been given a proper chance to be aroused, due to the deplorable fact that we had to fight with China, our sister nation, with no foreseeable conclusion to look forward to. ... While desperately fighting with a country which we made our enemy only reluctantly we were trying to find out a principle, an ethic based upon a new view of the world, which would justify our course of action. ... The China incident was not only insufficient to fulfill this goal but also met with insurmountable obstacles. Consequently, time and opportunity ripened to declare war against the United States and England....

...We would have nothing to say for ourselves if we were merely to follow the examples of the imperialistic and capitalistic exploitation of Greater East-Asia by Europe and the United States....

...It is true that the science of war is one manifestation of a nation's culture. But from this time on we have to realize the increasing responsibility on our part if we are to deserve the respect of the people of East-Asian countries as their leaders, in the sphere of culture in general (not only the mere fusion and continuance of Western and Oriental cultures but something surpassing and elevating them while making the most out of them) such as the formation of national character, refinement, intellect, training to become a world citizen, etc....

The sense of awe and respect with which the Orientals have held the white race, especially the Anglo-Saxons, for three hundred years is deep-rooted almost beyond our imagination. It is our task to realize this fact and deal with this servility at its root, find out why the white people became the objects of such reverence. It goes without saying that we cannot conclude simplemindedly that their shrewdness is the cause. Also we have to be very careful not to impose the *hakko ichiu* [the gathering of the whole world under one roof] spirit arbitrarily upon the Asians. If we make this kind of mistake we might antagonize those who could have become our compatriots and thus might also blaspheme our Imperial rule....

To sum up, we have finally witnessed the dawn of a new principle which we had been searching for over ten years....The phrase "Greater East-Asian Co-prosperity Sphere" is no longer a mere abstract idea.

QUESTIONS

1. Why, according to the author, did the Japanese effort in China sow confusion about Japan's wider aims?

2. What role was Japan to play in Southeast Asia if it was *not* merely to replace Western imperialistic exploitation with another form?

Source: From "Our Present War and Its Cultural Significance" by Nagayo Yashio, translated by Mitsuko Iriye, in *Modern Asia and Africa*, edited by William H. McNeill and Mitsuko Iriye (Oxford University Press, 1971).

Lend-Lease Act Act by the U.S. Congress authorizing President Franklin Roosevelt to lend or lease weapons or other aid to countries the president designated.

over the longer term. With the **Lend-Lease Act** of March 1941, intended to provide war materiel without the economic dislocations of World War I, the United States lined up on the side of Britain against the Axis powers. In August 1941, a meeting between Churchill and Roosevelt off the coast of Newfoundland produced the Atlantic Charter, the first tentative agreement about the aims of the anti-Axis war effort. The Americans extended lend-lease to the Soviet Union the next month.

But though Roosevelt was committed to the anti-Axis cause, isolationist sentiment remained strong in the United States. The Japanese attack on Pearl Harbor inflamed American opinion and enabled Roosevelt at last to bring his country into the war as an active belligerent. By May 1942, the United States had joined with Britain and the Soviet Union in a formal military alliance against the Axis powers.

From the start, mutual suspicions marked the relationship between the two democracies and the Soviet Union. Initially, Britain and the United States feared that the Soviets might even seek a separate peace, as Russia had in World War I. The Soviets, for their part, worried that these newfound allies, with their long-standing anticommunism, might hold back from full commitment or even seek to undermine the Soviet Union.

In response to pressure from Stalin, Britain and the United States agreed to open a second front in Europe as soon as possible. But the Nazis dominated the Continent, so opening such a front required landing troops from the outside. It proved far more difficult to mount an effective assault on Europe than either Churchill or Roosevelt anticipated in 1942. The resulting delays furthered Stalin's suspicions that his allies were only too eager to have the Soviets do the bulk of the fighting against Nazi Germany—and weaken themselves in the process.

The United States agreed with its new allies to give priority to the war in Europe. But because it had to respond to the direct Japanese assault in the Pacific, the United States was not prepared to act militarily in Europe right away. What it could do, however, was supply the British with the ships needed to overcome German submarines, which seriously threatened shipping to Britain by 1942.

In the Pacific theater, in contrast, it was immediately clear that the United States would bear the brunt of the fighting against Japan. Although the Japanese went from one success to another during the first months of the war, they lacked the long-term resources to exploit their initial victories. In May 1942, the Battle of Coral Sea—off New Guinea, north of Australia—ended in a stalemate, stopping the string of Japanese successes. Then in June, the United States defeated the Japanese navy for the first time in the Battle of Midway, northwest of Hawaii. After the United States stopped attempted Japanese advances in the Solomon Islands and New Guinea early in 1943, U.S. forces began steadily advancing across the islands of the Pacific toward Japan (see **Map 28.3**).

The Search for a Second Front in Europe

As the Soviet army fought the Germans in the Soviet Union, the United States and Britain tried to determine how they could help tip the scales in Europe, now an almost impregnable German fortress. Stalin kept urging a direct assault across the English Channel, which, if successful, would have the greatest immediate impact. Churchill, however, advocated attacking the underbelly of the Axis empire by way of the Mediterranean, which would first require winning control of North Africa. And it was that strategy the Allies tried first, starting in 1942.

By May 1943, step one of Churchill's plan had succeeded, but North Africa was valuable primarily as a staging ground for an Allied attempt to penetrate Europe from the south (see **Map 28.1**). Meeting at the Moroccan city of Casablanca in January 1943, Churchill and Roosevelt agreed that British and American forces would proceed from North Africa to Sicily and up through mainland Italy from there. The Soviets, still pushing for an invasion across the English Channel into France, objected that the Germans could easily block an Allied advance through the long, mountainous Italian peninsula.

Crossing from North Africa, Allied troops landed in Sicily in July 1943, prompting the arrest of Mussolini and the collapse of the fascist regime. Supported by King Victor Emmanuel III, the Italian military commander, Pietro Badoglio (bah-DOHL-yo), formed a new government to seek an armistice. Meanwhile, Allied forces moved on to the Italian mainland, but the Germans quickly occupied much of Italy in response. They even managed a daring rescue of Mussolini and promptly reestablished him as puppet leader of a new rump republic in northern Italy, now under German control. Just as the Soviets had warned, the Germans sought to block the Italian peninsula, and it was not until nine months later, in June 1944, that the Allies reached Rome. So Churchill's strategy of assaulting Europe from the south proved less than decisive.

Only when Churchill, Roosevelt, and Stalin met for the first time, at Teheran, Iran, in November 1943, did they agree that the next step would be to invade western Europe from Britain. Preparations had been underway since early 1942, but the operation was complex and hazardous. Finally, Allied troops crossed the English Channel to make an amphibious landing on the beaches of Normandy, in northern France, on June 6, 1944, known to history as **D-Day**. Partly by deceiving the Germans seeking to defend the area, they were quickly able to consolidate their positions.

The success of the D-Day invasion opened a major second front in Europe at last. Now, American-led forces from the west and Soviet forces from the east worked systematically toward Germany. The one substantial German counterattack in the west, the Battle of the Bulge in December 1944, slowed the Allies' advance, but on March 7, 1945, Allied troops crossed the Rhine River (see **Map 28.1**).

By June 1944, when Allied forces landed at Normandy, Soviet forces had already crossed the 1939 border with Poland as they moved steadily westward. But in August, the Soviets stopped before reaching Warsaw, allowing the Nazis to crush a notable uprising by the Polish resistance that took place from August to October. The Polish Home Army, as it was called, was seeking to liberate Warsaw on its own, without waiting for the Soviets, who seemed likely to impose communism on Poland. In putting down the uprising, the German occupying forces suffered

D-Day The complex Allied amphibious landings in Normandy, France, on June 6, 1944, that opened a second major European front in World War II.

SECTION SUMMARY

- Japan turned to a more aggressive, expansionist foreign policy during the 1930s, largely because its economy, heavily dependent on exports, proved especially vulnerable during the Great Depression.

- Although Japan and Nazi Germany joined in a military alliance, diplomatic and military coordination between them was minimal during World War II.

- Delays in opening a major second front in Europe furthered Stalin's suspicions that Britain and the United States were happy to let the Soviets bear the brunt of the burden in the fight against Nazi Germany.

- After the Allied invasion of Italy failed to make a conclusive difference on the continental level, Churchill, Roosevelt, and Stalin agreed in November 1943 that, as the next step, the democracies would invade western Europe from Britain.

- In making their continental landings in Italy and France, the Western democracies left it to the Soviets to drive the German forces from east-central Europe.

ten thousand casualties, and then destroyed much of the city in retaliation. Meanwhile, the major Soviet thrust began cutting south, through Romania, which surrendered in August, and on into the Danube Valley in Hungary and Yugoslavia during the fall. Only in January 1945, did the Soviets resume their advance, taking Warsaw and moving westward toward Germany.

Now, with the defeat of Germany simply a matter of time, Allied concern shifted to the postwar order. Churchill, especially, worried about the implications of the Soviet advances in east-central Europe and the Balkans. As a supplement to the D-Day landings, he wanted to strike from Italy through Yugoslavia into east-central Europe. But the Americans resisted; Churchill's priorities, they felt, reflected outmoded concerns over spheres of influence. So the Allies concentrated instead on a secondary landing in southern France in August 1944. This assault, in which Free French forces were prominent, led quickly to the liberation of Paris. But because the Allies made both their landings in France, and not in southeastern Europe, the Western democracies were involved only in the liberation of western Europe. It was the Soviets who drove the Germans from east-central Europe. This fact, and the resulting geographic distribution of military strength, fundamentally affected the postwar order.

D-Day, 1944 Allied forces land at Normandy, early in the morning of June 6, 1944, at last opening a major second front in Europe. (National Archives, Washington)

THE SHAPE OF THE ALLIED VICTORY, 1944–1945

How did the Allies manage to defeat Nazi Germany in World War II, after Germany's remarkable initial successes?

The leaders of the Soviet Union, Britain, and the United States sought to mold the postwar order at two notable conferences in 1945. Even as they brought different aspirations to the table, they had to deal together with the legacy of a war of unprecedented destructiveness. At the same time, they also had to face the hard military realities that had resulted from the fighting so far: Each country had forces in certain places but not in others. The result was an informal division of Europe into spheres of influence among the victors.

The most serious question the Allies faced concerned Germany, which was widely held responsible for the two world wars, as well as for Nazism with all its atrocities—including the concentration and extermination camps, discovered with shock and horror by the advancing Allied armies in 1945. Germany was to be forced to surrender unconditionally; there would be no negotiation or armistice. But what should be done with the country over the longer term?

In the Pacific theater, as in Europe, the way the war ended had major implications for the postwar world. The United States decided to use the atomic bomb, a weapon so destructive that it forced a quick Japanese surrender. The suddenness of the ending helped determine the fate of the European empires in Asia.

The Yalta Conference: Shaping the Postwar World

When Stalin, Roosevelt, and Churchill met at Yalta, a Soviet Black Sea resort, in February 1945, Allied victory was assured, and the three leaders accomplished a great deal. Yet controversy has long surrounded the **Yalta conference**. Western critics have charged that the concessions made to Stalin consigned east-central Europe to communist domination and opened the way to the dangerous cold war of the next forty years. At the time, however, the anticipation of victory produced a relatively cooperative spirit among the Allies. Thus, they firmed up plans for military occupation of Germany in separate zones, for joint occupation of Berlin, and for an Allied Control Council, composed of the military commanders-in-chief, which would make policy for all of Germany by unanimous agreement.

Each of the Allies had special concerns, but each got much of what it was seeking at Yalta. Roosevelt was eager for Soviet help against Japan as soon as possible. In exchange for territorial concessions in Asia and the Pacific, Stalin agreed to declare war on Japan within three months of the German surrender.

Churchill, meanwhile, worried about the future of Europe in light of the American intention, which Roosevelt announced at Yalta, to maintain occupation troops in Europe for only two years after the war. To help balance Soviet power on the Continent, Churchill felt it essential to restore France as a great power. To this end, he urged that France be granted a share in the occupation of Germany and a permanent seat on the Security Council of the proposed new international organization, the **United Nations** (see page 812). Roosevelt agreed, even though he had little use for Charles de Gaulle or what he viewed as the pretensions of the French.

It seemed to the Americans that both Britain and the Soviet Union remained too wedded to traditional conceptions of national interest as they sought to shape the postwar world. Hence, one of Roosevelt's major priorities was to secure British and Soviet commitment to the United Nations before the three allies began to disagree over particular issues. He won that commitment at Yalta, but only by giving in to Churchill on the sensitive matter of British colonies.

Because anti-imperial sentiment worked to Japan's advantage in Asia, the United States had pestered Britain on the colonial issue since early in the war. Roosevelt even asked Churchill in 1941 about British intentions in India. So prickly was Churchill that he proclaimed in 1942, "I have not become the King's First Minister in order to preside over the liquidation of the British Empire." The parties agreed at Yalta that the British Empire would be exempt from an anticipated measure to bring former colonies under United Nations trusteeship after the war.

Although it was not the only question on the table, the future of the former Axis territories was central to the seaside deliberations. By the time of the conference, those territories were already being divided into spheres of influence among the Allies, and in light of troop locations, the eventual alignment was probably inevitable. In Italy, where U.S. and British forces held sway,

Yalta conference
1945 meeting between Stalin, Roosevelt, and Churchill in which they began outlining plans for the postwar order, including the military occupation of Germany.

United Nations
International organization of nations founded in 1945 to encourage peace, cooperation, and recognition of human rights.

the two democracies had successfully resisted Stalin's claim for a share in the administration. In east-central Europe, however, the Soviet army was in control. Still, the United States, with its vision of a new world order, objected to spheres of influence and insisted that democratic principles be applied everywhere. At Yalta, this American priority led to an awkward compromise over east-central Europe: The new governments in the area were to be both democratic and friendly to the Soviet Union.

Most important to the Soviets was Poland, with its crucial location between the Soviet Union and Germany. Although they insisted that communists lead the new Polish government at the outset, the Soviets compromised by allowing a role for the noncommunist Polish government-in-exile in London and by promising free elections down the road. The Allies agreed that Poland would gain substantial German territory to its west to make up for the eastern territory it had already lost to the USSR (see **Map 28.4**).

In addition, the United States and Britain were to have a role in committees set up to engineer the transition to democracy in the rest of east-central Europe. However, only the Soviets had troops in the area, and those committees proved essentially powerless. The sources of future tension were already at work at Yalta, but they generally remained hidden by the high spirits of approaching victory.

Victory in Europe

Although the tide had turned in 1943, Germany managed to continue the war by exploiting its conquered territories and by more effectively allocating its domestic resources for war production. Thanks partly to the efforts of armaments minister Albert Speer, war production grew

![icon] Map 28.4—The Impact of World War II in Europe

As a result of World War II, the Soviet Union expanded its western borders and Poland shifted westward at the expense of Germany. Territorial changes added to the wartime disruption and produced a flood of refugees. The cold war division of Europe did not depend on immediate territorial changes, but soon Germany itself came to be divided on east-west lines.

sharply between 1941 and 1944, so Germany had plenty of weapons even as the war was ending. The Germans even proved able to withstand the systematic bombing of cities that the British, especially, had thought might prove decisive.

Beginning in 1942, British-led bombing attacks destroyed an average of half the built-up area of seventy German cities, sometimes producing huge firestorms. The bombing of the historic city of Dresden in February 1945 killed at least sixty thousand civilians in the most destructive air assault of the war in Europe. But despite this widespread destruction, such bombing did not undermine morale or disrupt production to the extent expected. Even in the face of steady Allied bombing, the Germans managed to increase their war production during 1943 and 1944.

But Germany encountered two crucial bottlenecks that finally crippled its military effort: It was running out of both oil and military personnel. Despite making effective use of synthetics, the Nazi war machine depended heavily on oil from Romania. And although the terror bombing of cities did not have the anticipated impact, the more precisely targeted bombing favored by U.S. strategists significantly affected the outcome. In May 1944, the United States began bombing oil fields in Romania and refineries and synthetic oil plants in Germany. Then, late in August 1944, Soviet troops crossed into Romania, taking control of the oil fields. Soon Germany lacked enough fuel even to train pilots. So serious were the bottlenecks by 1945 that the German air force could not use all the aircraft that German industry was producing.

Soviet troops moving westward finally met U.S. troops moving eastward at the Elbe River in Germany on April 26, 1945. With his regime now thoroughly defeated and much of his country in ruins, Hitler committed suicide in his underground military headquarters in Berlin on April 30. The war in Europe finally ended with the German surrender to General Dwight D. Eisenhower at Reims, France, on May 7 and to Marshal Zhukov at Berlin on May 8. The world celebrated the end of the fighting in Europe, but an element of uncertainty surrounded the Allied victory. East-West differences were increasingly coming to the fore within the anti-German alliance.

The Potsdam Conference and the Question of Germany

The immediate question for the victorious Allies was the fate of Germany, which they confronted at the last of their notable wartime conferences, at **Potsdam**, just outside Berlin, from July 17 to August 2, 1945. The circumstances were dramatically different from those at Yalta just months before. With Hitler dead and Germany defeated, no common military aim provided unity. And of the three Allied leaders who had been at Yalta, only Stalin remained. President Roosevelt had

Potsdam conference
A July–August 1945 meeting held at Potsdam, Germany, between the USSR, the United States, and Great Britain to implement their earlier agreements concerning the treatment of defeated Germany.

The Soviet Victory in Europe After forcing the Germans back for almost two years, Soviet troops reached Berlin in April 1945. After a day of heavy fighting and bombardment, the Soviets took the Reichstag building, in the heart of the devastated German capital, on April 30. Here two Soviet sergeants, Yegorov and Kantariya, plant the Soviet flag atop the Reichstag, symbolizing the Soviet victory in the decisive encounter of World War II in Europe. (ITAR-TASS/Sovfoto)

died in April, so his successor, Harry Truman (1884–1972), represented the United States. In Britain, Churchill's Conservatives lost the general election during the first days of the conference, so Clement Attlee (1883–1967), the new Labour prime minister, assumed the leadership of the British delegation.

At Potsdam, the Allies had to determine how to implement their earlier agreements about Germany, which, devastated by bombing and devoid of a government, depended on the Allied occupying forces even for day-to-day survival. For a time, U.S. policymakers had even considered destroying Germany's industrial capacity in perpetuity. However, cooler heads understood that the deindustrialization, or "pastoralization," of Germany would not be in anyone's economic interests. Moreover, as the democracies grew increasingly suspicious about Soviet intentions, an economically healthy Germany seemed necessary to help in the balance against the Soviet Union.

For their part, the Soviets had reason to take a much harder line against Germany. Having been ravaged by invading German forces twice within living memory, the Soviet Union wanted to weaken Germany both territorially and economically. And of the three victors, the Soviets had suffered a greatly disproportionate share of the wartime destruction and economic loss, so they also sought to exploit the remaining resources of Germany by exacting heavy reparations. Moreover, the British and the Americans accepted the Soviet proposal that Germany's eastern border with Poland be shifted substantially westward, to the line formed by the Oder and Neisse (NYE-suh) Rivers. But just as Poland gained at the expense of Germany, the Soviet Union kept a substantial slice of what had been eastern Poland (see **MAP 28.4**).

Each of the three Allies had responsibility for administering a particular zone of occupation, but they were supposed to coordinate their activities in a common policy toward Germany. This effort was to include de-Nazification, demilitarization, and an assault on concentrations of economic power—to root out what seemed to have been the sources of Germany's antidemocratic and aggressive tendencies. But East-West disagreements over economic policy soon undermined the pretense of joint government.

The Atomic Bomb and the Capitulation of Japan

In the Pacific, Japan had been forced onto the defensive by September 1943, and though it mounted two major counterattacks during 1944, the Japanese navy was crippled by shortages of ships and fuel by the end of the year. However, as the situation grew more desperate for Japan, Japanese ground soldiers battled ever more fiercely, often fighting to the death or taking their own lives rather than surrendering. Beginning late in 1944, aircraft pilots practiced *kamikaze* (kah-mih-KAH-zee), suicidally crashing planes filled with explosives into U.S. targets. The Japanese used this tactic especially as the Americans sought to take Okinawa in the spring of 1945. The U.S. forces finally prevailed in June, but only after the most bitter combat of the Pacific war (see **MAP 28.3**).

In conquering Okinawa, American forces got close enough for air raids on the Japanese home islands. But though the United States was now clearly in control, it seemed likely that an actual invasion of Japan would be necessary to force a Japanese surrender. Some estimated that, because the Japanese could be expected to fight even more desperately to defend their own soil, invasion might well cost the United States 1 million additional casualties. It was especially for this reason that the Americans decided to try to end the war in an altogether different way—by using an atomic bomb.

In 1939, scientists in several countries, including Germany, had started to advise their governments that new, immensely destructive weapons based on thermonuclear fission were theoretically possible. The German economics ministry began seeking uranium as early as 1939, but Hitler promoted jet- and rocket-propelled terror weaponry instead, especially the V-2 rocket bombs that the Germans began showering on England in the fall of 1944. Still, fear that the Nazis were developing atomic weapons lurked behind the Allied effort to produce the ultra-lethal bomb as quickly as possible.

Although the British were the first to initiate an atomic weapons program, by late 1941 the Americans were building on what they knew of British findings to develop their own crash program, known as the Manhattan Project. Constructing an atomic bomb proved far more difficult and costly than most had expected in 1941, and it took a concerted effort by the United States to have atomic weapons ready for use by mid-1945.

The U.S. decision to use the atomic bomb on Japanese civilians has been one of the most controversial of modern history. The decision fell to the new president, Harry Truman, who had known nothing of the bomb project when Roosevelt died in April 1945. During the next few months, Truman listened to spirited disagreement among American policymakers. Was it necessary actually to drop the bomb to force the Japanese to surrender? Since the ultimate victory of the United States was not in doubt, some argued that it would be enough simply to demonstrate the new weapon to the Japanese in a test firing.

By July, when the Allies met at Potsdam, the United States was prepared to use the bomb. But President Truman first warned Japan that if it did not surrender at once, it would be subjected to destruction immeasurably greater than Germany had just suffered. The Japanese ignored the warning, although the United States had begun area-bombing Japanese cities a few months before. The bombing of Tokyo in March produced a firestorm that gutted one-fourth of the city and killed over 80,000 people. In light of the Japanese refusal to surrender, the use of the atomic bomb seemed to Truman the logical next step.

At 8:15 on the morning of August 6, 1945, from a height of 32,000 feet above the Japanese city of Hiroshima, an American pilot released the first atomic bomb to be used against an enemy target. The bomb exploded after 45 seconds, 2,000 feet above the ground, killing 80,000 people outright and leaving tens of thousands more to die in the aftermath. Three days later, on August 9, the Americans exploded a second atomic bomb over Nagasaki, killing perhaps 50,000 people. Although sectors of the Japanese military held out for continued resistance, Emperor Hirohito (hee-roh-HEE-toh) (1901–1989) finally announced Japan's surrender on August 15. The bombing of civilians had discredited the Japanese military, which not only had proved unable to defend the country but had systematically misled the Japanese people about their country's prospects.

The war in the Pacific ended more suddenly than had seemed possible just a few months earlier (see **MAP 28.3**). This worked in favor of the various national liberation or decolonization movements that had developed in Asia during the war, for the Europeans had little opportunity to reestablish their dominance in the colonial territories they had earlier lost to the Japanese. In the Dutch East Indies, the Japanese had encouraged anticolonial sentiment, even helping local nationalists create patriotic militias. After the war, the Dutch were never able to reassert their control against this Indonesian nationalist movement. But though the war had severely weakened the old Western imperialism in Asia and the Pacific, what would replace it remained unclear.

Death, Disruption, and the Question of Guilt

World War II left as many as 60 million people dead—three times as many as World War I. The Soviet Union, Poland, and Germany suffered by far the highest casualty figures; for each, the figure was considerably higher than in World War I. An appalling 23 million Soviet citizens died, over half of them civilians. Poland lost over 6 million, the vast majority civilians, including 3 million Jews. Germany lost 5 million to 6 million, including perhaps 2 million civilians.

In contrast, casualty rates for Italy, Britain, and France were lower than in World War I. Italy suffered 200,000 military and 200,000 civilian deaths. Total British losses, including civilians, numbered 450,000, to which must be added 120,000 from the British Empire. Despite its quick defeat, France lost more lives than Britain because of the ravages of German occupation: the 350,000 deaths among French civilians considerably exceeded the British figure, closer to 100,000.

The United States lost 300,000 servicemen and 5,000 civilians. Figures for Japan are problematic, partly because the Japanese claim that 300,000 of those who surrendered to the Soviets in 1945 have remained unaccounted for. Apart from this number, 1.74 million Japanese servicemen died from 1941 to 1945, more from hunger and disease than from combat, and 300,000 civilians died in Japan, most from U.S. bombing.

During the war, Jews, Poles, and others deemed undesirable by the Nazis had been rounded up and shipped to ghettos or camps, where the great majority had died. Of those Jews who were still alive when the Nazi camps were liberated, almost half died within a few weeks. Even those who managed to return home sometimes faced pogroms during the difficult months that followed; forty Jews were killed in the worst of them, at Kielce (KYEL-tsuh), Poland, in 1946.

Late in the war, as German forces in the east retreated, ethnic Germans living in Poland, Czechoslovakia, Hungary, and elsewhere in east-central Europe began seeking refuge in Germany. They were fleeing the Soviet advance but also seeking to escape the growing wave of anti-German resentment in those countries. Once the war was over, the Poles began expelling ethnic Germans from the historically German areas that were now to become Polish. These Germans were sometimes sent to detention camps, and when they were shipped out, it was often in cattle cars. According to some estimates, as many as 2 million died in the process. At the same time, the uprooting of Poles that had begun during the war continued as Poles were systematically forced from the Polish territories incorporated into the Soviet Union.

In Czechoslovakia, the government expelled 3.5 million Germans from the Sudetenland area by 1947. All told, at least 7 million German refugees moved west into the shrunken territory of the new Germany by that year. They were among the 16 million Europeans who were permanently uprooted and transplanted during the war and its immediate wake. And the process continued at a diminished rate thereafter. By 1958, perhaps 10 million Germans had either left or been forced out of the new Poland, leaving only about 1 million Germans still living there.

As the end of the war approached, Europeans began attempting to assess guilt and to punish those responsible for the disasters of the era. In the climate of violence, resistance forces in France, Italy, and elsewhere often subjected fascists and collaborators to summary justice, sometimes through quick trials in ad hoc courts. In Italy, this process led to 15,000 executions, in France 10,000. French women accused of sleeping with German soldiers were shamed by having their heads shaved.

Nuremberg trials The war crimes trials conducted in Nuremberg, Germany. Most of the twenty-four defendants were convicted of war crimes and "crimes against humanity."

The most sensitive confrontation with the recent past took place in Germany, where the occupying powers imposed a systematic program of de-Nazification. In the western zones, German citizens were required to attend lectures on the virtues of democracy and to view the corpses of the victims of Nazism. In this context, the Allies determined to identify and bring to justice those responsible for the crimes of Hitler's regime. This effort led to the **Nuremberg trials** of 1945 and 1946, the most famous of a number of war crimes trials held in Germany and the occupied countries after the war.

Although Hitler, Himmler, and Goebbels had committed suicide, the occupying authorities apprehended for trial twenty-four individuals who had played important but very different roles in Hitler's Third Reich. All but three were convicted of war crimes and crimes against humanity. Twelve were sentenced to death; of those, two committed suicide, and the other ten were executed.

Questions about their legitimacy dogged the Nuremberg trials from the start. To a considerable extent, the accused were being judged according to law made after the fact. The notion of "crimes against humanity" remained vague. Moreover, even insofar as a measure of international law was in force, it was arguably binding only on states, not individuals. But in light of the unprecedented atrocities of the Nazi regime, there was widespread agreement among the victors that the Nazi leaders could not be treated simply as defeated adversaries.

SECTION SUMMARY

- The future of east-central Europe was but one of the items on the agenda at Yalta, where each of the Big Three achieved some of its major aims concerning the shape of the postwar world.

- As a result of the agreements at Yalta and Potsdam, the reconstituted Poland was shifted substantially westward at the expense of Germany.

- Although the terror bombing of cities did not undermine the German war effort, the more precisely targeted bombing of industrial and military targets hastened Germany's defeat, especially by cutting off oil supplies.

- Because the war in the Pacific ended so suddenly, as the result of the atomic bombing of Japan by the United States, the Europeans had little opportunity to reestablish their dominance in the colonial territories they had earlier lost to the Japanese.

- Of the twenty-four Germans charged with war crimes and crimes against humanity in the Nuremberg trials of 1945 and 1946, twenty-one were convicted, of whom twelve were sentenced to death.

INTO THE POSTWAR WORLD

What was the relationship between the Allied victory in World War II and the coming of the cold war?

Even after the fighting stopped in 1945, remarkable changes continued as the forces unleashed by the war played themselves out. In a number of war-torn countries, the legacies of wartime resistance movements helped shape the political order and priorities for beginning anew. At the same time, differences between the Soviets and the Western democracies began to undermine the wartime alliance, soon producing the division of Germany and a bipolar Europe. Thus, the conclusion of World War II led directly to the danger of a third world war, which might involve nuclear weapons and thus prove immeasurably more destructive than the last.

In addition to the dramatic changes in Europe, the wider effects of the war brought to the forefront a whole new set of issues, from anticolonialism to the Arab-Israeli conflict to the spread of communism in the non-Western world. These issues would remain central for decades. By 1949, however, it was already possible to discern the contours of the new postwar world, a world with new sources of hope, but also with conflicts and dangers hardly imaginable ten years earlier.

Resistance and Renewal

Though the Nazis had found some willing collaborators, the great majority of those living under German occupation came to despise the Nazis as their brutality became ever clearer. Nazi rule meant pillage, forced labor in Germany, and the random killing of hostages in reprisal for resistance activity. In one extreme case, the Germans destroyed the Czech village of Lidice (LIH-dyit-seh), killing all its inhabitants, in retaliation for the assassination of SS security chief Reinhard Heydrich in 1942.

Clandestine movements of resistance to the occupying Nazi forces gradually developed all over Europe. In western Europe, resistance was especially prominent in France and, beginning in 1943, northern Italy, which was subjected to German occupation after the Allies defeated Mussolini's regime. But the anti-German resistance was strongest in Yugoslavia, Poland, and the occupied portions of the Soviet Union, where full-scale guerrilla war against the Germans and their collaborators produced the highest civilian casualties of World War II.

The role of the resistance proved most significant in Yugoslavia, where the Croatian Marxist Josip Broz, taking the pseudonym Tito (1892–1980), forged the opponents of the Axis powers into a broadly based guerrilla army. Its initial foe was the inflated Croatian state that the Germans, early in 1941, carved from Yugoslavia and entrusted to the pro-Axis Croatian separatist movement, the Ustashe (oo-STAH-zhee). But Tito's forces soon came up against a rival resistance movement, led by Serb officers, that tended to be pro-Serb, monarchist, and anticommunist. By 1943, Tito led 250,000 men and women in what had become a vicious civil war, one that deepened ethnic divisions and left a legacy of bitterness. Tito's forces prevailed, enabling him to create a communist-led government in Yugoslavia late in the war.

In France and Italy as well, communists played leading roles in the wartime resistance movements. As a result, the Communist Party in each country overcame the disarray that followed from the Nazi-Soviet Pact of 1939, and after the war, each enjoyed a level of prestige that would have been unthinkable earlier.

In the French case, the indigenous resistance, with its significant communist component, generally worked well with de Gaulle and the Free French, operating outside France until August 1944. Still, de Gaulle took pains to cement his own leadership in the overall struggle. Among the measures to this end, he decreed women's suffrage for France, partly because women were playing a major role in the resistance. After the liberation of France in 1944, he sought to control a potentially volatile situation by disarming the resistance as quickly as possible.

The western European resistance movements are easily romanticized, their extent and importance overstated. Compared with regular troops, resistance forces were poorly trained, equipped, and disciplined. In France, fewer than 30 percent of the nearly 400,000 active resisters had firearms in 1944. But though the Allies never tried to use them in a systematic way, the resistance movements made at least some military contribution, especially through sabotage. And they boosted national self-esteem for the longer term, helping countries humiliated by defeat and occupation make a fresh start after the war.

But had governments and institutions outside Germany done all they could—especially as the dimensions of the Nazi exterminations began to come into focus? Especially controversial has been the response of Pope Pius XII (r. 1939–1958), who declined to take the moral high ground and denounce Nazi atrocities explicitly. He felt that he could not censure the Nazis without also censuring the Soviets, at that point allies in the anti-Nazi cause. He also feared for the fortunes of the Catholic Church as an institution in areas under German control, including Rome itself during the pivotal nine months from September 1943 to June 1944. The mission of the church was not merely to save lives, but above all to save souls—and for that, the institution was essential. Many felt, however, that stronger moral leadership by the Catholic Church would have stiffened resistance to the Nazis, stimulated aid to individual Jews, and enhanced the overall self-confidence of the West as it faced the post-Holocaust future.

Conflicting Visions and the Coming of the Cold War

Starting with the Atlantic Charter of 1941, Roosevelt had sought to ensure that the common effort against the Axis powers would lead to a firmer basis for peace, to be framed through a new international organization after the war. At a conference at Dumbarton Oaks in Washington, D.C., in September 1944, the United States proposed the structure for a new "United Nations." Meeting in San Francisco from April to June 1945, delegates from almost fifty anti-Axis countries translated that proposal into a charter for the new organization. As Roosevelt had envisioned, the major powers were given a privileged position as permanent members of the Security Council, each with veto power. To dramatize its departure from the Geneva-based League of Nations, which the United States had refused to join, the United Nations was headquartered in New York. In July 1945, the U.S. Senate approved U.S. membership in the international body almost unanimously.

By the end of the war, several international meetings had used the United Nations title. In July 1944, the United Nations Monetary and Financial Conference at Bretton Woods, New Hampshire, brought together delegates from forty-four nations to deal with problems of currency and exchange rates. The outcome of the conference, the Bretton Woods Agreement, laid the foundation for international economic exchange in the noncommunist world for the crucial quarter century of economic recovery after the war. In addition, the conference gave birth to the International Monetary Fund and the International Bank for Reconstruction and Development, which played major roles even into the twenty-first century.

Whereas the United States envisioned a world order based on the ongoing cooperation of the three victors, the Soviet Union had a different agenda. Its top priority was to create a buffer zone of friendly states in east-central Europe, especially as a bulwark against Germany. While seeking this sphere of influence, Stalin gave the British a free hand to settle the civil war between communists and anticommunists in Greece, and he did not push for revolution in western Europe. The strong communist parties that had emerged from the resistance movements in Italy and France were directed to work within broad-based democratic fronts rather than try to take power.

The Division of Germany

It was especially conflict over Germany that cemented the developing division of Europe. Neither the democracies nor the Soviets lived up to all their agreements concerning Germany, but in light of the fundamental differences in priorities, cooperation between the two sides was bound to be difficult at best.

At Potsdam, the West had accepted Soviet demands for German reparations, but the Soviets, rather than wait for payment, began removing German factories and equipment for reassembly in the Soviet Union. To ensure that they got their due, the Soviets wanted access to the economic resources not simply of the Russian occupation zone, but of the whole of Germany. The United States and Britain, in contrast, gave priority to economic reconstruction and quickly began integrating the economies of the Western zones for that purpose.

Finally, as part of their effort to spur economic recovery, the United States and Britain violated Allied agreements by introducing a new currency without Soviet consent. Stalin answered in June 1948 by blockading the city of Berlin, cutting its western sectors off from the main Western occupation zones, almost 200 miles west (see **Map 28.4**). The Western Allies responded with a massive airlift that kept their sectors of Berlin supplied for almost a year, until May 1949, when the Soviets finally backed down.

By 1948, two separate German states began emerging from the Allied occupation zones. With Allied support, a "parliamentary council" of West German leaders met during 1948 and 1949 and produced a document that, when ratified in September 1949, became the "Basic Law" of a new Federal Republic of Germany, with its capital at Bonn. This founding document was termed simply the Basic Law, as opposed to the constitution, to emphasize the provisional character of the new West German state. To create a state limited to the west was not to foreclose the future reunification of Germany. But as it became clear that a new state was being created in the Western zones, the Soviets settled for a new state in their zone, in eastern Germany. Thus, the Communist-led German Democratic Republic, with its capital in East Berlin, was born in October 1949.

The "Iron Curtain" and the Emergence of a Bipolar World

In east-central Europe, only Yugoslavia and Albania had achieved liberation on their own, and the communist leaders of their resistance movements had a plausible claim to political power. Elsewhere, the Soviet army had provided liberation, and the Soviet military presence remained the decisive political fact as the war ended. Under these circumstances, the Soviets were able to work with local communists to install new regimes, led by communists and friendly to the Soviet Union, in most of east-central Europe. But though Churchill warned as early as 1946 that an **"iron curtain"** was descending from the Baltic to the Adriatic, the process of Soviet power consolidation was not easy, and it took place gradually, in discrete steps over several years. By 1949, communist governments, relying on Soviet support, controlled Poland, Czechoslovakia, East Germany, Hungary, Romania, and Bulgaria, with Yugoslavia and Albania also communist but capable of a more independent line.

Communism might have spread still farther in Europe, and perhaps beyond, but the West drew the line at Greece. There, as in Yugoslavia, an indigenous, communist-led resistance movement had become strong enough to contend for political power by late 1944. But when it sought to oust the monarchical government that had just returned to Greece from exile, the British intervened, helping the monarchy put down the leftist uprising. Although Stalin gave the Greek communists little help, communist guerrilla activity continued, thanks partly to support from Tito's Yugoslavia. In 1946, a renewed communist insurgency escalated into civil war.

As U.S.-Soviet friction turned into a **cold war**, both countries began taking a more active interest in the Greek conflict, though Soviet intentions remained uncertain. After the financially strapped Labour government in Britain reduced its involvement early in 1947, the United States stepped in to support the Greek monarchy against the communists. American policymakers feared that communism would progress from the Balkans through Greece to the Middle East. Thus, in March 1947, President Truman announced the **Truman Doctrine**, which committed the United States to the "containment" of communism throughout the world. (See the feature, "The Written Record: 'Containment' as a Cold War Strategy.") American advisers now began reequipping the anticommunist forces in Greece. Faced with this determined opposition from the West, Stalin again pulled back, but the Greek communists, with their strong indigenous support, were not defeated until 1949.

Thus, the wartime marriage of expediency between the Soviet Union and the Western democracies gradually fell apart in the war's aftermath. Only in Austria, jointly occupied by the Soviets and the Western democracies, were the former Allies able to arrange the postwar transition in a

"iron curtain"   Term used by Winston Churchill in a speech on March 5, 1946, to warn that, thanks to Soviet policy, a formidable de facto barrier was emerging in Europe, cutting the Soviet sphere off from the West and threatening the long-term division of the Continent.

cold war   The hostile standoff between the Soviet Union and the United States that began after World War II, as Europe was divided into spheres of influence between the two superpowers and the United States vowed to resist the further spread of communism.

Truman Doctrine   The U.S. policy of containment, or limiting communist expansion, as outlined by President Harry Truman in 1947.

Gandhi and Anticolonialism   An apostle of nonviolence, Mohandas Gandhi became one of the most admired individuals of the century as he spearheaded the movement for Indian independence. He is pictured (*center*) in December 1942 with the British statesman Sir Stafford Cripps (*left*), who had come to India to offer a plan for Indian self-government. Despite the good spirit evident here, Cripps's mission failed; Gandhi and his movement held out for full independence. (Bettmann/Corbis)

"Containment" as a Cold War Strategy

As a foreign service officer, George F. Kennan (1904–2005) emerged as the U.S. government's leading authority on the dynamics of Soviet foreign policy by the later 1940s. After analyzing Soviet postwar objectives in his now-famous "long telegram" from Moscow to the U.S. State Department in 1946, Kennan returned to the United States to become director of the State Department's Policy Planning Staff from 1947 to 1949. With hawks pondering a preemptive strike on the Soviet Union and doves stressing mutual accommodation, Kennan forcefully advocated a middle position, a strategy of "containment," in an article published anonymously in the journal Foreign Affairs *in 1947. And his views prevailed. An uncertain experiment when it began in 1947, containment proved successful—arguably for the reasons Kennan anticipated.*

[The Soviet Union] is under no ideological compulsion to accomplish its purposes in a hurry. ... Thus the Kremlin has no compunction about retreating in the face of superior force. And being under the compulsion of no timetable, it does not get panicky under the necessity for such retreat. Its political action is a fluid stream which moves constantly, wherever it is permitted to move, toward a given goal....

...The patient persistence by which it is animated means that it can be effectively countered not by sporadic acts which represent the momentary whims of democratic opinion but only by intelligent long-range policies on the part of Russia's adversaries—policies no less steady in their purpose, and no less variegated and resourceful in their application, than those of the Soviet Union itself.

In these circumstances it is clear that the main element of any United States policy toward the Soviet Union must be that of a long-term, patient but firm and vigilant containment of Russian expansive tendencies. It is important to note, however, that such a policy has nothing to do with outward histrionics: with threats or blustering or superfluous gestures of outward "toughness." While the Kremlin is basically flexible in its reaction to political realities, it is by no means unamenable to considerations of prestige. ... It is a *sine qua non* of successful dealing with Russia that the foreign government in question should remain at all times cool and collected and that its demands on Russian policy should be put forward in such a manner as to leave the way open for a compliance not too detrimental to Russian prestige.

In the light of the above, it will be clearly seen that the Soviet pressure against the free institutions of the western world is something that can be contained by the adroit and vigilant application of counter-force at a series of constantly shifting geographical and political points, corresponding to the shifts and manoeuvres of Soviet policy, but which cannot be charmed or talked out of existence....

... Soviet power is only a crust concealing an amorphous mass of human beings among whom no independent organizational structure is tolerated. ... If, consequently, anything were ever to occur to disrupt the unity and efficacy of the Party as a political instrument, Soviet Russia might be changed overnight from one of the strongest to one of the weakest and most pitiable of national societies....

...It is...a question of the degree to which the United States can create among the peoples of the world generally the impression of a country which knows what it wants, which is coping successfully with the problems of its internal life and with the responsibilities of a World Power, and which has a spiritual vitality capable of holding its own among the major ideological currents of the time. To the extent that such an impression can be created and maintained, the aims of Russian Communism must appear sterile and quixotic, the hopes and enthusiasm of Moscow's supporters must wane, and added strain must be imposed on the Kremlin's foreign policies. For the palsied decrepitude of the capitalist world is the keystone of Communist philosophy....

...The United States has it in its power to increase enormously the strains under which Soviet policy must operate, to force upon the Kremlin a far greater degree of moderation and circumspection than it has had to observe in recent years, and in this way to promote tendencies which must eventually find their outlet in either the break-up or the gradual mellowing of Soviet power.

QUESTIONS

1. What conception of the Soviet Union and its aims led Kennan to propose a policy of containment?

2. What would containment actually entail on a practical level as a response to Soviet moves?

3. Why did Kennan believe that the United States had to be unified, consistent, and principled in everything it did if it was eventually to prevail in the cold war?

Source: Reprinted by permission of *Foreign Affairs*, 25, July 1947. Copyright 1947 by the Council on Foreign Relations, Inc. www.ForeignAffairs.com

reasonably amicable way. The Soviets accepted the neutralization of a democratic Austria as the occupying powers left in 1955. Elsewhere, Europe was divided into two antagonistic power blocs.

The antagonism between the two superpowers became more menacing when the Soviets exploded their first atomic bomb in August 1949, intensifying the postwar arms race. By then, in fact, the United States was on its way to the more destructive hydrogen bomb. The split between these two nations, unmistakable by 1949, established the framework for world affairs for the next forty years.

The West and the New World Agenda

At the same time, other dramatic changes around the world suggested that, with or without the cold war, the postwar political scene would be hard to manage. Events in India in 1947, in Israel in 1948, and in China in 1949 epitomized the wider new hopes and uncertainties spawned by World War II.

Although the British, under U.S. pressure, had reluctantly promised independence for India in order to elicit Indian support during the war, British authorities and Indian leaders had continued to skirmish. Mohandas Gandhi (see pages 729 and 760) was twice jailed for resisting British demands and threatening a massive program of nonviolent resistance to British rule. But by 1946, the British lacked the will and the financial resources to maintain their control on the subcontinent. Thus, Britain acquiesced as the new independent states of India and Pakistan emerged on August 15, 1947. Allowing independence to India, long the jewel of the British Empire, raised questions about Britain's role in the postwar world and portended a wider disintegration of the European colonial system.

INDEPENDENCE IN INDIA

Questions about the fate of the Jews, who had suffered so grievously during World War II, were inevitable as well. Almost two-thirds of the Jews of Europe had been killed, and many of the survivors either had no place to go or had decided that they could never again live as a minority in Europe. Many concluded that the Jews must have a homeland of their own. For decades, such Zionist sentiment (see page 714) had centered on the biblical area of Israel, in what had become, after World War I, the British mandate of Palestine. Jewish immigration to the area accelerated during the interwar period, causing friction with the Palestinian Arabs.

THE CREATION OF ISRAEL

Concerned about access to Middle Eastern oil, the British sought to cultivate good relations with the Arab world after World War II. Thus, they opposed further immigration of Jews to Palestine, as well as proposals to carve an independent Jewish state from the area. The United States, however, was considerably more sympathetic to the Zionist cause. As tensions grew, Jewish terrorists blew up the British headquarters in Jerusalem, and the British decided to abandon what seemed a no-win situation. In September 1947, they announced their intention to withdraw from Palestine, leaving its future to the United Nations. In November, the UN voted to partition Palestine, creating both a Jewish and a new Arab Palestinian state (see **MAP 28.5**).

Skirmishing between Jews and Arabs became full-scale war in December 1947, and in that context, the Jews declared their independence as the new state of Israel on May 14, 1948. When the fighting ended in 1949, the Israelis had conquered more territory than had been envisioned in the original partition plan, and the remaining Arab territories fell to Egypt and Jordan, rather than forming an independent Palestinian

🌐 **MAP 28.5—The Proposed Partition of Palestine and the Birth of the State of Israel**

In November 1947, the United Nations offered a plan to partition the British mandate of Palestine, but complications immediately arose. The Jews of the area won their own state, Israel, but the Palestinian Arabs were left stateless. Thus, tensions continued in the area.

SECTION SUMMARY

- Although it had spurned the League of Nations after World War I, the U.S. Senate approved U.S. membership in the United Nations almost unanimously in July 1945.

- Concerned primarily to win a secure sphere of influence in east-central Europe, especially as a bulwark against Germany, Stalin took a moderate position with regard to western Europe and did not seek to foment communist revolution.

- Disagreements over economic policy, especially, fed the split that led to the creation of two separate German states, one oriented toward the West, the other oriented toward the Soviet Union, in 1949.

- The communist challenge in Greece by 1947 prompted the Truman Doctrine, which committed the United States to the "containment" of communism throughout the world.

- The granting of independence to India in 1947, the creation of the state of Israel in 1948, and the communist takeover in China in 1949 indicated the new world agenda emerging after World War II.

state. Thus was born the new state of Israel, partly a product of the assault on the Jews during World War II. Yet it was born amid Arab hostility and Western concerns about oil, so its long-term prospects remained uncertain.

COMMUNISM IN CHINA

In 1949, the communist insurgency in China under Mao Zedong (Mao Tsetung) (see page 761) finally triumphed over the Chinese Nationalists under Jiang Jieshi (Chiang Kai-shek), who fled to the island of Taiwan. During the war, the Communists had done better than the Nationalists at identifying themselves with the Chinese cause against both Japanese and Western imperialism. After their victory, the Chinese Communists enjoyed great prestige among other "national liberation" movements struggling against Western colonialists. To many in the West, however, the outcome in China by 1949 simply intensified fears that communism was poised to infect the unsettled postwar world.

CHAPTER SUMMARY

Using an effective new offensive strategy, Germany quickly defeated Poland in 1939, but Britain and France refused Hitler's peace overtures in the aftermath. After France fell to German invasion eight months later, the Third Republic gave way to the authoritarian Vichy regime, which was obliged to collaborate with Nazi Germany. When the British again refused to come to terms, Hitler launched a sustained air assault on Britain. The British withstood it, but Hitler remained confident of containing Britain over the longer term. Even when the reckless intervention of Italy forced Hitler's attention to North Africa and the Balkans, the Germans won further successes, which suggested that the Soviet Union would fall in a matter of weeks in the wake of Germany's invasion of June 1941.

In dealing with their conquered territories first in Poland, then in the Soviet Union, the Nazis were concerned with population engineering and ideology; Jewish policy was distinctly secondary. Even when Jews were confined to ghettos in Poland, there was no plan to kill them. But ghettoization produced problems of its own, so Nazi forces were instructed to shoot Soviet Jews once the invasion of the Soviet Union began. Such shooting also proved to be problematic, so gradually the Nazi leadership decided on a more systematic method—mass extermination by gassing, to start with the Jews in the ghettos in Poland. Such a program could be envisioned, and implemented, especially because of the precedent of the "euthanasia" program in Germany. Once it began, the process of mass killing developed a momentum of its own, especially as it became clear that Germany was likely to lose the war.

FOCUS QUESTIONS

- What were the outcomes of the war as of late spring 1941, before the German invasion of the Soviet Union and the intervention of the United States?

- What was the place of the Holocaust in the Nazi effort to begin constructing a "new order" in eastern Europe?

- How did the Grand Alliance of Britain, the United States, and the Soviet Union come together against the Axis powers?

- How did the Allies manage to defeat Nazi Germany in World War II, after Germany's remarkable initial successes?

- What was the relationship between the Allied victory in World War II and the coming of the cold war?

After a disastrous start in the face of German invasion, Soviet forces stiffened in the fall of 1941, then, in December, mounted a formidable counterattack. That same month, the United States declared war on Germany in the aftermath of the bombing of Pearl Harbor by the Japanese. Meanwhile, the British, having withstood the German air assault, were regrouping for a protracted war. Common hostility to the Axis powers brought Britain, the Soviet Union, and the United States together in a "Grand Alliance" early in 1942, but mutual suspicions between the democracies, on the one hand, and the Soviet Union, on the other, marked the relationship. Above all, Stalin worried that Britain and the United States were dragging their feet in opening a major second front on the European continent. By the time of the D-Day landings in France in June 1944, the Soviets were steadily forcing the Germans back on the eastern front.

Even after all the upheavals of the 1930s, the Soviets proved able to spearhead the Allied victory in Europe, though they suffered incredibly heavy casualties in the process. Stalin managed to rally the Soviet people, and the Soviet military and industrial effort proved more effective than outside observers had thought possible. But the efforts of the democracies in North Africa, Italy, and France contributed to the final victory as well. And American-led bombing of military and industrial targets, especially oil refining facilities, seriously compromised Germany's capacity to wage war by the end.

The Grand Alliance began unraveling soon after the war was over, especially because the priorities of the Soviets differed considerably from those of the two democracies. Having been invaded, and devastated, by German forces twice in a generation, the Soviets were determined to have friendly states on their borders, especially in Poland. And having suffered from direct German military invasion as the other two victors had not, the Soviets were also determined to extract reparations from Germany, even including plant and equipment to be dismantled and carried back to the Soviet Union. By 1949, two competing German states had emerged, and Europe was clearly divided between East and West.

KEY TERMS

Vichy France   (p. 788)
Charles de Gaulle   (p. 788)
Winston Churchill   (p. 789)
Auschwitz-Birkenau   (p. 794)
Stalingrad   (p. 796)
"the Great Patriotic War"   (p. 797)

Franklin Delano Roosevelt   (p. 800)
Lend-Lease Act   (p. 802)
D-Day   (p. 803)
Yalta conference   (p. 805)
United Nations   (p. 805)

Potsdam conference   (p. 807)
Nuremberg trials   (p. 810)
"iron curtain"   (p. 813)
cold war   (p. 813)
Truman Doctrine   (p. 813)

 This icon will direct you to additional materials on the website: www .cengage.com/history/ noble/westciv6e.

NOTES

1. From Farrell's full account as related by General Leslie Groves in his "Memorandum to the Secretary of War," dated July 18, 1945, in *The American Atom: A Documentary History of Nuclear Policies from the Discovery of Fission to the Present*, ed. Philip L. Cantelon, Richard G. Hewlett, and Robert C. Williams, 2d ed. (Philadelphia: University of Pennsylvania Press, 1991), pp. 56–57.

2. Quoted in Karl Dietrich Bracher, *The German Dictatorship: The Origins, Structure, and Effects of National Socialism*, trans. Jean Steinberg (New York: Praeger, 1970), p. 423.

3. Christopher R. Browning, *Ordinary Men: Reserve Police Battalion 101 and the Final Solution in Poland*, with a new afterward (New York: HarperCollins, 1998); Daniel Jonah Goldhagen, *Hitler's Willing Executioners: Ordinary Germans and the Holocaust* (New York: Random House [Vintage], 1997).

4. Michael Burleigh, *Death and Deliverance: "Euthanasia" in Germany, c. 1900–1945* (Cambridge: Cambridge University Press, 1994), p. 221.

5. Michael Burleigh and Wolfgang Wippermann, *The Racial State: Germany, 1933–1945* (Cambridge: Cambridge University Press, 1991), p. 98.

6. Martin Broszat and Saul Friedländer, "A Controversy About the Historicization of National Socialism," in Peter Baldwin, ed., *Reworking the Past: Hitler, the Holocaust, and the Historians' Debate* (Boston: Beacon Press, 1990), pp. 120–121.

7. Goldhagen, *Hitler's Willing Executioners*, pp. 279–280.

8. Browning, *Ordinary Men*, p. 72.

See our interactive eBook for map and primary source activities.

29

Berlin Wall, November 1989
East Germans stream through the dismantled Berlin Wall into West Berlin. (AP Photo/Lionel Cironneau)

An Anxious Stability: The Age of the Cold War, 1949–1989

The atmosphere was festive, euphoric. Those who came to celebrate could hardly believe it was happening, for it had been unthinkable just a few months before. Yet happening it was, one of the defining events of the twentieth century, live on television. This was November 1989, and the Berlin Wall was coming down.

Erected to stop emigration from communist East Germany to the West in 1961, the wall had become an all-too-tangible symbol of the division of Europe, and much of the world, after World War II. As a physical barrier of concrete and barbed wire, the Berlin Wall had divided families and caused much human suffering. Indeed, 191 people died and 5,000 were arrested trying to cross it. But the East German government, desperate by 1989 to preserve its legitimacy, opened the wall on November 9 and began dismantling it within days. However, it proved too late. The communist regime in East Germany collapsed as part of a wider anticommunist revolution that finally enveloped even the Soviet Union itself in 1991. The anxious cold war era was suddenly over; virtually no one had foreseen its abrupt ending.

Although Berlin had been a particular hot spot, the cold war was global in scope. It seemed that confrontation between the Soviet Union and the United States might take place almost anywhere, sparking the cold war into a hot war threatening nuclear annihilation. And indeed confrontation came closest not over Berlin, but over Soviet missiles in Cuba in 1962. That crisis was surmounted, and East-West relations alternately warmed and cooled during the quarter century that followed.

Both halves of Europe had to operate within the bipolar framework, but the Western and Soviet blocs confronted different challenges and evolved in different ways. The countries of western Europe adjusted to a diminished international role as they recognized their dependence on U.S. leadership and gradually lost their overseas colonies. The change in scale led many politicians and intellectuals to advocate some form of European union, which might eventually enable the western Europeans to deal with the superpowers on a more equal basis. On the domestic level, the immediate postwar situation was so unsettled that few western European countries could simply return to the prewar norm. Postwar reconstruction rested on a new consensus that government must play a more active role in promoting economic growth and social welfare. By the 1960s, the promise of shared prosperity was realized to a remarkable extent. But changing circumstances by the early 1970s threatened the consensus that postwar prosperity had made possible.

FOCUS QUESTIONS

- What seemed the most likely overall cultural directions as western Europeans pondered priorities in light of all the disasters surrounding the era of the two world wars?

- What factors led to the surprisingly rapid restoration of democracy in much of continental western Europe after World War II?

- How did Soviet policy evolve after the death of Stalin in 1953?

- How did the place of western Europe in world affairs change during the cold war era?

- What led to the collapse of the communist system in the Soviet Union and its satellite states?

 This icon will direct you to additional materials on the website: www .cengage.com/history/ noble/westciv6e.

 See our interactive eBook for map and primary source activities.

Although the Soviet Union had suffered immensely in winning World War II, the communist regime emerged from the war with renewed legitimacy. During the 1950s and 1960s, the Soviet system achieved some significant successes, but its efforts to outgrow its Stalinist framework were halting. By 1980, the system was becoming rigid and stagnant. Thus, the dramatic changes in the Soviet bloc that came to a head in 1989, leading to the opening of the Berlin Wall and, by 1991, to the end of communism in Europe. Only as it was ending, more than four decades after World War II, was it possible to recognize that the anxious cold war era had been one of relative stability and peace.

THE SEARCH FOR CULTURAL BEARINGS

What seemed the most likely overall cultural directions as western Europeans pondered priorities in light of all the disasters surrounding the era of the two world wars?

The events from World War I to the cold war added up to an unprecedented period of disaster for Europe. Europeans were bound to ask what had gone wrong and what could be salvaged from the ruins of a culture that had made possible the most destructive wars in history, as well as fascism, totalitarianism, and the Holocaust.

The cold war framework crucially shaped responses all over the Western world. Some embraced the Soviet Union or sought a renewed Marxism. Opposition to communism helped stimulate others to return to religious or classical traditions or to embrace what seemed the American model. But the anxieties stemming from superpower rivalry, and especially the nuclear arms race, were bound to temper any renewed optimism.

Absurdity and Commitment in Existentialism

The postwar mood of exhaustion and despair found classic expression in the work of the Irish-born writer Samuel Beckett (1906–1989), especially in his plays *Waiting for Godot* (1952) and *Endgame* (1957). Through Beckett's characters, we see ourselves going through the motions, with nothing worth saying or doing. The only redeeming element is the comic pathos we feel as we watch ourselves ludicrously manipulating the husks of a worn-out culture.

existentialism A philosophical and cultural movement, often associated with Jean-Paul Sartre and Albert Camus, for whom an authentic human response to an apparently meaningless universe entailed commitment and responsibility.

The same sense of anxiety and despair led to the vogue of **existentialism**, a movement that marked philosophy, the arts, and popular culture from the later 1940s until well into the 1950s. The existentialists explored what it means to be human in a world cast adrift from its cultural moorings, with no mutually accepted guideposts, standards, or values. Although it developed from ideas that the German thinker Martin Heidegger (1889–1976) had developed in his *Being and Time* (1927), existentialism became influential especially through the works of two Frenchmen, Jean-Paul Sartre (SAH-truh) (1905–1980) and Albert Camus (ka-MOO) (1913–1960). Each had been involved in the French resistance, Camus in a particularly central role as editor of an underground newspaper. For both, an authentic human response to a world spinning out of control entails engagement, commitment, and responsibility—even though every action is fraught with risk.

Rather than accept the bleak, ludicrously comic vision of Beckett's plays, Camus sought to show how we might go on living in a positive, affirmative spirit, even in a world that seemed simply absurd in one sense, especially after the recent disasters in Europe. Conventional values like friendship and tolerance could be made usable again, based on the simple fact that we human beings are all caught up in this unmasterable situation together. People suffer and die, but as we come together to help as best we can, we might at least learn to stop killing one another.

Camus split from Sartre in a disagreement over the ongoing value of Marxism and the communist experiment in the Soviet Union. Though never an orthodox communist, Sartre found potential for human liberation in the working class, in communist political parties, even in the Soviet Union itself, which he saw as the strongest alternative to U.S. imperialism. By the 1950s, he was portraying existentialism as fundamentally a way to revitalize Marxism.

By contrast, Camus, who had started as a communist in the 1930s, had grown disillusioned with communism even before the war, and his major political tract, *The Rebel* (1951), was partly an attack on Marxism and communism. Establishing new bases for human happiness and solidarity meant recognizing limits to what human beings could accomplish, limits even to our demands for freedom and justice. These were precisely the limits that the new political movements of the century had so disastrously overstepped. Communism, like fascism, was part of the problem, not the solution.

Marxists and Traditionalists

Sartre was among the many European intellectuals who believed that Marxism had won a new lease on life from the wartime resistance. As they saw it, Marxism could be revamped for the West, without the Stalinist excesses of the Soviet Union. Marxism remained a significant strand in Western political culture throughout the cold war era, but it also attracted periodic waves of denunciation.

In Italy, as in France, the communists' major role in the resistance enhanced their prestige, preparing the way for the extraordinary posthumous influence of Antonio Gramsci (GRAHM-she) (1891–1937), a founder of the Italian Communist Party who had spent most of the fascist period in prison. His *Prison Notebooks*, published during the late 1940s, became influential throughout the world and helped make Marxism a powerful force in postwar Italian culture. Seeking to learn the lessons of the fascist triumph in Italy, Gramsci pointed Marxists toward a flexible political strategy, attuned to the special historical circumstances of each country. Thanks partly to Gramsci's legacy, Italy had the most innovative and important communist party outside the communist world for several decades after the war.

Loosely Marxist ideas were central to the renewal of political activism in the West by the late 1960s, although Marxism proved more effective as a critique of capitalism than as a blueprint for change. The best-known spokesman for that renewed radicalism was the German-born social thinker Herbert Marcuse (mar-KOO-zuh) (1898–1979), who explored the cultural mechanisms through which capitalism perpetuates itself in *One-Dimensional Man* (1964).

Even during the late 1940s, however, others, like Camus, denied that any recasting could overcome the inherent flaws in Marxism. Damaging revelations about the excesses of Stalinism during the 1930s seemed to confirm the view that communism was "the God that failed." By the mid-1970s, the disturbing portrait of the Soviet gulag, or forced-labor-camp system, by the exiled Soviet writer Alexander Solzhenitsyn (soul-zhen-EET-sin) (1918–2008) stimulated another wave of anticommunist thinking. And whether or not Marxism was necessarily Stalinist and repressive in implication, its relevance to the increasingly prosperous industrial democracies of western Europe seemed increasingly open to question.

Those hostile to Marxism often insisted that the West had to reconnect with older traditions if it were to

CHRONOLOGY

June 1947	Marshall Plan announced
April 1949	Formation of NATO
1951	Formation of the European Coal and Steel Community
March 5, 1953	Death of Stalin
June	Workers' revolt in East Germany
1955	West Germany joins NATO
	Warsaw Pact
February 1956	Khrushchev de-Stalinization speech
October–November 1956	Suez crisis
November 1956	Hungarian reform movement crushed
October 4, 1957	*Sputnik I* launched
January 1, 1958	Common Market launched
1958	Beginning of Fifth Republic in France
November 1959	Bad Godesberg congress: reorientation of German socialism
August 1961	Berlin Wall erected
March 1962	Algerian independence from France
October 1962	Cuban missile crisis
October 1964	Ouster of Khrushchev
May 1968	Days of May uprising in France
August 1968	"Prague Spring" reform movement crushed
October 1969	Brandt becomes West German chancellor
1973	First OPEC oil crisis
1975	Communist victory in Vietnam
October 1978	Election of Pope John Paul II
May 1979	Thatcher becomes prime minister of Britain
September 1980	Formation of Solidarity in Poland
April 1980	Formation of independent Zimbabwe from Southern Rhodesia
May 1981	Mitterrand becomes president of France
November 10, 1982	Death of Brezhnev
March 1985	Gorbachev comes to power in the Soviet Union
April 1986	Chernobyl disaster
1989	Collapse of communism in east-central Europe
1991	Collapse of communism in the Soviet Union
	Dissolution of the Soviet Union

Sartre and de Beauvoir Among the most influential intellectual couples of the century, Jean-Paul Sartre and Simone de Beauvoir emerged as leaders of French existentialism by the later 1940s. (Gianni Giansanti/Sygma/Corbis)

avoid further horrors. Especially in the first years after the war, many, like the French Catholic thinker Jacques Maritain (mar-eh-TAN) (1882–1973), held that only a return to religious traditions would suffice. For the American-born British writer T. S. Eliot (1888–1965), the essential return to tradition had to embrace family and locality, as well as religion. Without a return to tradition, Eliot warned, the West could expect more excesses such as fascism and totalitarianism in the future.

The Intellectual Migration and Americanism

The extraordinary migration of European artists and intellectuals to the United States to escape persecution during the 1930s and 1940s profoundly affected the cultural life of the postwar period. An array of luminaries arrived on American shores, from the composer Igor Stravinsky to the physicist Albert Einstein, from the architect Walter Gropius to the radical social theorist Herbert Marcuse.

Before this cross-fertilization, American culture had remained somewhat provincial, sometimes proudly and self-consciously so. All the direct contact with these Europeans by the 1940s helped propel the United States into the Western cultural mainstream. No longer could "Western" culture be identified primarily with Europe. In some spheres—painting, for example—Americans were now confident enough to claim the leadership for the first time.

But the American abstract expressionism emerging by the later 1940s owed something to European existentialism, and it became possible only because so many of the most innovative European painters had come to New York, where the Americans had been able to learn their lessons firsthand. At the same time, European painters, such as Jean Dubuffet (doo-boo-FAY) (1901–1985) in France and Francis Bacon (1910–1992) in Britain, created new forms of their own—sometimes playful, sometimes brutal—as they sought the new visual imagery that seemed appropriate to Western culture after decades of upheaval.

Even in the United States, artists began reacting against the deep seriousness of abstract expressionism during the mid-1950s. One new direction led by the early 1960s to "pop art," which was "American" in a different sense, featuring the ordinary objects and mass-produced images of modern consumerist culture. (See the feature, "The Visual Record: Pop Art.")

Some Europeans were eager to embrace what seemed distinctively American because America had remained relatively free of the political ideologies that seemed to have led Europe to totalitarianism and ruin. By the 1950s, there was much talk of "the end of ideology," with America offering a healthier alternative, combining technology, value-free social science, and scientific management. Whereas the old European way led either to mere theorizing, to political extremism, or to polarization and impasse, the American approach got results by tackling problems one at a time, so that they could be solved by experts.

Such Americanism fed the notion that Europe needed a clean break based on technological values. If such a break was necessary, however, what was to become of the European tradition, for centuries, the center of gravity of the West and until recently dominant in the world? Did anything distinctively European remain, or was Europe doomed to lick its wounds in the shadow of America? These questions lurked in the background as Europeans faced the difficult task of economic and political restoration.

SECTION SUMMARY

- Existentialism and the plays of Samuel Beckett expressed the sense of exhaustion and lack of bearings in Western culture after World War II.

- Cold war concerns helped fuel an often bitter debate between Marxists and anti-Marxists that continued, off and on, from the later 1940s well into the 1970s.

- Some held that a return to religious and other traditions offered the only antidote in light of the disasters surrounding the era of the two world wars.

- The migration of European artists and intellectuals to America profoundly affected cultural relations between America and western Europe, especially during the early years of the cold war era.

- As they sought a fresh start for Europe, many western Europeans sought to adapt what they took to be American practicality.

Dubuffet: *Spinning Round* Seeking to depart from the European tradition of sophisticated, well-made art, Jean Dubuffet developed imagery that was at once crude and primitive, playful and whimsical. (Tate, London/Art Resource, NY)

PROSPERITY AND DEMOCRACY IN WESTERN EUROPE

What factors led to the surprisingly rapid restoration of democracy in much of continental western Europe after World War II?

By 1941, democracy seemed to be dying on the European continent, yet it quickly revived in western Europe after World War II, taking root more easily than most had thought possible. The bipolar international framework helped. The United States actively encouraged democracy, and Europeans, fearing the spread of communism, were happy to follow the American lead. Success at economic reconstruction was important as well. Not only was there greater prosperity, but governments could afford to deliver on promises of enhanced security, social welfare, and equal opportunity. It also mattered that western Europeans learned from past mistakes.

Economic Reconstruction and the Atlantic Orientation

It is hard to imagine how desperate the situation in much of western Europe had become by 1945. Major cities, like Rotterdam, Hamburg, and Le Havre, lay largely in ruins. Production had declined to perhaps 25 percent of the prewar level in Italy, to 20 percent in France, and to a mere 5 percent in southern Germany. Cigarettes, often gained through barter from American soldiers, served widely as a medium of exchange.

Although the U.S. commitment to assist European economic reconstruction was not originally a cold war measure, the developing cold war context added urgency to the American effort. The key was the Marshall Plan, which U.S. secretary of state General George Marshall outlined in 1947 and which channeled $13.5 billion in aid to western Europe by 1951.

Cold war concerns deepened the partnership in April 1949, when the United States spearheaded a military alliance, the **North Atlantic Treaty Organization (NATO)**, that included much of western Europe. The Soviets were tightening their grip on their satellite states in east-central Europe, and the NATO alliance was intended to check any further Soviet expansion. The Soviets

North Atlantic Treaty Organization (NATO) An alliance for regional defense, created in 1949 by the United States, Canada, and western European nations, whose members agree to defend one another from attack by nonmember countries.

Pop Art

Hamburgers, comic strips, soup-can labels, familiar images of entertainment icons—such was the stuff of "pop art," which burst onto the New York art scene in the early 1960s and came to exert a widespread cultural influence. Indeed, with their imaginative renderings of familiar images and whimsical sculptures of everyday objects, artists like Andy Warhol (1928–1987), Roy Lichtenstein (1923–1997), and Claes Oldenburg (b. 1929) helped shape the experience of the later twentieth century. But was this serious art or simply a joke, a parody, a put-on? Were the pop artists poking fun at the triviality of modern society, or were they deepening our encounter with defining aspects of contemporary culture? Whatever their intent, what does this striking new art form tell us about the direction of Western culture in the decades after World War II?

The term *pop art* was coined in England in the 1950s, when a group of artists and critics became interested in bridging the cultural gap between "fine art" and the emerging popular culture of mass media and machine-produced images, of advertising and automobiles. Like everyone else, they associated that consumerist mass culture with America—the America of Hollywood, Detroit, and Madison Avenue. And they found it more vital than the conventional fine art of the period. The American pop artists were similarly fascinated by the impersonal, mass-produced, often expendable quality of the objects and images that have come to surround us.

Pop art was part of a wider reaction against the deeply serious abstract expressionist painting that emerged in New York just after the Second World War. By the early 1950s, abstract expressionists like Jackson Pollock (1912–1956) and Mark Rothko (1903–1970) had created images of unprecedented power, whether seeking to forge an artistic identity in the face of nothingness or to transcend selfhood in a cosmic wholeness. In the mid-1950s, however, younger artists, "tired of the stink of artists' egos," began reacting against the self-importance of abstract expressionism. For these younger artists, art did not have to be a vehicle for the psychological expression of the artist or a quest for "the tragic and timeless." Although the reaction took several forms, pop art proved the most influential. The pop movement emerged especially in the United States, and it interested Europeans as typically American—fresh and fascinating or garish and vulgar, depending on one's point of view.

Oldenburg: *Floor Burger*, 1962 (Claes Oldenburg [American, b. 1929], *Floor Burger*, 1962. Canvas filled with foam rubber and cardboard boxes, painted with acrylic paint, 132.1 x 213.4 cm. Art Gallery of Ontario, Toronto. Reproduced with permission of Claes Oldenburg.)

Whereas the abstract expressionists had sought to rise above the everyday world, Claes Oldenburg's sculptures played with the scale and context of the most ordinary objects—a mixer, a three-pronged plug, a lipstick, a hamburger—to deepen our involvement with the everyday things that surround us. In this sense, the aim of pop art was not simply to parody or satirize, but to affirm our relationship with the trappings of ordinary life. Hollywood, Detroit, and Madison Avenue were all right after all; indeed, they had become the centers of Western culture by the later twentieth century.

Though anonymous and impersonal, the modern world of mass production, mass consumption, and mass media is "popular" because its images and objects are accessible to us all. In fact, they bombard us from all directions, giving shared shape and definition to our everyday lives. This is our world, the pop artists were saying, and they were creating the art appropriate to our time. They invite us to relax and enjoy that world, but they also enhance our experience by making art from it, thereby awakening us to its novelty and vitality.

But some viewers have found an element of melancholy, nostalgia, even tragedy just beneath pop art's eye-catching

had considerable superiority in conventional forces, which had ready access to western Europe, but U.S. nuclear superiority provided a balance. Indeed, the American nuclear guarantee to western Europe was the cornerstone of the NATO alliance.

By the 1950s, economic recovery was so impressive in continental western Europe that many were referring to an "economic miracle." Western Europeans took advantage of the need to rebuild by adopting up-to-date methods and technologies, though economic strategies differed from one country to the next. The new German government intervened in the economy only to ensure free competition. In France, by contrast, many were determined to use government

Warhol: *Marilyn Diptych, 1962* (Tate Gallery, London/Art Resource, NY. © Artists Rights Society [ARS], New York/ADAGP, Paris)

surface. In a world of mass media and reproduced images, more of our experience becomes secondhand and literally superficial. Likewise, pop subjects, from fast food to billboards, have no deeper meaning, no expressive personal agenda. With his multiplied image of Marilyn Monroe, Andy Warhol dealt not with the actress herself but with the obsessive familiarity of her image. He cultivated a deadpan, detached style that reflected the machine-made quality of his subject matter—the quality that made the images he started with so familiar in the first place. But even as, on one level, he embraced aspects of the new mass culture, Warhol was exploring precisely the emotional detachment—and the accompanying trivialization of emotion—at work in the culture that had produced the images he adapted. Especially in his paintings treating impersonal newspaper images of disaster and death, Warhol bore witness to our indifference—and perhaps to a cosmic meaninglessness as well. One expert has noted that "in Warhol's pictures of the material objects and other false idols that most of us worship, the pain lies just below the bright surfaces of the images and waits passively to engage us."*

The advent of pop art provoked a series of questions that remain unanswered: Is the embrace of the mass-produced and commercial, at the expense of traditional "fine art" values, a symptom of exhaustion or a healthy affirmation of contemporary popular culture, so bound up with the commercial world? Or is pop art perhaps a valuable comment on the emptiness of that culture, with its impersonal conformity, garish commercialism, and mechanical repetition? In the final analysis, were the pop artists abandoning the artist's lofty mission and giving in to the ordinary? Or were they the first to show us what "Western civilization" had come to mean by the late twentieth century?

QUESTIONS

1. Does pop art seem to be embracing, or poking fun at, the modern world of consumerism and advertising?

2. What is "popular" about pop art?

* Eric Shanes, *Warhol* (New York: Portland House, 1991), p. 41.

to modernize the country, thereby overcoming the weakness that had led to defeat. So France adopted a flexible, pragmatic form of government-led economic planning, spearheaded by the technocrat Jean Monnet (moh-NAY) (1888–1979). By 1951, French industrial production had returned to its prewar peak, and by 1957, it had risen to twice the level of 1938. Indeed, strong and sustained rates of economic growth were achieved throughout much of western Europe until the late 1960s, although Britain lagged considerably.

As part of the new postwar consensus, labor was supposed to be brought more fully into economic decision making. Thus, for example, the trade unions participated in the planning

Ban the Bomb As nuclear tension escalated during the 1950s, some people built air-raid shelters; others took to the streets in antinuclear protests. The protest movement was especially prominent in Britain, where the noted philosopher Bertrand Russell (1872–1970) played a central role. Here, at the right of those seated, he awaits arrest during a sit-in demonstration outside the British Defense Ministry. (Jimmy Sime/Hulton Archive/Getty Images)

process in France. In Germany, the codetermination law of 1951 provided for labor participation in management decisions in heavy industry, and labor representatives were given access to company books and full voting memberships on boards of directors. This measure ultimately made little difference in the functioning of the affected firms, but it helped head off any return to trade-union radicalism.

Wages stayed relatively low at first. By the 1960s, however, labor began demanding—generally with success—to share more fully in the new prosperity. Now, rather abruptly, much of western Europe took on the look of a consumer society, with widespread ownership of automobiles, televisions, and other household appliances.

Social Welfare and the Issue of Gender

welfare state The concept, especially prevalent in Western countries after World War II, that government should adopt large-scale social welfare measures, while maintaining a primarily capitalistic economy.

Western governments began to adopt social welfare measures late in the nineteenth century (see page 648–649), and by the 1940s, a degree of governmental responsibility for unemployment insurance, workplace safety, and old-age pensions was widely accepted. Some Europeans, seeking renewal after the war, found attractive models in Sweden and Denmark, where the outlines of a **welfare state** had emerged by the 1930s (see page 758).

SWEDEN

Sweden's economy remained fundamentally capitalist, based on private ownership; even after World War II, its nationalized, or government-run, sector was not large by European standards. But the system of social insurance in Sweden was the most extensive in Europe, and the government worked actively with business to promote full employment and to steer the economy in directions deemed socially desirable. Moreover, the welfare state came to mean a major role for the Swedish trade unions, which won relatively high wages for workers and even enjoyed a quasi-veto power over legislation.

At the same time, the Swedish government began playing a more active role in spheres of life that had formerly been private, from sexuality to child rearing. Thus, for example, drugstores were required to carry contraceptives beginning in 1946. Sweden was the first country to provide sex education in the public schools; optional beginning in 1942, it became compulsory in 1955. By 1979, the Swedes were limiting corporal punishment—the right to spank—and prohibiting the sale of war toys. This deprivatization of the family stemmed from a sense, especially pronounced in Sweden, that society is collectively responsible for the well-being of its children.

BRITAIN

Although the Swedish model was extreme in certain respects, most of western Europe moved in the same direction in an effort to establish the foundations for democratic renewal after the war. In Britain, for example, it was widely assumed that greater collective responsibility for the well-being of all British citizens was appropriate, in light of the shared hardships the war had imposed. Moreover, the successes of government planning and control during the war suggested that once it was over, government could assume responsibility for the basic needs of the British people, guaranteeing full employment and providing a national health service. But the Labour Party, led by Clement Attlee, seemed better equipped to deliver on that promise than the Conservatives, whose leader, Winston Churchill, was hostile to welfare state notions.

When Britain held its first postwar elections, in July 1945, Churchill's Conservatives suffered a crushing loss to Labour, which promptly began creating the British welfare state. Although some expected, and others feared, that the result would be a form of socialism, the new direction did not undermine the capitalist economic system. The Labour government nationalized some key industries, but 80 percent of the British workforce remained employed in private firms in 1948. Moreover, even under Labour, the British government did not seek the kind of economic planning role that government was playing in France.

The core of the British departure was a set of government-sponsored social welfare measures that significantly affected the lives of ordinary people. These included old-age pensions; insurance against unemployment, sickness, and disability; and allowances for pregnancy, child rearing, widowhood, and burial. The heart of the system was free medical care, to be provided by the National Health Service, created in November 1946 and operating by 1948.

In Britain, as elsewhere, gender roles were inevitably at issue as government welfare measures were debated and adopted. Were married women to have access to the welfare system as individual citizens or as members of a family unit, responsible for child rearing and dependent on their husbands as breadwinners? Should government seek to enable women to be both mothers and workers, or should government help make it possible for mothers not to have to work outside the home?

As during the First World War, the percentage of women in the workforce had increased significantly during World War II, but both women and men proved eager to embrace the security of traditional domestic patterns once the war was over. So the war did not change gender patterns of work even to the extent that World War I had done. In Britain, women made up about 30 percent of the labor force in 1931, 31 percent in 1951. Thus, the embrace of welfare measures took place at a time of renewed conservatism in conceptions of gender roles.

British feminists initially welcomed provisions of the British welfare state that recognized the special role of women as mothers. The government was to ease burdens by providing family allowances, to be paid directly to mothers of more than one child to enable them to stay home with their children. This seemed a more progressive step than the long-standing British trade-union demand for a "family wage," sufficient to enable the male breadwinner to support a family. But though women were now to be compensated directly for their role as mothers, the assumptions about gender roles remained much the same.

FRANCE   In France, which had refused even to grant women the vote after World War I, the very different situation after 1945 stimulated an especially innovative response to gender and family issues. After the experience of defeat, collaboration, and resistance, the French were determined to pursue both economic dynamism and individual justice. But they also remained concerned with population growth, so they combined incentives to encourage large families with measures to promote equal opportunity and economic independence for women.

As they expanded the role of government after the war, the French tended, more than the British, to assume that paid employment for women was healthy and desirable. New laws gave French women equal access to civil service jobs and guaranteed equal pay for equal work. At the same time, the French recognized that women had special needs as mothers, but also that husbands shared the responsibility for parenting. So the French system provided benefits for women during and after pregnancy and then family allowances that treated the two parents as equally essential. At the same time, the system viewed women as individual citizens, regardless of marital or economic status. Thus, all were equally entitled to pensions, health services, and job-related benefits.

Although female participation in the paid labor force declined after the war, it began rising throughout the West during the 1950s, and then accelerated during the 1960s, reaching new highs in the 1970s and 1980s. Thanks partly to the expansion of government, the greatest job growth was in the service sector—in social work, health care, and education, for example—and many of these new jobs went to women. From about 1960 to 1988, the percentage of women aged 25 to 34 in the labor force rose from 38 to 67 in Britain, from 42 to 75 in France, and from 49 to 87 in Germany.

These statistics reflect significant changes in women's lives, but even as their choices expanded in some respects, women became more deeply aware of enduring limits to their opportunities. Thus, a new feminist movement emerged by the early 1970s, drawing intellectual inspiration from *The Second Sex*, a pioneering work published in 1949 by the French existentialist Simone de Beauvoir (1908–1986).

The Restoration of Democracy

Much of continental western Europe faced the challenge of rebuilding democracy after defeat and humiliation. With the developing cold war complicating the situation, the prospects for democracy were by no means certain in the late 1940s. Although the division of Germany weakened communism in the new Federal Republic, in France and Italy strong communist parties had emerged from the wartime resistance and claimed to point the way beyond conventional democracy altogether.

GERMANY   The new Federal Republic of Germany held its first election under the Basic Law in August 1949, launching what proved to be a stable and successful democracy. Partly to counter the Soviet Union, but also to avoid what seemed the disastrous mistake of the harsh peace settlement after World War I, the victors sought to help get West Germany back on its feet as quickly as possible. At the same time, West German political leaders, determined to avoid the mistakes of the Weimar years, now better understood the need to compromise, to take responsibility for governing the whole nation.

To prevent the instability that had plagued the Weimar Republic, the creators of the new government strengthened the chancellor in relation to the Bundestag, the lower house of parliament. In the same way, the Basic Law helped establish a stable party system by discouraging splinter parties and by empowering the courts to outlaw extremist parties. And the courts found reason to outlaw both the Communist Party and a Neo-Nazi Party during the formative years of the new German democracy.

The West German republic proved more stable than the earlier Weimar Republic, partly because the political party system was now considerably simpler. Two mass parties, the Christian Democratic Union (CDU) and the Social Democratic Party (SPD), were immediately predominant, although a third, the much smaller Free Democratic Party (FDP), proved important for coalition purposes.

Konrad Adenauer (1876–1967), head of the CDU, the largest party in 1949, immediately emerged as West Germany's leading statesman. A Catholic who had been mayor of Cologne under Weimar, he had withdrawn from active politics during the Nazi period, but he reemerged after the war to lead the council that drafted the Basic Law. As chancellor from 1949 to 1963, he oriented the new German democracy toward western Europe and the Atlantic bloc, led by the United States.

The new bipolar world confronted West Germany with a cruel choice. By accepting the bipolar framework, the country could become a full partner within the Atlantic bloc. But by straddling the fence instead, it could keep open the possibility that Germany could be reunified as a neutral and disarmed state. When the outbreak of war in Korea in 1950 intensified the cold war, the United States pressured West Germany to rearm and join the Western bloc. Although some West Germans resisted, Adenauer prevailed, committing the Federal Republic to NATO in 1955. Adenauer was eager to anchor the new Federal Republic to the West, partly to buttress the new democracy in West Germany, but also to cement U.S. support in the face of what seemed an ongoing Soviet threat to German security.

By the late 1950s, the West German economy was recovering nicely, and the country was a valued member of the Western alliance. Adenauer's CDU seemed so potent that the other major party, the SPD, appeared to be consigned to permanent—and sterile—opposition. Frustrated with its outsider status, the SPD began to shed its Marxist trappings in an effort to widen its appeal. Prominent among those pushing in this direction was **Willy Brandt** (1913–1992), who became mayor of West Berlin in 1957, and who would become the party's leader in 1963. At its watershed national congress at Bad Godesberg in 1959, the party officially gave up talk of the class struggle and adopted a more moderate program.

Franco-German Cooperation   French president Charles de Gaulle (*left*) and West German chancellor Konrad Adenauer (*right*) draw an enthusiastic crowd in Bonn in September 1963. De Gaulle was in the West German capital for the first formal meeting after France and West Germany had signed a friendship treaty in January. Each of the two leaders strongly advocated the new cooperation between their countries, and that cooperation proved a cornerstone of the unprecedented peace and prosperity in western Europe after World War II. (akg-images)

Adenauer stepped down in 1963 at the age of 87, after fourteen years as chancellor. The contrast with Weimar, which had known twenty-one different cabinets in a comparable fourteen-year period, could not be more striking. The Adenauer years proved to Germans that democracy could mean effective government, economic prosperity, and foreign policy success. Still, Adenauer had become somewhat authoritarian by his later years, and it was arguable that West Germany had become overly reliant on him and his party.

During the years from 1963 to 1969, the CDU proved it could govern without Adenauer, and the SPD came to seem ever more respectable, even joining as the junior partner in a government coalition with the CDU in 1966. Finally, in October 1969, new parliamentary elections brought Brandt to the chancellorship, and the SPD became responsible for governing West Germany for the first time since the war.

Brandt sought to provide a genuine alternative to the CDU without undermining the consensus that had developed around the new regime since 1949. He wanted especially to improve relations between West Germany and the Soviet bloc, but this required a more independent foreign policy than Adenauer and his successors had followed. Under Adenauer, the Federal Republic had refused to deal with East Germany at all. So Brandt's opening to the East, or *Ostpolitik* (OST-po-luh-teek), was risky for a socialist chancellor seeking to prove his respectability. But he pursued it with skill and success.

In treaties with the Soviet Union, Czechoslovakia, and Poland during the early 1970s, West Germany accepted the main lines of the postwar settlement. This was to abandon any claim to the former German territory east of the Oder-Neisse line, now in Poland. Brandt also managed to improve relations with East Germany. After the two countries finally agreed to mutual diplomatic recognition, each was admitted to the United Nations in 1973. Brandt's overtures made possible closer economic ties between them, and even broader opportunities for ordinary

Konrad Adenauer
Leading statesman of post–World War II Germany, who oriented the country toward western Europe and the United States and proved to Germans that democracy could mean effective government, economic prosperity, and foreign policy success.

Willy Brandt   Social Democratic West German chancellor whose policy of opening to the East, or *Ostpolitik*, made possible closer economic ties between West and East Germany and helped ordinary citizens interact across the east-west border.

citizens to interact across the east-west border. His *Ostpolitik* was widely popular and helped deepen the postwar consensus in West Germany.

FRANCE, ITALY, AND SOUTHERN EUROPE

In France and Italy, unlike West Germany, the communists constituted a potent force in light of their major roles in wartime resistance movements. The presence of Western troops in France and Italy gave the leverage to noncommunists, however, and Moscow directed the communists in both countries to settle for the moderate course of participation in broad political coalitions. Still, the United States intervened persistently in each nation to minimize the communists' role. Though support for the communists in France continued to grow until 1949, the French Communist Party settled into a particularly doctrinaire position, maintaining strict subservience to the Soviet Union, and found itself increasingly marginalized thereafter.

As the leader of the French resistance effort, Charles de Gaulle immediately assumed the dominant political role after the liberation of France in August 1944. But he withdrew, disillusioned, from active politics early in 1946, as the new Fourth Republic returned to the unstable multiparty coalitions that had marked the later years of the Third Republic. Still, governmental decision making changed significantly as the nonpolitical, technocratic side of the French state gained power in areas such as economic planning. And government technocrats survived the fall of the Fourth Republic in 1958, when de Gaulle returned to politics in a situation of crisis stemming from France's war to maintain control of Algeria (see page 839).

It was clear that de Gaulle's return signified a change of regime. After the French legislature gave him full powers for six months, his government drafted a new constitution, which was then approved by referendum in the fall of 1958. The result was the new Fifth Republic, which featured a stronger executive—and soon a president elected directly by the people and not dependent on the Chamber of Deputies. Only with the advent of de Gaulle's Fifth Republic did government in postwar France begin to assume definitive contours.

Italy's political challenge, after more than twenty years of fascism, was even more dramatic than France's. Shortly after the war, the Italians adopted a new democratic constitution and voted to end the monarchy, thereby making modern Italy a republic for the first time. But much depended on the balance of political forces, which quickly crystallized around the Christian Democratic Party (DC), oriented toward the Catholic Church, and the strong Communist Party. Many Italian moderates with little attachment to the church supported the Christian Democrats as the chief bulwark against communism. And though they consistently had to work with smaller parties to attain a parliamentary majority, the Christian Democrats promptly assumed the dominant role, which they maintained until the early 1990s.

The Communists continued to offer the major opposition, typically winning 25 to 35 percent of the vote in national elections. Taking their cue from Gramsci's writings, they adopted a proactive strategy to make their presence felt in Italian life and to demonstrate the superiority of their diagnoses and prescriptions. They found considerable success as they organized profit-making cooperatives for sharecroppers, ran local and regional governments, and garnered the support of intellectuals, journalists, and publishers. But though the Communists proved they could operate constructively within a democratic framework, their longer-term objective remained unclear into the 1970s. Could they function as part of a majority governing coalition within a democratic political system?

By the 1960s, the new democracies in Germany, France, and Italy seemed firmly rooted, and during the 1970s, Greece, Spain, and Portugal also established workable democracies after periods of dictatorial rule. Following the death of Francisco Franco in 1975, almost forty years after his triumph in the Spanish civil war, democracy returned to Spain more smoothly than most had dared hope. Franco ordained that a restoration of the monarchy would follow his death, and King Juan Carlos (b. 1938; r. 1975–) served as an effective catalyst in the transition to democracy. The new constitution of 1978 dismantled what was left of the Franco system so that, for example, Catholicism was no longer recognized as the official religion of the Spanish state.

New Discontents and New Directions

Even as democracy seemed to be thriving in western Europe, political disaffection began to threaten the consensus by the late 1960s. At that point, western Europe was at the height of the new prosperity, so the discontent did not stem from immediate economic circumstances. A new radicalism similarly emerged in the United States during the 1960s. Although this American radicalism developed especially from the civil rights movement and from opposition to the U.S. war in Vietnam, a sense that ordinary people were not truly empowered by contemporary democratic institutions fed the new radicalism on both sides of the Atlantic.

The most dramatic instance of radical protest in western Europe was the "Days of May" uprising of students and workers that shook France during May and June of 1968. The movement's aims were amorphous or utopian, and cooperation between students and workers proved sporadic. But the episode gave vent to growing discontent with the aloofness of the technocratic leaders and the unevenness of the modernization effort in de Gaulle's France. Despite impressive economic growth, many ordinary people were coming to feel left out as public services were neglected and problems worsened in such areas as housing and education.

In Italy, frustration with the stagnation of the political system bred radical labor unrest by 1969 and then a major wave of terrorism during the 1970s. By this time, many radical young people found the Communists too caught up in the system to be genuinely innovative, yet still too weak to break the Christian Democrats' lock on power. Because the Italian Communists, unlike the German Social Democrats, never established their credibility as a national governing party, the Christian Democrats grew ever more entrenched, becoming increasingly arrogant and corrupt.

In Germany, the Green movement, formed by peace and environmental activists during the late 1970s, took pains to avoid acting like a conventional party. Concerned that Germany, with its central location, would end up the devastated battleground in any superpower confrontation, the Greens opposed deployment of additional U.S. missiles on German soil and called for an alternative to the endless arms race. The SPD, as the governing party in an important NATO state, seemed unable to confront this issue and lost members as a result.

Prominent among the new political currents emerging by the early 1970s was the renewed feminist movement, which recalled the earlier movement for women's suffrage. This drive for "women's liberation" sought equal opportunities for women in education and employment. It was striking, for example, that despite major steps toward equal educational opportunity in postwar France, the country's prestigious engineering schools did not begin admitting women until the 1980s. But feminists also forced new issues onto the political stage as they worked, for example, to liberalize divorce and abortion laws.

The Energy Crisis and the Changing Economic Framework

As the political situation in western Europe became more volatile by the early 1970s, events outside Europe made it clear how interdependent the world had become—and that the West did not hold all the trump cards. In the fall of 1973, Egypt and Syria attacked Israel, seeking to recover the losses they had suffered in a brief war in 1967. Although the assault failed, the Arab nations of the oil-rich Middle East came together in the aftermath to retaliate against the Western bloc for supporting Israel. By restricting the output and distribution of oil, the Arab-led Organization of Petroleum Exporting Countries (OPEC) produced a sharp increase in oil prices and a severe economic disruption all over the industrialized world.

The 1970s proved to be an unprecedented period of "stagflation"—sharply reduced rates of growth, combined with inflation and rising unemployment. The economic miracle was over, partly because the process soon to be known as globalization was now taking off. The European economies were subject to growing competition from non-Western countries, most notably Japan. In light of increasing global competition and rising unemployment, the labor movement was suddenly on the defensive throughout the industrialized West. And the changing circumstances inevitably strained the social compact that had enabled western Europe to make a fresh start after the war.

Rethinking the Welfare State

In much of western Europe, the reach of government continued to expand into the 1970s, when reforms in Italy, for example, made available a wider range of state services—from kindergarten and medical care to sports and recreational facilities—than ever before. But during the 1970s, some began to question both the monetary costs of such measures and their implications for European competitiveness in the global economy.

Although much publicity surrounded the postwar British welfare state, by the early 1970s the percentage of the British economy devoted to public expenditure for welfare, housing, and education—18.2 percent—was about average for the industrialized nations of the West. Sweden had the highest figure at 23.7 percent, and by that point, 40 percent of Sweden's national income was devoted to taxes to finance the system—the highest rate of taxation in the world. But pressures on

Thatcher's Conservative Revolution As British prime minister from 1979 to 1990, Margaret Thatcher led an assault on the welfare state and a renewed embrace of free-market economics in Britain. Together with U.S. president Ronald Reagan, who greatly admired her, she came to symbolize the retreat from government that marked the 1980s. Thatcher is shown at a political rally in London in 1987. (D. Hudson/Sygma/Corbis)

the welfare state were especially striking in Sweden at the same time. Swedish opinion-makers grew increasingly doubtful that a welfare state could nurture the initiative and productivity needed for success in international economic competition. Sweden found itself less competitive, both because its wages were high and because it was not keeping abreast of technological developments.

In Britain, a dramatic assault on the welfare state began developing at the same time, especially because the postwar British economy, having lagged behind the others of the industrialized West, suffered especially with the more difficult economic circumstances of the 1970s. Between 1968 and 1976, the country lost one million manufacturing jobs.

Margaret Thatcher
Conservative prime minister of Britain from 1979 to 1990, she promoted privatization and free enterprise at the expense of the welfare state and the British labor unions.

During the 1970s, each of Britain's two major political parties made a serious effort to come to grips with the situation, but neither succeeded, especially because neither could deal effectively with Britain's strong trade unions. But when the militantly conservative **Margaret Thatcher** (b. 1925) became prime minister in 1979, it was clear that Britain was embarking on a radically different course.

Thatcher insisted that Britain could reverse its economic decline only by fostering a new "enterprise culture," restoring the individual initiative that had been sapped, as she saw it, by decades of dependence on government. So her government made substantial cuts in taxes and corresponding cuts in spending for education, national health, and public housing. It also fostered privatization, selling off an array of state-owned firms from Rolls-Royce to British Airways. The government even sold public housing to tenants, at as much as 50 percent below market value, a measure that helped win considerable working-class support.

At the same time, several new laws curtailed trade union power, and Thatcher refused to consult with union leaders as her predecessors had done since the war. A showdown was reached with the yearlong coal miners' strike of 1984–1985, one of the most bitter and violent European strikes of the century. Its failure in the face of government intransigence further discredited the labor movement and enhanced Thatcher's prestige.

Even critics admitted that Thatcher's policies had produced a significant change in British attitudes in favor of enterprise and competition. And Britain's economic performance certainly improved in the wake of the Thatcher revolution. But the gap between rich and poor widened, and the old industrial regions of the north were left further behind.

SECTION SUMMARY

- The continuing American commitment to western Europe, on both the economic and military diplomatic levels, helped provide a framework for democratic restoration.

- Government promises of enhanced social welfare and equality of opportunity were essential to a new social compact in the years of democratic reconstruction in western Europe.

- Konrad Adenauer led West Germany into the American-led Atlantic bloc as part of his effort to cement democratic institutions in the new West Germany.

- Discontent with the quality of democracy surfaced on both sides of the Atlantic by the 1960s, even before the economic downturn of the 1970s.

- The traditional socialist left, and even the welfare state, were on the defensive in many parts of western Europe by the 1980s.

THE COMMUNIST BLOC: FROM CONSOLIDATION TO STAGNATION

How did Soviet policy evolve after the death of Stalin in 1953?

By the late 1950s, policymakers in the West were increasingly concerned that the Soviet Union, though rigid and inhumane in important respects, might have significant advantages in the race with the capitalist democracies. Westerners worried especially about producing enough scientists and engineers to match the Soviets. With the Great Depression still in memory, some economists held that central planning might prove more efficient, and more likely to serve social justice, than capitalism. The sense that the communist system offered formidable competition added to the anxieties in the U.S.-led Atlantic bloc.

Nonetheless, the flawed political and economic order that had emerged under Stalin continued in the Soviet Union. And when it was imposed on the countries within the Soviet orbit after the war, it produced widespread resentment—and new dilemmas for Soviet leaders. Efforts to make communism more flexible after Stalin's death in 1953 proved sporadic. The Soviet suppression of the reform movement in Czechoslovakia during the "Prague Spring" of 1968 seemed to indicate the inherent rigidity of the Soviet system.

Dilemmas of the Soviet System in Postwar Europe, 1949–1955

Even in victory, the Soviet Union had suffered enormously in the war with Nazi Germany. Especially in the more developed western part of the country, thousands of factories, and even whole towns, lay destroyed, and there were severe shortages of everything from labor to housing. Yet the developing cold war seemed to require that military spending remain high.

At the same time, the Soviet Union faced the challenge of solidifying the new system of satellite states it had put together in east-central Europe. Partly in response to U.S. initiatives in western Europe, the Soviets sought to mold the new communist states into a secure, coordinated bloc of allies. In the economic sphere, the Soviets founded a new organization, COMECON, as part of their effort to lead the economies of the satellite states away from their earlier ties to the West and toward the Soviet Union (see **Map 29.1**). In the military-diplomatic sphere, the Soviets countered NATO in 1955 by bringing the Soviet bloc countries together in a formal alliance, the **Warsaw Pact**, which provided for a joint military command and mutual military assistance.

Warsaw Pact Military-diplomatic alliance of Soviet bloc countries, created to counter NATO.

From the start, Yugoslavia had been a point of vulnerability for the Soviet system. Communist-led partisans under Josip Tito had liberated Yugoslavia from the Axis on their own, and they had not needed the Red Army to begin constructing a new communist regime (see page 811). Tito was willing to work with the Soviets, but because he had his own legitimacy, he could be considerably more independent than those elsewhere whose power rested on Soviet support. Thus, the Soviets deemed it essential to bring Tito to heel, lest his example encourage too much independence in the other communist states.

But Tito broke with the Soviet Union in 1948, and Stalin responded by cracking down on potential opponents throughout the Soviet bloc. Though the terror did not approach the massive scale of 1937–1938 (see page 763), the secret police again executed those suspected of deviation, inspiring fear even among the top leadership. As such repression proceeded in the satellite states, opposition strikes and demonstrations developed as well, finally reaching a crisis point in East Germany in 1953.

In East Berlin, a workers' protest against a provision to increase output or face wage cuts promptly led to political demands, including free elections and the withdrawal of Soviet troops. Disturbances soon spread to the other East German cities. Though this spontaneous uprising was not well coordinated, Soviet military forces had to intervene to save the East German communist regime. But the East German protest helped stimulate strikes and antigovernment demonstrations elsewhere in the Soviet bloc as well, convincing Soviet leaders that adjustments were necessary. However, at this point, the leadership of the Soviet Union was again being sorted out, for Stalin had died early in 1953, a few months before the crisis in East Germany came to a head.

Map labels (as they appear):

- ICELAND — Reykjavik — Arctic Circle — 20°W
- U.S. loan of $3.5 billion, 1946 / Exploded first atomic bomb, 1952 / Joined Common Market, 1973 (NORWAY)
- NORWAY — Oslo
- SWEDEN — Stockholm
- FINLAND — Helsinki
- North Sea
- DENMARK — Copenhagen / Joined Common Market, 1973
- Baltic Sea
- IRELAND — Dublin
- Joined Common Market, 1973 (Ireland)
- UNITED KINGDOM — London — Amsterdam
- NETHERLANDS
- Brussels — BELGIUM
- West Berlin — East Berlin Uprising, 1953 / Berlin Wall erected, 1961 — East Berlin
- EAST GERMANY
- WEST GERMANY — Bonn
- POLAND — Warsaw
- Moscow
- UNION OF SOVIET SOCIALIST REPUBLICS — Exploded first atomic bomb, 1949
- Paris — LUX.
- Prague — Communist coup, 1948 / U.S.S.R. invasion, 1968
- CZECHOSLOVAKIA — Joined NATO, 1955
- Exploded first atomic bomb, 1960 / Withdrew from NATO, 1966
- Bern — SWITZ. — Vienna — AUSTRIA
- FRANCE — Budapest — HUNGARY
- Zones of occupation ended, 1955
- Revolution, 1956
- ROMANIA — Bucharest
- Joined Common Market, 1986
- Belgrade — YUGOSLAVIA — Tito-Stalin schism, 1948
- PORTUGAL — SPAIN — Madrid
- Lisbon
- ITALY — Rome
- BULGARIA — Sofia
- Black Sea
- Joined NATO, 1982 / Joined Common Market, 1986
- Corsica — Sardinia — Balearic Is.
- Left COMECON, 1961 / Withdrew from WP, 1968 — Tiranë — ALBANIA
- GREECE — Athens
- Mediterranean Sea — Sicily
- Ankara — TURKEY — Truman Doctrine, 1947 / Joined NATO, 1952
- Truman Doctrine, 1947 / Joined NATO, 1952 / Joined Common Market, 1981 — CYPRUS — Nicosia
- ATLANTIC OCEAN
- Dnieper R. — Don R. — Volga R. — Caspian Sea — Danube R.

Legend:
- $ Participants in the Marshall Plan
- Member of NATO,* formed in 1949
- Member of COMECON,** formed in 1949, and the Warsaw Pact, organized in 1955
- Member of the European Common Market, formed in 1958
- Iron Curtain
- * North Atlantic Treaty Organization
- ** Council for Mutual Economic Assistance
- 0 200 400 Km.
- 0 200 400 Mi.

🌐 MAP 29.1—Military Alliances and Multinational Economic Groupings, 1949–1989

The cold war split was reflected especially in the two military alliances: NATO, formed in 1949, and the Warsaw Pact, formed in 1955. Each side also had its own multinational economic organization, but the membership of the EEC, or Common Market, was not identical to that of NATO. Although communist, Yugoslavia remained outside Soviet-led organizations, as did Albania for part of the period.

De-Stalinization Under Khrushchev, 1955–1964

Although a struggle for succession followed Stalin's death, the political infighting involved a reasonable degree of give-and-take, as opposed to terror and violence. The winner, Nikita Khrushchev (KROOSH-choff) (1894–1971), was slightly crude, even something of a buffoon, but he outmaneuvered his rivals by 1955, partly because they repeatedly underestimated him. Although his period of leadership was brief, it was eventful indeed—and in some ways, the Soviet system's best chance for renewal.

At a closed session of the Soviet Communist Party's twentieth national congress in February 1956, Khrushchev made a dramatic late-night speech denouncing the criminal excesses of the Stalinist system and the "cult of personality" that had developed around Stalin himself. Khrushchev's immediate aim was to undercut his hard-line rivals, but he also insisted that key features of Stalinism had amounted to an unnecessary deviation from Marxism-Leninism. So the advent of Khrushchev suggested the possibility of liberalization and reform.

But could liberalization be contained within the framework of Soviet leadership, or was it likely to threaten the system itself? The test case proved to be Hungary, where reformers led by the moderate communist Imre Nagy had taken advantage of the liberalizing atmosphere by mid-1956 to begin dismantling collective farms and moving toward a multiparty political system. They even called for Soviet troops to withdraw, to enable Hungary to leave the Warsaw Pact and become neutral. These were not changes within the system, but challenges to the system itself. When a democratic coalition government was set up by November, the Soviets used tanks to crush the Hungarian reform movement. Thousands were killed during the fighting or subsequently executed, and 200,000 Hungarians fled to the West.

Yet even the crackdown in Hungary did not mean a return to the old days of Stalinist rigidity in the Soviet bloc. The Soviets understood that the system had to become more palatable, but liberalization was to be contained within certain limits. Above all, it could not challenge communist monopoly rule and the Warsaw Pact. After 1956, the satellites were granted greater leeway, and showed greater diversity, than had previously seemed possible. Hungary's new leader, János Kádár (1912–1989), collectivized agriculture more fully than before, but he also engineered a measure of economic decentralization, allowing scope for local initiatives and market mechanisms.

In East Germany, in contrast, Walter Ulbricht (1893–1973) concentrated on central planning and heavy industry in orthodox fashion. The East German economy became the most successful in the Soviet bloc, primarily because here the new communist regime fell heir to a skilled industrial labor force. Still, that economic growth was built on low wages, so East German workers were tempted to emigrate to West Germany as the West German economic miracle gleamed ever brighter during the 1950s. The special position of Berlin, in the heart of East Germany yet still divided among the occupying powers, made such emigration relatively easy, and 2.6 million East Germans left for the West between 1950 and 1962. With a population of only 17.1 million, East Germany could not afford to let this hemorrhaging continue. Thus, in August 1961, the Ulbricht regime erected the Berlin Wall, an ugly symbol of the cold war division of Europe.

From Liberalization to Stagnation

As a domestic leader, Khrushchev proved erratic, but he was an energetic innovator, willing to experiment. He jettisoned the worst features of the police state apparatus, including some of the infamous forced-labor camps, and offered several amnesties for prisoners. He also liberalized cultural life and gave workers greater freedom to move from one job to another. The economic planning apparatus was decentralized somewhat, affording more scope for local initiatives and placing greater emphasis on consumer goods. The government expanded medical and educational facilities and, between 1955 and 1964, doubled the nation's housing stock, substantially alleviating a severe housing shortage.

In 1957, the Soviets launched the first artificial satellite, *Sputnik I*, assuming the lead in the ensuing space race, and they sent the first human into space in 1961. Such achievements suggested that even ordinary Soviet citizens had reason for optimism. More generally, the communist regimes throughout the Soviet bloc entered the 1960s with confidence after achieving excellent rates of economic growth during the 1950s.

Yet Khrushchev had made enemies with his erratic reform effort, and this led to his forced retirement in October 1964. After the unending experiment in the economy, his opponents wanted to consolidate, to return to stability and predictability. But not until 1968 did it become clear that the liberalization and innovation of the Khrushchev era were over.

By early 1968, a significant reform movement had developed within the Communist Party in Prague, the capital of Czechoslovakia. Determined to avoid the fate of the Hungarian effort in 1956, the reformers emphasized that Czechoslovakia was to remain a communist state and a full member of the Warsaw Pact. But within that framework, they felt, it should be possible to invite freer cultural expression, to democratize the Communist Party's procedures, and to broaden participation in public life.

However, efforts to reassure the Soviets alienated some of the movement's supporters, who stepped up their demands. As earlier in Hungary, the desire for change seemed to outstrip the intentions of the movement's organizers. Finally, in August 1968, Soviet leaders sent tanks into Prague to crush the reform movement. This end of the **Prague Spring** closed the era of relative flexibility and cautious innovation in the Soviet bloc that had begun in 1953.

A period of relative stagnation followed under Leonid Brezhnev (BREZH-nef) (1906–1982), a careful, consensus-seeking bureaucrat. In dealing with the United States, Brezhnev helped engineer significant moves toward arms control and an easing of tensions. But despite this *détente*, the "Brezhnev Doctrine" made it clear that the Soviet Union would intervene as necessary to help established communist regimes remain in power. For the Soviet satellite states, there seemed no further hope of reform from within. But even as resignation marked the first years after 1968, forces soon emerged that undermined the whole communist system.

Prague Spring The attempt by Czechoslovakian reformers in 1968 to gain freer cultural expression, democratization of Communist Party procedures, and broader participation in public life within the framework of a communist state.

SECTION SUMMARY

- The imposition of Stalinist forms of governing in the new Soviet satellite states produced tensions that led the whole satellite system to a breaking point by 1953.

- Nikita Khrushchev's speech of February 1956, denouncing the excesses of Stalinism, opened the way to a measure of liberalization and reform in the Soviet Union.

- The Soviet suppression of the Hungarian revolution in the fall of 1956 indicated a strict set of limits, but the Soviet satellite states had some freedom to set their own course thereafter.

- The East German government erected the Berlin Wall in August 1961 to stop people from moving to West Berlin— and from there to other parts of West Germany.

- In light of the Soviet suppression of the Prague Spring reform movement in 1968, there seemed little scope for reforming the communist systems from within.

The End of the Prague Spring Moving tanks into Prague in August 1968, Soviet leaders ended the widely admired reform movement in Czechoslovakia. Though there were protests, as shown here on August 20, the outcome was a foregone conclusion once the Soviets decided to intervene. The ending of the Prague Spring proved a watershed for the fate of communism in Europe. (Josef Kondelka/Magnum Photos)

EUROPE, THE WEST, AND THE WORLD

How did the place of western Europe in world affairs change during the cold war era?

By the early 1950s, Europe seemed dwarfed by the two superpowers and, for the foreseeable future, divided by the conflict between them. The colonial networks that had manifested European predominance unraveled rapidly at the same time. One obvious response was some form of European integration. A unified Europe might eventually become a global superpower in its own right. Although the first steps toward European unity did not go as far as visionaries had hoped, a new group of leaders established lasting foundations by the late 1950s. Still, the cold war framework limited the new union's geographical extent and the scope of its activity for decades.

The Cold War Framework

That cold war tensions could produce dangerous military conflict quickly became clear as superpower divisions over Korea, which had been jointly liberated from the Japanese by the Americans and the Soviets, led to the complex Korean War (1950–1953). Although the United States had previously declared Korea outside the U.S. defense perimeter, it intervened in support of noncommunist South Korea in the face of an attempt by communist North Korea, encouraged by Stalin, to unify Korea as a communist state. The war was inconclusive, leaving the Korean peninsula divided more or less as before, but it prompted the United States to extend containment to the global level and to step up military production.

In retrospect, however, it is clear that the most intense phase of the cold war ended with Stalin's death in 1953. In his speech to the twentieth party congress in 1956, Khrushchev repudiated the previous Soviet tenet that a military showdown between the communist world and Western capitalist imperialism was inevitable. During a visit to the United States in 1959, he stressed that the ongoing competition between the two sides could be peaceful. However, despite summit conferences and sporadic efforts at better relations, friction between the Soviet Union and the United States continued to define the era.

Indeed, a new peak of tension was reached in October 1962, when the Soviets began placing missiles in Cuba, just 90 miles from the United States. Cuba had developed close ties with the Soviet Union after a 1959 revolution led by Fidel Castro (b. 1926). With Castro beginning to develop a communist system, a U.S.-supported force of Cuban exiles sought to invade Cuba and foment insurrection against the new regime in April 1961. This effort proved a fiasco, but it indicated to the Soviets that the new Cuban regime was vulnerable to overthrow from the United States.

Although the United States had placed offensive missiles in NATO member Turkey, adjacent to the Soviet Union, the Soviet attempt to base missiles in Cuba seemed an intolerable challenge to the U.S. administration. President John F. Kennedy (1917–1963) responded with a naval blockade of Cuba, and for several days, the superpowers seemed on the verge of military confrontation. Finally, the Soviets agreed to withdraw their missiles in exchange for a U.S. promise not to seek to overthrow the communist government of Cuba. The Americans also agreed informally to remove their offensive missiles from Turkey. Khrushchev's willingness to retreat antagonized hard-liners in the Soviet military and contributed to his ouster from power two years later. Yet Khrushchev himself viewed the outcome in Cuba as a victory. By challenging the United States with missiles, the Soviets had helped secure the survival of the Cuban communist regime, which was now less vulnerable to overthrow by the United States. The Cuban missile crisis was the closest the superpowers came to direct, armed confrontation during the cold war period.

At the same time, it became increasingly clear that international communism was not the monolithic force it had once seemed. The most dramatic indication was the Sino-Soviet split, which developed during the 1950s as the Chinese Communist Party, under Mao Zedong, solidified its power. In the long struggle that led to their victory in 1949, the Chinese Communists had often had no choice but to go their own way, and during the 1940s especially, Stalin had been willing to subordinate any concern for their cause to Soviet national interests. After taking power in 1949, the Chinese Communists pursued their own path to development without worrying about the Soviet model. Not without reason, the Soviets feared that the independent, innovative Chinese might be prepared to challenge Soviet leadership in international communism. By the early 1960s, the Chinese Communists' path had become appealing to many in the non-Western world, though it attracted dissident communists in the West as well.

The Varieties of Decolonization

The advent of a new world configuration, with a circumscribed place for Europe, found dramatic expression in the rapid disintegration of the European colonial empires after World War II (see **MAP 29.2**). The war itself had been a major catalyst for independence movements throughout the world. In southeast Asia and the Pacific, quick Japanese conquests revealed the tenuous hold of France, the Netherlands, and Britain on their domains. And it was not colonial reconquest that marked the end of the war, but the atomic bomb and the victory of the United States, which took a dim view of conventional European colonialism.

The effort of the Netherlands to regain control of the Dutch East Indies led to four years of military struggle against the Indonesian nationalist insurgency. Especially after the humiliations of defeat and occupation during World War II, many of the Dutch took pride in their imperial role. The struggle lasted from 1945 to 1949, when the Dutch finally had to yield as their former colony became independent Indonesia.

Britain was the most realistic of the European colonial powers, grasping the need to compromise and work with emerging national leaders in light of decolonization pressures. Nevertheless, British resistance in 1956 provoked an international crisis over the status of the Suez Canal in Egypt (see **MAP 28.1** on page 788). Once a British protectorate, Egypt had remained under British

THE SUEZ CRISIS

🌐 MAP 29.2—Decolonization, 1945–1980

During a thirty-five-year period after World War II, the European empires in Africa, Asia, and the Pacific gradually came apart as the former colonies became independent nations.

influence after nominally becoming sovereign in 1922. But a revolution in 1952 produced a new government of Arab nationalists, led by the charismatic Colonel Gamal Abdel Nasser (1918–1970). In 1954, Britain agreed with Egypt to leave the Suez Canal zone within twenty months, though the zone was to be international, not Egyptian, and Britain was to retain special rights there in the event of war. In 1956, however, Nasser announced the nationalization of the canal, partly so that Egypt could use its revenues to finance public works projects.

Determined to resist, the British won the support of Israel and France, each of which had reason to fear the pan-Arab nationalism that Nasser's Egypt was now spearheading. Late in 1956, Britain, Israel, and France orchestrated a surprise attack on Egypt. But their troops met stubborn Egyptian resistance, and the British and French encountered decisive defeat in the diplomatic maneuvering that accompanied the fighting. Both the United States and the Soviet Union opposed the attack, as did world opinion. The old European powers had sought to act on their own, by the old rules, but the outcome of this **Suez crisis** demonstrated how limited their reach had become.

Suez crisis   Crisis prompted by Egypt's nationalization of the British-owned Suez Canal. The effort of Britain, France, and Israel to seize the canal prompted a strong negative reaction in world opinion, forcing them to withdraw.

THE FRENCH IN VIETNAM

Still, the 1956 debacle did not convince France to abandon its struggle to retain Algeria. And that struggle proved the most wrenching experience that any European country was to have with decolonization. For the French, the process started not in North Africa, but in Indochina, in southeast Asia, during World War II.

Led by the communist Ho Chi Minh (1890–1969), the Indochinese anticolonialist movement gained strength resisting the Japanese during the war. Then, before the French could return, Ho established a political base in northern Vietnam in 1945. But in 1946, French authorities in Indochina deliberately provoked an incident to undercut negotiations and start hostilities. Eight years of difficult guerrilla war followed, creating a major drain on the French economy.

With its strongly anticolonialist posture, the United States was unsympathetic to the French cause at first. But the communist takeover in China in 1949 and the outbreak of war in Korea in 1950 made the French struggle in Indochina seem a battle in a larger war against communism in Asia. By 1954, the United States was covering 75 percent of the cost of the French effort. Nonetheless, when the fall of the fortified area at Dien Bien Phu in May 1954 signaled a decisive French defeat, the United States decided to pull back and accept a negotiated settlement. Partly at the urging of its European allies, the United States had concluded that the Soviet threat in Europe must remain its principal concern.

France worked out the terms of independence for Vietnam in 1955. The solution, however, entailed a North-South partition to separate the communist and anticommunist forces, pending elections to unify the country. The anticommunist regime the United States sponsored in the South resisted holding the elections, so the country remained divided (see **MAP 29.2**). With the Americans providing first advisers, then, beginning in 1964, active military support, South Vietnam sought unsuccessfully to defeat a guerrilla insurgency supported by the communist North. After defeating the United States and South Vietnam, the communist heirs of those who had fought the French assumed the leadership of a reunified Vietnam in 1975.

In France, the defeat in Indochina in 1954 left a legacy of bitterness, especially among army officers, many of whom felt that French forces could have won had they not been undercut by politicians at home. When the outcome in Indochina emboldened Arab nationalists in North Africa to take up arms against the French colonial power, the French army was anxious for a second chance—and the French government was willing to give it to them. Algeria had been under French control since 1830, and it had a substantial minority of ethnic Europeans, totaling over a million, or 10 percent of the population.

THE WAR IN ALGERIA

Although France gradually committed 500,000 troops to Algeria, the war bogged down into what threatened to become a lengthy stalemate, with increasing brutality on both sides. As it drained French lives and resources, the war became a highly contentious political issue in France. The situation came to a head during the spring of 1958, when the advent of a new ministry, rumored to favor a compromise settlement, led to violent demonstrations, engineered by the sectors of the French army in Algeria. Military intervention in France itself seemed likely to follow—and with it, the danger of civil war.

It was at this moment of genuine emergency that Charles de Gaulle returned to lead the change to the Fifth Republic. Those determined to hold Algeria welcomed him as their savior. But de Gaulle fooled them, working out a compromise with the Algerian rebels that ended the war and made Algeria independent in 1962. Only de Gaulle could have engineered this outcome without provoking still deeper political division in France.

INDEPENDENCE IN SUB-SAHARAN AFRICA

The outcomes of decolonization in sub-Saharan Africa depended on several factors: the number and intransigence of European settlers, the extent to which local elites had emerged, and the confidence of the Europeans that they could retain their influence if they agreed to independence. The transition was smoothest in British West Africa, where the Gold Coast achieved independence as Ghana, first as a dominion of the British Commonwealth in 1957, and then as a fully independent republic in 1960. Few British settlers lived in that part of Africa, and the small, relatively cohesive African elite favored a moderate transition, not revolution.

Where British settlers were relatively numerous, however, the transition to independence was much more difficult. The very presence of Europeans had impeded the development of cohesive local elites, so movements for independence in those areas tended to become more radical, threatening the expropriation of European-held property. In Southern Rhodesia, unyielding European settlers resisted the British government's efforts to promote a compromise. A white supremacist government declared its independence from Britain in 1965, fueling a guerrilla war. The Africans won independence as Zimbabwe only in 1980.

The reaction against Eurocentrism that accompanied the turn from colonialism was not confined to those who had been subjected to European imperialism. There was much interest among Westerners in the work of Frantz Fanon (1925–1961), a black intellectual from Martinique who became identified especially with the cause of the Algerian rebels. In *The Wretched of the Earth* (1961), Fanon found the West spiritually exhausted and called on the peoples of the non-Western world to go their own way, based on their own values and traditions. (See the feature, "The Global Record: The Legacy of European Colonialism.")

The process of decolonization led to a remarkable transformation in the thirty-five years after World War II. Forms of colonial rule that had been taken for granted before World War I stood discredited, virtually without defenders, by the late twentieth century. Europeans were

The Legacy of European Colonialism

In the following passages from The Wretched of the Earth *(1961), Frantz Fanon probes the negative consequences of colonialism—for both colonizers and colonized—and tries to show why a radical, even violent break from colonialism was necessary. In his conclusion, he offers a stirring call to the colonized world to repudiate the West, whose claims to offer universal values he finds hypocritical in the extreme.*

The violence which has ruled over the ordering of the colonial world, which has ceaselessly drummed the rhythm for the destruction of native social forms and broken up without reserve the systems of reference of the economy, the customs of dress and external life, that same violence will be claimed and taken over by the native at the moment when, deciding to embody history in his own person, he surges into the forbidden quarters....

...In the colonial context the settler only ends his work of breaking in the native when the latter admits loudly and intelligibly the supremacy of the white man's values. In the period of decolonization, the colonized masses mock at these very values, insult them, and vomit them up.

...All that the native has seen in his country is that they can freely arrest him, beat him, starve him: and no professor of ethics, no priest has ever come to be beaten in his place, nor to share their bread with him. As far as the native is concerned, morality is very concrete; it is to silence the settler's defiance, to break his flaunting violence—in a word, to put him out of the picture....

...The colonialist bourgeoisie, in its narcissistic dialogue, expounded by the members of its universities, had in fact deeply implanted in the minds of the colonized intellectual that the essential qualities remain eternal in spite of all the blunders men may make: the essential qualities of the West, of course....Now it so happens that during the struggle for liberation, at the moment that the native intellectual comes into touch again with his people,...[a]ll the Mediterranean values—the triumph of the human individual, of clarity, and of beauty...are revealed as worthless, simply because they have nothing to do with the concrete conflict in which the people is engaged.

Individualism is the first to disappear....The colonialist bourgeoisie had hammered into the native's mind the idea of a society of individuals where each person shuts himself up in his own subjectivity, and whose only wealth is individual thought. Now the native who has the opportunity to return to the people during the struggle for freedom will discover the falseness of this theory. The very forms of organization of the struggle will suggest to him a different vocabulary. Brother, sister, friend—these are words outlawed by the colonialist bourgeoisie, because for them my brother is my purse, my friend is part of my scheme for getting on. The native intellectual...will...discover the substance of village assemblies, the cohesion of people's committees, and the extraordinary fruitfulness of local meetings and groupments. Henceforward, the interests of one will be the interests of all, for in concrete fact *everyone* will be discovered by the troops, *everyone* will be massacred—or *everyone* will be saved....

Leave this Europe where they are never done talking of Man yet murder men everywhere they find them....For centuries they have stifled almost the whole of humanity in the name of a so-called spiritual experience. Look at them today swaying between atomic and spiritual disintegration....

Come then, comrades, the European game has finally ended; we must find something different. We today can do everything, so long as we do not imitate Europe, so long as we are not obsessed by the desire to catch up with Europe.

QUESTIONS

1. On what basis does Fanon believe that even native intellectuals who have embraced Western values can be won back for the anticolonialist cause?

2. What Western value does Fanon claim is the first to be repudiated—and why?

Source: Excerpts from *The Wretched of the Earth* by Frantz Fanon, copyright © 1963 by Presence Africaine. Used by permission of Grove/Atlantic, Inc.

---

now accepting the principle of national self-determination for non-Europeans. But decolonization hardly offered a neat and definitive solution. In formerly colonial territories, new political boundaries often stemmed from the ways Europeans had carved things up, rather than from indigenous ethnic or national patterns. Moreover, questions remained about the longer-term economic relationships between the Europeans and their former colonies.

Economic Integration and the Origins of the European Union

As the old colonialism increasingly fell into disrepute, many found in European unity the best prospect for the future. Although hopes for full-scale political unification were soon frustrated, the movement for European integration achieved significant successes in the economic sphere, especially through the European Economic Community, or Common Market, established in 1957.

The impetus for economic integration came especially from a new breed of "Eurocrats"—technocrats with a supranational, or pan-European, outlook. A notable example was Robert Schuman (1886–1963), a native of Lorraine, which had passed between France and Germany four times between 1870 and 1945. After serving as a German officer in World War I, he was elected to the French Chamber of Deputies in 1919 just after Lorraine was returned to France. As French foreign minister after World War II, Schuman was responsible for a 1950 plan to coordinate French and German production of coal and steel. The Schuman Plan quickly encompassed Italy, Belgium, the Netherlands, and Luxembourg to become the European Coal and Steel Community (ECSC) in 1951. Working closely with Schuman was Jean Monnet, who served as the ECSC's first president. From this position, he pushed for more thoroughgoing economic integration. The successes of the ECSC led the same six countries to agree to a wider "Common Market," officially known as the **European Economic Community (EEC)**, in 1957.

After the merger of the governing institutions of the several European supranational organizations in 1967, the term *European Community* (EC) and later *European Union* (EU) came to indicate the institutional web that had emerged since the launching of the European Coal and Steel Community in 1951. Meanwhile, its membership gradually expanded, encompassing, during the cold war era, Denmark, Ireland, and Britain in 1973, Greece in 1981, and Spain and Portugal in 1986 (see **Map 29.1**). For newly democratic countries like Spain, Portugal, and Greece, Common Market membership became a pillar of the solidifying democratic consensus.

The immediate aim of the original EEC was to facilitate trade by eliminating customs duties between its member countries and by establishing common tariffs on imports from the rest of the world. For each member of the EEC, tariff reduction meant access to wider markets abroad, but also the risks of new competition in its own domestic market. However, the EEC proved advantageous to so many that tariff reduction proceeded well ahead of schedule. By 1968, the last internal tariffs had been eliminated.

With tariffs dropping, trade among the member countries nearly doubled between 1958 and 1962. For example, French exports of automobiles and chemicals to Germany increased more than eightfold. Partly because the increasing competition stimulated initiative and productivity, industrial production within the EEC increased at a robust annual rate of 7.6 percent during those years.

Despite these successes, vigorous debate accompanied the development of the EEC during the 1960s. To enable goods, capital, and labor to move freely among the member countries, some coordination of social and economic policy was required. But were the member states prepared to give up some of their own sovereignty to the Common Market to make that coordination possible?

In the mid-1960s, French president de Gaulle forced some of the underlying uncertainties to the fore. Though he had willingly turned from the old colonialism, de Gaulle was not prepared to compromise French sovereignty, and he was not persuaded that supranational integration offered the best course for postwar Europe. With the end of the Algerian war in 1962, France began playing an assertively independent role in international affairs. Thus, for example, de Gaulle developed an independent French nuclear force, curtailed the French role in NATO, and recognized the communist People's Republic of China.

This determination to assert France's sovereignty led to friction between de Gaulle and the supranational Eurocrats of the Common Market. A dispute over agricultural policy brought matters to a head in 1965. The immediate result was a compromise, but de Gaulle's tough stance served to check the increasing supranationalism evident in the EEC until then. As the economic context became more difficult during the 1970s, it became still harder to maintain the EEC's cohesion. So, although the Common Market was an important departure, it did not overcome traditional national sovereignty or give western Europe a more muscular world role during the first decades after World War II.

European Economic Community (EEC)
Common market formed by Belgium, France, West Germany, Italy, Luxembourg, and the Netherlands to promote free trade.

SECTION SUMMARY

- Dependent on the United States for their security, the western European countries had limited freedom of action in world affairs during the cold war era.

- Though the decolonization process varied considerably from case to case, the long-standing European colonial networks gradually dissolved after World War II.

- Desires to remove the sources of war and to enhance Europe's economic competitiveness fueled the movement toward European integration, including the formation of the European Economic Community (Common Market) in 1957.

- French president Charles de Gaulle envisioned a more independent role for Europe from within the cold war framework, but that role was to be based on French leadership, not European integration.

THE COLLAPSE OF THE SOVIET SYSTEM, 1975–1991

What led to the collapse of the communist system in the Soviet Union and its satellite states?

Though the reasons were different, the Soviet bloc, like the West, encountered economic stagnation during the 1970s. The deteriorating situation finally produced a major Soviet reform effort by the mid-1980s. At the same time, new forms of opposition developed in the satellite states after the crushing of the Prague reform movement in 1968. The intersection of these forces led to the unraveling of the satellite system in 1989, and then to the collapse of the Soviet communist regime in 1991. This outcome stunned Western observers, who had come to take the anxious stability of the cold war framework for granted.

Economic Stagnation in the Soviet Bloc

The impressive rates of economic growth achieved in much of the Soviet bloc continued into the 1960s. However, such success came especially from adding labor—women and underemployed peasants—to the industrial workforce. By the end of the 1960s, that process was reaching its limits, so increasingly, the challenge for the Soviet bloc was to boost productivity through technological innovation.

By the late 1970s, however, the Soviets were falling seriously behind the West as a new technological revolution gathered force. Continuing development in high technology demanded the freedom to experiment and exchange ideas and the flexibility to anticipate innovation and shift resources. The Soviet system, with its direction from the top, proved too rigid. Moreover, as that system bogged down, the expense of the arms race with the United States dragged ever more seriously on the Soviet economy. Ordinary Soviet citizens grew increasingly frustrated as the communist economy proved erratic in providing even basic consumer goods. Yet major functionaries enjoyed access to special shops and other privileges.

In satellite countries, such as Poland and Hungary, the communist governments managed for a while to win mass support by borrowing from foreign banks to provide meat and other consumer goods at artificially low prices—"sausage-stuffing," some called it. But as the lending banks came to realize, by the end of the 1970s, that such loans were not being used to enhance productivity, these governments found it much harder to borrow. Thus, they began having to impose greater austerity.

Throughout the Soviet bloc, frustration grew, especially among women, who seemed to bear a disproportionate share of the burdens. Women were more likely to be employed outside the home in the communist countries than in the West. About 90 percent of adult women in the Soviet Union and East Germany had paid jobs by 1980. Yet, not only were these women concentrated in jobs with low pay and prestige, but they also still bore the major responsibility for child-care, housework, and shopping. They had few of the labor-saving devices available in the West, and they often had to spend hours in line to buy ordinary consumer items. Dissatisfaction among women fed an underground protest movement that began developing in the Soviet bloc in the mid-1970s—an indication of the growing strains in the overall system.

The Crisis of Communism in the Satellite States

For many intellectuals in the Soviet bloc, the Soviet suppression of the Prague Spring in 1968 ended any hope that communism could be made to work. The immediate outcome was a sense of hopelessness, but by the mid-1970s, a new opposition movement had begun to take shape, especially in Hungary, Poland, and Czechoslovakia. It centered initially on underground (or *samizdat*) publications, privately circulated writings that enabled dissidents to share ideas critical of the regime.

In one sense, these dissidents realized, intellectuals and ordinary people alike were powerless in the face of heavy-handed communist government. But they came to believe they could make a difference simply by "living the truth," ceasing to participate in the empty rituals of communist rule. And mere individual honesty could have political potential, especially because of the Helsinki Accords on human rights that the Soviet bloc countries had accepted in 1975.

The meeting of thirty-five countries in Helsinki, Finland, in 1975 was one of the most important fruits of the *Ostpolitik*, or opening to the East, that Willy Brandt began pursuing after becoming West Germany's chancellor in 1969 (see page 829). Eager to grasp Brandt's offer to regularize the status of East Germany and to confirm the western border of Poland, the Soviet bloc found it expedient to accept the detailed agreement on human rights included in the resulting **Helsinki Accords**.

Though merely symbolic, in one sense, the human rights agreement proved a touchstone for initiatives that would help bring the whole Soviet system crashing down. Through various "Helsinki Watch" groups monitoring civil liberties, anticommunists in the satellite states managed to assume moral leadership. By demanding that the communist governments live up to their agreements, and by noting the gap between idealistic pretense and grim reality, opposition intellectuals began to cast doubts on the very legitimacy of the communist regimes.

The most significant such group was Charter 77, which emerged in Czechoslovakia in response to the arrest of a rock group, "The Plastic People of the Universe." Long-haired and antiestablishment like their counterparts in the West, the Plastic People were deemed filthy, obscene, and disrespectful of society by the repressive Czechoslovak regime. In 1977, protesting the crackdown on the group, 243 individuals signed "Charter 77"—using their own names and addresses, living the truth, acting as if they were free to register such an opinion.

A leader in Charter 77 was the writer Václav Havel (HAH-vul) (b. 1936), who noted that, after 1968, the hope for change depended on people organizing themselves, outside the structures of the party-state, in diverse, independent social groupings. (See the feature, "The Written Record: Power from Below: Living the Truth.") Havel and a number of his associates were in and out of jail as the government sought to stave off this protest movement. Despite the efforts of Havel and his colleagues, however, government remained particularly repressive, and ordinary people relatively passive, in Czechoslovakia until the late 1980s. For quite different reasons, Hungary and Poland offered greater scope for change.

Even after the failed reform effort of 1956, Hungary proved the most innovative of the European communist countries. Partly because its government allowed small-scale initiatives outside the central planning apparatus, Hungary was able to respond more flexibly to the growing economic stagnation. This openness to economic experimentation enabled reformers within the Hungarian Communist Party to gain the upper hand. Amid growing talk of "socialist pluralism," the Hungarian elections of 1985 introduced an element of genuine democracy. Increasingly open to a variety of viewpoints, the Hungarian Communists gradually pulled back from their long-standing claim to a monopoly of power.

The reform effort that built gradually in Hungary stemmed especially from aspirations within the governing elite. More dramatic was the course of change in Poland, where workers and intellectuals, at odds even as recently as 1968, managed to come together during the 1970s. When Polish workers struck in 1976, in response to a cut in food subsidies, intellectuals formed a committee to defend them. This alliance had become possible because dissident intellectuals

Women's Work in the Soviet Union   This cartoon adapts the caryatid form from ancient sculpture to depict the special burdens that were coming to wear more heavily on women as the Soviet economy bogged down. Intended to commemorate International Women's Day, the image appeared in the Soviet magazine *Krokodil* in 1984.   (*Krokodil Magazine*, March 1984)

Helsinki Accords
Agreements signed by thirty-five countries in Helsinki, Finland, that committed the signatories to recognize existing borders, to increase economic and environmental cooperation, and to promote freedom of expression, religion, and travel.

were coming to emphasize the importance of grassroots efforts that challenged the logic of the communist system without attacking it directly.

An extra ingredient from an unexpected quarter also affected the situation in Poland, perhaps in a decisive way. In 1978, the College of Cardinals of the Roman Catholic Church departed from long tradition and, for the first time since 1522, elected a non-Italian pope. Even more startling was the fact that the new pope was from Poland, behind the iron curtain. He was Karol Cardinal Wojtyla (voy-TILL-ah) (1920–2005), the archbishop of Cracow, who took the name John Paul II.

After World War II, the Polish Catholic Church had been unique among the major churches of east-central Europe in maintaining and even enhancing its position. It worked just enough with the ruling Communists to be allowed to carve out a measure of autonomy. For many Poles, the church remained a tangible institutional alternative to communism and the focus of national consciousness in the face of Soviet domination. Thus, the new pope's visit to Poland in 1979 had an electrifying effect on ordinary Poles, who took to the streets by the millions to greet him—and found they were not alone. This boost in self-confidence provided the catalyst for the founding of a new trade union, **Solidarity**, in August 1980.

Led by a shipyard electrician, Lech Walesa (va-WEN-sah) (b. 1943), Solidarity emerged from labor discontent in the vast Lenin shipyard in Gdansk, on the Baltic Sea (see **Map 29.1**). Demanding the right to form their own independent unions, seventy thousand workers took over the shipyard, winning support both from their intellectual allies and from the Catholic Church. Support for Solidarity grew partly because the government, facing the crisis of its "sausage stuffing" strategy, was cutting subsidies and raising food prices. But the new union developed such force because it placed moral demands first—independent labor organizations, the right to strike, and freedom of expression. Reflecting the wider opposition thinking in east-central Europe, Solidarity was not to be bought off with lower meat prices, even had the government been able to deliver them.

After over a year of negotiation, compromise, and broken promises, the tense situation came to a head in December 1981, when the government under General Wojciech Jaruzelski (yah-roo-ZELL-skee) (b. 1923) declared martial law and outlawed Solidarity, imprisoning its leaders. Strikes in protest were crushed by military force. So much for that, it seemed: another lost cause, another reform effort colliding with inflexible communist power, as in 1953, 1956, and 1968. But this time, it was different, thanks especially to developments in the Soviet Union.

The Quest for Reform in the Soviet Union

The death of Leonid Brezhnev in 1982 paved the way for a reform effort that began in earnest when **Mikhail Gorbachev** (GOR-ba-choff) (b. 1931) became Soviet Communist Party secretary in 1985. Gorbachev's effort encompassed four intersecting initiatives: arms reduction; liberalization in the satellite states; *glasnost* (GLAHZ-nost), or "openness" to discussion and criticism; and *perestroika* (pair-es-TROY-kah), or economic "restructuring." This was to be a reform within the Soviet system. There was no thought of giving up the Communist Party's monopoly on power or embracing a free-market economy. The reformers still took it for granted that communism could point the way beyond Western capitalism, with its shallow consumerism. But they had to make communism work.

Gorbachev understood that "openness" was a prerequisite for "restructuring." The freedom to criticize was essential to check abuses of power, which, in turn, was necessary to overcome the cynicism of the workers and improve productivity. Openness was also imperative to gain the full participation of the country's most creative people, whose contributions were critical if the Soviet Union was to become competitive in advanced technology.

The main thrust of *perestroika* was to depart from the rigid economic planning mechanism by giving local managers more autonomy. But any restructuring was bound to encounter resistance, especially from those with careers tied to the central planning apparatus. And Gorbachev's program made only partial headway in this crucial sector.

The Anticommunist Revolution in East-Central Europe

Meanwhile, in Poland, repression continued, but Walesa, from prison, managed to keep his movement together, as the ideas of Solidarity continued to spread underground. Then the advent of Gorbachev in 1985 changed the overall framework, in light of his belief that reform

Solidarity A trade union formed in communist Poland, it became the nucleus of widespread demands for change—including independent labor organizations, the right to strike, and freedom of expression.

Mikhail Gorbachev Soviet Communist Party secretary who attempted to reform the Soviet communist system through arms reduction; liberalization in the satellite states; *glasnost*; and *perestroika*.

Power from Below: Living the Truth

Considering the scope for change in the communist world by the late 1970s, Václav Havel imagines a conformist grocer who routinely puts a sign in his window with the slogan "Workers of the world, unite!" simply because it is expected. That same grocer, says Havel, has the power to break the system, which rests on innumerable acts of everyday compliance. Havel finds this system "post-totalitarian" because it rests on neither the coercion nor the fanatical belief that, in some combination, had sustained the earlier totalitarian systems. At the same time, he senses that aspects of the "post-totalitarian" order reveal, in stark and garish terms, more general modern tendencies that are merely masked in the Western democracies. So the West did not offer an easy model; in fact, it might actually have something to learn from the forms of opposition that Havel saw emerging in the communist bloc.

The real meaning of the greengrocer's slogan has nothing to do with what the text of the slogan actually says. Even so, this real meaning is quite clear and generally comprehensible because the code is so familiar: the greengrocer declares his loyalty … in the only way the regime is capable of hearing; that is, by accepting the prescribed *ritual*, by accepting appearances as reality, by accepting the given rules of the game. In doing so, however, he has himself become a player in the game, thus making it possible for the game to go on, for it to exist in the first place. …

In the end, is not the greyness and emptiness of life in the post-totalitarian system only an inflated caricature of modern life in general? And do we not stand (although in the external measures of civilization, we are far behind) as a kind of warning to the West, revealing its own latent tendencies?

Let us now imagine that one day something in our greengrocer snaps and he stops putting up the slogans merely to ingratiate himself. He stops voting in elections he knows are a farce. He begins to say what he really thinks at political meetings. … He rejects the ritual and breaks the rules of the game. He discovers once more his suppressed identity and dignity. …

… By breaking the rules of the game, he has disrupted the game as such. He has exposed it as a mere game. He has shattered the world of appearance, the fundamental pillar of the system. … He has shown everyone that it *is* possible to live within the truth. Living within the lie can constitute the system only if it is universal. The principle must embrace and permeate everything. There are no terms whatsoever on which it can coexist with living within the truth, and therefore everyone who steps out of line *denies it in principle and threatens it in its entirety*. …

And since all genuine problems and matters of critical importance are hidden beneath a thick crust of lies, it is never quite clear when the proverbial last straw will fall, or what that straw will be. This … is why the regime prosecutes, almost as a reflex action preventively, even the most modest attempts to live within the truth.

… The crust presented by the life of lies is made of strange stuff. As long as it seals off hermetically the entire society, it appears to be made of stone. But the moment someone breaks through in one place, when one person cries out, "The emperor is naked!"—when a single person breaks the rules of the game, thus exposing it as a game—everything suddenly appears in another light and the whole crust seems then to be made of a tissue on the point of tearing and disintegrating uncontrollably. …

The post-totalitarian system is only one aspect … of this general inability of modern humanity to be the master of its own situation. The automatism of the post-totalitarian system is merely an extreme version of the global automatism of technological civilization. The human failure that it mirrors is only one variant of the general failure of modern humanity. …

It would appear that the traditional parliamentary democracies can offer no fundamental opposition to the automatism of technological civilization and the industrial-consumer society, for they, too, are being dragged helplessly along by it. People are manipulated in ways that are infinitely more subtle and refined than the brutal methods used in the post-totalitarian societies.

QUESTIONS

1. Why does Havel believe that small, everyday acts of conformity actually constitute the post-totalitarian system?

2. What relationship between the communist bloc and the Western democracies is Havel positing?

Source: From *The Power of the Powerless: Citizens Against the State in Central-Eastern Europe*, ed. Václav Havel et al.; John Keane, ed. (Armonk, NY: M. E. Sharpe, 1985). Copyright © 1985 by Palach Press. Reprinted with permission of M. E. Sharpe, Inc.

in the satellites was necessary to complement restructuring in the Soviet system. As the Polish economy, already in difficulty by 1980, reached a crisis in 1987, Solidarity began stepping up its efforts.

When proposed price increases were rejected in a referendum, the Polish government imposed them by fiat. Strikes demanding the relegalization of Solidarity followed during the spring of 1988. The government again responded with military force, but Solidarity-led strikes in August forced

Lech Walesa and Solidarity A shipyard electrician, Walesa spearheaded the dissident Polish trade union, Solidarity, formed in 1980, and then emerged from prison to lead the movement that eventually undercut the communist regime in Poland in 1989. Here he addresses a rally during a strike at the Lenin shipyard in Gdansk in August 1988. (Corbis Sygma)

government leaders to send signals that they might be prepared to negotiate. With the economy nearing collapse, the government recognized that it could no longer govern on its own.

The "Round Table" negotiations that followed early in 1989 proved pivotal. Not only did the government consent to legalize Solidarity, but it agreed to make the forthcoming elections free enough for the opposition genuinely to participate. The elections of June 1989 produced an overwhelming repudiation of Poland's communist government, forcing President Jaruzelski to give Solidarity a chance to lead. Not all members of the opposition felt it wise to accept government responsibility under such difficult economic circumstances, but finally Tadeusz Mazowiecki (mah-zo-VYETS-kee), Walesa's choice and one of the movement's most distinguished intellectuals, agreed to form a government.

The chain of events in Poland culminated in one of the extraordinary events of modern history—the negotiated end of communist rule. That a communist government might give up power voluntarily had been utterly unforeseen. It happened partly because the Soviet Union under Gorbachev was seeking reform and thus had become much less likely to intervene militarily. It also helped that the Polish Catholic Church was available to act as mediator, hosting meetings, reminding both sides of their shared responsibilities in the difficult situation facing their country. By some accounts, General Jaruzelski, who seemed for most of the 1980s to be just another military strongman and Soviet lackey, had proved to be a national hero for his grace, perhaps even ingenuity, in yielding power to the opposition. But most important was the courage, the persistence, and the vision of Solidarity itself.

Although the Hungarians were already breaking out of the communist mold, it was especially the Polish example that suggested to others in the Soviet bloc that the whole system was open to challenge. During 1989, demands for reform and, increasingly, for an end to communist rule spread through east-central Europe by means of the domino effect that had preoccupied the Soviets from the start. By the end of that year, the Soviet satellite system was in ruins (see **Map 30.1** on page 854).

A marked increase in illegal emigration from East Germany to the West had been one manifestation that the system was starting to unravel. During 1989, the reform-minded Hungarian Communists decided to stop impeding East Germans, many of whom vacationed in Hungary, from emigrating to the West at the Hungarian border with Austria. If the communist reformers in East Germany were to have any chance of turning the situation around, they had to relax restrictions on travel and even grant the right to emigrate. They began preparing to do both as part of a host of reforms intended to save the system. On November 9, 1989, the East German communist regime did the unthinkable and opened the Berlin Wall, which was promptly dismantled altogether. Germans now traveled freely back and forth between East and West. Although the fate of the Soviet Union itself remained uncertain, the opening of the wall signaled the end of the cold war. It was no longer a bipolar world.

By this point, discontented East Germans envisioned not simply reforming the communist system, but ending it altogether. Within weeks, it was clear that the rhythm of events was beyond the control of East Germany's reform communists, who opened the way for German reunification in 1990. Despite some nervousness, the four postwar occupying powers— the United States, Britain, France, and the Soviet Union—gave their blessing as the Federal Republic incorporated the five East German states. The communist system in East Germany simply dissolved.

Although some in West Germany were hesitant about immediate reunification, especially because of the economic costs that seemed likely, West German chancellor Helmut Kohl (KOLE) (b. 1930) sought to complete the process as quickly as possible. By early 1990, the emigration of East Germans to the West had become a flood. West German law treated these Germans as citizens, entitled to social benefits, so their arrival in such numbers presented a considerable financial burden. It seemed imperative for West Germany to regularize the situation as quickly as possible, assuming responsibility for the East and restoring its economy.

The division of Germany, symbolized by the Berlin Wall, had been central to the bipolar cold war world. Now Germany was a unified country for the first time since the Nazi era. What role would the new Germany play?

The End of the Soviet Union

Meanwhile, in the Soviet Union, what began as a restructuring of the communist system became a struggle for survival of the system itself. The much-trumpeted *glasnost* produced greater freedom in culture and politics, but Gorbachev sought to avoid alienating hard-line Communists, so he compromised, watering down the economic reforms essential to *perestroika*. The result proved a set of half measures that only made things worse. Because so little was done to force the entrenched Soviet bureaucracy to go along, the pace of economic reform was lethargic. The essential structures of the command economy weakened, but free-market forms of exchange among producers, distributors, and consumers did not emerge to replace them.

In 1986, an accidental explosion at the Soviet nuclear power plant at Chernobyl, in Ukraine (see **MAP 29.3**), released two hundred times as much radiation as the atomic bombs dropped on Hiroshima and Nagasaki combined. The accident contaminated food supplies and forced the abandonment of villages and thousands of square miles of formerly productive land. The radioactivity released would eventually hasten the deaths of at least 100,000 Soviet citizens. Despite his commitment to openness, Gorbachev reverted to old-fashioned Soviet secrecy for several weeks after the accident, in an effort to minimize what had happened. As a result, the eventual toll was far greater than it need have been. The accident and its aftermath seemed stark manifestation of all that was wrong with the Soviet system—its arrogance and secrecy, its premium on cutting corners to achieve targets imposed from above.

By the end of the 1980s, Soviet citizens felt betrayed by their earlier faith that Soviet communism was leading to a better future. A popular slogan spoke sarcastically of "seventy years on the road to nowhere." The economic situation was deteriorating, yet people were free to discuss alternatives as never before. As the discussion came to include once-unthinkable possibilities, such as privatization and a market economy, it became clear that the whole communist system was in jeopardy.

By mid-1990, moreover, the union of Soviet republics itself tottered on the verge of collapse. Lithuania led the way in calling for outright independence. But the stakes were raised enormously when the Russian republic, the most important in the USSR, followed Lithuania's lead. In June 1990, the newly elected chairman of Russia's parliament, Boris Yeltsin (1931–2007), persuaded the Russian republic to declare its sovereignty. Yeltsin had grown impatient with the slow pace of economic and political change. As a further challenge to Gorbachev, he dramatically resigned from the Communist Party during its televised national congress in July 1990. When, in June 1991, free elections in the Russian republic offered the first clear contest between communists determined to preserve the system and those seeking to replace it, the anticommunist Yeltsin was elected the republic's president by a surprising margin.

After tilting toward the hard-liners late in 1990, Gorbachev sought a return to reform after Yeltsin's election as Russia's president. He even engineered a new party charter that jettisoned much

30

CHAPTER OUTLINE

The Changing International Framework after the Cold War

Globalization and the Uncertainties of Democratic Capitalism

Lifestyles and Identities

The West in a Global Age

STABILITY | GROWTH | JOBS

A New World Order?

Meeting in London early in April 2009, leaders from around the world sought to coordinate responses to the most severe global economic crisis since the Great Depression of the 1930s. Despite the common aim, this meeting of leading economic powers and major multi-national financial organizations was notable for the range and diversity of the interests represented. Among the twenty-nine leaders who gathered for this photo are (first row, third through seventh from the left) French President Nicolas Sarkozy, Saudi Foreign Minister Prince Saud al-Faisal, Chinese President Hu Jintao, British Prime Minister Gordon Brown, and Brazilian President Lula Ignacio de Silva; (second row, second through fifth from the left) Indian Prime Minister Manmohan Singh, Turkish President Recep Tayyip Erdogan, U.S. President Barack Obama, and Russian President Dmitry Medvedev; (second row, second from the right) German Chancellor Angela Merkel; and (third row, fourth from the right) Japanese Prime Minister Taro Aso. (ERIC FEFERBERG/AFP/Getty Images)

A Continuing Experiment: The West and the World Since 1989

In April 2009 an entity known as the **Group of 20 (G-20)**, representing nineteen nations and the European Union (EU), met in London in its second attempt to deal with what was becoming the worst global economic crisis since the Great Depression of the 1930s. The group had met first in Washington the previous November, although signs of a financial and banking crisis had become evident by August 2007. That crisis stemmed most basically from a collapse in housing prices in a number of countries, including, most prominently, the United States, Britain, Ireland, Spain, and Iceland. But by April 2009 the financial crisis had led to a full-blown economic crisis: production and international trade were shrinking and unemployment was rapidly rising throughout the world.

Those involved in the G-20 represented almost 90 percent of the world's economy. In light of the magnitude of the crisis, a meeting of leaders of the world's largest economies was obviously essential. But these meetings marked a turning point in including such a wide array of countries, including several rapidly developing non-Western nations that had recently become major global economic players.

When, in the wake of depression and war, the Bretton Woods agreements of 1944 reworked the world's financial system (see page 812), it was largely the United States and Great Britain who called the shots. The economic problems of the 1970s, caused especially by rapid increases in oil prices (see page 831), led the world's seven largest economic powers (the United States, Japan, Germany, France, Britain, Italy, and Canada) to begin meeting regularly in an effort to coordinate economic policies. Seeking to avoid the isolation of Russia after the fall of communism, this **Group of Seven (G-7)** invited Russia to join, even though the size of the Russian economy did not warrant inclusion. So the G-7 became the G-8 (Group of 8).

By 2008, with such countries as China, India, and Brazil increasingly central to the world economy, the G-8 appeared anachronistic. The world's economies were so interconnected that response to the crisis clearly had to involve a much wider array of countries. The G-20 included, in addition to those in the G-8, Argentina, Australia, Brazil, China, India, Indonesia, Mexico, Saudi Arabia, South Africa, South Korea, and Turkey. The EU was also a member, even though four of its member nations were members of the G-20 as well. The emergence of the G-20 pointed to reform of the key institutions established at Bretton Woods—the World Bank and the International Monetary Fund—to give more say to the increasingly important economies outside the West.

FOCUS QUESTIONS

- Why and how did the relationship between western Europe and the United States change after the end of the cold war?

- What forces raised new questions about the effectiveness of Western-style democracy by the early years of the twenty-first century?

- How did the changes bound up with globalization affect identities in the West?

- What questions emerged as the West faced new crises all over the globe after the end of the cold war?

 This icon will direct you to additional materials on the website: www .cengage.com/history/ noble/westciv6e.

 See our interactive eBook for map and primary source activities.

Group of 20 (G-20) Informal grouping of twenty major economies, including a number from outside the West.

Group of Seven (G-7) This informal association of the world's seven largest economic powers (the United States, Japan, Germany, France, Britain, Italy, and Canada) began meeting during the 1970s in an effort to coordinate economic policies.

The turn to a new international economic order reflected the impact of the globalization process that, through the free flow of goods, credit, and currency, was drawing ever more of the world into a single competitive market economy. At the same time, however, a backlash against globalization had been growing since the later 1990s. Because the economic crisis seemed to demonstrate globalization's risks and dangers, it led to more insistent calls for financial controls and trade barriers to insulate national economies. So even as the G-20 summit meetings seemed to constitute a coordinated global response to the crisis, they also provoked fears and protests around the world.

At its two meetings, the G-20 sought to resist antiglobalization pressures by agreeing to promote still freer international trade. It also called for greater global uniformity in financial regulation and accounting standards. But even as national leaders sought to act in concert at these international meetings, they tended to go their own way on the national level, partly because the countries of the world found themselves caught up in the crisis in quite different ways. Some, like the United States, were net debtors, owing more to others than others owed to them. Others, like China, were net creditors. Some, like Germany, were more dependent on exports than were others, like France. Some were better able—or more willing—to stimulate their economies through deficit spending, itself a form of borrowing, and one that might threaten inflation down the road. Especially in light of such differences, the question was whether so large and heterogeneous a grouping as the G-20 could act effectively to coordinate responses to the economic crisis.

The economic crisis developed from within the wider new international framework that had emerged after the end of the cold war. That framework had quickly come to entail ethnic conflict in parts of Europe and tensions within the Western alliance. The former communist countries scrambled to institute Western-style democratic capitalism, and many of them were accepted into the European Union (EU) during the first decade of the twenty-first century. But even in the established Western democracies, unprecedented economic, technological, and demographic change raised new questions, some of which threatened the political consensus that had crystallized since World War II.

Quite apart from its economic effects, globalization seemed to make the world more unified and homogeneous, yet the backlash against it included the embrace of traditional cultural expressions, such as the headscarf worn by many Muslim women in Europe. But that backlash also included violence and terrorism. And it raised new questions about cultural pluralism, assimilation, and the meaning of citizenship all over the Western world.

THE CHANGING INTERNATIONAL FRAMEWORK AFTER THE COLD WAR

Why and how did the relationship between western Europe and the United States change after the end of the cold war?

The disintegration of the Soviet system by 1991 meant the swift, unexpected end of the bipolar cold war framework that had defined the era since World War II (see **Map 30.1**). An immediate and troubling outcome was renewed ethnic conflict in parts of Europe. Although Czechoslovakia divided peacefully into two nations, the Czech and Slovak Republics, on January 1, 1993, ethnic concerns elsewhere produced violence and massive human rights violations. Violence also found expression in increased international terrorism by the early twenty-first century. Efforts to address the unforeseen problems of the post–cold war world raised questions about the respective roles of multinational entities, such as NATO, the EU, and the UN.

New Power Relationships in the West

Although its role was less clear with the end of the Soviet threat, NATO began expanding in 1999 to encompass most of the former communist states of eastern Europe, from Poland to Bulgaria. To those countries, NATO membership meant the definitive repudiation of the cold war division of Europe.

Whereas the collapse of communism meant renewed pride and independence for the former satellite states, Russia initially felt humiliated as a onetime superpower that was now diminished in size, struggling economically, and was far less influential in world affairs. Russian leaders disliked the expansion of NATO, and they grew belligerent when, by 2008, NATO seemed poised to admit countries like Georgia and Ukraine, which had been part of the Soviet Union itself. As the Russians saw it, NATO had always been directed at Russia, and its expansion towards Russia could only threaten Russian security.

Germany, which promptly reunified as communism collapsed, seemed a major beneficiary of the end of the cold war. Whereas some worried that the new Germany might return to bullying and aggressiveness, others were eager to have Germany assume a stronger diplomatic and even military role, and thus, the responsibilities commensurate with its population and economic strength.

The Federal Republic officially moved its capital from provincial Bonn to Berlin in 1999, when a costly makeover of the old parliament (Reichstag) building had been completed. As it happened, precisely as the refurbished building was opened, German forces were involved in their first combat roles since World War II, participating in NATO air strikes in response to what seemed genocidal aggression in Yugoslavia. Still, though Germany contributed significantly to international peacekeeping efforts, many Germans remained reluctant to support an expanded international military role. German military spending remained low compared with that of the United States, Britain, and France.

The European Union

As the **European Union (EU)** continued to expand by the early twenty-first century, it became clear that it constituted one of the notable experiments in Western history. Though still very much in progress, that experiment had produced a complex web of institutional arrangements that was bizarre and complex in one sense, bold and innovative in another.

RENEWING THE UNION

After the oil crises of the 1970s, and amid concern over economic stagnation, the twelve members of the European Community committed themselves in 1985 to creating a true single market with genuinely free competition by the end of 1992. Meeting at Maastricht, in the Netherlands, in 1991, leaders of the member countries agreed to a new "Treaty on European Union," which,

CHRONOLOGY

October 3, 1990	Reunification of Germany
1991	Beginning of fighting in Yugoslavia
February 1992	Maastricht agreements signed, expanding scope of European Union
December 14, 1996	Bosnian peace accords signed
May 1997	Blair becomes prime minister of Britain
1998	UN establishes international criminal court in The Hague
1999	Euro launched as currency of European Union
	NATO bombing of Serbia in response to Serb policies in Kosovo
	Renewal of Russia's war with Chechnya
May 2000	Putin becomes president of Russia
2001	Milosevic put on trial for war crimes at The Hague
September 11, 2001	Terrorist attacks on United States
March–April 2003	U.S.- and British-led forces overthrow Saddam Hussein's regime in Iraq
September 2003	WTO meeting in Cancún, Mexico, breaks up amid protests
2004	EU adds ten new member countries, for a total of twenty-five
March 11, 2004	Terrorist bombings on commuter trains in Madrid
May–June 2005	EU draft constitution rejected in referenda in France and the Netherlands
July 7, 2005	Terrorist attack on the London public transportation system
October–November 2005	Riots by Muslim youth in Paris and other French cities
November 2005	Angela Merkel becomes German chancellor
2007	Beginnings of global finacial crisis
May 2007	Sarkozy becomes president of France
August 2008	Russia defeats Georgia in conflict over breakaway border regions
January 2009	Obama becomes U.S. president

🌐 **Map 30.1—Europe in the Early Twenty-First Century**

The reunification of Germany and the breakup of the Soviet Union, Yugoslavia, and Czechoslovakia fundamentally altered the map of Europe during the 1990s.

European Union (EU)
New name for the European Community after the Maastricht agreements of 1991. As of 2008, it consisted of twenty-seven member countries.

Maastricht agreements
1991 agreements among member states of the European Union. They agreed to expand cooperation on social, foreign, judicial, and security matters and adopted a timetable for common economic policies.

among other things, provided for a common policy on workers' rights and a common currency and central banking structure by 1999. Although the EU's members eventually ratified most of the **Maastricht agreements**, member countries could opt out of certain provisions. Even as the new common currency, the **euro**, was introduced in two major steps, in 1999 and 2002, four of the now-fifteen EU members, including Britain, remained outside the common currency mechanism. Still, the common currency facilitated a notable increase in supranational mergers and takeovers—a trend that threatened some, but promised greater international competitiveness for European firms.

So successful was the EU that others clamored to join. The EU added ten new member countries in 2004, and then two more in 2007, increasing the membership to twenty-seven. Ten of these twelve new members were formerly communist countries, where the lure of membership had significantly strengthened democracy. The EU had insisted on democratic institutions and alignment with EU procedures as a condition of membership. And just as EU membership had helped transform the economies of once-poor countries like Greece, Ireland, Spain, and Portugal, the new members from east-central Europe seemed poised to profit economically as well.

STRUCTURE AND ORGANIZATION

euro The common currency launched by the European Union in 1999 and 2002 to eliminate the cost of currency exchange and boost trade and economic interaction.

By the early twenty-first century, the EU included a network of five interlocking institutions, seated in Brussels, Strasbourg, Luxembourg, and Frankfurt. Much of its power was wielded by an unelected elite of technical experts in the EU's core body, the Commission in Brussels. Thus, critics charged that the EU suffered from a "democratic deficit," but defenders countered that only insofar as it was apolitical could the Commission pursue the wider interests of the community, rather than merely representing national interests.

By the early twenty-first century, "Europe" had become a kind of hybrid, at once a collection of sovereign states and a genuinely supranational entity, thanks to the gradual, incremental emergence

The Democratic Reichstag, Berlin The centerpiece of the renovation of the German parliament building, completed in 1999, was the addition of a glass dome, intended to manifest the openness of Germany's democracy as its capital moved from Bonn to Berlin. (Reimer Wulf/akg-images)

of the EU over more than fifty years. In spheres such as trade, agriculture, and the environment, the EU was dominant; national governments had little freedom of action. But other spheres, such as defense, taxation, and criminal justice, remained mostly national prerogatives. The question was whether the EU would continue to expand its sphere of competence—and in what directions.

The creation of an internal customs union, benign though it seemed, had never committed the EU to freer trade with nonmember countries—the United States, for example, or the developing nations of the non-Western world. Indeed, 40 percent of EU spending by 2008 went to the widely criticized **Common Agricultural Policy (CAP)**, entailing subsidies to protect farmers from outside competition. Political opposition to change remained strong, especially in France, which, by 2008, was receiving twice as much from these subsidies as any other EU member.

Especially with expansion coming in 2004, it seemed essential that the EU clarify and streamline its procedures through a formal constitution. But the EU's momentum was unexpectedly halted when, in May 2005, French voters rejected the EU's new draft constitution in a referendum. Voters in the Netherlands followed suit shortly thereafter. Most of the EU's member states required approval only by their elected parliaments, and such approval had, for the most part, been readily forthcoming. But the setbacks in France and the Netherlands indicated doubts and frustrations that could be found throughout Europe. Some felt that the recent expansion had itself been too radical a step, especially as discussion continued over further expansion to include, for example, Turkey, Albania, and Ukraine. Concerns about economic well-being were also at work; some worried that the recent eastward expansion of the EU had intensified competition from lower-wage countries, leading to downward pressures on living standards at home.

With the Lisbon Treaty of December 2007, the EU made a second try at systematic reorganization. If ratified, the treaty would, among other things, provide for a president and a foreign minister to represent the EU in world affairs. Although the vast majority of the members approved the Lisbon Treaty, Irish voters rejected it in June 2008. Efforts to reach a compromise followed, but the future of the Lisbon Treaty remained uncertain.

Common Agricultural Policy (CAP) A major pillar of the European Union, it entailed subsidies to protect farmers from outside competition. The CAP was widely criticized by advocates of freer world trade.

THE CONSTITUTION AND NEW MEMBER STATES

Ethnic Conflict and Peacekeeping Roles

As the members of the European Union struggled to create a supranational entity, forces in the opposite direction—subnational, religious, ethnic, tribal—grew more powerful in parts of the West, sometimes producing violent conflict. The most dramatic instance was in postcommunist

🌐 MAP 30.2—Ethnic Conflict in the Balkans and East-Central Europe

Much of east-central Europe, and particularly the Balkans, has long been an area of complex ethnic mixture. The end of communist rule opened the way to ethnic conflict, most tragically in what had been Yugoslavia. This map shows ethnic distribution in the region in the mid-1990s.

Yugoslavia, where ethnic and religious conflict led to the disintegration of the country in a series of brutal wars among Serbs, Croats, Bosnian Muslims, and ethnically Albanian Kosovars (see **MAP 30.2**). Defining events of the 1990s, these wars proved a major challenge for the new international order after the cold war.

THE WAR IN BOSNIA   Although much was made of ancient ethnic and religious differences once Yugoslavia began falling apart, the area had long traditions of pluralism and tolerance. Ethnic relations had been poisoned, however, by recent events, especially the civil war during World War II (see page 811). The situation had remained reasonably stable under Josip Tito's independent communist regime, which insisted on Yugoslav unity while affording some measure of regional autonomy. But within a few years of Tito's death in 1980, intellectuals concerned about cultural distinctiveness began undermining the wider Yugoslav identity that Tito had sought to foster.

After the fall of communism, Slovenia and Croatia declared themselves independent of Yugoslavia in May 1991. At the same time, the Serb leader of the remaining Yugoslavia, Slobodan Milosevic (mih-LOH-suh-vitch) (1941–2006), a former communist, embraced Serb nationalism at least partly to maintain his own power. His aim was to unite all the Serbs, two million of whom lived outside Serbia, mostly in Croatia and Bosnia-Herzegovina.

Starting in 1991, Milosevic proceeded with extreme brutality, fostering **ethnic cleansing**—forced relocation or mass killing to rid the territory in question of non-Serb inhabitants. In the Bosnian capital, Sarajevo, a culturally diverse city known for its tolerant, cosmopolitan atmosphere, more than 10,000 civilians, including 1,500 children, were killed by shelling and sniper fire during a Serb siege from 1992 to early 1996.

When a Serb mortar killed thirty-seven civilians in a marketplace in Sarajevo in August 1995, NATO forces responded with air strikes that led to peace accords and the end of fighting by early 1996. Although the peace agreement envisioned a unified Bosnian state, the contending Serbs, Croats, and Bosnian Muslims quickly began carving out separate spheres, violating agreements about repatriation and the rights of minorities. Even over a decade later, Bosnia remained ethnically divided and dependent on the international peacekeeping force stationed there.

ethnic cleansing An effort, through forced relocation or even mass killing, to remove an unwanted ethnic group from a particular geographical area. This tactic was implemented by Yugoslavian ruler Slobodan Milosevic to unite all Serbs.

THE WAR IN KOSOVO

The next phase of the Yugoslav tragedy centered on the province of Kosovo (KOH-suh-voh), which Serbs viewed as the cradle of their nationhood (see **MAP 30.2**). For complex historical reasons, however, Serbs had long constituted only a minority of its population. The majority were ethnic Albanians. The fissuring of Yugoslavia emboldened the Kosovars, who had come to envision full independence, as opposed to mere autonomy within the Serbian part of what remained of Yugoslavia.

When Milosevic struck against the Kosovars in the spring of 1999, ruthlessly pursuing ethnic cleansing, the Western powers again intervened, first convening a meeting with Serb and Kosovar leaders on Kosovo's future. When the Serb-led remnant of Yugoslavia refused to sign, NATO made good on its threats to bomb Serbia in retaliation. The bombing, concentrated on such economic targets as bridges and power stations, continued for eleven weeks in late 1999.

Critics argued that it set a dubious precedent to attack Serbia for refusing a settlement that would have ceded territory and opened the rest of the country to quasi-occupation by NATO. No one denied that Kosovo was part of Serbia, so the NATO action was an overt interference in the internal affairs of a sovereign state. Even the notion that the operation was a humanitarian response to genocide seemed hypocritical to some, who asked why the international community had done nothing in response to the far more systematic genocide in the African nation of Rwanda in 1994, when 800,000 people had been killed in a hundred days. Defenders countered that it was partly because of the soul-searching in the aftermath of Rwanda that the Western countries were now changing the rules and taking responsibility for concerted action.

Once the NATO bombing began, the Serbs intensified their ethnic cleansing of Kosovo, burning homes, forcing 800,000 refugees to flee into neighboring countries. But the bombing finally led both the Serbs and the Kosovars to pull back from their more extreme demands, and Russia joined in the multinational peacekeeping force in Kosovo in the aftermath. Still, the outcome bore little relationship to the multiethnic pluralism NATO had been seeking. As Kosovars came to dominate the now-ravaged territory, still nominally part of Serbia, they carried out ethnic cleansing of their own. Ethnic Albanians came to constitute over 90 percent of Kosovo's 2 million people, and ethnic separation became the rule. Finally, in February 2008, Kosovo declared its independence. Most of the world quickly recognized the new state, even in the face of fierce opposition from Serbia and Russia.

WAR CRIMES TRIALS

Although Milosevic was the first sitting head of state to be indicted for war crimes, he proved resilient, initially surviving his defeat in Kosovo in 1999. He lost the presidential election in September 2000, however, and the following year, under pressure from the international community, the Serbian government within the rump Yugoslav confederation turned him over to a UN war crimes tribunal in The Hague. There, as his trial dragged on, he died in prison in 2006.

Others accused of war crimes were the Bosnian Serb leader Radovan Karadžić (KA-rahdzich) and his top general, Ratko Mladic (MLAH-ditch), who was charged with the slaughter of as many as 8,000 Bosnian Muslim men when his forces took the town of Srebrenica (shreb-reh-NEET-sah) in 1995. Even after their indictments, each long evaded capture, partly because they were deemed heroes by many Serbs. Finally, however, Karadžić was apprehended and went on trial in The Hague in 2008. Like Milosevic, he denied the legitimacy of the court and refused to cooperate in its proceedings.

Mourning in Bosnia On July 11, 2009, a Muslim woman mourns by the grave of a relative during the reburial of 534 newly identified victims of the massacre of up to 8,000 Muslim men by Bosnian Serb forces at Srebrenica in 1995. Each year on July 11, the anniversary of the massacre, bones excavated from mass graves are matched to a name and reburied at the nearby Memorial Center of Potocari. As of the 2009 ceremony, over 4,000 of the victims had been reburied at the Memorial Center. (Damir Sagolj/Reuters/Landov)

Terror in New York City, September 11, 2001 With one of the twin towers of the World Trade Center burning from an attack at 8:45 A.M., a second hijacked plane crashed into the second tower less than an hour later. By the end of the morning, both towers had collapsed. (Chao Soi Cheong/AP/Wide World Photos)

Responding to Global Terrorism

Also complicating international relations was an increase in the scale and extent of terrorism, sometimes pitting non-Western-ers against the West. European venues ranged from Northern Ireland to the Basque region of northern Spain to the rebellious Russian republic of Chechnya to the subways of London.

With this new terror already erupting, a terrorist attack of unprecedented proportions shook the United States on September 11, 2001. Suicide hijackers seized four large airliners, crashing one into each of the towers of the World Trade Center in New York City and another into the Pentagon, just outside Washington, D.C. Passengers on the fourth plane, apparently also headed for Washington, forced it to crash in Pennsylvania. The World Trade Center crashes collapsed both towers, which had been among the world's most visible landmarks. The coor-dinated attacks claimed the lives of over three thousand people from eighty-two countries.

The United States proclaimed this assault an act of war, and the NATO alliance invoked Article 5 for the first time: The attack on one of its members was to be treated as an attack against all. U.S. leaders promptly assigned responsibility to al Qaeda, an international terrorist network led by the wealthy Saudi Arabian Osama bin Laden, who was living in exile in Afghanistan. There, he and others of his network were protected by the Taliban regime, whose extreme, radically fundamentalist version of Islam they shared in certain respects.

Led by President George W. Bush, the United States initiated military action against the Taliban regime later in 2001. Several weeks of U.S. bombing enabled Afghan opposition forces to oust the Taliban government and force al Qaeda onto the defensive. But both bin Laden and the Taliban survived, and the outcome in Afghanistan remained uncertain as of 2009. Al Qaeda regrouped sufficiently to launch terrorist attacks against Western interests in Morocco in 2002 and Saudi Arabia in 2003. Then, in March 2004, the network struck in Europe for the first time with a series of terrorist bombings on commuter trains in Madrid, killing over 200 people.

But terror could be bred in Western countries as well. The four terrorists who blew themselves up on the London public transportation system in July 2005, killing 52 others, were British citizens, Muslims of Pakistani descent, acting on their own. Whatever its sources, such terrorism posed an ongoing threat to Western security and complicated the West's relations with the non-Western world.

Divisions Over the Invasion of Iraq

The United States won widespread support for its effort to combat international terrorism. But the Americans encountered formidable opposition in 2002 when the Bush administration began to call for the overthrow of Saddam Hussein's regime in Iraq. The Iraqi dictator was charged with stockpiling chemical and biological weapons of mass destruction in violation of a UN agreement. Iraq was also accused of developing a nuclear weapons program and supporting terrorist networks like al Qaeda. Moreover, Saddam had long tyrannized the Iraqi people.

As it began to appear that the United States might be prepared to act unilaterally, the Iraq issue became one of the most divisive in recent history, seriously straining Western relations. An array of countries, with France, Germany, and Russia in the forefront, insisted that UN weapons inspectors be given more time to assess Iraqi compliance. Yet the American call for military action won a good deal of international support. Most notably, British prime minister Tony Blair made Britain a full partner of the United States. But even in countries like Britain, whose governments supported U.S. policy, the public tended to be strongly opposed to a military showdown in Iraq.

When it became clear they could not win UN endorsement, the United States and Britain sent military forces into Iraq in March 2003 and toppled Saddam Hussein's regime within six weeks. In the aftermath of the invasion, it had gradually become clear that Iraq had not been actively developing weapons of mass destruction. In addition, evidence suggested that both the U.S. and British governments had relied to some extent on faulty intelligence or had used intelligence selectively to justify the invasion.

The military success proved easier than most people had expected, but the tasks of reconstruction proved far more difficult than U.S. officials had envisioned, especially because an anti-occupation insurgency developed after the United States declared active hostilities ended on May 1, 2003. Sectarian and ethnic violence seriously complicated the effort of Iraqi leaders to develop a workable new government.

A "surge" in U.S. troop strength in 2007 helped reduce the violence, and in November 2008, the Iraqi parliament approved a troop withdrawal agreement with the United States. American forces were to withdraw to bases by the middle of 2009 and to leave Iraq altogether by the end of 2011. Whereas some found this outcome a vindication of the invasion, critics argued that America was being forced to leave, and that the outcome was not likely to be the unified, democratic, and stable Iraq that President Bush had said was the American aim. One possibility was a return to sectarian violence, which might spill over, inflaming religious and ethnic divisions in much of the Middle East. At the same time, the war had been hugely costly to all parties. As one measure, two million Iraqis had fled their country as refugees since 2003.

U.S. Unilateralism

A major source of friction between the United States and Europe was growing U.S. **unilateralism**— the country's willingness to go its own way in the world on the basis of what seemed its own interests. As the world's superpower, the United States was increasingly prone to such unilateralism during the 1990s, and then moved more decisively in that direction after the terrorist attacks of September 2001.

While an overwhelming majority of nations—120, to be exact—supported the establishment of the UN's International Criminal Court in The Hague in 1998, the United States was among only seven that opposed it. Then, as the court was being established, the United States sought an exemption for itself because it worried that American peacekeepers might be especially tempting targets of false accusations of war crimes. Such concerns were not groundless, and

unilateralism Term describing the increasing willingness of the United States to go its own way in world affairs after the end of the cold war, and especially after the terrorist attacks on the United States in September 2001.

they indicated the unique problems the United States faced as the world's undisputed, and often resented, superpower. But many found it disturbing that the United States did not want to play by the same rules as the vast majority.

SECTION SUMMARY

- The end of the cold war opened the way to a series of new issues that the West had to confront, even as it also changed power relationships within the West itself.

- The European Union expanded and gathered strength, but also encountered unforeseen setbacks.

- Ethnic conflict contributed to the breakup of Yugoslavia in a series of wars that included major human rights violations and significant dilemmas for peacekeepers.

- International terrorism, often reflecting tensions between the West and the Islamic world, became a major concern throughout the West.

- Increasing U.S. unilateralism, evident most dramatically in the U.S.-led invasion of Iraq, alienated many Europeans.

Some Europeans continued to look to the UN to check American hegemony, but others, including many non-Europeans, found a stronger European military and diplomatic presence the best potential balance to the United States. EU forces were prominent in peacekeeping missions in Macedonia, Bosnia, Kosovo, Afghanistan, and Congo. Yet the Europeans were much less willing than Americans to use force in the first place. As of early 2006, the United States was spending 3.4 percent of its gross domestic product (GDP) on defense, Europe 1.9 percent.

Still, some observers noted the scope for the United States and Europe to play complementary roles in world affairs. Americans were better at fighting wars, but Europeans might be better at preventing them. Precisely because they were not prone to threaten force, Europeans could play a constructive role of moral suasion, even if it was up to the Americans to provide the muscle.

Many Europeans welcomed the election of Barack Obama to the U.S. presidency in November 2008 because he seemed likely to adopt a more conciliatory and less unilateralist stance. But how, more specifically, Obama might renew or deepen the partnership between the United States and Europe remained to be seen.

GLOBALIZATION AND THE UNCERTAINTIES OF DEMOCRATIC CAPITALISM

What forces raised new questions about the effectiveness of Western style democracy by the early years of the twenty-first century?

Democracy had become the unchallenged norm in western Europe by the 1980s, and after the fall of communism, the former Soviet bloc countries seemed eager to adopt the western European model. But though patterns in several of the former communist countries came to approximate those of the mature democracies, the transition proved problematic in others, most dramatically in Russia. Even in the established democracies, globalization combined with technological and demographic changes to alter the socioeconomic framework, producing new challenges for governments and even threatening the socioeconomic compact that had emerged after World War II.

The Postcommunist Experiment

The former communist countries had little experience with the give-and-take of democratic politics, and their fragile new political systems had to engineer the difficult transition to a free-market economy. With their economies close to chaos as the transition began, the effort led to unemployment, inflation, and widespread corruption. No longer could ordinary people count on the subsidized consumer goods or the welfare safety net the communist regimes had provided. While many suffered great hardship, some former communist functionaries quickly got rich by taking over state-owned companies.

The case of Poland showed that strains and risks remained, even within the new framework of democratic governance and market economy. Although GDP grew by 50 percent from 1990 to 2005, as Poland attracted considerable foreign investment, the costs were high for those left out. In 2006, unemployment stood at 18 percent, ever more people were falling into poverty, and the gap between rich and poor was widening. The state was widely seen as weak, bloated, inefficient, and highly corrupt. Services were poor, and the tax system was full of loopholes. Low electoral turnouts manifested widespread disillusionment with the new political class—and even doubts about democracy itself.

🌐 MAP 30.3—GDP per Capita in Europe, 2008

Gross domestic product (GDP) per capita is a widely recognized measure of national economic success. By the early twenty first century, this measure varied dramatically among the European countries, revealing the wide disparity in economic well-being across the Continent. The former communist countries continued to lag, even as some were growing at impressive rates. The U.S. figure was $42,000, and Canada's was $32,900. (Figures are from 2008, before the worst of the economic crisis.)

In Russia, where communism had far deeper roots than elsewhere in the former Soviet bloc, the transition from communism proved even more difficult. Although privatization proceeded rapidly, it mostly benefited former Communist Party functionaries, some of whom became instant multimillionaires. By the mid-1990s, Russia had evolved a kind of "crony capitalism," with a small group of economic oligarchs manipulating much of the economy through dubious banking practices and outright extortion—and paying no taxes. After ten years, the postcommunist Russian economy had shrunk to perhaps half its former size. Especially sobering were the demographic effects: Russians were dying young and having few children. By 2001, the population had dropped to 143 million—a decline of 6 million people in ten years.

The combination of economic stringency and governmental weakness produced a chilling increase in street crime, from muggings to auto theft. Moreover, dozens of journalists, politicians, and business leaders were murdered gangland style, with the killers never apprehended. Particularly appalling was the 2006 assassination of the highly respected journalist Anna Politkovskaya (po-lit-koff-SKY-ah), who was killed in broad daylight, with her body left in the elevator of her apartment. In November 2008, the trial of three men suspected of involvement in her murder was suspended amid deepening controversy.

As Russia's president during the first postcommunist years, Boris Yeltsin seemed a committed reformer—surely the best hope for an orderly transition to democracy and a market economy. He enjoyed widespread support from the Western democracies, but among Russians, the difficult circumstances produced disenchantment with reform, nostalgia for the stability of communism, and much resentment of the West.

As it sought to engineer the transition to democratic capitalism, the Yeltsin government had to deal with the attempted defection of Chechnya (CHECH-nyah), a small, largely Muslim republic located in the Caucasus (see **Map 29.3** on page 848). Long restive under Russian control, the Chechens began demanding independence after the collapse of the Soviet Union in 1991, finally provoking war with Russia in 1994. In the aftermath of a compromise in 1996, Chechen hard-liners oppressed the Russian minority, kidnapping and enslaving some, and even killed journalists and international aid workers. When Chechnyan Islamic militants began spreading the anti-Russian message to adjacent Dagestan, Russia renewed full-scale war with Chechnya in 1999.

This renewed confrontation made possible the rise of **Vladimir Putin** (POO-tin), who had been director of Russia's secret police. Calling for a tough stance on Chechnya, Putin was Yeltsin's choice for prime minister in 1999, and he immediately delivered on his promise to clear Dagestan of Chechen terrorists. Whereas most Russians had disliked the earlier confrontation with Chechnya, by now they had had enough—not only of Chechen defiance, but also of Russian weakness. Putin's popularity soared as he talked tough and acted tougher. A brutal Russian assault late in 1999 left much of Chechnya, especially the capital, Grozny, in ruins.

In poor health and increasingly erratic, Yeltsin resigned at the end of 1999, essentially to make way for Putin, who was elected president in 2000, and then reelected in 2004. Although Putin was prohibited by law from running again in 2008, his hand-picked successor, Dmitry Medvedev (med-VYEH-dev), was elected easily, and Putin continued to wield power from his new post as prime minister.

As Russia's leader, Putin strengthened the Russian state against the forces of disintegration that emerged after communism, and he remained quite popular among Russians. Still, outside observers tended to give his performance decidedly mixed marks. In the economic sphere, the post-Soviet decline seemed at last to have been reversed by 2006, thanks in part to high prices for Russia's abundant oil and gas. Tax collection had improved, some well-run companies had emerged, and the Russian middle class was clearly expanding. But the political order suffered from secrecy and governmental inaccessibility. The media were increasingly concentrated and subject to restrictions and controls.

To counter demographic decline, Putin's government sought to promote a baby boom. A 2007 law expanded maternity leave benefits and granted mothers educational and other vouchers for a second child and for any children thereafter. Putin also increased spending on health and social programs. But more important, the economic upturn made child rearing a more plausible option for Russian couples. Still, though births began rising after 2006, deaths continued to outpace births, and Russian life expectancy was the lowest in Europe. Some demographic experts warned that because the number of women of childbearing age was still to decline, Russia was caught in a "demographic pit" that would be hard to escape.

Stinging from Russia's post-Soviet weakness, a considerable majority of Russians supported Putin as he sought to establish a Russian sphere of influence and to win international acceptance as a major international player. In the summer of 2008, a showdown between Russia and Georgia, a small, former Soviet republic (see **Map 30.1**), over two breakaway Georgian provinces produced controversy over Russia's place in the new international order.

Vladimir Putin Emerged in 1999 to become Russia's dominant political leader.

Under Vladimir Putin, Russia was sometimes aggressive in seeking to establish a leading role in a number of the states that were formerly part of the Soviet Union. Russian relations with Ukraine were particularly rocky as Ukraine angled for membership in NATO and even, eventually, the European Union. Putin is shown here speaking informally with Ukrainian prime minister Yulia Tymoshenko at a meeting of many of the former Soviet republics at Chisinau, the capital of Moldova, on November 14, 2008. (Alexei Nikolsky/RIA Novosti/Reuters/Landov)

After becoming independent with the breakup of the Soviet Union, Georgia developed close ties with the United States, especially after U.S.-educated Mikheil Saakashvili (sah-kahsh-VEE-lee) was elected president in 2004. As of August 2008, Georgia had 2,000 troops in Iraq, making it the third largest contributor to the coalition, after the United States and Britain. Georgia aspired to NATO membership, as did the much larger former Soviet republic of Ukraine, yet Russian authorities repeatedly asserted that they would not accept NATO membership for either. Still, Georgia and Ukraine were now sovereign states, in principle, free to make their own decisions about international alignments and foreign policy.

Dispute over NATO membership lay in the background as a confrontation between Russia and Georgia developed over the status of Abkhazia and South Ossetia, provinces that, though nominally part of Georgia, had never effectively been incorporated into the country after it became independent. Populated largely by ethnic groups that were neither Georgian nor Russian, both provinces sought to break definitively from Georgia. They looked for support to Russia, which warned repeatedly that it would send troops to block any Georgian effort to encompass the two provinces.

When Saakashvili used force against South Ossetia in July 2008, the Russians intervened as promised, quickly routing Georgia's troops early in August. Saakashvili seemed to have anticipated active support from the West, especially the United States, but the Americans were already involved in difficult wars in Afghanistan and Iraq, and it was not clear what more forceful response would have been possible in any case. So Georgia had to settle for strong protests against Russian belligerence from the United States and its NATO allies.

Other countries that had been part of the Soviet empire, especially Ukraine, but also the Baltic states and Poland, watched nervously, asking themselves what support they could expect from the West in the event of some comparable Russian threat. To be sure, those like Poland and the Baltic states that were now NATO members faced what seemed a very different situation. Still, the Poles and even the Czechs were eager to accept a U.S. missile shield, even in the face of Russian opposition, because of nervousness about the scope for renewed Russian expansionism.

Russia had clearly drawn a line over Georgia, but how far might its ambitions go? For some, Russia's belligerence suggested a return to cold war aspirations, but now with naked national self-interest replacing even the pretense of ideological aims. Especially at a time of record oil prices and growing concerns in the West over long-term sources of energy, Russia seemed to be returning to the struggle for spheres of influence and control of resources that had characterized the nineteenth century.

But others accented Russia's defensiveness. It was not unreasonable, they insisted, for Russia to worry that NATO expansion threatened Russian security, even that the presence of NATO on Russia's borders could destabilize the Russian Confederation itself. Moreover, the Russians had a plausible case in arguing that if the West was to allow Kosovo to break way from Serbia, it should also be prepared to allow the dissident provinces to break away from Georgia.

Two Models of Democratic Capitalism

By the 1980s, much of western Europe had caught up with the United States in standard of living, and it was increasingly clear that two models of democratic capitalism were at work—and to some extent in competition. The U.S. model, largely shared by Britain since the Thatcher period (see page 832), stressed free enterprise and the market, whereas continental western Europe had evolved a **social market economy,** with greater commitment to security, consensus, and communitarian values. The European model provided a more substantial safety net—in health care, for example—as well as a stronger commitment to subsidized transportation and day care.

In some respects, it was almost as if the Americans and Europeans had passed in the night in the decades since World War II. In the United States, which had long prided itself on its egalitarianism vis-à-vis class-bound Europe, disparities between rich and poor had become greater than anywhere in the developed world by the early twenty-first century. In business firms, the ratio of executive compensation to worker salaries was dramatically higher in the United States than in Europe.

Perhaps still more significant was the difference in attitudes toward such disparities. Wary of extreme inequalities of income, Europeans tended to view unrestricted competition more as a threat than an opportunity. Whereas most Europeans found the inequalities and insecurities of American life unacceptable, Americans accented the scope for upward mobility that their

social market economy A model of democratic capitalism, practiced in much of continental Europe, that seeks to temper free-market principles with communitarian values and a substantial social safety net.

system offered. As long as anyone could get rich, it did not matter that some were much richer than others. Americans were far more likely than Europeans to see themselves as moving up. In France, 75 percent of young people aspired to a civil service job, primarily because of the security such a job seemed to entail.

Americans had grown more skeptical than Europeans about government and its capacity to provide social services. Accustomed to a strong government role in society, Europeans had difficulty understanding how such measures as government-sponsored health care could cause waves of controversy among Americans.

New Economic Competitors

Just as the West became concerned with economic challenges from the Soviet Union in the 1950s, Japan by the later 1970s, and a wider array of East Asian "tigers" by the 1980s, it came to view China, and to a lesser extent India, as potential economic superpowers by the early twenty-first century. Although still nominally communist, China was increasingly willing to compete in the global economic marketplace and did well at manufacturing, thanks especially to a cheap, disciplined labor force. With its favorable trade balance, China came to hold such a large share of the U.S. national debt that it seemed capable, at least potentially, of compromising the independence of American foreign policy.

The former communist countries of east-central Europe proved tremendously appealing to manufacturing companies in the West, especially automakers. Although the communist system had not proved competitive over the long term, it had left a reasonably good infrastructure, as well as a skilled and disciplined labor force costing only about 20 percent as much as elsewhere in the EU. By 2006, major carmakers in France, Germany, and Italy were being forced to cut jobs and benefits at home in order to remain competitive. But it was not only the new EU members that were attracting such investment. Volkswagen was building new plants in Russia and China. Some were predicting that auto manufacture in western Europe would cease altogether in ten to fifteen years.

Responding to New Economic Challenges

As global economic competition intensified, governments throughout western Europe found it more difficult to pay for all the benefits they had gradually come to promise. By the early 1990s, some found the social compact all too generous—and unsustainable. Falling birthrates and aging populations meant that relatively fewer workers would have to foot the pension and health care bills for increasing numbers of older people. Although most agreed that reform was necessary, reform proposals led to protests, and governments found it difficult to address the problem.

Even with the renewed prosperity of the 1980s, unemployment in western Europe reached levels not seen since the Great Depression. During the 1990s, high unemployment persisted in much of Europe, even as it declined to postwar lows in the United States. The difference reflected differences in the structure of labor markets, which gave the U.S. economy greater flexibility. As a result of laws, labor agreements, and the postwar consensus now in place, European workers who had jobs were more secure than their American counterparts. But European employers were less able to adapt to changing conditions by laying off workers or hiring new ones with different skills. In this area, too, government reform efforts provoked strenuous protests in Europe.

Upon becoming Germany's first female chancellor in November 2005, the conservative Angela Merkel sought the measures necessary to streamline the German economy. But in light of the near dead heat in the national elections that September, she had to rely on an unstable "grand coalition" of the two largest parties—her own conservatives and the socialists. Though Merkel proved an effective international leader on several issues, her continued dependence on this coalition hampered her efforts at structural reform.

European Leaders French President Nicolas Sarkozy and German Chancellor Angela Merkel, both conservatives, proved popular, pragmatic, and highly visible leaders. Here Sarkozy welcomes Merkel as she arrives at the Elysée Palace in Paris, June 11, 2009. (Philippe Wojazer/Reuters/Landov)

Even as western Europe was finding it difficult to sustain its social market model in the face of increasing global competition, the financial crisis of 2008 led many Europeans to reaffirm the superiority of the European system. Critics charged that it was reckless borrowing and lax oversight in America that had brought the global financial system to the verge of collapse. They also noted the much higher savings rates in Europe. Whereas U.S. consumers had saved 9 percent of their disposable income from 1950 to 1985, the rate steadily declined thereafter to around zero by 2008.

As American leaders, responding to the crisis, appeared to vacillate on priorities, both French president **Nicolas Sarkozy** and British prime minister Gordon Brown sought to take the lead, especially in engineering state intervention to rescue faltering banks. Brown's strategy, especially, prompted the U.S. government to change course and follow his lead.

Nicolas Sarkozy Activist French president, from the political right, elected in 2007.

The Europeans could credibly lead in this direction because, despite a recent tendency toward privatization, they had a much stronger tradition of state intervention and ownership. At the same time, the more substantial safety net in Europe was likely to cushion the economic fall, at least up to a point. Moreover, both Sarkozy and Brown insisted that stronger and more uniform international standards of disclosure, accounting, transparency, and regulation would need to follow the present emergency measures. But it was not clear that European leadership in response to the crisis portended superior economic performance for the European system over the longer term.

Immigration, Assimilation, and Citizenship

By the first years of the new millennium, as globalization proceeded and immigration increased, concerns about national community, cultural diversity, and the meaning of citizenship were becoming central all over Europe. Although anti-immigrant politicians like Jean-Marie Le Pen in France and Jörg Haider (HY-dur) in Austria typically won only 15 to 20 percent of the vote, they articulated a wider sense among the public that immigrant communities were responsible not only for increasing crime, but also for a weakening of the common values necessary to sustain society.

The place of Muslims became especially controversial, partly because there were so many of them. Some countries did not count religion in the national census, so the number in western Europe was uncertain. Estimates ranged from 15 to 20 million, and the number was projected to grow to 15 percent of the population by 2050, because of both continued immigration and higher birthrates. But the place of Muslims caused controversy also because so many were religiously observant even as Europe, though Christian in its dominant tradition, was evidently becoming ever more secular; thus, especially, the scope for a clash of cultures.

It was striking that the Netherlands and Denmark, two small countries widely known for openness and tolerance, became flash points as controversy over the place of Muslims grew. In the Netherlands in 2004, a Dutch national of Moroccan descent brutally assassinated Theo Van Gogh for having made a film denouncing the treatment of women in Islamic societies. The screenplay was by Ayaan Hirsi Ali, a woman raised as a Muslim in Somalia, and by this point, an outspoken critic of the treatment of women by Muslim men. She was a member of the Dutch parliament, where she served from 2003 to 2006. And she herself remained under threat of death after the murder of Van Gogh.

Claiming that fears of violence against anyone perceived to be denigrating Islam were leading to self-censorship, the editor of a Danish newspaper, *Jyllands-Posten*, published twelve cartoons depicting the Islamic prophet Muhammad, one wearing a turban in the shape of a bomb, in September 2005. News of the cartoons gradually spread, provoking outrage across the Muslim world early in 2006. Scores of people were killed, and the cartoonists themselves received death threats and had to go into hiding. Any depiction of the prophet Muhammad would have offended Muslims, who traditionally have been particularly concerned to ward off idolatry, the worship of images. But Muslims found the Danish cartoons gratuitously offensive.

The largest Muslim population in western Europe was in France—by 2008 roughly 6 million, or 10 percent of the population. Many were French citizens, the second- or third-generation

Cartoon Protest On February 18, 2006, Muslims march through central London in an angry but peaceful protest against the publication in the Western press of cartoons seeming to caricature the prophet Muhammad. (AP Photos/Peter Willows)

descendants of immigrants who had begun coming to France from Algeria and other former French African colonies in the 1950s when, as the postwar economic miracle gathered force, France needed workers. But beginning in the early 1970s, jobs had become increasingly scarce.

With open citizenship central to the French self-understanding, French law accorded citizenship automatically to second-generation immigrants, on the assumption that these offspring would be readily assimilated. However, the Muslim community in France had not been well assimilated, and by the end of the 1980s, finger-pointing on all sides had begun. Whereas the French left defended cultural diversity and its compatibility with citizenship, the right complained that citizenship was being devalued as a mere convenience, requiring no real commitment to the national community. Critics, such as Le Pen, charged that many from recent immigrant families did not want to assimilate.

An especially symptomatic episode in 1989—the "affair of the scarves"—made it clear that the place of Muslims in France had become a central and volatile issue. Three teenaged Muslim girls were suspended from school on the grounds that, in wearing the traditional Muslim headscarf, they were violating a long-standing law banning religious displays in public schools. The girls insisted they were not seeking to flaunt their religion or to convert others; the point was simply that Islamic teaching required women to cover their heads in public as a sign of modesty. Yet in the eyes of some Westerners, that practice reflected the second-class status of women in Islamic civilization. To defend the right to wear the scarves was thus to condone the oppression of women.

An uncertain compromise resulted from this episode, and the issue continued to smolder as the Muslim presence in France increased. In 2004, the French National Assembly passed, by an overwhelming margin, a new law to ban conspicuous religious displays in French public schools, hospitals, and other government buildings. Although large Christian crosses and Jewish yarmulkes, or skullcaps, were also at issue, the law seemed especially to target the Muslim headscarf. The law was passed despite massive protest marches in cities throughout France and elsewhere.

Many non-Muslims supported the right of women to wear the scarf precisely on the grounds of pluralism, tolerance, and freedom of expression. Yet some of those opposing the new law sought not to preserve diversity, but to keep Muslim girls in the public schools to expose them to secular influence and to promote long-term assimilation. In the short term, they argued, any law restricting religious expression would spawn separate Islamic schools, thereby deepening the divisions already evident in France.

By the first decade of the new century, French Muslims were clustered in deteriorating high-rise ghetto suburbs ringing Paris and other cities. Whereas young Muslims were widely blamed for criminality, they themselves complained of police harassment and job discrimination. Certainly they experienced very high rates of unemployment, well over 40 percent in many areas. And thus, it was feared, they were increasingly prone to militancy or Islamic fundamentalism.

As the police sought to crack down on crime, an incident late in October 2005 provoked a riot among Muslim youth in the ghetto suburb of Clichy-sous-Bois. During the next few days, waves of looting and car-burning spread to cities throughout France. The rioting continued well into November, until the government declared a state of emergency and deployed sharply increased security forces. It was France's worst civil unrest since the Days of May in 1968 (see page 831). President Jacques Chirac admitted that the riots had dramatized problems that had to be addressed promptly. Some observers called for a form of affirmative action to bring French Muslims, or French citizens of North African descent, into positions of greater prominence in business, politics, and the media, spheres in which they were virtually absent.

In winning the French presidency in 2007, Nicolas Sarkozy promised a tough stance against illegal immigration and immigrant crime. Thus, he attracted some of the vote that had been going to Le Pen, reducing Le Pen's share to 11 percent, the lowest in twenty-five years. But once in office, Sarkozy proved pragmatic and practiced affirmative action for those with immigrant backgrounds. And though controversy had surrounded the ban on religious dress in public buildings when it went into effect in 2004, by 2008, it was widely accepted by all faiths. More generally, Muslims seemed increasingly prepared to say that they felt welcome in France, and many non-Muslims grew accustomed to having large mosques in their midst.

By the early twenty-first century, the tendency all over Europe was to push assimilation—the formation of citizens sharing the mainstream values of the national community. This meant a retreat from the multiculturalism that had been prevalent on the European left, and that had made the persistence of immigrant subcultures seem a virtue. Whereas some conflated the assimilationist impulse with racism, others insisted that, on the contrary, anyone could belong, regardless of race or ethnicity, but that belonging required adopting the dominant culture, not holding to cultural differences.

In the Netherlands, Muslims had often used the Internet to equate the country's pluralistic tolerance with mere decadence. In 2006, the Netherlands adopted a law, the first of its kind anywhere, requiring that prospective immigrants take a "civic integration examination" testing their willingness to accept the tolerant openness of Dutch culture. The chairman of a leading Dutch Muslim organization defended the measure, suggesting that all immigrants needed to be prepared to embrace modernity. It seemed significant evidence of a turning point in the Netherlands when a Moroccan-born immigrant, Ahmed Aboutaleb, was installed as mayor of Rotterdam early in 2009. He, too, insisted that immigrants must be prepared to adopt Dutch values.

SECTION SUMMARY

- Although the transition from communism to some variety of capitalism proved difficult throughout the former Soviet bloc, it proved especially problematic in Russia.

- From within the wider democratic concensus, there was a split between much of continental western Europe, with its "social market economy," and the United States, which had greater confidence in free-market capitalism and less confidence in government.

- Especially in continental western Europe, the challenges of globalization suggested the need for reforms—reforms that proved difficult to engineer through the democratic process.

- Concerns about the assimilation of immigrant communities in much of Europe raised new and volatile political issues.

LIFESTYLES AND IDENTITIES

How did the changes bound up with globalization affect identities in the West?

Even as matters of diversity and citizenship were becoming mainstream political concerns, they were very much bound up with wider issues of personal identity. And in that respect, they intersected in complex ways with other potential influences on identity, from consumerism to religion to gender.

By the mid-1960s, the remarkable postwar economic growth had created a secular, consumerist society throughout much of the West, establishing patterns of life that continued into the twenty-first century, when cell phones and personal computers were commonplace. But changing lifestyles dictated new choices, and the new affluence challenged traditional sources of personal identity in unexpected ways, producing new concerns—and sometimes conflict. Important groups of non-Westerners rejected Western secular consumerism altogether.

Supranational, National, and Subnational Identities

By the late 1980s, consumerism and the widening impact of American popular culture—from blue jeans and American TV to shopping malls and theme parks—suggested a growing homogenization in the capitalist democracies. But Americanization threatened long-standing European identities, and Europeans sometimes adopted special measures to preserve distinctiveness. The EU specified that EU television programming had to be at least 40 percent EU-made, while the French mandated that at least every third popular song played on the radio had to be French.

But were quotas and mandates really necessary to preserve distinctiveness? The American chain Starbucks, which had revolutionized the serving of coffee in the United States, found it hard to penetrate continental Europe, which had its own long traditions of coffee-making. Even as many were coming to assume that American pop culture was irresistible, it became clear that European viewers were increasingly picking local TV programming on their own, quite apart from quotas. By 2003, every EU country was well above the 40 percent minimum for local programming, with the average at 62 percent.

Meanwhile, the growing prominence of the supranational EU, and doubts about the significance of national politics, nourished a renewed premium on subnational identities in such European regions as Flanders, Corsica, Scotland, and Catalonia. Flemings and Corsicans, Scots and Catalans, actively sought to preserve some measure of their distinct cultures and languages in the face of contemporary pressures toward standardization. In Britain, Tony Blair fostered the "devolution" of powers from the central government in London to Scottish and Welsh assemblies in 1999. Those powers were limited, but a decade later, many Scots, especially, were calling for an enhanced role for their regional parliament.

National sentiment grew especially uncertain in Italy, which had had a relatively brief and problematic history as a unified nation. Although its movement for national unification had drawn widespread enthusiasm throughout the Western world in the nineteenth century (see pages 618–622), by the 1990s, disillusionment with national politics made many Italians particularly eager to embrace the EU. At the same time, some renewed their identification with region or locality. Resentful of the national government's ties to the less prosperous south, a new political movement, the Northern League, emerged during the 1990s to push for the north to become an independent nation. Whatever the seriousness of such literal separatism, the Northern League's persistent strength suggested that "Italian" had become less important as a basis of individual identity in Italy's relatively prosperous north.

Class Identities and Trade Unions

The advent of a media-driven consumerist society produced greater homogeneity of experience and taste and a corresponding de-emphasis on class as a basis of identity. One symptom was the decline of the trade-union movement, long central to working-class identity and advancement.

Changing labor patterns reinforced the decline of organized labor, which was decidedly on the defensive throughout western Europe and the United States by the 1980s. The increasing danger of unemployment undercut the leverage of the unions. And as the economy grew more complex, workers were less likely to think of themselves as members of a single, unified working class.

Still, union membership varied considerably from country to country, and some unions found new ways of exerting influence. In a survey of union membership as a percentage of the work force in twelve industrialized countries in 2001, Denmark and Sweden had the highest figures—around 80 percent. The figures for Italy, Germany, and Britain were all around 30 percent. The lowest figures were in France (10 percent) and the United States (14 percent). Despite some much publicized militancy in resisting government efforts at pension reform, the unions generally had moved beyond their earlier confrontational posture to an increasing pragmatism.

In Germany, local union councils made informal agreements with big companies that, while technically violating Germany's restrictive labor regulations, helped keep jobs in Germany. At the same time, some German-based multinational companies, such as Volkswagen, actively sought to head off trouble with German unions by agreeing to guidelines specifying how they would operate worldwide. By committing itself to giving its workers elsewhere proper pay and working conditions, as well as the right to unionize, Volkswagen was agreeing not merely to seek the lowest bidder, as globalization sometimes seemed to demand. In this respect, too, the unions were still making a difference.

Economic Growth and Environmental Concerns

The impact of rapid economic growth on the European landscape and cityscape provoked ever greater concern by the last third of the twentieth century. The number of automobiles in western Europe increased from 6 million in 1939 to 16 million by 1959 to 42 million by 1969. Almost overnight, traffic and air pollution fundamentally changed the face of Europe's old cities. In 1976, five statues that had supported the Eastern Portico of the Erectheum Temple on the Acropolis in Athens since the fifth century B.C. were replaced by replicas and put in a museum to save them from the rapid decay that air pollution was causing.

With the end of communist rule, it became obvious that the years of communism had produced environmental degradation on an appalling scale in the Soviet bloc. But even with the fall of communism, it was hard to break from the old, often polluting patterns because jobs and energy sources often depended on them. For years, Ukraine could not afford to replace the remaining nuclear reactors at Chernobyl, despite safety and environmental risks that the 1986 accident had only worsened (see page 847). International aid finally enabled Ukraine to close the plant in 2000.

The greater affluence in western Europe made possible, and sometimes dictated, more creative responses to pollution and other environmental side effects of economic growth. Many cities adopted pedestrian-only zones to restrict automobile traffic, and some experimented with road-pricing measures in an effort to reduce traffic in central cities.

The United States had joined the other industrialized nations in signing the Kyoto agreement of 1997, designed to limit emissions of the "greenhouse gases," widely held by scientists to be causing global warming, with potentially catastrophic consequences. But questioning the scientific evidence and citing concerns about economic growth, the United States pulled out of the agreement in 2001, causing much resentment in Europe and elsewhere. With 5 percent of the world's population, the United States was responsible for 25 percent of the world's greenhouse gas emissions per year.

Still, global warming was increasingly recognized, in the United States as elsewhere, as a serious issue. The question was what needed to be done, and how to muster the political will to do it. One possibility was the further use of nuclear power, long controversial because of safety, waste disposal, and other environmental concerns. Even as such countries as Germany and the United States pulled back during the 1970s, France continued to develop nuclear power until, by 2008, 77 percent of French electricity was nuclear-generated, as compared, for example, with 19 percent in the United States. The French took pride in their technical expertise in the nuclear area. By this point, however, support for nuclear power was increasing all over the Western world, in light of concern about global warming and high oil prices.

Religious Identities

Whereas religious affiliation and church or synagogue attendance remained relatively stable in the United States, Europeans abandoned churches in droves after the mid-1950s. As church attendance dropped, popular culture revolved less around religious festivals and holy days. Moreover, in assuming responsibility for social welfare, European governments had gradually taken over much of the charitable role that the churches had long played.

Seeking to change with the times, the Catholic Church undertook a notable modernization effort under the popular Pope John XXIII (r. 1958–1963). But under his more conservative successors, the church became caught up in controversy, especially over issues, such as abortion, that women had brought to the fore. By the 1990s, its conservative social policy had put the Catholic Church on the defensive. Still, the active, highly visible role of Pope John Paul II (r. 1978–2005) (see page 844) in a variety of spheres attracted widespread admiration. His death in 2005 led to an enormous outpouring of affection.

In such traditionally Catholic countries as France, Italy, and Spain, many people considered themselves "cultural Catholics" and ignored church rulings they found inappropriate, especially those concerning sexuality, marriage, and gender roles. In referenda in 1974 and 1981, two-thirds of Italians defied the Vatican by voting to legalize divorce and approve abortion rights. Even in heavily Catholic Ireland, the electorate approved, though narrowly, the legalization of divorce in 1995, after having defeated it overwhelmingly in a referendum just nine years before.

When surveys showed that 80 percent of Spaniards considered themselves Catholic by the twenty-first century, even the cardinal-bishop of Madrid admitted that for many, "Catholic" was not a way of life but merely a label, perhaps linked to national identity. Other surveys showed that whereas in 1975, the year of the dictator Francisco Franco's death, 61 percent of Spaniards reported regular church attendance, that figure had dropped to 19 percent by the early twenty-first century. Even 46 percent of those calling themselves Catholic admitted that they almost never went to church. By 2008, Christian Church attendance in many western European countries, including Britain, hovered at 5 percent. But while religious affiliations weakened in western Europe, the Russian Orthodox Church experienced a notable revival after the collapse of communism.

In parts of the West, religious and ethnic identities blurred, sometimes enhancing the potential for conflict. Even after the breakup of the wider Soviet Union gave independence to the predominantly Muslim central Asian republics, the remaining Russian Federation included more than twenty million Muslims, or about 15 percent of the overall population. In both absolute numbers and percentage terms, this was the largest Muslim population in Europe. Included were those who identified themselves as Muslims in cultural terms, even if they did not practice the Islamic religion.

A significant Islamic revival among Russian Muslims followed the collapse of communism, producing increasing friction with the central authorities. In 2002, the interior ministry banned women from wearing headscarves in photos for official documents. The Russian supreme court upheld the ban in response to an appeal by Islamic women that it violated Russia's constitutionally guaranteed freedom of religion. At the same time, the Russian army refused to allow Muslim services on military bases.

Family Life and Gender Roles

The new affluence significantly affected demographic patterns, partly because contraception became more readily available. Indeed, the advent of the birth control pill, widely obtainable by the late 1960s, fostered a secular lifestyle. At the same time, falling birthrates meant an aging population, and thus all the concerns about paying for the pensions and other welfare measures central to the postwar social compact.

In western Europe, as in the United States, a remarkable baby boom had followed the end of World War II and carried into the early 1960s. But the birthrate declined rapidly thereafter, so family size had diminished markedly by 1990. In Italy, the number of births in 1987 was barely half the number in 1964, when the postwar baby boom reached its peak. By 1995, the population was not sustaining itself in a number of European countries, including Italy (see **Map 30.4**). Thus, though some were reluctant to admit it, immigration was essential to sustain the working-age population. By 2008, Italy had the oldest population in Europe, with 20 percent of the population 65 or older. Germany was a close second. The figure for the United States was 12 percent, though the Americans, too, were aging rapidly.

The feminist movement that had reemerged in the late 1960s gradually expanded its focus beyond the quest for formal equality of opportunity. Examining subtle cultural obstacles to equality led feminists to the more general issue of gender—the way societies make sense of sexual difference and allocate social roles on that basis. By the late twentieth century, gender was central not only to public policy, but also to private relationships and life choices in much of the Western world.

By the 1970s, women sought measures, such as government-subsidized day care, that would enable them to combine paid employment with raising a family. At the same time, governments increasingly understood the value of policies to encourage both productive working parents and effective childhood development. Setting the pace was France, where the government began making quality day care available to all during the 1980s. Government subsidies kept costs within reach for ordinary working families. In addition, 95 percent of French children ages 3 to 6 were enrolled in the free public nursery schools available by the early 1990s.

The French model seemed to work well in combining child support with equal opportunity for paid employment. In simultaneously offering day care and allowances to concentrate on parenting, French government programs seemed to give French mothers a genuine choice as to whether to work outside the home. And French policy was sufficiently pro-baby to help give France Europe's highest birthrate. Overall, French family policy was widely popular; the key question was whether France could afford it.

Also much at issue by the early twenty-first century were the rights of homosexual couples—to adopt children, for example, or to have their partnerships legally recognized as marriage. Whether married or not, were homosexual partners entitled to job benefits, such as health care, which often were available to heterosexual couples?

The interrelationship of family, gender, sexuality, and personal self-realization, never static, was evolving in new ways—a crucial aspect of the ongoing experiment in the West.

SECTION SUMMARY

- The advent of a consumer society, increasingly on a global level, affected supranational, national, and subnational identities in complex, often unforeseen ways.

- The de-emphasis on class as a basis of identity contributed to the decline of the trade-union movement.

- Economic growth seemed to have adverse effects on the environment, though there was disagreement over how best to respond.

- The strength of religious identities diminished in much of Europe, though there was considerable variation from country to country.

- Affluence led to new ways of conceiving gender roles and family life.

Nelson Mandela and the Universality of Human Values

For all the admiration that continued to surround those who had helped undermine Soviet-style communism, the most revered person in the West and the world at the beginning of the twenty-first century was surely the black South African Nelson Mandela (b. 1918). As a militant in the African National Congress, which was seeking to overcome the brutally segregationist apartheid system in South Africa, he spent twenty-seven years in prison. He was released in 1990 as part of a wider amnesty granted by South Africa's new president, F. W. De Klerk (b. 1936). Responding to international pressures, including effective trade sanctions, De Klerk wanted Mandela's help in restructuring the South African system. The two were central to the ensuing negotiations that repealed apartheid and began the transition to a nonracial democracy in South Africa. When the first elections were held under the new system in 1994, Mandela was elected president of South Africa. In this passage from the conclusion to his autobiography, he articulates the idealism that inspired his remarkable achievement and made him a symbol of shared human values to Westerners and non-Westerners alike.

On the day of the inauguration, I was overwhelmed with a sense of history. In the first decade of the twentieth century, a few years after the bitter Anglo-Boer War and before my own birth, the white skinned peoples of South Africa patched up their differences and erected a system of racial domination against the dark-skinned peoples of their own land. The structure they created formed the basis of one of the harshest, most inhumane societies the world has ever known. Now, in the last decade of the twentieth century, and my own eighth decade as a man, that system had been overturned forever and replaced by one that recognized the rights and freedoms of all peoples regardless of the color of their skin.

That day had come about through the unimaginable sacrifices of thousands of my people, people whose suffering and courage can never be counted or repaid. I felt that day, as I have on so many other days, that I was simply the sum of all those African patriots who had gone before me. That long and noble line ended and now began again with me. I was pained that I was not able to thank them and that they were not able to see what their sacrifices had wrought....

I never lost hope that this great transformation would occur. Not only because of the great heroes I have already cited, but because of the courage of the ordinary men and women of my country. I always knew that deep down in every human heart, there is mercy and generosity. No one is born hating another person because of the color of his skin, or his background, or his religion. People must learn to hate, and if they can learn to hate, they can be taught to love, for love comes more naturally to the human heart than its opposite. Even in the grimmest times in prison, when my comrades and I were pushed to our limits, I would see a glimmer of humanity in one of the guards, perhaps just for a second, but it was enough to reassure me and keep me going....

I was not born with a hunger to be free. I was born free—free in every way that I could know....

But then I slowly saw that not only was I not free, but my brothers and sisters were not free. I saw that it was not just my freedom that was curtailed, but the freedom of everyone who looked like I did. That is when I joined the African National Congress, and that is when the hunger for my own freedom became the greater hunger for the freedom of my people. It was this desire for the freedom of my people to live their lives with dignity and self-respect that animated my life, that transformed a frightened young man into a bold one, that drove a law-abiding attorney to become a criminal, that turned a family-loving husband into a man without a home, that forced a life loving man to live like a monk. I am no more virtuous or self-sacrificing than the next man, but I found that I could not even enjoy the poor and limited freedoms I was allowed when I knew my people were not free. Freedom is indivisible; the chains on any one of my people were the chains on all of them, the chains on all of my people were the chains on me.

It was during those long and lonely years that my hunger for the freedom of my own people became a hunger for the freedom of all people, white and black. I knew as well as I knew anything that the oppressor must be liberated just as surely as the oppressed. A man who takes away another man's freedom is a prisoner of hatred, he is locked behind the bars of prejudice and narrow-mindedness. I am not truly free if I am taking away someone else's freedom, just as surely as I am not free when my freedom is taken from me. The oppressed and the oppressor alike are robbed of their humanity.

When I walked out of prison, that was my mission, to liberate the oppressed and the oppressor both. Some say that has now been achieved. But I know that that is not the case. The truth is that we are not yet free; we have merely achieved the freedom to be free, the right not to be oppressed. We have not taken the final step of our journey, but the first step on a longer and even more difficult road. For to be free is not merely to cast off one's chains, but to live in a way that respects and enhances the freedom of others. The true test of our devotion to freedom is just beginning.

...After climbing a great hill, one only finds that there are many more hills to climb. I have taken a moment here to rest, to steal a view of the glorious vista that surrounds me, to look back on the distance I have come. But I can rest only for a moment, for with freedom comes responsibilities, and I dare not linger, for my long walk is not yet ended.

QUESTIONS

1. In what sense is Mandela appealing to human values, as opposed to the values or special circumstances of a particular group?

2. Why does Mandela suggest that the struggle for freedom is essentially endless?

Source: From *Long Walk to Freedom* by Nelson Mandela. Copyright © 1994, 1995 by Nelson Rolihlahla Mandela. By permission of Little, Brown & Company.

THE WEST IN A GLOBAL AGE

What questions emerged as the West faced new crises all over the globe after the end of the cold war?

By the early twenty-first century, the West was part of a world that was, in one sense, dramatically less Eurocentric than it had been a century before, when European imperialism was at its peak. Events in the West competed for attention with OPEC oil prices, Chinese trade practices, and Iran's nuclear program. Decisions vitally affecting the industrialized West might be made anywhere. Just as capital and information flowed more quickly across national borders, so could epidemic diseases emerging in some distant jungle. This was the reverse side of the new interconnectedness of a global world. A planetary culture, a threatened environment, an interdependent economy, and an increasing sense of international responsibility required people to think in global terms as never before. (See the feature, "The Global Record: Nelson Mandela and the Universality of Human Values.")

Uniformity and Diversity in the "Global Village"

By the last decades of the twentieth century, a kind of global culture began to emerge for the first time. Indeed, talk of a single "global village" became commonplace. But just as "Americanization" produced concerns about preserving distinctiveness elsewhere in the West, "globalization" led to comparable concerns on a global level. Although the process promised a better life for many people in less developed countries, valuable diversity was seemingly being lost in an ever more uniform world. For instance, half the world's 6,500 languages were expected to disappear during the twenty-first century.

Skyscrapers in booming Asian cities looked much like skyscrapers in the West. Indeed, they were often designed by the same architects. Businessmen in conservative Western dress made postwar Japan the world's second-largest economy. American firms transferred billing and even customer service operations to lower-cost India, even as India was becoming a major player in computer technology. "Americanization" made such products as Coca-Cola and McDonald's burgers familiar not just in Europe, but worldwide. Especially among urban youth, a common style emerged that owed much to American popular culture. Meanwhile, for everyone from scientists to business leaders to airline pilots, English became the common language.

At work, however, was not simply Western or American cultural imperialism. What resulted in many spheres, from food to popular music, was a complex fusion, as elements from diverse cultures enriched one another even as distinctive features remained. The British tourist board declared Indian curry to be the official British dish, testimony to the number of Indian restaurants in Britain—itself testimony to the enduring impact of the Indian heritage on Britain.

Even multinational media conglomerates increasingly accented local content. When Viacom launched MTV in the 1980s, the producers assumed that since the pop music culture was universal, a single channel would succeed everywhere. But it quickly became evident that success required local variation. Between 2001 and 2003, MTV launched fourteen new channels, for a total of thirty-eight around the world. Each was tailored to local tastes, with no emphasis on an American link. One MTV executive observed, "we don't even call it an adaptation of American content: it's local content creation.... The American thing is irrelevant."[1] So whereas the advent of MTV had initially seemed an instance of cultural imperialism, the program's evolution manifested—and contributed to—the more complex global cross-fertilization in process.

Mutual Interdependence and Patterns of Development

The world's population had reached 1 billion in 1800, 2 billion in 1930. In 1999, it reached 6 billion, having doubled since 1960. This was the fastest rate of world population growth ever, and by the 1990s, virtually all of that growth was in the developing countries of Africa, Asia, and Latin America (see **Map 30.4**). As of mid-2008, world population stood at 6.7 billion and was projected to reach nearly 10 billion by 2050. But growth was expected to slow with the cultural

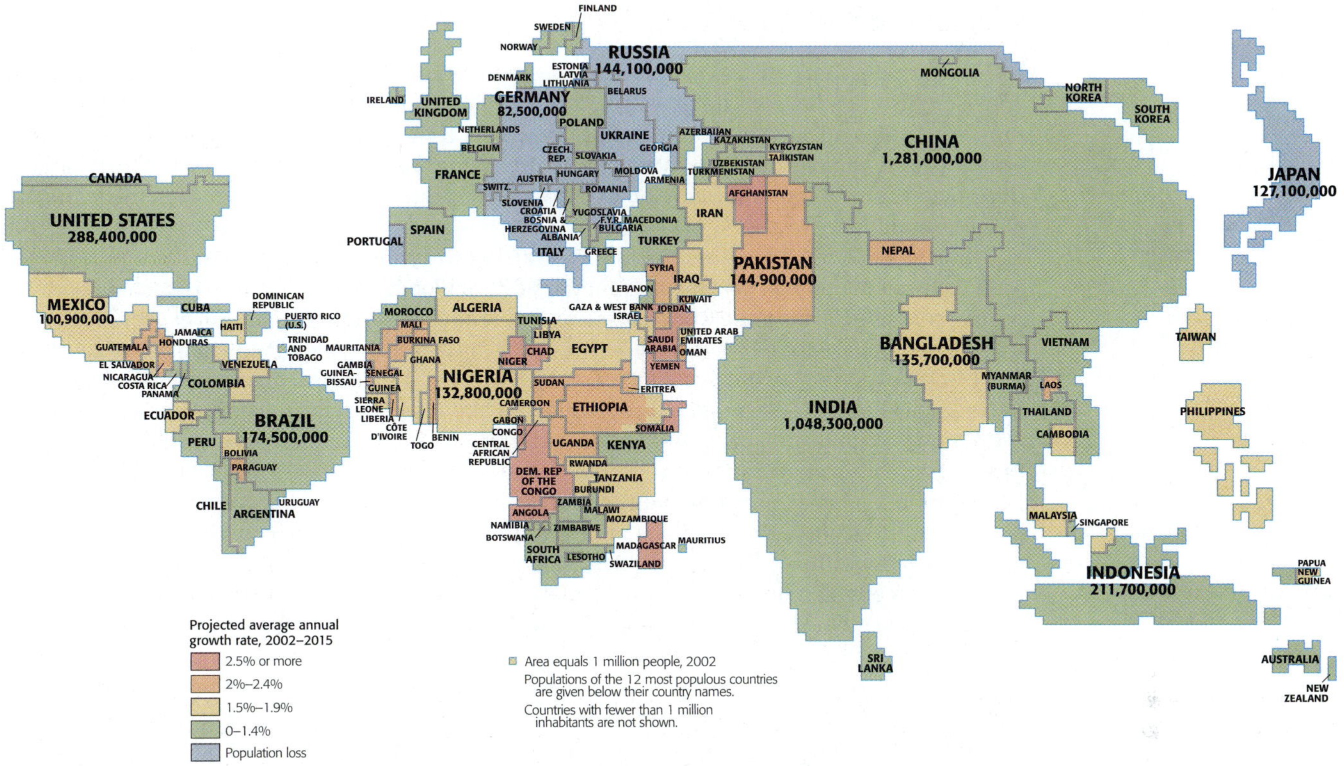

MAP 30.4—World Population Trends, 2002–2015

This map shows populations in 2002, as well as projected average annual growth rates from 2002 to 2015, in countries throughout the world. In the developed countries of the West, populations are relatively high but growing slowly, if at all. Most of the world's population growth is occurring in the less-developed countries outside the West.

(Source: Data from www.worldbank.org)

changes accompanying development, including the integration of more women into the workforce. Whereas world population was growing 1.2 percent a year as of 2008, growth was projected to decline to 0.5 percent by 2050.

Growing concern about the environment intensified the sense of global interdependence and pointed to the need for international cooperation. Such problems as global warming, the loss of biodiversity, and the deterioration of the ozone layer were inherently supranational in scope. Yet environmental concerns also complicated relations between the industrialized nations and the rest of the world. Countries seeking to industrialize encountered environmental constraints that had not been at issue when the West industrialized. The challenge for the West was to foster protection of the environment in poorer regions of the globe without imposing unfair limitations on economic growth.

Also bringing home mutual interdependence was the rapid spread of contagious, sometimes fatal diseases with the intensification of contacts around the world. Some of those diseases were apparently new, or at least previously unknown. As the world grew more crowded, humans intruded into previously untouched jungles and forests, intensifying interaction among species that had formerly remained largely separated. The crowding of animals for food production also fed the genesis and spread of new diseases. Officials of the UN's **World Health Organization (WHO)** stressed in 2005 that they lacked the global infrastructure to head off the sort of pandemic that might result, for example, from a further mutation in the "bird flu" virus.

AIDS (acquired immune deficiency syndrome), a sexually transmitted disease caused by the HIV virus, had apparently spread from chimpanzees to humans in Africa earlier in the twentieth century, although it began to be recognized only in the late 1970s. It then expanded throughout the world beginning in the 1980s. Particularly devastating in Africa, AIDS remained a major concern in the early twenty-first century.

World Health Organization (WHO) Established as a specialized agency of the United Nations in 1948, it serves as the coordinating authority on international public health. It is headquartered in Geneva, Switzerland.

Controversy Over Economic Globalization

Although many forces fed globalization, the most potent was international capitalism itself. The capitalist ideal of free and open markets sounded appealing, and economic models, based on comparative advantage, could explain how everybody wins through expanded economic exchange. The world economy was not a zero-sum game. But whatever the virtues of free markets in principle, experience showed globalization to be a multi-edged sword, producing complex, often-contradictory results.

The network of supranational agencies, starting with the World Bank and the International Monetary Fund, that had developed from the Bretton Woods Agreement of 1944 had long drawn praise for helping to keep the world economy stable and growing. Also central, especially in promoting free trade, was the **World Trade Organization (WTO)**, which grew from a 1947 multilateral trade agreement. By the late 1990s, however, these organizations, together with the G-8, had become focal points for the increasing concerns about globalization. Beginning with a meeting of the WTO in Seattle in 1999, large demonstrations, or even riots, routinely surrounded the meetings of these organizations.

Those protesting were often naive about economics and the benefits of free trade. But their protests raised significant questions about wages, working conditions, environmental impact, and international financial arrangements that were not always adequately addressed in the prevailing economic models. Most fundamentally at issue was whether it made sense to foster free trade and globalization without greater consistency in social and environmental policy. In the absence of common standards, free trade was not likely to be fair trade. Under present circumstances, trade agreements seemed to threaten a loss of jobs in the developed world and the exploitation of less-developed countries at the same time. Critics charged that globalization was not helping the poorer nations to catch up, as theory would have it, but leaving them ever further behind. The challenge was to find some balance between free trade and regulation within an increasingly global economy.

The Question of Global Responsibility

If people were forced to think in global terms as never before, how far did global responsibility extend in a world that remained divided into sovereign nation-states? The series of brutal, sometimes genocidal conflicts from Yugoslavia to Rwanda to Liberia that marked the post–cold war period fostered a growing sense of collective responsibility on the part of what was increasingly called "the international community." Amorphous though it was, that entity seemed to take on real existence by the end of the 1990s. But who or what constituted "the international community" and the conditions under which it should act remained uncertain.

Of course, a prominent international organization was already in place—the United Nations, the fruit of the hopes for a better world in light of World War II. By the 1990s, no one denied that it had achieved significant successes in areas such as nutrition, health, and education. But UN forces were often overburdened as they took on the often-incompatible objectives of peacekeeping and humanitarian relief—sometimes in areas where there was no real peace to keep. The need to seem impartial sometimes paralyzed UN peacekeepers. And the UN's members, especially its leaders on the Security Council, frequently disagreed over what should be done.

Still, the UN was a visible presence, even as concerns for national sovereignty compromised its ability to act. After ad hoc UN war crimes tribunals began dealing with the atrocities that had taken place in the Balkans and Rwanda, the UN established its permanent International Criminal Court in The Hague in 1998. Its charge was to bring to justice those responsible for war crimes or crimes against humanity. Supporters also cited the UN's successes in organizing relief in the wake of disasters, such as a devastating 2005 earthquake in Pakistan, and its at least partial successes in the war-torn Democratic Republic of Congo, where it disarmed militias, organized elections, and helped millions of people return to their homes.

Supplementing the efforts of governments and the supranational UN was a network of **nongovernmental organizations (NGOs)**, such as the Red Cross, Amnesty International, and Doctors Without Borders, that had emerged over the years to deal with humanitarian relief or human rights issues. Collectively, they were a major presence on the international scene by the early twenty-first century and central to the international community.

But those seeking to provide aid or maintain peace were often forced to deal with semicriminal elements who diverted humanitarian aid to buy weapons or who took peacekeepers

World Trade Organization (WTO)   Growing from a multilateral trade agreement in 1947, it sought, with mixed success, to promote freer trade throughout the world. By the early twenty-first century, WTO meetings tended to draw demonstrations by antiglobalization activists.

nongovernmental organizations (NGOs)   Private, independent organizations designed to deal with humanitarian relief and human rights issues. Though unaffiliated with governments or the United Nations, they became central to the international community.

The Question of Western Responsibility

The end of the cold war helped open the way to ethnic conflict, terrorism, and, in some areas, the breakdown of government as violent warlords fought for control. With the world more interconnected than ever before, it was increasingly assumed that "the international community," spearheaded by the rich countries of the West, ought to respond to tragedy anywhere. But quite apart from the difficult questions of leadership and coordination, it was not clear what level of risk, and expense, the West was prepared to assume. In the following excerpt, Brian Urquhart, born in Britain in 1919 and long a senior official of the United Nations, offers a pointed analysis of the issues that came to the fore as the West experimented with a more active response to tragedies around the world.

What is to be done when hundreds of thousands of people in a hitherto little-known region of the world are hounded from their homes, massacred, or starved to death in a brutal civil war, or even in a deliberate act of genocide? To our credit, we no longer turn away from the face of evil, but we still don't know how to control it. As the new century dawns, one of the biggest problems for international organizations and their member governments is to learn how to react to the great human emergencies that still seem to occur regularly in many parts of the world. . . .

The so-called "international community" is anything but a constitutional system. As far as it is organized at all, it is an institutional arrangement, unpredictable and slow to act. It usually responds only when disaster has already struck and when its members, usually in the UN Security Council, can agree to take action. Even then, since the UN has no standing forces or substantial resources of its own, its action, if it can be agreed upon, is likely to be too little and too late.

In his opening address to the General Assembly on September 20, 1999, Secretary-General Kofi Annan made an impassioned plea for UN intervention in cases of gross violations of human rights. The reactions of governments to Annan's remarks showed very clearly how far the world still has to go before evil can be systematically dealt with internationally. Most comments on Annan's speech were critical and stressed the paramount importance of national sovereignty; some even saw humanitarian intervention as a cloak for American or Western hegemony or neocolonialism. Only a small minority of Western countries supported Sweden's position that the collective conscience of mankind demands action.

A new idea of "human security" has now taken its place alongside the much older concept of "international peace and security." It has emerged as the result of a vaguely defined and fitful international conscience on the part of the liberal democracies, and it has been encouraged both by the prodigious growth of nongovernmental organizations and by the communications revolution. However, the rules and the means for protecting human security are still tentative and controversial, not least because virtually any situation threatening human security is likely to raise questions of national sovereignty. No government wants to set up a system which may, at some point in the future, be invoked against itself.

. . .Humanitarian action as it emerged in the aftermath of World War II was principally concerned with refugee resettlement and the reconstruction of war-shattered countries. In those innocent days, humanitarian relief was seen as a nonpolitical activity, dictated by the needs of the afflicted and by the resources and expertise available to meet them . . . . That relatively nonpolitical concept of humanitarianism has come to a brutal end with the rising importance of warlords and the conflicts within states of the post–cold war world. The international sponsors of humanitarian aid are no longer dealing with more or less responsible governments. . . .

. . . "The whole aid community has been overtaken by a new reality," the IRC [International Rescue Committee] stated. "Humanitarianism has become a resource . . . and people are manipulating it as never before. Sometimes we just shouldn't show up for a disaster." . . .

QUESTIONS

1. Why did the West find it so difficult to respond to the sorts of disasters that came to the fore after the cold war?

2. Why did even humanitarian aid come to seem increasingly ineffective under certain circumstances?

Source: "The Question of Western Responsibility" from Brian Urquhart, "In the Name of Humanity," *The New York Review of Books,* April 27, 2000, pp. 19–21.

and aid workers hostage—or even killed them. In 1994, for the first time, more UN civilian aid workers (twenty-four) than peacekeeping soldiers were killed in the line of duty. And the death toll for aid workers rose rapidly during the decade.

The conflicts that developed in hot spots around the world after the cold war spawned an increasing sense that it was up to the Western-led international community to "do something." But do what—and at what cost? What aims were realistic? During the first decade of the new century, the international community was widely called upon to end the apparent ongoing genocide in the Darfur region of Sudan. But there was no consensus on what degree of response was appropriate or on how it should be coordinated. (See the feature, "The Written Record: The Question of Western Responsibility.")

Questioning the Meaning of the West

Although in one sense "globalization" meant "Westernization" to advocates and critics alike, its accelerating pace bred deeper uncertainty about what was specifically Western—about the meaning and value of the Western tradition. Indeed, the need to respond both to the challenges of the competitive global economy and to the increasingly volatile international environment occasioned friction and fragmentation within the West.

Cultural differences between Europeans and Americans seemed to be deepening by the early twenty-first century. As a corollary of religious differences between the two, the United States experienced periodic controversy over the teaching of Darwinian evolution in the public schools—controversy that would have been unthinkable in Europe. In the same way, homosexuality and abortion tended to stir greater controversy in America than they did among Europeans.

In light of the disruptions of the twentieth century, the place of history became especially problematic in Europe. At the same time, the radical transformation in the half century since World War II in some ways cut Europeans off from their own traditions. The uneasy contemporary relationship with the past, especially the traumatic past of the earlier twentieth century, took especially pointed form in the neo-expressionist painting prominent in Germany and Italy by the late twentieth century.

For a generation after World War II, European artists, unsure of their direction, had tended to follow the lead of New York. But by the late 1960s, the new generation that included such painters as the German Anselm Kiefer (b. 1945) and the Italian Sandro Chia (KEE-ah) (b. 1946) sought to confront the recent past—and thus, the meaning of a tradition that now included fascism, total war, and the Holocaust. What did it mean to be German, Italian, or even European in light of this difficult past and the globalizing present and future? Wrestling with the interface of recent history and national identity, Kiefer and Chia conveyed the paradox and ambiguity that many felt as the rapidly changing West encountered the layers of its own cultural tradition.

The ongoing effort to come to terms with the recent past produced controversy and sometimes seemed to open old wounds, as earlier fascist or communist sympathies came under scrutiny. In Italy and France, questions about collaboration and resistance during World War II produced periodic waves of bitterness. Even how to remember and commemorate the Holocaust produced much dispute, although Berlin's Holocaust memorial, opened in 2005, indicated the widespread agreement that commemoration of some sort was essential.

By the early twenty-first century, bitter debate had raged for several decades over the legitimacy of "Western civilization" as a concept. Some critics highlighted the geographical imprecision of "the West" and claimed that the words *Western* and *civilization* had been juxtaposed simply to justify conquest and domination. Even among those who recognized a distinctive Western cultural tradition, some found it elitist and limiting. In their view, Western culture had defined itself around a group of artifacts—writings, paintings, monuments—that reflected the experience of a very restricted circle.

Others countered that imperialism and assumptions of superiority had not been confined to the West. Moreover, they continued, the West had been the source of ideas—the "rights of man," the scope for eliminating exploitation—that were now being eagerly embraced in the non-Western world. Even the charges of cultural elitism directed against the Western tradition stemmed from a democratic impulse that had itself grown from within that tradition. And by the last decades of the twentieth century, that impulse had prompted historians to focus on ordinary people and a far wider circle of cultural interpreters, thereby dramatically expanding the "canon"—the body of works considered worthy of attention.

Questions about the Western tradition and its contemporary relevance were bound up with the advent of *postmodernism*, a term widely used by the early 1990s for a cultural orientation that had been gathering force for decades. (See the feature, "The Visual Record: Postmodern Architecture.") Postmodernism reflected a certain conception of what *modernism* had meant, even a sense that modernism had defined an era that was ending. But what was ending—and how it was bound up with the debate over Western civilization—was not so clear.

Postmodernism emerged partly as confidence in the scope for a neutral, objective social science began to decline during the 1960s. That confidence had reflected the belief in reason that

Kiefer: Osiris and Isis The German artist Anselm Kiefer combined unusual materials to create haunting images that often suggested the horrors of recent history. In this work, dated 1985–1987, the interpenetrating layers of human culture include images of ruin and death, hope and resurrection. (Anselm Kiefer Osiris und Isis (Osiris and Isis), 1985–1987; painting; oil and acrylic emulsion with additional three-dimensional media, 150 in. × 220 $\frac{1}{2}$ in. × 6 $\frac{1}{2}$ in. (381 cm × 560.07 cm × 16.51 cm); Collection SFMOMA, Purchased through a gift of Jean Stein by exchange, the Mrs. Paul L. Wattis Fund, and the Doris and Donald Fisher Fund; © Anselm Kiefer)

had emerged from the Scientific Revolution and the Enlightenment. Reason had seemed universal, not limited to any particular culture, and it was assumed to be applicable to the human as well as the natural world.

To apply reason seemed "modern," and the West, apparently having progressed by applying reason, had long understood itself to be in the forefront of modernity. Everyone else was scrambling to catch up through the universal process of modernization. Such was the "master narrative" through which the West had understood its place in the world during the modern era.

But even as globalization proceeded during the late twentieth century, Western thinkers retreated from this long-standing master narrative. There was no question that capitalism had spread from Europe, but the West was not necessarily the model, the standard of development. Thus the growing interest in the non-Western world, and the increasing respect for its diverse traditions, that came to mark Western culture by the last decades of the twentieth century.

Postmodernists questioned claims of certainty, objective truth, and intrinsic meaning in language, in works of art, and ultimately in all cultural expressions. Some held that such claims were assertions of privilege in what was essentially a political struggle for power—the power to set the wider social agenda. Especially in the United States, the postmodernist reaction led by the 1980s to the vogue of the French philosopher and historian Michel Foucault (foo-KOH) (1926–1984), who had sought to show that the power to specify what counts as knowledge was the key to social or political power. Since, from this perspective, all knowledge was suspect, Foucault's accents invited mistrust and disruption.

Postmodern Architecture

Three building complexes, one by an Italian working in Japan, another by an American working in Germany, and a third by a Spaniard working in Spain: They look dramatically different, yet they were built at roughly the same time. Do they have anything in common? In fact, each was rejecting earlier "modern" architecture, and each expressed what came to be known as "postmodernism" by the last two decades of the twentieth century.

Modernism in architecture, design, and urban planning had emerged especially during the 1920s from sources like the German Bauhaus, which turned resolutely from tradition to embrace the modern industrial age (see page 751). During the first two decades after World War II, this modernist approach triumphed at last, transforming cities throughout the world. Now known as "the international style," it reflected the wider self-understanding of the modern world, centered in the West. "Modern" meant rationality and efficiency, clarity and regularity, machine precision and mass culture. Ornament, decoration, symbolism, and historical reference had little or no place.

At issue, in fact, was not just a particular style of building but a new relationship with history. As modern, we seemed to be living on the cutting edge of history, in the eternal present, endlessly being cut off from our past. Henry Ford, widely taken as the personification of modernity in his time, put the matter directly: "History is bunk."

But by the 1960s, a reaction began to develop in architecture and urban planning, reflecting deeper thinking about history, about what it meant to be modern, and about the contemporary relationship with cultural traditions, including older buildings. In 1977, the architectural critic Charles Jencks, in his book, *The Language of Post-Modern Architecture*, used the term *postmodernism* to characterize what now seemed to be a new movement or direction.

The earlier notion of modernity was coming to seem dubious in an emerging world of global interchange and plural perspectives. Memory, history, and the presence of the past were more, not less, important as accelerating technological change made possible instant communication and constant access to information across the globe. Yet, there was sometimes irony, uncertainty, or paradox in the coexistence of old and new.

Postmodernist architects did not merely reject the earlier modernism, and certainly their aim was not simply to revive previous styles, such as classical or Gothic, though elements of them, as embodiments of our living history, might be incorporated in postmodern buildings. For example, look at the photo above of the Palazzo Hotel, designed by the Italian Aldo Rossi (1931–1997). Set in a Japanese city, the hotel clearly recalls Italian buildings, even those of the fascist period, themselves ambiguously modern, with references to the classical tradition and especially ancient Rome. For the façade, constructed of red marble and brick crossed with green steel moldings, Rossi combined contrasting materials, uncertain scale, and historical reference in a striking, even uncanny way.

Aldo Rossi: Il Palazzo Hotel, Fukuoka, Japan (Courtesy, Nacasa & Partners, Inc.)

Moreover, postmodernist architects were just as committed to modern techniques and materials as the modernists. They reacted, however, against the modernist pretense of a single right way, the rejection of ornament and history, and the reduction of architecture to function and the logic of machines. Postmodernists did not simply accept but actively celebrated messiness, variety, mixture, and complexity. The American Frank Gehry (b. 1929) suggested impermanence as well as postmodern pluralism in his complex of three office buildings in Düsseldorf, Germany (opposite page, top). Notice how the project incorporates modernist elements—flat roofs, identical prefabricated windows—but provides remarkable variety and contrast by cladding one of the units in red brick, one in mirror-polished stainless steel, and the third in white plaster. At the same time, the uniform, angled windows contrast with the curved surfaces. None of the three is the right way; rather, they play evocatively against one another.

Santiago Calatrava (b. 1951) drew on an even wider frame of reference to create shapes that were never before part of our built environment. Calatrava used highly sculpted forms for the building shown here (opposite page, bottom)—the centerpiece of a science museum complex built in the bed of a diverted river in his native Valencia, Spain. Taking advantage of his engineering background,

Frank Gehry: Der Neue Zollhof (The New Customs House), Düsseldorf, Germany (Thomas Mayer, photographer)

he created unexpected spaces and sculptural surfaces that went beyond tradition altogether. With structures suggesting bones and tendons, he conveyed the dynamics of movement, of folding, opening, and closing—even the opening and closing of an eye.

Dramatically different though they appear, these three architectural statements share the wider postmodern framework. Rossi invokes the past to resist change; Gehry plays with the past, even the recent modernist past, while suggesting impermanence; Calatrava transcends the present outcome of the past, but without the limitations, the particular discipline, that modernism imposed. Rather than submit to the logic of the machine, he felt free to experiment more boldly, devising radically new forms. Each of the three architects represents a strand in the wider, complex, and contradictory postmodernist approach to history and tradition, including the tradition of modernism itself.

QUESTIONS

1. In what sense are the buildings we see here recognizably *post*modern, in the sense of consciously rejecting earlier modernist tenets?

2. How do Rossi, Gehry, and Calatrava differ in their approach to change and history?

Santiago Calatrava: City of Arts and Sciences, Valencia, Spain (Oliver Schuh, Palladium Photodesign)

Old and New in Contemporary Europe   Especially with the transformation of Europe since World War II, new styles intersect with living artifacts from the past to form sometimes ironic combinations. Here, in a neighborhood in Milan, Italy, teenagers wearing blue jeans and backpacks seem oblivious to the legacies of Roman antiquity and Christianity that are prominent around them.   (© 1999, George Steinmetz)

SECTION SUMMARY

- Although globalization meant cultural homogeneity in one sense, it also produced unforeseen forms of cultural fusion and a deeper appreciation of cultural diversity.

- Economic globalization produced a backlash, often targeting multinational entities like the World Trade Organization, on the grounds that free trade was too often exploitative and unfair.

- Even as it increasingly felt responsible for dealing with disasters around the world, the West, leading "the international community," was often unsure how best to respond.

- Cultural differences between Europeans and Americans, as reflected, for example, in attitudes toward religion or the role of government, seemed to be deepening by the early twenty-first century.

- Even as the concept of "Western civilization" was debated in the West, intellectual leaders sought to show how Western notions of reason and democracy could be given renewed relevance.

At the same time, however, an array of equally innovative thinkers, from the German Jürgen Habermas (b. 1929) to the American Richard Rorty (1931–2007), sought a more constructive orientation based on a renewed, no longer arrogant understanding of Western traditions, including the place of reason and democracy.

For those embracing this more constructive approach, the point was not to celebrate Western civilization but simply to understand it—as the framework that continued to shape the West and, less directly, the world. That tradition included much that might be criticized, and its present outcome entailed much that might be changed. Habermas, in particular, was a persistent and often radical critic of what he saw as the disparity between Western democratic ideals and contemporary social and political practices. But effective criticism had to rest on free inquiry and rational understanding, as opposed to prejudice or wishful thinking. The invitation to think freely about the Western tradition, to criticize and change it, rested on precisely that tradition; indeed, the scope for such criticism and change had been central to the Western belief in reason. That openness remained perhaps the West's most fundamental legacy.

CHAPTER SUMMARY

With the end of the cold war, the United States and the nations of western Europe no longer faced a common communist adversary, so close collaboration seemed less pressing to both sides. Greater freedom for Europe to set its own course stimulated the expansion and deepening of the European Union. And whereas the West was mostly united in response to increasing terrorism, Western nations split over the wisdom of the U.S.-led invasion of Iraq, which, to many Europeans, seemed to indicate an unwelcome unilateralism on the part of the United States.

Although democracy was the unquestioned norm, a variety of changes posed new challenges for governments and the political order more generally. In light of aging populations and increasing global competition, western European countries found it ever harder to pay for the benefits promised as part of the postwar social compact. Yet reform efforts provoked protests that led governments to back down. Adding to political volatility was growing concern over the assimilation of immigrants.

Increasing economic globalization expanded horizons, but also affected the self-understanding of individuals in complex ways. Skeptical Europeans often equated globalization with Americanization and promoted various measures to preserve distinctiveness. However, people disagreed over whether what was to be preserved was "European," national, or local. Ways of understanding class, gender, and the place of religion also changed, though in some countries more than others.

An array of challenges, from new diseases to genocidal aggression, called for coordinated multinational responses. Although the UN played more visible roles after the cold war, it was an unwieldy organization whose effectiveness was sometimes limited. Even its specialized entities, such as the World Health Organization, sometimes lacked the resources and the clout to coordinate multinational responses. In dealing with politically inspired humanitarian crises in the non-Western world, the West found it difficult to develop a consistent and workable policy of intervention.

Changing relationships between the West and the non-Western world prompted new questions about the meaning and ongoing relevance of "Western civilization" as a concept. Some suggested that the whole "modern" conception of history, which had assumed a privileged leadership role for the West, had fallen away. But wider cultural encounters helped bring home the centrality of Western notions of openness and pluralism.

FOCUS QUESTIONS

- Why and how did the relationship between western Europe and the United States change after the end of the cold war?

- What forces raised new questions about the effectiveness of Western-style democracy by the early years of the twenty-first century?

- How did the changes bound up with globalization affect identities in the West?

- What questions emerged as the West faced new crises all over the globe after the end of the cold war?

KEY TERMS

Group of 20 (G-20)   (p. 851)
Group of Seven (G-7)
   (p. 851)
European Union (EU)
   (p. 854)
Maastricht agreements
   (p. 854)
euro   (p. 854)

Common Agricultural
   Policy (CAP)   (p. 855)
ethnic cleansing   (p. 857)
unilateralism   (p. 859)
Vladimir Putin   (p. 862)
social market economy
   (p. 863)
Nicolas Sarkozy   (p. 865)

World Health Organization
   (WHO)   (p. 873)
World Trade Organization
   (WTO)   (p. 874)
nongovernmental
   organizations
   (NGOs)   (p. 874)

This icon will direct you to additional materials on the website: www.cengage.com/history/noble/westciv6e.

NOTES

1. Quoted in *The Economist*, April 5, 2003, p. 59.

 See our interactive eBook for map and primary source activities.

INDEX